New York State Criminal Law *Reference*

Looseleaf
Law Publications, Inc.

43-08 162nd Street
Flushing, NY 11358
www.LooseleafLaw.com   800-647-5547

This publication is not intended to replace, nor be a substitute for, any official procedural material issued by your agency of employment or other official source. Looseleaf Law Publications, Inc., the author and any associated advisors have made all possible efforts to ensure the accuracy and thoroughness of the information provided herein, but accept no liability whatsoever for injury, legal action or other adverse results following the application or adoption of the information contained in this book.

New York State Criminal Law Reference

978-1-932777-47-5

Current through Chapter 834 of the 2021 Legislative Session

New York State Criminal Law *Reference*

Table of Contents

Page #s

Part I

Penal Law i-224

Penal Law Index . . . . I-VIII

Part II

Criminal Procedure Law i-270

Criminal Procedure Law Index . . . . I-VI

Part III

Selected Laws of New York State i-218

Tables of Contents . . . . i-iv

Correction Law 1-36

Education Law 37-46

Executive Law 47-58

General Business Law 59-60

Public Health Law 61-90

Vehicle and Traffic Law 91-218

Selected Laws Index 219-224

Part IV

NYS Penal Offenses and Classifications 1

Felony Sentencing Guidelines 19

This page intentionally left blank.

PENAL
LAW
OF
NEW YORK STATE

Part I

43-08 162nd Street
Flushing, NY 11358
www.LooseleafLaw.com   800-647-5547

This page intentionally left blank.

STATE OF NEW YORK

SENATE and ASSEMBLY

Pursuant to the authority vested in us by section 70-b of the Public Officers Law and upon information and belief, I, Andrea Stewart-Cousins, Temporary President of the Senate and I, Carl E. Heastie, Speaker of the Assembly, hereby jointly certify that the text of the provisions of law contained in this publication is a correct transcript of the text of such law as last amended as of the date of execution of this certificate, and, in accordance with such section, is entitled to be read into evidence.

Given under my hand and seal of office, in the County of Albany, this 7th day of January 20 22 .

Temporary President of the Senate

Given under my hand and seal of office, in the County of Albany, this 7th day of January 20 22 .

Speaker of the Assembly

This certification is issued for: Looseleaf Law Publications, Inc.
Penal Law

Chapter 833/21 excepting §14 of Part O of Chapter 55/12, §19 of Part J of Chapter 56/12 and §10 of Part A of Chapter 60/12

LAW CHANGES BY THE 2021 LEGISLATURE WHICH AFFECT THE
PENAL LAW

Section	Subdivision	Change	Chapter	Eff. Date
30.00	3.(d)(ii)	Amended	809	12/29/21
60.04	7.	Amended	322	8/2/21
60.35	5.	Eff. Extended	55	4/19/21
60.35	5.(a)	Amended	322	8/2/21
60.35	5.	Amended	322	8/2/21
65.00	1.	Eff. Extended	55	4/19/21
65.15	3.	Eff. Extended	55	4/19/21
70.00	1., 6.	Eff. Extended	55	4/19/21
70.02	2. (a)	Eff. Extended	55	4/19/21
70.04	2., 3.	Eff. Extended	55	4/19/21
70.06	2., 3., 6., 7.	Eff. Extended	55	4/19/21
70.08	3.	Eff. Extended	55	4/19/21
70.20	1.(d)	Amended	322	8/2/21
70.20	1., 3.	Eff. Extended	55	4/19/21
70.25	1.(a), 2-a., 2-b.	Eff. Extended	55	4/19/21
70.25	5. (a), (b)	Eff. Extended	55	4/19/21
70.30	1., 3., 4., 7.	Eff. Extended	55	4/19/21
70.35		Eff. Extended	55	4/19/21
70.40	1. (a)	Eff. Extended	55	4/19/21
70.40	1. (b), (c)	Eff. Extended	55	4/19/21
70.40	3.	Amended	427	3/1/22
70.40	4.	New	427	3/1/22
70.45	5.(d)	Amended	427	3/1/22
70.70	1.(a),(b)	Amended	92	3/31/21
70.70	2.(b),(c)	Amended	92	3/31/21
70.70	3.(b),.(e)	Amended	92	3/31/21
70.70	4.(b)Op.Para.	Amended	92	3/31/21
85.15	1.	Eff. Extended	55	4/19/21
130.05	3.(e),(f)	Amended	322	8/2/21
135.60	Op.Para.	Amended	484	12/19/21
135.60	10.	New	447	11/7/21
155.05	2.(e)(iv)	Amended	447	11/7/21
156.25	4.	Amended	784	12/22/21
156.25	5.	New	784	12/22/21
170.00	1.	Amended	784	12/22/21
Art.179		Eff.Extended	92	3/31/21
179.00	Title plus	Amended	92	3/31/21

Section	Subdivision	Change	Chapter	Eff. Date
179.05	Title plus	Amended	92	3/31/21
179.10	Title plus	Amended	92	3/31/21
179.11	Title plus	Amended	92	3/31/21
179.15	Title plus	Amended	92	3/31/21
190.25	3. & 4.	Amended	739	12/22/21
190.25	5.	New	739	12/22/21
205.16		Eff. Extended	55	4/19/21
205.17		Eff. Extended	55	4/19/21
205.18		Eff. Extended	55	4/19/21
205.19		Eff. Extended	55	4/19/21
220.00	5.	Amended	92	3/31/21
220.00	6.	Repealed	92	3/31/21
220.00	9.	Amended	92	3/31/21
220.03	Op.Para.	Amended	433	10/7/21
220.06	4.	Repealed	92	3/31/21
220.09	10.	Repealed	92	3/31/21
220.34	3.	Repealed	92	3/31/21
220.45		Repealed	433	10/7/21
220.78		Amended	92	3/31/21
Art.221		Repealed	92	3/31/21
Art.222		New	92	3/31/21
230.01		Amended	23	2/2/21
240.32	Heading	Amended	322	8/2/21
240.32		Amended	322	8/2/21
240.37		Repealed	23	2/2/21
260.20		Amended	92	3/31/21
265.00	8-a.	New	520	4/26/22
265.00	20.	Amended	518	11/1/21
265.00	32.	New	519	2/25/22
265.00	32.	New	520	4/26/22
265.01	(8)	Amended	520	4/26/22
265.01	(9)	New	520	4/26/22
265.01	(9) & (10)	New	519	2/25/22
265.07		New	520	4/26/22
265.10	8.	New	518	11/1/21
265.17		Amended	236	7/1/21
265.60		New	520	4/26/22
265.61		New	520	4/26/22
265.63		New	519	2/25/22
265.64		New	519	2/25/22

Section	Subdivision	Change	Chapter	Eff. Date
270.40		New	274	7/16/21
480.00	7.(b),(c)	Amended	92	3/31/21

PUBLIC HEALTH LAW

Section	Subdivision	Change	Chapter	Eff. Date
3302		Amended	92	3/31/21
3306	Sch. I (d)(13) to (31)	Amended	92	3/31/21

I

PENAL LAW

TABLE OF CONTENTS

ARTICLE		SECTIONS
1	General Purposes	1.00 - 1.05
5	General Rules of Construction and Application	5.00 - 5.10
10	Definitions	10.00
15	Culpability	15.00 - 15.25
20	Parties to Offenses and Liability Through Accessorial Conduct	20.00 - 20.25
25	Defenses in General	25.00
30	Defense of Infancy	30.00
35	Defense of Justification	35.00 - 35.30
40	Other Defenses Involving Lack of Culpability	40.00 - 40.15
55	Classification and Designation of Offenses	55.00 - 55.10
60	Authorized Dispositions of Offenders	60.00 - 60.37
65	Sentences of Probation, Conditional Discharge and Unconditional Discharge	65.00 - 65.20
70	Sentences of Imprisonment	70.00 - 70.85
80	Fines	80.00 - 80.15
85	Sentence of Intermittent Imprisonment	85.00 - 85.15
100	Criminal Solicitation	100.00 - 100.20
105	Conspiracy	105.00 - 105.35
110	Attempt	110.00 - 110.10
115	Criminal Facilitation	115.00 - 115.20
120	Assault and Related Offenses	120.00 - 120.70
121	Strangulation and Related Offenses	121.11 - 121.14
125	Homicide and Related Offenses	125.00 - 125.27
130	Sex Offenses	130.00 - 130.96
135	Kidnapping, Coercion and Related Offenses	135.00 - 135.75
140	Burglary and Related Offenses	140.00 - 140.40
145	Criminal Mischief and Related Offenses	145.00 - 145.70
150	Arson	150.00 - 150.20
155	Larceny	155.00 - 155.45
156	Offenses Involving Computers; Definition of Terms	156.00 - 156.50
158	Welfare Fraud	158.00 - 158.50
160	Robbery	160.00 - 160.15
165	Other Offenses Relating to Theft	165.00 - 165.74
170	Forgery and Related Offenses	170.00 - 170.75
175	Offenses Involving False Written Statements	175.00 - 175.45
176	Insurance Fraud	176.00 - 176.80
177	Health Care Fraud	177.00 - 177.30
178	Criminal Diversion of Prescription Medications and Prescriptions	178.00 - 178.26
179	Criminal Diversion of Medical Marihuana	179.00 - 179.15

II

180   Bribery Not Involving Public Servants, and
         Related Offenses .... 180.00 - 180.57
185   Frauds on Creditors .... 185.00 - 185.15
187   Residential Mortgage Fraud .... 187.00 - 187.25
190   Other Frauds .... 190.00 - 190.89
195   Official Misconduct and Obstruction of Public
         Servants Generally .... 195.00 - 195.20
200   Bribery Involving Public Servants and
         Related Offenses .... 200.00 - 200.56
205   Escape and Other Offenses Relating to Custody . 205.00 - 205.65
210   Perjury and Related Offenses .... 210.00 - 210.50
215   Other Offenses Relating to Judicial and Other
         Proceedings .... 215.00 - 215.80
220   Controlled Substances Offenses .... 220.00 - 220.78
222   Cannabis .... 222.00 - 222.65
225   Gambling Offenses .... 225.00 - 225.95
230   Prostitution Offenses .... 230.00 - 230.40
235   Obscenity and Related Offenses .... 235.00 - 235.24
240   Offenses Against Public Order .... 240.00 - 240.77
241   Harassment of Rent Regulated Tenants ...... 241.00 - 241.05
242   Offenses Against Service Animals and Handlers . 242.00 - 242.15
245   Offenses Against Public Sensibilities .... 245.00 - 245.15
250   Offenses Against the Right to Privacy .... 250.00 - 250.65
255   Offenses Affecting the Marital Relationship .... 255.00 - 255.30
260   Offenses Relating to Children, Disabled
         Persons and Vulnerable Elderly Persons ..... 260.00 - 260.35
263   Sexual Performance by a Child .... 263.00 - 263.30
265   Firearms and Other Dangerous Weapons .... 265.00 - 265.55
270   Other Offenses Relating to Public Safety .... 270.00 - 270.35
275   Offenses Relating to Unauthorized Recording ... 275.00 - 275.45
400   Licensing and Other Provisions
         Relating to Firearms .... 400.00 - 400.20
405   Licensing and Other Provisions Relating
         to Fireworks .... 405.00 - 405.18
410   Seizure and Forfeiture of Equipment Used in
         Promoting Pornography 410.00
415   Seizure and Forfeiture of Vehicles, Vessels
         and Aircraft Used to Transport or
         Conceal Gambling Records 415.00
420   Seizure and Destruction of Unauthorized Recordings
         of Sound and Forfeiture of Equipment Used
         in the Production Thereof .... 420.00 - 420.05
450   Disposal of Stolen Property 450.10
460   Enterprise Corruption .... 460.00 - 460.80
470   Money Laundering .... 470.00 - 470.25
480   Criminal Forfeiture - Felony Controlled
         Substance Offenses .... 480.00 - 480.35
485   Hate Crimes .... 485.00 - 485.10
490   Terrorism .... 490.00 - 490.70
496   Corrupting the Government .... 496.01 - 496.07
500   Laws Repealed; Time of Taking Effect .... 500.05 - 500.10

PART ONE - GENERAL PROVISIONS

TITLE A - GENERAL PURPOSES, RULES OF CONSTRUCTION AND DEFINITIONS

ARTICLE 1. GENERAL PURPOSES

Section
1.00 Short title.
1.05 General purposes.

§1.00 Short title.
This chapter shall be known as the "Penal Law."

§1.05 General purposes.
The general purposes of the provisions of this chapter are:
1. To proscribe conduct which unjustifiably and inexcusably causes or threatens substantial harm to individual or public interests;
2. To give fair warning of the nature of the conduct proscribed and of the sentences authorized upon conviction;
3. To define the act or omission and the accompanying mental state which constitute each offense;
4. To differentiate on reasonable grounds between serious and minor offenses and to prescribe proportionate penalties therefor;
5. To provide for an appropriate public response to particular offenses, including consideration of the consequences of the offense for the victim, including the victim's family, and the community; and
6. To insure the public safety by preventing the commission of offenses through the deterrent influence of the sentences authorized, the rehabilitation of those convicted, the promotion of their successful and productive reentry and reintegration into society, and their confinement when required in the interests of public protection.

ARTICLE 5 - GENERAL RULES OF CONSTRUCTION AND APPLICATION

Section
5.00 Penal law not strictly construed.
5.05 Application of chapter to offenses committed before and after enactment.
5.10 Other limitations on applicability of this chapter.

§5.00 Penal law not strictly construed.
The general rule that a penal statute is to be strictly construed does not apply to this chapter, but the provisions herein must be construed according to the fair import of their terms to promote justice and effect the objects of the law.

§5.05 Application of chapter to offenses committed before and after enactment.
1. The provisions of this chapter shall govern the construction of and punishment for any offense defined in this chapter and committed after

the effective date hereof, as well as the construction and application of any defense to a prosecution for such an offense.

2. Unless otherwise expressly provided, or unless the context otherwise requires, the provisions of this chapter shall govern the construction of and punishment for any offense defined outside of this chapter and committed after the effective date thereof, as well as the construction and application of any defense to a prosecution for such an offense.

3. The provisions of this chapter do not apply to or govern the construction of and punishment for any offense committed prior to the effective date of this chapter, or the construction and application of any defense to a prosecution for such an offense. Such an offense must be construed and punished according to the provisions of law existing at the time of the commission thereof in the same manner as if this chapter had not been enacted.

§5.10 Other limitations on applicability of this chapter.

1. Except as otherwise provided, the procedure governing the accusation, prosecution, conviction and punishment of offenders and offenses is not regulated by this chapter but by the criminal procedure law.

2. This chapter does not affect any power conferred by law upon any court-martial or other military authority or officer to prosecute and punish conduct and offenders violating military codes or laws.

3. This chapter does not bar, suspend, or otherwise affect any right or liability to damages, penalty, forfeiture or other remedy authorized by law to be recovered or enforced in a civil action, regardless of whether the conduct involved in such civil action constitutes an offense defined in this chapter.

4. Sections 120.45, 120.50, 120.55, 120.60 and 240.25, subdivisions two and three of section 240.26, and sections 240.70 and 240.71 of this chapter (a) do not apply to conduct which is otherwise lawful under the provisions of the National Labor Relations Act as amended, the National Railway Labor Act as amended, or the Federal Employment Labor Management Act as amended, and (b) do not bar any conduct, including, but not limited to, peaceful picketing or other peaceful demonstration, protected from legal prohibition by the federal and state constitutions.

ARTICLE 10 - DEFINITIONS

Section
10.00   Definitions of terms of general use in this chapter.

§10.00 Definitions of terms of general use in this chapter.

Except where different meanings are expressly specified in subsequent provisions of this chapter, the following terms have the following meanings:

1. "Offense" means conduct for which a sentence to a term of imprisonment or to a fine is provided by any law of this state or

by any law, local law or ordinance of a political subdivision of this state, or by any order, rule or regulation of any governmental instrumentality authorized by law to adopt the same.

2. "Traffic infraction" means any offense defined as "traffic infraction" by section one hundred fifty-five of the vehicle and traffic law.

3. "Violation" means an offense, other than a "traffic infraction, " for which a sentence to a term of imprisonment in excess of fifteen days cannot be imposed.

4. "Misdemeanor" means an offense, other than a "traffic infraction, " for which a sentence to a term of imprisonment in excess of fifteen days may be imposed, but for which a sentence to a term of imprisonment in excess of one year cannot be imposed.

5. "Felony" means an offense for which a sentence to a term of imprisonment in excess of one year may be imposed.

6. "Crime" means a misdemeanor or a felony.

7. "Person" means a human being, and where appropriate, a public or private corporation, an unincorporated association, a partnership, a government or a governmental instrumentality.

8. "Possess" means to have physical possession or otherwise to exercise dominion or control over tangible property.

9. "Physical injury" means impairment of physical condition or substantial pain.

10. "Serious physical injury" means physical injury which creates a substantial risk of death, or which causes death or serious and protracted disfigurement, protracted impairment of health or protracted loss or impairment of the function of any bodily organ.

11. "Deadly physical force" means physical force which, under the circumstances in which it is used, is readily capable of causing death or other serious physical injury.

12. "Deadly weapon" means any loaded weapon from which a shot, readily capable of producing death or other serious physical injury, may be discharged, or a switchblade knife, pilum ballistic knife, metal knuckle knife, dagger, billy, blackjack, plastic knuckles, or metal knuckles.   *(Eff.5/30/19,Ch.34,L.2019)*

13. "Dangerous instrument" means any instrument, article or substance, including a "vehicle" as that term is defined in this section, which, under the circumstances in which it is used, attempted to be used or threatened to be used, is readily capable of causing death or other serious physical injury.

14. "Vehicle" means a "motor vehicle", "trailer" or "semi-trailer," as defined in the vehicle and traffic law, any snowmobile as defined in the parks and recreation law, any aircraft, or any vessel equipped for propulsion by mechanical means or by sail.

15. "Public servant" means (a) any public officer or employee of the state or of any political subdivision thereof or of any governmental instrumentality within the state, or (b) any person exercising the functions of any such public officer or employee. The term public servant includes a person who has been elected or designated to become a public servant.

16. "Juror" means any person who is a member of any jury, including a grand jury, impaneled by any court in this state or by any public servant authorized by law to impanel a jury. The term juror also includes a person who has been drawn or summoned to attend as a prospective juror.

17. "Benefit" means any gain or advantage to the beneficiary and includes any gain or advantage to a third person pursuant to the desire or consent of the beneficiary.

18. "Juvenile offender" means (1) a person thirteen years old who is criminally responsible for acts constituting murder in the second degree as defined in subdivisions one and two of section 125.25 of this chapter or such conduct as a sexually motivated felony, where authorized pursuant to section 130.91 of the penal law; and

(2) a person fourteen or fifteen years old who is criminally responsible for acts constituting the crimes defined in subdivisions one and two of section 125.25 (murder in the second degree) and in subdivision three of such section provided that the underlying crime for the murder charge is one for which such person is criminally responsible; section 135.25 (kidnapping in the first degree); 150.20 (arson in the first degree); subdivisions one and two of section 120.10 (assault in the first degree); 125.20 (manslaughter in the first degree); subdivisions one and two of section 130.35 (rape in the first degree); subdivisions one and two of section 130.50 (criminal sexual act in the first degree); 130.70 (aggravated sexual abuse in the first degree); 140.30 (burglary in the first degree); subdivision one of section 140.25 (burglary in the second degree); 150.15 (arson in the second degree); 160.15 (robbery in the first degree); subdivision two of section 160.10 (robbery in the second degree) of this chapter; or section 265.03 of this chapter, where such machine gun or such firearm is possessed on school grounds, as that phrase is defined in subdivision fourteen of section 220.00 of this chapter; or defined in this chapter as an attempt to commit murder in the second degree or kidnapping in the first degree, or such conduct as a sexually motivated felony, where authorized pursuant to section 130.91 of the penal law.

19. For the purposes of section 260.30 and 120.01 of this chapter the term "child day care provider" shall be defined as provided for in section three hundred ninety of the social services law.

20. For purposes of sections 120.13, 120.18, 125.11, 125.21 and 125.22 of this chapter, the term "peace officer" means a peace officer as defined in subdivision one, two, three, four, six, twelve, thirteen, fifteen, sixteen, seventeen, eighteen, nineteen, twenty, twenty-one, twenty-three, twenty-three-a, twenty-four, twenty-five, twenty-six, twenty-eight, twenty-nine, thirty, thirty-one, thirty-two, thirty-four, thirty-five, thirty-six, forty-three, forty-five, forty-seven, forty-eight, forty-nine, fifty-one, fifty-two, fifty-eight, sixty-one, as added by chapter two hundred fifty-seven of the laws of nineteen hundred ninety-two, sixty-one, as added by chapter three hundred twenty-one of the laws of nineteen hundred ninety-two, sixty-two, as added by chapter two hundred four of the laws of nineteen hundred ninety-three, sixty-two, as added by chapter six hundred eighty-seven of the laws of nineteen hundred ninety-three, sixty-three, as amended by chapter six hundred thirty-eight of the laws of two thousand three, sixty-four,

sixty-five, sixty-eight, as added by chapter one hundred sixty-eight of the laws of two thousand, sixty-eight, as added by chapter three hundred eighty-one of the laws of two thousand, seventy, seventy-one, seventy-four, as added by chapter five hundred forty-eight of the laws of two thousand one, seventy-five, as added by chapter three hundred twenty-one of the laws of two thousand two, seventy-five, as added by chapter six hundred twenty-three of the laws of two thousand two, seventy-seven, as added by chapter three hundred sixty-seven of the laws of two thousand four, seventy-eight or seventy-nine, as added by chapter two hundred forty-one of the laws of two thousand four, of section 2.10 of the criminal procedure law, as well as any federal law enforcement officer defined in section 2.15 of the criminal procedure law.

21. "Drug trafficking felony" means any of the following offenses defined in article two hundred twenty of this chapter: violation of use of a child to commit a controlled substance offense as defined in section 220.28; criminal sale of a controlled substance in the fourth degree as defined in section 220.34; criminal sale of a controlled substance in the third degree as defined in section 220.39; criminal sale of a controlled substance in the second degree as defined in section 220.41; criminal sale of a controlled substance in the first degree as defined in section 220.43; criminal sale of a controlled substance in or near school grounds as defined in section 220.44; unlawful manufacture of methamphetamine in the second degree as defined in section 220.74; unlawful manufacture of methamphetamine in the first degree as defined in section 220.75; or operating as a major trafficker as defined in section 220.77.

TITLE B - PRINCIPLES OF CRIMINAL LIABILITY
ARTICLE 15 - CULPABILITY

Section

15.00   Culpability; definitions of terms.
15.05   Culpability; definitions of culpable mental states.
15.10   Requirements for criminal liability in general and for offenses of strict liability and mental culpability.
15.15   Construction of statutes with respect to culpability requirements.
15.20   Effect of ignorance or mistake upon liability.
15.25   Effect of intoxication upon liability.

§15.00 Culpability; definitions of terms.

The following definitions are applicable to this chapter:

1. "Act" means a bodily movement.

2. "Voluntary act" means a bodily movement performed consciously as a result of effort or determination, and includes the possession of property if the actor was aware of his physical possession or control thereof for a sufficient period to have been able to terminate it.

This page intentionally left blank.

3. "Omission" means a failure to perform an act as to which a duty of performance is imposed by law.

4. "Conduct" means an act or omission and its accompanying mental state.

5. "To act" means either to perform an act or to omit to perform an act.

6. "Culpable mental state" means "intentionally" or "knowingly" or "recklessly" or with "criminal negligence," as these terms are defined in section 15.05.

§15.05 Culpability; definitions of culpable mental states.

The following definitions are applicable to this chapter:

1. "Intentionally." A person acts intentionally with respect to a result or to conduct described by a statute defining an offense when his conscious objective is to cause such result or to engage in such conduct.

2. "Knowingly." A person acts knowingly with respect to conduct or to a circumstance described by a statute defining an offense when he is aware that his conduct is of such nature or that such circumstance exists.

3. "Recklessly." A person acts recklessly with respect to a result or to a circumstance described by a statute defining an offense when he is aware of and consciously disregards a substantial and unjustifiable risk that such result will occur or that such circumstance exists. The risk must be of such nature and degree that disregard thereof constitutes a gross deviation from the standard of conduct that a reasonable person would observe in the situation. A person who creates such a risk but is unaware thereof solely by reason of voluntary intoxication also acts recklessly with respect thereto.

4. "Criminal negligence." A person acts with criminal negligence with respect to a result or to a circumstance described by a statute defining an offense when he fails to perceive a substantial and unjustifiable risk that such result will occur or that such circumstance exists. The risk must be of such nature and degree that the failure to perceive it constitutes a gross deviation from the standard of care that a reasonable person would observe in the situation.

§15.10 Requirements for criminal liability in general and for offenses of strict liability and mental culpability.

The minimal requirement for criminal liability is the performance by a person of conduct which includes a voluntary act or the omission to perform an act which he is physically capable of performing. If such conduct is all that is required for commission of a particular offense, or if an offense or some material element thereof does not require a culpable mental state on the part of the actor, such offense is one of "strict liability." If a culpable mental state on the part of the actor is required with respect to every material element of an offense, such offense is one of "mental culpability."

§15.15 Construction of statutes with respect to culpability requirements.

1. When the commission of an offense defined in this chapter, or some element of an offense, requires a particular culpable mental state, such mental state is ordinarily designated in the statute defining the offense by use of the terms "intentionally," "knowingly," "recklessly" or "criminal negligence," or by use of terms, such as "with intent to defraud" and "knowing it to be false," describing a specific kind of intent or knowledge. When one and only one of such terms appears in a statute defining an offense, it is presumed to apply to every element of the offense unless an intent to limit its application clearly appears.

2. Although no culpable mental state is expressly designated in a statute defining an offense, a culpable mental state may nevertheless be required for the commission of such offense, or with respect to some or all of the material elements thereof, if the proscribed conduct necessarily involves such culpable mental state. A statute defining a crime, unless clearly indicating a legislative intent to impose strict liability, should be construed as defining a crime of mental culpability. This subdivision applies to offenses defined both in and outside this chapter.

§15.20 Effect of ignorance or mistake upon liability.

1. A person is not relieved of criminal liability for conduct because he engages in such conduct under a mistaken belief of fact, unless:

    (a) Such factual mistake negatives the culpable mental state required for the commission of an offense; or

    (b) The statute defining the offense or a statute related thereto expressly provides that such factual mistake constitutes a defense or exemption; or

    (c) Such factual mistake is of a kind that supports a defense of justification as defined in article thirty-five of this chapter.

2. A person is not relieved of criminal liability for conduct because he engages in such conduct under a mistaken belief that it does not, as a matter of law, constitute an offense, unless such mistaken belief is founded upon an official statement of the law contained in (a) a statute or other enactment, or (b) an administrative order or grant of permission, or (c) a judicial decision of a state or federal court, or (d) an interpretation of the statute or law relating to the offense, officially made or issued by a public servant, agency or body legally charged or empowered with the responsibility or privilege of administering, enforcing or interpreting such statute or law.

3. Notwithstanding the use of the term "knowingly" in any provision of this chapter defining an offense in which the age of a child is an element thereof, knowledge by the defendant of the age of such child is not an element of any such offense and it is not, unless expressly so provided, a defense to a prosecution

therefor that the defendant did not know the age of the child or believed such age to be the same as or greater than that specified in the statute.

4. Notwithstanding the use of the term "knowingly" in any provision of this chapter defining an offense in which the aggregate weight of a controlled substance or marihuana is an element, knowledge by the defendant of the aggregate weight of such controlled substance or marihuana is not an element of any such offense and it is not, unless expressly so provided, a defense to a prosecution therefor that the defendant did not know the aggregate weight of the controlled substance or marihuana.

§15.25 Effect of intoxication upon liability.

Intoxication is not, as such, a defense to a criminal charge; but in any prosecution for an offense, evidence of intoxication of the defendant may be offered by the defendant whenever it is relevant to negative an element of the crime charged.

ARTICLE 20 - PARTIES TO OFFENSES AND LIABILITY THROUGH ACCESSORIAL CONDUCT

Section
20.00   Criminal liability for conduct of another.
20.05   Criminal liability for conduct of another; no defense.
20.10   Criminal liability for conduct of another; exemption.
20.15   Convictions for different degrees of offense.
20.20   Criminal liability of corporations.
20.25   Criminal liability of an individual for corporate conduct.

§20.00 Criminal liability for conduct of another.

When one person engages in conduct which constitutes an offense, another person is criminally liable for such conduct when, acting with the mental culpability required for the commission thereof, he solicits, requests, commands, importunes, or intentionally aids such person to engage in such conduct.

§20.05 Criminal liability for conduct of another; no defense.

In any prosecution for an offense in which the criminal liability of the defendant is based upon the conduct of another person pursuant to section 20.00, it is no defense that:

1. Such other person is not guilty of the offense in question owing to criminal irresponsibility or other legal incapacity or exemption, or to unawareness of the criminal nature of the conduct in question or of the defendant's criminal purpose or to other factors precluding the mental state required for the commission of the offense in question; or

2. Such other person has not been prosecuted for or convicted of any offense based upon the conduct in question, or has previously been acquitted thereof, or has legal immunity from prosecution therefor; or

3. The offense in question, as defined, can be committed only by a particular class or classes of persons, and the defendant, not belonging to such class or classes, is for that reason legally incapable of committing the offense in an individual capacity.

§20.10 Criminal liability for conduct of another; exemption.

Notwithstanding the provisions of sections 20.00 and 20.05, a person is not criminally liable for conduct of another person constituting an offense when his own conduct, though causing or aiding the commission of such offense, is of a kind that is necessarily incidental thereto. If such conduct constitutes a related but separate offense upon the part of the actor, he is liable for that offense only and not for the conduct or offense committed by the other person.

§20.15 Convictions for different degrees of offense.

Except as otherwise expressly provided in this chapter, when, pursuant to section 20.00, two or more persons are criminally liable for an offense which is divided into degrees, each person is guilty of such degree as is compatible with his own culpable mental state and with his own accountability for an aggravating fact or circumstance.

§20.20 Criminal liability of corporations.

1. As used in this section:
    (a) "Agent" means any director, officer or employee of a corporation, or any other person who is authorized to act in behalf of the corporation.
    (b) "High managerial agent" means an officer of a corporation or any other agent in a position of comparable authority with respect to the formulation of corporate policy or the supervision in a managerial capacity of subordinate employees.
2. A corporation is guilty of an offense when:
    (a) The conduct constituting the offense consists of an omission to discharge a specific duty of affirmative performance imposed on corporations by law; or
    (b) The conduct constituting the offense is engaged in, authorized, solicited, requested, commanded, or recklessly tolerated by the board of directors or by a high managerial agent acting within the scope of his employment and in behalf of the corporation; or
    (c) The conduct constituting the offense is engaged in by an agent of the corporation while acting within the scope of his employment and in behalf of the corporation, and the offense is (i) a misdemeanor or a violation, (ii) one defined by a statute which clearly indicates a legislative intent to impose such criminal liability on a corporation, or (iii) any offense set forth in title twenty-seven of article seventy-one of the environmental conservation law.

§20.25 Criminal liability of an individual for corporate conduct.

A person is criminally liable for conduct constituting an offense which he performs or causes to be performed in the name of or in behalf of a corporation to the same extent as if such conduct were performed in his own name or behalf.

TITLE C - DEFENSES
ARTICLE 25 - DEFENSES IN GENERAL

Section
25.00   Defenses; burden of proof.

§25.00 Defenses; burden of proof.

1. When a "defense," other than an "affirmative defense," defined by statute is raised at a trial, the people have the burden of disproving such defense beyond a reasonable doubt.
2. When a defense declared by statute to be an "affirmative defense" is raised at a trial, the defendant has the burden of establishing such defense by a preponderance of the evidence.

ARTICLE 30 - DEFENSE OF INFANCY

Section
30.00   Infancy.

§30.00   Infancy.

1. Except as provided in subdivisions two and three of this section, a person less than seventeen, or commencing October first, two thousand nineteen, a person less than eighteen years old is not criminally responsible for conduct.

2. A person thirteen, fourteen or, fifteen years of age is criminally responsible for acts constituting murder in the second degree as defined in subdivisions one and two of section 125.25 and in subdivision three of such section provided that the underlying crime for the murder charge is one for which such person is criminally responsible or for such conduct as a sexually motivated felony, where authorized pursuant to section 130.91 of this chapter; and a person fourteen or, fifteen years of age is criminally responsible for acts constituting the crimes defined in section 135.25 (kidnapping in the first degree); 150.20 (arson in the first degree); subdivisions one and two of section 120.10 (assault in the first degree); 125.20 (manslaughter in the first degree); subdivisions one and two of section 130.35 (rape in the first degree); subdivisions one and two of section 130.50 (criminal sexual act in the first degree); 130.70 (aggravated sexual abuse in the first degree); 140.30 (burglary in the first degree); subdivision one of section 140.25 (burglary in the second degree); 150.15 (arson in the second degree); 160.15 (robbery in the first degree); subdivision two of section 160.10 (robbery in the second degree) of this chapter; or section 265.03 of this chapter, where such machine gun or such firearm is possessed on school grounds, as that phrase is defined in subdivision fourteen of section 220.00 of this chapter; or defined in this chapter as an attempt to commit murder in the second degree or kidnapping in the first degree, or for such conduct as a sexually motivated felony, where authorized pursuant to section 130.91 of this chapter.

3. A person sixteen or commencing October first, two thousand nineteen, seventeen years of age is criminally responsible for acts constituting:

(a) a felony, as defined in subdivision five of section 10.00 of this chapter;

(b) a traffic infraction, as defined in subdivision two of section 10.00 of this chapter;

(c) a violation, as defined in subdivision three of section 10.00 of this chapter;

(d) a misdemeanor as defined in subdivision four of section 10.00 of this chapter, but only when the charge for such misdemeanor is:

(i) accompanied by a felony charge that is shown to have been committed as a part of the same criminal transaction, as defined in subdivision two of section 40.10 of the criminal procedure law;

(ii) results from reduction or dismissal in satisfaction of a charge for a felony offense, in accordance with a plea of guilty pursuant to subdivision four of section 220.10 of the criminal procedure law, unless the proceeding is removed to the family court pursuant to paragraph (g-1) of subdivision five of section 220.10 of the criminal procedure law; or   *(Eff.12/29/21,Ch.809,L.2021)*

(iii) a misdemeanor defined in the vehicle and traffic law.

4. In any prosecution for an offense, lack of criminal responsibility by reason of infancy, as defined in this section, is a defense.

ARTICLE 35 - DEFENSE OF JUSTIFICATION

Section
35.00   Justification; a defense.
35.05   Justification; generally.
35.10   Justification; use of physical force generally.
35.15   Justification; use of physical force in defense of a person.
35.20   Justification; use of physical force in defense of premises and in defense of a person in the course of burglary.
35.25   Justification; use of physical force to prevent or terminate larceny or criminal mischief.
35.27   Justification; use of physical force in resisting arrest prohibited.
35.30   Justification; use of physical force in making an arrest or in preventing an escape.

§35.00 Justification; a defense.

In any prosecution for an offense, justification, as defined in sections 35.05 through 35.30, is a defense.

§35.05 Justification; generally.

Unless otherwise limited by the ensuing provisions of this article defining justifiable use of physical force, conduct which would otherwise constitute an offense is justifiable and not criminal when:

1. Such conduct is required or authorized by law or by a judicial decree, or is performed by a public servant in the reasonable exercise of his official powers, duties or functions; or

2. Such conduct is necessary as an emergency measure to avoid an imminent public or private injury which is about to occur by reason of a situation occasioned or developed through no fault of the actor, and which is of such gravity that, according to ordinary standards of intelligence and morality, the desirability and urgency of avoiding such injury clearly outweigh the desirability of avoiding the injury sought to be prevented by the statute defining the offense in issue. The necessity and justifiability of such conduct may not rest upon considerations pertaining only to the morality and advisability of the statute, either in its general application or with respect to its application to a particular class of cases arising thereunder. Whenever evidence relating to the defense of justification under this subdivision is offered by the defendant, the court shall rule as a matter of law whether the claimed facts and circumstances would, if established, constitute a defense.

§35.10 Justification; use of physical force generally.

The use of physical force upon another person which would otherwise constitute an offense is justifiable and not criminal under any of the following circumstances:

1. A parent, guardian or other person entrusted with the care and supervision of a person under the age of twenty-one or an incompetent person, and a teacher or other person entrusted with the care and supervision of a person under the age of twenty-one for a special purpose, may use physical force, but not deadly physical force, upon such person when and to the extent that he reasonably believes it necessary to maintain discipline or to promote the welfare of such person.

This page intentionally left blank.

2. A warden or other authorized official of a jail, prison or correctional institution may, in order to maintain order and discipline, use such physical force as is authorized by the correction law.

3. A person responsible for the maintenance of order in a common carrier of passengers, or a person acting under his direction, may use physical force when and to the extent that he reasonably believes it necessary to maintain order, but he may use deadly physical force only when he reasonably believes it necessary to prevent death or serious physical injury.

4. A person acting under a reasonable belief that another person is about to commit suicide or to inflict serious physical injury upon himself may use physical force upon such person to the extent that he reasonably believes it necessary to thwart such result.

5. A duly licensed physician, or a person acting under a physician's direction, may use physical force for the purpose of administering a recognized form of treatment which he or she reasonably believes to be adapted to promoting the physical or mental health of the patient if (a) the treatment is administered with the consent of the patient or, if the patient is under the age of eighteen years or an incompetent person, with the consent of the parent, guardian or other person entrusted with the patient's care and supervision, or (b) the treatment is administered in an emergency when the physician reasonably believes that no one competent to consent can be consulted and that a reasonable person, wishing to safeguard the welfare of the patient, would consent.

6. A person may, pursuant to the ensuing provisions of this article, use physical force upon another person in self-defense or defense of a third person, or in defense of premises, or in order to prevent larceny of or criminal mischief to property, or in order to effect an arrest or prevent an escape from custody. Whenever a person is authorized by any such provision to use deadly physical force in any given circumstance, nothing contained in any other such provision may be deemed to negate or qualify such authorization.

§35.15 Justification; use of physical force in defense of a person.

1. A person may, subject to the provisions of subdivision two, use physical force upon another person when and to the extent he or she reasonably believes such to be necessary to defend himself, herself or a third person from what he or she reasonably believes to be the use or imminent use of unlawful physical force by such other person, unless:

(a) The latter's conduct was provoked by the actor with intent to cause physical injury to another person; or

(b) The actor was the initial aggressor; except that in such case the use of physical force is nevertheless justifiable if the actor has withdrawn from the encounter and effectively communicated such withdrawal to such other person but the latter persists in continuing the incident by the use or threatened imminent use of unlawful physical force; or

(c) The physical force involved is the product of a combat by agreement not specifically authorized by law.

2. A person may not use deadly physical force upon another person under circumstances specified in subdivision one unless:

(a) The actor reasonably believes that such other person is using or about to use deadly physical force. Even in such case, however, the actor may not use deadly physical force if he or she knows that with complete personal safety, to oneself and others he or she may avoid the necessity of so doing by retreating; except that the actor is under no duty to retreat if he or she is:

(i) in his or her dwelling and not the initial aggressor; or

(ii) a police officer or peace officer or a person assisting a police officer or a peace officer at the latter's direction, acting pursuant to section 35.30; or

(b) He or she reasonably believes that such other person is committing or attempting to commit a kidnapping, forcible rape, forcible criminal sexual act or robbery; or

(c) He or she reasonably believes that such other person is committing or attempting to commit a burglary, and the circumstances are such that the use of deadly physical force is authorized by subdivision three of section 35.20.

§35.20   Justification; use of physical force in defense of premises and in defense of a person in the course of burglary.

1. Any person may use physical force upon another person when he or she reasonably believes such to be necessary to prevent or terminate what he or she reasonably believes to be the commission or attempted commission by such other person of a crime involving damage to premises. Such person may use any degree of physical force, other than deadly physical force, which he or she reasonably believes to be necessary for such purpose, and may use deadly physical force if he or she reasonably believes such to be necessary to prevent or terminate the commission or attempted commission of arson.

2. A person in possession or control of any premises, or a person licensed or privileged to be thereon or therein, may use physical force upon another person when he or she reasonably believes such to be necessary to prevent or terminate what he or she reasonably believes to be the commission or attempted commission by such other person of a criminal trespass upon such premises. Such person may use any degree of physical force, other than deadly physical force, which he or she reasonably believes to be necessary for such purpose, and may use deadly physical force in order to prevent or terminate the commission or attempted commission of arson, as prescribed in subdivision one, or in the course of a burglary or attempted burglary, as prescribed in subdivision three.

3. A person in possession or control of, or licensed or privileged to be in, a dwelling or an occupied building, who reasonably believes that another person is committing or attempting to commit a burglary of such dwelling or building, may use deadly physical force upon such other person when he or she reasonably believes such to be necessary to prevent or terminate the commission or attempted commission of such burglary.

4. As used in this section, the following terms have the following meanings:

(a) The terms "premises," "building" and "dwelling" have the meanings prescribed in section 140.00;

(b) Persons "licensed or privileged" to be in buildings or upon other premises include, but are not limited to:

(i) police officers or peace officers acting in the performance of their duties; and

(ii) security personnel or employees of nuclear powered electric generating facilities located within the state who are employed as part of any security plan approved by the federal operating license agencies acting in the performance of their duties at such generating facilities. For purposes of this subparagraph, the term "nuclear powered electric generating facility" shall mean a facility that generates electricity using nuclear power for sale, directly or indirectly, to the public, including the land upon which the facility is located and the safety and security zones as defined under federal regulations.

§35.25 Justification; use of physical force to prevent or terminate larceny or criminal mischief.

A person may use physical force, other than deadly physical force, upon another person when and to the extent that he or she reasonably believes such to be necessary to prevent or terminate what he or she reasonably believes to be the commission or attempted commission by such other person of larceny or of criminal mischief with respect to property other than premises.

§35.27 Justification; use of physical force in resisting arrest prohibited.

A person may not use physical force to resist an arrest, whether authorized or unauthorized, which is being effected or attempted by a police officer or peace officer when it would reasonably appear that the latter is a police officer or peace officer.

§35.30 Justification; use of physical force in making an arrest or in preventing an escape.

1. A police officer or a peace officer, in the course of effecting or attempting to effect an arrest, or of preventing or attempting to prevent the escape from custody, of a person whom he or she reasonably believes to have committed an offense, may use physical force when and to the extent he or she reasonably believes such to be necessary to effect

the arrest, or to prevent the escape from custody, or in self-defense or to defend a third person from what he or she reasonably believes to be the use or imminent use of physical force; except that deadly physical force may be used for such purposes only when he or she reasonably believes that:

(a) The offense committed by such person was:

(i) a felony or an attempt to commit a felony involving the use or attempted use or threatened imminent use of physical force against a person; or

(ii) kidnapping, arson, escape in the first degree, burglary in the first degree or any attempt to commit such a crime; or

(b) The offense committed or attempted by such person was a felony and that, in the course of resisting arrest therefor or attempting to escape from custody, such person is armed with a firearm or deadly weapon; or

(c) Regardless of the particular offense which is the subject of the arrest or attempted escape, the use of deadly physical force is necessary to defend the police officer or peace officer or another person from what the officer reasonably believes to be the use or imminent use of deadly physical force.

2. The fact that a police officer or a peace officer is justified in using deadly physical force under circumstances prescribed in paragraphs (a) and (b) of subdivision one does not constitute justification for reckless conduct by such police officer or peace officer amounting to an offense against or with respect to innocent persons whom he or she is not seeking to arrest or retain in custody.

3. A person who has been directed by a police officer or a peace officer to assist such police officer or peace officer to effect an arrest or to prevent an escape from custody may use physical force, other than deadly physical force, when and to the extent that he or she reasonably believes such to be necessary to carry out such police officer's or peace officer's direction, unless he or she knows that the arrest or prospective arrest is not or was not authorized and may use deadly physical force under such circumstances when:

(a) He or she reasonably believes such to be necessary for self-defense or to defend a third person from what he or she reasonably believes to be the use or imminent use of deadly physical force; or

(b) He or she is directed or authorized by such police officer or peace officer to use deadly physical force unless he or she knows that the police officer or peace officer is not authorized to use deadly physical force under the circumstances.

4. A private person acting on his or her own account may use physical force, other than deadly physical force, upon another person when and to the extent that he or she reasonably believes such to be necessary to effect an arrest or to prevent the escape from custody of a person whom he or she reasonably believes to have committed an offense and who in fact has committed such offense; and may use deadly physical force for such purpose when he or she reasonably believes such to be necessary to:

(a) Defend himself, herself or a third person from what he or she reasonably believes to be the use or imminent use of deadly physical force; or

(b) Effect the arrest of a person who has committed murder, manslaughter in the first degree, robbery, forcible rape or forcible criminal sexual act and who is in immediate flight therefrom.

5. A guard, police officer or peace officer who is charged with the duty of guarding prisoners in a detention facility, as that term is defined in section 205.00, or while in transit to or from a detention facility, may use physical force when and to the extent that he or she reasonably believes such to be necessary to prevent the escape of a prisoner from a detention facility or from custody while in transit thereto or therefrom.

ARTICLE 40 - OTHER DEFENSES INVOLVING LACK OF CULPABILITY

Section
40.00   Duress.
40.05   Entrapment.
40.10   Renunciation.
40.15   Mental disease or defect.

§40.00 Duress.

1. In any prosecution for an offense, it is an affirmative defense that the defendant engaged in the proscribed conduct because he was coerced to do so by the use or threatened imminent use of unlawful physical force upon him or a third person, which force or threatened force a person of reasonable firmness in his situation would have been unable to resist.

2. The defense of duress as defined in subdivision one of this section is not available when a person intentionally or recklessly places himself in a situation in which it is probable that he will be subjected to duress.

§40.05 Entrapment.

In any prosecution for an offense, it is an affirmative defense that the defendant engaged in the proscribed conduct because he was induced or encouraged to do so by a public servant, or by a person acting in cooperation with a public servant, seeking to obtain evidence against him for purpose of criminal prosecution, and when the methods used to obtain such evidence were such as to create a substantial risk that the offense would be committed by a person not otherwise disposed to commit it. Inducement or encouragement to commit an offense means active inducement or encouragement. Conduct merely affording a person an opportunity to commit an offense does not constitute entrapment.

§40.10 Renunciation.

1. In any prosecution for an offense, other than an attempt to commit a crime, in which the defendant's guilt depends upon his criminal liability for the conduct of another person pursuant to section 20.00, it is an affirmative defense that, under circumstances manifesting a voluntary and complete renunciation of his criminal purpose, the defendant

withdrew from participation in such offense prior to the commission thereof and made a substantial effort to prevent the commission thereof.

2. In any prosecution for criminal facilitation pursuant to article one hundred fifteen, it is an affirmative defense that, prior to the commission of the felony which he facilitated, the defendant made a substantial effort to prevent the commission of such felony.

3. In any prosecution pursuant to section 110.00 for an attempt to commit a crime, it is an affirmative defense that, under circumstances manifesting a voluntary and complete renunciation of his criminal purpose, the defendant avoided the commission of the crime attempted by abandoning his criminal effort and, if mere abandonment was insufficient to accomplish such avoidance, by taking further and affirmative steps which prevented the commission thereof.

4. In any prosecution for criminal solicitation pursuant to article one hundred or for conspiracy pursuant to article one hundred five in which the crime solicited or the crime contemplated by the conspiracy was not in fact committed, it is an affirmative defense that, under circumstances manifesting a voluntary and complete renunciation of his criminal purpose, the defendant prevented the commission of such crime.

5. A renunciation is not "voluntary and complete" within the meaning of this section if it is motivated in whole or in part by (a) a belief that circumstances exist which increase the probability of detection or apprehension of the defendant or another participant in the criminal enterprise, or which render more difficult the accomplishment of the criminal purpose, or (b) a decision to postpone the criminal conduct until another time or to transfer the criminal effort to another victim or another but similar objective.

§40.15 Mental disease or defect.

In any prosecution for an offense, it is an affirmative defense that when the defendant engaged in the proscribed conduct, he lacked criminal responsibility by reason of mental disease or defect. Such lack of criminal responsibility means that at the time of such conduct, as a result of mental disease or defect, he lacked substantial capacity to know or appreciate either:

1. The nature and consequences of such conduct; or

2. That such conduct was wrong.

PART TWO - SENTENCES
TITLE E - SENTENCES
ARTICLE 55 - CLASSIFICATION AND
DESIGNATION OF OFFENSES

Section
55.00   Applicability of article.
55.05   Classifications of felonies and misdemeanors.
55.10   Designation of offenses.

§55.00 Applicability of article.

The provisions of this article govern the classification and designation of every offense, whether defined within or outside of this chapter.

§55.05 Classifications of felonies and misdemeanors.

1. Felonies. Felonies are classified, for the purpose of sentence, into five categories as follows:

(a) Class A felonies;

(b) Class B felonies

(c) Class C felonies;

(d) Class D felonies; and

(e) Class E felonies.

Class A felonies are subclassified, for the purpose of sentence, into two categories as follows: subclass I and subclass II, to be known as class A-I and class A-II felonies, respectively.

2. Misdemeanors. Misdemeanors are classified, for the purpose of sentence, into three categories as follows:

(a) Class A misdemeanors;

(b) Class B misdemeanors; and

(c) Unclassified misdemeanors.

§55.10 Designation of offenses.

1. Felonies.

(a) The particular classification or subclassification of each felony defined in this chapter is expressly designated in the section or article defining it.

(b) Any offense defined outside this chapter which is declared by law to be a felony without specification of the classification thereof, or for which a law outside this chapter provides a sentence to a term of imprisonment in excess of one year, shall be deemed a class E felony.

2. Misdemeanors.

(a) Each misdemeanor defined in this chapter is either a class A misdemeanor or a class B misdemeanor, as expressly designated in the section or article defining it.

(b) Any offense defined outside this chapter which is declared by law to be a misdemeanor without specification of the classification thereof or of the sentence therefor shall be deemed a class A misdemeanor.

(c) Except as provided in paragraph (b) of subdivision three, where an offense is defined outside this chapter and a sentence to a term of imprisonment in excess of fifteen days but not in excess of one year is provided in the law or ordinance defining it, such offense shall be deemed an unclassified misdemeanor.

3. Violations. Every violation defined in this chapter is expressly designated as such. Any offense defined outside this chapter which is not expressly designated a violation shall be deemed a violation if:

(a) Notwithstanding any other designation specified in the law or ordinance defining it, a sentence to a term of imprisonment which is not in excess of fifteen days as provided therein, or the only sentence provided therein is a fine; or

(b) A sentence to a term of imprisonment in excess of fifteen days is provided for such offense in a law or ordinance enacted prior to the effective date of this chapter but the offense was not a crime prior to that date.

4. Traffic infraction. Notwithstanding any other provision of this section, an offense which is defined as a "traffic infraction" shall not be deemed a violation or a misdemeanor by virtue of the sentence prescribed therefor.

ARTICLE 60 - AUTHORIZED DISPOSITIONS OF OFFENDERS

Section
60.00   Applicability of provisions.
60.01   Authorized dispositions; generally.
60.02   Authorized disposition; youthful offender.
60.04   Authorized disposition; controlled substances and marihuana felony offenses.
60.05   Authorized dispositions; other class A, B, certain C and D felonies and multiple felony offenders.
60.06   Authorized disposition; murder in the first degree offenders; aggravated murder offenders; certain murder in the second degree offenders; certain terrorism offenders; criminal possession of a chemical weapon or biological weapon offenders; criminal use of a chemical weapon or biological weapon offenders.
60.07   Authorized disposition; criminal attack on operators of for-hire vehicles.
60.08   Authorized dispositions; resentencing of certain controlled substance offenders.
60.09   Authorized dispositions; resentencing of certain persons convicted of specified controlled substance offenses.
60.10   Authorized disposition; juvenile offender.
60.10-a Authorized disposition; adolescent offender.
60.11   Authorized dispositions; criminal possession of a weapon in the fourth degree.
60.11-a Authorized dispositions; certain criminal possession of a weapon in the third degree offenders.
60.12   Authorized dispositions; alternative sentence; domestic violence cases.
60.13   Authorized dispositions; felony sex offenses.
60.20   Authorized dispositions; traffic infraction.
60.21   Authorized dispositions; driving while intoxicated or aggravated driving while intoxicated.
60.25   Authorized dispositions; corporation.
60.27   Restitution and reparation.
60.28   Authorized disposition; making graffiti and possession of graffiti instruments.
60.29   Authorized disposition; cemetery desecration.
60.30   Civil penalties.
60.35   Mandatory surcharge, sex offender registration fee, DNA databank fee, supplemental sex offender victim fee and crime victim assistance fee required in
60.36   Authorized dispositions; driving while intoxicated offenses.
60.37   Authorized disposition; certain offenses.

§60.00 Applicability of provisions.

1. The sentences prescribed by this article shall apply in the case of every offense, whether defined within or outside of this chapter.

2. The sole provision of this article that shall apply in the case of an offense committed by a juvenile offender is section 60.10 of this article and no other provisions of this article shall be deemed or construed to apply in any such case.

§60.01 Authorized dispositions; generally.

1. Applicability. Except as otherwise specified in this article when the court imposes sentence upon a person convicted of an offense, the court must impose a sentence prescribed by this section.

2. Revocable dispositions.

(a) The court may impose a revocable sentence as herein specified:

(i) the court, where authorized by article sixty-five, may sentence a person to a period of probation or to a period of conditional discharge as provided in that article; or

(ii) the court, where authorized by article eighty-five, may sentence a person to a term of intermittent imprisonment as provided in that article.

(b) A revocable sentence shall be deemed a tentative one to the extent that it may be altered or revoked in accordance with the provisions of the article under which it was imposed, but for all other purposes shall be deemed to be a final judgment of conviction.

(c) In any case where the court imposes a sentence of probation, conditional discharge, or a sentence of intermittent imprisonment, it may also impose a fine authorized by article eighty.

(d) In any case where the court imposes a sentence of imprisonment not in excess of sixty days, for a misdemeanor or not in excess of six months for a felony or in the case of a sentence of intermittent imprisonment not in excess of four months, it may also impose a sentence of probation or conditional discharge provided that the term of probation or conditional discharge together with the term of imprisonment shall not exceed the term of probation or conditional discharge authorized by article sixty-five of this chapter. The sentence of imprisonment shall be a condition of and run concurrently with the sentence of probation or conditional discharge.

3. Other dispositions. When a person is not sentenced as specified in subdivision two, or when a sentence specified in subdivision two is revoked, the sentence of the court must be as follows:

(a) A term of imprisonment; or

(b) A fine authorized by article eighty, provided, however, that when the conviction is of a class B felony or of any felony defined in article two hundred twenty, the sentence shall not consist solely of a fine; or

(c) Both imprisonment and a fine; or

(d) Where authorized by section 65.20, unconditional discharge as provided in that section; or

(e) Following revocation of a sentence of conditional discharge imposed pursuant to section 65.05 of this chapter or paragraph (d) of subdivision two of this section, probation as provided in section 65.00 of this chapter or to the sentence of imprisonment and probation as provided for in paragraph (d) of subdivision two of this section.

4. In any case where a person has been sentenced to a period of probation imposed pursuant to section 65.00 of this chapter, if the part of the sentence that provides for probation is revoked, the court must sentence such person to imprisonment or to the sentence of imprisonment and probation as provided for in paragraph (d) of subdivision two of this section.

§60.02 Authorized disposition; youthful offender.

When a person is to be sentenced upon a youthful offender finding, the court must impose a sentence as follows:

(1) If the sentence is to be imposed upon a youthful offender finding which has been substituted for a conviction of an offense other than a felony, the court must impose a sentence authorized for the offense for which the youthful offender finding was substituted, except that if the youthful offender finding was entered pursuant to paragraph (b) of subdivision one of section 720.20 of the criminal procedure law, the court must not impose a definite or intermittent sentence of imprisonment with a term of more than six months; or

(2) If the sentence is to be imposed upon a youthful offender finding which has been substituted for a conviction for any felony, the court must impose a sentence authorized to be imposed upon a person convicted of a class E felony provided, however, that the court must not impose a sentence of conditional discharge or unconditional discharge if the youthful offender finding was substituted for a conviction of a felony defined in article two hundred twenty of this chapter.

(3) *(Repealed, Eff.8/24/20,Ch.144,L.2020)*

(4) Notwithstanding any other provision of law in this section, if the sentence is to be imposed upon a youthful offender finding which has been substituted for a conviction of prostitution or loitering for the purposes of prostitution provided that the person does not stand charged with loitering for the purpose of patronizing a prostitute, and such offense occurred when the person was sixteen or seventeen years of age, the court must impose a sentence authorized to be imposed upon a person convicted of a violation as defined in subdivision three of section 10.00 of the penal law and where the court imposes a revocable sentence authorized for a violation may order any of the specialized services enumerated in title eight-A of article six of the social services law or other appropriate services made available to persons in need of supervision in accordance with article seven of the family court act.

§60.04 Authorized disposition; controlled substances and marihuana felony offenses.

1. Applicability. Notwithstanding the provisions of any law, this section shall govern the dispositions authorized when a person is to be sentenced upon a conviction of a felony offense defined in article two hundred twenty or two hundred twenty-one of this chapter or when a person is to be sentenced upon a conviction of such a felony as a multiple felony offender as defined in subdivision five of this section.

2. Class A felony. Every person convicted of a class A felony must be sentenced to imprisonment in accordance with section 70.71 of this title, unless such person is convicted of a class A-II felony and is sentenced to probation for life in accordance with section 65.00 of this title.

3. **Class B felonies.** Every person convicted of a class B felony must be sentenced to imprisonment in accordance with the applicable provisions of section 70.70 of this chapter, a definite sentence of imprisonment with a term of one year or less or probation in accordance with section 65.00 of this chapter provided, however, a person convicted of criminal sale of a controlled substance to a child as defined in section 220.48 of this chapter must be sentenced to a determinate sentence of imprisonment in accordance with the applicable provisions of section 70.70 of this chapter or to a sentence of probation in accordance with the opening paragraph of paragraph (b) of subdivision one of section 65.00 of this chapter.

4. **Alternative sentence.** Where a sentence of imprisonment or a sentence of probation as an alternative to imprisonment is not required to be imposed pursuant to subdivision two, three or five of this section, the court may impose any other sentence authorized by section 60.01 of this article, provided that when the court imposes a sentence of imprisonment, such sentence must be in accordance with section 70.70 of this title. Where the court imposes a sentence of imprisonment in accordance with this section, the court may also impose a fine authorized by article eighty of this title and in such case the sentence shall be both imprisonment and a fine.

5. **Multiple felony offender.** Where the court imposes a sentence pursuant to subdivision three of section 70.70 of this chapter upon a second felony drug offender, as defined in paragraph (b) of subdivision one of section 70.70 of this chapter, it must sentence such offender to imprisonment in accordance with the applicable provisions of section 70.70 of this chapter, a definite sentence of imprisonment with a term of one year or less, or probation in accordance with section 65.00 of this chapter, provided, however, that where the court imposes a sentence upon a class B second felony drug offender, it must sentence such offender to a determinate sentence of imprisonment in accordance with the applicable provisions of section 70.70 of this chapter or to a sentence of probation in accordance with the opening paragraph of paragraph (b) of subdivision one of section 65.00 of this chapter. When the court imposes sentence on a second felony drug offender pursuant to subdivision four of section 70.70 of this chapter, it must impose a determinate sentence of imprisonment in accordance with such subdivision.

6. **Substance abuse treatment.** When the court imposes a sentence of imprisonment which requires a commitment to the state department of corrections and community supervision upon a person who stands convicted of a controlled substance or marihuana offense, the court may, upon motion of the defendant in its discretion, issue an order directing that the department of corrections and community supervision enroll the defendant in the comprehensive alcohol and substance abuse treatment program in an alcohol and substance abuse correctional annex as defined in subdivision eighteen of section two of the correction law, provided that the defendant will satisfy the statutory eligibility criteria for participation in such program. Notwithstanding the foregoing provisions of this subdivision, any defendant to be enrolled in such program pursuant to this subdivision shall be governed by the same rules and regulations promulgated by the department of corrections and community supervision, including without limitation those rules and regulations establishing requirements for completion and those rules and

regulations governing discipline and removal from the program. No such period of court ordered corrections based drug abuse treatment pursuant to this subdivision shall be required to extend beyond the defendant's conditional release date.

7. a. Shock incarceration participation. When the court imposes a sentence of imprisonment which requires a commitment to the department of corrections and community supervision upon a person who stands convicted of a controlled substance or marihuana offense, upon motion of the defendant, the court may issue an order directing that the department of corrections and community supervision enroll the defendant in the shock incarceration program as defined in article twenty-six-A of the correction law, provided that the defendant is an eligible incarcerated individual, as described in subdivision one of section eight hundred sixty-five of the correction law. Notwithstanding the foregoing provisions of this subdivision, any defendant to be enrolled in such program pursuant to this subdivision shall be governed by the same rules and regulations promulgated by the department of corrections and community supervision, including without limitation those rules and regulations establishing requirements for completion and such rules and regulations governing discipline and removal from the program.

b. (i) In the event that an incarcerated individual designated by court order for enrollment in the shock incarceration program requires a degree of medical care or mental health care that cannot be provided at a shock incarceration facility, the department, in writing, shall notify the incarcerated individual, provide a proposal describing a proposed alternative-to-shock-incarceration program, and notify him or her that he or she may object in writing to placement in such alternative-to-shock-incarceration program. If the incarcerated individual objects in writing to placement in such alternative-to-shock-incarceration program, the department of corrections and community supervision shall notify the sentencing court, provide such proposal to the court, and arrange for the incarcerated individual's prompt appearance before the court. The court shall provide the proposal and notice of a court appearance to the people, the incarcerated individual and the appropriate defense attorney. After considering the proposal and any submissions by the parties, and after a reasonable opportunity for the people, the incarcerated individual and counsel to be heard, the court may modify its sentencing order accordingly, notwithstanding the provisions of section 430.10 of the criminal procedure law.

(ii) An incarcerated individual who successfully completes an alternative-to-shock-incarceration program within the department of corrections and community supervision shall be treated in the same manner as a person who has successfully completed the shock incarceration program, as set forth in subdivision four of section eight hundred sixty-seven of the correction law.   *(Eff.8/2/21,Ch.322,L.2021)*

§60.05 Authorized dispositions; other class A, B, certain C and D felonies and multiple felony offenders.

1. Applicability. Except as provided in section 60.04 of this article governing the authorized dispositions applicable to felony offenses

defined in article two hundred twenty or two hundred twenty-one of this chapter or in section 60.13 of this article governing the authorized dispositions applicable to felony sex offenses defined in paragraph (a) of subdivision one of section 70.80 of this title, this section shall govern the dispositions authorized when a person is to be sentenced upon a conviction of a class A felony, a class B felony or a class C, class D or class E felony specified herein, or when a person is to be sentenced upon a conviction of a felony as a multiple felony offender.

2. Class A felony. Except as provided in subdivisions three and four of section 70.06 of this chapter, every person convicted of a class A felony must be sentenced to imprisonment in accordance with section 70.00 of this title, unless such person is convicted of murder in the first degree and is sentenced in accordance with section 60.06 of this article.

3. Class B felony. Except as provided in subdivision six of this section, every person convicted of a class B violent felony offense as defined in subdivision one of section 70.02 of this title, must be sentenced to imprisonment in accordance with such section 70.02; and, except as provided in subdivision six of this section, every person convicted of any other class B felony must be sentenced to imprisonment in accordance with section 70.00 of this title.

4. Certain class C felonies. Except as provided in subdivision six, every person convicted of a class C violent felony offense as defined in subdivision one of section 70.02 of this title, must be sentenced to imprisonment in accordance with section 70.02 of this title; and, except as provided in subdivision six of this section, every person convicted of the class C felonies of: attempt to commit any of the class B felonies of bribery in the first degree as defined in section 200.04, bribe receiving in the first degree as defined in section 200.12, conspiracy in the second degree as defined in section 105.15 and criminal mischief in the first degree as defined in section 145.12; criminal usury in the first degree as defined in section 190.42, rewarding official misconduct in the first degree as defined in section 200.22, receiving reward for official misconduct in the first degree as defined in section 200.27, attempt to promote prostitution in the first degree as defined in section 230.32, promoting prostitution in the second degree as defined in section 230.30, arson in the third degree as defined in section 150.10 of this chapter, must be sentenced to imprisonment in accordance with section 70.00 of this title.

5. Certain class D felonies. Except as provided in subdivision six of this section, every person convicted of the class D felonies of assault in the second degree as defined in section 120.05, strangulation in the second degree as defined in section 121.12 or attempt to commit a class C felony as defined in section 230.30 of this chapter, must be sentenced in accordance with section 70.00 or 85.00 of this title.

6. Multiple felony offender. When the court imposes sentence upon a second violent felony offender, as defined in section 70.04, or a second felony offender, as defined in section 70.06, the court must impose a sentence of imprisonment in accordance with section 70.04 or 70.06, as the case may be, unless it imposes a sentence of imprisonment in accordance with section 70.08 or 70.10.

7. Fines. Where the court imposes a sentence of imprisonment in accordance with this section, the court also may impose a fine authorized by article eighty and in such case the sentence shall be both imprisonment and a fine.

8. Shock incarceration participation. (a) When the court imposes a determinate sentence of imprisonment pursuant to subdivision three of section 70.02 of this chapter or subdivision six of section 70.06 of this chapter upon a person who stands convicted either of burglary in the second degree as defined in subdivision two of section 140.25 of this chapter or robbery in the second degree as defined in subdivision one of section 160.10 of this chapter, or an attempt thereof, upon motion of the defendant, the court may issue an order directing that the department of corrections and community supervision enroll the defendant in the shock incarceration program as defined in article twenty-six-A of the correction law, provided that the defendant is an eligible inmate, as described in subdivision one of section eight hundred sixty-five of the correction law. Notwithstanding the foregoing provisions of this subdivision, any defendant to be enrolled in such program pursuant to this subdivision shall be governed by the same rules and regulations promulgated by the department of corrections and community supervision, including without limitation those rules and regulations establishing requirements for completion and such rules and regulations governing discipline and removal from the program.

(b) Paragraph (b) of subdivision seven of section 60.04 of this article shall apply in the event an inmate designated by court order for enrollment in the shock incarceration program requires a degree of medical care or mental health care that cannot be provided at a shock incarceration facility.   *(Eff.5/12/19,Ch.55,L.2019)*

§60.06 Authorized disposition; murder in the first degree offenders; aggravated murder offenders; certain murder in the second degree offenders; certain terrorism offenders; criminal possession of a chemical weapon or biological weapon offenders; criminal use of a chemical weapon or biological weapon offenders.

When a defendant is convicted of murder in the first degree as defined in section 125.27 of this chapter, the court shall, in accordance with the provisions of section 400.27 of the criminal procedure law, sentence the defendant to death, to life imprisonment without parole in accordance with subdivision five of section 70.00 of this title, or to a term of imprisonment for a class A-I felony other than a sentence of life imprisonment without parole, in accordance with subdivisions one through three of section 70.00 of this title. When a person is convicted of murder in the second degree as defined in subdivision five of section 125.25 of this chapter or of the crime of aggravated murder as defined in subdivision one of section 125.26 of this chapter, the court shall sentence the defendant to life imprisonment without parole in accordance with subdivision five of section 70.00 of this title. When a defendant is convicted of the crime of terrorism as defined in section 490.25 of this chapter, and the specified offense the defendant committed is a class A-I felony offense, or when a defendant is convicted of the crime of criminal possession of a chemical weapon or biological weapon in the first degree as defined in section 490.45 of this chapter, or when a defendant is convicted of the crime of criminal use of a chemical weapon or biological weapon in the first degree as defined in section 490.55 of this chapter, the court shall sentence the defendant to life imprisonment without parole in accordance with subdivision five of section 70.00 of this title; provided, however, that nothing in this section shall preclude or prevent a sentence of death when the defendant is also convicted of murder in the first degree as defined in section 125.27 of this chapter. When a defendant is convicted of aggravated murder as defined in subdivision two of section 125.26 of this chapter, the court shall sentence the defendant to life imprisonment without parole or to a term of imprisonment for a class A-I felony other than a sentence of life imprisonment without parole, in accordance with subdivisions one through three of section 70.00 of this title.

§60.07 Authorized disposition; criminal attack on operators of for-hire vehicles.

1. Notwithstanding any other provision of law to the contrary, when a court has found, pursuant to the provisions of section 200.61 of the criminal procedure law, both that a person has been convicted of a specified offense as defined in subdivision two of this section and the victim of such offense was operating a for-hire vehicle in the course of providing for-hire vehicle services at the time of the commission of such offense, the sentence of imprisonment imposed upon conviction for such offense shall be the sentence authorized by the applicable provisions of article seventy of this chapter, provided, however, that the minimum term of an indeterminate sentence or minimum determinate sentence shall be not less than three years nor more than five years greater than the minimum term or sentence otherwise required to be imposed pursuant to such provisions. The provisions of this subdivision shall not apply where the court, having regard to the nature and circumstances of the crime and the history and character of the defendant, finds on the record that such additional term or sentence would be unduly harsh and that not imposing such additional term or sentence would be consistent with the public safety and would not deprecate the seriousness of the crime.

2. For purposes of this section:
(a) the term "specified offense" shall mean an attempt to commit murder in the second degree as defined in section 125.25 of this chapter, gang assault in the first degree as defined in section 120.07 of this chapter, gang assault in the second degree as defined in section 120.06 of this chapter, assault in the first degree as defined in section 120.10 of this chapter, manslaughter in the first degree as defined in section 125.20 of this chapter, manslaughter in the second degree as defined in section 125.15 of this chapter, robbery in the first degree as defined in section 160.15 of this chapter, robbery in the second degree as defined in section 160.10 of this chapter, or the attempted commission of any of the following offenses: gang assault in the first degree as defined in section 120.07, assault in the first degree as defined in section 120.10,

manslaughter in the first degree as defined in section 125.20 or robbery in the first degree as defined in section 160.15;

(b) the term "for-hire vehicle" shall mean a vehicle designed to carry not more than five passengers for compensation and such vehicle is a taxicab, as defined in section one hundred forty-eight-a of the vehicle and traffic law, a livery, as such term is defined in section one hundred twenty-one-e of the vehicle and traffic law, or a "black car", as such term is defined in paragraph (g) of this subdivision;

(c) the term "livery car base" shall mean a central facility, wherever located, that dispatches a livery operator to both pick-up and discharge passengers in the state;

(d) "for-hire vehicle services" shall mean:

(i) with respect to a taxicab, the transport of passengers pursuant to a license or permit issued by a local authority by a person duly authorized to operate such taxicab;

(ii) with respect to a livery, the transport of passengers by a livery operator while affiliated with a livery car base; or

(iii) with respect to a "black car", the transport of passengers by a "black car operator" pursuant to dispatches from or by a central dispatch facility regardless of where the pick-up and discharge occurs, and, with respect to dispatches from or by a central dispatch facility located outside the state, all dispatches involving a pick-up in the state, regardless of where the discharge occurs.

(e) "livery operator" shall mean the registered owner of a livery, as such term is defined in section one hundred twenty-one-e of the vehicle and traffic law, or a driver designated by such registered owner to operate the registered owner's livery as the registered owner's authorized designee, where such registered owner or driver provides services while affiliated with a livery car base;

(f) "black car operator" shall mean the registered owner of a "black car" or a driver designated by such registered owner to operate the registered owner's black car as the registered owner's authorized designee; and

(g) "black car" shall mean a for-hire vehicle dispatched from a central facility, which has certified to the satisfaction of the department of state pursuant to article six-F of the executive law that more than ninety percent of the central facility's for-hire business is on a payment basis other than direct cash payment by a passenger.

§60.08 Authorized dispositions; resentencing of certain controlled substance offenders.

Any person convicted of an offense and sentenced to prison for an indeterminate sentence, the minimum of which was at least one year and the maximum of which was life imprisonment, which sentence was imposed pursuant to chapter two hundred seventy-six, two hundred seventy-seven, two hundred seventy-eight, or ten hundred fifty-one of the laws of nineteen hundred seventy-three, and for which such sentence was imposed upon conviction of the crime of criminal possession of a controlled substance in the first degree, criminal possession of a controlled substance in the second degree, criminal possession of a controlled substance in the third degree, criminal sale of a controlled substance in the first degree, criminal sale of a controlled substance in the second degree, or criminal sale of a controlled substance in the third degree, and the sole controlled substance involved was methadone, may apply upon notice to the appropriate district attorney, for resentencing in the court which originally imposed sentence.

Such resentencing shall, unless substantial justice dictates otherwise, be pursuant to the current provisions of the penal law, and shall include credit for any jail time incurred upon the subject conviction as well as credit for any period of incarceration incurred pursuant to the sentence originally imposed.

In cases where the proof before the court is not available or is not sufficiently reliable to determine the amount of methadone present in any preparation, compound, mixture or substance containing methadone, there shall exist a rebuttable presumption that each ounce of the preparation, compound, mixture or substance contained sixty milligrams of methadone.

§60.09 Authorized dispositions; resentencing of certain persons convicted of specified controlled substance offenses.

a. Any person convicted of an offense as defined in section 115.05, 220.16, 220.18, 220.39 or 220.41 of this chapter or of an attempt thereof, for an act committed on or after September first, nineteen hundred seventy-three but prior to the date on which the provisions of this section become effective, may, upon notice to the appropriate district attorney, apply for resentencing in the court which originally imposed sentence. Such resentencing shall be in accordance with the provisions of subdivision (b) of this section and shall include credit for any jail time incurred upon the subject conviction as well as credit for any period of incarceration incur red pursuant to the sentence originally imposed.

b. A court, upon an application specified in subdivision (a) of this section may resentence a person as follows:

(i) if the conviction was for a class A-III offense the court may impose a new maximum term which shall be no less than three times the amount of the minimum term imposed in the original sentence and no more than twenty-five years;

(ii) if the conviction was for a class A-II offense the court may impose a new minimum term which shall be no less than three years imprisonment and no more than eight and one-third years;

(iii) upon resentence of a person as specified in paragraph (i) of this subdivision the court shall resentence the person to the same minimum term previously imposed;

(iv) upon resentence of a person as specified in paragraph (ii) of this subdivision the court shall impose a maximum term of life imprisonment;

(v) if the conviction was for an offense as specified in section 115.05 of this chapter and the offense which was the object of the criminal facilitation was a class A-III felony then the court shall set aside the conviction and substitute it with a conviction for violation of section 115.01 or 115.00 of this chapter, whichever is appropriate under the facts of the case, and impose a sentence in accordance with those provisions.

c. Upon resentence as provided in this section the court may not impose a sentence greater than the sentence previously imposed.

§60.10 Authorized disposition; juvenile offender.

1. When a juvenile offender is convicted of a crime, the court shall sentence the defendant to imprisonment in accordance with section 70.05 or sentence him upon a youthful offender finding in accordance with section 60.02 of this chapter.

2. Subdivision one of this section shall apply when sentencing a juvenile offender notwithstanding the provisions of any other law that deals with the authorized sentence for persons who are not juvenile offenders. Provided, however, that the limitation prescribed by this section shall not be deemed or construed to bar use of a conviction of a juvenile offender, other than a juvenile offender who has been adjudicated a youthful offender pursuant to section 720.20 of the criminal procedure law, as a previous or predicate felony offender under section 70.04, 70.06, 70.08 or 70.10, when sentencing a person who commits a felony after he has reached the age of sixteen.

*§ 60.10-a Authorized disposition; adolescent offender.

When an adolescent offender is convicted of an offense, the court shall sentence the defendant to any sentence authorized to be imposed on a person who committed such offense at age eighteen or older. When a sentence is imposed, the court shall consider the age of the defendant in exercising its discretion at sentencing.
*(Eff.10/1/18; provided however, that when the applicability of such provisions are based on the conviction of a crime or an act committed by a person who was seventeen years of age at the time of such offense such provisions shall take effect 10/1/19,Ch.59,L.2017)

§60.11 Authorized dispositions: criminal possession of a weapon in the fourth degree.

When a person is to be sentenced upon conviction of the crime of criminal possession of a weapon in the fourth degree as defined in subdivision one of section 265.01 as a result of a plea of guilty entered in satisfaction of an indictment or count thereof charging the defendant with the class D violent felony offense of criminal possession of a weapon in the third degree as defined in subdivision four of section 265.02, the court must sentence the defendant in accordance with the provisions of section 70.15.

§60.11-a Authorized dispositions; certain criminal possession of a weapon in the third degree offenders.

When a person is to be sentenced upon conviction of the crime of criminal possession of a weapon in the third degree as defined in subdivision ten of section 265.02 of this chapter, the court must sentence such defendant to a determinate sentence as provided in subparagraph (ii) of paragraph (c) of subdivision three of section 70.02 of this chapter, unless a greater minimum sentence is otherwise required by another provision of this chapter.

§60.12 Authorized disposition; alternative sentence; domestic violence cases.

1. Notwithstanding any other provision of law, where a court is imposing sentence upon a person pursuant to section 70.00, 70.02, 70.06 or subdivision two or three of section 70.71 of this title, other than for an offense defined in section 125.26, 125.27, subdivision five of section 125.25, or article 490 of this chapter, or for an offense which would require such person to register as a sex offender pursuant to article six-C of the correction law, an attempt or conspiracy to commit any such offense, and is authorized or required pursuant to sections 70.00, 70.02, 70.06 or subdivision two or three of section 70.71 of this title to impose a sentence of imprisonment, the court, upon a determination following a hearing that (a) at the time of the instant offense, the defendant was a victim of domestic violence subjected to substantial physical, sexual or psychological abuse inflicted by a member of the same family or household as the defendant as such term is defined in subdivision one of section 530.11 of the criminal procedure law; (b) such abuse was a significant contributing factor to the defendant's criminal behavior; (c) having regard for the nature and circumstances of the crime and the history, character and condition of the defendant, that a sentence of imprisonment pursuant to section 70.00, 70.02, 70.06 or subdivision two or three of section 70.71 of this title would be unduly harsh may instead impose a sentence in accordance with this section. *(Eff.5/14/19,Ch.55,L.2019)*

A court may determine that such abuse constitutes a significant contributing factor pursuant to paragraph (b) of this subdivision regardless of whether the defendant raised a defense pursuant to article thirty-five, article forty, or subdivision one of section 125.25 of this chapter.

At the hearing to determine whether the defendant should be sentenced pursuant to this section, the court shall consider oral and written arguments, take testimony from witnesses offered by either party, and consider relevant evidence to assist in making its determination. Reliable hearsay shall be admissible at such hearings.

2. Where a court would otherwise be required to impose a sentence pursuant to section 70.02 of this title, the court may impose a definite sentence of imprisonment of one year or less, or probation in accordance with the provisions of section 65.00 of this title, or may fix a determinate term of imprisonment as follows:

(a) For a class B felony, the term must be at least one year and must not exceed five years;

(b) For a class C felony, the term must be at least one year and must not exceed three and one-half years;

(c) For a class D felony, the term must be at least one year and must not exceed two years; and

(d) For a class E felony, the term must be one year and must not exceed one and one-half years.

3. Where a court would otherwise be required to impose a sentence for a class A felony offense pursuant to section 70.00 of this title, the court may fix a determinate term of imprisonment of at least five years and not to exceed fifteen years.

4. Where a court would otherwise be required to impose a sentence for a class A felony offense pursuant to subparagraph (i) of paragraph (b) of subdivision two of section 70.71 of this title, the court may fix a determinate term of imprisonment of at least five years and not to exceed eight years.

5. Where a court would otherwise be required to impose a sentence for a class A felony offense pursuant to subparagraph (i) of paragraph (b) of subdivision three of section 70.71 of this title, the court may fix a determinate term of imprisonment of at least five years and not to exceed twelve years.

6. Where a court would otherwise be required to impose a sentence for a class A felony offense pursuant to subparagraph (ii) of paragraph (b) of subdivision two of section 70.71 of this title, the court may fix a determinate term of imprisonment of at least one year and not to exceed three years.

7. Where a court would otherwise be required to impose a sentence for a class A felony offense pursuant to subparagraph (ii) of paragraph (b) of subdivision three of section 70.71 of this title, the court may fix a determinate term of imprisonment of at least three years and not to exceed six years.

8. Where a court would otherwise be required to impose a sentence pursuant to subdivision six of section 70.06 of this title, the court may fix a term of imprisonment as follows:

(a) For a class B felony, the term must be at least three years and must not exceed eight years;

(b) For a class C felony, the term must be at least two and one-half years and must not exceed five years;

(c) For a class D felony, the term must be at least two years and must not exceed three years;

(d) For a class E felony, the term must be at least one and one-half years and must not exceed two years.

9. Where a court would otherwise be required to impose a sentence for a class B, C, D or E felony offense pursuant to section 70.00 of this title, the court may impose a sentence in accordance with the provisions of subdivision two of section 70.70 of this title.

10. Except as provided in subdivision seven of this section, where a court would otherwise be required to impose a sentence pursuant to subdivision three of section 70.06 of this title, the court may impose a sentence in accordance with the provisions of subdivision three of section 70.70 of this title.

11. Where a court would otherwise be required to impose a sentence pursuant to subdivision three of section 70.06 of this title, where the prior felony conviction was for a felony offense defined in section 70.02 of this title, the court may impose a sentence in accordance with the provisions of subdivision four of section 70.70 of this title.

(Eff.5/14/19,Ch.31,L.2019)

§60.13 Authorized dispositions; felony sex offenses.

When a person is to be sentenced upon a conviction for any felony defined in article one hundred thirty of this chapter, including a sexually motivated felony, or patronizing a person for prostitution in the first degree as defined in section 230.06 of this chapter, aggravated patronizing a minor for prostitution in the third degree as defined in section 230.11 of this chapter, aggravated patronizing a minor for prostitution in the second degree as defined in section 230.12 of this chapter, aggravated patronizing a minor for prostitution in the first degree as defined in section 230.13 of this chapter, incest in the second degree as defined in section 255.26 of this chapter, or incest in the first degree as defined in section 255.27 of this chapter, or a felony attempt or conspiracy to commit any of these crimes, the court must sentence the defendant in accordance with the provisions of section 70.80 of this title.

§60.20 Authorized dispositions; traffic infraction.

1. When a person is convicted of a traffic infraction, the sentence of the court shall be as follows:

(a) A period of conditional discharge, as provided in article sixty-five; or

(b) Unconditional discharge as provided in section 65.10; or

(c) A fine or a sentence to a term of imprisonment, or both, as prescribed in and authorized by the provision that defines the infraction; or

(d) A sentence of intermittent imprisonment, as provided in article eighty-five.

2. Where a sentence of conditional discharge is imposed for a traffic infraction, all incidents of the sentence shall be the same as would be applicable if the sentence were for a violation.

§60.21 Authorized dispositions; driving while intoxicated or aggravated driving while intoxicated.

Notwithstanding paragraph (d) of subdivision two of section 60.01 of this article, when a person is to be sentenced upon a conviction for a violation of subdivision two, two-a or three of section eleven hundred ninety-two of the vehicle and traffic law, the court may sentence such person to a period of imprisonment authorized by article seventy of this title and shall sentence such person to a period of probation or conditional discharge in accordance with the provisions of section 65.00 of this title and shall order the installation and maintenance of a functioning ignition interlock device. Such period of probation or conditional discharge shall run consecutively to any period of imprisonment and shall commence immediately upon such person's release from imprisonment.

§60.25 Authorized dispositions; corporation.

When a corporation is convicted of an offense, the sentence of the court shall be as follows:

(a) A fine authorized by section 80.10; or

(b) Where authorized by section 65.05, a period of conditional discharge as provided in that section; or

(c) Where authorized by section 65.20, unconditional discharge as provided in that section.

In any case where a corporation has been sentenced to a period of conditional discharge and such sentence is revoked, the court shall sentence the corporation to pay a fine.

§60.27 Restitution and reparation.

1. In addition to any of the dispositions authorized by this article, the court shall consider restitution or reparation to the victim of the crime and may require restitution or reparation as part of the sentence imposed upon a person convicted of an offense, and after providing the district attorney with an opportunity to be heard in accordance with the provisions of this subdivision, require the defendant to make restitution of the fruits of his or her offense or reparation for the actual out-of-pocket loss caused thereby and, in the case of a violation of section 190.78, 190.79, 190.80, 190.82 or 190.83 of this chapter, any costs or losses incurred due to any adverse action taken against the victim. The district attorney shall where appropriate, advise the court at or before the time of sentencing that the victim seeks restitution or reparation, the extent of injury or economic loss or damage of the victim, and the amount of restitution or reparation sought by the victim in accordance with his or her responsibilities under subdivision two of section 390.50 of the criminal procedure law and article twenty-three of the executive law. The court shall hear and consider the information presented by the district attorney in this regard. In that event, or when the victim impact statement reports that the victim seeks restitution or reparation, the court shall require, unless the interests of justice dictate otherwise, in addition to any of the dispositions authorized by this article that the defendant make restitution of the fruits of the offense and reparation for the actual out-of-pocket loss and, in the case of a violation of section 190.78, 190.79, 190.80, 190.82 or 190.83 of this chapter, any costs or losses incurred due to any adverse action, caused thereby to the victim. In the event that restitution or reparation are not ordered, the

court shall clearly state its reasons on the record. Adverse action as used in this subdivision shall mean and include actual loss incurred by the victim, including an amount equal to the value of the time reasonably spent by the victim attempting to remediate the harm incurred by the victim from the offense, and the consequential financial losses from such action.

2. Whenever the court requires restitution or reparation to be made, the court must make a finding as to the dollar amount of the fruits of the offense and the actual out-of-pocket loss to the victim caused by the offense. In making this finding, the court must consider any victim impact statement provided to the court. If the record does not contain sufficient evidence to support such finding or upon request by the defendant, the court must conduct a hearing upon the issue in accordance with the procedure set forth in section 400.30 of the criminal procedure law.

3. The provisions of sections 420.10, 420.20 and 420.30 of the criminal procedure law shall apply in the collection and remission of restitution and reparation.

4. For purposes of the imposition, determination and collection of restitution or reparation, the following definitions shall apply:

(a) the term "offense" shall include the offense for which a defendant was convicted, as well as any other offense that is part of the same criminal transaction or that is contained in any other accusatory instrument disposed of by any plea of guilty by the defendant to an offense.

(b) the term "victim" shall include the victim of the offense, the representative of a crime victim as defined in subdivision six of section six hundred twenty-one of the executive law, an individual whose identity was assumed or whose personal identifying information was used in violation of section 190.78, 190.79 or 190.80 of this chapter, or any person who has suffered a financial loss as a direct result of the acts of a defendant in violation of section 190.78, 190.79, 190.80, 190.82 or 190.83 of this chapter, a good samaritan as defined in section six hundred twenty-one of the executive law and the office of victim services or other governmental agency that has received an application for or has provided financial assistance or compensation to the victim. A victim shall also mean any owner or lawful producer of a master recording, or a trade association that represents such owner or lawful producer, that has suffered injury as a result of an offense as defined in article two hundred seventy-five of this chapter.

5. (a) Except upon consent of the defendant or as provided in paragraph (b) of this subdivision, or as a condition of probation or conditional discharge as provided in paragraph (g) of subdivision two of section 65.10 of this chapter, the amount of restitution or reparation required by the court shall not exceed fifteen thousand dollars in the case of a conviction for a felony, or ten thousand dollars in the case of a

conviction for any offense other than a felony. Notwithstanding the provisions of this subdivision, if an officer of a school district is convicted of violating any section of article one hundred fifty-five of this chapter where the victim of such crime is such officer's school district, the court may require an amount of restitution up to the full amount of the fruits of the offense or reparation up to the full amount of the actual out-of-pocket loss suffered by the victim, provided further that in such case the provisions of paragraph (b) of this subdivision shall not apply.

(b) The court in its discretion may impose restitution or reparation in excess of the amounts specified in paragraph (a) of this subdivision, provided however that the amount in excess must be limited to the return of the victim's property, including money, or the equivalent value thereof; and reimbursement for medical expenses actually incurred by the victim prior to sentencing as a result of the offense committed by the defendant.

6. Any payment made as restitution or reparation pursuant to this section shall not limit, preclude or impair any liability for damages in any civil action or proceeding for an amount in excess of such payment.

7. In the event that the court requires restitution or reparation to be made to a person and that person dies prior to the completion of said restitution or reparation, the remaining payments shall be made to the estate of the deceased.

8. The court shall in all cases where restitution or reparation is imposed direct as part of the disposition that the defendant pay a designated surcharge of five percent of the entire amount of a restitution or reparation payment to the official or organization designated pursuant to subdivision eight of section 420.10 of the criminal procedure law. The designated surcharge shall not exceed five percent of the amount actually collected. Upon the filing of an affidavit of the official or organization designated pursuant to subdivision eight of section 420.10 of the criminal procedure law demonstrating that the actual cost of the collection and administration of restitution or reparation in a particular case exceeds five percent of the entire amount of the payment or the amount actually collected, as the case may be, the court shall direct that the defendant pay an additional surcharge of not more than five percent of the entire amount of a restitution or reparation payment to such official or organization, or the actual cost of collection or administration, whichever is less unless, upon application of the defendant, the court determines that imposition of such additional surcharge would cause undue hardship to the defendant, or any other person who is financially supported by the defendant, or would other-wise not be in the interest of justice. Such additional surcharge, when added to the initial five percent surcharge, shall not exceed ten percent

of the amount actually collected.

9. If the offense of which a person is convicted is a class A, class B, class C, or class D felony involving the sale of a controlled substance, as defined in article two hundred twenty of this chapter, and no other victim who is a person is seeking restitution in the case, the term "victim" as used in this section, in addition to its ordinary meaning, shall mean any law enforcement agency of the state of New York or of any subdivision thereof which has expended funds in the purchase of any controlled substance from such person or his agent as part of the investigation leading to such conviction. Any restitution which may be required to be made to a law enforcement agency pursuant to this section shall be limited to the amount of funds expended in the actual purchase of such controlled substance by such law enforcement agency, less the amount of any funds which have been or will be recovered from any other source, and shall not include a designated surcharge pursuant to subdivision eight of this section. Any law enforcement agency seeking restitution pursuant to this section shall file with the court and the district attorney an affidavit stating that funds expended in the actual purchase of a controlled substance for which restitution is being sought have not been and will not be recovered from any other source or in any other civil or criminal proceeding. Any law enforcement agency receiving restitution pursuant to this section shall promptly transmit to the commissioner of the division of criminal justice services a report stating the dollar amount of the restitution received.

10. If the offense of which a person is convicted is defined in section 150.10, 150.15 or 150.20 of this chapter, and no other victim who is a person is seeking restitution in the case, the term "victim" as used in this section, in addition to its ordinary meaning, shall mean any municipality or volunteer fire company which has expended funds or will expend funds for the purpose of restoration, rehabilitation or clean-up of the site of the arson. Any restitution which may be required to be made to a municipality or volunteer fire company pursuant to this section shall be limited to the amount of funds reasonably expended or to be expended for the purpose of restoration, rehabilitation or clean-up of the site of the arson, less the amount of any funds which have been or will be recovered from any other source, and shall not include a designated surcharge pursuant to subdivision eight of this section. Any municipality or volunteer fire company seeking restitution pursuant to this section shall file with the court, district attorney and defense counsel an affidavit stating that the funds reasonably expended or to be expended for which restitution is being sought have not been and will not be recovered from any other source or in any other civil or criminal proceeding. For the purposes of this subdivision, "volunteer fire company" means a fire company as defined in paragraph a of subdivision two of section one hundred of the general municipal law.

11. Notwithstanding any other provision of this section to the contrary, when a person is convicted of harming an animal trained to aid a person with a disability in the second degree as defined in section 195.11 of this chapter, or harming an animal trained to aid a person with a disability in the first degree as defined in section 195.12 of this chapter, the court, in addition to any other sentence, shall order the payment of restitution to the person with a disability who was aided by such animal.

12. If the offense of which a person is convicted is defined in section 155.25, 155.30, 155.35, 155.40 or 155.42 of this chapter, and the property taken is timber, the court may upon conviction, in addition to any other sentence, direct the defendant to pay the rightful owner of such timber an amount equal to treble the stumpage value of the timber stolen as defined in section 71-0703 of the environmental conservation law and for any permanent and substantial damage caused to the land or the improvements thereon as a result of such violation. Such reparations shall be of such kind, nature and extent as will reasonably restore the lands affected by the violation to their condition immediately before the violation and may be made by physical restoration of such lands and/or by the assessment of monetary payment to make such restoration.

13. If the offense of which a person is convicted is defined in section 240.50, subdivision one or two of section 240.55, section 240.60, section 240.61, section 240.62 or section 240.63 of this chapter, and no other victim who is a person is seeking restitution in the case, the term "victim" as used in this subdivision, in addition to the ordinary meaning, shall mean any school, municipality, fire district, fire company, fire corporation, ambulance association, ambulance corporation, or other legal or public entity engaged in providing emergency services which has expended funds for the purpose of responding to a false report of an incident or false bomb as defined in section 240.50, subdivision one or two of section 240.55, section 240.60, section 240.61, section 240.62, or section 240.63 of this chapter. Any restitution which may be required to be made to a victim pursuant to this subdivision shall be limited to the amount of funds reasonably expended for the purpose of responding to such false report of incident or false bomb, less the amount of any funds which have been or will be recovered from any other source and shall not include a designated surcharge pursuant to subdivision eight of this section. Any victim seeking restitution pursuant to this subdivision shall file with the court, district attorney and defense counsel an affidavit stating that the funds reasonably expended for which restitution is being sought have not been and will not be recovered from any other source or in any other civil or criminal proceeding, except as provided for by section 3-112 of the general obligations law.

14. Where a transfer of probation has occurred pursuant to section 410.80 of the criminal procedure law and the probationer is subject to a restitution condition, the department of probation in the county in which the order of restitution was imposed shall notify the appropriate district attorney. Upon notification by the department of probation, such district attorney shall file a certified copy of the judgment with the clerk of the county in the receiving jurisdiction for purposes of establishing a first lien and to permit institution of civil proceedings pursuant to the provisions of subdivision six of section 420.10 of the criminal procedure law.

§60.28 Authorized disposition; making graffiti and possession of graffiti instruments.

When a person is convicted of an offense defined in section 145.60 or 145.65 of this chapter, or of an attempt to commit such offense, and the sentence imposed by the court for such conviction includes a sentence of probation or conditional discharge, the court shall, where appropriate, include as a condition of such sentence the defendant's successful participation in a graffiti removal program pursuant to paragraph (h) of subdivision two of section 65.10 of this chapter.

§60.29 Authorized disposition; cemetery desecration.

When a person is convicted of an offense defined in section 145.22 or 145.23 of this chapter or of an attempt to commit such an offense, and the sentence imposed by the court for such conviction includes a sentence of probation or conditional discharge, such sentence shall, where appropriate, be in accordance with paragraph (h) of subdivision two of section 65.10 of this article as such section relates to cemetery crime.

§60.30 Civil penalties.

This article does not deprive the court of any authority conferred by law to decree a forfeiture of property, suspend or cancel a license, remove a person from office, or impose any other civil penalty and any appropriate order exercising such authority may be included as part of the judgment of conviction.

§60.35 Mandatory surcharge, sex offender registration fee, DNA databank fee, supplemental sex offender victim fee and crime victim assistance fee required in certain cases.

1. (a) Except as provided in section eighteen hundred nine of the vehicle and traffic law and section 27.12 of the parks, recreation and historic preservation law, whenever proceedings in an administrative tribunal or a court of this state result in a conviction for a felony, a misdemeanor, or a violation, as these terms are defined in section 10.00 of this chapter, there shall be levied at sentencing a mandatory surcharge, sex offender registration fee, DNA databank fee and a crime victim assistance fee in addition to any sentence required or permitted by law, in accordance with the following schedule:

(i) a person convicted of a felony shall pay a mandatory surcharge of three hundred dollars and a crime victim assistance fee of twenty-five dollars;

(ii) a person convicted of a misdemeanor shall pay a mandatory surcharge of one hundred seventy-five dollars and a crime victim assistance fee of twenty-five dollars;

(iii) a person convicted of a violation shall pay a mandatory surcharge of ninety-five dollars and a crime victim assistance fee of twenty-five dollars;

(iv) a person convicted of a sex offense as defined by subdivision two of section one hundred sixty-eight-a of the correction law or a sexually violent offense as defined by subdivision three of section one hundred sixty-eight-a of the correction law shall, in addition to a mandatory surcharge and crime victim assistance fee, pay a sex offender registration fee of fifty dollars.

(v) a person convicted of a designated offense as defined by subdivision seven of section nine hundred ninety-five of the executive law shall, in addition to a mandatory surcharge and crime victim assistance fee, pay a DNA databank fee of fifty dollars.

(b) When the felony or misdemeanor conviction in subparagraphs (i), (ii) or (iv) of paragraph (a) of this subdivision results from an offense contained in article one hundred thirty of this chapter, incest in the third, second or first degree as defined in sections 255.25, 255.26 and 255.27 of this chapter or an offense contained in article two hundred sixty-three of this chapter, the person convicted shall pay a supplemental sex offender victim fee of one thousand dollars in addition to the mandatory surcharge and any other fee.

2. Where a person is convicted of two or more crimes or violations committed through a single act or omission, or through an act or omission which in itself constituted one of the crimes or violations and also was a material element of the other, the court shall impose a mandatory surcharge and a crime victim assistance fee, and where appropriate a supplemental sex offender victim fee, in accordance with the provisions of this section for the crime or violation which carries the highest classification, and no other sentence to pay a mandatory surcharge, crime victim assistance fee or supplemental sex offender victim fee required by this section shall be imposed. Where a person is convicted of two or more sex offenses or sexually violent offenses, as defined by subdivisions two and three of section one hundred sixty-eight-a of the correction law, committed through a single act or omission, or through an act or omission which in itself constituted one of the offenses and also was a material element of the other, the court shall impose only one sex offender registration fee. Where a person is convicted of two or more designated offenses, as defined by subdivision seven of section nine hundred ninety-five of the executive law, committed through a single act or omission, or through an act or omission which in itself constituted one of the offenses and also was a material element of the other, the court shall impose only one DNA databank fee.

3. The mandatory surcharge, sex offender registration fee, DNA databank fee, crime victim assistance fee, and supplemental sex offender victim fee provided for in subdivision one of this section shall be paid to the clerk of the court or administrative tribunal that rendered the conviction. Within the first ten days of the month following collection of the mandatory surcharge, crime victim assistance fee, and supplemental sex offender victim fee, the collecting authority shall determine the amount of mandatory surcharge, crime victim assistance fee, and supplemental sex offender victim fee collected and, if it is an administrative tribunal, or a town or village justice court, it shall then pay such money to the state comptroller who shall deposit such money in the state treasury pursuant to section one hundred twenty-one of the state finance law to the credit of the criminal justice improvement account established by section ninety-seven-bb of the state finance law. Within the first ten days of the month following collection of the sex offender registration fee and DNA databank fee, the collecting authority shall determine the amount of the sex offender registration fee and DNA databank fee collected and, if it is an administrative tribunal, or a

town or village justice court, it shall then pay such money to the state comptroller who shall deposit such money in the state treasury pursuant to section one hundred twenty-one of the state finance law to the credit of the general fund. If such collecting authority is any other court of the unified court system, it shall, within such period, pay such money attributable to the mandatory surcharge or crime victim assistance fee to the state commissioner of taxation and finance to the credit of the criminal justice improvement account established by section ninety-seven-bb of the state finance law. If such collecting authority is any other court of the unified court system, it shall, within such period, pay such money attributable to the sex offender registration fee and the DNA databank fee to the state commissioner of taxation and finance to the credit of the general fund.

4. Any person who has paid a mandatory surcharge, sex offender registration fee, DNA databank fee, a crime victim assistance fee or a supplemental sex offender victim fee under the authority of this section based upon a conviction that is subsequently reversed or who paid a mandatory surcharge, sex offender registration fee, DNA databank fee, a crime victim assistance fee or supplemental sex offender victim fee under the authority of this section which is ultimately determined not to be required by this section shall be entitled to a refund of such mandatory surcharge, sex offender registration fee, DNA databank fee, crime victim assistance fee or supplemental sex offender victim fee upon application, in the case of a town or village court, to the state comptroller. The state comptroller shall require such proof as is necessary in order to determine whether a refund is required by law. In all other cases, such application shall be made to the department, agency or court that collected such surcharge or fee. Such department, agency or court shall initiate the refund process and the state comptroller shall pay the refund pursuant to subdivision fifteen of section eight of the state finance law.

*5. (a) When a person who is convicted of a crime or violation and sentenced to a term of imprisonment has failed to pay the mandatory surcharge, sex offender registration fee, DNA databank fee, crime victim assistance fee or supplemental sex offender victim fee required by this section, the clerk of the court that rendered the conviction shall notify the superintendent or the municipal official of the facility where the person is confined. The superintendent or the municipal official shall cause any amount owing to be collected from such person during his or her term of imprisonment from moneys to the credit of an incarcerated individuals' fund or such moneys as may be earned by a person in a work release program pursuant to section eight hundred sixty of the correction law. Such moneys attributable to the mandatory surcharge or crime victim assistance fee shall be paid over to the state comptroller to the credit of the criminal justice improvement account established by section ninety-seven-bb of the state finance law and such moneys attributable to the sex offender registration fee or DNA databank fee shall be paid over to the state comptroller to the credit of the general fund, except that any such moneys collected which are surcharges, sex offender registration fees, DNA databank fees, crime victim assistance fees or supplemental sex offender victim fees levied in relation to convictions obtained in a town or village justice court shall be paid within thirty days after the receipt thereof by the superintendent or municipal official of the facility to the justice of the court in which the conviction was obtained. For the purposes of collecting such mandatory surcharge, sex offender registration fee, DNA databank fee, crime victim assistance fee, and supplemental sex offender victim fee, the state shall be legally entitled to the money to the credit of an incarcerated individuals' fund or money which is earned by an incarcerated individual in a work release program. For purposes of this subdivision, the term "incarcerated individuals' fund" shall mean moneys in the possession of an incarcerated individual at the time of his or her admission into such facility, funds earned by him or her as provided for in section one hundred eighty-seven of the correction law and any other funds received by him or her or on his or her behalf and deposited with such superintendent or municipal official.

(b) The incarceration fee provided for in subdivision two of section one hundred eighty-nine of the correction law shall not be assessed or collected if any order of restitution or reparation, fine, mandatory surcharge, sex offender registration fee, DNA databank fee, crime victim assistance fee or supplemental sex offender victim fee remains unpaid. In such circumstances, any monies which may lawfully be withheld from the compensation paid to a prisoner for work performed while housed in a general confinement facility in satisfaction of such an obligation shall first be applied toward satisfaction of such obligation.

*(Eff.8/2/21,Ch.322,L.2021) *(Eff. until 9/1/23,Ch.55,L.2021)*

*5. When a person who is convicted of a crime or violation and sentenced to a term of imprisonment has failed to pay the mandatory surcharge, sex offender registration fee, DNA databank fee, crime victim assistance fee or supplemental sex offender victim fee required by this section, the clerk of the court that rendered the conviction shall notify the superintendent or the municipal official of the facility where the person is confined. The superintendent or the municipal official shall cause any amount owing to be collected from such person during his or her term of imprisonment from moneys to the credit of an incarcerated individuals' fund or such moneys as may be earned by a person in a work release program pursuant to section eight hundred sixty of the correction law. Such moneys attributable to the mandatory surcharge or crime victim assistance fee shall be paid over to the state comptroller to the credit of the criminal justice improvement account established by section ninety-seven-bb of the state finance law and such moneys attributable to the sex offender registration fee or DNA databank fee shall be paid over to the state comptroller to the credit of the general fund, except that any such moneys collected which are surcharges, sex offender registration fees, DNA databank fees, crime victim assistance fees or supplemental sex offender victim fees levied in relation to convictions obtained in a town or village justice court shall be paid within thirty days after the receipt thereof by the superintendent or municipal official of the facility to the justice of the court in which the conviction was obtained. For the purposes of collecting such mandatory surcharge, sex offender registration fee, DNA databank fee, crime victim assistance fee and supplemental sex offender victim fee, the state shall be legally entitled to the money to the credit of an incarcerated individuals' fund or money which is earned by an incarcerated individual in a work release program. For purposes of this subdivision, the term "incarcerated individuals' fund" shall mean moneys in the possession of an incarcerated individual at the time of his or her admission into such facility, funds earned by him or her as provided for in section one hundred eighty-seven of the correction law and any other funds received by him or her or on his or her behalf and deposited with such superintendent or municipal official.

*(Amended, Ch.322,L.2021) *(Eff.9/1/23,Ch.55,L.2021)*

6. Notwithstanding any other provision of this section, where a person has made restitution or reparation pursuant to section 60.27 of this article, such person shall not be required to pay a mandatory surcharge or a crime victim assistance fee.

7. Notwithstanding the provisions of subdivision one of section 60.00 of this article, the provisions of subdivision one of this section shall not apply to a violation under any law other than this chapter.

8. Subdivision one of section 130.10 of the criminal procedure law notwithstanding, at the time that the mandatory surcharge, sex offender registration fee or DNA databank fee, crime victim assistance fee or supplemental sex offender victim fee is imposed a town or village court may, and all other courts shall, issue and cause to be served upon the person required to pay the mandatory surcharge, sex offender registration fee or DNA databank fee, crime victim assistance fee or supplemental sex offender victim fee, a summons directing that such person appear before the court regarding the payment of the mandatory surcharge, sex offender registration fee or DNA databank fee, crime victim assistance fee or supplemental sex offender victim fee, if after sixty days from the date it was imposed it remains unpaid. The designated date of appearance on the summons shall be set for the first day court is in session falling after the sixtieth day from the imposition of the mandatory surcharge, sex offender registration fee or DNA databank fee, crime victim assistance fee or supplemental sex offender victim fee. The summons shall contain the information required by subdivision two of section 130.10 of the criminal procedure law except that in substitution for the requirement of paragraph (c) of such subdivision the summons shall state that the person served must appear at a date, time and specific location specified in the summons if after sixty days from the date of issuance the mandatory surcharge, sex offender registration fee or DNA databank fee, crime victim assistance fee or supplemental sex offender victim fee remains unpaid. The court shall not issue a summons under this subdivision to a person who is

being sentenced to a term of confinement in excess of sixty days in jail or in the department of corrections and community supervision. The mandatory surcharges, sex offender registration fee and DNA databank fees, crime victim assistance fees and supplemental sex offender victim fees for those persons shall be governed by the provisions of section 60.30 of this article.

9. Notwithstanding the provisions of subdivision one of this section, in the event a proceeding is in a town or village court, such court shall add an additional five dollars to the surcharges imposed by such subdivision one.

§60.36 Authorized dispositions; driving while intoxicated offenses.

Where a court is imposing a sentence for a violation of subdivision two, two-a, or three of section eleven hundred ninety-two of the vehicle and traffic law pursuant to sections 65.00 or 65.05 of this title and, as a condition of such sentence, orders the installation and maintenance of an ignition interlock device, the court may impose any other penalty authorized pursuant to section eleven hundred ninety-three of the vehicle and traffic law.

§60.37 Authorized disposition; certain offenses.

When a person has been charged with an offense and the elements of such offense meet the criteria of an "eligible offense" and such person qualifies as an "eligible person" as such terms are defined in section four hundred fifty-eight-l of the social services law, the court may, as a condition of adjournment in contemplation of dismissal in accordance with section 170.55 of the criminal procedure law, or a condition of probation or a conditional discharge, direct that the defendant participate in an education reform program pursuant to subdivision two of section four hundred fifty-eight-l of the social services law.

ARTICLE 65 - SENTENCES OF PROBATION, CONDITIONAL DISCHARGE AND UNCONDITIONAL DISCHARGE

Section
65.00 Sentence of probation.
65.05 Sentence of conditional discharge.
65.10 Conditions of probation and of conditional discharge.
65.15 Calculation of periods of probation and of conditional discharge.
65.20 Sentence of unconditional discharge.

§65.00 Sentence of probation.

1. Criteria.

(a) Except as otherwise required by section 60.04 or 60.05 of this title, and except as provided by paragraph (b) hereof, the court may sentence a person to a period of probation upon conviction of any crime if the court, having regard to the nature and circumstances of the crime and to the history, character and condition of the defendant, is of the opinion that:

(i) Institutional confinement for the term authorized by law of the defendant is or may not be necessary for the protection of the public;

(ii) the defendant is in need of guidance, training or other assistance which, in his case, can be effectively administered through probation supervision; and

(iii) such disposition is not inconsistent with the ends of justice.

(b) The court, with the concurrence of either the administrative judge of the court or of the judicial district within which the court is situated or such administrative judge as the presiding justice of the appropriate appellate division shall designate, may sentence a person to a period of probation upon conviction of a class A-II felony defined in article two hundred twenty, the class B felony defined in section 220.48 of this chapter or any other class B felony defined in article two hundred twenty of this chapter where the person is a second felony drug offender as defined in paragraph (b) of subdivision one of section 70.70 of this chapter, if the prosecutor either orally on the record or in a writing filed with the indictment recommends that the court sentence such person to a period of probation upon the ground that such person has or is providing material assistance in the investigation, apprehension or prosecution of any person for a felony defined in article two hundred twenty or the attempt or the conspiracy to commit any such felony, and if the court, having regard to the nature and circumstances of the crime and to the history, character and condition of the defendant is of the opinion that:

(i) Institutional confinement of the defendant is not necessary for the protection of the public;

(ii) The defendant is in need of guidance, training or other assistance which, in his case, can be effectively administered through probation supervision;

(iii) The defendant has or is providing material assistance in the investigation, apprehension or prosecution of a person for a felony defined in article two hundred twenty or the attempt or conspiracy to commit any such felony; and

(iv) Such disposition is not inconsistent with the ends of justice.

*Provided, however, that the court shall not, except to the extent authorized by paragraph (d) of subdivision two of section 60.01 of this chapter, impose a sentence of probation in any case where it sentences a defendant for more than one crime and imposes a sentence of imprisonment for any one of the crimes, or where the defendant is subject to an undischarged indeterminate or determinate sentence of imprisonment which was imposed at a previous time by a court of this state and has more than one year to run.   *(Eff. until 9/1/23, Ch.55, L.2021)

*Provided, however, that the court shall not, except to the extent authorized by paragraph (d) of subdivision two of section 60.01 of this chapter, impose a sentence of probation in any case where it sentences a defendant for more than one crime and imposes a sentence of imprisonment for any one of the crimes, or where the defendant is subject to an undischarged indeterminate or reformatory sentence of imprisonment which was imposed at a previous time by a court of this state and has more than one year to run.   * (Eff. 9/1/23, Ch.55, L.2021)

2. Sentence. When a person is sentenced to a period of probation the court shall, except to the extent authorized by paragraph (d) of subdivision two of section 60.01 of this chapter, impose the period authorized by subdivision three of this section and shall specify, in accordance with section 65.10, the conditions to be complied with. The court may modify or enlarge the conditions or, if the defendant commits an additional offense or violates a condition, revoke the sentence at any time prior to the expiration or termination of the period of probation.

3. Periods of probation. Unless terminated sooner in accordance with the criminal procedure law, the period of probation shall be as follows:

(a) (i) For a felony, other than a class A-II felony defined in article two hundred twenty of this chapter or the class B felony defined in section 220.48 of this chapter, or any other class B felony defined in article two hundred twenty of this chapter committed by a second felony drug offender, or a sexual assault, the period of probation shall be a term of three, four or five years;

(ii) For a class A-II felony drug offender as defined in paragraph (a) of subdivision one of section 70.71 of this chapter as described in paragraph (b) of subdivision one of this section, or a class B felony committed by a second felony drug offender described in paragraph (b) of subdivision one of this section, the period of probation shall be life and for a class B felony defined in section 220.48 of this chapter, the period of probation shall be twenty-five years;

(iii) For a felony sexual assault, the period of probation shall be ten years.

(b) (i) For a class A misdemeanor, other than a sexual assault, the period of probation shall be a term of two or three years;

(ii) For a class A misdemeanor sexual assault, the period of probation shall be six years.

(c) For a class B misdemeanor, the period of probation shall be one year, except the period of probation shall be no less than one year and no more than three years for the class B misdemeanor of public lewdness as defined in section 245.00 of this chapter;

(d) For an unclassified misdemeanor, the period of probation shall be a term of two or three years if the authorized sentence of imprisonment is in excess of three months, otherwise the period of probation shall be one year.

For the purposes of this section, the term "sexual assault" means an offense defined in article one hundred thirty or two hundred sixty-three, or in section 255.25, 255.26 or 255.27 of this chapter, or an attempt to commit any of the foregoing offenses.

4. If during the periods of probation referenced in subparagraph (i) of paragraph (a), subparagraph (i) of paragraph (b) and paragraph (d) of subdivision three of this section an alleged violation is sustained following a hearing pursuant to section 410.70 of the criminal procedure law and the court continues or modifies the sentence, the court may extend the remaining period of probation up to the maximum term authorized by this section. Provided, however, a defendant shall receive credit for the time during which he or she was supervised under the original probation sentence prior to any declaration of delinquency and for any time spent in custody pursuant to this article for an alleged violation of probation.

5. In any case where a court pursuant to its authority under subdivision four of section 60.01 of this chapter revokes probation and sentences such person to imprisonment and probation, as provided in paragraph (d) of subdivision two of section 60.01 of this chapter, the period of probation shall be the remaining period of the original probation sentence or one year whichever is greater.

§65.05 Sentence of conditional discharge.

1. Criteria.

(a) Except as otherwise required by section 60.05, the court may impose a sentence of conditional discharge for an offense if the court, having regard to the nature and circumstances of the offense and to the history, character and condition of the defendant, is of the opinion that neither the public interest nor the ends of justice would be served by a sentence of imprisonment and that probation supervision is not appropriate.

(b) When a sentence of conditional discharge is imposed for a felony, the court shall set forth in the record the reasons for its action.

2. Sentence. Except to the extent authorized by paragraph (d) of subdivision two of section 60.01 of this chapter, when the court imposes a sentence of conditional discharge the defendant shall be released with respect to the conviction for which the sentence is imposed without imprisonment or probation supervision but subject, during the period of conditional discharge, to such conditions as the court may determine.

The court shall impose the period of conditional discharge authorized by subdivision three of this section and shall specify, in accordance with section 65.10, the conditions to be complied with. If a defendant is sentenced pursuant to paragraph (e) of subdivision two of section 65.10 of this chapter, the court shall require the administrator of the program to provide written notice to the court of any violation of program participation by the defendant. The court may modify or enlarge the conditions or, if the defendant commits an additional offense or violates a condition, revoke the sentence at any time prior to the expiration or termination of the period of conditional discharge.

3. Periods of conditional discharge. Unless terminated sooner in accordance with the criminal procedure law, the period of conditional discharge shall be as follows:

(a) Three years in the case of a felony; and
(b) One year in the case of a misdemeanor or a violation.

Where the court has required, as a condition of the sentence, that the defendant make restitution of the fruits of his or her offense or make reparation for the loss caused thereby and such condition has not been satisfied, the court, at any time prior to the expiration or termination of the period of conditional discharge, may impose an additional period. The length of the additional period shall be fixed by the court at the time it is imposed and shall not be more than two years. All of the incidents of the original sentence, including the authority of the court to modify or enlarge the conditions, shall continue to apply during such additional period.

§65.10 Conditions of probation and of conditional discharge.

1. In general. The conditions of probation and of conditional discharge shall be such as the court, in its discretion, deems reasonably necessary to insure that the defendant will lead a law-abiding life or to assist him to do so.

2. Conditions relating to conduct and rehabilitation. When imposing a sentence of probation or of conditional discharge, the court shall, as a condition of the sentence, consider restitution or reparation and may, as a condition of the sentence, require that the defendant:

(a) Avoid injurious or vicious habits;
(b) Refrain from frequenting unlawful or disreputable places or consorting with disreputable persons;
(c) Work faithfully at a suitable employment or faithfully pursue a course of study or of vocational training that will equip him for suitable employment;
(d) Undergo available medical or psychiatric treatment and remain in a specified institution, when required for that purpose;
(e) Participate in an alcohol or substance abuse program or an intervention program approved by the court after consultation with the local probation department having jurisdiction, or such other public or private agency as the court determines to be appropriate;
(e-1) Participate in a motor vehicle accident prevention course. The court may require such condition where a person has been convicted of a traffic infraction for a violation of article twenty-six of the vehicle and traffic law where the commission of such violation caused the serious

physical injury or death of another person. For purposes of this paragraph, the term "motor vehicle accident prevention course" shall mean a motor vehicle accident prevention course approved by the department of motor vehicles pursuant to article twelve-B of the vehicle and traffic law;

(f) Support his dependents and meet other family responsibilities;

(g) Make restitution of the fruits of his or her offense or make reparation, in an amount he can afford to pay, for the actual out-of-pocket loss caused thereby. When restitution or reparation is a condition of the sentence, the court shall fix the amount thereof, the manner of performance, specifically state the date when restitution is to be paid in full prior to the expiration of the sentence of probation and may establish provisions for the early termination of a sentence of probation or conditional discharge pursuant to the provisions of subdivision three of section 410.90 of the criminal procedure law after the restitution and reparation part of a sentence of probation or conditional discharge has been satisfied. The court shall provide that in the event the person to whom restitution or reparation is to be made dies prior to the completion of said restitution or reparation, the remaining payments shall be made to the estate of the deceased.

(h) Perform services for a public or not-for-profit corporation, association, institution or agency, including but not limited to services for the division of substance abuse services, services in an appropriate community program for removal of graffiti from public or private property, including any property damaged in the underlying offense, or services for the maintenance and repair of real or personal property maintained as a cemetery plot, grave, burial place or other place of interment of human remains. Provided however, that the performance of any such services shall not result in the displacement of employed workers or in the impairment of existing contracts for services, nor shall the performance of any such services be required or permitted in any establishment involved in any labor strike or lockout. The court may establish provisions for the early termination of a sentence of probation or conditional discharge pursuant to the provisions of subdivision three of section 410.90 of the criminal procedure law after such services have been completed. Such sentence may only be imposed upon conviction of a misdemeanor, violation, or class D or class E felony, or a youthful offender finding replacing any such conviction, where the defendant has consented to the amount and conditions of such service;

(i) If a person under the age of twenty-one years, (i) resides with his parents or in a suitable foster home or hostel as referred to in section two hundred forty-four of the executive law, (ii) attends school, (iii) spends such part of the period of the sentence as the court may direct, but not exceeding two years, in a facility made available by the division for youth pursuant to article nineteen-G of the executive law, provided that admission to such facility may be made only with the prior consent of the division for youth, (iv) attend a non-residential program for such hours and pursuant to a schedule prescribed by the court as suitable for a program of rehabilitation of youth, (v) contribute to his own support in any home, foster home or hostel;

(j) Post a bond or other security for the performance of any or all conditions imposed;

(k) Observe certain specified conditions of conduct as set forth in an order of protection issued pursuant to section 530.12 or 530.13 of the criminal procedure law.

(k-1) Install and maintain a functioning ignition interlock device, as that term is defined in section one hundred nineteen-a of the vehicle and traffic law, in any vehicle owned or operated by the defendant if the court in its discretion determines that such a condition is necessary to ensure the public safety. The court may require such condition only where a person has been convicted of a violation of subdivision two, two-a or three of section eleven hundred ninety-two of the vehicle and traffic law, or any crime defined by the vehicle and traffic law or this chapter of which an alcohol-related violation of any provision of section eleven hundred ninety-two of the vehicle and traffic law is an essential element. The offender shall be required to install and operate the ignition interlock device only in accordance with section eleven hundred ninety-eight of the vehicle and traffic law.

(k-2) (i) Refrain, upon sentencing for a crime involving unlawful sexual conduct committed against a metropolitan transportation authority passenger, customer, or employee or a crime involving assault against a metropolitan transportation authority employee, committed in or on any facility or conveyance of the metropolitan transportation authority or a subsidiary thereof or the New York city transit authority or a subsidiary thereof, from using or entering any of such authority's subways, trains, buses or other conveyances or facilities specified by the court for a period of up to three years, or a specified period of such probation or conditional discharge, whichever is less. For purposes of this section, a crime involving assault shall mean an offense described in article one hundred twenty of this chapter which has as an element the causing of physical injury or serious physical injury to another as well as the attempt thereof.

(ii) The court may, in its discretion, suspend, modify or cancel a condition imposed under this paragraph in the interest of justice at any time. If the person depends on the authority's subways, trains, buses, or other conveyances or facilities for trips of necessity, including, but not limited to, travel to or from medical or legal appointments, school or training classes or places of employment, obtaining food, clothing or necessary household items, or rendering care to family members, the court may modify such condition to allow for a trip or trips as in its discretion are necessary.

(iii) A person at liberty and subject to a condition under this paragraph who applies, within thirty days after the date such condition becomes effective, for a refund of any prepaid fare amounts rendered unusable in whole or in part by such condition including, but not limited to, a monthly pass, shall be issued a refund of the amounts so prepaid.

(Eff.7/2/20,Ch.56,L.2020)

(*l*) Satisfy any other conditions reasonably related to his rehabilitation.

3. Conditions relating to supervision. When imposing a sentence of probation the court, in addition to any conditions imposed pursuant to subdivision two of this section, shall require as conditions of the sentence, that the defendant:

(a) Report to a probation officer as directed by the court or the probation officer and permit the probation officer to visit him at his place of abode or elsewhere;

(b) Remain within the jurisdiction of the court unless granted permission to leave by the court or the probation officer. Where a defendant is granted permission to move or travel outside the jurisdiction of the court, the defendant shall sign a written waiver of extradition agreeing to waive extradition proceedings where such proceedings are the result of the issuance of a warrant by the court pursuant to subdivision two of section 410.40 of the criminal procedure law based on an alleged violation of probation. Where any county or the city of New York incurs costs associated with the return of any probationer based on the issuance of a warrant by the court pursuant to subdivision two of section 410.40 of the criminal procedure law, the jurisdiction may collect the reasonable and necessary expenses involved in connection with his or her transport, from the probationer; provided that where the sentence of probation is not revoked pursuant to section 410.70 of the criminal procedure law no such expenses may be collected.

(c) Answer all reasonable inquiries by the probation officer and notify the probation officer prior to any change in address or employment.

4. Electronic monitoring. When imposing a sentence of probation the court may, in addition to any conditions imposed pursuant to subdivisions two and three of this section, require the defendant to submit to the use of an electronic monitoring device and/or to follow a schedule that governs the defendant's daily movement. Such condition may be imposed only where the court, in its discretion, determines that requiring the defendant to comply with such condition will advance public safety, probationer control or probationer surveillance. Electronic monitoring shall be used in accordance with uniform procedures developed by the office of probation and correctional alternatives.

4-a. Mandatory conditions for sex offenders. (a) When imposing a sentence of probation or conditional discharge upon a person convicted of an offense defined in article one hundred thirty, two hundred thirty-five or two hundred sixty-three of this chapter, or section 255.25, 255.26 or 255.27 of this chapter, and the victim of such offense was under the age of eighteen at the time of such offense or such person has been designated a level three sex offender pursuant to subdivision six of section 168-l of the correction law, the court shall require, as a mandatory condition of such sentence, that such sentenced offender shall refrain from knowingly entering into or upon any school grounds, as that term is defined in subdivision fourteen of section 220.00 of this chapter, or any other facility or institution primarily used for the care or treatment of persons under the age of eighteen while one or more of such persons under the age of eighteen are present, provided however, that when such sentenced offender is a registered student or participant or an employee of such facility or institution or entity contracting therewith or has a family member enrolled in such facility or institution, such sentenced offender may, with the written authorization of his or her probation officer or the court and the superintendent or chief administrator of such facility, institution or grounds, enter such facility, institution or upon such grounds for the limited purposes authorized by the probation officer or the court and superintendent or chief officer. Nothing in this subdivision shall be construed as restricting any lawful condition of supervision that may be imposed on such sentenced offender.

(b) When imposing a sentence of probation or conditional discharge upon a person convicted of an offense for which registration as a sex offender is required pursuant to subdivision two or three of section one hundred sixty-eight-a of the correction law, and the victim of such offense was under the age of eighteen at the time of such offense or such person has been designated a level three sex offender pursuant to subdivision six of section one hundred sixty-eight-l of the correction law or the internet was used to facilitate the commission of the crime, the court shall require, as mandatory conditions of such sentence, that such sentenced offender be prohibited from using the internet to access pornographic material, access a commercial social networking website, communicate with other individuals or groups for the purpose of promoting sexual relations with persons under the age of eighteen, and communicate with a person under the age of eighteen when such offender is over the age of eighteen, provided that the court may permit an offender to use the internet to communicate with a person under the age of eighteen when such offender is the parent of a minor child and is not otherwise prohibited from communicating with such child. Nothing in this subdivision shall be construed as restricting any other lawful condition of supervision that may be imposed on such sentenced offender. As used in this subdivision, a "commercial social networking website" shall mean any business, organization or other entity operating a website that permits persons under eighteen years of age to be registered users for the purpose of establishing personal relationships with other users, where such persons under eighteen years of age may: (i) create web pages or profiles that provide information about themselves where such web pages or profiles are available to the public or to other users; (ii) engage in direct or real time communication with other users, such as a chat room or instant messenger; and (iii) communicate with persons over eighteen years of age; provided, however, that, for purposes of this subdivision, a commercial social networking website shall not include a website that permits users to engage in such other activities as are not enumerated herein.

5. Other conditions. When imposing a sentence of probation the court may, in addition to any conditions imposed pursuant to subdivisions two, three and four of this section, require that the defendant comply with any other reasonable condition as the court shall deter-

mine to be necessary or appropriate to ameliorate the conduct which gave rise to the offense or to prevent the incarceration of the defendant.

5-a. Other conditions for sex offenders. When imposing a sentence of probation upon a person convicted of an offense for which registration as a sex offender is required pursuant to subdivision two or three of section one hundred sixty-eight-a of the correction law, in addition to any conditions required under subdivisions two, three, four, four-a and five of this section, the court may require that the defendant comply with a reasonable limitation on his or her use of the internet that the court determines to be necessary or appropriate to ameliorate the conduct which gave rise to the offense or to protect public safety, provided that the court shall not prohibit such sentenced offender from using the internet in connection with education, lawful employment or search for lawful employment.

§65.15 Calculation of periods of probation and of conditional discharge.

1. A period of probation or a period or additional period of conditional discharge commences on the day it is imposed. Multiple periods, whether imposed at the same or at different times, shall run concurrently.

2. When a person has violated the conditions of his or her probation or conditional discharge and is declared delinquent by the court, the declaration of delinquency shall interrupt the period of the sentence as of the date of the delinquency and such interruption shall continue until a final determination as to the delinquency has been made by the court pursuant to a hearing held in accordance with the provisions of the criminal procedure law. Any order for the installation and maintenance of a functioning ignition interlock device imposed pursuant to section 60.21 of this title shall remain in effect throughout the delinquency and the court may extend the period of such installation and maintenance by the period of the delinquency; provided, however, that the defendant shall get credit for any period where the device was installed and maintained during the delinquency.

*3. In any case where a person who is under a sentence of probation or of conditional discharge is also under an indeterminate or determinate sentence of imprisonment, imposed for some other offense by a court of this state the service of the sentence of imprisonment shall satisfy the sentence of probation or of conditional discharge unless the sentence of probation or of conditional discharge is revoked prior to the next to occur of parole or conditional release under, or satisfaction of, the sentence of imprisonment. Provided, however, that the service of an indeterminate or determinate sentence of imprisonment shall not satisfy a sentence of probation if the sentence of probation was imposed at a time when the sentence of imprisonment had one year or less to run.

(Amendments deemed repealed 9/1/23, Ch.55,L.2021)

§65.20 Sentence of unconditional discharge.

1. Criteria. The court may impose a sentence of unconditional discharge in any case where it is authorized to impose a sentence of

conditional discharge under section 65.05 if the court is of the opinion that no proper purpose would be served by imposing any condition upon the defendant's release.

When a sentence of unconditional discharge is imposed for a felony, the court shall set forth in the record the reasons for its action.

2. Sentence. When the court imposes a sentence of unconditional discharge, the defendant shall be released with respect to the conviction for which the sentence is imposed without imprisonment, fine or probation supervision. A sentence of unconditional discharge is for all purposes a final judgment of conviction.

ARTICLE 70 - SENTENCES OF IMPRISONMENT

Section
70.00   Sentence of imprisonment for felony.
70.02   Sentence of imprisonment for a violent felony offense.
70.04   Sentence of imprisonment for second violent felony offender.
70.05   Sentence of imprisonment for juvenile offender.
70.06   Sentence of imprisonment for second felony offender.
70.07   Sentence of imprisonment for second child sexual assault felony offender.
70.08   Sentence of imprisonment for persistent violent felony offender; criteria.
70.10   Sentence of imprisonment for persistent felony offender.
70.15   Sentences of imprisonment for misdemeanors and violation.
70.20   Place of imprisonment.
70.25   Concurrent and consecutive terms of imprisonment.
70.30   Calculation of terms of imprisonment.
70.35   Merger of certain definite and indeterminate or determinate sentences.
70.40   Release on parole; conditional release; presumptive release.
70.45   Determinate sentence; post-release supervision.
70.70   Sentence of imprisonment for felony drug offender other than a class A felony.
70.71   Sentence of imprisonment for a class A felony drug offender.
70.80   Sentences of imprisonment for conviction of a felony sex offense.
70.85   Transitional exception to determinate sentencing laws.

§70.00 Sentence of imprisonment for felony.

1. Indeterminate sentence. Except as provided in subdivisions *four, five and six* of this section or section 70.80 of this article, a sentence of imprisonment for a felony, other than a felony defined in article two hundred twenty or two hundred twenty-one of this chapter, shall be an indeterminate sentence. When such a sentence is imposed, the court shall impose a maximum term in accordance with the provisions of subdivision two of this section and the minimum period of imprisonment shall be as provided in subdivision three of this section.
* *(Material in italic deemed repealed 9/1/23,as of that date becomes"four and five", Ch.55,L.2021)*

2. Maximum term of sentence. The maximum term of an indeterminate sentence shall be at least three years and the term shall be fixed as follows:

(a) For a class A felony, the term shall be life imprisonment;

(b) For a class B felony, the term shall be fixed by the court, and shall not exceed twenty-five years;

(c) For a class C felony, the term shall be fixed by the court, and shall not exceed fifteen years;

(d) For a class D felony, the term shall be fixed by the court, and shall not exceed seven years; and

(e) For a class E felony, the term shall be fixed by the court, and shall not exceed four years.

3. Minimum period of imprisonment. The minimum period of imprisonment under an indeterminate sentence shall be at least one year and shall be fixed as follows:

(a) In the case of a class A felony, the minimum period shall be fixed by the court and specified in the sentence.

(i) For a class A-I felony, such minimum period shall not be less than fifteen years nor more than twenty-five years; provided, however, that (A) where a sentence, other than a sentence of death or life imprisonment without parole, is imposed upon a defendant convicted of murder in the first degree as defined in section 125.27 of this chapter such minimum period shall be not less than twenty years nor more than twenty-five years, and, (B) where a sentence is imposed upon a defendant convicted of murder in the second degree as defined in subdivision five of section 125.25 of this chapter or convicted of aggravated murder as defined in section 125.26 of this chapter, the sentence shall be life imprisonment without parole, and, (C) where a sentence is imposed upon a defendant convicted of attempted murder in the first degree as defined in article one hundred ten of this chapter and subparagraph (i), (ii) or (iii) of paragraph (a) of subdivision one and paragraph (b) of subdivision one of section 125.27 of this chapter or attempted aggravated murder as defined in article one hundred ten of this chapter and section 125.26 of this chapter such minimum period shall be not less than twenty years nor more than forty years.

(ii) For a class A-II felony, such minimum period shall not be less than three years nor more than eight years four months, except that for the class A-II felony of predatory sexual assault as defined in section 130.95 of this chapter or the class A-II felony of predatory sexual assault against a child as defined in section 130.96 of this chapter, such minimum period shall be not less than ten years nor more than twenty-five years.

(b) For any other felony, the minimum period shall be fixed by the court and specified in the sentence and shall be not less than one year nor more than one-third of the maximum term imposed.

4. Alternative definite sentence for class D and E felonies. When a person, other than a second or persistent felony offender, is sentenced for a class D or class E felony, and the court, having regard to the nature and circumstances of the crime and to the history and character of the defendant, is of the opinion that a sentence of imprisonment is necessary but that it would be unduly harsh to impose an indeterminate or determinate sentence, the court may impose a definite sentence of imprisonment and fix a term of one year or less.

*5. Life imprisonment without parole. Notwithstanding any other provision of law, a defendant sentenced to life imprisonment without parole shall not be or become eligible for parole or conditional release. For purposes of commitment and custody, other than parole and conditional release, such sentence shall be deemed to be an indeterminate sentence. A defendant may be sentenced to life imprisonment without parole upon conviction for the crime of murder in the first degree as defined in section 125.27 of this chapter and in accordance with the procedures provided by law for imposing a sentence for such crime. A defendant *who was eighteen years of age or older at the time of the commission of the crime* must be sentenced to life imprisonment without parole upon conviction for the crime of terrorism as defined in section 490.25 of this chapter, where the specified offense the defendant committed is a class A-I felony; the crime of criminal possession of a chemical weapon or biological weapon in the first degree as defined in section 490.45 of this chapter; or the crime of criminal use of a chemical weapon or biological weapon in the first degree as defined in section 490.55 of this chapter; provided, however, that nothing in this subdivision shall preclude or prevent a sentence of death when the defendant is also convicted of the crime of murder in the first degree as defined in section 125.27 of this chapter. *A defendant who was seventeen years of age or younger at the time of the commission of the crime may be sentenced, in accordance with law, to the applicable indeterminate sentence with a maximum term of life imprisonment.* A defendant must be sentenced to life imprisonment without parole upon conviction for the crime of murder in the second degree as defined in subdivision five of section 125.25 of this chapter or for the crime of aggravated murder as defined in subdivision one of section 125.26 of this chapter. A defendant may be sentenced to life imprisonment without parole upon conviction for the crime of aggravated murder as defined in subdivision two of section 125.26 of this chapter.

(Material in Italics takes Eff.10/1/18; provided however, that when the applicability of such provisions are based on the conviction of a crime or an act committed by a person who was seventeen years of age at the time of such offense such provisions shall take effect 10/1/19,Ch.59,L.2017)

*6. Determinate sentence. Except as provided in subdivision four of this section and subdivisions two and four of section 70.02, when a person is sentenced as a violent felony offender pursuant to section 70.02 or as a second violent felony offender pursuant to section 70.04 or as a second felony offender on a conviction for a violent felony offense pursuant to section 70.06, the court must impose a determinate sentence of imprisonment in accordance with the provisions of such sections and such sentence shall include, as a part thereof, a period of post-release supervision in accordance with section 70.45. *(Repealed 9/1/23,Ch.55,L.2021)*

§70.02 Sentence of imprisonment for a violent felony offense.

1. Definition of a violent felony offense. A violent felony offense is a class B violent felony offense, a class C violent felony offense, a class D violent felony offense, or a class E violent felony offense, defined as follows:

(a) Class B violent felony offenses: an attempt to commit the class A-I felonies of murder in the second degree as defined in section 125.25, kidnapping in the first degree as defined in section 135.25, and arson in the first degree as defined in section 150.20; manslaughter in the first degree as defined in section 125.20, aggravated manslaughter in the first degree as defined in section 125.22, rape in the first degree as defined in section 130.35, criminal sexual act in the first degree as defined in section 130.50, aggravated sexual abuse in the first degree as defined in section 130.70, course of sexual conduct against a child in the first degree as defined in section 130.75; assault in the first degree as defined in section 120.10, kidnapping in the second degree as defined in section 135.20, burglary in the first degree as defined in section 140.30, arson in the second degree as defined in section 150.15, robbery in the first degree as defined in section 160.15, sex trafficking as defined in paragraphs (a) and (b) of subdivision five of section 230.34, sex trafficking of a child as defined in section 230.34-a, incest in the first degree as defined in section 255.27, criminal possession of a weapon in the first degree as defined in section 265.04, criminal use of a firearm in the first degree as defined in section 265.09, criminal sale of a firearm in the first degree as defined in section 265.13, aggravated assault upon a police officer or a peace officer as defined in section 120.11, gang assault in the first degree as defined in section 120.07, intimidating a victim or witness in the first degree as defined in section 215.17, hindering prosecution of terrorism in the first degree as defined in section 490.35, criminal possession of a chemical weapon or biological weapon in the second degree as defined in section 490.40, and criminal use of a chemical weapon or biological weapon in the third degree as defined in section 490.47.

(b) Class C violent felony offenses: an attempt to commit any of the class B felonies set forth in paragraph (a) of this subdivision; aggravated criminally negligent homicide as defined in section 125.11, aggravated manslaughter in the second degree as defined in section 125.21, aggravated sexual abuse in the second degree as defined in section 130.67, assault on a peace officer, police officer, firefighter or emergency medical services professional as defined in section 120.08, assault on a judge as defined in section 120.09, gang assault in the second degree as defined in section 120.06, strangulation in the first degree as defined in section 121.13, aggravated strangulation as defined in section 121.13-a, burglary in the second degree as defined in section 140.25, robbery in the second degree as defined in section 160.10, criminal possession of a weapon in the second degree as defined in section 265.03, criminal use of a firearm in the second degree as defined in section 265.08, criminal sale of a firearm in the second degree as defined in section 265.12, criminal sale of a firearm with the aid of a minor as defined in section 265.14, aggravated criminal possession of a weapon as defined in section 265.19, soliciting or providing support for an act of terrorism in the first degree as defined in section 490.15, hindering prosecution of terrorism in the second degree as defined in section 490.30, and criminal possession of a chemical weapon or biological weapon in the third degree as defined in section 490.37.

(c) Class D violent felony offenses: an attempt to commit any of the class C felonies set forth in paragraph (b); reckless assault of a child as defined in section 120.02, assault in the second degree as defined in section 120.05, menacing a police officer or peace officer as defined in section 120.18, stalking in the first degree, as defined in subdivision one of section 120.60, strangulation in the second degree as defined in section 121.12, rape in the second degree as defined in section 130.30, criminal sexual act in the second degree as defined in section 130.45, sexual abuse in the first degree as defined in section 130.65, course of sexual conduct against a child in the second degree as defined in section 130.80, aggravated sexual abuse in the third degree as defined in section 130.66, facilitating a sex offense with a controlled substance as defined in section 130.90, labor trafficking as defined in paragraphs (a) and (b) of subdivision three of section 135.35, criminal possession of a weapon in the third degree as defined in subdivision five, six, seven, eight, nine or ten of section 265.02, criminal sale of a firearm in the third degree as defined in section 265.11, intimidating a victim or witness in the second degree as defined in section 215.16, soliciting or providing support for an act of terrorism in the second degree as defined in section 490.10, and making a terroristic threat as defined in section 490.20, falsely reporting an incident in the first degree as defined in section 240.60, placing a false bomb or hazardous substance in the first degree as defined in section 240.62, placing a false bomb or hazardous substance in a sports stadium or arena, mass transportation facility or enclosed shopping mall as defined in section 240.63, aggravated unpermitted use of indoor pyrotechnics in the first degree as defined in section 405.18, and criminal manufacture, sale, or transport of an undetectable firearm, rifle or shotgun as defined in section 265.50.

(d) Class E violent felony offenses: an attempt to commit any of the felonies of criminal possession of a weapon in the third degree as defined in subdivision five, six, seven or eight of section 265.02 as a lesser included offense of that section as defined in section 220.20 of the criminal procedure law, persistent sexual abuse as defined in section

130.53, aggravated sexual abuse in the fourth degree as defined in section 130.65-a, falsely reporting an incident in the second degree as defined in section 240.55 and placing a false bomb or hazardous substance in the second degree as defined in section 240.61.

2. Authorized sentence.

*(a) Except as provided in subdivision six of section 60.05, the sentence imposed upon a person who stands convicted of a class B or class C violent felony offense must be a determinate sentence of imprisonment which shall be in whole or half years. The term of such sentence must be in accordance with the provisions of subdivision three of this section. *(Amendments deemed repealed 9/1/23,Ch.55,L.2021)*

(b) Except as provided in paragraph (b-1) of this subdivision, subdivision six of section 60.05 and subdivision four of this section, the sentence imposed upon a person who stands convicted of a class D violent felony offense, other than the offense of criminal possession of a weapon in the third degree as defined in subdivision five, seven or eight of section 265.02 or criminal sale of a firearm in the third degree as defined in section 265.11, must be in accordance with the applicable provisions of this chapter relating to sentencing for class D felonies provided, however, that where a sentence of imprisonment is imposed which requires a commitment to the state department of corrections and community supervision, such sentence shall be a determinate sentence in accordance with paragraph (c) of subdivision three of this section.

(b-1) Except as provided in subdivision six of section 60.05, the sentence imposed upon a person who stands convicted of the class D violent felony offense of menacing a police officer or peace officer as defined in section 120.18 of this chapter must be a determinate sentence of imprisonment.

(c) Except as provided in subdivision six of section 60.05, the sentence imposed upon a person who stands convicted of the class D violent felony offenses of criminal possession of a weapon in the third degree as defined in subdivision five, seven, eight or nine of section 265.02, criminal sale of a firearm in the third degree as defined in section 265.11, the class E violent felonies of attempted criminal possession of a weapon in the third degree as defined in subdivision five, seven, eight or nine of section 265.02, or criminal manufacture, sale, or transport of an undetectable firearm, rifle or shotgun as defined in section 265.50 must be a sentence to a determinate period of imprisonment, or, in the alternative, a definite sentence of imprisonment for a period of no less than one year, except that:

(i) the court may impose any other sentence authorized by law upon a person who has not been previously convicted in the five years immediately preceding the commission of the offense for a class A misdemeanor defined in this chapter, if the court having regard to the nature and circumstances of the crime and to the history and character of the defendant, finds on the record that such sentence would be unduly harsh and that the alternative sentence would be consistent with public safety and does not deprecate the seriousness of the crime; and

(ii) the court may apply the provisions of paragraphs (b) and (c) of subdivision four of this section when imposing a sentence upon a person who has previously been convicted of a class A misdemeanor defined in this chapter in the five years immediately preceding the commission of the offense.

3. Term of sentence. The term of a determinate sentence for a violent felony offense must be fixed by the court as follows:

(a) For a class B felony, the term must be at least five years and must not exceed twenty-five years, provided, however, that the term must be: (i) at least ten years and must not exceed thirty years where the sentence is for the crime of aggravated assault upon a police officer or peace officer as defined in section 120.11 of this chapter; and (ii) at least ten years and must not exceed thirty years where the sentence is for the crime of aggravated manslaughter in the first degree as defined in section 125.22 of this chapter;

(b) For a class C felony, the term must be at least three and one-half years and must not exceed fifteen years, provided, however, that the term must be: (i) at least seven years and must not exceed twenty years where the sentence is for the crime of aggravated manslaughter in the second degree as defined in section 125.21 of this chapter; (ii) at least seven years and must not exceed twenty years where the sentence is for the crime of attempted aggravated assault upon a police officer or peace officer as defined in section 120.11 of this chapter; (iii) at least three and one-half years and must not exceed twenty years where the sentence is for the crime of aggravated criminally negligent homicide as defined in section 125.11 of this chapter; and (iv) at least five years and must not exceed fifteen years where the sentence is imposed for the crime of aggravated criminal possession of a weapon as defined in section 265.19 of this chapter;

(c) For a class D felony, the term must be at least two years and must not exceed seven years, provided, however, that the term must be: (i) at least two years and must not exceed eight years where the sentence is for the crime of menacing a police officer or peace officer as defined in section 120.18 of this chapter; and (ii) at least three and one-half years and must not exceed seven years where the sentence is imposed for the crime of criminal possession of a weapon in the third degree as defined in subdivision ten of section 265.02 of this chapter;

(d) For a class E felony, the term must be at least one and one-half years and must not exceed four years.

4. (a) Except as provided in paragraph (b) of this subdivision, where a plea of guilty to a class D violent felony offense is entered pursuant to section 220.10 or 220.30 of the criminal procedure law in satisfaction of an indictment charging the defendant with an armed felony, as defined in subdivision forty-one of section 1.20 of the criminal procedure law, the court must impose a determinate sentence of imprisonment.

(b) In any case in which the provisions of paragraph (a) of this subdivision or the provisions of subparagraph (ii) of paragraph (c) of subdivision two of this section apply, the court may impose a sentence other than a determinate sentence of imprisonment, or a definite sentence of imprisonment for a period of no less than one year, if it finds that the alternate sentence is consistent with public safety and does not deprecate the seriousness of the crime and that one or more of the following factors exist:

(i) mitigating circumstances that bear directly upon the manner in which the crime was committed; or

(ii) where the defendant was not the sole participant in the crime, the defendant's participation was relatively minor although not so minor as to constitute a defense to the prosecution; or

(iii) possible deficiencies in proof of the defendant's commission of an armed felony.

(c) The defendant and the district attorney shall have an opportunity to present relevant information to assist the court in making a determination pursuant to paragraph (b) of this subdivision, and the court may, in its discretion, conduct a hearing with respect to any issue bearing upon such determination. If the court determines that a determinate sentence of imprisonment should not be imposed pursuant to the provisions of such paragraph (b), it shall make a statement on the record of the facts and circumstances upon which such determination is based. A transcript of the court's statement, which shall set forth the recommendation of the district attorney, shall be forwarded to the state division of criminal justice services along with a copy of the accusatory instrument.

§70.04 Sentence of imprisonment for second violent felony offender.

1. Definition of second violent felony offender.

(a) A second violent felony offender is a person who stands convicted of a violent felony offense as defined in subdivision one of section 70.02 after having previously been subjected to a predicate violent felony conviction as defined in paragraph (b) of this subdivision.

(b) For the purpose of determining whether a prior conviction is a predicate violent felony conviction the following criteria shall apply:

(i) The conviction must have been in this state of a class A felony (other than one defined in article two hundred twenty) or of a violent felony offense as defined in subdivision one of section 70.02, or of an offense defined by the penal law in effect prior to September first, nineteen hundred sixty-seven, which includes all of the essential elements of any such felony, or in any other jurisdiction of an offense which includes all of the essential elements of any such felony for which a sentence to a term of imprisonment in excess of one year or a sentence of death was authorized and is authorized in this state irrespective of whether such sentence was imposed;

(ii) Sentence upon such prior conviction must have been imposed before commission of the present felony;

(iii) Suspended sentence, suspended execution of sentence, a sentence of probation, a sentence of conditional discharge or of unconditional discharge, and a sentence of certification to the care and custody of the division of substance abuse services, shall be deemed to be a sentence;

(iv) Except as provided in subparagraph (v) of this paragraph, sentence must have been imposed not more than ten years before commission of the felony of which the defendant presently stands convicted;

    (v) In calculating the ten year period under subparagraph (iv), any period of time during which the person was incarcerated for any reason between the time of commission of the previous felony and the time of commission of the present felony shall be excluded and such ten year period shall be extended by a period or periods equal to the time served under such incarceration;

    (vi) An offense for which the defendant has been pardoned on the ground of innocence shall not be deemed a predicate violent felony conviction.

    2. Authorized sentence. When the court has found, pursuant to the provisions of the criminal procedure law, that a person is a second violent felony offender the court must impose a determinate sentence of imprisonment which shall be in whole or half years. Except where sentence is imposed in accordance with the provisions of section 70.10, the term of such sentence must be in accordance with the provisions of subdivision three of this section.(Amendments deemed repealed 9/1/23,Ch.55,2021)

    *3. Term of sentence. The term of a determinate sentence for a second violent felony offender must be fixed by the court as follows:

    (a) For a class B felony, the term must be at least ten years and must not exceed twenty-five years;

    (b) For a class C felony, the term must be at least seven years and must not exceed fifteen years; and

    (c) For a class D felony, the term must be at least five years and must not exceed seven years.

    (d) For a class E felony, the term must be at least three years and must not exceed four years.   *(Amendments deemed repealed 9/1/23,Ch.55,2021)

§70.05 Sentence of imprisonment for juvenile offender.

    1. Indeterminate sentence. A sentence of imprisonment for a felony committed by a juvenile offender shall be an indeterminate sentence. When such a sentence is imposed, the court shall impose a maximum term in accordance with the provisions of subdivision two of this section and the minimum period of imprisonment shall be as provided in subdivision three of this section. The court shall further provide that where a juvenile offender is under placement pursuant to article three of the family court act, any sentence imposed pursuant to this section which is to be served consecutively with such placement shall be served in a facility designated pursuant to subdivision four of section 70.20 of this article prior to service of the placement in any previously designated facility.

    2. Maximum term of sentence. The maximum term of an indeterminate sentence for a juvenile offender shall be at least three years and the term shall be fixed as follows:

    (a) For the class A felony of murder in the second degree, the term shall be life imprisonment;

(b) For the class A felony of arson in the first degree, or for the class A felony of kidnapping in the first degree the term shall be fixed by the court, and shall be at least twelve years but shall not exceed fifteen years;

(c) For a class B felony, the term shall be fixed by the court, and shall not exceed ten years;

(d) For a class C felony, the term shall be fixed by the court, and shall not exceed seven years; and

(e) For a class D felony, the term shall be fixed by the court and shall not exceed four years.

3. Minimum period of imprisonment. The minimum period of imprisonment under an indeterminate sentence for a juvenile offender shall be specified in the sentence as follows:

(a) For the class A felony of murder in the second degree, the minimum period of imprisonment shall be fixed by the court and shall be not less than five years but shall not exceed nine years provided, however, that where the sentence is for an offense specified in subdivision one or two of section 125.25 of this chapter and the defendant was fourteen or fifteen years old at the time of such offense, the minimum period of imprisonment shall be not less than seven and one-half years but shall not exceed fifteen years;

(b) For the class A felony of arson in the first degree, or for the class A felony of kidnapping in the first degree, the minimum period of imprisonment shall be fixed by the court and shall be not less than four years but shall not exceed six years; and

(c) For a class B, C or D felony, the minimum period of imprisonment shall be fixed by the court at one-third of the maximum term imposed.

§70.06 Sentence of imprisonment for second felony offender.

1. Definition of second felony offender.

(a) A second felony offender is a person, other than a second violent felony offender as defined in section 70.04, who stands convicted of a felony defined in this chapter, other than a class A-I felony, after having previously been subjected to one or more predicate felony convictions as defined in paragraph (b) of this subdivision.

(b) For the purpose of determining whether a prior conviction is a predicate felony conviction the following criteria shall apply:

(i) The conviction must have been in this state of a felony, or in any other jurisdiction of an offense for which a sentence to a term of imprisonment in excess of one year or a sentence of death was authorized and is authorized in this state irrespective of whether such sentence was imposed;

(ii) Sentence upon such prior conviction must have been imposed before commission of the present felony;

(iii) Suspended sentence, suspended execution of sentence, a sentence of probation, a sentence of conditional discharge or of unconditional discharge, and a sentence of certification to the care and custody of the division of substance abuse services, shall be deemed to be a sentence;

(iv) Except as provided in subparagraph (v) of this paragraph, sentence must have been imposed not more than ten years before commission of the felony of which the defendant presently stands convicted;

(v) In calculating the ten year period under subparagraph (iv), any period of time during which the person was incarcerated for any reason between the time of commission of the previous felony and the time of commission of the present felony shall be excluded and such ten year period shall be extended by a period or periods equal to the time served under such incarceration;

(vi) An offense for which the defendant has been pardoned on the ground of innocence shall not be deemed a predicate felony conviction.

*2. Authorized sentence. Except as provided in subdivision five *or six** of this section, or as provided in subdivision five of section 70.80 of this article, when the court has found, pursuant to the provisions of the criminal procedure law, that a person is a second felony offender the court must impose an indeterminate sentence of imprisonment. The maximum term of such sentence must be in accordance with the provisions of subdivision three of this section and the minimum period of imprisonment under such sentence must be in accordance with subdivision four of this section.

(Material in italic deemed repealed 9/1/23,Ch.55,L.2021)

*3. Maximum term of sentence. Except as provided in subdivision five *or six** of this section, or as provided in subdivision five of section 70.80 of this article, the maximum term of an indeterminate sentence for a second felony offender must be fixed by the court as follows:

(a) For a class A-II felony, the term must be life imprisonment;

(b) For a class B felony, the term must be at least nine years and must not exceed twenty-five years;

(c) For a class C felony, the term must be at least six years and must not exceed fifteen years;

(d) For a class D felony, the term must be at least four years and must not exceed seven years; and

(e) For a class E felony, the term must be at least three years and must not exceed four years; provided, however, that where the sentence is for the class E felony offense specified in section 240.32 of this chapter, the maximum term must be at least three years and must not exceed five years.   *(Material in italic deemed repealed 9/1/23,Ch.55,L.2021)*

4. Minimum period of imprisonment. (a) The minimum period of imprisonment for a second felony offender convicted of a class A-II felony must be fixed by the court at no less than six years and not to exceed twelve and one-half years and must be specified in the sentence,

except that for the class A-II felony of predatory sexual assault as defined in section 130.95 of this chapter or the class A-II felony of predatory sexual assault against a child as defined in section 130.96 of this chapter, such minimum period shall be not less than ten years nor more than twenty-five years.

(b) Except as provided in paragraph (a), the minimum period of imprisonment under an indeterminate sentence for a second felony offender must be fixed by the court at one-half of the maximum term imposed and must be specified in the sentence.

5. *(Repealed)*

*6. Determinate sentence. When the court has found, pursuant to the provisions of the criminal procedure law, that a person is a second felony offender and the sentence to be imposed on such person is for a violent felony offense, as defined in subdivision one of section 70.02, the court must impose a determinate sentence of imprisonment the term of which must be fixed by the court as follows:

(a) For a class B violent felony offense, the term must be at least eight years and must not exceed twenty-five years;

(b) For a class C violent felony offense, the term must be at least five years and must not exceed fifteen years;

(c) For a class D violent felony offense, the term must be at least three years and must not exceed seven years; and

(d) For a class E violent felony offense, the term must be at least two years and must not exceed four years.   *(Repealed 9/1/23,Ch.55,L.2021)*

*7. Notwithstanding any other provision of law, in the case of a person sentenced for a specified offense or offenses as defined in subdivision five of section 410.91 of the criminal procedure law, who stands convicted of no other felony offense, who has not previously been convicted of either a violent felony offense as defined in section 70.02 of this article, a class A felony offense or a class B felony offense, and is not under the jurisdiction of or awaiting delivery to the department of corrections and community supervision, the court may direct that such sentence be executed as a parole supervision sentence as defined in and pursuant to the procedures prescribed in section 410.91 of the criminal procedure law.   *(Repealed 9/1/23,Ch.55,L.2021)*

§70.07 Sentence of imprisonment for second child sexual assault felony offender.

1. A person who stands convicted of a felony offense for a sexual assault against a child, having been subjected to a predicate felony conviction for a sexual assault against a child, must be sentenced in accordance with the provisions of subdivision four or five of this section.

2. A "sexual assault against a child" means a felony offense, other than persistent sexual abuse as defined in section 130.53 of this chapter,

(a) the essential elements of which include the commission or attempted commission of sexual conduct, as defined in subdivision ten of section 130.00 of this chapter, (b) committed or attempted to be committed against a child less than fifteen years old.

3. For purposes of determining whether a person has been subjected to a predicate felony conviction under this section, the criteria set forth in paragraph (b) of subdivision one of section 70.06 shall apply provided however that for purposes of this subdivision, the terms "ten year" or "ten years", as provided in subparagraphs (iv) and (v) of paragraph (b) of subdivision one of such section 70.06, shall be "fifteen year" or "fifteen years". The provisions of section 400.19 of the criminal procedure law shall govern the procedures that must be followed to determine whether a person who stands convicted of a sexual assault against a child has been previously subjected to a predicate felony conviction for such a sexual assault and whether such offender was eighteen years of age or older at the time of the commission of the predicate felony.

4. Where the court has found pursuant to subdivision three of this section that a person who stands convicted of a felony offense defined in article one hundred thirty of this chapter for the commission or attempted commission of a sexual assault against a child has been subjected to a predicate felony conviction for a sexual assault against a child, the court shall sentence the defendant as follows:

(a) where the defendant stands convicted of such sexual assault against a child and such conviction is for a class A-II or class B felony offense, and the predicate conviction for such sexual assault against a child is for a class class A-II, B or class C felony offense, the court shall impose an indeterminate sentence of imprisonment, the maximum term of which shall be life and the minimum period of which shall be at least fifteen years and no more than twenty-five years;

(b) where the defendant stands convicted of such sexual assault against a child and the conviction is for a class C felony offense, and the predicate conviction for such sexual assault against a child is for a class A-II class B or class C felony offense, the court shall impose a determinate sentence of imprisonment, the term of which must be at least twelve years and must not exceed thirty years; provided however, that if the court determines that a longer sentence is warranted, the court shall set forth on the record the reasons for such determination and, in lieu of imposing such sentence of imprisonment, may impose an indeterminate sentence of imprisonment, the maximum term of which shall be life and the minimum period of which shall be at least fifteen years and no more than twenty-five years;

(c) where the defendant stands convicted of such sexual assault against a child and the conviction is for a class B felony offense, and the predicate conviction for such sexual assault against a child is for a class D or class E felony offense, the court shall impose a determinate sentence of imprisonment, the term of which must be at least twelve years and must not exceed thirty years;

(d) where the defendant stands convicted of such sexual assault against a child and the conviction is for a class C felony offense, and the predicate conviction for such sexual assault against a child is for a class D or class E felony offense, the court shall impose a determinate sentence of imprisonment, the term of which must be at least ten years and must not exceed twenty-five years;

(e) where the defendant stands convicted of such sexual assault against a child and the conviction is for a class D felony offense, and the predicate conviction for such sexual assault against a child is for a felony offense, the court shall impose a determinate sentence of imprisonment, the term of which must be at least five years and must not exceed fifteen years; and

(f) where the defendant stands convicted of such sexual assault against a child and the conviction is for a class E felony offense, and the predicate conviction for such sexual assault against a child is for a felony offense, the court shall impose a determinate sentence of imprisonment, the term of which must be at least four years and must not exceed twelve years.

5. Notwithstanding subdivision four of this section, where the court has found pursuant to subdivision three of this section that a person: (a) stands convicted of a felony offense defined in article one hundred thirty of this chapter for the commission or attempted commission of a sexual assault against a child; and (b) has been subjected to a predicate felony conviction for sexual assault against a child as defined in subdivision two of this section; and (c) who was under the age of eighteen years at the time of the commission of such predicate felony offense, then the court may, in lieu of the sentence authorized by subdivision four of this section, sentence the defendant to a term of imprisonment in accordance with the sentence authorized for the instant felony offense pursuant to subdivision three of section 70.04 of this article. The court shall set forth on the record the reasons for such determination.

§70.08 Sentence of imprisonment for persistent violent felony offender; criteria.

1. Definition of persistent violent felony offender.

(a) A persistent violent felony offender is a person who stands convicted of a violent felony offense as defined in subdivision one of section 70.02 or the offense of predatory sexual assault as defined in section 130.95 of this chapter or the offense of predatory sexual assault against a child as defined in section 130.96 of this chapter, after having previously been subjected to two or more predicate violent felony convictions as defined in paragraph (b) of subdivision one of section 70.04 of this article.

(b) For the purpose of determining whether a person has two or more predicate violent felony convictions, the criteria set forth in paragraph (b) of subdivision one of section 70.04 shall apply.

2. Authorized sentence. When the court has found, pursuant to the provisions of the criminal procedure law, that a person is a persistent violent felony offender the court must impose an indeterminate sentence of imprisonment, the maximum term of which shall be life imprisonment. The minimum period of imprisonment under such sentence must be in accordance with subdivision three of this section.

*3. Minimum period of imprisonment. The minimum period of imprisonment under an indeterminate life sentence for a persistent violent felony offender must be fixed by the court as follows:

(a) For the class A-II felony of predatory sexual assault as defined in section 130.95 of this chapter or the class A-II felony of predatory sexual assault against a child as defined in section 130.96 of this chapter, the minimum period must be twenty-five years;

(a-1) For a class B felony, the minimum period must be at least twenty years and must not exceed twenty-five years;

(b) For a class C felony, the minimum period must be at least sixteen years and must not exceed twenty-five years;

(c) For a class D felony, the minimum period must be at least twelve years and must not exceed twenty-five years.

(Amendments deemed repealed 9/1/23,Ch.55,L.2021)

§70.10 Sentence of imprisonment for persistent felony offender.

1. Definition of persistent felony offender.

(a) A persistent felony offender is a person, other than a persistent violent felony offender as defined in section 70.08, who stands convicted of a felony after having previously been convicted of two or more felonies, as provided in paragraphs (b) and (c) of this subdivision.

(b) A previous felony conviction within the meaning of paragraph (a) of this subdivision is a conviction of a felony in this state, or of a crime in any other jurisdiction, provided:

(i) that a sentence to a term of imprisonment in excess of one year, or a sentence to death, was imposed therefor; and

(ii) that the defendant was imprisoned under sentence for such conviction prior to the commission of the present felony; and

(iii) that the defendant was not pardoned on the ground of innocence; and

(iv) that such conviction was for a felony offense other than persistent sexual abuse, as defined in section 130.53 of this chapter.

(c) For the purpose of determining whether a person has two or more previous felony convictions, two or more convictions of crimes that were committed prior to the time the defendant was imprisoned under sentence for any of such convictions shall be deemed to be only one conviction.

2. Authorized sentence. When the court has found, pursuant to the provisions of the criminal procedure law, that a person is a persistent felony offender, and when it is of the opinion that the history and character of the defendant and the nature and circumstances of his

criminal conduct indicate that extended incarceration and life-time supervision will best serve the public interest, the court, in lieu of imposing the sentence of imprisonment authorized by section 70.00, 70.02, 70.04, 70.06 or subdivision five of section 70.80 for the crime of which such person presently stands convicted, may impose the sentence of imprisonment authorized by that section for a class A-I felony. In such event the reasons for the court's opinion shall be set forth in the record.

§70.15 Sentences of imprisonment for misdemeanors and violation.

1. Class A misdemeanor. A sentence of imprisonment for a class A misdemeanor shall be a definite sentence. When such a sentence is imposed the term shall be fixed by the court, and shall not exceed three hundred sixty-four days.   *(Eff.4/12/19,Ch.55,L.2019)*

1-a. (a) Notwithstanding the provisions of any other law, whenever the phrase "one year" or "three hundred sixty-five days" or "365 days" or any similar phrase appears in any provision of this chapter or any other law in reference to the definite sentence or maximum definite sentence of imprisonment that is imposed, or has been imposed, or may be imposed after enactment of this subdivision, for a misdemeanor conviction in this state, such phrase shall mean, be interpreted and be applied as three hundred sixty-four days.

(b) The amendatory provisions of this subdivision are ameliorative and shall apply to all persons who are sentenced before, on or after the effective date of this subdivision, for a crime committed before, on or after the effective date of this subdivision.

(c) Any sentence for a misdemeanor conviction imposed prior to the effective date of this subdivision that is a definite sentence of imprisonment of one year, or three hundred sixty-five days, shall, by operation of law, be changed to, mean and be interpreted and applied as a sentence of three hundred sixty-four days. In addition to any other right of a person to obtain a record of a proceeding against him or her, a person so sentenced prior to the effective date of this subdivision shall be entitled to obtain, from the criminal court or the clerk thereof, a certificate of conviction, as described in subdivision one of section 60.60 of the criminal procedure law, setting forth such sentence as the sentence specified in this paragraph.

(d) Any sentence for a misdemeanor conviction imposed prior to the effective date of this subdivision that is other than a definite sentence of imprisonment of one year may be set aside, upon motion of the defendant under section 440.20 of the criminal procedure law based on a showing that the judgment and sentence under the law in effect at the time of conviction imposed prior to the effective date of this subdivision is likely to result in collateral consequences, in order to permit the court to resentence the defendant in accordance with the amendatory provisions of this subdivision.   *(Eff.4/12/19,Ch.59,L.2019)*

(e) Resentence by operation of law is without prejudice to an individual seeking further relief pursuant to paragraph (j) of subdivision one of section 440.10 of the criminal procedure law. Nothing in this section is intended to diminish or abrogate any rights or remedies otherwise available to the individual. *(Eff.4/12/19,Chs.55 & 59,L.2019)*

2. Class B misdemeanor. A sentence of imprisonment for a class B misdemeanor shall be a definite sentence. When such a sentence is imposed the term shall be fixed by the court, and shall not exceed three months.

3. Unclassified misdemeanor. A sentence of imprisonment for an unclassified misdemeanor shall be a definite sentence. When such a sentence is imposed the term shall be fixed by the court, and shall be in accordance with the sentence specified in the law or ordinance that defines the crime but, in any event, it shall not exceed three hundred sixty-four days. *(Eff.4/12/19,Ch.55,L.2019)*

4. Violation. A sentence of imprisonment for a violation shall be a definite sentence. When such a sentence is imposed the term shall be fixed by the court, and shall not exceed fifteen days.

In the case of a violation defined outside this chapter, if the sentence is expressly specified in the law or ordinance that defines the offense and consists solely of a fine, no term of imprisonment shall be imposed.

§70.20 Place of imprisonment.

*1. (a) Indeterminate or determinate sentence. Except as provided in subdivision four of this section, when an indeterminate or determinate sentence of imprisonment is imposed, the court shall commit the defendant to the custody of the state department of corrections and community supervision for the term of his or her sentence and until released in accordance with the law; provided, however, that a defendant sentenced pursuant to subdivision seven of section 70.06 shall be committed to the custody of the state department of corrections and community supervision for immediate delivery to a reception center operated by the department.

(b) The court in committing a defendant who is not yet eighteen years of age to the department of corrections and community supervision shall inquire as to whether the parents or legal guardian of the defendant, if present, will grant to the minor the capacity to consent to routine medical, dental and mental health services and treatment.

(c) Notwithstanding paragraph (b) of this subdivision, where the court commits a defendant who is not yet eighteen years of age to the custody of the department of corrections and community supervision in accordance with this section and no medical consent has been obtained prior to said commitment, the commitment order shall be deemed to grant the capacity to consent to routine medical, dental and mental health services and treatment to the person so committed.

(d) Nothing in this subdivision shall preclude a parent or legal guardian of an incarcerated individual who is not yet eighteen years of age from making a motion on notice to the department of corrections and community supervision pursuant to article twenty-two of the civil practice law and rules and section one hundred forty of the correction law, objecting to routine medical, dental or mental health services and treatment being provided to such incarcerated individual under the provisions of paragraph (b) of this subdivision. *(Eff.8/2/21,Ch.322,L.2021)*

(e) Nothing in this section shall require that consent be obtained from the parent or legal guardian, where no consent is necessary or where the defendant is authorized by law to consent on his or her own behalf to any medical, dental, and mental health service or treatment.

*(Amendments deemed repealed 9/1/23,Ch.55,L.2021)

2. Definite sentence. Except as provided in subdivision four of this section, when a definite sentence of imprisonment is imposed, the court shall commit the defendant to the county or regional correctional institution for the term of his sentence and until released in accordance with the law.

2-a. Sentence of life imprisonment without parole. When a sentence of life imprisonment without parole is imposed, the court shall commit the defendant to the custody of the state department of corrections and community supervision for the remainder of the life of the defendant.

*3. Undischarged imprisonment in other jurisdiction. When a defendant who is subject to an undischarged term of imprisonment, imposed at a previous time by a court of another jurisdiction, is sentenced to an additional term or terms of imprisonment by a court of this state to run concurrently with such undischarged term, as provided in subdivision four of section 70.25, the return of the defendant to the custody of the appropriate official of the other jurisdiction shall be deemed a commitment for such portion of the term or terms of the sentence imposed by the court of this state as shall not exceed the said undischarged term. The defendant shall be committed to the custody of the state department of corrections and community supervision if the additional term or terms are indeterminate or determinate or to the appropriate county or regional correctional institution if the said term or terms are definite for such portion of the term or terms of the sentence imposed as shall exceed such undischarged term or until released in accordance with law. If such additional term or terms imposed shall run consecutively to the said undischarged term, the defendant shall be committed as provided in subdivisions one and two of this section.

*(Amendments deemed repealed 9/1/23,Ch.55,L.2021)

4. (a) Notwithstanding any other provision of law to the contrary, a juvenile offender, adolescent offender, or a juvenile offender or adolescent offender who is adjudicated a youthful offender, who is

given an indeterminate, determinate or a definite sentence, and who is under the age of twenty-one at the time of sentencing, shall be committed to the custody of the commissioner of the office of children and family services who shall arrange for the confinement of such offender in secure facilities of the office; provided, however if an adolescent offender who committed a crime on or after the youth's sixteenth birthday receives a definite sentence not exceeding one year, the judge may order that the adolescent offender serve such sentence in a specialized secure juvenile detention facility for older youth certified by the office of children and family services in conjunction with the state commission of correction and operated pursuant to section two hundred eighteen-a of the county law. The release or transfer of such juvenile offenders or adolescent offenders from the office of children and family services shall be governed by section five hundred eight of the executive law.

(a-1) *(Repealed, Eff.6/2/20,Ch.55,L.2020)*

(a-2) Notwithstanding any other provision of law to the contrary, a person sixteen years of age who commits a vehicle and traffic law offense that does not constitute an adolescent offender offense on or after October first, two thousand eighteen and a person seventeen years of age who commits such an offense on or after October first, two thousand nineteen who is sentenced to a term of imprisonment who is under the age of twenty-one at the time he or she is sentenced shall be committed to a specialized secure detention facility for older youth certified by the office of children and family services in conjunction with the state commission of correction.

(b) The court in committing a juvenile offender and youthful offender to the custody of the office of children and family services shall inquire as to whether the parents or legal guardian of the youth, if present, will consent for the office of children and family services to provide routine medical, dental and mental health services and treatment.

(c) Notwithstanding paragraph (b) of this subdivision, where the court commits an offender to the custody of the office of children and family services in accordance with this section and no medical consent has been obtained prior to said commitment, the commitment order shall be deemed to grant consent for the office of children and family services to provide for routine medical, dental and mental health services and treatment to the offender so committed.

(d) Nothing in this subdivision shall preclude a parent or legal guardian of an offender who is not yet eighteen years of age from making a motion on notice to the office of children and family services pursuant to article twenty-two of the civil practice law and rules objecting to routine medical, dental or mental health services and treatment being provided to such offender under the provisions of paragraph (b) of this subdivision.

(e) Nothing in this section shall require that consent be obtained from the parent or legal guardian, where no consent is necessary or where the offender is authorized by law to consent on his or her own behalf to any medical, dental and mental health service or treatment.

5. Subject to regulations of the department of health, routine medical, dental and mental health services and treatment is defined for the purposes of this section to mean any routine diagnosis or treatment, including without limitation the administration of medications or nutrition, the extraction of bodily fluids for analysis, and dental care performed with a local anesthetic. Routine mental health treatment shall not include psychiatric administration of medication unless it is part of an ongoing mental health plan or unless it is otherwise authorized by law.

§70.25 Concurrent and consecutive terms of imprisonment.

1. Except as provided in subdivisions two, two-a and five of this section, when multiple sentences of imprisonment are imposed on a person at the same time, or when a person who is subject to any undischarged term of imprisonment imposed at a previous time by a court of this state is sentenced to an additional term of imprisonment, the sentence or sentences imposed by the court shall run either concurrently or consecutively with respect to each other and the undischarged term or terms in such manner as the court directs at the time of sentence. If the court does not specify the manner in which a sentence imposed by it is to run, the sentence shall run as follows:

(a) An indeterminate *or determinate** sentence shall run concurrently with all other terms; and

*(Material in italic deemed repealed 9/1/23,Ch.55,L.2021)

(b) A definite sentence shall run concurrently with any sentence imposed at the same time and shall be consecutive to any other term.

2. When more than one sentence of imprisonment is imposed on a person for two or more offenses committed through a single act or omission, or through an act or omission which in itself constituted one of the offenses and also was a material element of the other, the

sentences, except if one or more of such sentences is for a violation of section 270.20 of this chapter, must run concurrently.

2-a. When an indeterminate or determinate sentence of imprisonment is imposed pursuant to section 70.04, 70.06, 70.07, 70.08, 70.10, subdivision three or four of section 70.70, subdivision three or four of section 70.71 or subdivision five of section 70.80 of this article, or is imposed for a class A-I felony pursuant to section 70.00 of this article, and such person is subject to an undischarged indeterminate *or determinate** sentence of imprisonment imposed prior to the date on which the present crime was committed, the court must impose a sentence to run consecutively with respect to such undischarged sentence. **(Material in italic deemed repealed 9/1/23,Ch.55,L.2021)*

2-b. When a person is convicted of a violent felony offense committed after arraignment and while released on recognizance or bail, but committed prior to the imposition of sentence on a pending felony charge, and if an indeterminate *or determinate** sentence of imprisonment is imposed in each case, such sentences shall run consecutively. Provided, however, that the court may, in the interest of justice, order a sentence to run concurrently in a situation where consecutive sentences are required by this subdivision if it finds either mitigating circumstances that bear directly upon the manner in which the crime was committed or, where the defendant was not the sole participant in the crime, the defendant's participation was relatively minor although not so minor as to constitute a defense to the prosecution. The defendant and the district attorney shall have an opportunity to present relevant information to assist the court in making this determination and the court may, in its discretion, conduct a hearing with respect to any issue bearing upon such determination. If the court determines that consecutive sentences should not be ordered, it shall make a statement on the record of the facts and circumstances upon which such determination is based. **(Material in italic deemed repealed 9/1/23,Ch.55,L.2021)*

2-c. When a person is convicted of bail jumping in the second degree as defined in section 215.56 or bail jumping in the first degree as defined in section 215.57 committed after arraignment and while released on recognizance or bail in connection with a pending indictment or information charging one or more felonies, at least one of which he is subsequently convicted, and if an indeterminate sentence of imprisonment is imposed in each case, such sentences shall run consecutively. Provided, however, that the court may, in the interest of justice, order a sentence to run concurrently in a situation where consecutive sentences are required by this subdivision if it finds mitigating circumstances that bear directly upon the manner in which the crime was committed. The defendant and the district attorney shall have an opportunity to present relevant information to assist the court in making this determination and the court may, in its discretion, conduct a hearing with respect to any issue bearing upon such determination. If the court determines that consecutive sentences should not be ordered, it shall make a statement on the record of the facts and circumstances upon which such determination is based.

2-d. When a person is convicted of escape in the second degree as defined in section 205.10 or escape in the first degree as defined in section 205.15 committed after issuance of a securing order, as defined in subdivision five of section 500.10 of the criminal procedure law, in connection with a pending indictment or information charging one or more felonies, at least one of which he is subsequently convicted, and if an indeterminate sentence of imprisonment is imposed in each case, such sentences shall run consecutively. Provided, however, that the court may, in the interest of justice, order a sentence to run concurrently in a situation where consecutive sentences are required by this subdivision if it finds mitigating circumstances that bear directly upon the manner in which the crime was committed. The defendant and the district attorney shall have an opportunity to present relevant information to assist the court in making this determination and the court may, in its discretion, conduct a hearing with respect to any issue bearing upon such determination. If the court determines that consecutive sentences should not be ordered, it shall make a statement on the record of the facts and circumstances upon which such determination is based.

2-e. Whenever a person is convicted of course of sexual conduct against a child in the first degree as defined in section 130.75 or course of sexual conduct against a child in the second degree as defined in section 130.80 and any other crime under article one hundred thirty committed against the same child and within the period charged under section 130.75 or 130.80, the sentences must run concurrently.

2-f. Whenever a person is convicted of facilitating a sex offense with a controlled substance as defined in section 130.90 of this chapter, the sentence imposed by the court for such offense may be ordered to run consecutively to any sentence imposed upon conviction of an offense defined in article one hundred thirty of this chapter arising from the same criminal transaction.

2-g. Whenever a person is convicted of unlawful manufacture of methamphetamine in the third degree as defined in section 220.73 of this chapter, unlawful manufacture of methamphetamine in the second degree as defined in section 220.74 of this chapter, or unlawful manufacture of methamphetamine in the first degree as defined in section 220.75 of this chapter, or any attempt to commit any of such offenses, and such person is also convicted, with respect to such unlawful methamphetamine laboratory, of unlawful disposal of methamphetamine laboratory material as defined in section 220.76 of this chapter, the sentences must run concurrently.

3. Where consecutive definite sentences of imprisonment are not prohibited by subdivision two of this section and are imposed on a person for offenses which were committed as parts of a single incident or transaction, the aggregate of the terms of such sentences shall not exceed one year.

4. When a person, who is subject to any undischarged term of imprisonment imposed at a previous time by a court of another jurisdiction, is sentenced to an additional term or terms of imprisonment by a court of this state, the sentence or sentences imposed by the court of this state, subject to the provisions of subdivisions one, two and three of this section, shall run either concurrently or consecutively with respect to such undischarged term in such manner as the court directs at the time of sentence. If the court of this state does not specify the manner in which a sentence imposed by it is to run, the sentence or sentences shall run consecutively.

5. *(a) Except as provided in paragraph (c) of this subdivision, when a person is convicted of assault in the second degree, as defined in subdivision seven of section 120.05 of this chapter, any definite, indeterminate or determinate term of imprisonment which may be imposed as a sentence upon such conviction shall run consecutively to any undischarged term of imprisonment to which the defendant was subject and for which he was confined at the time of the assault.

(Amendments deemed repealed 9/1/23,Ch.55,L.2021)

*(b) Except as provided in paragraph (c) of this subdivision, when a person is convicted of assault in the second degree, as defined in subdivision seven of section 120.05 of this chapter, any definite, indeterminate or determinate term of imprisonment which may be imposed as a sentence upon such conviction shall run consecutively to any term of imprisonment which was previously imposed or which may be prospectively imposed where the person was confined within a detention facility at the time of the assault upon a charge which culminated in such sentence of imprisonment.

(Amendments deemed repealed 9/1/23,Ch.55,L.2021)

(c) Notwithstanding the provisions of paragraphs (a) and (b) of this subdivision, a term of imprisonment imposed upon a conviction to assault in the second degree as defined in subdivision seven of section 120.05 of this chapter may run concurrently to any other term of imprisonment, in the interest of justice, provided the court sets forth in the record its reasons for imposing a concurrent sentence. Nothing in this section shall require the imposition of a sentence of imprisonment where it is not otherwise required by law.

§70.30 Calculation of terms of imprisonment.

*1. Indeterminate or determinate sentences. An indeterminate or determinate sentence of imprisonment commences when the prisoner is received in an institution under the jurisdiction of the state department of corrections and community supervision. Where a person is under more than one indeterminate or determinate sentence, the sentences shall be calculated as follows:

(a) If the sentences run concurrently, the time served under imprisonment on any of the sentences shall be credited against the minimum periods of all the concurrent indeterminate sentences and against the terms of all the concurrent determinate sentences. The maximum term or terms of the indeterminate sentences and the term or terms of the determinate sentences shall merge in and be satisfied by discharge of the term which has the longest unexpired time to run;

(b) If the defendant is serving two or more indeterminate sentences which run consecutively, the minimum periods of imprisonment are added to arrive at an aggregate minimum period of imprisonment equal to the sum of all the minimum periods, and the maximum terms are added to arrive at an aggregate maximum term equal to the sum of all the maximum terms, provided, however, that both the aggregate maximum term and the aggregate minimum period of imprisonment shall be subject to the limitations set forth in paragraphs (e) and (f) of this subdivision, where applicable;

(c) If the defendant is serving two or more determinate sentences of imprisonment which run consecutively, the terms of the determinate sentences are added to arrive at an aggregate maximum term of imprisonment, provided, however, that the aggregate maximum term of imprisonment shall be subject to the limitations set forth in paragraphs (e) and (f) of this subdivision, where applicable.

(d) If the defendant is serving one or more indeterminate sentences of imprisonment and one or more determinate sentence of imprisonment which run consecutively, the minimum term or terms of the indeterminate sentence or sentences and the term or terms of the determinate sentence or sentences are added to arrive at an aggregate maximum term of imprisonment, provided, however, (i) that in no event shall the aggregate maximum so calculated be less than the term or maximum term of imprisonment of the sentence which has the longest unexpired time to run; and (ii) that the aggregate maximum term of imprisonment shall be subject to the limitations set forth in paragraphs (e) and (f) of this subdivision, where applicable.

(e) (i) Except as provided in subparagraph (ii), (iii), (iv), (v), (vi) or (vii) of this paragraph, the aggregate maximum term of consecutive sentences, all of which are indeterminate sentences or all of which are determinate sentences, imposed for two or more crimes, other than two or more crimes that include a class A felony, committed prior to the time the person was imprisoned under any of such sentences shall, if it exceeds twenty years, be deemed to be twenty years, unless one of the sentences was imposed for a class B felony, in which case the aggregate maximum term shall, if it exceeds thirty years, be deemed to be thirty years. Where the aggregate maximum term of two or more indeterminate consecutive sentences is reduced by calculation made pursuant to this paragraph, the aggregate minimum period of imprisonment, if it exceeds one-half of the aggregate maximum term as so reduced, shall be deemed to be one-half of the aggregate maximum term as so reduced;

(ii) Where the aggregate maximum term of two or more consecutive sentences, one or more of which is a determinate sentence and one or more of which is an indeterminate sentence, imposed for two or more crimes, other than two or more crimes that include a class A felony, committed prior to the time the person was imprisoned under any of such sentences, exceeds twenty years, and none of the sentences was imposed for a class B felony, the following rules shall apply:

(A) if the aggregate maximum term of the determinate sentence or sentences exceeds twenty years, the defendant shall be deemed to be serving to a determinate sentence of twenty years.

(B) if the aggregate maximum term of the determinate sentence or sentences is less than twenty years, the defendant shall be deemed to be serving an indeterminate sentence the maximum term of which shall be deemed to be twenty years. In such instances, the minimum sentence shall be deemed to be ten years or six-sevenths of the term or aggregate maximum term of the determinate sentence or sentences, whichever is greater.

(iii) Where the aggregate maximum term of two or more consecutive sentences, one or more of which is a determinate sentence and one or more of which is an indeterminate sentence, imposed for two or more crimes, other than two or more crimes that include a class A felony, committed prior to the time the person was imprisoned under any of such sentences, exceeds thirty years, and one of the sentences was imposed for a class B felony, the following rules shall apply:

(A) if the aggregate maximum term of the determinate sentence or sentences exceeds thirty years, the defendant shall be deemed to be serving a determinate sentence of thirty years;

(B) if the aggregate maximum term of the determinate sentence or sentences is less than thirty years, the defendant shall be deemed to be serving an indeterminate sentence the maximum term of which shall be deemed to be thirty years. In such instances, the minimum sentence shall be deemed to be fifteen years or six-sevenths of the term or aggregate maximum term of the determinate sentence or sentences, whichever is greater.

(iv) Notwithstanding subparagraph (i) of this paragraph, the aggregate maximum term of consecutive sentences, all of which are indeterminate sentences or all of which are determinate sentences, imposed for the conviction of two violent felony offenses committed prior to the time the person was imprisoned under any of such sentences and one of which is a class B violent felony offense, shall, if it exceeds forty years, be deemed to be forty years

(v) Notwithstanding subparagraphs (ii) and (iii) of this paragraph, where the aggregate maximum term of two or more consecutive sentences, one or more of which is a determinate sentence and one or more of which is an indeterminate sentence, and where such sentences are imposed for the conviction of two violent felony offenses committed prior to the time the person was imprisoned under any such sentences and where one of which is a class B violent felony offense, the following rules shall apply:

(A) if the aggregate maximum term of the determinate sentence or sentences exceeds forty years, the defendant shall be deemed to be serving a determinate sentence of forty years;

(B) if the aggregate maximum term of the determinate sentence or sentences is less than forty years, the defendant shall be deemed to be serving an indeterminate sentence the maximum term of which shall be deemed to be forty years. In such instances, the minimum sentence shall be deemed to be twenty years or six-sevenths of the term or aggregate maximum term of the determinate sentence or sentences, whichever is greater.

(vi) Notwithstanding subparagraphs (i) and (iv) of this paragraph, the aggregate maximum term of consecutive sentences, all of which are indeterminate or all of which are determinate sentences, imposed for the conviction of three or more violent felony offenses committed prior to the time the person was imprisoned under any of such sentences and one of which is a class B violent felony offense, shall, if it exceeds fifty years, be deemed to be fifty years;

(vii) Notwithstanding subparagraphs (ii), (iii) and (v) of this paragraph, where the aggregate maximum term of two or more consecutive sentences, one or more of which is a determinate sentence and one or more of which is an indeterminate sentence, and where such sentences are imposed for the conviction of three or more violent felony offenses committed prior to the time the person was imprisoned under any such sentences and one of which is a class B violent felony offense, the following rules shall apply:

(A) if the aggregate maximum term of the determinate sentence or sentences exceeds fifty years, the defendant shall be deemed to be serving a determinate sentence of fifty years.

(B) if the aggregate maximum term of the determinate sentence or sentences is less than fifty years, the defendant shall be deemed to be serving an indeterminate sentence the maximum term of which shall be deemed to be fifty years. In such instances, the minimum sentence shall be deemed to be twenty-five years or six-sevenths of the term or aggregate maximum term of the determinate sentence or sentences, whichever is greater.

(viii) Notwithstanding any provision of this subdivision to the contrary where a person is serving two or more consecutive sentences, one or more of which is an indeterminate sentence and one or more of which is a determinate sentence, and if he would be eligible for a reduction provision pursuant to this subdivision if the maximum term or aggregate maximum term of the indeterminate sentence or sentences were added to the term or aggregate maximum term of the determinate sentence or sentences, the person shall be deemed to be eligible for the applicable reduction provision and the rules set forth in this subdivision shall apply.

(f) The aggregate maximum term of consecutive sentences imposed upon a juvenile offender for two or more crimes, not including a class A felony, committed before he has reached the age of sixteen, shall, if it exceeds ten years, be deemed to be ten years. If consecutive indeterminate sentences imposed upon a juvenile offender include a sentence for the class A felony of arson in the first degree or for the class A felony of kidnapping in the first degree, then the aggregate maximum term of such sentences shall, if it exceeds fifteen years, be deemed to be fifteen years. Where the aggregate maximum term of two or more consecutive sentences is reduced by a calculation made pursuant to this paragraph, the aggregate minimum period of imprisonment, if it exceeds one-half of the aggregate maximum term as so reduced, shall be deemed to be one-half of the aggregate maximum term as so reduced. *(Amendments deemed repealed 9/1/23,Ch.55,L.2021)*

2. Definite sentences. A definite sentence of imprisonment commences when the prisoner is received in the institution named in the commitment. Where a person is under more than one definite sentence, the sentences shall be calculated as follows:

(a) If the sentences run concurrently and are to be served in a single institution, the terms merge in and are satisfied by discharge of the term which has the longest unexpired time to run;

(b) If the sentences run consecutively and are to be served in a single institution, the terms are added to arrive at an aggregate term and are satisfied by discharge of such aggregate term, or by service of two years imprisonment plus any term imposed for an offense committed while the person is under the sentences, whichever is less;

(c) If the sentences run concurrently and are to be served in more than one institution, the term of each such sentence shall be credited with the portion of any concurrent term served after that sentence was imposed;

(d) If the sentences run consecutively and are to be served in more than one institution, the aggregate of the time served in all of the institutions shall not exceed two years plus any term imposed for an offense committed while the person is under the sentences.

2-a. Undischarged imprisonment in other jurisdiction. Where a person who is subject to an undischarged term of imprisonment imposed at a previous time by a court of another jurisdiction is sentenced to an additional term or terms of imprisonment by a court of this state, to run concurrently with such undischarged term, such additional term or terms shall be deemed to commence when the said person is returned to the custody of the appropriate official of such other jurisdiction where the undischarged term of imprisonment is being served. If the additional term or terms imposed shall run consecutively to the said undischarged term, such additional term or terms shall commence when the prisoner is received in the appropriate institution as provided in subdivisions one and two of this section. The term or terms of such imprisonment shall be calculated and such other pertinent provisions of this section applied in the same manner as where a person is under more than one sentence in this state as provided in this section.

*3. Jail time. The term of a definite sentence, a determinate sentence, or the maximum term of an indeterminate sentence imposed on a person shall be credited with and diminished by the amount of time the person spent in custody prior to the commencement of such sentence as a result of the charge that culminated in the sentence. In the case of an indeterminate sentence, if the minimum period of imprisonment has been fixed by the court or by the board of parole, the credit shall also be applied against the minimum period. The credit herein provided shall be calculated from the date custody under the charge commenced to the date the sentence commences and shall not include any time that is credited against the term or maximum term of any previously imposed sentence or period of post-release supervision to which the person is subject. Where the charge or charges culminate in more than one sentence, the credit shall be applied as follows:

(a) If the sentences run concurrently, the credit shall be applied against each such sentence;

(b) If the sentences run consecutively, the credit shall be applied against the aggregate term or aggregate maximum term of the sentences and against the aggregate minimum period of imprisonment.

In any case where a person has been in custody due to a charge that culminated in a dismissal or an acquittal, the amount of time that would have been credited against a sentence for such charge, had one been imposed, shall be credited against any sentence that is based on a charge for which a warrant or commitment was lodged during the pendency of such custody.   *(Eff. until 9/1/23,Ch.55,L.2021)

*4.Good behavior time. Time allowances earned for good behavior, pursuant to the provisions of the correction law, shall be computed and applied as follows:

(a) In the case of a person serving an indeterminate or determinate sentence, the total of such allowances shall be calculated as provided in section eight hundred three of the correction law and the allowances shall be applied as provided in paragraph (b) of subdivision one of section 70.40;

(b) In the case of a person serving a definite sentence, the total of such allowances shall not exceed one-third of his term or aggregate term and the allowances shall be applied as a credit against such term.

*(Eff. until 9/1/23,Ch.55,L.2021)

5. Time served under vacated sentence. When a sentence of imprisonment that has been imposed on a person is vacated and a new sentence is imposed on such person for the same offense, or for an offense based upon the same act, the new sentence shall be calculated as if it had commenced at the time the vacated sentence commenced, and all time credited against the vacated sentence shall be credited against the new sentence. In any case where a vacated sentence also includes a period of post-release supervision, all time credited against the period of post-release supervision shall be credited against the period of post-release supervision included with the new sentence. In the event a period of post-release supervision is not included with the new sentence, such period shall be credited against the new sentence.

6. Escape. When a person who is serving a sentence of imprisonment escapes from custody, the escape shall interrupt the sentence and such interruption shall continue until the return of the person to the institution in which the sentence was being served or, if the sentence was being served in an institution under the jurisdiction of the state department of corrections and community supervision, to an institution under the jurisdiction of that department. Any time spent by such person in custody from the date of escape to the date the sentence resumes shall be credited against the term or maximum term of the interrupted sentence, provided:

(a) That such custody was due to an arrest or surrender based upon the escape; or

(b) That such custody arose from an arrest on another charge which culminated in a dismissal or an acquittal; or

(c) That such custody arose from an arrest on another charge which culminated in a conviction, but in such case, if a sentence of imprisonment was imposed, the credit allowed shall be limited to the portion of the time spent in custody that exceeds the period, term or maximum term of imprisonment imposed for such conviction.

*7. Absconding from temporary release or furlough program. When a person who is serving a sentence of imprisonment is permitted to leave an institution to participate in a program of work release or furlough program as such term is defined in section six hundred thirty-one of the correction law, or in the case of an institution under the jurisdiction of the state department of corrections and community supervision or a facility under the jurisdiction of the state office of children and family services to participate in a program of temporary release, fails to return to the institution or facility at or before the time prescribed for his or her return, such failure shall interrupt the sentence and such interruption shall continue until the return of the person to the institution in which the sentence was being served or, if the sentence was being served in an institution under the jurisdiction of the state department of corrections and community supervision or a facility under the jurisdiction of the state office of children and family services to an institution under the jurisdiction of that department or a facility under the jurisdiction of that office. Any time spent by such person in an institution from the date of his or her failure to return to the date his or her sentence resumes shall be credited against the term or maximum term of the interrupted sentence, provided:

(a) That such incarceration was due to an arrest or surrender based upon the failure to return; or

(b) That such incarceration arose from an arrest on another charge which culminated in a dismissal or an acquittal; or

(c) That such custody arose from an arrest on another charge which culminated in a conviction, but in such case, if a sentence of imprisonment was imposed, the credit allowed shall be limited to the portion of the time spent in custody that exceeds the period, term or maximum term of imprisonment imposed for such conviction.

*(Expires 9/1/23, Ch.55, L.2021)

*§70.35   Merger of certain definite and indeterminate or
           determinate sentences.

The service of an indeterminate or determinate sentence of imprisonment shall satisfy any definite sentence of imprisonment imposed on a person for an offense committed prior to the time the indeterminate or determinate sentence was imposed, except as provided in paragraph (b) of subdivision five of section 70.25 of this article. A person who is serving a definite sentence at the time an indeterminate or determinate sentence is imposed shall be delivered to the custody of the state department of corrections and community supervision to commence service of the indeterminate or determinate sentence immediately unless the person is serving a definite sentence pursuant to paragraph (b) of subdivision five of section 70.25 of this article. In any case where the indeterminate or determinate sentence is revoked or vacated, the person shall receive credit against the definite sentence for each day spent in the custody of the state department of corrections and community supervision. *(Expires 9/1/23,Ch.55,L.2021)*

§70.40 Release on parole; conditional release; presumptive release.

1. Indeterminate sentence.

*(a) Release on parole shall be in the discretion of the state board of parole, and such person shall continue service of his or her sentence or sentences while on parole, in accordance with and subject to the provisions of the executive law and the correction law.

*(i) A person who is serving one or more than one indeterminate sentence of imprisonment may be paroled from the institution in which he or she is confined at any time after the expiration of the minimum or the aggregate minimum period of the sentence or sentences or, where applicable, the minimum or aggregate minimum period reduced by the merit time allowance granted pursuant to paragraph (d) of subdivision one of section eight hundred three of the correction law.

(Expires 9/1/23, Ch.55,L.2021)

(ii) A person who is serving one or more than one determinate sentence of imprisonment shall be ineligible for discretionary release on parole.

(iii) A person who is serving one or more than one indeterminate sentence of imprisonment and one or more than one determinate sentence of imprisonment, which run concurrently may be paroled at any time after the expiration of the minimum period of imprisonment of the indeterminate sentence or sentences, or upon the expiration of six-sevenths of the term of imprisonment of the determinate sentence or sentences, whichever is later.

(iv) A person who is serving one or more than one indeterminate sentence of imprisonment and one or more than one determinate sentence of imprisonment which run consecutively may be paroled at any time after the expiration of the sum of the minimum or aggregate minimum period of the indeterminate sentence or sentences and six-sevenths of the term or aggregate term of imprisonment of the determinate sentence or sentences.

(v) Notwithstanding any other subparagraph of this paragraph, a person may be paroled from the institution in which he or she is confined at any time on medical parole pursuant to section two hundred fifty-nine-r or section two hundred fifty-nine-s of the executive law or for deportation pursuant to paragraph (d) of subdivision two of section two hundred fifty-nine-i of the executive law or after the successful completion of a shock incarceration program pursuant to article twenty-six-A of the correction law. *(Expires 9/1/23,Ch.55,L.2021)*

*(b) A person who is serving one or more than one indeterminate or determinate sentence of imprisonment shall, if he or she so requests, be conditionally released from the institution in which he or she is confined when the total good behavior time allowed to him or her, pursuant to the provisions of the correction law, is equal to the unserved portion of his or her term, maximum term or aggregate maximum term; provided, however, that (i) in no event shall a person serving one or more indeterminate sentence of imprisonment and one or more determinate sentence of imprisonment which run concurrently be conditionally released until serving at least six-sevenths of the determinate term of imprisonment which has the longest unexpired time to run and (ii) in no event shall a person be conditionally released prior to the date on which such person is first eligible for discretionary parole release. The conditions of release, including those governing post-release supervision, shall be such as may be imposed by the state board of parole in accordance with the provisions of the executive law.

Every person so released shall be under the supervision of the state department of corrections and community supervision for a period equal to the unserved portion of the term, maximum term, aggregate maximum term, or period of post-release supervision.

(Amendments deemed repealed, 9/1/23, Ch.55, L.2021)

*(c) A person who is serving one or more than one indeterminate sentence of imprisonment shall, if he or she so requests, be released from the institution in which he or she is confined if granted presumptive release pursuant to section eight hundred six of the correction law. The conditions of release shall be such as may be imposed by the state board of parole in accordance with the provisions of the executive law. Every person so released shall be under the supervision of the department of corrections and community supervision for a period equal to the unserved portion of his or her maximum or aggregate maximum term unless discharged in accordance with law.

(Repealed 9/1/23, Ch.55, L.2021)

2. Definite sentence. A person who is serving one or more than one definite sentence of imprisonment with a term or aggregate term in excess of ninety days, and is eligible for release according to the criteria set forth in paragraphs (a), (b) and (c) of subdivision one of section two hundred seventy-three of the correction law, may, if he or she so requests, be conditionally released from the institution in which he or she is confined at any time after service of sixty days of that term, exclusive of credits allowed under subdivisions four and six of section 70.30. In computing service of sixty days, the credit allowed for jail time under subdivision three of section 70.30 shall be calculated as time served. Conditional release from such institution shall be in the discretion of the parole board, or a local conditional release commission established pursuant to article twelve of the correction law, provided, however that where such release is by a local conditional release commission, the person must be serving a definite sentence with a term in excess of one hundred twenty days and may only be released after service of ninety days of such term. In computing service of ninety days,

the credit allowed for jail time under subdivision three of section 70.30 of this article shall be calculated as time served. A conditional release granted under this subdivision shall be upon such conditions as may be imposed by the parole board, in accordance with the provisions of the executive law, or a local conditional release commission in accordance with the provisions of the correction law.

Conditional release shall interrupt service of the sentence or sentences and the remaining portion of the term or aggregate term shall be held in abeyance. Every person so released shall be under the supervision of the department of corrections and community supervision or a local probation department and in the custody of the local conditional release commission in accordance with article twelve of the correction law, for a period of one year. The local probation department shall cause complete records to be kept of every person released to its supervision pursuant to this subdivision. The department of corrections and community supervision may supply to a local probation department and the local conditional release commission custody information and records maintained on persons under the supervision of such local probation department to aid in the performance of its supervision responsibilities. Compliance with the conditions of release during the period of supervision shall satisfy the portion of the term or aggregate term that has been held in abeyance.

3. Delinquency. (a) When a person is alleged to have violated the terms of presumptive release or parole by absconding, and the state board of parole has declared such person to be delinquent, the declaration of delinquency shall interrupt the person's sentence as of the date of the delinquency and such interruption shall continue until the releasee's appearance in response to a notice of violation or the date of the execution of a warrant, whichever is earlier.

(b) When a person is alleged to have violated the terms of his or her conditional release or post-release supervision by absconding and has been declared delinquent by the parole board or the local conditional release commission having supervision over such person, the declaration of delinquency shall interrupt the period of supervision or post-release supervision as of the date of the delinquency. For a conditional release, such interruption shall continue until the releasee's appearance in response to a notice of violation or the date of the execution of a warrant, whichever is earlier. For a person released to post-release supervision, the provisions of section 70.45 of this article shall apply.

(c) Any time spent by a person in custody from the time of execution of a warrant pursuant to paragraph (a) of subdivision three of section two hundred fifty-nine-i of the executive law to the time service of the sentence resumes shall be credited against the term or maximum term of the interrupted sentence. *(Eff.3/1/22,Ch.427,L.2021)*

4. Earned time credits. (a) Any person subject to community supervision shall be awarded earned time credits. The calculation of earned time credit periods shall begin on the releasee's first day of community supervision and shall be awarded after each completed thirty day period in compliance with the terms of their community supervision.

Any such awarded earned time credits shall be applied against such person's unserved portion of the maximum term, aggregate maximum term or period of post-release supervision for any current sentence. Persons subject to a sentence with a maximum term of life imprisonment or lifetime supervision shall not be eligible to receive earned time credits under this section.

(b) After a person has begun a period of community supervision pursuant to this section and section 70.45 of this article, such period of community supervision shall be reduced by thirty days for every thirty days that such person does not violate a condition of and remains in compliance with all conditions of his or her community supervision, provided, however, that the person is not subject to any sentence with a maximum term of life imprisonment or lifetime supervision. When a person is subject to more than one period of community supervision, the reduction authorized in this subdivision shall be applied to every such period of parole or conditional release to which the person is subject.

(c) Retroactive earned time credits shall be awarded to eligible persons subject to community supervision at the time this legislation becomes effective, provided, however, that the maximum allowable retroactive earned time credit awarded shall not exceed a period of two years. Retroactive earned time credits shall not be awarded to any releasee serving a term of reincarceration for a sustained parole violation at the time of the effective date of the chapter of the laws of two thousand twenty-one that added this subdivision until the releasee is returned to community supervision. Persons subject to a sentence with a maximum term of life imprisonment or lifetime supervision shall not be eligible to receive retroactive earned time credits under this section.

(d) If a releasee's current period of community supervision has been interrupted by a period of reincarceration prior to the effective date of the chapter of the laws of two thousand twenty-one that added this subdivision, no earned time credits shall be awarded for such period of reincarceration. The department shall calculate retroactive earned time credits within one year after the bill shall have become law and shall prioritize earned time credit calculations for releasees whose terms of community supervision are due to terminate before June first, two thousand twenty-two.

(e) Earned time credits may be withheld or revoked for the thirty-day period commencing from the date of violative behavior as sustained at a final revocation hearing, or for the period during which a releasee absconded from supervision, as sustained at a final revocation hearing. Earned time credits may not be earned and shall be suspended: (i) during a period of reincarceration imposed for any sustained violation; (ii) during the period in which the individual has absconded; or (iii) pending the outcome of a preliminary or final revocation hearing. If, at the preliminary hearing, there is no finding by a preponderance of the evidence of a violation of a condition of release in an important respect or a violation is not sustained at the final revocation hearing, then the individual shall be deemed to have been in compliance with the terms of release and shall be awarded earned time credits from the period in which the accrual was suspended. If a violation is sustained, the calculation of an earned time credit period shall recommence on the thirty-first day after the date of the violative behavior or, if the sustained violation or conviction resulted in a term of reincarceration, on the day the releasee is restored to community supervision, whichever is later.

(f) At least every one hundred eighty days from the first date of a person's release to community supervision, and every one hundred eighty days thereafter, the department of corrections and community supervision shall provide each person on community supervision a report indicating the total earned time credits received, the total earned time credits received in the prior one hundred eighty days, the total earned time credits withheld, the total earned time credits withheld in the prior one hundred eighty days, the total amount of time reduced from the person's sentence, and the person's earliest release date based on the amount of earned time credits received. The department shall provide the report in written or electronic form.   *(Eff.3/1/22,Ch.427,L.2021)*

§70.45 Determinate sentence; post-release supervision.
1. In general. When a court imposes a determinate sentence it shall in each case state not only the term of imprisonment, but also an additional period of post-release supervision as determined pursuant to this article. Such period shall commence as provided in subdivision five of this section and a violation of any condition of supervision occurring at any time during such period of post-release supervision shall subject the defendant to a further period of imprisonment up to the balance of the remaining period of post-release supervision, not to exceed five years; provided, however, that a defendant serving a term of post-release supervision for a conviction of a felony sex offense, as defined in section 70.80 of this article, may be subject to a further period of imprisonment up to the balance of the remaining period of post-release supervision. Such maximum limits shall not preclude a longer period of further imprisonment for a violation where the defendant is subject to indeterminate and determinate sentences.

1-a. When, following a final hearing, a time assessment has been imposed upon a person convicted of a felony sex offense who owes three years or more on a period of post-release supervision, imposed pursuant to subdivision two-a of this section, such defendant, after serving three years of the time assessment, shall be reviewed by the board of parole and may be re-released to post-release supervision only upon a determination by the board of parole made in accordance with subdivision two of section two hundred fifty-nine-i of the executive law. If re-release is not granted, the board shall specify a date not more than twenty-four months from such determination for reconsideration, and the procedures to be followed upon reconsideration shall be the same. If a time assessment of less than three years is imposed upon such a defendant, the defendant shall be released upon the expiration of such time assessment, unless he or she is subject to further imprisonment or confinement under any provision of law.

2. Period of post-release supervision for other than felony sex offenses. The period of post-release supervision for a determinate sentence, other than a determinate sentence imposed for a felony sex offense as defined in paragraph (a) of subdivision one of section 70.80 of this article, shall be five years except that:

(a) such period shall be one year whenever a determinate sentence of imprisonment is imposed pursuant to subdivision two of section 70.70 of this article or subdivision nine of section 60.12 of this title upon a conviction of a class D or class E felony offense;

(b) such period shall be not less than one year nor more than two years whenever a determinate sentence of imprisonment is imposed pursuant to subdivision two of section 70.70 of this article or subdivision nine of section 60.12 of this title upon a conviction of a class B or class C felony offense;

(c) such period shall be not less than one year nor more than two years whenever a determinate sentence of imprisonment is imposed pursuant to subdivision three or four of section 70.70 of this article upon conviction of a class D or class E felony offense or subdivision ten of section 60.12 of this title;

(d) such period shall be not less than one and one-half years nor more than three years whenever a determinate sentence of imprisonment is imposed pursuant to subdivision three or four of section 70.70 of this article upon conviction of a class B felony or class C felony offense or subdivision eleven of section 60.12 of this title;

(e) such period shall be not less than one and one-half years nor more than three years whenever a determinate sentence of imprisonment is imposed pursuant to subdivision three of section 70.02 of this article or subdivision two or eight of section 60.12 of this title upon a conviction of a class D or class E violent felony offense or subdivision four, five, six, or seven of section 60.12 of this title;

(f) such period shall be not less than two and one-half years nor more than five years whenever a determinate sentence of imprisonment is imposed pursuant to subdivision three of section 70.02 of this article or subdivision two or eight of section 60.12 of this title upon a conviction of a class B or class C violent felony offense.

2-a. Periods of post-release supervision for felony sex offenses. The period of post-release supervision for a determinate sentence imposed for a felony sex offense as defined in paragraph (a) of subdivision one of section 70.80 of this article shall be as follows:

(a) not less than three years nor more than ten years whenever a determinate sentence of imprisonment is imposed pursuant to subdivision four of section 70.80 of this article upon a conviction of a class D or class E felony sex offense;

(b) not less than five years nor more than fifteen years whenever a determinate sentence of imprisonment is imposed pursuant to subdivision four of section 70.80 of this article upon a conviction of a class C felony sex offense;

(c) not less than five years nor more than twenty years whenever a determinate sentence of imprisonment is imposed pursuant to subdivision four of section 70.80 of this article upon a conviction of a class B felony sex offense;

(d) not less than three years nor more than ten years whenever a determinate sentence is imposed pursuant to subdivision three of section 70.02 of this article upon a conviction of a class D or class E violent felony sex offense as defined in paragraph (b) of subdivision one of section 70.80 of this article;

(e) not less than five years nor more than fifteen years whenever a determinate sentence is imposed pursuant to subdivision three of section 70.02 of this article upon a conviction of a class C violent felony sex offense as defined in section 70.80 of this article;

(f) not less than five years nor more than twenty years whenever a determinate sentence is imposed pursuant to subdivision three of section 70.02 of this article upon a conviction of a class B violent felony sex offense as defined in section 70.80 of this article;

(g) not less than five years nor more than fifteen years whenever a determinate sentence of imprisonment is imposed pursuant to either section 70.04, section 70.06, or subdivision five of section 70.80 of this article upon a conviction of a class D or class E violent or non-violent felony sex offense as defined in section 70.80 of this article;

(h) not less than seven years nor more than twenty years whenever a determinate sentence of imprisonment is imposed pursuant to either section 70.04, section 70.06, or subdivision five of section 70.80 of this article upon a conviction of a class C violent or non-violent felony sex offense as defined in section 70.80 of this article;

(i) such period shall be not less than ten years nor more than twenty-five years whenever a determinate sentence of imprisonment is imposed pursuant to either section 70.04, section 70.06, or subdivision five of section 70.80 of this article upon a conviction of a class B violent or non-violent felony sex offense as defined in section 70.80 of this article; and

(j) such period shall be not less than ten years nor more than twenty years whenever any determinate sentence of imprisonment is imposed pursuant to subdivision four of section 70.07 of this article.

3. Conditions of post-release supervision. The board of parole shall establish and impose conditions of post-release supervision in the same manner and to the same extent as it may establish and impose conditions in accordance with the executive law upon persons who are granted parole or conditional release; provided that, notwithstanding any other provision of law, the board of parole may impose as a condition of post-release supervision that for a period not exceeding six months immediately following release from the underlying term of imprisonment the person be transferred to and participate in the programs of a residential treatment facility as that term is defined in subdivision six of section two of the correction law. Upon release from the underlying term of imprisonment, the person shall be furnished with a written statement setting forth the conditions of post-release

supervision in sufficient detail to provide for the person's conduct and supervision.

4. Revocation of post-release supervision. An alleged violation of any condition of post-release supervision shall be initiated, heard and determined in accordance with the provisions of subdivisions three and four of section two hundred fifty-nine-i of the executive law.

5. Calculation of service of period of post-release supervision. A period or periods of post-release supervision shall be calculated and served as follows:

(a) A period of post-release supervision shall commence upon the person's release from imprisonment to supervision by the department of corrections and community supervision and shall interrupt the running of the determinate sentence or sentences of imprisonment and the indeterminate sentence or sentences of imprisonment, if any. The remaining portion of any maximum or aggregate maximum term shall then be held in abeyance until the successful completion of the period of post-release supervision or the person's return to the custody of the department of corrections and community supervision, whichever occurs first.

(b) Upon the completion of the period of post-release supervision, the running of such sentence or sentences of imprisonment shall resume and only then shall the remaining portion of any maximum or aggregate maximum term previously held in abeyance be credited with and diminished by such period of post-release supervision. The person shall then be under the jurisdiction of the department of corrections and community supervision for the remaining portion of such maximum or aggregate maximum term.

(c) When a person is subject to two or more periods of post-release supervision, such periods shall merge with and be satisfied by discharge of the period of post-release supervision having the longest unexpired time to run; provided, however, any time served upon one period of post-release supervision shall not be credited to any other period of post-release supervision except as provided in subdivision five of section 70.30 of this article.

(d) When a person is alleged to have violated a condition of post-release supervision by absconding and the department of corrections and community supervision has declared such person to be delinquent: (i) the declaration of delinquency shall interrupt the period of post-release supervision; (ii) such interruption shall continue until the person is restored to post-release supervision; (iii) if the person is restored to post-release supervision without being returned to the department of corrections and community supervision, any time spent in custody from the date of delinquency until restoration to post-release supervision shall first be credited to the maximum or aggregate maximum term of the sentence or sentences of imprisonment, but only to the extent authorized by subdivision three of section 70.40 of this article. Any time spent in custody solely pursuant to such delinquency after completion of the maximum or aggregate maximum term of the sentence or sentences of imprisonment shall be credited to the period of post-release supervision, if any; and (iv) if the person is ordered returned to the department of corrections and community supervision, the person shall be required to serve the time assessment before being re-released to post-release supervision. If the person is detained pursuant to paragraph (a) of subdivision three of section two hundred fifty-nine-i of the executive law pending a preliminary or final revocation hearing, the time assessment imposed following such hearing shall commence upon the execution of the warrant. If a warrant was executed pursuant to paragraph (a) of subdivision three of section two hundred fifty-nine-i of the executive law but a court released the person pending a preliminary or final revocation hearing, the time assessment shall commence upon the issuance of a determination after a final hearing that the person has violated one or more conditions of community supervision in an important respect, and shall include the time period between execution of the warrant and release of the person pending a preliminary or final revocation hearing. If a releasee is committed to the custody of the sheriff pursuant to article five hundred thirty of the criminal procedure law, the time assessment, if any, shall include any time the releasee spent in such custody. If a notice of violation was issued pursuant to subdivision three of section two hundred fifty-nine-i of the executive law, the time assessment shall commence upon the issuance of a determination after a final hearing that the person has violated one or more conditions of supervision. While serving such assessment, the person shall not receive any good behavior allowance pursuant to section eight hundred three of the correction law. Any time spent in custody from the date of delinquency until return to the department of corrections and community supervision shall first be credited to the maximum or aggregate maximum term of the sentence or sentences of imprisonment, but only to the extent authorized by subdivision three of section 70.40 of this article. The maximum or aggregate maximum term of the sentence or sentences of imprisonment shall run while the person is serving such time assessment in the custody of the department of corrections and community supervision. Any time spent in custody solely pursuant to such delinquency after completion of the maximum or aggregate maximum term of the sentence or sentences of imprisonment shall be credited to the period of post-release supervision, if any.

(Eff.3/1/22,Ch.427,L.2021)

(e) Notwithstanding paragraph (d) of this subdivision, in the event a person is sentenced to one or more additional indeterminate or determinate term or terms of imprisonment prior to the completion of the period of post-release supervision, such period of post-release supervision shall be held in abeyance and the person shall be committed to the custody of the department of corrections and community supervision in accordance with the requirements of the prior and additional terms of imprisonment.

(f) When a person serving a period of post-release supervision is returned to the department of corrections and community supervision pursuant to an additional consecutive sentence of imprisonment and without a declaration of delinquency, such period of post-release supervision shall be held in abeyance while the person is in the custody of the department of corrections and community supervision. Such period of post-release supervision shall resume running upon the person's re-release.

§70.70 Sentence of imprisonment for felony drug offender other than a class A felony.

1. For the purposes of this section, the following terms shall mean:

(a) "Felony drug offender" means a defendant who stands convicted of any felony, defined in article two hundred twenty or two hundred twenty-two of this chapter other than a class A felony.

(Eff.3/31/21,Ch.92,L.2021)

(b) "Second felony drug offender" means a second felony offender as that term is defined in subdivision one of section 70.06 of this article, who stands convicted of any felony, defined in article two hundred twenty or two hundred twenty-two of this chapter other than a class A felony.   *(Eff.3/31/21,Ch.92,L.2021)*

(c) "Violent felony" shall have the same meaning as that term is defined in subdivision one of section 70.02 of this article.

2. Except as provided in subdivision three or four of this section, a sentence of imprisonment for a felony drug offender shall be a determinate sentence as provided in paragraph (a) of this subdivision.

(a) Term of determinate sentence. Except as provided in paragraph (b) or (c) of this subdivision, the court shall impose a determinate term of imprisonment upon a felony drug offender which shall be imposed by the court in whole or half years, which shall include as a part thereof a period of post-release supervision in accordance with section 70.45 of this article. The terms of imprisonment authorized for such determinate sentences are as follows:

(i) for a class B felony, the term shall be at least one year and shall not exceed nine years, except that for the class B felony of criminal sale of a controlled substance in or near school grounds as defined in subdivision two of section 220.44 of this chapter or on a school bus as defined in subdivision seventeen of section 220.00 of this chapter or criminal sale of a controlled substance to a child as defined in section 220.48 of this chapter, the term shall be at least two years and shall not exceed nine years;

(ii) for a class C felony, the term shall be at least one year and shall not exceed five and one-half years;

(iii) for a class D felony, the term shall be at least one year and shall not exceed two and one-half years; and

(iv) for a class E felony, the term shall be at least one year and shall not exceed one and one-half years.

(b) Probation. Notwithstanding any other provision of law, the court may sentence a defendant convicted of a class B, class C, class D or class E felony offense defined in article two hundred twenty or two hundred twenty-two of this chapter to probation in accordance with the provisions of sections 60.04 and 65.00 of this chapter.

(Eff.3/31/21,Ch.92,L.2021)

(c) Alternative definite sentence for class B, class C, class D, and class E felonies. If the court, having regard to the nature and circumstances of the crime and to the history and character of the defendant, is of the opinion that a sentence of imprisonment is necessary but that it would be unduly harsh to impose a determinate sentence upon a person convicted of a class C, class D or class E felony offense defined in article two hundred twenty or two hundred twenty-two of this chapter, or a class B felony defined in article two hundred twenty of this chapter, other than the class B felony defined in section 220.48 of this chapter, as added by a chapter of the laws of two thousand nine the court may impose a definite sentence of imprisonment and fix a term of one year or less. *(Eff.3/31/21,Ch.92,L.2021)*

(d) The court may direct that a determinate sentence imposed on a defendant convicted of a class B felony, other than the class B felony defined in section 220.48 of this chapter, pursuant to this subdivision be executed as a sentence of parole supervision in accordance with section 410.91 of the criminal procedure law.

3. Sentence of imprisonment for second felony drug offender.

(a) Applicability. This subdivision shall apply to a second felony drug offender whose prior felony conviction was not a violent felony.

(b) Except as provided in paragraphs (c), (d) and (e) of this subdivision, when the court has found pursuant to the provisions of section 400.21 of the criminal procedure law that a defendant is a second felony drug offender who stands convicted of a class B, class C, class D or class E felony offense defined in article two hundred twenty or two hundred twenty-two of this chapter the court shall impose a determinate sentence of imprisonment. Such determinate sentence shall include as a part thereof a period of post-release supervision in accordance with section 70.45 of this article. The terms of such determinate sentence shall be imposed by the court in whole or half years as follows:

(i) for a class B felony, the term shall be at least two years and shall not exceed twelve years;

(ii) for a class C felony, the term shall be at least one and one-half years and shall not exceed eight years;

(iii) for a class D felony, the term shall be at least one and one-half years and shall not exceed four years; and

(iv) for a class E felony, the term shall be at least one and one-half years and shall not exceed two years. *(Eff.3/31/21,Ch.92,L.2021)*

(c) Probation. Notwithstanding any other provision of law, the court may sentence a second felony drug offender convicted of a class B felony to lifetime probation in accordance with the provisions of section 65.00 of this chapter and may sentence a second felony drug offender convicted of a class C, class D or class E felony to probation in accordance with the provisions of section 65.00 of this chapter.

(d) Sentence of parole supervision. In the case of a person sentenced for a specified offense or offenses as defined in subdivision five of section 410.91 of the criminal procedure law, who stands convicted of no other felony offense, who has not previously been convicted of either

a violent felony offense as defined in section 70.02 of this article, a class
A felony offense or a class B felony offense, and is not under the
jurisdiction of or awaiting delivery to the department of corrections and
community supervision, the court may direct that a determinate sentence
imposed pursuant to this subdivision shall be executed as a parole
supervision sentence as defined in and pursuant to the procedures
prescribed in section 410.91 of the criminal procedure law.

(e) Alternate definite sentence for class C, class D and class E
felonies. If the court, having regard to the nature and circumstances of
the crime and to the history and character of the defendant, is of the
opinion that a sentence of imprisonment is necessary but that it would
be unduly harsh to impose a determinate sentence upon a person
convicted of a class C, class D or class E felony offense defined in
article two hundred twenty or two hundred twenty-two of this chapter,
the court may impose a definite sentence of imprisonment and fix a term
of one year or less.   *(Eff.3/31/21,Ch.92,L.2021)*

4. Sentence of imprisonment for second felony drug offender
previously convicted of a violent felony.

(a) Applicability. This subdivision shall apply to a second felony
drug offender whose prior felony conviction was a violent felony.

(b) Authorized sentence. When the court has found pursuant to the
provisions of section 400.21 of the criminal procedure law that a
defendant is a second felony drug offender whose prior felony
conviction was a violent felony, who stands convicted of a class B, class
C, class D or class E felony offense defined in article two hundred
twenty or two hundred twenty-two of this chapter, the court shall impose
a determinate sentence of imprisonment. Such determinate sentence
shall include as a part thereof a period of post-release supervision in
accordance with section 70.45 of this article. The terms of such
determinate sentence shall be imposed by the court in whole or half
years as follows: *(Eff.3/31/21,Ch.92,L.2021)*

(i) for a class B felony, the term shall be at least six years and
shall not exceed fifteen years;

(ii) for a class C felony, the term shall be at least three and
one-half years and shall not exceed nine years;

(iii) for a class D felony, the term shall be at least two and
one-half years and shall not exceed four and one-half years; and

(iv) for a class E felony, the term shall be at least two years and
shall not exceed two and one-half years.

§70.71 Sentence of imprisonment for a class A felony drug offender.

1. For the purposes of this section, the following terms shall mean:

(a) "Felony drug offender" means a defendant who stands convicted
of any class A felony as defined in article two hundred twenty of this
chapter.

(b) "Second felony drug offender" means a second felony offender
as that term is defined in subdivision one of section 70.06 of this article,

who stands convicted of and is to be sentenced for any class A felony as defined in article two hundred twenty of this chapter.

(c) "Violent felony offense" shall have the same meaning as that term is defined in subdivision one of section 70.02 of this article.

2. Sentence of imprisonment for a first felony drug offender.

(a) Applicability. Except as provided in subdivision three, four or five of this section, this subdivision shall apply to a person convicted of a class A felony as defined in article two hundred twenty of this chapter.

(b) Authorized sentence. The court shall impose a determinate term of imprisonment which shall be imposed by the court in whole or half years and which shall include as a part thereof a period of post-release supervision in accordance with section 70.45 of this article. The terms authorized for such determinate sentences are as follows:

(i) for a class A-I felony, the term shall be at least eight years and shall not exceed twenty years;

(ii) for a class A-II felony, the term shall be at least three years and shall not exceed ten years.

(c) Lifetime probation. Notwithstanding any other provision of law, the court may sentence a defendant convicted of a class A-II felony defined in article two hundred twenty of this chapter to lifetime probation in accordance with the provisions of section 65.00 of this chapter.

3. Sentence of imprisonment for a second felony drug offender.

(a) Applicability. This subdivision shall apply to a second felony drug offender whose prior felony conviction or convictions did not include one or more violent felony offenses.

(b) Authorized sentence. When the court has found pursuant to the provisions of section 400.21 of the criminal procedure law that a defendant is a second felony drug offender who stands convicted of a class A felony as defined in article two hundred twenty or two hundred twenty-one of this chapter, the court shall impose a determinate sentence of imprisonment. Such determinate sentence shall include as a part thereof a period of post-release supervision in accordance with section 70.45 of this article. Such determinate sentence shall be imposed by the court in whole or half years as follows:

(i) for a class A-I felony, the term shall be at least twelve years and shall not exceed twenty-four years;

(ii) for a class A-II felony, the term shall be at least six years and shall not exceed fourteen years.

(c) Lifetime probation. Notwithstanding any other provision of law, the court may sentence a defendant convicted of a class A-II felony defined in article two hundred twenty of this chapter to lifetime probation in accordance with the provisions of section 65.00 of this chapter.

4. Sentence of imprisonment for a second felony drug offender previously convicted of a violent felony offense.

(a) Applicability. This subdivision shall apply to a second felony drug offender whose prior felony conviction was a violent felony.

(b) Authorized sentence. When the court has found pursuant to the provisions of section 400.21 of the criminal procedure law that a defendant is a second felony drug offender whose prior felony conviction was a violent felony, who stands convicted of a class A felony as defined in article two hundred twenty or two hundred twenty-one of this chapter, the court shall impose a determinate sentence of imprisonment. Such determinate sentence shall include as a part thereof a period of post-release supervision in accordance with section 70.45 of this article. Such determinate sentence shall be imposed by the court in whole or half years as follows:

(i) for a class A-I felony, the term shall be at least fifteen years and shall not exceed thirty years;

(ii) for a class A-II felony, the term shall be at least eight years and shall not exceed seventeen years.

5. Sentence of imprisonment for operating as a major trafficker.

(a) Applicability. This subdivision shall apply to a person convicted of the class A-I felony of operating as a major trafficker as defined in section 220.77 of this chapter.

(b) Authorized sentence. Except as provided in paragraph (c) of this subdivision, the court shall impose an indeterminate term of imprisonment for an A-I felony, in accordance with the provisions of section 70.00 of this article.

(c) Alternative determinate sentence. If a defendant stands convicted of violating section 220.77 of this chapter, and if the court, having regard to the nature and circumstances of the crime and the history and character of the defendant, is of the opinion that a sentence of imprisonment is necessary but that it would be unduly harsh to impose the indeterminate sentence for a class A-I felony specified under section 70.00 of this article, the court may instead impose the determinate sentence of imprisonment authorized by clause (i) of subparagraph (b) of subdivision two of this section for a class A-I drug felony; in such case, the reasons for the court's opinion shall be set forth on the record.

§70.80 Sentences of imprisonment for conviction of a felony sex offense.

1. Definitions.

(a) For the purposes of this section, a "felony sex offense" means a conviction of any felony defined in article one hundred thirty of this chapter, including a sexually motivated felony, or patronizing a person for prostitution in the first degree as defined in section 230.06 of this chapter, patronizing a person for prostitution in the second degree as defined in section 230.05 of this chapter, aggravated patronizing a minor for prostitution in the third degree as defined in section 230.11 of this chapter, aggravated patronizing a minor for prostitution in the second degree as defined in section 230.12 of this chapter, aggravated patronizing a minor for prostitution in the first degree as defined in section 230.13 of this chapter, incest in the second degree as defined in section 255.26 of this chapter, or incest in the first degree as defined in section 255.27 of this chapter, or a felony attempt or conspiracy to commit any of the above.

(b) A felony sex offense shall be deemed a "violent felony sex offense" if it is for an offense defined as a violent felony offense in section 70.02 of this article, or for a sexually motivated felony as defined in section 130.91 of this chapter where the specified offense is a violent felony offense as defined in section 70.02 of this article.

(c) For the purposes of this section, a "predicate felony sex offender" means a person who stands convicted of any felony sex offense as defined in paragraph (a) of this subdivision, other than a class A-I felony, after having previously been subjected to one or more predicate felony convictions as defined in subdivision one of section 70.06 or subdivision one of section 70.04 of this article.

(d) For purposes of this section, a "violent felony offense" is any felony defined in subdivision one of section 70.02 of this article, and a "non-violent felony offense" is any felony not defined therein.

2. In imposing a sentence within the authorized statutory range for any felony sex offense, the court may consider all relevant factors set forth in section 1.05 of this chapter, and in particular, may consider the defendant's criminal history, if any, including any history of sex offenses; any mental illness or mental abnormality from which the defendant may suffer; the defendant's ability or inability to control his sexual behavior; and, if the defendant has difficulty controlling such behavior, the extent to which that difficulty may pose a threat to society.

3. Except as provided by subdivision four, five, six, seven or eight of this section, or when a defendant is being sentenced for a conviction of the class A-II felonies of predatory sexual assault and predatory sexual assault against a child as defined in sections 130.95 and 130.96 of this chapter, or for any class A-I sexually motivated felony for which a life sentence or a life without parole sentence must be imposed, a sentence imposed upon a defendant convicted of a felony sex offense shall be a determinate sentence. The determinate sentence shall be imposed by the court in whole or half years, and shall include as a part thereof a period of post-release supervision in accordance with subdivision two-a of section 70.45 of this article. Persons eligible for sentencing under section 70.07 of this article governing second child sexual assault felonies shall be sentenced under such section and paragraph (j) of subdivision two-a of section 70.45 of this article.

4. (a) Sentences of imprisonment for felony sex offenses. Except as provided in subdivision five, six, seven, or eight of this section, the term of the determinate sentence must be fixed by the court as follows:

(i) for a class B felony, the term must be at least five years and must not exceed twenty-five years;

(ii) for a class C felony, the term must be at least three and one-half years and must not exceed fifteen years;

(iii) for a class D felony, the term must be at least two years and must not exceed seven years; and

(iv) for a class E felony, the term must be at least one and one-half years and must not exceed four years.

(b) Probation. The court may sentence a defendant convicted of a class D or class E felony sex offense to probation in accordance with the provisions of section 65.00 of this title.

(c) Alternative definite sentences for class D and class E felony sex offenses. If the court, having regard to the nature and circumstances of the crime and to the history and character of the defendant, is of the opinion that a sentence of imprisonment is necessary but that it would be unduly harsh to impose a determinate sentence upon a person convicted of a class D or class E felony sex offense, the court may impose a definite sentence of imprisonment and fix a term of one year or less.

5. Sentence of imprisonment for a predicate felony sex offender. (a) Applicability. This subdivision shall apply to a predicate felony sex offender who stands convicted of a non-violent felony sex offense and who was previously convicted of one or more felonies.

(b) Non-violent predicate felony offense. When the court has found, pursuant to the provisions of the criminal procedure law, that a person is a predicate felony sex offender, and the person's predicate conviction was for a non-violent felony offense, the court must impose a determinate sentence of imprisonment, the term of which must be fixed by the court as follows:

(i) for a class B felony, the term must be at least eight years and must not exceed twenty-five years;

(ii) for a class C felony, the term must be at least five years and must not exceed fifteen years;

(iii) for a class D felony, the term must be at least three years and must not exceed seven years; and

(iv) for a class E felony, the term must be at least two years and must not exceed four years.

(c) Violent predicate felony offense. When the court has found, pursuant to the provisions of the criminal procedure law, that a person is a predicate felony sex offender, and the person's predicate conviction was for a violent felony offense, the court must impose a determinate sentence of imprisonment, the term of which must be fixed by the court as follows:

(i) for a class B felony, the term must be at least nine years and must not exceed twenty-five years;

(ii) for a class C felony, the term must be at least six years and must not exceed fifteen years;

(iii) for a class D felony, the term must be at least four years and must not exceed seven years; and

(iv) for a class E felony, the term must be at least two and one-half years and must not exceed four years.

(d) A defendant who stands convicted of a non-violent felony sex offense, other than a class A-I or class A-II felony, who is adjudicated a persistent felony offender under section 70.10 of this article, shall be sentenced pursuant to the provisions of section 70.10 or pursuant to this subdivision.

6. Sentence of imprisonment for a violent felony sex offense. Except as provided in subdivisions seven and eight of this section, a defendant who stands convicted of a violent felony sex offense must be sentenced pursuant to the provisions of section 70.02, section 70.04, subdivision six of section 70.06, section 70.08, or section 70.10 of this article, as applicable.

7. Sentence for a class A felony sex offense. When a person stands convicted of a sexually motivated felony pursuant to section 130.91 of this chapter and the specified offense is a class A felony, the court must sentence the defendant in accordance with the provisions of:

(a) section 60.06 of this chapter and section 70.00 of this article, as applicable, if such offense is a class A-I felony; and

(b) section 70.00, 70.06 or 70.08 of this article, as applicable, if such offense is a class A-II felony.

8. Whenever a juvenile offender stands convicted of a felony sex offense, he or she must be sentenced pursuant to the provisions of sections 60.10 and 70.05 of this chapter.

9. Every determinate sentence for a felony sex offense, as defined in paragraph (a) of subdivision one of this section, imposed pursuant to any section of this article, shall include as a part thereof a period of post-release supervision in accordance with subdivision two-a of section 70.45 of this article.

§70.85 Transitional exception to determinate sentencing laws.

This section shall apply only to cases in which a determinate sentence was imposed between September first, nineteen hundred ninety-eight, and the effective date of this section, and was required by law to include a term of post-release supervision, but the court did not explicitly state such a term when pronouncing sentence. When such a case is again before the court pursuant to section six hundred one-d of the correction law or otherwise, for consideration of whether to resentence, the court may, notwithstanding any other provision of law but only on consent of the district attorney, re-impose the originally imposed determinate sentence of imprisonment without any term of post-release supervision, which then shall be deemed a lawful sentence.

ARTICLE 80 - FINES

Section
80.00   Fine for felony.
80.05   Fines for misdemeanors and violation.
80.10   Fines for corporations.
80.15   Multiple offenses.

§80.00   Fine for felony.

1. A sentence to pay a fine for a felony shall be a sentence to pay an amount, fixed by the court, not exceeding the higher of
   a. five thousand dollars; or
   b. double the amount of the defendant's gain from the commission of the crime or, if the defendant is convicted of a crime defined in article four hundred ninety-six of this chapter, any higher amount not exceeding three times the amount of the defendant's gain from the commission of such offense; or
   c. if the conviction is for any felony defined in article two hundred twenty or two hundred twenty-one of this chapter, according to the following schedule:
      (i) for A-I felonies, one hundred thousand dollars;
      (ii) for A-II felonies, fifty thousand dollars;
      (iii) for B felonies, thirty thousand dollars;
      (iv) for C felonies, fifteen thousand dollars. When imposing a fine pursuant to the provisions of this paragraph, the court shall consider the profit gained by defendant's conduct, whether the amount of the fine is disproportionate to the conduct in which defendant engaged, its impact on any victims, and defendant's economic circumstances, including the defendant's ability to pay, the effect of the fine upon his or her immediate family or any other persons to whom the defendant owes an obligation of support.

2. As used in this section the term "gain" means the amount of money or the value of property derived from the commission of the crime, less the amount of money or the value of property returned to the victim of the crime or seized by or surrendered to lawful authority prior to the time sentence is imposed.

3. When the court imposes a fine for a felony pursuant to paragraph b of subdivision one of this section, the court shall make a finding as to the amount of the defendant's gain from the crime. If the record does not contain sufficient evidence to support such a finding or to permit adequate consideration of the matters specified in paragraph c of subdivision one of this section, the court may conduct a hearing upon such issues.

4. Exception. The provisions of this section shall not apply to a corporation.

5. All moneys in excess of five thousand dollars received or collected in payment of a fine imposed pursuant to paragraph c of subdivision one of this section are the property of the state and the state comptroller shall deposit all such fines to the rehabilitative alcohol and substance treatment fund established pursuant to section ninety-seven-cc of the state finance law.

6. Notwithstanding any inconsistent provision of subdivision one of this section a sentence to pay a fine for a felony set forth in the vehicle and traffic law shall be a sentence to pay an amount fixed by the court in accordance with the provisions of the law that defines the crime.

7. When the court imposes a fine pursuant to section 145.22 or 145.23 of this chapter, the court shall direct that no less than ten percent of such fine be credited to the state cemetery vandalism restoration and administration fund created pursuant to section ninety-seven-r of the state finance law.

§80.05 Fines for misdemeanors and violation.

1. Class A misdemeanor. A sentence to pay a fine for a class A misdemeanor shall be a sentence to pay an amount, fixed by the court, not exceeding one thousand dollars, provided, however, that a sentence imposed for a violation of section 215.80 of this chapter may include a fine in an amount equivalent to double the value of the property unlawfully disposed of in the commission of the crime.

2. Class B misdemeanor. A sentence to pay a fine for a class B misdemeanor shall be a sentence to pay an amount, fixed by the court, not exceeding five hundred dollars.

3. Unclassified misdemeanor. A sentence to pay a fine for an unclassified misdemeanor shall be a sentence to pay an amount, fixed by the court, in accordance with the provisions of the law or ordinance that defines the crime.

4. Violation. A sentence to pay a fine for a violation shall be a sentence to pay an amount, fixed by the court, not exceeding two hundred fifty dollars.

In the case of a violation defined outside this chapter, if the amount of the fine is expressly specified in the law or ordinance that defines the offense, the amount of the fine shall be fixed in accordance with that law or ordinance.

5. Alternative sentence. If a person has gained money or property through the commission of any misdemeanor or violation then upon conviction thereof, the court, in lieu of imposing the fine authorized for the offense under one of the above subdivisions, may sentence the defendant to pay an amount, fixed by the court, not exceeding double the amount of the defendant's gain from the commission of the offense; provided, however, that the amount fixed by the court pursuant to this subdivision upon a conviction under section 11-1904 of the environmental conservation law shall not exceed five thousand dollars. In such event the provisions of subdivisions two and three of section 80.00 shall be applicable to the sentence.

6. Exception. The provisions of this section shall not apply to a corporation.

§80.10 Fines for corporations.

1. In general. A sentence to pay a fine, when imposed on a corporation for an offense defined in this chapter or for an offense defined outside this chapter for which no special corporate fine is specified, shall be a sentence to pay an amount, fixed by the court, not exceeding:

(a) Ten thousand dollars, when the conviction is of a felony;

(b) Five thousand dollars, when the conviction is of a class A misdemeanor or of an unclassified misdemeanor for which a term of imprisonment in excess of three months is authorized;

(c) Two thousand dollars, when the conviction is of a class B misdemeanor or of an unclassified misdemeanor for which the authorized term of imprisonment is not in excess of three months;

(d) Five hundred dollars, when the conviction is of a violation;

(e) Any higher amount not exceeding double the amount of the corporation's gain from the commission of the offense or, if the corporation is convicted of a crime defined in article four hundred ninety-six of this chapter, any higher amount not exceeding three times the amount of the corporation's gain from the commission of such offense.

2. Exception. In the case of an offense defined outside this chapter, if a special fine for a corporation is expressly specified in the law or ordinance that defines the offense, the fine fixed by the court shall be as follows:

(a) An amount within the limits specified in the law or ordinance that defines the offense; or

(b) Any higher amount not exceeding double the amount of the corporation's gain from the commission of the offense.

3. Determination of amount or value. When the court imposes the fine authorized by paragraph (e) of subdivision one or paragraph (b) of subdivision two for any offense the provisions of subdivision three of section 80.00 shall be applicable to the sentence.

§80.15 Multiple offenses.

Where a person is convicted of two or more offenses committed through a single act or omission, or through an act or omission which in itself constituted one of the offenses and also was a material element of the other, and the court imposes a sentence of imprisonment or a fine or both for one of the offenses, a fine shall not be imposed for the other. The provisions of this section shall not apply to any offense or offenses set forth in the vehicle and traffic law.

ARTICLE 85. SENTENCE OF INTERMITTENT IMPRISONMENT

Section

85.00   Sentence of intermittent imprisonment.
85.05   Modification and revocation of sentences of intermittent imprisonment.
85.10   Commitment; notifications; warrants.
85.15   Subsequent sentences.

§85.00 Sentence of intermittent imprisonment.

1. Definition. A sentence of intermittent imprisonment is a revocable sentence of imprisonment to be served on days or during certain periods of days, or both, specified by the court as part of the sentence. A person who receives a sentence of intermittent imprisonment shall be incarcerated in the institution to which he

is committed at such times as are specified by the court in the sentence.

2. Authorization for use of sentence. The court may impose a sentence of intermittent imprisonment in any case where:

(a) the court is imposing sentence, upon a person other than a second or persistent felony offender, for a class D or class E felony or for any offense that is not a felony; and

(b) the court is not imposing any other sentence of imprisonment upon the defendant at the same time; and

(c) the defendant is not under any other sentence of imprisonment with a term in excess of fifteen days imposed by any other court; and

3. Duration of sentence. A sentence of intermittent imprisonment may be for any term that could be imposed as a definite sentence of imprisonment for the offense for which such sentence is imposed. The term of the sentence shall commence on the day it is imposed and shall be calculated upon the basis of the duration of its term, rather than upon the basis of the days spent in confinement, so that no person shall be subject to any such sentence for a period that is longer than a period that commences on the date the sentence is imposed and ends on the date the term of the longest definite sentence for the offense would have expired, after deducting the credit that would have been applicable to a definite sentence for jail time but without regard to any credit authorized to be allowed against the term of a definite sentence for good behavior. The provisions of section five hundred-l of the correction law shall not be applicable to a sentence of intermittent imprisonment.

4. Imposition of sentence.

(a) When the court imposes a sentence of intermittent imprisonment the court shall specify in the sentence:

(i) that the court is imposing a sentence of intermittent imprisonment;

(ii) the term of such sentence;

(iii) the days or parts of days on which the sentence is to be served, but except as provided in paragraph (iv) hereof such specification need not include the dates on which such days fall; and

(iv) the first and last dates on which the defendant is to be incarcerated under the sentence.

(b) The court, in its discretion, may specify any day or days or parts thereof on which the defendant shall be confined and may specify a period to commence at the commencement of the sentence and not to exceed fifteen days during which the defendant is to be continuously confined.

§85.05 Modification and revocation of sentences of intermittent imprisonment.

1. Authorization. A sentence of intermittent imprisonment may be modified by the court in its discretion upon application of the defendant; and the court on its own motion may modify or revoke any such sentence if:

(a) the court is satisfied during the term of the sentence that the defendant has committed another offense during such term;

(b) the defendant has failed to report to the institution to which he has been committed, or to the institution designated by the head of the agency to which he has been committed, on a day or dates specified in the commitment and is unable or unwilling to furnish a reasonable and acceptable explanation for such failure; or

(c) the defendant has violated a rule or regulation of the institution or agency to which he has been committed and the head of such institution or agency or someone delegated by him has reported such violation in writing to the court.

2. Interruption of sentence. In any case where the defendant fails to report to the institution or to an institution of the agency to which he has been committed, the term of the sentence shall be interrupted and such interruption shall continue until the defendant either reports to such institution or appears before the court that imposed the sentence, whichever occurs first. If the defendant reports to the institution before he appears before the court, he shall be brought before the court.

3. Action by court. The court shall not modify or revoke a sentence of intermittent imprisonment unless the defendant has been afforded an opportunity to be heard. Any modification of a sentence of intermittent imprisonment:

(a) may provide (i) for different or additional or fewer days or parts of days on which the defendant is to be confined, or (ii) where the defendant has failed to report as specified in the sentence, an extension of the term of the sentence for the period during which it was interrupted, or (iii) for both; and

(b) shall be by written order of the court and shall be delivered and filed in the same manner as the original sentence, as specified in subdivision two of section 85.10 of this article.

4. Jail time. Where a sentence of intermittent imprisonment is revoked and a sentence of imprisonment is imposed in its place for the same offense, time spent in confinement under the sentence of intermittent imprisonment shall be calculated as jail time under subdivision three of section 70.30 of this chapter and shall be added to any jail time accrued against such sentence prior to imposition thereof.

§85.10 Commitment; notifications; warrants.

1. Commitment. Commitment under a sentence of intermittent imprisonment and execution of the judgment shall be in accordance with the procedure applicable to a definite sentence of imprisonment, except that:

(a) detention of the defendant under the judgment shall be executed during the times specified in the sentence; and

(b) the court may provide that the defendant is to report to a specified institution on a specified date at a specified time to commence service of the sentence and in such case the defendant need not be taken into or retained in custody when sentence is imposed.

2. Notifications. A written copy of the sentence imposed by the court signed by the judge who imposed the sentence shall be delivered to the defendant and shall be annexed to the commitment and to each copy of the commitment required to be delivered or filed. When the defendant is not taken into or retained in custody at the time sentence is imposed, the commitment and copy of the sentence shall forthwith be delivered to the person whose duty it is to execute the judgment. If at any time the defendant fails to report for confinement as provided in the sentence the officer in charge of the institution or department to which such commitment is made or someone designated by such officer shall forthwith notify the court in writing of such failure to report.

3. Warrants. Upon receipt of any such notification the court may issue a warrant to an appropriate police officer or peace officer directing him to take the defendant into custody and bring him before the court. The court may then commit such person to custody or fix bail or release him on his own recognizance for future appearance before the court.

§85.15 Subsequent sentences.

*1. Indeterminate and determinate sentences. The service of an indeterminate or a determinate sentence of imprisonment shall satisfy any sentence of intermittent imprisonment imposed on a person for an offense committed prior to the time the indeterminate or determinate sentence was imposed. A person who is serving a sentence of intermittent imprisonment at the time an indeterminate or a determinate sentence of imprisonment is imposed shall be delivered to the custody of the state department of corrections and community supervision to commence service of the indeterminate or determinate sentence immediately.   *(Amendments deemed repealed 9/1/23,Ch.55,L.2021)

2. Definite sentences. If a definite sentence of imprisonment is imposed on a person who is under a previously imposed sentence of intermittent imprisonment, such person shall commence service of the

definite sentence immediately. Where such definite sentence is for a term in excess of thirty days, the service of such sentence shall satisfy the sentence of intermittent imprisonment unless the sentence of intermittent imprisonment is revoked, or a warrant is issued pursuant to subdivision three of section 85.10 of this article and prior to satisfaction of, or conditional release under, such definite sentence of imprisonment.

PART THREE - SPECIFIC OFFENSES

TITLE G - ANTICIPATORY OFFENSES

ARTICLE 100 - CRIMINAL SOLICITATION

Section
100.00 Criminal solicitation in the fifth degree.
100.05 Criminal solicitation in the fourth degree.
100.08 Criminal solicitation in the third degree.
100.10 Criminal solicitation in the second degree.
100.13 Criminal solicitation in the first degree.
100.15 Criminal solicitation; no defense.
100.20 Criminal solicitation; exemption.

§100.00 Criminal solicitation in the fifth degree.

A person is guilty of criminal solicitation in the fifth degree when, with intent that another person engage in conduct constituting a crime, he solicits, requests, commands, importunes or otherwise attempts to cause such other person to engage in such conduct.

Criminal solicitation in the fifth degree is a violation.

§100.05 Criminal solicitation in the fourth degree.

A person is guilty of criminal solicitation in the fourth degree when:

1. with intent that another person engage in conduct constituting a felony, he solicits, requests, commands, importunes or otherwise attempts to cause such other person to engage in such conduct; or

2. being over eighteen years of age, with intent that another person under sixteen years of age engage in conduct that would constitute a crime, he solicits, requests, commands, importunes or otherwise attempts to cause such other person to engage in such conduct.

Criminal solicitation in the fourth degree is a class A misdemeanor.

§100.08 Criminal solicitation in the third degree.

A person is guilty of criminal solicitation in the third degree when, being over eighteen years of age, with intent that another person under sixteen years of age engage in conduct that would constitute a felony, he solicits, requests, commands, importunes or otherwise attempts to cause such other person to engage in such conduct.

Criminal solicitation in the third degree is a class E felony.

§100.10 Criminal solicitation in the second degree.

A person is guilty of criminal solicitation in the second degree when, with intent that another person engage in conduct constituting a class A felony, he solicits, requests, commands, importunes or otherwise attempts to cause such other person to engage in such conduct.

Criminal solicitation in the second degree is a class D felony.

§100.13 Criminal solicitation in the first degree.

A person is guilty of criminal solicitation in the first degree when, being over eighteen years of age, with intent that another person under sixteen years of age engage in conduct that would constitute a class A felony, he solicits, requests, commands, importunes or otherwise attempts to cause such other person to engage in such conduct.

Criminal solicitation in the first degree is a class C felony.

§100.15 Criminal solicitation; no defense.

It is no defense to a prosecution for criminal solicitation that the person solicited could not be guilty of the crime solicited owing to criminal irresponsibility or other legal incapacity or exemption, or to unawareness of the criminal nature of the conduct solicited or of the defendant's criminal purpose or to other factors precluding the mental state required for the commission of the crime in question.

§100.20 Criminal solicitation; exemption.

A person is not guilty of criminal solicitation when his solicitation constitutes conduct of a kind that is necessarily incidental to the commission of the crime solicited. When under such circumstances the solicitation constitutes an offense other than criminal solicitation which is related to but separate from the crime solicited, the actor is guilty of such related and separate offense only and not of criminal solicitation.

ARTICLE 105 - CONSPIRACY

Section
105.00 Conspiracy in the sixth degree.
105.05 Conspiracy in the fifth degree.
105.10 Conspiracy in the fourth degree.
105.13 Conspiracy in the third degree.
105.15 Conspiracy in the second degree.
105.17 Conspiracy in the first degree.
105.20 Conspiracy; pleading and proof; necessity of overt act.
105.25 Conspiracy; jurisdiction and venue.
105.30 Conspiracy; no defense.
105.35 Conspiracy; enterprise corruption: applicability.

§105.00 Conspiracy in the sixth degree.

A person is guilty of conspiracy in the sixth degree when, with intent that conduct constituting a crime be performed, he agrees with one or more persons to engage in or cause the performance of such conduct.

Conspiracy in the sixth degree is a class B misdemeanor.

§105.05 Conspiracy in the fifth degree.

A person is guilty of conspiracy in the fifth degree when, with intent that conduct constituting:

1. a felony be performed, he agrees with one of more persons to engage in or cause the performance of such conduct; or

2. a crime be performed, he, being over eighteen years of age, agrees with one or more persons under sixteen years of age to engage in or cause the performance of such conduct.

Conspiracy in the fifth degree is a class A misdemeanor.

§105.10 Conspiracy in the fourth degree.

A person is guilty of conspiracy in the fourth degree when, with intent that conduct constituting:

1. a class B or class C felony be performed, he or she agrees with one or more persons to engage in or cause the performance of such conduct; or

2. a felony be performed, he or she, being over eighteen years of age, agrees with one or more persons under sixteen years of age to engage in or cause the performance of such conduct; or

3. the felony of money laundering in the third degree as defined in section 470.10 of this chapter, be performed, he or she agrees with one or more persons to engage in or cause the performance of such conduct.

Conspiracy in the fourth degree is a class E felony.

§105.13 Conspiracy in the third degree.

A person is guilty of conspiracy in the third degree when, with intent that conduct constituting a class B or a class C felony be performed, he, being over eighteen years of age, agrees with one or more persons under sixteen years of age to engage in or cause the performance of such

Conspiracy in the third degree is a class D felony.

§105.15 Conspiracy in the second degree.

A person is guilty of conspiracy in the second degree when, with intent that conduct constituting a class A felony be performed, he agrees with one or more persons to engage in or cause the performance of such conduct.

Conspiracy in the second degree is a class B felony.

§105.17 Conspiracy in the first degree.

A person is guilty of conspiracy in the first degree when, with intent that conduct constituting a class A felony be performed, he, being over eighteen years of age, agrees with one or more persons under sixteen years of age to engage in or cause the performance of such conduct.

Conspiracy in the first degree is a class A-I felony.

§105.20 Conspiracy; pleading and proof; necessity of overt act.

A person shall not be convicted of conspiracy unless an overt act is alleged and proved to have been committed by one of the conspirators in furtherance of the conspiracy.

§105.25 Conspiracy; jurisdiction and venue.

1. A person may be prosecuted for conspiracy in the county in which he entered into such conspiracy or in any county in which an overt act in furtherance thereof was committed.

2. An agreement made within this state to engage in or cause the performance of conduct in another jurisdiction is punishable herein as a conspiracy only when such conduct would constitute a crime both under the laws of this state if performed herein and under the laws of the other jurisdiction if performed therein.

3. An agreement made in another jurisdiction to engage in or cause the performance of conduct within this state, which would constitute a crime herein, is punishable herein only when an overt act in furtherance of such conspiracy is committed within this state. Under such circumstances, it is no defense to a prosecution for conspiracy that the conduct which is the objective of the conspiracy would not constitute a crime under the laws of the other jurisdiction if performed therein.

§105.30 Conspiracy; no defense.

It is no defense to a prosecution for conspiracy that, owing to criminal irresponsibility or other legal incapacity or exemption, or to unawareness of the criminal nature of the agreement or the object conduct or of the defendant's criminal purpose or to other factors precluding the mental state required for the commission of conspiracy or the object crime, one or more of the defendant's co-conspirators could not be guilty of conspiracy or the object crime.

§105.35 Conspiracy; enterprise corruption: applicability.

For purposes of this article, conspiracy to commit the crime of enterprise corruption in violation of section 460.20 of this chapter shall not constitute an offense.

ARTICLE 110 - ATTEMPT

Section
110.00 Attempt to commit a crime.
110.05 Attempt to commit a crime; punishment.
110.10 Attempt to commit a crime; no defense.

§110.00 Attempt to commit a crime.

A person is guilty of an attempt to commit a crime when, with intent to commit a crime, he engages in conduct which tends to effect the commission of such crime.

§110.05 Attempt to commit a crime; punishment.

An attempt to commit a crime is a:

1. Class A-I felony when the crime attempted is the A-I felony of murder in the first degree, aggravated murder as defined in subdivision one of section 125.26 of this chapter, criminal possession of a controlled substance in the first degree, criminal sale of a controlled substance in the first degree, criminal possession of a chemical or biological weapon in the first degree or criminal use of a chemical or biological weapon in the first degree;

2. Class A-II felony when the crime attempted is a class A-II felony;

3. Class B felony when the crime attempted is a class A-I felony except as provided in subdivision one hereof;

4. Class C felony when the crime attempted is a class B felony;

5. Class D felony when the crime attempted is a class C felony;

6. Class E felony when the crime attempted is a class D felony;

7. Class A misdemeanor when the crime attempted is a class E felony;

8. Class B misdemeanor when the crime attempted is a misdemeanor;

9. Class D felony when the crime attempted is bribery in the third degree as defined in section 200.00 of this chapter, a class C felony when the crime attempted is bribery in the second degree as defined in section 200.03 of this chapter and a class B felony when the crime attempted is bribery in the first degree as defined in subdivision two of section 200.04 of this chapter.

§110.10 Attempt to commit a crime; no defense.

If the conduct in which a person engages otherwise constitutes an attempt to commit a crime pursuant to section 110.00, it is no defense to a prosecution for such attempt that the crime charged to have been attempted was, under the attendant circumstances, factually or legally impossible of commission, if such crime could have been committed had the attendant circumstances been as such person believed them to be.

ARTICLE 115 - CRIMINAL FACILITATION

Section
115.00 Criminal facilitation in the fourth degree.
115.01 Criminal facilitation in the third degree.
115.05 Criminal facilitation in the second degree.
115.08 Criminal facilitation in the first degree.
115.10 Criminal facilitation; no defense.
115.15 Criminal facilitation; corroboration.
115.20 Criminal facilitation; definitions and construction.

§115.00 Criminal facilitation in the fourth degree.

A person is guilty of criminal facilitation in the fourth degree when, believing it probable that he is rendering aid:

1. to a person who intends to commit a crime, he engages in conduct which provides such person with means or opportunity for the commission thereof and which in fact aids such person to commit a felony; or

2. to a person under sixteen years of age who intends to engage in conduct which would constitute a crime, he, being over eighteen years of age, engages in conduct which provides such person with means or opportunity for the commission thereof and which in fact aids such person to commit a crime.

Criminal facilitation in the fourth degree is a class A misdemeanor.

§115.01 Criminal facilitation in the third degree.

A person guilty of criminal facilitation in the third degree, when believing it probable that he is rendering aid to a person under sixteen years of age who intends to engage in conduct that would constitute a felony, he, being over eighteen years of age, engages in conduct which provides such person with means or opportunity for the commission thereof and which in fact aids such person to commit a felony.

Criminal facilitation in the third degree is a class E felony.

§115.05 Criminal facilitation in the second degree.

A person is guilty of criminal facilitation in the second degree when, believing it probable that he is rendering aid to a person who intends to commit a class A felony, he engages in conduct which provides such person with means or opportunity for the commission thereof and which in fact aids such person to commit such class A felony.

Criminal facilitation in the second degree is a class C felony.

§115.08 Criminal facilitation in the first degree.

A person is guilty of criminal facilitation in the first degree when, believing it probable that he is rendering aid to a person under sixteen years of age who intends to engage in conduct that would constitute a class A felony, he, being over eighteen years of age, engages in conduct which provides such person with means or opportunity for the commission thereof and which in fact aids such person to commit such a class A felony.

Criminal facilitation in the first degree is a class B felony.

§115.10 Criminal facilitation; no defense.

It is no defense to a prosecution for criminal facilitation that:

1. The person facilitated was not guilty of the underlying felony owing to criminal irresponsibility or other legal incapacity or exemption, or to unawareness of the criminal nature of the conduct in question or to other factors precluding the mental state required for the commission of such felony; or

2. The person facilitated has not been prosecuted for or convicted of the underlying felony, or has previously been acquitted thereof; or

3. The defendant himself is not guilty of the felony which he facilitated because he did not act with the intent or other culpable mental state required for the commission thereof.

§115.15 Criminal facilitation; corroboration.

A person shall not be convicted of criminal facilitation upon the testimony of a person who has committed the felony charged to have been facilitated unless such testimony be corroborated by such other evidence as tends to connect the defendant with such facilitation.

§115.20 Criminal facilitation; definitions and construction.

For purposes of this article, such conduct shall include, but not be limited to, making available, selling, exchanging, giving or disposing of a community gun, which in fact, aids a person to commit a crime. "Community gun" shall mean a firearm that is actually shared, made available, sold, exchanged, given or disposed of among or between two or more persons, at least one of whom is not authorized pursuant to law to possess such firearm. "Dispose of" shall have the same meaning as that term is defined in section 265.00 of this chapter. "Share" and "make available" shall, in the case of a firearm, be construed to include knowingly placing such firearm at a location accessible and known to one or more other persons.

TITLE H - OFFENSES AGAINST THE PERSON INVOLVING PHYSICAL INJURY, SEXUAL CONDUCT, RESTRAINT AND INTIMIDATION

ARTICLE 120 - ASSAULT AND RELATED OFFENSES

Setion
120.00 Assault in the third degree.
120.01 Reckless assault of a child by a child day care provider.
120.02 Reckless assault of a child.
120.03 Vehicular assault in the second degree.
120.04 Vehicular assault in the first degree.
120.04-a Aggravated vehicular assault.
120.05 Assault in the second degree.
120.06 Gang assault in the second degree.
120.07 Gang assault in the first degree.
120.08 Assault on a peace officer, police officer, firefighter or emergency medical services professional.
120.09 Assault on a judge.
120.10 Assault in the first degree.
120.11 Aggravated assault upon a police officer or a peace officer.
120.12 Aggravated assault upon a person less than eleven years old.
120.13 Menacing in the first degree.
120.14 Menacing in the second degree.
120.15 Menacing in the third degree.
120.16 Hazing in the first degree.
120.17 Hazing in the second degree.
120.18 Menacing a police officer or peace officer.
120.20 Reckless endangerment in the second degree.
120.25 Reckless endangerment in the first degree.
120.30 Promoting a suicide attempt.
120.35 Promoting a suicide attempt; when punishable as attempt to commit murder.
120.40 Definitions.
120.45 Stalking in the fourth degree.
120.50 Stalking in the third degree.
120.55 Stalking in the second degree.
120.60 Stalking in the first degree.
120.70 Luring a child.

§120.00 Assault in the third degree.

A person is guilty of assault in the third degree when:

1. With intent to cause physical injury to another person, he causes such injury to such person or a third person; or

2. He recklessly causes physical injury to another person; or

3. With criminal negligence, he causes physical injury to another person by means of a deadly weapon or a dangerous instrument.

Assault in the third degree is a class A misdemeanor.

§120.01 Reckless assault of a child by a child day care provider.

A person is guilty of reckless assault of a child when, being a child day care provider or an employee thereof, he or she recklessly causes serious physical injury to a child under the care of such provider or employee who is less than eleven years of age.

Reckless assault of a child by a child day care provider is a class E felony.

§120.02 Reckless assault of a child.

1. A person is guilty of reckless assault of a child when, being eighteen years of age or more, such person recklessly causes serious physical injury to the brain of a child less than five years old by shaking the child, or by slamming or throwing the child so as to impact the child's head on a hard surface or object.

2. For purposes of subdivision one of this section, the following shall constitute "serious physical injury":

a. "serious physical injury" as defined in subdivision ten of section 10.00 of this chapter; or

b. extreme rotational cranial acceleration and deceleration and one or more of the following: (i) subdural hemorrhaging; (ii) intracranial hemorrhaging; or (iiii) retinal hemorrhaging.

Reckless assault of a child is a class D felony.

§120.03 Vehicular assault in the second degree.

A person is guilty of vehicular assault in the second degree when he or she causes serious physical injury to another person, and either:

(1) operates a motor vehicle in violation of subdivision two, three, four or four-a of section eleven hundred ninety-two of the vehicle and traffic law or operates a vessel or public vessel in violation of paragraph (b), (c), (d) or (e) of subdivision two of section forty-nine-a of the navigation law, and as a result of such intoxication or impairment by the use of a drug, or by the combined influence of drugs or of alcohol and any drug or drugs, operates such motor vehicle, vessel or public vessel in a manner that causes such serious physical injury to such other person, or

(2) operates a motor vehicle with a gross vehicle weight rating of more than eighteen thousand pounds which contains flammable gas, radioactive materials or explosives in violation of subdivision one of section eleven hundred ninety-two of the vehicle and traffic law, and such flammable gas, radioactive materials or explosives is the cause of such serious physical injury, and as a result of such impairment by the use of alcohol, operates such motor vehicle in a manner that causes such serious physical injury to such other person, or

(3) operates a snowmobile in violation of paragraph (b), (c) or (d) of subdivision one of section 25.24 of the parks, recreation and historic preservation law or operates an all terrain vehicle as defined in paragraph (a) of subdivision one of section twenty-two hundred eighty-one of the vehicle and traffic law and in violation of subdivision two, three, four, or four-a of section eleven hundred ninety-two of the vehicle and traffic law, and as a result of such intoxication or impairment by the use of a drug, or by the combined influence of

drugs or of alcohol and any drug or drugs, operates such snowmobile or all terrain vehicle in a manner that causes such serious physical injury to such other person.

If it is established that the person operating such motor vehicle, vessel, public vessel, snowmobile or all terrain vehicle caused such serious physical injury while unlawfully intoxicated or impaired by the use of alcohol or a drug, then there shall be a rebuttable presumption that, as a result of such intoxication or impairment by the use of alcohol or a drug, or by the combined influence of drugs or of alcohol and any drug or drugs, such person operated the motor vehicle, vessel, public vessel, snowmobile or all terrain vehicle in a manner that caused such serious physical injury, as required by this section.

Vehicular assault in the second degree is a class E felony.

§120.04 Vehicular assault in the first degree.

A person is guilty of vehicular assault in the first degree when he or she commits the crime of vehicular assault in the second degree as defined in section 120.03 of this article, and either:

(1) commits such crime while operating a motor vehicle while such person has .18 of one per centum or more by weight of alcohol in such person's blood as shown by chemical analysis of such person's blood, breath, urine or saliva made pursuant to the provisions of section eleven hundred ninety-four of the vehicle and traffic law;

(2) commits such crime while knowing or having reason to know that: (a) his or her license or his or her privilege of operating a motor vehicle in another state or his or her privilege of obtaining a license to operate a motor vehicle in another state is suspended or revoked and such suspension or revocation is based upon a conviction in such other state for an offense which would, if committed in this state, constitute a violation of any of the provisions of section eleven hundred ninety-two of the vehicle and traffic law; or (b) his or her license or his or her privilege of operating a motor vehicle in the state or his or her privilege of obtaining a license issued by the commissioner of motor vehicles is suspended or revoked and such suspension or revocation is based upon either a refusal to submit to a chemical test pursuant to section eleven hundred ninety-four of the vehicle and traffic law or following a conviction for a violation of any of the provisions of section eleven hundred ninety-two of the vehicle and traffic law;

(3) has previously been convicted of violating any of the provisions of section eleven hundred ninety-two of the vehicle and traffic law within the preceding ten years, provided that, for the purposes of this subdivision, a conviction in any other state or jurisdiction for an offense which, if committed in this state, would constitute a violation of section eleven hundred ninety-two of the vehicle and traffic law, shall be treated as a violation of such law;

(4) causes serious physical injury to more than one other person;

(5) has previously been convicted of violating any provision of this article or article one hundred twenty-five of this title involving the operation of a motor vehicle, or was convicted in any other state or jurisdiction of an offense involving the operation of a motor vehicle which, if committed in this state, would constitute a violation of this article or article one hundred twenty-five of this title; or

(6) commits such crime while operating a motor vehicle while a child who is fifteen years of age or less is a passenger in such motor vehicle and causes serious physical injury to such child.

If it is established that the person operating such motor vehicle caused such serious physical injury or injuries while unlawfully intoxicated or impaired by the use of alcohol or a drug, or by the combined influence of drugs or of alcohol and any drug or drugs, then there shall be a rebuttable presumption that, as a result of such intoxication or impairment by the use of alcohol or a drug, or by the combined influence of drugs or of alcohol and any drug or drugs, such person operated the motor vehicle in a manner that caused such serious physical injury or injuries, as required by this section and section 120.03 of this article.

Vehicular assault in the first degree is a class D felony.

§120.04-a   Aggravated vehicular assault.

A person is guilty of aggravated vehicular assault when he or she engages in reckless driving as defined by section twelve hundred twelve of the vehicle and traffic law, and commits the crime of vehicular assault in the second degree as defined in section 120.03 of this article, and either:

(1) commits such crimes while operating a motor vehicle while such person has .18 of one per centum or more by weight of alcohol in such person's blood as shown by chemical analysis of such person's blood, breath, urine or saliva made pursuant to the provisions of section eleven hundred ninety-four of the vehicle and traffic law;

(2) commits such crimes while knowing or having reason to know that: (a) his or her license or his or her privilege of operating a motor vehicle in another state or his or her privilege of obtaining a license to operate a motor vehicle in another state is suspended or revoked and such suspension or revocation is based upon a conviction in such other state for an offense which would, if committed in this state, constitute a violation of any of the provisions of section eleven hundred ninety-two of the vehicle and traffic law; or (b) his or her license or his or her privilege of operating a motor vehicle in this state or his or her privilege of obtaining a license issued by the commissioner of motor vehicles is suspended or revoked and such suspension or revocation is based upon either a refusal to submit to a chemical test pursuant to section eleven hundred ninety-four of the vehicle and traffic law or following a conviction for a violation of any of the provisions of section eleven hundred ninety-two of the vehicle and traffic law;

(3) has previously been convicted of violating any of the provisions of section eleven hundred ninety-two of the vehicle and traffic law within the preceding ten years, provided that, for the purposes of this subdivision, a conviction in any other state or jurisdiction for an offense which, if committed in this state, would constitute a violation of section eleven hundred ninety-two of the vehicle and traffic law, shall be treated as a violation of such law;

(4) causes serious physical injury to more than one other person;

(5) has previously been convicted of violating any provision of this article or article one hundred twenty-five of this title involving the operation of a motor vehicle, or was convicted in any other state or jurisdiction of an offense involving the operation of a motor vehicle which, if committed in this state, would constitute a violation of this article or article one hundred twenty-five of this title; or

(6) commits such crime while operating a motor vehicle while a child who is fifteen years of age or less is a passenger in such motor vehicle and causes serious physical injury to such child.

If it is established that the person operating such motor vehicle caused such serious physical injury or injuries while unlawfully intoxicated or impaired by the use of alcohol or a drug, or by the combined influence of drugs or of alcohol and any drug or drugs, then there shall be a rebuttable presumption that, as a result of such intoxication or impairment by the use of alcohol or a drug, or by the combined influence of drugs or of alcohol and any drug or drugs, such person operated the motor vehicle in a manner that caused such serious physical injury or injuries, as required by this section and section 120.03 of this article.

Aggravated vehicular assault is a class C felony.

§120.05 Assault in the second degree.

A person is guilty of assault in the second degree when:

1. With intent to cause serious physical injury to another person, he causes such injury to such person or to a third person; or

2. With intent to cause physical injury to another person, he causes such injury to such person or to a third person by means of a deadly weapon or a dangerous instrument; or

*3. With intent to prevent a peace officer, a police officer, prosecutor as defined in subdivision thirty-one of section 1.20 of the criminal procedure law, registered nurse, licensed practical nurse, public health sanitarian, New York city public health sanitarian, sanitation enforcement agent, New York city sanitation worker, a firefighter, including a firefighter acting as a paramedic or emergency medical technician administering first aid in the course of performance of duty as such firefighter, an emergency medical service paramedic or emergency medical service technician, or medical or related personnel in a hospital emergency department, a city marshal, a school crossing guard appointed pursuant to section two hundred eight-a of the general municipal law, a traffic enforcement officer, traffic enforcement agent or employee of any entity governed by the public service law in the course of performing an essential service, from performing a lawful duty, by means including releasing or failing to control an animal under circumstances evincing the actor's intent that the animal obstruct the lawful activity of such peace officer, police officer, prosecutor as defined in subdivision thirty-one of section 1.20 of the criminal procedure law, registered nurse, licensed practical nurse, public health sanitarian, New York city public health sanitarian, sanitation

enforcement agent, New York city sanitation worker, firefighter, paramedic, technician, city marshal, school crossing guard appointed pursuant to section two hundred eight-a of the general municipal law, traffic enforcement officer, traffic enforcement agent or employee of an entity governed by the public service law, he or she causes physical injury to such peace officer, police officer, prosecutor as defined in subdivision thirty-one of section 1.20 of the criminal procedure law, registered nurse, licensed practical nurse, public health sanitarian, New York city public health sanitarian, sanitation enforcement agent, New York city sanitation worker, firefighter, paramedic, technician or medical or related personnel in a hospital emergency department, city marshal, school crossing guard, traffic enforcement officer, traffic enforcement agent; or employee of an entity governed by the public service law; or   *(Eff.11/1/16,Ch.267,L.2016)

3-a. With intent to prevent an employee of a local social services district directly involved in investigation of or response to alleged abuse or neglect of a child, a vulnerable elderly person or an incompetent or physically disabled person, from performing such investigation or response, the actor, not being such child, vulnerable elderly person or incompetent or physically disabled person, or with intent to prevent an employee of a local social services district directly involved in providing public assistance and care from performing his or her job, causes physical injury to such employee including by means of releasing or failing to control an animal under circumstances evincing the actor's intent that the animal obstruct the lawful activities of such employee; or

3-b. With intent to prevent an employee of the New York city housing authority from performing his or her lawful duties while located on housing project grounds, real property, or a building owned, managed, or operated by such authority he or she causes physical injury to such employee; or

3-c. With intent to prevent an employee providing direct patient care, who is not a nurse pursuant to title eight of the education law, whose principal employment responsibility is to carry out direct patient care for one or more patients in any hospital, nursing home, residential health care facility, general hospital, government agency including any chronic disease hospital, maternity hospital, outpatient department, emergency center or surgical center under article twenty-eight of the public health law, from performing a lawful duty, he or she causes physical injury to such employee providing direct patient care; or

4. He recklessly causes serious physical injury to another person by means of a deadly weapon or a dangerous instrument; or

4-a. He recklessly causes physical injury to another person who is a child under the age of eighteen by intentional discharge of a firearm, rifle or shotgun; or

5. For a purpose other than lawful medical or therapeutic treatment, he intentionally causes stupor, unconsciousness or other physical impairment or injury to another person by administering to him, without his consent, a drug, substance or preparation capable of producing the same; or

6. In the course of and in furtherance of the commission or attempted commission of a felony, other than a felony defined in article one hundred thirty which requires corroboration for conviction, or of immediate flight therefrom, he, or another participant if there be any, causes physical injury to a person other than one of the participants; or

7. Having been charged with or convicted of a crime and while confined in a correctional facility, as defined in subdivision three of

section forty of the correction law, pursuant to such charge or conviction, with intent to cause physical injury to another person, he causes such injury to such person or to a third person; or

8. Being eighteen years old or more and with intent to cause physical injury to a person less than eleven years old, the defendant recklessly causes serious physical injury to such person; or

9. Being eighteen years old or more and with intent to cause physical injury to a person less than seven years old, the defendant causes such injury to such person; or

10. Acting at a place the person knows, or reasonably should know, is on school grounds and with intent to cause physical injury, he or she:

    (a) causes such injury to an employee of a school or public school district; or

    (b) not being a student of such school or public school district, causes physical injury to another, and such other person is a student of such school who is attending or present for educational purposes. For purposes of this subdivision the term "school grounds" shall have the meaning set forth in subdivision fourteen of section 220.00 of this chapter; or

11. With intent to cause physical injury to a train operator, ticket inspector, conductor, signalperson, bus operator, or station agent, station cleaner or terminal cleaner employed by any transit agency, authority or company, public or private, whose operation is authorized by New York state or any of its political subdivisions, a city marshal, a school crossing guard appointed pursuant to section two hundred eight-a of the general municipal law, a traffic enforcement officer, traffic enforcement agent, prosecutor as defined in subdivision thirty-one of section 1.20 of the criminal procedure law, sanitation enforcement agent, New York city sanitation worker, public health sanitarian, New York city public health sanitarian, registered nurse, licensed practical nurse, emergency medical service paramedic, or emergency medical service technician, he or she causes physical injury to such train operator, ticket inspector, conductor, signalperson, bus operator, station agent, station cleaner or terminal cleaner, city marshal, school crossing guard appointed pursuant to section two hundred eight-a of the general municipal law, traffic enforcement officer, traffic enforcement agent, prosecutor as defined in subdivision thirty-one of section 1.20 of the criminal procedure law, registered nurse, licensed practical nurse, public health sanitarian, New York city public health sanitarian, sanitation enforcement agent, New York city sanitation worker, emergency medical service paramedic, or emergency medical service technician, while such employee is performing an assigned duty on, or directly related to, the operation of a train or bus, including the cleaning of a train or bus station or terminal, or such city marshal, school crossing guard, traffic enforcement officer, traffic enforcement agent, prosecutor as defined in subdivision thirty-one of section 1.20 of the criminal procedure law, registered nurse, licensed practical nurse, public health sanitarian, New York city public health sanitarian, sanitation enforcement agent, New York city sanitation worker, emergency medical service paramedic, or emergency medical service technician is performing an assigned duty;

11-a. With intent to cause physical injury to an employee of a local social services district directly involved in investigation of or response to alleged abuse or neglect of a child, vulnerable elderly person or an incompetent or physically disabled person, the actor, not being such child, vulnerable elderly person or incompetent or physically disabled person, or with intent to prevent an employee of a local social services district directly involved in providing public assistance and care from performing his or her job, causes physical injury to such employee; or

11-b. With intent to cause physical injury to an employee of the New York city housing authority performing his or her lawful duties while located on housing project grounds, real property, or a building owned, managed, or operated by such authority he or she causes physical injury to such employee; or

11-c. With intent to cause physical injury to an employee providing direct patient care, who is not a nurse pursuant to title eight of the education law, whose principal employment responsibility is to carry out direct patient care for one or more patients in any hospital, nursing home, residential health care facility, general hospital, government agency including any chronic disease hospital, maternity hospital, outpatient department, emergency center or surgical center under article twenty-eight of the public health law, he or she causes physical injury to such employee providing direct patient care while such employee is performing a lawful duty; or

12. With intent to cause physical injury to a person who is sixty-five years of age or older, he or she causes such injury to such person, and the actor is more than ten years younger than such person; or

13. Being confined to a secure treatment facility, as such term is defined in subdivision (o) of section 10.03 of the mental hygiene law, and with intent to cause physical injury to an employee of such secure treatment facility performing his or her duties, he or she causes such injury to such person; or

14. With intent to prevent or obstruct a process server, as defined in section eighty-nine-t of the general business law, from performing a lawful duty pursuant to article three of the civil practice law and rules, or intentionally, as retaliation against such a process server for the performance of the process server's duties pursuant to such article, including by means of releasing or failing to control an animal evincing the actor's intent that the animal prevent or obstruct the lawful duty of the process server or as retaliation against the process server, he or she causes physical injury to such process server.

Assault in the second degree is a class D felony.

§120.06 Gang assault in the second degree.

A person is guilty of gang assault in the second degree when, with intent to cause physical injury to another person and when aided by two or more other persons actually present, he causes serious physical injury to such person or to a third person.

Gang assault in the second degree is a class C felony.

§120.07 Gang assault in the first degree.

A person is guilty of gang assault in the first degree when, with intent to cause serious physical injury to another person and when aided by two or more other persons actually present, he causes serious physical injury to such person or to a third person.

Gang assault in the first degree is a class B felony.

§120.08 Assault on a peace officer, police officer, firefighter or emergency medical services professional.

A person is guilty of assault on a peace officer, police officer, firefighter or emergency medical services professional when, with intent to prevent a peace officer, police officer, a firefighter, including a firefighter acting as a paramedic or emergency medical technician administering first aid in the course of performance of duty as such firefighter, or an emergency medical service paramedic or emergency medical service technician, from performing a lawful duty, he or she causes serious physical injury to such peace officer, police officer, firefighter, paramedic or technician.

Assault on a peace officer, police officer, firefighter or emergency medical services professional is a class C felony. *(Eff.12/28/18,Ch.476,L.2018)*

§120.09 Assault on a judge.
A person is guilty of assault on a judge when, with intent to cause serious physical injury and prevent a judge from performing official judicial duties, he or she causes serious physical injury to such judge. For the purposes of this section, the term judge shall mean a judge of a court of record or a justice court.

Assault on a judge is a class C felony.

§120.10 Assault in the first degree.
A person is guilty of assault in the first degree when:
1. With intent to cause serious physical injury to another person, he causes such injury to such person or to a third person by means of a deadly weapon or a dangerous instrument; or
2. With intent to disfigure another person seriously and permanently, or to destroy, amputate or disable permanently a member or organ of his body, he causes such injury to such person or to a third person; or
3. Under circumstances evincing a depraved indifference to human life, he recklessly engages in conduct which creates a grave risk of death to another person, and thereby causes serious physical injury to another person; or
4. In the course of and in furtherance of the commission or attempted commission of a felony or of immediate flight therefrom, he, or another participant if there be any, causes serious physical injury to a person other than one of the participants.

Assault in the first degree is a class B felony.

§120.11 Aggravated assault upon a police officer or a peace officer.
A person is guilty of aggravated assault upon a police officer or a peace officer when, with intent to cause serious physical injury to a person whom he knows or reasonably should know to be a police officer or a peace officer engaged in the course of performing his official duties, he causes such injury by means of a deadly weapon or dangerous instrument.

Aggravated assault upon a police officer or a peace officer is a class B felony.

§120.12 Aggravated assault upon a person less than eleven years old.
A person is guilty of aggravated assault upon a person less than eleven years old when being eighteen years old or more the defendant commits the crime of assault in the third degree as defined in section 120.00 of this article upon a person less than eleven years old and has been previously convicted of such crime upon a person less than eleven years old within the preceding ten years.

Aggravated assault upon a person less than eleven years old is a class E felony.

§120.13 Menacing in the first degree.
A person is guilty of menacing in the first degree when he or she commits the crime of menacing in the second degree and has been previously convicted of the crime of menacing in the second degree or the crime of menacing a police officer or peace officer within the preceding ten years.
Menacing in the first degree is a class E felony.

§120.14 Menacing in the second degree.
A person is guilty of menacing in the second degree when:
1. He or she intentionally places or attempts to place another person in reasonable fear of physical injury, serious physical injury or death by displaying a deadly weapon, dangerous instrument or what appears to be a pistol, revolver, rifle, shotgun, machine gun or other firearm; or
2. He or she repeatedly follows a person or engages in a course of conduct or repeatedly commits acts over a period of time intentionally placing or attempting to place another person in reasonable fear of physical injury, serious physical injury or death; or
3. He or she commits the crime of menacing in the third degree in violation of that part of a duly served order of protection, or such order which the defendant has actual knowledge of because he or she was present in court when such order was issued, pursuant to article eight of the family court act, section 530.12 of the criminal procedure law, or an order of protection issued by a court of competent jurisdiction in another state, territorial or tribal jurisdiction, which directed the respondent or defendant to stay away from the person or persons on whose behalf the order was issued.
Menacing in the second degree is a class A misdemeanor.

§120.15 Menacing in the third degree.
A person is guilty of menacing in the third degree when, by physical menace, he or she intentionally places or attempts to place another person in fear of death, imminent serious physical injury or physical injury.
Menacing in the third degree is a class B misdemeanor.

§120.16 Hazing in the first degree.
A person is guilty of hazing in the first degree when, in the course of another person's initiation into or affiliation with any organization, he intentionally or recklessly engages in conduct, including, but not limited to, making physical contact with or requiring physical activity of such other person, which creates a substantial risk of physical injury to such other person or a third person and thereby causes such injury.
Hazing in the first degree is a class A misdemeanor. *(Eff.8/13/18,Ch.188,L.2018)*

§120.17 Hazing in the second degree.
A person is guilty of hazing in the second degree when, in the course of another person's initiation or affiliation with any organization, he intentionally or recklessly engages in conduct, including, but not limited to, making physical contact with or requiring physical activity of such other person, which creates a substantial risk of physical injury to such other person or a third person.
Hazing in the second degree is a violation. *(Eff.8/13/18,Ch.188,L.2018)*

§120.18 Menacing a police officer or peace officer.
A person is guilty of menacing a police officer or peace officer

when he or she intentionally places or attempts to place a police officer or peace officer in reasonable fear of physical injury, serious physical injury or death by displaying a deadly weapon, knife, pistol, revolver, rifle, shotgun, machine gun or other firearm, whether operable or not, where such officer was in the course of performing his or her official duties and the defendant knew or reasonably should have known that such victim was a police officer or peace officer.

Menacing a police officer or peace officer is a class D felony.

§120.20 Reckless endangerment in the second degree.

A person is guilty of reckless endangerment in the second degree when he recklessly engages in conduct which creates a substantial risk of serious physical injury to another person.

Reckless endangerment in the second degree is a class A misdemeanor.

§120.25 Reckless endangerment in the first degree.

A person is guilty of reckless endangerment in the first degree when, under circumstances evincing a depraved indifference to human life, he recklessly engages in conduct which creates a grave risk of death to another person.

Reckless endangerment in the first degree is a class D felony.

§120.30 Promoting a suicide attempt.

A person is guilty of promoting a suicide attempt when he intentionally causes or aids another person to attempt suicide.

Promoting a suicide attempt is a class E felony.

§120.35 Promoting a suicide attempt; when punishable as attempt to commit murder.

A person who engages in conduct constituting both the offense of promoting a suicide attempt and the offense of attempt to commit murder may not be convicted of attempt to commit murder unless he causes or aids the suicide attempt by the use of duress or deception.

§120.40 Definitions.

For purposes of sections 120.45, 120.50, 120.55 and 120.60 of this article:

1. "Kidnapping" shall mean a kidnapping crime defined in article one hundred thirty-five of this chapter.

2. "Unlawful imprisonment" shall mean an unlawful imprisonment felony crime defined in article one hundred thirty-five of this chapter.

3. "Sex offense" shall mean a felony defined in article one hundred thirty of this chapter, sexual misconduct, as defined in section 130.20 of this chapter, sexual abuse in the third degree as defined in section 130.55 of this chapter or sexual abuse in the second degree as defined in section 130.60 of this chapter.

4. "Immediate family" means the spouse, former spouse, parent, child, sibling, or any other person who regularly resides or has regularly resided in the household of a person.

5. "Specified predicate crime" means:

   a. a violent felony offense;

   b. a crime defined in section 130.20, 130.25, 130.30, 130.40, 130.45, 130.55, 130.60, 130.70, 255.25, 255.26 or 255.27;

c. assault in the third degree, as defined in section 120.00; menacing in the first degree, as defined in section 120.13; menacing in the second degree, as defined in section 120.14; coercion in the first degree, as defined in section 135.65; coercion in the second degree, as defined in section 135.61; coercion in the third degree, as defined in section 135.60; aggravated harassment in the second degree, as defined in section 240.30; harassment in the first degree, as defined in section 240.25; menacing in the third degree, as defined in section 120.15; criminal mischief in the third degree, as defined in section 145.05; criminal mischief in the second degree, as defined in section 145.10, criminal mischief in the first degree, as defined in section 145.12; criminal tampering in the first degree, as defined in section 145.20; arson in the fourth degree, as defined in section 150.05; arson in the third degree, as defined in section 150.10; criminal contempt in the first degree, as defined in section 215.51; endangering the welfare of a child, as defined in section 260.10; or   *(Eff.11/1/18,Ch.55,L.2018)*

d. stalking in the fourth degree, as defined in section 120.45; stalking in the third degree, as defined in section 120.50; stalking in the second degree, as defined in section 120.55; or

e. an offense in any other jurisdiction which includes all of the essential elements of any such crime for which a sentence to a term of imprisonment in excess of one year or a sentence of death was authorized and is authorized in this state irrespective of whether such sentence was imposed.

§120.45 Stalking in the fourth degree.

A person is guilty of stalking in the fourth degree when he or she intentionally, and for no legitimate purpose, engages in a course of conduct directed at a specific person, and knows or reasonably should know that such conduct:

1. is likely to cause reasonable fear of material harm to the physical health, safety or property of such person, a member of such person's immediate family or a third party with whom such person is acquainted; or

2. causes material harm to the mental or emotional health of such person, where such conduct consists of following, telephoning or initiating communication or contact with such person, a member of such person's immediate family or a third party with whom such person is acquainted, and the actor was previously clearly informed to cease that conduct; or

3. is likely to cause such person to reasonably fear that his or her employment, business or career is threatened, where such conduct consists of appearing, telephoning or initiating communication or contact at such person's place of employment or business, and the actor was previously clearly informed to cease that conduct.

For the purposes of subdivision two of this section, "following" shall include the unauthorized tracking of such person's movements or location through the use of a global positioning system or other device.

Stalking in the fourth degree is a class B misdemeanor.

§120.50 Stalking in the third degree.

A person is guilty of stalking in the third degree when he or she:

1. Commits the crime of stalking in the fourth degree in violation

of section 120.45 of this article against three or more persons, in three or more separate transactions, for which the actor has not been previously convicted; or

2. Commits the crime of stalking in the fourth degree in violation of section 120.45 of this article against any person, and has previously been convicted, within the preceding ten years of a specified predicate crime, as defined in subdivision five of section 120.40 of this article, and the victim of such specified predicate crime is the victim, or an immediate family member of the victim, of the present offense; or

3. With intent to harass, annoy or alarm a specific person, intentionally engages in a course of conduct directed at such person which is likely to cause such person to reasonably fear physical injury or serious physical injury, the commission of a sex offense against, or the kidnapping, unlawful imprisonment or death of such person or a member of such person's immediate family; or

4. Commits the crime of stalking in the fourth degree and has previously been convicted within the preceding ten years of stalking in the fourth degree.

Stalking in the third degree is a class A misdemeanor.

§120.55 Stalking in the second degree.

A person is guilty of stalking in the second degree when he or she:

1. Commits the crime of stalking in the third degree as defined in subdivision three of section 120.50 of this article and in the course of and in furtherance of the commission of such offense: (i) displays, or possesses and threatens the use of, a firearm, pistol, revolver, rifle, shotgun, machine gun, electronic dart gun, electronic stun gun, cane sword, billy, blackjack, bludgeon, plastic knuckles, metal knuckles, chuka stick, sand bag, sandclub, slingshot, slungshot, shirken, "Kung Fu Star", dagger, dangerous knife, dirk, razor, stiletto, imitation pistol, dangerous instrument, deadly instrument or deadly weapon; or (ii) displays what appears to be a pistol, revolver, rifle, shotgun, machine gun or other firearm; or

2. Commits the crime of stalking in the third degree in violation of subdivision three of section 120.50 of this article against any person, and has previously been convicted, within the preceding five years, of a specified predicate crime as defined in subdivision five of section 120.40 of this article, and the victim of such specified predicate crime is the victim, or an immediate family member of the victim, of the present offense; or

3. Commits the crime of stalking in the fourth degree and has previously been convicted of stalking in the third degree as defined in subdivision four of section 120.50 of this article against any person; or

4. Being twenty-one years of age or older, repeatedly follows a person under the age of fourteen or engages in a course of conduct or repeatedly commits acts over a period of time intentionally placing or attempting to place such person who is under the age of fourteen in reasonable fear of physical injury, serious physical injury or death; or

5. Commits the crime of stalking in the third degree, as defined in subdivision three of section 120.50 of this article, against ten or more persons, in ten or more separate transactions, for which the actor has not been previously convicted.

Stalking in the second degree is a class E felony.

§120.60 Stalking in the first degree.

A person is guilty of stalking in the first degree when he or she commits the crime of stalking in the third degree as defined in subdivision three of section 120.50 or stalking in the second degree as defined in section 120.55 of this article and, in the course and furtherance thereof, he or she:

1. intentionally or recklessly causes physical injury to the victim of such crime; or

2. commits a class A misdemeanor defined in article one hundred thirty of this chapter, or a class E felony defined in section 130.25, 130.40 or 130.85 of this chapter, or a class D felony defined in section 130.30 or 130.45 of this chapter.

Stalking in the first degree is a class D felony.

§120.70 Luring a child.

1. A person is guilty of luring a child when he or she lures a child into a motor vehicle, aircraft, watercraft, isolated area, building, or part thereof, for the purpose of committing against such child any of the following offenses: an offense as defined in section 70.02 of this chapter; an offense as defined in section 125.25 or 125.27 of this chapter; a felony offense that is a violation of article one hundred thirty of this chapter; an offense as defined in section 135.25 of this chapter; an offense as defined in sections 230.30, 230.33, 230.34 or 230.34-a of this chapter; an offense as defined in sections 255.25, 255.26, or 255.27 of this chapter; or an offense as defined in sections 263.05, 263.10, or 263.15 of this chapter. For purposes of this subdivision "child" means a person less than seventeen years of age. Nothing in this section shall be deemed to preclude, if the evidence warrants, a conviction for the commission or attempted commission of any crime, including but not limited to a crime defined in article one hundred thirty-five of this chapter. *(Eff.11/13/18,Ch.189,L.2018)*

2. Luring a child is a class E felony, provided, however, that if the underlying offense the actor intended to commit against such child constituted a class A or a class B felony, then the offense of luring a child in violation of this section shall be deemed respectively, a class C felony or class D felony.

ARTICLE 121 - STRANGULATION AND RELATED OFFENSES

Section
121.11   Criminal obstruction of breathing or blood circulation.
121.12   Strangulation in the second degree.
121.13   Strangulation in the first degree.
121.13-a Aggravated strangulation.
121.14   Medical or dental purpose.

§121.11 Criminal obstruction of breathing or blood circulation.

A person is guilty of criminal obstruction of breathing or blood circulation when, with intent to impede the normal breathing or circulation of the blood of another person, he or she:

a. applies pressure on the throat or neck of such person; or

b. blocks the nose or mouth of such person.

Criminal obstruction of breathing or blood circulation is a class A misdemeanor.

§121.12 Strangulation in the second degree.

A person is guilty of strangulation in the second degree when he or she commits the crime of criminal obstruction of breathing or blood circulation, as defined in section 121.11 of this article, and thereby causes stupor, loss of consciousness for any period of time, or any other physical injury or impairment.

Strangulation in the second degree is a class D felony.

§121.13 Strangulation in the first degree.

A person is guilty of strangulation in the first degree when he or she commits the crime of criminal obstruction of breathing or blood circulation, as defined in section 121.11 of this article, and thereby causes serious physical injury to such other person.

Strangulation in the first degree is a class C felony.

§121.13-a Aggravated strangulation.

A person is guilty of aggravated strangulation when, being a police officer as defined in subdivision thirty-four of section 1.20 of the criminal procedure law or a peace officer as defined in section 2.10 of the criminal procedure law, he or she commits the crime of criminal obstruction of breathing or blood circulation, as defined in section 121.11 of this article, or uses a chokehold or similar restraint, as described in paragraph b of subdivision one of section eight hundred thirty-seven-t of the executive law, and thereby causes serious physical injury or death to another person.

Aggravated strangulation is a class C felony.   *(Eff.6/12/20,Ch.94,L.2020)*

§121.14 Medical or dental purpose.

For purposes of section 121.11, 121.12, 121.13 or 121.13-a of this article, it shall be an affirmative defense that the defendant performed such conduct for a valid medical or dental purpose.

(Eff.6/12/20,Ch.94,L.2020)

ARTICLE 125 - HOMICIDE AND RELATED OFFENSES

Section
125.00   Homicide defined.
125.05   Homicide and related offenses; definition.
125.10   Criminally negligent homicide.
125.11   Aggravated criminally negligent homicide.
125.12   Vehicular manslaughter in the second degree.
125.13   Vehicular manslaughter in the first degree.
125.14   Aggravated vehicular homicide.
125.15   Manslaughter in the second degree.
125.20   Manslaughter in the first degree.
125.21   Aggravated manslaughter in the second degree.
125.22   Aggravated manslaughter in the first degree.
125.25   Murder in the second degree.
125.26   Aggravated murder.
125.27   Murder in the first degree.

§125.00 Homicide defined.

Homicide means conduct which causes the death of a person under circumstances constituting murder, manslaughter in the first degree, manslaughter in the second degree, or criminally negligent homicide.

§125.05 Homicide and related offenses; definition.

The following definition is applicable to this article:

"Person," when referring to the victim of a homicide, means a human being who has been born and is alive.

§125.10 Criminally negligent homicide.

A person is guilty of criminally negligent homicide when, with criminal negligence, he causes the death of another person.

Criminally negligent homicide is a class E felony.

§125.11 Aggravated criminally negligent homicide.

A person is guilty of aggravated criminally negligent homicide when, with criminal negligence, he or she causes the death of a police officer or peace officer where such officer was in the course of performing his or her official duties and the defendant knew or reasonably should have known that such victim was a police officer or peace officer.

Aggravated criminally negligent homicide is a class C felony.

§125.12 Vehicular manslaughter in the second degree.

A person is guilty of vehicular manslaughter in the second degree when he or she causes the death of another person, and either:

(1) operates a motor vehicle in violation of subdivision two, three, four or four-a of section eleven hundred ninety-two of the vehicle and traffic law or operates a vessel or public vessel in violation of paragraph (b), (c), (d) or (e) of subdivision two of section forty-nine-a of the navigation law, and as a result of such intoxication or impairment by the use of a drug, or by the combined influence of drugs or of alcohol and any drug or drugs, operates such motor vehicle, vessel or public vessel in a manner that causes the death of such other person, or

(2) operates a motor vehicle with a gross vehicle weight rating of more than eighteen thousand pounds which contains flammable gas, radioactive materials or explosives in violation of subdivision one of section eleven hundred ninety-two of the vehicle and traffic law, and such flammable gas, radioactive materials or explosives is the cause of such death, and as a result of such impairment by the use of alcohol, operates such motor vehicle in a manner that causes the death of such other person, or

(3) operates a snowmobile in violation of paragraph (b), (c) or (d) of subdivision one of section 25.24 of the parks, recreation and historic preservation law or operates an all terrain vehicle as defined in paragraph (a) of subdivision one of section twenty-two hundred eighty-one of the vehicle and traffic law in violation of subdivision two, three, four, or four-a of section eleven hundred ninety-two of the vehicle and traffic law, and as a result of such intoxication or impairment by the use of a drug, or by the combined influence of drugs or of alcohol and any drug or drugs, operates such snowmobile or all terrain vehicle in a manner that causes the death of such other person.

If it is established that the person operating such motor vehicle, vessel, public vessel, snowmobile or all terrain vehicle caused such death while unlawfully intoxicated or impaired by the use of alcohol or a drug, then there shall be a rebuttable presumption that, as a result of such intoxication or impairment by the use of alcohol or a drug, or by the combined influence of drugs or of alcohol and any drug or drugs, such person operated the motor vehicle, vessel, public vessel, snowmobile or all terrain vehicle in a manner that caused such death, as required by this section.

Vehicular manslaughter in the second degree is a class D felony.

§125.13 Vehicular manslaughter in the first degree.

A person is guilty of vehicular manslaughter in the first degree when he or she commits the crime of vehicular manslaughter in the second degree as defined in section 125.12 of this article, and either:

(1) commits such crime while operating a motor vehicle while such person has .18 of one per centum or more by weight of alcohol in such person's blood as shown by chemical analysis of such person's blood, breath, urine or saliva made pursuant to the provisions of section eleven hundred ninety-four of the vehicle and traffic law;

(2) commits such crime while knowing or having reason to know that: (a) his or her license or his or her privilege of operating a motor vehicle in another state or his or her privilege of obtaining a license to operate a motor vehicle in another state is suspended or revoked and such suspension or revocation is based upon a conviction in such other state for an offense which would, if committed in this state, constitute a violation of any of the provisions of section eleven hundred ninety-two of the vehicle and traffic law; or (b) his or her license or his or her privilege of operating a motor vehicle in the state or his or her privilege of obtaining a license issued by the commissioner of motor vehicles is suspended or revoked and such suspension or revocation is based upon either a refusal to submit to a chemical test pursuant to section eleven hundred ninety-four of the vehicle and traffic law or following a conviction for a violation of any of the provisions of section eleven hundred ninety-two of the vehicle and traffic law;

(3) has previously been convicted of violating any of the provisions of section eleven hundred ninety-two of the vehicle and traffic law within the preceding ten years, provided that, for the purposes of this subdivision, a conviction in any other state or jurisdiction for an offense which, if committed in this state, would constitute a violation of section eleven hundred ninety-two of the vehicle and traffic law, shall be treated as a violation of such law;

(4) causes the death of more than one other person;

(5) has previously been convicted of violating any provision of this article or article one hundred twenty of this title involving the operation of a motor vehicle, or was convicted in any other state or

jurisdiction of an offense involving the operation of a motor vehicle which, if committed in this state, would constitute a violation of this article or article one hundred twenty of this title; or

(6) commits such crime while operating a motor vehicle while a child who is fifteen years of age or less is a passenger in such motor vehicle and causes the death of such child.

If it is established that the person operating such motor vehicle caused such death or deaths while unlawfully intoxicated or impaired by the use of alcohol or a drug, or by the combined influence of drugs or of alcohol and any drug or drugs, then there shall be a rebuttable presumption that, as a result of such intoxication or impairment by the use of alcohol or a drug, or by the combined influence of drugs or of alcohol and any drug or drugs, such person operated the motor vehicle in a manner that caused such death or deaths, as required by this section and section 125.12 of this article.

Vehicular manslaughter in the first degree is a class C felony.

§125.14 Aggravated vehicular homicide.

A person is guilty of aggravated vehicular homicide when he or she engages in reckless driving as defined by section twelve hundred twelve of the vehicle and traffic law, and commits the crime of vehicular manslaughter in the second degree as defined in section 125.12 of this article, and either:

(1) commits such crimes while operating a motor vehicle while such person has .18 of one per centum or more by weight of alcohol in such person's blood as shown by chemical analysis of such person's blood, breath, urine or saliva made pursuant to the provisions of section eleven hundred ninety-four of the vehicle and traffic law;

(2) commits such crimes while knowing or having reason to know that: (a) his or her license or his or her privilege of operating a motor vehicle in another state or his or her privilege of obtaining a license to operate a motor vehicle in another state is suspended or revoked and such suspension or revocation is based upon a conviction in such other state for an offense which would, if committed in this state, constitute a violation of any of the provisions of section eleven hundred ninety-two of the vehicle and traffic law; or (b) his or her license or his or her privilege of operating a motor vehicle in this state or his or her privilege of obtaining a license issued by the commissioner of motor vehicles is suspended or revoked and such suspension or revocation is based upon either a refusal to submit to a chemical test pursuant to section eleven hundred ninety-four of the vehicle and traffic law or following a conviction for a violation of any of the provisions of section eleven hundred ninety-two of the vehicle and traffic law;

(3) has previously been convicted of violating any of the provisions of section eleven hundred ninety-two of the vehicle and traffic law within the preceding ten years, provided that, for the purposes of this subdivision, a conviction in any other state or jurisdiction for an offense which, if committed in this state, would constitute a violation of section eleven hundred ninety-two of the vehicle and traffic law, shall be treated as a violation of such law;

(4) causes the death of more than one other person;

(5) causes the death of one person and the serious physical injury of at least one other person;

(6) has previously been convicted of violating any provision of this article or article one hundred twenty of this title involving the operation of a motor vehicle, or was convicted in any other state or jurisdiction of an offense involving the operation of a motor vehicle which, if committed in this state, would constitute a violation of this article or article one hundred twenty of this title; or

(7) commits such crime while operating a motor vehicle while a child who is fifteen years of age or less is a passenger in such motor vehicle and causes the death of such child.

 If it is established that the person operating such motor vehicle caused such death or deaths while unlawfully intoxicated or impaired by the use of alcohol or a drug, or by the combined influence of drugs or of alcohol and any drug or drugs, then there shall be a rebuttable presumption that, as a result of such intoxication or impairment by the use of alcohol or a drug, or by the combined influence of drugs or of alcohol and any drug or drugs, such person operated the motor vehicle in a manner that caused such death or deaths, as required by this section and section 125.12 of this article.

Aggravated vehicular homicide is a class B felony.

§125.15 Manslaughter in the second degree.

A person is guilty of manslaughter in the second degree when:

1. He recklessly causes the death of another person; or

2. *(Repealed, Eff.1/22/19,Ch.1,L.2019)*

3. He intentionally causes or aids another person to commit suicide.

Manslaughter in the second degree is a class C felony.

§125.20 Manslaughter in the first degree.

A person is guilty of manslaughter in the first degree when:

1. With intent to cause serious physical injury to another person, he causes the death of such person or of a third person; or

2. With intent to cause the death of another person, he causes the death of such person or of a third person under circumstances which do not constitute murder because he acts under the influence of extreme

emotional disturbance, as defined in paragraph (a) of subdivision one of section 125.25. The fact that homicide was committed under the influence of extreme emotional disturbance constitutes a mitigating circumstance reducing murder to manslaughter in the first degree and need not be proved in any prosecution initiated under this subdivision; or

3. *(Repealed, Eff.1/22/19,Ch.1,L.2019)*

4. Being eighteen years old or more and with intent to cause physical injury to a person less than eleven years old, the defendant recklessly engages in conduct which creates a grave risk of serious physical injury to such person and thereby causes the death of such person.

Manslaughter in the first degree is a class B felony.

§125.21 Aggravated manslaughter in the second degree.

A person is guilty of aggravated manslaughter in the second degree when he or she recklessly causes the death of a police officer or peace officer where such officer was in the course of performing his or her official duties and the defendant knew or reasonably should have known that such victim was a police officer or peace officer.

Aggravated manslaughter in the second degree is a class C felony.

§125.22 Aggravated manslaughter in the first degree.

A person is guilty of aggravated manslaughter in the first degree when:

1. with intent to cause serious physical injury to a police officer or peace officer, where such officer was in the course of performing his or her official duties and the defendant knew or reasonably should have known that such victim was a police officer or a peace officer, he or she causes the death of such officer or another police officer or peace officer; or

2. with intent to cause the death of a police officer or peace officer, where such officer was in the course of performing his or her official duties and the defendant knew or reasonably should have known that such victim was a police officer or peace officer, he or she causes the death of such officer or another police officer or peace officer under circumstances which do not constitute murder because he or she acts under the influence of extreme emotional disturbance, as defined in paragraph (a) of subdivision one of section 125.25. The fact that homicide was committed under the influence of extreme emotional disturbance constitutes a mitigating circumstance reducing murder to aggravated manslaughter in the first degree or manslaughter in the first degree and need not be proved in any prosecution initiated under this subdivision.

Aggravated manslaughter in the first degree is a class B felony.

§125.25 Murder in the second degree.

A person is guilty of murder in the second degree when:

1. With intent to cause the death of another person, he causes the death of such person or of a third person; except that in any prosecution under this subdivision, it is an affirmative defense that:

(a) (i) The defendant acted under the influence of extreme emotional disturbance for which there was a reasonable explanation or excuse, the reasonableness of which is to be determined from the viewpoint of a person in the defendant's situation under the circumstances as the defendant believed them to be. Nothing contained in this paragraph shall constitute a defense to a prosecution for, or preclude a conviction of, manslaughter in the first degree or any other crime. (ii) It shall not be a "reasonable explanation or excuse" pursuant to subparagraph (i) of this paragraph when the defendant's conduct resulted from the discovery, knowledge or disclosure of the victim's sexual orientation, sex, gender, gender identity, gender expression or sex assigned at birth; or   *(Eff.6/30/19,Ch.45,L.2019)*

(b) The defendant's conduct consisted of causing or aiding, without the use of duress or deception, another person to commit suicide. Nothing contained in this paragraph shall constitute a defense to a prosecution for, or preclude a conviction of, manslaughter in the second degree or any other crime; or

2. Under circumstances evincing a depraved indifference to human life, he recklessly engages in conduct which creates a grave risk of death to another person, and thereby causes the death of another person; or

3. Acting either alone or with one or more other persons, he commits or attempts to commit robbery, burglary, kidnapping, arson, rape in the first degree, criminal sexual act in the first degree, sexual abuse in the first degree, aggravated sexual abuse, escape in the first degree, or escape in the second degree, and, in the course of and in furtherance of such crime or of immediate flight therefrom, he, or another participant, if there be any, causes the death of a person other than one of the participants; except that in any prosecution under this subdivision, in which the defendant was not the only participant in the underlying crime, it is an affirmative defense that the defendant:

(a) Did not commit the homicidal act or in any way solicit, request, command, importune, cause or aid the commission thereof; and

(b) Was not armed with a deadly weapon, or any instrument, article or substance readily capable of causing death or serious physical injury and of a sort not ordinarily carried in public places by law-abiding persons; and

(c) Had no reasonable ground to believe that any other participant was armed with such a weapon, instrument, article or substance; and

(d) Had no reasonable ground to believe that any other participant intended to engage in conduct likely to result in death or serious physical injury; or

4. Under circumstances evincing a depraved indifference to human life, and being eighteen years old or more the defendant recklessly engages in conduct which creates a grave risk of serious physical injury or death to another person less than eleven years old and thereby causes the death of such person; or

5. Being eighteen years old or more, while in the course of committing rape in the first, second or third degree, criminal sexual act in the first, second or third degree, sexual abuse in the first degree, aggravated sexual abuse in the first, second, third or fourth degree, or incest in the first, second or third degree, against a person less than fourteen years old, he or she intentionally causes the death of such person.

Murder in the second degree is a class A-I felony.

§125.26 Aggravated murder.

A person is guilty of aggravated murder when:

1. With intent to cause the death of another person, he or she causes the death of such person, or of a third person who was a person described in subparagraph (i), (ii), (ii-a) or (iii) of paragraph (a) of this subdivision engaged at the time of the killing in the course of performing his or her official duties; and

(a) Either:

(i) the intended victim was a police officer as defined in subdivision thirty-four of section 1.20 of the criminal procedure law who was at the time of the killing engaged in the course of performing his or her official duties, and the defendant knew or reasonably should have known that the victim was a police officer; or

(ii) the intended victim was a peace officer as defined in paragraph a of subdivision twenty-one, subdivision twenty-three, twenty-four or sixty-two (employees of the division for youth) of section 2.10 of the criminal procedure law who was at the time of the killing engaged in the course of performing his or her official duties, and the defendant knew or reasonably should have known that the victim was such a uniformed court officer, parole officer, probation officer, or employee of the division for youth; or

(ii-a) the intended victim was a firefighter, emergency medical technician, ambulance driver, paramedic, physician or registered nurse involved in a first response team, or any other individual who, in the course of official duties, performs emergency response activities and was engaged in such activities at the time of killing and the defendant knew or reasonably should have known that the intended victim was such firefighter, emergency medical technician, ambulance driver, paramedic, physician or registered nurse; or

(iii) the intended victim was an employee of a state correctional institution or was an employee of a local correctional facility as defined in subdivision two of section forty of the correction law, who was at the time of the killing engaged in the course of performing his or her official duties, and the defendant knew or reasonably should have known that the victim was an employee of a state correctional institution or a local correctional facility; and

(b) The defendant was more than eighteen years old at the time of the commission of the crime; or

2. (a) With intent to cause the death of a person less than fourteen years old, he or she causes the death of such person, and the defendant acted in an especially cruel and wanton manner pursuant to a course of conduct intended to inflict and inflicting torture upon the victim prior to the victim's death. As used in this subdivision, "torture" means the intentional and depraved infliction of extreme physical pain that is separate and apart from the pain which otherwise would have been associated with such cause of death; and

(b) The defendant was more than eighteen years old at the time of the commission of the crime.

3. In any prosecution under subdivision one or two of this section, it is an affirmative defense that:

(a) (i) The defendant acted under the influence of extreme emotional disturbance for which there was a reasonable explanation or excuse, the reasonableness of which is to be determined from the viewpoint of a person in the defendant's situation under the circumstances as the defendant believed them to be. Nothing contained in this paragraph shall constitute a defense to a prosecution for, or preclude a conviction of, aggravated manslaughter in the first degree, manslaughter in the first degree or any other crime except murder in the second degree. (ii) It shall not be a "reasonable explanation or excuse" pursuant to subparagraph (i) of this paragraph when the defendant's conduct resulted from the discovery, knowledge or disclosure of the victim's sexual orientation, sex, gender, gender identity, gender expression or sex assigned at birth; or   *(Eff.6/30/19,Ch.45,L.2019)*

(b) The defendant's conduct consisted of causing or aiding, without the use of duress or deception, another person to commit suicide. Nothing contained in this paragraph shall constitute a defense to a prosecution for, or preclude a conviction of, aggravated manslaughter in the second degree, manslaughter in the second degree or any other crime except murder in the second degree.

Aggravated murder is a class A-I felony.

§125.27 Murder in the first degree.

A person is guilty of murder in the first degree when:

1. With intent to cause the death of another person, he causes the death of such person or of a third person; and

 (a) Either:

  (i) the intended victim was a police officer as defined in subdivision 34 of section 1.20 of the criminal procedure law who was at the time of the killing engaged in the course of performing his official duties, and the defendant knew or reasonably should have known that the intended victim was a police officer; or

  (ii) the intended victim was a peace officer as defined in paragraph a of subdivision twenty-one, subdivision twenty-three, twenty-four or sixty-two (employees of the division for youth) of section 2.10 of the criminal procedure law who was at the time of the killing engaged in the course of performing his official duties, and the defendant knew or reasonably should have known that the intended victim was such a uniformed court officer, parole officer, probation officer, or employee of the division for youth; or

  (ii-a) the intended victim was a firefighter, emergency medical technician, ambulance driver, paramedic, physician or registered nurse involved in a first response team, or any other individual who, in the course of official duties, performs emergency response activities and was engaged in such activities at the time of killing and the defendant knew or reasonably should have known that the intended victim was such firefighter, emergency medical technician, ambulance driver, paramedic, physician or registered nurse; or

  (iii) the intended victim was an employee of a state correctional institution or was an employee of a local correctional facility as defined in subdivision two of section forty of the correction law, who was at the time of the killing engaged in the course of performing his official duties, and the defendant knew or reasonably should have known that the intended victim was an employee of a state correctional institution or a local correctional facility; or

  (iv) at the time of the commission of the killing, the defendant was confined in a state correctional institution or was otherwise in custody upon a sentence for the term of his natural life, or upon a sentence commuted to one of natural life, or upon a sentence for an indeterminate term the minimum of which was at least fifteen years and the maximum of which was natural life, or at the time of the commission of the killing, the defendant had escaped from such confinement or custody while serving such a sentence and had not yet been returned to such confinement or custody; or

  (v) the intended victim was a witness to a crime committed on a prior occasion and the death was caused for the purpose of preventing the intended victim's testimony in any criminal action or proceeding whether or not such action or proceeding had been commenced, or the intended victim had previously testified in a criminal action or proceeding and the killing was committed for the purpose of exacting retribution for such prior testimony, or the intended victim was an immediate family member of a witness to a crime committed on a prior occasion and the killing was committed for the purpose of preventing or influencing the testimony of such witness, or the intended victim was an immediate family member of a witness who had previously testified in a criminal action or proceeding and the killing was committed for the purpose of exacting retribution upon such witness for such prior testimony. As used in this subparagraph "immediate family member" means a husband, wife, father, mother, daughter, son, brother, sister, stepparent, grandparent, stepchild or grandchild; or

(vi) the defendant committed the killing or procured commission of the killing pursuant to an agreement with a person other than the intended victim to commit the same for the receipt, or in expectation of the receipt, of anything of pecuniary value from a party to the agreement or from a person other than the intended victim acting at the direction of a party to such agreement; or

(vii) the victim was killed while the defendant was in the course of committing or attempting to commit and in furtherance of robbery, burglary in the first degree or second degree, kidnapping in the first degree, arson in the first degree or second degree, rape in the first degree, criminal sexual act in the first degree, sexual abuse in the first degree, aggravated sexual abuse in the first degree or escape in the first degree, or in the course of and furtherance of immediate flight after committing or attempting to commit any such crime or in the course of and furtherance of immediate flight after attempting to commit the crime of murder in the second degree; provided however, the victim is not a participant in one of the aforementioned crimes and, provided further that, unless the defendant's criminal liability under this subparagraph is based upon the defendant having commanded another person to cause the death of the victim or intended victim pursuant to section 20.00 of this chapter, this subparagraph shall not apply where the defendant's criminal liability is based upon the conduct of another pursuant to section 20.00 of this chapter; or

(viii) as part of the same criminal transaction, the defendant, with intent to cause serious physical injury to or the death of an additional person or persons, causes the death of an additional person or persons; provided, however, the victim is not a participant in the criminal transaction; or

(ix) prior to committing the killing, the defendant had been convicted of murder as defined in this section or section 125.25 of this article, or had been convicted in another jurisdiction of an offense which, if committed in this state, would constitute a violation of either of such sections; or

(x) the defendant acted in an especially cruel and wanton manner pursuant to a course of conduct intended to inflict and inflicting torture upon the victim prior to the victim's death. As used in this subparagraph, "torture" means the intentional and depraved infliction of extreme physical pain; "depraved" means the defendant relished the infliction of extreme physical pain upon the victim evidencing debasement or perversion or that the defendant evidenced a sense of pleasure in the infliction of extreme physical pain; or

(xi) the defendant intentionally caused the death of two or more additional persons within the state in separate criminal transactions within a period of twenty-four months when committed in a similar fashion or pursuant to a common scheme or plan; or

(xii) the intended victim was a judge as defined in subdivision twenty-three of section 1.20 of the criminal procedure law and the defendant killed such victim because such victim was, at the time of the killing, a judge; or

(xiii) the victim was killed in furtherance of an act of terrorism, as defined in paragraph (b) of subdivision one of section 490.05 of this chapter; and

(b) The defendant was more than eighteen years old at the time of the commission of the crime.

2. In any prosecution under subdivision one, it is an affirmative defense that:

(a) (i) The defendant acted under the influence of extreme emotional disturbance for which there was a reasonable explanation or excuse, the reasonableness of which is to be determined from the viewpoint of a person in the defendant's situation under the circumstances as the defendant believed them to be. Nothing contained in this paragraph shall constitute a defense to a prosecution for, or preclude a conviction of, manslaughter in the first degree or any other crime except murder in the second degree. (ii) It shall not be a "reasonable explanation or excuse" pursuant to subparagraph (i) of this paragraph when the defendant's conduct resulted from the discovery, knowledge or disclosure of the victim's sexual orientation, sex, gender, gender identity, gender expression or sex assigned at birth; or

(Eff.6/30/19,Ch.45,L.2019)

(b) The defendant's conduct consisted of causing or aiding, without the use of duress or deception, another person to commit suicide. Nothing contained in this paragraph shall constitute a defense to a prosecution for, or preclude a conviction of, manslaughter in the second degree or any other crime except murder in the second degree.

Murder in the first degree is a class A-I felony.

§125.40 through §125.60   *(Repealed, Eff.1/22/19,Ch.1,L.2019)*

ARTICLE 130 - SEX OFFENSES

Section
130.00   Sex offenses; definitions of terms.
130.05   Sex offenses; lack of consent.
130.10   Sex offenses; limitation; defenses.
130.16   Sex offenses; corroboration.
130.20   Sexual misconduct.
130.25   Rape in the third degree.
130.30   Rape in the second degree.
130.35   Rape in the first degree.
130.40   Criminal sexual act in the third degree.
130.45   Criminal sexual act in the second degree.
130.50   Criminal sexual act in the first degree.
130.52   Forcible touching.
130.53   Persistent sexual abuse.
130.55   Sexual abuse in the third degree.
130.60   Sexual abuse in the second degree.
130.65   Sexual abuse in the first degree.
130.65-a Aggravated sexual abuse in the fourth degree.
130.66   Aggravated sexual abuse in the third degree.
130.67   Aggravated sexual abuse in the second degree.
130.70   Aggravated sexual abuse in the first degree.
130.75   Course of sexual conduct against a child in the first degree.
130.80   Course of sexual conduct against a child in the second degree.
130.85   Female genital mutilation.
130.90   Facilitating a sex offense with a controlled substance.
130.91   Sexually motivated felony.
130.92   Sentencing.
130.95   Predatory sexual assault.
130.96   Predatory sexual assault against a child.

§130.00 Sex offenses; definitions of terms.

The following definitions are applicable to this article:

1. "Sexual intercourse" has its ordinary meaning and occurs upon any penetration, however slight.

2. (a) "Oral sexual conduct" means conduct between persons consisting of contact between the mouth and the penis, the mouth and the anus, or the mouth and the vulva or vagina.

(b) "Anal sexual conduct" means conduct between persons consisting of contact between the penis and anus.

3. "Sexual contact" means any touching of the sexual or other intimate parts of a person for the purpose of gratifying sexual desire of either party. It includes the touching of the actor by the victim, as well as the touching of the victim by the actor, whether directly or through clothing, as well as the emission of ejaculate by the actor upon any part of the victim, clothed or unclothed.

4. For the purposes of this article "married" means the existence of the relationship between the actor and the victim as spouses which is recognized by law at the time the actor commits an offense proscribed by this article against the victim.

5. "Mentally disabled" means that a person suffers from a mental disease or defect which renders him or her incapable of appraising the nature of his or her conduct.

6. "Mentally incapacitated" means that a person is rendered temporarily incapable of appraising or controlling his conduct owing to the influence of a narcotic or intoxicating substance administered to him

without his consent, or to any other act committed upon him without his consent.

7. "Physically helpless" means that a person is unconscious or for any other reason is physically unable to communicate unwillingness to an act.

8. "Forcible compulsion" means to compel by either:
a. use of physical force; or
b. a threat, express or implied, which places a person in fear of immediate death or physical injury to himself, herself or another person, or in fear that he, she or another person will immediately be kidnapped.

9. "Foreign object" means any instrument or article which, when inserted in the vagina, urethra, penis, rectum or anus, is capable of causing physical injury.

10. "Sexual conduct" means sexual intercourse, oral sexual conduct, anal sexual conduct, aggravated sexual contact, or sexual contact.

11. "Aggravated sexual contact" means inserting, other than for a valid medical purpose, a foreign object in the vagina, urethra, penis, rectum or anus of a child, thereby causing physical injury to such child.

12. "Health care provider" means any person who is, or is required to be, licensed or registered or holds himself or herself out to be licensed or registered, or provides services as if he or she were licensed or registered in the profession of medicine, chiropractic, dentistry or podiatry under any of the following: article one hundred thirty-one, one hundred thirty-two, one hundred thirty-three, or one hundred forty-one of the education law.

13. "Mental health care provider" shall mean a licensed physician, licensed psychologist, registered professional nurse, licensed clinical social worker or a licensed master social worker under the supervision of a physician, psychologist or licensed clinical social worker.

§130.05 Sex offenses; lack of consent.

1. Whether or not specifically stated, it is an element of every offense defined in this article that the sexual act was committed without consent of the victim.

2. Lack of consent results from:
(a) Forcible compulsion; or
(b) Incapacity to consent; or
(c) Where the offense charged is sexual abuse or forcible touching, any circumstances, in addition to forcible compulsion or incapacity to consent, in which the victim does not expressly or impliedly acquiesce in the actor's conduct; or
(d) Where the offense charged is rape in the third degree as defined in subdivision three of section 130.25, or criminal sexual act in the third degree as defined in subdivision three of section 130.40, in addition to forcible compulsion, circumstances under which, at the time of the act of intercourse, oral sexual conduct or anal sexual conduct, the victim clearly expressed that he or she did not consent to engage in such act, and a reasonable person in the actor's situation would have understood such person's words and acts as an expression of lack of consent to such act under all the circumstances.

3. A person is deemed incapable of consent when he or she is:
   (a) less than seventeen years old; or
   (b) mentally disabled; or
   (c) mentally incapacitated; or
   (d) physically helpless; or
   (e) committed to the care and custody or supervision of the state
department of corrections and community supervision or a hospital, as
such term is defined in subdivision two of section four hundred of the
correction law, and the actor is an employee who knows or reasonably
should know that such person is committed to the care and custody or
supervision of such department or hospital. For purposes of this
paragraph, "employee" means (i) an employee of the state department of
corrections and community supervision who, as part of his or her
employment, performs duties: (A) in a state correctional facility in
which the victim is confined at the time of the offense consisting of
providing custody, medical or mental health services, counseling
services, educational programs, vocational training, institutional parole
services or direct supervision to incarcerated individuals; or

   (B) of supervising persons released on community supervision
and supervises the victim at the time of the offense or has supervised the
victim and the victim is still under community supervision at the time of
the offense; or

   (ii) an employee of the office of mental health who, as part of his
or her employment, performs duties in a state correctional facility or
hospital, as such term is defined in subdivision two of section four
hundred of the correction law in which the incarcerated individual is
confined at the time of the offense, consisting of providing custody,
medical or mental health services, or direct supervision to such
incarcerated individuals; or

   (iii) a person, including a volunteer, providing direct services to
incarcerated individuals in a state correctional facility in which the
victim is confined at the time of the offense pursuant to a contractual
arrangement with the state department of corrections and community
supervision or, in the case of a volunteer, a written agreement with such
department, provided that the person received written notice concerning
the provisions of this paragraph; or   *(Eff.8/2/21,Ch.322,L.2021)*

   (f) committed to the care and custody of a local correctional facility,
as such term is defined in subdivision two of section forty of the
correction law, and the actor is an employee, not married to such person,
who knows or reasonably should know that such person is committed to
the care and custody of such facility. For purposes of this paragraph,
"employee" means an employee of the local correctional facility where
the person is committed who performs professional duties consisting of
providing custody, medical or mental health services, counseling
services, educational services, or vocational training for incarcerated
individuals. For purposes of this paragraph, "employee" shall also mean
a person, including a volunteer or a government employee of the state
department of corrections and community supervision or a local health,
education or probation agency, providing direct services to incarcerated
individuals in the local correctional facility in which the victim is

confined at the time of the offense pursuant to a contractual arrangement with the local correctional department or, in the case of such a volunteer or government employee, a written agreement with such department, provided that such person received written notice concerning the provisions of this paragraph; or *(Eff.8/2/21,Ch.322,L.2021)*

(g) committed to or placed with the office of children and family services and in residential care, and the actor is an employee, not married to such person, who knows or reasonably should know that such person is committed to or placed with such office of children and family services and in residential care. For purposes of this paragraph, "employee" means an employee of the office of children and family services or of a residential facility in which such person is committed to or placed at the time of the offense who, as part of his or her employment, performs duties consisting of providing custody, medical or mental health services, counseling services, educational services, vocational training, or direct supervision to persons committed to or placed in a residential facility operated by the office of children and family services; or

(h) a client or patient and the actor is a health care provider or mental health care provider charged with rape in the third degree as defined in section 130.25, criminal sexual act in the third degree as defined in section 130.40, aggravated sexual abuse in the fourth degree as defined in section 130.65-a, or sexual abuse in the third degree as defined in section 130.55, and the act of sexual conduct occurs during a treatment session, consultation, interview, or examination; or

(i) a resident or inpatient of a residential facility operated, licensed or certified by (i) the office of mental health; (ii) the office for people with developmental disabilities; or (iii) the office of alcoholism and substance abuse services, and the actor is an employee of the facility not married to such resident or inpatient. For purposes of this paragraph, "employee" means either: an employee of the agency operating the residential facility, who knows or reasonably should know that such person is a resident or inpatient of such facility and who provides direct care services, case management services, medical or other clinical services, habilitative services or direct supervision of the residents in the facility in which the resident resides; or an officer or other employee, consultant, contractor or volunteer of the residential facility, who knows or reasonably should know that the person is a resident of such facility and who is in direct contact with residents or inpatients; provided, however, that the provisions of this paragraph shall only apply to a consultant, contractor or volunteer providing services pursuant to a contractual arrangement with the agency operating the residential facility or, in the case of a volunteer, a written agreement with such facility, provided that the person received written notice concerning the provisions of this paragraph; provided further, however, "employee" shall not include a person with a developmental disability who is or was receiving services and is also an employee of a service provider and who has sexual contact with another service recipient who is a consenting adult who has consented to such contact; or

(j) detained or otherwise in the custody of a police officer, peace officer, or other law enforcement official and the actor is a police officer, peace officer or other law enforcement official who either: (i) is detaining or maintaining custody of such person; or (ii) knows, or reasonably should know, that at the time of the offense, such person was detained or in custody.

§130.10 Sex offenses; limitation; defenses.

1. In any prosecution under this article in which the victim's lack of consent is based solely upon his or her incapacity to consent because he or she was mentally disabled, mentally incapacitated or physically helpless, it is an affirmative defense that the defendant, at the time he or she engaged in the conduct constituting the offense, did not know of the facts or conditions responsible for such incapacity to consent.

2. Conduct performed for a valid medical or mental health care purpose shall not constitute a violation of any section of this article in which incapacity to consent is based on the circumstances set forth in paragraph (h) of subdivision three of section 130.05 of this article.

3. In any prosecution for the crime of rape in the third degree as defined in section 130.25, criminal sexual act in the third degree as defined in section 130.40, aggravated sexual abuse in the fourth degree as defined in section 130.65-a, or sexual abuse in the third degree as defined in section 130.55 in which incapacity to consent is based on the circumstances set forth in paragraph (h) of subdivision three of section 130.05 of this article it shall be an affirmative defense that the client or patient consented to such conduct charged after having been expressly advised by the health care or mental health care provider that such conduct was not performed for a valid medical purpose.

4. In any prosecution under this article in which the victim's lack of consent is based solely on his or her incapacity to consent because he or she was less than seventeen years old, mentally disabled, a client or patient and the actor is a health care provider, detained or otherwise in custody of law enforcement under the circumstances described in paragraph (j) of subdivision three of section 130.05 of this article, or committed to the care and custody or supervision of the state department of corrections and community supervision or a hospital and the actor is an employee, it shall be a defense that the defendant was married to the victim as defined in subdivision four of section 130.00 of this article.

§130.16 Sex offenses; corroboration.

A person shall not be convicted of any offense defined in this article of which lack of consent is an element but results solely from incapacity to consent because of the victim's mental defect, or mental incapacity, or an attempt to commit the same, solely on the testimony of the victim, unsupported by other evidence tending to:

(a) Establish that an attempt was made to engage the victim in sexual intercourse, oral sexual conduct, anal sexual conduct, or sexual contact, as the case may be, at the time of the occurrence; and

(b) Connect the defendant with the commission of the offense or attempted offense.

§130.20 Sexual misconduct.

A person is guilty of sexual misconduct when:

1. He or she engages in sexual intercourse with another person without such person's consent; or

2. He or she engages in oral sexual conduct or anal sexual conduct with another person without such person's consent; or

3. He or she engages in sexual conduct with an animal or a dead human body.

Sexual misconduct is a class A misdemeanor.

§130.25 Rape in the third degree.

A person is guilty of rape in the third degree when:

1. He or she engages in sexual intercourse with another person who is incapable of consent by reason of some factor other than being less than seventeen years old;

2. Being twenty-one years old or more, he or she engages in sexual intercourse with another person less than seventeen years old; or

3. He or she engages in sexual intercourse with another person without such person's consent where such lack of consent is by reason of some factor other than incapacity to consent.

Rape in the third degree is a class E felony.

§130.30 Rape in the second degree.

A person is guilty of rape in the second degree when:

1. being eighteen years old or more, he or she engages in sexual intercourse with another person less than fifteen years old; or

2. he or she engages in sexual intercourse with another person who is incapable of consent by reason of being mentally disabled or mentally incapacitated.

It shall be an affirmative defense to the crime of rape in the second degree as defined in subdivision one of this section that the defendant was less than four years older than the victim at the time of the act.

Rape in the second degree is a class D felony.

§130.35 Rape in the first degree.

A person is guilty of rape in the first degree when he or she engages in sexual intercourse with another person:

1. By forcible compulsion; or

2. Who is incapable of consent by reason of being physically helpless; or

3. Who is less than eleven years old; or

4. Who is less than thirteen years old and the actor is eighteen years old or more.

Rape in the first degree is a class B felony.

§130.40 Criminal sexual act in the third degree.

A person is guilty of criminal sexual act in the third degree when:

1. He or she engages in oral sexual conduct or anal sexual conduct with a person who is incapable of consent by reason of some factor other than being less than seventeen years old;

2. Being twenty-one years old or more, he or she engages in oral sexual conduct or anal sexual conduct with a person less than seventeen years old; or

3. He or she engages in oral sexual conduct or anal sexual conduct with another person without such person's consent where such lack of consent is by reason of some factor other than incapacity to consent.

Criminal sexual act in the third degree is a class E felony.

§130.45 Criminal sexual act in the second degree.

A person is guilty of criminal sexual act in the second degree when:

1. being eighteen years old or more, he or she engages in oral sexual conduct or anal sexual conduct with another person less than fifteen years old; or

2. he or she engages in oral sexual conduct or anal sexual conduct with another person who is incapable of consent by reason of being mentally disabled or mentally incapacitated.

It shall be an affirmative defense to the crime of criminal sexual act in the second degree as defined in subdivision one of this section that the defendant was less than four years older than the victim at the time of the act.

Criminal sexual act in the second degree is a class D felony.

§130.50 Criminal sexual act in the first degree.

A person is guilty of criminal sexual act in the first degree when he or she engages in oral sexual conduct or anal sexual conduct with another person:

1. By forcible compulsion; or
2. Who is incapable of consent by reason of being physically helpless; or
3. Who is less than eleven years old; or
4. Who is less than thirteen years old and the actor is eighteen years old or more.

Criminal sexual act in the first degree is a class B felony.

§130.52 Forcible touching.

A person is guilty of forcible touching when such person intentionally, and for no legitimate purpose:

1. forcibly touches the sexual or other intimate parts of another person for the purpose of degrading or abusing such person, or for the purpose of gratifying the actor's sexual desire; or
2. subjects another person to sexual contact for the purpose of gratifying the actor's sexual desire and with intent to degrade or abuse such other person while such other person is a passenger on a bus, train, or subway car operated by any transit agency, authority or company, public or private, whose operation is authorized by New York state or any of its political subdivisions.

For the purposes of this section, forcible touching includes squeezing, grabbing or pinching.

Forcible touching is a class A misdemeanor.

§130.53 Persistent sexual abuse.

A person is guilty of persistent sexual abuse when he or she commits the crime of forcible touching, as defined in section 130.52 of this article, sexual abuse in the third degree, as defined in section 130.55 of this article, or sexual abuse in the second degree, as defined in section 130.60 of this article, and, within the previous ten year period, excluding any time during which such person was incarcerated for any reason, has been convicted two or more times, in separate criminal transactions for which sentence was imposed on separate occasions, of forcible touching, as defined in section 130.52 of this article, sexual abuse in the third degree as defined in section 130.55 of this article, sexual abuse in the second degree, as defined in section 130.60 of this article, or any offense defined in this article, of which the commission or attempted commission thereof is a felony.

Persistent sexual abuse is a class E felony.

§130.55 Sexual abuse in the third degree.

A person is guilty of sexual abuse in the third degree when he or she subjects another person to sexual contact without the latter's consent; except that in any prosecution under this section, it is an affirmative defense that (a) such other person's lack of consent was due solely to incapacity to consent by reason of being less than seventeen years old, and (b) such other person was more than fourteen years old, and (c) the defendant was less than five years older than such other person.

Sexual abuse in the third degree is a class B misdemeanor.

§130.60 Sexual abuse in the second degree.

A person is guilty of sexual abuse in the second degree when he or she subjects another person to sexual contact and when such other person is:

1. Incapable of consent by reason of some factor other than being less than seventeen years old; or

2. Less than fourteen years old.

Sexual abuse in the second degree is a class A misdemeanor

§130.65 Sexual abuse in the first degree.

A person is guilty of sexual abuse in the first degree when he or she subjects another person to sexual contact:

1. By forcible compulsion; or

2. When the other person is incapable of consent by reason of being physically helpless; or

3. When the other person is less than eleven years old; or

4. When the other person is less than thirteen years old and the actor is twenty-one years old or older.

Sexual abuse in the first degree is a class D felony.

§130.65-a Aggravated sexual abuse in the fourth degree.

1. A person is guilty of aggravated sexual abuse in the fourth degree when:

(a) He or she inserts a foreign object in the vagina, urethra, penis, rectum or anus of another person and the other person is incapable of consent by reason of some factor other than being less than seventeen years old; or

(b) He or she inserts a finger in the vagina, urethra, penis, rectum or anus of another person causing physical injury to such person and such person is incapable of consent by reason of some factor other than being less than seventeen years old.

2. Conduct performed for a valid medical purpose does not violate the provisions of this section.

Aggravated sexual abuse in the fourth degree is a class E felony.

§130.66 Aggravated sexual abuse in the third degree.

1. A person is guilty of aggravated sexual abuse in the third degree when he or she inserts a foreign object in the vagina, urethra, penis, rectum or anus of another person:

(a) By forcible compulsion; or

(b) When the other person is incapable of consent by reason of being physically helpless; or

(c) When the other person is less than eleven years old.

2. A person is guilty of aggravated sexual abuse in the third degree when he or she inserts a foreign object in the vagina, urethra, penis, rectum or anus of another person causing physical injury to such person and such person is incapable of consent by reason of being mentally disabled or mentally incapacitated.

3. Conduct performed for a valid medical purpose does not violate the provisions of this section.

Aggravated sexual abuse in the third degree is a class D felony.

§130.67 Aggravated sexual abuse in the second degree.

1. A person is guilty of aggravated sexual abuse in the second degree when he or she inserts a finger in the vagina, urethra, penis, rectum or anus of another person causing physical injury to such person:

(a) By forcible compulsion; or

(b) When the other person is incapable of consent by reason of being physically helpless; or

(c) When the other person is less than eleven years old.

2. Conduct performed for a valid medical purpose does not violate the provisions of this section.

Aggravated sexual abuse in the second degree is a class C felony.

§130.70 Aggravated sexual abuse in the first degree.

1. A person is guilty of aggravated sexual abuse in the first degree when he or she inserts a foreign object in the vagina, urethra, penis, rectum or anus of another person causing physical injury to such person:

(a) By forcible compulsion; or

(b) When the other person is incapable of consent by reason of being physically helpless; or

(c) When the other person is less than eleven years old.

2. Conduct performed for a valid medical purpose does not violate the provisions of this section.

Aggravated sexual abuse in the first degree is a class B felony.

§130.75 Course of sexual conduct against a child in the first degree

1. A person is guilty of course of sexual conduct against a child in the first degree when, over a period of time not less than three months in duration:

(a) he or she engages in two or more acts of sexual conduct, which includes at least one act of sexual intercourse, oral sexual conduct, anal sexual conduct or aggravated sexual contact, with a child less than eleven years old; or

(b) he or she, being eighteen years old or more, engages in two or more acts of sexual conduct, which include at least one act of sexual intercourse, oral sexual conduct, anal sexual conduct or aggravated sexual contact, with a child less than thirteen years old.

2. A person may not be subsequently prosecuted for any other sexual offense involving the same victim unless the other charged offense occurred outside the time period charged under this section.

Course of sexual conduct against a child in the first degree is a class B felony.

§130.80 Course of sexual conduct against a child in the second degree

1. A person is guilty of course of sexual conduct against a child in the second degree when, over a period of time not less than three months in duration:

(a) he or she engages in two or more acts of sexual conduct with a child less than eleven years old; or

(b) he or she, being eighteen years old or more, engages in two or more acts of sexual conduct with a child less than thirteen years old.

2. A person may not be subsequently prosecuted for any other sexual offense involving the same victim unless the other charged offense occurred outside the time period charged under this section.

Course of sexual conduct against a child in the second degree is a class D felony.

§130.85 Female genital mutilation.

1. A person is guilty of female genital mutilation when:

(a) a person knowingly circumcises, excises, or infibulates the whole or any part of the labia majora or labia minora or clitoris of another person who has not reached eighteen years of age; or

(b) being a parent, guardian or other person legally responsible and charged with the care or custody of a child less than eighteen years old, he or she knowingly consents to the circumcision, excision or infibulation of whole or part of such child's labia majora or labia minora or clitoris.

2. Such circumcision, excision, or infibulation is not a violation of this section if such act is:

(a) necessary to the health of the person on whom it is performed, and is performed by a person licensed in the place of its performance as a medical practitioner; or

(b) performed on a person in labor or who has just given birth and is performed for medical purposes connected with that labor or birth by a person licensed in the place it is performed as a medical practitioner, midwife, or person in training to become such a practitioner or midwife.

3. For the purposes of paragraph (a) of subdivision two of this section, no account shall be taken of the effect on the person on whom such procedure is to be performed of any belief on the part of that or any other person that such procedure is required as a matter of custom or ritual.

Female genital mutilation is a class E felony.

§130.90 Facilitating a sex offense with a controlled substance.

A person is guilty of facilitating a sex offense with a controlled substance when he or she:

1. knowingly and unlawfully possesses a controlled substance or any preparation, compound, mixture or substance that requires a prescription to obtain and administers such substance or preparation, compound, mixture or substance that requires a prescription to obtain to another person without such person's consent and with intent to commit against such person conduct constituting a felony defined in this article; and

2. commits or attempts to commit such conduct constituting a felony defined in this article.

Facilitating a sex offense with a controlled substance is a class D felony.

§130.91 Sexually motivated felony.

1. A person commits a sexually motivated felony when he or she commits a specified offense for the purpose, in whole or substantial part, of his or her own direct sexual gratification.

2. A "specified offense" is a felony offense defined by any of the following provisions of this chapter: assault in the second degree as defined in section 120.05, assault in the first degree as defined in section 120.10, gang assault in the second degree as defined in section 120.06, gang assault in the first degree as defined in section 120.07, stalking in the first degree as defined in section 120.60, strangulation in the second degree as defined in section 121.12, strangulation in the first degree as defined in section 121.13, manslaughter in the second degree as defined in subdivision one of section 125.15, manslaughter in the first degree as defined in section 125.20, murder in the second degree as defined in section 125.25, aggravated murder as defined in section 125.26, murder in the first degree as defined in section 125.27, kidnapping in the second degree as defined in section 135.20, kidnapping in the first degree as defined in section 135.25, burglary in the third degree as defined in section 140.20, burglary in the second degree as defined in section 140.25, burglary in the first degree as defined in section 140.30, arson in the second degree as defined in section 150.15, arson in the first degree as defined in section 150.20, robbery in the third degree as defined in section 160.05, robbery in the second degree as defined in section 160.10, robbery in the first degree as defined in section 160.15, promoting prostitution in the second degree as defined in section 230.30, promoting prostitution in the first degree as defined in section 230.32, compelling prostitution as defined in section 230.33, sex trafficking of a child as defined in section 230.34-a, disseminating indecent material to minors in the first degree as defined in section 235.22, use of a child in a sexual performance as defined in section 263.05, promoting an obscene sexual performance by a child as defined in section 263.10, promoting a sexual performance by a child as defined in section 263.15, or any felony attempt or conspiracy to commit any of the foregoing offenses. *(Eff.11/13/18,Ch.189,L.2018)*

§130.92 Sentencing.

1. When a person is convicted of a sexually motivated felony pursuant to this article, and the specified felony is a violent felony offense, as defined in section 70.02 of this chapter, the sexually motivated felony shall be deemed a violent felony offense.

2. When a person is convicted of a sexually motivated felony pursuant to this article, the sexually motivated felony shall be deemed to be the same offense level as the specified offense the defendant committed.

3. Persons convicted of a sexually motivated felony as defined in

section 130.91 of this article, must be sentenced in accordance with the provisions of section 70.80 of this chapter.

§130.95 Predatory sexual assault.

A person is guilty of predatory sexual assault when he or she commits the crime of rape in the first degree, criminal sexual act in the first degree, aggravated sexual abuse in the first degree, or course of sexual conduct against a child in the first degree, as defined in this article, and when:

1. In the course of the commission of the crime or the immediate flight therefrom, he or she:

    (a) Causes serious physical injury to the victim of such crime; or

    (b) Uses or threatens the immediate use of a dangerous instrument; or

2. He or she has engaged in conduct constituting the crime of rape in the first degree, criminal sexual act in the first degree, aggravated sexual abuse in the first degree, or course of sexual conduct against a child in the first degree, as defined in this article, against one or more additional persons; or

3. He or she has previously been subjected to a conviction for a felony defined in this article, incest as defined in section 255.25 of this chapter or use of a child in a sexual performance as defined in section 263.05 of this chapter.

Predatory sexual assault is a class A-II felony.

§130.96 Predatory sexual assault against a child.

A person is guilty of predatory sexual assault against a child when, being eighteen years old or more, he or she commits the crime of rape in the first degree, criminal sexual act in the first degree, aggravated sexual abuse in the first degree, or course of sexual conduct against a child in the first degree, as defined in this article, and the victim is less than thirteen years old.

Predatory sexual assault against a child is a class A-II felony.

ARTICLE 135 - KIDNAPPING, COERCION AND RELATED OFFENSES

Section
135.00   Unlawful imprisonment, kidnapping and custodial interference; definitions of terms.
135.05   Unlawful imprisonment in the second degree.
135.10   Unlawful imprisonment in the first degree.
135.15   Unlawful imprisonment; defense.
135.20   Kidnapping in the second degree.
135.25   Kidnapping in the first degree.
135.30   Kidnapping; defense.
135.35   Labor trafficking.
135.36   Labor trafficking; accomplice.
135.37   Aggravated labor trafficking.
135.45   Custodial interference in the second degree.
135.50   Custodial interference in the first degree.
135.55   Substitution of children.
135.60   Coercion in the third degree.
135.61   Coercion in the second degree.
135.65   Coercion in the first degree.
135.70   Coercion; no defense.
135.75   Coercion; defense.

§135.00 Unlawful imprisonment, kidnapping and custodial interference; definitions of terms.

The following definitions are applicable to this article:

1. "Restrain" means to restrict a person's movements intentionally and unlawfully in such manner as to interfere substantially with his liberty by moving him from one place to another, or by confining him either in the place where the restriction commences or in a place to

which he has been moved, without consent and with knowledge that the restriction is unlawful. A person is so moved or confined "without consent" when such is accomplished by (a) physical force, intimidation or deception, or (b) any means whatever, including acquiescence of the victim, if he is a child less than sixteen years old or an incompetent person and the parent, guardian or other person or institution having lawful control or custody of him has not acquiesced in the movement or confinement.

2. "Abduct" means to restrain a person with intent to prevent his liberation by either (a) secreting or holding him in a place where he is not likely to be found, or (b) using or threatening to use deadly physical force.

3. "Relative" means a parent, ancestor, brother, sister, uncle or aunt.

§135.05 Unlawful imprisonment in the second degree.

A person is guilty of unlawful imprisonment in the second degree when he restrains another person.

Unlawful imprisonment in the second degree is a class A misdemeanor.

§135.10 Unlawful imprisonment in the first degree.

A person is guilty of unlawful imprisonment in the first degree when he restrains another person under circumstances which expose the latter to a risk of serious physical injury.

Unlawful imprisonment in the first degree is a class E felony.

§135.15 Unlawful imprisonment; defense.

In any prosecution for unlawful imprisonment, it is an affirmative defense that (a) the person restrained was a child less than sixteen years old, and (b) the defendant was a relative of such child, and (c) his sole purpose was to assume control of such child.

§135.20 Kidnapping in the second degree.

A person is guilty of kidnapping in the second degree when he abducts another person.

Kidnapping in the second degree is a class B felony.

§135.25 Kidnapping in the first degree.

A person is guilty of kidnapping in the first degree when he abducts another person and when:

1. His intent is to compel a third person to pay or deliver money or property as ransom, or to engage in other particular conduct, or to refrain from engaging in particular conduct; or

2. He restrains the person abducted for a period of more than twelve hours with intent to:

(a) Inflict physical injury upon him or violate or abuse him sexually; or

(b) Accomplish or advance the commission of a felony; or

(c) Terrorize him or a third person; or

(d) Interfere with the performance of a governmental or political function; or

3. The person abducted dies during the abduction or before he is able to return or to be returned to safety. Such death shall be presumed, in a case where such person was less than sixteen years old or an incompetent person at the time of the abduction, from evidence that his parents, guardians or other lawful custodians did not see or hear from him following the termination of the abduction and prior to trial and received no reliable information during such period persuasively indicating that he was alive. In all other cases, such death shall be presumed from evidence that a person whom the person abducted would have been extremely likely to visit or communicate with during the specified period were he alive and free to do so did not see or hear from him during such period and received no reliable information during such period persuasively indicating that he was alive.

Kidnapping in the first degree is a class A-I felony.

§135.30 Kidnapping; defense.

In any prosecution for kidnapping, it is an affirmative defense that (a) the defendant was a relative of the person abducted, and (b) his sole purpose was to assume control of such person.

§135.35 Labor trafficking.

A person is guilty of labor trafficking if he or she compels or induces another to engage in labor or recruits, entices, harbors, or transports such other person by means of intentionally:

1. requiring that the labor be performed to retire, repay, or service a real or purported debt that the actor has caused by a systematic ongoing course of conduct with intent to defraud such person;

2. withholding, destroying, or confiscating any actual or purported passport, immigration document, or any other actual or purported government identification document, of another person with intent to impair said person's freedom of movement; provided, however, that this subdivision shall not apply to an attempt to correct a social security administration record or immigration agency record in accordance with any local, state, or federal agency requirement, where such attempt is not made for the purpose of any express or implied threat;

3. using force or engaging in any scheme, plan or pattern to compel or induce such person to engage in or continue to engage in labor activity by means of instilling a fear in such person that, if the demand is not complied with, the actor or another will do one or more of the following:

(a) cause physical injury, serious physical injury, or death to a person; or

(b) cause damage to property, other than the property of the actor; or

(c) engage in other conduct constituting a felony or unlawful imprisonment in the second degree in violation of section 135.05 of this article; or

(d) accuse some person of a crime or cause criminal charges or deportation proceedings to be instituted against such person; provided, however, that it shall be an affirmative defense to this subdivision that the defendant reasonably believed the threatened charge to be true and that his or her sole purpose was to compel or induce the victim to take reasonable action to make good the wrong which was the subject of such threatened charge; or

(e) expose a secret or publicize an asserted fact, whether true or false, tending to subject some person to hatred, contempt or ridicule; or

(f) testify or provide information or withhold testimony or information with respect to another's legal claim or defense; or

(g) use or abuse his or her position as a public servant by performing some act within or related to his or her official duties, or by failing or refusing to perform an official duty, in such manner as to affect some person adversely.

Labor trafficking is a class D felony.

§135.36 Labor trafficking; accomplice.

In a prosecution for labor trafficking, a person who has been compelled or induced or recruited, enticed, harbored or transported to engage in labor shall not be deemed to be an accomplice.

§135.37 Aggravated labor trafficking.

A person is guilty of aggravated labor trafficking if he or she compels or induces another to engage in labor or recruits, entices, harbors, or transports such other person to engage in labor by means of intentionally unlawfully providing a controlled substance to such person with intent to impair said person's judgment.

Aggravated labor trafficking is a class C felony.

§135.45 Custodial interference in the second degree.

A person is guilty of custodial interference in the second degree when:

1. Being a relative of a child less than sixteen years old, intending to hold such child permanently or for a protracted period, and knowing that he has no legal right to do so, he takes or entices such child from his lawful custodian; or

2. Knowing that he has no legal right to do so, he takes or entices from lawful custody any incompetent person or other person entrusted by authority of law to the custody of another person or institution.

Custodial interference in the second degree is a class A misdemeanor.

§135.50 Custodial interference in the first degree.

A person is guilty of custodial interference in the first degree when he commits the crime of custodial interference in the second degree:

1. With intent to permanently remove the victim from this state, he removes such person from the state; or

2. Under circumstances which expose the victim to a risk that his safety will be endangered or his health materially impaired.

It shall be an affirmative defense to a prosecution under subdivision one of this section that the victim had been abandoned or that the taking was necessary in an emergency to protect the victim because he has been subjected to or threatened with mistreatment or abuse.

Custodial interference in the first degree is a class E felony.

§135.55 Substitution of children.

A person is guilty of substitution of children when, having been temporarily entrusted with a child less than one year old and intending to deceive a parent, guardian or other lawful custodian of such child, he substitutes, produces or returns to such parent, guardian or custodian a child other than the one entrusted.

Substitution of children is a class E felony.

§135.60 Coercion in the third degree.

A person is guilty of coercion in the third degree when he or she compels or induces a person to engage in conduct which the latter has a legal right to abstain from engaging in, or to abstain from engaging in conduct in which he or she has a legal right to engage, or compels or induces a person to join a group, organization or criminal enterprise which such latter person has a right to abstain from joining, or compels or induces a person to produce, disseminate, or otherwise display an image or images depicting nudity of such person or depicting such person engaged in sexual conduct as defined in subdivisions two and three of section 235.20 of this chapter, by means of instilling in him or her a fear that, if the demand is not complied with, the actor or another will: *(Eff.12/19/21,Ch.484,L.2021)*

1. Cause physical injury to a person; or

2. Cause damage to property; or

3. Engage in other conduct constituting a crime; or

4. Accuse some person of a crime or cause criminal charges to be instituted against him or her; or

5. Expose a secret or publicize an asserted fact, whether true or false, tending to subject some person to hatred, contempt or ridicule; or

6. Cause a strike, boycott or other collective labor group action injurious to some person's business; except that such a threat shall not be deemed coercive when the act or omission compelled is for the benefit of the group in whose interest the actor purports to act; or

7. Testify or provide information or withhold testimony or information with respect to another's legal claim or defense; or

8. Use or abuse his or her position as a public servant by performing some act within or related to his or her official duties, or by failing or refusing to perform an official duty, in such manner as to affect some person adversely; or

9. Perform any other act which would not in itself materially benefit the actor but which is calculated to harm another person materially with respect to his or her health, safety, business, calling, career, financial condition, reputation or personal relationships.

10. Report his or her immigration status or suspected immigration status.   *(Eff.11/7/21,Ch.447,L.2021)*

Coercion in the third degree is a class A misdemeanor.

§135.61 Coercion in the second degree.

A person is guilty of coercion in the second degree when he or she commits the crime of coercion in the third degree as defined in section 135.60 of this article and thereby compels or induces a person to engage in sexual intercourse, oral sexual conduct or anal sexual conduct as such terms are defined in section 130 of the penal law.

Coercion in the second degree is a class E felony.

§135.65 Coercion in the first degree.

A person is guilty of coercion in the first degree when he or she commits the crime of coercion in the third degree, and when:

1. He or she commits such crime by instilling in the victim a fear that he or she will cause physical injury to a person or cause damage to property; or

2. He or she thereby compels or induces the victim to:

    (a) Commit or attempt to commit a felony; or

    (b) Cause or attempt to cause physical injury to a person; or

    (c) Violate his or her duty as a public servant.

Coercion in the first degree is a class D felony.

§135.70 Coercion; no defense.

The crimes of (a) coercion and attempt to commit coercion, and (b) bribe receiving by a labor official as defined in section 180.20, and bribe receiving as defined in section 200.05, are not mutually exclusive, and it is no defense to a prosecution for coercion or an attempt to commit coercion that, by reason of the same conduct, the defendant also committed one of such specified crimes of bribe receiving.

§135.75 Coercion; defense.

In any prosecution for coercion committed by instilling in the victim a fear that he or another person would be charged with a crime, it is an affirmative defense that the defendant reasonably believed the threatened charge to be true and that his sole purpose was to compel or induce the victim to take reasonable action to make good the wrong which was the subject of such threatened charge.

TITLE I - OFFENSES INVOLVING DAMAGE TO AND INTRUSION UPON PROPERTY

ARTICLE 140 - BURGLARY AND RELATED OFFENSES

Section
140.00 Criminal trespass and burglary; definitions of terms.
140.05 Trespass.
140.10 Criminal trespass in the third degree.
140.15 Criminal trespass in the second degree.
140.17 Criminal trespass in the first degree.
140.20 Burglary in the third degree.
140.25 Burglary in the second degree.
140.30 Burglary in the first degree.
140.35 Possession of burglar's tools.
140.40 Unlawful possession of radio devices.

§140.00 Criminal trespass and burglary; definitions of terms.

The following definitions are applicable to this article:

1. "Premises" includes the term "building," as defined herein, and any real property.

2. "Building" in addition to its ordinary meaning, includes any structure, vehicle or watercraft used for overnight lodging of persons, or used by persons for carrying on business therein, or used as an elementary or secondary school, or an enclosed motor truck, or an enclosed motor truck trailer. Where a building consists of two or more units separately secured or occupied, each unit shall be deemed both a separate building in itself and a part of the main building.

3. "Dwelling" means a building which is usually occupied by a person lodging therein at night.

4. "Night means the period between thirty minutes after sunset and thirty minutes before sunrise.

5. "Enter or remain unlawfully." A person "enters or remains unlawfully" in or upon premises when he is not licensed or privileged to do so. A person who, regardless of his intent, enters or remains in or upon premises which are at the time open to the public does so with license and privilege unless he defies a lawful order not to enter or remain, personally communicated to him by the owner of such premises or other authorized person. A license or privilege to enter or remain in a building which is only partly open to the public is not a license or privilege to enter or remain in that part of the building which is not open to the public. A person who enters or remains upon unimproved and apparently unused land, which is neither fenced nor otherwise enclosed in a manner designed to exclude intruders, does so with license and privilege unless notice against trespass is personally communicated to him by the owner of such land or other authorized person, or unless such notice is given by posting in a conspicuous manner. A person who enters or remains in or about a school building without written permission from someone authorized to issue such permission or without a legitimate reason which includes a relationship involving custody of or responsibility for a pupil or student enrolled in the school or without legitimate business or a purpose relating to the operation of the school does so without license and privilege.

§140.05 Trespass.

A person is guilty of trespass when he knowingly enters or remains unlawfully in or upon premises.

Trespass is a violation.

§140.10 Criminal trespass in the third degree.

A person is guilty of criminal trespass in the third degree when he knowingly enters or remains unlawfully in a building or upon real property

(a) which is fenced or otherwise enclosed in a manner designed to exclude intruders; or

(b) where the building is utilized as an elementary or secondary school or a children's overnight camp as defined in section one thousand three hundred ninety-two of the public health law or a summer day camp as defined in section one thousand three hundred ninety-two of the public health law in violation of conspicuously posted rules or regulations governing entry and use thereof; or

(c) located within a city with a population in excess of one million and where the building or real property is utilized as an elementary or secondary school in violation of a personally communicated request to leave the premises from a principal, custodian or other person in charge thereof; or

(d) located outside of a city with a population in excess of one million and where the building or real property is utilized as an elementary or secondary school in violation of a personally communicated request to leave the premises from a principal, custodian, school board member or trustee, or other person in charge thereof; or

(e) where the building is used as a public housing project in violation of conspicuously posted rules or regulations governing entry and use thereof; or

(f) where a building is used as a public housing project in violation of a personally communicated request to leave the premises from a housing police officer or other person in charge thereof; or

(g) where the property consists of a right-of-way or yard of a railroad or rapid transit railroad which has been designated and conspicuously posted as a no-trespass railroad zone.

Criminal trespass in the third degree is a class B misdemeanor.

§140.15 Criminal trespass in the second degree.

A person is guilty of criminal trespass in the second degree when:

1. he or she knowingly enters or remains unlawfully in a dwelling; or

2. being a person required to maintain registration under article six-C of the correction law and designated a level two or level three offender pursuant to subdivision six of section one hundred sixty-eight-l of the correction law, he or she enters or remains in a public or private elementary, parochial, intermediate, junior high, vocational or high school knowing that the victim of the offense for which such registration is required attends or formerly attended such school. It shall not be an offense subject to prosecution under this subdivision if: the person is a lawfully registered student at such school; the person is a lawful student participant in a school sponsored event; the person is a parent or a legal guardian of a lawfully registered student at such school and enters the school for the purpose of attending their child's or dependent's event or activity; such school is the person's designated polling place and he or she enters such school building for the limited purpose of voting; or if the person enters such school building for the limited purposes authorized by the superintendent or chief administrator of such school.

Criminal trespass in the second degree is a class A misdemeanor.

§140.17 Criminal trespass in the first degree.

A person is guilty of criminal trespass in the first degree when he knowingly enters or remains unlawfully in a building, and when, in the course of committing such crime, he:

1. Possesses, or knows that another participant in the crime possesses, an explosive or a deadly weapon; or

2. Possesses a firearm, rifle or shotgun, as those terms are defined in section 265.00, and also possesses or has readily accessible a quantity of ammunition which is capable of being discharged from such firearm, rifle or shotgun; or

3. Knows that another participant in the crime possesses a firearm, rifle or shotgun under circumstances described in subdivision two.

Criminal trespass in the first degree is a class D felony.

§140.20 Burglary in the third degree.

A person is guilty of burglary in the third degree when he knowingly enters or remains unlawfully in a building with intent to commit a crime therein.

Burglary in the third degree is a class D felony.

§140.25 Burglary in the second degree.

A person is guilty of burglary in the second degree when he knowingly enters or remains unlawfully in a building with intent to commit a crime therein, and when:

1. In effecting entry or while in the building or in immediate flight therefrom, he or another participant in the crime:

(a) Is armed with explosives or a deadly weapon; or

(b) Causes physical injury to any person who is not a participant in the crime; or

(c) Uses or threatens the immediate use of a dangerous instrument; or

(d) Displays what appears to be a pistol, revolver, rifle, shotgun, machine gun or other firearm; or

2. The building is a dwelling.

Burglary in the second degree is a class C felony.

§140.30 Burglary in the first degree.

A person is guilty of burglary in the first degree when he knowingly enters or remains unlawfully in a dwelling with intent to commit a crime therein, and when, in effecting entry or while in the dwelling or in immediate flight therefrom, he or another participant in the crime:

1. Is armed with explosives or a deadly weapon; or

2. Causes physical injury to any person who is not a participant in the crime; or

3. Uses or threatens the immediate use of a dangerous instrument; or

4. Displays what appears to be a pistol, revolver, rifle, shotgun, machine gun or other firearm; except that in any prosecution under this subdivision, it is an affirmative defense that such pistol, revolver, rifle, shotgun, machine gun or other firearm was not a loaded weapon from which a shot, readily capable of producing death or other serious physical injury, could be discharged. Nothing contained in this subdivision shall constitute a defense to a

prosecution for, or preclude a conviction of, burglary in the second degree, burglary in the third degree or any other crime.

Burglary in the first degree is a class B felony.

§140.35 Possession of burglar's tools.

A person is guilty of possession of burglar's tools when he possesses any tool, instrument or other article adapted, designed or commonly used for committing or facilitating offenses involving forcible entry into premises, or offenses involving larceny by a physical taking, or offenses involving theft of services as defined in subdivisions four, five and six of section 165.15, under circumstances evincing an intent to use or knowledge that some person intends to use the same in the commission of an offense of such character.

Possession of burglar's tools is a class A misdemeanor.

§140.40 Unlawful possession of radio devices.

As used in this section, the term "radio device" means any device capable of receiving a wireless voice transmission on any frequency allocated for police use, or any device capable of transmitting and receiving a wireless voice transmission. A person is guilty of unlawful possession of a radio device when he possesses a radio device with the intent to use that device in the commission of robbery, burglary, larceny, gambling or a violation of any provision of article two hundred twenty of the penal law.

Unlawful possession of a radio device is a class B misdemeanor.

ARTICLE 145 - CRIMINAL MISCHIEF
AND RELATED OFFENSES

Section
145.00 Criminal mischief in the fourth degree.
145.05 Criminal mischief in the third degree.
145.10 Criminal mischief in the second degree.
145.12 Criminal mischief in the first degree.
145.13 Definitions.
145.14 Criminal tampering in the third degree.
145.15 Criminal tampering in the second degree.
145.20 Criminal tampering in the first degree.
145.22 Cemetery desecration in the second degree.
145.23 Cemetery desecration in the first degree.
145.25 Reckless endangerment of property.
145.26 Aggravated cemetery desecration in the second degree.
145.27 Aggravated cemetery desecration in the first degree.
145.30 Unlawfully posting advertisements.
145.35 Tampering with a consumer product; consumer product defined.
145.40 Tampering with a consumer product in the second degree.
145.45 Tampering with a consumer product in the first degree.
145.50 Penalties for littering on railroad tracks and rights-of-way.
145.60 Making graffiti.
145.65 Possession of graffiti instruments.
145.70 Criminal possession of a taximeter accelerating device.

§145.00 Criminal mischief in the fourth degree.

A person is guilty of criminal mischief in the fourth degree when, having no right to do so nor any reasonable ground to believe that he or she has such right, he or she:

1. Intentionally damages property of another person; or

2. Intentionally participates in the destruction of an abandoned building as defined in section one thousand nine hundred seventy-one-a of the real property actions and proceedings law; or

3. Recklessly damages property of another person in an amount exceeding two hundred fifty dollars; or

4. With intent to prevent a person from communicating a request for emergency assistance, intentionally disables or removes telephonic, TTY or similar communication sending equipment while that person: (a) is attempting to seek or is engaged in the process of seeking emergency assistance from police, law enforcement, fire or emergency medical services personnel; or (b) is attempting to seek or is engaged in the process of seeking emergency assistance from another person or entity in order to protect himself, herself or a third person from imminent physical injury. The fact that the defendant has an ownership interest in such equipment shall not be a defense to a charge pursuant to this subdivision.

Criminal mischief in the fourth degree is a class A misdemeanor.

§145.05 Criminal mischief in the third degree.

A person is guilty of criminal mischief in the third degree when, with intent to damage property of another person, and having no right to do so nor any reasonable ground to believe that he or she has such right, he or she:

1. damages the motor vehicle of another person, by breaking into such vehicle when it is locked with the intent of stealing property, and within the previous ten year period, has been convicted three or more times, in separate criminal transactions for which sentence was imposed on separate occasions, of criminal mischief in the fourth degree as defined in section 145.00, criminal mischief in the third degree as defined in this section, criminal mischief in the second degree as defined in section 145.10, or criminal mischief in the first degree as defined in section 145.12 of this article; or

2. damages property of another person in an amount exceeding two hundred fifty dollars.

Criminal mischief in the third degree is a class E felony.

§145.10 Criminal mischief in the second degree.

A person is guilty of criminal mischief in the second degree when with intent to damage property of another person, and having no right to do so nor any reasonable ground to believe that he has such right, he damages property of another person in an amount exceeding one thousand five hundred dollars.

Criminal mischief in the second degree is a class D felony.

§145.12 Criminal mischief in the first degree.

A person is guilty of criminal mischief in the first degree when with intent to damage property of another person, and having no right to do so nor any reasonable ground to believe that he has such right, he damages property of another person by means of an explosive.

Criminal mischief in the first degree is a class B felony.

§145.13 Definitions.

For the purposes of sections 145.00, 145.05, 145.10 and 145.12 of this article:

"Property of another" shall include all property in which another person has an ownership interest, whether or not a person who damages such property, or any other person, may also have an interest in such property.

§145.14 Criminal tampering in the third degree.

A person is guilty of criminal tampering in the third degree when, having no right to do so nor any reasonable ground to believe that he has such right, he tampers with property of another person with intent to cause substantial inconvenience to such person or to a third person.

Criminal tampering in the third degree is a class B misdemeanor.

§145.15 Criminal tampering in the second degree.

A person is guilty of criminal tampering in the second degree when, having no right to do so nor any reasonable ground to believe that he has such right, he or she tampers or makes connection with property of a gas, electric, sewer, steam or water-works corporation, telephone or telegraph corporation, common carrier, nuclear powered electric generating facility, or public utility operated by a municipality or district; except that in any prosecution under this section, it is an affirmative defense that the defendant did not engage in such conduct for a larcenous or otherwise unlawful or wrongful purpose.

Criminal tampering in the second degree is a class A misdemeanor.

§145.20 Criminal tampering in the first degree.

A person is guilty of criminal tampering in the first degree when, with intent to cause a substantial interruption or impairment of a service rendered to the public, and having no right to do so nor any reasonable ground to believe that he or she has such right, he or she damages or tampers with property of a gas, electric, sewer, steam or water-works corporation, telephone or telegraph corporation, common carrier, nuclear powered electric generating facility, or public utility operated by a municipality or district, and thereby causes such substantial interruption or impairment of service.

Criminal tampering in the first degree is a class D felony.

§145.22 Cemetery desecration in the second degree.

A person is guilty of cemetery desecration in the second degree when:

(a) with intent to damage property of another person, and having no right to do so nor any reasonable ground to believe that he has such right, he damages any real or personal property maintained as a cemetery plot, grave, burial place or other place of interment of human remains; or

(b) with intent to steal personal property, he steals personal property which is located at a cemetery plot, grave, burial place or other place of interment of human remains and which property is owned by the person or organization which maintains or owns such place or the estate, next-of-kin or representatives of the deceased person interred there.

Cemetery desecration in the second degree is a class A misdemeanor.

§145.23 Cemetery desecration in the first degree.

A person is guilty of cemetery desecration in the first degree when with intent to damage property of another person, and having no right to do so nor any reasonable ground to believe that he has such right, he:

(a) damages any real or personal property maintained as a cemetery plot, grave, burial place or other place of interment of human remains in an amount exceeding two hundred fifty dollars; or

(b) with intent to steal personal property, he steals personal property, the value of which exceeds two hundred fifty dollars, which is located at a cemetery plot, grave, burial place or other place of interment of human remains and which property is owned by the person or organization which maintains or owns such place or the estate, next-of-kin or representatives of the deceased person interred there; or

(c) commits the crime of cemetery desecration in the second degree as defined in section 145.22 of this article and has been previously convicted of the crime of cemetery desecration in the second degree within the preceding five years.

Cemetery desecration in the first degree is a class E felony.

§145.25 Reckless endangerment of property.

A person is guilty of reckless endangerment of property when he recklessly engages in conduct which creates a substantial risk of damage to the property of another person in an amount exceeding two hundred fifty dollars.

Reckless endangerment of property is a class B misdemeanor.

§145.26 Aggravated cemetery desecration in the second degree.

A person is guilty of aggravated cemetery desecration in the second degree when, having no right to do so nor any reasonable ground to believe that he or she has such right, he or she opens a casket, crypt, or similar vessel containing a human body or human remains which has been buried or otherwise interred in a cemetery and unlawfully removes therefrom a body, bodily part, any human remains or any object contained in such casket, crypt or similar vessel for the purpose of obtaining unlawful possession of such body, bodily part, human remains or object for such person or a third person.

Aggravated cemetery desecration in the second degree is a class E felony.

§145.27 Aggravated cemetery desecration in the first degree.

A person is guilty of aggravated cemetery desecration in the first degree when such person commits the crime of aggravated cemetery desecration in the second degree and has been previously convicted within the past five years of the crime of cemetery desecration in the second degree as defined in section 145.22 of this article, cemetery desecration in the first degree as defined in section 145.23 of this article or aggravated cemetery desecration in the second degree as defined in section 145.26 of this article.

Aggravated cemetery desecration in the first degree is a class D felony.

§145.30 Unlawfully posting advertisements.

1. A person is guilty of unlawfully posting advertisements when, having no right to do so nor any reasonable ground to believe that he has such right, he posts, paints or otherwise affixes to the property of another person any advertisement, poster, notice or other matter designed to benefit a person other than the owner of the property.

2. Where such matter consists of a commercial advertisement, it shall be presumed that the vendor of the specified product, service or entertainment is a person who placed such advertisement or caused it to be placed upon the property.

Unlawfully posting advertisements is a violation.

§145.35 Tampering with a consumer product; consumer product defined.

For the purposes of sections 145.40 and 145.45 of this article, "consumer product" means any drug, food, beverage or thing which is displayed or offered for sale to the public, for administration into or ingestion by a human being or for application to any external surface of a human being.

§145.40 Tampering with a consumer product in the second degree.

A person is guilty of tampering with a consumer product in the second degree when, having no right to do so nor any reasonable ground to believe that he has such right, and with intent to cause physical injury to another or with intent to instill in another a fear that he will cause such physical injury, he alters, adulterates or otherwise contaminates a consumer product.

Tampering with a consumer product in the second degree is a class A misdemeanor.

§145.45 Tampering with a consumer product in the first degree.

A person is guilty of tampering with a consumer product in the first degree when, having no right to do so nor any reasonable ground to believe that he has such right, and with intent to cause physical injury to another or with intent to instill in another a fear that he will cause such physical injury, he alters, adulterates or otherwise contaminates a consumer product and thereby creates a substantial risk of serious physical injury to one or more persons.

Tampering with a consumer product in the first degree is a class E felony.

§145.50 Penalties for littering on railroad tracks and rights-of-way.

1. No person shall throw, dump, or cause to be thrown, dumped, deposited or placed upon any railroad tracks, or within the limits of the rights-of-way of any railroad, any refuse, trash, garbage, rubbish, litter or any nauseous or offensive matter.

2. Where a highway or road lies in whole or part within a railroad rights-of-way, nothing in this section shall be construed as prohibiting the use in a reasonable manner of ashes, sand, salt or other material for the purpose of reducing the hazard of, or providing traction on snow, ice or sleet situated on such highway or road.

3. A violation of the provisions of subdivision one of this section shall be punishable by a fine not to exceed two hundred fifty dollars and/or a requirement to perform services for a public or not-for-profit corporation, association, institution or agency not to exceed eight hours and for any second or subsequent violation by a fine not to exceed five hundred dollars and/or a requirement to perform services for a public or not-for-profit corporation, association, institution or agency not to exceed eight hours.

4. Nothing in this section shall be deemed to apply to a railroad or its employees when matter deposited by them on the railroad tracks or rights-of-way is done pursuant to railroad rules, regulations or procedures.

§145.60 Making graffiti.

1. For purposes of this section, the term "graffiti" shall mean the etching, painting, covering, drawing upon or otherwise placing of a mark upon public or private property with intent to damage such property.

2. No person shall make graffiti of any type on any building, public or private, or any other property real or personal owned by any person, firm or corporation or any public agency or instrumentality, without the express permission of the owner or operator of said property.

Making graffiti is a class A misdemeanor.

§145.65 Possession of graffiti instruments.

A person is guilty of possession of graffiti instruments when he possesses any tool, instrument, article, substance, solution or other compound designed or commonly used to etch, paint, cover, draw upon or otherwise place a mark upon a piece of property which that person has no permission or authority to etch, paint, cover, draw upon or otherwise mark, under circumstances evincing an intent to use same in order to damage such property.

Possession of graffiti instruments is a class B misdemeanor.

§145.70 Criminal possession of a taximeter accelerating device.

1. For purposes of this section, a "taximeter" means an instrument or device that automatically calculates and displays the charge to a passenger in a vehicle that is licensed to transport members of the public for hire pursuant to local law.

2. For purposes of this section, a "taximeter accelerating device" means an instrument or device that causes a taximeter to increase the charge displayed by such taximeter to an amount greater than the maximum amount permitted by local law.

3. A person is guilty of criminal possession of a taximeter accelerating device when he knowingly possesses, with intent to use unlawfully, a taximeter accelerating device. If such a device is knowingly possessed there is a rebuttable presumption that it is intended to be used unlawfully.

Criminal possession of a taximeter accelerating device is a class A misdemeanor.

ARTICLE 150 - ARSON

Section
150.00 Arson; definitions.
150.01 Arson in the fifth degree.
150.05 Arson in the fourth degree.
150.10 Arson in the third degree.
150.15 Arson in the second degree.
150.20 Arson in the first degree.

§150.00 Arson; definitions.

As used in this article,

1. "Building", in addition to its ordinary meaning, includes any structure, vehicle or watercraft used for overnight lodging of persons, or used by persons for carrying on business therein. Where a building consists of two or more units separately secured or occupied, each unit shall not be deemed a separate building.

2. "Motor vehicle", includes every vehicle operated or driven upon a public highway which is propelled by any power other than muscular power, except (a) electrically-driven invalid chairs being operated or driven by an invalid, (b) vehicles which run only upon rails or tracks, and (c) snowmobiles as defined in article forty-seven of the vehicle and traffic law.

§150.01 Arson in the fifth degree.

A person is guilty of arson in the fifth degree when he or she intentionally damages property of another without consent of the owner by intentionally starting a fire or causing an explosion.

Arson in the fifth degree is a class A misdemeanor.

§150.05 Arson in the fourth degree.

1. A person is guilty of arson in the fourth degree when he recklessly damages a building or motor vehicle by intentionally starting a fire or causing an explosion.

2. In any prosecution under this section, it is an affirmative defense that no person other than the defendant had a possessory or proprietary interest in the building or motor vehicle.

Arson in the fourth degree is a class E felony.

§150.10 Arson in the third degree.

1. A person is guilty of arson in the third degree when he intentionally damages a building or motor vehicle by starting a fire or causing an explosion.

2. In any prosecution under this section, it is an affirmative defense that (a) no person other than the defendant had a possessory or proprietary interest in the building or motor vehicle, or if other persons had such interests, all of them consented to the defendant's conduct, and

(b) the defendant's sole intent was to destroy or damage the building or motor vehicle for a lawful and proper purpose, and (c) the defendant had no reasonable ground to believe that his conduct might endanger the life or safety of another person or damage another building or motor vehicle.

Arson in the third degree is a class C felony.

§150.15 Arson in the second degree.

A person is guilty of arson in the second degree when he intentionally damages a building or motor vehicle by starting a fire, and when (a) another person who is not a participant in the crime is present in such building or motor vehicle at the time, and (b) the defendant knows that fact or the circumstances are such as to render the presence of such a person therein a reasonable possibility.

Arson in the second degree is a class B felony.

§150.20 Arson in the first degree.

1. A person is guilty of arson in the first degree when he intentionally damages a building or motor vehicle by causing an explosion or a fire and when (a) such explosion or fire is caused by an incendiary device propelled, thrown or placed inside or near such building or motor vehicle; or when such explosion or fire is caused by an explosive; or when such explosion or fire either (i) causes serious physical injury to another person other than a participant, or (ii) the explosion or fire was caused with the expectation or receipt of financial advantage or pecuniary profit by the actor; and when (b) another person who is not a participant in the crime is present in such building or motor vehicle at the time; and (c) the defendant knows that fact or the circumstances are such as to render the presence of such person therein a reasonable possibility.

2. As used in this section, "incendiary device" means a breakable container designed to explode or produce uncontained combustion upon impact, containing flammable liquid and having a wick or a similar device capable of being ignited.

Arson in the first degree is a class A-I felony.

TITLE J - OFFENSES INVOLVING THEFT
ARTICLE 155 - LARCENY

Section
155.00 Larceny; definitions of terms.
155.05 Larceny; defined.
155.10 Larceny; no defense.
155.15 Larceny; defenses.
155.20 Larceny; value of stolen property.
155.25 Petit larceny.
155.30 Grand Larceny in the fourth degree.
155.35 Grand larceny in the third degree.
155.40 Grand larceny in the second degree.
155.42 Grand larceny in the first degree.
155.43 Aggravated grand larceny of an automated teller machine.
155.45 Larceny; pleading and proof.

§155.00 Larceny; definitions of terms.

The following definitions are applicable to this title:

1. "Property" means any money, personal property, real property, computer data, computer program, thing in action, evidence of debt or contract, or any article, substance or thing of value, including any gas, steam, water or electricity, which is provided for a charge or compensation.

2. "Obtain" includes, but is not limited to, the bringing about of a transfer or purported transfer of property or of a legal interest therein, whether to the obtainer or another.

3. "Deprive." To "deprive" another of property means (a) to withhold it or cause it to be withheld from him permanently or for so extended a period or under such circumstances that the major portion of its economic value or benefit is lost to him, or (b) to dispose of the property in such manner or under such circumstances as to render it unlikely that an owner will recover such property.

4. "Appropriate." To "appropriate" property of another to oneself or a third person means (a) to exercise control over it, or to aid a third person to exercise control over it, permanently or for so extended a period or under such circumstances as to acquire the major portion of its economic value or benefit, or (b) to dispose of the property for the benefit of oneself or a third person.

5. "Owner." When property is taken, obtained or withheld by one person from another person, an "owner" thereof means any person who has a right to possession thereof superior to that of the taker, obtainer or withholder.

A person who has obtained possession of property by theft or other illegal means shall be deemed to have a right of possession superior to that of a person who takes, obtains or withholds it from him by larcenous means.

A joint or common owner of property shall not be deemed to have a right of possession thereto superior to that of any other joint or common owner thereof.

In the absence of a specific agreement to the contrary, a person in lawful possession of property shall be deemed to have a right of possession superior to that of a person having only a security interest therein, even if legal title lies with the holder of the security interest pursuant to a conditional sale contract or other security agreement.

6. "Secret scientific material" means a sample, culture, microorganism, specimen, record, recording, document, drawing or any other article, material, device or substance which constitutes, represents, evidences, reflects, or records a scientific or technical process, invention or formula or any part or phase thereof, and which is not, and is not intended to be, available to anyone other than the person or persons rightfully in possession thereof or selected persons having access thereto with his or their consent, and when it accords or may accord such rightful possessors an advantage over competitors or other persons who do not have knowledge or the benefit thereof.

7. "Credit card" means any instrument or article defined as a credit card in section five hundred eleven of the general business law.

7-a. "Debit card" means any instrument or article defined as a debit card in section five hundred eleven of the general business law.

7-b. "Public benefit card" means any medical assistance card, food stamp assistance card, public assistance card, or any other identification, authorization card or electronic access device issued by the state or a social services district as defined in subdivision seven of section two of the social services law, which entitles a person to obtain public assistance benefits under a local, state or federal program administered by the state, its political subdivisions or social services districts.

7-c. "Access device" means any telephone calling card number, credit card number, account number, mobile identification number, electronic serial number or personal identification number that can be used to obtain telephone service.

8. "Service" includes, but is not limited to, labor, professional service, a computer service, transportation service, the supply of hotel accommodations, restaurant services, entertainment, the supplying of equipment for use, and the supplying of commodities of a public utility nature such as gas, electricity, steam and water. A ticket or equivalent instrument which evidences a right to receive a service is not in itself service but constitutes property within the meaning of subdivision one.

9. "Cable television service" means any and all services provided by or through the facilities of any cable television system or closed circuit coaxial cable communications system, or any microwave or similar transmission service used in connection with any cable television system or other similar closed circuit coaxial cable communications system.

§155.05 Larceny; defined.

1. A person steals property and commits larceny when, with intent to deprive another of property or to appropriate the same to himself or to a third person, he wrongfully takes, obtains or withholds such property from an owner thereof.

2. Larceny includes a wrongful taking, obtaining or withholding of another's property, with the intent prescribed in subdivision one of this section, committed in any of the following ways:

(a) By conduct heretofore defined or known as common law larceny by trespassory taking, common law larceny by trick, embezzlement, or obtaining property by false pretenses;

(b) By acquiring lost property. A person acquires lost property when he exercises control over property of another which he knows to have been lost or mislaid, or to have been delivered under a mistake as to the identity of the recipient or the nature or amount of the property, without taking reasonable measures to return such property to the owner;

(c) By committing the crime of issuing a bad check, as defined in section l90.05;

(d) By false promise. A person obtains property by false promise when, pursuant to a scheme to defraud, he obtains property of another by means of a representation, express or implied, that he or a third person will in the future engage in particular conduct, and when he does not intend to engage in such conduct or, as the case may be, does not believe that the third person intends to engage in such conduct.

In any prosecution for larceny based upon a false promise, the defendant's intention or belief that the promise would not be performed may not be established by or inferred from the fact alone that such promise was not performed. Such a finding may be based only upon evidence establishing that the facts and circumstances of the case are wholly consistent with guilty intent or belief and wholly inconsistent with innocent intent or belief, and excluding to a moral certainty every hypothesis except that of the defendant's intention or belief that the promise would not be performed;

(e) By extortion. A person obtains property by extortion when he compels or induces another person to deliver such property to himself or to a third person by means of instilling in him a fear that, if the property is no so delivered, the actor or another will:

(i) Cause physical injury to some person in the future; or

(ii) Cause damage to property; or

(iii) Engage in other conduct constituting a crime; or

(iv) Accuse some person of a crime or cause criminal charges or removal proceedings to be instituted against him or her; or

(Eff.11/7/21,Ch.447,L.2021)

(v) Expose a secret or publicize an asserted fact, whether true or false, tending to subject some person to hatred, contempt or ridicule; or

(vi) Cause a strike, boycott or other collective labor group action injurious to some person's business; except that such a threat shall not be deemed extortion when the property is demanded or received for the benefit of the group in whose interest the actor purports to act; or

(vii) Testify of provide information or withhold testimony or information with respect to another's legal claim or defense; or

(viii) Use or abuse his position as a public servant by performing some act within or related to his official duties, or by failing or refusing to perform an official duty, in such manner as to affect some person adversely; or

(ix) Perform any other act which would not in itself materially benefit the actor but which is calculated to harm another person materially with respect to his health, safety, business, calling, career, financial condition, reputation or personal relationships.

§155.10 Larceny; no defense.

The crimes of (a) larceny committed by means of extortion and an attempt to commit the same, and (b) bribe receiving by a labor official as defined in section 180.20, and bribe receiving as defined in section 200.05, are not mutually exclusive, and it is no defense to a prosecution for larceny committed by means of extortion or for an attempt to commit the same that, by reason of the same conduct, the defendant also committed one of such specified crimes of bribe receiving.

§155.15 Larceny; defenses.

1. In any prosecution for larceny committed by trespassory taking or embezzlement, it is an affirmative defense that the property was appropriated under a claim of right made in good faith.

2. In any prosecution for larceny by extortion committed by instilling in the victim a fear that he or another person would be charged with a crime, it is an affirmative defense that the defendant reasonably believed the threatened charge to be true and that his sole purpose was to compel or induce the victim to take reasonable action to make good the wrong which was the subject of such threatened charge.

§155.20 Larceny; value of stolen property.

For the purposes of this title, the value of property shall be ascertained as follows:

1. Except as otherwise specified in this section, value means the market value of the property at the time and place of the crime, or if such cannot be satisfactorily ascertained, the cost of replacement of the property within a reasonable time after the crime.

2. Whether or not they have been issued or delivered, certain written instruments, not including those having a readily ascertainable market value such as some public and corporate bonds and securities, shall be evaluated as follows:

(a) The value of an instrument constituting an evidence of debt, such as a check, draft or promissory note, shall be deemed the amount due or collectable thereon or thereby, such figure ordinarily being the face amount of the indebtedness less any portion thereof which has been satisfied.

(b) The value of a ticket or equivalent instrument which evidences a right to receive a transportation, entertainment or other service shall be deemed the price stated thereon, if any; and if no price is stated thereon the value shall be deemed the price of such ticket or equivalent instrument which the issuer charges the general public.

(c) The value of any other instrument which creates, releases, discharges or otherwise affects any valuable legal right, privilege or obligation shall be deemed the greatest amount of economic loss which the owner of the instrument might reasonably suffer by virtue of the loss of the instrument.

3. Where the property consists of gas, steam, water or electricity, which is provided for charge or compensation, the value shall be the value of the property stolen in any consecutive twelvemonth period.

4. When the value of property cannot be satisfactorily ascertained pursuant to the standards set forth in subdivisions one and two of this section, its value shall be deemed to be an amount less than two hundred fifty dollars.

§155.25 Petit larceny.

A person is guilty of petit larceny when he steals property.

Petit larceny is a class A misdemeanor.

§155.30 Grand larceny in the fourth degree.

A person is guilty of grand larceny in the fourth degree when he steals property and when:

1. The value of the property exceeds one thousand dollars; or

2. The property consists of a public record, writing or instrument kept, filed or deposited according to law with or in the keeping of any public office or public servant; or

3. The property consists of secret scientific material; or

4. The property consists of a credit card or debit card; or

5. The property, regardless of its nature and value, is taken from the person of another; or

6. The property, regardless of its nature and value, is obtained by extortion; or

7. The property consists of one or more firearms, rifles or shotguns, as such terms are defined in section 265.00 of this chapter; or

8. The value of the property exceeds one hundred dollars and the property consists of a motor vehicle, as defined in section one hundred twenty-five of the vehicle and traffic law, other than a motorcycle, as defined in section one hundred twenty-three of such law; or

9. The property consists of a scroll, religious vestment, a vessel, an item comprising a display of religious symbols which forms a representative expression of faith, or other miscellaneous item of property which:

(a) has a value of at least one hundred dollars; and

(b) is kept for or used in connection with religious worship in any building, structure or upon the curtilage of such building or structure used as a place of religious worship by a religious corporation, as incorporated under the religious corporations law or the education law.

10. The property consists of an access device which the person intends to use unlawfully to obtain telephone service.

11. The property consists of anhydrous ammonia or liquified ammonia gas and the actor intends to use, or knows another person intends to use, such anhydrous ammonia or liquified ammonia gas to manufacture methamphetamine.

Grand larceny in the fourth degree is a class E felony.

§155.35 Grand larceny in the third degree.

A person is guilty of grand larceny in the third degree when he or she steals property and:

1. when the value of the property exceeds three thousand dollars, or

2. the property is an automated teller machine or the contents of an automated teller machine.

Grand larceny in the third degree is a class D felony.

§155.40 Grand larceny in the second degree.

A person is guilty of grand larceny in the second degree when he steals property and when:

1. The value of the property exceeds fifty thousand dollars; or

2. The property, regardless of its nature and value, is obtained by extortion committed by instilling in the victim a fear that the actor or another person will (a) cause physical injury to some person in the future, or (b) cause damage to property, or (c) use or abuse his position as a public servant by engaging in conduct within or related to his official duties, or by failing or refusing to perform an official duty, in such manner as to affect some person adversely.

Grand larceny in the second degree is a class C felony.

§155.42 Grand larceny in the first degree.

A person is guilty of grand larceny in the first degree when he steals

property and when the value of the property exceeds one million dollars.
Grand larceny in the first degree is a class B felony.

§155.43 Aggravated grand larceny of an automated teller machine.

A person is guilty of aggravated grand larceny of an automated teller
machine when he or she commits the crime of grand larceny in the third
degree, as defined in subdivision two of section 155.35 of this article
and has been previously convicted of grand larceny in the third degree
within the previous five years.

Aggravated grand larceny of an automated teller machine is a class C felony.

§155.45 Larceny; pleading and proof.

1. Where it is an element of the crime charged that property was taken
from the person or obtained by extortion, an indictment for larceny must
so specify. In all other cases, an indictment, information or complaint
for larceny is sufficient if it alleges that the defendant stole property of
the nature or value required for the commission of the crime charged
without designating the particular way or manner in which said property
was stolen or the particular theory of larceny involved.

2. Proof that the defendant engaged in any conduct constituting
larceny as defined in section 155.05 is sufficient to support any
indictment, information or complaint for larceny other than one charging
larceny by extortion. An indictment charging larceny by extortion must
be supported by proof establishing larceny by extortion.

ARTICLE 156 - OFFENSES INVOLVING COMPUTERS; DEFINITION OF TERMS

Section
156.00 Offenses involving computers; definition of terms.
156.05 Unauthorized use of a computer.
156.10 Computer trespass.
156.20 Computer tampering in the fourth degree.
156.25 Computer tampering in the third degree.
156.26 omputer tampering in the second degree.
156.27 Computer tampering in the first degree.
156.29 Unlawful duplication of computer related material in the
        second degree.
156.30 Unlawful duplication of computer related material in the first
        degree.
156.35 Criminal possession of computer related material.
156.40 Operating an unlawful electronic sweepstakes.
156.50 Offenses involving computers; defenses.

§156.00 Offenses involving computers; definition of terms.

The following definitions are applicable to this chapter except where
different meanings are expressly specified:

1. "Computer" means a device or group of devices which, by
manipulation of electronic, magnetic, optical or electrochemical impulses,
pursuant to a computer program, can automatically perform arithmetic,
logical, storage or retrieval operations with or on computer data, and
includes any connected or directly related device, equipment or facility
which enables such computer to store, retrieve or communicate to or from
a person, another computer or another device the

results of computer operations, computer programs or computer data.

2. "Computer program" is property and means an ordered set of data representing coded instructions or statements that, when executed by computer, cause the computer to process data or direct the computer to perform one or more computer operations or both and may be in any form, including magnetic storage media, punched cards, or stored internally in the memory of the computer.

3. "Computer data" is property and means a representation of information, knowledge, facts, concepts or instructions which are being processed, or have been processed in a computer and may be in any form, including magnetic storage media, punched cards, or stored internally in the memory of the computer.

4. "Computer service" means any and all services provided by or through the facilities of any computer communication system allowing the input, output, examination, or transfer, of computer data or computer programs from one computer to another.

5. "Computer material" is property and means any computer data or computer program which:

(a) contains records of the medical history or medical treatment of an identified or readily identifiable individual or individuals. This term shall not apply to the gaining access to or duplication solely of the medical history or medical treatment records of a person by that person or by another specifically authorized by the person whose records are gained access to or duplicated; or

(b) contains records maintained by the state or any political subdivision thereof or any governmental instrumentality within the state which contains any information concerning a person, as defined in subdivision seven of section 10.00 of this chapter, which because of name, number, symbol, mark or other identifier, can be used to identify the person and which is otherwise prohibited by law from being disclosed. This term shall not apply to the gaining access to or duplication solely of records of a person by that person or by another specifically authorized by the person whose records are gained access to or duplicated; or

(c) is not and is not intended to be available to anyone other than the person or persons rightfully in possession thereof or selected persons having access thereto with his, her or their consent and which accords or may accord such rightful possessors an advantage over competitors or other persons who do not have knowledge or the benefit thereof.

6. "Computer network" means the interconnection of hardwire or wireless communication lines with a computer through remote terminals, or a complex consisting of two or more interconnected computers.

7. "Access" means to instruct, communicate with, store data in, retrieve from, or otherwise make use of any resources of a computer, physically, directly or by electronic means.

8. "Without authorization" means to use or to access a computer, computer service or computer network without the permission of the owner or lessor or someone licensed or privileged by the owner or lessor where such person knew that his or her use or access was without permission or after actual notice to such person that such use or access was without permission. It shall also mean the access of a computer service by a person without permission where such person knew that such access was without permission or after actual notice to such person, that such access was without permission.

Proof that such person used or accessed a computer, computer service or computer network through the knowing use of a set of instructions, code or computer program that bypasses, defrauds or otherwise circumvents a security measure installed or used with the user's authorization on the computer, computer service or computer network shall be presumptive evidence that such person used or accessed such computer, computer service or computer network without authorization.

9. "Felony" as used in this article means any felony defined in the laws of this state or any offense defined in the laws of any other jurisdiction for which a sentence to a term of imprisonment in excess of one year is authorized in this state.

§156.05 Unauthorized use of a computer.

A person is guilty of unauthorized use of a computer when he or she knowingly uses, causes to be used, or accesses a computer, computer service, or computer network without authorization.

Unauthorized use of a computer is a class A misdemeanor.

§156.10 Computer trespass.

A person is guilty of computer trespass when he or she knowingly uses, causes to be used, or accesses a computer, computer service, or computer network without authorization and:

1. he or she does so with an intent to commit or attempt to commit or further the commission of any felony; or

2. he or she thereby knowingly gains access to computer material.

Computer trespass is a class E felony.

§156.20 Computer tampering in the fourth degree.

A person is guilty of computer tampering in the fourth degree when he or she uses, causes to be used, or accesses a computer, computer service, or computer network without authorization and he or she intentionally alters in any manner or destroys computer data or a computer program of another person.

Computer tampering in the fourth degree is a class A misdemeanor.

§156.25 Computer tampering in the third degree.

A person is guilty of computer tampering in the third degree when he commits the crime of computer tampering in the fourth degree and:

1. he does so with an intent to commit or attempt to commit or further the commission of any felony; or

2. he has been previously convicted of any crime under this article or subdivision eleven of section 165.15 of this chapter; or

3. he intentionally alters in any manner or destroys computer material; or

4. he intentionally alters in any manner or destroys computer data or a computer program so as to cause damages in an aggregate amount exceeding one thousand dollars; or

5. he intentionally alters in any manner or destroys computer material indicating that a person did or did not receive a vaccination against COVID-19.   *(Eff.12/22/21,Ch.784,L.2021)*

Computer tampering in the third degree is a class E felony.

§156.26 Computer tampering in the second degree.

A person is guilty of computer tampering in the second degree when he or she commits the crime of computer tampering in the fourth degree and he or she intentionally alters in any manner or destroys:

1. computer data or a computer program so as to cause damages in an aggregate amount exceeding three thousand dollars; or

2. computer material that contains records of the medical history or medical treatment of an identified or readily identifiable individual or individuals and as a result of such alteration or destruction, such individual or individuals suffer serious physical injury, and he or she is aware of and consciously disregards a substantial and unjustifiable risk that such serious physical injury may occur.

Computer tampering in the second degree is a class D felony.

§156.27 Computer tampering in the first degree.

A person is guilty of computer tampering in the first degree when he commits the crime of computer tampering in the fourth degree and he intentionally alters in any manner or destroys computer data or a computer program so as to cause damages in an aggregate amount exceeding fifty thousand dollars.

Computer tampering in the first degree is a class C felony.

§156.29 Unlawful duplication of computer related material in the second degree.

A person is guilty of unlawful duplication of computer related material in the second degree when having no right to do so, he or she copies, reproduces or duplicates in any manner computer material that contains records of the medical history or medical treatment of an identified or readily identifiable individual or individuals with an intent to commit or further the commission of any crime under this chapter.

Unlawful duplication of computer related material in the second degree is a class B misdemeanor.

§156.30 Unlawful duplication of computer related material in the first degree.

A person is guilty of unlawful duplication of computer related * in the first degree material** when having no right to do so, he or she copies, reproduces or duplicates in any manner:

1. any computer data or computer program and thereby intentionally and wrongfully deprives or appropriates from an owner thereof an economic value or benefit in excess of two thousand five hundred dollars; or

2. any computer data or computer program with an intent to commit or attempt to commit or further the commission of any felony.

Unlawful duplication of computer related material in the first degree is a class E felony.

(So in original, "material" inadvertently omitted)
**(So in original, "material" inadvertently included)*

§156.35 Criminal possession of computer related material.

A person is guilty of criminal possession of computer related material when having no right to do so, he knowingly possesses, in any form, any copy, reproduction or duplicate of any computer data or computer program which was copied, reproduced or duplicated in violation of section 156.30 of this article, with intent to benefit himself or a person other than an owner thereof.

Criminal possession of computer related material is a class E felony.

§156.40 Operating an unlawful electronic sweepstakes.

1. As used in this section the following words and terms shall have the following meanings:

(a) "Electronic machine or device" means a mechanically, electrically or electronically operated machine or device that is owned, leased or otherwise possessed by a sweepstakes sponsor or promoter, or any sponsors, promoters, partners, affiliates, subsidiaries or contractors thereof; that is intended to be used by a sweepstakes entrant; that uses energy; and that displays the results of a game entry or game outcome to a participant on a screen or other mechanism at a business location, including a private club; provided, that an electronic machine or device may, without limitation:

(1) be server-based;

(2) use a simulated game terminal as a representation of the prizes associated with the results of the sweepstakes entries;

(3) utilize software such that the simulated game influences or determines the winning or value of the prize;

(4) select prizes from a predetermined finite pool of entries;

(5) utilize a mechanism that reveals the content of a predetermined sweepstakes entry;

(6) predetermine the prize results and stores those results for delivery at the time the sweepstakes entry results are revealed;

(7) utilize software to create a game result;

(8) require deposit of any money, coin or token, or the use of any credit card, debit card, prepaid card or any other method of payment to activate the electronic machine or device;

(9) require direct payment into the electronic machine or device, or remote activation of the electronic machine or device;

(10) require purchase of a related product having legitimate value;

(11) reveal the prize incrementally, even though it may not influence if a prize is awarded or the value of any prize awarded;

(12) determine and associate the prize with an entry or entries at the time the sweepstakes is entered; or

(13) be a slot machine or other form of electrical, mechanical, or computer game.

(b) "Enter" or "entry" means the act or process by which a person becomes eligible to receive any prize offered in a sweepstakes.

(c) "Entertaining display" means any visual information, capable of being seen by a sweepstakes entrant, that takes the form of actual game play or simulated game play.

(d) "Prize" means any gift, award, gratuity, good, service, credit or anything else of value, which may be transferred to a person, whether possession of the prize is actually transferred, or placed on an account or other record as evidence of the intent to transfer the prize.

(e) "Sweepstakes" means any game, advertising scheme or plan, or other promotion, which, with or without payment of any consideration, a person may enter to win or become eligible to receive any prize, the determination of which is based upon chance.

2. A person is guilty of operating an unlawful electronic sweepstakes when he or she knowingly possesses with the intent to operate, or place into operation, an electronic machine or device to:

(a) conduct a sweepstakes through the use of an entertaining display, including the entry process or the reveal of a prize; or

(b) promote a sweepstakes that is conducted through the use of an entertaining display, including the entry process or the reveal of a prize.

3. Nothing in this section shall be construed to make illegal any activity which is lawfully conducted as the New York state lottery for education as authorized by article thirty-four of the tax law; pari-mutuel wagering on horse races as authorized by articles two, three, four, five-A, and ten of the racing, pari-mutuel wagering and breeding law; the game of bingo as authorized pursuant to article fourteen-H of the general municipal law; games of chance as authorized pursuant to article nine-A of the general municipal law; gaming as authorized by article thirteen of the racing, pari-mutuel wagering and breeding law; or pursuant to the federal Indian Gaming Regulatory Act.

Operating an unlawful electronic sweepstakes is a class E felony.

§156.50 Offenses involving computers; defenses.

In any prosecution:

1. under section 156.05 or 156.10 of this article, it shall be a defense that the defendant had reasonable grounds to believe that he had authorization to use the computer;

2. under section 156.20, 156.25, 156.26 or 156.27 of this article it shall be a defense that the defendant had reasonable grounds to believe that he had the right to alter in any manner or destroy the computer data or the computer program;

3. under section 156.29 or 156.30 of this article it shall be a defense that the defendant had reasonable grounds to believe that he had the right to copy, reproduce or duplicate in any manner the computer data or the computer program.

ARTICLE 158 - WELFARE FRAUD

Section
158.00 Definitions; presumption; limitation.
158.05 Welfare fraud in the fifth degree.
158.10 Welfare fraud in the fourth degree.
158.15 Welfare fraud in the third degree.
158.20 Welfare fraud in the second degree.
158.25 Welfare fraud in the first degree.
158.30 Criminal use of a public benefit card in the second degree.
158.35 Criminal use of a public benefit card in the first degree.
158.40 Criminal possession of public benefit cards in the third degree.
158.45 Criminal possession of public benefit cards in the second degree.
158.50 Criminal possession of public benefit cards in the first degree.

§158.00 Definitions; presumption; limitation.

1. Definitions. The following definitions are applicable to this article:

(a) "Public benefit card" means any medical assistance card, food stamp assistance card, public assistance card, or any other identification, authorization card or electronic access device issued by the state or a social services district, as defined in subdivision seven of section two of the social services law, which entitles a person to obtain public assistance benefits under a local, state, or federal program administered by the state, its political subdivisions, or social services districts.

(b) "Fraudulent welfare act" means knowingly and with intent to defraud, engaging in an act or acts pursuant to which a person:

(1) offers, presents or causes to be presented to the state, any of its political subdivisions or social services districts, or any employee or agent thereof, an oral or written application or request for public assistance benefits or for a public benefit card with knowledge that the application or request contains a false statement or false information, and such statement or information is material, or

(2) holds himself or herself out to be another person, whether real or fictitious, for the purpose of obtaining public assistance benefits, or

(3) makes a false statement or provides false information for the purpose of (i) establishing or maintaining eligibility for public assistance benefits or (ii) increasing or preventing reduction of public assistance benefits, and such statement or information is material.

(c) "Public assistance benefits" means money, property or services provided directly or indirectly through programs of the federal government, the state government or the government of any political subdivision within the state and administered by the department of social services or social services districts.

2. Rebuttable presumption.

(a) A person who possesses five or more public benefit cards in a name or names other than his or her own is presumed to possess the same with intent to defraud, deceive or injure another.

(b) The presumption established by this subdivision shall not apply to:

(1) any employee or agent of the department of social services to the extent that he or she possesses such cards in the course of his or her official duties; or

(2) any person to the extent that he she* possesses a public benefit card or cards issued to a member or members of his or her immediate family or household with the consent of the cardholder; or

(3) any person providing home health services or personal care services pursuant to title eleven of article five of the social services law, or any agent or employee of a congregate care or residential treatment facility or foster care provider, to the extent that in the course of his or her duties, he or she possesses public assistance cards issued to persons under his or her care.

(c) The presumption established by this subdivision is rebuttable by evidence tending to show that the defendant did not possess such public benefit card or cards with intent to defraud, deceive or injure another. In any action tried before a jury, the jury shall be so instructed.

(d) The foregoing presumption shall apply to prosecutions for criminal possession of public benefit cards.

3. Limitation. Nothing contained in this article shall be construed to prohibit a recipient of public assistance benefits from pledging his or her public assistance benefits or using his or her public benefit card as collateral for a loan.

* *(So in original. Probably should read "he or she".)*

§158.05 Welfare fraud in the fifth degree.

A person is guilty of welfare fraud in the fifth degree when he or she commits a fraudulent welfare act and thereby takes or obtains public assistance benefits.

Welfare fraud in the fifth degree is a class A misdemeanor.

§158.10 Welfare fraud in the fourth degree.

A person is guilty of welfare fraud in the fourth degree when he or she commits a fraudulent welfare act and thereby takes or obtains public assistance benefits, and when the value of the public assistance benefits exceeds one thousand dollars.

Welfare fraud in the fourth degree is a class E felony.

§158.15 Welfare fraud in the third degree.

A person is guilty of welfare fraud in the third degree when he or she commits a fraudulent welfare act and thereby takes or obtains public assistance benefits, and when the value of the public assistance benefits exceeds three thousand dollars.

Welfare fraud in the third degree is a class D felony.

§158.20 Welfare fraud in the second degree.

A person is guilty of welfare fraud in the second degree when he or she commits a fraudulent welfare act and thereby takes or obtains public assistance benefits, and when the value of the public assistance benefits exceeds fifty thousand dollars.

Welfare fraud in the second degree is a class C felony.

§158.25 Welfare fraud in the first degree.

A person is guilty of welfare fraud in the first degree when he or she commits a fraudulent welfare act and thereby takes or obtains public assistance benefits, and when the value of the public assistance benefits exceed one million dollars.

Welfare fraud in the first degree is a class B felony.

§158.30 Criminal use of a public benefit card in the second degree.

A person is guilty of criminal use of a public benefit card in the second degree when he or she knowingly:

1. Loans money or otherwise provides property or services on credit, and accepts a public benefit card as collateral or security for the repayment of such loan or for the provision of such property or services;

2. Obtains a public benefit card in exchange for a benefit; or

3. Transfers or delivers a public benefit card to another (a) in exchange for money or a controlled substance as defined in subdivision five of section 220.00, or (b) for the purpose of committing an unlawful act.

Criminal use of a public benefit card in the second degree is a class A misdemeanor.

§158.35 Criminal use of a public benefit card in the first degree.

A person is guilty of criminal use of a public benefit card in the first degree when he or she, pursuant to an act or a series of acts, knowingly (i) obtains three or more public benefit cards from another or others in exchange for a benefit, or (ii) transfers or delivers three or more public benefit cards to another or others in exchange for money or a controlled substance as defined in subdivision five of section 220.00 of this chapter.

Criminal use of a public benefit card in the first degree is a class E felony.

§158.40 Criminal possession of public benefit cards in the third degree.

A person is guilty of criminal possession of public benefit cards in the third degree when he or she with intent to defraud, deceive or injure another, knowingly possesses five or more public benefit cards in a name or names other than the person's own name.

Criminal possession of public benefit cards in the third degree is a class E felony.

§158.45 Criminal possession of public benefit cards in the second degree.

A person is guilty of criminal possession of public benefit cards in the second degree when he or she with intent to defraud, deceive or injure another, knowingly possesses ten or more public benefit cards in a name or names other than the person's own name.

Criminal possession of public benefit cards in the second degree is a class D felony.

§158.50 Criminal possession of public benefit cards in the first degree.

A person is guilty of criminal possession of public benefit cards in the first degree when he or she with intent to defraud, deceive or injure another, knowingly possesses twenty-five or more public benefit cards in a name or names other than the person's own name.

Criminal possession of public benefit cards in the first degree is a class C felony.

ARTICLE 160 - ROBBERY

Section
160.00 Robbery; defined.
160.05 Robbery in the third degree.
160.10 Robbery in the second degree.
160.15 Robbery in the first degree.

§160.00 Robbery; defined.

Robbery is forcible stealing. A person forcibly steals property and commits robbery when, in the course of committing a larceny, he uses or threatens the immediate use of physical force upon another person for the purpose of:

1. Preventing or overcoming resistance to the taking of the property or to the retention thereof immediately after the taking; or

2. Compelling the owner of such property or another person to deliver up the property or to engage in other conduct which aids in the commission of the larceny.

§160.05 Robbery in the third degree.

A person is guilty of robbery in the third degree when he forcibly steals property.

Robbery in the third degree is a class D felony.

§160.10 Robbery in the second degree.

A person is guilty of robbery in the second degree when he forcibly steals property and when:

1. He is aided by another person actually present; or

2. In the course of the commission of the crime or of immediate flight therefrom, he or another participant in the crime:

(a) Causes physical injury to any person who is not a participant in the crime; or

(b) Displays what appears to be a pistol, revolver, rifle, shotgun, machine gun or other firearm; or

3. The property consists of a motor vehicle, as defined in section one hundred twenty-five of the vehicle and traffic law.

Robbery in the second degree is a class C felony.

§160.15 Robbery in the first degree.

A person is guilty of robbery in the first degree when he forcibly steals property and when, in the course of the commission of the crime or of immediate flight therefrom, he or another participant in the crime:

1. Causes serious physical injury to any person who is not a participant in the crime; or

2. Is armed with a deadly weapon; or

3. Uses or threatens the immediate use of a dangerous instrument; or

4. Displays what appears to be a pistol, revolver, rifle, shotgun, machine gun or other firearm; except that in any prosecution under this subdivision, it is an affirmative defense that such pistol, revolver, rifle, shotgun, machine gun or other firearm was not a loaded weapon from which a shot, readily capable of producing death or other serious physical injury, could be discharged. Nothing contained in this subdivision shall constitute a defense to a prosecution for, or preclude a conviction of, robbery in the second degree, robbery in the third degree or any other crime.

Robbery in the first degree is a class B felony.

ARTICLE 165 - OTHER OFFENSES RELATING TO THEFT

Section
165.00 Misapplication of property.
165.05 Unauthorized use of a vehicle in the third degree.
165.06 Unauthorized use of a vehicle in the second degree.
165.07 Unlawful use of secret scientific material.
165.08 Unauthorized use of a vehicle in the first degree.
165.09 Auto stripping in the third degree.
165.10 Auto stripping in the second degree.
165.11 Auto stripping in the first degree.
165.15 Theft of services.
165.16 Unauthorized sale of certain transportation services.
165.17 Unlawful use of credit card, debit card or public benefit card.
165.20 Fraudulently obtaining a signature.
165.25 Jostling.
165.30 Fraudulent accosting.
165.35 Fortune telling.
165.40 Criminal possession of stolen property in the fifth degree.
165.45 Criminal possession of stolen property in the fourth degree.
165.50 Criminal possession of stolen property in the third degree.
165.52 Criminal possession of stolen property in the second degree.
165.54 Criminal possession of stolen property in the first degree.
165.55 Criminal possession of stolen property; presumptions.
165.60 Criminal possession of stolen property; no defense.
165.65 Criminal possession of stolen property; corroboration.
165.70 Definitions.
165.71 Trademark counterfeiting in the third degree.
165.72 Trademark counterfeiting in the second degree.
165.73 Trademark counterfeiting in the first degree.
165.74 Seizure and distribution or destruction of goods bearing counterfeit trademarks.

§165.00 Misapplication of property.

1. A person is guilty of misapplication of property when, knowingly possessing personal property of another pursuant to an agreement that the same will be returned to the owner at a future time,

(a) he loans, leases, pledges, pawns or otherwise encumbers such property without the consent of the owner thereof in such manner as to create a risk that the owner will not be able to recover it or will suffer pecuniary loss; or

(b) he intentionally refuses to return personal property valued in excess of one hundred dollars to the owner pursuant to the terms of the rental agreement provided that the owner shall have made a written demand for the return of such personal property in person or by certified mail at an address indicated in the rental agreement and he intentionally refuses to return such personal property for a period of thirty days after such demand has been received or should reasonably have been received by him. Such written demand shall state: (i) the date and time at which the personal property was to have been returned under the rental agreement; (ii) that the owner does not consent to the continued withholding or retaining of such personal property and demands its return; and (iii) that the continued withholding or retaining of the property may constitute a class A misdemeanor punishable by a fine of up to one thousand dollars or by a sentence to a term of imprisonment for a period of up to one year or by both such fine and imprisonment.

(c) as used in paragraph (b) of this subdivision and in subdivision three of this section, the terms owner, personal property, and rental agreement shall be defined as in subdivision one of section three hundred ninety-nine-w of the general business law.

2. In any prosecution under paragraph (a) of subdivision one of this section, it is a defense that, at the time the prosecution was commenced,

(a) the defendant had recovered possession of the property, unencumbered as a result of the unlawful disposition, and (b) the owner had suffered no material economic loss as a result of the unlawful disposition.

3. In any prosecution under paragraph (b) of subdivision one of this section, it is a defense that at the time the prosecution was commenced, (a) the owner had recovered possession of the personal property and suffered no material economic loss as a result of the unlawful retention; or (b) the defendant is unable to return such personal property because it has been accidentally destroyed or stolen; or (c) the owner failed to comply with the provisions of section three hundred ninety-nine-w of the general business law.

Misapplication of property is a class A misdemeanor.

§165.05 Unauthorized use of a vehicle in the third degree.
A person is guilty of unauthorized use of a vehicle in the third degree when:

1. Knowing that he does not have the consent of the owner, he takes, operates, exercises control over, rides in or otherwise uses a vehicle. A person who engages in any such conduct without the consent of the owner is presumed to know that he does not have such consent; or

2. Having custody of a vehicle pursuant to an agreement between himself or another and the owner thereof whereby he or another is to perform for compensation a specific service for the owner involving the maintenance, repair or use of such vehicle, he intentionally uses or operates the same, without the consent of the owner, for his own purposes in a manner constituting a gross deviation from the agreed purpose; or

3. Having custody of a vehicle pursuant to an agreement with the owner thereof whereby such vehicle is to be returned to the owner at a specified time, he intentionally retains or withholds possession thereof, without the consent of the owner, for so lengthy a period beyond the specified time as to render such retention or possession a gross deviation from the agreement.

For the purposes of this section "a gross deviation from the agreement" shall consist of, but not be limited to, circumstances wherein a person who having had custody of a vehicle for a period of fifteen days or less pursuant to a written agreement retains possession of such vehicle for at least seven days beyond the period specified in the agreement, and continues such possession for a period of more than two days after service or refusal of attempted service of a notice in person or by certified mail at an address indicated in the agreement stating (i) the date and time at which the vehicle was to have been returned under the agreement; (ii) that the owner does not consent to the continued withholding or retaining of such vehicle and demands its return; and that continued withholding or retaining of the vehicle may constitute a class A misdemeanor punishable by a fine of up to one thousand dollars or by a sentence to a term of imprisonment for a period of up to one year or by both such fine and imprisonment.

Unauthorized use of a vehicle in the third degree is a class A misdemeanor.

§165.06 Unauthorized use of a vehicle in the second degree.

A person is guilty of unauthorized use of a vehicle in the second degree when:

He commits the crime of unauthorized use of a vehicle in the third degree as defined in subdivision one of section 165.05 of this article and has been previously convicted of the crime of unauthorized use of a vehicle in the third degree as defined in subdivision one of section 165.05 or second degree within the preceding ten years.

Unauthorized use of a vehicle in the second degree is a class E felony.

§165.07 Unlawful use of secret scientific material.

A person is guilty of unlawful use of secret scientific material when, with intent to appropriate to himself or another the use of secret scientific material, and having no right to do so and no reasonable ground to believe that he has such right, he makes a tangible reproduction or representation of such secret scientific material by means of writing, photographing, drawing, mechanically or electronically reproducing or recording such secret scientific material.

Unlawful use of secret scientific material is a class E felony.

§165.08 Unauthorized use of a vehicle in the first degree.

A person is guilty of unauthorized use of a vehicle in the first degree when knowing that he does not have the consent of the owner, he takes, operates, exercises control over, rides in or otherwise uses a vehicle with the intent to use the same in the course of or the commission of a class A, class B, class C or class D felony or in the immediate flight therefrom. A person who engages in any such conduct without the consent of the owner is presumed to know that he does not have such consent.

Unauthorized use of a vehicle in the first degree is a class D felony.

§165.09 Auto stripping in the third degree.

A person is guilty of auto stripping in the third degree when:

1. He or she removes or intentionally destroys or defaces any part of a vehicle, other than an abandoned vehicle, as defined in subdivision one of section one thousand two hundred twenty-four of the vehicle and traffic law, without the permission of the owner; or

2. He or she removes or intentionally destroys or defaces any part of an abandoned vehicle, as defined in subdivision one of section one thousand two hundred twenty-four of the vehicle and traffic law, except that it is a defense to such charge that such person was authorized to do so pursuant to law or by permission of the owner.

Auto stripping in the third degree is a class A misdemeanor.

§165.10 Auto stripping in the second degree.

A person is guilty of auto stripping in the second degree when:

1. He or she commits the offense of auto stripping in the third degree and when he or she has been previously convicted within the last five years of having violated the provisions of section 165.09 or this section; or

2. He or she removes or intentionally destroys, defaces, disguises, or alters any part of two or more vehicles, other than abandoned vehicles, as defined in subdivision one of section one thousand two hundred twenty-four of the vehicle and traffic law, without the permission of the owner, and the value of the parts of vehicles removed, destroyed, defaced, disguised, or altered exceeds an aggregate value of one thousand dollars.

Auto stripping in the second degree is a class E felony.

§165.11 Auto stripping in the first degree.

A person is guilty of auto stripping in the first degree when he or she removes or intentionally destroys, defaces, disguises, or alters any part of three or more vehicles, other than abandoned vehicles, as defined in subdivision one of section one thousand two hundred twenty-four of the vehicle and traffic law, without the permission of the owner, and the value of the parts of vehicles removed, destroyed, defaced, disguised, or altered exceeds an aggregate value of three thousand dollars.

Auto stripping in the first degree is a class D felony.

§165.15 Theft of services.

A person is guilty of theft of services when:

1. He obtains or attempts to obtain a service, or induces or attempts to induce the supplier of a rendered service to agree to payment therefor on a credit basis, by the use of a credit card or debit card which he knows to be stolen.

2. With intent to avoid payment for restaurant services rendered, or for services rendered to him as a transient guest at a hotel, motel, inn,

tourist cabin, rooming house or comparable establishment, he avoids or attempts to avoid such payment by unjustifiable failure or refusal to pay, by stealth, or by any misrepresentation of fact which he knows to be false. A person who fails or refuses to pay for such services is presumed to have intended to avoid payment therefor; or

3. With intent to obtain railroad, subway, bus, air, taxi, or any other public transportation service without payment of the lawful charge therefor, or to avoid payment of the lawful charge for such transportation service which has been rendered to him, he obtains or attempts to obtain such service or avoids or attempts to avoid payment therefor by force, intimidation, stealth, deception or mechanical tampering, or by unjustifiable failure or refusal or pay; or

4. With intent to avoid payment by himself or another person of the lawful charge for any telecommunications service, including, without limitation, cable television service, or any gas, steam, sewer, water, electrical, telegraph or telephone service which is provided for a charge or compensation, he obtains or attempts to obtain such service for himself or another person or avoids or attempts to avoid payment therefor by himself or another person by means of (a) tampering or making connection with the equipment of the supplier, whether by mechanical, electrical, acoustical or other means, or (b) offering for sale or otherwise making available, to anyone other than the provider of a telecommunications service for such service provider's own use in the provision of its service, any telecommunications decoder or descrambler, a principal function of which defeats a mechanism of electronic signal encryption, jamming or individually addressed switching imposed by the provider of any such telecommunications service to restrict the delivery of such service, or (c) any misrepresentation of fact which he knows to be false, or (d) any other artifice, trick, deception, code or device. For the purposes of this subdivision the telecommunications decoder or descrambler described in paragraph (b) above or the device described in paragraph (d) above shall not include any non-decoding and non-descrambling channel frequency converter or any television receiver type-accepted by the federal communications commission. In any prosecution under this subdivision, proof that telecommunications equipment, including, without limitation, any cable television converter, descrambler, or related equipment, has been tampered with or otherwise intentionally prevented from performing its functions of control of service delivery without the consent of the supplier of the service, or that telecommunications equipment, including, without limitation, any cable television converter, descrambler, receiver, or related equipment, has been connected to the equipment of the supplier of the service without the consent of the supplier of the service, shall be presumptive evidence that the resident to whom the service which is at the time being furnished by or through such equipment has, with intent to avoid payment by himself or another person for a prospective or already rendered service, created or caused to be created with reference to such equipment, the condition so existing. A person who tampers with such a device or equipment without the

consent of the supplier of the service is presumed to do so with intent to avoid, or to enable another to avoid, payment for the service involved. In any prosecution under this subdivision, proof that any telecommunications decoder or descrambler, a principal function of which defeats a mechanism of electronic signal encryption, jamming or individually addressed switching imposed by the provider of any such telecommunications service to restrict the delivery of such service, has been offered for sale or otherwise made available by anyone other than the supplier of such service shall be presumptive evidence that the person offering such equipment for sale or otherwise making it available has, with intent to avoid payment by himself or another person of the lawful charge for such service, obtained or attempted to obtain such service for himself or another person or avoided or attempted to avoid payment therefor by himself or another person; or

5. With intent to avoid payment by himself or another person of the lawful charge for any telephone service which is provided for a charge or compensation he (a) sells, offers for sale or otherwise makes available, without consent, an existing, canceled or revoked access device; or (b) uses, without consent, an existing, canceled or revoked access device; or (c) knowingly obtains any telecommunications service with fraudulent intent by use of an unauthorized, false, or fictitious name, identification, telephone number, or access device. For purposes of this subdivision access device means any telephone calling card number, credit card number, account number, mobile identification number, electronic serial number or personal identification number that can be used to obtain telephone service.

6. With intent to avoid payment by himself or another person for a prospective or already rendered service the charge or compensation for which is measured by a meter or other mechanical device, he tampers with such device or with other equipment related thereto, or in any manner attempts to prevent the meter or device from performing its measuring function, without the consent of the supplier of the service. In any prosecution under this subdivision, proof that a meter or related equipment has been tampered with or otherwise intentionally prevented from performing its measuring function without the consent of the supplier of the service shall be presumptive evidence that the person to whom the service which is at the time being furnished by or through such meter or related equipment has, with intent to avoid payment by himself or another person for a prospective or already rendered service, created or caused to be created with reference to such meter or related equipment, the condition so existing. A person who tampers with such a device or equipment without the consent of the supplier of the service is presumed to do so with intent to avoid, or to enable another to avoid, payment for the service involved; or

7. He knowingly accepts or receives the use and benefit of service, including gas, steam or electricity service, which should pass through a meter but has been diverted therefrom, or which has been prevented from being correctly registered by a meter provided therefor, or which has been diverted from the pipes, wires or conductors of the supplier thereof. In any prosecution under this subdivision proof that service has been intentionally diverted from passing through a meter, or has been intentionally prevented from being correctly registered by a meter

provided therefor, or has been intentionally diverted from the pipes, wires or conductors of the supplier thereof, shall be presumptive evidence that the person who accepts or receives the use and benefit of such service has done so with knowledge of the condition so existing; or

8. With intent to obtain, without the consent of the supplier thereof, gas, electricity, water, steam or telephone service, he tampers with any equipment designed to supply or to prevent the supply of such service either to the community in general or to particular premises; or

9. With intent to avoid payment of the lawful charge for admission to any theater or concert hall, or with intent to avoid payment of the lawful charge for admission to or use of a chair lift, AL gondola, rope-tow or similar mechanical device utilized in assisting skiers in transportation to a point of ski arrival or departure, he obtains or attempts to obtain such admission without payment of the lawful charge therefor.

10. Obtaining or having control over labor in the employ of another person, or of business, commercial or industrial equipment or facilities of another person, knowing that he is not entitled to the use thereof, and with intent to derive a commercial or other substantial benefit for himself or a third person, he uses or diverts to the use of himself or a third person such labor, equipment or facilities.

11. With intent to avoid payment by himself, herself, or another person of the lawful charge for use of any computer, computer service, or computer network which is provided for a charge or compensation he or she uses, causes to be used, accesses, or attempts to use or access a computer, computer service, or computer network and avoids or attempts to avoid payment therefor. In any prosecution under this subdivision proof that a person overcame or attempted to overcome any device or coding system a function of which is to prevent the unauthorized use of said computer or computer service shall be presumptive evidence of an intent to avoid payment for the computer or computer service.

12. With intent to avoid payment for services rendered by a barbershop, salon or beauty shop, he or she avoids or attempts to avoid such payment by unjustifiable failure or refusal to pay, by stealth, or by any misrepresentation of fact which he or she knows to be false.

Theft of services is a class A misdemeanor, provided, however, that theft of cable television service as defined by the provisions of paragraphs (a), (c) and (d) of subdivision four of this section, and having a value in excess of one hundred dollars by a person who has not been previously convicted of theft of services under subdivision four of this section is a violation, that theft of services under subdivision nine of this section by a person who has not been previously convicted of theft of services under subdivision nine of this section is a violation, that theft of services under subdivision twelve of this section by a person who has not previously been convicted of theft of services under subdivision twelve of this section is a violation, and provided further, however, that theft of services of any telephone service under paragraph (a) or (b) of subdivision five of this section having a value in excess of one thousand dollars or by a person who has been previously convicted within five years of theft of services under paragraph (a) of subdivision five of this section is a class E felony.   *(Eff.12/24/18,Ch.275,L.2018)*

§165.16 Unauthorized sale of certain transportation services.

1. A person is guilty of unauthorized sale of certain transportation services when, with intent to avoid payment by another person to the metropolitan transportation authority, New York city transit authority or a subsidiary or affiliate of either such authority of the lawful charge for transportation services on a railroad, subway, bus or mass transit service operated by either such authority or a subsidiary or affiliate thereof, he or she, in exchange for value, sells access to such transportation services to such person, without authorization, through the use of an unlimited farecard or doctored farecard. This section shall apply only to such sales that occur in a transportation facility, as such term is defined in subdivision two of section 240.00 of this chapter, operated by such metropolitan transportation authority, New York city transit authority or subsidiary or affiliate of such authority, when public notice of the prohibitions of its section and the exemptions thereto appears on the face of the farecard or is conspicuously posted in transportation facilities operated by such metropolitan transportation authority, New York city transit authority or such subsidiary or affiliate of such authority.

2. It shall be a defense to a prosecution under this section that a person, firm, partnership, corporation, or association: (a) selling a farecard containing value, other than a doctored farecard, relinquished all rights and privileges thereto upon consummation of the sale; or (b) sold access to transportation services through the use of a farecard, other than a doctored farecard, when such sale was made at the request of the purchaser as an accommodation to the purchaser at a time when a farecard was not immediately available to the purchaser, provided, however, that the seller lawfully acquired the farecard and did not, by means of an unlawful act, contribute to the circumstances that caused the purchaser to make such request.

3. For purposes of this section:

(a) "farecard" means a value-based, magnetically encoded card containing stored monetary value from which a specified amount of value is deducted as payment of a fare;

(b) "unlimited farecard" means a farecard that is time-based, magnetically encoded and which permits entrance an unlimited number of times into facilities and conveyances for a specified period of time; and

(c) "doctored farecard" means a farecard that has been bent or manipulated or altered so as to facilitate a person's access to transportation services without paying the lawful charge.

Unauthorized sale of transportation service is a class B misdemeanor.

§165.17 Unlawful use of credit card, debit card or public benefit card.

A person is guilty of unlawful use of credit card, debit card or public benefit card when in the course of obtaining or attempting to obtain property or a service, he uses or displays a credit card, debit card or public benefit card which he knows to be revoked or cancelled.

Unlawful use of a credit card, debit card or public benefit card is a class A misdemeanor.

§165.20 Fraudulently obtaining a signature.

A person is guilty of fraudulently obtaining a signature when, with intent to defraud or injure another or to acquire a substantial benefit for himself or a third person, he obtains the signature of a person to a written instrument by means of any misrepresentation of fact which he knows to be false.

Fraudulently obtaining a signature is a class A misdemeanor.

§165.25 Jostling.

A person is guilty of jostling when, in a public place, he intentionally and unnecessarily:

1. Places his hand in the proximity of a person's pocket or handbag; or
2. Jostles or crowds another person at a time when a third person's hand is in the proximity of such person's pocket or handbag.

Jostling is a class A misdemeanor.

§165.30 Fraudulent accosting.

1. A person is guilty of fraudulent accosting when he accosts a person in a public place with intent to defraud him of money or other property by means of a trick, swindle or confidence game.

2. A person who, either at the time he accosts another in a public place or at some subsequent time or at some other place, makes statements to him or engages in conduct with respect to him of a kind commonly made or performed in the perpetration of a known type of confidence game, is presumed to intend to defraud such person of money or other property.

Fraudulent accosting is a class A misdemeanor.

§165.35 Fortune telling.

A person is guilty of fortune telling when, for a fee or compensation which he directly or indirectly solicits or receives, he claims or pretends to tell fortunes, or holds himself out as being able, by claimed or pretended use of occult powers, to answer questions or give advice on personal matters or to exorcise, influence or affect evil spirits or curses; except that this section does not apply to a person who engages in the afore described conduct as part of a show or exhibition solely for the purpose of entertainment or amusement.

Fortune telling is a class B misdemeanor.

§165.40 Criminal possession of stolen property in the fifth degree.

A person is guilty of criminal possession of stolen property in the fifth degree when he knowingly possesses stolen property, with intent to benefit himself or a person other than an owner thereof or to impede the recovery by an owner thereof.

Criminal possession of stolen property in the fifth degree is class A misdemeanor.

§165.45 Criminal possession of stolen property in the fourth degree.

A person is guilty of criminal possession of stolen property in the fourth degree when he knowingly possesses stolen property, with intent to benefit himself or a person other than an owner thereof or to impede the recovery by an owner thereof, and when:

1. The value of the property exceeds one thousand dollars; or

2. The property consists of a credit card, debit card or public benefit card; or

3. He is a collateral loan broker or is in the business of buying, selling or otherwise dealing in property; or

4. The property consists of one of more firearms, rifles and shotguns, as such terms are defined in section 265.00 of this chapter; or

5. The value of the property exceeds one hundred dollars and the property consists of a motor vehicle, as defined in section one hundred twenty-five of the vehicle and traffic law, other than a motorcycle, as defined in section one hundred twenty-three of such law; or

6. The property consists of a scroll, religious vestment, vessel or other item of property having a value of at least one hundred dollars kept for or used in connection with religious worship in any building or structure used as a place of religious worship by a religious corporation, as incorporated under the religious corporations law or the education law.

7. The property consists of anhydrous ammonia or liquified ammonia gas and the actor intends to use, or knows another person intends to use, such anhydrous ammonia or liquified ammonia gas to manufacture methamphetamine.

Criminal possession of stolen property in the fourth degree is a class E felony.

§165.50 Criminal possession of stolen property in the third degree.

A person is guilty of criminal possession of stolen property in the third degree when he knowingly possesses stolen property, with intent to benefit himself or a person other than an owner thereof or to impede the recovery by an owner thereof, and when the value of the property exceeds three thousand dollars.

Criminal possession of stolen property in the third degree is a class D felony.

§165.52 Criminal possession of stolen property in the second degree.

A person is guilty of criminal possession of stolen property in the second degree when he knowingly possesses stolen property, with intent to benefit himself or a person other than an owner thereof or to impede the recovery by an owner thereof, and when the value of the property exceeds fifty thousand dollars.

Criminal possession of stolen property in the second degree is a class C felony.

§165.54 Criminal possession of stolen property in the first degree.

A person is guilty of criminal possession of stolen property in the first degree when he knowingly possesses stolen property, with intent to benefit himself or a person other than an owner thereof or to impede the recovery by an owner, and when the value of the property exceeds one million dollars.

Criminal possession of stolen property in the first degree is a class B felony.

§165.55 Criminal possession of stolen property; presumptions.

1. A person who knowingly possesses stolen property is presumed to possess it with intent to benefit himself or a person other than an owner thereof or to impede the recovery by an owner thereof.

2. A collateral loan broker or a person in the business of buying, selling or otherwise dealing in property who possesses stolen property is presumed to know that such property was stolen if he obtained it without having ascertained by reasonable inquiry that the person from whom he obtained it had a legal right to possess it.

3. A person who possesses two or more stolen credit cards, debit cards or public benefit cards is presumed to know that such credit cards, debit cards or public benefit cards were stolen.

4. A person who possesses three or more tickets or equivalent instrument for air transportation service, which tickets or instruments were stolen by reason of having been obtained from the issuer or agent thereof by the use of one or more stolen or forged credit cards, is presumed to know that such tickets or instruments were stolen.

§165.60 Criminal possession of stolen property; no defense.

In any prosecution for criminal possession of stolen property, it is no defense that:

1. The person who stole the property has not been convicted, apprehended or identified; or

2. The defendant stole or participated in the larceny of the property; or

3. The larceny of the property did not occur in this state.

§165.65 Criminal possession of stolen property; corroboration.

1. A person charged with criminal possession of stolen property who participated in the larceny thereof may not be convicted of criminal possession of such stolen property solely upon the testimony of an accomplice in the larceny unsupported by corroborative evidence tending to connect the defendant with such criminal possession.

2. Unless inconsistent with the provisions of subdivision one of this section, a person charged with criminal possession of stolen property may be convicted thereof solely upon the testimony of one from whom he obtained such property or solely upon the testimony of one to whom he disposed of such property.

§165.70 Definitions.

As used in sections 165.71, 165.72, 165.73 and 165.74, the following terms have the following definitions:

1. The term "trademark" means (a) any word, name, symbol, or device, or any combination thereof adopted and used by a person to identify goods made by a person and which distinguish them from those manufactured or sold by others which is in use and which is registered, filed or recorded under the laws of this state or of any other state or is registered in the principal register of the United States patent and trademark office; or (b) the symbol of the International Olympic Committee, consisting of five interlocking rings; the emblem of the United States Olympic Committee, consisting of an escutcheon having a blue chief and vertically extending red and white bars on the base with five interlocking rings displayed on the chief; any trademark, trade name, sign, symbol, or insignia falsely representing association with, or authorization by, the International Olympic Committee or the United States Olympic Committee; or the words "Olympic", "Olympiad", "Citius Altius Fortius", or any combination thereof tending to cause confusion, to cause mistake, to deceive, or to falsely suggest a connection with the United States Olympic Committee or any International Olympic Committee or United States Olympic Committee activity.

2. The term "counterfeit trademark" means a spurious trademark or an imitation of a trademark that is:

(a) used in connection with trafficking in goods; and

(b) used in connection with the sale, offering for sale or distribution of goods that are identical with or substantially indistinguishable from a trademark as defined in subdivision one of this section.

The term "counterfeit trademark" does not include any mark used in connection with goods for which the person using such mark was authorized to use the trademark for the type of goods so manufactured or produced by the holder of the right to use such mark or designation, whether or not such goods were manufactured or produced in the United States or in another country, and does not include imitations of trade dress or packaging such as color, shape and the like unless those features have been registered as trademarks as defined in subdivision one of this section.

3. The term "traffic" means to transport, transfer, or otherwise dispose of, to another, as consideration for anything of value, or to obtain control of with intent to so transport, transfer, or otherwise dispose of.

4. The term "goods" means any products, services, objects, materials, devices or substances which are identified by the use of a trademark.

§165.71 Trademark counterfeiting in the third degree.

A person is guilty of trademark counterfeiting in the third degree when, with the intent to deceive or defraud some other person or with the intent to evade a lawful restriction on the sale, resale, offering for sale, or distribution of goods, he or she manufactures, distributes, sells, or offers for sale goods which bear a counterfeit trademark, or possesses a trademark knowing it to be counterfeit for the purpose of affixing it to any goods.

Trademark counterfeiting in the third degree is a class A misdemeanor.

§165.72 Trademark counterfeiting in the second degree.

A person is guilty of trademark counterfeiting in the second degree when, with the intent to deceive or defraud some other person or with the intent to evade a lawful restriction on the sale, resale, offering for sale, or distribution of goods, he or she manufactures, distributes, sells, or offers for sale goods which bear a counterfeit trademark, or possesses a trademark knowing it to be counterfeit for the purpose of affixing it to any goods, and the retail value of all such goods bearing counterfeit trademarks exceeds one thousand dollars.

Trademark counterfeiting in the second degree is a class E felony.

§165.73 Trademark counterfeiting in the first degree.

A person is guilty of trademark counterfeiting in the first degree when, with the intent to deceive or defraud some other person, or with the intent to evade a lawful restriction on the sale, resale, offering for sale, or distribution of goods, he or she manufactures, distributes, sells, or offers for sale goods which bear a counterfeit trademark, or possesses a trademark knowing it to be counterfeit for the purpose of affixing it to any goods, and the retail value of all such goods bearing counterfeit trademarks exceeds one hundred thousand dollars.

Trademark counterfeiting in the first degree is a class C felony.

§165.74 Seizure and distribution or destruction of goods bearing counterfeit trademarks.

Any goods manufactured, sold, offered for sale, distributed or produced in violation of this article may be seized by any police officer. The magistrate must, within forty-eight hours after arraignment of the defendant, determine whether probable cause exists to believe that the goods had been manufactured, sold, offered for sale, distributed or produced in violation of this article, and upon a finding that probable cause exists to believe that the goods had been manufactured, sold, offered for sale, distributed, or produced in violation of this article, the court shall authorize such articles to be retained as evidence pending the trial of the defendant. Upon conviction of the defendant, the articles in respect whereof the defendant stands convicted shall be destroyed or donated. Destruction shall not include auction, sale or distribution of the items in their original form. Donation of the items shall be made at the court's discretion upon the request of any law enforcement agency and pursuant to the restrictions and procedures of section three hundred sixty-m of the general business law, for the benefit of indigent individuals.

TITLE K - OFFENSES INVOLVING FRAUD
ARTICLE 170 - FORGERY AND RELATED OFFENSES

Section
170.00 Forgery; definitions of terms.
170.05 Forgery in the third degree.
170.10 Forgery in the second degree.
170.15 Forgery in the first degree.
170.20 Criminal possession of a forged instrument in the third degree.
170.25 Criminal possession of a forged instrument in the second degree.
170.27 Criminal possession of a forged instrument in the second degree; presumption.
170.30 Criminal possession of a forged instrument in the first degree.
170.35 Criminal possession of a forged instrument; no defense.
170.40 Criminal possession of forgery devices.
170.45 Criminal simulation.
170.47 Criminal possession of an anti-security item.
170.50 Unlawfully using slugs; definitions of terms.
170.55 Unlawfully using slugs in the second degree.
170.60 Unlawfully using slugs in the first degree.
170.65 Forgery of a vehicle identification number.
170.70 Illegal possession of a vehicle identification number.
170.71 Illegal possession of a vehicle identification number; presumptions.
170.75 Fraudulent making of an electronic access device in the second degree.

§170.00 Forgery; definitions of terms.

1. "Written instrument" means any instrument or article, including computer data or a computer program, containing written or printed matter or the equivalent thereof, used for the purpose of reciting, embodying, conveying or recording information, or constituting a symbol or evidence of value, right, privilege or identification, which is capable of being used to the advantage or disadvantage of some person. For the purposes of this article, a card provided to a person by a vaccine provider indicating the date a person received a vaccination against COVID-19, the type of vaccine and its lot number, and bearing a government logo or other indication that it is created by a governmental instrumentality, shall be considered a written instrument.

(Eff.12/22/21,Ch.784,L.2021)

2. "Complete written instrument" means one which purports to be a genuine written instrument fully drawn with respect to every essential feature thereof. An endorsement, attestation, acknowledgment or other similar signature or statement is deemed both a complete written instrument in itself and a part of the main instrument in which it is contained or to which it attaches.

3. "Incomplete written instrument" means one which contains some matter by way of content or authentication but which requires additional matter in order to render it a complete written instrument.

4. "Falsely make." A person "falsely makes" a written instrument when he makes or draws a complete written instrument in its entirety, or an incomplete written instrument, which purports to be an authentic creation of its ostensible maker or drawer, but which is not such either because the ostensible maker or drawer is fictitious or because, if real, he did not authorize the making or drawing thereof.

5. "Falsely complete." A person "falsely completes" a written instrument when, by adding, inserting or changing matter, he transforms an incomplete written instrument into a complete one, without the authority of anyone entitled to grant it, so that such complete instrument

appears or purports to be in all respects an authentic creation of or fully
authorized by its ostensible maker or drawer.

6. "Falsely alter." A person "falsely alters" a written instrument when,
without the authority of anyone entitled to grant it, he changes a written
instrument, whether it be in complete or incomplete form, by means of
erasure, obliteration, deletion, insertion of new matter, transposition of
matter, or in any other manner, so that such instrument in its thus altered
form appears or purports to be in all respects an authentic creation of or
fully authorized by its ostensible maker or drawer.

7. "Forged instrument" means a written instrument which has been
falsely made, completed or altered.

8. "Electronic access device" means a mobile identification number or
electronic serial number that can be used to obtain telephone service.

§170.05 Forgery in the third degree.

A person is guilty of forgery in the third degree when, with intent to
defraud, deceive or injure another, he falsely makes, completes or alters
a written instrument.

Forgery in the third degree is a class A misdemeanor.

§170.10 Forgery in the second degree.

A person is guilty of forgery in the second degree when, with intent to
defraud, deceive or injure another, he falsely makes, completes or alters
a written instrument which is or purports to be, or which is calculated to
become or to represent if completed:

1. A deed, will, codicil, contract, assignment, commercial instrument,
credit card, as that term is defined in subdivision seven of section
155.00, or other instrument which does or may evidence, create,
transfer, terminate or otherwise affect a legal right, interest, obligation
or status; or

2. A public record, or an instrument filed or required or authorized by
law to be filed in or with a public office or public servant; or

3. A written instrument officially issued or created by a public office,
public servant or governmental instrumentality; or

4. Part of an issue of tokens, public transportation transfers,
certificates or other articles manufactured and designed for use as
symbols of value usable in place of money for the purchase of property
or services; or

5. A prescription of a duly licensed physician or other person
authorized to issue the same for any drug or any instrument or device
used in the taking or administering of drugs for which a prescription is
required by law.

Forgery in the second degree is a class D felony.

§170.15 Forgery in the first degree.

A person is guilty of forgery in the first degree when, with intent to
defraud, deceive or injure another, he falsely makes, completes or alters
a written instrument which is or purports to be, or which is calculated to
become or to represent if completed:

1. Part of an issue of money, stamps, securities or other valuable instruments issued by a government or governmental instrumentality; or

2. Part of an issue of stock, bonds or other instruments representing interests in or claims against a corporate or other organization or its property.

Forgery in the first degree is a class C felony.

§170.20 Criminal possession of a forged instrument in the third degree.

A person is guilty of criminal possession of a forged instrument in the third degree when, with knowledge that it is forged and with intent to defraud, deceive or injure another, he utters or possesses a forged instrument.

Criminal possession of a forged instrument in the third degree is a class A misdemeanor.

§170.25 Criminal possession of a forged instrument in the second degree.

A person is guilty of criminal possession of a forged instrument in the second degree when, with knowledge that it is forged and with intent to defraud, deceive or injure another, he utters or possesses any forged instrument of a kind specified in section 170.10.

Criminal possession of a forged instrument in the second degree is a class D felony.

§170.27 Criminal possession of a forged instrument in the second degree; presumption.

A person who possesses two or more forged instruments, each of which purports to be a credit card or debit card, as those terms are defined in subdivisions seven and seven-a of section 155.00, is presumed to possess the same with knowledge that they are forged and with intent to defraud, deceive or injure another.

§170.30 Criminal possession of a forged instrument in the first degree.

A person is guilty of criminal possession of a forge instrument in the first degree when, with knowledge that it is forged and with intent to defraud, deceive or injure another, he utters or possesses any forged instrument of a kind specified in section 170.15.

Criminal possession of a forged instrument in the first degree is a class C felony.

§170.35 Criminal possession of a forged instrument; no defense.

In any prosecution for criminal possession of a forged instrument, it is no defense that the defendant forged or participated in the forgery of the instrument in issue; provided that a person may not be convicted of both criminal possession of a forged instrument and forgery with respect to the same instrument.

§170.40 Criminal possession of forgery devices.

A person is guilty of criminal possession of forgery devices when:

1. He makes or possesses with knowledge of its character any plate, die or other device, apparatus, equipment, or article specifically designed for use in counterfeiting or otherwise forging written instruments; or

2. With intent to use, or to aid or permit another to use, the same for purposes of forgery, he makes or possesses any device, apparatus, equipment or article capable of or adaptable to such use.

Criminal possession of forgery devices is a class D felony.

§170.45 Criminal simulation.

A person is guilty of criminal simulation when:

1. With intent to defraud, he makes or alters any object in such manner that it appears to have an antiquity, rarity, source or authorship which it does not in fact possess; or

2. With knowledge of its true character and with intent to defraud, he utters or possesses an object so simulated.

Criminal simulation is a class A misdemeanor.

§170.47 Criminal possession of an anti-security item.

A person is guilty of criminal possession of an anti-security item, when with intent to steal property at a retail mercantile establishment as defined in article twelve-B of the general business law, he knowingly possesses in such an establishment an item designed for the purpose of overcoming detection of security markings or attachments placed on property offered for sale at such an establishment.

Criminal possession of an anti-security item is a class B misdemeanor.

§170.50 Unlawfully using slugs; definitions of terms.

The following definitions are applicable to sections 170.55 and 170.60:

1. "Coin machine" means a coin box, turnstile, vending machine or other mechanical or electronic device or receptacle designed (a) to receive a coin or bill or a token made for the purpose, and (b) in return for the insertion or deposit thereof, automatically to offer, to provide, to assist in providing or to permit the acquisition of some property or some service.

2. "Slug" means an object or article which, by virtue of its size, shape or any other quality, is capable of being inserted or deposited in a coin machine as an improper substitute for a genuine coin, bill or token.

3. "Value" of a slug means the value of the coin, bill or token for which it is capable of being substituted.

§170.55 Unlawfully using slugs in the second degree.

A person is guilty of unlawfully using slugs in the second degree when:

1. With intent to defraud the owner of a coin machine, he inserts or deposits a slug in such machine; or

2. He makes, possesses or disposes of a slug with intent to enable a person to insert or deposit it in a coin machine.

Unlawfully using slugs in the second degree is a class B misdemeanor.

§170.60 Unlawfully using slugs in the first degree.

A person is guilty of unlawfully using slugs in the first degree when he makes, possesses or disposes of slugs with intent to enable a person to insert or deposit them in a coin machine, and the value of such slugs exceeds one hundred dollars.

Unlawfully using slugs in the first degree is a class E felony.

§170.65 Forgery of a vehicle identification number.

A person is guilty of forgery of a vehicle identification number when:

(1) He knowingly destroys, covers, defaces, alters or otherwise changes the form or appearance of a vehicle identification number on any vehicle or component part thereof, except tires; or

(2) He removes any such number from a vehicle or component part thereof, except as required by the provisions of the vehicle and traffic law; or

(3) He affixes a vehicle identification number to a vehicle, except in accordance with the provisions of the vehicle and traffic law.

(4) He or she, with intent to defraud, knowingly manufactures, produces or reproduces a vehicle identification number label, sticker or plate which was not manufactured, produced or reproduced in accordance with the rules and regulations promulgated by the United States National Highway Safety Administration and/or in accordance with the provisions of the state vehicle and traffic law.

Forgery of a vehicle identification number is a class E felony.

§170.70 Illegal possession of a vehicle identification number.

A person is guilty of illegal possession of a vehicle identification number when:

(1) He knowingly possesses a vehicle identification number label, sticker or plate which has been removed from the vehicle or vehicle part to which such label, sticker or plate was affixed by the manufacturer in accordance with 49 U.S.C. section 32101, et seq. and regulations promulgated thereunder or in accordance with the provisions of the vehicle and traffic law; or

(2) He knowingly possesses a vehicle or vehicle part to which is attached a vehicle identification number label, sticker or plate or on which is stamped or embossed a vehicle identification number which has been destroyed, covered, defaced, altered or otherwise changed, or a vehicle or vehicle part from which a vehicle identification number label, sticker or plate has been removed, which label, sticker or plate was affixed in accordance with 49 U.S.C. section 32101, et seq. or regulations promulgated thereunder, except when he has complied with the provisions of the vehicle and traffic law and regulations promulgated thereunder; or

(3) He knowingly possesses a vehicle, or part of a vehicle to which by law or regulation must be attached a vehicle identification number, either (a) with a vehicle identification number label, sticker, or plate which was not affixed by the manufacturer in accordance with 49 U.S.C. section 32101, et seq. or regulations promulgated thereunder, or in accordance with the provisions of the vehicle and traffic law or regulations promulgated thereunder, or (b) on which is affixed, stamped or embossed a vehicle identification number which was not affixed, stamped or embossed by the manufacturer, or in accordance with 49 U.S.C. section 32101, et seq. or regulations promulgated thereunder or in accordance with the provisions of the vehicle and traffic law or regulations promulgated thereunder.

Illegal possession of a vehicle identification number is a class E felony.

§170.71 Illegal possession of a vehicle identification number; presumptions.

(1) A person is presumed to knowingly possess a vehicle or vehicle part in violation of subdivision two of section 170.70, when he possesses any combination of five such whole vehicles or individual

vehicle parts, none of which are attached to or contained in the same vehicle.

(2) A person is presumed to knowingly possess a vehicle or vehicle part in violation of subdivision three of section 170.70, when he possesses any combination of five such whole vehicles or individual vehicle parts, none of which are attached to or contained in the same vehicle.

§170.75 Fraudulent making of an electronic access device in the second degree.

A person is guilty of fraudulent making of an electronic access device in the second degree when, with intent to defraud, deceive or injure another, he falsely makes, completes or alters two or more electronic access devices, as that term is defined in subdivision eight of section 170.00 of this article.

Fraudulent making of an electronic access device in the second degree is a class D felony.

ARTICLE 175 - OFFENSES INVOLVING FALSE WRITTEN STATEMENTS

Section
175.00 Definitions of terms.
175.05 Falsifying business records in the second degree.
175.10 Falsifying business records in the first degree.
175.15 Falsifying business records; defense.
175.20 Tampering with public records in the second degree.
175.25 Tampering with public records in the first degree.
175.30 Offering a false instrument for filing in the second degree.
175.35 Offering a false instrument for filing in the first degree.
175.40 Issuing a false certificate.
175.45 Issuing a false financial statement.

§175.00 Definitions of terms.

The following definitions are applicable to this article:

1. "Enterprise" means any entity of one or more persons, corporate or otherwise, public or private, engaged in business, commercial, professional, industrial, eleemosynary, social, political or governmental activity.

2. "Business record" means any writing or article, including computer data or a computer program, kept or maintained by an enterprise for the purpose of evidencing or reflecting its condition or activity.

3. "Written instrument" means any instrument or article, including computer data or a computer program, containing written or printed matter or the equivalent thereof, used for the purpose of reciting, embodying, conveying or recording information, or constituting a symbol or evidence of value, right, privilege or identification, which is capable of being used to the advantage or disadvantage of some person.

§175.05 Falsifying business records in the second degree.

A person is guilty of falsifying business records in the second degree when, with intent to defraud, he:

1. Makes or causes a false entry in the business records of an enterprise; or

2. Alters, erases, obliterates, deletes, removes or destroys a true entry in the business records of an enterprise; or

3. Omits to make a true entry in the business records of an enterprise in violation of a duty to do so which he knows to be imposed upon him by law or by the nature of his position; or

4. Prevents the making of a true entry or causes the omission thereof in the business records of an enterprise.

Falsifying business records in the second degree is a class A misdemeanor.

§175.10 Falsifying business records in the first degree.

A person is guilty of falsifying business records in the first degree when he commits the crime of falsifying business records in the second degree, and when his intent to defraud includes an intent to commit another crime or to aid or conceal the commission thereof.

Falsifying business records in the first degree is a class E felony.

§175.15 Falsifying business records; defense.

In any prosecution for falsifying business records, it is an affirmative defense that the defendant was a clerk, bookkeeper or other employee who, without personal benefit, merely executed the orders of his employer or of a superior officer or employee generally authorized to direct his activities.

§175.20 Tampering with public records in the second degree.

A person is guilty of tampering with public records in the second degree when, knowing that he does not have the authority of anyone entitled to grant it, he knowingly removes, mutilates, destroys, conceals, makes a false entry in or falsely alters any record or other written instrument filed with, deposited in, or otherwise constituting a record of a public office or public servant.

Tampering with public records in the second degree is a class A misdemeanor.

§175.25 Tampering with public records in the first degree.

A person is guilty of tampering with public records in the first degree when, knowing that he does not have the authority of anyone entitled to grant it, and with intent to defraud, he knowingly removes, mutilates, destroys, conceals, makes a false entry in or falsely alters any record or other written instrument filed with, deposited in, or otherwise constituting a record of a public office or public servant.

Tampering with public records in the first degree is a class D felony.

§175.30 Offering a false instrument for filing in the second degree.

A person is guilty of offering a false instrument for filing in the second degree when, knowing that a written instrument contains a false statement or false information, he offers or presents it to a public office or public servant with the knowledge or belief that it will be filed with, registered or recorded in or otherwise become a part of the records of such public office or public servant.

Offering a false instrument for filing in the second degree is a class A misdemeanor.

§175.35 Offering a false instrument for filing in the first degree.

A person is guilty of offering a false instrument for filing in the first degree when:

1. knowing that a written instrument contains a false statement or false information, and with intent to defraud the state or any political subdivision, public authority or public benefit corporation of the state, he or she offers or presents it to a public office, public servant, public authority or public benefit corporation with the knowledge or belief that it will be filed with, registered or recorded in or otherwise become a part of the records of such public office, public servant, public authority or public benefit corporation; or

2. (a) he or she commits the crime of offering a false instrument for filing in the second degree; and

(b) such instrument is a financing statement the contents of which are prescribed by section 9--502 of the uniform commercial code, the collateral asserted to be covered in such statement is the property of a person who is a state or local officer as defined by section two of the public officers law or who otherwise is a judge or justice of the unified court system, such financing statement does not relate to an actual transaction, and he or she filed such financing statement in retaliation for the performance of official duties by such person.

Offering a false instrument for filing in the first degree is a class E felony.

§175.40 Issuing a false certificate.

A person is guilty of issuing a false certificate when, being a public servant authorized by law to make or issue official certificates or other official written instruments, and with intent to defraud, deceive or injure another person, he issues such an instrument, or makes the same with intent that it be issued, knowing that it contains a false statement or false information.

Issuing a false certificate is a class E felony.

§175.45 Issuing a false financial statement.

A person is guilty of issuing a false financial statement when, with intent to defraud:

1. He knowingly makes or utters a written instrument which purports to describe the financial condition or ability to pay of some person and which is inaccurate in some material respect; or

2. He represents in writing that a written instrument purporting to describe a person's financial condition or ability to pay as of a

prior date is accurate with respect to such person's current financial condition or ability to pay, whereas he knows it is materially inaccurate in that respect.

Issuing a false financial statement is a class A misdemeanor.

ARTICLE 176 - INSURANCE FRAUD

Section
176.00 Insurance fraud; definition of terms.
176.05 Insurance fraud; defined.
176.10 Insurance fraud in the fifth degree.
176.15 Insurance fraud in the fourth degree.
176.20 Insurance fraud in the third degree.
176.25 Insurance fraud in the second degree.
176.30 Insurance fraud in the first degree.
176.35 Aggravated insurance fraud.
176.40 Fraudulent life settlement act; defined.
176.45 Life settlement fraud in the fifth degree.
176.50 Life settlement fraud in the fourth degree.
176.55 Life settlement fraud in the third degree.
176.60 Life settlement fraud in the second degree.
176.65 Life settlement fraud in the first degree.
176.70 Aggravated life settlement fraud.
176.75 Staging a motor vehicle accident in the second degree.
176.80 Staging a motor vehicle accident in the first degree.

§176.00 Insurance fraud; definition of terms.

The following definitions are applicable to this article:

1. "Insurance policy" has the meaning assigned to insurance contract by subsection (a) of section one thousand one hundred one of the insurance law except it shall include reinsurance contracts, purported insurance policies and purported reinsurance contracts.

2. "Statement" includes, but is not limited to, any notice, proof of loss, bill of lading, invoice, account, estimate of property damages, bill for services, diagnosis, prescription, hospital or doctor records, x-ray, test result, and other evidence of loss, injury or expense.

3. "Person" includes any individual, firm, association or corporation.

4. "Personal insurance" means a policy of insurance insuring a natural person against any of the following contingencies:

(a) loss of or damage to real property used predominantly for residential purposes and which consists of not more than four dwelling units, other than hotels, motels and rooming houses;

(b) loss of or damage to personal property which is not used in the conduct of a business;

(c) losses or liabilities arising out of the ownership, operation, or use of a motor vehicles, predominantly used for non-business purposes;

(d) other liabilities for loss of, damage to, or injury to persons or property, not arising from the conduct of a business;

(e) death, including death by personal injury, or the continuation of life, or personal injury by accident, or sickness, disease or ailment, excluding insurance providing disability benefits pursuant to article nine of the workers' compensation law.

A policy of insurance which insures any of the contingencies listed in paragraphs (a) through (e) of this subdivision as well as other contingencies shall be personal insurance if that portion of the annual premium attributable to the listed contingencies exceeds that portion attributable to other contingencies.

5. "Commercial insurance" means insurance other than personal insurance, and shall also include insurance providing disability benefits

pursuant to article nine of the workers' compensation law, insurance providing workers' compensation benefits pursuant to the provisions of the workers' compensation law and any program of self insurance providing similar benefits.

§176.05 Insurance fraud; defined.

A fraudulent insurance act is committed by any person who, knowingly and with intent to defraud presents, causes to be presented, or prepares with knowledge or belief that it will be presented to or by an insurer, self insurer, or purported insurer, or purported self insurer, or any agent thereof:

1. any written statement as part of, or in support of, an application for the issuance of, or the rating of a commercial insurance policy, or certificate or evidence of self insurance for commercial insurance or commercial self insurance, or a claim for payment or other benefit pursuant to an insurance policy or self insurance program for commercial or personal insurance that he or she knows to:

(a) contain materially false information concerning any fact material thereto; or

(b) conceal, for the purpose of misleading, information concerning any fact material thereto; or

2. any written statement or other physical evidence as part of, or in support of, an application for the issuance of a health insurance policy, or a policy or contract or other authorization that provides or allows coverage for, membership or enrollment in, or other services of a public or private health plan, or a claim for payment, services or other benefit pursuant to such policy, contract or plan that he or she knows to:

(a) contain materially false information concerning any material fact thereto; or

(b) conceal, for the purpose of misleading, information concerning any fact material thereto.

Such policy or contract or plan or authorization shall include, but not be limited to, those issued or operating pursuant to any public or governmentally-sponsored or supported plan for health care coverage or services or those otherwise issued or operated by entities authorized pursuant to the public health law. For purposes of this subdivision an "application for the issuance of a health insurance policy" shall not include (i) any application for a health insurance policy or contract approved by the superintendent of financial services pursuant to the provisions of sections three thousand two hundred sixteen, four thousand three hundred four, four thousand three hundred twenty-one or four thousand three hundred twenty-two of the insurance law or any other application for a health insurance policy or contract approved by the superintendent of financial services in the individual or direct payment market; or (ii) any application for a certificate evidencing coverage under a self-insured plan or under a group contract approved by the superintendent of financial services.

§176.10 Insurance fraud in the fifth degree.

A person is guilty of insurance fraud in the fifth degree when he commits a fraudulent insurance act.

Insurance fraud in the fifth degree is a class A misdemeanor.

§176.15 Insurance fraud in the fourth degree.

A person is guilty of insurance fraud in the fourth degree when he commits a fraudulent insurance act and thereby wrongfully takes, obtains or withholds, or attempts to wrongfully take, obtain or withhold property with a value in excess of one thousand dollars.

Insurance fraud in the fourth degree is a class E felony.

§176.20 Insurance fraud in the third degree.

A person is guilty of insurance fraud in the third degree when he commits a fraudulent insurance act and thereby wrongfully takes, obtains or withholds, or attempts to wrongfully take, obtain or withhold property with a value in excess of three thousand dollars.

Insurance fraud in the third degree is a class D felony.

§176.25 Insurance fraud in the second degree.

A person is guilty of insurance fraud in the second degree when he commits a fraudulent insurance act and thereby wrongfully takes, obtains or withholds, or attempts to wrongfully take, obtain or withhold property with a value in excess of fifty thousand dollars.

Insurance fraud in the second degree is a class C felony.

§176.30 Insurance fraud in the first degree.

A person is guilty of insurance fraud in the first degree when he commits a fraudulent insurance act and thereby wrongfully takes, obtains or withholds, or attempts to wrongfully take, obtain or withhold property with a value in excess of one million dollars.

Insurance fraud in the first degree is a class B felony.

§176.35 Aggravated insurance fraud.

A person is guilty of aggravated insurance fraud in the fourth degree when he commits a fraudulent insurance act, and has been previously convicted within the preceding five years of any offense, an essential element of which is the commission of a fraudulent insurance act.

Aggravated insurance fraud in the fourth degree is a class D felony.

§176.40 Fraudulent life settlement act; defined.

A fraudulent life settlement act is committed by any person who, knowingly and with intent to defraud, presents, causes to be presented, or prepares with knowledge or belief that it will be presented to, or by, a life settlement provider, life settlement broker, life settlement intermediary, or any agent thereof, or to any owner any written statement or other physical evidence as part of, or in support of, an application for a life settlement contract, a claim for payment or other benefit under a life settlement contract, which the person knows to:

(1) contain materially false information concerning any material fact thereto; or

(2) conceal, for the purpose of misleading, information concerning any fact material thereto.

§176.45 Life settlement fraud in the fifth degree.
A person is guilty of life settlement fraud in the fifth degree when he or she commits a fraudulent life settlement act.
Life settlement fraud in the fifth degree is a class A misdemeanor.

§176.50 Life settlement fraud in the fourth degree.
A person is guilty of life settlement fraud in the fourth degree when he or she commits a fraudulent life settlement act and thereby wrongfully takes, obtains or withholds, or attempts to wrongfully take, obtain or withhold property with a value in excess of twenty-five thousand dollars.
Life settlement fraud in the fourth degree is a class E felony.

§176.55 Life settlement fraud in the third degree.
A person is guilty of life settlement fraud in the third degree when he or she commits a fraudulent life settlement act and thereby wrongfully takes, obtains or withholds, or attempts to wrongfully take, obtain or withhold property with a value in excess of fifty thousand dollars.
Life settlement fraud in the third degree is a class D felony.

§176.60 Life settlement fraud in the second degree.
A person is guilty of life settlement fraud in the second degree when he or she commits a fraudulent life settlement act and thereby wrongfully takes, obtains or withholds, or attempts to wrongfully take, obtain or withhold property with a value in excess of one hundred thousand dollars.
Life settlement fraud in the second degree is a class C felony.

§176.65 Life settlement fraud in the first degree.
A person is guilty of life settlement fraud in the first degree when he or she commits a fraudulent life settlement act and thereby wrongfully takes, obtains or withholds, or attempts to wrongfully take, obtain or withhold property with a value in excess of one million dollars.
Life settlement fraud in the first degree is a class B felony.

§176.70 Aggravated life settlement fraud.
A person is guilty of aggravated life settlement fraud when he or she commits a fraudulent life settlement act, and has been previously convicted within the preceding five years of any offense, an essential element of which is the commission of a fraudulent life settlement act.
Aggravated life settlement fraud is a class D felony.

§176.75 Staging a motor vehicle accident in the second degree.
A person is guilty of staging a motor vehicle accident in the second degree when, with intent to commit and in furtherance of a fraudulent insurance act, he or she operates a motor vehicle and intentionally causes a collision involving a motor vehicle.
Staging a motor vehicle accident in the second degree is a class E felony.
(Eff.11/1/19,Ch.151,L.2019)

§176.80 Staging a motor vehicle accident in the first degree.
A person is guilty of staging a motor vehicle accident in the first degree when he or she commits the offense of staging a motor vehicle accident in the second degree and thereby causes serious physical injury or death to another person, other than a participant in such offense.
Staging a motor vehicle accident in the first degree is a class D felony.
(Eff.11/1/19,Ch.151,L.2019)

ARTICLE 177 - HEALTH CARE FRAUD

Section
177.00 Definitions.
177.05 Health care fraud in the fifth degree.
177.10 Health care fraud in the fourth degree.
177.15 Health care fraud in the third degree.
177.20 Health care fraud in the second degree.
177.25 Health care fraud in the first degree.
177.30 Health care fraud; affirmative defense.

§177.00 Definitions.

The following definitions are applicable to this article:

1. "Health plan" means any publicly or privately funded health insurance or managed care plan or contract, under which any health care item or service is provided, and through which payment may be made to the person who provided the health care item or service. The state's medical assistance program (Medicaid) shall be considered a single health plan. For purposes of this article, a payment made pursuant to the state's managed care program as defined in paragraph (c) of subdivision one of section three hundred sixty-four-j of the social services law shall be deemed a payment by the state's medical assistance program (Medicaid).

2. "Person" means any individual or entity, other than a recipient of a health care item or service under a health plan unless such recipient acts as an accessory to such an individual or entity.

§177.05 Health care fraud in the fifth degree.

A person is guilty of health care fraud in the fifth degree when, with intent to defraud a health plan, he or she knowingly and willfully provides materially false information or omits material information for the purpose of requesting payment from a health plan for a health care item or service and, as a result of such information or omission, he or she or another person receives payment in an amount that he, she or such other person is not entitled to under the circumstances.

Health care fraud in the fifth degree is a class A misdemeanor.

§177.10 Health care fraud in the fourth degree.

A person is guilty of health care fraud in the fourth degree when such person, on one or more occasions, commits the crime of health care fraud in the fifth degree and the payment or portion of the payment wrongfully received, as the case may be, from a single health plan, in a period of not more than one year, exceeds three thousand dollars in the aggregate.

Health care fraud in the fourth degree is a class E felony.

§177.15 Health care fraud in the third degree.

A person is guilty of health care fraud in the third degree when such person, on one or more occasions, commits the crime of health care fraud in the fifth degree and the payment or portion of the payment wrongfully received, as the case may be, from a single health plan, in a period of not more than one year, exceeds ten thousand dollars in the aggregate.

Health care fraud in the third degree is a class D felony.

§177.20 Health care fraud in the second degree.

A person is guilty of health care fraud in the second degree when such person, on one or more occasions, commits the crime of health care fraud in the fifth degree and the payment or portion of the payment wrongfully received, as the case may be, from a single health plan, in a period of not more than one year, exceeds fifty thousand dollars in the aggregate.

Health care fraud in the second degree is a class C felony.

§177.25 Health care fraud in the first degree.

A person is guilty of health care fraud in the first degree when such person, on one or more occasions, commits the crime of health care fraud in the fifth degree and the payment or portion of the payment wrongfully received, as the case may be, from a single health plan, in a period of not more than one year, exceeds one million dollars in the aggregate.

Health care fraud in the first degree is a class B felony.

§177.30 Health care fraud; affirmative defense.

In any prosecution under this article, it shall be an affirmative defense that the defendant was a clerk, bookkeeper or other employee, other than an employee charged with the active management and control, in an executive capacity, of the affairs of the corporation, who, without personal benefit, merely executed the orders of his or her employer or of a superior employee generally authorized to direct his or her activities.

ARTICLE 178 - CRIMINAL DIVERSION OF PRESCRIPTION MEDICATIONS AND PRESCRIPTIONS

Section
178.00 Criminal diversion of prescription medications and prescriptions; definitions.
178.05 Criminal diversion of prescription medications and prescriptions; limitation.
178.10 Criminal diversion of prescription medications and prescriptions in the fourth degree.
178.15 Criminal diversion of prescription medications and prescriptions in the third degree.
178.20 Criminal diversion of prescription medications and prescriptions in the second degree.
178.25 Criminal diversion of prescription medications and prescriptions in the first degree.
178.26 Fraud and deceit related to controlled substances.

§178.00 Criminal diversion of prescription medications and prescriptions; definitions.

The following definitions are applicable to this article:

1. "Prescription medication or device" means any article for which a prescription is required in order to be lawfully sold, delivered or distributed by any person authorized by law to engage in the practice of the profession of pharmacy.

2. "Prescription" means a direction or authorization by means of a written prescription form or an oral prescription which permits a person to lawfully obtain a prescription medication or device from any person authorized to dispense such prescription medication or device.

3. "Criminal diversion act" means an act or acts in which a person knowingly:

(a) transfers or delivers, in exchange for anything of pecuniary value, a prescription medication or device with knowledge or reasonable grounds to know that the recipient has no medical need for it; or

(b) receives, in exchange for anything of pecuniary value, a prescription medication or device with knowledge or reasonable grounds to know that the seller or transferor is not authorized by law to sell or transfer such prescription medication or device; or

(c) transfers or delivers a prescription in exchange for anything of pecuniary value; or

(d) receives a prescription in exchange for anything of pecuniary value.

§178.05 Criminal diversion of prescription medications and prescriptions; limitation.

1. The provisions of this article shall not apply to:

(a) a duly licensed physician or other person authorized to issue a prescription acting in good faith in the lawful course of his or her profession; or

(b) a duly licensed pharmacist acting in good faith in the lawful course of the practice of pharmacy; or

(c) a person acting in good faith seeking treatment for a medical condition or assisting another person to obtain treatment for a medical condition.

2. No provision of this article relating to the sale of a prescription medication or device shall be deemed to authorize any act prohibited by article thirty-three of the public health law or article two hundred twenty of this chapter.

§178.10 Criminal diversion of prescription medications and prescriptions in the fourth degree.

A person is guilty of criminal diversion of prescription medications and prescriptions in the fourth degree when he or she commits a criminal diversion act.

Criminal diversion of prescription medications and prescriptions in the fourth degree is a class A misdemeanor.

§178.15 Criminal diversion of prescription medications and prescriptions in the third degree.

A person is guilty of criminal diversion of prescription medications and prescriptions in the third degree when he or she:

1. commits a criminal diversion act, and the value of the benefit exchanged is in excess of one thousand dollars; or

2. commits the crime of criminal diversion of prescription medications and prescriptions in the fourth degree, and has previously been convicted of the crime of criminal diversion of prescription medications and prescriptions in the fourth degree.

Criminal diversion of prescription medications and prescriptions in the third degree is a class E felony.

§178.20 Criminal diversion of prescription medications and prescriptions in the second degree.

A person is guilty of criminal diversion of prescription medications and prescriptions in the second degree when he or she commits a criminal diversion act, and the value of the benefit exchanged is in excess of three thousand dollars.

Criminal diversion of prescription medications and prescriptions in the second degree is a class D felony.

§178.25 Criminal diversion of prescription medications and prescriptions in the first degree.

A person is guilty of criminal diversion of prescription medications and prescriptions in the first degree when he or she commits a criminal diversion act, and the value of the benefit exchanged is in excess of fifty thousand dollars.

Criminal diversion of prescription medications and prescriptions in the first degree is a class C felony.

§178.26 Fraud and deceit related to controlled substances.

1. No person shall willfully:
(a) obtain or attempt to obtain a controlled substance, a prescription for a controlled substance or an official New York state prescription form,
(i) by fraud, deceit, misrepresentation or subterfuge; or
(ii) by the concealment of a material fact; or
(iii) by the use of a false name or the giving of a false address;
(b) make a false statement in any prescription, order, application, report or record required by article thirty-three of the public health law;
(c) falsely assume the title of, or represent himself or herself to be a licensed manufacturer, distributor, pharmacy, pharmacist, practitioner, researcher, approved institutional dispenser, owner or employee of a registered outsourcing facility or other authorized person, for the purpose of obtaining a controlled substance as these terms are defined in article thirty-three of the public health law;
(d) make or utter any false or forged prescription or false or forged written order;
(e) affix any false or forged label to a package or receptacle containing controlled substances; or
(f) imprint on or affix to any controlled substance a false or forged code number or symbol.
2. Possession of a false or forged prescription for a controlled substance by any person other than a pharmacist in the lawful pursuance of his or her profession shall be presumptive evidence of his or

her intent to use the same for the purpose of illegally obtaining a controlled substance.

3. Possession of a blank official New York state prescription form by any person to whom it was not lawfully issued shall be presumptive evidence of such person's intent to use same for the purpose of illegally obtaining a controlled substance.

4. Any person who, in the course of treatment, is supplied with a controlled substance or a prescription therefor by one practitioner and who with the intent to deceive, intentionally withholds or intentionally fails to disclose the fact, is supplied during such treatment with a controlled substance or a prescription therefor by another practitioner shall be guilty of a violation of this article.

5. The provisions of subdivision one of section thirty-three hundred ninety-six of the public health law shall apply to this section.

Fraud and deceit related to controlled substances is a class A misdemeanor.

ARTICLE 179 - CRIMINAL DIVERSION OF MEDICAL MARIHUANA

(Repealed 7/5/28,Ch,92,L.2021)

Section
179.00 Criminal diversion of medical cannabis; definitions.
179.05 Criminal diversion of medical cannabis; limitations.
179.10 Criminal diversion of medical cannabis in the first degree.
179.11 Criminal diversion of medical cannabis in the second degree.
179.15 Criminal retention of medical cannabis.

§179.00 Criminal diversion of medical cannabis; definitions.

The following definitions are applicable to this article:

1. "Medical cannabis" means medical cannabis as defined in section three of the cannabis law.

2. "Certification" means a certification, made under section thirty of the cannabis law. *(Eff.3/31/21,Ch.92,L.2021)*

§179.05 Criminal diversion of medical cannabis; limitations.

The provisions of this article shall not apply to:

1. a practitioner authorized to issue a certification who acted in good faith in the lawful course of his or her profession; or

2. a registered organization as that term is defined in section thirty-four of the cannabis law who acted in good faith in the lawful course of the practice of pharmacy; or

3. a person who acted in good faith seeking treatment for a medical condition or assisting another person to obtain treatment for a medical condition. *(Eff.3/31/21,Ch.92,L.2021)*

§179.10 Criminal diversion of medical cannabis in the first degree.

A person is guilty of criminal diversion of medical cannabis in the first degree when he or she is a practitioner, as that term is defined in section three of the cannabis law, who issues a certification with knowledge of reasonable grounds to know that (i) the recipient has no medical need for it, or (ii) it is for a purpose other than to treat a condition as defined in section three of the cannabis law.

Criminal diversion of medical cannabis in the first degree is a class E felony.

(Eff.3/31/21,Ch.92,L.2021)

§179.11 Criminal diversion of medical cannabis in the second degree.

A person is guilty of criminal diversion of medical cannabis in the second degree when he or she sells, trades, delivers, or otherwise provides medical cannabis to another with knowledge or reasonable grounds to know that the recipient is not registered under article three of the cannabis law.

Criminal diversion of medical cannabis in the second degree is a class B misdemeanor.   *(Eff.3/31/21,Ch.92,L.2021)*

§179.15 Criminal retention of medical cannabis.

A person is guilty of criminal retention of medical cannabis when, being a certified patient or designated caregiver, as those terms are defined in section three of the cannabis law, he or she knowingly obtains, possesses, stores or maintains an amount of cannabis in excess of the amount he or she is authorized to possess under the provisions of article three of the cannabis law.

Criminal retention of medical cannabis shall be punishable as provided in section 222.25 of this chapter.   *(Eff.3/31/21,Ch.92,L.2021)*

ARTICLE 180 - BRIBERY NOT INVOLVING PUBLIC SERVANTS, AND RELATED OFFENSES

Section
180.00 Commercial bribing in the second degree.
180.03 Commercial bribing in the first degree.
180.05 Commercial bribe receiving in the second degree.
180.08 Commercial bribe receiving in the first degree.
180.10 Bribery of labor official; definition of term.
180.15 Bribing a labor official.
180.20 Bribing a labor official; defense.
180.25 Bribe receiving by a labor official.
180.30 Bribe receiving by a labor official; no defense.
180.35 Sports bribery and tampering; definitions of terms.
180.40 Sports bribing.
180.45 Sports bribe receiving.
180.50 Tampering with a sports contest in the second degree.
180.51 Tampering with a sports contest in the first degree.
180.52 Impairing the integrity of a pari-mutuel betting system in the second degree.
180.53 Impairing the integrity of a pari-mutuel betting system in the first degree.
180.54 Rent gouging; definition of term.
180.55 Rent gouging in the third degree.
180.56 Rent gouging in the second degree.
180.57 Rent gouging in the first degree.

§180.00 Commercial bribing in the second degree.

A person is guilty of commercial bribing in the second degree when he confers, or offers or agrees to confer, any benefit upon any employee, agent or fiduciary without the consent of the latter's employer or principal, with intent to influence his conduct in relation to his employer's or principal's affairs.

Commercial bribing in the second degree is a class A misdemeanor.

§180.03 Commercial bribing in the first degree.

A person is guilty of commercial bribing in the first degree when he confers, or offers or agrees to confer, any benefit upon any employee, agent or fiduciary without the consent of the latter's employer or principal, with intent to influence his conduct in relation to his employer's or principal's affairs, and when the value of the benefit conferred or offered or agreed to be conferred exceeds one thousand dollars and causes economic harm to the employer or principal in an amount exceeding two hundred fifty dollars.

Commercial bribing in the first degree is a class E felony.

§180.05 Commercial bribe receiving in the second degree.

An employee, agent or fiduciary is guilty of commercial bribe receiving in the second degree when, without the consent of his employer or principal, he solicits, accepts or agrees to accept any benefit from another person upon an agreement or understanding that such benefit will influence his conduct in relation to his employer's or principal's affairs.

Commercial bribe receiving in the second degree is a class A misdemeanor.

§180.08 Commercial bribe receiving in the first degree.

An employee, agent or fiduciary is guilty of commercial bribe receiving in the first degree when, without the consent of his employer or principal, he solicits, accepts or agrees to accept any benefit from another person upon an agreement or understanding that such benefit will influence his conduct in relation to his employer or principal's affairs, and when the value of the benefit solicited, accepted or agreed to be accepted exceeds one thousand dollars and causes economic harm to the employer or principal in an amount exceeding two hundred fifty dollars.

Commercial bribe receiving in the first degree is a class E felony.

§180.10 Bribery of labor official; definition of term.

As used in this article, "labor official" means any duly appointed representative of a labor organization or any duly appointed trustee or representative of an employee welfare trust fund.

§180.15 Bribing a labor official.

A person is guilty of bribing a labor official when, with intent to influence a labor official in respect to any of his acts, decisions or duties as such labor official, he confers, or offers or agrees to confer, any benefit upon him.

Bribing a labor official is a class D felony.

§180.20 Bribing a labor official; defense.

In any prosecution for bribing a labor official, it is a defense that the defendant conferred or agreed to confer the benefit involved upon the labor official as a result of conduct of the latter constituting larceny committed by means of extortion, or an attempt to commit the same, or coercion, or an attempt to commit coercion.

§180.25 Bribe receiving by a labor official.

A labor official is guilty of bribe receiving by a labor official when he solicits, accepts or agrees to accept any benefit from another person upon an agreement or understanding that such benefit will influence him in respect to any of his acts, decisions, or duties as such labor official.

Bribe receiving by a labor official is a class D felony.

§180.30 Bribe receiving by a labor official; no defense.

The crimes of (a) bribe receiving by a labor official, and (b) larceny committed by means of extortion, attempt to commit the same, coercion or attempt to commit coercion, are not mutually exclusive, and it is no defense to a prosecution for bribe receiving by a labor official that, by reason of the same conduct, the defendant also committed one of such other specified crimes.

§180.35 Sports bribery and tampering; definitions of terms.

As used in this article:

1. "Sports contest" means any professional or amateur sport or athletic game or contest viewed by the public.

2. "Sports participant" means any person who participates or expects to participate in a sports contest as a player, contestant or member of a team, or as a coach, manager, trainer or other person directly associated with a player, contestant or team.

3. "Sports official" means any person who acts or expects to act in a sports contest as an umpire, referee, judge or otherwise to officiate at a sports contest.

4. "Pari-mutuel betting" is such betting as is authorized under the provisions of the pari-mutuel revenue law as set forth in chapter 254 of the laws of 1940 with amendments.

5. "Pari-mutuel horse race" means any horse race upon which betting is conducted under the provisions of the pari-mutuel revenue law as set forth in chapter 254 of the laws of 1940.

§180.40 Sports bribing.

A person is guilty of sports bribing when he:

1. Confers, or offers or agrees to confer, any benefit upon a sports participant with intent to influence him not to give his best efforts in a sports contest; or

2. Confers, or offers or agrees to confer, any benefit upon a sports official with intent to influence him to perform his duties improperly.

Sports bribing is a class D felony.

§180.45 Sports bribe receiving.

A person is guilty of sports bribe receiving when:

1. Being a sports participant, he solicits, accepts or agrees to accept any benefit from another person upon an agreement or understanding that he will thereby be influenced not to give his best efforts in a sports contest; or

2. Being a sports official, he solicits, accepts or agrees to accept any benefit from another person upon an agreement or understanding that he will perform his duties improperly.

Sports bribe receiving is a class E felony.

§180.50 Tampering with a sports contest in the second degree.

A person is guilty of tampering with a sports contest when, with intent to influence the outcome of a sports contest, he tampers with any sports participant, sports official or with any animal or equipment or other thing involved in the conduct or operation of a sports contest in a manner contrary to the rules and usages purporting to govern such a contest.

Tampering with a sports contest in the second degree is class A misdemeanor.

§180.51 Tampering with a sports contest in the first degree.

A person is guilty of tampering with a sports contest in the first degree when, with intent to influence the outcome of a parimutuel horse race:

1. He affects any equine animal involved in the conduct or operation of a pari-mutuel horse race by administering to the animal in any manner whatsoever any controlled substance listed in section thirty-three hundred six of the public health law; or

2. He knowingly enters or furnishes to another person for entry or brings into this state for entry into a pari-mutuel horse race, or rides or drives in any pari-mutuel horse race any running, trotting or pacing horse, mare, gelding, colt or filly under an assumed name, or deceptively out of its proper class, or that has been painted or disguised or represented to be any other or different horse, mare, gelding, colt or filly from that which it actually is; or

3. He knowingly and falsely registers with the jockey club, United States trotting association, American quarterhorse association or national steeplechase and hunt association a horse, mare, gelding, colt or filly previously registered under a different name; or

4. He agrees with one or more persons to enter such misrepresented or drugged animal in a pari-mutuel horse race. A person shall not be convicted of a violation of this subdivision unless an overt act is alleged and proved to have been committed by one of said persons in furtherance of said agreement.

Tampering with a sports contest in the first degree is a class E felony.

§180.52 Impairing the integrity of a pari-mutuel betting system in the second degree.

A person is guilty of impairing the integrity of a pari-mutuel betting system in the second degree when, with the intent to obtain either any payment for himself or for a third person or with the intent to defraud any person he:

1. Alters, changes or interferes with any equipment or device used in connection with pari-mutuel betting; or

2. Causes any false, inaccurate, delayed or unauthorized data, impulse or signal to be fed into, or transmitted over, or registered in or displayed upon any equipment or device used in connection with pari-mutuel betting.

Impairing the integrity of a pari-mutuel betting system in the second degree is a class E felony.

§180.53 Impairing the integrity of a pari-mutuel betting system in the first degree.

A person is guilty of impairing the integrity of a pari-mutuel betting system in the first degree when, with the intent to obtain either any payment for himself or for a third person or with the intent to defraud any person, and when the value of the payment exceeds one thousand five hundred dollars he:

1. Alters, changes or interferes with any equipment or device used in connection with pari-mutuel betting; or

2. Causes any false, inaccurate, delayed or unauthorized data, impulse or signal to be fed into, or transmitted over, or registered in or displayed upon any equipment or device used in connection with pari-mutuel betting.

Impairing the integrity of a pari-mutuel system in the first degree is a class D felony.

§180.54 Rent gouging; definition of term.

As used in this article, "lawful rental and other lawful charges" means registered, reported or contracted for rent pursuant to chapter four hundred three of the laws of nineteen hundred eighty-three, article two of the private housing finance law or section eight of the federal housing act of nineteen hundred sixty-eight, or, rent contained in a court approved stipulation of settlement, even if such rent or charges are subsequently decreased by order of the department of housing and community renewal or a court of competent jurisdiction.

§180.55 Rent gouging in the third degree.

A person is guilty of rent gouging in the third degree when, in connection with the leasing, rental or use of real property, he solicits, accepts or agrees to accept from a person some consideration of value, less than two hundred fifty dollars, in addition to lawful rental and other lawful charges, upon an agreement or understanding that the furnishing of such consideration will increase the possibility that any person may obtain or renew the lease, rental or use of such property, or that a failure to furnish it will decrease the possibility that any person may obtain or renew the same.

Rent gouging in the third degree is a class B misdemeanor.

§180.56 Rent gouging in the second degree.

A person is guilty of rent gouging in the second degree when, in connection with the leasing, rental or use of real property, he solicits, accepts or agrees to accept from a person some consideration of value, of two hundred fifty dollars or more, in addition to lawful rental and other lawful charges, upon an agreement or understanding that the furnishing of such consideration will increase the possibility that any person may obtain or renew the lease, rental or use of such property, or that a failure to furnish it will decrease the possibility that any person may obtain or renew the same.

Rent gouging in the second degree is a class A misdemeanor.

§180.57 Rent gouging in the first degree.

A person is guilty of rent gouging in the first degree when, in the course of a scheme constituting a systematic ongoing course of conduct in connection with the leasing, rental or use of three or more apartment units, the rental price of which is regulated pursuant to the provisions of federal, state or local law, he solicits, accepts or agrees to accept from one or more persons in three separate transactions some consideration of value, knowing that such consideration is in addition to lawful rental and other lawful charges established pursuant to the provisions of such federal, state or local law, and upon an agreement or understanding that the furnishing of such consideration will increase the possibility that any person may obtain or renew the lease, rental or use of such property, or that a failure to furnish it will decrease the possibility that any person may obtain or renew same, and thereby obtains such consideration from one or more persons.

Rent gouging in the first degree is a class E felony.

ARTICLE 185 - FRAUDS ON CREDITORS

Section
185.00 Fraud in insolvency.
185.05 Fraud involving a security interest.
185.10 Fraudulent disposition of mortgaged property.
185.15 Fraudulent disposition of property subject to a conditional sale contract.

§185.00 Fraud in insolvency.

1. As used in this section, "administrator" means an assignee or trustee for the benefit of creditors, a liquidator, a receiver or any other person entitled to administer property for the benefit of creditors.

2. A person is guilty of fraud in insolvency when, with intent to defraud any creditor and knowing that proceedings have been or are about to be instituted for the appointment of an administrator, or knowing that a composition agreement or other arrangement for the benefit of creditors has been or is about to be made, he

(a) conveys,transfers, removes, conceals, destroys, encumbers or otherwise disposes of any part of or any interest in the debtor's estate; or

(b) obtains any substantial part of or interest in the debtor's estate; or

(c) presents to any creditor or to the administrator any writing or record relating to the debtor's estate knowing the same to contain a false material statement; or

(d) misrepresents or fails or refuses to disclose to the administrator the existence, amount or location of any part of or any interest in the debtor's estate, or any other information which he is legally required to furnish to such administrator.

Fraud in insolvency is a class A misdemeanor.

§185.05 Fraud involving a security interest.

A person is guilty of fraud involving a security interest when, having executed a security agreement creating a security interest in personal property securing a monetary obligation owed to a secured party, and:

1. Having under the security agreement both the right of sale or other disposition of the property and the duty to account to the secured party for the proceeds of disposition, he sells or otherwise disposes of the property and wrongfully fails to account to the secured party for the proceeds of disposition; or

2. Having under the security agreement no right of sale or other disposition of the property, he knowingly secretes, withholds or disposes of such property in violation of the security agreement.

Fraud involving a security interest is a class A misdemeanor.

§185.10 Fraudulent disposition of mortgaged property.

A person is guilty of fraudulent disposition of mortgaged property when, having theretofore executed a mortgage of real or personal property or any instrument intended to operate as such, he sells, assigns, exchanges, secretes, injures, destroys or otherwise disposes of any part of the property, upon which the mortgage or other instrument is at the time a lien, with intent thereby to defraud the mortgagee or a purchaser thereof.

Fraudulent disposition of mortgaged property is a class A misdemeanor.

§185.15 Fraudulent disposition of property subject to a conditional sale contract.

A person is guilty of fraudulent disposition of property subject to a conditional sale contract when, prior to the performance of the condition of a conditional sale contract and being the buyer or any legal successor in interest of the buyer, he sells, assigns, mortgages, exchanges, secretes, injures, destroys or otherwise disposes of the goods subject to the conditional sale contract under claim of full ownership, with intent thereby to defraud another.

Fraudulent disposition of property subject to a conditional sale contract is a class A misdemeanor.

ARTICLE 187 - RESIDENTIAL MORTGAGE FRAUD
Section
187.00 Definitions.
187.01 Limitation on prosecution.
187.05 Residential mortgage fraud in the fifth degree.
187.10 Residential mortgage fraud in the fourth degree.
187.15 Residential mortgage fraud in the third degree.
187.20 Residential mortgage fraud in the second degree.
187.25 Residential mortgage fraud in the first degree.

§187.00 Definitions.
As used in this article:
1. "Person" means any individual or entity.
2. "Residential mortgage loan" means a loan or agreement to extend credit, including the renewal, refinancing or modification of any such loan, made to a person, which loan is primarily secured by either a mortgage, deed of trust, or other lien upon any interest in residential real property or any certificate of stock or other evidence of ownership in, and a proprietary lease from, a corporation or partnership formed for the purpose of cooperative ownership of residential real property.
3. "Residential real property" means real property improved by a one-to-four family dwelling, or a residential unit in a building including units owned as condominiums or on a cooperative basis, used or occupied, or intended to be used or occupied, wholly or partly, as the home or residence of one or more persons, but shall not refer to unimproved real property upon which such dwellings are to be constructed.
4. "Residential mortgage fraud" is committed by a person who, knowingly and with intent to defraud, presents, causes to be presented, or prepares with knowledge or belief that it will be used in soliciting an applicant for, applying for, underwriting or closing a residential mortgage loan, or filing with a county clerk of any county in the state arising out of and related to the closing of a residential mortgage loan, any written statement which:
(a) contains materially false information concerning any fact material thereto; or
(b) conceals, for the purpose of misleading, information concerning any fact material thereto.

§187.01 Limitation on prosecution.
No individual who applies for a residential mortgage loan and intends to occupy such residential property which such mortgage secures shall be held liable under this article provided, however, any such individual who acts as an accessory to an individual or entity in committing any crime defined in this article may be charged as an accessory to such crime.

§187.05 Residential mortgage fraud in the fifth degree.
A person is guilty of residential mortgage fraud in the fifth degree when he or she commits residential mortgage fraud.
Residential mortgage fraud in the fifth degree is a class A misdemeanor.

§187.10 Residential mortgage fraud in the fourth degree.
A person is guilty of residential mortgage fraud in the fourth degree when he or she commits residential mortgage fraud and thereby receives

proceeds or any other funds in the aggregate in excess of one thousand dollars.

Residential mortgage fraud in the fourth degree is a class E felony.

§187.15 Residential mortgage fraud in the third degree.

A person is guilty of residential mortgage fraud in the third degree when he or she commits residential mortgage fraud and thereby receives proceeds or any other funds in the aggregate in excess of three thousand dollars.

Residential mortgage fraud in the third degree is a class D felony.

§187.20 Residential mortgage fraud in the second degree.

A person is guilty of residential mortgage fraud in the second degree when he or she commits residential mortgage fraud and thereby receives proceeds or any other funds in the aggregate in excess of fifty thousand dollars.

Residential mortgage fraud in the second degree is a class C felony.

§187.25 Residential mortgage fraud in the first degree.

A person is guilty of residential mortgage fraud in the first degree when he or she commits residential mortgage fraud and thereby receives proceeds or any other funds in the aggregate in excess of one million dollars.

Residential mortgage fraud in the first degree is a class B felony.

ARTICLE 190 - OTHER FRAUDS

Section
190.00   Issuing a bad check; definitions of terms.
190.05   Issuing a bad check.
190.10   Issuing a bad check; presumptions.
190.15   Issuing a bad check; defenses.
190.20   False advertising.
190.23   False personation.
190.25   Criminal impersonation in the second degree.
190.26   Criminal impersonation in the first degree.
190.27   Criminal sale of a police uniform.
190.30   Unlawfully concealing a will.
190.35   Misconduct by corporate official.
190.40   Criminal usury in the second degree.
190.42   Criminal usury in the first degree.
190.45   Possession of usurious loan records.
190.50   Unlawful collection practices.
190.55   Making a false statement of credit terms.
190.60   Scheme to defraud in the second degree.
190.65   Scheme to defraud in the first degree.
190.70   Scheme to defraud the state by unlawfully selling prescriptions.
190.72   Unauthorized radio transmission.
190.75   Criminal use of an access device in the second degree.
190.76   Criminal use of an access device in the first degree.
190.77   Offenses involving theft of identity; definitions.
190.78   Identity theft in the third degree.
190.79   Identity theft in the second degree.
190.80   Identity theft in the first degree.
190.80-a Aggravated identity theft.
190.81   Unlawful possession of personal identification information in the third degree.
190.82   Unlawful possession of personal identification information in the second degree.
190.83   Unlawful possession of personal identification information in the first degree.
190.84   Defenses.
190.85   Unlawful possession of a skimmer device in the second degree.
190.86   Unlawful possession of a skimmer device in the first degree.
190.87   Immigrant assistant* services fraud in the second degree.
190.89   Immigrant assistance services fraud in the first degree.

§190.00 Issuing a bad check; definitions of terms.

The following definitions are applicable to this article:

1. "Check" means any check, draft or similar sight order for the payment of money which is not post-dated with respect to the time of utterance.

2. "Drawer" of a check means a person whose name appears thereon as the primary obligor, whether the actual signature be that of himself or of a person purportedly authorized to draw the check in his behalf.

3. "Representative drawer" means a person who signs a check as drawer in a representative capacity or as agent of the person whose name appears thereon as the principal drawer or obligor.

4. "Utter." A person "utters" a check when, as a drawer or representative drawer thereof, he delivers it or causes it to be delivered to a person who thereby acquires a right against the drawer with respect to such check. One who draws a check with intent that it be so delivered is deemed to have uttered it if the delivery occurs.

5. "Pass." A person "passes" a check when, being a payee, holder or bearer of a check which previously has been or purports to have been drawn and uttered by another, he delivers it, for a purpose other than collection, to a third person who thereby acquires a right with respect thereto.

6. "Funds" means money or credit.

(So in original, "assistant" should be "assistance".)

7. "Insufficient funds." A drawer has "insufficient funds" with a drawee to cover a check when he has no funds or account whatever, or funds in an amount less than that of the check; and a check dishonored for "no account" shall also be deemed to have been dishonored for "insufficient funds."

§190.05 Issuing a bad check.

A person is guilty of issuing a bad check when:

1. (a) As a drawer or representative drawer, he utters a check knowing that he or his principal, as the case may be, does not then have sufficient funds with the drawee to cover it, and (b) he intends or believes at the time of utterance that payment will be refused by the drawee upon presentation, and (c) payment is refused by the drawee upon presentation; or

2. (a) He passes a check knowing that the drawer thereof does not then have sufficient funds with the drawee to cover it, and (b) he intends or believes at the time the check is passed that payment will be refused by the drawee upon presentation, and (c) payment is refused by the drawee upon presentation.

Issuing a bad check is a class B misdemeanor.

§190.10 Issuing a bad check; presumptions.

1. When the drawer of a check has insufficient funds with the drawee to cover it at the time of utterance, the subscribing drawer or representative drawer, as the case may be, is presumed to know of such insufficiency.

2. A subscribing drawer or representative drawer, as the case may be, of an ultimately dishonored check is presumed to have intended or believed that the check would be dishonored upon presentation when:

(a) The drawer had no account with the drawee at the time of utterance; or

(b) (i) The drawer had insufficient funds with the drawee at the time of utterance, and (ii) the check was presented to the drawee for payment not more than thirty days after the date of utterance, and (iii) the drawer had insufficient funds with the drawee at the time of presentation.

3. Dishonor of a check by the drawee and insufficiency of the drawer's funds at the time of presentation may properly be proved by introduction in evidence of a notice of protest of the check, or of a certificate under oath of an authorized representative of the drawee declaring the dishonor and insufficiency, and such proof shall constitute presumptive evidence of such dishonor and insufficiency.

§190.15 Issuing a bad check; defenses.

In any prosecution for issuing a bad check, it is an affirmative defense that:

1. The defendant or a person acting in his behalf made full satisfaction of the amount of the check within ten days after dishonor by the drawee; or

2. The defendant, in acting as a representative drawer, did so as an employee who, without personal benefit, merely executed the orders of his employer or of a superior officer or employee generally authorized to direct his activities.

§190.20 False advertising.

A person is guilty of false advertising when, with intent to promote the sale or to increase the consumption of property or services, he makes or causes to be made a false or misleading statement in any advertisement or publishes any advertisement in violation of chapter three of the act of congress entitled "Truth in Lending Act" and the regulations thereunder, as such act and regulations may from time to time be amended, addressed to the public or to a substantial number of persons; except that, in any prosecution under this section, it is an affirmative defense that the allegedly false or misleading statement was not knowingly or recklessly made or caused to be made.

False advertising is a class A misdemeanor.

§190.23 False personation.

A person is guilty of false personation when after being informed of the consequences of such act, he or she knowingly misrepresents his or her actual name, date of birth or address to a police officer or peace officer with intent to prevent such police officer or peace officer from ascertaining such information.

False personation is a class B misdemeanor.

§190.25 Criminal impersonation in the second degree.

A person is guilty of criminal impersonation in the second degree when he:

1. Impersonates another and does an act in such assumed character with intent to obtain a benefit or to injure or defraud another; or

2. Pretends to be a representative of some person or organization and does an act in such pretended capacity with intent to obtain a benefit or to injure or defraud another; or

3. (a) Pretends to be a public servant, or wears or displays without authority any uniform, badge, insignia or facsimile thereof by which such public servant is lawfully distinguished, or falsely expresses by his words or actions that he is a public servant or is acting with approval or authority of a public agency or department; and (b) so acts with intent to induce another to submit to such pretended official authority, to solicit funds or to otherwise cause another to act in reliance upon that pretense; or

4. Impersonates another by communication by internet website or electronic means with intent to obtain a benefit or injure or defraud another, or by such communication pretends to be a public servant in order to induce another to submit to such authority or act in reliance on such pretense; or

5. Impersonates another person, without such other person's permission, by using the other person's electronic signature with intent to obtain a benefit or injure or defraud the other person or another person. For the purposes of this subdivision, electronic signature shall have the same meaning as set forth in subdivision three of section three hundred two of the state technology law. *(Eff.12/22/21,Ch.739,L.2021)*

Criminal impersonation in the second degree is a class A misdemeanor.

§190.26 Criminal impersonation in the first degree.

A person is guilty of criminal impersonation in the first degree when he:

1. Pretends to be a police officer or a federal law enforcement officer as enumerated in section 2.15 of the criminal procedure law, or wears or displays without authority, any uniform, badge or other insignia or facsimile thereof, by which such police officer or federal law enforcement officer is lawfully distinguished or expresses by his or her words or actions that he or she is acting with the approval or authority of any police department or acting as a federal law enforcement officer with the approval of any agency that employs federal law enforcement officers as enumerated in section 2.15 of the criminal procedure law; and

2. So acts with intent to induce another to submit to such pretended official authority or otherwise to act in reliance upon said pretense and in the course of such pretense commits or attempts to commit a felony; or

3. Pretending to be a duly licensed physician or other person authorized to issue a prescription for any drug or any instrument or device used in the taking or administering of drugs for which a prescription is required by law, communicates to a pharmacist an oral prescription which is required to be reduced to writing pursuant to section thirty-three hundred thirty-two of the public health law.

Criminal impersonation in the first degree is a class E felony.

§190.27 Criminal sale of a police uniform.

A person is guilty of criminal sale of a police uniform when he or she sells or offers for sale the uniform of any police officer to any person, unless presented with a valid photo identification card showing the purchaser to be a member of the police department which has authorized the requested uniform or an authorization to purchase specified uniforms signed by the police chief or the police commissioner of such police department accompanied by a personal photo identification. For purposes of this section, "police officer" shall include federal law enforcement officers, as defined in section 2.15 of the criminal procedure law; and "uniform" shall include all or any part of the uniform which identifies the wearer as a member of a police department, such as the uniform, shield, badge, numbers or other identifying insignias or emblems.

Criminal sale of a police uniform is a class A misdemeanor.

§190.30 Unlawfully concealing a will.

A person is guilty of unlawfully concealing a will when, with intent to defraud, he conceals, secretes, suppresses, mutilates or destroys a will, codicil or other testamentary instrument.

Unlawfully concealing a will is a class E felony.

§190.35 Misconduct by corporate official.

A person is guilty of misconduct by corporate official when:

1. Being a director of a stock corporation, he knowingly concurs in any vote or act of the directors of such corporation, or any of them, by which it is intended:

(a) To make a dividend except in the manner provided by law; or

(b) To divide, withdraw or in any manner pay to any stockholder any part of the capital stock of the corporation except in the manner provided by law; or

(c) To discount or receive any note or other evidence of debt in payment of an installment of capital stock actually called in and required to be paid, or with intent to provide the means of making such payment; or

(d) To receive or discount any note or other evidence of debt with intent to enable any stockholder to withdraw any part of the money paid in by him on his stock; or

(e) To apply any portion of the funds of such corporation, directly or indirectly, to the purchase of shares of its own stock, except in the manner provided by law; or

2. Being a director or officer of a stock corporation:

(a) He issues, participates in issuing, or concurs in a vote to issue any increase of its capital stock beyond the amount of the capital stock thereof, duly authorized by or in pursuance of law; or

(b) He sells, or agrees to sell, or is directly or indirectly interested in the sale of any share of stock of such corporation, or in any agreement to sell the same, unless at the time of such sale or agreement he is an actual owner of such share, provided that the foregoing shall not apply to a sale by or on behalf of an underwriter or dealer in connection with a bona fide public offering of shares of stock of such corporation.

Misconduct by corporation official is a class B misdemeanor.

§190.40 Criminal usury in the second degree.

A person is guilty of criminal usury in the second degree when, not being authorized or permitted by law to do so, he knowingly charges, takes or receives any money or other property as interest on the loan or forbearance of any money or other property, at a rate exceeding twenty-five per centum per annum or the equivalent rate for a longer or shorter period.

Criminal usury in the second degree is a class E felony.

§190.42 Criminal usury in the first degree.

A person is guilty of criminal usury in the first degree when, not being authorized or permitted by law to do so, he knowingly charges, takes or receives any money or other property as interest on the loan or forbearance of any money or other property, at a rate exceeding twenty-five per cent per annum or the equivalent rate for a longer or shorter period and either the actor had previously been convicted of the crime of criminal usury or of the attempt to commit such crime, or the actor's conduct was part of a scheme or business of making or collecting usurious loans.

Criminal usury in the first degree is a class C felony.

§190.45 Possession of usurious loan records.

A person is guilty of possession of usurious loan records when, with knowledge of the contents thereof, he possesses any writing, paper, instrument or article used to record criminally usurious transactions prohibited by section 190.40.

Possession of usurious loan records is a class A misdemeanor.

§190.50 Unlawful collection practices.

A person is guilty of unlawful collection practices when, with intent to enforce a claim or judgment for money or property, he knowingly sends, mails or delivers to another person a notice, document or other instrument which has no judicial or official sanction and which in its format or appearance, simulates a summons, complaint, court order or process, or an insignia, seal or printed form of a federal, state or local government or an instrumentality thereof, or is otherwise calculated to induce a belief that such notice, document or instrument has a judicial or official sanction.

Unlawful collection practices is a class B misdemeanor.

§190.55 Making a false statement of credit terms.

A person is guilty of making a false statement of credit terms when he knowingly and willfully violates the provisions of chapter two of the act of congress entitled "Truth in Lending Act" and the regulations thereunder, as such act and regulations may from time to time be amended, by understating or failing to state the interest rate required to be disclosed, or by failing to make or by making a false or inaccurate or incomplete statement of other credit terms in violation of such act.

Making a false statement of credit terms if a class A misdemeanor.

§190.60 Scheme to defraud in the second degree.

1. A person is guilty of a scheme to defraud in the second degree when he engages in a scheme constituting a systematic ongoing course of conduct with intent to defraud more than one person or to obtain property from more than one person by false or fraudulent pretenses, representations or promises, and so obtains property from one or more of such persons.

2. In any prosecution under this section, it shall be necessary to prove the identity of at least one person from whom the defendant so obtained property, but it shall not be necessary to prove the identity of any other intended victim.

Scheme to defraud in the second degree is a class A misdemeanor.

§190.65 Scheme to defraud in the first degree.

1. A person is guilty of a scheme to defraud in the first degree when he or she: (a) engages in a scheme constituting a systematic ongoing course of conduct with intent to defraud ten or more persons or to obtain property from ten or more persons by false or fraudulent pretenses, representations or promises, and so obtains property from one or more of such persons; or (b) engages in a scheme constituting a systematic ongoing course of conduct with intent to defraud more than one person or to obtain property from more than one person by false or fraudulent pretenses, representations or promises, and so obtains property with a value in excess of one thousand dollars from one or more such persons; or (c) engages in a scheme constituting a systematic ongoing course of conduct with intent to defraud more than one person, more than one of whom is a vulnerable elderly person as defined in subdivision three of section 260.31 of this chapter or to obtain property from more than one person, more than one of whom is a vulnerable elderly person as defined in subdivision three of section 260.31 of this chapter, by false or fraudulent pretenses, representations or promises, and so obtains property from one or more such persons; or (d) engages in a systematic ongoing course of conduct, with intent to defraud more than one person by false or fraudulent pretenses, representations or promises, by disposing of solid waste as defined in section 27-0701 of the environmental conservation law on such persons' property, and so

damages the property of one or more of such persons in an amount in excess of one thousand dollars.

2. In any prosecution under this section, it shall be necessary to prove the identity of at least one person from whom the defendant so obtained property, but it shall not be necessary to prove the identity of any other intended victim, provided that in any prosecution under paragraph (c) of subdivision one of this section, it shall be necessary to prove the identity of at least one such vulnerable elderly person as defined in subdivision three of section 260.31 of this chapter.

3. In any prosecution under paragraph (d) of subdivision one of this section, it shall be necessary to prove the identity of at least one person on whose property the defendant fraudulently disposed of solid waste pursuant to such paragraph (d), but it shall not be necessary to prove the identity of any other victim or intended victim.

Scheme to defraud in the first degree is a class E felony.

(Eff.1/1/21,Ch.332,L.2020)

§190.70 Scheme to defraud the state by unlawfully selling prescriptions.

A person is guilty of a scheme to defraud the state by unlawfully selling prescriptions when he or she engages, with intent to defraud the state, in a scheme constituting a systematic, ongoing course of conduct to make, sell, deliver for sale or offer for sale one or more prescriptions and so obtains goods or services from the state with a value in excess of one thousand dollars or causes the state to reimburse another in excess of one thousand dollars for the delivery of such goods or services.

Scheme to defraud the state by unlawfully selling prescriptions is a class A misdemeanor.

§190.72 Unauthorized radio transmission.

A person is guilty of an unauthorized radio transmission when such person knowingly makes or causes to be made a radio transmission in this state, on a radio frequency assigned and licensed by the federal communications commission for use by amplitude modulation (AM) radio stations between the frequencies of five hundred thirty kilohertz (kHz) to seventeen hundred kilohertz (kHz), or frequency modulation (FM) radio stations between the frequencies of eighty-eight megahertz (MHz) to one hundred eight megahertz (MHz), without authorization or having first obtained a license from the federal communications commission or duly authorized federal agency, in violation of federal law.

Unauthorized radio transmission is a class A misdemeanor.

§190.75 Criminal use of an access device in the second degree.

A person is guilty of criminal use of an access device in the second degree when he knowingly uses an access device without consent of an owner thereof with intent to unlawfully obtain telecommunications services on behalf of himself or a third person. As used in this section, access device shall have the meaning set forth in subdivision seven-c of section 155.00 of this chapter.

Criminal use of an access device in the second degree is a class A misdemeanor.

§190.76 Criminal use of an access device in the first degree.

A person is guilty of criminal use of an access device in the first degree when he knowingly uses an access device without consent of an owner thereof with intent to unlawfully obtain telecommunications services on behalf of himself or a third person, and so obtains such services with a value in excess of one thousand dollars. As used in this section, access device shall have the meaning set forth in subdivision seven-c of section 155.00 of this chapter.

Criminal use of an access device in the first degree is a class E felony.

§190.77 Offenses involving theft of identity; definitions.

1. For the purposes of sections 190.78, 190.79, 190.80 and 190.80-a and 190.85 of this article "personal identifying information" means a person's name, address, telephone number, date of birth, driver's license number, social security number, place of employment, mother's maiden name, financial services account number or code, savings account number or code, checking account number or code, brokerage account number or code, credit card account number or code, debit card number or code, automated teller machine number or code, taxpayer identification number, computer system password, signature or copy of a signature, electronic signature, unique biometric data that is a fingerprint, voice print, retinal image or iris image of another person, telephone calling card number, mobile identification number or code, electronic serial number or personal identification number, or any other name, number, code or information that may be used alone or in conjunction with other such information to assume the identity of another person.

2. For the purposes of sections 190.78, 190.79, 190.80, 190.80-a, 190.81, 190.82 and 190.83 of this article:

   a. "electronic signature" shall have the same meaning as defined in subdivision three of section three hundred two of the state technology law.

   b. "personal identification number" means any number or code which may be used alone or in conjunction with any other information to assume the identity of another person or access financial resources or credit of another person.

   c. "member of the armed forces" shall mean a person in the military service of the United States or the military service of the state, including but not limited to, the armed forces of the United States, the army national guard, the air national guard, the New York naval militia, the New York guard, and such additional forces as may be created by the federal or state government as authorized by law.

§190.78 Identity theft in the third degree.

A person is guilty of identity theft in the third degree when he or she knowingly and with intent to defraud assumes the identity of another person by presenting himself or herself as that other person, or by acting as that other person or by using personal identifying information of that other person, and thereby:

1. obtains goods, money, property or services or uses credit in the name of such other person or causes financial loss to such person or to another person or persons; or

2. commits a class A misdemeanor or higher level crime.
Identity theft in the third degree is a class A misdemeanor.

§190.79 Identity theft in the second degree.

A person is guilty of identify* theft in the second degree when he or she knowingly and with intent to defraud assumes the identity of another person by presenting himself or herself as that other person, or by acting as that other person or by using personal identifying information of that other person, and thereby:

1. obtains goods, money, property or services or uses credit in the name of such other person in an aggregate amount that exceeds five hundred dollars; or

2. causes financial loss to such person or to another person or persons in an aggregate amount that exceeds five hundred dollars; or

3. commits or attempts to commit a felony or acts as an accessory to the commission of a felony; or

4. commits the crime of identity theft in the third degree as defined in section 190.78 of this article and has been previously convicted within the last five years of identity theft in the third degree as defined in section 190.78, identity theft in the second degree as defined in this section, identity theft in the first degree as defined in section 190.80, unlawful possession of personal identification information in the third degree as defined in section 190.81, unlawful possession of personal identification information in the second degree as defined in section 190.82, unlawful possession of personal identification information in the first degree as defined in section 190.83, unlawful possession of a skimmer device in the second degree as defined in section 190.85, unlawful possession of a skimmer device in the first degree as defined in section 190.86, grand larceny in the fourth degree as defined in section 155.30, grand larceny in the third degree as defined in section 155.35, grand larceny in the second degree as defined in section 155.40 or grand larceny in the first degree as defined in section 155.42 of this chapter.

Identity theft in the second degree is a class E felony.

§190.80 Identity theft in the first degree.

A person is guilty of identity theft in the first degree when he or she knowingly and with intent to defraud assumes the identity of another person by presenting himself or herself as that other person, or by acting as that other person or by using personal identifying information of that other person, and thereby:

1. obtains goods, money, property or services or uses credit in the name of such other person in an aggregate amount that exceeds two thousand dollars; or

2. causes financial loss to such person or to another person or persons in an aggregate amount that exceeds two thousand dollars; or

(So in original, "identify" should be "identity".)

3. commits or attempts to commit a class D felony or higher level crime or acts as an accessory in the commission of a class D or higher level felony; or

4. commits the crime of identity theft in the second degree as defined in section 190.79 of this article and has been previously convicted within the last five years of identity theft in the third degree as defined in section 190.78, identity theft in the second degree as defined in section 190.79, identity theft in the first degree as defined in this section, unlawful possession of personal identification information in the third degree as defined in section 190.81, unlawful possession of personal identification information in the second degree as defined in section 190.82, unlawful possession of personal identification information in the first degree as defined in section 190.83, unlawful possession of a skimmer device in the second degree as defined in section 190.85, unlawful possession of a skimmer device in the first degree as defined in section 190.86, grand larceny in the fourth degree as defined in section 155.30, grand larceny in the third degree as defined in section 155.35, grand larceny in the second degree as defined in section 155.40 or grand larceny in the first degree as defined in section 155.42 of this chapter.

Identity theft in the first degree is a class D felony.

§190.80-a   Aggravated identity theft.

A person is guilty of aggravated identity theft when he or she knowingly and with intent to defraud assumes the identity of another person by presenting himself or herself as that other person, or by acting as that other person or by using personal identifying information of that other person, and knows that such person is a member of the armed forces, and knows that such member is presently deployed outside of the continental United States and:

1. thereby obtains goods, money, property or services or uses credit in the name of such member of the armed forces in an aggregate amount that exceeds five hundred dollars; or

2. thereby causes financial loss to such member of the armed forces in an aggregate amount that exceeds five hundred dollars.

Aggravated identity theft is a class D felony.

§190.81   Unlawful possession of personal identification information in the third degree.

A person is guilty of unlawful possession of personal identification information in the third degree when he or she knowingly possesses a person's financial services account number or code, savings account number or code, checking account number or code, brokerage account number or code, credit card account number or code, debit card number or code, automated teller machine number or code, personal identification number, mother's maiden name, computer system password, electronic signature or unique biometric data that is a fingerprint, voice print, retinal image or iris image of another person knowing such information is intended to be used in furtherance of the commission of a crime defined in this chapter.

Unlawful possession of personal identification information in the third degree is a class A misdemeanor.

§190.82 Unlawful possession of personal identification information in the second degree.

A person is guilty of unlawful possession of personal identification information in the second degree when he or she knowingly possesses two hundred fifty or more items of personal identification information of the following nature: a person's financial services account number or code, savings account number or code, checking account number or code, brokerage account number or code, credit card account number or code, debit card number or code, automated teller machine number or code, personal identification number, mother's maiden name, computer system password, electronic signature or unique biometric data that is a fingerprint, voice print, retinal image or iris image of another person knowing such information is intended to be used in furtherance of the commission of a crime defined in this chapter.

Unlawful possession of personal identification information in the second degree is a class E felony.

§190.83 Unlawful possession of personal identification information in the first degree.

A person is guilty of unlawful possession of personal identification information in the first degree when he or she commits the crime of unlawful possession of personal identification information in the second degree and:

1. with intent to further the commission of identity theft in the second degree, he or she supervises more than three accomplices; or

2. he or she has been previously convicted within the last five years of identity theft in the third degree as defined in section 190.78, identity theft in the second degree as defined in section 190.79, identity theft in the first degree as defined in section 190.80, unlawful possession of personal identification information in the third degree as defined in section 190.81, unlawful possession of personal identification information in the second degree as defined in section 190.82, unlawful possession of personal identification information in the first degree as defined in this section, unlawful possession of a skimmer device in the second degree as defined in section 190.85, unlawful possession of a skimmer device in the first degree as defined in section 190.86, grand larceny in the fourth degree as defined in section 155.30, grand larceny in the third degree as defined in section 155.35, grand larceny in the second degree as defined in section 155.40 or grand larceny in the first degree as defined in section 155.42 of this chapter; or

3. with intent to further the commission of identity theft in the second degree:

(a) he or she supervises more than two accomplices, and

(b) he or she knows that the person whose personal identification information that he or she possesses is a member of the armed forces, and

(c) he or she knows that such member of the armed forces is presently deployed outside of the continental United States.

Unlawful possession of personal identification information in the first degree is a class D felony.

§190.84 Defenses.

In any prosecution for identity theft or unlawful possession of personal identification information pursuant to this article, it shall be an affirmative defense that the person charged with the offense:

1. was under twenty-one years of age at the time of committing the offense and the person used or possessed the personal identifying or identification information of another solely for the purpose of purchasing alcohol;

2. was under eighteen years of age at the time of committing the offense and the person used or possessed the personal identifying or identification information of another solely for the purpose of purchasing tobacco products; or

3. used or possessed the personal identifying or identification information of another person solely for the purpose of misrepresenting the person's age to gain access to a place the access to which is restricted based on age.

§190.85 Unlawful possession of a skimmer device in the second degree.

1. A person is guilty of unlawful possession of a skimmer device in the second degree when he or she possesses a skimmer device with the intent that such device be used in furtherance of the commission of the crime of identity theft or unlawful possession of personal identification information as defined in this article.

2. For purposes of this article, "skimmer device" means a device designed or adapted to obtain personal identifying information from a credit card, debit card, public benefit card, access card or device, or other card or device that contains personal identifying information.

Unlawful possession of a skimmer device in the second degree is a class A misdemeanor.

§190.86 Unlawful possession of a skimmer device in the first degree.

A person is guilty of unlawful possession of a skimmer device in the first degree when he or she commits the crime of unlawful possession of a skimmer device in the second degree and he or she has been previously convicted within the last five years of identity theft in the third degree as defined in section 190.78, identity theft in the second degree as defined in section 190.79, identity theft in the first degree as defined in section 190.80, unlawful possession of personal identification information in the third degree as defined in section 190.81, unlawful possession of personal identification information in the second degree as defined in section 190.82, unlawful possession of personal identification information in the first degree as defined in section 190.83, unlawful possession of a skimmer device in the second degree as defined in section 190.85, unlawful possession of a skimmer device in the first degree as defined in this section, grand larceny in the fourth degree as defined in section 155.30, grand larceny in the third degree as defined in section 155.35, grand larceny in the second degree as defined in section 155.40 or grand larceny in the first degree as defined in section 155.42 of this chapter.

Unlawful possession of a skimmer device in the first degree is a class E felony.

§190.87 Immigrant assistant* services fraud in the second degree.

A person is guilty of immigrant assistance services fraud in the second degree when, with intent to defraud another person seeking immigrant assistance services, as defined in article twenty-eight-C of the general business law, from such person, he or she violates section four hundred sixty-d of the general business law with intent to obtain property from such other person by false or fraudulent pretenses, representations or promises, and thereby wrongfully obtains such property.

Immigrant assistance services fraud in the second degree is a class A misdemeanor.

§190.89 Immigrant assistance services fraud in the first degree.

A person is guilty of immigrant assistance services fraud in the first degree when, with intent to defraud another person seeking immigrant assistance services, as defined in article twenty-eight-C of the general business law, from such person, he or she violates section four hundred sixty-d of the general business law with intent to obtain property from such other person by false or fraudulent pretenses, representations or promises, and thereby wrongfully obtains such property with a value in excess of one thousand dollars.

Immigrant assistance services fraud in the first degree is a class E felony.

(So in original "assistant" should be "assistance".)

TITLE L - OFFENSES AGAINST PUBLIC ADMINISTRATION
ARTICLE 195 - OFFICIAL MISCONDUCT AND OBSTRUCTION OF PUBLIC SERVANTS GENERALLY

Section
195.00   Official misconduct.
195.02   Concealment of a human corpse.
195.05   Obstructing governmental administration in the second degree.
195.06   Killing or injuring a police animal.
195.06-a   Killing a police work dog or police work horse.
195.07   Obstructing governmental administration in the first degree.
195.08   Obstructing governmental administration by means of a self-defense spray device.
195.10   Refusing to aid a peace or a police officer.
195.11   Harming an animal trained to aid a person with a disability in the second degree.
195.12   Harming an animal trained to aid a person with a disability in the first degree.
195.15   Obstructing firefighting operations.
195.16   Obstructing emergency medical services.
195.17   Obstruction of governmental duties by means of a bomb, destructive device, explosive, or hazardous substance.
195.20   Defrauding the government.

§195.00 Official misconduct.

A public servant is guilty of official misconduct when, with intent to obtain a benefit or deprive another person of a benefit:

1. He commits an act relating to his office but constituting an unauthorized exercise of his official functions, knowing that such act is unauthorized; or

2. He knowingly refrains from performing a duty which is imposed upon him by law or is clearly inherent in the nature of his office.

Official misconduct is a class A misdemeanor.

§195.02 Concealment of a human corpse.

A person is guilty of concealment of a human corpse when, having a reasonable expectation that a human corpse or a part thereof will be produced for or used as physical evidence in: (a) an official proceeding; (b) an autopsy as part of a criminal investigation; or (c) an examination by law enforcement personnel as part of a criminal investigation; such person, alone or in concert with another, conceals, alters or destroys such corpse or part thereof with the intent to prevent its production, use or discovery.

Concealment of a human corpse is a class E felony.

§195.05 Obstructing governmental administration in the second degree.

A person is guilty of obstructing governmental administration when he intentionally obstructs, impairs or perverts the administration of law or other governmental function or prevents or attempts to prevent a public servant from performing an official function, by means of intimidation, physical force or interference, or by means of any independently unlawful act, or by means of interfering, whether or not physical force is involved, with radio, telephone, television or other telecommunications systems owned or operated by the state, or a county, city, town, village, fire district or emergency medical service or by means of releasing a dangerous animal under circumstances evincing the actor's intent that the animal obstruct governmental administration.

Obstructing governmental administration is a class A misdemeanor.

§195.06 Killing or injuring a police animal.

A person is guilty of killing or injuring a police animal when such person intentionally kills or injures any animal while such animal is in the performance of its duties and under the supervision of a police or peace officer.

Killing or injuring a police animal is a class A misdemeanor.

§195.06-a Killing a police work dog or police work horse.

A person is guilty of killing a police work dog or police work horse when such person intentionally kills a police work dog or police work horse while such dog or horse is in the performance of its duties and under the supervision of a police officer. For purposes of this section, "police work dog" or "police work horse," as the case may be, shall mean any dog or horse owned or harbored by any state or municipal police department or any state or federal law enforcement agency, which has been trained to aid law enforcement officers and is actually being used for police work purposes.

Killing a police work dog or police work horse is a class E felony.

§195.07 Obstructing governmental administration in the first degree.

A person is guilty of obstructing governmental administration in the first degree when he commits the crime of obstructing governmental administration in the second degree by means of interfering with a telecommunications system thereby causing serious physical injury to another person.

Obstructing governmental administration in the first degree is a class E felony.

§195.08 Obstructing governmental administration by means of a self-defense spray device.

A person is guilty of obstructing governmental administration by means of a self-defense spray device when, with the intent to prevent a police officer or peace officer from performing a lawful duty, he causes temporary physical impairment to a police officer or peace officer by intentionally discharging a self-defense spray device, as defined in paragraph fourteen of subdivision a of section 265.20 of this chapter, thereby causing such temporary physical impairment.

Obstructing governmental administration by means of a self-defense spray device is a class D felony.

§195.10 Refusing to aid a peace or a police officer.

A person is guilty of refusing to aid a peace or a police officer when, upon command by a peace or a police officer identifiable or identified to him as such he unreasonably fails or refuses to aid such peace or a police officer in effecting an arrest, or in preventing the commission by another person of any offense.

Refusing to aid a peace or a police officer is a class B misdemeanor.

This page intentionally left blank.

§195.11 Harming an animal trained to aid a person with a disability in the second degree.

A person is guilty of harming an animal trained to aid a person with a disability in the second degree when such person intentionally causes physical injury to such animal while it is in the performance of aiding a person with a disability, and thereby renders such animal incapable of providing such aid to such person, or to another person with a disability. For purposes of this section and section 195.12 of this article, the term "disability" means "disability" as defined in subdivision twenty-one of section two hundred ninety-two of the executive law.

Harming an animal trained to aid a person with a disability in the second degree is a class B misdemeanor.

§195.12 Harming an animal trained to aid a person with a disability in the first degree.

A person is guilty of harming an animal trained to aid a person with a disability in the first degree when such person:

1. intentionally causes physical injury to such animal while it is in the performance of aiding a person with a disability, and thereby renders such animal permanently incapable of providing such aid to such person, or to another person with a disability; or

2. intentionally kills such animal while it is in the performance of aiding a person with a disability.

Harming an animal trained to aid a person with a disability in the first degree is a class A misdemeanor.

§195.15 Obstructing firefighting operations.

A person is guilty of obstructing firefighting operations when he or she intentionally and unreasonably obstructs the efforts of any:

1. firefighter in extinguishing a fire, or prevents or dissuades another from extinguishing or helping to extinguish a fire;

2. firefighter, police officer or peace officer in performing his or her duties in circumstances involving an imminent danger created by an explosion, threat of explosion or the presence of toxic fumes or gases; or

3. firefighter performing emergency medical care on a sick or injured person. *(Eff.11/1/17,Ch.124,L.2017)*

Obstructing firefighting operations is a class A misdemeanor.

§195.16 Obstructing emergency medical services.

A person is guilty of obstructing emergency medical services when he or she intentionally and unreasonably obstructs the efforts of any service, technician, personnel, system or unit specified in section three thousand one of the public health law in the performance of their duties.

Obstructing emergency medical services is a class A misdemeanor.

§195.17 Obstruction of governmental duties by means of a bomb, destructive device, explosive, or hazardous substance.

A person is guilty of obstruction of governmental duties by means of a bomb, destructive device, explosive, or hazardous substance when he or she, in furtherance of a felony offense, knowingly and unlawfully installs or causes to be installed a bomb, destructive device, explosive, or hazardous substance, in any object, place, or compartment that is subject to a search so as to obstruct, prevent, hinder or delay the administration of law or performance of a government function.

Obstruction of governmental duties by means of a bomb, destructive device, explosive, or hazardous substance is a class D felony.

§195.20 Defrauding the government.

A person is guilty of defrauding the government when, being a public servant or party officer, he or she:

(a) engages in a scheme constituting a systematic ongoing course of conduct with intent to:

(i) defraud the state or a political subdivision of the state or a governmental instrumentality within the state or to obtain property, services or other resources from the state or a political subdivision of the state or a governmental instrumentality within the state by false or fraudulent pretenses, representations or promises; or

(ii) defraud the state or a political subdivision of the state or a governmental instrumentality within the state by making use of property, services or resources of the state, political subdivision of the state or a governmental instrumentality within the state for private business purposes or other compensated non-governmental purposes; and

(b) so obtains property, services or other resources with a value in excess of one thousand dollars from such state, political subdivision or governmental instrumentality.

Defrauding the government is a class E felony.

ARTICLE 200 - BRIBERY INVOLVING PUBLIC SERVANTS AND RELATED OFFENSES

Section
200.00   **Bribery in the third degree.**
200.03   **Bribery in the second degree.**
200.04   **Bribery in the first degree.**
200.05   **Bribery; defense.**
200.10   **Bribe receiving in the third degree.**
200.11   **Bribe receiving in the second degree.**
200.12   **Bribe receiving in the first degree.**
200.15   **Bribe receiving; no defense.**
200.20   **Rewarding official misconduct in the second degree.**
200.22   **Rewarding official misconduct in the first degree.**
200.25   **Receiving reward for official misconduct in the second degree.**
200.27   **Receiving reward for official misconduct in the first degree.**
200.30   **Giving unlawful gratuities.**
200.35   **Receiving unlawful gratuities.**
200.40   **Bribe giving and bribe receiving for public office; definition of term.**
200.45   **Bribe giving for public office.**
200.50   **Bribe receiving for public office.**
200.55   **Impairing the integrity of a government licensing examination.**
200.56   **Corrupt use of position or authority.**

§200.00 Bribery in the third degree.

A person is guilty of bribery in the third degree when he confers, or offers or agrees to confer, any benefit upon a public servant upon an agreement or understanding that such public servant's vote, opinion, judgment, action, decision or exercise of discretion as a public servant will thereby be influenced.

Bribery in the third degree is a class D felony.

§200.03 Bribery in the second degree.

A person is guilty of bribery in the second degree when he confers, or offers or agrees to confer, any benefit valued in excess of five thousand dollars upon a public servant upon an agreement or understanding that such public servant's vote, opinion, judgment, action, decision or exercise of discretion as a public servant will thereby be influenced.

Bribery in the second degree is a class C felony.

§200.04 Bribery in the first degree.

A person is guilty of bribery in the first degree when the person confers, or offers or agrees to confer: (1) any benefit upon a public servant upon an agreement or understanding that such public servant's vote, opinion, judgment, action, decision or exercise of discretion as a public servant will thereby be influenced in the investigation, arrest, detention, prosecution or incarceration of any person for the commission or alleged commission of a class A felony defined in article two hundred twenty of this part or an attempt to commit any such class A felony; or (2) any benefit valued in excess of one hundred thousand dollars upon a public servant upon an agreement or understanding that such public servant's vote, opinion, judgment, action, decision or exercise of discretion as a public servant will thereby be influenced.

Bribery in the first degree is a class B felony.

§200.05 Bribery; defense.

In any prosecution for bribery, it is a defense that the defendant conferred or agreed to confer the benefit involved upon the public servant involved as a result of conduct of the latter constituting larceny committed by means of extortion, or an attempt to commit the same, or coercion, or an attempt to commit coercion.

§200.10 Bribe receiving in the third degree.

A public servant is guilty of bribe receiving in the third degree when he or she solicits, accepts or agrees to accept any benefit from another person upon an agreement or understanding that his or her vote, opinion, judgment, action, decision or exercise of discretion as a public servant will thereby be influenced.

Bribe receiving in the third degree is a class D felony.

§200.11 Bribe receiving in the second degree.

A public servant is guilty of bribe receiving in the second degree when he or she solicits, accepts or agrees to accept any benefit valued in excess of five thousand dollars from another person upon an agreement or understanding that his or her vote, opinion, judgment, action, decision or exercise of discretion as a public servant will thereby be influenced.

Bribe receiving in the second degree is a class C felony.

§200.12 Bribe receiving in the first degree.

A public servant is guilty of bribe receiving in the first degree when he or she solicits, accepts or agrees to accept: (a) any benefit from another person upon an agreement or understanding that his or her vote, opinion, judgment, action, decision or exercise of discretion as a public servant will thereby be influenced in the investigation, arrest, detention, prosecution or incarceration of any person for the commission or alleged commission of a class A felony defined in article two hundred twenty of this part or an attempt to commit any such class A felony; or (b) any benefit valued in excess of one hundred thousand dollars from another person upon an agreement or understanding that such public servant's vote, opinion, judgment, action, decision or exercise of discretion as a public servant will thereby be influenced.

Bribe receiving in the first degree is a class B felony.

§200.15 Bribe receiving; no defense.

1. The crimes of (a) bribe receiving, and (b) larceny committed by means of extortion, attempt to commit the same, coercion and attempt to commit coercion, are not mutually exclusive, and it is no defense to a prosecution for bribe receiving that, by reason of the same conduct, the defendant also committed one of such other specified crimes.

2. It is no defense to a prosecution pursuant to the provisions of this article that the public servant did not have power or authority to perform the act or omission for which the alleged bribe, gratuity or reward was given.

§200.20 Rewarding official misconduct in the second degree.

A person is guilty of rewarding official misconduct in the second degree when he knowingly confers, or offers or agrees to confer, any benefit upon a public servant for having violated his duty as a public servant.

Rewarding official misconduct in the second degree is a class E felony.

§200.22 Rewarding official misconduct in the first degree.

A person is guilty of rewarding official misconduct in the first degree when he knowingly confers, or offers or agrees to confer, any benefit upon a public servant for having violated his duty as a public servant in the investigation, arrest, detention, prosecution, or incarceration of any person for the commission or alleged commission of a class A felony defined in article two hundred twenty of the penal law or the attempt to commit any such class A felony.

Rewarding official misconduct in the first degree is a class C felony.

§200.25 Receiving reward for official misconduct in the second degree.

A public servant is guilty of receiving reward for official misconduct in the second degree when he solicits, accepts or agrees to accept any benefit from another person for having violated his duty as a public servant.

Receiving reward for official misconduct in the second degree is a class E felony.

§200.27 Receiving reward for official misconduct in the first degree.

A public servant is guilty of receiving reward for official misconduct in the first degree when he solicits, accepts or agrees to accept any benefit from another person for having violated his duty as a public servant in the investigation, arrest, detention, prosecution, or incarceration of any person for the commission or alleged commission of a class A felony defined in article two hundred twenty of the penal law or the attempt to commit any such class A felony.

Receiving reward for official misconduct in the first degree is a class C felony.

§200.30 Giving unlawful gratuities.

A person is guilty of giving unlawful gratuities when he knowingly confers, or offers or agrees to confer, any benefit upon a public servant for having engaged in official conduct which he was required or authorized to perform, and for which he was not entitled to any special or additional compensation.

Giving unlawful gratuities is a class A misdemeanor.

§200.35 Receiving unlawful gratuities.

A public servant is guilty of receiving unlawful gratuities when he solicits, accepts or agrees to accept any benefit for having engaged in official conduct which he was required or authorized to perform, and for which he was not entitled to any special or additional compensation.

Receiving unlawful gratuities is a class A misdemeanor.

§200.40 Bribe giving and bribe receiving for public office; definition of term.

As used in sections 200.45 and 200.50, "party officer" means a person who holds any position or office in a political party, whether by election, appointment or otherwise.

§200.45 Bribe giving for public office.

A person is guilty of bribe giving for public office when he confers, or offers or agrees to confer, any money or other property upon a public servant or a party officer upon an agreement or understanding that some person will or may be appointed to a public office or designated or nominated as a candidate for public office.

Bribe giving for public office is a class D felony.

§200.50 Bribe receiving for public office.

A public servant or a party officer is guilty of bribe receiving for public office when he solicits, accepts or agrees to accept any money or other property from another person upon an agreement or understanding that some person will or may be appointed to a public office or designated or nominated as a candidate for public office.

Bribe receiving for public office is a class D felony.

§200.55 Impairing the integrity of a government licensing examination.

A person is guilty of impairing the integrity of a government licensing examination when, with intent to obtain a benefit for himself or herself, or for another person, he or she:

1. Wrongfully alters or changes an applicant's grade on a government licensing examination; or

2. Causes any false or inaccurate grade to be entered into a government licensing registry; or

3. Provides answers, with an intent to wrongfully benefit another, to current questions on a pending government licensing examination; or

4. Wrongfully provides a copy of a current test used to determine competence in a licensed profession, trade, craft or other vocation.

Impairing the integrity of a government licensing examination is a class D felony.

§200.56 Corrupt use of position or authority.

A person is guilty of corrupt use of position or authority if such person:

1. While holding public office, or being nominated or seeking a nomination therefor, corruptly uses or promises to use, directly, or indirectly, any official authority or influence possessed or anticipated, in the way of conferring upon any person, or in order to secure, or aid any person in securing, any office or public employment, or any nomination, confirmation, promotion or increase of salary, upon consideration that the vote or political influence or action of the person so to be benefited or of any other person, shall be given or used in behalf of any candidate, officer or party or upon any other corrupt condition or consideration; or

2. Being a public officer or employee of the state or a political subdivision having, or claiming to have, any authority or influence affecting the nomination, public employment, confirmation, promotion, removal or increase or decrease of salary of any public officer or employee, corruptly promises or threatens to use any such authority or influence, directly or indirectly to affect the vote or political action of any such public officer or employee, or on account of the vote or political action of such officer or employee; or

3. Corruptly makes, tenders or offers to procure, or cause any nomination or appointment for any public office or place, or accepts or requests any such nomination or appointment, upon the payment or contribution of any valuable consideration, or upon an understanding or promise thereof; or

4. Corruptly makes any gift, promise or contribution to any person, upon the condition or consideration of receiving an appointment or election to a public office or a position of public employment, or for receiving or retaining any such office or position, or promotion, privilege, increase of salary or compensation therein, or exemption from removal or discharge therefrom.

Corrupt use of position or authority is a class E felony.

ARTICLE 205 - ESCAPE AND OTHER OFFENSES RELATING TO CUSTODY

Section
205.00 Escape and other offenses relating to custody; definitions of terms.
205.05 Escape in the third degree.
205.10 Escape in the second degree.
205.15 Escape in the first degree.
205.16 Absconding from temporary release in the second degree.
205.17 Absconding from temporary release in the first degree.
205.18 Absconding from a furlough program.
205.19 Absconding from a community treatment facility.
205.20 Promoting prison contraband in the second degree.
205.25 Promoting prison contraband in the first degree.
205.30 Resisting arrest.
205.50 Hindering prosecution; definition of term.
205.55 Hindering prosecution in the third degree.
205.60 Hindering prosecution in the second degree.
205.65 Hindering prosecution in the first degree.

§205.00 Escape and other offenses relating to custody; definitions of terms.

The following definitions are applicable to this article:

1. "Detention Facility" means any place used for the confinement, pursuant to an order of a court, of a person (a) charged with or convicted of an offense, or (b) charged with being or adjudicated a youthful offender, person in need of supervision or juvenile delinquent, or (c) held for extradition or as a material witness, or (d) otherwise confined pursuant to an order of a court.

2. "Custody" means restraint by a public servant pursuant to an authorized arrest or an order of a court.

3. "Contraband" means any article or thing which a person confined in a detention facility is prohibited from obtaining or possessing by statute, rule, regulation or order.

4. "Dangerous contraband" means contraband which is capable of such use as may endanger the safety or security of a detention facility or any person therein.

§205.05 Escape in the third degree.

A person is guilty of escape in the third degree when he escapes from custody.

Escape in the third degree is a class A misdemeanor.

§205.10 Escape in the second degree.

A person is guilty of escape in the second degree when:

1. He escapes from a detention facility; or

2. Having been arrested for, charged with or convicted of a class C, class D or class E felony, he escapes from custody; or

3. Having been adjudicated a youthful offender, which finding was substituted for the conviction of a felony, he escapes from custody.

Escape in the second degree is a class E felony.

§205.15 Escape in the first degree.

A person is guilty of escape in the first degree when:

1. Having been charged with or convicted of a felony, he escapes from a detention facility; or

2. Having been arrested for, charged with or convicted of a class A or class B felony, he escapes from custody; or

3. Having been adjudicated a youthful offender, which finding was substituted for the conviction of a felony, he escapes from a detention facility.

Escape in the first degree is a class D felony.

*§205.16 Absconding from temporary release in the second degree.

A person is guilty of absconding from temporary release in the second degree when having been released from confinement in a correctional institution or division for youth facility to participate in a program of work release, he intentionally fails to return to the institution or facility of his confinement at or before the time prescribed for his return.

Absconding from temporary release in the second degree is a class A misdemeanor.   *(Expires 9/1/23, Ch.55,L.2021)*

*§205.17 Absconding from temporary release in the first degree.

A person is guilty of absconding from temporary release in the first degree when having been released from confinement in a correctional institution under the jurisdiction of the state department of corrections and community supervision or a facility under the jurisdiction of the state office of children and family services to participate in a program of temporary release, he or she intentionally fails to return to the institution or facility of his or her confinement at or before the time prescribed for his or her return.

Absconding from temporary release in the first degree is a class E felony.   *(Expires 9/1/23, Ch.55,L.2021)*

*§205.18 Absconding from a furlough program.

A person is guilty of absconding from a furlough program when, having been released from confinement in an institution under the jurisdiction of the commissioner of correction in a city having a population of one million or more or of a county which elects to have this article apply thereto to participate in a furlough program, he intentionally fails to return to the institution of his confinement at or before the time prescribed for his return.

Absconding from a furlough program is a class A misdemeanor.
                                                  (Expires 9/1/23, Ch.55,L.2021)

*§205.19 Absconding from a community treatment facility.

A person is guilty of absconding from a community treatment facility when having been released from confinement from a correctional institution under the jurisdiction of the state department of corrections and community supervision by transfer to a community treatment facility, he or she leaves such facility without authorization or he or she intentionally fails to return to the community treatment facility at or before the time prescribed for his or her return.

Absconding from a community treatment facility is a class E felony.
                                                  (Expires 9/1/23, Ch.55,L.2021)

§205.20 Promoting prison contraband in the second degree.

A person is guilty of promoting prison contraband in the second degree when:

1. He knowingly and unlawfully introduces any contraband into a detention facility; or

2. Being a person confined in a detention facility, he knowingly and unlawfully makes, obtains or possesses any contraband.

Promoting prison contraband in the second degree is a class A misdemeanor.

§205.25 Promoting prison contraband in the first degree.

A person is guilty of promoting prison contraband in the first degree when:

1. He knowingly and unlawfully introduces any dangerous contraband into a detention facility; or

2. Being a person confined in a detention facility, he knowingly and unlawfully makes, obtains or possesses any dangerous contraband.

Promoting prison contraband in the first degree is a class D felony.

§205.30 Resisting arrest.

A person is guilty of resisting arrest when he intentionally prevents or attempts to prevent a police officer or peace officer from effecting an authorized arrest of himself or another person.

Resisting arrest is a class A misdemeanor.

§205.50 Hindering prosecution; definition of term.

As used in sections 205.55, 205.60 and 205.65, a person "renders criminal assistance" when, with intent to prevent, hinder or delay the discovery or apprehension of, or the lodging of a criminal charge against, a person who he knows or believes has committed a crime or is being sought by law enforcement officials for the commission of a crime, or with intent to assist a person in profiting or benefiting from the commission of a crime, he:

1. Harbors or conceals such person; or

2. Warns such person of impending discovery or apprehension; or

3. Provides such person with money, transportation, weapon, disguise or other means of avoiding discovery or apprehension; or

4. Prevents or obstructs, by means of force, intimidation or deception, anyone from performing an act which might aid in the discovery or apprehension of such person or in the lodging of a criminal charge against him; or

5. Suppresses, by any act of concealment, alteration or destruction, any physical evidence which might aid in the discovery or apprehension of such person or in the lodging of a criminal charge against him; or

6. Aids such person to protect or expeditiously profit from an advantage derived from such crime.

§205.55 Hindering prosecution in the third degree.

A person is guilty of hindering prosecution in the third degree when he renders criminal assistance to a person who has committed a felony.

Hindering prosecution in the third degree is a class A misdemeanor.

§205.60 Hindering prosecution in the second degree.

A person is guilty of hindering prosecution in the second degree when he renders criminal assistance to a person who has committed a class B or class C felony.

Hindering prosecution in the second degree is a class E felony.

§205.65 Hindering prosecution in the first degree.

A person is guilty of hindering prosecution in the first degree when he renders criminal assistance to a person who has committed a class A felony, knowing or believing that such person has engaged in conduct constituting a class A felony.

Hindering prosecution in the first degree is a class D felony.

ARTICLE 210 - PERJURY AND RELATED OFFENSES

Section
210.00 Perjury and related offenses; definitions of terms.
210.05 Perjury in the third degree.
210.10 Perjury in the second degree.
210.15 Perjury in the first degree.
210.20 Perjury; pleading and proof where inconsistent statements involved.
210.25 Perjury; defense.
210.30 Perjury; no defense.
210.35 Making an apparently sworn false statement in the second degree.
210.40 Making an apparently sworn false statement in the first degree.
210.45 Making a punishable false written statement.
210.50 Perjury and related offenses; requirement of corroboration.

§210.00 Perjury and related offenses; definitions of terms.

The following definitions are applicable to this article:

1. "Oath" includes an affirmation and every other mode authorized by law of attesting to the truth of that which is stated.

2. "Swear" means to state under oath.

3. "Testimony" means an oral statement made under oath in a proceeding before any court, body, agency, public servant or other person authorized by law to conduct such proceeding and to administer the oath or cause it to be administered.

4. "Oath required by law." An affidavit, deposition or other subscribed written instrument is one for which an "oath is required by law" when, absent an oath or swearing thereto, it does not or would not, according to statute or appropriate regulatory provisions, have legal efficacy in a court of law or before any public or governmental body, agency or public servant to whom it is or might be submitted.

5. "Swear falsely." A person "swears falsely" when he intentionally makes a false statement which he does not believe to be true (a) while giving testimony, or (b) under oath in a subscribed written instrument. A false swearing in a subscribed written

instrument shall not be deemed complete until the instrument is delivered by its subscriber, or by someone acting in his behalf, to another person with intent that it be uttered or published as true.

6. "Attesting officer" means any notary public or other person authorized by law to administer oaths in connection with affidavits, depositions and other subscribed written instruments, and to certify that the subscriber of such an instrument has appeared before him and has sworn to the truth of the contents thereof.

7. "Jurat" means a clause wherein an attesting officer certifies, among other matters, that the subscriber has appeared before him and sworn to the truth of the contents thereof.

§210.05 Perjury in the third degree.

A person is guilty of perjury in the third degree when he swears falsely.

Perjury in the third degree is a class A misdemeanor.

§210.10 Perjury in the second degree.

A person is guilty of perjury in the second degree when he swears falsely and when his false statement is (a) made in a subscribed written instrument for which an oath is required by law, and (b) made with intent to mislead a public servant in the performance of his official functions, and (c) material to the action, proceeding or matter involved.

Perjury in the second degree is a class E felony.

§210.15 Perjury in the first degree.

A person is guilty of perjury in the first degree when he swears falsely and when his false statement (a) consists of testimony, and (b) is material to the action, proceeding or matter in which it is made.

Perjury in the first degree is a class D felony.

§210.20 Perjury; pleading and proof where inconsistent statements involved.

Where a person has made two statements under oath which are inconsistent to the degree that one of them is necessarily false, where the circumstances are such that each statement, if false, is perjuriously so, and where each statement was made within the jurisdiction of this state and within the period of the statute of limitations for the crime charged, the inability of the people to establish specifically which of the two statements is the false one does not preclude a prosecution for perjury, and such prosecution may be conducted as follows:

1. The indictment or information may set forth the two statements and, without designating either, charge that one of them is false and perjuriously made.

2. The falsity of one or the other of the two statements may be established by proof or a showing of their irreconcilable inconsistency.

3. The highest degree of perjury of which the defendant may be convicted is determined by hypothetically assuming each statement to be false and perjurious. If under such circumstances perjury of the same degree would be established by the making of each statement, the defendant may be convicted of that degree at most. If perjury of different degrees would be established by the making of the two statements, the defendant may be convicted of the lesser degree at most.

§210.25 Perjury; defense.

In any prosecution for perjury, it is an affirmative defense that the defendant retracted his false statement in the course of the proceeding in which it was made before such false statement substantially affected the proceeding and before it became manifest that its falsity was or would be exposed.

§210.30 Perjury; no defense.

It is no defense to a prosecution for perjury that:

1. The defendant was not competent to make the false statement alleged; or

2. The defendant mistakenly believed the false statement to be immaterial; or

3. The oath was administered or taken in an irregular manner or that the authority or jurisdiction of the attesting officer who administered the oath was defective, if such defect was excusable under any statute or rule of law.

§210.35 Making an apparently sworn false statement in the second degree.

A person is guilty of making an apparently sworn false statement in the second degree when (a) he subscribes a written instrument knowing that it contains a statement which is in fact false and which he does not believe to be true, and (b) he intends or believes that such instrument will be uttered or delivered with a jurat affixed thereto, and (c) such instrument is uttered or delivered with a jurat affixed thereto.

Making an apparently sworn false statement in the second degree is a class A misdemeanor.

§210.40 Making an apparently sworn false statement in the first degree.

A person is guilty of making an apparently sworn false statement in the first degree when he commits the crime of making an apparently sworn false statement in the second degree, and when (a) the written instrument involved is one for which an oath is required by law, and (b) the false statement contained therein is made with intent to mislead a public servant in the performance of his official functions, and (c) such false statement is material to the action, proceeding or matter involved.

Making an apparently sworn false statement in the first degree is a class E felony.

§210.45 Making a punishable false written statement.

A person is guilty of making a punishable false written statement when he knowingly makes a false statement, which he does not believe to be true, in a written instrument bearing a legally authorized form notice to the effect that false statements made therein are punishable.

Making a punishable false written statement is a class A misdemeanor.

§210.50 Perjury and related offenses; requirements of corroboration.

In any prosecution for perjury, except a prosecution based upon inconsistent statements pursuant to section 210.20, or in any prosecution for making an apparently sworn false statement, or making a punishable false written statement, falsity of a statement may not be established by the uncorroborated testimony of a single witness.

ARTICLE 215 - OTHER OFFENSES RELATING TO JUDICIAL AND OTHER PROCEEDINGS

Section
215.00 Bribing a witness.
215.05 Bribe receiving by a witness.
215.10 Tampering with a witness in the fourth degree.
215.11 Tampering with a witness in the third degree.
215.12 Tampering with a witness in the second degree.
215.13 Tampering with a witness in the first degree.
215.14 Employer unlawfully penalizing witness or victim.
215.15 Intimidating a victim or witness in the third degree.
215.16 Intimidating a victim or witness in the second degree.
215.17 Intimidating a victim or witness in the first degree.
215.19 Bribing a juror.
215.20 Bribe receiving by a juror.
215.22 Providing a juror with a gratuity.
215.23 Tampering with a juror in the second degree.
215.25 Tampering with a juror in the first degree.
215.28 Misconduct by a juror in the second degree.
215.30 Misconduct by a juror in the first degree.
215.35 Tampering with physical evidence; definitions of terms.
215.40 Tampering with physical evidence.
215.45 Compounding a crime.
215.50 Criminal contempt in the second degree.
215.51 Criminal contempt in the first degree.
215.52 Aggravated criminal contempt.
215.54 Criminal contempt; prosecution and punishment.
215.55 Bail jumping in the third degree.
215.56 Bail jumping in the second degree.
215.57 Bail jumping in the first degree.
215.58 Failing to respond to an appearance ticket.
215.59 Bail jumping and failing to respond to an appearance ticket; defense.
215.60 Criminal contempt of the legislature.
215.65 Criminal contempt of a temporary state commission.
215.66 Criminal contempt of the state commission on judicial conduct.
215.70 Unlawful grand jury disclosure.
215.75 Unlawful disclosure of an indictment.
215.80 Unlawful disposition of assets subject to forfeiture.

§215.00 Bribing a witness.

A person is guilty of bribing a witness when he confers, or offers or agrees to confer, any benefit upon a witness or a person about to be called as a witness in any action or proceeding upon an agreement or understanding that (a) the testimony of such witness will thereby be influenced, or (b) such witness will absent himself from, or otherwise avoid or seek to avoid appearing or testifying at, such action or proceeding.

Bribing a witness is a class D felony.

§215.05 Bribe receiving by a witness.

A witness or a person about to be called as a witness in any action or proceeding is guilty of bribe receiving by a witness when he solicits, accepts or agrees to accept any benefit from another person upon an agreement or understanding that (a) his testimony will thereby be influenced, or (b) he will absent himself from, or otherwise avoid or seek to avoid appearing or testifying at, such action or proceeding.

Bribe receiving by a witness is a class D felony.

§215.10 Tampering with a witness in the fourth degree.

A person is guilty of tampering with a witness when, knowing that a person is or is about to be called as a witness in an action or proceeding, (a) he wrongfully induces or attempts to induce such person to absent himself from, or otherwise to avoid or seek to avoid appearing or testifying at, such action or proceeding, or (b) he knowingly makes any false statement or practices any fraud or deceit with intent to affect the testimony of such person.

Tampering with a witness is a class A misdemeanor.

§215.11 Tampering with a witness in the third degree.

A person is guilty of tampering with a witness in the third degree when, knowing that a person is about to be called as a witness in a criminal proceeding:

1. He wrongfully compels or attempts to compel such person to absent himself from, or otherwise to avoid or seek to avoid appearing or testifying at such proceeding by means of instilling in him a fear that the actor will cause physical injury to such person or another person; or

2. He wrongfully compels or attempts to compel such person to swear falsely by means of instilling in him a fear that the actor will cause physical injury to such person or another person.

Tampering with a witness in the third degree is a class E felony.

§215.12 Tampering with a witness in the second degree.

A person is guilty of tampering with a witness in the second degree when he:

1. Intentionally causes physical injury to a person for the purpose of obstructing, delaying, preventing or impeding the giving of testimony in a criminal proceeding by such person or another person or for the purpose of compelling such person or another person to swear falsely; or

2. He intentionally causes physical injury to a person on account of such person or another person having testified in a criminal proceeding.

Tampering with a witness in the second degree is a class D felony.

§215.13 Tampering with a witness in the first degree.

A person is guilty of tampering with a witness in the first degree when:

1. He intentionally causes serious physical injury to a person for the purpose of obstructing, delaying, preventing or impeding the giving of testimony in a criminal proceeding by such person or another person or for the purpose of compelling such person or another person to swear falsely; or

2. He intentionally causes serious physical injury to a person on account of such person or another person having testified in a criminal proceeding.

Tampering with a witness in the first degree is a class B felony.

§215.14 Employer unlawfully penalizing witness or victim.

1. Any person who is the victim of an offense upon which an accusatory instrument is based or, is subpoenaed to attend a criminal proceeding as a witness pursuant to article six hundred ten of the criminal procedure law or who exercises his rights as a victim as provided by section 380.50 or 390.30 of the criminal procedure law or subdivision two of section two hundred fifty-nine-i of the executive law and who notifies his employer or agent of his intent to appear as a witness, to consult with the district attorney, or to exercise his rights as provided in the criminal procedure law, the family court act and the executive law prior to the day of his attendance, shall not on account of his absence from employment by reason of such service be subject to discharge or penalty except as hereinafter provided. Upon request of the employer or agent, the party who sought the attendance or testimony shall provide verification of the employee's service. An employer may, however, withhold wages of any such employee during the period of such attendance. The subjection of an employee to discharge or penalty on account of his absence from employment by reason of his required attendance as a witness at a criminal proceeding or consultation with the district attorney or exercise of his rights as provided under law shall constitute a class B misdemeanor.

2. For purposes of this section, the term "victim" shall include the aggrieved party or the aggrieved party's next of kin, if the aggrieved party is deceased as a result of the offense, the representative of a victim as defined in subdivision six of section six hundred twenty-one of the executive law, a good samaritan as defined in subdivision seven of section six hundred twenty-one of such law or a person pursuing an application or enforcement of an order of protection under the criminal procedure law or the family court act.

§215.15 Intimidating a victim or witness in the third degree.

A person is guilty of intimidating a victim or witness in the third degree when, knowing that another person possesses information relating to a criminal transaction and other than in the course of that criminal transaction or immediate flight therefrom,he:

1. Wrongfully compels or attempts to compel such other person to refrain from communicating such information to any court, grand jury, prosecutor, police officer or peace officer by means of instilling in him a fear that the actor will cause physical injury to such other person or another person; or

2. Intentionally damages the property of such other person or another person for the purpose of compelling such other person or another person to refrain from communicating, or on account of such other person or another person having communicated, information relating to that criminal transaction to any court, grand jury, prosecutor, police officer or peace officer.

Intimidating a victim or witness in the third degree is a class E felony.

§215.16 Intimidating a victim or witness in the second degree.

A person is guilty of intimidating a victim or witness in the second degree when, other than in the course of that criminal transaction or immediate flight therefrom, he:

1. Intentionally causes physical injury to another person for the purpose of obstructing, delaying, preventing or impeding the communication by such other person or another person of information relating to a criminal transaction to any court, grand jury, prosecutor, police officer or peace officer or for the purpose of compelling such other person or another person to swear falsely; or

2. Intentionally causes physical injury to another person on account of such other person or another person having communicated information relating to a criminal transaction to any court, grand jury, prosecutor, police officer or peace officer; or

3. Recklessly causes physical injury to another person by intentionally damaging the property of such other person or another person, for the purpose of obstructing, delaying, preventing or impeding such other person or another person from communicating, or on account of such other person or another person having communicated, information relating to a criminal transaction to any court, grand jury, prosecutor, police officer or peace officer.

Intimidating a victim or witness in the second degree is a class D felony.

§215.17 Intimidating a victim or witness in the first degree.

A person is guilty of intimidating a victim or witness in the first degree when, other than in the course of that criminal transaction or immediate flight therefrom, he:

1. Intentionally causes serious physical injury to another person for the purpose of obstructing, delaying, preventing or impeding the communication by such other person or another person of information relating to a criminal transaction to any court, grand jury, prosecutor, police officer or peace officer or for the purpose of compelling such other person or another person to swear falsely; or

2. Intentionally causes serious physical injury to another person on account of such other person or another person having communicated information relating to a criminal transaction to any court, grand jury, prosecutor, police officer or peace officer.

Intimidating a victim or witness in the first degree is a class B felony.

§215.19 Bribing a juror.

A person is guilty of bribing a juror when he confers, or offers or agrees to confer, any benefit upon a juror upon an agreement or understanding that such juror's vote, opinion, judgment, decision or other action as a juror will thereby be influenced.

Bribing a juror is a class D felony.

§215.20 Bribe receiving by a juror.

A juror is guilty of bribe receiving by a juror when he solicits, accepts or agrees to accept any benefit from another person upon an agreement or understanding that his vote, opinion, judgment, decision or other action as a juror will thereby be influenced.

Bribe receiving by a juror is a class D felony.

§215.22 Providing a juror with a gratuity.

A person is guilty of providing a juror with a gratuity when he or she, having been a party in a concluded civil or criminal action or proceeding or having been a person with regard to whom a grand jury has taken action pursuant to any subdivision of section 190.60 of the criminal procedure law (or acting on behalf of such a party or such a person), directly or indirectly confers, offers to confer or agrees to confer upon a person whom he or she knows has served as a juror in such action or proceeding or on such grand jury any benefit with intent to reward such person for such service.

Providing a juror with a gratuity is a class A misdemeanor.

§215.23 Tampering with a juror in the second degree.

A person is guilty of tampering with a juror in the second degree when, prior to discharge of the jury, he:

1. confers, or offers or agrees to confer, any payment or benefit upon a juror or upon a third person acting on behalf of such juror, in consideration for such juror or third person supplying information in relation to an action or proceeding pending or about to be brought before such juror; or

2. acting on behalf of a juror, accepts or agrees to accept any payment or benefit for himself or for such juror, in consideration for supplying any information in relation to an action or proceeding pending or about to be brought before such juror and prior to his discharge.

Tampering with a juror in the second degree is a class B misdemeanor.

§215.25 Tampering with a juror in the first degree.

A person is guilty of tampering with a juror in the first degree when, with intent to influence the outcome of an action or proceeding, he communicates with a juror in such action or proceeding, except as authorized by law.

Tampering with a juror in the first degree is a class A misdemeanor.

§215.28 Misconduct by a juror in the second degree.

A person is guilty of misconduct by a juror in the second degree when, in relation to an action or proceeding pending or about to be brought before him and prior to discharge, he accepts or agrees to accept any payment or benefit for himself or for a third person in consideration for supplying any information concerning such action or proceeding.

Misconduct by a juror in the second degree is a violation.

§215.30 Misconduct by a juror in the first degree.

A juror is guilty of misconduct by a juror in the first degree when, in relation to an action or proceeding pending or about to be brought before him, he agrees to give a vote, opinion, judgment, decision or report for or against any party to such action or proceeding.

Misconduct by a juror in the first degree is a class A misdemeanor.

§215.35 Tampering with physical evidence; definitions of terms.
The following definitions are applicable to section 215.40:

1. "Physical evidence" means any article, object, document, record or other thing of physical substance which is or is about to be produced or used as evidence in an official proceeding.

2. "Official proceeding" means any action or proceeding conducted by or before a legally constituted judicial, legislative, administrative or other governmental agency or official, in which evidence may properly be received.

§215.40 Tampering with physical evidence.
A person is guilty of tampering with physical evidence when:

1. With intent that it be used or introduced in an official proceeding or a prospective official proceeding, he (a) knowingly makes, devises or prepares false physical evidence, or (b) produces or offers such evidence at such a proceeding knowing it to be false; or

2. Believing that certain physical evidence is about to be produced or used in an official proceeding or a prospective official proceeding, and intending to prevent such production or use, he suppresses it by any act of concealment, alteration or destruction, or by employing force, intimidation or deception against any person.

Tampering with physical evidence is a class E felony.

§215.45 Compounding a crime.
1. A person is guilty of compounding a crime when:

(a) He solicits, accepts or agrees to accept any benefit upon an agreement or understanding that he will refrain from initiating a prosecution for a crime; or

(b) He confers, or offers or agrees to confer, any benefit upon another person upon an agreement or understanding that such other person will refrain from initiating a prosecution for a crime.

2. In any prosecution under this section, it is an affirmative defense that the benefit did not exceed an amount which the defendant reasonably believed to be due as restitution or indemnification for harm caused by the crime.

Compounding a crime is a class A misdemeanor.

§215.50 Criminal contempt in the second degree.
A person is guilty of criminal contempt in the second degree when he engages in any of the following conduct:

1. Disorderly, contemptuous, or insolent behavior, committed during the sitting of a court, in its immediate view and presence and directly tending to interrupt its proceedings or to impair the respect due to its authority; or

2. Breach of the peace, noise, or other disturbance, directly tending to interrupt a court's proceedings; or

3. Intentional disobedience or resistance to the lawful process or other mandate of a court except in cases involving or growing out of labor disputes as defined by subdivision two of section seven hundred fifty-three-a of the judiciary law; or

4. Contumacious and unlawful refusal to be sworn as a witness in any court proceeding or, after being sworn, to answer any legal and proper interrogatory; or

5. Knowingly publishing a false or grossly inaccurate report of a court's proceedings; or

6. Intentional failure to obey any mandate, process or notice, issued pursuant to articles sixteen, seventeen, eighteen, or eighteen-a of the judiciary law, or to rules adopted pursuant to any such statute or to any special statute establishing commissioners of jurors and prescribing their duties or who refuses to be sworn as provided therein; or

7. On or along a public street or sidewalk within a radius of two hundred feet of any building established as a courthouse, he calls aloud, shouts, holds or displays placards or signs containing written or printed matter, concerning the conduct of a trial being held in such courthouse or the character of the court or jury engaged in such trial or calling for or demanding any specified action or determination by such court or jury in connection with such trial.

Criminal contempt in the second degree is a class A misdemeanor.

§215.51 Criminal contempt in the first degree.

A person is guilty of criminal contempt in the first degree when:

(a) he contumaciously and unlawfully refuses to be sworn as a witness before a grand jury, or, when after having been sworn as a witness before a grand jury, he refuses to answer any legal and proper interrogatory; or

(b) in violation of a duly served order of protection, or such order of which the defendant has actual knowledge because he or she was present in court when such order was issued, or an order of protection issued by a court of competent jurisdiction in this or another state, territorial or tribal jurisdiction, he or she:

(i) intentionally places or attempts to place a person for whose protection such order was issued in reasonable fear of physical injury, serious physical injury or death by displaying a deadly weapon, dangerous instrument or what appears to be a pistol, revolver, rifle, shotgun, machine gun or other firearm or by means of a threat or threats; or

(ii) intentionally places or attempts to place a person for whose protection such order was issued in reasonable fear of physical injury, serious physical injury or death by repeatedly following such person or engaging in a course of conduct or repeatedly committing acts over a period of time; or

(iii) intentionally places or attempts to place a person for whose protection such order was issued in reasonable fear of physical injury, serious physical injury or death when he or she communicates or causes a communication to be initiated with such person by mechanical or electronic means or otherwise, anonymously or otherwise, by telephone, or by telegraph, mail or any other form of written communication; or

(iv) with intent to harass, annoy, threaten or alarm a person for whose protection such order was issued, repeatedly makes telephone calls to such person, whether or not a conversation ensues, with no purpose of legitimate communication; or

(v) with intent to harass, annoy, threaten or alarm a person for whose protection such order was issued, strikes, shoves, kicks or otherwise subjects such other person to physical contact or attempts or threatens to do the same; or

(vi) by physical menace, intentionally places or attempts to place a person for whose protection such order was issued in reasonable fear of death, imminent serious physical injury or physical injury.

(c) he or she commits the crime of criminal contempt in the second degree as defined in subdivision three of section 215.50 of this article by violating that part of a duly served order of protection, or such order of which the defendant has actual knowledge because he or she was present in court when such order was issued, under sections two hundred forty and two hundred fifty-two of the domestic relations law, articles four, five, six and eight of the family court act and section 530.12 of the criminal procedure law, or an order of protection issued by a court of competent jurisdiction in another state, territorial or tribal jurisdiction, which requires the respondent or defendant to stay away from the person or persons on whose behalf the order was issued, and where the defendant has been previously convicted of the crime of aggravated criminal contempt or criminal contempt in the first or second degree for violating an order of protection as described herein within the preceding five years; or

(d) in violation of a duly served order of protection, or such order of which the defendant has actual knowledge because he or she was present in court when such order was issued, or an order issued by a court of competent jurisdiction in this or another state, territorial or tribal jurisdiction, he or she intentionally or recklessly damages the property of a person for whose protection such order was issued in an amount exceeding two hundred fifty dollars.

Criminal contempt in the first degree is a class E felony.

§215.52 Aggravated criminal contempt.

A person is guilty of aggravated criminal contempt when:

1. in violation of a duly served order of protection, or such order of which the defendant has actual knowledge because he or she was present in court when such order was issued, or an order of protection issued by a court of competent jurisdiction in another state, territorial or tribal jurisdiction, he or she intentionally or recklessly causes physical injury or serious physical injury to a person for whose protection such order was issued; or

2. he or she commits the crime of criminal contempt in the first degree as defined in subdivision (b) or (d) of section 215.51 of this article and has been previously convicted of the crime of aggravated criminal contempt; or

3. he or she commits the crime of criminal contempt in the first degree, as defined in paragraph (i), (ii), (iii), (v) or (vi) of subdivision (b) or subdivision (c) of section 215.51 of this article, and has been previously been convicted of the crime of criminal contempt in the first degree, as defined in such subdivision (b), (c) or (d) of section 215.51 of this article, within the preceding five years.

Aggravated criminal contempt is a class D felony.

§215.54 Criminal contempt; prosecution and punishment.

Adjudication for criminal contempt under subdivision A of section seven hundred fifty of the judiciary law shall not bar a prosecution for the crime of criminal contempt under section 215.50 based upon the same conduct but, upon conviction thereunder, the court, in sentencing the defendant shall take the previous punishment into consideration.

§215.55 Bail jumping in the third degree.

A person is guilty of bail jumping in the third degree when by court order he has been released from custody or allowed to remain at liberty, either upon bail or upon his own recognizance, upon condition that he will subsequently appear personally in connection with a criminal action or proceeding, and when he does not appear personally on the required date or voluntarily within thirty days thereafter.

Bail jumping in the third degree is a class A misdemeanor.

§215.56 Bail jumping in the second degree.

A person is guilty of bail jumping in the second degree when by court order he has been released from custody or allowed to remain at liberty, either upon bail or upon his own recognizance, upon condition that he will subsequently appear personally in connection with a charge against him of committing a felony, and when he does not appear personally on the required date or voluntarily within thirty days thereafter.

Bail jumping in the second degree is a class E felony.

§215.57 Bail jumping in the first degree.

A person is guilty of bail jumping in the first degree when by court order he has been released from custody or allowed to remain at liberty, either upon bail or upon his own recognizance, upon condition that he will subsequently appear personally in connection with an indictment pending against him which charges him with the commission of a class A or class B felony, and when he does not appear personally on the required date or voluntarily within thirty days thereafter.

Bail jumping in the first degree is a class D felony.

§215.58 Failing to respond to an appearance ticket.

1. A person is guilty of failing to respond to an appearance ticket when, having been personally served with an appearance ticket, as defined in subdivision two, based upon his alleged commission of a crime, he does not appear personally in the court in which such appearance ticket is returnable on the return date thereof or voluntarily within thirty days thereafter.

2. As used in this section, an appearance ticket means a written notice, whether referred to as a summons or by any other name, issued by a police officer, peace officer or other non-judicial public servant authorized by law to issue the same, directing a designated person to appear in a designated court at a designated future time in connection with a criminal action to be instituted in such court with respect to his alleged commission of a designated offense.

3. This section does not apply to any case in which an alternative to response to an appearance ticket is authorized by law and the actor complies with such alternative procedure.

Failing to respond to an appearance ticket is a violation.

§215.59 Bail jumping and failing to respond to an appearance ticket; defense.

In any prosecution for bail jumping or failing to respond to an appearance ticket, it is an affirmative defense that:

1. The defendant's failure to appear on the required date or within thirty days thereafter was unavoidable and due to circumstances beyond his control; and

2. During the period extending from the expiration of the thirty day period to the commencement of the action, the defendant either:

(a) appeared voluntarily as soon as he was able to do so, or

(b) although he did not so appear, such failure of appearance was unavoidable and due to circumstances beyond his control.

§215.60 Criminal contempt of the legislature.

A person is guilty of criminal contempt of the legislature when, having been duly subpoenaed to attend as a witness before either house of the legislature or before any committee thereof, he:

1. Fails or refuses to attend without lawful excuse; or

2. Refuses to be sworn; or

3. Refuses to answer any material and proper question; or

4. Refuses, after reasonable notice, to produce books, papers, or documents in his possession or under his control which constitute material and proper evidence.

Criminal contempt of the legislature is a class A misdemeanor.

§215.65 Criminal contempt of a temporary state commission.

A person is guilty of criminal contempt of a temporary state commission when, having been duly subpoenaed to attend as a witness at an investigation or hearing before a temporary state commission, he fails or refuses to attend without lawful excuse.

Criminal contempt of a temporary state commission is a class A misdemeanor.

§215.66 Criminal contempt of the state commission on judicial conduct.

A person is guilty of criminal contempt of the state commission on judicial conduct when, having been duly subpoenaed to attend as a witness at an investigation or hearing before the commission or a referee designated by the commission, he fails or refuses to attend without lawful excuse.

Criminal contempt of the state commission on judicial conduct is a class A misdemeanor.

§215.70 Unlawful grand jury disclosure.

A person is guilty of unlawful grand jury disclosure when, being a grand juror, a public prosecutor, a grand jury stenographer, a grand jury interpreter, a police officer or a peace officer guarding a witness in a grand jury proceeding, or a clerk, attendant, warden or other public servant having official duties in or about a grand jury room or proceeding, or a public officer or public employee, he intentionally discloses to another the nature or substance of any grand jury testimony, or any decision, result or other matter attending a grand jury proceeding which is required by law to be kept secret, except in the proper discharge of his official duties or upon written order of the court. Nothing contained herein shall prohibit a witness from disclosing his own testimony.

Unlawful grand jury disclosure is a class E felony.

§215.75 Unlawful disclosure of an indictment.

A public servant is guilty of unlawful disclosure of an indictment when, except in the proper discharge of his official duties, he intentionally discloses the fact that an indictment has been found or filed before the accused person is in custody.

Unlawful disclosure of an indictment is a class B misdemeanor.

§215.80 Unlawful disposition of assets subject to forfeiture.

Any defendant in a forfeiture action pursuant to article thirteen-A of the civil practice law and rules who knowingly and intentionally conceals, destroys, dissipates, alters, removes from the jurisdiction, or otherwise disposes of, property specified in a provisional remedy ordered by the court or in a judgment of forfeiture in knowing contempt of said order shall be guilty of a class A misdemeanor.

TITLE M - OFFENSES AGAINST PUBLIC HEALTH AND MORALS
ARTICLE 220 - CONTROLLED SUBSTANCES OFFENSES

Section
220.00 Controlled substances; definitions.
220.03 Criminal possession of a controlled substance in the seventh degree.
220.06 Criminal possession of a controlled substance in the fifth degree.
220.09 Criminal possession of a controlled substance in the fourth degree.
220.16 Criminal possession of a controlled substance in the third degree.
220.18 Criminal possession of a controlled substance in the second degree.
220.21 Criminal possession of a controlled substance in the first degree.
220.25 Criminal possession of a controlled substance; presumption.
220.28 Use of a child to commit a controlled substance offense.
220.31 Criminal sale of a controlled substance in the fifth degree.
220.34 Criminal sale of a controlled substance in the fourth degree.
220.39 Criminal sale of a controlled substance in the third degree.
220.41 Criminal sale of a controlled substance in the second degree.
220.43 Criminal sale of a controlled substance in the first degree.
220.44 Criminal sale of a controlled substance in or near school grounds.
220.46 Criminal injection of a narcotic drug.
220.48 Criminal sale of a controlled substance to a child.
220.50 Criminally using drug paraphernalia in the second degree.
220.55 Criminally using drug paraphernalia in the first degree.
220.60 Criminal possession of precursors of controlled substances.
220.65 Criminal sale of a prescription for a controlled substance or of a controlled substance by a practitioner or pharmacist.
220.70 Criminal possession of methamphetamine manufacturing material in the second degree.
220.71 Criminal possession of methamphetamine manufacturing material in the first degree.
220.72 Criminal possession of precursors of methamphetamine.
220.73 Unlawful manufacture of methamphetamine in the third degree.
220.74 Unlawful manufacture of methamphetamine in the second degree.
220.75 Unlawful manufacture of methamphetamine in the first degree.
220.76 Unlawful disposal of methamphetamine laboratory material.
220.77 Operating as a major trafficker.
220.78 Witness or victim of drug or alcohol overdose.

§220.00   **120**

§220.00 Controlled substances; definitions.

1. "Sell" means to sell, exchange, give or dispose of to another, or to offer or agree to do the same.

2. "Unlawfully" means in violation of article thirty-three of the public health law.

3. "Ounce" means an avoirdupois ounce as applied to solids or semisolids, and a fluid ounce as applied to liquids.

4. "Pound" means an avoirdupois pound.

5. "Controlled substance" means any substance listed in schedule I, II, III, IV or V of section thirty-three hundred six of the public health law.

(Eff.3/31/21,Ch.92,L.2021)

6. *(Repealed, Eff.3/31/21,Ch.92,L.2021)*

7. "Narcotic drug" means any controlled substance listed in schedule I(b), I(c), II(b) or II(c) other than methadone.

8. "Narcotic preparation" means any controlled substance listed in schedule II(b-1), III(d) or III(e).

9. "Hallucinogen" means any controlled substance listed in paragraphs (5), (17), (18), (19), (20) and (21) of subdivision (d) of schedule I of section thirty-three hundred six of the public health law.

(Eff.3/31/21,Ch.92,L.2021)

10. "Hallucinogenic substance" means any controlled substance listed in schedule I(d) other than concentrated cannabis, lysergic acid diethylamide, or an hallucinogen.

11. "Stimulant" means any controlled substance listed in schedule I(f),II(d).

12. "Dangerous depressant" means any controlled substance listed in schedule I(e)(2), (3), II(e), III(c)(3) or IV(c)(2), (31), (32), (40).

13. "Depressant" means any controlled substance listed in schedule IV(c) except (c)(2), (31), (32), (40).

14. "School grounds" means (a) in or on or within any building, structure, athletic playing field, playground or land contained within the real property boundary line of a public or private elementary, parochial, intermediate, junior high, vocational, or high school, or (b) any area accessible to the public located within one thousand feet of the real property boundary line comprising any such school or any parked automobile or other parked vehicle located within one thousand feet of the real property boundary line comprising any such school. For the purposes of this section an "area accessible to the public" shall mean sidewalks, streets, parking lots, parks, playgrounds, stores and restaurants.

15. "Prescription for a controlled substance" means a direction or authorization, by means of an official New York state prescription form, a written prescription form or an oral prescription, which will permit a person to lawfully obtain a controlled substance from any person authorized to dispense controlled substances.

16. For the purposes of sections 220.70, 220.71, 220.72, 220.73, 220.74, 220.75 and 220.76 of this article:

(a) "Precursor" means ephedrine, pseudoephedrine, or any salt, isomer or salt of an isomer of such substances.

(b) "Chemical reagent" means a chemical reagent that can be used in the manufacture, production or preparation of methamphetamine.

(c) "Solvent" means a solvent that can be used in the manufacture, production or preparation of methamphetamine.

(d) "Laboratory equipment" means any items, components or materials that can be used in the manufacture, preparation or production of methamphetamine.

(e) "Hazardous or dangerous material" means any substance, or combination of substances, that results from or is used in the manufacture, preparation or production of methamphetamine which, because of its quantity, concentration, or physical or chemical characteristics, poses a substantial risk to human health or safety, or a substantial danger to the environment.

17. "School bus" means every motor vehicle owned by a public or governmental agency or private school and operated for the transportation of pupils, teachers and other persons acting in a supervisory capacity, to or from school or school activities or privately owned and operated for compensation for the transportation of pupils, children of pupils, teachers and other persons acting in a supervisory capacity to or from school or school activities.

18. "Controlled substance organization" means four or more persons sharing a common purpose to engage in conduct that constitutes or advances the commission of a felony under this article.

19. "Director" means a person who is the principal administrator, organizer, or leader of a controlled substance organization or one of several principal administrators, organizers, or leaders of a controlled substance organization.

20. "Profiteer" means a person who: (a) is a director of a controlled substance organization; (b) is a member of a controlled substance organization and has managerial responsibility over one or more other members of that organization; or (c) arranges, devises or plans one or more transactions constituting a felony under this article so as to obtain profits or expected profits. A person is not a profiteer if he or she is acting only as an employee; or if he or she is acting as an accommodation to a friend or relative; or if he or she is acting only under the direction and control of others and exercises no substantial, independent role in arranging or directing the transactions in question.

§220.03 Criminal possession of a controlled substance in the seventh degree.

A person is guilty of criminal possession of a controlled substance in the seventh degree when he or she knowingly and unlawfully possesses a controlled substance; provided, however, that it shall not be a violation of this section when a person possesses a residual amount of a controlled substance and that residual amount is in or on a hypodermic syringe or hypodermic needle; nor shall it be a violation of this section when a person's unlawful possession of a controlled substance is discovered as a result of seeking immediate health care as defined in paragraph (b) of subdivision three of section 220.78 of this article, for either another person or him or herself because such person is experiencing a drug or alcohol overdose or other life threatening medical emergency as defined in paragraph (a) of subdivision three of section 220.78 of this article.   *(Eff.10/7/21,Ch.433,L.2021)*

Criminal possession of a controlled substance in the seventh degree is a class A misdemeanor.

§220.06 Criminal possession of a controlled substance in the fifth degree.

A person is guilty of criminal possession of a controlled substance in the fifth degree when he knowingly and unlawfully possesses:

1. a controlled substance with intent to sell it; or

2. one or more preparations, compounds, mixtures or substances containing a narcotic preparation and said preparations, compounds, mixtures or substances are of an aggregate weight of one-half ounce or more; or

3. phencyclidine and said phencyclidine weighs fifty milligrams or more; or

4. *(Repealed, Eff.3/31/21,Ch.92,L.2021)*

5. cocaine and said cocaine weighs five hundred milligrams or more.

6. ketamine and said ketamine weighs more than one thousand milligrams; or

7. ketamine and has previously been convicted of possession or the attempt to commit possession of ketamine in any amount; or

8. one or more preparations, compounds, mixtures or substances containing gamma hydroxybutyric acid, as defined in paragraph four of subdivision (e) of schedule I of section thirty-three hundred six of the public health law, and said preparations, compounds, mixtures or substances are of an aggregate weight of twenty-eight grams or more.

Criminal possession of a controlled substance in the fifth degree is a class D felony.

§220.09 Criminal possession of a controlled substance in the fourth degree.

A person is guilty of criminal possession of a controlled substance in the fourth degree when he knowingly and unlawfully possesses:

1. one or more preparations, compounds, mixtures or substances containing a narcotic drug and said preparations, compounds, mixtures or substances are of an aggregate weight of one-eighth ounce or more; or

2. one or more preparations, compounds, mixtures or substances containing methamphetamine, its salts, isomers or salts of isomers and said preparations, compounds, mixtures or substances are of an aggregate weight of one-half ounce or more; or

3. one or more preparations, compounds, mixtures or substances containing a narcotic preparation and said preparations, compounds, mixtures or substances are of an aggregate weight of two ounces or more; or

4. a stimulant and said stimulant weighs one gram or more; or

5. lysergic acid diethylamide and said lysergic acid diethylamide weighs one milligram or more; or

6. a hallucinogen and said hallucinogen weighs twenty-five milligrams or more; or

7. a hallucinogenic substance and said hallucinogenic substance weighs one gram or more; or

8. a dangerous depressant and such dangerous depressant weighs ten ounces or more; or

9. a depressant and such depressant weighs two pounds or more; or

10. *(Repealed, Eff.3/31/21,Ch.92,L.2021)*

11. phencyclidine and said phencyclidine weighs two hundred fifty milligrams or more; or

12. methadone and said methadone weighs three hundred sixty milligrams or more; or

13. phencyclidine and said phencyclidine weighs fifty milligrams or more with intent to sell it and has previously been convicted of an offense defined in this article or the attempt or conspiracy to commit any such offense; or

14. ketamine and said ketamine weighs four thousand milligrams or more; or

15. one or more preparations, compounds, mixtures or substances containing gamma hydroxybutyric acid, as defined in paragraph four of subdivision (e) of schedule I of section thirty-three hundred six of the public health law, and said preparations, compounds, mixtures or substances are of an aggregate weight of two hundred grams or more.

Criminal possession of a controlled substance in the fourth degree is a class C felony.

§220.16 Criminal possession of a controlled substance in the third degree.

A person is guilty of criminal possession of a controlled substance in the third degree when he knowingly and unlawfully possesses:

1. a narcotic drug with intent to sell it; or

2. a stimulant, hallucinogen, hallucinogenic substance, or lysergic acid diethylamide, with intent to sell it and has previously been convicted of an offense defined in article two hundred twenty or the attempt or conspiracy to commit any such offense; or

3. a stimulant with intent to sell it and said stimulant weighs one gram or more; or

4. lysergic acid diethylamide with intent to sell it and said lysergic acid diethylamide weighs one milligram or more; or

5. a hallucinogen with intent to sell it and said hallucinogen weighs twenty-five milligrams or more; or

6. a hallucinogenic substance with intent to sell it and said hallucinogenic substance weighs one gram or more; or

7. one or more preparations, compounds, mixtures or substances containing methamphetamine, its salts, isomers or salts of isomers with intent to sell it and said preparations, compounds, mixtures or substances are of an aggregate weight of one-eighth ounce or more; or

8. a stimulant and said stimulant weighs five grams or more; or

9. lysergic acid diethylamide and said lysergic acid diethylamide weighs five milligrams or more; or

10. a hallucinogen and said hallucinogen weighs one hundred twenty-five milligrams or more; or

11. a hallucinogenic substance and said hallucinogenic substance weighs five grams or more; or

12. one or more preparations, compounds, mixtures or substances containing a narcotic drug and said preparations, compounds, mixtures or substances are of an aggregate weight of one-half ounce or more; or

13. phencyclidine and said phencyclidine weighs one thousand two hundred fifty milligrams or more.

Criminal possession of a controlled substance in the third degree is a class B felony.

§220.18 Criminal possession of a controlled substance in the second degree.

A person is guilty of criminal possession of a controlled substance in the second degree when he or she knowingly and unlawfully possesses:

1. one or more preparations, compounds, mixtures or substances containing a narcotic drug and said preparations, compounds, mixtures or substances are of an aggregate weight of four ounces or more; or

2. one or more preparations, compounds, mixtures or substances containing methamphetamine, its salts, isomers or salts of isomers and said preprations, compounds, mixtures or substances are of an aggregate weight of two ounces or more; or

3. a stimulant and said stimulant weighs ten grams or more; or

4. lysergic acid diethylamide and said lysergic acid diethylamide weighs twenty-five milligrams or more; or

5. a hallucinogen and said hallucinogen weighs six hundred twenty-five milligrams or more; or

6. a hallucinogenic substance and said hallucinogenic substance weighs twenty-five grams or more; or

7. methadone and said methadone weighs two thousand eight hundred eighty milligrams or more.

Criminal possession of a controlled substance in the second degree is a class A-II felony.

§220.21 Criminal possession of a controlled substance in the first degree.

A person is guilty of criminal possession of a controlled substance in the first degree when he or she knowingly and unlawfully possesses:

1. one or more preparations, compounds, mixtures or substances containing a narcotic drug and said preparations, compounds, mixtures or substances are of an aggregate weight of eight ounces or more; or

2. methadone and said methadone weighs five thousand seven hundred sixty milligrams or more.

Criminal possession of a controlled substance in the first degree is a class A-I felony.

§220.25 Criminal possession of a controlled substance; presumption.

1. The presence of a controlled substance in an automobile, other than a public omnibus, is presumptive evidence of knowing possession thereof by each and every person in the automobile at the time such controlled substance was found; except that such presumption does not apply (a) to a duly licensed operator of an automobile who is at the time operating it for hire in the lawful and proper pursuit of his trade, or (b) to any person in the automobile if one of them, having obtained the controlled substance and not being under duress, is authorized to possess it and such controlled substance is in the same container as when he received possession thereof, or (c) when the controlled substance is concealed upon the person of one of the occupants.

2. The presence of a narcotic drug, narcotic preparation, marihuana or phencyclidine in open view in a room, other than a public place, under circumstances evincing an intent to unlawfully mix, compound, package or otherwise prepare for sale such controlled substance is presumptive evidence of knowing possession thereof by each and every person in close proximity to such controlled substance at the time such controlled substance was found; except that such presumption does not apply to any such persons if (a) one of them, having obtained such controlled substance and not being under duress, is authorized to possess it and such controlled substance is in the same container as when he received possession thereof, or (b) one of them has such controlled substance upon his person.

§220.28 Use of a child to commit a controlled substance offense.

1. A person is guilty of use of a child to commit a controlled substance offense when, being eighteen years old or more, he or she commits a felony sale or felony attempted sale of a controlled substance in violation of this article and, as part of that criminal transaction, knowingly uses a child to effectuate such felony sale or felony attempted sale of such controlled substance.

2. For purposes of this section, "uses a child to effectuate the felony sale or felony attempted sale of such controlled substance" means conduct by which the actor: (a) conceals such controlled substance on or about the body or person of such child for the purpose of effectuating the criminal sale or attempted sale of such controlled substance to a third person; or (b) directs, forces or otherwise requires such child to sell or attempt to sell or offer direct assistance to the defendant in selling or attempting to sell such controlled substance to a third person.

For purposes of this section, "child" means a person less than sixteen years of age.

Use of a child to commit a controlled substance offense is a class E felony.

§220.31 Criminal sale of a controlled substance in the fifth degree.

A person is guilty of criminal sale of a controlled substance in the fifth degree when he knowingly and unlawfully sells a controlled substance.

Criminal sale of a controlled substance in the fifth degree is a class D felony.

§220.34 Criminal sale of a controlled substance in the fourth degree.

A person is guilty of criminal sale of a controlled substance in the fourth degree when he knowingly and unlawfully sells:

1. a narcotic preparation; or
2. a dangerous depressant or a depressant and the dangerous depressant weighs ten ounces or more, or the depressant weighs two pounds or more; or
3. *(Repealed, Eff.3/31/21,Ch.92,L.2021)*
4. phencyclidine and the phencyclidine weighs fifty milligrams or more; or
5. methadone; or
6. any amount of phencyclidine and has previously been convicted of an offense defined in this article or the attempt or conspiracy to commit any such offense; or
6-a. ketamine and said ketamine weighs four thousand milligrams or more.
7. a controlled substance in violation of section 220.31 of this article, when such sale takes place upon school grounds or on a school bus; or
8. a controlled substance in violation of section 220.31 of this article, when such sale takes place upon the grounds of a child day care or educational facility under circumstances evincing knowledge by the defendant that such sale is taking place upon such grounds. As used in this subdivision, the phrase "the grounds of a child day care or educational facility" shall have the same meaning as provided for in subdivision five of section 220.44 of this article. For the purposes of this subdivision, a rebuttable presumption shall be established that a person has knowledge that they are within the grounds of a child day care or educational facility when notice is conspicuously posted of the presence or proximity of such facility; or
9. one or more preparations, compounds, mixtures or substances containing gamma hydroxybutyric acid, as defined in paragraph four of subdivision (e) of schedule I of section thirty-three hundred six of the public health law, and said preparations, compounds, mixtures or substances are of an aggregate weight of twenty-eight grams or more.

Criminal sale of a controlled substance in the fourth degree is a class C felony.

§220.39 Criminal sale of a controlled substance in the third degree.

A person is guilty of criminal sale of a controlled substance in the third degree when he knowingly and unlawfully sells:

1. a narcotic drug; or

2. a stimulant, hallucinogen, hallucinogenic substance, or lysergic acid diethylamide and has previously been convicted of an offense defined in article two hundred twenty or the attempt or conspiracy to commit any such offense; or

3. a stimulant and the stimulant weighs one gram or more; or

4. lysergic acid diethylamide and the lysergic acid diethylamide weighs one milligram or more; or

5. a hallucinogen and the hallucinogen weighs twenty-five milligrams or more; or

6. a hallucinogenic substance and the hallucinogenic substance weighs one gram or more; or

7. one or more preparations, compounds, mixtures or substances containing methamphetamine, its salts, isomers or salts of isomers and the preparations, compounds, mixtures or substances are of an aggregate weight of one-eighth ounce or more; or

8. phencyclidine and the phencyclidine weighs two hundred fifty milligrams or more; or

9. a narcotic preparation to a person less than twenty-one years old.

Criminal sale of a controlled substance in the third degree is a class B felony.

§220.41 Criminal sale of a controlled substance in the second degree.

A person is guilty of criminal sale of a controlled substance in the second degree when he knowingly and unlawfully sells:

1. one or more preparations, compounds, mixtures or substances containing a narcotic drug and the preparations, compounds, mixtures or substances are of an aggregate weight of one-half ounce or more; or

2. one or more preparations, compounds, mixtures or substances containing methamphetamine, its salts, isomers or salts of isomers and the preparations, compounds, mixtures or substances are of an aggregate weight of one-half ounce or more; or

3. a stimulant and the stimulant weighs five grams or more; or

4. lysergic acid diethylamide and the lysergic acid diethylamide weighs five milligrams or more; or

5. a hallucinogen and the hallucinogen weighs one hundred twenty-five milligrams or more; or

6. a hallucinogenic substance and the hallucinogenic substance weighs five grams or more; or

7. methadone and the methadone weighs three hundred sixty milligrams or more.

Criminal sale of a controlled substance in the second degree is a class A-II felony.

§220.43 Criminal sale of a controlled substance in the first degree.

A person is guilty of criminal sale of a controlled substance in the first degree when he knowingly and unlawfully sells:

1. one or more preparations, compounds, mixtures or substances containing a narcotic drug and the preparations, compounds, mixtures or substances are of an aggregate weight of two ounces or more; or

2. methadone and the methadone weighs two thousand eight hundred eighty milligrams or more.

Criminal sale of a controlled substance in the first degree is a class A-I felony.

§220.44 Criminal sale of a controlled substance in or near school grounds.

A person is guilty of criminal sale of a controlled substance in or near school grounds when he knowingly and unlawfully sells:

1. a controlled substance in violation of any one of subdivisions one through six-a of section 220.34 of this article, when such sale takes place upon school grounds or on a school bus; or

2. a controlled substance in violation of any one of subdivisions one through eight of section 220.39 of this article, when such sale takes place upon school grounds or on a school bus; or

3. a controlled substance in violation of any one of subdivisions one through six of section 220.34 of this article, when such sale takes place upon the grounds of a child day care or educational facility under circumstances evincing knowledge by the defendant that such sale is taking place upon such grounds; or

4. a controlled substance in violation of any one of subdivisions one through eight of section 220.39 of this article, when such sale takes place upon the grounds of a child day care or educational facility under circumstances evincing knowledge by the defendant that such sale is taking place upon such grounds.

5. For purposes of subdivisions three and four of this section, "the grounds of a child day care or educational facility" means (a) in or on or within any building, structure, athletic playing field, a playground or land contained within the real property boundary line of a public or private child day care center as such term is defined in paragraph (c) of subdivision one of section three hundred ninety of the social services law, or nursery, pre-kindergarten or kindergarten, or (b) any area accessible to the public located within one thousand feet of the real property boundary line comprising any such facility or any parked automobile or other parked vehicle located within one thousand feet of the real property boundary line comprising any such facility. For the purposes of this section an "area accessible to the public" shall mean sidewalks, streets, parking lots, parks, playgrounds, stores and restaurants.

6. For the purposes of this section, a rebuttable presumption shall be established that a person has knowledge that they are within the grounds of a child day care or educational facility when notice is conspicuously posted of the presence or proximity of such facility.

Criminal sale of a controlled substance in or near school grounds is a class B felony.

§220.45 Criminally possessing a hypodermic instrument.

(REPEALED, Eff.10/7/21,Ch.433,L.2021)

§220.46 Criminal injection of a narcotic drug.

A person is guilty of criminal injection of a narcotic drug when he knowingly and unlawfully possesses a narcotic drug and he intentionally injects by means of a hypodermic syringe or hypodermic needle all or any portion of that drug into the body of another person with the latter's consent.

Criminal injection of a narcotic drug is a class E felony.

§220.48 Criminal sale of a controlled substance to a child.

A person is guilty of criminal sale of a controlled substance to a child when, being over twenty-one years old, he or she knowingly and unlawfully sells a controlled substance in violation of section 220.34 or 220.39 of this article to a person less than seventeen years old.

Criminal sale of a controlled substance to a child is a class B felony.

§220.50 Criminally using drug paraphernalia in the second degree.

A person is guilty of criminally using drug paraphernalia in the second degree when he knowingly possesses or sells:

1. Diluents, dilutants or adulterants, including but not limited to, any of the following: quinine hydrochloride, mannitol, mannite, lactose or dextrose, adapted for the dilution of narcotic drugs or stimulants under circumstances evincing an intent to use, or under circumstances evincing knowledge that some person intends to use, the same for purposes of unlawfully mixing, compounding, or otherwise preparing any narcotic drug or stimulant; or

2. Gelatine capsules, glassine envelopes, vials, capsules or any other material suitable for the packaging of individual quantities of narcotic drugs or stimulants under circumstances evincing an intent to use, or under circumstances evincing knowledge that some person intends to use, the same for the purpose of unlawfully manufacturing, packaging or dispensing of any narcotic drug or stimulant; or

3. Scales and balances used or designed for the purpose of weighing or measuring controlled substances, under circumstances evincing an intent to use, or under circumstances evincing knowledge that some person intends to use, the same for purpose of unlawfully manufacturing, packaging or dispensing of any narcotic drug or stimulant.

Criminally using drug paraphernalia in the second degree is a class A misdemeanor.

§220.55 Criminally using drug paraphernalia in the first degree.

A person is guilty of criminally using drug paraphernalia in the first degree when he commits the crime of criminally using drug paraphernalia in the second degree and he has previously been convicted of criminally using drug paraphernalia in the second degree.

Criminally using drug paraphernalia in the first degree is a class D felony.

§220.60 Criminal possession of precursors of controlled substances.

A person is guilty of criminal possession of precursors of controlled substances when, with intent to manufacture a controlled substance unlawfully, he possesses at the same time:

(a) carbamide (urea) and propanedioc and malonic acid or its derivatives; or

(b) ergot or an ergot derivative and diethylamine or dimethylformamide or diethylamide; or

(c) phenylaceton (1-phenyl-2 propanone) and hydroxylamine or ammonia or formamide or benzaldehyde or nitroethane or methylamine.

(d) pentazocine and methyliodid; or

(e) phenylacetonitrile and dichlorodiethyl methylamine or dichlorodiethyl benzylamine; or

(f) diphenylacetonitrile and dimethylaminoisopropyl chloride; or

(g) piperidine and cyclohexanone and bromobenzene and lithium or magnesium; or

(h) 2,5-dimethoxy benzaldehyde and nitroethane and a reducing agent.

Criminal possession of precursors of controlled substances is a class E felony.

§220.65 Criminal sale of a prescription for a controlled substance or of a controlled substance by a practitioner or pharmacist.

A person is guilty of criminal sale of a prescription for a controlled substance or of a controlled substance by a practitioner or pharmacist when:

1. being a practitioner, as that term is defined in section thirty-three hundred two of the public health law, he or she knowingly and unlawfully sells a prescription for a controlled substance. For the purposes of this section, a person sells a prescription for a controlled substance unlawfully when he or she does so other than in good faith in the course of his or her professional practice; or

2. being a practitioner or pharmacist, as those terms are defined in section thirty-three hundred two of the public health law, he or she, acting other than in good faith, while purporting to act within the scope of the power, authority and privileges of his or her license, as that term is defined in section thirty-three hundred two of the public health law, knowingly and unlawfully sells a controlled substance.

Criminal sale of a prescription for a controlled substance or of a controlled substance by a practitioner or pharmacist is a class C felony.

§220.70 Criminal possession of methamphetamine manufacturing material in the second degree.

A person is guilty of criminal possession of methamphetamine manufacturing material in the second degree when he or she possesses a precursor, a chemical reagent or a solvent with the intent to use or knowing another intends to use such precursor, chemical reagent, or solvent to unlawfully produce, prepare or manufacture methamphetamine.

Criminal possession of methamphetamine manufacturing material in the second degree is a class A misdemeanor.

§220.71 Criminal possession of methamphetamine manufacturing material in the first degree.

A person is guilty of criminal possession of methamphetamine manufacturing material in the first degree when he or she commits the offense of criminal possession of methamphetamine manufacturing material in the second degree, as defined in section 220.70 of this article, and has previously been convicted within the preceding five years of criminal possession of methamphetamine manufacturing material in the second degree, as defined in section 220.70 of this article, or a violation of this section.

Criminal possession of methamphetamine manufacturing material in the first degree is a class E felony.

§220.72 Criminal possession of precursors of methamphetamine.

A person is guilty of criminal possession of precursors of methamphetamine when he or she possesses at the same time a precursor and a solvent or chemical reagent, with intent to use or knowing that another intends to use each such precursor, solvent or chemical reagent to unlawfully manufacture methamphetamine.

Criminal possession of precursors of methamphetamine is a class E felony.

§220.73 Unlawful manufacture of methamphetamine in the third degree.

A person is guilty of unlawful manufacture of methamphetamine in the third degree when he or she possesses at the same time and location, with intent to use, or knowing that another intends to use each such product to unlawfully manufacture, prepare or produce methamphetamine:

1. Two or more items of laboratory equipment and two or more precursors, chemical reagents or solvents in any combination; or

2. One item of laboratory equipment and three or more precursors, chemical reagents or solvents in any combination; or

3. A precursor:
   (a) mixed together with a chemical reagent or solvent; or
   (b) with two or more chemical reagents and/or solvents mixed together.

Unlawful manufacture of methamphetamine in the third degree is a class D felony.

§220.74 Unlawful manufacture of methamphetamine in the second degree.

A person is guilty of unlawful manufacture of methamphetamine in the second degree when he or she:

1. Commits the offense of unlawful manufacture of methamphetamine in the third degree as defined in section 220.73 of this article in the presence of another person under the age of sixteen, provided, however, that the actor is at least five years older than such other person under the age of sixteen; or

2. Commits the crime of unlawful manufacture of methamphetamine in the third degree as defined in section 220.73 of this article and has previously been convicted within the preceding five years of the offense of criminal possession of precursors of methamphetamine as defined in section 220.72 of this article, criminal possession of methamphetamine

manufacturing material in the first degree as defined in section 220.71 of this article, unlawful disposal of methamphetamine laboratory material as defined in section 220.76 of this article, unlawful manufacture of methamphetamine in the third degree as defined in section 220.73 of this article, unlawful manufacture of methamphetamine in the second degree as defined in this section, or unlawful manufacture of methamphetamine in the first degree as defined in section 220.75 of this article.

Unlawful manufacture of methamphetamine in the second degree is a class C felony.

§220.75 Unlawful manufacture of methamphetamine in the first degree.

A person is guilty of unlawful manufacture of methamphetamine in the first degree when such person commits the crime of unlawful manufacture of methamphetamine in the second degree, as defined in subdivision one of section 220.74 of this article, after having previously been convicted within the preceding five years of unlawful manufacture of methamphetamine in the third degree, as defined in section 220.73, unlawful manufacture of methamphetamine in the second degree, as defined in section 220.74 of this article, or unlawful manufacture of methamphetamine in the first degree, as defined in this section.

Unlawful manufacturer* of methamphetamine in the first degree is a class B felony.

*(So in original. Probably should read "manufacture".)

§220.76 Unlawful disposal of methamphetamine laboratory material.

A person is guilty of unlawful disposal of methamphetamine laboratory material when, knowing that such actions are in furtherance of a methamphetamine operation, he or she knowingly disposes of, or possesses with intent to dispose of, hazardous or dangerous material under circumstances that create a substantial risk to human health or safety or a substantial danger to the environment.

Unlawful disposal of methamphetamine laboratory material is a class E felony.

§220.77 Operating as a major trafficker.

A person is guilty of operating as a major trafficker when:

1. Such person acts as a director of a controlled substance organization during any period of twelve months or less, during which period such controlled substance organization sells one or more controlled substances, and the proceeds collected or due from such sale or sales have a total aggregate value of seventy-five thousand dollars or more; or

2. As a profiteer, such person knowingly and unlawfully sells, on one or more occasions within six months or less, a narcotic drug, and the proceeds collected or due from such sale or sales have a total aggregate value of seventy-five thousand dollars or more.

3. As a profiteer, such person knowingly and unlawfully possesses, on one or more occasions within six months or less, a narcotic drug with intent to sell the same, and such narcotic drugs have a total aggregate value of seventy-five thousand dollars or more.

Operating as a major trafficker is a class A-I felony.

§220.78 Witness or victim of drug or alcohol overdose.

1. A person who, in good faith, seeks health care for someone who is experiencing a drug or alcohol overdose or other life threatening medical emergency shall not be charged or prosecuted for a controlled substance offense under this article or a cannabis offense under article two hundred twenty-two of this title, other than an offense involving sale for consideration or other benefit or gain, or charged or prosecuted for possession of alcohol by a person under age twenty-one years under section sixty-five-c of the alcoholic beverage control law, or for possession of drug paraphernalia under article thirty-nine of the general business law, with respect to any controlled substance, cannabis, alcohol or paraphernalia that was obtained as a result of such seeking or receiving of health care.

2. A person who is experiencing a drug or alcohol overdose or other life threatening medical emergency and, in good faith, seeks health care for himself or herself or is the subject of such a good faith request for health care, shall not be charged or prosecuted for a controlled substance offense under this article or a cannabis offense under article two hundred twenty-two of this title, other than an offense involving sale for consideration or other benefit or gain, or charged or prosecuted for possession of alcohol by a person under age twenty-one years under section sixty-five-c of the alcoholic beverage control law, or charged or prosecuted for possession of cannabis or concentrated cannabis by a person under the age of twenty-one under section one hundred thirty-two of the cannabis law, or for possession of drug paraphernalia under article thirty-nine of the general business law, with respect to any substance, cannabis, alcohol or paraphernalia that was obtained as a result of such seeking or receiving of health care.

3. Definitions. As used in this section the following terms shall have the following meanings:

(a) "Drug or alcohol overdose" or "overdose" means an acute condition including, but not limited to, physical illness, coma, mania, hysteria or death, which is the result of consumption or use of a controlled substance or alcohol and relates to an adverse reaction to or the quantity of the controlled substance or alcohol or a substance with which the controlled substance or alcohol was combined; provided that a patient's condition shall be deemed to be a drug or alcohol overdose if a prudent layperson, possessing an average knowledge of medicine and health, could reasonably believe that the condition is in fact a drug or alcohol overdose and (except as to death) requires health care.

(b) "Health care" means the professional services provided to a person experiencing a drug or alcohol overdose by a health care professional licensed, registered or certified under title eight of the education law or article thirty of the public health law who, acting within his or her lawful scope of practice, may provide diagnosis, treatment or emergency services for a person experiencing a drug or alcohol overdose.

4. It shall be an affirmative defense to a criminal sale controlled substance offense under this article or a criminal sale of cannabis offense under article two hundred twenty-two of this title, not covered by subdivision one or two of this section, with respect to any controlled substance or cannabis which was obtained as a result of such seeking or receiving of health care, that:

(a) the defendant, in good faith, seeks health care for someone or for him or herself who is experiencing a drug or alcohol overdose or other life threatening medical emergency; and

(b) the defendant has no prior conviction for the commission or attempted commission of a class A-I, A-II or B felony under this article.

5. Nothing in this section shall be construed to bar the admissibility of any evidence in connection with the investigation and prosecution of a crime with regard to another defendant who does not independently qualify for the bar to prosecution or for the affirmative defense; nor with regard to other crimes committed by a person who otherwise qualifies under this section; nor shall anything in this section be construed to bar any seizure pursuant to law, including but not limited to pursuant to section thirty-three hundred eighty-seven of the public health law.

6. The bar to prosecution described in subdivisions one and two of this section shall not apply to the prosecution of a class A-I felony under this article, and the affirmative defense described in subdivision four of this section shall not apply to the prosecution of a class A-I or A-II felony under this article.   *(Eff.3/31/21,Ch.92,L.2021)*

ARTICLE 221 - OFFENSES INVOLVING MARIHUANA
(Repealed, Eff.3/31/21,Ch.92,L.2021)

ARTICLE 222 - CANNABIS
(Eff.3/31/21,Ch.92,L.2021)

Section
222.00 Cannabis; definitions.
222.05 Personal use of cannabis.
222.10 Restrictions on cannabis use.
222.15 Personal cultivation and home possession of cannabis.
222.20 Licensing of cannabis production and distribution; defense.
222.25 Unlawful possession of cannabis.
222.30 Criminal possession of cannabis in the third degree.
222.35 Criminal possession of cannabis in the second degree.
222.40 Criminal possession of cannabis in the first degree.
222.45 Unlawful sale of cannabis.
222.50 Criminal sale of cannabis in the third degree.
222.55 Criminal sale of cannabis in the second degree.
222.60 Criminal sale of cannabis in the first degree.
222.65 Aggravated criminal sale of cannabis.

§222.00 Cannabis; definitions.

1. "Cannabis" means all parts of the plant of the genus Cannabis, whether growing or not; the seeds thereof; the resin extracted from any part of the plant; and every compound, manufacture, salt, derivative,

mixture, or preparation of the plant, its seeds or resin. It does not include the mature stalks of the plant, fiber produced from the stalks, oil or cake made from the seeds of the plant, any other compound, manufacture, salt, derivative, mixture, or preparation of the mature stalks (except the resin extracted therefrom), fiber, oil, or cake, or the sterilized seed of the plant which is incapable of germination. It does not include hemp, cannabinoid hemp or hemp extract as defined in section three of the cannabis law or drug products approved by the Federal Food and Drug Administration.

2. "Concentrated cannabis" means:

(a) the separated resin, whether crude or purified, obtained from a plant of the genus Cannabis; or

(b) a material, preparation, mixture, compound or other substance which contains more than three percent by weight of delta-9 tetrahydrocannabinol, or its isomer, delta-8 dibenzopyran numbering system, or delta-1 tetrahydrocannabinol or its isomer, delta 1 (6) monoterpene numbering system.

3. For the purposes of this article, "sell" shall mean to sell, exchange or dispose of for compensation. "Sell" shall not include the transfer of cannabis or concentrated cannabis between persons twenty-one years of age or older without compensation in the quantities authorized in paragraph (b) of subdivision one of section 222.05 of this article.

4. For the purposes of this article, "smoking" shall have the same meaning as that term is defined in section three of the cannabis law.

§222.05 Personal use of cannabis.

Notwithstanding any other provision of law to the contrary:

1. The following acts are lawful for persons twenty-one years of age or older: (a) possessing, displaying, purchasing, obtaining, or transporting up to three ounces of cannabis and up to twenty-four grams of concentrated cannabis;

(b) transferring, without compensation, to a person twenty-one years of age or older, up to three ounces of cannabis and up to twenty-four grams of concentrated cannabis;

(c) using, smoking, ingesting, or consuming cannabis or concentrated cannabis unless otherwise prohibited by state law;

(d) possessing, using, displaying, purchasing, obtaining, manufacturing, transporting or giving to any person twenty-one years of age or older cannabis paraphernalia or concentrated cannabis paraphernalia;

(e) planting, cultivating, harvesting, drying, processing or possessing cultivated cannabis in accordance with section 222.15 of this article; and

(f) assisting another person who is twenty-one years of age or older, or allowing property to be used, in any of the acts described in paragraphs (a) through (e) of this subdivision.

2. Cannabis, concentrated cannabis, cannabis paraphernalia or concentrated cannabis paraphernalia involved in any way with conduct deemed lawful by this section are not contraband nor subject to seizure or forfeiture of assets under article four hundred eighty of this chapter, section thirteen hundred eleven of the civil practice law and rules, or other applicable law, and no conduct deemed lawful by this section shall constitute the basis for approach, search, seizure, arrest or detention.

3. Except as provided in subdivision four of this section, in any criminal proceeding including proceedings pursuant to section 710.20 of the criminal procedure law, no finding or determination of reasonable cause to believe a crime has been committed shall be based solely on evidence of the following facts and circumstances, either individually or in combination with each other:

(a) the odor of cannabis;

(b) the odor of burnt cannabis;

(c) the possession of or the suspicion of possession of cannabis or concentrated cannabis in the amounts authorized in this article;

(d) the possession of multiple containers of cannabis without evidence of concentrated cannabis in the amounts authorized in this article;

(e) the presence of cash or currency in proximity to cannabis or concentrated cannabis; or

(f) the planting, cultivating, harvesting, drying, processing or possessing cultivated cannabis in accordance with section 222.15 of this article.

4. Paragraph (b) of subdivision three of this section shall not apply when a law enforcement officer is investigating whether a person is operating a motor vehicle, vessel or snowmobile while impaired by drugs or the combined influence of drugs or of alcohol and any drug or drugs in violation of subdivision four or subdivision four-a of section eleven hundred ninety-two of the vehicle and traffic law, or paragraph (e) of subdivision two of section forty-nine-a of the navigation law, or paragraph (d) of subdivision one of section 25.24 of the parks, recreation and historic preservation law. During such investigations, the odor of burnt cannabis shall not provide probable cause to search any area of a vehicle that is not readily accessible to the driver and reasonably likely to contain evidence relevant to the driver's condition.

§222.10 Restrictions on cannabis use.

Unless otherwise authorized by law or regulation, no person shall:

1. smoke or vape cannabis in a location where smoking or vaping cannabis is prohibited pursuant to article thirteen-E of the public health law; or

2. smoke, vape or ingest cannabis or concentrated cannabis in or upon the grounds of a school, as defined in subdivision ten of section eleven hundred twenty-five of the education law or in or on a school bus, as defined in section one hundred forty-two of the vehicle and traffic law;

provided, however, provisions of this subdivision shall not apply to acts that are in compliance with article three of the cannabis law.

Notwithstanding any other section of law, violations of restrictions on cannabis use are subject to a civil penalty not exceeding twenty-five dollars or an amount of community service not exceeding twenty hours.

§222.15 Personal cultivation and home possession of cannabis.

1. Except as provided for in section forty-one of the cannabis law, and unless otherwise authorized by law or regulation, no person may:

(a) plant, cultivate, harvest, dry, process or possess more than three mature cannabis plants and three immature cannabis plants at any one time; or

(b) plant, cultivate, harvest, dry, process or possess, within his or her private residence, or on the grounds of his or her private residence, more than three mature cannabis plants and three immature cannabis plants at any one time; or

(c) being under the age of twenty-one, plant, cultivate, harvest, dry, process or possess cannabis plants.

2. No more than six mature and six immature cannabis plants may be cultivated, harvested, dried, or possessed within any private residence, or on the grounds of a person's private residence.

3. The personal cultivation of cannabis shall only be permitted within, or on the grounds of, a person's private residence.

4. Any mature or immature cannabis plant described in paragraph (a) or (b) of subdivision one of this section, and any cannabis produced by any such cannabis plant or plants cultivated, harvested, dried, processed or possessed pursuant to paragraph (a) or (b) of subdivision one of this section shall, unless otherwise authorized by law or regulation, be stored within such person's private residence or on the grounds of such person's private residence. Such person shall take reasonable steps designed to ensure that such cultivated cannabis is in a secured place and not accessible to any person under the age of twenty-one.

5. Notwithstanding any law to the contrary, a person may lawfully possess up to five pounds of cannabis in their private residence or on the grounds of such person's private residence. Such person shall take reasonable steps designed to ensure that such cannabis is in a secured place not accessible to any person under the age of twenty-one.

6. A county, town, city or village may enact and enforce regulations to reasonably regulate the actions and conduct set forth in subdivision one of this section; provided that:

(a) a violation of any such a regulation, as approved by such county, town, city or village enacting the regulation, may constitute no more than an infraction and may be punishable by no more than a discretionary civil penalty of two hundred dollars or less; and

(b) no county, town, city or village may enact or enforce any such regulation or regulations that may completely or essentially prohibit a person from engaging in the action or conduct authorized by subdivision one of this section.

A violation of this section, other than paragraph (a) of subdivision six of this section, may be subject to a civil penalty of up to one hundred twenty-five dollars per violation.

7. The office of cannabis management shall issue regulations for the home cultivation of cannabis. The office of cannabis management shall enact, and may enforce, regulations to regulate the actions and conduct set forth in this section including requirements for, or restrictions and prohibitions on, the use of any compressed flammable gas solvents such as propane, butane, or other hexane gases for cannabis processing; or other forms of home cultivation, manufacturing, or cannabinoid production and processing, which the office determines poses a danger to public safety; and to ensure the home cultivation of cannabis is for personal use by an adult over the age of twenty-one in possession of cannabis plants, and not utilized for unlicensed commercial or illicit activity, provided any regulations issued by the office shall not completely or essentially prohibit a person from engaging in the action or conduct authorized by this section.

8. The office of cannabis management may issue guidance or advisories for the education and promotion of safe practices for activities and conduct authorized in subdivision one of this section.

9. Subdivisions one through five of this section shall not take effect until such a time as the office of cannabis management has issued regulations governing the home cultivation of cannabis. The office shall issue rules and regulations governing the home cultivation of cannabis by certified patients as defined in section three of the cannabis law, no later than six months after the effective date of this article and shall issue rules and regulations governing the home cultivation of cannabis for cannabis consumers as defined by section three of the cannabis law no later than eighteen months following the first authorized retail sale of adult-use cannabis products to a cannabis consumer.

§222.20 Licensing of cannabis production and distribution; defense.
In any prosecution for an offense involving cannabis under this article or an authorized local law, it is a defense that the defendant was engaged in such activity in compliance with the cannabis law.

§222.25 Unlawful possession of cannabis.
A person is guilty of unlawful possession of cannabis when he or she knowingly and unlawfully possesses cannabis and such cannabis weighs more than three ounces or concentrated cannabis and such concentrated cannabis weighs more than twenty-four grams.

Unlawful possession of cannabis is a violation punishable by a fine of not more than one hundred twenty-five dollars.

§222.30 Criminal possession of cannabis in the third degree.

A person is guilty of criminal possession of cannabis in the third degree when he or she knowingly and unlawfully possesses:

1. cannabis and such cannabis weighs more than sixteen ounces; or
2. concentrated cannabis and such concentrated cannabis weighs more than five ounces.

Criminal possession of cannabis in the third degree is a class A misdemeanor.

§222.35 Criminal possession of cannabis in the second degree.

A person is guilty of criminal possession of cannabis in the second degree when he or she knowingly and unlawfully possesses:

1. cannabis and such cannabis weighs more than five pounds; or
2. concentrated cannabis and such concentrated cannabis weighs more than two pounds.

Criminal possession of cannabis in the second degree is a class E felony.

§222.40 Criminal possession of cannabis in the first degree.

A person is guilty of criminal possession of cannabis in the first degree when he or she knowingly and unlawfully possesses:

1. cannabis and such cannabis weighs more than ten pounds; or
2. concentrated cannabis and such concentrated cannabis weighs more than four pounds.

Criminal possession of cannabis in the first degree is a class D felony.

§222.45 Unlawful sale of cannabis.

A person is guilty of unlawful sale of cannabis when he or she knowingly and unlawfully sells cannabis or concentrated cannabis.

Unlawful sale of cannabis is a violation punishable by a fine of not more than two hundred fifty dollars.

§222.50 Criminal sale of cannabis in the third degree.

A person is guilty of criminal sale of cannabis in the third degree when:

1. he or she knowingly and unlawfully sells more than three ounces of cannabis or more than twenty-four grams of concentrated cannabis; or
2. being twenty-one years of age or older, he or she knowingly and unlawfully sells or gives, or causes to be given or sold, cannabis or concentrated cannabis to a person less than twenty-one years of age; except that in any prosecution under this subdivision, it is a defense that the defendant was less than three years older than the person under the age of twenty-one at the time of the offense. This subdivision shall not apply to designated caregivers, practitioners, employees of a registered organization or employees of a designated caregiver facility acting in compliance with article three of the cannabis law.

Criminal sale of cannabis in the third degree is a class A misdemeanor.

§222.55 Criminal sale of cannabis in the second degree.

A person is guilty of criminal sale of cannabis in the second degree when:

1. he or she knowingly and unlawfully sells more than sixteen ounces of cannabis or more than five ounces of concentrated cannabis; or

2. being twenty-one years of age or older, he or she knowingly and unlawfully sells or gives, or causes to be given or sold, more than three ounces of cannabis or more than twenty-four grams of concentrated cannabis to a person less than eighteen years of age. This subdivision shall not apply to designated caregivers, practitioners, employees of a registered organization or employees of a designated caregiver facility acting in compliance with article three of the cannabis law.

Criminal sale of cannabis in the second degree is a class E felony.

§222.60 Criminal sale of cannabis in the first degree.

A person is guilty of criminal sale of cannabis in the first degree when he or she knowingly and unlawfully sells more than five pounds of cannabis or more than two pounds of concentrated cannabis.

Criminal sale of cannabis in the first degree is a class D felony.

§222.65 Aggravated criminal sale of cannabis.

A person is guilty of aggravated criminal sale of cannabis when he or she knowingly and unlawfully sells cannabis or concentrated cannabis weighing one hundred pounds or more.

Aggravated criminal sale of cannabis is a class C felony.

ARTICLE 225 - GAMBLING OFFENSES

Section
225.00 Gambling offenses; definitions of terms.
225.05 Promoting gambling in the second degree.
225.10 Promoting gambling in the first degree.
225.15 Possession of gambling records in the second degree.
225.20 Possession of gambling records in the first degree.
225.25 Possession of gambling records; defense.
225.30 Possession of a gambling device.
225.32 Possession of a gambling device; defenses.
225.35 Gambling offenses; presumptions.
225.40 Lottery offenses; no defense.
225.55 Gaming fraud in the second degree.
225.60 Gaming fraud in the first degree.
225.65 Use of counterfeit, unapproved or unlawful wagering instruments.
225.70 Possession of unlawful gaming property in the third degree.
225.75 Possession of unlawful gaming property in the second degree.
225.80 Possession of unlawful gaming property in the first degree.
225.85 Use of unlawful gaming property.
225.90 Manipulation of gaming outcomes at an authorized gaming establishment.
225.95 Unlawful manufacture, sale, distribution, marking, altering or modification of equipment and devices associated with gaming.

§225.00 Gambling offenses; definitions of terms.

The following definitions are applicable to this article:

1. "Contest of chance" means any contest, game, gaming scheme or gaming device in which the outcome depends in a material degree upon an element of chance, notwithstanding that skill of the contestants may also be a factor therein.

2. "Gambling." A person engages in gambling when he stakes or risks something of value upon the outcome of a contest of chance or a future contingent event not under his control or influence, upon an agreement or understanding that he will receive something of value in the event of a certain outcome.

3. "Player" means a person who engages in any form of gambling solely as a contestant or bettor, without receiving or becoming entitled to receive any profit therefrom other than personal gambling winnings, and without otherwise rendering any material assistance to the establishment, conduct or operation of the particular gambling activity. A person who gambles at a social game of chance on equal terms with the other participants therein does not otherwise render material assistance to the establishment, conduct or operation thereof by performing, without fee or remuneration, acts directed toward the arrangement or facilitation of the game, such as inviting persons to play, permitting the use of premises therefor and supplying cards or other equipment used therein. A person who engages in "bookmaking", as defined in this section is not a "player."

4. "Advance gambling activity." A person "advances gambling activity" when, acting other than as a player, he engages in conduct which materially aids any form of gambling activity. Such conduct includes but is not limited to conduct directed toward the creation or establishment of the particular game, contest, scheme, device or activity involved, toward the acquisition or maintenance of premises, paraphernalia, equipment or apparatus therefor, toward the solicitation or inducement of persons to participate therein, toward the actual conduct of the playing phases thereof, toward the arrangement of any of its financial or recording phases, or toward any other phase of its

operation. One advances gambling activity when, having substantial proprietary or other authoritative control over premises being used with his knowledge for purposes of gambling activity, he permits such to occur or continue or makes no effort to prevent its occurrence or continuation.

5. "Profit from gambling activity." A person "profits from gambling activity" when, other than as a player, he accepts or receives money or other property pursuant to an agreement or understanding with any person whereby he participates or is to participate in the proceeds of gambling activity.

6. "Something of value" means any money or property, any token, object or article exchangeable for money or property, or any form of credit or promise directly or indirectly contemplating transfer of money or property or of any interest therein, or involving extension of a service, entertainment or a privilege of playing at a game or scheme without charge.

7. "Gambling device" means any device, machine, paraphernalia or equipment which is used or usable in the playing phases of any gambling activity, whether such activity consists of gambling between persons or gambling by a person involving the playing of a machine. Notwithstanding the foregoing, lottery tickets, policy slips and other items used in the playing phases of lottery and policy schemes are not gambling devices.

7-a. A "coin operated gambling device" means a gambling device which operates as a result of the insertion of something of value. A device designed, constructed or readily adaptable or convertible for such use is a coin operated gambling device notwithstanding the fact that it may require adjustment, manipulation or repair in order to operate as such. A machine which awards free or extended play is not a gambling device merely because such free or extended play may constitute something of value provided that the outcome depends upon the skill of the player and not in a material degree upon an element of chance.

8. "Slot machine" means a gambling device which, as a result of the insertion of a coin or other object, operates, either completely automatically or with the aid of some physical act by the player, in such manner that, depending upon elements of chance, it may eject something of value. A device so constructed, or readily adaptable or convertible to such use, is no less a slot machine because it is not in working order or because some mechanical act of manipulation or repair is required to accomplish its adaptation, conversion or workability. Nor is it any less a slot machine because, apart from its use or adaptability as such, it may also sell or deliver something of value on a basis other than chance. A machine which sells items of merchandise which are of equivalent value, is not a slot machine merely because such items differ from each other in composition, size, shape or color.

9. "Bookmaking" means advancing gambling activity by unlawfully accepting bets from members of the public as a business, rather than in a casual or personal fashion, upon the outcomes of future contingent events.

10. "Lottery" means an unlawful gambling scheme in which (a) the

players pay or agree to pay something of value for chances, represented and differentiated by numbers or by combinations of numbers or by some other media, one or more of which chances are to be designated the winning ones; and (b) the winning chances are to be determined by a drawing or by some other method based upon the element of chance; and (c) the holders of the winning chances are to receive something of value provided, however, that in no event shall the provisions of this subdivision be construed to include a raffle as such term is defined in subdivision three-b of section one hundred eighty-six of the general municipal law.

11. "Policy" or "the numbers game" means a form of lottery in which the winning chances or plays are not determined upon the basis of a drawing or other act on the part of persons conducting or connected with the scheme, but upon the basis of the outcome or outcomes of a future contingent event or events otherwise unrelated to the particular scheme.

12. "Unlawful" means not specifically authorized by law.

13. "Authorized gaming establishment" means any structure, structure and adjacent or attached structure, or grounds adjacent to a structure in which casino gaming, conducted pursuant to article thirteen of the racing, pari-mutuel wagering and breeding law, or Class III gaming, as authorized pursuant to a compact reached between the state of New York and a federally recognized Indian nation or tribe under the federal Indian Gaming Regulatory Act of 1988, is conducted and shall include all public and non-public areas of any such building, except for such areas of a building where either Class I or II gaming are conducted or any building or grounds known as a video gaming entertainment facility, including facilities where food and drink are served, as well as those areas not normally open to the public, such as where records related to video lottery gaming operations are kept, except shall not include the racetracks or such areas where such video lottery gaming operations or facilities do not take place or exist, such as racetrack areas or fairgrounds which are wholly unrelated to video lottery gaming operations, pursuant to section sixteen hundred seventeen-a and paragraph five of subdivision a of section sixteen hundred twelve of the tax law, as amended and implemented.

14. "Authorized gaming operator" means an enterprise or business entity authorized by state or federal law to operate casino or video lottery gaming.

15. "Casino gaming" means games authorized to be played pursuant to a license granted under article thirteen of the racing, pari-mutuel wagering and breeding law or by federally recognized Indian nations or tribes pursuant to a gaming compact reached in accordance with the federal Indian Gaming Regulatory Act of 1988, Pub. L. 100-497, 102 Stat. 2467, codified at 25 U.S.C. Sections 2701-21 and 18 U.S.C. Sections 1166-68.

16. "Cash equivalent" means a treasury check, a travelers check, wire transfer of funds, transfer check, money order, certified check, cashiers check, payroll check, a check drawn on the account of the authorized gaming operator payable to the patron or to the authorized gaming establishment, a promotional coupon, promotional chip, promotional cheque, promotional token, or a voucher recording cash drawn against a credit card or charge card.

17. "Cheques" or "chips" or "tokens" means nonmetal, metal or partly metal representatives of value, redeemable for cash or cash equivalent,

and issued and sold by an authorized casino operator for use at an authorized gaming establishment. The value of such cheques or chips or tokens shall be considered equivalent in value to the cash or cash equivalent exchanged for such cheques or chips or tokens upon purchase or redemption.

18. "Class I gaming" and "Class II gaming" means those forms of gaming that are not Class III gaming, as defined in subsection eight of section four of the federal Indian Gaming Regulatory Act, 25 U.S.C. §2703.

19. "Class III gaming" means those forms of gaming that are not Class I or Class II gaming, as defined in subsections six and seven of section four of the federal Indian Gaming Regulatory Act, 25 U.S.C. §2703 and those games enumerated in the Appendix of a gaming compact.

20. "Compact" or "gaming compact" means the agreement between a federally recognized Indian tribe and the state of New York regarding Class III gaming activities entered into pursuant to the federal Indian Gaming Regulatory Act, Pub. L. 100-497, 102 Stat. 2467, codified at 25 U.S.C. Sections 2701-21 and 18 U.S.C. Sections 1166-68 (1988 & Supp. II).

21. "Gaming equipment or device" means any machine or device which is specially designed or manufactured for use in the operation of any Class III or video lottery game.

22. "Gaming regulatory authority" means, with respect to any authorized gaming establishment on Indian lands, territory or reservation, the Indian nation or tribal gaming commission, its authorized officers, agents and representatives acting in their official capacities or such other agency of a nation or tribe as the nation or tribe may designate as the agency responsible for the regulation of Class III gaming, jointly with the state gaming agency, conducted pursuant to a gaming compact between the nation or tribe and the state of New York, or with respect to any casino gaming authorized pursuant to article thirteen of the racing, pari-mutuel wagering and breeding law or video lottery gaming conducted pursuant to section sixteen hundred seventeen-a and paragraph five of subdivision a of section sixteen hundred twelve of the tax law, as amended and implemented.

23. "Premises" includes any structure, parking lot, building, vehicle, watercraft, and any real property.

24. "Sell" means to sell, exchange, give or dispose of to another.

25. "State gaming agency" shall mean the New York state gaming commission, its authorized officials, agents, and representatives acting in their official capacities as the regulatory agency of the state which has responsibility for regulation with respect to video lottery gaming or casino gaming.

26. "Unfair gaming equipment" means loaded dice, marked cards, substituted cards or dice, or fixed roulette wheels or other gaming equipment which has been altered in a way that tends to deceive or tends to alter the elements of chance or normal random selection which determine the result of the game or outcome, or the amount or frequency of the payment in a game.

27. "Unlawful gaming property" means:
   (a) any device, not prescribed for use in casinio* gaming by its
*(So in original "casinio" should be "casino".)

rules, which is capable of assisting a player:

(i) to calculate any probabilities material to the outcome of a contest of chance; or

(ii) to receive or transmit information material to the outcome of a contest of chance; or

(b) any object or article which, by virtue of its size, shape or any other quality, is capable of being used in casino gaming as an improper substitute for a genuine chip, cheque, token, betting coupon, debit instrument, voucher or other instrument or indicia of value; or

(c) any unfair gaming equipment.

28. "Video lottery gaming" has the meaning set forth in subdivision six of section sixteen hundred two of the tax law.

29. "Voucher" means an instrument of value generated by a video lottery terminal representing a monetary amount and/or play value owed to a customer at a specific video lottery terminal based on video lottery gaming winnings and/or amounts not wagered.

§225.05 Promoting gambling in the second degree.

A person is guilty of promoting gambling in the second degree when he knowingly advances or profits from unlawful gambling activity.

Promoting gambling in the second degree is a class A misdemeanor.

§225.10 Promoting gambling in the first degree.

A person is guilty of promoting gambling in the first degree when he knowingly advances or profits from unlawful gambling activity by:

1. Engaging in bookmaking to the extent that he receives or accepts in any one day more than five bets totaling more than five thousand dollars; or

2. Receiving, in connection with a lottery or policy scheme or enterprise, (a) money or written records from a person other than a player whose chances or plays are represented by such money or records, or (b) more than five hundred dollars in any one day of money played in such scheme or enterprise.

Promoting gambling in the first degree is a class E felony.

§225.15 Possession of gambling records in the second degree.

A person is guilty of possession of gambling records in the second degree when, with knowledge of the contents or nature thereof, he possesses any writing, paper, instrument or article:

1. Of a kind commonly used in the operation or promotion of a bookmaking scheme or enterprise; or

2. Of a kind commonly used in the operation, promotion or playing of a lottery or policy scheme or enterprise; except that in any prosecution under this subdivision, it is a defense that the writing, paper, instrument or article possessed by the defendant constituted, reflected or represented plays, bets or chances of the defendant himself in a number not exceeding ten.

3. Of any paper or paper product in sheet form chemically converted to nitrocellulose having explosive characteristics.

4. Of any water soluble paper or paper derivative in sheet form.

Possession of gambling records in the second degree is a class A misdemeanor.

§225.20 Possession of gambling records in the first degree.

A person is guilty of possession of gambling records in the first degree when, with knowledge of the contents thereof, he possesses any writing, paper, instrument or article:

1. Of a kind commonly used in the operation or promotion of a bookmaking scheme or enterprise, and constituting, reflecting or representing more than five bets totaling more than five thousand dollars; or

2. Of a kind commonly used in the operation, promotion or playing of a lottery or policy scheme or enterprise, and constituting, reflecting or representing more than five hundred plays or chances therein.

Possession of gambling records in the first degree is a class E felony.

§225.25 Possession of gambling records; defense.

In any prosecution for possession of gambling records, it is a defense that the writing, paper, instrument or article possessed by the defendant was neither used nor intended to be used in the operation or promotion of a bookmaking scheme or enterprise, or in the operation, promotion or playing of a lottery or policy scheme or enterprise.

§225.30 Possession of a gambling device.

a. A person is guilty of possession of a gambling device when, with knowledge of the character thereof, he or she manufactures, sells, transports, places or possesses, or conducts or negotiates any transaction affecting or designed to affect ownership, custody or use of:

1. A slot machine, unless such possession is permitted pursuant to article nine-A of the general municipal law; or

2. Any other gambling device, believing that the same is to be used in the advancement of unlawful gambling activity; or

3. A coin operated gambling device with intent to use such device in the advancement of unlawful gambling activity.

b. Possession of a slot machine shall not be unlawful where such possession and use is pursuant to a gaming compact, duly executed by the governor and an Indian tribe or Nation, under the Indian Gaming Regulatory Act, as codified at 25 U.S.C. Sections 2701-2721 and 18 U.S.C Sections 1166-1168, where the use of such slot machine or machines is consistent with such gaming compact and where the state receives a negotiated percentage of the net drop (defined as gross money wagered after payout, but before expenses) from any such slot machine or machines.

c. Transportation and possession of a slot machine shall not be unlawful where such transportation and possession is necessary to facilitate the training of persons in the repair and reconditioning of such machines as are used or are to be used for operations in those casinos authorized pursuant to a tribal-state compact as provided for pursuant to section eleven hundred seventy-two of title fifteen of the United States Code in the state of New York.

d. Transportation and possession of a slot machine shall not be unlawful where such slot machine was transported into this state in a sealed container and possessed for the purpose of product development, research, or additional manufacture or assembly, and such slot machine will be or has been transported in a sealed container to a jurisdiction outside of this state for purposes which are lawful in such outside jurisdiction.

e. Transportation and possession of a gambling device shall not be unlawful where (i) the manufacturer or distributor of the gambling device has filed a statement with the state gaming commission required by subdivision twenty-one of section one hundred four of the racing, pari-mutuel wagering and breeding law, (ii) such gambling device was transported into this state in a sealed container and possessed for the purpose of exhibition or marketing in accordance with such statement, and (iii) such device is thereafter transported in a sealed container to a jurisdiction outside of this state for purposes that are lawful in such outside jurisdiction.

Possession of a gambling device is a class A misdemeanor.

§225.32 Possession of a gambling device; defenses.

1. In any prosecution for possession of a gambling device specified in subdivision one of section 225.30 of this article, it is an affirmative defense that: (a) the slot machine possessed by the defendant was neither used nor intended to be used in the operation or promotion of unlawful gambling activity or enterprise and that such slot machine is an antique; for purposes of this section proof that a slot machine was manufactured prior to nineteen hundred forty-one shall be conclusive proof that such a machine is an antique; (b) the slot machine possessed by the defendant was manufactured or assembled by the defendant for the sole purpose of transporting such slot machine in a sealed container to a jurisdiction outside this state for purposes which are lawful in such outside jurisdiction; or (c) the slot machine possessed by the defendant was neither used nor intended to be used in the operation or promotion of unlawful gambling activity or enterprise, is more than thirty years old, and such possession takes place in the defendant's home.

2. Where a defendant raises an affirmative defense provided by subdivision one hereof, any slot machine seized from the defendant shall not be destroyed, or otherwise altered until a final court determination is rendered. In a final court determination rendered in favor of said defendant, such slot machine shall be returned, forthwith, to said defendant, notwithstanding any provisions of law to the contrary.

§225.35 Gambling offenses; presumptions.

1. Proof of possession of any gambling device or of any gambling record specified in sections 225.15 and 225.20, is presumptive evidence of possession thereof with knowledge of its character or contents.

2. In any prosecution under this article in which it is necessary to prove the occurrence of a sporting event, a published report of its occurrence in any daily newspaper, magazine or other periodically printed publication of general circulation shall be admissible in evidence and shall constitute presumptive proof of the occurrence of such event.

3. Possession of three or more coin operated gambling devices or possession of a coin operated gambling device in a public place shall be presumptive evidence of intent to use in the advancement of unlawful gambling activity.

§225.40 Lottery offenses; no defense.

Any offense defined in this article which consists of the commission of acts relating to a lottery is no less criminal because the lottery itself is drawn or conducted without the state and is not violative of the laws of the jurisdiction in which it was so drawn or conducted.

§225.55 Gaming fraud in the second degree.

A person is guilty of gaming fraud in the second degree when he or she:

1. with intent to defraud and in violation of the rules of the casino gaming, misrepresents, changes the amount bet or wagered on, or the outcome or possible outcome of the contest or event which is the subject of the bet or wager, or the amount or frequency of payment in the casino gaming; or

2. with intent to defraud, obtains anything of value from casino gaming without having won such amount by a bet or wager contingent thereon.

Gaming fraud in the second degree is a class A misdemeanor.

§225.60 Gaming fraud in the first degree.

A person is guilty of gaming fraud in the first degree when he or she commits a gaming fraud in the second degree, and:

1. The value of the benefit obtained exceeds one thousand dollars; or

2. He or she has been previously convicted within the preceding five years of any offense of which an essential element is the commission of a gaming fraud.

Gaming fraud in the first degree is a class E felony.

§225.65 Use of counterfeit, unapproved or unlawful wagering instruments.

A person is guilty of use of counterfeit, unapproved or unlawful wagering instruments when in playing or using any casino gaming designed to be played with, received or be operated by chips, cheques, tokens, vouchers or other wagering instruments approved by the appropriate gaming regulatory authority, he or she knowingly uses chips, cheques, tokens, vouchers or other wagering instruments other than those approved by the appropriate gaming regulating authority and the state gaming agency or lawful coin or legal tender of the United States of America.

Possession of more than one counterfeit, unapproved or unlawful wagering instrument described in this section is presumptive evidence of possession thereof with knowledge of its character or contents.

Use of counterfeit, unapproved or unlawful wagering instruments is a class A misdemeanor.

§225.70 Possession of unlawful gaming property in the third degree.

A person is guilty of possession of unlawful gaming property in the third degree when he or she possesses, with intent to use such property to commit gaming fraud, unlawful gaming property at a premises being used for casino gaming.

Possession of unlawful gaming property in the third degree is a class A misdemeanor.

§225.75 Possession of unlawful gaming property in the second degree.

A person is guilty of possession of unlawful gaming property in the second degree when:

1. He or she makes, sells, or possesses with intent to sell, any unlawful gaming property at a casino gaming facility, the value of which exceeds three hundred dollars, with intent that it be made available to a person for unlawful use; or

2. He or she commits possession of unlawful gaming property in the third degree as defined in section 225.70 of this article, and the face value of the improper substitute property exceeds five hundred dollars; or

3. He or she commits the offense of possession of unlawful gaming property in the third degree and has been previously convicted within the preceding five years of any offense of which an essential element is possession of unlawful gaming property.

Possession of unlawful gaming property in the second degree is a class E felony.

§225.80 Possession of unlawful gaming property in the first degree.

A person is guilty of possession of unlawful gaming property in the first degree when:

1. He or she commits the crime of unlawful possession of gaming property in the third degree as defined in section 225.70 of this article and the face value of the improper substitute property exceeds one thousand dollars; or

2. He or she commits the offense of possession of unlawful gaming property in the second degree as defined in subdivision one or two of section 225.75 of this article and has been previously convicted within the preceding five years of any offense of which an essential element is possession of unlawful gaming property.

Possession of unlawful gaming property in the first degree is a class D felony.

§225.85 Use of unlawful gaming property.

A person is guilty of use of unlawful gaming property when he or she knowingly with intent to defraud uses unlawful gaming property at a premises being used for casino gaming.

Use of unlawful gaming property is a class E felony.

§225.90 Manipulation of gaming outcomes at an authorized gaming establishment.

A person is guilty of manipulation of gaming outcomes at an authorized gaming establishment when he or she:

1. Knowingly conducts, operates, deals or otherwise manipulates, or knowingly allows to be conducted, operated, dealt or otherwise manipulated, cards, dice or gaming equipment or device, for themselves or for another, through any trick or sleight of hand performance, with the intent of deceiving or altering the elements of chance or normal random selection which determines the result or outcome of the game, or the amount or frequency of the payment in a game; or

2. Knowingly uses, conducts, operates, deals, or exposes for play, or knowingly allows to be used, conducted, operated, dealt or exposed for play any cards, dice or gaming equipment or device, or any combination of gaming equipment or devices, which have in any manner been altered, marked or tampered with, or placed in a condition, or operated in a manner, the result of which tends to deceive or tends to alter the elements of chance or normal random selection which determine the result of the game or outcome, or the amount or frequency of the payment in a game; or

3. Knowingly uses, or possesses with the intent to use, any cards, dice or other gaming equipment or devices other than that provided by an authorized gaming operator for current use in a permitted gaming activity; or

4. Alters or misrepresents the outcome of a game or other event on which bets or wagers have been made after the outcome is made sure but before it is revealed to players.

Possession of altered, marked or tampered with dice, cards, or gaming equipment or devices at an authorized gambling establishment is presumptive evidence of possession thereof with knowledge of its character or contents and intention to use such altered, marked or tampered with dice, cards, or gaming equipment or devices in violation of this section.

Manipulation of gaming outcomes at an authorized gaming establishment is a class A misdemeanor provided, however, that if the person has previously been convicted of this crime within the past five years this crim* shall be a class E felony.

*(So in original "crim" should be "crime")

§225.95 Unlawful manufacture, sale, distribution, marking, altering or modification of equipment and devices associated with gaming.

A person is guilty of unlawful manufacture, sale, distribution, marking, altering or modification of equipment and devices associated with gaming when if* he or she:

1. Manufactures, sells or distributes any cards, chips, cheques, tokens, dice, vouchers, game or device and he or she knew or reasonably should have known it was intended to be used to violate any provision of this article; or

2. Marks, alters or otherwise modifies any associated gaming equipment or device in a manner that either affects the result of the wager by determining win or loss or alters the normal criteria of random selection in a manner that affects the operation of a game or determines the outcome of a game, and he or she knew or reasonably should have known that it was intended to be used to violate any provision of this article.

Unlawful manufacture, sale, distribution, marking, altering or modification of equipment and devices associated with gaming is a class A misdemeanor provided, however, that if the person has previously been convicted of this crime within the past five years this crim** shall be a class E felony.

*(So in original, "if" inadvertently added.) **(So in original, "crim" should be "crime".)*

ARTICLE 230 - PROSTITUTION OFFENSES

Section
230.00   Prostitution.
230.01   Prostitution; affirmative defense.
230.02   Patronizing a person for prostitution; definitions.
230.03   Prostitution in a school zone.
230.04   Patronizing a person for prostitution in the third degree.
230.05   Patronizing a person for prostitution in the second degree.
230.06   Patronizing a person for prostitution in the first degree.
230.07   Patronizing a person for prostitution; defense.
230.08   Patronizing a person for prostitution in a school zone.
230.10   Prostitution and patronizing a person for prostitution; no defense.
230.11   Aggravated patronizing a minor for prostitution in the third degree.
230.12   Aggravated patronizing a minor for prostitution in the second degree.
230.13   Aggravated patronizing a minor for prostitution in the first degree.
230.15   Promoting prostitution; definitions of terms.
230.19   Promoting prostitution in a school zone.
230.20   Promoting prostitution in the fourth degree.
230.25   Promoting prostitution in the third degree.
230.30   Promoting prostitution in the second degree.
230.32   Promoting prostitution in the first degree.
230.33   Compelling prostitution.
230.34   Sex trafficking.
230.34-a   Sex trafficking of a child.
230.35   Promoting or compelling prostitution; accomplice.
230.36   Sex trafficking; accomplice.
230.40   Permitting prostitution.

§230.00 Prostitution.

A person is guilty of prostitution when such person engages or agrees or offers to engage in sexual conduct with another person in return for a fee.

Prostitution is a class B misdemeanor.

§230.01 Prostitution; affirmative defense.

In any prosecution under section 230.00, section 230.03, section 230.19, section 230.20, subdivision 2 of section 230.25, subdivision 2 of section 230.30 or section 230.34-a of this article, it is an affirmative defense that the defendant's participation in the offense was a result of having been a victim of compelling prostitution under section 230.33 of this article, a victim of sex trafficking under section 230.34 of this article, a victim of sex trafficking of a child under section 230.34-a of this article or a victim of trafficking in persons under the trafficking victims protection act (United States Code, Title 22, Chapter 78).

(Eff.3//21,Ch.23,L.2021)

§230.02 Patronizing a person for prostitution; definitions.

1. A person patronizes a person for prostitution when:

(a) Pursuant to a prior understanding, he or she pays a fee to another person as compensation for such person or a third person having engaged in sexual conduct with him or her; or

(b) He or she pays or agrees to pay a fee to another person pursuant to an understanding that in return therefor such person or a third person will engage in sexual conduct with him or her; or

(c) He or she solicits or requests another person to engage in sexual conduct with him or her in return for a fee.

2. As used in this article, "person who is patronized" means the person with whom the defendant engaged in sexual conduct or was to have engaged in sexual conduct pursuant to the understanding, or the person who was solicited or requested by the defendant to engage in sexual conduct.

§230.03 Prostitution in a school zone.

1. A person is guilty of prostitution in a school zone when, being nineteen years of age or older, and acting during the hours that school is in session, he or she commits the crime of prostitution in violation of section 230.00 of this article at a place that he or she knows, or reasonably should know, is in a school zone, and he or she knows, or reasonably should know, that such act of prostitution is within the direct view of children attending such school.

2. For the purposes of this section, section 230.08 and section 230.19 of this article, "school zone" means (a) in or on or within any building, structure, athletic playing field, playground or land contained within the real property boundary line of a public or private elementary, parochial, intermediate, junior high, vocational, or high school, or (b) any public sidewalk, street, parking lot, park, playground or private land, located immediately adjacent to the boundary line of such school.

Prostitution in a school zone is a class A misdemeanor.

§230.04 Patronizing a person for prostitution in the third degree.

A person is guilty of patronizing a person for prostitution in the third degree when he or she patronizes a person for prostitution.

Patronizing a person for prostitution in the third degree is a class A misdemeanor.

§230.05 Patronizing a person for prostitution in the second degree.

A person is guilty of patronizing a person for prostitution in the second degree when, being eighteen years old or more, he or she patronizes a person for prostitution and the person patronized is less than fifteen years old.

Patronizing a person for prostitution in the second degree is a class E felony.

§230.06 Patronizing a person for prostitution in the first degree.

A person is guilty of patronizing a person for prostitution in the first degree when:

1. He or she patronizes a person for prostitution and the person patronized is less than eleven years old; or

2. Being eighteen years old or more, he or she patronizes a person for prostitution and the person patronized is less than thirteen years old.

Patronizing a person for prostitution in the first degree is a class D felony.

§230.07 Patronizing a person for prostitution; defense.

In any prosecution for patronizing a person for prostitution in the first or second degrees or patronizing a person for prostitution in a school zone, it is a defense that the defendant did not have reasonable grounds to believe that the person was less than the age specified.

§230.08 Patronizing a person for prostitution in a school zone.

1. A person is guilty of patronizing a person for prostitution in a school zone when, being twenty-one years old or more, he or she patronizes a person for prostitution and the person patronized is less than eighteen years old at a place that he or she knows, or reasonably should know, is in a school zone.

2. For purposes of this section, "school zone" shall mean "school zone" as defined in subdivision two of section 230.03 of this article.

Patronizing a person for prostitution in a school zone is a class E felony.

§230.10 Prostitution and patronizing a person for prostitution; no defense.

In any prosecution for prostitution or patronizing a person for prostitution, the sex of the two parties or prospective parties to the sexual conduct engaged in, contemplated or solicited is immaterial, and it is no defense that:

1. Such persons were of the same sex; or

2. The person who received, agreed to receive or solicited a fee was a male and the person who paid or agreed or offered to pay such fee was a female.

§230.11 Aggravated patronizing a minor for prostitution in the third degree.

A person is guilty of aggravated patronizing a minor for prostitution in the third degree when, being twenty-one years old or more, he or she patronizes a person for prostitution and the person patronized is less than seventeen years old and the person guilty of patronizing engages in sexual intercourse, oral sexual conduct, anal sexual conduct, or aggravated sexual conduct as those terms are defined in section 130.00 of this part, with the person patronized.

Aggravated patronizing a minor for prostitution in the third degree is a class E felony.

§230.12 Aggravated patronizing a minor for prostitution in the second degree.

A person is guilty of aggravated patronizing a minor for prostitution in the second degree when, being eighteen years old or more, he or she patronizes a person for prostitution and the person patronized is less than fifteen years old and the person guilty of patronizing engages in sexual intercourse, oral sexual conduct, anal sexual conduct, or aggravated sexual conduct as those terms are defined in section 130.00 of this part, with the person patronized.

Aggravated patronizing a minor for prostitution in the second degree is a class D felony.

§230.13 Aggravated patronizing a minor for prostitution in the first degree.

A person is guilty of aggravated patronizing a minor for prostitution in the first degree when he or she patronizes a person for prostitution and the person patronized is less than eleven years old, or being eighteen years old or more, he or she patronizes a person for prostitution and the person patronized is less than thirteen years old, and the person guilty of patronizing engages in sexual intercourse, oral sexual conduct, anal sexual conduct, or aggravated sexual conduct as those terms are defined in section 130.00 of this part, with the person patronized.

Aggravated patronizing a minor for prostitution in the first degree is a class B felony.

§230.15 Promoting prostitution; definitions of terms.

The following definitions are applicable to this article:

1. "Advance prostitution." A person "advances prostitution" when, acting other than as a person in prostitution or as a patron thereof, he or she knowingly causes or aids a person to commit or engage in prostitution, procures or solicits patrons for prostitution, provides persons or premises for prostitution purposes, operates or assists

in the operation of a house of prostitution or a prostitution enterprise, or engages in any other conduct designed to institute, aid or facilitate an act or enterprise of prostitution.

2. "Profit from prostitution." A person "profits from prostitution" when, acting other than as a person in prostitution receiving compensation for personally rendered prostitution services, he or she accepts or receives money or other property pursuant to an agreement or understanding with any person whereby he or she participates or is to participate in the proceeds of prostitution activity.

§230.19 Promoting prostitution in a school zone.

1. A person is guilty of promoting prostitution in a school zone when, being nineteen years old or more, he or she knowingly advances or profits from prostitution that he or she knows or reasonably should know is or will be committed in violation of section 230.03 of this article in a school zone during the hours that school is in session.

2. For purposes of this section, "school zone" shall mean "school zone" as defined in subdivision two of section 230.03 of this article.

Promoting prostitution in a school zone is a class E felony.

§230.20 Promoting prostitution in the fourth degree.

A person is guilty of promoting prostitution in the fourth degree when he or she knowingly:

1. Advances or profits from prostitution; or

2. With intent to advance or profit from prostitution, distributes or disseminates to ten or more people in a public place obscene material, as such terms are defined by subdivisions one and two of section 235.00 of this title, or material that depicts nudity, as such term is defined by subdivision one of section 245.10 of this part.

Promoting prostitution in the fourth degree is a class A misdemeanor.

§230.25 Promoting prostitution in the third degree.

A person is guilty of promoting prostitution in the third degree when he or she knowingly:

1. Advances or profits from prostitution by managing, supervising, controlling or owning, either alone or in association with others, a house of prostitution or a prostitution business or enterprise involving prostitution activity by two or more persons in prostitution, or a business that sells travel-related services knowing that such services include or are intended to facilitate travel for the purpose of patronizing a person for prostitution, including to a foreign jurisdiction and regardless of the legality of prostitution in said foreign jurisdiction; or

2. Advances or profits from prostitution of a person less than nineteen years old.

Promoting prostitution in the third degree is a class D felony.

§230.30 Promoting prostitution in the second degree.

A person is guilty of promoting prostitution in the second degree when he or she knowingly:

1. Advances prostitution by compelling a person by force or intimidation to engage in prostitution, or profits from such coercive conduct by another; or

2. Advances or profits from prostitution of a person less than eighteen years old.

Promoting prostitution in the second degree is a class C felony.

§230.32 Promoting prostitution in the first degree.

A person is guilty of promoting prostitution in the first degree when he or she:

1. knowingly advances or profits from prostitution of a person less than thirteen years old; or

2. being twenty-one years old or more, he or she knowingly advances or profits from prostitution of a person less than fifteen years old.

Promoting prostitution in the first degree is a class B felony.

§230.33 Compelling prostitution.

A person is guilty of compelling prostitution when, being eighteen years old or more, he or she knowingly advances prostitution by compelling a person less than eighteen years old, by force or intimidation, to engage in prostitution.

Compelling prostitution is a class B felony.

§230.34 Sex trafficking.

A person is guilty of sex trafficking if he or she intentionally advances or profits from prostitution by:

1. unlawfully providing to a person who is patronized, with intent to impair said person's judgment: (a) a narcotic drug or a narcotic preparation; (b) concentrated cannabis as defined in paragraph (a) of subdivision four of section thirty-three hundred two of the public health law; (c) methadone; or (d) gamma-hydroxybutyrate (GHB) or flunitrazepan, also known as Rohypnol;

2. making material false statements, misstatements, or omissions to induce or maintain the person being patronized to engage in or continue to engage in prostitution activity;

3. withholding, destroying, or confiscating any actual or purported passport, immigration document, or any other actual or purported government identification document of another person with intent to impair said person's freedom of movement; provided, however, that this subdivision shall not apply to an attempt to correct a social security administration record or immigration agency record in accordance with any local, state, or federal agency requirement, where such attempt is not made for the purpose of any express or implied threat;

4. requiring that prostitution be performed to retire, repay, or service a real or purported debt;

5. using force or engaging in any scheme, plan or pattern to compel or induce the person being patronized to engage in or continue to engage in prostitution activity by means of instilling a fear in the person being patronized that, if the demand is not complied with, the actor or another will do one or more of the following:

(a) cause physical injury, serious physical injury, or death to a person; or

(b) cause damage to property, other than the property of the actor; or

(c) engage in other conduct constituting a felony or unlawful imprisonment in the second degree in violation of section 135.05 of this chapter; or

(d) accuse some person of a crime or cause criminal charges or deportation proceedings to be instituted against some person; provided, however, that it shall be an affirmative defense to this subdivision that the defendant reasonably believed the threatened charge to be true and that his or her sole purpose was to compel or induce the victim to take reasonable action to make good the wrong which was the subject of such threatened charge; or

(e) expose a secret or publicize an asserted fact, whether true or false, tending to subject some person to hatred, contempt or ridicule; or

(f) testify or provide information or withhold testimony or information with respect to another's legal claim or defense; or

(g) use or abuse his or her position as a public servant by performing some act within or related to his or her official duties, or by failing or refusing to perform an official duty, in such manner as to affect some person adversely; or

(h) perform any other act which would not in itself materially benefit the actor but which is calculated to harm the person who is patronized materially with respect to his or her health, safety, or immigration status.

Sex trafficking is a class B felony*   *(So in original, period omitted.)*

§230.34-a Sex trafficking of a child.

1. A person is guilty of sex trafficking of a child when he or she, being twenty-one years old or more, intentionally advances or profits from prostitution of another person and such person is a child less than eighteen years old. Knowledge by the defendant of the age of such child is not an element of this offense and it is not a defense to a prosecution therefor that the defendant did not know the age of the child or believed such age to be eighteen or over.

2. For purposes of this section:

(a) A person "advances prostitution" when, acting other than as a person in prostitution or as a patron thereof, and with intent to cause prostitution, he or she directly engages in conduct that facilitates an act or enterprise of prostitution.

(b) A person "profits from prostitution" when, acting other than as a person in prostitution receiving compensation for personally rendered prostitution services, and with intent to facilitate prostitution, he or she accepts or receives money or other property pursuant to an agreement or understanding with any person whereby he or she participates in the proceeds of prostitution activity.

Sex trafficking of a child is a class B felony.   *(Eff.11/13/18,Ch.189,L.2018)*

This page intentionally left blank

§230.35 Promoting or compelling prostitution; accomplice.

In a prosecution for promoting prostitution or compelling prostitution, a person less than eighteen years old from whose prostitution activity another person is alleged to have advanced or attempted to advance or profited or attempted to profit shall not be deemed to be an accomplice.

§230.36 Sex trafficking; accomplice.

In a prosecution for sex trafficking, a person from whose prostitution activity another person is alleged to have advanced or attempted to advance or profited or attempted to profit shall not be deemed to be an accomplice.

§230.40 Permitting prostitution.

A person is guilty of permitting prostitution when, having possession or control of premises or vehicle which he or she knows are being used for prostitution purposes or for the purpose of advancing prostitution, he or she fails to make reasonable effort to halt or abate such use.

Permitting prostitution is a class B misdemeanor.

ARTICLE 235 - OBSCENITY AND RELATED OFFENSES

Section
235.00 Obscenity; definitions of terms.
235.05 Obscenity in the third degree.
235.06 Obscenity in the second degree.
235.07 Obscenity in the first degree.
235.10 Obscenity; presumptions.
235.15 Obscenity or disseminating indecent material to minors in the second degree; defense.
235.20 Disseminating indecent material to minors; definitions of terms.
235.21 Disseminating indecent material to minors in the second degree.
235.22 Disseminating indecent material to minors in the first degree.
235.23 Disseminating indecent material to minors; presumption and defenses.
235.24 Disseminating indecent material to minors; limitations.

§235.00 Obscenity; definitions of terms.

The following definitions are applicable to sections 235.05, 235.10 and 235.15:

1. "Obscene." Any material or performance is "obscene" if (a) the average person, applying contemporary community standards, would find that considered as a whole, its predominant appeal is to the prurient interest in sex, and (b) it depicts or describes in a patently offensive manner, actual or simulated: sexual intercourse, criminal sexual act, sexual bestiality, masturbation, sadism, masochism, excretion or lewd exhibition of the genitals, and (c) considered as a whole, it lacks serious literary, artistic, political, and scientific value. Predominant appeal shall be judged with reference to ordinary adults unless it appears from the

character of the material or the circumstances of its dissemination to be designed for children or other specially susceptible audience.

2. "Material" means anything tangible which is capable of being used or adapted to arouse interest, whether through the medium of reading, observation, sound or in any other manner.

3. "Performance" means any play, motion picture, dance or other exhibition performed before an audience.

4. "Promote" means to manufacture, issue, sell, give, provide, lend, mail, deliver, transfer, transmute, publish, distribute, circulate, disseminate, present, exhibit or advertise, or to offer or agree to do the same.

5. "Wholesale promote" means to manufacture, issue, sell, provide, mail, deliver, transfer, transmute, publish, distribute, circulate, disseminate or to offer or agree to do the same for purposes of resale.

6. "Simulated" means the explicit depiction or description of any of the types of conduct set forth in clause (b) of subdivision one of this section, which creates the appearance of such conduct.

7. " Criminal sexual act" means any of the types of sexual conduct defined in subdivision two of section 130.00 provided, however, that in any prosecution under this article the marital status of the persons engaged in such conduct shall be irrelevant and shall not be considered.

§235.05 Obscenity in the third degree.

A person is guilty of obscenity in the third degree when, knowing its content and character, he:

1. Promotes, or possesses with intent to promote, any obscene material; or

2. Produces, presents or directs an obscene performance or participates in a portion thereof which is obscene or which contributes to its obscenity.

Obscenity in the third degree is a class A misdemeanor.

§235.06 Obscenity in the second degree.

A person is guilty of obscenity in the second degree when he commits the crime of obscenity in the third degree as defined in subdivisions one and two of section 235.05 of this chapter and has been previously convicted of obscenity in the third degree.

Obscenity in the second degree is a class E felony.

§235.07 Obscenity in the first degree.

A person is guilty of obscenity in the first degree when, knowing its content and character, he wholesale promotes or possesses with intent to wholesale promote, any obscene material.

Obscenity in the first degree is a class D felony.

§235.10 Obscenity; presumptions.

1. A person who promotes or wholesale promotes obscene material, or possesses the same with intent to promote or wholesale promote it, in the course of his business is presumed to do so with knowledge of its content and character.

2. A person who possesses six or more identical or similar obscene articles is presumed to possess them with intent to promote the same.

The provisions of this section shall not apply to public libraries or association libraries as defined in subdivision two of section two hundred fifty-three of the education law, or trustees or employees of such public libraries or association libraries when acting in the course and scope of their duties or employment.

§235.15 Obscenity or disseminating indecent material to minors in the second degree; defense.

1. In any prosecution for obscenity, or disseminating indecent material to minors in the second degree in violation of subdivision three of section 235.21 of this article, it is an affirmative defense that the persons to whom allegedly obscene or indecent material was disseminated, or the audience to an allegedly obscene performance, consisted of persons or institutions having scientific, educational, governmental or other similar justification for possessing, disseminating or viewing the same.

2. In any prosecution for obscenity, it is an affirmative defense that the person so charged was a motion picture projectionist, stage employee or spotlight operator, cashier, doorman, usher, candy stand attendant, porter or in any other non-managerial or non-supervisory capacity in a motion picture theater; provided he has no financial interest, other than his employment, which employment does not encompass compensation based upon any proportion of the gross receipts, in the promotion of obscene material for sale, rental or exhibition or in the promotion, presentation or direction of any obscene performance, or is in any way responsible for acquiring obscene material for sale, rental or exhibition.

§235.20 Disseminating indecent material to minors; definitions of terms.

The following definitions are applicable to sections 235.21, 235.22, 235.23 and 235.24 of this article:

1. "Minor" means any person less than seventeen years old.

2. "Nudity" means the showing of the human male or female genitals, pubic area or buttocks with less than a full opaque covering or the showing of the female breast with less than a fully opaque covering of any portion thereof below the top of the nipple, or the depiction of covered male genitals in a discernably turgid state.

3. "Sexual conduct" means acts of masturbation, homosexuality, sexual intercourse, or physical contact with a person's clothed or unclothed genitals, pubic area, buttocks or, if such person be a female, breast.

4. "Sexual excitement" means the condition of human male or female genitals when in a state of sexual stimulation or arousal.

5. "Sado-masochistic abuse" means flagellation or torture by or upon a person clad in undergarments, a mask or bizarre costume, or the condition of being fettered, bound or otherwise physically restrained on the part of one so clothed.

6. "Harmful to minors" means that quality of any description or representation, in whatever form, of nudity, sexual conduct, sexual excitement, or sado-masochistic abuse, when it:

(a) Considered as a whole, appeals to the prurient interest in sex of minors; and

(b) Is patently offensive to prevailing standards in the adult community as a whole with respect to what is suitable material for minors; and

(c) Considered as a whole, lacks serious literary, artistic, political and scientific value for minors.

7. The term "access software" means software (including client or server software) or enabling tools that do not create or provide the content of the communication but that allow a user to do any one or more of the following:

(a) filter, screen, allow or disallow content;

(b) pick, choose, analyze or digest content; or

(c) transmit, receive, display, forward, cache, search, subset, organize, reorganize or translate content.

§235.21 Disseminating indecent material to minors in the second degree.

A person is guilty of disseminating indecent material to minors in the second degree when:

1. With knowledge of its character and content, he sells or loans to a minor for monetary consideration:

(a) Any picture, photograph, drawing, sculpture, motion picture film, or similar visual representation or image of a person or portion of the human body which depicts nudity, sexual conduct or sado-masochistic abuse and which is harmful to minors; or

(b) Any book, pamphlet, magazine, printed matter however reproduced, or sound recording which contains any matter enumerated in paragraph (a) hereof, or explicit and detailed verbal descriptions or narrative accounts of sexual excitement, sexual conduct or sado-masochistic abuse and which, taken as a whole, is harmful to minors; or

2. Knowing the character and content of a motion picture, show or other presentation which, in whole or in part, depicts nudity, sexual conduct or sado-masochistic abuse, and which is harmful to minors, he:

(a) Exhibits such motion picture, show or other presentation to a minor for a monetary consideration; or

(b) Sells to a minor an admission ticket or pass to premises whereon there is exhibited or to be exhibited such motion picture, show or other presentation; or

(c) Admits a minor for a monetary consideration to premises whereon there is exhibited or to be exhibited such motion picture show or other presentation; or

3. Knowing the character and content of the communication which, in whole or in part, depicts actual or simulated nudity, sexual conduct or sado-masochistic abuse, and which is harmful to minors, he intentionally uses any computer communication system allowing the input, output, examination or transfer, of computer data or computer programs from one computer to another, to initiate or engage in such communication with a person who is a minor.

Disseminating indecent material to minors in the second degree is a class E felony.

§235.22 Disseminating indecent material to minors in the first degree.

A person is guilty of disseminating indecent material to minors in the first degree when:

1. knowing the character and content of the communication which, in whole or in part, depicts or describes, either in words or images actual or simulated nudity, sexual conduct or sado-masochistic abuse, and which is harmful to minors, he intentionally uses any computer communication system allowing the input, output, examination or transfer, of computer data or computer programs from one computer to another, to initiate or engage in such communication with a person who is a minor; and

2. by means of such communication he importunes, invites or induces a minor to engage in sexual intercourse, oral sexual conduct or anal sexual conduct, or sexual contact with him, or to engage in a sexual performance, obscene sexual performance, or sexual conduct for his benefit.

Disseminating indecent material to minors in the first degree is a class D felony.

§235.23 Disseminating indecent material to minors; presumption and defenses.

1. A person who engages in the conduct proscribed by section 235.21 is presumed to do so with knowledge of the character and content of the material sold or loaned, or the motion picture, show or presentation exhibited or to be exhibited.

2. In any prosecution for disseminating indecent material to minors in the second degree pursuant to subdivision one or two of section 235.21 of this article, it is an affirmative defense that:

(a) The defendant had reasonable cause to believe that the minor involved was seventeen years old or more; and

(b) Such minor exhibited to the defendant a draft card, driver's license, birth certificate or other official or apparently official document purporting to establish that such minor was seventeen years old or more.

3. In any prosecution for disseminating indecent material to minors in the second degree pursuant to subdivision three of section 235.21 of this article or disseminating indecent material to minors in the first degree pursuant to section 235.22 of this article, it shall be a defense that:

(a) The defendant made a reasonable effort to ascertain the true age of the minor and was unable to do so as a result of actions taken by the minor; or

(b) The defendant has taken, in good faith, reasonable, effective and appropriate actions under the circumstances to restrict or prevent access by minors to materials specified in such subdivision, which may involve any appropriate measures to restrict minors from access to such communications, including any method which is feasible under available technology; or

(c) The defendant has restricted access to such materials by requiring use of a verified credit card, debit account, adult access code or adult personal identification number; or

(d) The defendant has in good faith established a mechanism such that the labelling, segregation or other mechanism enables such material to be automatically blocked or screened by software or other capabilities reasonably available to responsible adults wishing to effect such blocking or screening and the defendant has not otherwise solicited minors not subject to such screening or blocking capabilities to access that material or to circumvent any such screening or blocking.

§235.24 Disseminating indecent material to minors; limitations.

In any prosecution for disseminating indecent material to minors in the second degree pursuant to subdivision three of section 235.21 of this article or disseminating indecent material to minors in the first degree pursuant to section 235.22 of this article:

1. No person shall be held to have violated such provisions solely for providing access or connection to or from a facility, system, or network not under that person's control, including transmission, downloading, intermediate storage, access software, or other related capabilities that are incidental to providing such access or connection that do not include the creation of the content of the communication.

(a) The limitations provided by this subdivision shall not be applicable to a person who is a conspirator with an entity actively involved in the creation or knowing distribution of communications that violate such provisions, or who knowingly advertises the availability of such communications.

(b) The limitations provided by this subdivision shall not be applicable to a person who provides access or connection to a facility, system, or network engaged in the violation of such provisions that is owned or controlled by such person.

2. No employer shall be held liable under such provisions for the actions of an employee or agent unless the employee's or agent's conduct is within the scope of his employment or agency and the employer having knowledge of such conduct, authorizes or ratifies such conduct, or recklessly disregards such conduct.

TITLE N - OFFENSES AGAINST PUBLIC ORDER, PUBLIC SENSIBILITIES AND THE RIGHT TO PRIVACY
ARTICLE 240 - OFFENSES AGAINST PUBLIC ORDER

Section
240.00 Offenses against public order; definitions of terms.
240.05 Riot in the second degree.
240.06 Riot in the first degree.
240.08 Inciting to riot.
240.10 Unlawful assembly.
240.15 Criminal anarchy.
240.20 Disorderly conduct.
240.21 Disruption or disturbance of a religious service, funeral, burial or memorial service.
240.25 Harassment in the first degree.
240.26 Harassment in the second degree.
240.30 Aggravated harassment in the second degree.
240.31 Aggravated harassment in the first degree.

Section
240.32 Aggravated harassment of an employee by an incarcerated individual.
240.35 Loitering.
240.36 Loitering in the first degree.
240.40 Appearance in public under the influence of narcotics or a drug other than alcohol.
240.45 Criminal nuisance in the second degree.
240.46 Criminal nuisance in the first degree.
240.48 Disseminating a false registered sex offender notice.
240.50 Falsely reporting an incident in the third degree.
240.55 Falsely reporting an incident in the second degree.
240.60 Falsely reporting an incident in the first degree.
240.61 Placing a false bomb or hazardous substance in the second degree.
240.62 Placing a false bomb or hazardous substance in the first degree.
240.63 Placing a false bomb or hazardous substance in a sports stadium or arena, mass transportation facility or enclosed shopping mall.
240.65 Unlawful prevention of public access to records.
240.70 Criminal interference with health care services or religious worship in the second degree.
240.71 Criminal interference with health care services or religious worship in the first degree.
240.72 Aggravated interference with health care services in the second degree.
240.73 Aggravated interference with health care services in the first degree.
240.75 Aggravated family offense.
240.76 Directing a laser at an aircraft in the second degree.
240.77 Directing a laser at an aircraft in the first degree.

§240.00 Offenses against public order; definitions of terms.

The following definitions are applicable to this article:

1. "Public place" means a place to which the public or a substantial group of persons has access, and includes, but is not limited to, highways, transportation facilities, schools, places of amusement, parks, playgrounds, community centers, and hallways, lobbies and other portions of apartment houses and hotels not constituting rooms or apartments designed for actual residence.

2. "Transportation facility" means any conveyance, premises or place used for or in connection with public passenger transportation, whether by air, railroad, motor vehicle or any other method. It includes aircraft, watercraft, railroad cars, buses, school buses as defined in section one hundred forty-two of the vehicle and traffic law, and air, boat, railroad and bus terminals and stations and all appurtenances thereto.

3. "School grounds" means in or on or within any building, structure, school bus as defined in section one hundred forty-two of the vehicle and traffic law, athletic playing field, playground or land contained within the real property boundary line of a public or private elementary, parochial, intermediate, junior high, vocational or high school.

4. "Hazardous substance" shall mean any physical, chemical, microbiological or radiological substance or matter which, because of its quantity, concentration, or physical, chemical or infectious characteristics, may cause or significantly contribute to an increase in mortality or an increase in serious irreversible or incapacitating reversible illness, or pose a substantial present or potential hazard to human health.

5. "Age" means sixty years old or more.

6. "Disability" means a physical or mental impairment that substantially limits a major life activity.

7. "Gender identity or expression" means a person's actual or perceived gender-related identity, appearance, behavior, expression, or other gender-related characteristic regardless of the sex assigned to that person at birth, including, but not limited to, the status of being transgender.

§240.05 Riot in the second degree.

A person is guilty of riot in the second degree when, simultaneously with four or more other persons, he engages in tumultuous and violent conduct and thereby intentionally or recklessly causes or creates a grave risk of causing public alarm.

Riot in the second degree is a class A misdemeanor.

§240.06 Riot in the first degree.

A person is guilty of riot in the first degree when he:

1. Simultaneously with ten or more other persons, engages in tumultuous and violent conduct and thereby intentionally or recklessly causes or creates a grave risk of causing public alarm, and in the course of and as a result of such conduct, a person other than one of the participants suffers physical injury or substantial property damage occurs; or

2. While in a correctional facility or a local correctional facility, as those terms are defined in subdivisions four and sixteen, respectively, of section two of the correction law, simultaneously with ten or more other persons, engages in tumultuous and violent conduct and thereby intentionally or recklessly causes or creates a grave risk of causing alarm within such correctional facility or local correctional facility and in the course of and as a result of such conduct, a person other than one of the participants suffers physical injury or substantial property damage occurs.

Riot in the first degree is a class E felony.

§240.08 Inciting to riot.

A person is guilty of inciting to riot when he urges ten or more persons to engage in tumultuous and violent conduct of a kind likely to create public alarm.

Inciting to riot is a class A misdemeanor.

§240.10 Unlawful assembly.

A person is guilty of unlawful assembly when he assembles with four or more other persons for the purpose of engaging or preparing to engage with them in tumultuous and violent conduct likely to cause public alarm, or when, being present at an assembly which either has or develops such purpose, he remains there with intent to advance that purpose.

Unlawful assembly is a class B misdemeanor.

§240.15 Criminal anarchy.

A person is guilty of criminal anarchy when (a) he advocates the overthrow of the existing form of government of this state by violence, or (b) with knowledge of its contents, he publishes, sells or distributes any document which advocates such violent overthrow, or (c) with knowledge of its purpose, he becomes a member of any organization which advocates such violent overthrow.

Criminal anarchy is a class E felony.

§240.20 Disorderly conduct.

A person is guilty of disorderly conduct when, with intent to cause public inconvenience, annoyance or alarm, or recklessly creating a risk thereof:

1. He engages in fighting or in violent, tumultuous or threatening behavior; or
2. He makes unreasonable noise; or
3. In a public place, he uses abusive or obscene language, or makes an obscene gesture; or
4. Without lawful authority, he disturbs any lawful assembly or meeting of persons; or
5. He obstructs vehicular or pedestrian traffic; or
6. He congregates with other persons in a public place and refuses to comply with a lawful order of the police to disperse; or
7. He creates a hazardous or physically offensive condition by any act which serves no legitimate purpose.

Disorderly conduct is a violation.

§240.21 Disruption or disturbance of a religious service, funeral, burial or memorial service.

A person is guilty of disruption or disturbance of a religious service, funeral, burial or memorial service when he or she makes unreasonable noise or disturbance while at a lawfully assembled religious service, funeral, burial or memorial service, or within three hundred feet thereof, with intent to cause annoyance or alarm or recklessly creating a risk thereof.

Disruption or disturbance of a religious service, funeral, burial or memorial service is a class A misdemeanor.

§240.25 Harassment in the first degree.

A person is guilty of harassment in the first degree when he or she intentionally and repeatedly harasses another person by following such person in or about a public place or places or by engaging in a course of conduct or by repeatedly committing acts which places such person in reasonable fear of physical injury. This section shall not apply to activities regulated by the national labor relations act, as amended, the railway labor act, as amended, or the federal employment labor management act, as amended.

Harassment in the first degree is a class B misdemeanor.

§240.26 Harassment in the second degree.

A person is guilty of harassment in the second degree when, with intent to harass, annoy or alarm another person:

1. He or she strikes, shoves, kicks or otherwise subjects such other person to physical contact, or attempts or threatens to do the same; or

2. He or she follows a person in or about a public place or places; or

3. He or she engages in a course of conduct or repeatedly commits acts which alarm or seriously annoy such other person and which serve no legitimate purpose. Subdivisions two and three of this section shall not apply to activities regulated by the national labor relations act, as amended, the railway labor act, as amended, or the federal employment labor management act, as amended.

Harassment is a violation.

§240.30 Aggravated harassment in the second degree.

A person is guilty of aggravated harassment in the second degree when:

1. With intent to harass another person, the actor either:

(a) communicates, anonymously or otherwise, by telephone, by computer or any other electronic means, or by mail, or by transmitting or delivering any other form of communication, a threat to cause physical harm to, or unlawful harm to the property of, such person, or a member of such person's same family or household as defined in subdivision one of section 530.11 of the criminal procedure law, and the actor knows or reasonably should know that such communication will cause such person to reasonably fear harm to such person's physical safety or property, or to the physical safety or property of a member of such person's same family or household; or

(b) causes a communication to be initiated anonymously or otherwise, by telephone, by computer or any other electronic means, or by mail, or by transmitting or delivering any other form of communication, a threat to cause physical harm to, or unlawful harm to the property of, such person, a member of such person's same family or household as defined in subdivision one of section 530.11 of the criminal procedure law, and the actor knows or reasonably should know that such communication will cause such person to reasonably fear harm to such person's physical safety or property, or to the physical safety or property of a member of such person's same family or household; or

2. With intent to harass or threaten another person, he or she makes a telephone call, whether or not a conversation ensues, with no purpose of legitimate communication; or

3. With the intent to harass, annoy, threaten or alarm another person, he or she strikes, shoves, kicks, or otherwise subjects another person to physical contact, or attempts or threatens to do the same because of a belief or perception regarding such person's race, color, national origin, ancestry, gender, gender identity or expression, religion, religious practice, age, disability or sexual orientation, regardless of whether the belief or perception is correct; or   *(Eff.11/1/19,Ch.8,L.2019)*

4. With the intent to harass, annoy, threaten or alarm another person, he or she strikes, shoves, kicks or otherwise subjects another person to physical contact thereby causing physical injury to such person or to a family or household member of such person as defined in section 530.11 of the criminal procedure law; or

5. He or she commits the crime of harassment in the first degree and has previously been convicted of the crime of harassment in the first degree as defined by section 240.25 of this article within the preceding ten years.

Aggravated harassment in the second degree is a class A misdemeanor.

§240.31 Aggravated harassment in the first degree.

A person is guilty of aggravated harassment in the first degree when with intent to harass, annoy, threaten or alarm another person, because of a belief or perception regarding such person's race, color, national origin, ancestry, gender, gender identity or expression, religion, religious practice, age, disability or sexual orientation, regardless of whether the belief or perception is correct, he or she:

1. Damages premises primarily used for religious purposes, or acquired pursuant to section six of the religious corporation law and maintained for purposes of religious instruction, and the damage to the premises exceeds fifty dollars; or

2. Commits the crime of aggravated harassment in the second degree in the manner proscribed by the provisions of subdivision three of section 240.30 of this article and has been previously convicted of the crime of aggravated harassment in the second degree for the commission of conduct proscribed by the provisions of subdivision three of section 240.30 or he or she has been previously convicted of the crime of aggravated harassment in the first degree within the preceding ten years; or

3. Etches, paints, draws upon or otherwise places a swastika, commonly exhibited as the emblem of Nazi Germany, on any building or other real property, public or private, owned by any person, firm or corporation or any public agency or instrumentality, without express permission of the owner or operator of such building or real property;

4. Sets on fire a cross in public view; or

5. Etches, paints, draws upon or otherwise places or displays a noose, commonly exhibited as a symbol of racism and intimidation, on any building or other real property, public or private, owned by any person, firm or corporation or any public agency or instrumentality, without express permission of the owner or operator of such building or real property.

Aggravated harassment in the first degree is a class E felony.

§240.32 Aggravated harassment of an employee by an incarcerated individual.

An incarcerated individual or respondent is guilty of aggravated harassment of an employee by an incarcerated individual when, with intent to harass, annoy, threaten or alarm a person in a facility whom he or she knows or reasonably should know to be an employee of such facility or the board of parole or the office of mental health, or a probation department, bureau or unit or a police officer, he or she causes or attempts to cause such employee to come into contact with blood, seminal fluid, urine, feces, or the contents of a toilet bowl, by throwing, tossing or expelling such fluid or material.

For purposes of this section, "incarcerated individual" means an incarcerated individual or detainee in a correctional facility, local correctional facility or a hospital, as such term is defined in subdivision two of section four hundred of the correction law. For purposes of this section, "respondent" means a juvenile in a secure facility operated and maintained by the office of children and family services who is placed with or committed to the office of children and family services. For purposes of this section, "facility" means a correctional facility or local correctional facility, hospital, as such term is defined in subdivision two of section four hundred of the correction law, or a secure facility operated and maintained by the office of children and family services.

Aggravated harassment of an employee by an incarcerated individual is a class E felony.   *(Eff.8/2/21,Ch.322,L.2021)*

§240.35 Loitering.

A person is guilty of loitering when he:

1. *(Repealed.)*
2. Loiters or remains in a public place for the purpose of gambling with cards, dice or other gambling paraphernalia; or
3. *(Repealed.)*
4. *(Repealed, Eff.6/13/20,Ch.98,L.2020)*
5. Loiters or remains in or about school grounds, a college or university building or grounds or a children's overnight camp as defined in section one thousand three hundred ninety-two of the public health law or a summer day camp as defined in section one thousand three hundred ninety-two of the public health law, or loiters, remains in or enters a school bus as defined in section one hundred forty-two of the vehicle and traffic law, not having any reason or relationship

involving custody of or responsibility for a pupil or student, or any other specific, legitimate reason for being there, and not having written permission from anyone authorized to grant the same or loiters or remains in or about such children's overnight camp or summer day camp in violation of conspicuously posted rules or regulations governing entry and use thereof; or

6. Loiters or remains in any transportation facility, unless specifically authorized to do so, for the purpose of soliciting or engaging in any business, trade or commercial transactions involving the sale of merchandise or services, or for the purpose of entertaining persons by singing, dancing or playing any musical instrument; or*

Loitering is a violation.   **(So in original "7." repealed)*

§240.36 Loitering in the first degree.

A person is guilty of loitering in the first degree when he loiter or remains in any place with one or more persons for the purpose of unlawfully using or possessing a controlled substance, as defined in section 220.00 of this chapter.

Loitering in the first degree is a class B misdemeanor.

§240.37 Loitering for the purpose of engaging in a prostitution offense.   *(Repealed, Eff.2/2/21,Ch.23,L.2021)*

§240.40 Appearance in public under the influence of narcotics or a drug other than alcohol.

A person is guilty of appearance in public under the influence of narcotics or a drug other than alcohol when he appears in a public place under the influence of narcotics or a drug other than alcohol to the degree that he may endanger himself or other persons or property, or annoy persons in his vicinity.

Appearance in public under the influence of narcotics or a drug other than alcohol is a violation.

§240.45 Criminal nuisance in the second degree.

A person is guilty of criminal nuisance in the second degree when:

1. By conduct either unlawful in itself or unreasonable under all the circumstances, he knowingly or recklessly creates or maintains a condition which endangers the safety or health of a considerable number of persons; or

2. He knowingly conducts or maintains any premises, place or resort where persons gather for purposes of engaging in unlawful conduct.

Criminal nuisance in the second degree is a class B misdemeanor.

This page intentionally left blank.

§240.46 Criminal nuisance in the first degree.

A person is guilty of criminal nuisance in the first degree when he knowingly conducts or maintains any premises, place or resort where persons come or gather for purposes of engaging in the unlawful sale of controlled substances in violation of section 220.39, 220.41, or 220.43 of this chapter, and thereby derives the benefit from such unlawful conduct.

Criminal nuisance in the first degree is a class E felony.

§240.48 Disseminating a false registered sex offender notice.

A person is guilty of disseminating a false registered sex offender notice when, knowing the information he or she disseminates or causes to be disseminated to be false or baseless, such person disseminates or causes to be disseminated any notice which purports to be an official notice from a government agency or a law enforcement agency and such notice asserts that an individual is a registered sex offender.

Disseminating a false registered sex offender notice is a class A misdemeanor.

§240.50 Falsely reporting an incident in the third degree.

A person is guilty of falsely reporting an incident in the third degree when, knowing the information reported, conveyed or circulated to be false or baseless, he or she:

1. Initiates or circulates a false report or warning of an alleged occurrence or impending occurrence of a crime, catastrophe or emergency under circumstances in which it is not unlikely that public alarm or inconvenience will result; or

2. Reports, by word or action, to an official or quasi-official agency or organization having the function of dealing with emergencies involving danger to life or property, an alleged occurrence or impending occurrence of a catastrophe or emergency which did not in fact occur or does not in fact exist; or

3. Gratuitously reports to a law enforcement officer or agency (a) the alleged occurrence of an offense or incident which did not in fact occur; or (b) an allegedly impending occurrence of an offense or incident which in fact is not about to occur; or (c) false information relating to an actual offense or incident or to the alleged implication of some person therein; or

4. Reports, by word or action, an alleged occurrence or condition of child abuse or maltreatment or abuse or neglect of a vulnerable person which did not in fact occur or exist to:

(a) the statewide central register of child abuse and maltreatment, as defined in title six of article six of the social services law or the vulnerable persons' central register as defined in article eleven of such law, or

(b) any person required to report cases of suspected child abuse or maltreatment pursuant to subdivision one of section four hundred thirteen of the social services law or to report cases of suspected abuse or neglect of a vulnerable person pursuant to section four hundred ninety-one of such law, knowing that the person is required to report such cases, and with the intent that such an alleged occurrence be reported to the statewide central register or vulnerable persons' central register.

Falsely reporting an incident in the third degree is a class A misdemeanor.

§240.55 Falsely reporting an incident in the second degree.
A person is guilty of falsely reporting an incident in the second degree when, knowing the information reported, conveyed or circulated to be false or baseless, he or she:
1. Initiates or circulates a false report or warning of an alleged occurrence or impending occurrence of a fire, explosion, or the release of a hazardous substance under circumstances in which it is not unlikely that public alarm or inconvenience will result;
2. Reports, by word or action, to any official or quasi-official agency or organization having the function of dealing with emergencies involving danger to life or property, an alleged occurrence or impending occurrence of a fire, explosion, or the release of a hazardous substance which did not in fact occur or does not in fact exist; or
3. Knowing the information reported, conveyed or circulated to be false or baseless and under circumstances in which it is likely public alarm or inconvenience will result, he or she initiates or circulates a report or warning of an alleged occurrence or an impending occurrence of a fire, an explosion, or the release of a hazardous substance upon any private premises.
    Falsely reporting an incident in the second degree is a class E felony.

§240.60 Falsely reporting an incident in the first degree.
A person is guilty of falsely reporting an incident in the first degree when he:
1. commits the crime of falsely reporting an incident in the second degree as defined in section 240.55 of this article, and has previously been convicted of that crime; or
2. commits the crime of falsely reporting an incident in the third degree as defined in subdivisions one and two of section 240.50 of this article or falsely reporting an incident in the second degree as defined in subdivisions one and two of section 240.55 of this article and another person who is an employee or member of any official or quasi-official agency having the function of dealing with emergencies involving danger to life or property; or who is a volunteer firefighter with a fire department, fire company, or any unit thereof as defined in the volunteer firefighters' benefit law; or who is a volunteer ambulance worker with a volunteer ambulance corporation or any unit thereof as defined in the volunteer ambulance workers' benefit law suffers serious physical injury or is killed in the performance of his or her official duties in traveling to or working at or returning to a firehouse, police station, quarters or other base facility from the location identified in such report; or
3. commits the crime of falsely reporting an incident in the third degree as defined in subdivisions one and two of section 240.50 of this article or falsely reporting an incident in the second degree as defined in subdivisions one and two of section 240.55 of this article and another person suffers serious physical injury or is killed as a result of any vehicular or other accident involving any emergency vehicle which is responding to, operating at, or returning from the location identified in such report.
4. An emergency vehicle as referred to in subdivision three of this section shall include any vehicle operated by any employee or member of any official or quasi-official agency having the function of dealing with emergencies involving danger to life or property and shall in-

clude, but not necessarily be limited to, an emergency vehicle which is operated by a volunteer firefighter with a fire department, fire company, or any unit thereof as defined in the volunteer firefighters' benefit law; or by a volunteer ambulance worker with a volunteer ambulance corporation, or any unit thereof as defined in the volunteer ambulance workers' benefit law.

5. Knowing the information reported, conveyed or circulated to be false or baseless and under circumstances in which it is likely public alarm or inconvenience will result, he or she initiates or circulates a report or warning of an alleged occurrence or an impending occurrence of a fire, an explosion, or the release of a hazardous substance upon school grounds and it is likely that persons are present on said grounds.

6. Knowing the information reported, conveyed or circulated to be false or baseless and under circumstances in which it is likely public alarm or inconvenience will result, he or she initiates or circulates a report or warning of an alleged occurrence or impending occurrence of a fire, explosion or the release of a hazardous substance in or upon a sports stadium or arena, mass transportation facility, enclosed shopping mall, any public building or any public place, and it is likely that persons are present. For purposes of this subdivision, the terms "sports stadium or arena, mass transportation facility or enclosed shopping mall" shall have their natural meaning and the term "public building" shall have the meaning set forth in section four hundred one of the executive law.

Falsely reporting an incident in the first degree is a class D felony.

§240.61 Placing a false bomb or hazardous substance in the second degree.

A person is guilty of placing a false bomb or hazardous substance in the second degree when he or she places, or causes to be placed, any device or object that by its design, construction, content or characteristics appears to be or to contain, a bomb, destructive device, explosive or hazardous substance, but is, in fact, an inoperative facsimile or imitation of such a bomb, destructive device, explosive or hazardous substance and which he or she knows, intends or reasonably believes will appear to be a bomb, destructive device, explosive or hazardous substance under circumstances in which it is likely to cause public alarm or inconvenience.

Placing a false bomb or hazardous substance in the second degree is a class E felony.

§240.62 Placing a false bomb or hazardous substance in the first degree.

A person is guilty of placing a false bomb or hazardous substance in the first degree when he or she places, or causes to be placed, in or upon school grounds, a public building, or a public place any device or object that by its design, construction, content or characteristics appears to be or to contain, a bomb, destructive device, explosive or hazardous substance, but is, in fact, an inoperative facsimile or imitation of such a bomb, destructive device, explosive or hazardous substance and which he or she knows, intends or reasonably believes will appear to be a bomb, destructive device, explosive or hazardous substance under circumstances in which it is likely to cause public alarm or inconvenience. For purposes of this section the term "public building" shall have the meaning set forth in section four hundred one of the executive law.

Placing a false bomb or hazardous substance in the first degree is a class D felony.

§240.63 Placing a false bomb or hazardous substance in a sports stadium or arena, mass transportation facility or enclosed shopping mall.

A person is guilty of placing a false bomb or hazardous substance in a sports stadium or arena, mass transportation facility or enclosed shopping mall when he or she places, or causes to be placed, in a sports stadium or arena, mass transportation facility or enclosed shopping mall, in which it is likely that persons are present, any device or object that by its design, construction, content or characteristics appears to be or to contain a bomb, destructive device, explosive or hazardous substance, but is, in fact, an inoperative facsimile or imitation of such a bomb, destructive device, explosive or hazardous substance and which he or she knows, intends or reasonably believes will appear to be a bomb, destructive device, explosive or hazardous substance under circumstances in which it is likely to cause public alarm or inconvenience. For purposes of this section, "sports stadium or arena, mass transportation facility or enclosed shopping mall" shall have its natural meaning.

Placing a false bomb or hazardous substance in a sports stadium or arena, mass transportation facility or enclosed shopping mall is a class D felony.

§240.65 Unlawful prevention of public access to records.

A person is guilty of unlawful prevention of public access to records when, with intent to prevent the public inspection of a record pursuant to article six of the public officers law, he willfully conceals or destroys any such record.

Unlawful prevention of public access to records is a violation.

§240.70 Criminal interference with health care services or religious worship in the second degree.

1. A person is guilty of criminal interference with health services or religious worship in the second degree when:

(a) by force or threat of force or by physical obstruction, he or she intentionally injures, intimidates or interferes with, or attempts to injure, intimidate or interfere with, another person because such other person was or is obtaining or providing reproductive health services; or

(b) by force or threat of force or by physical obstruction, he or she intentionally injures, intimidates or interferes with, or attempts to injure, intimidate or interfere with, another person in order to discourage such other person or any other person or persons from obtaining or providing reproductive health services; or

(c) by force or threat of force or by physical obstruction, he or she intentionally injures, intimidates or interferes with, or attempts to injure, intimidate or interfere with, another person because such person was or is seeking to exercise the right of religious freedom at a place of religious worship; or

(d) he or she intentionally damages the property of a health care facility, or attempts to do so, because such facility provides reproductive health services, or intentionally damages the property of a place of religious worship.

2. A parent or legal guardian of a minor shall not be subject to prosecution for conduct otherwise prohibited by paragraph (a) or (b) of subdivision one of this section which is directed exclusively at such minor.

3. For purposes of this section:

(a) the term "health care facility" means a hospital, clinic, physician's office or other facility that provides reproductive health services, and includes the building or structure in which the facility is located;

(b) the term "interferes with" means to restrict a person's freedom of movement;

(c) the term "intimidates" means to place a person in reasonable apprehension of physical injury to himself or herself or to another person;

(d) the term "physical obstruction" means rendering impassable ingress to or egress from a facility that provides reproductive health services or to or from a place of religious worship, or rendering passage to or from such a facility or place of religious worship unreasonably difficult or hazardous; and

(e) the term "reproductive health services" means health care services provided in a hospital, clinic, physician's office or other facility and includes medical, surgical, counseling or referral services relating to the human reproductive system, including services relating to pregnancy or the termination of a pregnancy.

Criminal interference with health care services or religious worship in the second degree is a class A misdemeanor.

§240.71 Criminal interference with health care services or religious worship in the first degree.

A person is guilty of criminal interference with health care services or religious worship in the first degree when he or she commits the crime of criminal interference with health care services or religious worship in the second degree and has been previously convicted of the crime of criminal interference with health care services or religious worship in the first or second degree or aggravated interference with health care services in the first or second degree.

Criminal interference with health care services or religious worship in the first degree is a class E felony.

§240.72 Aggravated interference with health care services in the second degree.

A person is guilty of the crime of aggravated interference with health care services in the second degree when he or she commits the crime of criminal interference with health care services or religious worship in violation of paragraph (a) of subdivision one of section 240.70 of this article and thereby causes physical injury to such other person who was obtaining or providing, or was assisting another person to obtain or provide reproductive health services.

Aggravated interference with health care services in the second degree is a class E felony.

§240.73 Aggravated interference with health care services in the first degree.

A person is guilty of the crime of aggravated interference with health care services in the first degree when he or she commits the crime of criminal interference with health care services or religious worship in violation of paragraph (a) of subdivision one of section 240.70 of this article and thereby causes serious physical injury to such other person who was obtaining or providing, or who was assisting another person to obtain or provide reproductive health services.

Aggravated interference with health care services in the first degree is a class C felony.

§240.75 Aggravated family offense.

1. A person is guilty of aggravated family offense when he or she commits a misdemeanor defined in subdivision two of this section as a specified offense and he or she has been convicted of one or more specified offenses within the immediately preceding five years. For the purposes of this subdivision, in calculating the five year period, any period of time during which the defendant was incarcerated for any reason between the time of the commission of any of such previous offenses and the time of commission of the present crime shall be excluded and such five year period shall be extended by a period or periods equal to the time served under such incarceration.

2. A "specified offense" is an offense defined in section 120.00 (assault in the third degree); section 120.05 (assault in the second degree); section 120.10 (assault in the first degree); section 120.13 (menacing in the first degree); section 120.14 (menacing in the second degree); section 120.15 (menacing in the third degree); section 120.20 (reckless endangerment in the second degree); section 120.25 (reckless endangerment in the first degree); section 120.45 (stalking in the fourth degree); section 120.50 (stalking in the third degree); section 120.55 (stalking in the second degree); section 120.60 (stalking in the first degree); section 121.11 (criminal obstruction of breathing or blood circulation); section 121.12 (strangulation in the second degree); section 121.13 (strangulation in the first degree); subdivision one of section 125.15 (manslaughter in the second degree); subdivision one, two or four of section 125.20 (manslaughter in the first degree); sec-

tion 125.25 (murder in the second degree); section 130.20 (sexual misconduct); section 130.30 (rape in the second degree); section 130.35 (rape in the first degree); section 130.40 (criminal sexual act in the third degree); section 130.45 (criminal sexual act in the second degree); section 130.50 (criminal sexual act in the first degree); section 130.52 (forcible touching); section 130.53 (persistent sexual abuse); section 130.55 (sexual abuse in the third degree); section 130.60 (sexual abuse in the second degree); section 130.65 (sexual abuse in the first degree); section 130.66 (aggravated sexual abuse in the third degree); section 130.67 (aggravated sexual abuse in the second degree); section 130.70 (aggravated sexual abuse in the first degree); section 130.91 (sexually motivated felony); section 130.95 (predatory sexual assault); section 130.96 (predatory sexual assault against a child); section 135.05 (unlawful imprisonment in the second degree); section 135.10 (unlawful imprisonment in the first degree); section 135.60 (coercion in the third degree); section 135.61 (coercion in the second degree); section 135.65 (coercion in the first degree); section 140.20 (burglary in the third degree); section 140.25 (burglary in the second degree); section 140.30 (burglary in the first degree); section 145.00 (criminal mischief in the fourth degree); section 145.05 (criminal mischief in the third degree); section 145.10 (criminal mischief in the second degree); section 145.12 (criminal mischief in the first degree); section 145.14 (criminal tampering in the third degree); section 215.50 (criminal contempt in the second degree); section 215.51 (criminal contempt in the first degree); section 215.52 (aggravated criminal contempt); section 240.25 (harassment in the first degree); subdivision one, two or four of section 240.30 (aggravated harassment in the second degree); aggravated family offense as defined in this section or any attempt or conspiracy to commit any of the foregoing offenses where the defendant and the person against whom the offense was committed were members of the same family or household as defined in subdivision one of section 530.11 of the criminal procedure law.

3. The person against whom the current specified offense is committed may be different from the person against whom the previous specified offense was committed and such persons do not need to be members of the same family or household.

Aggravated family offense is a class E felony.

§240.76 Directing a laser at an aircraft in the second degree.

A person is guilty of directing a laser at an aircraft in the second degree when, with intent to disrupt safe air travel, he or she directs the beam of a laser:

1. onto a specific aircraft intending to thereby disrupt or interfere with such aircraft in the special aircraft jurisdiction of the United States; or

2. in the immediate vicinity of an aircraft in the special aircraft jurisdiction of the United States, and:

(a) the calculated or measured beam irradiance on the aircraft, or in the immediate vicinity of the aircraft, exceeds limits set by the FAA for the FAA-specified laser flight zone (normal, sensitive, critical, or laser-free) where the aircraft was located; and (b) a pilot in the illuminated aircraft files a laser incident report with the FAA.

3. As used in this section:

(a) the term "laser" shall mean any device designed or used to amplify electromagnetic radiation by stimulated emission that emits a beam; and

(b) the term "FAA" shall mean the Federal Aviation Administration.

4. This section does not prohibit directing a laser beam at an aircraft, or in the immediate vicinity of an aircraft, by:

(a) an authorized individual in the conduct of research and development or flight test operations conducted by an aircraft manufacturer, the FAA, or any other person authorized by the FAA to conduct such research and development or flight test operations; or

(b) members or elements of the United States department of defense or the United States department of homeland security acting in an official capacity for the purpose of research, development, operations, testing or training; or

(c) an individual in an emergency situation using a laser to attract the attention of an aircraft for bona fide rescue purposes; or

(d) an individual whose laser operations have been submitted to and reviewed by the FAA, when:

(i) the FAA has issued a letter not objecting to the laser use; and

(ii) the laser is operated in conformity with the FAA submission.

Directing a laser at an aircraft * is a class A misdemeanor.

§240.77 Directing a laser at an aircraft in the first degree.

A person is guilty of directing a laser at an aircraft in the first degree when he or she commits the crime of directing a laser at an aircraft in the second degree in violation of section 240.76 of this article and thereby causes a significant change of course or other serious disruption to the safe travel of an aircraft that threatens the physical safety of the aircraft's passengers or crew.

Directing a laser at an aircraft in the first degree is a class E felony.

(So in original "in the second degree" inadvertently omitted.)

ARTICLE 241 - HARASSMENT OF RENT REGULATED TENANTS

Section
241.00   **Harassment of a rent regulated tenant; definition of terms.**
241.02   **Harassment of a rent regulated tenant in the second degree.**
241.05   **Harassment of a rent regulated tenant in the first degree.**

§241.00   Harassment of a rent regulated tenant; definition of terms.

As used in this article:

1. "Rent regulated tenant" shall mean a person occupying a housing accommodation or any lawful successor to the tenancy which is subject to the regulations and control of residential rents and evictions pursuant to the emergency housing rent control law, the local emergency housing rent control act, the emergency tenant protection act of nineteen seventy-four, the New York city rent and rehabilitation law or the New York city rent stabilization law of nineteen hundred sixty-nine, and such person is either a party to a lease or rental agreement for such housing accommodation, a statutory tenant or a person who lawfully occupies such housing accommodation with such party to a lease or rental agreement or with such statutory tenant. The definition of "rent regulated tenant" as used in this subdivision shall be applicable only to the provisions of this article and shall not be applicable to any other provision of law.   *(Eff.5/31/20,Ch.573,L.2019)*

2. "Housing accommodations" shall mean housing accommodations which are subject to the regulations and control of residential rents and evictions pursuant to the emergency housing rent control law, the local emergency housing rent control act, the emergency tenant protection act of nineteen seventy-four, the New York city rent and rehabilitation law or the New York city rent stabilization law of nineteen hundred sixty-nine.

3. "Owner" shall mean an owner, lessor, sublessor, assignee, net lessee, or a proprietary lessee of a housing accommodation in a structure or premises owned by a cooperative corporation or association, or an owner of a condominium unit or the sponsor of such cooperative corporation or association or condominium development, or any other person or entity receiving or entitled to receive rent for the use or occupation of any housing accommodation, or an agent of or any person acting on behalf of any of the foregoing

§241.02 Harassment of a rent regulated tenant in the second degree.

An owner is guilty of harassment of a rent regulated tenant in the second degree when, with intent to induce a rent regulated tenant to vacate a housing accommodation, such owner intentionally engages in a course of conduct that:

1. impairs the habitability of a housing accommodation; or

2. creates or maintains a condition which endangers the safety or health of the dwelling's tenant; or

3. is reasonably likely to interfere with or disturb, and does interfere with or disturb, the comfort, repose, peace or quiet of such rent regulated tenant in his or her use and occupancy of such housing

accommodation including, but not limited to, the interruption or discontinuance of essential services. The good faith commencement and pursuit of a lawful eviction action by an owner against a rent regulated tenant in a court of competent jurisdiction shall not, by itself, constitute a "course of conduct" in violation of this subdivision.

Harassment of a rent regulated tenant in the second degree is a class A misdemeanor. *(Eff.5/31/20,Ch.573,L.2019)*

§241.05 Harassment of a rent regulated tenant in the first degree.

An owner is guilty of harassment of a rent regulated tenant in the first degree when:

1. With intent to induce a rent regulated tenant to vacate a housing accommodation, such owner:

(a) With intent to cause physical injury to such tenant, causes such injury to such tenant or to a third person; or

(b) Recklessly causes physical injury to such tenant or to a third person; or

2. With intent to induce two or more rent regulated tenants occupying different housing accommodations to vacate such housing accommodations, such owner intentionally engages in a systematic ongoing course of conduct that:

(a) impairs the habitability of such housing accommodations; or

(b) creates or maintains a condition which endangers the safety or health of one or more of the dwellings' rent regulated tenants; or

(c) is reasonably likely to interfere with or disturb, and does interfere with or disturb, the comfort, repose, peace or quiet of one or more of such rent regulated tenants in their use and occupancy of such housing accommodations including, but not limited to, the interruption or discontinuance of essential services; or

3. Such owner commits the crime of harassment of a rent regulated tenant in the second degree as defined in section 241.02 of this article and has previously been convicted within the preceding five years of such crime or the crime of harassment of a rent regulated tenant in the first degree.

The good faith commencement and pursuit of a lawful eviction action by an owner against a rent regulated tenant in a court of competent jurisdiction shall not, by itself, constitute a "systematic ongoing course of conduct" in violation of paragraph (c) of subdivision two of this section.

Harassment of a rent regulated tenant in the first degree is a class E felony.

(Eff.5/31/20,Ch.573,L.2019)

ARTICLE 242 - OFFENSES AGAINST SERVICE ANIMALS AND HANDLERS

Section
242.00 Definitions.
242.05 Interference, harassment or intimidation of a service animal.
242.10 Harming a service animal in the second degree.
242.15 Harming a service animal in the first degree.

§242.00 Definitions.

For purposes of this article:

1. "Service animal" shall mean any animal that has been partnered with a person who has a disability and has been trained or is being trained, by a qualified person, to aid or guide a person with a disability.

2. "Disability" shall have the same meaning as provided in section two hundred ninety-two of the executive law.

3. "Handler" shall mean a disabled person using a service animal.

4. "Formal training program" or "certified trainer" shall mean an institution, group or individual who has documentation and community recognition as a provider of service animals.

§242.05 Interference, harassment or intimidation of a service animal.

A person is guilty of interference, harassment or intimidation of a service animal when he or she commits an act with intent to and which does make it impractical, dangerous or impossible for a service animal to perform its assigned responsibilities of assisting a person with a disability.

Interference, harassment or intimidation of a service animal is a class B misdemeanor.

§242.10 Harming a service animal in the second degree.

A person is guilty of harming a service animal in the second degree when, with the intent to do so, he or she causes physical injury, or causes such injury that results in the death, of a service animal.

Harming a service animal in the second degree is a class A misdemeanor.

§242.15 Harming a service animal in the first degree.

A person is guilty of harming a service animal in the first degree when, he or she commits the crime of harming a service animal in the second degree, and has been convicted of harming a service animal in the first or second degree within the prior five years.

Harming a service animal in the first degree is a class E felony.

ARTICLE 245 - OFFENSES AGAINST PUBLIC SENSIBILITIES

Section
245.00 Public lewdness.
245.01 Exposure of a person.
245.02 Promoting the exposure of a person.
245.03 Public lewdness in the first degree.
245.05 Offensive exhibition.
245.10 Public display of offensive sexual material; definitions of terms.
245.11 Public display of offensive sexual material.
245.15 Unlawful dissemination or publication of an intimate image.

§245.00 Public lewdness.

A person is guilty of public lewdness when he or she intentionally exposes the private or intimate parts of his or her body in a lewd manner or commits any other lewd act: (a) in a public place, or (b) (i) in private premises under circumstances in which he or she may readily be observed from either a public place or from other private premises, and with intent that he or she be so observed, or (ii) while trespassing, as defined in section 140.05 of this part, in a dwelling as defined in subdivision three of section 140.00 of this part, under circumstances in which he or she is observed by a lawful occupant.

Public lewdness is a class B misdemeanor.

§245.01 Exposure of a person.

A person is guilty of exposure if he appears in a public place in such a manner that the private or intimate parts of his body are unclothed or exposed. For purposes of this section, the private or intimate parts of a female person shall include that portion of the breast which is below the top of the areola. This section shall not apply to the breast-feeding of infants or to any person entertaining or performing in a play, exhibition, show or entertainment.

Exposure of a person is a violation.

Nothing in this section shall prevent the adoption by a city, town or village of a local law prohibiting exposure of a person as herein defined in a public place, at any time, whether or not such person is entertaining or performing in a play, exhibition, show or entertainment.

§245.02 Promoting the exposure of a person.

A person is guilty of promoting the exposure of a person when he knowingly conducts, maintains, owns, manages, operates or furnishes any public premise or place where a person in a public place appears in such a manner that the private or intimate parts of his body are unclothed or exposed. For purposes of this section, the private or intimate parts of a female person shall include that portion of the breast which is below the top of the areola. This section shall not apply to the breast-feeding of infants or to any person entertaining or performing in a play, exhibition, show or entertainment.

Promoting the exposure of a person is a violation.

Nothing in this section shall prevent the adoption by a city, town or village of a local law prohibiting the exposure of a person substantially as herein defined in a public place, at any time, whether or not such person is entertaining or performing in a play, exhibition, show or entertainment.

§245.03 Public lewdness in the first degree.

A person is guilty of public lewdness in the first degree when:

1. being nineteen years of age or older and intending to be observed by a person less than sixteen years of age in a place described in subdivision (a) or (b) of section 245.00 of this article, he or she intentionally exposes the private or intimate parts of his or her body in a lewd manner for the purpose of alarming or seriously annoying such person, and he or she is thereby observed by such person in such place; or

2. he or she commits the crime of public lewdness, as defined in section 245.00 of this article, and within the preceding year has been convicted of an offense defined in such section 245.00 or this section.

Public lewdness in the first degree is a class A misdemeanor.

§245.05 Offensive exhibition.

A person is guilty of offensive exhibition when he knowingly produces, operates, manages or furnishes premises for, or in any way promotes or participates in, an exhibition in the nature of public entertainment or amusement in which:

1. A person competes continuously without respite for a period of more than eight consecutive hours in a dance contest, bicycle race or other contest involving physical endurance; or

2. A person is held up to ridicule or contempt by voluntarily submitting to indignities such as the throwing of balls or other articles at his head or body; or

3. A firearm is discharged or a knife, arrow or other sharp or dangerous instrument is thrown or propelled at or toward a person.

Offensive exhibition is a violation.

§245.10 Public display of offensive sexual material; definitions of terms.

The following definitions are applicable to section 245.11:

1. "Nudity" means the showing of the human male or female genitals, pubic area or buttocks with less than a full opaque covering, or the showing of the female breast with less than a fully opaque covering of

any portion thereof below the top of the nipple, or the depiction of covered male genitals in a discernibly turgid state.

2. "Sexual conduct" means an act of masturbation, homosexuality, sexual intercourse, or physical contact with a person's clothed or unclothed genitals, pubic area, buttocks or, if such person be a female, breast.

3. "Sado-masochistic abuse" means flagellation or torture by or upon a person clad in undergarments, a mask or bizarre costume, or the condition of being fettered, bound or otherwise physically restrained on the part of one so clothed.

4. "Transportation facility" means any conveyance, premises or place used for or in connection with public passenger transportation, whether by air, railroad, motor vehicle or any other method. It includes aircraft, watercraft, railroad cars, buses, and air, boat, railroad and bus terminals and stations and all appurtenances thereto.

§245.11 Public display of offensive sexual material.

A person is guilty of public display of offensive sexual material when, with knowledge of its character and content, he displays or permits to be displayed in or on any window, showcase, newsstand, display rack, wall, door, billboard, display board, viewing screen, moving picture screen, marquee or similar place, in such manner that the display is easily visible from or in any: public street, sidewalk or thoroughfare; transportation facility; or any place accessible to members of the public without fee or other limit or condition of admission such as a minimum age requirement and including but not limited to schools, places of amusement, parks and playgrounds but excluding rooms or apartments designed for actual residence; any pictorial three-dimensional or other visual representation of a person or a portion of the human body that predominantly appeals to prurient interest in sex, and that:

(a) depicts nudity, or actual or simulated sexual conduct or sado-masochistic abuse; or

(b) depicts or appears to depict nudity, or actual or simulated sexual conduct or sado-masochistic abuse, with the area of the male or female subject's unclothed or apparently unclothed genitals, public area or buttocks, or of the female subject's unclothed or apparently unclothed breast, obscured by a covering or mark placed or printed on or in front of the material displayed, or obscured or altered in any other manner.

Public display of offensive sexual material is a Class A misdemeanor.

§245.15 Unlawful dissemination or publication of an intimate image.

1. A person is guilty of unlawful dissemination or publication of an intimate image when:

(a) with intent to cause harm to the emotional, financial or physical welfare of another person, he or she intentionally disseminates or publishes a still or video image of such other person, who is identifiable from the still or video image itself or from information displayed in connection with the still or video image, without such other person's consent, which depicts:

(i) an unclothed or exposed intimate part of such other person; or

(ii) such other person engaging in sexual conduct as defined in subdivision ten of section 130.00 of this chapter with another person; and

(b) such still or video image was taken under circumstances when the person depicted had a reasonable expectation that the image would remain private and the actor knew or reasonably should have known the person depicted intended for the still or video image to remain private, regardless of whether the actor was present when the still or video image was taken.

2. For purposes of this section "intimate part" means the naked genitals, pubic area, anus or female nipple of the person.

2-a. For purposes of this section "disseminate" and "publish" shall have the same meaning as defined in section 250.40 of this title.

3. This section shall not apply to the following:

(a) the reporting of unlawful conduct;

(b) dissemination or publication of an intimate image made during lawful and common practices of law enforcement, legal proceedings or medical treatment;

(c) images involving voluntary exposure in a public or commercial setting; or

(d) dissemination or publication of an intimate image made for a legitimate public purpose.

4. Nothing in this section shall be construed to limit, or to enlarge, the protections that 47 U.S.C § 230 confers on an interactive computer service for content provided by another information content provider, as such terms are defined in 47 U.S.C. § 230.

Unlawful dissemination or publication of an intimate image is a class A misdemeanor.

(Eff.9/21/19,Ch.109,L.2019)

ARTICLE 250 - OFFENSES AGAINST THE RIGHT TO PRIVACY

Section
250.00 Eavesdropping; definitions of terms.
250.05 Eavesdropping.
250.10 Possession of eavesdropping devices.
250.15 Failure to report wiretapping.
250.20 Divulging an eavesdropping warrant.
250.25 Tampering with private communications.
250.30 Unlawfully obtaining communications information.
250.35 Failing to report criminal communications.
250.40 Unlawful surveillance; definitions.
250.45 Unlawful surveillance in the second degree.
250.50 Unlawful surveillance in the first degree.
250.55 Dissemination of an unlawful surveillance image in the second degree.
250.60 Dissemination of an unlawful surveillance image in the first degree.
250.65 Additional provisions.

§250.00 Eavesdropping; definitions of terms.

The following definitions are applicable to this article:

1. "Wiretapping" means the intentional overhearing or recording of a telephonic or telegraphic communication by a person other than a sender or receiver thereof, without the consent of either the sender or receiver, by means of any instrument, device or equipment. The normal operation of a telephone or telegraph corporation and the normal use of the services and facilities furnished by such corporation pursuant to its tariffs or necessary to protect the rights or property of said corporation shall not be deemed "wiretapping."

2. "Mechanical overhearing of a conversation" means the intentional overhearing or recording of a conversation or discussion, without the consent of at least one party thereto, by a person not present thereat, by means of any instrument, device or equipment.

3. "Telephonic communication" means any aural transfer made in whole or in part through the use of facilities for the transmission of communications by the aid of wire, cable or other like connection between the point of origin and the point of reception (including the use of such connection in a switching station) furnished or operated by any person engaged in providing or operating such facilities for the transmission of communications and such term includes any electronic storage of such communications.

4. "Aural transfer" means a transfer containing the human voice at any point between and including the point of origin and the point of reception.

5. "Electronic communication" means any transfer of signs, signals, writing, images, sounds, data, or intelligence of any nature transmitted in whole or in part by a wire, radio, electromagnetic, photoelectronic or photo-optical system, but does not include:

(a) any telephonic or telegraphic communication; or

(b) any communication made through a tone only paging device; or

(c) any communication made through a tracking device consisting of an electronic or mechanical device which permits the tracking of the movement of a person or object; or

(d) any communication that is disseminated by the sender through a method of transmission that is configured so that such communication is readily accessible to the general public.

6. "Intercepting or accessing of an electronic communication" and "intentionally intercepted or accessed" mean the intentional acquiring, receiving, collecting, overhearing, or recording of an electronic communication, without the consent of the sender or intended receiver thereof, by means of any instrument, device or equipment, except when used by a telephone company in the ordinary course of its business or when necessary to protect the rights or property of such company.

7. "Electronic communication service" means any service which provides to users thereof the ability to send or receive wire or electronic communications.

8. "Unlawfully" means not specifically authorized pursuant to article seven hundred or seven hundred five of the criminal procedure law for the purposes of this section and sections 250.05, 250.10, 250.15, 250.20, 250.25, 250.30 and 250.35 of this article.

§250.05 Eavesdropping.

A person is guilty of eavesdropping when he unlawfully engages in wiretapping, mechanical overhearing of a conversation, or intercepting or accessing of an electronic communication.

Eavesdropping is a class E felony.

§250.10 Possession of eavesdropping devices.

A person is guilty of possession of eavesdropping devices when, under circumstances evincing an intent to use or to permit the same to be used in violation of section 250.05, he possesses any instrument, device or equipment designed for, adapted to or commonly used in wiretapping or mechanical overhearing of a conversation.

Possession of eavesdropping devices is a class A misdemeanor.

§250.15 Failure to report wiretapping.

A telephone or telegraph corporation is guilty of failure to report wiretapping when, having knowledge of the occurrence of unlawful wiretapping, it does not report such matter to an appropriate law enforcement officer or agency.

Failure to report wiretapping is a class B misdemeanor.

§250.20 Divulging an eavesdropping warrant.

A person is guilty of divulging an eavesdropping warrant when, possessing information concerning the existence or content of an eavesdropping warrant issued pursuant to article seven hundred of the criminal procedure law, or concerning any circumstances attending an application for such a warrant, he discloses such information to another person; except that such disclosure is not criminal or unlawful when permitted by section 700.65 of the criminal procedure law or when made to a state or federal agency specifically authorized by law to receive reports concerning eavesdropping warrants, or when made in a legal proceeding, or to a law enforcement officer or agency connected with the application for such warrant, or to a legislative committee or temporary state commission, or to the telephone or telegraph corporation whose facilities are involved, or to any entity operating an electronic communications service whose facilities are involved.

Divulging an eavesdropping warrant is a class A misdemeanor.

§250.25 Tampering with private communications.

A person is guilty of tampering with private communications when:

1. Knowing that he does not have the consent of the sender or receiver, he opens or reads a sealed letter or other sealed private communication; or

2. Knowing that a sealed letter or other sealed private communication has been opened or read in violation of subdivision one of this section, he divulges without the consent of the sender or receiver, the contents of such letter or communication, in whole or in part, or a resume of any portion of the contents thereof; or

3. Knowing that he does not have the consent of the sender or receiver, he obtains or attempts to obtain from an employee, officer or representative of a telephone or telegraph corporation, by connivance, deception, intimidation or in any other manner, information with respect to the contents or nature thereof of a telephonic or telegraphic communication; except that the provisions of this subdivision do not apply to a law enforcement officer who obtains information from a telephone or telegraph corporation pursuant to section 250.35; or

4. Knowing that he does not have the consent of the sender or receiver, and being an employee, officer or representative of a telephone or telegraph corporation, he knowingly divulges to another person the

contents or nature thereof of a telephonic or telegraphic communication; except that the provisions of this subdivision do not apply to such person when he acts pursuant to section 250.35.

Tampering with private communications is a class B misdemeanor.

§250.30 Unlawfully obtaining communications information.

A person is guilty of unlawfully obtaining communications information when, knowing that he does not have the authorization of a telephone or telegraph corporation, he obtains or attempts to obtain, by deception, stealth or in any other manner, from such corporation or from any employee, officer or representative thereof:

1. Information concerning identification or location of any wires, cables, lines, terminals or other apparatus used in furnishing telephone or telegraph service; or

2. Information concerning a record of any communication passing over telephone or telegraph lines of any such corporation.

Unlawfully obtaining communications information is a class B misdemeanor.

§250.35 Failing to report criminal communications.

1. It shall be the duty of a telephone or telegraph corporation, or an entity operating an electronic communications service, and of any employee, officer or representative thereof having knowledge that the facilities of such corporation or entity are being used to conduct any criminal business, traffic or transaction, to furnish or attempt to furnish to an appropriate law enforcement officer or agency all pertinent information within his possession relating to such matter, and to cooperate fully with any law enforcement officer or agency investigating such matter.

2. A person is guilty of failing to report criminal communications when he knowingly violates any duty prescribed in subdivision one of this section.

Failing to report criminal communications is a class B misdemeanor.

§250.40 Unlawful surveillance; definitions.

The following definitions shall apply to sections 250.45, 250.50, 250.55 and 250.60 of this article:

1. "Place and time when a person has a reasonable expectation of privacy" means a place and time when a reasonable person would believe that he or she could fully disrobe in privacy.

2. "Imaging device" means any mechanical, digital or electronic viewing device, camera, cellular phone or any other instrument capable of recording, storing or transmitting visual images that can be utilized to observe a person.

3. "Sexual or other intimate parts" means the human male or female genitals, pubic area or buttocks, or the female breast below the top of the nipple, and shall include such part or parts which are covered only by an undergarment.

4. "Broadcast" means electronically transmitting a visual image with the intent that it be viewed by a person.

5. "Disseminate" means to give, provide, lend, deliver, mail, send,

forward, transfer or transmit, electronically or otherwise to another person.

6. "Publish" means to (a) disseminate, as defined in subdivision five of this section, with the intent that such image or images be disseminated to ten or more persons; or (b) disseminate with the intent that such images be sold by another person; or (c) post, present, display, exhibit, circulate, advertise or allows access, electronically or otherwise, so as to make an image or images available to the public; or (d) disseminate with the intent that an image or images be posted, presented, displayed, exhibited, circulated, advertised or made accessible, electronically or otherwise and to make such image or images available to the public.

7. "Sell" means to disseminate to another person, as defined in subdivision five of this section, or to publish, as defined in subdivision six of this section, in exchange for something of value.

§250.45 Unlawful surveillance in the second degree.

A person is guilty of unlawful surveillance in the second degree when:

1. For his or her own, or another person's amusement, entertainment, or profit, or for the purpose of degrading or abusing a person, he or she intentionally uses or installs, or permits the utilization or installation of an imaging device to surreptitiously view, broadcast or record a person dressing or undressing or the sexual or other intimate parts of such person at a place and time when such person has a reasonable expectation of privacy, without such person's knowledge or consent; or

2. For his or her own, or another person's sexual arousal or sexual gratification, he or she intentionally uses or installs, or permits the utilization or installation of an imaging device to surreptitiously view, broadcast or record a person dressing or undressing or the sexual or other intimate parts of such person at a place and time when such person has a reasonable expectation of privacy, without such person's knowledge or consent; or

3. (a) For no legitimate purpose, he or she intentionally uses or installs, or permits the utilization or installation of an imaging device to surreptitiously view, broadcast or record a person in a bedroom, changing room, fitting room, restroom, toilet, bathroom, washroom, shower or any room assigned to guests or patrons in a motel, hotel or inn, without such person's knowledge or consent.

(b) For the purposes of this subdivision, when a person uses or installs, or permits the utilization or installation of an imaging device in a bedroom, changing room, fitting room, restroom, toilet, bathroom, washroom, shower or any room assigned to guests or patrons in a hotel, motel or inn, there is a rebuttable presumption that such person did so for no legitimate purpose; or

4. Without the knowledge or consent of a person, he or she intentionally uses or installs, or permits the utilization or installation of an imaging device to surreptitiously view, broadcast or record, under the clothing being worn by such person, the sexual or other intimate parts of such person; or

5. For his or her own, or another individual's amusement, entertainment, profit, sexual arousal or gratification, or for the purpose

of degrading or abusing a person, the actor intentionally uses or installs or permits the utilization or installation of an imaging device to surreptitiously view, broadcast, or record such person in an identifiable manner:

(a) engaging in sexual conduct, as defined in subdivision ten of section 130.00 of this part;

(b) in the same image with the sexual or intimate part of any other person; and

(c) at a place and time when such person has a reasonable expectation of privacy, without such person's knowledge or consent.

Unlawful surveillance in the second degree is a class E felony.

§250.50 Unlawful surveillance in the first degree.

A person is guilty of unlawful surveillance in the first degree when he or she commits the crime of unlawful surveillance in the second degree and has been previously convicted within the past ten years of unlawful surveillance in the first or second degree.

Unlawful surveillance in the first degree is a class D felony.

§250.55 Dissemination of an unlawful surveillance image in the second degree.

A person is guilty of dissemination of an unlawful surveillance image in the second degree when he or she, with knowledge of the unlawful conduct by which an image or images of the sexual or other intimate parts of another person or persons were obtained and such unlawful conduct would satisfy the essential elements of the crime of unlawful surveillance in the first or second degree, as defined, respectively, in section 250.50 or 250.45 of this article, intentionally disseminates such image or images.

Dissemination of an unlawful surveillance image in the second degree is a class A misdemeanor.

§250.60 Dissemination of an unlawful surveillance image in the first degree.

A person is guilty of dissemination of an unlawful surveillance image in the first degree when:

1. He or she, with knowledge of the unlawful conduct by which an image or images of the sexual or other intimate parts of another person or persons were obtained and such unlawful conduct would satisfy the essential elements of the crime of unlawful surveillance in the first or second degree, as defined, respectively, in section 250.50 or 250.45 of this article, sells or publishes such image or images; or

2. Having created a surveillance image in violation of section 250.45 or 250.50 of this article, or in violation of the law in any other jurisdiction which includes all of the essential elements of either such crime, or having acted as an accomplice to such crime, or acting as an agent to the person who committed such crime, he or she intentionally disseminates such unlawfully created image; or

3. He or she commits the crime of dissemination of an unlawful surveillance image in the second degree and has been previously convicted within the past ten years of dissemination of an unlawful surveillance image in the first or second degree.

Dissemination of an unlawful surveillance image in the first degree is a class E felony.

§250.65 Additional provisions.

1. The provisions of sections 250.45, 250.50, 250.55 and 250.60 of this article do not apply with respect to any: (a) law enforcement personnel engaged in the conduct of their authorized duties; (b) security system wherein a written notice is conspicuously posted on the premises stating that a video surveillance system has been installed for the purpose of security; or (c) video surveillance devices installed in such a manner that their presence is clearly and immediately obvious.

2. With respect to sections 250.55 and 250.60 of this article, the provisions of subdivision two of section 235.15 and subdivisions one and two of section 235.24 of this chapter shall apply.

TITLE O - OFFENSES AGAINST MARRIAGE , THE FAMILY, AND THE WELFARE OF CHILDREN AND INCOMPETENTS
ARTICLE 255 - OFFENSES AFFECTING THE MARITAL RELATIONSHIP

Section
255.00 Unlawfully solemnizing a marriage.
255.05 Unlawfully issuing a dissolution decree.
255.10 Unlawfully procuring a marriage license.
255.15 Bigamy.
255.17 Adultery.
255.20 Unlawfully procuring a marriage license, bigamy, adultery: defense.
255.25 Incest in the third degree.
255.26 Incest in the second degree.
255.27 Incest in the first degree.
255.30 Adultery and incest; corroboration.

§255.00 Unlawfully solemnizing a marriage.

A person is guilty of unlawfully solemnizing a marriage when:

1. Knowing that he is not authorized by the laws of this state to do so, he performs a marriage ceremony or presumes to solemnize a marriage; or

2. Being authorized by the laws of this state to perform marriage ceremonies and to solemnize marriages, he performs a marriage ceremony or solemnizes a marriage knowing that a legal impediment to such marriage exists.

Unlawfully solemnizing a marriage is a class A misdemeanor.

§255.05 Unlawfully issuing a dissolution decree.

A person is guilty of unlawfully issuing a dissolution decree when, not being a judicial officer authorized to issue decrees of divorce or annulment, he issues a written instrument reciting or certifying that he or some other purportedly but not actually authorized person has issued a valid decree of civil divorce, annulment or other dissolution of a marriage.

Unlawfully issuing a dissolution decree is a class A misdemeanor.

§255.10 Unlawfully procuring a marriage license.

A person is guilty of unlawfully procuring a marriage license when he procures a license to marry another person at a time when he has a living spouse, or the other person has a living spouse.

Unlawfully procuring a marriage license is a class A misdemeanor.

§255.15 Bigamy.

A person is guilty of bigamy when he contracts or purports to contract a marriage with another person at a time when he has a living spouse, or the other person has a living spouse.

Bigamy is a class E felony.

§255.17 Adultery.

A person is guilty of adultery when he engages in sexual intercourse with another person at a time when he has a living spouse, or the other person has a living spouse.

Adultery is a class B misdemeanor.

§255.20 Unlawfully procuring a marriage license, bigamy, adultery; defense.

In any prosecution for unlawfully procuring a marriage license, bigamy, or adultery, it is an affirmative defense that the defendant acted under a reasonable belief that both he and the other person to the marriage or prospective marriage or to the sexual intercourse, as the case may be, were unmarried.

§255.25 Incest in the third degree.

A person is guilty of incest in the third degree when he or she marries or engages in sexual intercourse, oral sexual conduct or anal sexual conduct with a person whom he or she knows to be related to him or her, whether through marriage or not, as an ancestor, descendant, brother or sister of either the whole or the half blood, uncle, aunt, nephew or niece.

Incest in the third degree is a class E felony.

§255.26 Incest in the second degree.

A person is guilty of incest in the second degree when he or she commits the crime of rape in the second degree, as defined in section 130.30 of this part, or criminal sexual act in the second degree, as defined in section 130.45 of this part, against a person whom he or she knows to be related to him or her, whether through marriage or not, as an ancestor, descendant, brother or sister of either the whole or the half blood, uncle, aunt, nephew or niece.

Incest in the second degree is a class D felony.

§255.27 Incest in the first degree.

A person is guilty of incest in the first degree when he or she commits the crime of rape in the first degree, as defined in subdivision three or four of section 130.35 of this part, or criminal sexual act in the first degree, as defined in subdivision three or four of section 130.50 of this part, against a person whom he or she knows to be related to him or her, whether through marriage or not, as an ancestor, descendant, brother or sister of either the whole or half blood, uncle, aunt, nephew or niece.

Incest in the first degree is a class B felony.

§255.30 Adultery and incest; corroboration.

1. A person shall not be convicted of adultery or of an attempt to commit adultery solely upon the testimony of the other party to the adulterous act or attempted act, unsupported by other evidence tending to establish that the defendant attempted to engage with the other party in sexual intercourse, and that the defendant or the other party had a living spouse at the time of the adulterous act or attempted act.

2. A person shall not be convicted of incest or of an attempt to commit incest solely upon the testimony of the other party unsupported by other evidence tending to establish that the defendant married the other party, or that the defendant was a relative of the other party of a kind specified in section 255.25.

ARTICLE 260 - OFFENSES RELATING TO CHILDREN, DISABLED PERSONS AND VULNERABLE ELDERLY PERSONS

Section
260.00 Abandonment of a child.
260.05 Non-support of a child in the second degree.
260.06 Non-support of a child in the first degree.
260.10 Endangering the welfare of a child.
260.11 Endangering the welfare of a child; corroboration.
260.15 Endangering the welfare of a child; defense.
260.20 Unlawfully dealing with a child in the first degree.
260.21 Unlawfully dealing with a child in the second degree.
260.22 Facilitating female genital mutilation.
260.24 Endangering the welfare of an incompetent or physically disabled person in the second degree.
260.25 Endangering the welfare of an incompetent or physically disabled person in the first degree.
260.31 Vulnerable elderly persons; definitions.
260.31 Misrepresentation by a child day care provider.
260.31 Endangering the welfare of a vulnerable elderly person, or an incompetent or physically disabled person in the second degree.
260.34 Endangering the welfare of a vulnerable elderly person, or an incompetent or physically disabled person in the first degree.
260.35 Misrepresentation by, or on behalf of, a caregiver for a child or children.

§260.00 Abandonment of a child.

1. A person is guilty of abandonment of a child when, being a parent, guardian or other person legally charged with the care or custody of a child less than fourteen years old, he or she deserts such child in any place with intent to wholly abandon such child.

2. A person is not guilty of the provisions of this section when he or she engages in the conduct described in subdivision one of this section: (a) with the intent that the child be safe from physical injury and cared for in an appropriate manner; (b) the child is left with an appropriate person, or in a suitable location and the person who leaves the child promptly notifies an appropriate person of the child's location; and (c) the child is not more than thirty days old.

Abandonment of a child is a class E felony.

§260.05 Non-support of a child in the second degree.

A person is guilty of non-support of a child when:

1. being a parent, guardian or other person legally charged with the care or custody of a child less than sixteen years old, he or she fails or

refuses without lawful excuse to provide support for such child when he or she is able to do so, or becomes unable to do so, when, though employable, he or she voluntarily terminates his or her employment, voluntarily reduces his or her earning capacity, or fails to diligently seek employment; or

2. being a parent, guardian or other person obligated to make child support payments by an order of child support entered by a court of competent jurisdiction for a child less than eighteen years old, he or she knowingly fails or refuses without lawful excuse to provide support for such child when he or she is able to do so, or becomes unable to do so, when, though employable, he or she voluntarily terminates his or her employment, voluntarily reduces his or her earning capacity, or fails to diligently seek employment.

Non-support of a child in the second degree is a class A misdemeanor.

§260.06 Non-support of a child in the first degree.

A person is guilty of non-support of a child in the first degree when:

1. (a) being a parent, guardian or other person legally charged with the care or custody of a child less than sixteen years old, he or she fails or refuses without lawful excuse to provide support for such child when he or she is able to do so; or

(b) being a parent, guardian or other person obligated to make child support payments by an order of child support entered by a court of competent jurisdiction for a child less than eighteen years old, he or she fails or refuses without lawful excuse to provide support for such child when he or she is able to do so; and

2. he or she has previously been convicted in the preceding five years of a crime defined in section 260.05 of this article or a crime defined by the provisions of this section.

Non-support of a child in the first degree is a class E felony.

§260.10 Endangering the welfare of a child.

A person is guilty of endangering the welfare of a child when:

1. He or she knowingly acts in a manner likely to be injurious to the physical, mental or moral welfare of a child less than seventeen years old or directs or authorizes such child to engage in an occupation involving a substantial risk of danger to his or her life or health; or

2. Being a parent, guardian or other person legally charged with the care or custody of a child less than eighteen years old, he or she fails or refuses to exercise reasonable diligence in the control of such child to prevent him or her from becoming an "abused child," a "neglected child," a "juvenile delinquent" or a "person in need of supervision," as those terms are defined in articles ten, three and seven of the family court act.

3. A person is not guilty of the provisions of this section when he or she engages in the conduct described in subdivision one of section 260.00 of this article: (a) with the intent to wholly abandon the child by relinquishing responsibility for and right to the care and custody of such child; (b) with the intent that the child be safe from physical injury and cared for in an appropriate manner; (c) the child is left with an appropriate person, or in a suitable location and the person who leaves

the child promptly notifies an appropriate child's location; and (d) the child is not more than thirty days old.

Endangering the welfare of a child is a class A misdemeanor.

§260.11 Endangering the welfare of a child; corroboration.

A person shall not be convicted of endangering the welfare of a child, or of an attempt to commit the same, upon the testimony of a victim who is incapable of consent because of mental defect or mental incapacity as to conduct that constitutes an offense or an attempt to commit an offense referred to in section 130.16, without additional evidence sufficient pursuant to section 130.16 to sustain a conviction of an offense referred to in section 130.16, or of an attempt to commit the same.

§260.15 Endangering the welfare of a child; defense.

In any prosecution for endangering the welfare of a child, pursuant to section 260.10 of this article, based upon an alleged failure or refusal to provide proper medical care or treatment to an ill child, it is an affirmative defense that the defendant (a) is a parent, guardian or other person legally charged with the care or custody of such child; and (b) is a member or adherent of an organized church or religious group the tenets of which prescribe prayer as the principal treatment for illness; and (c) treated or caused such ill child to be treated in accordance with such tenets.

§260.20 Unlawfully dealing with a child in the first degree.

A person is guilty of unlawfully dealing with a child in the first degree when:

1. He knowingly permits a child less than eighteen years old to enter or remain in or upon a place, premises or establishment where sexual activity as defined by article one hundred thirty, two hundred thirty or two hundred sixty-three of this part or activity involving controlled substances as defined by article two hundred twenty of this part is maintained or conducted, and he knows or has reason to know that such activity is being maintained or conducted; or

2. He gives or sells or causes to be given or sold any alcoholic beverage, as defined by section three of the alcoholic beverage control law, to a person less than twenty-one years old; except that this subdivision does not apply to the parent or guardian of such a person or to a person who gives or causes to be given any such alcoholic beverage to a person under the age of twenty-one years, who is a student in a curriculum licensed or registered by the state education department, where the tasting or imbibing of alcoholic beverages is required in courses that are part of the required curriculum, provided such alcoholic beverages are given only for instructional purposes during classes conducted pursuant to such curriculum.

It is no defense to a prosecution pursuant to subdivision two of this section that the child acted as the agent or representative of another person or that the defendant dealt with the child as such.

It is an affirmative defense to a prosecution pursuant to subdivision two of this section that the defendant who sold, caused to be sold or attempted to sell such alcoholic beverage to a person less than twenty-one years old, had not been, at the time of such sale or attempted sale, convicted of a violation of this section or section 260.21 of this article within the preceding five years, and such defendant, subsequent to the commencement of the present prosecution, has completed an alcohol training awareness program established pursuant to subdivision twelve of section seventeen of the alcoholic beverage control law. A defendant otherwise qualifying pursuant to this paragraph may request and shall be afforded a reasonable adjournment of the proceedings to enable him or her to complete such alcohol training awareness program.

Unlawfully dealing with a child in the first degree is a class A misdemeanor.

(Eff.3/31/21,Ch.92,L.2021)

§260.21 Unlawfully dealing with a child in the second degree.

A person is guilty of unlawfully dealing with a child in the second degree when:

1. Being an owner, lessee, manager or employee of a place where alcoholic beverages are sold or given away, he permits a child less than sixteen years old to enter or remain in such place unless:

(a) The child is accompanied by his parent, guardian or an adult authorized by a parent or guardian; or

(b) The entertainment or activity is being conducted for the benefit or under the auspices of a non-profit school, church or other educational or religious institution; or

(c) Otherwise permitted by law to do so; or

(d) The establishment is closed to the public for a specified period of time to conduct an activity or entertainment, during which the child is in or remains in such establishment, and no alcoholic beverages are sold, served, given away or consumed at such establishment during such period. The state liquor authority shall be notified in writing by the licensee of such establishment, of the intended closing of such establishment, to conduct any such activity or entertainment, not less than ten days prior to any such closing; or

2. He marks the body of a child less than eighteen years old with indelible ink or pigments by means of tattooing; or

3. He or she sells or causes to be sold tobacco in any form to a child less than twenty-one years old.

It is no defense to a prosecution pursuant to subdivision three of this section that the child acted as the agent or representative of another person or that the defendant dealt with the child as such.

Unlawfully dealing with a child in the second degree is a class B misdemeanor.

§260.22 Facilitating female genital mutilation.

A person is guilty of facilitating female genital mutilation when, knowing that a person intends to engage in the circumcising, excising or infibulating of the whole or any part of the labia majora or labia minora or clitoris of a person under eighteen years of age, and except as provided in subdivision two of section 130.85 of this chapter, he or she intentionally aids the commission or attempted commission of such conduct.

Facilitating female genital mutilation is a class A misdemeanor.

§260.24 Endangering the welfare of an incompetent or physically disabled person in the second degree.

A person is guilty of endangering the welfare of an incompetent or physically disabled person in the second degree when he or she recklessly engages in conduct which is likely to be injurious to the physical, mental or moral welfare of a person who is unable to care for himself or herself because of physical disability, mental disease or defect.

Endangering the welfare of an incompetent or physically disabled person in the second degree is a class A misdemeanor.

§260.25 Endangering the welfare of an incompetent or physically disabled person in the first degree.

A person is guilty of endangering the welfare of an incompetent or physically disabled person in the first degree when he knowingly acts in a manner likely to be injurious to the physical, mental or moral welfare of a person who is unable to care for himself or herself because of physical disability, mental disease or defect.

Endangering the welfare of an incompetent or physically disabled person in the first degree is a class E felony.

*§260.31 Misrepresentation by a child day care provider.

A person is guilty of misrepresentation by a child day care provider when, being a child day care provider or holding himself or herself out as such, he or she makes any willful and intentional misrepresentation, by act or omission, to a parent or guardian of a child in the care of such provider (or a child whose prospective placement in such care is being considered by such parent or guardian) to any state or local official having jurisdiction over child day care providers, or to any police officer or peace officer as to the facts pertaining to such child day care provider, including, but not limited to: (i) the number of children in the facility or home where such number is in violation of the provisions of section three hundred ninety of the social services law, (ii) the area of the facility, home, or center used for child day care, or (iii) the credentials or qualifications of any child day care provider, assistant, employee, or volunteer. A misrepresentation subject to the provisions of this section must substantially place at risk the health or safety of a child in the care of a child day care provider.

Misrepresentation by a child day care provider is a class A misdemeanor.

(There are two §260.31's)

*§260.31 Vulnerable elderly persons; definitions.

For the purpose of sections 260.32 and 260.34 of this article, the following definitions shall apply:

1. "Caregiver" means a person who (i) assumes responsibility for the care of a vulnerable elderly person, or an incompetent or physically disabled person pursuant to a court order; or (ii) receives monetary or other valuable consideration for providing care for a vulnerable elderly person, or an incompetent or physically disabled person.

2. "Sexual contact" means any touching of the sexual or other intimate parts of a person for the purpose of gratifying sexual desire of either party. It includes the touching of the actor by the victim, as well as the touching of the victim by the actor, whether directly or through clothing,

as well as the emission of ejaculate by the actor upon any part of the victim, clothed or unclothed.

3. "Vulnerable elderly person" means a person sixty years of age or older who is suffering from a disease or infirmity associated with advanced age and manifested by demonstrable physical, mental or emotional dysfunction to the extent that the person is incapable of adequately providing for his or her own health or personal care.

4. "Incompetent or physically disabled person" means an individual who is unable to care for himself or herself because of physical disability, mental disease or defect.   *(There are two §260.31's)*

§260.32 Endangering the welfare of a vulnerable elderly person, or an incompetent or physically disabled person in the second degree.

A person is guilty of endangering the welfare of a vulnerable elderly person, or an incompetent or physically disabled person in the second degree when, being a caregiver for a vulnerable elderly person, or an incompetent or physically disabled person:

1. With intent to cause physical injury to such person, he or she causes such injury to such person; or

2. He or she recklessly causes physical injury to such person; or

3. With criminal negligence, he or she causes physical injury to such person by means of a deadly weapon or a dangerous instrument; or

4. He or she subjects such person to sexual contact without the latter's consent. Lack of consent under this subdivision results from forcible compulsion or incapacity to consent, as those terms are defined in article one hundred thirty of this chapter, or any other circumstances in which the vulnerable elderly person, or an incompetent or physically disabled person does not expressly or impliedly acquiesce in the caregiver's conduct. In any prosecution under this subdivision in which the victim's alleged lack of consent results solely from incapacity to consent because of the victim's mental disability or mental incapacity, the provisions of section 130.16 of this chapter shall apply. In addition, in any prosecution under this subdivision in which the victim's lack of consent is based solely upon his or her incapacity to consent because he or she was mentally disabled, mentally incapacitated or physically helpless, it is an affirmative defense that the defendant, at the time he or she engaged in the conduct constituting the offense, did not know of the facts or conditions responsible for such incapacity to consent.

Endangering the welfare of a vulnerable elderly person, or an incompetent or physically disabled person in the second degree is a class E felony.

§260.34 Endangering the welfare of a vulnerable elderly person, or an incompetent or physically disabled person in the first degree.

A person is guilty of endangering the welfare of a vulnerable elderly person, or an incompetent or physically disabled person in the first degree when, being a caregiver for a vulnerable elderly person, or an incompetent or physically disabled person:

1. With intent to cause physical injury to such person, he or she causes serious physical injury to such person; or

2. He or she recklessly causes serious physical injury to such person.

Endangering the welfare of a vulnerable elderly person, or an incompetent or physically disabled person in the first degree is a class D felony.

§260.35 Misrepresentation by, or on behalf of, a caregiver for a child or children.

1. A person is guilty of misrepresentation by, or on behalf of, a caregiver for a child or children when he or she:

(a) intentionally makes a false written statement about himself, herself, or another person while he or she, or such other person, is being considered for employment, or while under employment as a caregiver to a parent or guardian of a child or children, or the agent of a parent or guardian, and

(b) such statement contains a materially false representation regarding the caregiver's background related to the ability to safely care for a child or children, and

(c) a reasonable person would have relied upon such statement in making an employment decision.

2. For the purposes of this section, "caregiver" shall mean a person employed by or being considered for employment to provide fifteen or more hours of care per week to a child or children in the home of such child or children or in the home of such caregiver, provided that such term shall not apply to a child day care provider required to be licensed pursuant to the social services law.

Misrepresentation by, or on behalf of, a caregiver for a child or children is a class A misdemeanor, provided, however, that if any sentence of imprisonment is imposed for a conviction under this section, term of imprisonment shall not exceed six months.   *(Eff.10/15/18,Ch.195,L.2018)*

ARTICLE 263 - SEXUAL PERFORMANCE BY A CHILD

Section
263.00   Definitions.
263.05   Use of a child in a sexual performance.
263.10   Promoting an obscene sexual performance by a child.
263.11   Possessing an obscene sexual performance by a child.
263.15   Promoting a sexual performance by a child.
263.16   Possessing a sexual performance by a child.
263.20   Sexual performance by a child; affirmative defenses.
263.25   Proof of age of child.
263.30   Facilitating a sexual performance by a child with a controlled substance or alcohol.

§263.00 Definitions.

As used in this article the following definitions shall apply:

1. "Sexual performance" means any performance or part thereof which, for purposes of section 263.16 of this article, includes sexual conduct by a child less than sixteen years of age or, for purposes of section 263.05 or 263.15 of this article, includes sexual conduct by a child less than seventeen years of age.

2. "Obscene sexual performance" means any performance which, for purposes of section 263.11 of this article, includes sexual conduct by a child less than sixteen years of age or, for purposes of section 263.10 of this article, includes sexual conduct by a child less than seventeen years of age, in any material which is obscene, as such term is defined in section 235.00 of this chapter.

3. "Sexual conduct" means actual or simulated sexual intercourse, oral sexual conduct, anal sexual conduct, sexual bestiality, masturbation, sado-masochistic abuse, or lewd exhibition of the genitals.

4. "Performance" means any play, motion picture, photograph or dance. Performance also means any other visual representation exhibited before an audience.

5. "Promote" means to procure, manufacture, issue, sell, give, provide, lend, mail, deliver, transfer, transmute, publish, distribute,

circulate, disseminate, present, exhibit or advertise, or to offer or agree to do the same.

6. "Simulated" means the explicit depiction of any of the conduct set forth in subdivision three of this section which creates the appearance of such conduct and which exhibits any uncovered portion of the breasts, genitals or buttocks.

7. "Oral sexual conduct" and "anal sexual conduct" mean the conduct defined by subdivision two of section 130.00 of this chapter.

8. "Sado-masochistic abuse" means the conduct defined in subdivision five of section 235.20 of this chapter.

9. For purposes of sections 263.10, 263.11, 263.15 and 263.16 of this article, the terms "possession," "control" and "promotion" shall not include conduct by an attorney when the performance was provided to such attorney in relation to the representation of a person under investigation or charged under this chapter or as a respondent pursuant to the family court act, and is limited in use for the purpose of representation for the period of such representation.

§263.05 Use of a child in a sexual performance.

A person is guilty of the use of a child in a sexual performance if knowing the character and content thereof he employs, authorizes or induces a child less than seventeen years of age to engage in a sexual performance or being a parent, legal guardian or custodian of such child, he consents to the participation by such child in a sexual performance.

Use of a child in a sexual performance is a class C felony.

§263.10 Promoting an obscene sexual performance by a child.

A person is guilty of promoting an obscene sexual performance by a child when, knowing the character and content thereof, he produces, directs or promotes any obscene performance which includes sexual conduct by a child less than seventeen years of age.

Promoting an obscene sexual performance by a child is a class D felony.

§263.11 Possessing an obscene sexual performance by a child.

A person is guilty of possessing an obscene sexual performance by a child when, knowing the character and content thereof, he knowingly has in his possession or control, or knowingly accesses with intent to view, any obscene performance which includes sexual conduct by a child less than sixteen years of age.

Possessing an obscene sexual performance by a child is a class E felony.

§263.15 Promoting a sexual performance by a child.

A person is guilty of promoting a sexual performance by a child when, knowing the character and content thereof, he produces, directs or promotes any performance which includes sexual conduct by a child less than seventeen years of age.

Promoting a sexual performance by a child is a class D felony.

§263.16 Possessing a sexual performance by a child.

A person is guilty of possessing a sexual performance by a child when, knowing the character and content thereof, he knowingly has in his possession or control, or knowingly accesses with intent to view, any performance which includes sexual conduct by a child less than sixteen years of age.

Possessing a sexual performance by a child is a class E felony.

§263.20 Sexual performance by a child; affirmative defenses.

1. Under this article, it shall be an affirmative defense that the defendant in good faith reasonably believed the person appearing in the performance was, for purposes of section 263.11 or 263.16 of this article, sixteen years of age or over or, for purposes of section 263.05, 263.10 or 263.15 of this article, seventeen years of age or over.

2. In any prosecution for any offense pursuant to this article, it is an affirmative defense that the person so charged was a librarian engaged in the normal course of his employment, a motion picture projectionist, stage employee or spotlight operator, cashier, doorman, usher, candy stand attendant, porter or in any other non-managerial or non-supervisory capacity in a motion picture theatre; provided he has no financial interest, other than his employment, which employment does not encompass compensation based upon any proportion of the gross receipts, in the promotion of a sexual performance for sale, rental or exhibition or in the promotion, presentation or direction of any sexual performance, or is in any way responsible for acquiring such material for sale, rental or exhibition.

§263.25 Proof of age of child.

Whenever it becomes necessary for the purposes of this article to determine whether a child who participated in a sexual performance was under an age specified in this article, the court or jury may make such determination by any of the following: personal inspection of the child; inspection of a photograph or motion picture which constituted the sexual performance; oral testimony by a witness to the sexual performance as to the age of the child based upon the child's appearance; expert medical testimony based upon the appearance of the child in the sexual performance; and any other method authorized by any applicable provision of law or by the rules of evidence at common law.

§263.30 Facilitating a sexual performance by a child with a controlled substance or alcohol.

1. A person is guilty of facilitating a sexual performance by a child with a controlled substance or alcohol when he or she:

(a) (i) knowingly and unlawfully possesses a controlled substance as defined in section thirty-three hundred six of the public health law or any controlled substance that requires a prescription to obtain, (ii) administers that substance to a person under the age of seventeen without such person's consent, (iii) intends to commit against such person conduct constituting a felony as defined in section 263.05, 263.10, or 263.15 of this article, and (iv) does so commit or attempt to commit such conduct against such person; or

(b) (i) administers alcohol to a person under the age of seventeen without such person's consent, (ii) intends to commit against such person conduct constituting a felony defined in section 263.05, 263.10, or 263.15 of this article, and (iii) does so commit or attempt to commit such conduct against such person.

2. For the purposes of this section, "controlled substance" means any substance or preparation, compound, mixture, salt, or isomer of any substance defined in section thirty-three hundred six of the public health law.

Facilitating a sexual performance by a child with a controlled substance or alcohol is a class B felony.

TITLE P - OFFENSES AGAINST PUBLIC SAFETY
ARTICLE 265 - FIREARMS AND OTHER DANGEROUS WEAPONS

Section
265.00   Definitions.
265.01   Criminal possession of a weapon in the fourth degree.
265.01-a   Criminal possession of a weapon on school grounds.
265.01-b   Criminal possession of a firearm.
265.01-c   Criminal possession of a rapid-fire modification device.
265.02   Criminal possession of a weapon in the third degree.
265.03   Criminal possession of a weapon in the second degree.
265.04   Criminal possession of a weapon in the first degree.
265.05   Unlawful possession of weapons by persons under sixteen.
265.06   Unlawful possession of a weapon upon school grounds.
265.07   Registration and serialization of firearms, rifles, shotguns, finished frames or receivers, and unfinished frames or receivers.
265.08   Criminal use of a firearm in the second degree.
265.09   Criminal use of a firearm in the first degree.
265.10   Manufacture, transport, disposition and defacement of weapons and dangerous instruments and appliances.
265.11   Criminal sale of a firearm in the third degree.
265.12   Criminal sale of a firearm in the second degree.
265.13   Criminal sale of a firearm in the first degree.
265.14   Criminal sale of a firearm with the aid of a minor.
265.15   Presumptions of possession, unlawful intent and defacement.
265.16   Criminal sale of a firearm to a minor.
265.17   Criminal purchase or disposal of a weapon.
265.19   Aggravated criminal possession of a weapon.
265.20   Exemptions.
265.25   Certain wounds to be reported.
265.26   Burn injury and wounds to be reported.
265.30   Certain convictions to be reported.
265.35   Prohibited use of weapons.
265.36   Unlawful possession of a large capacity ammunition feeding device.
265.37   Unlawful possession of certain ammunition feeding devices.
265.40   Purchase of rifles and/or shotguns in contiguous states.
265.45   Failure to safely store rifles, shotguns, and firearms in the first degree.
265.50   Criminal manufacture, sale, or transport of an undetectable firearm, rifle or shotgun.
265.50   Failure to safely store rifles, shotguns, and firearms in the second degree.
265.55   Criminal possession of an undetectable firearm, rifle or shotgun.
265.60   Criminal sale of a ghost gun in the second degree.
265.61   Criminal sale of a ghost gun in the first degree.
265.63   Criminal sale of an unfinished frame or receiver in the second degree.
265.64   Criminal sale of an unfinished frame or receiver in the first degree.

§265.00 Definitions.

As used in this article and in article four hundred, the following terms shall mean and include:

1. "Machine-gun" means a weapon of any description, irrespective of size, by whatever name known, loaded or unloaded, from which a number of shots or bullets may be rapidly or automatically discharged from a magazine with one continuous pull of the trigger and includes a sub-machine gun.

2. "Firearm silencer" means any instrument, attachment, weapon or appliance for causing the firing of any gun, revolver, pistol or other firearms to be silent, or intended to lessen or muffle the noise of the firing of any gun, revolver, pistol or other firearms.

3. "Firearm" means (a) any pistol or revolver; or (b) a shotgun having one or more barrels less than eighteen inches in length; or (c) a rifle having one or more barrels less than sixteen inches in length; or (d) any weapon made from a shotgun or rifle whether by alteration, modification, or otherwise if such weapon as altered, modified, or otherwise has an overall length of less than twenty-six inches; or (e) an assault weapon. For the purpose of this subdivision the length of the barrel on a shotgun or rifle shall be determined by measuring the distance between the muzzle and the face of the bolt, breech, or breechlock when closed and when the shotgun or rifle is cocked; the overall length of a weapon made from a shotgun or rifle is the distance between the extreme ends of the weapon measured along a line parallel to the center line of the bore. Firearm does not include an antique firearm.

3-a. "Major component of a firearm, rifle or shotgun" means the barrel, the slide or cylinder, the frame, or receiver of the firearm, rifle, or shotgun.

4. "Switchblade knife" means any knife which has a blade which opens automatically by hand pressure applied to a button, spring or other device in the handle of the knife.

5. "Gravity knife" means any knife which has a blade which is released from the handle or sheath thereof by the force of gravity or the application of centrifugal force which, when released, is locked in place by means of a button, spring, lever or other device.

5-a. "Pilum ballistic knife" means any knife which has a blade which can be projected from the handle by hand pressure applied to a button, lever, spring or other device in the handle of the knife.

5-b. "Metal knuckle knife" means a weapon that, when closed, cannot function as a set of plastic knuckles or metal knuckles, nor as a knife and when open, can function as both a set of plastic knuckles or metal knuckles as well as a knife.

5-c. "Automatic knife" includes a stiletto, a switchblade knife, a cane sword, a pilum ballistic knife, and a metal knuckle knife.

5-d. "Undetectable knife" means any knife or other instrument, which does not utilize materials that are detectable by a metal detector or magnetometer when set at a standard calibration, that is capable of ready use as a stabbing or cutting weapon and was commercially manufactured to be used as a weapon.

6. "Dispose of" means to dispose of, give, give away, lease, loan, keep for sale, offer, offer for sale, sell, transfer and otherwise dispose of.

7. "Deface" means to remove, deface, cover, alter or destroy the manufacturer's serial number or any other distinguishing number or identification mark.

8. "Gunsmith" means any person, firm, partnership, corporation or company who engages in the business of repairing, altering, assembling, manufacturing, cleaning, polishing, engraving or trueing, or who performs any mechanical operation on, any firearm, large capacity ammunition feeding device or machine-gun.

8-a. "Serialized" means bearing a visible identification number and/or symbol in accordance with the requirements imposed on licensed importers and licensed manufacturers pursuant to subsection (i) of Section 923 of Title 18 of the United States Code and regulations issued pursuant thereto in effect at the time of assembly, except for antique firearms as defined in subdivision fourteen of this section, as added by chapter nine hundred eighty-six of the laws of nineteen hundred seventy-four, or any firearm, rifle or shotgun manufactured prior to nineteen hundred sixty-eight. *(Eff.4/26/22,Ch.520,L.2021)*

9. "Dealer in firearms" means any person, firm, partnership, corporation or company who engages in the business of purchasing, selling, keeping for sale, loaning, leasing, or in any manner disposing of, any assault weapon, large capacity ammunition feeding device, pistol or revolver.

10. "Licensing officer" means in the city of New York the police commissioner of that city; in the county of Nassau the commissioner of police of that county; in the county of Suffolk the sheriff of that county except in the towns of Babylon, Brookhaven, Huntington, Islip and Smithtown, the commissioner of police of that county; for the purposes of section 400.01 of this chapter the superintendent of state police; and elsewhere in the state a judge or justice of a court of record having his office in the county of issuance.

11. "Rifle" means a weapon designed or redesigned, made or remade, and intended to be fired from the shoulder and designed or redesigned and made or remade to use the energy of the explosive in a fixed metallic cartridge to fire only a single projectile through a rifled bore for each single pull of the trigger.

12. "Shotgun" means a weapon designed or redesigned, made or remade, and intended to be fired from the shoulder and designed or redesigned and made or remade to use the energy of the explosive in a fixed shotgun shell to fire through a smooth bore either a number of ball shot or a single projectile for each single pull of the trigger.

13. "Cane Sword" means a cane or swagger stick having concealed within it a blade that may be used as a sword or stilletto.*

(So in original should read "stileto".)

*14. "Antique firearm" means:
Any unloaded muzzle loading pistol or revolver with a matchlock, flintlock, percussion cap, or similar type of ignition system, or a pistol or revolver which uses fixed cartridges which are no longer available in the ordinary channels of commercial trade. *(There are 2 sb 14's)*

*14. "Chuka stick" means any device designed primarily as a weapon, consisting of two or more lengths of a rigid material joined together by a thong, rope or chain in such a manner as to allow free movement of a portion of the device while held in the hand and capable of being rotated in such a manner as to inflict serious injury upon a person by striking or choking. These devices are also known as nunchakus and centrifugal force sticks. *(There are 2 sb 14's)*

15. "Loaded firearm" means any firearm loaded with ammunition or any firearm which is possessed by one who, at the same time, possesses a quantity of ammunition which may be used to discharge such firearm.

15-a. "Electronic dart gun" means any device designed primarily as a weapon, the purpose of which is to momentarily stun, knock out or paralyze a person by passing an electrical shock to such person by means of a dart or projectile.

15-b. "Kung Fu star" means a disc-like object with sharpened points on the circumference thereof and is designed for use primarily as a weapon to be thrown.

15-c. "Electronic stun gun" means any device designed primarily as a weapon, the purpose of which is to stun, cause mental disorientation, knock out or paralyze a person by passing a high voltage electrical shock to such person.

16. "Certified not suitable to possess a self-defense spray device, a rifle or shotgun" means that the director or physician in charge of any hospital or institution for mental illness, public or private, has certified to the superintendent of state police or to any organized police department of a county, city, town or village of this state, that a person who has been judicially adjudicated incompetent, or who has been confined to such institution for mental illness pursuant to judicial authority, is not suitable to possess a self-defense spray device, as defined in section 265.20 of this article, or a rifle or shotgun.

17. "Serious offense" means (a) any of the following offenses defined in the current penal law and any offense in any jurisdiction or the former penal law that includes all of the essential elements of any of the following offenses: illegally using, carrying or possessing a pistol or other dangerous weapon; possession of burglar's tools; criminal possession of stolen property in the third degree; escape in the third degree; jostling; fraudulent accosting; endangering the welfare of a child; obscenity in the third degree; issuing abortional articles; permitting prostitution; promoting prostitution in the third degree; stalking in the fourth degree; stalking in the third degree; sexual misconduct; forcible touching; sexual abuse in the third degree; sexual abuse in the second degree; criminal possession of a controlled substance in the seventh degree; criminally possessing a hypodermic instrument; criminally using drug paraphernalia in the second degree; criminal possession of methamphetamine manufacturing material in the second degree; and a hate crime defined in article four hundred eighty-five of this chapter.

(b) any of the following offenses defined in the current penal law and any offense in any jurisdiction or in the former penal law that includes all of the essential elements of any of the following offenses, where the defendant and the person against whom the offense was committed were members of the same family or household as defined in subdivision one of section 530.11 of the criminal procedure law and as established pursuant to section 370.15 of the criminal procedure law: assault in the third degree; menacing in the third degree; menacing in the second degree; criminal obstruction of breathing or blood circulation; unlawful imprisonment in the second degree; coercion in the third degree; criminal tampering in the third degree; criminal contempt in the second degree; harassment in the first degree; aggravated harassment in the second degree; criminal trespass in the third degree; criminal trespass in the second degree; arson in the fifth degree; or attempt to commit any of the above-listed offenses.

(c) any misdemeanor offense in any jurisdiction or in the former penal law that includes all of the essential elements of a felony offense as defined in the current penal law.

18. "Armor piercing ammunition" means any ammunition capable of being used in pistols or revolvers containing a projectile or projectile core, or a projectile or projectile core for use in such ammunition, that is constructed entirely (excluding the presence of traces of other substances) from one or a combination of any of the following: tungsten alloys, steel, iron, brass, bronze, beryllium copper, or uranium.

19. "Duly authorized instructor" means (a) a duly commissioned officer of the United States army, navy, marine corps or coast guard, or of the national guard of the state of New York; or (b) a duly qualified adult citizen of the United States who has been granted a certificate as an instructor in small arms practice issued by the United States army, navy or marine corps, or by the adjutant general of this state, or by the national rifle association of America, a not-for-profit corporation duly organized under the laws of this state; (c) by a person duly qualified and designated by the department of environmental conservation under paragraph c of subdivision three of section 11-0713 of the environmental conservation law as its agent in the giving of instruction and the making of certifications of qualification in responsible hunting practices; or (d) a New York state 4-H certified shooting sports instructor.

20. "Disguised gun" means any weapon or device capable of being concealed on the person from which a shot can be discharged through the energy of an explosive and is designed and intended to appear to be either; (a) something other than a gun; or (b) a toy gun that shall include, but not be limited to, any rifle, pistol, shotgun or machine-gun displaying a color finish other than the original manufacture color, a decorative pattern or plastic like surface; provided, however, that any rifle or shotgun displaying a camouflage color finish or pattern that is intended for hunting, as defined by article eleven of the environmental conservation law, shall not be considered a "disguised gun" for purposes of this section. *(Eff.11/1/21,Ch.518,L.2021)*

21. "Semiautomatic" means any repeating rifle, shotgun or pistol, regardless of barrel or overall length, which utilizes a portion of the energy of a firing cartridge or shell to extract the fired cartridge case or spent shell and chamber the next round, and which requires a separate pull of the trigger to fire each cartridge or shell.

22. "Assault weapon" means

(a) a semiautomatic rifle that has an ability to accept a detachable magazine and has at least one of the following characteristics:

(i) a folding or telescoping stock;

(ii) a pistol grip that protrudes conspicuously beneath the action of the weapon;

(iii) a thumbhole stock;

(iv) a second handgrip or a protruding grip that can be held by the non-trigger hand;

(v) a bayonet mount;

(vi) a flash suppressor, muzzle break, muzzle compensator, or threaded barrel designed to accommodate a flash suppressor, muzzle break, or muzzle compensator;

(vii) a grenade launcher; or

(b) a semiautomatic shotgun that has at least one of the following characteristics:

(i) a folding or telescoping stock;

(ii) a thumbhole stock;

(iii) a second handgrip or a protruding grip that can be held by the non-trigger hand;

(iv) a fixed magazine capacity in excess of seven rounds;

(v) an ability to accept a detachable magazine; or

(c) a semiautomatic pistol that has an ability to accept a detachable magazine and has at least one of the following characteristics:

(i) a folding or telescoping stock;

(ii) a thumbhole stock;

(iii) a second handgrip or a protruding grip that can be held by the non-trigger hand;

(iv) capacity to accept an ammunition magazine that attaches to the pistol outside of the pistol grip;

(v) a threaded barrel capable of accepting a barrel extender, flash suppressor, forward handgrip, or silencer;

(vi) a shroud that is attached to, or partially or completely encircles, the barrel and that permits the shooter to hold the firearm with the non-trigger hand without being burned;

(vii) a manufactured weight of fifty ounces or more when the pistol is unloaded; or

(viii) a semiautomatic version of an automatic rifle, shotgun or firearm;

(d) a revolving cylinder shotgun;

(e) a semiautomatic rifle, a semiautomatic shotgun or a semiautomatic pistol or weapon defined in subparagraph (v) of paragraph (e) of subdivision twenty-two of section 265.00 of this chapter as added by chapter one hundred eighty-nine of the laws of two thousand and otherwise lawfully possessed pursuant to such chapter of the laws of two thousand prior to September fourteenth, nineteen hundred ninety-four;

(f) a semiautomatic rifle, a semiautomatic shotgun or a semiautomatic pistol or weapon defined in paragraph (a), (b) or (c) of this subdivision, possessed prior to the date of enactment of the chapter of the laws of two thousand thirteen which added this paragraph;

(g) provided, however, that such term does not include:

(i) any rifle, shotgun or pistol that (A) is manually operated by bolt, pump, lever or slide action; (B) has been rendered permanently inoperable; or (C) is an antique firearm as defined in 18 U.S.C. 921(a)(16);

(ii) a semiautomatic rifle that cannot accept a detachable magazine that holds more than five rounds of ammunition;

(iii) a semiautomatic shotgun that cannot hold more than five rounds of ammunition in a fixed or detachable magazine; or

(iv) a rifle, shotgun or pistol, or a replica or a duplicate thereof, specified in Appendix A to 18 U.S.C. 922 as such weapon was manufactured on October first, nineteen hundred ninety-three. The mere fact that a weapon is not listed in Appendix A shall not be construed to mean that such weapon is an assault weapon;

(v) any weapon validly registered pursuant to subdivision sixteen-a of section 400.00 of this chapter. Such weapons shall be subject to the provisions of paragraph (h) of this subdivision;

(vi) any firearm, rifle, or shotgun that was manufactured at least fifty years prior to the current date, but not including replicas thereof that is validly registered pursuant to subdivision sixteen-a of section 400.00 of this chapter;

(h) Any weapon defined in paragraph (e) or (f) of this subdivision and any large capacity ammunition feeding device that was legally possessed by an individual prior to the enactment of the chapter of the laws of two thousand thirteen which added this paragraph, may only be sold to, exchanged with or disposed of to a purchaser authorized to possess such weapons or to an individual or entity outside of the state provided that any such transfer to an individual or entity outside of the state must be reported to the entity wherein the weapon is registered within seventy-two hours of such transfer. An individual who transfers any such weapon or large capacity ammunition device to an individual inside New York state or without complying with the provisions of this paragraph shall be guilty of a class A misdemeanor unless such large capacity ammunition feeding device, the possession of which is made illegal by the chapter of the laws of two thousand thirteen which added this paragraph, is transferred within one year of the effective date of the chapter of the laws of two thousand thirteen which added this paragraph.

23. "Large capacity ammunition feeding device" means a magazine, belt, drum, feed strip, or similar device, that (a) has a capacity of, or that can be readily restored or converted to accept, more than ten rounds of ammunition, or (b)* contains more than seven rounds of ammunition, or (c)* is obtained after the effective date of the chapter of the laws of two thousand thirteen which amended this subdivision and has a capacity of, or that can be readily restored or converted to accept, more than seven rounds of ammunition provided, however, that such term does not include an attached tubular device designed to accept, and capable of operating only with, .22 caliber rimfire ammunition or a feeding device that is a curio or relic. A feeding device that is a curio or relic is defined as a device that (i) was manufactured at least fifty years prior to the current date, (ii) is only capable of being used exclusively in a firearm, rifle, or shotgun that was manufactured at least fifty years prior to the current date, but not including replicas thereof, (iii) is possessed by an individual who is not prohibited by state or federal law from possessing a firearm and (iv) is registered with the division of state police pursuant to subdivision sixteen-a of section 400.00 of this chapter, except such feeding devices transferred into the state may be registered at any time, provided they are registered within thirty days of their transfer into the state. Notwithstanding paragraph (h) of subdivision twenty-two of this

section, such feeding devices may be transferred provided that such transfer shall be subject to the provisions of section 400.03 of this chapter including the check required to be conducted pursuant to such section.

(Deemed Eff.4/15/13, paragraphs (b) and (c) subdivision 23. are suspended and NOT effective Ch. 57, L.2013)

24. "Seller of ammunition" means any person, firm, partnership, corporation or company who engages in the business of purchasing, selling or keeping ammunition.

25. "Qualified retired New York or federal law enforcement officer" means an individual who is a retired police officer as police officer is defined in subdivision thirty-four of section 1.20 of the criminal procedure law, a retired peace officer as peace officer is defined in section 2.10 of the criminal procedure law or a retired federal law enforcement officer as federal law enforcement officer is defined in section 2.15 of the criminal procedure law, who: (a) separated from service in good standing from a public agency located in New York state in which such person served as either a police officer, peace officer or federal law enforcement officer; and (b) before such separation, was authorized by law to engage in or supervise the prevention, detection, investigation, or prosecution of, or the incarceration of any person for, any violation of law, and had statutory powers of arrest, pursuant to their official duties, under the criminal procedure law; and (c) (i) before such separation, served as either a police officer, peace officer or federal law enforcement officer for five years or more and at the time of separation, is such an officer; or (ii) separated from service with such agency, after completing any applicable probationary period of such service, due to a service-connected disability, as determined by such agency at or before the time of separation; and (d)(i) has not been found by a qualified medical professional employed by such agency to be unqualified for reasons relating to mental health; or (ii) has not entered into an agreement with such agency from which the individual is separating from service in which that individual acknowledges he or she is not qualified for reasons relating to mental health; and (e) is not otherwise prohibited by New York or federal law from possessing any firearm.

26. "Rapid-fire modification device" means any bump stock, trigger crank, binary trigger system, burst trigger system, or any other device that is designed to accelerate the rate of fire of a semi-automatic firearm, rifle or shotgun.

27. "Bump stock" means any device or instrument that increases the rate of fire achievable with a semi-automatic firearm, rifle or shotgun by using energy from the recoil of the weapon to generate a reciprocating action that facilitates repeated activation of the trigger.

28. "Trigger crank" means any device or instrument that repeatedly activates the trigger of a semi-automatic firearm, rifle or shotgun through the use of a lever or other part that is turned in a circular motion and thereby accelerates the rate of fire of such firearm, rifle or shotgun, provided, however, that "trigger crank" shall not include any weapon initially designed and manufactured to fire through the use of a crank or lever.

29. "Binary trigger system" means any device that, when installed in or attached to a semi-automatic firearm rifle, or shotgun causes that weapon to fire once when the trigger is pulled and again when the trigger is released.

30. "Burst trigger system" means any device that, when installed in or attached to a semi-automatic firearm, rifle, or shot gun, allows that weapon to discharge two or more shots with a single pull or the trigger by altering the trigger reset.

31. "New York state 4-H certified shooting instructor" means a certified shooting sports instructor of the National 4-H Shooting Sports, a non-profit organization, engaged in shooting education and youth development programming that is administered by the National Institute of Food and Agriculture of the United States department of agriculture.

*32. "Unfinished frame or receiver" means any material that does not constitute the frame or receiver of a firearm, rifle or shotgun but that has been shaped or formed in any way for the purpose of becoming the frame or receiver of a firearm, rifle or shotgun, and which may readily be made into a functional frame or receiver through milling, drilling or other means. The term shall not include material that has had its size or external shape altered to facilitate transportation or storage or has had its chemical composition altered. *(Eff.2/25/22,Ch.519,L.2021)*

*32. "Ghost gun" means a firearm, rifle or shotgun that does not comply with the provisions of section 265.07 of this article and is not serialized. *(Eff.4/26/22,Ch.520,L.2021) *(There are Two 32's)*

§265.01 Criminal possession of a weapon in the fourth degree.

A person is guilty of criminal possession of a weapon in the fourth degree when:

(1) He or she possesses any firearm, electronic dart gun, electronic stun gun, switchblade knife, pilum ballistic knife, metal knuckle knife, cane sword, billy, blackjack, bludgeon, plastic knuckles, metal knuckles, chuka stick, sand bag, sandclub, wrist-brace type slingshot or slungshot, shirken, or "Kung Fu star";

(2) He or she possesses any dagger, dangerous knife, dirk, machete, razor, stiletto, imitation pistol, undetectable knife or any other dangerous or deadly instrument or weapon with intent to use the same unlawfully against another; or

*(3); or   *(So in original.)*

(4) He possesses a rifle, shotgun, antique firearm, black powder rifle, black powder shotgun, or any muzzle-loading firearm, and has been convicted of a felony or serious offense; or

(5) He possesses any dangerous or deadly weapon and is not a citizen of the United States; or

(6) He is a person who has been certified not suitable to possess a rifle or shotgun, as defined in subdivision sixteen of section 265.00, and refuses to yield possession of such rifle or shotgun upon the demand of a police officer. Whenever a person is certified not suitable to possess a rifle or shotgun, a member of the police department to which such certification is made, or of the state police, shall forthwith seize any rifle or shotgun possessed by such person. A rifle or shotgun seized as herein

provided shall not be destroyed, but shall be delivered to the headquarters of such police department, or state police, and there retained until the aforesaid certificate has been rescinded by the director or physician in charge, or other disposition of such rifle or shotgun has been ordered or authorized by a court of competent jurisdiction.

(7) He knowingly possesses a bullet containing an explosive substance designed to detonate upon impact.

(8) Such person possesses any armor piercing ammunition with intent to use the same unlawfully against another. *(Eff.4/26/22,Ch.520,L.2021)*

*(9) Such person possesses a major component of a firearm, rifle, or shotgun and such person is prohibited from possessing a shotgun or rifle pursuant to:

(i) this article;

(ii) subsection (g) of section 922 of title 18 of the United States Code; or

(iii) a temporary or final extreme risk protection order issued under article sixty-three-A of the civil practice law and rules; or

(Eff.2/25/22,Ch.519,L.2021)

*(9) Such person is not required to be a gunsmith licensed pursuant to section 400.00 of this chapter and, knowing it is a ghost gun, such person possesses a ghost gun, provided that a person shall not be guilty under this subdivision when he or she (a) voluntarily surrenders such ghost gun to any law enforcement official designated pursuant to subparagraph (f) of paragraph one of subdivision (a) of section 265.20 of this article; or (b) for a period of six months after the effective date of this section possesses a ghost gun prior to serialization and registration of such ghost gun pursuant to section 265.07 of this article.

(Eff.4/26/22,Ch.520,L.2021)

(10) Such person is not required to be a gunsmith licensed pursuant to section 400.00 of this chapter and, knowing it is an unfinished frame or receiver, such person possesses an unfinished frame or receiver, provided that for a period of six months after the effective date of this subdivision, a person shall not be guilty under this subdivision when such person: (a) voluntarily surrenders such unfinished frame or receiver to any law enforcement official designated pursuant to subparagraph (f) of paragraph one of subdivision (a) of section 265.20 of this article; or (b) possesses such unfinished frame or receiver prior to serialization of such unfinished frame or receiver in accordance with the requirements imposed on licensed importers and licensed manufacturers pursuant to subsection (i) of Section 923 of Title 18 of the United States Code and regulations issued pursuant thereto, except for antique firearms as defined in subdivision fourteen of section 265.00 of this article, as added by chapter nine hundred eighty-six of the laws of nineteen hundred seventy-four, or any firearm, rifle or shotgun manufactured prior to nineteen hundred sixty-eight. *(Eff.2/25/22,Ch.519,L.2021)*

Criminal possession of a weapon in the fourth degree is a class A misdemeanor.

* (There are two (9)'s)

§265.01-a Criminal possession of a weapon on school grounds.

A person is guilty of criminal possession of a weapon on school grounds when he or she knowingly has in his or her possession a rifle, shotgun, or firearm in or upon a building or grounds, used for educational purposes, of any school, college, or university, except the forestry lands, wherever located, owned, maintained or held in trust for the benefit of the New York State College of Forestry at Syracuse University, now known as the State University of New York college of environmental science and forestry, or upon a school bus as defined in section one hundred forty-two of the vehicle and traffic law, without the written authorization of such educational institution; provided, however no school, as defined in subdivision ten of section eleven hundred twenty-five of the education law, shall issue such written authorization to any teacher, school administrator, or other person employed at the school who is not primarily employed as a school resource officer, police officer, peace officer, or security guard who has been issued a special armed guard registration card as defined in section eighty-nine-f of the general business law, regardless of whether the person is employed directly by such school or by a third party.

Criminal possession of a weapon on school grounds is a class E felony.

§265.01-b Criminal possession of a firearm.

A person is guilty of criminal possession of a firearm when he or she: (1) possesses any firearm or; (2) lawfully possesses a firearm prior to the effective date of the chapter of the laws of two thousand thirteen which added this section subject to the registration requirements of subdivision sixteen-a of section 400.00 of this chapter and knowingly fails to register such firearm pursuant to such subdivision.

Criminal possession of a firearm is a class E felony.

§265.01-c Criminal possession of a rapid-fire modification device.

A person is guilty of criminal possession of a rapid-fire modification device when he or she knowingly possesses any rapid-fire modification device.

Criminal possession of a rapid-fire modification device is a class A misdemeanor.

§265.02 Criminal possession of a weapon in the third degree.

A person is guilty of criminal possession of a weapon in the third degree when:

(1) Such person commits the crime of criminal possession of a weapon in the fourth degree as defined in subdivision one, two, three or five of section 265.01, and has been previously convicted of any crime; or

(2) Such person possesses any explosive or incendiary bomb, bombshell, firearm silencer, machine-gun or any other firearm or weapon simulating a machine-gun and which is adaptable for such use; or

(3) Such person knowingly possesses a machine-gun, firearm, rifle or shotgun which has been defaced for the purpose of concealment or

prevention of the detection of a crime or misrepresenting the identity of such machine-gun, firearm, rifle or shotgun; or

(4) *(Repealed)*

(5) (i) Such person possesses three or more firearms; or (ii) such person possesses a firearm and has been previously convicted of a felony or a class A misdemeanor defined in this chapter within the five years immediately preceding the commission of the offense and such possession did not take place in the person's home or place of business; or

(6) Such person knowingly possesses any disguised gun; or

(7) Such person possesses an assault weapon; or

(8) Such person possesses a large capacity ammunition feeding device. For purposes of this subdivision, a large capacity ammunition feeding device shall not include an ammunition feeding device lawfully possessed by such person before the effective date of the chapter of the laws of two thousand thirteen which amended this subdivision, that has a capacity of, or that can be readily restored or converted to accept more than seven but less than eleven rounds of ammunition, or that was manufactured before September thirteenth, nineteen hundred ninety-four, that has a capacity of, or that can be readily restored or converted to accept, more than ten rounds of ammunition; or

(9) Such person possesses an unloaded firearm and also commits a drug trafficking felony as defined in subdivision twenty-one of section 10.00 of this chapter as part of the same criminal transaction; or

(10) Such person possesses an unloaded firearm and also commits any violent felony offense as defined in subdivision one of section 70.02 of this chapter as part of the same criminal transaction.

Criminal possession of a weapon in the third degree is a class D felony.

§265.03 Criminal possession of a weapon in the second degree.

A person is guilty of criminal possession of a weapon in the second degree when:

(1) with intent to use the same unlawfully against another, such person:

(a) possesses a machine-gun; or

(b) possesses a loaded firearm; or

(c) possesses a disguised gun; or

(2) such person possesses five or more firearms; or

(3) such person possesses any loaded firearm. Such possession shall not, except as provided in subdivision one or seven of section 265.02 of this article, constitute a violation of this subdivision if such possession takes place in such person's home or place of business.

Criminal possession of a weapon in the second degree is a class C felony.

§265.04 Criminal possession of a weapon in the first degree.

A person is guilty of criminal possession of a weapon in the first degree when such person:

(1) possesses any explosive substance with intent to use the same unlawfully against the person or property of another; or

(2) possesses ten or more firearms.

Criminal possession of a weapon in the first degree is a class B felony.

§265.05 Unlawful possession of weapons by persons under sixteen.

It shall be unlawful for any person under the age of sixteen to possess any air-gun, spring-gun or other instrument or weapon in which the propelling force is a spring or air, or any gun or any instrument or weapon in or upon which any loaded or blank cartridges may be used, or any loaded or blank cartridges or ammunition therefor, or any dangerous knife; provided that the possession of rifle or shotgun or ammunition therefor by the holder of a hunting license or permit issued pursuant to article eleven of the environmental conservation law and used in accordance with said law shall not be governed by this section.

A person who violates the provisions of this section shall be adjudged a juvenile delinquent.

§265.06 Unlawful possession of a weapon upon school grounds.

It shall be unlawful for any person age sixteen or older to knowingly possess any air-gun, spring-gun or other instrument or weapon in which the propelling force is a spring, air, piston or co2 cartridge in or upon a building or grounds, used for educational purposes, of any school, college or university, without the written authorization of such educational institution.

Unlawful possession of a weapon upon school grounds is a violation.

§265.07 Registration and serialization of firearms, rifles, shotguns, finished frames or receivers, and unfinished frames or receivers.

(1) For the purposes of this section, "unfinished frame or receiver" means any material that does not constitute the frame or receiver of a firearm, rifle or shotgun but that has been shaped or formed in any way for the purpose of becoming the frame or receiver of a firearm, rifle or shotgun, and which may readily be made into a functional frame or receiver through milling, drilling or other means. The term shall not include material that has had its size or external shape altered to facilitate transportation or storage or has had its chemical composition altered.

(2) On or before the effective date of this section, and promptly upon taking possession thereof at any time thereafter, any person required to be a gunsmith licensed pursuant to section 400.00 of this chapter, who is in possession of an unserialized firearm, rifle, shotgun, finished frame or receiver, or unfinished frame or receiver shall:

(a) engrave, cast, stamp or otherwise conspicuously place both a unique serial number and his or her name (or recognized abbreviation) on such firearm, rifle, shotgun, finished frame or receiver, or unfinished frame or receiver, in a manner that satisfies or exceeds the requirements imposed on licensed importers and manufacturers pursuant to section (i) of Section 923 of Title 18 of the United States Code and regulations issued pursuant thereto at the time of such assembly; and

(b) register with the division of state police any such firearm, rifle or shotgun, finished frame or receiver, or unfinished frame or receiver.

Any person required to be a gunsmith licensed pursuant to section 400.00 of this chapter who fails to comply with the provisions of this section shall be guilty of a class E felony.   *(Eff.4/26/22,Ch.520,L.2021)*

§265.08　Criminal use of a firearm in the second degree.

A person is guilty of criminal use of a firearm in the second degree when he commits any class C violent felony offense as defined in paragraph (b) of subdivision one of section 70.02 and he either:

(1) possesses a deadly weapon, if the weapon is a loaded weapon from which a shot, readily capable of producing death or other serious injury may be discharged; or

(2) displays what appears to be a pistol, revolver, rifle, shotgun, machine gun or other firearm.

Criminal use of a firearm in the second degree is a class C felony.

§265.09　Criminal use of a firearm in the first degree.

(1) A person is guilty of criminal use of a firearm in the first degree when he commits any class B violent felony offense as defined in paragraph (a) of subdivision one of section 70.02 and he either:

(a) possesses a deadly weapon, if the weapon is a loaded weapon from which a shot, readily capable of producing death or other serious injury may be discharged; or

(b) displays what appears to be a pistol, revolver, rifle, shotgun, machine gun or other firearm.

Criminal use of a firearm in the first degree is a class B felony.

(2) Sentencing. Notwithstanding any other provision of law to the contrary, when a person is convicted of criminal use of a firearm in the first degree as defined in subdivision one of this section, the court shall impose an additional consecutive sentence of five years to the sentence imposed on the underlying class B violent felony offense where the person convicted of such crime displays a loaded weapon from which a shot, readily capable of producing death or other serious injury may be discharged, in furtherance of the commission of such crime, provided, however, that such additional sentence shall not be imposed if the court, having regard to the nature and circumstances of the crime and to the history and character of the defendant, finds on the record that such additional consecutive sentence would be unduly harsh and that not imposing such sentence would be consistent with the public safety and would not deprecate the seriousness of the crime. Notwithstanding any other provision of law to the contrary, the aggregate of the five year consecutive term imposed pursuant to this subdivision and the minimum term of the indeterminate sentence imposed on the underlying class B violent felony shall constitute the new aggregate minimum term of imprisonment, and a person subject to such term shall be required to serve the entire aggregate minimum term and shall not be eligible for release on parole or conditional release during such term. This subdivision shall not apply where the defendant's criminal liability for displaying a loaded weapon from which a shot, readily capable of producing death or other serious injury may be discharged, in furtherance of the commission of crime is based on the conduct of another pursuant to section 20.00 of this chapter.

§265.10 Manufacture, transport, disposition and defacement of weapons and dangerous instruments and appliances.

1. Any person who manufactures or causes to be manufactured any machine-gun, assault weapon, large capacity ammunition feeding device or disguised gun is guilty of a class D felony. Any person who manufactures or causes to be manufactured any rapid-fire modification device is guilty of a class E felony. Any person who manufactures or causes to be manufactured any switchblade knife, pilum ballistic knife, metal knuckle knife, undetectable knife, billy, blackjack, bludgeon, plastic knuckles, metal knuckles, Kung Fu star, chuka stick, sandbag, sandclub or slungshot is guilty of a class A misdemeanor.

2. Any person who transports or ships any machine-gun, firearm silencer, assault weapon or large capacity ammunition feeding device or disguised gun, or who transports or ships as merchandise five or more firearms, is guilty of a class D felony. Any person who transports or ships any rapid-fire modification device is guilty of a class E felony. Any person who transports or ships as merchandise any firearm, other than an assault weapon, switchblade knife, pilum ballistic knife, undetectable knife, billy, blackjack, bludgeon, plastic knuckles, metal knuckles, Kung Fu star, chuka stick, sandbag or slungshot is guilty of a class A misdemeanor.

3. Any person who disposes of any machine-gun, assault weapon, large capacity ammunition feeding device or firearm silencer is guilty of a class D felony. Any person who disposes of any rapid-fire modification device is guilty of a class E felony. Any person who knowingly buys, receives, disposes of, or conceals a machine-gun, firearm, large capacity ammunition feeding device, rifle or shotgun which has been defaced for the purpose of concealment or prevention of the detection of a crime or misrepresenting the identity of such machine-gun, firearm, large capacity ammunition feeding device, rifle or shotgun is guilty of a class D felony.

4. Any person who disposes of any of the weapons, instruments or appliances specified in subdivision one of section 265.01, except a firearm, is guilty of a class A misdemeanor, and he is guilty of a class D felony if he has previously been convicted of any crime.

5. Any person who disposes of any of the weapons, instruments, appliances or substances specified in section 265.05 to any other person under the age of sixteen years is guilty of a class A misdemeanor.

6. Any person who wilfully defaces any machine-gun, large capacity ammunition feeding device or firearm is guilty of a class D felony.

7. Any person, other than a wholesale dealer, or gunsmith or dealer in firearms duly licensed pursuant to section 400.00, lawfully in possession of a firearm, who disposes of the same without first notifying in writing the licensing officer in the city of New York and counties of Nassau and Suffolk and elsewhere in the state the executive department, division of state police, Albany, is guilty of a class A misdemeanor.

8. Any person, dealer, firm, partnership or corporation who intentionally designs or transforms a rifle, pistol, shotgun or machine-gun to resemble a toy gun by either altering or concealing the

original color or surface of the gun with the purpose of selling such weapon is guilty of a class D felony. *(Eff.11/1/21,Ch.518,L.2021)*

§265.11 Criminal Sale of a firearm in the third degree.

A person is guilty of criminal sale of a firearm in the third degree when such person is not authorized pursuant to law to possess a firearm and such person unlawfully either:

(1) sells, exchanges, gives or disposes of a firearm or large capacity ammunition feeding device to another person; or

(2) possesses a firearm with the intent to sell it.

Criminal sale of a firearm in the third degree is a class D felony.

§265.12 Criminal sale of a firearm in the second degree.

A person is guilty of criminal sale of a firearm in the second degree when such person:

(1) unlawfully sells, exchanges, gives or disposes of to another five or more firearms; or

(2) unlawfully sells, exchanges, gives or disposes of to another person or persons a total of five or more firearms in a period of not more than one year.

Criminal sale of a firearm in the second degree is a class C felony.

§265.13 Criminal sale of a firearm in the first degree.

A person is guilty of criminal sale of a firearm in the first degree when such person:

(1) unlawfully sells, exchanges, gives or disposes of to another ten or more firearms; or

(2) unlawfully sells, exchanges, gives or disposes of to another person or persons a total of ten or more firearms in a period of not more than one year.

Criminal sale of a firearm in the first degree is a class B felony.

§265.14 Criminal sale of a firearm with the aid of a minor.

A person over the age of eighteen years of age is guilty of criminal sale of a weapon with the aid of a minor when a person under sixteen years of age knowingly and unlawfully sells, exchanges, gives or disposes of a firearm in violation of this article, and such person over the age of eighteen years of age, acting with the mental culpability required for the commission thereof, solicits, requests, commands, importunes or intentionally aids such person under sixteen years of age to engage in such conduct.

Criminal sale of a firearm with the aid of a minor is a class C felony.

§265.15 Presumptions of possession, unlawful intent and defacement.

1. The presence in any room, dwelling, structure or vehicle of any machine-gun is presumptive evidence of its unlawful possession by all persons occupying the place where such machine-gun is found.

2. The presence in any stolen vehicle of any weapon, instrument, appliance or substance specified in sections 265.01, 265.02, 265.03,

265.04 and 265.05 is presumptive evidence of its possession by all persons occupying such vehicle at the time such weapon, instrument, appliance or substance is found.

3. The presence in an automobile, other than a stolen one or a public omnibus, of any firearm, large capacity ammunition feeding device, defaced firearm, defaced rifle or shotgun, defaced large capacity ammunition feeding device, firearm silencer, explosive or incendiary bomb, bombshell, switchblade knife, pilum ballistic knife, metal knuckle knife, dagger, dirk, stiletto, billy, blackjack, plastic knuckles, metal knuckles, chuka stick, sandbag, sandclub or slungshot is presumptive evidence of its possession by all persons occupying such automobile at the time such weapon, instrument or appliance is found, except under the following circumstances: (a) if such weapon, instrument or appliance is found upon the person of one of the occupants therein; (b) if such weapon, instrument or appliance is found in an automobile which is being operated for hire by a duly licensed driver in the due, lawful and proper pursuit of his or her trade, then such presumption shall not apply to the driver; or (c) if the weapon so found is a pistol or revolver and one of the occupants, not present under duress, has in his or her possession a valid license to have and carry concealed the same.   *(Eff.5/30/19,Ch.34,L.2019)*

4. The possession by any person of the substance as specified in section 265.04 is presumptive evidence of possessing such substance with intent to use the same unlawfully against the person or property of another if such person is not licensed or otherwise authorized to possess such substance. The possession by any person of any dagger, dirk, stiletto, dangerous knife or any other weapon, instrument, appliance or substance designed, made or adapted for use primarily as a weapon, is presumptive evidence of intent to use the same unlawfully against another.

5. The possession by any person of a defaced machine-gun, firearm, rifle or shotgun is presumptive evidence that such person defaced the same.

6. The possession of five or more firearms by any person is presumptive evidence that such person possessed the firearms with the intent to sell same.

§265.16 Criminal sale of a firearm to a minor.

A person is guilty of criminal sale of a firearm to a minor when he is not authorized pursuant to law to possess a firearm and he unlawfully sells, exchanges, gives or disposes of a firearm to another person who is or reasonably appears to be less than nineteen years of age who is not licensed pursuant to law to possess a firearm.

Criminal sale of a firearm to a minor is a class C felony.

§265.17 Criminal purchase or disposal of a weapon.

A person is guilty of criminal purchase or disposal of a weapon when:

1. Knowing that he or she is prohibited by law from possessing a firearm, rifle or shotgun because of a prior conviction or because of some other disability which would render him or her ineligible to

lawfully possess a firearm, rifle or shotgun in this state, or knowing that he or she is the subject of an outstanding warrant of arrest issued upon the alleged commission of a felony or serious offense, such person purchases or otherwise acquires a firearm, rifle or shotgun from another person; or

2. Knowing that it would be unlawful for another person to possess a firearm, rifle or shotgun, or knowing that another person is the subject of an outstanding warrant of arrest issued upon the alleged commission of a felony or serious offense, he or she purchases or otherwise acquires a firearm, rifle or shotgun for, on behalf of, or for the use of such other person; or

3. Knowing that another person is prohibited by law from possessing a firearm, rifle or shotgun because of a prior conviction or because of some other disability which would render him or her ineligible to lawfully possess a firearm, rifle or shotgun in this state, or knowing that another person is the subject of an outstanding warrant of arrest issued upon the alleged commission of a felony or serious offense, a person disposes of a firearm, rifle or shotgun to such other person.

    Criminal purchase or disposal of a weapon is a class D felony.

(Eff.7/1/21,Ch.236,L.2021)

§265.19 Aggravated criminal possession of a weapon.

A person is guilty of aggravated criminal possession of a weapon when he or she commits the crime of criminal possession of a weapon in the second degree as defined in subdivision three of section 265.03 of this article and also commits any violent felony offense as defined in subdivision one of section 70.02 of this chapter or a drug trafficking felony as defined in subdivision twenty-one of section 10.00 of this chapter arising out of the same criminal transaction.

    Aggravated criminal possession of a weapon is a class C felony.

§265.20 Exemptions.

a. Paragraph (h) of subdivision twenty-two of section 265.00 and sections 265.01, 265.01-a, 265.01-b, 265.01-c, 265.02, 265.03, 265.04, 265.05, 265.10, 265.11, 265.12, 265.13, 265.15, 265.36, 265.37, 265.50, 265.55 and 270.05 shall not apply to:

1. Possession of any of the weapons, instruments, appliances or substances specified in sections 265.01, 265.01-c, 265.02, 265.03, 265.04, 265.05, 265.50, 265.55 and 270.05 by the following:

(a) Persons in the military service of the state of New York when duly authorized by regulations issued by the adjutant general to possess the same.

(b) Police officers as defined in subdivision thirty-four of section 1.20 of the criminal procedure law.

(c) Peace officers as defined by section 2.10 of the criminal procedure law.

(d) Persons in the military or other service of the United States, in pursuit of official duty or when duly authorized by federal law, regulation or order to possess the same.

(e) Persons employed in fulfilling defense contracts with the government of the United States or agencies thereof when possession of the same is necessary for manufacture, transport, installation and testing under the requirements of such contract.

(f) A person voluntarily surrendering such weapon, instrument, appliance or substance, provided that such surrender shall be made to the superintendent of the division of state police or a member thereof designated by such superintendent, or to the sheriff of the county in which such person resides, or in the county of Nassau or in the towns of Babylon, Brookhaven, Huntington, Islip and Smithtown in the county of Suffolk to the commissioner of police or a member of the police department thereof designated by such commissioner, or if such person resides in a city, town other than one named in this subparagraph, or village to the police commissioner or head of the police force or department thereof or to a member of the force or department designated by such commissioner or head; and provided, further, that the same shall be surrendered by such person in accordance with such terms and conditions as may be established by such superintendent, sheriff, police force or department. Nothing in this paragraph shall be construed as granting immunity from prosecution for any crime or offense except that of unlawful possession of such weapons, instruments, appliances or substances surrendered as herein provided. A person who possesses any such weapon, instrument, appliance or substance as an executor or administrator or any other lawful possessor of such property of a decedent may continue to possess such property for a period not over fifteen days. If such property is not lawfully disposed of within such period the possessor shall deliver it to an appropriate official described in this paragraph or such property may be delivered to the superintendent of state police. Such officer shall hold it and shall thereafter deliver it on the written request of such executor, administrator or other lawful possessor of such property to a named person, provided such named person is licensed to or is otherwise lawfully permitted to possess the same. If no request to deliver the property is received by such official within one year of the delivery of such property, such official shall dispose of it in accordance with the provisions of section 400.05 of this chapter.

2. Possession of a machine-gun, large capacity ammunition feeding device, rapid-fire modification device, firearm, switchblade knife, pilum ballistic knife, billy or blackjack by a warden, superintendent, headkeeper or deputy of a state prison, penitentiary, workhouse, county jail or other institution for the detention of persons convicted or accused of crime or detained as witnesses in criminal cases, in pursuit of official duty or when duly authorized by regulation or order to possess the same.

3. Possession of a pistol or revolver by a person to whom a license therefor has been issued as provided under section 400.00 or 400.01 of this chapter or possession of a weapon as defined in paragraph (e) or (f) of subdivision twenty-two of section 265.00 of this article which is registered pursuant to paragraph (a) of subdivision sixteen-a of section 400.00 of this chapter or is included on an amended license issued pursuant to section 400.00 of this chapter. In the event such license is revoked, other than because such licensee is no longer permitted to possess a firearm, rifle or shotgun under federal or state law, information sufficient to satisfy the requirements of subdivision sixteen-a of section 400.00 of this chapter, shall be transmitted by the licensing officer to the state police, in a form as determined by the superintendent of state police. Such transmission shall constitute a valid registration under such section. Further provided, notwithstanding any other section of this title, a failure to register such weapon by an individual who possesses such weapon before the enactment of the chapter of the laws of two thousand thirteen which amended this paragraph and may so lawfully possess it thereafter upon registration, shall only be subject to punishment pursuant to paragraph (c) of subdivision sixteen-a of section 400.00 of this chapter; provided, that such a license or registration shall not preclude a conviction for the offense defined in subdivision three of section 265.01 of this article or section 265.01-a of this article.

4. Possession of a rifle, shotgun, crossbow or longbow for use while hunting, trapping or fishing, by a person, not a citizen of the United States, carrying a valid license issued pursuant to section 11-0713 of the environmental conservation law.

5. Possession of a rifle or shotgun by a person other than a person who has been convicted of a class A-I felony or a violent felony offense, as defined in subdivision one of section 70.02 of this chapter, who has been convicted as specified in subdivision four of section 265.01 to whom a certificate of good conduct has been issued pursuant to section seven hundred three-b of the correction law.

6. Possession of a switchblade for use while hunting, trapping or fishing by a person carrying a valid license issued to him pursuant to section 11-0713 of the environmental conservation law.

7. Possession, at an indoor or outdoor shooting range for the purpose of loading and firing, of a rifle or shotgun, the propelling force of which is gunpowder by a person under sixteen years of age but not under twelve, under the immediate supervision, guidance and instruction of (a) a duly commissioned officer of the United States army, navy, air force, marine corps or coast guard, or of the national guard of the state of New York; or (b) a duly qualified adult citizen of the United States who has been granted a certificate as an instructor in small arms practice issued by the United States army, navy, air force or marine corps, or by the adjutant general of this state, by the national rifle association of America, a not-for-profit corporation duly organized under the laws of this state, or by a New York state 4-H certified shooting sports instructor; or (c) a parent, guardian, or a person over the age of eighteen designated in writing by such parent or guardian who shall have a

certificate of qualification in responsible hunting, including safety, ethics, and landowner relations-hunter relations, issued or honored by the department of environmental conservation; or (d) an agent of the department of environmental conservation appointed to conduct courses in responsible hunting practices pursuant to article eleven of the environmental conservation law. *(Eff.8/24/20,Ch.150,L.2020)*

7-a. Possession and use, at an indoor or outdoor pistol range located in or on premises owned or occupied by a duly incorporated organization organized for conservation purposes or to foster proficiency in small arms or at a target pistol shooting competition under the auspices of or approved by the national rifle association for the purpose of loading and firing the same, by a person duly licensed to possess a pistol or revolver pursuant to section 400.00 or 400.01 of this chapter of a pistol or revolver duly so licensed to another person who is present at the time.

7-b. Possession and use, at an indoor or outdoor pistol range located in or on premises owned or occupied by a duly incorporated organization organized for conservation purposes or to foster proficiency in small arms or at a target pistol shooting competition under the auspices of or approved by the national rifle association for the purpose of loading and firing the same, by a person who has applied for a license to possess a pistol or revolver and pre-license possession of same pursuant to section 400.00 or 400.01 of this chapter, who has not been previously denied a license, been previously convicted of a felony or serious offense, and who does not appear to be, or pose a threat to be, a danger to himself or to others, and who has been approved for possession and use herein in accordance with section 400.00 or 400.01 of this chapter; provided however, that such possession shall be of a pistol or revolver duly licensed to and shall be used under the supervision, guidance and instruction of, a person specified in paragraph seven of this subdivision and provided further that such possession and use be within the jurisdiction of the licensing officer with whom the person has made application therefor or within the jurisdiction of the superintendent of state police in the case of a retired sworn member of the division of state police who has opted to make an application pursuant to section 400.01 of this chapter.

7-c. Possession for the purpose of loading and firing, of a rifle, pistol or shotgun, the propelling force of which may be either air, compressed gas or springs, by a person under sixteen years of age but not under twelve, under the immediate supervision, guidance and instruction of (a) a duly commissioned officer of the United States army, navy, marine corps or coast guard, or of the national guard of the state of New York; or (b) a duly qualified adult citizen of the United States who has been granted a certificate as an instructor in small arms practice issued by the United States army, navy or marine corps, or by the adjutant general of this state, by the national rifle association of America, a not-for-profit corporation duly organized under the laws of this state, or by a New York state 4-H certified shooting sports instructor; or (c) a parent, guardian, or a person over the age of eighteen designated in writing by such parent or guardian who shall have a certificate of qualification in responsible hunting, including safety, ethics, and landowner relations-hunter relations, issued or honored by the department of environmental conservation. *(Eff.8/24/20,Ch.150,L.2020)*

7-d. Possession, at an indoor or outdoor shooting range for the purpose of loading and firing, of a rifle, pistol or shotgun, the propelling force of which may be either air, compressed gas or springs, by a person under twelve years of age, under the immediate supervision, guidance and instruction of (a) a duly commissioned officer of the United States army, navy, marine corps or coast guard, or of the national guard of the state of New York; or (b) a duly qualified adult citizen of the United States who has been granted a certificate as an instructor in small arms practice issued by the United States army, navy or marine corps, or by the adjutant general of this state, by the national rifle association of America, a not-for-profit corporation duly organized under the laws of this state, or by a New York state 4-H certified shooting sports instructor; or (c) a parent, guardian, or a person over the age of eighteen designated in writing by such parent or guardian who shall have a certificate of qualification in responsible hunting, including safety, ethics, and landowner relations-hunter relations, issued or honored by the department of environmental conservation. *(Eff.8/24/20,Ch.150,L.2020)*

7-e. Possession and use of a pistol or revolver, at an indoor or outdoor pistol range located in or on premises owned or occupied by a duly incorporated organization organized for conservation purposes or to foster proficiency in small arms or at a target pistol shooting competition under the auspices of or approved by an association or organization described in paragraph 7-a of this subdivision for the purpose of loading and firing the same by a person at least fourteen years of age but under the age of twenty-one who has not been previously convicted of a felony or serious offense, and who does not appear to be, or pose a threat to be, a danger to himself or to others; provided however, that such possession shall be of a pistol or revolver duly licensed to and shall be used under the immediate supervision, guidance and instruction of, a person specified in paragraph seven of this subdivision.

7-f. Possession and use of a magazine, belt, feed strip or similar device, that contains more than seven rounds of ammunition, but that does not have a capacity of or can readily be restored or converted to accept more than ten rounds of ammunition, at an indoor or outdoor firing range located in or on premises owned or occupied by a duly incorporated organization organized for conservation purposes or to foster proficiency in arms; at an indoor or outdoor firing range for the purpose of firing a rifle or shotgun; at a collegiate, olympic or target shooting competition under the auspices of or approved by the national rifle association; or at an organized match sanctioned by the International Handgun Metallic Silhouette Association.

8. The manufacturer of machine-guns, firearm silencers, assault weapons, large capacity ammunition feeding devices, rapid-fire modification devices, disguised guns, pilum ballistic knives, switchblade or gravity knives, billies or blackjacks as merchandise, or as a transferee recipient of the same for repair, lawful distribution or research and

development, and the disposal and shipment thereof direct to a regularly constituted or appointed state or municipal police department, sheriff, police officer or other peace officer, or to a state prison, penitentiary, workhouse, county jail or other institution for the detention of persons convicted or accused of crime or held as witnesses in criminal cases, or to the military service of this state or of the United States; or for the repair and return of the same to the lawful possessor or for research and development.

9. The regular and ordinary transport of firearms as merchandise, provided that the person transporting such firearms, where he knows or has reasonable means of ascertaining what he is transporting, notifies in writing the police commissioner, police chief or other law enforcement officer performing such functions at the place of delivery, of the name and address of the consignee and the place of delivery, and withholds delivery to the consignee for such reasonable period of time designated in writing by such police commissioner, police chief or other law enforcement officer as such official may deem necessary for investigation as to whether the consignee may lawfully receive and possess such firearms.

9-a. a. Except as provided in subdivision b hereof, the regular and ordinary transport of pistols or revolvers by a manufacturer of firearms to whom a license as a dealer in firearms has been issued pursuant to section 400.00 of this chapter, or by an agent or employee of such manufacturer of firearms who is otherwise duly licensed to carry a pistol or revolver and who is duly authorized in writing by such manufacturer of firearms to transport pistols or revolvers on the date or dates specified, directly between places where the manufacturer of firearms regularly conducts business provided such pistols or revolvers are transported unloaded, in a locked opaque container. For purposes of this subdivision, places where the manufacturer of firearms regularly conducts business includes, but is not limited to places where the manufacturer of firearms regularly or customarily conducts development or design of pistols or revolvers, or regularly or customarily conducts tests on pistols or revolvers, or regularly or customarily participates in the exposition of firearms to the public.

b. The transportation of such pistols or revolvers into, out of or within the city of New York may be done only with the consent of the police commissioner of the city of New York. To obtain such consent, the manufacturer must notify the police commissioner in writing of the name and address of the transporting manufacturer, or agent or employee of the manufacturer who is authorized in writing by such manufacturer to transport pistols or revolvers, the number, make and model number of the firearms to be transported and the place where the manufacturer regularly conducts business within the city of New York and such other information as the commissioner may deem necessary. The manufacturer must not transport such pistols and revolvers between the designated places of business for such reasonable period of time designated in writing by the police commissioner as such official may deem necessary for investigation and to give consent. The police commissioner may not unreasonably withhold his consent.

10. Engaging in the business of gunsmith or dealer in firearms by a person to whom a valid license therefor has been issued pursuant to section 400.00.

11. Possession of a firearm or large capacity ammunition feeding device by a police officer or sworn peace officer of another state while conducting official business within the state of New York.

12. Possession of a pistol or revolver by a person who is a member or coach of an accredited college or university target pistol team while transporting the pistol or revolver into or through New York state to participate in a collegiate, olympic or target pistol shooting competition under the auspices of or approved by the national rifle association, provided such pistol or revolver is unloaded and carried in a locked carrying case and the ammunition therefor is carried in a separate locked container.

12-a. Possession and use of a pistol or revolver, at an indoor or outdoor shooting range, by a registered student of a higher education institution chartered by the state of New York, who is participating in a course in gun safety and proficiency offered by such institution, under the immediate supervision, guidance, and instruction of a person specified in paragraph seven of this subdivision.

13. Possession of pistols and revolvers by a person who is a nonresident of this state while attending or traveling to or from, an organized competitive pistol match or league competition under auspices of, or approved by, the National Rifle Association and in which he is a competitor, within forty-eight hours of such event or by a person who is a non-resident of the state while attending or traveling to or from an organized match sanctioned by the International Handgun Metallic Silhouette Association and in which he is a competitor, within forty-eight hours of such event, provided that he has not been previously convicted of a felony or a crime which, if committed in New York, would constitute a felony, and further provided that the pistols or revolvers are transported unloaded in a locked opaque container together with a copy of the match program, match schedule or match registration card. Such documentation shall constitute prima facie evidence of exemption, providing that such person also has in his possession a pistol license or firearms registration card issued in accordance with the laws of his place of residence. For purposes of this subdivision, a person licensed in a jurisdiction which does not authorize such license by a person who has been previously convicted of a felony shall be presumed to have no prior conviction. The superintendent of state police shall annually review the laws of jurisdictions within the United States and Canada with respect to the applicable requirements for licensing or registration of firearms and shall publish a list of those jurisdictions which prohibit possession of a firearm by a person previously convicted of a felony or crimes which if committed in New York state would constitute a felony.

13-a. Except in cities not wholly contained within a single county of the state, possession of pistols and revolvers by a person who is a nonresident of this state while attending or traveling to or from, an organized convention or exhibition for the display of or education about firearms, which is conducted under auspices of, or approved by, the National Rifle Association and in which he is a registered participant, within forty-eight hours of such event, provided that he has not been previously convicted of a felony or a crime which, if committed in New York, would constitute a felony, and further provided that the pistols or revolvers are transported unloaded in a locked opaque container together with a copy of the convention or exhibition program, convention or exhibition schedule or convention or exhibition registration card. Such documentation shall constitute prima facie evidence of exemption, providing that such person also has in his possession a pistol license or firearms registration card issued in accordance with the laws of his place of residence. For purposes of this paragraph, a person licensed in a jurisdiction which does not authorize such license by a person who has been previously convicted of a felony shall be presumed to have no prior conviction. The superintendent of state police shall annually review the laws of jurisdictions within the United States and Canada with respect to the applicable requirements for licensing or registration of firearms and shall publish a list of those jurisdictions which prohibit possession of a firearm by a person previously convicted of a felony or crimes which if committed in New York state would constitute a felony.

14. Possession in accordance with the provisions of this paragraph of a self-defense spray device as defined herein for the protection of a person or property and use of such self-defense spray device under circumstances which would justify the use of physical force pursuant to article thirty-five of this chapter.

(a) As used in this section "self-defense spray device" shall mean a pocket sized spray device which contains and releases a chemical or organic substance which is intended to produce temporary physical discomfort or disability through being vaporized or otherwise dispensed in the air or any like device containing tear gas, pepper or similar disabling agent

(b) The exemption under this paragraph shall not apply to a person who:

(i) is less than eighteen years of age; or

(ii) has been previously convicted in this state of a felony or any assault; or

(iii) has been convicted of a crime outside the state of New York which if committed in New York would constitute a felony or any assault crime.

(c) The department of health, with the cooperation of the division of criminal justice services and the superintendent of state police, shall develop standards and promulgate regulations regarding the type of self-defense spray device which may lawfully be purchased, possessed and used pursuant to this paragraph. The regulations shall include a requirement that every self-defense spray device which may be lawfully purchased, possessed or used pursuant to this paragraph have a label which states: "WARNING: The use of this substance or device for any purpose other than self-defense is a criminal offense under the law. The contents are dangerous - use with care. This device shall not be sold by anyone other than a licensed or authorized dealer. Possession of this device by any person under the age of eighteen or by anyone who has been convicted of a felony or assault is illegal. Violators may be prosecuted under the law."

15. Possession and sale of a self-defense spray device as defined in paragraph fourteen of this subdivision by a dealer in firearms licensed pursuant to section 400.00 of this chapter, a pharmacist licensed pursuant to article one hundred thirty-seven of the education law or by such other vendor as may be authorized and approved by the superintendent of state police.

(a) Every self-defense spray device shall be accompanied by an insert or inserts which include directions for use, first aid information, safety and storage information and which shall also contain a toll free telephone number for the purpose of allowing any purchaser to call and receive additional information regarding the availability of local courses in self-defense training and safety in the use of a self-defense spray device.

(b) Before delivering a self-defense spray device to any person, the licensed or authorized dealer shall require proof of age and a sworn statement on a form approved by the superintendent of state police that such person has not been convicted of a felony or any crime involving an assault. Such forms shall be forwarded to the division of state police at such intervals as directed by the superintendent of state police. Absent any such direction the forms shall be maintained on the premises of the vendor and shall be open at all reasonable hours for inspection by any peace officer or police officer, acting pursuant to his or her special duties. No more than two self-defense spray devices may be sold at any one time to a single purchaser.

16. The terms "rifle," "shotgun," "pistol," "revolver," and "firearm" as used in paragraphs three, four, five, seven, seven-a, seven-b, nine, nine-a, ten, twelve, thirteen and thirteen-a of this subdivision shall not include a disguised gun or an assault weapon.

b. Section 265.01 shall not apply to possession of that type of billy commonly known as a "police baton" which is twenty-four to twenty-six inches in length and no more than one and one-quarter inches in thickness by members of an auxiliary police force of a city with a population in excess of one million persons or the county of Suffolk when duly authorized by regulation or order issued by the police commissioner of such city or such county respectively. Such regulations shall require training in the use of the police baton including but not limited to the defensive use of the baton and instruction in the legal use of deadly physical force pursuant to article thirty-five of this chapter. Notwithstanding the provisions of this section or any other provision of law, possession of such baton shall not be authorized when used intentionally to strike another person except in those situations when the use of deadly physical force is authorized by such article thirty-five.

c. Sections 265.01, 265.10 and 265.15 shall not apply to possession of billies or blackjacks by persons:

1. while employed in fulfilling contracts with New York state, its agencies or political subdivisions for the purchase of billies or blackjacks; or

2. while employed in fulfilling contracts with sister states, their agencies or political subdivisions for the purchase of billies or blackjacks; or

3. while employed in fulfilling contracts with foreign countries, their agencies or political subdivisions for the purchase of billies or blackjacks as permitted under federal law.

d. Subdivision one of section 265.01 and subdivision four of section 265.15 of this article shall not apply to possession or ownership of automatic knives by any cutlery and knife museum established pursuant to section two hundred sixteen-c of the education law or by any director, officer, employee, or agent thereof when he or she is in possession of an automatic knife and acting in furtherance of the business of such museum.

e. Subdivision eight of section 265.02 and sections 265.36 and 265.37 of this chapter shall not apply to a qualified retired New York or federal law enforcement officer as defined in subdivision twenty-five of section 265.00 of this article, with respect to large capacity ammunition feeding devices issued to such officer or purchased by such officer in the course of his or her official duties and owned by such officer at the time of his or her retirement or comparable replacements for such devices, if: (i) the agency that employed the officer qualified such officer in the use of the weapon which accepts such device in accordance with applicable state or federal standards for active duty law enforcement officers within twelve months prior to his or her retirement; and (ii) such retired officer meets, at his or her own expense, such applicable standards for such weapon at least once within three years after his or her retirement date and at least once every three years thereafter, provided, however, that any such qualified officer who has been retired for eighteen months or more on the effective date of this subdivision shall have eighteen months from such effective date to qualify in the use of the weapon which accepts such large capacity ammunition feeding device according to the provisions of this subdivision, notwithstanding that such officer did not qualify within three years after his or her retirement date, provided that such officer is otherwise qualified and maintains compliance with the provisions of this subdivision.

§265.25 Certain wounds to be reported.

Every case of a bullet wound, gunshot wound, powder burn or any other injury arising from or caused by the discharge of a gun or firearm, and every case of a wound which is likely to or may result in death and is actually or apparently inflicted by a knife, ice-pick or other sharp or pointed instrument, shall be reported at once to the police authorities of the city, town or village where the person reporting is located by: (a) the physician attending or treating the case; or (b) the manager, superintendent or other person in charge, whenever such case is treated in a hospital, sanitarium or other institution. Failure to make such report is a class A misdemeanor. This subdivision shall not apply to such wounds, burns or injuries received by a member of the armed forces of the United States or the state of New York while engaged in the actual performance of duty.

§265.26 Burn injury and wounds to be reported.

Every case of a burn injury or wound, where the victim sustained second or third degree burns to five percent or more of the body and/or any burns to the upper respiratory tract or laryngeal edema due to the inhalation of super-heated air, and every case of a burn injury or wound which is likely to or may result in death, shall be reported at once to the office of fire prevention and control. The state fire administrator shall accept the report and notify the proper investigatory agency. A written report shall also be provided to the office of fire prevention and control within seventy-two hours. The report shall be made by (a) the physician attending or treating the case; or (b) the manager, superintendent or other person in charge, whenever such case is treated in a hospital, sanitarium, institution or other medical facility.

The intentional failure to make such report is a class A misdemeanor.

§265.30 Certain convictions to be reported.

Every conviction under this article or section 400.00, of a person who is not a citizen of the United States, shall be certified to the proper officer of the United States government by the district attorney of the county in which such conviction was had.

§265.35 Prohibited use of weapons.

1. Any person hunting with a dangerous weapon in any county wholly embraced within the territorial limits of a city is guilty of a class A misdemeanor.

2. Any person who wilfully discharges a loaded firearm or any other gun, the propelling force of which is gunpowder, at an aircraft while such aircraft is in motion in the air or in motion or stationary upon the ground, or at any railway or street railroad train as defined by the public service law, or at a locomotive, car, bus or vehicle standing or moving upon such railway, railroad or public highway, is guilty of a class D felony if thereby the safety of any person is endangered, and in every other case, of a class E felony.

3. Any person who, otherwise than in self defense or in the discharge of official duty, (a) wilfully discharges any species of firearms, air-gun or other weapon, or throws any other deadly missile, either in a public place, or in any place where there is any person to be endangered thereby, or, in Putnam county, within one-quarter mile of any occupied school building other than under supervised instruction by properly authorized instructors although no injury to any person ensues; (b) intentionally, without malice, points or aims any firearm or any other gun, the propelling force of which is gunpowder, at or toward any other person; (c) discharges, without injury to any other person, firearms or any other guns, the propelling force of which is gunpowder, while intentionally without malice, aimed at or toward any person; or (d) maims or injures any other person by the discharge of any firearm or any other gun, the propelling force of which is gunpowder, pointed or aimed intentionally, but without malice, at any such person is guilty of a class A misdemeanor.

§265.36 Unlawful possession of a large capacity ammunition feeding device.

It shall be unlawful for a person to knowingly possess a large capacity ammunition feeding device manufactured before September thirteenth, nineteen hundred ninety-four, and if such person lawfully possessed such large capacity feeding device before the effective date of the chapter of the laws of two thousand thirteen which added this section, that has a capacity of, or that can be readily restored or converted to accept, more than ten rounds of ammunition.

An individual who has a reasonable belief that such device is of such a character that it may lawfully be possessed and who surrenders or lawfully disposes of such device within thirty days of being notified by law enforcement or county licensing officials that such possession is unlawful shall not be guilty of this offense. It shall be a rebuttable presumption that such person knows that such large capacity ammunition feeding device may not be lawfully possessed if he or she has been contacted by law enforcement or county licensing officials and informed that such device may not be lawfully possessed.

Unlawful possession of a large capacity ammunition feeding device is a class A misdemeanor.

§265.37 Unlawful possession of certain ammunition feeding devices.

It shall be unlawful for a person to knowingly possess an ammunition feeding device where such device contains more than seven rounds of ammunition.

If such device containing more than seven rounds of ammunition is possessed within the home of the possessor, the person so possessing the device shall, for a first offense, be guilty of a violation and subject to a fine of two hundred dollars, and for each subsequent offense, be guilty of a class B misdemeanor and subject to a fine of two hundred dollars and a term of up to three months imprisonment.

If such device containing more than seven rounds of ammunition is possessed in any location other than the home of the possessor, the person so possessing the device shall, for a first offense, be guilty of a class B misdemeanor and subject to a fine of two hundred dollars and a term of up to six months imprisonment, and for each subsequent offense, be guilty of a class A misdemeanor.

§265.40 Purchase of rifles and/or shotguns in contiguous states.

Definitions. As used in this act:

1. "Contiguous state" shall mean any state having any portion of its border in common with a portion of the border of the state of New York;

2. All other terms herein shall be given the meaning prescribed in Public Law 90-618 known as the "Gun Control Act of 1968" (18 U.S.C. 921).

It shall be lawful for a person or persons residing in this state, to purchase or otherwise obtain a rifle and/or shotgun in a contiguous state, and to receive or transport such rifle and/or shotgun into this state; provided, however, such person is otherwise eligible to possess a rifle and/or shotgun under the laws of this state.

§265.45 Failure to safely store rifles, shotguns, and firearms in the first degree.

No person who owns or is custodian of a rifle, shotgun or firearm who resides with an individual who: (i) is under sixteen years of age; (ii) such person knows or has reason to know is prohibited from possessing a rifle, shotgun or firearm pursuant to a temporary or final extreme risk protection order issued under article sixty-three-A of the civil practice law and rules or 18 U.S.C. § 922(g) (1), (4), (8) or (9); or (iii) such person knows or has reason to know is prohibited from possessing a rifle, shotgun or firearm based on a conviction for a felony or a serious offense, shall store or otherwise leave such rifle, shotgun or firearm out of his or her immediate possession or control without having first securely locked such rifle, shotgun or firearm in an appropriate safe storage depository or rendered it incapable of being fired by use of a gun locking device appropriate to that weapon. For purposes of this section "safe storage depository" shall mean a safe or other secure container which, when locked, is incapable of being opened without the key, combination or other unlocking mechanism and is capable of preventing an unauthorized person from obtaining access to and possession of the weapon contained therein. Nothing in this section shall be deemed to affect, impair or supersede any special or local act relating to the safe storage of rifles, shotguns or firearms which impose additional requirements on the owner or custodian of such weapons.

It shall not be a violation of this section to allow a person less than sixteen years of age access to: (i) a firearm, rifle or shotgun for lawful use as authorized under paragraph seven or seven-e of subdivision a of section 265.20 of this article, or (ii) a rifle or shotgun for lawful use as authorized by article eleven of the environmental conservation law when such person less than sixteen years of age is the holder of a hunting license or permit and such rifle or shotgun is used in accordance with such law.

Failure to safely store rifles, shotguns, and firearms in the first degree is a class A misdemeanor.

*§265.50 Criminal manufacture, sale, or transport of an undetectable firearm, rifle or shotgun.

A person is guilty of criminal manufacture, sale, or transport of an undetectable firearm, rifle or shotgun when he or she knowingly manufactures, causes to be manufactured, sells, exchanges, gives, disposes of, transports, ships, or possesses with the intent to sell:

1. any firearm, rifle or shotgun that, after the removal of grips, stocks and magazines, is not detectable by a metal detector calibrated to detect the Security Exemplar, as defined pursuant to 18 U.S.C. § 922(p); or

2. any major component of a firearm, rifle or shotgun that, if subject to the types of detection devices commonly used at airports for security screening, does not generate an image that adequately displays the shape of the component.

Criminal manufacture, sale, or transport of an undetectable firearm, rifle or shotgun is a class D felony. *(There are 2 §265.50's)*

*§265.50 Failure to safely store rifles, shotguns, and firearms in the second degree.

No person who owns or is custodian of a rifle, shotgun or firearm and knows, or has reason to know, that a person less than sixteen years of age is likely to gain access to such rifle, shotgun or firearm shall store or otherwise leave such rifle, shotgun or firearm out of his or her immediate possession or control without having first securely locked such rifle, shotgun or firearm in an appropriate safe storage depository or rendered it incapable of being fired by use of a gun locking device appropriate to that weapon. For purposes of this section "safe storage depository" shall have the same meaning as such term is defined in section 265.45 of this article. Nothing in this section shall be deemed to affect, impair or supersede any special or local act relating to the safe storage of rifles, shotguns or firearms which impose additional requirements on the owner or custodian of such weapons.

It shall not be a violation of this section to allow a person less than sixteen years of age access to: (i) a firearm, rifle or shotgun for lawful use as authorized under paragraph seven or seven-e of subdivision a of section 265.20 of this article, or (ii) a rifle or shotgun for lawful use as authorized by article eleven of the environmental conservation law when such person less than sixteen years of age is the holder of a hunting license or permit and such rifle or shotgun is used in accordance with such law.

Failure to safely store rifles, shotguns, and firearms in the second degree is a violation punishable only by a fine of not more than two hundred fifty dollars.

(There are 2 §265.50's)

§265.55 Criminal possession of an undetectable firearm, rifle or shotgun.

A person is guilty of criminal possession of an undetectable firearm, rifle or shotgun when he or she knowingly possesses:

1. any firearm, rifle or shotgun that, after the removal of grips, stocks and magazines, is not detectable by a metal detector calibrated to detect the Security Exemplar, as defined pursuant to 18 U.S.C. § 922(p); or

2. any major component of a firearm, rifle or shotgun that, if subject to the types of detection devices commonly used at airports for security screening, does not generate an image that adequately displays the shape of the component.

Criminal possession of an undetectable firearm, rifle or shotgun is a class E felony.

§265.60 Criminal sale of a ghost gun in the second degree.

1. A person is guilty of criminal sale of a ghost gun in the second degree when, knowing or having reason to know it is a ghost gun, he or she sells, exchanges, gives or disposes of a ghost gun to another person.

2. Notwithstanding subdivision one of this section, a person shall not be guilty of criminal sale of a ghost gun in the second degree when such person: (a) voluntarily surrenders such ghost gun to any law enforcement official designated pursuant to subparagraph (f) of paragraph one of subdivision (a) of section 265.20 of this article; or (b) within a period of six months after the effective date of this section sells, exchanges, gives, or disposes of such ghost gun to a gunsmith licensed pursuant to section 400.00 of this chapter.

Criminal sale of a ghost gun in the second degree is a class E felony.

(Eff.4/26/22,Ch.520,L.2021)

§265.61 Criminal sale of a ghost gun in the first degree.

1. A person is guilty of criminal sale of a ghost gun in the first degree when, knowing or having reason to know they are ghost guns, he or she sells, exchanges, gives or disposes of ten or more ghost guns to another person or persons.

2. Notwithstanding subdivision one of this section, a person shall not be guilty of criminal sale of a ghost gun in the first degree if he or she: (a) voluntarily surrenders such ghost guns to any law enforcement official designated pursuant to subparagraph (f) of paragraph one of subdivision (a) of section 265.20 of this article; or (b) within a period of six months after the effective date of this section sells, exchanges, gives, or disposes of such ghost guns to a gunsmith licensed pursuant to section 400.00 of this chapter.

Criminal sale of a ghost gun in the first degree is a class D felony.

(Eff.4/26/22,Ch.520,L.2021)

§265.63 Criminal sale of an unfinished frame or receiver in the second degree.

A person is guilty of criminal sale of an unfinished frame or receiver in the second degree when, knowing it is an unfinished frame or receiver, such person unlawfully sells, exchanges, gives or disposes of an unfinished frame or receiver, provided that for a period of six months after the effective date of this section, a person shall not be guilty of criminal sale of an unfinished frame or receiver in the second degree if such person: (a) voluntarily surrenders such unfinished frame or receiver to any law enforcement official designated pursuant to subparagraph (f) of paragraph one of subdivision (a) of section 265.20 of this article; or (b) sells, exchanges, gives, or disposes of such unfinished frame or receiver to a gunsmith licensed pursuant to section 400.00 of this chapter.

Criminal sale of an unfinished frame or receiver in the second degree is a class E felony.
(Eff.2/25/22,Ch.519,L.2021)

§265.64 Criminal sale of an unfinished frame or receiver in the first degree.

A person is guilty of criminal sale of an unfinished frame or receiver in the first degree when, knowing they are unfinished frames or receivers, such person unlawfully sells, exchanges, gives or disposes of a total of ten or more unfinished frames or receivers in a period of not more than one year, provided that for a period of six months after the effective date of this section, a person shall not be guilty of criminal sale of an unfinished frame or receiver in the first degree if such person: (a) voluntarily surrenders such unfinished frames or receivers to any law enforcement official designated pursuant to subparagraph (f) of paragraph one of subdivision (a) of section 265.20 of this article; or (b) sells, exchanges, gives or disposes of such unfinished frames or receivers to a gunsmith licensed pursuant to section 400.00 of this chapter.

Criminal sale of an unfinished frame or receiver in the first degree is a class D felony.   *(Eff.2/25/22,Ch.519,L.2021)*

ARTICLE 270 - OTHER OFFENSES RELATING TO PUBLIC SAFETY

Section
270.00 Unlawfully dealing with fireworks and dangerous fireworks.
270.05 Unlawfully possessing or selling noxious material.
270.10 Creating a hazard.
270.15 Unlawfully refusing to yield a party line.
270.20 Unlawful wearing of a body vest.
270.25 Unlawful fleeing a police officer in a motor vehicle in the third degree.
270.30 Unlawful fleeing a police officer in a motor vehicle in the second degree.
270.35 Unlawful fleeing a police officer in a motor vehicle in the first degree.
270.40 Unlawfully installing a gas meter.

§270.00 Unlawfully dealing with fireworks and dangerous fireworks.

1. Definition of "fireworks" and "dangerous fireworks". (a) The term "fireworks," as used in this section, includes:

(i) display fireworks, which means fireworks devices in a finished state, exclusive of mere ornamentation, primarily intended for commercial displays which are designed to produce visible and/or audible effects by combustion, deflagration or detonation, including, but not limited to, salutes containing more than one hundred thirty milligrams (two grains) of explosive composition, aerial shells containing more than forty grams of chemical composition exclusive of lift charge, and other exhibition display items that exceed the limits of consumer fireworks contained in the American Pyrotechnic Association (APA) Standard 87-1, 2001 edition;

(ii) articles pyrotechnic, which means pyrotechnic devices for professional use similar to consumer fireworks in chemical composition and construction but not intended for consumer use and which articles meet the weight limits for consumer fireworks but are not labeled as such and are classified by the United States department of transportation in 49 CFR 172.101 as UN0431;

(iii) special effects, which means any combination of chemical elements or chemical compounds capable of burning independently of the oxygen of the atmosphere, and designed and intended to produce an audible, visual, mechanical, or thermal effect as an integral part of a motion picture, radio, television, theatrical, or opera production, or live entertainment;

(iv) consumer fireworks which are aerial in performance and are commonly referred to as sky rockets, bottle rockets, missile type rockets, helicopters, aerial spinners, roman candles, mines, shell devices, aerial shell kits, reloadables and audible ground devices which are commonly referred to as firecrackers and chasers, as well as metal wire handheld sparklers;

(v) any blank cartridge, blank cartridge pistol, or toy cannon in which explosives are used, firecrackers, or any preparation containing any explosive or inflammable compound or any tablets or other device commonly used and sold as fireworks containing nitrates, chlorates, oxalates, sulphides of lead, barium, antimony, arsenic, mercury, nitroglycerine, phosphorus or any compound containing any of the same or other explosives, or any substance or combination of substances, or article prepared for the purpose of producing a visible or an audible effect by combustion, explosion, deflagration or detonation, or other device containing any explosive substance, other than sparkling devices as defined in subparagraph (vi) of this paragraph; and

(vi) "sparkling devices," as used in this section, includes:

(1) sparkling devices which are ground-based or hand-held devices that produce a shower of white, gold, or colored sparks as their primary pyrotechnic effect. Additional effects may include a colored flame, an audible crackling effect, an audible whistle effect, and smoke. These devices do not rise into the air, do not fire inserts or projectiles into the air, and do not explode or produce a report (an audible crackling-type effect is not considered to be a report). Ground-based or hand-held devices that produce a cloud of smoke as their sole pyrotechnic effect are also included in this category. Types of devices in this category include:

(A) cylindrical fountain: cylindrical tube containing not more than seventy-five grams of pyrotechnic composition that may be contained in a different shaped exterior such as a square, rectangle, cylinder or other shape but the interior tubes are cylindrical in shape. Upon ignition, a shower of colored sparks, and sometimes a whistling effect or smoke, is produced. This device may be provided with a spike for insertion into the ground (spike fountain), a wood or plastic base for placing on the ground (base fountain), or a wood or cardboard handle to be hand held (handle fountain). When more than one tube is mounted on a common base, total pyrotechnic composition may not exceed two hundred grams, and when tubes are securely attached to a base and the tubes are separated from each other on the base by a distance of at least half an inch (12.7 millimeters), a maximum total weight of five hundred grams of pyrotechnic composition shall be allowed.

(B) cone fountain: cardboard or heavy paper cone containing not more than fifty grams of pyrotechnic composition. The effect is the same as that of a cylindrical fountain. When more than one cone is mounted on a common base, total pyrotechnic composition may not exceed two hundred grams, as is outlined in this subparagraph.

(C) wooden sparkler/dipped stick: these devices consist of a wood dowel that has been coated with pyrotechnic composition. Upon ignition of the tip of the device, a shower of sparks is produced. Sparklers may contain up to one hundred grams of pyrotechnic composition per item.

(2) novelties which do not require approval from the United States department of transportation and are not regulated as explosives, provided that they are manufactured and packaged as described below:

(A) party popper: small devices with paper or plastic exteriors that are actuated by means of friction (a string or trigger is typically pulled to actuate the device). They frequently resemble champagne bottles or toy pistols in shape. Upon activation, the device expels flame-resistant paper streamers, confetti, or other novelties and produces a small report. Devices may contain not more than sixteen milligrams (0.25 grains) of explosive composition, which is limited to potassium chlorate and red phosphorus. These devices must be packaged in an inner packaging which contains a maximum of seventy-two devices.

(B) snapper: small, paper-wrapped devices containing not more than one milligram of silver fulminate coated on small bits of sand or gravel. When dropped, the device explodes, producing a small report. Snappers must be in inner packages not to exceed fifty devices each, and the inner packages must contain sawdust or a similar, impact-absorbing material.

(b) The term "dangerous fireworks" means any fireworks capable of causing serious physical injury and which are: firecrackers containing more than fifty milligrams of any explosive substance, torpedoes, skyrockets and rockets including all devices which employ any combustible or explosive substance and which rise in the air during discharge, Roman candles, and bombs, provided, however, that in cities with a population of one million or more, the term "dangerous fireworks" shall also include sparklers more than ten inches in length or one-fourth of one inch in diameter, or chasers including all devices which dart or travel about the surface of the ground during discharge.

(c) "Fireworks" and "dangerous fireworks" shall not be deemed to include the following nor shall the purchase and use of any items listed below be subject to the provisions of section 61 of title 12 of the New York state codes, rules and regulations or section four hundred eighty, four hundred eighty-one, four hundred eighty-two or four hundred eighty-three of the general business law:

(i) flares of the type used by railroads or any warning lights commonly known as red flares, or marine distress signals of a type approved by the United States coast guard, or

(ii) toy pistols, toy canes, toy guns or other devices in which paper caps containing twenty-five hundredths grains or less of explosive compound are used, providing they are so constructed that the hand cannot come in contact with the cap when in place for use, and toy pistol paper caps which contain less than twenty-hundredths grains of explosive mixture, the sale and use of which shall be permitted at all times, or

(iii) bank security devices which contain not more than fifty grams of any compound or substance or any combination thereof, together with an igniter not exceeding 0.2 gram, capable of producing a lachrymating and/or visible or audible effect, where such device is stored or used only by banks, national banking associations, trust companies, savings banks, savings and loan associations, industrial banks, or credit unions, or by any manufacturer, wholesaler, dealer, jobber or common carrier for such devices and where the total storage on any one premises does not exceed one hundred devices, or

(iv) except in cities with a population of one million or more, "fireworks" and "dangerous fireworks" shall not be deemed to include "sparkling devices" as defined in subparagraph (vi) of paragraph (a) of this subdivision. The storage and retail sale of sparkling devices shall be regulated in a manner that is not in conflict with the provisions of NFPA 1124, 2006 edition.

2. Offense. (a) Except as herein otherwise provided, or except where a permit is obtained pursuant to section 405.00 of this chapter:

(i) any person who shall offer or expose for sale, sell or furnish, any fireworks or dangerous fireworks is guilty of a class B misdemeanor;

(ii) any person who shall offer or expose for sale, sell or furnish any fireworks or dangerous fireworks valued at five hundred dollars or more shall be guilty of a class A misdemeanor;

(iii) any person who shall possess, use, explode or cause to explode any fireworks or dangerous fireworks is guilty of a violation;

(iv) any person who shall offer or expose for sale, sell or furnish, any dangerous fireworks, fireworks or sparkling devices to any person who is under the age of eighteen is guilty of a class A misdemeanor.

(b) A person who has previously been convicted of a violation of subparagraph (iv) of paragraph (a) of this subdivision within the preceding five years and who shall offer or expose for sale, sell or furnish, any dangerous fireworks to any person who is under the age of eighteen, shall be guilty of a class E felony.

(c) Possession of fireworks or dangerous fireworks valued at one hundred fifty dollars or more shall be a presumption that such fireworks were intended to be offered or exposed for sale.

3. Exceptions. (a) The provisions of this section shall not apply to:

(i) fireworks, dangerous fireworks, and sparkling devices while in possession of railroads, common or contract carriers, retailers, wholesalers, distributors, jobbers and transportation companies or transportation agencies for the purpose of transportation to points without the state, the shipment of which is not prohibited by interstate commerce commission regulations as formulated and published from time to time, unless they be held voluntarily by such railroads, common or contract carriers, retailers, wholesalers, distributors, jobbers and transportation agencies or transporting companies as warehousemen for delivery to points within the state;

(ii) signaling devices used by railroad companies or motor vehicles referred to in subdivision seventeen of section three hundred seventy-five of the vehicle and traffic law;

(iii) high explosives for blasting or similar purposes;

(iv) fireworks, dangerous fireworks and sparkling devices for the use thereof by the United States military, and departments of the state and federal government;

(v) the use, transportation and storage of fireworks, dangerous fireworks and sparkling devices and special effects materials in connection with the production of motion pictures, television programs, commercials, and all entertainment media recorded in any current or to be designed format when such use, transportation and storage has been appropriately permitted by the local governmental subdivision having jurisdiction.

(b) Nothing in this article shall be construed to prohibit:

(i) any manufacturer, wholesaler, retailer, dealer or jobber from manufacturing, possessing or selling at wholesale a sparkling device to municipalities, religious or civic organizations, fair associations, amusement parks, or other organizations authorized by the state to store, transport, possess and use or to individuals to store, transport, possess and use;

(ii) the sale or use of blank cartridges for a motion picture, television program, commercial and all entertainment media, or for signal purposes in athletic sports, or for dog trials or dog training;

(iii) the use, storage, transportation or sale or transfer for use of fireworks and sparkling devices in the preparation for or in connection with motion pictures, television programs, commercials, and all entertainment media recorded in any current or to be designed format when such use, transportation and storage has been appropriately permitted by the local governmental subdivision having jurisdiction;

(iv) the manufacture or sale of sparkling devices provided they are to be shipped directly out of such city and any such items are sold in accordance with the provisions of this article; or

(v) except in cities with a population of one million or more, possession of sparkling devices lawfully obtained in another jurisdiction.

4. Sales of ammunition not prohibited. Nothing contained in this section shall be construed to prevent, or interfere in any way with, the sale of ammunition for revolvers or pistols of any kind, or for rifles, shot guns, or other arms, belonging or which may belong to any persons whether as sporting or hunting weapons or for the purpose of protection to them in their homes, or, as they may go abroad; and manufacturers are authorized to continue to manufacture, and wholesalers and dealers to continue to deal in and freely to sell ammunition to all such persons for such purposes.

5. Notwithstanding the provisions of subdivision four of this section, it shall be unlawful for any dealer in firearms to sell any ammunition designed exclusively for use in a pistol or revolver to any person, not authorized to possess a pistol or revolver. The violation of this section shall constitute a class B misdemeanor.

§270.05 Unlawfully possessing or selling noxious material.

1. As used in this section, "noxious material" means any container which contains any drug or other substance capable of generating offensive, noxious or suffocating fumes, gases or vapors, or capable of immobilizing a person.

2. A person is guilty of unlawfully possessing noxious material when he possesses such material under circumstances evincing an intent to use it to or cause it to be used to inflict physical injury upon or to cause annoyance to a person, or to damage property of another, or to disturb the public peace.

3. Possession of noxious material is presumptive evidence of intent to use it or cause it to be used in violation of this section.

4. Bank security devices not prohibited. Notwithstanding the provisions of subdivision one of this section, it shall not be unlawful for any bank, national banking association, trust company, savings bank, savings and loan association, industrial bank, or credit union to store, possess, transport, use or cause to discharge any bank security device as described in subdivision one of section 270.00 of this chapter; nor shall it be unlawful for any manufacturer, wholesaler, dealer, jobber or common carrier to manufacture, store, possess, transport, or sell such a device to banks, national banking associations, trust companies, savings banks, savings and loan associations, industrial banks or credit unions.

5. Self-defense spray devices not prohibited. Notwithstanding the provisions of subdivisions two and three of this section, it shall not be

unlawful for a person eighteen years of age or older to possess a self-defense spray device as defined in paragraph fourteen of subdivision a of section 265.20 of this chapter in accordance with the provisions set forth therein.

6. A person is guilty of unlawfully selling a noxious material when he or she sells a self-defense spray device as defined in paragraph fourteen of subdivision a of section 265.20 of this chapter and such sale was not authorized in accordance with the provisions of paragraph fifteen of subdivision a of section 265.20 of this chapter.

Unlawfully possessing or selling noxious material is a class B misdemeanor.

§270.10 Creating a hazard.

A person is guilty of creating a hazard when:

1. Having discarded in any place where it might attract children, a container which has a compartment of more than one and one-half cubic feet capacity and a door or lid which locks or fastens automatically when closed and which cannot easily be opened from the inside, he fails to remove the door, lid, locking or fastening device; or

2. Being the owner or otherwise having possession of property upon which an abandoned well or cesspool is located, he fails to cover the same with suitable protective construction.

Creating a hazard is a class B misdemeanor.

§270.15 Unlawfully refusing to yield a party line.

1. As used in this section:

(a) "Party line" means a subscriber's line telephone circuit, consisting of two or more main telephone stations connected therewith, each station with a distinctive ring or telephone number.

(b) "Emergency call" means a telephone call to a police or fire department, or for medical aid or ambulance service, necessitated by a situation in which human life or property is in jeopardy and prompt summoning of aid is essential.

2. A person is guilty of unlawfully refusing to yield a party line when being informed that a party line is needed for an emergency call, he refuses immediately to relinquish such line.

Unlawfully refusing to yield a party line is a class B misdemeanor.

§270.20 Unlawful wearing of a body vest.

1. A person is guilty of the unlawful wearing of a body vest when acting either alone or with one or more other persons he commits any violent felony offense defined in section 70.02 while possessing a firearm, rifle or shotgun and in the course of and in furtherance of such crime he wears a body vest.

2. For the purposes of this section a "body vest" means a bullet-resistant soft body armor providing, as a minimum standard, the level of protection known as threat level I which shall mean at least seven layers of bullet-resistant material providing protection from three shots of one hundred fifty-eight grain lead ammunition fired from a .38 calibre handgun at a velocity of eight hundred fifty feet per second.

The unlawful wearing of a body vest is a class E felony.

§270.25 Unlawful fleeing a police officer in a motor vehicle in the third degree.

A person is guilty of unlawful fleeing a police officer in a motor vehicle in the third degree when, knowing that he or she has been directed to stop his or her motor vehicle by a uniformed police officer or a marked police vehicle by the activation of either the lights or the lights and siren of such vehicle, he or she thereafter attempts to flee such officer or such vehicle by driving at speeds which equal or exceed twenty-five miles per hour above the speed limit or engaging in reckless driving as defined by section twelve hundred twelve of the vehicle and traffic law.

Unlawful fleeing a police officer in a motor vehicle in the third degree is a class A misdemeanor.

§270.30 Unlawful fleeing a police officer in a motor vehicle in the second degree.

A person is guilty of unlawful fleeing a police officer in a motor vehicle in the second degree when he or she commits the offense of unlawful fleeing a police officer in a motor vehicle in the third degree, as defined in section 270.25 of this article, and as a result of such conduct a police officer or a third person suffers serious physical injury.

Unlawful fleeing a police officer in a motor vehicle in the second degree is a class E felony.

§270.35 Unlawful fleeing a police officer in a motor vehicle in the first degree.

A person is guilty of unlawful fleeing a police officer in a motor vehicle in the first degree when he or she commits the offense of unlawful fleeing a police officer in a motor vehicle in the third degree, as defined in section 270.25 of this article, and as a result of such conduct a police officer or a third person is killed.

Unlawful fleeing a police officer in a motor vehicle in the first degree is a class D felony.

§270.40 Unlawfully installing a gas meter.

1. As used in this section "gas meter" means any gas meter that measures usage of any end use customer of gas services.

2. A person is guilty of unlawfully installing a gas meter when he or she installs the gas meter or is the owner of the premises where the meter is unlawfully installed and knows that such gas meter was unlawfully installed. A gas meter is unlawfully installed when it is installed by any person other than a person acting on behalf of a utility corporation subject to the jurisdiction of the public service commission, unless such person has received a permit to install the gas meter from the appropriate permitting authority.

Unlawfully installing a gas meter is a class B misdemeanor.

(Eff.7/16/21,Ch.274,L.2021)

ARTICLE 275 - OFFENSES RELATING TO
UNAUTHORIZED RECORDING

Section
275.00 Definitions.
275.05 Manufacture of unauthorized recordings in the second degree.
275.10 Manufacture of unauthorized recordings in the first degree.
275.15 Manufacture or sale of an unauthorized recording of a performance in the second degree.
275.20 Manufacture or sale of an unauthorized recording of a performance in the first degree.
275.25 Advertisement or sale of unauthorized recordings in the second degree.
275.30 Advertisement or sale of unauthorized recordings in the first degree.
275.32 Unlawful operation of a recording device in a motion picture or live theater in the third degree.
275.33 Unlawful operation of a recording device in a motion picture or live theater in the second degree.
275.34 Unlawful operation of a recording device in a motion picture or live theater in the first degree.
275.35 Failure to disclose the origin of a recording in the second degree.
275.40 Failure to disclose the origin of a recording in the first degree.
275.45 Limitations of application.

§275.00 Definitions.

The following definitions are applicable to this article:

1. "Person" means any individual, firm, partnership, corporation or association.

2. "Owner" means (a) the person who owns, or has the exclusive license in the United States to reproduce or the exclusive license in the United States to distribute to the public copies of the sounds fixed in a master phonograph record, master disc, master tape, master film or any other device used for reproducing sounds on phonograph records, discs, tapes, films, videocassettes, or any other articles upon which sound is recorded, and from which the transferred recorded sounds are directly derived; or (b) the person who owns the rights to record or authorize the recording of a live performance.

3. "Fixed" means embodied in a recording by or under the authority of the author, so that the matter embodied is sufficiently permanent or stable to permit it to be perceived, reproduced, or otherwise communicated for a period of more than transitory duration.

4. "Performer" means the person or persons appearing in a performance.

5. "Performance" means, whether live before an audience or transmitted by wire or through the air by radio or television, a recitation, rendering, or playing of a series of images, musical, spoken, or other sounds, or a combination of images and sounds, in an audible sequence.

6. "Recording" means an original phonograph record, disc, tape, audio or video cassette, wire, film, hard drive, flash drive, memory card or other data storage device or any other medium on which such sounds, images, or both sounds and images are or can be recorded or otherwise stored, or a copy or reproduction that duplicates in whole or in part the original.

§275.05 Manufacture of unauthorized recordings in the second degree.

A person is guilty of the manufacture of unauthorized recordings in the second degree when such person:

1. knowingly, and without the consent of the owner, transfers or causes to be transferred any sound recording, with the intent to rent or sell, or cause to be rented or sold for profit, or used to promote the sale of any product, such article to which such recording was transferred, or

2. transports within this state, for commercial advantage or private financial gain, a recording, knowing that the sounds have been reproduced or transferred without the consent of the owner; provided, however, that this section shall only apply to sound recordings initially fixed prior to February fifteenth, nineteen hundred seventy-two.

Manufacture of unauthorized recordings in the second degree is a class A misdemeanor.

§275.10 Manufacture of unauthorized recordings in the first degree.

A person is guilty of manufacture of unauthorized recordings in the first degree when he commits the crime of manufacture of unauthorized recordings in the second degree as defined in section 275.05 of this article and either:

1. has previously been convicted of that crime within the past five years; or

2. commits that crime by the manufacture of one thousand unauthorized sound recordings; provided, however, that this section shall only apply to sound recordings initially fixed prior to February fifteenth, nineteen hundred seventy-two.

Manufacture of unauthorized recordings in the first degree is a class E felony.

§275.15 Manufacture or sale of an unauthorized recording of a performance in the second degree.

A person commits the crime of manufacture or sale of an unauthorized recording of a performance in the second degree when he knowingly, and without the consent of the performer, records or fixes or causes to be recorded or fixed on a recording a performance, with the intent to sell or rent or cause to be sold or rented such recording, or with the intent to use such recording to promote the sale of any product; or when he knowingly possesses, transports or advertises, for purposes of sale, resale or rental or sells, resells, rents or offers for rental, sale or resale, any recording that the person knows has been produced in violation of this section.

Manufacture or sale of an unauthorized recording of a performance in the second degree is a class A misdemeanor.

§275.20 Manufacture or sale of an unauthorized recording of a performance in the first degree.

A person commits the crime of unauthorized recording of a performance in the first degree when he commits the crime of manufacture or sale of an unauthorized recording of a performance in the second degree as defined in section 275.15 of this article and either:

1. such person has previously been convicted of that crime within the past five years; or

2. commission of that crime involves at least one thousand unauthorized sound recordings or at least one hundred unauthorized audiovisual recordings.

Unauthorized recording of a performance in the first degree is a class E felony.

§275.25 Advertisement or sale of unauthorized recordings in the second degree.

A person is guilty of the advertisement or sale of unauthorized recordings in the second degree when such person knowingly advertises, offers for sale, resale, or rental, or sells, resells, rents, distributes or possesses for any such purposes, any recording that has been produced or transferred without the consent of the owner; provided, however, that this section shall only apply to sound recordings initially fixed prior to February fifteenth, nineteen hundred seventy-two.

Advertisement or sale of unauthorized recordings in the second degree is a class A misdemeanor.

§275.30 Advertisement or sale of unauthorized recordings in the first degree.

A person is guilty of the advertisement or sale of unauthorized recordings in the first degree when such person commits the crime of advertisement or sale of unauthorized recordings in the second degree as defined in section 275.25 of this article and either:

1. such person has previously been convicted of that crime within the past five years; or

2. commission of that crime involves at least one thousand unauthorized sound recordings or at least one hundred unauthorized audiovisual recordings.

Advertisement and sale of unauthorized recordings in the first degree is a class E felony.

§275.32 Unlawful operation of a recording device in a motion picture or live theater in the third degree.

1. A person is guilty of unlawful operation of a recording device in a motion picture or live theater in the third degree when without authority or written permission from the operator of a motion picture theater or live theater, the person operates a recording device in such theater.

2. As used in this section (a) "recording device" means a photographic or video camera, or any audiovisual recording function of any device used for recording the sound or picture of a motion picture;

(b) "operator" means the owner or lessee of a motion picture theater or live theater or the authorized agent or employee of such owner or lessee;

(c) "motion picture theater" means a theater, screening room, auditorium or other venue that is being utilized primarily for the exhibition of a motion picture at the time of the offense; and

(d) "live theater" means a concert hall, recital hall, theater, or auditorium in which a presentation is rendered, consisting in whole or in part of a musical, dramatic, dance, or other stage rendition by one or more professional performers who appear in person in the immediate presence of their audiences, and admission to which is limited by its operator to persons holding an admission ticket or who have other authority or written permission to enter. Live theater shall not mean or include a musical, dramatic, dance, or other stage rendition that is performed by students enrolled in a school or college or as a part of a children's camp or similar program.

Unlawful operation of a recording device in a motion picture or live theater in the third degree is a violation.

§275.33 Unlawful operation of a recording device in a motion picture or live theater in the second degree.

A person is guilty of unlawful operation of a recording device in a motion picture or live theater in the second degree when he or she violates section 275.32 of this article:

1. for financial profit or commercial purposes; or

2. in circumstances where the material recorded is fifteen or more minutes, or all or a substantial portion, of the motion picture or live theatrical performance; or

3. in circumstances where such person has previously been convicted within the past five years of violating section 275.32 or 275.34 of this article or this section.

Unlawful operation of a recording device in a motion picture or live theater in the second degree is a class A misdemeanor.

§275.34 Unlawful operation of a recording device in a motion picture or live theater in the first degree.

A person is guilty of unlawful operation of a recording device in a motion picture or live theater in the first degree when he or she commits the crime of unlawful operation of a recording device in a motion picture or live theater in the second degree as defined in section 275.33 of this article and has previously been convicted within the past ten years of violating section 275.33 of this article or this section.

Unlawful operation of a recording device in a motion picture or live theatre in the first degree is a class E felony.

§275.35 Failure to disclose the origin of a recording in the second degree.

A person is guilty of failure to disclose the origin of a recording in the second degree when, for commercial advantage or private financial gain, he knowingly advertises or offers for sale, resale, or rental, or sells, resells, or rents, or possesses for such purposes, a recording the cover,

box, jacket or label does not clearly and conspicuously disclose the
actual name and address of the manufacturer or the name of the
performer or principal artist. The omission of the actual name and
address of the manufacturer, or the omission of the name of the
performer or principal artise, or the omission of both, shall constitute the
failure to disclose the origin of a recording.

**Failure to disclose the origin of a recording in the second degree is a class A
misdemeanor.**

§275.40 Failure to disclose the origin of a recording in the first degree.

A person is guilty of failure to disclose the origin of a recording in the
first degree when such person commits the crime of failure to disclose
the origin of a recording in the second degree as defined in section
275.35 of this article and either:

1. such person has been convicted of failure to disclose the origin of a
recording in the first or second degree within the past five years; or

2. commission of the crime involves at least one hundred
unauthorized sound recordings or at least one hundred unauthorized
audiovisual recordings.

**Failure to disclose the origin of a recording in the first degree is a class E
felony.**

§275.45 Limitations of application.

1. This article does not apply to:

(a) any broadcaster who, in connection with or as part of a radio,
television, or cable broadcast transmission, or for the purposes of
archival preservation, transfers any such recorded sounds or images; or

(b) any person who transfers such sounds or images for personal
use, and without profit for such transfer.

2. This article shall neither enlarge nor diminish the rights of parties in
civil litigation.

**PART IV - ADMINISTRATIVE PROVISIONS
TITLE W - PROVISIONS RELATING TO FIREARMS,
FIREWORKS, PORNOGRAPHY EQUIPMENT AND VEHICLES
USED IN THE TRANSPORTATION OF GAMBLING RECORDS
ARTICLE 400 - LICENSING AND OTHER PROVISIONS
RELATING TO FIREARMS**

Section
400.00 Licenses to carry, possess, repair and dispose of firearms.
400.01 License to carry and possess firearms for retired sworn members of the division
of state police.
400.02 Statewide license and record database.
400.03 Sellers of ammunition.
400.05 Disposition of weapons and dangerous instruments, appliances and substances.
400.10 Report of theft or loss of a firearm, rifle or shotgun.
400.20 Waiting period in connection with the sale or transfer of a rifle or shotgun.

§400.00 Licenses to carry, possess, repair and dispose of firearms.

1. Eligibility. No license shall be issued or renewed pursuant to this section except by the licensing officer, and then only after investigation and finding that all statements in a proper application for a license are true. No license shall be issued or renewed except for an applicant (a) twenty-one years of age or older, provided, however, that where such applicant has been honorably discharged from the United States army, navy, marine corps, air force or coast guard, or the national guard of the state of New York, no such age restriction shall apply; (b) of good moral character; (c) who has not been convicted anywhere of a felony or a serious offense or who is not the subject of an outstanding warrant of arrest issued upon the alleged commission of a felony or serious offense; (d) who is not a fugitive from justice; (e) who is not an unlawful user of or addicted to any controlled substance as defined in section 21 U.S.C. 802; (f) who being an alien (i) is not illegally or unlawfully in the United States or (ii) has not been admitted to the United States under a nonimmigrant visa subject to the exception in 18 U.S.C. 922(y)(2); (g) who has not been discharged from the Armed Forces under dishonorable conditions; (h) who, having been a citizen of the United States, has not renounced his or her citizenship; (i) who has stated whether he or she has ever suffered any mental illness; (j) who has not been involuntarily committed to a facility under the jurisdiction of an office of the department of mental hygiene pursuant to article nine or fifteen of the mental hygiene law, article seven hundred thirty or section 330.20 of the criminal procedure law, section four hundred two or five hundred eight of the correction law, section 322.2 or 353.4 of the family court act, or has not been civilly confined in a secure treatment facility pursuant to article ten of the mental hygiene law; (k) who has not had a license revoked or who is not under a suspension or ineligibility order issued pursuant to the provisions of section 530.14 of the criminal procedure law or section eight hundred forty-two-a of the family court act; (l) in the county of Westchester, who has successfully completed a firearms safety course and test as evidenced by a certificate of completion issued in his or her name and endorsed and affirmed under the penalties of perjury by a duly authorized instructor, except that: (i) persons who are honorably discharged from the United States army, navy, marine corps or coast guard, or of the national guard of the state of New York, and produce evidence of official qualification in firearms during the term of service are not required to have completed those hours of a firearms safety course pertaining to the safe use, carrying, possession, maintenance and storage of a firearm; and (ii) persons who were licensed to possess a pistol or revolver prior to the effective date of this paragraph are not required to have completed a firearms safety course and test; (m) who has not had a guardian appointed for him or her pursuant to any provision of state law, based on a determination that as a result of marked subnormal intelligence, mental illness, incapacity, condition or disease, he or she lacks the mental capacity to contract or manage his or her own affairs; and (n) concerning whom no good cause

exists for the denial of the license. No person shall engage in the business of gunsmith or dealer in firearms unless licensed pursuant to this section. An applicant to engage in such business shall also be a citizen of the United States, more than twenty-one years of age and maintain a place of business in the city or county where the license is issued. For such business, if the applicant is a firm or partnership, each member thereof shall comply with all of the requirements set forth in this subdivision and if the applicant is a corporation, each officer thereof shall so comply.

*1-a. For purposes of subdivision one of this section, serious offense shall include an offense in any jurisdiction or the former penal law that includes all of the essential elements of a serious offense as defined by subdivision seventeen of section 265.00 of this chapter. Nothing in this subdivision shall preclude the denial of a license based on the commission of, arrest for or conviction of an offense in any other jurisdiction which does not include all of the essential elements of a serious offense.   *(Eff.4/3/21,Ch.55,L.2020)*

2. Types of licenses. A license for gunsmith or dealer in firearms shall be issued to engage in such business. A license for a pistol or revolver, other than an assault weapon or a disguised gun, shall be issued to (a) have and possess in his dwelling by a householder; (b) have and possess in his place of business by a merchant or storekeeper; (c) have and carry concealed while so employed by a messenger employed by a banking institution or express company; (d) have and carry concealed by a justice of the supreme court in the first or second judicial departments, or by a judge of the New York city civil court or the New York city criminal court; (e) have and carry concealed while so employed by a regular employee of an institution of the state, or of any county, city, town or village, under control of a commissioner of correction of the city or any warden, superintendent or head keeper of any state prison, penitentiary, workhouse, county jail or other institution for the detention of persons convicted or accused of crime or held as witnesses in criminal cases, provided that application is made therefor by such commissioner, warden, superintendent or head keeper; (f) have and carry concealed, without regard to employment or place of possession, by any person when proper cause exists for the issuance thereof; and (g) have, possess, collect and carry antique pistols which are defined as follows: (i) any single shot, muzzle loading pistol with a matchlock, flintlock, percussion cap, or similar type of ignition system manufactured in or before 1898, which is not designed for using rimfire or conventional centerfire fixed ammunition; and (ii) any replica of any pistol described in clause (i) hereof if such replica-

(1) is not designed or redesigned for using rimfire or conventional centerfire fixed ammunition, or

(2) uses rimfire or conventional centerfire fixed ammunition which is no longer manufactured in the United States and which is not readily available in the ordinary channels of commercial trade.

3. Applications. (a) Applications shall be made and renewed, in the case of a license to carry or possess a pistol or revolver, to the licensing officer in the city or county, as the case may be, where the applicant resides, is principally employed or has his or her principal place of business as merchant or storekeeper; and, in the case of a license as gunsmith or dealer in firearms, to the licensing officer where such place of business is located. Blank applications shall, except in the city of New York, be approved as to form by the superintendent of state police. An application shall state the full name, date of birth, residence, present occupation of each person or individual signing the same, whether or not he or she is a citizen of the United States, whether or not he or she complies with each requirement for eligibility specified in subdivision one of this section and such other facts as may be required to show the good character, competency and integrity of each person or individual signing the application. An application shall be signed and verified by the applicant. Each individual signing an application shall submit one photograph of himself or herself and a duplicate for each required copy of the application. Such photographs shall have been taken within thirty days prior to filing the application. In case of a license as gunsmith or dealer in firearms, the photographs submitted shall be two inches square, and the application shall also state the previous occupation of each individual signing the same and the location of the place of such business, or of the bureau, agency, subagency, office or branch office for which the license is sought, specifying the name of the city, town or village, indicating the street and number and otherwise giving such apt description as to point out reasonably the location thereof. In such case, if the applicant is a firm, partnership or corporation, its name, date and place of formation, and principal place of business shall be stated. For such firm or partnership, the application shall be signed and verified by each individual composing or intending to compose the same, and for such corporation, by each officer thereof.

(b) Application for an exemption under paragraph seven-b of subdivision a of section 265.20 of this chapter. Each applicant desiring to obtain the exemption set forth in paragraph seven-b of subdivision a of section 265.20 of this chapter shall make such request in writing of the licensing officer with whom his application for a license is filed, at the time of filing such application. Such request shall include a signed and verified statement by the person authorized to instruct and supervise the applicant, that has met with the applicant and that he has determined that, in his judgment, said applicant does not appear to be or poses a threat to be, a danger to himself or to others. He shall include a copy of his certificate as an instructor in small arms, if he is required to be certified, and state his address and telephone number. He shall specify the exact location by name, address and telephone number where such instruction will take place. Such licensing officer shall, no later than ten business days after such filing, request the duly constituted police authorities of the locality where such application is made to investigate and ascertain any previous criminal record of the applicant pursuant to subdivision four of this section. Upon completion of this investigation, the police authority shall report the results to the licensing officer without unnecessary delay. The licensing officer shall no later than ten business days after the receipt of such investigation, determine if the applicant has been previously denied a license, been convicted of a felony, or been convicted of a serious offense, and either approve or disapprove the applicant for exemption purposes based upon such determinations. If the applicant is approved for the exemption, the licensing officer shall notify the appropriate duly constituted police authorities and the applicant. Such exemption shall terminate if the application for the license is denied, or at any earlier time based upon any information obtained by the licensing officer or the appropriate police authorities which would cause the license to be denied. The applicant and appropriate police authorities shall be notified of any such terminations.

4. Investigation. Before a license is issued or renewed, there shall be an investigation of all statements required in the application by the duly constituted police authorities of the locality where such application is made, including but not limited to such records as may be accessible to the division of state police or division of criminal justice services pursuant to section 400.02 of this article. For that purpose, the records of the appropriate office of the department of mental hygiene concerning previous or present mental illness of the applicant shall be available for inspection by the investigating officer of the police authority. Where the applicant is domiciled in a foreign state, the investigation shall include inquiry of the foreign state for records concerning the previous or present mental illness of the applicant, and, to the extent necessary for inspection by the investigating officer, the applicant shall execute a waiver of confidentiality of such record in such form as may be required by the foreign state. In order to ascertain any previous criminal record, the investigating officer shall take the fingerprints and physical descriptive data in quadruplicate of each individual by whom the application is signed and verified. Two copies of such fingerprints shall be taken on standard fingerprint cards eight inches square, and one copy may be taken on a card supplied for that purpose by the federal bureau of investigation; provided, however, that in the case of a corporate applicant that has already been issued a dealer in firearms license and seeks to operate a firearm dealership at a second or subsequent location, the original fingerprints on file may be used to ascertain any criminal record in the second or subsequent application unless any of the corporate officers have changed since the prior application, in which case the new corporate officer shall comply with procedures governing an initial application for such license. When completed, one standard card shall be forwarded to and retained by the division of criminal justice services in the executive department, at Albany. A search of the files of such division and written notification of the results of the search to the investigating officer shall be made without unnecessary delay. Thereafter, such division shall notify the licensing officer and the executive department, division of state police, Albany, of any criminal record of the applicant filed therein subsequent to the search of its files. A second standard card, or the one supplied by the federal bureau of investigation, as the case may be, shall be forwarded to that bureau at Washington with a request that the files of the bureau be searched and notification of the results of the search be made to the investigating police authority. Of the remaining two fingerprint cards, one shall be filed with the executive department,

division of state police, Albany, within ten days after issuance of the license, and the other remain on file with the investigating police authority. No such fingerprints may be inspected by any person other than a peace officer, who is acting pursuant to his or her special duties, or a police officer, except on order of a judge or justice of a court of record either upon notice to the licensee or without notice, as the judge or justice may deem appropriate. Upon completion of the investigation, the police authority shall report the results to the licensing officer without unnecessary delay. *(Eff.11/2/19,Ch.242,L.2019)*

4-a. Processing of license applications. Applications for licenses shall be accepted for processing by the licensing officer at the time of presentment. Except upon written notice to the applicant specifically stating the reasons for any delay, in each case the licensing officer shall act upon any application for a license pursuant to this section within six months of the date of presentment of such an application to the appropriate authority. Such delay may only be for good cause and with respect to the applicant. In acting upon an application, the licensing officer shall either deny the application for reasons specifically and concisely stated in writing or grant the application and issue the license applied for.

4-b. Westchester county firearms safety course certificate. In the county of Westchester, at the time of application, the licensing officer to which the license application is made shall provide a copy of the safety course booklet to each license applicant. Before such license is issued, such licensing officer shall require that the applicant submit a certificate of successful completion of a firearms safety course and test issued in his or her name and endorsed and affirmed under the penalties of perjury by a duly authorized instructor.

5. Filing of approved applications. (a) The application for any license, if granted, shall be filed by the licensing officer with the clerk of the county of issuance, except that in the city of New York and, in the counties of Nassau and Suffolk, the licensing officer shall designate the place of filing in the appropriate division, bureau or unit of the police department thereof, and in the county of Suffolk the county clerk is hereby authorized to transfer all records or applications relating to firearms to the licensing authority of that county. Except as provided in paragraphs (b) through (f) of this subdivision, the name and address of any person to whom an application for any license has been granted shall be a public record. Upon application by a licensee who has changed his place of residence such records or applications shall be transferred to the appropriate officer at the licensee's new place of residence. A duplicate copy of such application shall be filed by the licensing officer in the executive department, division of state police, Albany, within ten days after issuance of the license. The superintendent of state police may designate that such application shall be transmitted to the division of state police electronically. In the event the superintendent of the division of state police determines that it lacks any of the records required to be filed with the division, it may request that such records be provided to it by the appropriate clerk, department or authority and such clerk, department or authority shall provide the division with such records. In the event such clerk, department or authority lacks such records, the division may request the license holder

provide information sufficient to constitute such record and such license holder shall provide the division with such information. Such information shall be limited to the license holder's name, date of birth, gender, race, residential address, social security number and firearms possessed by said license holder. Nothing in this subdivision shall be construed to change the expiration date or term of such licenses if otherwise provided for in law. Records assembled or collected for purposes of inclusion in the database established by this section shall be released pursuant to a court order. Records assembled or collected for purposes of inclusion in the database created pursuant to section 400.02 of this chapter shall not be subject to disclosure pursuant to article six of the public officers law.

(b) Each application for a license pursuant to paragraph (a) of this subdivision shall include, on a separate written form prepared by the division of state police within thirty days of the effective date of the chapter of the laws of two thousand thirteen, which amended this section, and provided to the applicant at the same time and in the same manner as the application for a license, an opportunity for the applicant to request an exception from his or her application information becoming public record pursuant to paragraph (a) of this subdivision. Such forms, which shall also be made available to individuals who had applied for or been granted a license prior to the effective date of the chapter of the laws of two thousand thirteen which amended this section, shall notify applicants that, upon discovery that an applicant knowingly provided false information, such applicant may be subject to penalties pursuant to section 175.30 of this chapter, and further, that his or her request for an exception shall be null and void, provided that written notice containing such determination is provided to the applicant. Further, such forms shall provide each applicant an opportunity to specify the grounds on which he or she believes his or her application information should not be publicly disclosed. These grounds, which shall be identified on the application with a box beside each for checking, as applicable, by the applicant, shall be as follows:

(i) the applicant's life or safety may be endangered by disclosure because:

(A) the applicant is an active or retired police officer, peace officer, probation officer, parole officer, or corrections officer;

(B) the applicant is a protected person under a currently valid order of protection;   (C) the applicant is or was a witness in a criminal proceeding involving a criminal charge;

(D) the applicant is participating or previously participated as a juror in a criminal proceeding, or is or was a member of a grand jury; or

(E) the applicant is a spouse, domestic partner or household member of a person identified in this subparagraph or subparagraph (ii) of this paragraph, specifying which subparagraph or subparagraphs and clauses apply.

(ii) the applicant has reason to believe his or her life or safety may be endangered by disclosure due to reasons stated by the applicant.

(iii) the applicant has reason to believe he or she may be subject to unwarranted harassment upon disclosure of such information.

(c) Each form provided for recertification pursuant to paragraph (b) of subdivision ten of this section shall include an opportunity for the applicant to request an exception from the information provided on such form becoming public record pursuant to paragraph (a) of this subdivision. Such forms shall notify applicants that, upon discovery that an applicant knowingly provided false information, such applicant may be subject to penalties pursuant to section 175.30 of this chapter, and further, that his or her request for an exception shall be null and void, provided that written notice containing such determination is provided to the applicant. Further, such forms shall provide each applicant an opportunity to either decline to request the grant or continuation of an exception, or specify the grounds on which he or she believes his or her information should not be publicly disclosed. These grounds, which shall be identified in the application with a box beside each for checking, as applicable, by the applicant, shall be the same as provided in paragraph (b) of this subdivision.

(d) Information submitted on the forms described in paragraph (b) of this subdivision shall be excepted from disclosure and maintained by the entity retaining such information separate and apart from all other records.

(e) (i) Upon receiving a request for exception from disclosure, the licensing officer shall grant such exception, unless the request is determined to be null and void, pursuant to paragraph (b) or (c) of this subdivision.

(ii) A request for an exception from disclosure may be submitted at any time, including after a license or recertification has been granted.

(iii) If an exception is sought and granted pursuant to paragraph (b) of this subdivision, the application information shall not be public record, unless the request is determined to be null and void. If an exception is sought and granted pursuant to paragraph (c) of this subdivision, the information concerning such recertification application shall not be public record, unless the request is determined to be null and void. Notwithstanding the foregoing provisions of this subparagraph, local and state law enforcement shall, upon request, be granted access to and copies of such application information provided that such information obtained by law enforcement pursuant to this subparagraph shall not be considered a public record of such law enforcement agency. *(Eff.9/3/19,Ch.244,L.2019)*

(f) The information of licensees or applicants for a license shall not be disclosed to the public during the first one hundred twenty days following the effective date of the chapter of the laws of two thousand thirteen, which amended this section. After such period, the information of those who had applied for or been granted a license prior to the preparation of the form for requesting an exception, pursuant to paragraph (b) of this subdivision, may be released only if such individuals did not file a request for such an exception during the first sixty days following such preparation; provided, however, that no information contained in an application for licensure or recertification shall be disclosed by an entity that has not completed processing any such requests received during such sixty days.

(g) If a request for an exception is determined to be null and void pursuant to paragraph (b) or (c) of this subdivision, an applicant may request review of such determination pursuant to article seventy-eight of the civil practice laws and rules. Such proceeding must commence within thirty days after service of the written notice containing the adverse determination. Notice of the right to commence such a petition, and the time period therefor, shall be included in the notice of the determination. Disclosure following such a petition shall not be made prior to the disposition of such review.

6. License: validity. Any license issued pursuant to this section shall be valid notwithstanding the provisions of any local law or ordinance. No license shall be transferable to any other person or premises. A license to carry or possess a pistol or revolver, not otherwise limited as to place or time of possession, shall be effective throughout the state, except that the same shall not be valid within the city of New York unless a special permit granting validity is issued by the police commissioner of that city. Such license to carry or possess shall be valid within the city of New York in the absence of a permit issued by the police commissioner of that city, provided that (a) the firearms covered by such license have been purchased from a licensed dealer within the city of New York and are being transported out of said city forthwith and immediately from said dealer by the licensee in a locked container during a continuous and uninterrupted trip; or provided that (b) the firearms covered by such license are being transported by the licensee in a locked container and the trip through the city of New York is continuous and uninterrupted; or provided that (c) the firearms covered by such license are carried by armored car security guards transporting money or other valuables, in, to, or from motor vehicles commonly known as armored cars, during the course of their employment; or provided that (d) the licensee is a retired police officer as police officer is defined pursuant to subdivision thirty-four of section 1.20 of the criminal procedure law or a retired federal law enforcement officer, as defined in section 2.15 of the criminal procedure law, who has been issued a license by an authorized licensing officer as defined in subdivision ten of section 265.00 of this chapter; provided, further, however, that if such license was not issued in the city of New York it must be marked "Retired Police Officer" or "Retired Federal Law Enforcement Officer", as the case may be, and, in the case of a retired officer the license shall be deemed to permit only police or federal law enforcement regulations weapons; or provided that (e) the licensee is a peace officer described in subdivision four of section 2.10 of the criminal procedure law and the license, if issued by other than the city of New York, is marked "New York State Tax Department Peace Officer" and in such case the exemption shall apply only to the firearm issued to such licensee by the department of taxation and finance. A license as gunsmith or dealer in firearms shall not be valid outside the city or county, as the case may be, where issued. Notwithstanding any inconsistent provision of state or local law or rule or regulation, the premises limitation set forth in any license to have and possess a pistol or revolver in the licensee's dwelling or place of business pursuant to paragraph (a) or (b) of subdivision two of this section shall not prevent

the transport of such pistol or revolver directly to or from (i) another dwelling or place of business of the licensee where the licensee is authorized to have and possess such pistol or revolver, (ii) an indoor or outdoor shooting range that is authorized by law to operate as such, (iii) a shooting competition at which the licensee may possess such pistol or revolver consistent with the provisions of subdivision a of section 265.20 of this chapter or consistent with the law applicable at the place of such competition, or (iv) any other location where the licensee is lawfully authorized to have and possess such pistol or revolver; provided however, that during such transport to or from a location specified in clauses (i) through (iv) of this paragraph, the pistol or revolver shall be unloaded and carried in a locked container, and the ammunition therefor shall be carried separately; provided further, however, that a license to have and possess a pistol or revolver in the licensee's dwelling or place of business pursuant to paragraph (a) or (b) of subdivision two of this section that is issued by a licensing officer other than the police commissioner of the city of New York shall not authorize transport of a pistol or revolver into the city of New York in the absence of written authorization to do so by the police commissioner of that city. The term "locked container" shall not include the glove compartment or console of a vehicle. *(Eff. 7/16/19, Ch. 104, L. 2019)*

7. License: form. Any license issued pursuant to this section shall, except in the city of New York, be approved as to form by the superintendent of state police. A license to carry or possess a pistol or revolver shall have attached the licensee's photograph, and a coupon which shall be removed and retained by any person disposing of a firearm to the licensee. Such license shall specify the weapon covered by calibre, make, model, manufacturer's name and serial number, or if none, by any other distinguishing number or identification mark, and shall indicate whether issued to carry on the person or possess on the premises, and if on the premises shall also specify the place where the licensee shall possess the same. If such license is issued to an alien, or to a person not a citizen of and usually a resident in the state, the licensing officer shall state in the license the particular reason for the issuance and the names of the persons certifying to the good character of the applicant. Any license as gunsmith or dealer in firearms shall mention and describe the premises for which it is issued and shall be valid only for such premises.

8. License: exhibition and display. Every licensee while carrying a pistol or revolver shall have on his or her person a license to carry the same. Every person licensed to possess a pistol or revolver on particular premises shall have the license for the same on such premises. Upon demand, the license shall be exhibited for inspection to any peace officer, who is acting pursuant to his or her special duties, or police officer. A license as gunsmith or dealer in firearms shall be prominently displayed on the licensed premises. A gunsmith or dealer of firearms may conduct business temporarily at a location other than the location specified on the license if such temporary location is the location for a gun show or event sponsored by any national, state, or local organization, or any affiliate of any such organization devoted to the collection, competitive use or other sporting use of firearms. Any sale or

transfer at a gun show must also comply with the provisions of article thirty-nine-DD of the general business law. Records of receipt and disposition of firearms transactions conducted at such temporary location shall include the location of the sale or other disposition and shall be entered in the permanent records of the gunsmith or dealer of firearms and retained on the location specified on the license. Nothing in this section shall authorize any licensee to conduct business from any motorized or towed vehicle. A separate fee shall not be required of a licensee with respect to business conducted under this subdivision. Any inspection or examination of inventory or records under this section at such temporary location shall be limited to inventory consisting of, or records related to, firearms held or disposed at such temporary locations. Failure of any licensee to so exhibit or display his or her license, as the case may be, shall be presumptive evidence that he or she is not duly licensed.

9. License: amendment. Elsewhere than in the city of New York, a person licensed to carry or possess a pistol or revolver may apply at any time to his or her licensing officer for amendment of his or her license to include one or more such weapons or to cancel weapons held under license. If granted, a record of the amendment describing the weapons involved shall be filed by the licensing officer in the executive department, division of state police, Albany. The superintendent of state police may authorize that such amendment be completed and transmitted to the state police in electronic form. Notification of any change of residence shall be made in writing by any licensee within ten days after such change occurs, and a record of such change shall be inscribed by such licensee on the reverse side of his or her license. Elsewhere than in the city of New York, and in the counties of Nassau and Suffolk, such notification shall be made to the executive department, division of state police, Albany, and in the city of New York to the police commissioner of that city, and in the county of Nassau to the police commissioner of that county, and in the county of Suffolk to the licensing officer of that county, who shall, within ten days after such notification shall be received by him or her, give notice in writing of such change to the executive department, division of state police, at Albany.

10. License: expiration, certification and renewal. (a) Any license for gunsmith or dealer in firearms and, in the city of New York, any license to carry or possess a pistol or revolver, issued at any time pursuant to this section or prior to the first day of July, nineteen hundred sixty-three and not limited to expire on an earlier date fixed in the license, shall expire not more than three years after the date of issuance. In the counties of Nassau, Suffolk and Westchester, any license to carry or possess a pistol or revolver, issued at any time pursuant to this section or prior to the first day of July, nineteen hundred sixty-three and not limited to expire on an earlier date fixed in the license, shall expire not more than five years after the date of issuance; however, in the county of Westchester, any such license shall be certified prior to the first day of April, two thousand, in accordance with a schedule to be contained in regulations promulgated by the commissioner of the division of criminal justice services, and every such license shall be recertified every five

years thereafter. For purposes of this section certification shall mean that the licensee shall provide to the licensing officer the following information only: current name, date of birth, current address, and the make, model, caliber and serial number of all firearms currently possessed. Such certification information shall be filed by the licensing officer in the same manner as an amendment. Elsewhere than in the city of New York and the counties of Nassau, Suffolk and Westchester, any license to carry or possess a pistol or revolver, issued at any time pursuant to this section or prior to the first day of July, nineteen hundred sixty-three and not previously revoked or cancelled, shall be in force and effect until revoked as herein provided. Any license not previously cancelled or revoked shall remain in full force and effect for thirty days beyond the stated expiration date on such license. Any application to renew a license that has not previously expired, been revoked or cancelled shall thereby extend the term of the license until disposition of the application by the licensing officer. In the case of a license for gunsmith or dealer in firearms, in counties having a population of less than two hundred thousand inhabitants, photographs and fingerprints shall be submitted on original applications and upon renewal thereafter only at six year intervals. Upon satisfactory proof that a currently valid original license has been despoiled, lost or otherwise removed from the possession of the licensee and upon application containing an additional photograph of the licensee, the licensing officer shall issue a duplicate license.

(b) All licensees shall be recertified to the division of state police every five years thereafter. Any license issued before the effective date of the chapter of the laws of two thousand thirteen which added this paragraph shall be recertified by the licensee on or before January thirty-first, two thousand eighteen, and not less than one year prior to such date, the state police shall send a notice to all license holders who have not recertified by such time. Such recertification shall be in a form as approved by the superintendent of state police, which shall request the license holder's name, date of birth, gender, race, residential address, social security number, firearms possessed by such license holder, email address at the option of the license holder and an affirmation that such license holder is not prohibited from possessing firearms. The form may be in an electronic form if so designated by the superintendent of state police. Failure to recertify shall act as a revocation of such license. If the New York state police discover as a result of the recertification process that a licensee failed to provide a change of address, the New York state police shall not require the licensing officer to revoke such license.

11. License: revocation and suspension. (a) The conviction of a licensee anywhere of a felony or serious offense or a licensee at any time becoming ineligible to obtain a license under this section shall operate as a revocation of the license. A license may be revoked or suspended as provided for in section 530.14 of the criminal procedure law or section eight hundred forty-two-a of the family court act. Except for a license issued pursuant to section 400.01 of this article, a license may be revoked and cancelled at any time in the city of New York, and in the counties of Nassau and Suffolk, by the licensing officer, and elsewhere than in the city of New York by any judge or justice of a

court of record; a license issued pursuant to section 400.01 of this article may be revoked and cancelled at any time by the licensing officer or any judge or justice of a court of record. The official revoking a license shall give written notice thereof without unnecessary delay to the executive department, division of state police, Albany, and shall also notify immediately the duly constituted police authorities of the locality.

(b) Whenever the director of community services or his or her designee makes a report pursuant to section 9.46 of the mental hygiene law, the division of criminal justice services shall convey such information, whenever it determines that the person named in the report possesses a license issued pursuant to this section, to the appropriate licensing official, who shall issue an order suspending or revoking such license.

(c) In any instance in which a person's license is suspended or revoked under paragraph (a) or (b) of this subdivision, such person shall surrender such license to the appropriate licensing official and any and all firearms, rifles, or shotguns owned or possessed by such person shall be surrendered to an appropriate law enforcement agency as provided in subparagraph (f) of paragraph one of subdivision a of section 265.20 of this chapter. In the event such license, firearm, shotgun, or rifle is not surrendered, such items shall be removed and declared a nuisance and any police officer or peace officer acting pursuant to his or her special duties is authorized to remove any and all such weapons.

12. Records required of gunsmiths and dealers in firearms. Any person licensed as gunsmith or dealer in firearms shall keep a record book approved as to form, except in the city of New York, by the superintendent of state police. In the record book shall be entered at the time of every transaction involving a firearm the date, name, age, occupation and residence of any person from whom a firearm is received or to whom a firearm is delivered, and the calibre, make, model, manufacturer's name and serial number, or if none, any other distinguishing number or identification mark on such firearm. Before delivering a firearm to any person, the licensee shall require him to produce either a license valid under this section to carry or possess the same, or proof of lawful authority as an exempt person pursuant to section 265.20 of this chapter and either (a) the National Instant Criminal Background Check System (NICS) or its successor has issued a "proceed" response to the licensee, or (b) thirty calendar days have elapsed since the date the licensee contacted NICS to initiate a national instant criminal background check and NICS has not notified the licensee that the transfer of the firearm to such person should be denied. In addition, before delivering a firearm to a peace officer, the licensee shall verify that person's status as a peace officer with the division of state police. After completing the foregoing, the licensee shall remove and retain the attached coupon and enter in the record book the date of such license, number, if any, and name of the licensing officer, in the case of the holder of a license to carry or possess, or the shield or other number, if any, assignment and department, unit or agency, in the case of an exempt person. The original transaction report shall be forwarded

to the division of state police within ten days of delivering a firearm to any person, and a duplicate copy shall be kept by the licensee. The superintendent of state police may designate that such record shall be completed and transmitted in electronic form. A dealer may be granted a waiver from transmitting such records in electronic form if the superintendent determines that such dealer is incapable of such transmission due to technological limitations that are not reasonably within the control of the dealer, or other exceptional circumstances demonstrated by the dealer, pursuant to a process established in regulation, and at the discretion of the superintendent. Records assembled or collected for purposes of inclusion in the database created pursuant to section 400.02 of this article shall not be subject to disclosure pursuant to article six of the public officers law. The record book shall be maintained on the premises mentioned and described in the license and shall be open at all reasonable hours for inspection by any peace officer, acting pursuant to his special duties, or police officer. In the event of cancellation or revocation of the license for gunsmith or dealer in firearms, or discontinuance of business by a licensee, such record book shall be immediately surrendered to the licensing officer in the city of New York, and in the counties of Nassau and Suffolk, and elsewhere in the state to the executive department, division of state police. *(Eff.9/12/19,Ch.129,L.2019)*

12-a. State police regulations applicable to licensed gunsmiths engaged in the business of assembling or manufacturing firearms. The superintendent of state police is hereby authorized to issue such rules and regulations as he deems reasonably necessary to prevent the manufacture and assembly of unsafe firearms in the state. Such rules and regulations shall establish safety standards in regard to the manufacture and assembly of firearms in the state, including specifications as to materials and parts used, the proper storage and shipment of firearms, and minimum standards of quality control. Regulations issued by the state police pursuant to this subdivision shall apply to any person licensed as a gunsmith under this section engaged in the business of manufacturing or assembling firearms, and any violation thereof shall subject the licensee to revocation of license pursuant to subdivision eleven of this section.

12-c. Firearms records. (a) Every employee of a state or local agency, unit of local government, state or local commission, or public or private organization who possesses a firearm or machine-gun under an exemption to the licensing requirements under this chapter, shall promptly report in writing to his employer the make, model, calibre and serial number of each such firearm or machine-gun. Thereafter, within ten days of the acquisition or disposition of any such weapon, he shall furnish such information to his employer, including the name and address of the person from whom the weapon was acquired or to whom it was disposed.

(b) Every head of a state or local agency, unit of local government, state or local commission, public authority or public or private organization to whom an employee has submitted a report pursuant to paragraph (a) of this subdivision shall promptly forward such report to the superintendent of state police.

(c) Every head of a state or local agency, unit of local government, state or local commission, public authority, or any other agency, firm or corporation that employs persons who may lawfully possess firearms or machine-guns without the requirement of a license therefor, or that employs persons licensed to possess firearms or machine-guns, shall promptly report to the superintendent of state police, in the manner prescribed by him, the make, model, calibre and serial number of every firearm or machine-gun possessed by it on the effective date of this act for the use of such employees or for any other use. Thereafter, within ten days of the acquisition or disposition of any such weapon, such head shall report such information to the superintendent of the state police, including the name and address of the person from whom the weapon was acquired or to whom it was disposed.

13. Expenses. The expense of providing a licensing officer with blank applications, licenses and record books for carrying out the provisions of this section shall be a charge against the county, and in the city of New York against the city.

14. Fees. In the city of New York and the county of Nassau, the annual license fee shall be twenty-five dollars for gunsmiths and fifty dollars for dealers in firearms. In such city, the city council and in the county of Nassau the Board of Supervisors shall fix the fee to be charged for a license to carry or possess a pistol or revolver and provide for the disposition of such fees. Elsewhere in the state, the licensing officer shall collect and pay into the county treasury the following fees: for each license to carry or possess a pistol or revolver, not less than three dollars nor more than ten dollars as may be determined by the legislative body of the county; for each amendment thereto, three dollars, and five dollars in the county of Suffolk; and for each license issued to a gunsmith or dealer in firearms, ten dollars. The fee for a duplicate license shall be five dollars. The fee for processing a license transfer between counties shall be five dollars. The fee for processing a license or renewal thereof for a qualified retired police officer as defined under subdivision thirty-four of section 1.20 of the criminal procedure law, or a qualified retired sheriff, undersheriff, or deputy sheriff of the city of New York as defined under subdivision two of section 2.10 of the criminal procedure law, or a qualified retired bridge and tunnel officer, sergeant or lieutenant of the triborough bridge and tunnel authority as defined under subdivision twenty of section 2.10 of the criminal procedure law, or a qualified retired uniformed court officer in the unified court system, or a qualified retired court clerk in the unified court system in the first and second judicial departments, as defined in paragraphs a and b of subdivision twenty-one of section 2.10 of the criminal procedure law or a retired correction officer as defined in subdivision twenty-five of section 2.10 of the criminal procedure law shall be waived in all counties throughout the state.

15. Any violation by any person of any provision of this section is a class A misdemeanor.

16. Unlawful disposal. No person shall except as otherwise authorized pursuant to law dispose of any firearm unless he is licensed as gunsmith or dealer in firearms.

16-a. Registration. (a) An owner of a weapon defined in paragraph (e) or (f) of subdivision twenty-two of section 265.00 of this chapter, possessed before the date of the effective date of the chapter of the laws of two thousand thirteen which added this paragraph, must make an application to register such weapon with the superintendent of state police, in the manner provided by the superintendent, or by amending a license issued pursuant to this section within one year of the effective date of this subdivision except any weapon defined under subparagraph (vi) of paragraph (g) of subdivision twenty-two of section 265.00 of this chapter transferred into the state may be registered at any time, provided such weapons are registered within thirty days of their transfer into the state. Registration information shall include the registrant's name, date of birth, gender, race, residential address, social security number and a description of each weapon being registered. A registration of any weapon defined under subparagraph (vi) of paragraph (g) of subdivision twenty-two of section 265.00 or a feeding device as defined under subdivision twenty-three of section 265.00 of this chapter shall be transferable, provided that the seller notifies the state police within seventy-two hours of the transfer and the buyer provides the state police with information sufficient to constitute a registration under this section. Such registration shall not be valid if such registrant is prohibited or becomes prohibited from possessing a firearm pursuant to state or federal law. The superintendent shall determine whether such registrant is prohibited from possessing a firearm under state or federal law. Such check shall be limited to determining whether the factors in 18 USC 922 (g) apply or whether a registrant has been convicted of a serious offense as defined in subdivision sixteen-b of section 265.00 of this chapter, so as to prohibit such registrant from possessing a firearm, and whether a report has been issued pursuant to section 9.46 of the mental hygiene law. All registrants shall recertify to the division of state police every five years thereafter. Failure to recertify shall result in a revocation of such registration.

(a-1) Notwithstanding any inconsistent provisions of paragraph (a) of this subdivision, an owner of an assault weapon as defined in subdivision twenty-two of section 265.00 of this chapter, who is a qualified retired New York or federal law enforcement officer as defined in subdivision twenty-five of section 265.00 of this chapter, where such weapon was issued to or purchased by such officer prior to retirement and in the course of his or her official duties, and for which such officer was qualified by the agency that employed such officer within twelve months prior to his or her retirement, must register such weapon within sixty days of retirement.

(b) The superintendent of state police shall create and maintain an internet website to educate the public as to which semiautomatic rifle, semiautomatic shotgun or semiautomatic pistol or weapon that are illegal as a result of the enactment of the chapter of the laws of two thousand thirteen which added this paragraph, as well as such assault weapons which are illegal pursuant to article two hundred sixty-five of this chapter. Such website shall contain information to assist the public in recognizing the relevant features proscribed by such article two hundred sixty-five, as well as which make and model of weapons that require registration.

(c) A person who knowingly fails to apply to register such weapon, as required by this section, within one year of the effective date of the chapter of the laws of two thousand thirteen which added this paragraph shall be guilty of a class A misdemeanor and such person who unknowingly fails to validly register such weapon within such one year period shall be given a warning by an appropriate law enforcement authority about such failure and given thirty days in which to apply to register such weapon or to surrender it. A failure to apply or surrender such weapon within such thirty-day period shall result in such weapon being removed by an appropriate law enforcement authority and declared a nuisance.

16-b. The cost of the software, programming and interface required to transmit any record that must be electronically transmitted by the dealer or licensing officer to the division of state police pursuant to this chapter shall be borne by the state.

17. Applicability of section. The provisions of article two hundred sixty-five of this chapter relating to illegal possession of a firearm, shall not apply to an offense which also constitutes a violation of this section by a person holding an otherwise valid license under the provisions of this section and such offense shall only be punishable as a class A misdemeanor pursuant to this section. In addition, the provisions of such article two hundred sixty-five of this chapter shall not apply to the possession of a firearm in a place not authorized by law, by a person who holds an otherwise valid license or possession of a firearm by a person within a one year period after the stated expiration date of an otherwise valid license which has not been previously cancelled or revoked shall only be punishable as a class A misdemeanor pursuant to this section.

18. Notice. Upon the issuance of a license, the licensing officer shall issue therewith the following notice in conspicuous and legible twenty-four point type on eight and one-half inches by eleven inches paper stating in bold print the following:

WARNING: RESPONSIBLE FIREARM STORAGE IS THE LAW IN NEW YORK STATE. FIREARMS MUST EITHER BE STORED WITH A GUN LOCKING DEVICE OR IN A SAFE STORAGE DEPOSITORY OR NOT BE LEFT OUTSIDE THE IMMEDIATE POSSESSION AND CONTROL OF THE OWNER OR OTHER LAWFUL POSSESSOR IF A CHILD RESIDES IN THE HOME OR

IS PRESENT, OR IF THE OWNER OR POSSESSOR RESIDES
WITH A PERSON PROHIBITED FROM POSSESSING A FIREARM
UNDER STATE OR FEDERAL LAW. FIREARMS SHOULD BE
STORED UNLOADED AND LOCKED IN A LOCATION
SEPARATE FROM AMMUNITION. LEAVING FIREARMS
ACCESSIBLE TO A CHILD OR OTHER PROHIBITED PERSON
MAY SUBJECT YOU TO IMPRISONMENT, FINE, OR BOTH.

Nothing in this subdivision shall be deemed to affect, impair or
supersede any special or local law relating to providing notice regarding
the safe storage of rifles, shotguns or firearms.   *(Eff.9/28/19,Ch.135,L.2019)*

§400.01 License to carry and possess firearms for retired sworn members of the division of state police.

1. A license to carry or possess a firearm for a retired sworn member
of the division of state police shall be granted in the same manner and
upon the same terms and conditions as licenses issued under section
400.00 of this article provided, however, that applications for such
license may be made to, and the licensing officer may be, the
superintendent of state police.

2. For purposes of this section, a "retired sworn member of the
division of state police" shall mean a former sworn member of the
division of state police, who upon separation from the division of state
police was immediately entitled to receive retirement benefits under the
provisions of the retirement and social security law.

3. The provisions of this section shall only apply to license
applications made or renewals which must be made on or after the
effective date of this section. A license to carry or possess a pistol or
revolver issued pursuant to the provisions of section 400.00 of this
article to a person covered by the provisions of this section shall be valid
until such license would have expired pursuant to the provisions of
section 400.00 of this article; provided that, on or after the effective date
of this section, an application or renewal of such license shall be made
pursuant to the provisions of this section.

4. Except for the designation of the superintendent of state police as
the licensing officer for retired sworn members of the division of state
police who have opted to obtain such license under this section, all of
the provisions and requirements of section 400.00 of this article and any
other provision of law shall be applicable to individuals licensed
pursuant to this section. In addition all provisions of section 400.00 of
this article, except for the designation of the superintendent of state
police as licensing officer are hereby deemed applicable to individuals
licensed pursuant to this section.

§400.02 Statewide license and record database.

There shall be a statewide license and record database which shall be created and maintained by the division of state police the cost of which shall not be borne by any municipality. Records assembled or collected for purposes of inclusion in such database shall not be subject to disclosure pursuant to article six of the public officers law. Records containing granted license applications shall be periodically checked by the division of criminal justice services against criminal conviction, mental health, and all other records as are necessary to determine their continued accuracy as well as whether an individual is no longer a valid license holder. The division of criminal justice services shall also check pending applications made pursuant to this article against such records to determine whether a license may be granted. All state agencies shall cooperate with the division of criminal justice services, as otherwise authorized by law, in making their records available for such checks. The division of criminal justice services, upon determining that an individual is ineligible to possess a license, or is no longer a valid license holder, shall notify the applicable licensing official of such determination and such licensing official shall not issue a license or revoke such license and any weapons owned or possessed by such individual shall be removed consistent with the provisions of subdivision eleven of section 400.00 of this article. Local and state law enforcement shall have access to such database in the performance of their duties. Records assembled or collected for purposes of inclusion in the database established by this section shall be released pursuant to a court order.   *(Eff.9/3/19,Ch.244,L.2019)*

§400.03 Sellers of ammunition.

1. A seller of ammunition as defined in subdivision twenty-four of section 265.00 of this chapter shall register with the superintendent of

state police in a manner provided by the superintendent. Any dealer in firearms that is validly licensed pursuant to section 400.00 of this article shall not be required to complete such registration.

2. Any seller of ammunition or dealer in firearms shall keep a record book approved as to form by the superintendent of state police. In the record book shall be entered at the time of every transaction involving ammunition the date, name, age, occupation and residence of any person from whom ammunition is received or to whom ammunition is delivered, and the amount, calibre, manufacturer's name and serial number, or if none, any other distinguishing number or identification mark on such ammunition. The record book shall be maintained on the premises mentioned and described in the license and shall be open at all reasonable hours for inspection by any peace officer, acting pursuant to his or her special duties, or police officer. Any record produced pursuant to this section and any transmission thereof to any government agency shall not be considered a public record for purposes of article six of the public officers law.

3. No later than thirty days after the superintendent of the state police certifies that the statewide license and record database established pursuant to section 400.02 of this article is operational for the purposes of this section, a dealer in firearms licensed pursuant to section 400.00 of this article, a seller of ammunition as defined in subdivision twenty-four of section 265.00 of this chapter shall not transfer any ammunition to any other person who is not a dealer in firearms as defined in subdivision nine of such section 265.00 or a seller of ammunition as defined in subdivision twenty-four of section 265.00 of this chapter, unless:

(a) before the completion of the transfer, the licensee or seller contacts the statewide license and record database and provides the database with information sufficient to identify such dealer or seller, transferee based on information on the transferee's identification document as defined in paragraph (c) of this subdivision, as well as the amount, calibre, manufacturer's name and serial number, if any, of such ammunition;

(b) the system provides the licensee or seller with a unique identification number; and

(c) the transferor has verified the identity of the transferee by examining a valid state identification document of the transferee issued by the department of motor vehicles or if the transferee is not a resident of the state of New York, a valid identification document issued by the transferee's state or country of residence containing a photograph of the transferee.

4. If the database determines that the purchaser of ammunition is eligible to possess ammunition pursuant to state and federal laws, the system shall:

(a) assign a unique identification number to the transfer; and

(b) provide the licensee or seller with the number.

5. If the statewide license and record database notifies the licensee or seller that the information available to the database does not

demonstrate that the receipt of ammunition by such other person would violate 18 U.S.C. 922(g) or state law, and the licensee transfers ammunition to such other person, the licensee shall indicate to the database that such transaction has been completed at which point a record of such transaction shall be created which shall be accessible by the division of state police and maintained for no longer than one year from point of purchase, which shall not be incorporated into the database established pursuant to section 400.02 of this article or the registry established pursuant to subdivision sixteen-a of section 400.00 of this article. The division of state police may share such information with a local law enforcement agency. Evidence of the purchase of ammunition is not sufficient to establish probable cause to believe that the purchaser has committed a crime absent other information tending to prove the commission of a crime. Records assembled or accessed pursuant to this section shall not be subject to disclosure pursuant to article six of the public officers law. This requirement of this section shall not apply (i) if a background check cannot be completed because the system is not operational as determined by the superintendent of state police, or where it cannot be accessed by the practitioner due to a temporary technological or electrical failure, as set forth in regulation, or (ii) a dealer or seller has been granted a waiver from conducting such background check if the superintendent of state police determines that such dealer is incapable of such check due to technological limitations that are not reasonably within the control of the dealer, or other exceptional circumstances demonstrated by the dealer, pursuant to a process established in regulation, and at the discretion of such superintendent.

    6. If the superintendent of state police certifies that background checks of ammunition purchasers may be conducted through the national instant criminal background check system, use of that system by a dealer or seller shall be sufficient to satisfy subdivisions four and five of this section and such checks shall be conducted through such system, provided that a record of such transaction shall be forwarded to the state police in a form determined by the superintendent.

    7. No commercial transfer of ammunition shall take place unless a licensed dealer in firearms or registered seller of ammunition acts as an intermediary between the transferor and the ultimate transferee of the ammunition for the purposes of contacting the statewide license and record database pursuant to this section. Such transfer between the dealer or seller, and transferee must occur in person.

    8. A seller of ammunition who fails to register pursuant to this section and sells ammunition, for a first offense, shall be guilty of a violation and subject to the fine of one thousand dollars and for a second offense, shall be guilty of a class A misdemeanor.

    A seller of ammunition that fails to keep any record required pursuant to this section, for a first offense shall be guilty of a violation and subject to a fine of five hundred dollars, and for a second offense shall be guilty of a class B misdemeanor, and the registration of such seller shall be revoked.

§400.05 Disposition of weapons and dangerous instruments, appliances and substances.

1. Any weapon, instrument, appliance or substance specified in article two hundred sixty-five, when unlawfully possessed, manufactured, transported or disposed of, or when utilized in the commission of an offense, is hereby declared a nuisance. When the same shall come into the possession of any police officer or peace officer, it shall be surrendered immediately to the official mentioned in paragraph (f) of subdivision one of section 265.20, except that such weapon, instrument, appliance or substance coming into the possession of the state police shall be surrendered to the superintendent of state police.

2. The official to whom the weapon, instrument, appliance or substance which has subsequently been declared a nuisance pursuant to subdivision one of this section is so surrendered shall, at any time but at least once each year, destroy the same or cause it to be destroyed, or render the same or cause it to be rendered ineffective and useless for its intended purpose and harmless to human life.

3. Notwithstanding subdivision two of this section, the official to whom the weapon, instrument, appliance or substance is so surrendered shall not destroy the same if (a) a judge or justice of a court of record, or a district attorney, shall file with the official a certificate that the non-destruction thereof is necessary or proper to serve the ends of justice; or (b) the official directs that the same be retained in any laboratory conducted by any police or sheriff's department for the purpose of research, comparison, identification or other endeavor toward the prevention and detection of crime.

4. In the case of any machine-gun or firearm taken from the possession of any person, the official to whom such weapon is surrendered pursuant to subdivision one of this section shall immediately notify the executive department, division of state police, Albany, giving the calibre, make, model, manufacturer's name and serial number, or if none, any other distinguishing number or identification mark. A search of the files of such division and notification of the results of the search to such official shall immediately be made.

5. Before any machine-gun or firearm is destroyed pursuant to subdivision two of this section, (a) the official to whom the same has been surrendered shall forward to the executive department, division of state police, Albany, a notice of intent to destroy and the calibre, make, model, manufacturer's name and serial number, or if none, any other distinguishing number or identification mark of the machine-gun or firearm; (b) such division shall make and keep a record of such description together with the name and address of the official reporting the same and the date such notice was received; and (c) a search of the files of such division and notification of the results of the search to such official shall be made without unnecessary delay.

6. A firearm or other weapon which is surrendered, or is otherwise voluntarily delivered pursuant to section 265.20 of this chapter and which has not been declared a nuisance pursuant to subdivision one of this section, shall be retained by the official to whom it was delivered for a period not to exceed one year. Prior to the expiration of such time

period, a person who surrenders a firearm shall have the right to arrange for the sale, or transfer, of such firearm to a dealer in firearms licensed in accordance with this chapter or for the transfer of such firearm to himself or herself provided that a license therefor has been issued in accordance with this chapter. If no lawful disposition of the firearm or other weapon is made within the time provided, the firearm or weapon concerned shall be declared a nuisance and shall be disposed of in accordance with the provisions of this section.

§400.10 Report of theft or loss of a firearm, rifle or shotgun.

1. (a) Any owner or other person lawfully in possession of: (i) a firearm, rifle or, shotgun who suffers the loss or theft of said weapon; (ii) ammunition as well as a firearm, rifle or shotgun who suffers the loss or theft of such ammunition as well as a firearm, rifle or shotgun; or (iii) ammunition and is a dealer in firearms or seller of ammunition who suffers the loss or theft of such ammunition shall within twenty-four hours of the discovery of the loss or theft report the facts and circumstances of the loss or theft to a police department or sheriff's office.

(b) Whenever a person reports the theft or loss of a firearm, rifle, shotgun or ammunition to any police department or sheriff's office, the officer or department receiving such report shall forward notice of such theft or loss to the division of state police via the New York Statewide Police Information Network. The notice shall contain information in compliance with the New York Statewide Police Information Network Operating Manual, including the caliber, make, model, manufacturer's name and serial number, if any, and any other distinguishing number or identification mark on the weapon.

2. The division of state police shall receive, collect and file the information referred to in subdivision one of this section. The division shall cooperate, and undertake to furnish or make available to law enforcement agencies this information, for the purpose of coordinating law enforcement efforts to locate such weapons.

3. Notwithstanding any other provision of law, a violation of paragraph (a) of subdivision one of this section shall be a class A misdemeanor.

§400.20 Waiting period in connection with the sale or transfer of a rifle or shotgun.

When a national instant criminal background check is required pursuant to state or federal law to be conducted through the National Instant Criminal Background Check System (NICS) or its successor in connection with the sale or transfer of a rifle or shotgun to any person, before delivering a rifle or shotgun to such person, either (a) NICS has issued a "proceed" response to the seller or transferor, or (b) thirty calendar days shall have elapsed since the date the seller or transferor contacted NICS to initiate a national instant criminal background check and NICS has not notified the seller or transferor that the transfer of the rifle or shotgun to such person should be denied. *(Eff. 9/12/19, Ch.129, L.2019)*

ARTICLE 405 - LICENSING AND OTHER PROVISIONS RELATING TO FIREWORKS

Section
405.00 Permits for public displays of fireworks.
405.05 Seizure and destruction of fireworks.
405.10 Permits for indoor pyrotechnics.
405.12 Unpermitted use of indoor pyrotechnics in the second degree.
405.14 Unpermitted use of indoor pyrotechnics in the first degree.
405.16 Aggravated unpermitted use of indoor pyrotechnics in the second degree.
405.18 Aggravated unpermitted use of indoor pyrotechnics in the first degree.

§405.00 Permits for public displays of fireworks.

1. Definition of "permit authority." The term "permit authority," as used in this section, means and includes the agency authorized to grant and issue the permits provided in this section. The permit authority on or within state property shall be the office of fire prevention and control. The permit authority for territory within a county park shall be the county park commission, or such other agency having jurisdiction, control and/or operation of the parks or parkways within which any fireworks are to be displayed. The permit authority in a city shall be the duly constituted licensing agency thereof and, in the absence of such agency, shall be an officer designated for the purpose by the legislative body thereof. The permit authority in a village shall be an officer designated for the purpose by the board of trustees thereof and the permit authority in the territory of a town outside of villages shall be an officer designated for the purpose by the town board thereof.

2. Permits for fireworks displays. Notwithstanding the provisions of section 270.00 of this chapter, the permit authority for state property, county parks, cities, villages, or towns may grant a permit for the display of fireworks to municipalities, fair associations, amusement parks, persons, or organizations of individuals that submit an application in writing. The application for such permit shall set forth:

(a) The name of the body sponsoring the display and the names of the persons actually to be in charge of the firing of the display who shall possess a valid certificate of competence as a pyrotechnician as required under the general business law and article sixteen of the labor law. The permit application shall further contain a verified statement from the applicant identifying the individuals who are authorized to fire the display including their certificate numbers, and that such individuals possess a valid certificate of competence as a pyrotechnician.

(b) The date and time of day at which the display is to be held.

(c) The exact location planned for the display.

(d) The number and kind of fireworks to be discharged.

(e) The manner and place of storage of such fireworks prior to the display.

(f) A diagram of the grounds on which the display is to be held showing the point at which the fireworks are to be discharged, the location of all buildings, highways and other lines of communication, the lines behind which the audience will be restrained and the location of all nearby trees, telegraph or telephone lines or other overhead obstructions.

(g) Such other information as the permit authority may deem necessary to protect persons or property.

3. Applications for permits. All applications for permits for the display of fireworks shall be made at least five days in advance of the date of the display and the permit shall contain provisions that the actual point at which the fireworks are to be fired be in accordance with the rules promulgated by the commissioner of labor pursuant to section four hundred sixty-two of the labor law and that all the persons in actual charge of firing the fireworks shall be over the age of eighteen years, competent and physically fit for the task, that there shall be at least two such operators constantly on duty during the discharge and that at least two approved type fire extinguishers shall be kept at as widely separated points as possible within the actual area of the display. For any applications made for the display of fireworks on state property, the state fire administrator shall coordinate the issuance of such permits with the head of the police or fire department or both, where there are such departments. The legislative body of a county park, city, village or town may provide for approval of such permit by the head of the police or fire department or both where there are such departments. No permit granted and issued hereunder shall be transferable. After such permit shall have been granted, sales, possession, use and distribution of fireworks for such display shall be lawful solely therefor.

3-a. Notwithstanding the provisions of subdivision three of this section, no permit may be issued to conduct a display of fireworks upon any property where the boundary line of such property is less than five hundred yards from the boundary line of any property which is owned, leased or operated by any breeder as defined in subdivision four of section two hundred fifty-one of the racing, pari-mutuel wagering and breeding law.

4. Bonds. Before granting and issuing a permit for a display of fireworks as herein provided, the permit authority shall require an adequate bond from the applicant therefor, unless it is a state entity, county park, city, village or town, in a sum to be fixed by the permit authority, which, however, shall not be less than one million dollars, conditioned for the payment of all damages, which may be caused to a person or persons or to property, by reason of the display so permitted and arising from any acts of the permittee, his or her agents, employees, contractors or subcontractors. Such bond shall run to the state if the permit is granted for a display on state property, or to the county park, city, village or town in which the permit is granted and issued and shall be for the use and benefit of any person or persons or any owner or owners of any property so injured or damaged, and such person or persons or such owner or owners are hereby authorized to maintain an action thereon, which right of action also shall accrue to the heirs, executors, administrators, successors or assigns of such person

or persons or such owner or owners. The permit authority may accept, in lieu of such bond, an indemnity insurance policy with liability coverage and indemnity protection equivalent to the terms and conditions upon which such bond is predicated and for the purposes provided in this section.

5. Local ordinances superseded. (a) All local ordinances regulating or prohibiting the display of fireworks are hereby superseded by the provisions of this section. Every city, town or village shall have the power to enact ordinances or local laws regulating or prohibiting the use, or the storage, transportation or sale for use of fireworks in the preparation for or in connection with television broadcasts.

(b) Notwithstanding any inconsistent provision of law, a county may enact a local law to prohibit the sale and use of "sparkling devices", as such term is defined in section 270.00 of this chapter, provided, however, any such local law shall not establish:

(i) an offense greater than a violation for a person who shall use, explode or cause to be exploded a sparkling device; or

(ii) an offense greater than a class B misdemeanor for a person who shall offer or expose for sale, sell or furnish a sparkling device valued at less than five hundred dollars unless such offer, sale or furnishing is to a person less than eighteen years of age.   *(Eff.1/21/18,Ch.371,L.2017)*

(c) Notwithstanding paragraph (b) of this subdivision, any city wholly contained within the county of Orange may enact a local law to prohibit the sale and use of "sparkling devices" as defined in section 270.00 of this chapter, in accordance with subparagraphs (i) and (ii) of paragraph (b) of this subdivision, notwithstanding that such county has not enacted a local law to prohibit the sale and use of such sparkling devices.   *(Eff.1/21/18,Ch.371,L.2017)*

§405.05 Seizure and destruction of fireworks.

Fireworks possessed unlawfully may be seized by any peace officer, acting pursuant to his special duties, or police officer, who must deliver the same to the magistrate before whom the person arrested is required to be taken. The magistrate must, upon the examination of the defendant, or if such examination is delayed or prevented, without awaiting such examination, determine whether the fireworks had been possessed by the defendant in violation of the provisions of section 270.00; and if he finds that the fireworks had been so possessed by the defendant, he must cause such fireworks to be destroyed, in a way safe for the particular type of such fireworks, or to be delivered to the district attorney of the county in which the defendant is liable to indictment or trial, as the interests of justice and public safety may, in his opinion, require. Upon the conviction of the defendant, the district attorney must cause to be destroyed, in a way safe for the particular type of such fireworks, the fireworks in respect whereof the defendant stands convicted, and which remain in the possession or under the control of the district attorney.

§405.10 Permits for indoor pyrotechnics.

1. Definitions. For the purposes of this section, the following terms have the following meanings:

a. Airburst. A pyrotechnic device that is suspended in the air to simulate outdoor aerial fireworks shells without producing hazardous debris.

b. Areas of public assembly. All buildings or portions of buildings used for gathering together fifty or more persons for amusement, athletic, civic, dining, educational, entertainment, patriotic, political, recreational, religious, social, or similar purposes, the entire fire area of which they are a part, and the means of egress therefrom.

c. Assistant. A person who works under the supervision of the pyrotechnic operator.

d. Audience. Spectators whose primary purpose is to view a performance.

e. Building. A combination of any materials, whether portable or fixed, having a roof, to form a structure affording shelter for persons, animals, or property. The word "building" shall be construed for the purposes of this section as though followed by the words "or part or parts thereof", unless the context clearly requires a different meaning.

f. Concussion mortar. A device specifically designed and constructed to produce a loud noise and a violent jarring shock for dramatic effect without producing any damage.

g. Fallout area. The area in which any hazardous debris falls after a pyrotechnic device is fired. The fallout area is defined as a circle that, in turn, is defined by the fallout radius.

h. Fallout radius. A line that defines the fallout area of a pyrotechnic device. The line is defined by two points. The first point is at the center of a pyrotechnic device. The second point is the point most distant from the center of the pyrotechnic device at which any hazardous debris from the device can fall.

i. Fire area. The floor area of a story of a building within exterior walls, party walls, fire walls, or any combination thereof.

j. Hazardous debris. Any debris, produced or expelled by the functioning of a pyrotechnic device, that is capable of causing personal injury or unpredicted property damage. This includes, but is not limited to, hot sparks, heavy casing fragments, and unignited components. Materials such as confetti, lightweight foam pieces, feathers, or novelties are not to be construed as hazardous debris.

k. Owner. Any person, agent, firm, association, limited liability company, partnership, or corporation having a legal or equitable interest in the property.

l. Performance. The enactment of a musical, dramatic, operatic, or other entertainment production. The enactment may begin and progress to its end according to a script, plan, or other preconceived list of events, or deviate therefrom. A performance includes any encores.

m. Performer. Any person active in a performance during which pyrotechnics are used and who is not part of the audience or support personnel. Among others, performers include, but are not limited to, actors, singers, musicians, and acrobats.

n. Permit authority. The agency authorized to grant and issue the permits provided for in this section on or within state property shall be the office of fire prevention and control, in the territory within a county park shall be the county park commission, or such other agency having jurisdiction, control, and/or operation of the parks or parkways within which any pyrotechnics are to be used, in a city shall be the duly constituted licensing agency thereof and, in the absence of such agency, shall be an officer designated for the purpose by the legislative body thereof, in a village shall be an officer designated for the purpose by the board of trustees thereof, and, in the territory of a town outside of villages, shall be an officer designated for the purpose by the town board thereof.

o. Permittee. (1) The person or persons who are responsible, as provided in subparagraph two of this paragraph, for obtaining the necessary permit or permits for the use of indoor pyrotechnics in areas of public assembly or for a production, or who are responsible for obtaining such permit or permits under an applicable local law or ordinance authorized pursuant to subdivision five of this section.

(2) The owner of a place of public assembly or building in which pyrotechnics are to be used shall be responsible for obtaining such permit or permits; provided, however, that such owner, in writing, by agreement or lease, may require or otherwise authorize a lessee, licensee, pyrotechnic operator, or other party to be responsible for obtaining such permit or permits, in which case such other party or parties shall be deemed responsible for obtaining such permit or permits and shall be the permittee for purposes of this article; provided further that the structure is otherwise appropriate for such use under the New York state fire prevention and building code or other such applicable code.

p. Producer. An individual who has overall responsibility for the operation and management of the performance where the pyrotechnics are to be used. Generally, the producer is an employee of the promotion company, entertainment company, festival, theme park, or other entertainment group.

q. Production. All the performances of a musical, dramatic, operatic, or other show or series of shows.

r. Pyrotechnic device. Any device containing pyrotechnic materials and capable of producing a special effect as defined in this subdivision.

s. Pyrotechnic material (Pyrotechnic special effects material). A chemical mixture used in the entertainment industry to produce visible or audible effects by combustion, deflagration, or detonation. Such a chemical mixture consists predominantly of solids capable of producing a controlled, self-sustaining, and self-contained exothermic chemical reaction that results in heat, gas, sound, light, or a combination of these effects. The chemical reaction functions without external oxygen.

t. Pyrotechnic operator (Special effects operator). An individual who has responsibility for pyrotechnic safety and who controls, initiates, or otherwise creates special effects.

u. Pyrotechnic special effect. A special effect created through the use of pyrotechnic materials and devices.

v. Pyrotechnics. Controlled exothermic chemical reactions that are timed to create the effects of heat, gas, sound, dispersion of aerosols, emission of visible electromagnetic radiation, or a combination of these effects to provide the maximum effect from the least volume.

w. Rocket. A pyrotechnic device that moves by the ejection of matter produced by the internal combustion of propellants.

x. Special effect. A visual or audible effect used for entertainment purposes, often produced to create an illusion. For example, smoke might be produced to create the impression of fog being present, or a puff of smoke, a flash of light, and a loud sound might be produced to create the impression that a cannon has been fired.

y. Support personnel. Any individual who is not a performer or member of the audience. Among others, support personnel include the road crew of any production, stage hands, property masters, security guards, fire watch officers, janitors, or any other employee.

z. Venue manager. An individual who has overall responsibility for the operation and management of the facility where pyrotechnics are to be used in a performance.

2. Permit requirements. a. All uses of all pyrotechnics in areas of public assembly shall be approved by the permit authority. The permit authority shall determine that appropriate measures are established to provided* acceptable crowd management, security, fire protection, (including sprinklers), and other emergency services. All planning and use of pyrotechnics shall be coordinated with the venue manager and producer.

b. Before the performance of any production, the permittee shall submit a plan for the use of pyrotechnics to the permit authority. After a permit has been granted, the permittee shall keep the plan available at the site for safety inspectors or other designated agents of the permit authority. Any addition of pyrotechnics to a performance or any significant change in the presentation of pyrotechnics shall require approval by the permit authority, except that reducing the number or size of pyrotechnics to be used in a performance shall not be considered to be a significant change in the presentation.

c. (1) The plan for the use of pyrotechnics shall be made in writing or such other form as is required or approved by the permit authority.

(2) The plan shall provide the following:

(a) Name of the person, group, organization, or other entity sponsoring the production.

(b) Date and time of day of the production.

(c) Exact location of the production.

(d) Name of the person actually in charge of firing the pyrotechnics (i.e., the pyrotechnic operator).

(e) Number, names, and ages of all assistants who are to be present.

(f) Qualifications of the pyrotechnic operator.

(g) Pyrotechnic experience of the operator.

(h) Confirmation of any applicable local, state, and federal licenses held by the operator or assistant.

(i) Evidence of the permittee's insurance carrier or financial responsibility.

(j) Number and types of pyrotechnic devices and materials to be used, the operator's experience with those devices and effects, and a definition of the general responsibilities of assistants.

*(So in original, should be "provide")

(k) Diagram of the grounds or facilities where the production is to be held. This diagram shall show the point at which the pyrotechnic devices are to be fired, the fallout radius for each pyrotechnic device used in the performance, the lines behind which the audience shall be restrained, and the placement of sprinkler systems.

(*l*) Point of on-site assembly of pyrotechnic devices.

(m) Manner and place of storage of the pyrotechnic materials and devices.

(n) Material safety data sheet (MSDS) for the pyrotechnic materials to be used.

(o) Certification that the set, scenery, and rigging materials are inherently flame-retardant or have been treated to achieve flame retardancy.

(p) Certification that all materials worn by performers in the fallout area during use of pyrotechnic effects shall be inherently flame-retardant or have been treated to achieve flame retardancy.

(3) All plans shall be submitted as soon as is possible so that the permit authority has time to be present and to notify other interested parties. In no event shall such advance notice be less than five business days.

d. A walk-through and a representative demonstration of the pyrotechnics shall be approved by the permit authority before a permit is approved. The permit authority may waive this requirement based on past history, prior knowledge, and other factors; provided that the authority is confident that the discharge of pyrotechnics can be conducted safely. The demonstration shall be scheduled with sufficient time allowed to reset/reload the pyrotechnics before the arrival of the audience.

e. All pyrotechnic operators shall be at least twenty-one years old and licensed or approved by the permit authority in accordance with all applicable laws, if any. All assistants shall be at least eighteen years old.

3. Conduct of pyrotechnic performances. a. Two or more fire extinguishers of the proper classification and size as approved by the permit authority shall be readily accessible while the pyrotechnics are being loaded, prepared for firing, or fired. In all cases, at least two pressurized water or pump extinguishers shall be available. Additional fire extinguishing equipment shall be provided as required by the permit authority. Personnel who have a working knowledge of the use of the applicable fire extinguishers shall be present while the pyrotechnics are being handled, used, or removed. No personnel shall use or handle pyrotechnic materials or devices while under the influence of intoxicating beverages, narcotics, controlled substances, and prescription or nonprescription drugs that can impair judgment. Fire detection and life safety systems shall not be interrupted during the operation of pyrotechnic effects.

b. (1) All pyrotechnic devices shall be mounted in a secure manner to maintain their proper positions and orientations so that, when they are fired, the pyrotechnic effects described in the plan submitted by the permittee are produced. Pyrotechnicdevices shall be mounted so that no fallout from the device endangers human lives, results in personal injury, or damages property. Pyrotechnic materials shall be fired only from equipment specifically constructed for the purpose of firing pyrotechnic materials. The pyrotechnic operator shall be responsible for selecting equipment and materials that are compatible.

(2) Where rockets are launched before an audience, performers, or support personnel, the rockets shall be attached securely to a guide wire or cable with both ends securely attached and placed on an impact-resistant surface located at the terminal end of the guide. This guide wire or cable shall be of sufficient strength and flame resistance to withstand the exhaust from the rocket. An effective arrangement to stop the rocket shall be provided.

(3) Pyrotechnics shall be: (a) placed so that any hazardous debris falls into a safe, flame-resistant area; (b) fired so that the trajectory of their pyrotechnic material is not carried over the audience; and (c) placed for firing so that no flammable materials are within their fallout area.

(4) Pyrotechnic devices and materials used indoors shall be specifically manufactured and marked for indoor use by the manufacturer.

(5) Airbursts shall be permitted to be fired above the assembled audience, subject to the following conditions:

(a) The airburst shall be suspended by a minimum 30-gauge metal wire that is attached securely to a secure support acceptable to the authority having jurisdiction.

(b) The airburst shall occur at a minimum height of three times the diameter of the effect.

(c) Where the effect is demonstrated, there shall be no burning or glowing particles below the fifteen-foot level above the floor.

c. Each pyrotechnic device fired during a performance shall be separated from the audience by at least fifteen feet but not by less than twice the fallout radius of the device. Concussion mortars shall be separated from the audience by a minimum of twenty-five feet. There shall be no glowing or flaming particles within ten feet of the audience.

d. (1) The facility where pyrotechnic materials and devices are handled and used shall be maintained in a neat and orderly condition and shall be kept free of any conditions that can create a fire hazard.

(2) Smoking shall not be permitted within twenty-five feet of the area where pyrotechnics are being handled or fired; provided that smoking by performers as part of the performance shall be permitted as blocked in rehearsals and if expressly approved by the pyrotechnic operator and the permit authority.

e. (1) The pyrotechnic effect operator shall advise all performers and support personnel that they are exposed to a potentially hazardous situation when performing or otherwise carrying out their responsibilities in the vicinity of a pyrotechnic effect. Performers and support personnel familiar and experienced with the pyrotechnic effects being used shall be permitted to be in the area of a pyrotechnic effect, but only voluntarily and in the performance of their duties.

(2) No part, projectile, or debris from the pyrotechnic material or device shall be propelled so that it damages overhead properties, overhead equipment, or the ceiling and walls of the facility.

(3) Immediately before any performance, the pyrotechnic operator shall make a final check of wiring, positions, hook-ups, and pyrotechnic devices to ensure that they are in proper working order. The pyrotechnic operator also shall verify safety distances.

(4) The placement and wiring of all pyrotechnic devices shall be designed to minimize the possibility of performers and support personnel disturbing the devices during a performance.

(5) The pyrotechnic operator shall exercise extreme care throughout the performance to ensure that the pyrotechnic devices function correctly and that the performers, support personnel, and audience are clear of the devices.

(6) When pyrotechnics are fired, the quantity of smoke developed shall be controlled so as not to obscure the visibility of exit signs or paths of egress.

4. Bonds. Before granting and issuing a permit for a use of pyrotechnics as provided in this section, the permit authority shall require an adequate bond from the applicant therefor, unless such applicant is a state entity, county park, city, village, or town, or from the person to whom a contract for such use shall be awarded, in a sum to be fixed by the permit authority, which, however, shall not be less than five hundred thousand dollars, conditioned for the payment of all damages which may be caused to a person or persons or to property by reason of the use so permitted and arising from any acts of the permittee, his or her agents, employees, contractors, or subcontractors. Such bond shall run to the owner of the facility for which the permit is granted and issued and shall be for the use and benefit of any person or persons or any owner or owners of any property so injured or damaged, and such person or persons or such owner or owners are hereby authorized to maintain an action thereon, which right of action also shall accrue to the heirs, executors, administrators, successors, or assigns of such person or persons or such owner or owners. The permit authority may accept, in lieu of such bond, an indemnity insurance policy with liability coverage and indemnity protection equivalent to the terms and conditions upon which such bond is predicated and for the purposes herein provided.

5. Local laws or ordinances superseded. All local laws or ordinances regulating the use of pyrotechnics within the contemplation of this section are hereby superseded by the provisions of this section, with the exception of:

a. all laws or ordinances enacted by a city of one million or more; and

b. other local laws or ordinances that prohibit the use of indoor pyrotechnics.

§405.12 Unpermitted use of indoor pyrotechnics in the second degree.

A person is guilty of unpermitted use of indoor pyrotechnics in the second degree when he or she is responsible for obtaining a necessary permit to use indoor pyrotechnics, as required by paragraph o of subdivision one of section 405.10 of this article, and, without obtaining such permit or knowing that he or she is not in compliance with the terms of a permit, he or she intentionally ignites or detonates pyrotechnics for which such permit is required, or knowingly permits another to ignite or detonate such pyrotechnics, in a building, as defined in paragraph e of subdivision one of section 405.10 of this article.

Unpermitted use of indoor pyrotechnics in the second degree is a class A misdemeanor.

§405.14 Unpermitted use of indoor pyrotechnics in the first degree.

A person is guilty of unpermitted use of indoor pyrotechnics in the first degree when he or she commits the crime of unpermitted use of indoor pyrotechnics in the second degree, as defined in section 405.12 of this article, and, within the previous five year period, he or she has been convicted one or more times of the crime of unpermitted use of indoor pyrotechnics in the second degree, as defined in section 405.12 of this article, or unpermitted use of indoor pyrotechnics in the first degree, as defined in this section.

Unpermitted use of indoor pyrotechnics in the first degree is a class E felony.

§405.16 Aggravated unpermitted use of indoor pyrotechnics in the second degree.

A person is guilty of aggravated unpermitted use of indoor pyrotechnics in the second degree when he or she commits the crime of unpermitted use of indoor pyrotechnics in the second degree, as defined in section 405.12 of this article, and, by means of igniting or detonating such indoor pyrotechnics, he or she recklessly: (1) causes physical injury to another person; or (2) damages the property of another person in an amount that exceeds two hundred fifty dollars.

Aggravated unpermitted use of indoor pyrotechnics in the second degree is a class E felony.

§405.18 Aggravated unpermitted use of indoor pyrotechnics in the first degree.

A person is guilty of aggravated unpermitted use of indoor pyrotechnics in the first degree when he or she commits the crime of unpermitted use of indoor pyrotechnics in the second degree, as defined in section 405.12 of this article, and, by means of igniting or detonating such indoor pyrotechnics, he or she recklessly causes serious physical injury or death to another person.

Aggravated unpermitted use of indoor pyrotechnics in the first degree is a class D felony.

ARTICLE 410 - SEIZURE AND FORFEITURE OF EQUIPMENT USED IN PROMOTING PORNOGRAPHY

Section
410.00 Seizure and forfeiture of equipment used in photographing, filming, producing, manufacturing, projecting or distributing pornographic still or motion pictures.

§410.00 Seizure and forfeiture of equipment used in photographing, filming, producing, manufacturing, projecting or distributing pornographic still or motion pictures.

1. Any peace officer, acting pursuant to his special duties, or police officer of this state may seize any equipment used in the photographic, filming, printing, producing, manufacturing or projecting of pornographic still or motion pictures and may seize any vehicle or other means of transportation, other than a vehicle or other means of transportation used by any person as a common carrier in the transaction of business as such common carrier, used in the distribution of such obscene prints and articles and such equipment or vehicle or other means of transportation shall be subject to forfeiture as hereinafter in this section provided.

2. The seized property shall be delivered by the police officer or peace officer having made the seizure to the custody of the district attorney of the county wherein the seizure was made, except that in the cities of New York, Yonkers and Buffalo, the seized property shall be delivered to the custody of the police department of such cities, together with a report of all the facts and circumstances of the seizure.

3. It shall be the duty of the district attorney of the county wherein the seizure was made, if elsewhere than in the cities of New York or Buffalo, and where the seizure is made in either such city it shall be the duty of the corporation counsel of the city, to inquire into the facts of the

seizure so reported to him and if it appears probable that a forfeiture has been incurred, for the determination of which the institution of proceedings in the supreme court is necessary, to cause the proper proceedings to be commenced and prosecuted, at any time after thirty days from the date of seizure, to declare such forfeiture, unless, upon inquiry and examination such district attorney or corporation counsel decides that such proceedings cannot probably be sustained or that the ends of public justice do not require that they should be instituted or prosecuted, in which case, the district attorney or corporation counsel shall cause such seized property to be returned to the owner thereof.

4. Notice of the institution of the forfeiture proceeding shall be served either (a) personally on the owners of the seized property or (b) by registered mail to the owners' last known address and by publication of the notice once a week for two successive weeks in a newspaper published or circulated in the county wherein the seizure was made.

5. Forfeiture shall not be adjudged where the owners established by preponderance of the evidence that (a) the use of such seized property was not intentional on the part of any owner, or (b) said seized property was used by any person other than an owner thereof, while such seized property was unlawfully in the possession of a person who acquired possession thereof in violation of the criminal laws of the United States, or of any state.

6. The district attorney or the police department having custody of the seized property, after such judicial determination of forfeiture, shall, by a public notice of at least five days, sell such forfeited property at public sale. The net proceeds of any such sale, after deduction of the lawful expenses incurred, shall be paid into the general fund of the county wherein the seizure was made except that the net proceeds of the sale of property seized in the cities of New York and Buffalo shall be paid into the respective general funds of such cities.

7. Whenever any person interested in any property which is seized and declared forfeited under the provisions of this section files with a justice of the supreme court a petition for the recovery of such forfeited property, the justice of the supreme court may restore said forfeited property upon such terms and conditions as he deems reasonable and just, if the petitioner establishes either of the affirmative defenses set forth in subdivision five of this section and that the petitioner was without personal or actual knowledge of the forfeiture proceeding. If the petition be filed after the sale of the forfeited property, any judgment in favor of the petitioner shall be limited to the net proceeds of such sale, after deduction of the lawful expenses and costs incurred by the district attorney, police department or corporation counsel.

8. No suit or action under this section for wrongful seizure shall be instituted unless such suit or action is commenced within two years after the time when the property was seized.

9. For the purposes of this section only, a pornographic still or motion picture, is defined as a still or motion picture showing acts of sexual intercourse or acts of sexual perversion. This section shall not be construed as applying to bona fide medical photographs or films.

ARTICLE 415 - SEIZURE AND FORFEITURE OF VEHICLES, VESSELS AND AIRCRAFT USED TO TRANSPORT OR CONCEAL GAMBLING RECORDS

Section
415.00 Seizure and forfeiture of vehicles, vessels and aircraft used to transport or conceal gambling records.

§415.00 Seizure and forfeiture of vehicles, vessels and aircraft used to transport or conceal gambling records.

1. It shall be unlawful to transport, carry, convey or conceal in, upon or by means of any vehicles, vessel or aircraft, with knowledge of the contents thereof, any writing, paper, instrument or article:

(a) Of a kind commonly used in the operation or promotion of a bookmaking scheme or enterprise, and constituting, reflecting or representing more than five bets totaling more than five thousand dollars; or

(b) Of a kind commonly used in the operation, promotion or playing of a lottery or policy scheme or enterprise, and constituting, reflecting or representing more than five hundred plays or chances therein.

2. Any vehicle, vessel or aircraft which has been or is being used in violation of subdivision one by a person other than a bettor, player or

shareholder whose bets, plays or shares are represented by all such writings, papers, instruments or articles, shall be seized by any peace officer, who is acting pursuant to his special duties, or police officer, and forfeited as provided in this section. However, such forfeiture and seizure provisions shall not apply to any vehicle, vessel or aircraft used by any person as a common carrier in the transaction of business as such common carrier.

3. The seized property shall be delivered by the police officer or peace officer having made the seizure to the custody of the district attorney of the county wherein the seizure was made, except that in the cities of New York, Yonkers and Buffalo, the seized property shall be delivered to the custody of the police department of such cities, together with a report of all the facts and circumstances of the seizure.

4. It shall be the duty of the district attorney of the county wherein the seizure is made, if elsewhere than in the cities of New York, Yonkers or Buffalo, and where the seizure is made in either such city it shall be the duty of the corporation counsel of the city to inquire into the facts of the seizure so reported to him and if it appears probable that a forfeiture has been incurred by reason of a violation of this section, for the determination of which the institution of proceedings in the supreme court is necessary, to cause the proper proceedings to be commenced and prosecuted, at any time after thirty days from the date of seizure, to declare such forfeiture, unless, upon inquiry and examination, such district attorney or corporation counsel decides that such proceedings cannot probably be sustained or that the ends of public justice do not require that they should be instituted or prosecuted, in which case, the district attorney or corporation counsel shall cause such seized property to be returned to the owner thereof.

5. Notice of the institution of the forfeiture proceeding shall be served either (a) personally on the owners of the seized property, or (b) by registered mail to the owners' last known address and by publication of the notice once a week for two successive weeks in a newspaper published or circulated in the county wherein the seizure was made.

6. Forfeiture shall not be adjudged where the owners establish by preponderance of the evidence that (a) the use of such seized property, in violation of subdivision one of this section, was not intentional on the part of any owner, or (b) said seized property was used in violation of subdivision one of this section by any person other than an owner thereof, while such seized property was unlawfully in the possession of a person who acquired possession thereof in violation of the criminal laws of the United States, or of any state.

7. The district attorney or the police department having custody

of the seized property, after such judicial determination of forfeiture, shall, at their discretion, either retain such seized property for the official use of their office or department, or, by a public notice of at least five days, sell such forfeited property at public sale. The net proceeds of any such sale, after deduction of the lawful expenses incurred, shall be paid into the general fund of the county wherein the seizure was made except that the net proceeds of the sale of property seized in the cities of New York, Yonkers and Buffalo shall be paid into the respective general funds of such cities.

8. Whenever any person interested in any property which is seized and declared forfeited under the provisions of this section files with a justice of the supreme court a petition for the recovery of such forfeited property, the justice of the supreme court may restore such forfeited property upon such terms and conditions as he deems reasonable and just, if the petitioner establishes either of the affirmative defenses set forth in subdivision six of this section and that the petitioner was without personal or actual knowledge of the forfeiture proceeding. If the petition be filed after the sale of the forfeited property, any judgment in favor of the petitioner shall be limited to the net proceeds of such sale after deduction of the lawful expenses and costs incurred by the district attorney, police department or corporation counsel.

9. No suit or action under this section for wrongful seizure shall be instituted unless such suit or action is commenced within two years after the time when the property was seized

ARTICLE 420 - SEIZURE AND DESTRUCTION OF UNAUTHORIZED RECORDINGS OF SOUND AND FORFEITURE OF EQUIPMENT USED IN THE PRODUCTION THEREOF

Section
420.00 Seizure and destruction of unauthorized recordings.
420.05 Seizure and forfeiture of equipment used in the production of unauthorized recordings.

§420.00 Seizure and destruction of unauthorized recordings.

Any article produced in violation of article two hundred seventy-five of this chapter may be seized by any police officer upon the arrest of any individual in possession of same. Upon final determination of the charges, the court shall, upon proper notice by the district attorney or representative of the crime victim or victims, after prior notice to the district attorney and custodian of the seized property, enter an order preserving any goods manufactured, sold, offered for sale, distributed or produced in violation of this article, as evidence for use in other cases, including a civil action. This notice must be received within thirty days of final determination of the charges. The cost of storage, security, and destruction of goods so ordered for preservation and use as evidence in a civil action, other than a civil action under article thirteen-A of the civil practice law and rules initiated by the district attorney, shall be paid by the party seeking preservation of the evidence for a civil action. If no such order is entered within the thirty day period, the district attorney or custodian of the seized property must cause such articles to be destroyed. Destruction shall not include auction, sale, or distribution of the items in their original form.

§420.05 Seizure and forfeiture of equipment used in the production of unauthorized recordings.

1. Any police officer of this state may seize any equipment, or components, used in the manufacture or production of unauthorized recordings and may seize any vehicle or other means of transportation, other than a vehicle or means of transportation used by any person as a common carrier in the transaction of business as such common carrier, used in the distribution of such unauthorized recordings and such equipment or vehicle or other means of transportation shall be subject to forfeiture as provided in this section.

2. The seized property shall be delivered by the police officer having made the seizure to the custody of the district attorney of the county wherein the seizure was made, except that in the cities of New York, Yonkers and Buffalo, the seized property shall be delivered to the custody of the police department of such cities, together with a report of all the facts and circumstances of the seizure.

3. It shall be the duty of the district attorney of the county wherein the seizure was made, if elsewhere than in the city of New York, Yonkers or Buffalo, and where the seizure is made in either such city, it shall be the duty of the corporation counsel of the city, to inquire into the facts of the seizure so reported to him and if it appears probable that a forfeiture has been incurred for the determination of which the institution of proceedings in the supreme court is necessary, to cause the proper proceedings to be commenced and prosecuted, at any time after thirty days from the date of seizure, to declare such forfeiture, unless, upon inquiry and examination such district attorney or corporation counsel decides that such proceedings cannot probably be sustained or that the ends of public justice do not require that they should be instituted or prosecuted, in which case, the district attorney or corporation counsel shall cause such seized property to be returned to the owner thereof.

4. Notice of the institution of the forfeiture proceeding shall be served either:

(a) personally on the owners of the seized property; or

(b) by registered mail to the owners' last known address and by publication of the notice once a week for two successive weeks in a newspaper published or circulated in the county wherein the seizure was made.

5. Forfeiture shall not be adjudged where the owners established by preponderance of the evidence that:

(a) the use of such seized property was not intentional on the part of any owner; or

(b) said seized property was used by any person other than an owner thereof, while such seized property was unlawfully in the possession of a person who acquired possession thereof in violation of the criminal laws of the United States, or of any state.

6. The district attorney or the police department having custody of the seized property, after such judicial determination of forfeiture, shall, by a public notice of at least five days, sell such forfeited property at public sale. The net proceeds of any such sale, after deduction of the lawful expenses incurred, shall be paid into the general fund of the county wherein the seizure was made except that the net proceeds of the sale of property seized in the cities of New York, Yonkers and Buffalo shall be paid into the respective general funds of such cities.

7. Whenever any person interested in any property which is seized and declared forfeited under the provisions of this section files with a justice of the supreme court a petition for the recovery of such forfeited property, the justice of the supreme court may restore said forfeited property upon such terms and conditions as he deems reasonable and just, if the petitioner establishes either of the affirmative defenses set forth in subdivision five of this section and that the petitioner was without personal or actual knowledge of the forfeiture proceeding. If the petition be filed after the sale of the forfeited property, any judgment in favor of the petitioner shall be limited to the net proceeds of such sale, after deduction of the lawful expenses and costs incurred by the district attorney, police department or corporation counsel.

8. No suit or action under this section for wrongful seizure shall be instituted unless such suit or action is commenced within two years after the time when the property was seized.

ARTICLE 450 - DISPOSAL OF STOLEN PROPERTY
Section
450.10 Disposal of stolen property.

§450.10 Disposal of stolen property.
1. When property, other than contraband including but not limited to those items subject to the provisions of sections 410.00, 415.00, 420.00 and 420.05 of this chapter, alleged to have been stolen is in the custody of a police officer, a peace officer or a district attorney and a request for its release is made prior to or during the criminal proceeding, it may not be released except as provided in subdivisions two, three and four of this section. When a request is made for the return of stolen property under this section, the police officer, peace officer or district attorney in possession of such property must provide written notice to the defendant or his counsel of such request as soon as practicable. Such notice shall advise the defendant or his counsel of the date on which the property will be released and the name and address of a person with whom arrangements can be made for the examination, testing, photographing, photocopying or other reproduction of said property.

2. Both the defendant's counsel and the prosecutor thereafter shall make a diligent effort to examine, test and photograph, photocopy or otherwise reproduce the property. Either party may apply to the court for an extension of any period allowed for examination, testing, photographing, photocopying or otherwise reproducing the property. For good cause shown the court may order retention of the property for use as evidence by either party. Unless extended by a court order sought by

either party on notice to the other, the property shall be released no later than the time periods for retention set forth in subdivisions three and four of this section to the person making such request after satisfactory proof of such person's entitlement to the possession thereof. Unless a court, upon application of either party with notice to the other, orders otherwise, the release of property in accordance with the provisions of this section shall be unconditional.

3. Except as provided in subdivision four of this section, when a request is made for the release of property described in subdivision one of this section, the property shall be retained until either the expiration of a fifteen day period from receipt by the defendant or his counsel of the notice of the request, or the examination testing and photographing, photocopying or other reproduction of such property, by the parties, whichever event occurs first. The fifteen day period may be extended by up to five additional days by agreement between the parties.

4. (a) Except as provided in paragraphs (b) and (c) of this subdivision and in subdivision eleven of this section, when a request is made for the release of property described in subdivision one of this section, and the property shall consist of perishables, fungible retail items, motor vehicles or any other property release of which is necessary for either the operation of a business or the health or welfare of any person, the property shall be retained until either the expiration of a forty-eight hour period from the receipt by the defendant's counsel of the notice of the request, or the examination, testing and photocopying, photographing or other reproduction of such property, by the parties whichever event occurs first. The forty-eight hour period may be extended by up to twenty-four additional hours by agreement between the parties. For the purposes of this section, perishables shall mean any property likely to spoil or decay or diminish significantly in value within twenty days of the initial retention of the property.

(b) If, upon oral or written application by the district attorney with notice to the defendant or his counsel, a court determines that immediate release of property described in paragraph (a) of this subdivision is required under the attendant circumstances, the court shall issue an order releasing the property and, if requested by either party, setting, as a part of such order, any condition appropriate in the furtherance of justice.

(c) A motor vehicle alleged to have been stolen but not alleged to have been used in connection with any crime or criminal transaction other than the theft or unlawful use of said motor vehicle, which is in the custody of a police officer, a peace officer or a district attorney, may be released expeditiously to its registered owner or the owner's representative without prior notice to the defendant. Before such release, evidentiary photographs shall be taken of such motor vehicle. Such photographs shall include the vehicle identification number, registration on windshield, license plates, each side of the vehicle, including vent windows, door locks and handles, the front and back of the vehicle, the interior of the vehicle, including ignition lock, seat to floor clearance, center console, radio receptacle and dashboard area, the motor, and any other interior or exterior surfaces showing any and all damage to the vehicle. Notice of such release, and the photographs taken of said vehicle, shall be furnished to the defendant within fifteen days after arraignment or after counsel initially appears on behalf of the defendant or respondent, whichever occurs later.

5. If stolen property comes into the custody of a court, it must, unless temporary retention be deemed necessary in furtherance of justice, be delivered to the owner, on satisfactory proof of his title, and on his paying the necessary expenses incurred in its preservation, to be certified by the court.

6. If stolen property has not been delivered to the owner, the court before which a trial is had for stealing it, may, on proof of his title, order it to be restored to the owner.

7. If stolen property is not claimed by the owner, before the expiration of six months from the conviction of a person for stealing it, the court or other officer having it in custody must, on payment of the necessary expenses incurred in its preservation, deliver it to the county commissioner of social services, or in the city of New York, to the commissioner of social services, to be applied for the benefit of the poor of the county or city, as the case may be.

8. Except in the city of New York, when money or other property is taken from a defendant, arrested upon a charge of an offense, the officer taking it must, at the time, give duplicate receipts therefor, specifying particularly the amount of property taken, one of which receipts he must deliver to the defendant, and the other of which he must forthwith file with the court in which the criminal action is pending.

9. The commissioners of police of the city of New York may designate some person to take charge of all property alleged to be stolen, and which may be brought into the police office, and all property taken from the person of a prisoner, and may prescribe regulations in regard to the duties of the clerk or clerks so designated, and to require and take security for the faithful performance of the duties imposed by this subdivision, and it shall be the duty of every officer into whose possession such property may come, to deliver the same forthwith to the person so designated.

10. Where there has been a failure to comply with the provisions of this section, and where the district attorney does not demonstrate to the satisfaction of the court that such failure has not caused the defendant prejudice, the court shall instruct the jury that it may consider such failure in determining the weight to be given such evidence and may also impose any other sanction set forth in subdivision one of section 245.80 of the criminal procedure law; provided, however, that unless the defendant has convinced the court that such failure has caused him undue prejudice, the court shall not preclude the district attorney from introducing into evidence the property, photographs, photocopies, or other reproductions of the property or, where appropriate, testimony concerning its value and condition, where such evidence is otherwise properly authenticated and admissible under the rules of evidence. Failure to comply with any one or more of the provisions of this section

shall not for that reason alone be grounds for dismissal of the accusatory instrument.   *(Eff.1/1/20,Ch.59,L.2019)*

11. When a request for the release of stolen property is made pursuant to paragraph (a) of subdivision four of this section and the defendant is not represented by counsel the notice required pursuant to subdivision one of this section shall be personally delivered to the defendant and release of said property shall not occur for a period less than five days: from (a) the delivery of such notice; or (b) in the case of delivery to such person in custody, from the first appearance before the court, whichever is later.

TITLE X - ORGANIZED CRIME CONTROL ACT
ARTICLE 460 - ENTERPRISE CORRUPTION

Section
460.00 Legislative findings.
460.10 Definitions.
460.20 Enterprise corruption.
460.22 Aggravated enterprise corruption.
460.25 Enterprise corruption; limitations.
460.30 Enterprise corruption; forfeiture.
460.40 Enterprise corruption; jurisdiction.
460.50 Enterprise corruption; prosecution.
460.60 Enterprise corruption; consent to prosecute.
460.70 Provisional remedies.
460.80 Court ordered disclosure.

§460.00 Legislative findings.

The legislature finds and determines as follows:

Organized crime in New York state involves highly sophisticated, complex and widespread forms of criminal activity. The diversified illegal conduct engaged in by organized crime, rooted in the illegal use of force, fraud, and corruption, constitutes a major drain upon the state's economy, costs citizens and businesses of the state billions of dollars each year, and threatens the peace, security and general welfare of the people of the state.

Organized crime continues to expand its corrosive influence in the state through illegal enterprises engaged in such criminal endeavors as the theft and fencing of property, the importation and distribution of narcotics and other dangerous drugs, arson for profit, hijacking, labor racketeering, loansharking, extortion and bribery, the illegal disposal of hazardous wastes, syndicated gambling, trafficking in stolen securities, insurance and investment frauds, and other forms of economic and social exploitation.

The money and power derived by organized crime through its illegal enterprises and endeavors is increasingly being used to infiltrate and corrupt businesses, unions and other legitimate enterprises and to corrupt our democratic processes. This infiltration takes several forms with legitimate enterprises being employed as instrumentalities, injured as victims, or taken as prizes. Through such infiltration the power of an enterprise can be diverted to criminal ends, its resources looted, or it can be taken over entirely, either on paper or de facto. Thus, for purposes of making both criminal and civil remedies available to deal with the corruption of such enterprises, the concept of criminal enterprise should not be limited to traditional criminal syndicates or crime families, and may include persons who join together in a criminal enterprise, as defined by subdivision three of section 460.10 of this article, for the purpose of corrupting such legitimate enterprises or infiltrating and illicitly influencing industries.

One major cause of the continuing growth of organized criminal activities within the state is the inadequacy and limited nature of sanctions and remedies available to state and local law enforcement officials to deal with this intricate and varied criminal conduct. Existing penal law provisions are primarily concerned with the commission of specific and limited criminal acts without regard to the relationships of particular criminal acts or the illegal profits derived therefrom, to legitimate or illicit enterprises operated or controlled by organized crime. Further, traditional penal law provisions only provide for the imposition of conventional criminal penalties, including imprisonment, fines and probation, for entrenched organized crime enterprises. Such penalties are not adequate to enable the state to effectively fight organized crime. Instead, new penal prohibitions and enhanced sanctions, and new civil and criminal remedies are necessary to deal with the unlawful activities of persons and enterprises engaged in organized crime. Comprehensive statutes enacted at the federal level and in a number of other states with significant organized crime problems, have provided law enforcement agencies with an effective tool to fight organized crime. Such laws permit law enforcement authorities (i) to charge and prove patterns of criminal activity and their connection to ongoing enterprises, legitimate or illegal, that are controlled or operated by organized crime, and (ii) to apply criminal and civil penalties designed to prevent and eliminate organized crime's involvement with such enterprises. The organized crime control act is a statute of comparable purpose but tempered by reasonable limitations on its applicability, and by due regard for the rights of innocent persons. Because of its more rigorous definitions, this act will not apply to some situations encompassed within comparable statutes in other jurisdictions. This act is vital to the peace, security and general welfare of the state.

In part because of its highly diverse nature, it is impossible to precisely define what organized crime is. This article, however, does attempt to define and criminalize what organized crime does. This article focuses upon criminal enterprises because their sophistication and organization make them more effective at their criminal purposes and because their structure and insulation protect their leadership from detection and prosecution.

At the same time, this article is not intended to be employed to prosecute relatively minor or isolated acts of criminality which, while related to an enterprise and arguably part of a pattern as defined in this article, can be adequately and more fairly prosecuted as separate offenses. Similarly, particular defendants may play so minor a role in a criminal enterprise that their culpability would be unfairly distorted by prosecution and punishment for participation in the enterprise.

The balance intended to be struck by this act cannot readily be codified in the form of restrictive definitions or a categorical list of exceptions. General, yet carefully drawn definitions of the terms "pattern of criminal activity" and "criminal enterprise" have been employed. Notwithstanding the provisions of section 5.00 of this chapter these definitions should be given their plain meaning, and should not be construed either liberally or strictly, but in the context of the legislative purposes set forth in these findings. Within the confines of these and other applicable definitions, discretion ought still be exercised. Once the letter of the law is complied with, including the essential showing that there is a pattern of conduct which is criminal under existing statutes, the question whether to prosecute under those statutes or for the pattern itself is essentially one of fairness. The answer will depend on the particular situation, and is best addressed by those institutions of government which have traditionally exercised that function: the grand jury, the public prosecutor, and an independent judiciary.

§460.10 Definitions.
The following definitions are applicable to this article.
1. "Criminal act" means conduct constituting any of the following crimes, or conspiracy or attempt to commit any of the following felonies:
(a) Any of the felonies set forth in this chapter: sections 120.05, 120.10 and 120.11 relating to assault; sections 121.12 and 121.13 relating to strangulation; sections 125.10 to 125.27 relating to homicide; sections 130.25, 130.30 and 130.35 relating to rape; sections 135.20 and 135.25 relating to kidnapping; sections 135.35 and 135.37 relating to labor trafficking; section 135.65 relating to coercion; sections 140.20, 140.25 and 140.30 relating to burglary; sections 145.05, 145.10 and 145.12 relating to criminal mischief; article one hundred fifty relating to arson; sections 155.30, 155.35, 155.40 and 155.42 relating to grand larceny; sections 177.10, 177.15, 177.20 and 177.25 relating to health care fraud; article one hundred sixty relating to robbery; sections 165.45, 165.50, 165.52 and 165.54 relating to criminal possession of stolen property; sections 165.72 and 165.73 relating to trademark counterfeiting; sections 170.10, 170.15, 170.25, 170.30, 170.40, 170.65 and 170.70 relating to forgery; sections 175.10, 175.25, 175.35, 175.40 and 210.40 relating to false statements; sections 176.15, 176.20, 176.25 and 176.30 relating to insurance fraud; sections 178.20 and 178.25 relating to criminal diversion of prescription medications and prescriptions; sections 180.03, 180.08, 180.15, 180.25, 180.40, 180.45, 200.00, 200.03, 200.04, 200.10, 200.11, 200.12, 200.20, 200.22, 200.25, 200.27, 200.56, 215.00, 215.05 and 215.19 relating to bribery; sections 187.10, 187.15, 187.20 and 187.25 relating to residential mortgage fraud, sections 190.40 and 190.42 relating to criminal usury; section 190.65 relating to schemes to defraud; any felony defined in article four hundred ninety-six; sections 205.60 and 205.65 relating to hindering prosecution; sections 210.10, 210.15, and 215.51 relating to perjury and contempt; section 215.40 relating to tampering with physical evidence; sections 220.06, 220.09, 220.16, 220.18, 220.21, 220.31, 220.34, 220.39, 220.41, 220.43, 220.46, 220.55, 220.60, 220.65 and 220.77 relating to controlled substances; sections 225.10 and 225.20

relating to gambling; sections 230.25, 230.30, and 230.32 relating to promoting prostitution; section 230.34 relating to sex trafficking; section 230.34-a relating to sex trafficking of a child; sections 235.06, 235.07, 235.21 and 235.22 relating to obscenity; sections 263.10 and 263.15 relating to promoting a sexual performance by a child; sections 265.02, 265.03, 265.04, 265.11, 265.12, 265.13 and the provisions of section 265.10 which constitute a felony relating to firearms and other dangerous weapons; sections 265.14 and 265.16 relating to criminal sale of a firearm; section 265.50 relating to the criminal manufacture, sale or transport of an undetectable firearm, rifle or shotgun; section 275.10, 275.20, 275.30, or 275.40 relating to unauthorized recordings; and sections 470.05, 470.10, 470.15 and 470.20 relating to money laundering; or section 275.10, 275.20, 275.30, or 275.40 relating to unauthorized recordings; and sections 470.05, 470.10, 470.15 and 470.20 relating to money laundering; or *(Eff.1/26/20,Ch.134,L.2019)*

(b) Any felony set forth elsewhere in the laws of this state and defined by the tax law relating to alcoholic beverage, cigarette, gasoline and similar motor fuel taxes; article seventy-one of the environmental conservation law relating to water pollution, hazardous waste or substances hazardous or acutely hazardous to public health or safety of the environment; article twenty-three-A of the general business law relating to prohibited acts concerning stocks, bonds and other securities, article twenty-two of the general business law concerning monopolies.

2. "Enterprise" means either an enterprise as defined in subdivision one of section 175.00 of this chapter or criminal enterprise as defined in subdivision three of this section.

3. "Criminal enterprise" means a group of persons sharing a common purpose of engaging in criminal conduct, associated in an ascertainable structure distinct from a pattern of criminal activity, and with a continuity of existence, structure and criminal purpose beyond the scope of individual criminal incidents.

4. "Pattern of criminal activity" means conduct engaged in by persons charged in an enterprise corruption count constituting three or more criminal acts that:

(a) were committed within ten years of the commencement of the criminal action;

(b) are neither isolated incidents, nor so closely related and connected in point of time or circumstance of commission as to constitute a criminal offense or criminal transaction, as those terms are defined in section 40.10 of the criminal procedure law; and

(c) are either: (i) related to one another through a common scheme or plan or (ii) were committed, solicited, requested, importuned or intentionally aided by persons acting with the mental culpability required for the commission thereof and associated with or in the criminal enterprise.

§460.20 Enterprise corruption.

1. A person is guilty of enterprise corruption when, having knowledge of the existence of a criminal enterprise and the nature of its activities, and being employed by or associated with such enterprise, he:

(a) intentionally conducts or participates in the affairs of an enterprise by participating in a pattern of criminal activity; or

(b) intentionally acquires or maintains any interest in or control of an enterprise by participating in a pattern of criminal activity; or

(c) participates in a pattern of criminal activity and knowingly invests any proceeds derived from that conduct, or any proceeds derived from the investment or use of those proceeds, in an enterprise.

2. For purposes of this section, a person participates in a pattern of criminal activity when, with intent to participate in or advance the affairs of the criminal enterprise, he engages in conduct constituting, or, is criminally liable for pursuant to section 20.00 of this chapter, at least three of the criminal acts included in the pattern, provided that:

(a) Two of his acts are felonies other than conspiracy;

(b) Two of his acts, one of which is a felony, occurred within five years of the commencement of the criminal action; and

(c) Each of his acts occurred within three years of a prior act.

3. For purposes of this section, the enterprise corrupted in violation of subdivision one of this section need not be the criminal enterprise by which the person is employed or with which he is associated, and may be a legitimate enterprise.

Enterprise corruption is a class B felony.

§460.22 Aggravated enterprise corruption.

A person is guilty of aggravated enterprise corruption when he or she commits the crime of enterprise corruption and two or more of the acts that constitute his or her pattern of criminal activity are class B felonies or higher, and at least two acts are armed felonies as defined in paragraph (a) of subdivision forty-one of section 1.20 of the criminal procedure law or one act is such an armed felony and one act is a violation of subdivision two of section 265.17 of this chapter or one act is a class B violent felony and two are violations of subdivision two of section 265.17 of this chapter.

Aggravated enterprise corruption is a class A-I felony.

§460.25 Enterprise corruption; limitations.

1. For purposes of subdivision one of section 460.20 of this article, a person does not acquire or maintain an interest in an enterprise by participating in a pattern of criminal activity when he invests proceeds derived from a pattern of criminal activity in such enterprise.

2. For purposes of subdivision one of section 460.20 of this article, it shall not be unlawful to:

(a) purchase securities on the open market with intent to make an investment, and without the intent of controlling or participating in the control of the issuer, or of assisting another to do so, if the securities of the issuer held by the purchaser, the members of his immediate family, and his or their accomplices in any pattern of criminal activity do not amount in the aggregate to five percent of the outstanding securities of any one class and do not confer, either in the law or in fact, the power to elect one or more directors of the issuer;

(b) make a deposit in an account maintained in a savings and loan association, or a deposit in any other such financial institution, that creates an ownership interest in that association or institution;

(c) purchase shares in co-operatively owned residential or commercial property;

(d) purchase non-voting shares in a limited partnership, with intent to make an investment, and without the intent of controlling or participating in the control of the partnership.

§460.30 Enterprise corruption; forfeiture.

1. Any person convicted of enterprise corruption may be required pursuant to this section to criminally forfeit to the state:

(a) any interest in, security of, claim against or property or contractual right of any kind affording a source of influence over any enterprise whose affairs he has controlled or in which he has participated in violation of subdivision one of section 460.20 of this article and for which he was convicted and the use of which interest, security, claim or right by him contributed directly and materially to the crime for which he was convicted unless such forfeiture is disproportionate to the defendant's gain from his association or employment with the enterprise, in which event the jury may recommend forfeiture of a portion thereof;

(b) any interest, including proceeds, he has acquired or maintained in an enterprise in violation of subdivision one of section 460.20 of this article and for which he was convicted unless such forfeiture is disproportionate to the conduct he engaged in and on which the forfeiture is based, in which event the jury may recommend forfeiture of a portion thereof; or

(c) any interest, including proceeds he has derived from an investment of proceeds in an enterprise in violation of subdivision one of section 460.20 of this article and for which he was convicted unless such forfeiture is disproportionate to the conduct he engaged in and on which the forfeiture is based, in which event the jury may recommend forfeiture of a portion thereof.

2. (a) Forfeiture may be ordered when the grand jury returning an indictment charging a person with enterprise corruption has received evidence legally sufficient to establish, and providing reasonable cause to believe, that the property or other interest is subject to forfeiture under this section. In that event, the grand jury shall file a special information, not to be disclosed to the jury in the criminal action prior to verdict on the criminal charges, specifying the property or other interest for which forfeiture is sought and containing a plain and concise factual statement which sets forth the basis for the forfeiture. Alternatively, where the defendant has waived indictment and consented to be prosecuted by superior court information pursuant to article one hundred ninety-five of the criminal procedure law, the prosecutor may file, in addition to the superior court information charging enterprise corruption, a special information specifying the property or other interest for which forfeiture is sought and containing a plain and concise factual statement which sets forth the basis for the forfeiture.

(b) After returning a verdict of guilty on an enterprise corruption count or counts, the jury shall be given the special information and hear any additional evidence which is relevant and legally admissible upon the forfeiture count or counts of the special information. After hearing such evidence, the jury shall then deliberate upon the forfeiture count or counts and, based upon all the evidence received in connection with the

indictment or superior court information and the special information,
may, if satisfied by proof beyond a reasonable doubt that the property or
other interest, or a portion thereof, is subject to forfeiture under this
section return a verdict determining such property or other interest, or
portion thereof, is subject to forfeiture, provided, however, where a
defendant has waived a jury trial pursuant to article three hundred
twenty of the criminal procedure law, the court may hear and receive all
of the evidence upon the indictment or superior court information and
the special information and render a verdict upon the enterprise
corruption count or counts and the forfeiture count or counts.

(c) After the verdict of forfeiture, the court shall hear arguments and
may receive additional evidence upon a motion of the defendant that the
verdict of forfeiture (i) is against the weight of the evidence, or (ii) is,
with respect to a forfeiture pursuant to paragraph (a) of subdivision one
of this section, disproportionate to the defendant's gain from his
association or employment with the enterprise, or, with respect to a
forfeiture pursuant to paragraph (b) or (c) of subdivision one of this
section, disproportionate to the conduct he engaged in on which the
forfeiture is based. Upon such a finding the court may in the interests of
justice set aside, modify, limit or otherwise condition an order of
forfeiture.

3. (a) An order of criminal forfeiture shall authorize the prosecutor to
seize all property or other interest declared forfeited under this section
upon such terms and conditions as the court shall deem proper. If a
property right or other interest is not exercisable or transferable for
value by the prosecutor, it shall expire and shall not revert to the
convicted person. The court ordering any forfeiture may remit such
forfeiture or any portion thereof.

(b) No person shall forfeit any right, title or interest in any property
or enterprise under this article who has not been convicted of a violation
of section 460.20 of this article. Any person other than the convicted
person claiming an interest in forfeited property or other interest may
bring a special proceeding to determine that claim, before or after trial,
pursuant to section thirteen hundred twenty-seven of the civil practice
law and rules, provided, however, that if such an action is brought
before trial, it may, upon motion of the prosecutor, and in the court's
discretion, be postponed by the court until completion of the trial. In
addition, any person claiming an interest in property subject to forfeiture
may petition for remission as provided in subdivision seven of section
thirteen hundred eleven of such law and rules.

4. All property and other interests which are criminally forfeited
following the commencement of an action under this article, whether by
plea, verdict or other agreement, shall be disposed of in accordance with
the provisions of section thirteen hundred forty-nine of the civil practice
law and rules. In any case where one or more of the counts upon which
a person is convicted specifically includes as a criminal act a violation
of any offense defined in article two hundred twenty of this chapter, the
court

shall determine what portion of that property or interest derives from or relates to such criminal act, and direct that distribution of that portion be conducted in the manner prescribed for actions grounded upon offenses in violation of article two hundred twenty.

5. Any person convicted of a violation of section 460.20 of this article through which he derived pecuniary value, or by which he caused personal injury or property damage or other loss, may be sentenced to pay a fine not in excess of three times the gross value he gained or three times the gross loss he caused, whichever is greater. Moneys so collected shall be paid as restitution to victims of the crime for medical expenses actually incurred, loss of earnings or property loss or damage caused thereby. Any excess after restitution shall be paid to the state treasury. In any case where one or more of the counts upon which a person is convicted specifically includes as a criminal act a violation of any offense defined in article two hundred twenty of this chapter, the court shall determine what proportion of the entire pattern such criminal acts constitute and distribute such portion in the manner prescribed by section three hundred forty-nine of the civil practice law and rules for forfeiture actions grounded upon offenses in violation of article two hundred twenty. When the court imposes a fine pursuant to this subdivision, the court shall make a finding as to the amount of the gross value gained or the gross loss caused. If the record does not contain sufficient evidence to support such a finding the court may conduct a hearing upon the issue. In imposing a fine, the court shall consider the seriousness of the conduct, whether the amount of the fine is disproportionate to the conduct in which he engaged, its impact on victims and the enterprise corrupted by that conduct, as well as the economic circumstances of the convicted person, including the effect of the imposition of such a fine upon his immediate family.

6. The imposition of an order of criminal forfeiture pursuant to subdivision one of this section, a judgment of civil forfeiture pursuant to article thirteen-A of the civil practice law and rules, or a fine pursuant to subdivision five of this section or paragraph (b) of subdivision one of section 80.00 of this chapter, shall preclude the imposition of any other such order or judgment of forfeiture or fine based upon the same criminal conduct, provided, however that where an order of criminal forfeiture is imposed pursuant to subdivision one of this section, an action pursuant to article thirteen-A of the civil practice law and rules may nonetheless be brought, and an order imposed in that action, for forfeiture of the proceeds of a crime or the substituted proceeds of a crime where such proceeds are not subject to criminal forfeiture pursuant to subdivision one of this section. The imposition of a fine pursuant to subdivision five of this section or paragraph (b) of subdivision one of section 80.00 of this chapter, shall preclude the imposition of any other fine pursuant to any other provision of this chapter.

7. Other than as provided in subdivision six, the imposition of a criminal penalty, forfeiture or fine under this section shall not preclude the application of any other criminal penalty or civil remedy under this article or under any other provision of law.

8. Any payment made as restitution to victims pursuant to this section shall not limit, preclude or impair any liability for damages in any civil action or proceeding for an amount in excess of such payment.

§460.40 Enterprise corruption; jurisdiction.

A person may be prosecuted for enterprise corruption:

1. in any county in which the principal place of business, if any, of the enterprise was located at the time of the offense, and, if the enterprise had a principal place or business located in more than one county, then in any such county in which any conduct occurred constituting or requisite to the completion of the offense of enterprise corruption; or

2. in any county in which any act included in the pattern of criminal activity could have been prosecuted pursuant to article twenty of the criminal procedure law; provided, however, that such person may not be prosecuted for enterprise corruption in such county based on this subdivision if the jurisdiction of such county is based solely on section 20.60 of the criminal procedure law; or

3. in any county in which he:

(a) conducts or participates in the affairs of the enterprise in violation of subdivision one of section 460.20 of this article,

(b) acquires or maintains an interest in or control of the enterprise in violation of subdivision one of section 460.20 of this article,

(c) invests proceeds in an enterprise in violation of subdivision one of section 460.20 of this article; or

4. in any county in which the conduct of the actor had or was likely to have a particular effect upon such county or a political subdivision or part thereof, and was performed with intent that it would, or with knowledge that it was likely to, have such particular effect therein.

§460.50 Enterprise corruption; prosecution.

1. Subject to the provisions of section 460.60 of this article, a charge of enterprise corruption may be prosecuted by: (a) the district attorney of any county with jurisdiction over the offense pursuant to section 460.40 of this article; (b) the deputy attorney general in charge of the statewide organized crime task force when authorized by subdivision seven of section seventy-a of the executive law; or (c) the attorney general when he is otherwise authorized by law to prosecute each of the criminal acts specifically included in the pattern of criminal activity alleged in the enterprise corruption charge.

2. For purposes of paragraph (c) of subdivision one of this section, a criminal act or an offense is specifically included in a pattern of criminal activity when the count of the accusatory instrument charging a person with enterprise corruption alleges a pattern of criminal activity and the act is alleged to be a criminal act within the pattern of criminal activity.

§460.60 Enterprise corruption; consent to prosecute.

1. For purposes of this section, when a grand jury proceeding concerns a possible charge of enterprise corruption, or when an accusatory instrument includes a count charging a person with enterprise corruption, the affected district attorneys are the district attorneys otherwise empowered to prosecute any of the underlying acts of criminal activity in a county with jurisdiction over the offense of enterprise corruption pursuant to section 460.40 of this article, in which:

(a) there has been substantial and significant activity by the particular enterprise; or

(b) conduct occurred constituting a criminal act specifically included in the pattern of criminal activity charged in the accusatory instrument and not previously prosecuted; or

(c) the particular enterprise has its principal place of business.

2. A grand jury proceeding concerning a possible charge of enterprise corruption may be instituted only with the consent of the affected district attorneys. Should the possibility of such a charge develop after a grand jury proceeding has been instituted, the consent of the affected district attorneys shall be sought as soon as is practical, and an indictment charging a person with enterprise corruption may not be voted upon by the grand jury without such consent.

3. A person may be charged in an accusatory instrument with enterprise corruption only with the consent of the affected district attorneys. When it is impractical to obtain the consent specified in subdivision two of this section prior to the filing of the accusatory instrument, then that consent must be secured within twenty days thereafter.

4. When the prosecutor is the deputy attorney general in charge of the statewide organized crime task force, the consent required by subdivisions two and three of this section shall be in addition to that required by subdivision seven of section seventy-a of the executive law.

5. Within fifteen days after the arraignment of any person on an indictment charging a person with the crime of enterprise corruption the prosecutor shall provide a copy of the indictment to those district attorneys whose consent was required pursuant to subdivision three of this section, and shall notify the court and defendant of those district attorneys whose consent the prosecutor has secured. The court shall then review the indictment and the grand jury minutes, notify any district attorney whose consent under subdivision one of this section should have been but was not obtained, direct that the prosecutor provide that district attorney with the portion of the indictment and grand jury minutes that are relevant to a determination whether that district attorney is an "affected district attorney" within the meaning of subdivision one of this section.

6. The failure to obtain from any district attorney the consent required by subdivision two or three of this section shall not be grounds for dismissal of the accusatory instrument or for any other relief upon motion of a defendant in the criminal action.

Upon motion of a district attorney whose consent, pursuant to subdivision three of this section, the court determines was required but not obtained, the court may not dismiss the accusatory instrument or any count thereof but may grant any appropriate relief. Such relief may include, but is not limited to:

(a) ordering that any money forfeited by a defendant in the criminal action, or the proceeds from the sale of any other property forfeited in the criminal action by a defendant, which would have been paid to the county of that district attorney pursuant to section thirteen hundred forty-nine of the civil practice law and rules had the forfeiture action been prosecuted in the county of that district attorney, be paid in whole or in part to the county of that district attorney; or

(b) upon consent of the defendant, ordering the transfer of the prosecution, or any part thereof, to that district attorney or to any other prosecutor with jurisdiction over the prosecution, of the part thereof to be transferred. However, prior to ordering any transfer of the prosecution, the court shall provide to those district attorneys who have previously consented to the prosecution an opportunity to intervene and be heard concerning such transfer.

7. A district attorney whose consent, pursuant to subdivision three of this section, the court determines was required but not obtained may seek the relief described in subdivision six of this section exclusively by a pre-trial motion in the criminal action based on the indictment charging the crime of enterprise corruption. Such relief must be sought without forty-five days of the receipt of notice from the court pursuant to subdivision five of this section.

§460.70 Provisional remedies.

1. The provisional remedies authorized by article thirteen-A of the civil practice law and rules shall be available in all criminal actions in which criminal forfeiture or a fine pursuant to section 460.60 is sought to the extent and under the same terms and conditions as provided in article thirteen-A of such law and rules.

2. Upon the filing of an indictment and special information seeking criminal forfeiture under this article all further proceedings with respect to provisional remedies shall be heard by the judge or justice in the criminal part to which the indictment and special information are assigned.

3. For purposes of this section, the indictment and special information seeking criminal forfeiture shall constitute the summons and complaint referred to in article thirteen-A of the civil practice law and rules.

§460.80 Court ordered disclosure.

Notwithstanding the provisions of article two hundred forty-five of the criminal procedure law, when forfeiture is sought pursuant to section 460.30 of this article, the court may order discovery of any property not otherwise disclosed which is material and reasonably necessary for preparation by the defendant with respect to the forfeiture proceeding pursuant to such section. The court may issue a protective order denying, limiting, conditioning, delaying or regulating such discovery where a danger to the integrity of physical evidence or a substantial risk of physical harm, intimidation, economic reprisal, bribery or unjustified annoyance or embarrassment to any person or an adverse effect upon the legitimate needs of law enforcement, including the protection of the confidentiality of informants, or any other factor or set of factors outweighs the usefulness of the discovery.   *(Eff.1/1/20,Ch.59,L.2019)*

ARTICLE 470 - MONEY LAUNDERING

Section
470.00 **Definitions.**
470.03 **Money laundering: aggregation of value; other matters.**
470.05 **Money laundering in the fourth degree.**
470.10 **Money laundering in the third degree.**
470.15 **Money laundering in the second degree.**
470.20 **Money laundering in the first degree.**
470.21 **Money laundering in support of terrorism in the fourth degree.**
470.22 **Money laundering in support of terrorism in the third degree.**
470.23 **Money laundering in support of terrorism in the second degree.**
470.24 **Money laundering in support of terrorism in the first degree.**
470.25 **Money laundering; fines.**

§470.00 Definitions.

The following definitions are applicable to this article.

1. "Monetary instrument" means coin and currency of the United States or of any other country; personal checks; bank checks; traveler's checks; money orders; and investment securities and negotiable instruments, in bearer form or otherwise, in such form that title thereto passes on delivery, except that "monetary instrument" shall not include payments to attorneys for legal services.

2. "Conducts" includes initiating, concluding or participating in initiating or concluding a transaction.

3. "Transaction" includes a payment, purchase, sale, loan, pledge, gift, transfer, or delivery, and with respect to a financial institution includes a deposit, withdrawal, transfer between accounts, exchange of currency, loan, extension of credit, purchase or sale of any stock, bond,certificate of deposit, or other monetary instrument, use of a safe deposit box, or any other payment, transfer, or delivery by, through, or to a financial institution, by whatever means effected, except that "transaction" shall not include payments to attorneys for legal services.

4. "Criminal conduct" means conduct which is a crime under the laws of this state or conduct committed in any other jurisdiction which is or would be a crime under the laws of this state.

5. "Specified criminal conduct" means criminal conduct committed in this state constituting a criminal act, as the term criminal act is defined in section 460.10 of this chapter, or constituting the crime of enterprise

corruption, as defined in section 460.20 of this chapter, or conduct committed in any other jurisdiction which is or would be specified criminal conduct if committed in this state.

  6. "Financial institution" means:

  (a) an insured bank, as defined in section 3(b) of the Federal Deposit Insurance Act, 12 U.S.C. 1813(h);

  (b) a commercial bank or trust company;

  (c) a private banker;

  (d) an agency or branch of a foreign bank in the United States;

  (e) a credit union;

  (f) a thrift institution;

  (g) a broker or dealer registered with the Securities and Exchange Commission under the Securities and Exchange Act of 1934, U.S.C. 78a et seq.;

  (h) a broker or dealer in securities or commodities;

  (i) an investment banker or investment company;

  (j) a currency exchange;

  (k) an issuer, redeemer, or cashier of travelers' checks, checks, money orders, or similar instruments;

  (l) an operator of a credit card system;

  (m) an insurance company;

  (n) a dealer in precious metals, stones, or jewels;

  (o) a pawnbroker;

  (p) a loan or finance company;

  (q) a travel agency;

  (r) a person licensed to engage in the business of receiving money for transmission or transmitting the same by whatever means, or any other person engaged in such business as an agent of a licensee or engaged in such business without a license;

  (s) a telegraph company;

  (t) a business engaged in vehicle sales, including automobile, airplane and boat sales;

  (u) persons involved in real estate closings and settlements;

  (v) the United States Postal Service;

  (w) an agency of the United States government or of a state or local government carrying out a duty or power of a business described in this subdivision;

  (x) a casino, gambling casino, or gaming establishment with an annual gaming revenue of more than a million dollars which:

  (i) is licensed as a casino, gambling casino or gaming establishment under the laws of any state or any political subdivision of any state; or

  (ii) is an Indian gaming operation conducted under or pursuant to the Indian Gaming Regulatory Act other than an operation which is limited to class 1 gaming as defined in subdivision six of section four of such act; or

  (y) any business or agency engaged in any activity which the superintendent of financial services or the United States Secretary of the Treasury determines, by regulation, to be an activity which is similar to, related to, or a substitute for activity which any business as described in this subdivision is authorized to engage.

7. "Financial transaction" means a transaction involving:

(a) the movement of funds by wire or other means; or

(b) one or more monetary instruments; or

(c) the transfer of title to any real property, vehicle, vessel or aircraft; or

(d) the use of a financial institution.

8. "Represented" means any representation made by a law enforcement officer, or by another person at the direction of, or with the approval of, such law enforcement officer.

9. "Law enforcement officer" means any public servant, federal or state, who is authorized to conduct an investigation, prosecute or make an arrest for a criminal offense.

10. For the purpose of this article, each of the five counties in the city of New York shall be considered as a separate county.

§470.03 Money laundering: aggregation of value; other matters.

1. For purposes of subdivisions one and three of sections 470.05, 470.10, 470.15, 470.21, 470.22 and 470.23, and for purposes of subdivisions one and two of sections 470.20 and 470.24 of this article, financial transactions may be considered together and the value of the property involved may be aggregated, provided that the transactions are all part of a single "criminal transaction" as defined in subdivision two of section 40.10 of the criminal procedure law.

2. For purposes of subdivision two of sections 470.05, 470.10, 470.15, 470.21, 470.22 and 470.23 of this article, separate occasions involving the transport, transmittal or transfer of monetary instruments may be considered together and the value of the monetary instruments involved may be aggregated, provided that the occasions are all part of a single "criminal transaction" as defined in subdivision two of section 40.10 of the criminal procedure law.

3. Nothing in sections 470.05, 470.21, 470.22, 470.23 and 470.24; paragraph (b) of subdivision one, paragraph (b) of subdivision two and paragraph (b) of subdivision three of section 470.10; paragraph (b) of subdivision one, paragraph (b) of subdivision two and paragraph (b) of subdivision three of section 470.15; or paragraph (b) of subdivision one and paragraph (b) of subdivision two of section 470.20 of this article shall make it unlawful to return funds held in escrow:

(a) as a portion of a purchase price for real property pursuant to a contract of sale; or

(b) to satisfy the tax or other lawful obligations arising out of an administrative or judicial proceeding concerning the person who provided the escrow funds.

§470.05 Money laundering in the fourth degree.

A person is guilty of money laundering in the fourth degree when:

1. Knowing that the property involved in one or more financial transactions represents the proceeds of criminal conduct:

(a) he or she conducts one or more such financial transactions which in fact involve the proceeds of specified criminal conduct:

(i) With intent to:

(A) promote the carrying on of criminal conduct; or

(B) engage in conduct constituting a felony as set forth in section eighteen hundred three, eighteen hundred four, eighteen hundred five, or eighteen hundred six of the tax law; or

(ii) Knowing that the transaction or transactions in whole or in part are designed to:

(A) conceal or disguise the nature, the location, the source, the ownership or the control of the proceeds of criminal conduct; or

(B) avoid any transaction reporting requirement imposed by law; and

(b) The total value of the property involved in such financial transaction or transactions exceeds five thousand dollars; or

2. Knowing that one or more monetary instruments represents the proceeds of criminal conduct:

(a) he or she transports, transmits, or transfers on one or more occasions, monetary instruments which in fact represent the proceeds of specified criminal conduct:

(i) With intent to promote the carrying on of criminal conduct; or

(ii) Knowing that such transportation, transmittal, or transfer is designed in whole or in part to:

(A) conceal or disguise the nature, the location, the source, the ownership, or the control of the proceeds of criminal conduct; or

(B) avoid any transaction reporting requirement imposed by law; and

(b) The total value of such monetary instrument or instruments exceeds ten thousand dollars; or

3. He or she conducts one or more financial transactions:

(a) involving property represented to be the proceeds of specified criminal conduct, or represented to be property used to conduct or facilitate specified criminal conduct, with intent to:

(i) promote the carrying on of specified criminal conduct; or

(ii) conceal or disguise the nature, the location, the source, the ownership or the control of property believed to be the proceeds of specified criminal conduct; or

(iii) avoid any transaction reporting requirement imposed by law; and

(b) the total value of the property involved in such financial transaction or transactions exceeds ten thousand dollars.

Money laundering in the fourth degree is a class E felony.

§470.10   Money laundering in the third degree.

A person is guilty of money laundering in the third degree when:

1. Knowing that the property involved in one or more financial transactions represents:

(a) the proceeds of the criminal sale of a controlled substance, he or she conducts one or more such financial transactions which in fact involve the proceeds of the criminal sale of a controlled substance:

(i) With intent to:

(A) promote the carrying on of specified criminal conduct; or

(B) engage in conduct constituting a felony as set forth in section eighteen hundred three, eighteen hundred four, eighteen hundred five, or eighteen hundred six of the tax law; or

(ii) Knowing that the transaction or transactions in whole or in part are designed to:

(A) conceal or disguise the nature, the location, the source, the ownership or the control of the proceeds of specified criminal conduct; or

(B) avoid any transaction reporting requirement imposed by law; and

(iii) The total value of the property involved in such financial transaction or transactions exceeds ten thousand dollars; or

(b) the proceeds of criminal conduct, he or she conducts one or more such financial transactions which in fact involve the proceeds of specified criminal conduct:

(i) With intent to:

(A) promote the carrying on of criminal conduct; or

(B) engage in conduct constituting a felony as set forth in section eighteen hundred three, eighteen hundred four, eighteen hundred five, or eighteen hundred six of the tax law; or

(ii) knowing that the transaction or transactions in whole or in part are designed to:

(A) conceal or disguise the nature, the location, the source, the ownership or the control of the proceeds of criminal conduct; or

(B) avoid any transaction reporting requirement imposed by law; and

(iii) The total value of the property involved in such financial transaction or transactions exceeds fifty thousand dollars; or

2. Knowing that one or more monetary instruments represent:

(a) the proceeds of the criminal sale of a controlled substance, he or she transports, transmits, or transfers or attempts to transport, transmit or transfer, on one or more occasions, monetary instruments which in fact represent the proceeds of the criminal sale of a controlled substance from a place in any county in this state to or through a place outside that county or to a place in any county in this state from or through a place outside that county:

(i) With intent to promote the carrying on of specified criminal conduct; or

(ii) Knowing that such transportation, transmittal or transfer is designed in whole or in part to:

(A) conceal or disguise the nature, the location, the source, the ownership or the control of the proceeds of specified criminal conduct; or

(B) avoid any transaction reporting requirement imposed by law; and

(iii) The total value of such monetary instrument or instruments exceeds ten thousand dollars; or

(b) the proceeds of criminal conduct, he or she transports, transmits, or transfers or attempts to transport, transmit or transfer, on one or more occasions monetary instruments which in fact represent the proceeds of specified criminal conduct from a place in any county in this state to or through a place outside that county or to a place in any county in this state from or through a place outside that county:

(i) With intent to promote the carrying on of criminal conduct; or

(ii) Knowing that such transportation, transmittal or transfer is designed in whole or in part to:

(A) conceal or disguise the nature, the location, the source, the ownership, or the control of the proceeds of criminal conduct; or

(B) avoid any transaction reporting requirement imposed by law; and

(iii) The total value of such monetary instrument or instruments exceeds fifty thousand dollars; or

3. He or she conducts one or more financial transactions involving property represented to be:

(a) the proceeds of the criminal sale of a controlled substance, or represented to be property used to conduct or facilitate the criminal sale of a controlled substance:

(i) With intent to:

(A) promote the carrying on of specified criminal conduct; or

(B) conceal or disguise the nature, the location, the source, the ownership or the control of property believed to be the proceeds of specified criminal conduct; or

(C) avoid any transaction reporting requirement imposed by law; and

(ii) The total value of the property involved in such financial transaction or transactions exceeds ten thousand dollars; or

(b) the proceeds of specified criminal conduct, or represented to be property used to conduct or facilitate specified criminal conduct:

(i) With intent to:

(A) promote the carrying on of specified criminal conduct; or

(B) conceal or disguise the nature, the location, the source, the ownership or the control of property believed to be the proceeds of specified criminal conduct; or

(C) avoid any transaction reporting requirement imposed by law; and

(ii) The total value of the property involved in such financial transaction or transactions exceeds fifty thousand dollars.

Money laundering in the third degree is a class D felony.

§470.15 Money laundering in the second degree.

A person is guilty of money laundering in the second degree when:

1. Knowing that the property involved in one or more financial transactions represents:

(a) the proceeds of the criminal sale of a controlled substance, he or she conducts one or more such financial transactions which in fact involve the proceeds of the criminal sale of a controlled substance:

(i) With intent to:

(A) promote the carrying on of specified criminal conduct; or

(B) engage in conduct constituting a felony as set forth in section eighteen hundred three, eighteen hundred four, eighteen hundred five, or eighteen hundred six of the tax law; or

(ii) Knowing that the transaction or transactions in whole or in part are designed to:

(A) conceal or disguise the nature, the location, the source, the ownership or the control of the proceeds of specified criminal conduct; or

(B) avoid any transaction reporting requirement imposed by law; and

(iii) The total value of the property involved in such financial transaction or transactions exceeds fifty thousand dollars; or

(b) the proceeds of specified criminal conduct, he or she conducts one or more such financial transactions which in fact involve the proceeds of specified criminal conduct:

(i) With intent to:

(A) promote the carrying on of specified criminal conduct; or

(B) engage in conduct constituting a felony as set forth in section eighteen hundred three, eighteen hundred four, eighteen hundred five, or eighteen hundred six of the tax law; or

(ii) Knowing that the transaction or transactions in whole or in part are designed to:

(A) conceal or disguise the nature, the location, the source, the ownership or the control of the proceeds of specified criminal conduct; or

(B) avoid any transaction reporting requirement imposed by law; and

(iii) The total value of the property involved in such financial transaction or transactions exceeds one hundred thousand dollars; or

2. Knowing that one or more monetary instruments represent:

(a) the proceeds of the criminal sale of a controlled substance, he or she transports, transmits, or transfers or attempts to transport, transmit or transfer, on one or more occasions, monetary instruments which in fact represent the proceeds of the criminal sale of a controlled substance from a place in any county in this state to or through a place outside that county or to a place in any county in this state from or through a place outside that county:

(i) With intent to promote the carrying on of specified criminal conduct; or

(ii) Knowing that such transportation, transmittal or transfer is designed in whole or in part to:

(A) conceal or disguise the nature, the location, the source, the ownership or the control of the proceeds of specified criminal conduct; or

(B) avoid any transaction reporting requirement imposed by law; and

(iii) The total value of such monetary instrument or instruments exceeds fifty thousand dollars; or

(b) the proceeds of specified criminal conduct, he or she transports, transmits, or transfers or attempts to transport, transmit or transfer, on one or more occasions, monetary instruments which in fact represent the proceeds of specified criminal conduct from a place in any county in this state to or through a place outside that county or to a place in any county in this state from or through a place outside that county:

(i) With intent to promote the carrying on of specified criminal conduct; or

(ii) Knowing that such transportation, transmittal or transfer is designed in whole or in part to:

(A) conceal or disguise the nature, the location, the source, the ownership or the control of the proceeds of specified criminal conduct; or

(B) avoid any transaction reporting requirement imposed by law; and

(iii) The total value of such monetary instrument or instruments exceeds one hundred thousand dollars; or

3. He or she conducts one or more financial transactions involving property represented to be:

(a) the proceeds of the criminal sale of a controlled substance, or represented to be property used to conduct or facilitate the criminal sale of a controlled substance:
(i) With intent to:
(A) promote the carrying on of specified criminal conduct; or
(B) conceal or disguise the nature, the location, the source, the ownership or the control of property believed to be the proceeds of specified criminal conduct; or
(C) avoid any transaction reporting requirement imposed by law; and
(ii) The total represented value of the property involved in such financial transaction or transactions exceeds fifty thousand dollars; or
(b) the proceeds of specified criminal conduct, or represented to be property used to conduct or facilitate specified criminal conduct:
(i) With intent to:
(A) promote the carrying on of specified criminal conduct;
(B) conceal or disguise the nature, the location, the source, the ownership or the control of property believed to be the proceeds of specified criminal conduct; or
(C) avoid any transaction reporting requirement imposed by law; and
(ii) The total represented value of the property involved in such financial transaction or transactions exceeds one hundred thousand dollars.
Money laundering in the second degree is a class C felony.

§470.20 Money laundering in the first degree.
A person is guilty of money laundering in the first degree when:
1. Knowing that the property involved in one or more financial transactions represents:
(a) the proceeds of the criminal sale of a controlled substance, he or she conducts one or more such financial transactions which in fact involve the proceeds of the criminal sale of a controlled substance:
(i) With intent to:
(A) promote the carrying on of specified criminal conduct; or
(B) engage in conduct constituting a felony as set forth in section eighteen hundred three, eighteen hundred four, eighteen hundred five, or eighteen hundred six of the tax law; or
(ii) Knowing that the transaction or transactions in whole or in part are designed to:
(A) conceal or disguise the nature, the location, the source, the ownership or the control of the proceeds of specified criminal conduct; or
(B) avoid any transaction reporting requirement imposed by law; and
(iii) The total value of the property involved in such financial transaction or transactions exceeds five hundred thousand dollars; or
(b) the proceeds of a class A, B or C felony, or of a crime in any other jurisdiction that is or would be a class A, B or C felony under the laws of this state, he or she conducts one or more such financial transactions which in fact involve the proceeds of any such felony:

(i) With intent to:

(A) promote the carrying on of specified criminal conduct; or

(B) engage in conduct constituting a felony as set forth in section eighteen hundred three, eighteen hundred four, eighteen hundred five,* eighteen hundred six of the tax law; or

(ii) Knowing that the transaction or transactions in whole or in part are designed to:

(A) conceal or disguise the nature, the location, the source, the ownership or the control of the proceeds of specified criminal conduct; or

(B) avoid any transaction reporting requirement imposed by law; and

(iii) The total value of the property involved in such financial transaction or transactions exceeds one million dollars.

2. He or she conducts one or more financial transactions involving property represented to be:

(a) the proceeds of the criminal sale of a controlled substance, or represented to be property used to conduct or facilitate the criminal sale of a controlled substance:

(i) With intent to:

(A) promote the carrying on of specified criminal conduct; or

(B) conceal or disguise the nature, the location, the source, the ownership or the control of property believed to be the proceeds of specified criminal conduct; or

(C) avoid any transaction reporting requirement imposed by law; and

(ii) The total represented value of the property involved in such financial transaction or transactions exceeds five hundred thousand dollars; or

(b) the proceeds of a class A, B or C felony or of a crime in any other jurisdiction that is or would be a class A, B or C felony under the laws of this state, or represented to be property used to conduct or facilitate such crimes:

(i) With intent to:

(A) promote the carrying on of specified criminal conduct; or

(B) conceal or disguise the nature, the location, the source, the ownership or the control of property believed to be the proceeds of specified criminal conduct; or

(C) avoid any transaction reporting requirement imposed by law; and

(ii) The total represented value of the property involved in such financial transaction or transactions exceeds one million dollars.

Money laundering in the first degree is a class B felony.

§470.21 Money laundering in support of terrorism in the fourth degree.

A person is guilty of money laundering in support of terrorism in the fourth degree when:

*("or" inadvertently omitted.)

1. Knowing that the property involved in one or more financial transactions represents either the proceeds of an act of terrorism as defined in subdivision one of section 490.05 of this part, or a monetary instrument given, received or intended to be used to support a violation of article four hundred ninety of this part:

(a) he or she conducts one or more such financial transactions which in fact involve either the proceeds of an act of terrorism as defined in subdivision one of section 490.05 of this part, or a monetary instrument given, received or intended to be used to support a violation of article four hundred ninety of this part:

(i) With intent to:

(A) promote the carrying on of criminal conduct; or

(B) engage in conduct constituting a felony as set forth in section eighteen hundred three, eighteen hundred four, eighteen hundred five, or eighteen hundred six of the tax law; or

(ii) Knowing that the transaction or transactions in whole or in part are designed to:

(A) conceal or disguise the nature, the location, the source, the ownership or the control of either the proceeds of an act of terrorism as defined in subdivision one of section 490.05 of this part, or a monetary instrument given, received or intended to be used to support a violation of article four hundred ninety of this part; or

(B) avoid any transaction reporting requirement imposed by law; and

(b) the total value of the property involved in such financial transaction or transactions exceeds one thousand dollars; or

2. Knowing that one or more monetary instruments represents either the proceeds of an act of terrorism as defined in subdivision one of section 490.05 of this part, or a monetary instrument given, received or intended to be used to support a violation of article four hundred ninety of this part:

(a) he or she transports, transmits, or transfers on one or more occasions, monetary instruments which in fact represent either the proceeds of an act of terrorism as defined in subdivision one of section 490.05 of this part, or a monetary instrument given, received or intended to be used to support a violation of article four hundred ninety of this part:

(i) With intent to promote the carrying on of criminal conduct; or

(ii) Knowing that such transportation, transmittal, or transfer is designed in whole or in part to:

(A) conceal or disguise the nature, the location, the source, the ownership, or the control of either the proceeds of an act of terrorism as defined in subdivision one of section 490.05 of this part, or a monetary instrument given, received or intended to be used to support a violation of article four hundred ninety of this part; or

(B) avoid any transaction reporting requirement imposed by law; and

(b) the total value of such monetary instrument or instruments exceeds two thousand dollars; or

3. He or she conducts one or more financial transactions:

(a) involving property represented to be either the proceeds of an act of terrorism as defined in subdivision one of section 490.05 of this part, or a monetary instrument given, received or intended to be used to support a violation of article four hundred ninety of this part, with intent to:

(i) promote the carrying on of specified criminal conduct; or

(ii) conceal or disguise the nature, the location, the source, the ownership or the control of property believed to be either the proceeds of an act of terrorism as defined in subdivision one of section 490.05 of this part, or a monetary instrument given, received or intended to be used to support a violation of article four hundred ninety of this part; or

(iii) avoid any transaction reporting requirement imposed by law; and

(b) the total value of the property involved in such financial transaction or transactions exceeds two thousand dollars.

Money laundering in support of terrorism in the fourth degree is a class E felony.

§470.22 Money laundering in support of terrorism in the third degree.

A person is guilty of money laundering in support of terrorism in the third degree when:

1. Knowing that the property involved in one or more financial transactions represents either the proceeds of an act of terrorism as defined in subdivision one of section 490.05 of this part, or a monetary instrument given, received or intended to be used to support a violation of article four hundred ninety of this part:

(a) he or she conducts one or more such financial transactions which in fact involve either the proceeds of an act of terrorism as defined in subdivision one of section 490.05 of this part, or a monetary instrument given, received or intended to be used to support a violation of article four hundred ninety of this part:

(i) With intent to:

(A) promote the carrying on of specified criminal conduct; or

(B) engage in conduct constituting a felony as set forth in section eighteen hundred three, eighteen hundred four, eighteen hundred five, or eighteen hundred six of the tax law; or

(ii) Knowing that the transaction or transactions in whole or in part are designed to:

(A) conceal or disguise the nature, the location, the source, the ownership or the control of either the proceeds of an act of terrorism as

defined in subdivision one of section 490.05 of this part, or a monetary
instrument given, received or intended to be used to support a violation
of article four hundred ninety of this part; or

    (B) avoid any transaction reporting requirement imposed by law;
and

    (b) the total value of the property involved in such financial
transaction or transactions exceeds five thousand dollars; or

  2. Knowing that one or more monetary instruments represent either
the proceeds of an act of terrorism as defined in subdivision one of
section 490.05 of this part, or a monetary instrument given, received or
intended to be used to support a violation of article four hundred ninety
of this part:

    (a) he or she transports, transmits, or transfers or attempts to
transport, transmit or transfer, on one or more occasions, monetary
instruments which in fact represent either the proceeds of an act of
terrorism as defined in subdivision one of section 490.05 of this part, or
a monetary instrument given, received or intended to be used to support
a violation of article four hundred ninety of this part from a place in any
county in this state to or through a place outside that county or to a place
in any county in this state from or through a place outside that county:

    (i) With intent to promote the carrying on of specified criminal
conduct; or

    (ii) Knowing that such transportation, transmittal or transfer is
designed in whole or in part to:

    (A) conceal or disguise the nature, the location, the source, the
ownership or the control of either the proceeds of an act of terrorism as
defined in subdivision one of section 490.05 of this part, or a monetary
instrument given, received or intended to be used to support a violation
of article four hundred ninety of this part; or

    (B) avoid any transaction reporting requirement imposed by law;
and

    (b) The total value of such monetary instrument or instruments
exceeds five thousand dollars; or

  3. He or she conducts one or more financial transactions involving
property represented to be either the proceeds of an act of terrorism as
defined in subdivision one of section 490.05 of this part, or a monetary
instrument given, received or intended to be used to support a violation
of article four hundred ninety of this part:

    (a) With intent to:

    (i) promote the carrying on of specified criminal conduct; or

    (ii) conceal or disguise the nature, the location, the source, the
ownership or the control of property believed to be either the proceeds
of an act of terrorism as defined in subdivision one of section 490.05 of
this part, or a monetary instrument given, received or intended to be
used to support a violation of article four hundred ninety of this part; or

    (iii) avoid any transaction reporting requirement imposed by law;
and

(b) The total value of the property involved in such financial transaction or transactions exceeds five thousand dollars.

Money laundering in support of terrorism in the third degree is a class D felony.

§470.23 Money laundering in support of terrorism in the second degree.

A person is guilty of money laundering in support of terrorism in the second degree when:

1. Knowing that the property involved in one or more financial transactions represents either the proceeds of an act of terrorism as defined in subdivision one of section 490.05 of this part, or a monetary instrument given, received or intended to be used to support a violation of article four hundred ninety of this part:

(a) he or she conducts one or more such financial transactions which in fact involve either the proceeds of an act of terrorism as defined in subdivision one of section 490.05 of this part, or a monetary instrument given, received or intended to be used to support a violation of article four hundred ninety of this part:

(i) With intent to:

(A) promote the carrying on of specified criminal conduct; or

(B) engage in conduct constituting a felony as set forth in section eighteen hundred three, eighteen hundred four, eighteen hundred five, or eighteen hundred six of the tax law; or

(ii) Knowing that the transaction or transactions in whole or in part are designed to:

(A) conceal or disguise the nature, the location, the source, the ownership or the control of either the proceeds of an act of terrorism as defined in subdivision one of section 490.05 of this part, or a monetary instrument given, received or intended to be used to support a violation of article four hundred ninety of this part; or

(B) avoid any transaction reporting requirement imposed by law; and

(b) the total value of the property involved in such financial transaction or transactions exceeds twenty-five thousand dollars; or

2. Knowing that one or more monetary instruments represent either the proceeds of an act of terrorism as defined in subdivision one of section 490.05 of this part, or a monetary instrument given, received or intended to be used to support a violation of article four hundred ninety of this part:

(a) he or she transports, transmits, or transfers or attempts to transport, transmit or transfer, on one or more occasions, monetary instruments which in fact represent either the proceeds of an act of terrorism as defined in subdivision one of section 490.05 of this part, or a monetary instrument given, received or intended to be used to support a violation of article four hundred ninety of this part from a place in any county in this state to or through a place outside that county or to a place in any county in this state from or through a place outside that county:

(i) With intent to promote the carrying on of specified criminal conduct; or

(ii) Knowing that such transportation, transmittal or transfer is designed in whole or in part to:

(A) conceal or disguise the nature, the location, the source, the ownership or the control of either the proceeds of an act of terrorism as defined in subdivision one of section 490.05 of this part, or a monetary instrument given, received or intended to be used to support a violation of article four hundred ninety of this part; or

(B) avoid any transaction reporting requirement imposed by law; and

(b) the total value of such monetary instrument or instruments exceeds twenty-five thousand dollars; or

3. He or she conducts one or more financial transactions involving property represented to be either the proceeds of an act of terrorism as defined in subdivision one of section 490.05 of this part, or a monetary instrument given, received or intended to be used to support a violation of article four hundred ninety of this part:

(a) With intent to:

(i) promote the carrying on of specified criminal conduct; or

(ii) conceal or disguise the nature, the location, the source, the ownership or the control of property believed to be either the proceeds of an act of terrorism as defined in subdivision one of section 490.05 of this part, or a monetary instrument given, received or intended to be used to support a violation of article four hundred ninety of this part; or

(iii) avoid any transaction reporting requirement imposed by law; and

(b) The total value of the property involved in such financial transaction or transactions exceeds twenty-five thousand dollars.

Money laundering in support of terrorism in the second degree is a class C felony.

§470.24 Money laundering in support of terrorism in the first degree.

A person is guilty of money laundering in support of terrorism in the first degree when:

1. Knowing that the property involved in one or more financial transactions represents either the proceeds of an act of terrorism as defined in subdivision one of section 490.05 of this part, or a monetary instrument given, received or intended to be used to support a violation of article four hundred ninety of this part:

(a) he or she conducts one or more financial transactions which in fact involve either the proceeds of an act of terrorism as defined in subdivision one of section 490.05 of this part, or a monetary instrument given, received or intended to be used to support a violation of article four hundred ninety of this part:

    (i) With intent to:

      (A) promote the carrying on of specified criminal conduct; or

      (B) engage in conduct constituting a felony as set forth in section eighteen hundred three, eighteen hundred four, eighteen hundred five, or eighteen hundred six of the tax law; or

    (ii) Knowing that the transaction or transactions in whole or in part are designed to:

      (A) conceal or disguise the nature, the location, the source, the ownership or the control of the proceeds of either the proceeds of an act of terrorism as defined in subdivision one of section 490.05 of this part, or a monetary instrument given, received or intended to be used to support a violation of article four hundred ninety of this part; or

      (B) avoid any transaction reporting requirement imposed by law; and

    (iii) The total value of the property involved in such financial transaction or transactions exceeds seventy-five thousand dollars.

2. He or she conducts one or more financial transactions involving property represented to be either the proceeds of an act of terrorism as defined in subdivision one of section 490.05 of this part, or a monetary instrument given, received or intended to be used to support a violation of article four hundred ninety of this part:

    (a) With intent to:

    (i) promote the carrying on of specified criminal conduct; or

    (ii) conceal or disguise the nature, the location, the source, the ownership or the control of property believed to be either the proceeds of an act of terrorism as defined in subdivision one of section 490.05 of this part, or a monetary instrument given, received or intended to be used to support a violation of article four hundred ninety of this part; or

    (iii) avoid any transaction reporting requirement imposed by law; and

    (b) The total represented value of the property involved in such financial transaction or transactions exceeds one hundred twenty-five thousand dollars.

Money laundering in support of terrorism in the first degree is a class B felony.

§470.25 Money laundering; fines.

1. Any person convicted of a violation of section 470.05, 470.10, 470.15, or 470.20 of this article may be sentenced to pay a fine not in excess of two times the value of the monetary instruments which are the proceeds of specified criminal activity. When a fine is imposed pursuant to this subdivision, the court shall make a finding as to the value of such monetary instrument or instruments. If the record does not contain sufficient evidence to support such a finding the court may conduct a hearing upon the issue. In imposing a fine, the court shall consider the seriousness of the conduct, whether the amount of the fine is disproportionate to the conduct in which he engaged, its impact on victims, as well as the economic circumstances of the convicted person, including the effect of the imposition of such a fine upon his immediate family.

2. The imposition of a fine pursuant to subdivision one of this section or paragraph b of subdivision one of section 80.00 of this chapter, shall preclude the imposition of any other order or judgment of forfeiture or fine based upon the same criminal conduct.

ARTICLE 480 - CRIMINAL FORFEITURE - FELONY CONTROLLED SUBSTANCE OFFENSES

Section
480.00 **Definitions.**
480.05 **Felony controlled substance offenses; forfeiture.**
480.10 **Procedure.**
480.20 **Disposal of property.**
480.25 **Election of remedies.**
480.30 **Provisional remedies.**
480.35 **Rebuttable presumption.**

§480.00 Definitions.

The following definitions are applicable to this article.

1. "Felony offense" means only a felony defined in article two hundred twenty of this chapter, or an attempt or conspiracy to commit any such felony, provided such attempt or conspiracy is punishable as a felony, or solicitation of any such felony provided such solicitation is punishable as a felony.

2. "Property" means real property, personal property, money, negotiable instruments, securities, or anything of value or an interest in a thing of value.

3. "Proceeds" means any property obtained by a defendant through the commission of a felony controlled substance offense, and includes any appreciation in value of such property.

4. "Substituted proceeds" means any property obtained by a defendant by the sale or exchange of proceeds of a felony controlled substance offense, and any gain realized by such sale or exchange.

5. "Instrumentality of a felony controlled substance offense" means any property, other than real property and any buildings,

fixtures, appurtenances, and improvements thereon, whose use contributes directly and materially to the commission of a felony controlled substance offense.

6. "Real property instrumentality of a crime" means an interest in real property the use of which contributes directly and materially to the commission of a specified felony offense.

7. "Specified felony offense" means:

(a) a conviction of a person for a violation of section 220.18, 220.21, 220.41, 220.43, or 220.77 of this chapter, or where the accusatory instrument charges one or more of such offenses, conviction upon a plea of guilty to any of the felonies for which such plea is otherwise authorized by law or a conviction of a person for conspiracy to commit a violation of section 220.18, 220.21, 220.41, 220.43, or 220.77 of this chapter, where the controlled substances which are the object of the conspiracy are located in the real property which is the subject of the forfeiture action; or

(b) three or more violations of any of the felonies defined in section 220.09, 220.16, 220.18, 220.21, 220.31, 220.34, 220.39, 220.41, 220.43 or 220.77 of this chapter, which violations do not constitute a single criminal offense as defined in subdivision one of section 40.10 of the criminal procedure law, or a single criminal transaction, as defined in paragraph (a) of subdivision two of section 40.10 of the criminal procedure law, and at least one of which resulted in a conviction of such offense, or where the accusatory instrument charges one or more of such felonies, conviction upon a plea of guilty to a felony for which such plea is otherwise authorized by law; or

(c) a conviction of a person for a violation of section 220.09, 220.16, 220.34 or 220.39 of this chapter, or where the accusatory instrument charges any such felony, conviction upon a plea of guilty to a felony for which the plea is otherwise authorized by law, together with evidence which: (i) provides substantial indicia that the defendant used the real property to engage in a continual, ongoing course of conduct involving the unlawful mixing, compounding, manufacturing, warehousing, or packaging of controlled substances as part of an illegal trade or business for gain; and (ii) establishes, where the conviction is for possession of a controlled substance, that such possession was with the intent to sell it.

(Eff.3/31/21,Ch.92,L.2021)

§480.05 Felony controlled substance offenses; forfeiture.

1. When any person is convicted of a felony offense, the following property is subject to forfeiture pursuant to this article:

(a) any property constituting the proceeds or substituted proceeds of such offense, unless the forfeiture is disproportionate to the defendant's gain from or participation in the offense, in which event the trier of fact may direct forfeiture of a portion thereof; and

(b) any property constituting an instrumentality of such offense, other than a real property instrumentality of a crime, unless such forfeiture is disproportionate to the defendant's gain from or participation in the offense, in which event the trier of fact may direct forfeiture of a portion thereof.

2. When any person is convicted of a specified offense, the real property instrumentality of such specified offense is subject to forfeiture pursuant to this article, unless such forfeiture is disproportionate to the defendant's gain from or participation in the offense, in which event the trier of fact may direct forfeiture of a portion thereof.

3. Property acquired in good faith by an attorney as payment for the reasonable and bona fide fees of legal services or reimbursement of reasonable and bona fide expenses related to the representation of a defendant in connection with a civil or criminal forfeiture proceeding or a related criminal matter, shall be exempt from a judgment of forfeiture. For purposes of this subdivision, "bona fide" means that the attorney who acquired such property had no reasonable basis to believe that the fee transaction was a fraudulent or sham transaction designed to shield property from forfeiture, hide its existence from governmental investigative agencies, or was conducted for any purpose other than legitimate.

§480.10 Procedure.

1. After the grand jury votes to file an indictment charging a person with a felony offense as that term is defined in section 480.00 of this article, it may subsequently receive evidence that property is subject to forfeiture under this article. If such evidence is legally sufficient and provides reasonable cause to believe that such property is subject to forfeiture under this article, the grand jury shall file together with the indictment a special forfeiture information specifying the property for which forfeiture is sought and containing a plain and concise factual statement which sets forth the basis for the forfeiture. Alternatively, where the defendant has waived indictment and has consented to be prosecuted for a felony offense by superior court information pursuant to article one hundred ninety-five of the criminal procedure law, the prosecutor may, in addition to the superior court information, file a special forfeiture information specifying the property for which the forfeiture is sought and containing a plain and concise factual statement which sets forth the basis for the forfeiture.

2. At any time before entry of a plea of guilty to an indictment or commencement of a trial thereof, the prosecutor may file a superseding special forfeiture information in the same court in accordance with the provisions of subdivision one of this section. Upon the filing of such a superseding forfeiture information the court must, upon application of the defendant, order any adjournment of the proceedings which may, by reason of such superseding

special forfeiture information, be necessary to accord the defendant adequate opportunity to prepare his defense of the forfeiture action.

3. A motion to inspect and reduce made pursuant to section 210.20 of the criminal procedure law may seek modification of a special forfeiture information dismissing a claim with respect to any property interest therein where the court finds the evidence before the grand jury was legally insufficient to support a claim against such interest.

4. The prosecutor shall promptly file a copy of the special forfeiture information, including the terms thereof, with the state division of criminal justice services and with the local agency responsible for criminal justice planning. Failure to file such information shall not be grounds for any relief under this chapter. The prosecutor shall also report such demographic data as required by the state division of criminal justice services when filing a copy of the special forfeiture information with the state division of criminal justice services.

(Eff.10/9/19,Ch.55,L.2019)

5. In addition to information required to be disclosed pursuant to article two hundred forty-five of the criminal procedure law, when forfeiture is sought pursuant to this article, and following the defendant's arraignment on the special forfeiture information, the court shall order discovery of any information not otherwise disclosed which is material and reasonably necessary for preparation by the defendant with respect to a forfeiture proceeding brought pursuant to this article. Such material shall include those portions of the grand jury minutes and such other information which pertain solely to the special forfeiture information and shall not include information which pertains to the criminal charges. Upon application of the prosecutor, the court may issue a protective order pursuant to section 245.70 of the criminal procedure law with respect to any information required to be disclosed pursuant to this subdivision.   *(Eff.1/1/20,Ch.59,L.2019)*

6. (a) Trial of forfeiture counts by jury or by the court. Evidence which relates solely to the issue of forfeiture shall not be presented during the trial on the underlying felony offense or specified felony offense, and the defendant shall not be required to present such evidence prior to the verdict on such offense. A defendant who does not present evidence in his defense with respect to the trial of the underlying offense is not precluded on account thereof from presenting evidence during the trial of the forfeiture count or counts.

(b) Trial of forfeiture counts by the jury. After returning a verdict of guilty of a felony offense or specified felony offense, or where the defendant has pled guilty to a felony offense or a specified felony offense and has not waived a jury trial of the forfeiture count or counts pursuant to article three hundred twenty of the criminal procedure law, the jury shall be given the forfeiture information and shall hear any additional evidence which is relevant and legally admissible upon the forfeiture count or counts. After hearing such evidence, the jury shall then deliberate upon the forfeiture count or counts, and based upon all the evidence admitted in connection with the indictment or superior court information and the forfeiture information, may, if satisfied by proof beyond a reasonable doubt that the property, or a portion thereof, is subject to forfeiture pursuant to this article, return a verdict directing that such property, or portion thereof, is subject to forfeiture.

(c) Trial of forfeiture counts by the court. Where a defendant has waived a jury trial of the forfeiture count or counts pursuant to article three hundred twenty of the criminal procedure law, the court shall hear all evidence upon the forfeiture information and may, if satisfied by proof beyond a reasonable doubt that the property, or a portion thereof, is subject to forfeiture under this article, render a verdict determining that such property, or a portion thereof, is subject to forfeiture under this article.

(d) After the verdict of forfeiture, the court shall hear arguments and may receive additional evidence upon a motion of the defendant that the verdict of forfeiture (i) is against the weight of the evidence, or (ii) is, with respect to a forfeiture pursuant to this article, disproportionate to the defendant's gain from the offense, or the defendant's interest in the property, or the defendant's participation in the conduct upon which the forfeiture is based. Upon such a finding, the court may in the interest of justice set aside, modify, limit or otherwise condition the verdict of forfeiture.

7. A final judgment or order of forfeiture issued pursuant to this article shall authorize the prosecutor to seize all property directed to be forfeited under this article upon such terms and conditions as the court deems proper. If a property right is not exercisable or transferable for value by the prosecutor, it shall expire and shall not revert to the convicted person.

8. Where the forfeited property consists of real property, the court may at any time prior to a verdict of forfeiture, enter an order pursuant to subdivision four-a of section thirteen hundred eleven of the civil practice law and rules.

9. No person shall forfeit any right, title, or interest in any property under this article who has not been convicted of a felony offense or specified felony offense, as the case may be. Any person claiming an interest in property subject to forfeiture may institute a special proceeding to determine that claim, before or after the trial, pursuant to section thirteen hundred twenty-seven of the civil practice law and rules; provided, however, that if such special proceeding is initiated before trial on the forfeiture count or counts, it may, upon written motion of the prosecutor, and in the court's discretion, be postponed by the court until completion of the trial. In addition, any person claiming an interest in property subject to forfeiture may petition for remission as provided for in subdivision seven of section thirteen hundred eleven of the civil practice law and rules.

10. Testimony of the defendant or evidence derived therefrom introduced in the trial of the forfeiture count may not be used by the prosecution in any post-trial motion proceedings, appeals, or

retrials relating to the defendant's criminal liability for the underlying criminal offense unless the defendant has previously referred to such evidence in such post-trial proceeding, appeal, or retrial relating to the underlying offense and the evidence is presented by the prosecutor in response thereto. Upon vacatur or reversal on appeal of a judgment of conviction upon which a verdict of forfeiture is based, any verdict of forfeiture which is based upon such conviction shall also be vacated or reversed.

§480.20 Disposal of property.

All property which is forfeited pursuant to this article shall be disposed of in accordance with the provisions of section thirteen hundred forty-nine of the civil practice law and rules. All reports required to be filed pursuant to article thirteen-A of such law and rules by a claiming authority shall be filed by the prosecutor in a forfeiture action brought pursuant to this article.

§480.25 Election of remedies.

The imposition of a judgment or order of forfeiture pursuant to this article with respect to a defendant's interest in property shall preclude the imposition of a judgment or order of forfeiture with respect to such interest in property pursuant to the provisions of any other state or local law based upon the same criminal conduct.

§480.30 Provisional remedies.

1. The provisional remedies authorized by article thirteen-A of the civil practice law and rules shall be available in an action for criminal forfeiture pursuant to this article to the extent and under the same terms, conditions and limitations as provided in article thirteen-A of such law and rules, except as specifically provided herein.

2. Upon the filing of an indictment and special forfeiture information, or a superior court information and special forfeiture information, seeking forfeiture pursuant to this article, all further proceedings with respect to provisional remedies shall be heard by the judge or justice in the criminal part to which the criminal action is assigned.

3. For purposes of this section, the indictment and special forfeiture information or superior court information and special forfeiture information seeking criminal forfeiture shall constitute the summons with notice or summons and verified complaint referred to in article thirteen-A of the civil practice law and rules.

§480.35 Rebuttable presumption.

1. In a criminal forfeiture proceeding commenced pursuant to this article, the following rebuttable presumption shall apply: all currency or negotiable instruments payable to the bearer shall be presumed to be the proceeds of a felony offense when such currency or negotiable

instruments are (i) found in close proximity to a controlled substance unlawfully possessed by the defendant in an amount sufficient to constitute a violation of section 220.18 or 220.21 of the penal law, or (ii) found in close proximity to any quantity of a controlled substance or marihuana unlawfully possessed by such defendant in a room, other than a public place, under circumstances evincing an intent to unlawfully mix, compound, package, distribute or otherwise prepare for sale such controlled substance or marihuana.

2. The presumption established by this section shall be rebutted by credible and reliable evidence which tends to show that such currency or negotiable instruments payable to the bearer is not the proceeds of a felony offense. In an action tried before a jury, the jury shall be so instructed. Any sworn testimony of a defendant offered to rebut the presumption and any other evidence which is obtained as a result of such testimony, shall be inadmissible in any subsequent proceeding relating to the forfeiture action, or in any other civil or criminal action, except in a prosecution for a violation of article two hundred ten of this chapter. In an action tried before a jury, at the commencement of the trial, or at such other time as the court reasonably directs, the prosecutor shall provide notice to the court and to the defendant of its intent to request that the court charge such presumption.

TITLE Y - HATE CRIMES ACT OF 2000
ARTICLE 485 - HATE CRIMES

Section
485.00 Legislative findings.
485.05 Hate crimes.
485.10 Sentencing.

§485.00 Legislative findings.

The legislature finds and determines as follows: criminal acts involving violence, intimidation and destruction of property based upon bias and prejudice have become more prevalent in New York state in recent years. The intolerable truth is that in these crimes, commonly and justly referred to as "hate crimes", victims are intentionally selected, in whole or in part, because of their race, color, national origin, ancestry, gender, gender identity or expression, religion, religious practice, age, disability or sexual orientation. Hate crimes do more than threaten the safety and welfare of all citizens. They inflict on victims incalculable physical and emotional damage and tear at the very fabric of free society. Crimes motivated by invidious hatred toward particular groups not only harm individual victims but send a powerful message of intolerance and discrimination to all members of the group to which the victim belongs. Hate crimes can and do intimidate and disrupt entire communities and vitiate the civility that is essential to healthy democratic processes. In a democratic society, citizens cannot be required to approve of the beliefs and practices of others, but must never commit criminal acts on account of them. However, these criminal acts do occur and are occurring more and more frequently. Quite often, these crimes of hate are also acts of terror. The recent attacks in Monsey, New York as well as the shootings in El Paso, Texas; Pittsburgh, Pennsylvania; Sutherland Springs, Texas; Orlando, Florida; and Charleston, South Carolina illustrate that mass killings are often apolitical, motivated by the hatred of a specific group coupled with a desire to inflict mass casualties. The current law emphasizes the political motivation of an act over its catastrophic effect and does not adequately recognize the harm to public order and individual safety that hate crimes cause. Therefore, our laws must be strengthened to provide clear recognition of the gravity of hate crimes and the compelling importance of preventing their recurrence. *(Eff.11/1/20,Ch.55,L.2020)*

Accordingly, the legislature finds and declares that hate crimes should be prosecuted and punished with appropriate severity.

§485.05 Hate crimes.

1. A person commits a hate crime when he or she commits a specified offense and either:

(a) intentionally selects the person against whom the offense is committed or intended to be committed in whole or in substantial part because of a belief or perception regarding the race, color, national origin, ancestry, gender, gender identity or expression, religion, religious practice, age, disability or sexual orientation of a person, regardless of whether the belief or perception is correct, or

(b) intentionally commits the act or acts constituting the offense in whole or in substantial part because of a belief or perception regarding the race, color, national origin, ancestry, gender, gender identity or expression, religion, religious practice, age, disability or sexual orientation of a person, regardless of whether the belief or perception is correct.

2. Proof of race, color, national origin, ancestry, gender, gender identity or expression, religion, religious practice, age, disability or sexual orientation of the defendant, the victim or of both the defendant and the victim does not, by itself, constitute legally sufficient evidence satisfying the people's burden under paragraph (a) or (b) of subdivision one of this section.

3. A "specified offense" is an offense defined by any of the following provisions of this chapter: section 120.00 (assault in the third degree); section 120.05 (assault in the second degree); section 120.10 (assault in the first degree); section 120.12 (aggravated assault upon a person less than eleven years old); section 120.13 (menacing in the first degree); section 120.14 (menacing in the second degree); section 120.15 (menacing in the third degree); section 120.20 (reckless endangerment in the second degree); section 120.25 (reckless endangerment in the first

degree); section 121.12 (strangulation in the second degree); section 121.13 (strangulation in the first degree); subdivision one of section 125.15 (manslaughter in the second degree); subdivision one, two or four of section 125.20 (manslaughter in the first degree); section 125.25 (murder in the second degree); section 120.45 (stalking in the fourth degree); section 120.50 (stalking in the third degree); section 120.55 (stalking in the second degree); section 120.60 (stalking in the first degree); subdivision one of section 130.35 (rape in the first degree); subdivision one of section 130.50 (criminal sexual act in the first degree); subdivision one of section 130.65 (sexual abuse in the first degree); paragraph (a) of subdivision one of section 130.67 (aggravated sexual abuse in the second degree); paragraph (a) of subdivision one of section 130.70 (aggravated sexual abuse in the first degree); section 135.05 (unlawful imprisonment in the second degree); section 135.10 (unlawful imprisonment in the first degree); section 135.20 (kidnapping in the second degree); section 135.25 (kidnapping in the first degree); section 135.60 (coercion in the third degree); section 135.61 (coercion in the second degree); section 135.65 (coercion in the first degree); section 140.10 (criminal trespass in the third degree); section 140.15 (criminal trespass in the second degree); section 140.17 (criminal trespass in the first degree); section 140.20 (burglary in the third degree); section 140.25 (burglary in the second degree); section 140.30 (burglary in the first degree); section 145.00 (criminal mischief in the fourth degree); section 145.05 (criminal mischief in the third degree); section 145.10 (criminal mischief in the second degree); section 145.12 (criminal mischief in the first degree); section 150.05 (arson in the fourth degree); section 150.10 (arson in the third degree); section 150.15 (arson in the second degree); section 150.20 (arson in the first degree); section 155.25 (petit larceny); section 155.30 (grand larceny in the fourth degree); section 155.35 (grand larceny in the third degree); section 155.40 (grand larceny in the second degree); section 155.42 (grand larceny in the first degree); section 160.05 (robbery in the third degree); section 160.10 (robbery in the second degree); section 160.15 (robbery in the first degree); section 240.25 (harassment in the first degree); subdivision one, two or four of section 240.30 (aggravated harassment in the second degree); section 490.10 (soliciting or providing support for an act of terrorism in the second degree); section 490.15 (soliciting or providing support for an act of terrorism in the first degree); section 490.20 (making a terroristic threat); section 490.25 (crime of terrorism); section 490.30 (hindering prosecution of terrorism in the second degree); section 490.35 (hindering prosecution of terrorism in the first degree); section 490.37 (criminal possession of a chemical weapon or biological weapon in the third degree); section 490.40 (criminal possession of a chemical weapon or biological weapon in the second degree); section 490.45 (criminal possession of a chemical weapon or biological weapon in the first degree); section 490.47

(criminal use of a chemical weapon or biological weapon in the third degree); section 490.50 (criminal use of a chemical weapon or biological weapon in the second degree); section 490.55 (criminal use of a chemical weapon or biological weapon in the first degree); or any attempt or conspiracy to commit any of the foregoing offenses.

(Eff.11/1/20,Ch.55,L.2020)

4. For purposes of this section:

(a) the term "age" means sixty years old or more;

(b) the term "disability" means a physical or mental impairment that substantially limits a major life activity;

(c) the term "gender identity or expression" means a person's actual or perceived gender-related identity, appearance, behavior, expression, or other gender-related characteristic regardless of the sex assigned to that person at birth, including, but not limited to, the status of being transgender.

§485.10 Sentencing.

1. When a person is convicted of a hate crime pursuant to this article, and the specified offense is a violent felony offense, as defined in section 70.02 of this chapter, the hate crime shall be deemed a violent felony offense.

2. When a person is convicted of a hate crime pursuant to this article and the specified offense is a misdemeanor or a class C, D or E felony, the hate crime shall be deemed to be one category higher than the specified offense the defendant committed, or one category higher than the offense level applicable to the defendant's conviction for an attempt or conspiracy to commit a specified offense, whichever is applicable.

3. Notwithstanding any other provision of law, when a person is convicted of a hate crime pursuant to this article and the specified offense is a class B felony:

(a) the maximum term of the indeterminate sentence must be at least six years if the defendant is sentenced pursuant to section 70.00 of this chapter;

(b) the term of the determinate sentence must be at least eight years if the defendant is sentenced pursuant to section 70.02 of this chapter;

(c) the term of the determinate sentence must be at least twelve years if the defendant is sentenced pursuant to section 70.04 of this chapter;

(d) the maximum term of the indeterminate sentence must be at least four years if the defendant is sentenced pursuant to section 70.05 of this chapter; and

(e) the maximum term of the indeterminate sentence or the term of the determinate sentence must be at least ten years if the defendant is sentenced pursuant to section 70.06 of this chapter.

4. Notwithstanding any other provision of law, when a person is convicted of a hate crime pursuant to this article and the specified

offense is a class A-1 felony, the minimum period of the indeterminate sentence shall be not less than twenty years.

5. In addition to any of the dispositions authorized by this chapter, the court may require as part of the sentence imposed upon a person convicted of a hate crime pursuant to this article, that the defendant complete a program, training session or counseling session directed at hate crime prevention and education, where the court determines such program, training session or counseling session is appropriate, available and was developed or authorized by the court or local agencies in cooperation with organizations serving the affected community.

TITLE Y - 1
ARTICLE 490 - TERRORISM

Section
490.00 Legislative findings.
490.01 Liability protection.
490.05 Definitions.
490.10 Soliciting or providing support for an act of terrorism in the second degree.
490.15 Soliciting or providing support for an act of terrorism in the first degree.
490.20 Making a terroristic threat.
490.25 Crime of terrorism.
490.27 Domestic act of terrorism motivated by hate in the second degree.
490.28 Domestic act of terrorism motivated by hate in the first degree.
490.30 Hindering prosecution of terrorism in the second degree.
490.35 Hindering prosecution of terrorism in the first degree.
490.37 Criminal possession of a chemical weapon or biological weapon in the third degree.
490.40 Criminal possession of a chemical weapon or biological weapon in the second degree.
490.45 Criminal possession of a chemical weapon or biological weapon in the first degree.
490.47 Criminal use of a chemical weapon or biological weapon in third degree.
490.50 Criminal use of a chemical weapon or biological weapon in the second degree.
490.55 Criminal use of a chemical weapon or biological weapon in the first degree.
490.70 Limitations.

§490.00 Legislative findings.

The devastating consequences of the recent barbaric attack on the World Trade Center and the Pentagon underscore the compelling need for legislation that is specifically designed to combat the evils of terrorism. Indeed, the bombings of American embassies in Kenya and Tanzania in 1998, the federal building in Oklahoma City in 1995, Pan Am Flight number 103 in Lockerbie in 1988, the 1997 shooting atop the Empire State Building, the 1994 murder of Ari Halberstam on the Brooklyn Bridge and the 1993 bombing of the World Trade Center, will forever serve to remind us that terrorism is a serious and deadly problem that disrupts public order and threatens individual safety both at home and around the world. Terrorism is inconsistent with civilized society and cannot be tolerated.

Although certain federal laws seek to curb the incidence of terrorism, there are no corresponding state laws that facilitate the prosecution and punishment of terrorists in state courts. Inexplicably, there is also no criminal penalty in this state for a person who solicits or raises funds for, or provides other material support or resources to, those who commit or encourage the commission of horrific and cowardly acts of terrorism. Nor do our criminal laws proscribe the making of terrorist threats or punish with appropriate severity those who hinder the prosecution of terrorists. Finally, our death penalty statute must be strengthened so that the cold-blooded execution of an individual for terrorist purposes is a capital offense.

A comprehensive state law is urgently needed to complement federal laws in the fight against terrorism and to better protect all citizens against terrorist acts. Accordingly, the legislature finds that our laws must be strengthened to ensure that terrorists, as well as those who solicit or provide financial and other support to terrorists, are prosecuted and punished in state courts with appropriate severity.

§490.01 Liability protection.

1. Any person who makes a qualified disclosure of suspicious behavior shall be immune from civil and criminal liability for reporting such behavior.

2. For purposes of this article, "qualified disclosure of suspicious behavior" means any disclosure of allegedly suspicious behavior of another individual or individuals to any person that is made in good faith and with the reasonable belief that such suspicious behavior constitutes, is indicative of, or is in furtherance of a crime or an act of terrorism.

3. An action alleging that a statement or disclosure by a person of any suspicious transaction, activity or occurrence indicating that an individual may be engaging in or preparing to engage in suspicious behavior which constitutes, is indicative of, or is in furtherance of, a crime or an act of terrorism was not made in good faith and with the reasonable belief that such suspicious behavior constitutes, is indicative of, or is in furtherance of, a crime or an act of terrorism must be pled with particularity pursuant to subdivision (b) of rule three thousand sixteen of the civil practice law and rules.

§490.05 Definitions.

As used in this article, the following terms shall mean and include:

1. "Act of terrorism":

(a) for purposes of this article means an act or acts consituting a specified offense as defined in subdivision three of this section for which a person may be convicted in the criminal courts of this state pursuant to article twenty of the criminal procedure law, or an act or acts constituting an offense in any other jurisdiction within or outside the territorial boundaries of the United States which contains all of the essential elements of a specified offense, that is intended to:

(i) intimidate or coerce a civilian population;

(ii) influence the policy of a unit of government by intimidation or coercion; or

(iii) affect the conduct of a unit of government by murder, assassination or kidnapping; or

(b) for purposes of subparagraph (xiii) of paragraph (a) of subdivision one of section 125.27 of this chapter means activities that involve a violent act or acts dangerous to human life that are in violation of the criminal laws of this state and are intended to:

(i) intimidate or coerce a civilian population;

(ii) influence the policy of a unit of government by intimidation or coercion; or

(iii) affect the conduct of a unit of government by murder, assassination or kidnapping.

2. "Material support or resources" means currency or other financial securities, financial services, lodging, training, safehouses, false documentation or identification, communications equipment, facilities, weapons, lethal substances, explosives, personnel, transportation, and other physical assets, except medicine or religious materials.

3. (a) "Specified offense" for purposes of this article means a class A felony offense other than an offense as defined in article two hundred twenty, a violent felony offense as defined in section 70.02, manslaughter in the second degree as defined in section 125.15, criminal tampering in the first degree as defined in section 145.20, identity theft in the second degree as defined in section 190.79, identity theft in the first degree as defined in section 190.80, unlawful possession of personal identification information in the second degree as defined in section 190.82, unlawful possession of personal identification information in the first degree as defined in section 190.83, money laundering in support of terrorism in the fourth degree as defined in section 470.21, money laundering in support of terrorism in the third degree as defined in section 470.22, money laundering in support of terrorism in the second degree as defined in section 470.23, money laundering in support of terrorism in the first degree as defined in section 470.24 of this chapter, and includes an attempt or conspiracy to commit any such offense.

(b) Notwithstanding the provisions of paragraph (a) of this subdivision, a specified offense shall not mean an offense defined in sections 490.37, 490.40, 490.45, 490.47, 490.50, and 490.55 of this article, nor shall a specified offense mean an attempt to commit any such offense.

4. "Renders criminal assistance" for purposes of sections 490.30 and 490.35 of this article shall have the same meaning as in section 205.50 of this chapter.

5. "Biological agent" means any micro-organism, virus, infectious substance, or biological product that may be engineered as a result of biotechnology, or any naturally occurring or bioengineered component

of any such micro-organism, virus, infectious substance, or biological product, capable of causing:

(a) death, disease, or other biological malfunction in a human, an animal, a plant, or another living organism;

(b) deterioration of food, water, equipment, supplies, or material of any kind; or

(c) deleterious alteration of the environment.

6. "Toxin" means the toxic material of plants, animals, micro-organisms, viruses, fungi, or infectious substances, or a recombinant molecule, whatever its origin or method of production, including:

(a) any poisonous substance or biological product that may be engineered as a result of biotechnology produced by a living organism; or

(b) any poisonous isomer or biological product, homolog, or derivative of such a substance.

7. "Delivery system" means:

(a) any apparatus, equipment, device, or means of delivery specifically designed to deliver or disseminate a biological agent, toxin, or vector; or

(b) any vector.

8. "Vector" means a living organism, or molecule, including a recombinant molecule, or biological product that may be engineered as a result of biotechnology, capable of carrying a biological agent or toxin to a host.

9. "Biological weapon" means any biological agent, toxin, vector, or delivery system or combination thereof.

10. "Chemical weapon" means the following, together or separately:

(a) a toxic chemical or its precursors;

(b) a munition or device specifically designed to cause death or other harm through the toxic properties of a toxic chemical or its precursors, which would be released as a result of the employment of such munition or device;

(c) any equipment specifically designed for use directly in connection with the employment of munitions or devices; or

(d) any device that is designed to release radiation or radioactivity at a level dangerous to human life.

11. "Precursor" means any chemical reactant that takes part at any stage in the production by whatever method of a toxic chemical, including any key component of a binary or multicomponent chemical system, and includes precursors which have been identified for application of verification measures under article VI of the convention in schedules contained in the annex on chemicals of the chemical weapons convention.

12. "Key component of a binary or multicomponent chemical system" means the precursor which plays the most important role in determining the toxic properties of the final product and reacts rapidly with other chemicals in the binary or multicomponent system.

13. "Toxic chemical" means any chemical which through its chemical action on life processes can cause death, serious physical injury or permanent harm to humans or animals, including all such chemicals, regardless of their origin or of their method of production, and regardless of whether they are produced in facilities, in munitions or elsewhere, and includes toxic chemicals which have been identified by the commissioner of health and included on the list of toxic chemicals pursuant to subdivision twenty of section two hundred six of the public health law.

14. The terms "biological agent", "toxin", and "toxic chemical" do not include any biological agent, toxin or toxic chemical that is in its naturally occurring environment, if the biological agent, toxin or toxic chemical has not been cultivated, collected, or otherwise extracted from its natural source.

15. "Select chemical agent" shall mean a chemical weapon which has been identified in regulations promulgated pursuant to subdivision twenty of section two hundred six of the public health law.

16. "Select biological agent" shall mean a biological weapon which has been identified in regulations promulgated pursuant to subdivision twenty-one of section two hundred six of the public health law.

17. "Chemical weapons convention" and "convention" mean the convention on the prohibition of the development, production, stockpiling and use of chemical weapons and on their destruction, opened for signature on January thirteenth, nineteen hundred ninety-three.

§490.10. Soliciting or providing support for an act of terrorism in the second degree.

A person commits soliciting or providing support for an act of terrorism in the second degree when, with intent that material support or resources will be used, in whole or in part, to plan, prepare, carry out or aid in either an act of terrorism or the concealment of, or an escape from, an act of terrorism, he or she raises, solicits, collects or provides material support or resources.

Soliciting or providing support for an act of terrorism in the second degree is a class D felony.

§490.15 Soliciting or providing support for an act of terrorism in the first degree.

A person commits soliciting or providing support for an act of terrorism in the first degree when he or she commits the crime of soliciting or providing support for an act of terrorism in the second degree and the total value of material support or resources exceeds one thousand dollars.

Soliciting or providing support for an act of terrorism in the first degree is a class C felony.

§490.20 Making a terroristic threat.

1. A person is guilty of making a terroristic threat when with intent to intimidate or coerce a civilian population, influence the policy of a unit of government by itimidation or coercion, or affect the conduct of a unit of government by murder, assassination or kidnapping, he or she threatens to commit or cause to be committed a specified offense and thereby causes a reasonable expectation or fear of the imminent commission of such offense.

2. It shall be no defense to a prosecution pursuant to this section that the defendant did not have the intent or capability of committing the specified offense or that the threat was not made to a person who was a subject thereof.

Making a terroristic threat is a class D felony

§490.25 Crime of terrorism.

1. A person is guilty of a crime of terrorism when, with intent to intimidate or coerce a civilian population, influence the policy of a unit of government by intimidation or coercion, or affect the conduct of a unit of government by murder, assassination or kidnapping, he or she commits a specified offense.

2. Sentencing.

(a) When a person is convicted of a crime of terrorism pursuant to this section, and the specified offense is a class B, C, D or E felony offense, the crime of terrorism shall be deemed a violent felony offense.

(b) When a person is convicted of a crime of terrorism pursuant to this section, and the specified offense is a class C, D or E felony offense, the crime of terrorism shall be deemed to be one category higher than the specified offense the defendant committed, or one category higher than the offense level applicable to the defendant's conviction for an attempt or conspiracy to commit the offense, whichever is applicable.

(c) When a person is convicted of a crime of terrorism pursuant to this section, and the specified offense is a class B felony offense, the crime of terrorism shall be deemed a class A-I felony offense and the sentence imposed upon conviction of such offense shall be in accordance with section 70.00 of this chapter.

(d) Notwithstanding any other provision of law, when a person is convicted of a crime of terrorism pursuant to this section, and the specified offense is a class A-I felony offense, the sentence upon conviction of such offense shall be life imprisonment without parole; provided, however, that nothing herein shall preclude or prevent a sentence of death when the specified offense is murder in the first degree as defined in section 125.27 of this chapter.

§490.27 Domestic act of terrorism motivated by hate in the second degree.

A person is guilty of the crime of domestic act of terrorism motivated by hate in the second degree when, acting with the intent to cause the death of, or serious physical injury to, five or more other persons, in whole or in substantial part because of the perceived race, color, national origin, ancestry, gender, gender identity or expression, religion, religious practice, age, disability, or sexual orientation of such other persons, regardless of whether that belief or perception is correct, he or she, as part of the same criminal transaction, attempts to cause the death of, or serious physical injury to, such five or more persons, provided that the victims are not participants in the criminal transaction.

Domestic act of terrorism motivated by hate in the second degree is a class A-I felony.   *(Eff.11/1/20,Ch.55,L.2020)*

§490.28 Domestic act of terrorism motivated by hate in the first degree.

A person is guilty of the crime of domestic act of terrorism motivated by hate in the first degree when, acting with the intent to cause the death of, or serious physical injury to, five or more other persons, in whole or in substantial part because of the perceived race, color, national origin, ancestry, gender, gender identity or expression, religion, religious practice, age, disability, or sexual orientation of such other person or persons, regardless of whether that belief or perception is correct, he or she, as part of the same criminal transaction:

1. causes the death of at least one other person, provided that the victim or victims are not a participant in the criminal transaction; and

2. causes or attempts to cause the death of four or more additional other persons, provided that the victims are not a participant in the criminal transaction; and

3. the defendant was more than eighteen years old at the time of the commission of the crime.

Domestic act of terrorism motivated by hate in the first degree is a class A-I felony.

Notwithstanding any other provision of law, when a person is convicted of domestic act of terrorism motivated by hate in the first degree, the sentence shall be life imprisonment without parole.

(Eff.11/1/20,Ch.55,L.2020)

§490.30 Hindering prosecution of terrorism in the second degree.

A person is guilty of hindering prosecution of terrorism in the second degree when he or she renders criminal assistance to a person who has committed an act of terrorism, knowing or believing that such person engaged in conduct constituting an act of terrorism.

Hindering prosecution of terrorism in the second degree is a class C felony.

§490.35 Hindering prosecution of terrorism in the first degree.

A person is guilty of hindering prosecution of terrorism in the first degree when he or she renders criminal assistance to a person who has committed an act of terrorism that resulted in the death of a person other than one of the participants, knowing or believing that such person engaged in conduct constituting an act of terrorism.

Hindering prosecution of terrorism in the first degree is a class B felony.

§490.37 Criminal possession of a chemical weapon or biological weapon in the third degree.

A person is guilty of criminal possession of a chemical weapon or biological weapon in the third degree when he or she possesses any select chemical agent or select biological agent under circumstances evincing an intent by the defendant to use such weapon to cause serious physical injury or death to another person.

Criminal possession of a chemical weapon or biological weapon in the third degree is a class C felony.

§490.40 Criminal possession of a chemical weapon or biological weapon in the second degree.

A person is guilty of criminal possession of a chemical weapon or biological weapon in the second degree when he or she possesses any chemical weapon or biological weapon with intent to use such weapon to:

1. (a) cause serious physical injury to, or the death of, another person; and

   (b) (i) intimidate or coerce a civilian population;

   (ii) influence the policy of a unit of government by intimidation or coercion; or

   (iii) affect the conduct of a unit of government by murder, assassination, or kidnapping.

2. cause serious physical injury to, or the death of, more than two persons.

Criminal possession of a chemical weapon or biological weapon in the second degree is a class B felony.

§490.45 Criminal possession of a chemical weapon or biological weapon in the first degree.

A person is guilty of criminal possession of a chemical weapon or biological weapon in the first degree when he or she possesses:

1. any select chemical agent, with intent to use such agent to:

   (a) cause serious physical injury to, or the death of, another person; and

   (b) (i) intimidate or coerce a civilian population;

   (ii) influence the policy of a unit of government by intimidation or coercion; or

   (iii) affect the conduct of a unit of government by murder, assassination, or kidnapping.

2. any select chemical agent, with intent to use such agent to cause serious physical injury to, or the death of, more than two other persons; or

3. any select biological agent, with intent to use such agent to cause serious physical injury to, or the death of, another person.

Criminal possession of a chemical weapon or biological weapon in the first degree is a class A-I felony.

§490.47 Criminal use of a chemical weapon or biological weapon in the third degree.

A person is guilty of criminal use of a chemical weapon or biological weapon in the third degree when, under circumstances evincing a depraved indifference to human life, he or she uses, deploys, releases, or causes to be used, deployed, or released any select chemical agent or select biological agent, and thereby creates a grave risk of death or serious physical injury to another person not a participant in the crime.

Criminal use of a chemical weapon or biological weapon in the third degree is a class B felony.

§490.50 Criminal use of a chemical weapon or biological weapon in the second degree.

A person is guilty of criminal use of a chemical weapon or biological weapon in the second degree when he or she uses, deploys, releases, or causes to be used, deployed, or released, any chemical weapon or biological weapon, with intent to:

1. cause serious physical injury to, or the death of, another person; and

2. (a) intimidate or coerce a civilian population;

(b) influence the policy of a unit of government by intimidation or coercion; or

(c) to affect the conduct of a unit of government by murder, assassination, or kidnapping.

Criminal use of a chemical weapon or biological weapon in the second degree is a class A-II felony.

§490.55 Criminal use of a chemical weapon or biological weapon in the first degree.

A person is guilty of criminal use of a chemical weapon or biological weapon in the first degree when:

1. with intent to:

(a) cause serious physical injury to, or the death of, another person; and

(b) (i) intimidate or coerce a civilian population;

(ii) influence the policy of a unit of government by intimidation or coercion; or

(iii) affect the conduct of a unit of government by murder, assassination, or kidnapping;
he or she uses, deploys, releases, or causes to be used, deployed, or released any select chemical agent and thereby causes serious physical injury to, or the death of, another person who is not a participant in the crime.

2. with intent to cause serious physical injury to, or the death of, more than two persons, he or she uses, deploys, releases, or causes to be used, deployed, or released any select chemical agent and thereby causes serious physical injury to, or the death of, more than two persons who are not participants in the crime; or

3. with intent to cause serious physical injury to, or the death of, another person, he or she uses, deploys, releases, or causes to be used, deployed, or released any select biological agent and thereby causes serious physical injury to, or the death of, another person who is not a participant in the crime.

Criminal use of a chemical weapon or biological weapon in the first degree is a class A-I felony.

§490.70 Limitations.

1. The provisions of sections 490.37, 490.40, 490.45, 490.47, 490.50, and 490.55 of this article shall not apply where the defendant possessed or used:

(a) any household product generally available for sale to consumers in this state in the quantity and concentration available for such sale;

(b) a self-defense spray device in accordance with the provisions of paragraph fourteen of subdivision a of section 265.20 of this chapter;

(c) a chemical weapon solely for a purpose not prohibited under this chapter, as long as the type and quantity is consistent with such a purpose; or

(d) a biological agent, toxin, or delivery system solely for prophylactic, protective, bona fide research, or other peaceful purposes.

2. For the purposes of this section, the phrase "purposes not prohibited by this chapter" means the following:

(a) any peaceful purpose related to an industrial, agricultural, research, medical, or pharmaceutical activity or other peaceful activity;

(b) any purpose directly related to protection against toxic chemicals and to protection against chemical weapons;

(c) any military purpose of the United States that is not connected with the use of a chemical weapon or that is not dependent on the use of the toxic or poisonous properties of the chemical weapon to cause death or other harm; and

(d) any law enforcement purpose, including any domestic riot control purpose and including imposition of capital punishment.

TITLE Y - 2 - CORRUPTING THE GOVERNMENT
ARTICLE 496 - CORRUPTING THE GOVERNMENT

Section
496.01 Definitions.
496.02 Corrupting the government in the fourth degree.
496.03 Corrupting the government in the third degree.
496.04 Corrupting the government in the second degree.
496.05 Corrupting the government in the first degree.
496.06 Public corruption.
496.07 Sentencing.

§496.01 Definitions.

For the purposes of this article, "scheme" means any plan, pattern, device, contrivance, or course of action.

§496.02 Corrupting the government in the fourth degree.

A person is guilty of corrupting the government in the fourth degree when, being a public servant, or acting in concert with a public servant, he or she engages in a scheme constituting a systematic ongoing course of conduct with intent to defraud the state or one or more political subdivisions of the state or one or more governmental instrumentalities within the state to obtain property, actual services or other resources, or obtain property, actual services or other resources from the state, or any political subdivision or governmental instrumentality of the state by false or fraudulent pretenses, representations or promises, and thereby wrongfully obtains such property, actual services or other resources.

Corrupting the government in the fourth degree is a class E felony.

§496.03 Corrupting the government in the third degree.

A person is guilty of corrupting the government in the third degree when, being a public servant, or acting in concert with a public servant, he or she engages in a scheme constituting a systematic ongoing course of conduct with intent to defraud the state or one or more political subdivisions of the state or one or more governmental instrumentalities within the state to obtain property, actual services or other resources, or obtain property, actual services or other resources from the state, or any political subdivision or governmental instrumentality of the state by false or fraudulent pretenses, representations or promises, and thereby wrongfully obtains such property, actual services or other resources with a value in excess of one thousand dollars.

Corrupting the government in the third degree is a class D felony.

§496.04 Corrupting the government in the second degree.

A person is guilty of corrupting the government in the second degree when, being a public servant, or acting in concert with a public servant, he or she engages in a scheme constituting a systematic ongoing course of conduct with intent to defraud the state or one or more political subdivisions of the state or one or more governmental instrumentalities within the state to obtain property, actual services or other resources, or obtain property, actual services or other resources from the state, or any political subdivision or governmental instrumentality of the state by false or fraudulent pretenses, representations or promises, and thereby wrongfully obtains such property, actual services or other resources with a value in excess of twenty thousand dollars.

Corrupting the government in the second degree is a class C felony.

§496.05 Corrupting the government in the first degree.

A person is guilty of corrupting the government in the first degree when, being a public servant, or acting in concert with a public servant, he or she engages in a scheme constituting a systematic ongoing course of conduct with intent to defraud the state or one or more political subdivisions of the state or one or more governmental instrumentalities within the state to obtain property, actual services or other resources, or to obtain property, actual services or other resources from the state, or any political subdivision or governmental instrumentality of the state by false or fraudulent pretenses, representations or promises, and thereby wrongfully obtains such property, actual services or other resources with a value in excess of one hundred thousand dollars.

Corrupting the government in the first degree is a class B felony.

§496.06 Public corruption.

1. A person commits the crime of public corruption when: (a) (i) being a public servant he or she commits a specified offense through the use of his or her public office, or (ii) being a person acting in concert with such public servant he or she commits a specified offense, and (b) the state or any political subdivision thereof or any governmental instrumentality within the state is the owner of the property.

2. A "specified offense" is an offense defined by any of the following provisions of this chapter: section 155.25 (petit larceny); section 155.30 (grand larceny in the fourth degree); section 155.35 (grand larceny in the third degree); section 155.40 (grand larceny in the second degree); section 155.42 (grand larceny in the first degree); section 190.60 (scheme to defraud in the second degree); or section 190.65 (scheme to defraud in the first degree).

§496.07 Sentencing.

When a person is convicted of the crime of public corruption pursuant to section 496.06 of this article and the specified offense is a class C, D or E felony, the crime shall be deemed to be one category higher than the specified offense the defendant committed, or one category higher than the offense level applicable to the defendant's conviction for an attempt or conspiracy to commit a specified offense, whichever is applicable.

TITLE Z - LAWS REPEALED; TIME OF TAKING EFFECT

ARTICLE 500 - LAWS REPEALED; TIME OF TAKING EFFECT

Section
500.05 Laws repealed.
500.10 Time of taking effect.

§500.05 Laws repealed

Chapter eighty-eight of the laws of nineteen hundred nine, entitled "An act providing for the punishment of crime, constituting chapter forty of the consolidated laws," and all acts amendatory thereof and supplemental thereto, constituting the penal law as heretofore in force, are hereby repealed.

§500.10 Time of taking effect.

This act shall take effect September first, nineteen hundred sixty-seven.

APPENDIX
TO
NYS PENAL LAW

To facilitate the use of the Penal Law, Sections 3302 and 3306 of the Public Health Law have been added.

43-08 162nd Street
Flushing, NY 11358
www.LooseleafLaw.com 800-647-5547

§3302. Definitions of terms of general use in this article.

Except where different meanings are expressly specified in subsequent provisions of this article, the following terms have the following meanings:

1. "Addict" means a person who habitually uses a controlled substance for a non-legitimate or unlawful use, and who by reason of such use is dependent thereon.

2. "Administer" means the direct application of a controlled substance, whether by injection, inhalation, ingestion, or any other means, to the body of a patient or research subject.

3. "Agent" means an authorized person who acts on behalf of or at the direction of a manufacturer, distributor, or dispenser. No person may be authorized to so act if under title VIII of the education law such person would not be permitted to engage in such conduct. It does not include a common or contract carrier, public warehouseman, or employee of the carrier or warehouseman when acting in the usual and lawful course of the carrier's or warehouseman's business.

4. "Controlled substance" means a substance or substances listed in section thirty-three hundred six of this title.

5. "Commissioner" means commissioner of health of the state of New York.

6. "Deliver" or "delivery" means the actual, constructive or attempted transfer from one person to another of a controlled substance, whether or not there is an agency relationship.

7. "Department" means the department of health of the state of New York.

8. "Dispense" means to deliver a controlled substance to an ultimate user or research subject by lawful means, including by means of the internet, and includes the packaging, labeling, or compounding necessary to prepare the substance for such delivery.

9. "Distribute" means to deliver a controlled substance, including by means of the internet, other than by administering or dispensing.

10. "Distributor" means a person who distributes a controlled substance.

11. "Diversion" means manufacture, possession, delivery or use of a controlled substance by a person or in a manner not specifically authorized by law.

12. "Drug" means

(a) substances recognized as drugs in the official United States Pharmacopoeia, official Homeopathic Pharmacopoeia of the United States, or official National Formulary, or any supplement to any of them;

(b) substances intended for use in the diagnosis, cure, mitigation, treatment, or prevention of disease in man or animals; and

(c) substances (other than food) intended to affect the structure or a function of the body of man or animal. It does not include devices or their components, parts, or accessories.

13. "Federal agency" means the Drug Enforcement Administration, United States Department of Justice, or its successor agency.

14. "Federal controlled substances act" means the Comprehensive Drug Abuse Prevention and Control Act of 1970, Public Law 91-513, and any act or acts amendatory or supplemental thereto or regulations promulgated thereunder.

15. "Federal registration number" means such number assigned by the Federal agency to any person authorized to manufacture, distribute, sell, dispense or administer controlled substances.

16. "Habitual user" means any person who is, or by reason of repeated use of any controlled substance for non-legitimate or unlawful use is in danger of becoming, dependent upon such substance.

17. "Institutional dispenser" means a hospital, veterinary hospital, clinic, dispensary, maternity home, nursing home, mental hospital or similar facility approved and certified by the department as authorized to obtain controlled substances by distribution and to dispense and administer such substances pursuant to the order of a practitioner.

18. "License" means a written authorization issued by the department or the New York state department of education permitting persons to engage in a specified activity with respect to controlled substances.

19. "Manufacture" means the production, preparation, propagation, compounding, cultivation, conversion or processing of a controlled substance, either directly or indirectly or by extraction from substances of natural origin, or independently by means of chemical synthesis, or by a combination of extraction and chemical synthesis, and includes any packaging or repackaging of the substance or labeling or relabeling of its container, except that this term does not include the preparation, compounding, packaging or labeling of a controlled substance:

(a) by a practitioner as an incident to his administering or dispensing of a controlled substance in the course of his professional practice; or

(b) by a practitioner, or by his authorized agent under his supervision, for the purpose of, or as an incident to, research, teaching, or chemical analysis and not for sale; or

(c) by a pharmacist as an incident to his dispensing of a controlled substance in the course of his professional practice.

20. "Narcotic drug" means any of the following, whether produced directly or indirectly by extraction from substances of vegetable origin, or independently by means of chemical synthesis, or by a combination of extraction and chemical synthesis:

(a) opium and opiate, and any salt, compound, derivative, or preparation of opium or opiate;

(b) any salt, compound, isomer, derivative, or preparation thereof which is chemically equivalent or identical with any of the substances referred to in paragraph (a) of this subdivision, but not including the isoquinoline alkaloids of opium;

(c) opium poppy and poppy straw.

21. "Opiate" means any substance having an addiction-forming or addiction-sustaining liability similar to morphine or being capable of conversion into a drug having addiction-forming or addiction-sustaining liability. It does not include, unless specifically designated as controlled under section thirty-three hundred six of this title, the dextrorotatory isomer of 3-methoxy-n-methylmorphinan and its salts (dextromethorphan). It does include its racemic and levorotatory forms.

22. "Opium poppy" means the plant of the species Papaver somniferum L., except its seeds.

23. "Person" means individual, institution, corporation, government or governmental subdivision or agency, business trust, estate, trust, partnership or association, or any other legal entity.

24. "Pharmacist" means any person licensed by the state department of education to practice pharmacy.

25. "Pharmacy" means any place registered as such by the New York state board of pharmacy and registered with the Federal agency pursuant to the federal controlled substances act.

26. "Poppy straw" means all parts, except the seeds, of the opium poppy, after mowing.

27. "Practitioner" means:

A physician, dentist, podiatrist, veterinarian, scientific investigator, or other person licensed, or otherwise permitted to dispense, administer or conduct research with respect to a controlled substance in the course of a licensed professional practice or research licensed pursuant to this article. Such person shall be deemed a "practitioner" only as to such substances, or conduct relating to such substances, as is permitted by his license, permit or otherwise permitted by law.

28. "Prescribe" means a direction or authorization, by prescription, permitting an ultimate user lawfully to obtain controlled substances from any person authorized by law to dispense such substances.

29. "Prescription" shall mean an official New York state prescription, an electronic prescription, an oral prescription or an out-of-state prescription.

30. "Sell" means to sell, exchange, give or dispose of to another, or offer or agree to do the same.

31. "Ultimate user" means a person who lawfully obtains and possesses a controlled substance for his own use or the use by a member of his household or for an animal owned by him or in his custody. It shall also mean and include a person designated, by a practitioner on a prescription, to obtain such substance on behalf of the patient for whom such substance is intended.

32. "Internet" means collectively computer and telecommunications facilities which comprise the worldwide network of networks that employ a set of industry standards and protocols, or any predecessor or successor protocol to such protocol, to exchange information of all kinds. "Internet," as used in this article, also includes other networks, whether private or public, used to transmit information by electronic means.

33. "By means of the internet" means any sale, delivery, distribution, or dispensing of a controlled substance that uses the internet, is initiated by use of the internet or causes the internet to be used.

34. "Online dispenser" means a practitioner, pharmacy, or person in the United States that sells, delivers or dispenses, or offers to sell, deliver, or dispense, a controlled substance by means of the internet.

35. "Electronic prescription" means a prescription issued with an electronic signature and transmitted by electronic means in accordance with regulations of the commissioner and the commissioner of education and consistent with federal requirements. A prescription generated on an electronic system that is printed out or transmitted via facsimile is not considered an electronic prescription and must be manually signed.

36. "Electronic" means of or relating to technology having electrical, digital, magnetic, wireless, optical, electromagnetic or similar capabilities. "Electronic" shall not include facsimile.

37. "Electronic record" means a paperless record that is created, generated, transmitted, communicated, received or stored by means of electronic equipment and includes the preservation, retrieval, use and disposition in accordance with regulations of the commissioner and the commissioner of education and in compliance with federal law and regulations.

38. "Electronic signature" means an electronic sound, symbol, or process, attached to or logically associated with an electronic record and executed or adopted by a person with the intent to sign the record, in accordance with regulations of the commissioner and the commissioner of education.

39. "Registry" or "prescription monitoring program registry" means the prescription monitoring program registry established pursuant to section thirty-three hundred forty-three-a of this article.

40. "Compounding" means the combining, admixing, mixing, diluting, pooling, reconstituting, or otherwise altering of a drug or bulk drug substance to create a drug with respect to an outsourcing facility under section 503B of the federal Food, Drug and Cosmetic Act and further defined in this section.

41. "Outsourcing facility" means a facility that:

(a) is engaged in the compounding of sterile drugs as defined in section sixty-eight hundred two of the education law;

(b) is currently registered as an outsourcing facility pursuant to article one hundred thirty-seven of the education law; and

(c) complies with all applicable requirements of federal and state law, including the Federal Food, Drug and Cosmetic Act.

Notwithstanding any other provision of law to the contrary, when an outsourcing facility distributes or dispenses any drug to any person pursuant to a prescription, such outsourcing facility shall be deemed to be providing pharmacy services and shall be subject to all laws, rules and regulations governing pharmacies and pharmacy services.

(Eff.3/31/21,Ch.92,L.2021)

§3306.   Schedules of controlled substances.
There are hereby established five schedules of controlled substances, to be known as schedules I, II, III, IV and V respectively. Such schedules shall consist of the following substances by whatever name or chemical designation known:

Schedule I.
(a) Schedule I shall consist of the drugs and other substances, by whatever official name, common or usual name, chemical name, or brand name designated, listed in this section.
(b) Opiates. Unless specifically excepted or unless listed in another schedule, any of the following opiates, including their isomers, esters, ethers, salts, and salts of isomers, esters, and ethers, whenever the existence of such isomers, esters, ethers and salts is possible within the specific chemical designation (for purposes of 3-methylfentanyl only, the term isomer includes the optical and geometric isomers): (1) Acetyl-alpha-methylfentanyl (N-{1-(-methyl-2-phenethyl)-4-piperidinyl} -N-phenylacetamide. (2) Acetylmethadol. (3) Allylprodine. (4) Alphacetylmethadol (except levoalphacetylmethadol also known as levo-alpha-acetylmethadol, levomethadylacetate or LAAM). (5) Alphameprodine. (6) Alphamethadol. (7) Alpha-methylfentanyl (N-{1-(alpha-methyl-beta-phenyl) ethyl-4-piperidyl} propionanilide; 1-(1-methyl-2-phenyl ethyl) -4-(N-propanilido) piperidine), (8) Alpha-methylthiofentanyl (N-{1-methyl -2)2-thienyl) ethyl-4-piperidinyl} -N-phenylpropanamide), (9) Beta-hydroxyfentanyl (N-{1-2 (2-hydroxy-2-phenethyl)- 4-piperidinyl} -N-phenylpropanamide), (10) Beta-hydroxy-3-methylfentanyl (other name: N-{1-(2-hydroxy-2-phenethyl) -3-methyl -4-piperidinyl} -N-phenylpropanamide, (11) Benzethidine, (12) Betacetylmethadol, (13) Betameprodine, (14) Betamethadol, (15) Betaprodine, (16) Clonitazene, (17) Dextromoramide, (18) Diampromide, (19) Diethylthiambutene, (20) Difenoxin, (21) Dimenoxadol (22) Dimepheptanol, (23) Dimethylthiambutene, (24) Dioxaphetyl butyrate, (25) Dipipanone, (26) Ethylmethylthiambutene, (27) Etonitazene, (28) Etoxeridine, (29) Furethidine, (30) Hydroxypethidine, (31) Ketobemidone, (32) Levomoramide, (33) Levophenacylmorphan, (34) 3-Methylfentanyl (N-{3-methyl-1-1-(2- phenylethyl -4-piperidyl} -N-phenylpropanamide), (35) 3-Methylthiofentanyl (N-{3-methyl-1-(2-thienyl)ethyl -4-piperidinyl} -N-phenylpropanamide), (36) Morpheridine, (37) MPPP (1-methyl -4-phenyl -4-propionoxypiperidine), (38) Noracymethadol, (39) Norlevorphanol, (40) Normethadone, (41) Norpipanone, (42) Para-fluorofentanyl (N- (4-fluorophenyl) -N-{1-(2-phenethyl) -4-piperidinyl} -propanamide, (43) PEPAP (1-(-2-phenethyl) -4-phenyl -4-acetoxypiperidine, (44) Phenadoxone, (45) Phenampromide, (46) Phenomorphan, (47) Phenoperidine, (48) Piritramide, (49) Proheptazine, (50) Properidine, (51) Propiram, (52) Racemoramide, (53) Thiofentanyl (N-phenyl-N-{1-(2-thienyl) ethyl -4- piperidinyl} -propanamide, (54) Tilidine, (55) Trimeperidine, (56) 3,4-dichloro-N-{(1-dimethylamino)cyclohexylmethyl}benzamide. Some trade or other names: AH-7921. (57) N-(1-phenethylpiperidin-4-yl)-N-phenylacetamide. Some trade or other names: Acetyl Fentanyl. (58) N-(1-phenethyl-piperidin-4-yl)-N-phenylbutyramide. Other name: Butyryl Fentanyl. (59) N-{1-{2-hydroxy-2-(thiophen-2-yl)ethyl} piperidin-4-yl}-N-phenylp- ropionamide. Other name: Beta-Hydroxythiofentanyl. (60) N-(1-phenethylpiperidin-4-yl)-N-phenylfuran-2-carboxamide. Other name: Furanyl Fentanyl. (61) 3,4-Dichloro-N-{2-(dimethylamino) cyclohexyl}-N-methylbenzamide. Other name: U-47700. (62) N-(1-phenethylpiperidin-4-yl)-N-phenylacrylamide. Other names: Acryl Fentanyl or Acryloylfentanyl. (63) N-(4-fluorophenyl)-N-(1-phenethyl-piperidin-4-yl)isobutyramide. Other names: 4-fluoroisobutyryl fentanyl, para-fluoro-isobutyryl fentanyl. (64) N-(2-fluorophenyl)-N-(1-phenethylpiperidin-4-yl)propionamide. Other names: ortho-fluorofentanyl or 2-fluorofentanyl. (65) N-(1-phenethylpiperidin-4-yl)-N-phenyltetrahydrofuran-2-carbox- amide. Other name: tetrahydro-furanyl fentanyl. (66) 2-methoxy-N-(1-phenethylpiperidin-4-yl)-N-phenylacetamide. Other name: methoxyacetyl fentanyl. (67) N-(1-phenethylpiperidin-4-yl)-N-phenyl-cyclopropanecarboxamide. Other name: cyclopropyl fentanyl. (68) N-(4-fluorophenyl)-N-(1-phenethylpiperidin-4-yl)butyramide. Other name: para-fluoro-butyrylfentanyl. (69) N-(2-fluorophenyl)-2-methoxy-N-(1-phenethylpiperidin-4-yl)

acetam- ide. Other name: Ocfentanil. (70) 1-cyclohexyl-4-(1,2-diphenylethyl)piper-azine. Other name: MT-45.

(c) Opium derivatives. Unless specifically excepted or unless listed in another schedule, any of the following opium derivatives, its salts, isomers, and salts of isomers whenever the existence of such salts, isomers, and salts of isomers is possible within the specific chemical designation: (1) Acetorphine, (2) Acetyldihydrocodeine, (3) Benzylmorphine, (4) Codeine methylbromide, (5) Codeine-N-oxide, (6) Cyprenorphine, (7) Desomorphine, (8) Dihydromorphine, (9) Drotebanol, (10) Etorphine (except hydrochloride salt), (11) Heroin, (12) Hydromorphinol, (13) Methyldesorphine, (14) Methyldihydromorphine, (15) Morphine methylbromide, (16) Morphine methylsulfonate, (17) Morphine-N-oxide, (18) Myrophine, (19) Nicocodeine, (20) Nicomorphine, (21) Normorphine, (22) Pholcodine, (23) Thebacon.

(d) Hallucinogenic substances. Unless specifically excepted or unless listed in another schedule, any material, compound, mixture, or preparation, which contains any quantity of the following hallucinogenic substances, or which contains any of its salts, isomers, and salts of isomers whenever the existence of such salts, isomers, and salts of isomers is possible within the specific chemical designation (for purposes of this paragraph only, the term "isomer" includes the optical, position and geometric isomers):

(EXPLANATION--Within the following chemical designations, character symbol substitutions were made from the original text: "@" = Greek alpha, "&" = Greek beta, "'" = prime mark and "/\" = triangle.)

(1) 4-bromo-2, 5-dimethoxy-amphetamine. Some trade or other names: 4-bromo-2, 5-dimethoxy-@-methylphenethylamine; 4-bromo-2, 5-DMA. (2) 2, 5-dimethoxyam-phetamine Some trade or other names: 2, 5-dimethoxy-@-methylphenethylamine; 2, 5-DMA, (3) 4-methoxyamphetamine Some trade or other names: 4-methoxy-@-methylphenethylamine; paramethoxyamphetamine, PMA, (4) 5-methoxy-3, 4-methyl enedioxy - amphetamine, (5) 4-methyl-2, 5-dimethoxy-amphetamine Some trade and other names: 4-methyl-2, 5-dimethoxy-@-methylphenethylamine; "DOM"; and "STP", (6) 3, 4-methylenedioxy amphetamine, (7) 3, 4, 5-trimethoxy amphetamine, (8) Bufo-tenine Some trade and other names: 3-(&-dimethylaminoethyl)-5 hydroxindole; 3-(2-dimethylaminoethyl)- 5-indolol; N, N-dimethylserotonin; -5-hydroxy-N, N-dime-thyltryptamine; mappine, (9) Diethyltryptamine Some trade and other names: N, N-diethyltryptamine; DET, (10) Dimethyltryptamine Some trade or other names: DMT, (11) Ibogane Some trade and other names: 7-ethyl-6, 6&, 7, 8, 9, 10, 12, 13-octa-hydro-2-methoxy-6, 9-methano-5h-pyrido {1',2':1,2} azepino {5,4-b} indole: tabernanthe iboga, (12) Lysergic acid diethylamide, (13) Mescaline. (14) Parahexyl. Some trade or other names: 3-Hexyl-1-hydroxy- 7,8,9,10-tetra hydro-6,6,9-trimethyl-6H-dibenfo{b,d} pyran. (15) Peyote. Meaning all parts of the plant presently classified botanically as Lophophora williamsii Lemaire, whether growing or not, the seeds thereof, any extract from any part of such plant, and every compound, manufacture, salts, derivative, mixture, or preparation of such plant, its seeds or extracts. (16) N-ethyl-3-piperidyl benzilate. (17) N-methyl-3-piperidyl benzilate. (18) Psilocybin. (19) Psilocyn. (20) Tetrahydrocannabinols. Synthetic tetrahydrocannabinols not derived from the cannabis plant that are equivalents of the substances contained in the plant, or in the resinous extractives of cannabis, sp. and/or synthetic substances, derivatives, and their isomers with similar chemical structure and pharmacological activity such as the following:

delta 1 cis or trans tetrahydrocannabinol, and their optical isomers

delta 6 cis or trans tetrahydrocannabinol, and their optical isomers

delta 3, 4 cis or trans tetrahydrocannabinol, and its optical isomers (since nomenclature of these substances is not internationally standardized, compounds of these structures, regardless of numerical designation of atomic positions covered). Any Federal Food and Drug Administration approved product containing tetrahydrocannabinol shall not be considered a synthetic tetrahydrocannabinol. (21) Ethylamine analog of phencyclidine. Some trade or other names:

N-ethyl-1-phenylcyclohexylamine, (1-phenylcyclohexyl) ethylamine, N-(1-phenylcyclohexyl) ethylamine cyclohexamine, PCE. (22) Pyrrolidine analog of phencyclidine. Some trade or other names 1-(1-phenylcyclohexyl)-pyrrolidine; PCPy, PHP. (23) Thiophene analog of phencyclidine. Some trade or other names: 1-{1-(2-thienyl)-cyclohexyl}-piperidine, 2-thienylanalog of phencyclidine, TPCP, TCP. (24) 3,4-methylenedioxymethamphetamine (MDMA). (25) 3,4-methylendioxy-N-ethylamphetamine (also known as N-ethyl-alpha-methyl-3,4 (methylenedioxy) phenethylamine, N-ethyl MDA, MDE, MDEA. (26) N-hydroxy-3,4-methylenedioxyamphetamine (also known as N-hydroxy-alpha-methyl-3,4 (methylenedioxy) phenethylamine, and N-hydroxy MDA. (27) 1-{1- (2-thienyl) cyclohexyl} pyrrolidine. Some other names: TCPY. (28) Alpha-ethyltryptamine. Some trade or other names: etryptamine; Monase; Alpha-ethyl-1H-indole-3-ethanamine; 3- (2-aminobutyl) indole; Alpha-ET or AET. (29) 2,5-dimethoxy-4-ethylamphetamine. Some trade or other names: DOET. (30) 4-Bromo-2,5-dimethoxyphenethylamine. Some trade or other names: 2-(4-bromo-2,5-dimethoxyphenyl)-1-aminoethane; alpha-desmethyl DOB; 2C-B, Nexus. (31) 2,5-dimethoxy-4-(n)-propylthiophenethylamine (2C-T-7), its optical isomers, salts and salts of isomers. * (33) 2-(4-iodo-2,5-dimethoxyphenyl)-N-(2-methoxybenzyl)ethanamine, also known as 25I-NBOMe; 2C-I-NBOMe; 25I; or Cimbi-5. (34) 2-(4-chloro-2,5-dimethoxyphenyl)-N-(2-methoxybenzyl)ethanamine, also known as 25 CNBOMe; 2C-C-NBOMe; 25C; or Cimbi-82. (35) 2-(4-bromo-2,5-dimethoxyphenyl)-N-(2-methoxybenzyl)ethanamine, also known as, 25 BNBOMe; 2C-B-NBOMe; Cimbi-36. (36) 5-methoxy-N,N-dimethyltryptamine. (37) Alpha-methyltryptamine. Some trade or other names: AMT. (38) 5-methoxy-N,N-diisopropyltryptamine. Some trade or other names: 5-MeO-DIPT.

(Eff.3/31/21,Ch.92,L.2021)(There is no (32) in law.)

(e) Depressants. Unless specifically excepted or unless listed in another schedule, any material, compound, mixture, or preparation which contains any quantity of the following substances having a depressant effect on the central nervous system, including its salts, isomers, and salts of isomers whenever the existence of such salts, isomers, and salts of isomers is possible within the specific chemical designation: (1) Mecloqualone, (2) Methaqualone, (3) Phencyclidine, (4) Gamma hydroxybutyric acid, and salt, hydroxybutyric compound, derivative or preparation of gamma hydroxybutyric acid, including any isomers, esters and ethers and salts of isomers, esters and ethers of gamma hydroxybutyric acid, except gamma-butyrolactone, whenever the existence of such isomers, esters and ethers and salts is possible within the specific chemical, (5) Gamma-butyrolactone, including butyrolactone; butyrolactone gamma; 4-butyrolactone; 2(3H)-furanone dihydro; dihydro-2(3H)-furanone; tetrahydro-2-furanone; 1,2-butanolide; 1,4-butanolide; 4-butanolide; gamma-hydroxybutyric acid lactone; 3-hydroxybutyric acid lactone and 4-hydroxybutanoic acid lactone with Chemical Abstract Service number (96-48-0) when any such substance is intended for human consumption, (6) 1,4 butanediol, including butanediol; butane-1,4-diol; 1,4-butylene glyco; butylene glycol; 1,4-dihydroxybutane; 1,4-tetramethylene glycol; tetramethylene glycol; tetramethylene 1,4-diol with Chemical Abstract Service number (110-63-4) when any such substance is intended for human consumption.

(f) Stimulants. Unless specifically excepted or unless listed in another schedule, any material, compound, mixture, or preparation which contains any quantity of the following substances having a stimulant effect on the central nervous system, including its salts, isomers, and salts of isomers: (1) Fenethylline, (2) N-ethylamphetamine, (3) (+-)cis-4-methylaminorex ((+-)cis-4,5-dihydro-4-methyl -5-phenyl -2-oxazolamine), (4) N,N-dimethylamphetamine (also known as N,N-alpha- trimethyl-benzeneethanamine; N,N-alpha- trimethylphenethylamine), (5) Methcathinone (some other names: 2-(methylamino) - propiophenone; alpha-(methylamino) propiophenone; 2-(methylamino)-1-phenylpropan-1-one; alpha-N- methylaminopropiophenone; monomethylpropion; ephedrone, N-methylcathinone, methylcathinone; AL-464; AL-422; AL-463 and UR1432), its salts, optical isomers and salts of optical isomers, (6) Aminorex.

Some other names: aminoxaphen; 2-amino-5-phenyl -2-oxazoline; or 4,5-dihydro-5-phenyl-2-oxazolamine, (7) Cathinone. Some trade or other names: 2-amino-1-phenyl-1-propanone, alpha-aminopropiophenone, 2-aminopropiophenone, and norephedrone, (8) N-benzylpiperazine (some other names: BZP; 1-benzylpiperazine), its optical isomers, salts and salts of isomers. (9) 4-methyl-N-methylcathinone or 4-Methylmethcathinone, also known as Mephedrone. (10) 3,4-methylenedioxypyrovalerone or Methylenedioxypyrovalerone, also known as MDPV. (11) 3,4-methylenedioxy-N-methylcathinone (some other names: methylone). (12) 4-Methoxymethcathinone. (13) 3-Fluoromethcathinone. (14) 4-Fluoromethcathinone. (15) Ethylpropion (Ethcathinone). (16) 2-(2,5-Dimethoxy-4-ethylphenyl)ethanamine (2C-E). (17) 2-(2,5-Dimethoxy-4-methylphenyl)ethanamine (2C-D). (18) 2-(4-Chloro-2,5-dimethoxyphenyl)ethanamine (2C-C). (19) 2-(4-Iodo-2,5-dimethoxyphenyl)ethanamine (2C-I). (20) 2-{4-(Ethylthio)-2,5-dimethoxyphenyl}ethanamine (2C-T-2). (21) 2-{4-(Isopropylthio)-2,5-dimethoxyphenyl}ethanamine (2C-T-4). (22) 2-(2,5-Dimethoxyphenyl)ethanamine (2C-H). (23) 2-(2,5-Dimethoxy-4-nitro-phenyl)ethanamine (2C-N). (24) 2-(2,5-Dimethoxy-4-(n)-propylphenyl)ethanamine (2C-P).

(g) Synthetic cannabinoids. Unless specifically excepted or unless listed in another schedule, any material, compound, mixture, or preparation, which contains any quantity of the following synthetic cannabinoid substances, or which contains any of its salts, isomers, and salts of isomers whenever the existence of such salts, isomers, and salts of isomers is possible within the specific chemical designation (for purposes of this paragraph only, the term "isomer" includes the optical, position and geometric isomers):

(1) (1-pentyl-1H-indol-3-yl)(2,2,3,3-tetramethylcyclopropyl) methanone. Some trade or other names: UR-144.

(2) {1-(5-fluro-pentyl)-1H-indol-3-yl}(2,2,3,3-tetramethylcyclopropyl) methanone. Some trade names or other names: 5-fluoro-UR-144, XLR11.

(3) N-(1-adamantyl)-1-pentyl-1H-indazole-3-carboxamide. Some trade or other names: APINACA, AKB48.

(4) quinolin-8-yl 1-pentyl-1H-indole-3-carboxylate. Some trade or other names: PB-22; QUPIC.

(5) quinolin-8-yl 1-(5-fluoropentyl)-1H-indole-3-carboxylate. Some trade or other names: 5-fluoro-PB-22; 5F-PB-22.

(6) N-(1-amino-3-methyl-1-oxobutan-2-yl)-1-(4-fluorobenzyl)-1H-indazole-3-carboxamide. Some trade or other names: AB-FUBINACA.

(7) N-(1-amino-3,3-dimethyl-1-oxobutan-2-yl)-1-pentyl-1H-indazole-3-carboxamide. Some trade or other names: ADB-PINACA.

(8) N-(1-amino-3-methyl-1-oxobutan-2-yl)-1-(cyclohexylmethyl)-1H-indazole-3-carboxamide. Some trade or other names: AB-CHMINACA.

(9) N-(1-amino-3-methyl-1-oxobutan-2-yl)-1-pentyl-1H-indazole-3-carboxamide. Some trade or other names: AB-PINACA.

(10) {1-(5-fluoropentyl)-1H-indazol-3-yl}(naphthalen-1-yl)methanone. Some trade or other names: THJ-2201.

(h) (1) Cannabimimetic agents. Unless specifically exempted or unless listed in another schedule, any material, compound, mixture, or preparation that is not approved by the federal food and drug administration (FDA) which contains any quantity of cannabimimetic agents, or which contains their salts, isomers, and salts of isomers whenever the existence of such salts, isomers, and salts of isomers is possible within the specific chemical designation.

(2) As used in this subdivision, the term "cannabimimetic agents" means any substance that is a cannabinoid receptor type 1 (CB1 receptor) agonist as demonstrated by binding studies and functional assays within any of the following structural classes:

(i) 2-(3-hydroxycyclohexyl)phenol with substitution at the 5-position of the phenolic ring by alkyl or alkenyl, whether or not substituted on the cyclohexyl ring to any extent.

(ii) 3-(1-naphthoyl)indole or 3-(1-naphthylmethane)indole by substitution at the nitrogen atom of the indole ring, whether or not further substituted on the indole ring to any extent, whether or not substituted on the naphthoyl or naphthyl ring to any extent.

(iii) 3-(1-naphthoyl)pyrrole by substitution at the nitrogen atom of the pyrrole ring, whether or not further substituted in the pyrrole ring to any extent, whether or not substituted on the naphthoyl ring to any extent.

(iv) 1-(1-naphthylmethylene)indene by substitution of the 3-position of the indene ring, whether or not further substituted in the indene ring to any extent, whether or not substituted on the naphthyl ring to any extent.

(v) 3-phenylacetylindole or 3-benzoylindole by substitution at the nitrogen atom of the indole ring, whether or not further substituted in the indole ring to any extent, whether or not substituted on the phenyl ring to any extent.

(3) Such term includes:

(i) 5-(1,1-dimethylheptyl)-2-{(1R,3S)-3-hydroxycyclohexyl}-phenol (CP-47,497);

(ii) 5-(1,1-dimethyloctyl)-2-{(1R,3S)-3-hydroxycyclohexyl}-phenol (cannabicyclohexanol or CP-47,497 C8-homolog);

(iii) 1-pentyl-3-(1-naphthoyl)indole (JWH-018 and AM678);

(iv) 1-butyl-3-(1-naphthoyl)indole (JWH-073);

(v) 1-hexyl-3-(1-naphthoyl)indole (JWH-019);

(vi) 1-{2-(4-morpholinyl)ethyl}-3-(1-naphthoyl)indole (JWH-200);

(vii) 1-pentyl-3-(2-methoxyphenylacetyl)indole (JWH-250);

(viii) 1-pentyl-3-{1-(4-methoxynaphthoyl)}indole (JWH-081);

(ix) 1-pentyl-3-(4-methyl-1-naphthoyl)indole (JWH-122);

(x) 1-pentyl-3-(4-chloro-1-naphthoyl)indole (JWH-398);

(xi) 1-(5-fluoropentyl)-3-(1-naphthoyl)indole (AM2201);

(xii) 1-(5-fluoropentyl)-3-(2-iodobenzoyl)indole (AM694);

(xiii) 1-pentyl-3-{(4-methoxy)-benzoyl}indole (SR-19 and RCS-4);

(xiv) 1-cyclohexylethyl-3-(2-methoxyphenylacetyl)indole (SR-18 and RCS-8); and

(xv) 1-pentyl-3-(2-chlorophenylacetyl)indole (JWH-203).

Schedule II.

(a) Schedule II shall consist of the drugs and other substances, by whatever official name, common or usual name, chemical name, or brand name designated, listed in this section.

(b) Substances, vegetable origin or chemical synthesis. Unless specifically excepted or unless listed in another schedule, any of the following substances whether produced directly or indirectly by extraction from substances of vegetable origin, or independently by means of chemical synthesis, or by a combination of extraction and chemical synthesis:

(1) Opium and opiate, and any salt, compound, derivative, or preparation of opium or opiate, excluding apomorphine, dextrorphan, nalbuphine, nalmefene, naloxone, and naltrexone, and their respective salts, but including the following:

1. Raw opium, 2. Opium extracts, 3. Opium fluid, 4. Powdered opium, 5. Granulated opium, 6. Tincture of opium, 7. Codeine, 8. Ethylmorphine, 9. Etorphine hydrochloride, 10. Hydrocodone (also known as dihydrocodeinone), 11. Hydromorphone, 12. Metopon, 13. Morphine, 14. Oxycodone, 15. Oxymorphone, 16. Thebaine, 17. Dihydroetorphine, 18. Oripavine.

(2) Any salt, compound, derivative, or preparation thereof which is chemically equivalent or identical with any of the substances referred to in this section, except that these substances shall not include the isoquinoline alkaloids of opium.

(3) Opium poppy and poppy straw.

(4) Coca leaves and any salt, compound, derivative, or preparation of coca leaves, and any salt, compound, derivative, or preparation thereof which is chemically equivalent or identical with any of these substances including cocaine and ecgonine, their salts, isomers, and salts of isomers, except that the substances shall not include:

(A) decocainized coca leaves or extraction of coca leaves, which extractions do not contain cocaine or ecgonine; or (B) (123I) ioflupane.

(5) Concentrate of poppy straw (the crude extract of poppy straw in either liquid, solid or powder form which contains the phenanthrene alkaloids of the opium poppy).

(b-1) Unless specifically excepted or unless listed in another schedule, any material, compound, mixture, or preparation containing any of the following, or their salts calculated as the free anhydrous base or alkaloid, in limited quantities as set forth below:

(1) Not more than three hundred milligrams of dihydrocodeinone (hydrocodone) per one hundred milliliters or not more than fifteen milligrams per dosage unit, with a fourfold or greater quantity of an isoquinoline alkaloid of opium.

(2) Not more than three hundred milligrams of dihydrocodeinone (hydroodone) per one hundred milliliters or not more than fifteen milligrams per dosage unit, with one or more active nonnarcotic ingredients in recognized therapeutic amounts.

(c) Opiates. Unless specifically excepted or unless in another schedule any of the following opiates, including its isomers, esters, ethers, salts and salts of isomers, esters and ethers whenever the existence of such isomers, esters, ethers, and salts is possible within the specific chemical designation, dextrorphan and levopropoxyphene excepted:

(1) Alfentanil, (2) Alphaprodine, (3) Anileridine, (4) Bezitramide, (5) Bulk dextropropoxyphene (non-dosage forms), (6) Carfentanil, (7) Dihydrocodeine, (8) Diphenoxylate, (9) Fentanyl, (10) Isomethadone, (11) Levo-alphacetylmethadol (also known as levo-alpha-acetylmethadol, levomethadylacetate or LAAM), (12) Levomethorphan, (13) Levorphanol, (14) Metazocine, (15) Methadone, (16) Methadone-intermediate, 4-cyano-2-dimethylamino-4, 4-diphenyl butane, (17) Moramide-intermediate, 2-methyl-3-morpholino-1, 1-diphenylpropane-carboxylic, (18) Pethidine (meperidine), (19) Pethidine-intermediate-A, 4-cyano-1-methyl-4-phenylpiperidine. (20) Pethidine-intermediate-B, ethyl-4-phenylpiperidine-4-carboxylate, (21) Pethidine-intermediate-C, 1-methyl-4- phenylpiperidine-4-carboxylic acid, (22) Phenazocine, (23) Piminodine, (24) Racemethorphan, (25) Racemorphan, (26) Sufentanil, (27) Remifentanil; (28) Tapentadol. (29) Thiafentanil. *(Eff.7/2/20,Ch.56,L.2020)*

(d) Stimulants. Unless specifically excepted or unless listed in another schedule, any material, compound, mixture, or preparation which contains any quantity of the following substances having a stimulant effect on the central nervous system, including its salts, isomers, and salts of isomers:

(1) Amphetamine.
(2) Methamphetamine.
(3) Phenmetrazine.
(4) Methylphenidate.

(5) Lisdexamfetamine.

(e) Depressants. Unless specifically excepted or unless listed in another schedule, any material, compound, mixture, or preparation which contains any quantity of the following substances having a depressant effect on the central nervous system, including its salts, isomers, and salts of isomers whenever the existence of such salts, isomers, and salts of isomers is possible within the specific chemical designation: (1) Amobarbital, (2) Glutethimide, (3) Pentobarbital, (4) Secobarbital.

(f) Hallucinogenic substances.

Nabilone: Another name for nabilone: (+,-)-trans-3-(1,1-dimethylheptyl)-6, 6a, 7, 8, 10, 10a-hexahydro-1-hydroxy-6, 6-dimethyl-9H-dibenzo{b,d}pyran-9-one.

(g) Immediate precursors. Unless specifically excepted or unless listed in another schedule, any material, compound, mixture or preparation which contains any quantity of the following substances:

(1) Immediate precursor to amphetamine and methamphetamine:

(i) Phenylacetone Some trade or other names: phenyl-2-propanone; P2P; benzyl methyl ketone; methyl benzyl ketone;

(2) Immediate precursors to phencyclidine (PCP):

(i) 1-phenylcyclohexylamine;

(ii) 1-piperidinocyclohexanecarbonitrile (PCC).

(3) Immediate precursor to fentanyl:

(i) 4-anilino-N-phenethyl-4-piperidine (ANPP).

(h) Anabolic steroids. Unless specifically excepted or unless listed in another schedule, "anabolic steroid" shall mean any drug or hormonal substance, chemically and pharmacologically related to testosterone (other than estrogens, progestins, corticosteroids and dehydroepiandrosterone) and includes:

(1) 3{beta}, 17-dihydroxy-5a-androstane.

(2) 3{alpha}, 17{beta}-dihydroxy-5a-androstane.

(3) 5{alpha}-androstan-3,17-dione.

(4) 1-androstenediol (3{beta},17{beta}-dihydroxy-5{alpha}-androst-1-ene).

(5) 1-androstenediol (3{alpha},17{beta}-dihydroxy-5{alpha}-androst-1-ene).

(6) 4-androstenediol (3{beta}, 17{beta}-dihydroxy-androst-4-ene).

(7) 5-androstenediol (3{beta}, 17{beta}-dihydroxy-androst-5-ene).

(8) 1-androstenedione ({5{alpha}}-androst-1-en-3,17-dione).

(9) 4-androstenedione (androst-4-en-3,17-dione).

(10) 5-androstenedione (androst-5-en-3,17-dione).

(11) Bolasterone (7{alpha},17{alpha}-dimethyl-17{beta}-hydroxyandrost-4-en-3-one).

(12) Boldenone (17{beta}-hydroxyandrost-1, 4,-diene-3-one).

(13) Boldione (androsta-1,4-diene-3,17-dione).

(14) Calusterone (7{beta}, 17{alpha}-dimethyl-17{beta}-hydroxyandrost-4-en-3-one).

(15) Clostebol (4-chloro-17{beta}-hydroxyandrost-4-en-3-one).

(16) Dehydrochloromethyltestosterone(4-chloro-17{beta}-hydroxy-17 {alpha}-methyl-androst-1, 4-dien-3-one).

(17) {Delta} 1-dihydrotestosterone (a.k.a. '1-testosterone') (17 {beta}-hydroxy-5 {alpha}-androst-1-en-3-one).

(18) 4-dihydrotestosterone (17{beta}-hydroxy-androstan-3-one).

(19) Drostanolone (17{beta}-hydroxy-2{alpha}-methyl-5{alpha}-androstan-3-one).

(20) Ethylestrenol (17{alpha}-ethyl-17{beta}-hydroxyestr-4-ene).

(21) Fluoxymesterone (9-fluoro-17{alpha}-methyl-11{beta}, 17 {beta}-dihydroxy-androst-4-en-3-one).

(22) Formebolone (2-formyl-17{alpha}- methyl-11{alpha}, 17{beta}- dihydroxy androst-1, 4-dien-3-one).

(23) Furazabol (17{alpha}-methyl-17{beta}-hydroxyandrostano{2, 3-c}-furazan).

(24) 13{beta}-ethyl-17{beta}-hyroxygon-4-en-3-one.

(25) 4-hydroxytestosterone (4, 17{beta}-dihydroxy-androst-4-en-3-one).

(26) 4-hydroxy-19-nortestosterone (4,17{beta}-dihydroxy-estr-4-en-3-one).

(27) desoxymethyltestosterone (17{alpha}-methyl-5{alpha}-androst-2-en-17{beta}-ol) (a.k.a., madol).

(28) Mestanolone (17{alpha}-methyl-17{beta}-hydroxy-5-androstan-3-one).

(29) Mesterolone (1{alpha}-methyl-17{beta}-hydroxy-{5{alpha}}-androstan-3-one).

(30) Methandienone (17{alpha}-methyl-17{beta}-hydroxyandrost-1,4-dien-3-one).

(31) Methandriol (17{alpha}-methyl-3{beta}, 17{beta}- dihydroxyandrost-5-ene).

(32) Methenolone (1-methyl-17{beta}-hydroxy-5{alpha}-androst-1-en-3-one).

(33) 17{alpha}-methyl-3{beta}, 17{beta}-dihydroxy-5a-androstane.

(34) 17{alpha}-methyl-3{alpha}, 17{beta}-dihydroxy-5a-androstane.

(35) 17{alpha}-methyl-3{beta}, 17{beta}-dihydroxyandrost-4-ene.

(36) 17{alpha}-methyl-4-hydroxynandrolone (17{alpha}-methyl-4-hydroxy-17{beta}-hydroxyestr-4-en-3-one).

(37) Methyldienolone (17{alpha}-methyl-17{beta}-hydroxyestra-4,9(10)-dien-3-one).

(38) Methyltrienolone (17{alpha}-methyl-17{beta}-hydroxyestra-4,9-11-trien-3-one).

(39) Methyltestosterone (17{alpha}-methyl-17{beta}- hydroxyandrost-4-en-3-one).

(40) Mibolerone (7{alpha},17{alpha}-dimethyl-17{beta}-hydroxyestr-4-en-3-one).

(41) 17{alpha}-methyl-{Delta} 1-dihydrotestosterone (17b{beta}-hydroxy-17{alpha}-methyl-5{alpha}-androst-1-en-3-one)(a.k.a. '17-{alpha}-methyl-1-testosterone').

(42) Nandrolone (17{beta}-hydroxyestr-4-en-3-one).

(43) 19-nor-4-androstenediol (3{beta},17{beta}-dihydroxyestr-4-ene).

(44) 19-nor-4-androstenediol (3{alpha},17{beta}-dihydroxyestr-4-ene).

(45) 19-nor-5-androstenediol (3{beta},17{beta}-dihydroxyestr-5-ene).

(46) 19-nor-5-androstenediol (3{alpha},17{beta}-dihydroxyestr-5-ene).

(47) 19-nor-4,9(10)-androstadienedione (estra-4,9(10)-diene-3,17-dione).

(48) 19-nor-4-androstenedione (estr-4-en-3,17-dione).

(49) 19-nor-5-androstenedione (estr-5-en-3,17-dione).

(50) Norbolethone (13{beta}, 17{alpha}-diethyl-17{beta}-hydroxygon-4-en-3-one).

(51) Norclostebol (4-chloro-17{beta}-hydroxyestr-4-en-3-one).

(52) Norethandrolone (17{alpha}-ethyl-17{beta}-hydroxyestr-4-en-3-one).

(53) Normethandrolone (17{alpha}-methyl-17{beta}-hydroxyestr-4-en-3-one).

(54) Oxandrolone (17{alpha}-methyl-17{beta}-hydroxy-2-oxa- {5{alpha}}-androstan-3-one).

(55) Oxymesterone (17{alpha}-methyl-4, 17{beta}-dihydroxy-androst-4-en-3-one).

(56) Oxymetholone (17 {alpha}-methyl-2-hydroxymethylene-17 {beta}-hydroxy-{5{alpha}}- androstan-3-one).

(57) Stanozolol (17{alpha}-methyl-17{beta}-hydroxy-{5{alpha}}-androst-2-eno{3, 2-c}-pyrazole).

(58) Stenbolone (17{beta}-hydroxy-2-methyl-{5{alpha}}-androst-1-en-3-one).

(59) Testolactone (13-hydroxy-3-oxo-13, 17-secoandrosta-1, 4-dien-17-oic acid lactone).

(60) Testosterone (17{beta}-hydroxyandrost-4-en-3-one).

(61) Tetrahydrogestrinone (13{beta}, 17{alpha}-diethyl-17{beta}-hydroxygon-4, 9, 11-trien-3-one).

(62) Trenbolone (17{beta}-hydroxyestr-4, 9, 11-trien-3-one).

(63) Any salt, ester or ether of a drug or substance described or listed in this subdivision.

(i) Subdivision (h) of this section shall not include any substance containing anabolic steroids expressly intended for administration through implants to cattle or other nonhuman species and that are approved by the federal food and drug administration solely for such use. Any individual who knowingly and willfully administers to himself or another person, prescribes, dispenses or distributes such substances for other than implantation to cattle or nonhuman species shall be subject to the same penalties as a practitioner who violates the provisions of this section or any other penalties prescribed by law.

Schedule III.

(a) Schedule III shall consist of the drugs and other substances, by whatever official name, common or usual name, chemical name, or brand name designated, listed in this section.

(b) Stimulants. Unless specifically excepted or unless listed in another schedule, any material, compound, mixture, or preparation which contains any quantity of the following substances having a stimulant effect on the central nervous system, including its salts, isomers (whether optical, position, or geometric), and salts of such isomers whenever the existence of such salts, isomers, and salts of isomers is possible within the specific chemical designation:

(1) Those compounds, mixtures, or preparations in dosage unit form containing any stimulant substances listed in schedule II which compounds, mixtures, or preparations were listed on August twenty-five, nineteen hundred seventy-one, as excepted compounds under title twenty-one, section 308.32 of the code of federal regulations and any other drug of the quantitive composition shown in that list for those drugs or which is the same except that it contains a lesser quantity of controlled substances.

(2) Benzphetamine.

(3) Chlorphentermine.

(4) Clortermine.

(6) Phendimetrazine.

(c) Depressants. Unless specifically excepted or unless listed in another schedule, any material, compound, mixture, or preparation which contains any quantity of the following substances having a depressant effect on the central nervous system, including its salts, isomers, and salts of isomers:

(1) Any compound, mixture or preparation containing:

(i) Amobarbital; (ii) Secobarbital; (iii) Pentobarbital; or any salt thereof and one or more other active medicinal ingredients which are not listed in any schedule.

(2) Any suppository dosage form containing:

(i) Amobarbital; (ii) Secobarbital; (iii) Pentobarbital; or any salt of any of these drugs and approved by the federal food and drug administration for marketing only as a suppository.

(3) Any substance which contains any quantity of a derivative of barbituric acid or any salt thereof.

(4) Chlorhexadol.

(5) Lysergic acid.

(6) Lysergic acid amide.

(7) Methyprylon.

(8) Sulfondiethylmethane.

(9) Sulfonethylmethane.

(10) Sulfonmethane.

(11) Tiletamine and zolazepam or any salt thereof. Some trade or other names for a tiletamine-zolazepam combination product: Telazol. Some trade or other names for tiletamine: 2-(ethylamino) -2-(2-thienyl) -cyclohexanone. Some trade or other names for zolazepam: 4-(2-fluorophenyl) -6,8-dihydro -1, 3, 8i-trimethylpyrazolo-{3,4-e} {1,4} -diazepin-7(1H)-one, flupyrazapon.

(12) Gamma hydroxybutyric acid, and salt, hydroxybutyric compound, derivative or preparation of gamma hydroxybutyric acid, including any isomers, esters and ethers and salts of isomers, esters and ethers of gamma hydroxybutyric acid, contained in a

drug product for which an application has been approved under section 505 of the federal food, drug and cosmetic act.

(13) Ketamine, its salts, isomers and salts of isomers (some other names for ketamine: (±)-2-(2-chlorophenyl)-2-(methylamino)-cyclohexanone).

(14) Embutramide.

(d) Nalorphine.

(e) Narcotic drugs. Unless specifically excepted or unless listed in another schedule, any material, compound, mixture, or preparation containing any of the following narcotic drugs, or their salts calculated as the free anhydrous base or alkaloid, in limited quantities as set forth below:

(1) Not more than 1.8 grams of codeine per one hundred milliliters or not more than ninety milligrams per dosage unit, with an equal or greater quantity of an isoquinoline alkaloid of opium.

(2) Not more than 1.8 grams of codeine per one hundred milliliters or not more than ninety milligrams per dosage unit, with one or more active, nonnarcotic ingredients in recognized therapeutic amounts.

(3) Not more than 1.8 grams of dihydrocodeine per one hundred milliliters or not more than ninety milligrams per dosage unit, with one or more active nonnarcotic ingredients in recognized therapeutic amounts.

(4) Not more than three hundred milligrams of ethylmorphine per one hundred milliliters or not more than fifteen milligrams per dosage unit, with one or more active, nonnarcotic ingredients in recognized therapeutic amounts.

(5) Not more than five hundred milligrams of opium per one hundred milliliters or per one hundred grams or not more than twenty-five milligrams per dosage unit, with one or more active, nonnarcotic ingredients in recognized therapeutic amounts.

(6) Not more than fifty milligrams of morphine per one hundred milliliters or per one hundred grams, with one or more active, nonnarcotic ingredients in recognized therapeutic amounts.

(7) Buprenorphine in any quantities.

(f) Dronabinol (synthetic) in sesame oil and encapsulated in a soft gelatin capsule in a U.S. Food and Drug Administration approved product.

Some other names for dronabinol include: (6aR-trans)-6a, 7, 8, 10a-tetrahydro-6, 6, 9-trimethyl-3-pentyl-6H-dibenzo{b,d} pyran-1-o1, or delta-9-(trans) - tetrahydrocannabinol.

(g) Chorionic gonadotropin.

(1) Unless specifically excepted or unless listed in another schedule any material, compound, mixture, or preparation which contains any amount of chorionic gonadotropin.

(2) Paragraph one of this subdivision shall not include any substance containing chorionic gonadotropin expressly intended for administration through implants or injection to cattle or other nonhuman species and that are approved by the federal food and drug administration solely for such use. Any individual who knowingly and willfully administers to himself or another person, prescribes, dispenses or distributes such substances for other than implantation or injection to cattle or nonhuman species shall be subject to the same penalties as a practitioner who violates the provisions of this section or any other penalties prescribed by law.   *(Eff.6/19/19,Ch.428,L.2018)*

Schedule IV.

(a) Schedule IV shall consist of the drugs and other substances, by whatever official name, common or usual name, chemical name, or brand name designated, listed in this section.

(b) Narcotic drugs. Unless specifically excepted or unless listed in another schedule, any material, compound, mixture, or preparation containing any of the following narcotic drugs, or their salts calculated as the free anhydrous base or alkaloid, in limited quantities as set forth below:

(1) Not more than one milligram of difenoxin and not less than twenty-five micrograms of atropine sulfate per dosage unit.

(2) Dextropropoxyphene (alpha-(+)-4-dimethylamino-1, 2-diphenyl-3-methyl-2-propionoxybutane).

(c) Depressants. Unless specifically excepted or unless listed in another schedule, any material, compound, mixture, or preparation which contains any quantity of the following substances, including its salts, isomers, and salts of isomers whenever the existence of such salts, isomers, and salts of isomers is possible within the specific chemical designation:

(1) Alprazolam, (2) Barbital, (3) Bromazepam, (4) Camazepam, (5) Chloral betaine, (6) Chloral hydrate, (7) Chlordiazepoxide, (8) Clobazam, (9) Clonazepam, (10) Clorazepate, (11) Clotiazepam, (12) Cloxazolam, (13) Delorazepam, (14) Diazepam, (15) Estazolam, (16) Ethchlorvynol, (17) Ethinamate, (18) Ethyl Loflazepate, (19) Fludiazepam, (20) Flunitrazepam, (21) Flurazepam, (22) Halazepam, (23) Haloxazolam, (24) Ketazolam, (25) Loprazolam, (26) Lorazepam, (27) Lormetazepam, (28) Mebutamate, (29) Medazepam, (30) Meprobamate, (31) Methohexital, (32) Methylphenobarbital (mephobarbital), (33) Nimetazepam, (34) Nitrazepam, (35) Nordiazepam, (36) Oxazepam, (37) Oxazolam, (38) Paraldehyde, (39) Petrichoral, (40) Phenobarbital, (41) Pinazepam, (42) Prazepam, (43) Temazepam, (44) Tetrazepam, (45) Triazolam, (46) Midazolam, (47) Quazepam, (48) Zolpidem, (49) Dichloralphenazone, (50) Zaleplon, (51) Zopiclone (eszopiclone), (52) Fospropofol, (53) Carisoprodol.

* (d) Fenfluramine. Any material, compound, mixture, or preparation which contains any quantity of the following substances, including its salts, isomers (whether optical, position, or geometric), and salts of such isomers, whenever the existence of such salts, isomers and salts of isomers is possible:

(1) Fenfluramine.

Repealed upon the removal of fenfluramine and its salts and isomers from Schedule IV of the federal Controlled Substances Act

(e) Stimulants. Unless specifically excepted or unless listed in another schedule, any material, compound, mixture, or preparation which contains any quantity of the following substances having a stimulant effect on the central nervous system, including its salts, isomers, and salts of such isomers:

(1) Cathine ((+) - norpseudoephedrine), (2) Diethylpropion, (3) Fencamfamin, (4) Fenproporex, (5) Mazindol, (6) Mefenorex, (7) Pemoline (including organometallic complexes and chelates thereof), (8) Phentermine, (9) Pipradrol, (10) SPA ((-))-1-dimethylamino-1, 2-diphenylethane), (11) Modafinil, (12) Sibutramine.

(f) Other substances. Unless specifically excepted or unless listed in another schedule, any material, compound, mixture or preparation which contains any quantity of the following substances, including its salts:

(1) Pentazocine.

(2) Butorphanol (including its optical isomers).

(3) Tramadol in any quantities.

Schedule V.

(a) Schedule V shall consist of the drugs and other substances, by whatever official name, common or usual name, chemical name, or brand name designated, listed in this section.

(b) Narcotic drugs containing nonnarcotic active medicinal ingredients. Any compound, mixture, or preparation containing any of the following narcotic drugs, or their salts calculated as the free anhydrous base or alkaloid, in limited quantities as set forth below, which shall include one or more nonnarcotic active medicinal ingredients in sufficient proportion to confer upon the compound, mixture, or preparation valuable medicinal qualities other than those possessed by narcotic drugs alone:

(1) Not more than two hundred milligrams of codeine per one hundred milliliters or per one hundred grams.

(2) Not more than one hundred milligrams of dihydrocodeine per one hundred milliliters or per one hundred grams.

(3) Not more than one hundred milligrams of ethylmorphine per one hundred milliliters or per one hundred grams.

(4) Not more than 2.5 milligrams of diphenoxylate and not less than twenty-five micrograms of atropine sulfate per dosage unit.

(5) Not more than one hundred milligrams of opium per one hundred milliliters or per one hundred grams.

(6) Not more than 0.5 milligram of difenoxin and not less than twenty-five micrograms of atropine sulfate per dosage unit.

(c) Stimulants. Unless specifically exempted or excluded or unless listed in another schedule, any material, compound, mixture, or preparation which contains any quantity of the following substances having a stimulant effect on the central nervous system, including its salts, isomers and salts of isomers:

(1) Pyrovalerone.

(d) Depressants. Unless specifically exempted or excluded or unless listed in another schedule, any material, compound, mixture, or preparation which contains any quantity of the following substances having a depressant effect on the central nervous system, including its salts, isomers, and salts of isomers:

(1) Ezogabine {N-{2-amino-4-(4-fluorobenzylamino)-phenyl}-carbamic acid ethyl ester}.

(2) Lacosamide {(R)-2-acetoamido-N-benzyl-3-methoxy-propionamide}.

(3) Pregabalin {(S)-3-(aminomethyl)-5-methylhexanoic acid)}.

INDEX

Controlled substances
  Schedule I A-5
  Schedule II A-7
  Schedule III A-11
  Schedule IV A-12
  Schedule V A-13
  schedules of A-5
Definitions of terms A-2

PENAL LAW INDEX
Sections

A

Abandonment of child 260.00
Abduct, defined 135.00
Absconding from
  community treatment center 205.19
  furlough program 205.18
  temporary release 205.16,.17
Access device, criminal use of . . 190.75,.76
  defined 155.00
Accosting, fraudulent 165.30
Act, defined 15.00
Adultery 255.17,.20,.30
Advertisements, unlawfully posting . 145.30
Advertising, false 190.20
Affirmative defense 25.00
Aggravated
  assault 120.11,.12
  cemetery desecration 145.26,.27
  criminal contempt 215.52
  criminal pos/weapon 265.19
  criminally negligent homicide . . . 125.11
  family offense 240.75
  grand larceny, ATM 155.43
  harassment 240.30–.32
  insurance fraud 176.35
  labor trafficking 135.37
  manslaughter 125.21, 125.22
  murder 125.26
  patronizing minor/prostitution 230.11-.13
  sexual abuse 130.65–a,.70
  strangulation 121.13-a
  vehicular assault 120.04-a
  vehicular homicide 125.14
Aircraft, directing laser at 240.76,–.77
Alcohol overdose, witness/victim of 220.78
Ammunition, armor piercing 265.00
  sellers of 400.03
Anarchy, criminal 240.15
Animal, harming 195.11,.12
Animal, service . . . . Article 242
Anti-security item,
  criminal possession of 170.47
Antique firearm 265.00
Appearance ticket, failing to respond 215.58
Arrest, resisting 205.30
Arson . . . . Art. 150
Assault 120.00–.12
  by day care provider 120.01
  on a judge 120.09
Assault weapon, defined 265.00
Assembly, unlawful 240.10
Assets subject to forfeiture
  unlawful disposition 215.80
ATM, aggravated grand larceny . . . 155.43
Attempt 110.00–.10
Auto stripping 165.09–.11

B

Bad check, issuing 190.00–.15
Bail jumping 215.55–.59
Benefit, defined 10.00
Bigamy 255.15,.20
Biological weapon
  criminal possession of 60.06, 490.37–.45
  criminal use of 490.47–.55
Blood circulation
  criminal obstruction 121.11
  strangulation . . . . 121.12 -.13
Body vest, unlawful wearing of 270.20
Bomb, placing a false 240.61,.62
Breathing
  criminal obstruction 121.11
  strangulation . . . . 121.12 -.13
Bribe, giving, public office 200.40,.45
Bribe, receiving 200.10–.15
  commercial 180.05
  juror 215.20
  labor official 180.25,.30
  public office 200.40,.50
  sports 180.45
  witness 215.05
Bribery 200.00–.05
Bribing
  commercial 180.00–.08
  juror 215.19
  labor official 180.10–.20
  sports 180.35,.40
  witness 215.00
Broadcast, defined 250.40
Building, defined 140.00, 150.00
Burglar's tools 140.35
Burglary 140.20–.30
  definitions 140.00
Burn injury to be reported 265.26
Business records, falsifying . . . 175.00–.15

C

Cane sword, defined 265.00
Cannabis . . . . Art. 222
  criminal possession of . . . . . 222.30 - .40
  criminal sale of . . . . 222.50 - .65
  definitions 222.00
  defense, licensing of production
    and distribution 222.20
  personal possession, cultivation
    & home 222.15
  personal use 222.05
  restrictions on use 222.10
  unlawful sale 222.45
Cemetery, desecration 145.22,.23
  aggravated 145.26,.27
  authorized disposition 60.29
Check, bad 190.00–.15

Sections

Chemical reagent, defined 220.00
Chemical weapon
  criminal possession of 60.06,490.37–.45
  criminal use of 490.47–.55
Child
  abandonment 260.00
  assault by day care provider 120.01
  course of sexual conduct
    against 130.75–.80
  endangering welfare 260.10–.15
  luring of 120.70
  misrepresentation
    by a caregiver 260.35
    by day care provider 260.31
  non-support 260.05,.06
  predatory sexual assault 130.96
  reckless assault 120.02
  sex trafficking of 230.34-a
  sexual performance by .... Art. 263
  substitution 135.55
  unlawfully dealing with 260.20,.21
  use of, to commit controlled
    substance offense 220.28
Chuka stick, defined 265.00
Coercion 135.60–.75
Collection practices, unlawful 190.50
Commercial bribing 180.00–.08
Commit a crime, attempt .... Art. 110
Communications information,
  unlawfully obtaining 250.30
Community guns, defined 115.20
Compounding a crime 215.45
Computer related material
  criminal possession of 156.35
  unlawful duplication of .... 156.29, .30
Computers, offenses involving . 156.00–.50
Concealment of human corpse 195.02
Conditional and unconditional
  discharge .... Art. 65
Conduct, defined 15.00
Consent, lack of 130.05–.35
Conspiracy 105.00–.35
Contraband, defined 205.00
  dangerous, defined 205.00
Controlled substance organization;
  defined 220.00
Controlled substances
  authorized disposition 60.04
  deceit 178.26
  definitions 220.00
  drug/alcohol overdose 220.78
  facilitating sex offense 130.90
  fraud 178.26
  offenses .... Art. 220
  possession 220.03–.25
  precursors 220.60
  sale 220.31–.43

Sections

sale to a child 220.48
school grounds, near 220.44
under influence, in public 240.40
use of child 220.28
Convictions to be reported 265.30
Corporate official, misconduct by . 190.35
Corpse, human concealment of ... 195.02
Corroboration 115.15, 130.16,
.... 165.65, 260.11
Corrupt use of position or authority 200.56
Counterfeiting, trademark 165.70–.74
Credit card, unlawful use 165.17
Credit terms, false statement 190.55
Crime, defined 10.00
Crime victim assistance fee 60.35
Criminal act, defined 460.10
Criminal anarchy 240.15
Criminal communications,
  failing to report 250.35
Criminal contempt 215.50–.54
  legislature 215.60
  state commission on judicial
    conduct 215.66
  temporary state commission 215.65
Criminal facilitation 115.00–.20
Criminal forfeiture .... Art. 480
Criminal impersonation ...... 190.25, .26
Criminal injection-narcotic drug .. 220.46
Criminal liability 20.00–.25
Criminal mischief 145.00–.12
Criminal negligence 15.05
Criminal nuisance .... 240.45, .46
Criminal obstruction
  affirmative defense 121.14
  blood circulation 121.11
  breathing 121.11
Criminal possession
  anti-security item 170.47
  controlled substance 220.03–.25
  controlled substances, precursors 220.60
  forged instrument 170.20–.35
  forgery devices 170.40
  hypodermic instrument 220.03
  methamphetamine manufacturing
    material 220.70,–.71
  stolen property 165.40–.65
  weapon 265.01–.04
  weapon, aggravated 265.19
Criminal sale of
  cannabis .... 222.50 - .60
  controlled substance 220.48
  ghost gun .... 265.60, .61
  unfinished frame .... 265.63, .64
Criminal sexual act 130.40–.50
Criminal simulation 170.45
Criminal solicitation 100.00–.20
Criminal tampering 145.14–.20

Sections

Criminal trespass 140.00–.17
  defined 140.00
Criminal use, defined
Criminal usury 190.40.–.42
Culpability . . . . Art. 15
  lack of; other defenses involving . Art. 40
Custodial interference 135.45–.50
Custody, defined 205.00

D

Dangerous instrument/
  deadly weapon definitions 10.00
Dangerous material, defined 220.00
Dangerous weapons and firearms . Art. 265
Day care provider/child,
  misrepresentation by 260.31
Deadly physical force, defined 10.00
Deadly weapon, defined 10.00
Debit card, unlawful use of 165.17
Defenses 25.00–40.15
Defraud, scheme to 190.60–.70
Defrauding the government 195.20
Depressant/stimulant drug, defined . 220.00
Detention facility, defined 205.00
Determinate sentencing,
  transitional exception 70.85
Deviate sexual intercourse, defined . 130.00
Director, defined 220.00
Discharge . . . . Art. 65
Disclosure, unlawful . . . . 215.70, .75
Disorderly conduct 240.20
Disposal of stolen property 450.10
Disposition of offenders . . . . Art. 60
Disposition of weapons 400.05
Disseminate, defined 250.40
Dissolution decree,
  unlawfully issuing 255.05
Domestic act of terrorism . . . . 490.27, .28
DNA databank fee 60.35
Driving while intoxicated
  authorized dispositions 60.21
  offenses 60.36
Drug overdose, witness/victim of . . 220.78
Drug paraphernalia, using . 220.50, 220.55
Drug trafficking felony, defined 10.00
Drugs, dangerous
  see Controlled substances 220.00
Drugs, public appearance
  under influence 240.40
Duress 40.00

E

Eavesdropping 250.00–.20
  devices, possession of 250.10
  warrant, divulging 250.20

Sections

Elderly person
  endangering welfare of . . . . 260.32, .34
  vulnerable, definitions 260.31
Electronic
  dart gun, defined 265.00
  monitoring 65.10
  sweepstakes, unlawful operating . 156.40
  stun gun, defined 265.00
Electronic access device,
  fraudulent making of 170.75
  defined 170.00
Emergency medical services 195.16
  obstructing 195.16
Endangering welfare of
  child 260.10–.15
  incompetent person 1° 260.25
  incompetent person 2° 260.24
  physically disabled person 1° . . . 260.34
  physically disabled person 2° . . . 260.32
  vulnerable elderly person . . . 260.32, .34
Enter or remain unlawfully 140.00
Enterprise corruption . . . . 105.35, Art. 460
Entrapment 40.05
Escape 205.00–.15
Evidence, tampering with . . . . 215.35, .40
Examination, government licensing,
  impairing integrity of 200.55
Exhibition, offensive 245.05
Exposure of person 245.01
  promoting 245.02

F

Facilitation, criminal 115.00–.15
False
  advertising 190.20
  bomb, placing a . . . . 240.61, .63
  certificate issuing 175.40
  financial statement, issuing 175.45
  instrument, offering for filing 175.30,.35
  personation 190.23
  reporting 240.50–60
  statement of credit terms 190.55
False statement
  credit terms 190.55
  making apparently sworn . . 210.35, .40
  written, making a punishable . . . 210.45
Falsely reporting an incident . . 240.50–.60
Falsifying business records . . . 175.00–.15
Felony, defined 10.00
Female, defined 130.00
Financial statement, issuing false . . 175.45
Fines 80.00–.15
Firearms . . . . Arts. 265 & 400
  destruction 400.05
  ghost gun, criminal sale . . . . 265.60, .61

Sections

licensing provisions 400.00
registration and serialization of . 265.07
report of theft or loss 400.10
safely store, failure to ...... 265.45, .50
toy gun, manufacture 265.10
undetectable 265.55
unfinished frame or receiver 265.63, .64
statewide license & record database 400.02
Firefighting operations, obstructing 195.15
Fireworks
permits for display 405.00
seizure and destruction 405.05
unlawfully, dealing with 270.00
Fleeing a police officer 270.25–.35
For-hire vehicles, criminal attack on 60.07
Force, use of 35.10–.30
Forcible compulsion, defined 130.00
Forcible touching 130.52
Foreign object, defined 130.00
Forfeiture
felony controlled substances
offense Art.480
unlawful disposition of assets .. 215.80
Forged instrument
criminal possession of 170.20–.35
defined 170.00
Forgery 170.00–.15
devices, criminal possession of . 170.40
of v.i.n. 170.65
Fortune telling 165.35
Fraud
controlled substances 178.26
health care .... Art. 177
in insolvency 185.00
involving a security interest 185.05
welfare .... Art. 158
Fraudulent
accosting 165.30
disposition of mortgaged property 185.10
disposition of property,
conditional sale 185.15
Fraudulently obtaining signature .. 165.20
Fraudulent life settlement act 176.40

G

Gambling .... Art. 225
device, possession of ...... 225.30, .32
offenses, terms defined 225.00
records, possession of 225.15–.25
seizure/forfeiture of vehicle/
vessel/aircraft 415.00
Gaming
equipment, unlawful 225.95
fraud .... 225.55, .60
outcomes, manipulation 225.90

Sections

property, unlawful poss. 225.70-.85
Gang assault 120.06,. 07
Gas meter, unlawful installing 270.40
Genitals, female, mutilation of 130.85
facilitating 260.22
Ghost gun
criminal sale .... 265.60, .61
Government, defrauding 195.20
Government licensing examination,
impairing the integrity of 200.55
Governmental administration,
obstructing 195.05
Governmental duties, obstruction of 195.17
Graffiti, making 145.60
possession of instruments 145.65
removal program, disposition of . 60.28
Grand jury, disclosure 215.70
Grand larceny 155.30–.43
Gratuities, unlawful .... 200.30, .35
Gravity knife, defined 265.00
Gunsmiths 400.00

H

Hallucinogen, defined 220.00
Harassment .... 240.25, .26
aggravated .... 240.30, .32
rent regulated tenants 241.00-.05
Hate crimes .... Art. 485
Hazard creating 270.10
Hazardous material, defined 220.00
Hazardous substance,
placing of 240.61–.63
Hazing .... 120.16, .17
Health care fraud .... Art. 177
Health care provider, defined 130.00
Health care services, criminal
interference with ...... 240.70, .71-.73
Hinder prosecution 205.50–.65
Homicide, definitions 125.00–.10
criminally negligent 125.10, 125.11
vehicular 125.12-.14
Hypodermic instrument,
criminally possessing 220.03

I

Identity theft crimes 190.77-.80-a
Ignition interlock device 65.15
Ignorance of law 15.20
Imaging device, defined 250.40
Immediate family, defined 120.40
Immigrant assistant
services fraud 190.87,-.89
Impersonation, criminal 190.25
Imprisonment, sentences of ...... Art. 70
Imprisonment, unlawful 135.00–.15
defined 120.40

Sections

Incest 255.25.–30
Inciting a riot 240.08
Incompetent person,
    defined 260.31
    endangering welfare 260.25
Indecent materials,
    disseminating to minors ... 235.20–.24
Indeterminate sentence 70.00
Indictment, unlawful disclosure 215.75
Infancy, defense of 30.00
Injection, narcotic drug 220.46
Insurance fraud 176.00–.35
Intentionally, defined 15.05
Intermittent imprisonment .... Art. 85

J

Jostling 165.25
Jurat, defined 210.00
Juror
    bribing; tampering with,
        misconduct by 215.15–.30
    defined 10.00
Justification, defense of .... Art. 35
Juvenile delinquent,
    possession of weapons 265.05
Juvenile offender, defined 10.00

K

Kidnapping 135.00–.30
    defined 120.40
Knives .... Art. 265
Knowingly, defined 15.05
Kung Fu star, defined 265.00

L

Labor trafficking 135.35
    accomplice 135.36
    aggravated 135.37
Laboratory equipment, defined 220.00
Larceny 155.00–.45
Laser, directing at aircraft 240.76,-.77
Lewdness, public 245.00
Licensing firearms 400.00
Life settlement fraud
    aggravated 176.70
    fifth degree 176.45
    first degree 176.65
    fourth degree 176.50
    second degree 176.60
    third degree 176.55
Littering, on RR tracks and
    rights-of-way 145.50
Loitering .... 240.35, .36
Lotteries 225.00–.40
Lottery offenses 225.40

Sections

Luring a child 120.70

M

Manslaughter 125.15,.20
    aggravated 125.21, 125.22
    vehicular .... 125.12, .13
Marihuana (see Cannabis) ....
    authorized disposition 60.04
    medical
        criminal diversion .. 179.00–179.11
        criminal retention 179.15
Marriage
    license, unlawfully procuring ... 255.10
    unlawfully solemnizing 255.00
Mechanical overhearing, defined ... 250.00
Menacing 120.13–.15
    police / peace officer 120.18
Mental disease or defect 40.15
Mental health care provider, defined 130.00
Mentally disabled, defined 130.00
Mentally incapacitated, defined 130.00
Metal knuckle knife, defined 265.00
Metal knuckles, defined 10.00
Methamphetamine - See *Possession of*
Misapplication of property 165.00
Mischief, criminal 145.00–.12
Misconduct by corporate official ... 190.35
Misconduct by juror .... 215.28, .30
Misconduct, official 195.00
Misdemeanor, defined 10.00
Misrepresentation
    by a caregiver 260.35
    by day care provider 260.31
Monetary instrument, defined 470.00
Money laundering ...... 105.10, Art. 470
Mortgage, fraud; residential ... 187.00–.25
Mortgaged property,
    fraudulent disposition 185.10
Motor vehicle, defined 150.00
Murder 125.25–.27
Mutilation, female genitals 130.85
    facilitating 260.22

N

Narcotic drug, defined 220.00
    criminal injection, narcotic 220.46
Non-support of child .... 260.05, .06
Noxious materials
    unlawfully possessing/selling ... 270.05
Nuisance, criminal .... 240.45, .46

O

Oath, defined 210.00
Obscenity 235.00–.15
    minors 235.15

Sections | Sections

Obstructing
  emergency medical services 195.16
  firefighting operations 195.15
  governmental
    administration ..... 195.05, .07, .08
Obtain, defined 155.00
Offense, defined 10.00
  against public order .... Art. 240
  classification .... Art. 55
Official misconduct 195.00
Omission, defined 15.00
Organized Crime Control
  Act .... Arts. 460, 470, 480
Owner, defined 155.00

P

Pari-mutuel betting system,
  impair integrity .... 180.52, .53
Party line, unlawfully refusing
  to yield 270.15
Pattern of criminal act, defined ... 460.10
Peace officer, refusing to aid 195.10
Perjury 210.00–.50
Permit for fireworks 405.00
Permit for indoor pyrotechnics 405.10
Persistent felony offender, defined .. 70.10
Person, defined 10.00
Petit larceny 155.25
Physical evidence,
  tampering with .... 215.35, .40
Physical force, use of .... Art. 35
Physical injury, defined 10.00
Physically
  disabled person, defined 260.31
  helpless, defined 130.00
Pilum ballistic knife, defined 265.00
Plastic knuckles, defined 10.00
Police, animal killing/injuring 195.06,.06-a
Police officer, refusal to aid 195.10
Police officer, fleeing 270.25–.35
Police uniform, criminal sale of ... 190.27
Pornography,
  seizure and forfeiture
    of equipment 410.00
Possession, defined 10.00
Possession of
  ammunition feeding device . 265.36,.37
  burglar's tools 140.35
  controlled substance 220.03–.25
  firearms .... Arts. 265, 400
  forged instrument 170.20–.35
  forgery devices 170.40
  gambling device .... 225.30, .35
  gambling records .. 225.15–.25, 415.00
  methamphetamine

mfg material 220.70,71
precursors 220.72
unlawful disposal of meth. lab 220.76
unlawful manufacture of . 220.73–.75
stolen property 165.40–.65
usurious loan records 190.45
weapons .... Art. 265
Precursor, defined 220.00
Predatory sexual assault 130.95
  against a child 130.96
Premises, defined 140.00
Prescription, criminal sale 220.65
Prescription medications & prescriptions
  criminal diversion of 178.00–.25
  definitions 178.00
Prison
  contraband, promoting ..... 205.20, .25
Private communications,
  tampering with 250.25
Probation .... Art. 65
Profiteer, defined 220.00
Promoting prostitution 230.15–.35
Promoting suicide, attempt .... 120.30, .35
Property, misapplication of 165.00
Property, reckless endangerment of 145.25
  defined 155.00
Property, stolen
  criminal possession of 165.40–.65
Property of another, defined 145.13
Prosecution, hindering 205.50–.65
Prostitution 230.00–.40
  affirmative defense 230.01
  in a school zone 230.03
  patronizing 230.02–.10
    aggravated 230.11-.13
  permitting 230.40
  promoting 230.15–.35
    in a school zone 230.19
Public appearance under influence
  of drugs 240.40
Public benefit card
  criminal possession 158.40–.50
  criminal use .... 158.30, .35
  definition 158.00
  unlawful use of 165.17
Public display of offensive
  sexual material .... 245.10, .11
Public lewdness .... 245.00, .03
Public office,
  bribing and bribe receiving . 200.40–.50
Public records, tampering with . 175.20, .25
Public servants, defined 10.00
Publish, defined 250.40
Punishment and sentence .... Arts. 55–85
Pyrotechnics, indoor .... 405.10 to .18

Sections

R

Radio device, unlawful possession . 140.40
Radio transmission, unauthorized . . 190.72
Railroad tracks, littering 145.50
Rape 130.25–.35
Receiving
  reward for official
    misconduct . . . . 200.25, .27
  unlawful gratuities 200.35
Reckless assault by child
  care provider 120.01
Reckless assault of a child 120.02
Reckless endangerment . . . . . . 120.20, .25
  of property 145.25
Recklessly, defined 15.05
Recording device,
  unauthorized operation 275.32-.34
Recordings, unauthorized
  advertisement/sale . . . . 275.25, .30
  failure to disclose origin . . . 275.35, .40
  in motion picture or
    live theater 275.33,.34
  manufacture . . . . 275.05, .10
  performance . . . . 275.15, .20
  seizure/destruction of 420.00
  seizure/forfeiture of equipment . . 420.05
Refusing
  aid to peace/police officer 195.10
  to yield party line 270.15
Relative, defined 135.00
Religious service
  criminal interference with . . 240.70, .71
  disruption or disturbance of 240.21
Rent gouging 180.54–.57
Renunciation 40.10
Representative drawer, defined 190.00
Resisting arrest 205.30
Restitution and reparation 60.27
Restrain, defined 135.00
Rewarding official misconduct 200.20, .22
Rifle . . . . Art. 265.00
  transfer, waiting period 400.20
Rights-of-way, littering 145.50
Riot 240.00–.06
  inciting 240.08
Robbery 160.00–.15

S

Sadism/masochism, defined 235.20
Scheme to defraud 190.60–.70
School, criminal sale of
  controlled substance 220.44
School bus, defined 220.00
Secret scientific material,
  unlawful use of 165.07
Sell, defined 250.40
Sentence and punishment . . . 55.00–85.00

Sections

Sentence of probation . . . . Art. 65
Serious physical injury, defined 10.00
Service animal, offenses against . . Art. 242
Services, theft of 165.15
Sex offender
  registration fee 60.35
Sex offense, defined 120.40
  with controlled substance 130.90
    defined 235.00
Sex offenses 130.00–.16
Sex trafficking 230.34
Sex trafficking of child 230.34-a
Sexual abuse 130.53–.70
Sexual act, criminal 130.40–.50
Sexual assault, predatory 130.95
  against child 130.96
Sexual conduct
  against child . . . . 130.75, .80
  aggravated, defined 130.00
  defined 130.00
Sexual contact, defined 130.00
Sexual intercourse, defined 130.00
Sexual material,
  offensive public display . . . 245.10, .11
Sexual misconduct 130.20
Sexual performance, by child . . . . Art. 263
Sexually motivated felony 130.91
Shock incarceration,
  participation 60.05
Shotgun . . . . Arts. 265 & 400
  transfer, waiting period 400.20
Signature, fraudulently obtaining . . 165.20
Simulation, criminal 170.45
Skimmer device, defined 190.85
  unlawful possession 190.85,.86
Slot machine, defined 225.00
Slugs, unlawful 170.50–.60
Sodomy *(See Criminal Sexual Act)*
Solemnizing marriage, unlawfully . . 255.00
Solicitation, criminal . . . . Art. 100
Solvent, defined 220.00
Sound recordings . . . . Art. 275
Specified predicate crime, defined . . 120.40
Sports arena, placing false bomb . . 240.63
Sports bribery and receiving . . 180.35–.45
Sports contest, tampering with 180.50, .51
Staging a motor vehicle accident 176.75,.80
Stalking 120.45–.60
Stimulant, defined 220.00
Stolen property
  criminal possession 165.40–.65
  disposal 450.10
Strangulation . . . . 121.12, .13, .13-a
Substitution of children 135.55
Suicide, promoting attempt . . . 120.30, .35
Swear, defined 210.00
Swear falsely, defined 210.00

Sections

Sweepstakes, unlawful 156.40
Switchblade knife, defined 265.00
Syringe, criminally
   possessing 220.03

T

Tampering, criminal 145.14–.20
Tampering with
   computer .... 156.20, .27
   consumer product 145.35–.45
   juror 215.25
   physical evidence .... 215.35, .40
   private communications 250.25
   public records .... 175.20, .25
   sports contest .... 180.50, .51
   witness 215.10–.13
Taximeter accelerating device,
   criminal possession of 145.70
Tenant, harassment of 241.00-.05
Terrorism .... Art. 490
   domestic act of .... 490.27, .28
   hindering prosecution of ... 490.30,.35
   liability protection 490.01
   money laundering 470.21–.24
   offenders 60.06
Terroristic threat, making a 490.20
Testimony 210.00
Theft of services 165.15
Touching, forcible 130.52
Trademark, counterfeiting 165.71–.73
   definitions 165.70
   goods bearing, seizure of 165.74
Traffic infraction, defined 10.00
Trafficker, operating as major 220.77
Trafficking, labor 135.35
   accomplice 135.36
   aggravated 135.37
   sex 230.34
   sex, accomplice 230.36
Transportation services,
   unauthorized sale of 165.16
Trespass, criminal 140.00–.17

U

Unauthorized use of vehicle ... 165.05, .06
Unlawful dissemination or publication
   of an intimate image 245.15
Unlawful surveillance, definitions . 250.40
   1st degree 250.50
   2nd degree 250.45

image, dissemination of, 2nd deg. 250.55
Use of force 35.10–.30
Usurious loan records, possession . 190.45
Usury, criminal .... 190.40, .42
Uttering bad check 190.00–.15

V

Vehicle
   defined 10.00
   forgery 170.65
   identification,
     illegal possession 170.70,.71
     unauthorized use ..... 165.05, .06, .08
Vehicular assault 120.03-.04-a
Vehicular homicide 125.14
Vehicular manslaughter ...... 125.12, .13
Victim
   intimidating a 215.15–.17
   employer unlawfully penalizing . 215.14
Violation, defined 10.00
Voluntary act, defined 15.00
Vulnerable elderly persons 260.31
   endangering welfare of 260.34

W

Wagering instruments, unlawful use 225.65
Weapon, criminal possession .. 265.01–.04
   aggravated criminal pos 265.19
   criminal disposal 265.17
   criminal purchase 265.17
Weapons .... Arts. 265 & 400
Welfare, endangering
   child 260.10–.15
   incompetent person 260.25
   vulnerable elderly person ... 260.32, .34
Welfare fraud 158.00–.25
Will, unlawfully concealing 190.30
Wiretapping
   defined 250.00
   failure to report 250.15
Witness
   bribing and bribe receiving . 215.00, .05
   employer unlawfully penalizing . 215.14
   intimidating 215.15–.17
   tampering with 215.10–.13
Wounds to be reported ...... 265.25, .26
Written instrument, defined 170.00

Y

Youthful offender, sentencing 60.02

CRIMINAL
PROCEDURE
LAW

OF
NEW YORK STATE

Part II

43-08 162nd Street
Flushing, NY 11358
www.LooseleafLaw.com   800-647-5547

This page intentionally left blank.

STATE OF NEW YORK

SENATE and ASSEMBLY

Pursuant to the authority vested in us by section 70-b of the Public Officers Law and upon information and belief, I, Andrea Stewart-Cousins, Temporary President of the Senate and I, Carl E. Heastie, Speaker of the Assembly, hereby jointly certify that the text of the provisions of law contained in this publication is a correct transcript of the text of such law as last amended as of the date of execution of this certificate, and, in accordance with such section, is entitled to be read into evidence.

Given under my hand and seal of office, in the County of Albany this 7th day of January 20 22.

_____
Temporary President of the Senate

Given under my hand and seal of office, in the County of Albany this 7th day of January 20 22.

_____
Speaker of the Assembly

This certification is issued for: Looseleaf Law Publications, Inc.
Criminal Procedure Law

Chapter 833/21 excepting §14 of Part O of Chapter 55/12, §19 of Part J of Chapter 56/12 and §10 of Part A of Chapter 60/12

LAW CHANGES BY THE 2021 LEGISLATURE WHICH AFFECT THE
CRIMINAL PROCEDURE LAW

Section	Subdivision	Change	Chapter	Eff. Date
1.20	34. (b),(c),(d),(e), (f),(j),(k),(*l*),(o), (p),(s),(u)	Amended	59	10/16/23
1.20	34-a.(a)	Eff. Extended	55	4/19/21
2.10	7-a.	Eff.Extended	175	6/29/21
10.40		Eff.Extended	118	6/11/21
60.47		Amended	23	2/2/21
60.49		New	431	12/6/21
Art. 65		Eff. Extended	55	4/19/21
95.00		Eff. Extended	55	4/19/21
140.10	4.	Eff. Extended	55	4/19/21
160.10	1.(c)	Amended	23	2/2/21
160.10	1.(d)	Deleted	23	2/2/21
160.50	3.(k)(iii)	Amended	23	2/2/21
160.50	3.(k)(iv)	New	23	2/2/21
160.50	3.(k)	Amended	92	3/31/21
160.55	1.,2.,3.	Amended	23	2/2/21
170.15	5.	Amended	91	4/28/21
170.30	4.	Amended	23	2/2/21
170.56	1.	Amended	92	3/31/21
170.80	1. Op.Para.	Amended	23	2/2/21
180.20	4.	Amended	91	4/28/21
Art. 182		Eff. Extended	55	4/19/21
216.00	1.	Eff.Extended	92	3/31/21
216.00	Op.Para. & 2.	Amended	435	10/7/21
216.05		Amended	435	10/7/21
220.10	5.(g-1)	New	809	12/29/21
220.10	5.(h)	Amended	322	8/2/21
220.50	7.	Eff. Extended	55	4/19/21
220.50	8.	New	103	9/1/23
230.11		New	91	4/28/21
340.40		Amended	806	7/1/22
380.50	5.	Amended	210	7/31/21

Section	Subdivision	Change	Chapter	Eff. Date
380.55		Amended	616	1/14/22
380.70		Eff. Extended	55	4/19/21
390.20	4.(a) Cl. Para.	Eff. Extended	55	4/19/21
Art. 410	Heading	Eff. Extended	55	4/19/21
410.10	4.	New	487	10/22/21
410.91		Eff. Extended	55	4/19/21
410.91	5.	Eff.Extended	92	3/31/21
420.10	5. Cls.Para.	Amended	322	8/2/21
420.35	2.	Amended	23	2/2/21
430.20	2. & 4.	Eff. Extended	55	4/19/21
440.10	1.(i) Op.Para.	Amended	629	11/16/21
440.10	1.(i) Subs. (ii)	Amended	629	1/15/22
440.10	1.(i) Sub.(i), (iii)	Amended	629	11/16/21
440.10	1.(k)	Amended	92	3/31/21
440.10	2. (b) & (c)	Amended	501	10/25/21
440.10	6.	Amended	629	11/16/21
440.46-a		New	92	3/31/21
440.50	1.	Amended	322	8/2/21
460.90		Eff.Extended	118	6/11/21
510.15	1.	Amended	813	12/29/21
530.12	5.	Eff. Extended	55	4/19/21
530.13	4.	Eff. Extended	55	4/19/21
580.20	Art. VIII	Amended	322	8/2/21
580.20	Art.IX 5.	Amended	322	8/2/21
700.05	8.(c)	Amended	92	3/31/21
720.15	4.	Amended	23	2/2/21
720.20	5.	New	552	11/2/21
720.35	1.	Amended	23	2/2/21
725.05	7.	Amended	809	12/29/21
725.10	1.	Amended	809	12/29/21

This page intentionally left blank.

CRIMINAL PROCEDURE LAW

TABLE OF CONTENTS

ARTICLE		SECTIONS
1	Short Title, Applicability and Definitions	1.00 - 1.20
2	Peace Officers	2.10 - 2.30
10	The Criminal Courts	10.10 - 10.40
20	Geographical Jurisdiction of Offenses	20.10 - 20.60
30	Timeliness of Prosecutions and Speedy Trial	30.10 - 30.30
40	Exemption from Prosecution by Reason of Previous Prosecution	40.10 - 40.51
50	Compulsion of Evidence by Offer of Immunity	50.10 - 50.30
60	Rules of Evidence and Related Matters	60.10 - 60.76
65	Use of Closed-circuit Television for Certain Child Witnesses	65.00 - 65.30
70	Standards of Proof	70.10 - 70.20
95	Pre-Criminal Proceeding Settlements	95.00
100	Commencement of Action in Local Criminal Court or Youth Part of a Superior Court–Accusatory Instruments	100.05 - 100.60
110	Requiring Defendant's Appearance in Local Criminal Court or Youth Part of Superior Court for Arraignment	110.10 - 110.20
120	Warrant of Arrest	120.10 - 120.90
130	The Summons	130.10 - 130.60
140	Arrest Without a Warrant	140.05 - 140.55
150	The Appearance Ticket	150.10 - 150.80
160	Fingerprinting and Photographing of Defendant After Arrest–Criminal Identification Records and Statistics	160.10 - 160.60
170	Proceedings Upon Information, Simplified Traffic Information, Prosecutor's Information and Misdemeanor Complaint from Arraignment to Plea	170.10 - 170.80
180	Proceedings upon Felony Complaint from Arraignment Thereon Through Disposition Thereof	180.10 - 180.85
182	Alternate Method of Court Appearance	182.10 - 182.40
190	The Grand Jury and its Proceedings	190.05 - 190.90

II

ARTICLE		SECTIONS
195	Waiver of Indictment	195.10 - 195.40
200	Indictment and Related Instruments	200.10 - 200.95
210	Proceedings in Superior Court from Filing of Indictment to Plea	210.05 - 210.50
215	Adjournment in Contemplation of Dismissal for Purposes of Referring Selected Felonies to Dispute Resolution	215.10 - 215.40
216	Judicial Diversion Program for Certain Felony Offenders	216.00 - 216.05
220	The Plea	220.10 - 220.60
230	Removal of Action	230.10 - 230.40
245	Discovery	245.10 - 245.85
250	Pre-trial Notices of Defenses	250.10 - 250.40
255	Pre-trial Motions	255.10 - 255.20
260	Jury Trial–Generally	260.10 - 260.30
270	Jury Trial–Formation and Conduct of Jury	270.05 - 270.55
280	Jury Trial—Motion for a Mistrial	280.10 - 280.20
290	Jury Trial–Trial Order of Dismissal	290.10
300	Jury Trial–Court's Charge and Instructions to Jury	300.10 - 300.50
310	Jury Trial–Deliberation and Verdict of Jury	310.10 - 310.85
320	Waiver of Jury Trial and Conduct of Non-Jury Trial	320.10 - 320.20
330	Proceedings from Verdict to Sentence	330.10 - 330.50
340	Pre-Trail Proceedings	340.10 - 340.50
350	Non-Jury Trials	350.10 - 350.20
360	Jury Trial	360.05 - 360.55
370	Proceedings from Verdict to Sentence	370.10 - 370.25
380	Sentencing in General	380.10 - 380.97
390	Pre-sentence Reports	390.10 - 390.60
400	Pre-sentence Proceedings	400.10 - 400.40
410	Sentences of Probation, Conditional Discharge and Parole Supervision	410.10 - 410.91
420	Fines, Restitution and Reparation	420.05 - 420.45
430	Sentences of Imprisonment	430.10 - 430.30
440	Post-Judgment Motions	440.10 - 440.70
450	Appeals-In What Cases Authorized and to What Courts Taken	450.10 - 450.90
460	Appeals-Taking and Perfection Thereof and Stays During Pendency Thereof	460.10 - 460.90

ARTICLE

470   Appeals–Determination Thereof .... 470.05 - 470.60

500   Recognizance, Bail and Commitment–Definitions
      of Terms 500.10

510   Recognizance, Bail and Commitment-Determination
      of Application for Recognizance or Bail, Issuance
      of Securing Orders, and Related Matters ..... 510.10 - 510.50

520   Bail and Bail Bonds .... 520.10 - 520.40

530   Orders of Recognizance or Bail with Respect to
      Defendants in Criminal Actions and Proceedings-
      When and by What Courts Authorized .... 530.10 - 530.80

540   Forfeiture of Bail and Remission Thereof ...... 540.10 - 540.30

550   Securing Attendance of Defendants-in General 550.10

560   Securing Attendance of Defendants Confined in
      Institutions Within the State 560.10

570   Securing Attendance of Defendants Who Are Outside
      the State but Within the United States-Rendition
      to Other Jurisdictions of Defendants Within the
      State-Uniform Criminal Extradition Act ...... 570.02 - 570.66

580   Securing Attendance of Defendants Confined as
      Prisoners in Institutions of Other Jurisdictions of
      the United States-Rendition to Other Jurisdictions
      of Persons Confined as Prisoners in this
      State-Agreement on Detainers .... 580.10 - 580.30

590   Securing Attendance of Defendants Who Are
      Outside the United States 590.10

600   Securing Attendance of Corporate Defendants
      and Related Matters .... 600.10 - 600.20

610   Securing Attendance of Witnesses by Subpoena . 610.10 - 610.50

620   Securing Attendance of Witnesses by Material
      Witness Order .... 620.10 - 620.80

630   Securing Attendance as Witnesses of Persons
      Confined in Institutions Within the State ..... 630.10 - 630.20

640   Securing Attendance as Witnesses of Persons at
      Liberty Outside the State-Rendition to Other
      Jurisdictions of Witnesses at Liberty Within the
      State-Uniform Act to Secure Attendance of
      Witnesses From Without the State in Criminal Cases ... 640.10

IV

650   Securing Attendance as Witnesses of Prisoners
      Confined in Institutions of Other Jurisdictions
      of the United States-Rendition to Other
      Jurisdictions of Prisoners Confined
      In Institutions Within the State . . . . 650.10 - 650.30
660   Securing Testimony for Use in a Subsequent
      Proceeding–Examination of Witnesses
      Conditionally . . . . 660.10 - 660.60
670   Use in a Criminal Proceeding of Testimony Given
      in a Previous Proceeding . . . . 670.10 - 670.20
680   Securing Testimony Outside the State for Use in
      Proceeding Within the State-Examination of
      Witnesses on Commission . . . . 680.10 - 680.80
690   Search Warrants . . . . 690.05 - 690.55
700   Eavesdropping and Video Surveillance Warrants . 700.05 - 700.70
705   Pen Registers and Trap and Trace Devices . . . . . 705.00 - 705.35
710   Motion to Suppress Evidence . . . . 710.10 - 710.70
715   Destruction of Dangerous Drugs . . . . 715.05 - 715.50
720   Youthful Offender Procedure . . . . 720.10 - 720.35
722   Proceedings Against Juvenile Offenders and
      Adolescent Offenders; Establishment of Youth
      Part and Related Procedures . . . . 722.00 - 722.24
725   Removal of Proceeding Against Juvenile Offender
      to Family Court . . . . 725.00 - 725.20
730   Mental Disease or Defect Excluding
      Fitness to Proceed . . . . 730.10 - 730.70

PART ONE - GENERAL PROVISIONS
TITLE A - SHORT TITLE, APPLICABILITY AND DEFINITIONS
ARTICLE 1 - SHORT TITLE, APPLICABILITY
AND DEFINITIONS

Section
1.00 Short title.
1.10 Applicability of chapter to actions and matter occurring before and after effective date.
1.20 Definitions of terms of general use in this chapter.

§1.00 Short title.

This chapter shall be known as the criminal procedure law, and may be cited as "CPL".

§1.10 Applicability of chapter to actions and matter occurring before and after effective date.

1. The provisions of this chapter apply exclusively to:

(a) All criminal actions and proceedings commenced upon or after the effective date thereof and all appeals and other post-judgment proceedings relating or attaching thereto; and

(b) All matters of criminal procedure prescribed in this chapter which do not constitute a part of any particular action or case, occurring upon or after such effective date.

2. The provisions of this chapter apply to (a) all criminal actions and proceedings commenced prior to the effective date thereof but still pending on such date, and (b) all appeals and other post-judgment proceedings commenced upon or after such effective date which relate or attach to criminal actions and proceedings commenced or concluded prior to such effective date; provided that, if application of such provisions in any particular case would not be feasible or would work injustice, the provisions of the code of criminal procedure apply thereto.

3. The provisions of this chapter do not impair or render ineffectual any proceedings or procedural matters which occurred prior to the effective date thereof.

§1.20 Definitions of terms of general use in this chapter.

Except where different meanings are expressly specified in subsequent provisions of this chapter, the term definitions contained in section 10.00 of the penal law are applicable to this chapter, and, in addition, the following terms have the following meanings:

1. "Accusatory instrument" means: (a) an indictment, an indictment ordered reduced pursuant to subdivision one-a of section 210.20 of this chapter, an information, a simplified information, a prosecutor's information, a superior court information, a misdemeanor complaint or a felony complaint. Every accusatory instrument, regardless of the person designated therein as accuser, constitutes an accusation on behalf of the state as plaintiff and must be entitled "the people of the state of New York" against a designated person, known as the defendant; and

(b) an appearance ticket issued for a parking infraction when (i) such ticket is based on personal knowledge or information and belief of the police officer or other public servant who issues the ticket, (ii) the police officer or other public servant who issues such ticket verifies that false statements made therein are punishable as a class A misdemeanor, (iii) the infraction or infractions contained therein are stated in detail and not in conclusory terms so as to provide the defendant with sufficient notice including, but not limited, to the applicable provision of law allegedly violated, and the date, time and particular place of the alleged infraction, and (iv) such ticket contains: (1) the license plate designation of the ticketed vehicle, (2) the license plate type of the ticketed vehicle, (3) the expiration of the ticketed vehicle's registration, (4) the make or model of the ticketed vehicle, and (5) the body type of the ticketed vehicle, provided, however, that where the plate type or the expiration date are not shown on either the registration plates or sticker of a vehicle or where the registration sticker is covered, faded, defaced or mutilated so that it is unreadable, the plate type or the expiration date may be omitted, provided, further, however, that such condition must be so described and inserted on the instrument.

(Eff.11/8/19,Ch.450,L.2019)

2. "Local criminal court accusatory instrument" means any accusatory instrument other than an indictment or a superior court information.

3. "Indictment" means a written accusation by a grand jury, more fully defined and described in article two hundred, filed with a superior court, which charges one or more defendants with the commission of one or more offenses, at least one of which is a crime, and which serves as a basis for prosecution thereof.

3-a. "Superior court information" means a written accusation by a district attorney more fully defined and described in articles one hundred ninety-five and two hundred, filed with a superior court pursuant to article one hundred ninety-five, which charges one or more defendants with the commission of one or more offenses, at least one of which is a crime, and which serves as a basis for prosecution thereof.

4. "Information" means a verified written accusation by a person, more fully defined and described in article one hundred, filed with a local criminal court, which charges one or more defendants with the commission of one or more offenses, none of which is a felony, and which may serve both to commence a criminal action and as a basis for prosecution thereof.

*5. (a) "Simplified information" means a simplified traffic information, a simplified parks information, or a simplified environmental conservation information.

(b) "Simplified traffic information" means a written accusation by a police officer, or other public servant authorized by law to issue same, more fully defined and described in article one hundred, filed with a local criminal court, which, being in a brief or simplified form prescribed by the commissioner of motor vehicles, charges a person with one or more traffic infractions or misdemeanors relating to traffic, and which may serve both to commence a criminal action for such offense and as a basis for prosecution thereof.

(c) "Simplified parks information" means a written accusation by a police officer, or other public servant authorized by law to issue same, filed with a local criminal court, which, being in a brief or simplified form prescribed by the commissioner of parks and recreation, charges a person with one or more offenses, other than a felony, for which a uniform simplified parks information may be issued pursuant to the parks and recreation law and the navigation law, and which may serve both to commence a criminal action for such offense and as a basis for prosecution thereof.

(d) "Simplified environmental conservation information" means a written accusation by a police officer, or other public servant authorized by law to issue same, filed with a local criminal court, which being in a brief or simplified form prescribed by the commissioner of environmental conservation, charges a person with one or more offenses, other than a felony, for which a uniform simplified environmental conservation simplified** information may be issued pursuant to the environmental conservation law, and which may serve both to commence a criminal action for such offense and as a basis for prosecution thereof.

(There are 2 sb 5's -- cannot be put together.)**(So in original.)

* 5. "Simplified traffic information" means a written accusation, more fully defined and described in article one hundred, by a police officer or other public servant authorized by law to issue same, filed with a local criminal court, which, being in a brief or simplified form prescribed by the commissioner of motor vehicles, charges a person with one or more traffic infractions or misdemeanors relating to traffic, and which may serve both to commence a criminal action for such offense and as a basis for prosecution thereof. *(There are 2 sb 5's -- cannot be put together.)*

6. "Prosecutor's information" means a written accusation by a district attorney, more fully defined and described in article one hundred, filed with a local criminal court, which charges one or more defendants with the commission of one or more offenses, none of which is a felony, and which serves as a basis for prosecution thereof.

7. "Misdemeanor complaint" means a verified written accusation by a person, more fully defined and described in article one hundred, filed with a local criminal court, which charges one or more defendants with the commission of one or more offenses, at least one of which is a misdemeanor and none of which is a felony, and which serves to commence a criminal action but which may not, except upon the defendant's consent, serve as a basis for prosecution of the offenses charged therein.

8. "Felony complaint" means a verified written accusation by a person, more fully defined and described in article one hundred, filed with a local criminal court, which charges one or more defendants with the commission of one or more felonies and which serves to commence a criminal action but not as a basis for prosecution thereof.

9. "Arraignment" means the occasion upon which a defendant against whom an accusatory instrument has been filed appears before the court in which the criminal action is pending for the purpose of having such court acquire and exercise control over his person with respect to such accusatory instrument and of setting the course of further proceedings in the action.

10. "Plea," in addition to its ordinary meaning as prescribed in sections 220.10 and 340.20, means, where appropriate, the occasion upon which a defendant enters such a plea to an accusatory instrument.

11. "Trial." A jury trial commences with the selection of the jury and includes all further proceedings through the rendition of a verdict. A non-jury trial commences with the first opening address, if there be any, and, if not, when the first witness is sworn, and includes all further proceedings through the rendition of a verdict.

12. "Verdict" means the announcement by a jury in the case of a jury trial, or by the court in the case of a non-jury trial, of its decision upon the defendant's guilt or innocence of the charges submitted to or considered by it.

13. "Conviction" means the entry of a plea of guilty to, or a verdict of guilty upon, an accusatory instrument other than a felony complaint, or to one or more counts of such instrument.

14. "Sentence" means the imposition and entry of sentence upon a conviction.

15. "Judgment." A judgment is comprised of a conviction and the sentence imposed thereon and is completed by imposition and entry of the sentence.

16. "Criminal action." A criminal action (a) commences with the filing of an accusatory instrument against a defendant in a criminal court, as specified in subdivision seventeen; (b) includes the filing of all further accusatory instruments directly derived from the initial one, and all proceedings, orders and motions conducted or made by a criminal court in the course of disposing of any such accusatory instrument, or which, regardless of the court in which they occurred or were made, could properly be considered as a part of the record of the case by an appellate court upon an appeal from a judgment of conviction; and (c) terminates with the imposition of sentence or some other final disposition in a criminal court of the last accusatory instrument filed in the case.

17. "Commencement of criminal action." A criminal action is commenced by the filing of an accusatory instrument against a defendant in a criminal court, and, if more than one accusatory instrument is filed in the course of the action, it commences when the first of such instruments is filed.

18. "Criminal proceeding" means any proceeding which (a) constitutes a part of a criminal action or (b) occurs in a criminal court and is related to a prospective, pending or completed criminal action, either of this state or of any other jurisdiction, or involves a criminal investigation.

19. "Criminal court" means any court defined as such by section 10.10.

20. "Superior court" means any court defined as such by subdivision two of section 10.10.

21. "Local criminal court" means any court defined as such by subdivision three of section 10.10.

22. "Intermediate appellate court" means any court possessing appellate jurisdiction, other than the court of appeals.

23. "Judge" means any judicial officer who is a member of or constitutes a court, whether referred to in another provision of law as a justice or by any other title.

24. "Trial jurisdiction." A criminal court has "trial jurisdiction" of an offense when an indictment or an information charging such offense may properly be filed with such court, and when such court has authority to accept a plea to, try or otherwise finally dispose of such accusatory instrument.

25. "Preliminary jurisdiction." A criminal court has "preliminary jurisdiction" of an offense when, regardless of whether it has trial jurisdiction thereof, a criminal action for such offense may be commenced therein, and when such court may conduct proceedings with respect thereto which lead or may lead to prosecution and final disposition of the action in a court having trial jurisdiction thereof.

26. "Appearance ticket" means a written notice issued by a public servant, more fully defined in section 150.10, requiring a person to appear before a local criminal court in connection with an accusatory instrument to be filed against him therein.

27. "Summons" means a process of a local criminal court or superior court, more fully defined in section 130.10, requiring a defendant to appear before such court for the purpose of arraignment upon an accusatory instrument filed therewith by which a criminal action against him has been commenced.

28. "Warrant of arrest" means a process of a local criminal court, more fully defined in section 120.10, directing a police officer to arrest a defendant and to bring him before such court for the purpose of arraignment upon an accusatory instrument filed therewith by which a criminal action against him has been commenced.

29. "Superior court warrant of arrest" means a process of a superior court directing a police officer to arrest a defendant and to bring him before such

---

court for the purpose of arraignment upon an indictment filed therewith by which a criminal action against him has been commenced.

30. "Bench warrant" means a process of a criminal court in which a criminal action is pending, directing a police officer, or a uniformed court officer, pursuant to paragraph b of subdivision two of section 530.70 of this chapter, to take into custody a defendant in such action who has previously been arraigned upon the accusatory instrument by which the action was commenced, and to bring him before such court. The function of a bench warrant is to achieve the court appearance of a defendant in a pending criminal action for some purpose other than his initial arraignment in the action.

31. "Prosecutor" means a district attorney or any other public servant who represents the people in a criminal action.

32. "District attorney" means a district attorney, an assistant district attorney or a special district attorney, and, where appropriate, the attorney general, an assistant attorney general, a deputy attorney general, a special deputy attorney general, or the special prosecutor and inspector general for the protection of people with special needs or his or her assistants when acting pursuant to their duties in matters arising under article twenty of the executive law, or the inspector general of New York for transportation or his or her deputies when acting pursuant to article four-B of the executive law.

33. "Peace officer" means a person listed in section 2.10 of this chapter.

34. "Police officer." The following persons are police officers:

(a) A sworn member of the division of state police;

*(b) Sheriffs, under-sheriffs and deputy sheriffs of counties outside of New York City;   *(Eff. Until 10/16/23, Ch.59, L.2021)

*(b) Sheriffs, under-sheriffs and deputy sheriffs of counties outside of New York City where such department is certified in accordance with paragraph (d) of subdivision one of section eight hundred forty-six-h of the executive law;   *(Eff. 10/16/23, Ch.59, L.2021)

*(c) A sworn officer of an authorized county or county parkway police department;   *(Eff. Until 10/16/23, Ch.59, L.2021)

*(c) A sworn officer of an authorized county or county parkway police department where such department is certified in accordance with paragraph (d) of subdivision one of section eight hundred forty-six-h of the executive law;   *(Eff. 10/16/23, Ch.59, L.2021)

*(d) A sworn officer of an authorized police department or force of a city, town, village or police district;   *(Eff. Until 10/16/23, Ch.59, L.2021)

*(d) A sworn officer of an authorized police department or force of a city, town, village or police district where such department or force is certified in accordance with paragraph (d) of subdivision one of section eight hundred forty-six-h of the executive law;   *(Eff. 10/16/23, Ch.59, L.2021)

*(e) A sworn officer of an authorized police department of an authority or a sworn officer of the state regional park police in the office of parks and recreation;   *(Eff. Until 10/16/23, Ch.59, L.2021)

*(e) A sworn officer of an authorized police department of an authority or a sworn officer of the state regional park police in the office of parks and recreation where such department or force is certified in accordance with

paragraph (d) of subdivision one of section eight hundred forty-six-h of the executive law;   *(Eff. 10/16/23,Ch.59,L.2021)

*(f) A sworn officer of the capital police force of the office of general services;   *(Eff. Until 10/16/23,Ch.59,L.2021)

*(f) A sworn officer of the capital police force of the office of general services where such force is certified in accordance with paragraph (d) of subdivision one of section eight hundred forty-six-h of the executive law;
*(Eff. 10/16/23,Ch.59,L.2021)

(g) An investigator employed in the office of a district attorney;

(h) An investigator employed by a commission created by an interstate compact who is, to a substantial extent, engaged in the enforcement of the criminal laws of this state;

(i) The chief and deputy fire marshals, the supervising fire marshals and the fire marshals of the bureau of fire investigation of the New York City fire department;

*(j) A sworn officer of the division of law enforcement in the department of environmental conservation;   *(Eff. Until 10/16/23,Ch.59,L.2021)

*(j) A sworn officer of the division of law enforcement in the department of environmental conservation where such division is certified in accordance with paragraph (d) of subdivision one of section eight hundred forty-six-h of the executive law;   *(Eff. Until 10/16/23,Ch.59,L.2021)

*(k) A sworn officer of a police force of a public authority created by an interstate compact;   *(Eff. Until 10/16/23,Ch.59,L.2021)

*(k) A sworn officer of a police force of a public authority created by an interstate compact where such force is certified in accordance with paragraph (d) of subdivision one of section eight hundred forty-six-h of the executive law;   *(Eff. 10/16/23,Ch.59,L.2021)

*(l) Long Island railroad police.   *(Eff. Until 10/16/23,Ch.59,L.2021)

*(l) Long Island railroad police where such department or force is certified in accordance with paragraph (d) of subdivision one of section eight hundred forty-six-h of the executive law;   *(Eff.10/16/23,Ch.59,L.2021)

(m) A special investigator employed in the statewide organized crime task force, while performing his assigned duties pursuant to section seventy-a of the executive law.

(n) A sworn officer of the Westchester county department of public safety services who, on or prior to June thirtieth, nineteen hundred seventy-nine was appointed as a sworn officer of the division of Westchester county parkway police or who was appointed on or after July first, nineteen hundred seventy-nine to the title of police officer, sergeant, lieutenant, captain or inspector or who, on or prior to January thirty-first, nineteen hundred eighty-three, was appointed as a Westchester county deputy sheriff.

*(o) A sworn officer of the water-supply police employed by the city of New York, appointed to protect the sources, works, and transmission of water supplied to the city of New York, and to protect persons on or in the vicinity of such water sources, works, and transmission.
*(Eff. Until 10/16/23,Ch.59,L.2021)

*(o) A sworn officer of the New York city department of environmental protection police, employed by the city of New York, appointed to protect the sources, works, and transmission of water supplied to the city of New York, and to protect persons on or in the vicinity of such water sources, works, and transmission where such department is certified in accordance with paragraph (d) of subdivision one of section eight hundred forty-six-h of the executive law; *(Eff. 10/16/23,Ch.59,L.2021)*

*(p) Persons appointed as railroad police officers pursuant to section eighty-eight of the railroad law. *(Eff. Until 10/16/23,Ch.59,L.2021)*

*(p) Persons appointed as railroad police officers pursuant to section eighty-eight of the railroad law where such department or force is certified in accordance with paragraph (d) of subdivision one of section eight hundred forty-six-h of the executive law; *(Eff. 10/16/23,Ch.59,L.2021)*

(q) An employee of the department of taxation and finance (i) assigned to enforcement of the taxes imposed under or pursuant to the authority of article twelve-A of the tax law and administered by the commissioner of taxation and finance, taxes imposed under or pursuant to the authority of article eighteen of the tax law and administered by the commissioner, taxes imposed under article twenty of the tax law, or sales or compensating use taxes relating to petroleum products or cigarettes imposed under article twenty-eight or pursuant to the authority of article twenty-nine of the tax law and administered by the commissioner or (ii) designated as a revenue crimes specialist and assigned to the enforcement of the taxes described in paragraph (c) of subdivision four of section 2.10 of this title, for the purpose of applying for and executing search warrants under article six hundred ninety of this chapter, for the purpose of acting as a claiming agent under article thirteen-A of the civil practice law and rules in connection with the enforcement of the taxes referred to above and for the purpose of executing warrants of arrest relating to the respective crimes specified in subdivision four of section 2.10 of this title.

(r) Any employee of the Suffolk county department of parks who is appointed as a Suffolk county park police officer.

*(s) A university police officer appointed by the state university pursuant to paragraph 1 of subdivision two of section three hundred fifty-five of the education law. *(Eff. Until 10/16/23,Ch.59,L.2021)*

*(s) A university police officer appointed by the state university pursuant to paragraph 1 of subdivision two of section three hundred fifty-five of the education law where such department or force is certified in accordance with paragraph (d) of subdivision one of section eight hundred forty-six-h of the executive law; *(Eff. 10/16/23,Ch.59,L.2021)*

(t) A sworn officer of the department of public safety of the Buffalo municipal housing authority who has achieved or been granted the status of sworn police officer and has been certified by the division of criminal justice services as successfully completing an approved basic course for police officers.

*(u) Persons appointed as Indian police officers pursuant to section one hundred fourteen of the Indian law. *(Eff. Until 10/16/23,Ch.59,L.2021)*

*(u) Persons appointed as Indian police officers pursuant to section one hundred fourteen of the Indian law where such department or force is certified in accordance with paragraph (d) of subdivision one of section eight hundred forty-six-h of the executive law;   *(Eff. 10/16/23,Ch.59,L.2021)

(v) Supervisor of forest ranger services; assistant supervisor of forest ranger services; forest ranger 3; forest ranger 2; forest ranger 1 employed by the state department of environmental conservation or sworn officer of the division of forest protection and fire management in the department of environmental conservation responsible for wild land search and rescue, wild land fire management in the state as prescribed in subdivision eighteen of section 9-0105 and title eleven of article nine of the environmental conservation law, exercising care, custody and control of state lands administered by the department of environmental conservation.

34-a. "Geographical area of employment." The "geographical area of employment" of certain police officers is as follows:

* (a) Except as provided in paragraph (d) of this subdivision, New York state constitutes the "geographical area of employment" of any police officer employed as such by an agency of the state or by an authority which functions throughout the state, or a police officer designated by the superintendent of state police pursuant to section two hundred twenty-three of the executive law;   * (Revisions REPEALED 9/1/23,Ch.55,L.2021)

(b) A county, city, town or village, as the case may be, constitutes the "geographical area of employment" of any police officer employed as such by an agency of such political subdivision or by an authority which functions only in such political subdivision; and

(c) Where an authority functions in more than one county, the "geographical area of employment" of a police officer employed thereby extends through all of such counties.

(d) The geographical area of employment of a police officer appointed by the state university is the campuses and other property of the state university, including any portion of a public highway which crosses or abuts such property.

(e) The geographical area of employment of a police officer appointed pursuant to section one hundred fourteen of the Indian law is within the county of Franklin, and within that county, only within the boundary of the St. Regis reservation, except that if the superintendent of state police has certified such officer with expanded jurisdiction within the county of Franklin, pursuant to subdivision eight-a of such section, the geographical area of employment of such police officer shall also include the area of expanded jurisdiction set forth in that subdivision.

35. "Commitment to the custody of the sheriff," when referring to an order of a court located in a county or city which has established a department of correction, means commitment to the commissioner of correction of such county or city.

36. "County" ordinarily means (a) any county outside of New York City or (b) New York City in its entirety. Unless the context requires a different construction, New York City, despite its five counties, is deemed a single

county within the meaning of the provisions of this chapter in which that term appears.

37. "Lesser included offense." When it is impossible to commit a particular crime without concomitantly committing, by the same conduct, another offense of lesser grade or degree, the latter is, with respect to the former, a "lesser included offense." In any case in which it is legally possible to attempt to commit a crime, an attempt to commit such crime constitutes a lesser included offense with respect thereto.

38. "Oath" includes an affirmation and every other mode authorized by law of attesting to the truth of that which is stated.

39. "Petty offense" means a violation or a traffic infraction.

40. "Evidence in chief" means evidence, received at a trial or other criminal proceeding in which a defendant's guilt or innocence of an offense is in issue, which may be considered as a part of the quantum of substantive proof establishing or tending to establish the commission of such offense or an element thereof or the defendant's connection therewith.

41. "Armed felony" means any violent felony offense defined in section 70.02 of the penal law that includes as an element either:

(a) possession, being armed with or causing serious physical injury by means of a deadly weapon, if the weapon is a loaded weapon from which a shot, readily capable of producing death or other serious physical injury may be discharged; or

(b) display of what appears to be a pistol, revolver, rifle, shotgun, machine gun or other firearm.

42. "Juvenile offender" means (1) a person, thirteen years old who is criminally responsible for acts constituting murder in the second degree as defined in subdivisions one and two of section 125.25 of the penal law, or such conduct as a sexually motivated felony, where authorized pursuant to section 130.91 of the penal law; and (2) a person fourteen or fifteen years old who is criminally responsible for acts constituting the crimes defined in subdivisions one and two of section 125.25 (murder in the second degree) and in subdivision three of such section provided that the underlying crime for the murder charge is one for which such person is criminally responsible; section 135.25 (kidnapping in the first degree); 150.20 (arson in the first degree); subdivisions one and two of section 120.10 (assault in the first degree); 125.20 (manslaughter in the first degree); subdivisions one and two of section 130.35 (rape in the first degree); subdivisions one and two of section 130.50 (criminal sexual act in the first degree); 130.70 (aggravated sexual abuse in the first degree); 140.30 (burglary in the first degree); subdivision one of section 140.25 (burglary in the second degree); 150.15 (arson in the second degree); 160.15 (robbery in the first degree); subdivision two of section 160.10 (robbery in the second degree) of the penal law; or section 265.03 of the penal law, where such machine gun or such firearm is possessed on school grounds, as that phrase is defined in subdivision fourteen of section 220.00 of the penal law; or defined in the penal law as an attempt to commit murder in the second degree or kidnapping in the first degree, or such conduct as a sexually motivated felony, where authorized pursuant to section 130.91 of the penal law.

43. "Judicial hearing officer" means a person so designated pursuant to provisions of article twenty-two of the judiciary law.

44. "Adolescent offender" means a person charged with a felony committed on or after October first, two thousand eighteen when he or she was sixteen years of age or on or after October first, two thousand nineteen, when he or she was seventeen years of age.

45. "Expunge" means, where an arrest and any enforcement activity connected with that arrest, including prosecution and any disposition in any New York state court, is deemed a nullity and the accused is restored, in contemplation of the law, to the status such individual occupied before the arrest, prosecution and/or disposition; that records of such arrest, prosecution and/or disposition shall be marked as expunged or shall be destroyed as set forth in section 160.50 of this chapter. Neither the arrest nor prosecution and/or disposition, if any, of a matter deemed a nullity shall operate as a disqualification of any person so accused to pursue or engage in any lawful activity, occupation, profession or calling. Except where specifically required or permitted by statute or upon specific authorization of a superior court, no such person shall be required to divulge information pertaining to the arrest, prosecution and/or disposition of such a matter.

ARTICLE 2 - PEACE OFFICERS

Section
2.10 Persons designated as peace officers.
2.15 Federal law enforcement officers; powers.
2.16 Watershed protection and enforcement officers; powers, duties, jurisdiction for
      arrests.
2.20 Powers of peace officers.
2.30 Training requirements for peace officers.

§2.10 Persons designated as peace officers.

Notwithstanding the provisions of any general, special or local law or charter to the contrary, only the following persons shall have the powers of, and shall be peace officers:

1. Constables or police constables of a town or village, provided such designation is not inconsistent with local law.

2. The sheriff, undersheriff and deputy sheriffs of New York city and sworn officers of the Westchester county department of public safety services appointed after January thirty-first, nineteen hundred eighty-three to the title of public safety officer and who perform the functions previously performed by a Westchester county deputy sheriff on or prior to such date.

3. Investigators of the office of the state commission of investigation.

4. Employees of the department of taxation and finance designated by the commissioner of taxation and finance as peace officers and assigned by the commissioner of taxation and finance (a) to the enforcement of any of the criminal or seizure and forfeiture provisions of the tax law relating to (i) taxes imposed under or pursuant to the authority of article twelve-A of the tax law and administered by the commissioner, (ii) taxes imposed under or pursuant to the authority of article eighteen of the tax law and administered by the commissioner, (iii) taxes imposed under article twenty of the tax law, or (iv) sales or compensating use taxes relating to petroleum products or cigarettes imposed under article twenty-eight or pursuant to the authority of article twenty-nine of the tax law and administered by the commissioner or

(b) to the enforcement of any provision of the penal law relating to any of the taxes described in paragraph (a) of this subdivision and relating to crimes effected through the use of a statement or document filed with the department in connection with the administration of such taxes or

(c) as revenue crimes specialist and assigned to the enforcement of any of the criminal provisions of the tax law relating to taxes administered by the commissioner of taxation and finance other than those taxes set forth in paragraph (a) of this subdivision or any provision of the penal law relating to such taxes, and those provisions of the penal law (i) relating to any of the foregoing taxes and (ii) relating to crimes effected through the use of a statement or document filed with the department in connection with the administration of such foregoing taxes or

(d) to the enforcement of any provision of law which is subject to enforcement by criminal penalties and which relates to the performance by persons employed by the department of taxation and finance of the duties of their employment.

Provided, however, that nothing in this subdivision shall be deemed to authorize any such employee designated as a peace officer after November first, nineteen hundred eighty-five to carry, possess, repair or dispose of a firearm unless the appropriate license therefor has been issued pursuant to section 400.00 of the penal law, and further provided that, prior to such designation by the commissioner each such employee shall have successfully completed the training requirements specified in section 2.30 of this article. Provided, further, that any license issued to such employee pursuant to such peace officer designation by the commissioner shall relate only to the firearm issued to such employee by the department of taxation and finance and such permit shall not cover any other firearms. The foregoing sentence shall not be deemed to prohibit such peace officer from applying for a separate permit relating to non-departmental firearms.

5. Employees of the New York city department of finance assigned to enforcement of the tax on cigarettes imposed by title D of chapter forty-six of the administrative code of the city of New York by the commissioner of finance.

6. Confidential investigators and inspectors, as designated by the commissioner, of the department of agriculture and markets, pursuant to rules of the department.

7. Officers or agents of a duly incorporated society for the prevention of cruelty to animals.

* 7-a. Officers or agents of a duly incorporated society for the prevention of cruelty to children in Rockland county; provided, however, that nothing in this subdivision shall be deemed to authorize such officer or agent to carry, possess, repair, or dispose of a firearm unless the appropriate license therefor has been issued pursuant to section 400.00 of the penal law; and provided further that such officer or agent shall exercise the powers of a peace officer only when he is acting pursuant to his special duties.

(Deemed Repealed 8/11/23,Ch.175,L.2021)

8. Inspectors and officers of the New York city department of health when acting pursuant to their special duties as set forth in section 564-11.0 of the administrative code of the city of New York; provided, however, that nothing in this subdivision shall be deemed to authorize such officer to carry, possess, repair or dispose of a firearm unless the appropriate license therefor has been issued pursuant to section 400.00 of the penal law.

9. Park rangers in Suffolk county, who shall be authorized to issue appearance tickets, simplified traffic informations, simplified parks informations and simplified environmental conservation informations.

10. Broome county park rangers who shall be authorized to issue appearance tickets, simplified traffic informations, simplified parks informations, and simplified environmental conservation informations; provided, however, that nothing in this subdivision shall be deemed to authorize such officer to carry, possess, repair or dispose of a firearm unless the appropriate license therefor has been issued pursuant to section 400.00 of the penal law.

11. Park rangers in Onondaga and Cayuga counties, who shall be authorized to issue appearance tickets, simplified traffic informations, simplified parks informations and simplified environmental conservation informations, within the respective counties of Onondaga and Cayuga.

12. Special police officers designated by the commissioner and the directors of in-patient facilities in the office of mental health pursuant to section 7.25 of the mental hygiene law, and special police officers designated by the commissioner and the directors of facilities under his or her jurisdiction in the office for people with developmental disabilities pursuant to section 13.25 of the mental hygiene law; provided, however, that nothing in this subdivision shall be deemed to authorize such officers to carry, possess, repair or dispose of a firearm unless the appropriate license therefor has been issued pursuant to section 400.00 of the penal law.

13. Persons designated as special police officers by the director of a hospital in the department of health pursuant to section four hundred fifty-five of the public health law; provided, however, that nothing in this subdivision shall be deemed to authorize such officer to carry, possess, repair or dispose of a firearm unless the appropriate license therefor has been issued pursuant to section 400.00 of the penal law.

14. *(Repealed.)*

15. Uniformed enforcement forces of the New York state thruway authority, when acting pursuant to subdivision two of section three hundred sixty-one of the public authorities law; provided, however, that nothing in this subdivision shall be deemed to authorize such officer to carry, possess, repair or dispose of a firearm unless the appropriate license therefor has been issued pursuant to section 400.00 of the penal law.

16. Employees of the department of health designated pursuant to section thirty-three hundred eighty-five of the public health law; provided, however, that nothing in this subdivision shall be deemed to authorize such officer to carry, possess, repair or dispose of a firearm unless the appropriate license therefor has been issued pursuant to section 400.00 of the penal law.

17. Uniformed housing guards of the Buffalo municipal housing authority.

18. Bay constable of the city of Rye, the villages of Mamaroneck, South Nyack and bay constables of the towns of East Hampton, Hempstead, Oyster Bay, Riverhead, Southampton, Southold, Islip, Shelter Island, Brookhaven, Babylon, Smithtown, Huntington and North Hempstead; provided, however, that nothing in this subdivision shall be deemed to authorize the bay constables in the city of Rye, the village of South Nyack or the towns of Brookhaven, Babylon, Southold, East Hampton, Riverhead, Islip, other than a bay constable of the town of Islip who prior to April third, nineteen hundred ninety-eight served as harbormaster for such town and whose

position was reclassified as bay constable for such town prior to such date, Smithtown, Huntington and Shelter Island to carry, possess, repair or dispose of a firearm unless the appropriate license therefor has been issued pursuant to section 400.00 of the penal law.

19. Harbor masters appointed by a county, city, town or village.

20. Bridge and tunnel officers, sergeants and lieutenants of the Triborough bridge and tunnel authority.

21. a. Uniformed court officers of the unified court system.

b. Court clerks of the unified court system in the first and second departments.

c. Marshall, deputy marshall, clerk or uniformed court officer of a district court.

d. Marshalls or deputy marshalls of a city court, provided, however, that nothing in this subdivision shall be deemed to authorize such officer to carry, possess, repair or dispose of a firearm unless the appropriate license therefor has been issued pursuant to section 400.00 of the penal law.

e. Uniformed court officers of the city of Mount Vernon.

f. Uniformed court officers of the city of Jamestown.

22. Patrolmen appointed by the Lake George park commission; provided however that nothing in this subdivision shall be deemed to authorize such officer to carry, possess, repair or dispose of a firearm unless the appropriate license therefor has been issued pursuant to section 400.00 of the penal law.

23. Parole officers or warrant officers in the department of corrections and community supervision.

23-a. Parole revocation specialists in the department of corrections and community supervision; provided, however, that nothing in this subdivision shall be deemed to authorize such employee to carry, possess, repair or dispose of a firearm unless the appropriate license therefor has been issued pursuant to section 400.00 of the penal law.

24. Probation officers.

25. Officials, as designated by the commissioner of the department of corrections and community supervision pursuant to rules of the department, and correction officers of any state correctional facility or of any penal correctional institution.

26. Peace officers designated pursuant to the provisions of the New York state defense emergency act, as set forth in chapter seven hundred eighty-four of the laws of nineteen hundred fifty-one, as amended, when acting pursuant to their special duties during a period of attack or imminent attack by enemy forces, or during official drills called to combat natural or man-made disasters, or during official drills in preparation for an attack by enemy forces or in preparation for a natural or man-made disaster; provided, however, that nothing in this subdivision shall be deemed to authorize such officer to carry, possess, repair or dispose of a firearm unless the appropriate license therefor has been issued pursuant to section 400.00 of the penal law; and provided further, that such officer shall have the powers set forth in section 2.20 of this article only during a period of imminent or actual attack by enemy forces and during drills authorized under section twenty-nine-b of article two-B of the executive law, providing for the use of civil defense forces in disasters. Notwithstanding any other provision of law, such officers shall have the power to direct and control traffic during official drills in preparation for an attack by enemy forces or in preparation for combating natural or man-made disasters; however, this

grant does not include any of the other powers set forth in section 2.20 of this article.

27. New York city special patrolmen appointed by the police commissioner pursuant to subdivision c or e of section 434a-7.0 or subdivision c or e of section 14-106 of the administrative code of the city of New York; provided, however, that nothing in this subdivision shall be deemed to authorize such officer to carry, possess, repair or dispose of a firearm unless the appropriate license therefor has been issued pursuant to section 400.00 of the penal law and the employer has authorized such officer to possess a firearm during any phase of the officers on-duty employment. Special patrolmen shall have the powers set forth in section 2.20 of this article only when they are acting pursuant to their special duties; provided, however, that the following categories of New York city special patrolmen shall have such powers whether or not they are acting pursuant to their special duties: school safety officers employed by the board of education of the city of New York; parking control specialists, taxi and limousine inspectors, urban park rangers and evidence and property control specialists employed by the city of New York; and further provided that, with respect to the aforementioned categories of New York city special patrolmen, where such a special patrolman has been appointed by the police commissioner and, upon the expiration of such appointment the police commissioner has neither renewed such appointment nor explicitly determined that such appointment shall not be renewed, such appointment shall remain in full force and effect indefinitely, until such time as the police commissioner expressly determines to either renew or terminate such appointment.

28. All officers and members of the uniformed force of the New York city fire department as set forth and subject to the limitations contained in section 487a-15.0 of the administrative code of the city of New York; provided, however, that nothing in this subdivision shall be deemed to authorize such officer to carry, possess, repair or dispose of a firearm unless the appropriate license therefor has been issued pursuant to section 400.00 of the penal law.

29. Special police officers for horse racing, appointed pursuant to the provisions of the pari-mutuel revenue law as set forth in chapter two hundred fifty-four of the laws of nineteen hundred forty, as amended; provided, however, that nothing in this subdivision shall be deemed to authorize such officer to carry, possess, repair or dispose of a firearm unless the appropriate license therefor has been issued pursuant to section 400.00 of the penal law.   *(Eff.12/28/18,Ch.476,L.2018)*

31. *(Repealed)*

30. Supervising fire inspectors, fire inspectors, the fire marshal and assistant fire marshals, all of whom are full-time employees of the county of Nassau fire marshal's office.

32. Investigators of the department of motor vehicles, pursuant to section three hundred ninety-two-b of the vehicle and traffic law; provided, however, that nothing in this subdivision shall be deemed to authorize such officer to carry, possess, repair or dispose of a firearm unless the appropriate license therefor has been issued pursuant to section 400.00 of the penal law.

33. A city marshall of the city of New York who has received training in firearms handling from the federal bureau of investigation or in the New

York city police academy, or in the absence of the available training programs from the federal bureau of investigation and the New York city police academy, from another law enforcement agency located in the state of New York, and who has received a firearms permit from the license division of the New York city police department.

34. Waterfront and airport investigators, pursuant to subdivision four of section ninety-nine hundred six of the unconsolidated laws; provided, however, that nothing in this subdivision shall be deemed to authorize such officer to carry, possess, repair or dispose of a firearm unless the appropriate license therefor has been issued pursuant to section 400.00 of the penal law.

35. Special investigators appointed by the state board of elections, pursuant to secton* 3-107 of the election law. *(So in original, shold be section.)

36. Investigators appointed by the state liquor authority, pursuant to section fifteen of the alcoholic beverage control law; provided, however, that nothing in this subdivision shall be deemed to authorize such officer to carry, possess, repair or dispose of a firearm unless the appropriate license therefor has been issued pursuant to section 400.00 of the penal law.

37. Special patrolmen of a political subdivision, appointed pursuant to section two hundred nine-v of the general municipal law; provided, however, that nothing in this subdivision shall be deemed to authorize such officer to carry, possess, repair or dispose of a firearm unless the appropriate license therefor has been issued pursuant to section 400.00 of the penal law.

38. A special investigator of the New York city department of investigation who has received training in firearms handling in the New York police academy and has received a firearms permit from the license division of the New York city police department.

39. Broome county special patrolman, appointed by the Broome county attorney; provided, however, that nothing in this subdivision shall be deemed to authorize such officer to carry, possess, repair or dispose of a firearm unless the appropriate license therefor has been issued pursuant to section 400.00 of the penal law.

40. Special officers employed by the city of New York or by the New York city health and hospitals corporation; provided, however, that nothing in this subdivision shall be deemed to authorize such officer to carry, possess, repair or dispose of a firearm unless the appropriate license therefor has been issued pursuant to section 400.00 of the penal law. The New York city health and hospitals corporation shall employ peace officers appointed pursuant to this subdivision to perform the patrol, investigation, and maintenance of the peace duties of special officer, senior special officer and hospital security officer, provided however that nothing in this subdivision shall prohibit managerial, supervisory, or state licensed or certified professional employees of the corporation from performing such duties where they are incidental to their usual duties, or shall prohibit police officers employed by the city of New York from performing these duties.

41. Fire police squads organized pursuant to section two hundred nine-c of the general municipal law, at such times as the fire department, fire company or an emergency rescue and first aid squad of the fire department or fire company are on duty, or when, on orders of the chief of the fire department or fire company of which they are members, they are separately engaged in response to a call for assistance pursuant to the provisions of section two hundred nine of the general municipal law; provided, however, that nothing in this subdivision shall be deemed to authorize such officer to carry, possess, repair or dispose of a firearm unless the appropriate license therefor has been issued pursuant to section 400.00 of the penal law.

42. Special deputy sheriffs appointed by the sheriff of a county within which any part of the grounds of Cornell university or the grounds of any state institution constituting a part of the educational and research plants owned or under the supervision, administration or control of said university are located pursuant to section fifty-seven hundred nine of the education law; provided, however, that nothing in this subdivision shall be deemed to authorize such officer to carry, possess, repair or dispose of a firearm unless the appropriate license therefor has been issued pursuant to section 400.00 of the penal law.

43. Housing patrolmen of the Mount Vernon housing authority, acting pursuant to rules of the Mount Vernon housing authority; provided, however, that nothing in this subdivision shall be deemed to authorize such officer to carry, possess, repair or dispose of a firearm unless the appropriate license therefor has been issued pursuant to section 400.00 of the penal law.

44. The officers, employees and members of the New York city division of fire prevention, in the bureau of fire, as set forth and subject to the limitations contained in subdivision one of section 487a-1.0 of the administrative code of the city of New York; provided, however, that nothing in this subdivision shall be deemed to authorize such officer to carry, possess, repair or dispose of a firearm unless the appropriate license therefor has been issued pursuant to section 400.00 of the penal law.

45. Persons appointed and designated as peace officers by the Niagara frontier transportation authority, pursuant to subdivision thirteen of section twelve hundred ninety-nine-e of the public authorities law.

46. Persons appointed as peace officers by the Sea Gate Association pursuant to the provisions of chapter three hundred ninety-one of the laws of nineteen hundred forty, provided, however, that nothing in this subdivision shall be deemed to authorize such officer to carry, possess, repair or dispose of a firearm unless the appropriate license therefor has been issued pursuant to section 400.00 of the penal law.

47. Employees of the department of financial services when designated as peace officers by the superintendent of financial services and acting pursuant to their special duties as set forth in article four of the financial services law; provided, however, that nothing in this subdivision shall be deemed to authorize such officer to carry, possess, repair or dispose of a firearm unless the appropriate license therefor has been issued pursuant to section 400.00 of the penal law.

48. New York state air base security guards when they are designated as peace officers under military regulations promulgated by the chief of staff to the governor and when performing their duties as air base security guards pursuant to orders issued by appropriate military authority; provided, however, that nothing in this subdivision shall be deemed to authorize such guards to carry, possess, repair or dispose of a firearm unless the appropriate license therefor has been issued pursuant to section 400.00 of the penal law.

49. Members of the army national guard military police and air national guard security personnel belonging to the organized militia of the state of New York when they are designated as peace officers under military regulations promulgated by the adjutant general and when performing their duties as military police officers or air security personnel pursuant to orders issued by appropriate military authority; provided, however, that nothing in this subdivision shall be deemed to authorize such military police or air security personnel to carry, possess, repair or dispose of a firearm unless the appropriate license therefor has been issued pursuant to section 400.00 of the penal law.   *(Eff. 12/28/18, Ch. 476, L. 2018)*

50. Transportation supervisors in the city of White Plains appointed by the commissioner of public safety in the city of White Plains; provided, however, that nothing in this subdivision shall be deemed to authorize such officer to carry, possess, repair or dispose of a firearm unless the appropriate license therefor has been issued pursuant to section 400.00 of the penal law.

51. Officers and members of the fire investigation division of the fire department of the city of Rochester, the city of Binghamton and the city of Utica, when acting pursuant to their special duties in matters arising under the laws relating to fires, the extinguishment thereof and fire perils; provided, however, that nothing in this subdivision shall be deemed to authorize such officer to carry, possess, repair or dispose of a firearm unless the appropriate license therefor has been issued pursuant to section 400.00 of the penal law.

52. Security hospital treatment assistants, as so designated by the commissioner of the office of mental health while performing duties in or arising out of the course of their employment; provided, however, that nothing in this subdivision shall be deemed to authorize such employee to carry, possess, repair or dispose of a firearm unless the appropriate license therefor has been issued pursuant to section 400.00 of the penal law.

53. Authorized agents of the municipal directors of weights and measures in the counties of Suffolk, Nassau and Westchester when acting pursuant to their special duties as set forth in section one hundred eighty-one of the agriculture and markets law; provided, however, that nothing in this subdivision shall be deemed to authorize such officer to carry, possess, repair or dispose of a firearm unless the appropriate license therefor has been issued pursuant to section 400.00 of the penal law.

54. Special police officers appointed pursuant to section one hundred fifty-eight of the town law; provided, however, that nothing in this subdivision shall be deemed to authorize such officer to carry, possess, repair or dispose of a firearm unless the appropriate license therefor has been issued pursuant to section 400.00 of the penal law. *(Eff.12/28/18,Ch.476,L.2018)*

55. *(Expired)*

56. Dog control officers of the town of Brookhaven, who at the discretion of the town board may be designated as constables for the purpose of enforcing article twenty-six of the agriculture and markets law and for the purpose of issuing appearance tickets permitted under article seven of such law; provided, however, that nothing in this subdivision shall be deemed to authorize such officer to carry, possess, repair or dispose of a firearm unless the appropriate license therefor has been issued pursuant to section 400.00 of the penal law.

57. Harbor Park rangers employed by the Snug Harbor cultural center in Richmond county and appointed as New York city special patrolmen by the police commissioner pursuant to subdivision c of section 14-106 of the administrative code of the city of New York. Notwithstanding any provision of law, rule or regulation, such officers shall be authorized to issue appearance tickets pursuant to section 150.20 of this chapter, and shall have such other powers as are specified in section 2.20 of this article only when acting pursuant to their special duties. Nothing in this subdivision shall be deemed to authorize such officers to carry, possess, repair or dispose of a firearm unless the appropriate license therefor has been issued pursuant

to section 400.00 of the penal law and the employer has authorized such officer to possess a firearm during any phase of the officer's on-duty employment.

*57-a. Seasonal park rangers of the Westchester county department of public safety while employed as authorized by the commissioner of public safety/sheriff of the county of Westchester; provided, however, that nothing in this subdivision shall be deemed to authorize such officer to carry, possess, repair or dispose of a firearm unless the appropriate license therefor has been issued pursuant to section 400.00 of the penal law.

(There are 2 sub 57-a's)

*57-a. Officers of the Westchester county public safety emergency force, when activated by the commissioner of public safety/sheriff of the county of Westchester; provided, however that nothing in this subdivision shall be deemed to authorize such officer to carry, possess, repair or dispose of a firearm unless the appropriate license therefor has been issued pursuant to section 400.00 of the penal law.   *(There are 2 sub 57-a's)*

58. Uniformed members of the security force of the Troy housing authority provided, however, that nothing in this subdivision shall be deemed to authorize such officer to carry, possess, repair or dispose of a firearm unless the appropriate license therefor has been issued pursuant to section 400.00 of the penal law.

59. Officers and members of the sanitation police of the department of sanitation of the city of New York, duly appointed and designated as peace officers by such department; provided, however, that nothing in this subdivision shall be deemed to authorize such officer to carry, possess, repair or dispose of a firearm unless the appropriate license therefor has been issued pursuant to section 400.00 of the penal law. Provided, further, that nothing in this subdivision shall be deemed to apply to officers and members of the sanitation police regularly and exclusively assigned to enforcement of such city's residential recycling laws.

60. *(Repealed)*

61. Chief fire marshall, assistant chief fire marshall, fire marshall II and fire marshall I, all of whom are full-time employees of the Suffolk county department of fire, rescue and emergency services, when acting pursuant to their special duties in matters arising under the laws relating to fires, the extinguishment thereof and fire perils; provided, however, that nothing in this subdivision shall be deemed to authorize such officer to carry, possess, repair or dispose of a firearm unless the appropriate license therefor has been issued pursuant to section 400.00 of the penal law.

* 62. Chief fire marshall, assistant chief fire marshall, fire marshall II and fire marshall I, all of whom are full-time employees of the town of Babylon, when acting pursuant to their special duties in matters arising under the laws relating to fires, the extinguishment thereof and fire perils; provided, however, that nothing in this subdivision shall be deemed to authorize such officer to carry, possess, repair or dispose of a firearm unless the appropriate license therefor has been issued pursuant to section 400.00 of the penal law.   * *(There are 2 sub 62's)*

*62. Employees of the division for youth assigned to transport and warrants units who are specifically designated by the director in accordance with section five hundred four-b of the executive law, provided, however, that nothing in this subdivision shall be deemed to authorize such employees to carry, possess, repair or dispose of a firearm unless the appropriate license therefor has been issued pursuant to section 400.00 of the penal law. * *(There are 2 sub 62's)*

* 63. Uniformed members of the fire marshal's office in the town of Southampton and the town of Riverhead, when acting pursuant to their special duties in matters arising under the laws relating to fires, the extinguishment thereof and fire perils; provided, however that nothing in this subdivision shall be deemed to authorize such officer to carry, possess, repair or dispose of a firearm unless the appropriate license therefor has been issued pursuant to section 400.00 of the penal law.

* *(There are 2 sub 63s)*

* 63. Employees of the town court of the town of Greenburgh serving as a security officer; provided, however, that nothing in this subdivision will be deemed to authorize such officer to carry, possess, repair or dispose of a firearm unless the appropriate license therefor has been issued pursuant to section 400.00 of the penal law or to authorize such officer to carry or possess a firearm except while on duty. * *(There are 2 sub 63s)*

64. Cell block attendants employed by the city of Buffalo police department; provided, however, that nothing in this subdivision shall be deemed to authorize such officer to carry, possess, repair or dispose of a firearm unless the appropriate license therefor has been issued pursuant to section 400.00 of the penal law.

65. Chief fire marshall, assistant chief fire marshall, fire marshall II and fire marshall I, all of whom are full-time employees of the town of Brookhaven, when acting pursuant to their special duties in matters arising under the laws relating to fires, the extinguishment thereof and fire perils; provided, however, that nothing in this subdivision shall be deemed to authorize such officer to carry, possess, repair or dispose of a firearm unless the appropriate license thereof has been issued pursuant to section 400.00 of the penal law.

66. Employees of the village court of the village of Spring Valley serving as security officers at such village court; provided, however, that nothing in this subdivision shall be deemed to authorize such officer to carry, possess, repair or dispose of a firearm unless the appropriate license therefor has been issued pursuant to section 400.00 of the penal law.

67. Employees of the town court of the town of Putnam Valley serving as a security officer; provided, however, that nothing in this subdivision will be deemed to authorize such officer to carry, possess, repair or dispose of a firearm unless the appropriate license therefor has been issued pursuant to section 400.00 of the penal law or to authorize such officer to carry or possess a firearm except while on duty.

* 68. The state inspector general and investigators designated by the state inspector general; provided, however, that nothing in this subdivision shall be deemed to authorize the state inspector general or such investigators to carry, possess, repair or dispose of a firearm unless the appropriate license therefor has been issued pursuant to section 400.00 of the penal law. * *(There are 5 sub 68's)*

* 68. Dog control officers of the town of Arcadia, who at the discretion of the town board may be designated as constables for the purpose of enforcing article twenty-six of the agriculture and markets law and for the purpose of issuing appearance tickets permitted under article seven of such law; provided, however, that nothing in this subdivision shall be deemed to authorize such officer to carry, possess, repair or dispose of a firearm

unless the appropriate license therefor has been issued pursuant to section 400.00 of the penal law.   *(There are 5 sub 68's)

* 68. Employees appointed by the sheriff of Livingston county, when acting pursuant to their special duties serving as uniformed marine patrol officers; provided, however, that nothing in this subdivision shall be deemed to authorize such officer to carry, possess, repair or dispose of a firearm unless the appropriate license has been issued pursuant to section 400.00 of the penal law or to authorize such officer to carry or possess a firearm except while on duty.   *(There are 5 sub 68's)

* 68. Employees of the town court of the town of Southampton serving as uniformed court officers at such town court; provided, however, that nothing in this subdivision shall be deemed to authorize such officer to carry, possess, repair or dispose of a firearm unless the appropriate license therefor has been issued pursuant to section 400.00 of the penal law.
                                                      *(There are 5 sub 68's)

* 68. Persons employed by the Chautauqua county sheriff's office serving as court security officers; provided, however, that nothing in this subdivision shall be deemed to authorize such officer to carry, possess, repair or dispose of a firearm unless the appropriate license therefor has been issued pursuant to section 400.00 of the penal law.   *(There are 5 sub 68's)

69. Employees of the village court of the village of Amityville serving as uniformed court officers at such village court; provided, however, that nothing in this subdivision shall be deemed to authorize such officer to carry, possess, repair or dispose of a firearm unless the appropriate license therefor has been issued pursuant to section 400.00 of the penal law.

70. Employees appointed by the sheriff of Yates county, pursuant to their special duties serving as uniformed marine patrol officers; provided, however, that nothing in this subdivision shall be deemed to authorize such officer to carry, possess, repair or dispose of a firearm unless the appropriate license has been issued pursuant to section 400.00 of the penal law or to authorize such officer to carry or possess a firearm except while on duty.

71. Town of Smithtown fire marshalls when acting pursuant to their special duties in matters arising under the laws relating to fires, the extinguishment thereof and fire perils; provided, however, that nothing in this subdivision shall be deemed to authorize such officers to carry, possess, repair or dispose of a firearm unless the appropriate license therefor has been issued pursuant to section 400.00 of the penal law.

72. Persons employed by Canisius college as members of the security force of such college; provided, however, that nothing in this subdivision shall be deemed to authorize such officer to carry, possess, repair or dispose of a firearm unless the appropriate license therefor has been issued pursuant to section 400.00 of the penal law.

73. Employees of the town court of the town of Newburgh serving as uniformed court officers at such town court; provided, however, that nothing in this subdivision shall be deemed to authorize such officer to carry, possess, repair or dispose of a firearm unless the appropriate license therefor has been issued pursuant to section 400.00 of the penal law.

* 74. a. Special deputy sheriffs appointed by the sheriff of Tompkins county pursuant to paragraphs b and c of this subdivision; provided, however, that nothing in this subdivision shall be deemed to authorize such officer to carry, possess, repair or dispose of a firearm unless the appropriate license therefor has been issued pursuant to section 400.00 of the penal law.

b. For the protection of the grounds, buildings and property of Ithaca college the prevention of crime and the enforcement of law and order, and for the enforcement of such rules and regulations as the board of trustees of Ithaca college shall from time to time make, the sheriff of Tompkins county may appoint and remove following consultation with Ithaca college such number of special deputy sheriffs as is determined by the sheriff to be necessary for the maintenance of public order at Ithaca college, such appointments to be made from persons nominated by the president of Ithaca college. Such special deputy sheriffs shall comply with requirements as established by the sheriff and shall act only within Tompkins county. Such special deputy sheriffs so appointed shall be employees of the college and subject to its supervision and control as outlined in the terms and conditions to be mutually agreed upon between the sheriff and Ithaca college. Such special deputy sheriffs shall have the powers of peace officers and shall act solely within the said grounds or premises owned or administered by Ithaca college, except in those rare and special situations when requested by the sheriff to provide assistance on any public highway which crosses or adjoins such property. Ithaca college will provide legal defense and indemnification, and hold harmless the county of Tompkins, its officers and employees and the Tompkins county sheriff, its officers and employees, from all claims arising out of conduct by or injury to, such personnel while carrying out their law enforcement functions except in those situations when they are acting under the direct supervision and control of the county or sheriff's department.

c. Every special deputy sheriff so appointed shall, before entering upon the duties of his or her office, take and subscribe the oath of office prescribed by article thirteen of the constitution of the state of New York which oath shall be filed in the office of the county clerk of Tompkins county. Every special deputy sheriff appointed under this subdivision when on regular duty shall wear conspicuously a metallic shield with a designating number and the words "Special Deputy Sheriff Ithaca College" thereon.

(There are 4 sub 74's)

* 74. Parks and recreation forest rangers employed by the office of parks, recreation and historic preservation; provided, however, that nothing in this subdivision shall be deemed to authorize such individuals to carry, possess, repair or dispose of a firearm unless the appropriate license therefor has been issued pursuant to section 400.00 of the penal law

(There are 4 sub 74's)

* 74. Employees of the village court of the village of Quogue, town of Southampton serving as uniformed court officers at such village court; provided, however, that nothing in this subdivision shall be deemed to authorize such officer to carry, possess, repair or dispose of a firearm unless the appropriate license therefor has been issued pursuant to section 400.00 of the penal law.

* 74. Employees of the town court of the town of East Hampton serving as uniformed court officers at such town court; provided, however, that nothing in this subdivision shall be deemed to authorize such officer to carry, possess, repair or dispose of a firearm unless the appropriate license therefor has been issued pursuant to section 400.00 of the penal law.

(There are 4 sub 74's)

* 75. Dog control officers of the town of Clarence, who at the discretion of the town board may be designated as constables for the purpose of enforcing article twenty-six of the agriculture and markets law and for the purpose of issuing appearance tickets permitted under article seven of the agriculture and markets law; provided, however, that nothing in this subdivision shall be deemed to authorize such officers to carry, possess, repair or dispose of a firearm unless the appropriate license therefor has been issued pursuant to section 400.00 of the penal law.

(There are 3 sub 75's)

* 75. Airport security guards, senior airport security guards, airport security supervisors, retired police officers, and supervisors of same, who are designated by resolution of the town board of the town of Islip to provide security at Long Island MacArthur Airport when acting pursuant to their duties as such, and such authority being specifically limited to the grounds of the said airport. However, nothing in this subdivision shall be deemed to authorize such officer to carry, possess, repair or dispose of a firearm unless the appropriate license therefor has been issued pursuant to section 400.00 of the penal law.   *(There are 3 sub 75's)*

* 75. Officers and members of the fire investigation unit of the fire department of the city of Buffalo when acting pursuant to their special duties in matters arising under the laws relating to fires, the extinguishment thereof and fire perils; provided, however, that nothing in this subdivision shall be deemed to authorize such officer to carry, possess, repair or dispose of a firearm unless the appropriate license therefor has been issued pursuant to section 400.00 of the penal law.   *(There are 3 sub 75's)*

* 76. Employees of the village court of the village of Southampton, town of Southampton serving as uniformed court officers at such village court; provided, however, that nothing in this subdivision shall be deemed to authorize such officer to carry, possess, repair or dispose of a firearm unless the appropriate license therefor has been issued pursuant to section 400.00 of the penal law.   *(There are 2 sub 76's)*

* 76. Animal control officers employed by the city of Peekskill; provided, however, that nothing in this subdivision shall be deemed to authorize such individuals to carry, possess, repair or dispose of a firearm unless the appropriate license therefor has been issued pursuant to section 400.00 of the penal law.   *(There are 2 sub 76's)*

* 77. (a) Syracuse University peace officers appointed by the chief law enforcement officer of the city of Syracuse pursuant to paragraphs (b), (c) and (d) of this subdivision, who shall be authorized to issue appearance tickets and simplified traffic informations; provided, however, that nothing in this subdivision shall be deemed to authorize any such officer to carry, possess, repair or dispose of a firearm unless the appropriate license therefor has been issued pursuant to section 400.00 of the penal law.

(b) For the protection of the grounds, buildings and property of Syracuse University, the prevention of crime and the enforcement of law and order, and for the enforcement of such rules and regulations as Syracuse University shall from time to time establish, the chief law enforcement officer of the city of Syracuse may appoint and remove, following consultations with Syracuse University; such number of Syracuse University peace officers as is determined by the chief law enforcement officer of the city of Syracuse to be necessary for the maintenance of public order at such university, such appointments to be made from persons nominated by the chancellor of Syracuse University. Such peace officers shall comply with such requirements as shall be established by the chief law enforcement officer of the city of Syracuse. Such Syracuse University peace officers so appointed shall be employees of such university, and subject to its supervision and control and the terms and conditions to be mutually agreed upon between the chief law enforcement officer of the city of Syracuse and Syracuse University. Nothing in this paragraph shall limit the authority of Syracuse University to remove such peace officers. Such Syracuse University peace officers shall have the powers of peace officers within the geographical area of employment of the grounds or premises owned, controlled or administrated by Syracuse University within the county of Onondaga, except in those situations when requested by the chief law enforcement officer of the city of Syracuse or his or her designee, including by means of written protocols agreed to by the chief law enforcement officer of the city of Syracuse and Syracuse University, to provide assistance on any public highway which crosses or adjoins such grounds or premises. Syracuse University shall provide legal defense and indemnification, and hold harmless the city of Syracuse, and its officers and employees from all claims arising out of conduct by or injury to, such peace officers while carrying out their law enforcement functions, except in those situations when they are acting under the direct supervision and control of the chief law enforcement officer of the city of Syracuse, or his or her designee.

(c) Every Syracuse University peace officer so appointed shall, before entering upon the duties of his or her office, take and subscribe the oath of office prescribed by article thirteen of the state constitution, which oath shall be filed in the office of the county clerk of the county of Onondaga. Every such peace officer appointed pursuant to this subdivision when on regular duty shall conspicuously wear a metallic shield with a designating number and the words "Syracuse University Peace Officer" engraved thereon.

(d) To become eligible for appointment as a Syracuse University peace officer a candidate shall, in addition to the training requirements as set forth in section 2.30 of this article, complete the course of instruction in public and private law enforcement established pursuant to paragraph (c) of subdivision five of section sixty-four hundred fifty of the education law.

(There are 2 sub 77's)

* 77. Chief fire marshal, assistant chief fire marshal, and fire marshals, all of whom are full-time employees of the town of East Hampton, when acting pursuant to their special duties in matters arising under the laws relating to fires, the extinguishment thereof and fire perils; provided, however, that nothing in this subdivision shall be deemed to authorize such officer to carry, possess, repair or dispose of a firearm unless the appropriate license therefor has been issued pursuant to section 400.00 of the penal law.

(There are 2 sub 77's)

78. A security officer employed by a community college who is specifically designated as a peace officer by the board of trustees of a community college pursuant to subdivision five-a of section sixty-three hundred six of the education law, or by a community college regional board of trustees pursuant to subdivision four-a of section sixty-three hundred ten of the education law; provided, however, that nothing in this subdivision shall be deemed to authorize such officer to carry, possess, repair or dispose of a firearm unless the appropriate license therefor has been issued pursuant to section 400.00 of the penal law.

* 79. Court security officers employed by the Wayne county sheriff's office; provided however, that nothing in this subdivision shall be deemed to authorize such officer to carry, possess, repair or dispose of a firearm unless the appropriate license therefor has been issued pursuant to section 400.00 of the penal law.

(There are 4 sub 79's)

* 79. Supervisors and members of the arson investigation bureau and fire inspection bureau of the office of fire prevention and control when acting pursuant to their special duties in matters arising under the laws relating to fires, their prevention, extinguishment, investigation thereof, and fire perils; provided, however, that nothing in this subdivision shall be deemed to authorize such employees to carry, possess, repair, or dispose of a firearm unless the appropriate license therefor has been issued pursuant to section 400.00 of the penal law.

(There are 4 sub 79's)

* 79. Peace officers appointed by the city university of New York pursuant to subdivision sixteen of section sixty-two hundred six of the education law, who shall have the powers set forth in section 2.20 of this article whether or not they are acting pursuant to their special duties; provided, however, that nothing in this subdivision shall be deemed to authorize such officer to carry, possess, repair or dispose of a firearm unless the appropriate license therefor has been issued pursuant to section 400.00 of the penal law.

(There are 4 sub 79's)

 * 79. Animal control officers of the city of Elmira, who at the discretion of the city council of the city of Elmira may be designated as constables for the purpose of enforcing article twenty-six of the agriculture and markets law, and for the purpose of issuing appearance tickets permitted under article seven of such law; provided, however, that nothing in this subdivision shall be deemed to authorize such officer to carry, possess, repair or dispose of a firearm unless the appropriate license therefor has been issued pursuant to section 400.00 of the penal law.   *(There are 4 sub 79's)*

80. Employees of the Onondaga county sheriff's department serving as uniformed court security officers at Onondaga county court facilities; provided, however, that nothing in this subdivision shall be deemed to authorize such officers to carry, possess, repair or dispose of a firearm unless the appropriate license therefor has been issued pursuant to section 400.00 of the penal law.

 * 81. Members of the security force employed by Erie County Medical Center; provided however, that nothing in this subdivision shall be deemed to authorize such officer to carry, possess, repair or dispose of a firearm unless the appropriate license therefor has been issued pursuant to section 400.00 of the penal law.   *(There are 6 sb 81's)*

 * 81. Employees of the town of Riverhead serving as court officers at town of Riverhead court facilities; provided, however, that nothing in this subdivision shall be deemed to authorize such officers to carry, possess, repair or dispose of a firearm unless the appropriate license therefor has been issued pursuant to section 400.00 of the penal law. *(There are 6 sb 81's)*

 * 81. Employees of the town court of the town of Southold serving as uniformed court officers at such town court; provided, however, that nothing in this subdivision shall be deemed to authorize such officer to carry, possess, repair or dispose of a firearm unless the appropriate license therefor has been issued pursuant to section 400.00 of the penal law.

(There are 6 sb 81's)

 * 81. Commissioners of and court officers in the department of public safety for the town of Rye when acting pursuant to their special duties in matters arising under the laws relating to maintaining the safety and security of citizens, judges and court personnel in the town court, and effecting the safe and secure transport of persons under the custody of said department; provided, however, that nothing in this subdivision shall be deemed to authorize such employees to carry, possess, repair, or dispose of a firearm unless the appropriate license therefor has been issued pursuant to section 400.00 of the penal law.*   *(There are 6 sb 81's)*

 * 81. Employees of the town of Yorktown serving as court attendants at town of Yorktown court facilities; provided, however, that nothing in this subdivision shall be deemed to authorize such employees to carry, possess, repair or dispose of a firearm unless the appropriate license therefor has been issued pursuant to section 400.00 of the penal law. *(There are 6 sb 81's)*

 * 81. Employees of the Lewis county sheriff's department serving as uniformed court security officers at Lewis county court facilities; provided, however, that nothing in this subdivision shall be deemed to authorize such officers to carry, possess, repair or dispose of a firearm unless the appropriate license therefor has been issued pursuant to section 400.00 of the penal law.   *(There are 6 sb 81's)*

82. Employees of the New York city business integrity commission designated as peace officers by the chairperson of such commission; provided, however, that nothing in this subdivision shall be deemed to authorize such officer to carry, possess, repair or dispose of a firearm unless the appropriate license therefor has been issued pursuant to section 400.00 of the penal law.

83. Members of the security force employed by Kaleida Health within and directly adjacent to the hospital buildings on the medical campus located between East North Street, Goodell Street, Main Street and Michigan Avenue. These officers shall only have the powers listed in paragraph (c) of subdivision one of section 2.20 of this article, as well as the power to detain an individual for a reasonable period of time while awaiting the arrival of law enforcement, provided that the officer has actual knowledge, or probable cause to believe, that such individual has committed an offense; provided however, that nothing in this subdivision shall be deemed to authorize such officer to carry, possess, repair or dispose of a firearm unless the appropriate license therefor has been issued pursuant to section 400.00 of the penal law.

84. (a) Public safety officers employed by the University of Rochester who are designated as peace officers by the board of trustees of the University of Rochester pursuant to paragraphs (b), (c), and (d) of this subdivision; provided, however, that nothing in this subdivision shall be deemed to authorize any such officer to carry, possess, repair or dispose of a firearm unless the appropriate license therefor has been issued pursuant to section 400.00 of the penal law.

(b) For the protection of the grounds, buildings and property of the University of Rochester, the prevention of crime and the enforcement of law and order, the board of trustees of the University of Rochester may appoint and remove such number of public safety officers designated as peace officers as is determined by the board of trustees to be necessary for the maintenance of public order consistent with this subdivision. Such peace officers shall comply with such requirements as shall be mutually agreed upon between the chief law enforcement officers of the applicable local law enforcement jurisdictions and the University of Rochester. Such University of Rochester peace officers so appointed shall be employees of the University of Rochester and subject to its supervision and control. Such University of Rochester peace officers shall have the powers of peace officers within the geographic area of employment of the grounds or premises owned, controlled or administered by the University of Rochester within the county of Monroe, on any public street and sidewalk that abuts the grounds, buildings or property of such university, and beyond such geographic area upon the request of the chief law enforcement officer of the local law enforcement jurisdiction or his or her designee, for the purpose of transporting an individual who has been arrested in accordance with section 140.27 of this chapter and when no local law enforcement officer is available for transporting such individual in a timely manner.

(c) The University of Rochester shall provide legal defense and indemnification to applicable municipality and its officers and employees, and hold them harmless, against all claims arising out of conduct by or injury to such peace officers while carrying out their special duties, except in those situations when they are acting as agents of the chief law enforcement officer of the applicable local law enforcement jurisdiction or his or her designee.

(d) To become eligible for designation as a University of Rochester peace officer, a candidate shall, in addition to the training requirements as set forth in section 2.30 of this article, complete the course of instruction in public and private law enforcement established pursuant to subdivision three of section sixty-four hundred thirty-five of the education law.

85. Uniformed members of the bureau of fire prevention of the town of Islip, when acting pursuant to their special duties in matters arising under laws relating to fires, the extinguishment thereof and fire perils; provided, however, that nothing in this subdivision shall be deemed to authorize such members to carry, possess, repair or dispose of a firearm unless the appropriate license therefor has been issued pursuant to section 400.00 of the penal law.   *(Eff.12/12/19,Ch.632,L.2019)*

§2.15 Federal law enforcement officers; powers.

The following federal law enforcement officers shall have the powers set forth in paragraphs (a) (with the exception of the powers provided by paragraph (b) of subdivision one and paragraph (b) of subdivision three of section 140.25 of this chapter), (b), (c) and (h) of subdivision one of section 2.20 of this article:

1. Federal Bureau of Investigation special agents.
2. United States Secret Service special agents.
3. Immigration and Customs Enforcement special agents, deportation officers, and detention and deportation officers.
4. United States Marshals and Marshals Service deputies.
5. Drug Enforcement Administration special agents.
6. Federal Protective Officers, including law enforcement security officers, criminal investigators and police officers of the Federal Protective Service.
7. United States Customs and Border Protection Officers and United States Customs and Border Protection Border Patrol agents.
8. United States Postal Service police officers and inspectors.
9. United States park police; provided, however that, notwithstanding any provision of this section to the contrary, such park police shall also have the powers set forth in paragraph (b) of subdivision one of section 140.25 of this chapter and the powers set forth in paragraphs (d), (e) and (g) of subdivision one of section 2.20 of this article.
10. United States probation officers.
11. United States General Services Administration special agents.
12. United States Department of Agriculture special agents.
13. Bureau of Alcohol, Tobacco and Firearms special agents.
14. Internal Revenue Service special agents and inspectors.
15. Officers of the United States bureau of prisons.
16. United States Fish and Wildlife special agents.
17. United States Naval Investigative Service special agents.
18. United States Department of State special agents.
19. Special agents of the defense criminal investigative service of the United States department of defense.
20. United States Department of Commerce, Office of Export Enforcement, special agents.
21. United States Department of Veterans Administration police officers employed at the Veterans Administration Medical Center in Batavia.
22. Federal Reserve law enforcement officers.
23. Federal air marshal program special agents.
*24. United States department of transportation federal police officers and police supervisors assigned to the United States Merchant Marine Academy in Kings Point, New York; provided, however that, notwithstanding any provision of this section to the contrary, such police shall also have the powers set forth in paragraph (b) of subdivision one of section 140.25 of this chapter and the powers set forth in paragraphs (d), (e) and (g) of subdivision one of section 2.20 of this article when acting pursuant to their special duties within the geographical area of their employment or within one hundred yards of such geographical area.   * *(There are 2 sb 24's)*

*24. United States Coast Guard Investigative Service special agents.

* *(There are 2 sb 24's)*

25. United States Department of Commerce, special agents and enforcement officers of the National Oceanic and Atmospheric Administration's Fisheries Office for Law Enforcement.

26. Department of the Army special agents, detectives and police officers.

27. United States Department of Interior, park rangers with law enforcement authority.

28. United States Environmental Protection Agency special agents with law enforcement authority.

29. United States mint police.

§2.16 Watershed protection and enforcement officers; powers, duties, jurisdiction for arrests.

1. Watershed protection and enforcement officers appointed by the city of Peekskill shall have the powers set forth in paragraphs (a), (b), (c), (f), (g), (h) of subdivision one of section 2.20 of this article; provided, however, that nothing in this section shall be deemed to authorize such officer to carry, possess, repair, or dispose of a firearm unless the appropriate license therefor has been issued pursuant to section 400.00 of the penal law. Watershed protection and enforcement officers shall complete the training requirements set forth in section 2.30 of this article.

2. The city of Peekskill may appoint the following persons as watershed protection and enforcement officers:

    (a) the water superintendent;

    (b) the deputy assistant to the water superintendent; and

    (c) the watershed inspector or inspectors.

3. The duties of the watershed protection and enforcement officers shall be to enforce those provisions of the environmental conservation law and the penal law which relate to the contamination of water in those areas of the Hollow Brook watershed located within the city of Peekskill, including its reservoirs, shoreline, and tributaries, and those areas of the Hollow Brook watershed and Wiccopee reservoir located outside of the city of Peekskill in the counties of Putnam and Westchester, including its reservoirs, shoreline, and tributaries.

4. Notwithstanding paragraph (b) of subdivision thirty-four-a of section 1.20 of this title and paragraph (b) of subdivision five of section 140.25 of this chapter, watershed protection and enforcement officers are authorized to make arrests and issue appearance tickets in those areas of the Hollow Brook watershed and Wiccopee reservoir located outside of the city of Peekskill in the counties of Putnam and Westchester, including along its reservoirs, shoreline, and tributaries.

§2.20 Powers of peace officers.

1. The persons designated in section 2.10 of this article shall have the following powers:

    (a) The power to make warrantless arrests pursuant to section 140.25 of this chapter.

    (b) The power to use physical force and deadly physical force in making an arrest or preventing an escape pursuant to section 35.30 of the penal law.

    (c) The power to carry out warrantless searches whenever such searches are constitutionally permissible and acting pursuant to their special duties.

(d) The power to issue appearance tickets pursuant to subdivision three of section 150.20 of this chapter, when acting pursuant to their special duties. New York city special patrolmen shall have the power to issue an appearance ticket only when it is pursuant to rules and regulations of the police commissioner of the city of New York.

(e) The power to issue uniform appearance tickets pursuant to article twenty-seven of the parks, recreation and historic preservation law and to issue simplified traffic informations pursuant to section 100.25 of this chapter and section two hundred seven of the vehicle and traffic law whenever acting pursuant to their special duties.

(f) The power to issue a uniform navigation summons and/or complaint pursuant to section nineteen of the navigation law whenever acting pursuant to their special duties.

(g) The power to issue uniform appearance tickets pursuant to article seventy-one of the environmental conservation law, whenever acting pursuant to their special duties.

(h) The power to possess and take custody of firearms not owned by the peace officer for the purpose of disposing, guarding, or any other lawful purpose, consistent with his duties as a peace officer.

(i) Any other power which a particular peace officer is otherwise authorized to exercise by any general, special or local law or charter whenever acting pursuant to his special duties, provided such power is not inconsistent with the provisions of the penal law or this chapter.

(j) Uniformed court officers shall have the power to issue traffic summonses and complaints for parking, standing, or stopping violations pursuant to the vehicle and traffic law whenever acting pursuant to their special duties.

2. For the purposes of this section a peace officer acts pursuant to his special duties when he performs the duties of his office, pursuant to the specialized nature of his particular employment, whereby he is required or authorized to enforce any general, special or local law or charter, rule, regulation, judgment or order.

3. A peace officer, whether or not acting pursuant to his special duties, who lawfully exercises any of the powers conferred upon him pursuant to this section, shall be deemed to be acting within the scope of his public employment for purposes of defense and indemnification rights and benefits that he may be otherwise entitled to under the provisions of section fifty-k of the general municipal law, section seventeen or eighteen of the public officers law, or any other applicable section of law.

§2.30 Training requirements for peace officers.

1. Every peace officer in the state of New York must successfully complete a training program, a portion of which shall be prescribed by the municipal police training council and a portion of which shall be prescribed by his or her employer. The portion prescribed by the municipal police training council shall be comprised of subjects, and the hours each is to be taught, that shall be required of all types or classes of peace officers. The hours of instruction required by the municipal police training council shall

not exceed one hundred eighty, unless a greater amount is either required by law or regulation, or is requested by the employer.

The segment prescribed by the employer for its employees shall be comprised of subjects, and the hours each is to be taught, relating to the special nature of the duties of the peace officers employed by it provided, however, that when the subjects prescribed by the employer are identical to the subjects in the training program required by the municipal police training council, the employer shall not be required to provide duplicate training for those subjects.

2. Each state or local agency, unit of local government, state or local commission, or public authority, or public or private organization which employs peace officers shall provide the training mandated by this section, the cost of which will be borne by the employer. Each peace officer satisfactorily completing the course prescribed by the municipal police training council shall be awarded a certificate by the division of criminal justice services attesting to that effect, and no person appointed as a peace officer shall exercise the powers of a peace officer, unless he or she has received such certification within twelve months of appointment.

3. No employer shall allow any peace officer it employs to carry or use a weapon during any phase of the officer's official duties, which constitutes on-duty employment, unless the officer has satisfactorily completed a course of training approved by the municipal police training council in the use of deadly physical force and firearms and other weapons, and annually receives instruction in deadly physical force and the use of firearms and other weapons as approved by the municipal police training council.

4. Upon the failure or refusal to comply with the requirements of this section, the commissioner of the division of criminal justice services shall apply to the supreme court for an order directed to the person responsible requiring compliance. Upon such application, the court may issue such order as may be just, and a failure to comply with the order of the court shall be a contempt of court and punishable as such.

5. Every employer of peace officers shall report to the division of criminal justice services, in such form and at such time as the division may by regulation require, the names of all peace officers who have satisfactorily completed any of the training requirements prescribed by this section.

6. A certificate attesting to satisfactory completion of the training requirements imposed under this section awarded to any peace officer by the executive director of the municipal police training council pursuant to this section shall remain valid:

(a) during the holder's continuous service as a peace officer; and

(b) for two years after the date of the commencement of an interruption in such service where the holder had, immediately prior to such interruption, served as a peace officer for less than two consecutive years; or

(c) for four years after the date of the commencement of an interruption in such service where the holder had, immediately prior to such interruption, served as a peace officer for two consecutive years or longer.

As used in this subdivision, the term "interruption" shall mean a period of separation from employment as a peace officer by reason of such officer's leave of absence, resignation or removal, other than removal for cause.

TITLE B - THE CRIMINAL COURTS
ARTICLE 10 - THE CRIMINAL COURTS

Section
10.10   The criminal courts; enumeration and definitions.
10.20   Superior courts; jurisdiction.
10.30   Local criminal courts; jurisdiction.
10.40   Chief administrator to prescribe forms and to authorize use of electronic filing.

§10.10   The criminal courts; enumeration and definitions.

1. The "criminal courts" of this state are comprised of the superior courts and the local criminal courts.

2. "Superior court" means:
   (a) The supreme court; or
   (b) A county court.

3. "Local criminal court" means:
   (a) A district court; or
   (b) The New York City criminal court; or
   (c) A city court; or
   (d) A town court; or
   (e) A village court; or
   (f) A supreme court justice sitting as a local criminal court; or
   (g) A county judge sitting as a local criminal court.

4. "City court" means any court for a city, other than New York City, having trial jurisdiction of offenses of less than felony grade only committed within such city, whether such court is entitled a city court, a municipal court, a police court, a recorder's court or is known by any other name or title.

5. "Town court." A "town court" is comprised of all the town justices of a town.

6. "Village court." A "village court" is comprised of the justice of a village, or all the justices thereof if there be more than one, or, at a time when he or they are absent, an associate justice of a village who is authorized to perform the functions of a village justice during his absence.

7. Notwithstanding any other provision of this section, a court specified herein which possesses civil as well as criminal jurisdiction does not act as a criminal court when acting solely in the exercise of its civil jurisdiction, and an order or determination made by such a court in its civil capacity is not an order or determination of a criminal court even though it may terminate or otherwise control or affect a criminal action or proceeding.

§10.20   Superior courts; jurisdiction.

1. Superior courts have trial jurisdiction of all offenses. They have:
   (a) Exclusive trial jurisdiction of felonies; and
   (b) Trial jurisdiction of misdemeanors concurrent with that of the local criminal courts; and
   (c) Trial jurisdiction of petty offenses, but only when such an offense is charged in an indictment which also charges a crime.

2. Superior courts have preliminary jurisdiction of all offenses, but they exercise such jurisdiction only by reason of and through the agency of their grand juries.

3. Superior court judges may, in their discretion, sit as local criminal courts for the following purposes:
   (a) conducting arraignments, as provided in subdivision two of section 170.15 and subdivision two of section 180.20 of this chapter;
   (b) issuing warrants of arrests, as provided in subdivision one of section 120.70 of this chapter; and
   (c) issuing search warrants, as provided in article six hundred ninety of this chapter.

§10.30   Local criminal courts; jurisdiction.

1. Local criminal courts have trial jurisdiction of all offenses other than felonies. They have:

(a) Exclusive trial jurisdiction of petty offenses except for the superior court jurisdiction thereof prescribed in paragraph (c) of subdivision one of section 10.20; and

(b) Trial jurisdiction of misdemeanors concurrent with that of the superior courts but subject to divestiture thereof by the latter in any particular case.

2. Local criminal courts have preliminary jurisdiction of all offenses subject to divestiture thereof in any particular case by the superior courts and their grand juries.

3. Notwithstanding the provisions of subdivision one, a superior court judge sitting as a local criminal court does not have trial jurisdiction of any offense, but has preliminary jurisdiction only, as provided in subdivision two.

*§10.40   Chief administrator to prescribe forms and to authorize use of electronic filing.

1. The chief administrator of the courts shall have the power to adopt, amend and rescind forms for the efficient and just administration of this chapter. Such forms shall include, without limitation, the forms described in paragraph (z-1) of subdivision two of section two hundred twelve of the judiciary law. A failure by any party to submit papers in compliance with forms authorized by this section shall not be grounds for that reason alone for denial or granting of any motion.   *(Eff.12/12/20,Ch.102,L.2020)*

2. (a) Notwithstanding any other provision of law, the chief administrator, with the approval of the administrative board of the courts, may promulgate rules authorizing a program in the use of electronic means ("e-filing") in the supreme court and in the county court for (i) the filing with a court of an accusatory instrument for the purpose of commencement of a criminal action or proceeding in a superior court, as provided by articles one hundred ninety-five and two hundred of this chapter, and (ii) the filing and service of papers in pending criminal actions and proceedings. Provided, however, the chief administrator shall consult with the county clerk of a county outside the city of New York before the use of electronic means is to be authorized in the supreme court or county court of such county, afford him or her the opportunity to submit comments with respect thereto, consider any such comments and obtain the agreement thereto of such county clerk.

(b) (i) Except as otherwise provided in this paragraph, participation in this program shall be strictly voluntary and will take place only upon consent of all parties in the criminal action or proceeding; except that a party's failure to consent to participation shall not bar any other party to the action from filing and serving papers by electronic means upon the court or any other party to such action or proceeding who has consented to participation. Filing an accusatory instrument by electronic means with the court for the purpose of commencement of a criminal action or proceeding shall not require the consent of any other party; provided, however, that upon such filing any person who is the subject of such accusatory instrument and any attorney for such person shall be permitted to immediately review and obtain copies of such instrument if such person or attorney would have been authorized by law to review or copy such instrument if it had been filed with the court in paper form.

No party shall be compelled, directly or indirectly, to participate in e-filing. All parties shall be notified clearly, in plain language, about their options to participate in e-filing. Where a party is not represented by counsel, the clerk shall explain such party's options for electronic filing in plain language, including the option for expedited processing, and shall inquire whether he or she wishes to participate, provided however the unrepresented litigant may participate in the program only upon his or her request, which shall be documented in the case file, after said party has been presented with sufficient information in plain language concerning the program.

(ii) The chief administrator may eliminate the requirement of consent to participation in this program in supreme and county courts of not more than six counties provided he or she may not eliminate such requirement for a court without the consent of the district attorney, the consent of the criminal defense bar as defined in subdivision three of this section and the consent of the county clerk of the county in which such court presides. Notwithstanding the foregoing provisions of this subparagraph, the chief administrator shall not eliminate the requirement of consent to participation in a county hereunder until he or she shall have provided all persons and organizations, or their representative or representatives, who regularly appear in criminal actions or proceedings in the superior court of such county with reasonable notice and opportunity to submit comments with respect thereto and shall have given due consideration to all such comments, nor until he or she shall have consulted with the members of the advisory committee specified in subparagraph (v) of paragraph (u) of subdivision two of section two hundred twelve of the judiciary law.

(c) Where the chief administrator eliminates the requirement of consent as provided in subparagraph (ii) of paragraph (b) of this subdivision, he or she shall afford counsel the opportunity to opt out of the program, via presentation of a prescribed form to be filed with the court where the criminal action is pending. Said form shall permit an attorney to opt out of participation in the program under any of the following circumstances, in which event, he or she will not be compelled to participate:

(i) Where the attorney certifies in good faith that he or she lacks appropriate computer hardware and/or connection to the internet and/or scanner or other device by which documents may be converted to an electronic format; or

(ii) Where the attorney certifies in good faith that he or she lacks the requisite knowledge in the operation of such computers and/or scanners necessary to participate. For the purposes of this subparagraph, the knowledge of any employee of an attorney, or any employee of the attorney's law firm, office or business who is subject to such attorney's direction, shall be imputed to the attorney.

Notwithstanding the foregoing provisions of this paragraph: (A) where a party is not represented by counsel, the clerk shall explain such party's options for electronic filing in plain language, including the option for expedited processing, and shall inquire whether he or she wishes to participate, provided however the unrepresented litigant may participate in the program only upon his or her request, which shall be documented in the case file, after said party has been presented with sufficient information in plain language concerning the program; (B) a party not represented by counsel who has chosen to participate in the program shall be afforded the opportunity to opt out of the program for any reason via presentation of a prescribed form to be filed with the clerk of the court where the proceeding is pending; and (C) a court may exempt any attorney from being required to participate in the program upon application for such exemption, showing good cause therefor.

(d) (i) Nothing in this section shall affect or change any existing laws governing the sealing and confidentiality of court records in criminal proceedings or access to court records by the parties to such proceedings,nor shall this section be construed to compel a party to file a sealed document by electronic means.

(ii) Notwithstanding any other provision of this section, no paper or document that is filed by electronic means in a criminal proceeding in supreme court or county court shall be available for public inspection on-line. Subject to the provisions of existing laws governing the sealing and confidentiality of court records, nothing herein shall prevent the unified court system from sharing statistical information that does not include any papers or documents filed with the action; and, provided further, that this paragraph shall not prohibit the chief administrator, in the exercise of his or her discretion, from posting papers or documents that have not been sealed pursuant to law on a public website maintained by the unified court system where: (A) the website is not the website established by the rules promulgated pursuant to paragraph (a) of this subdivision, and (B) to do so would be in the public interest. For purposes of this subparagraph, the chief administrator, in determining whether posting papers or documents on a public website is in the public interest, shall, at a minimum, take into account for each posting the following factors: (A) the type of case involved; (B) whether such posting would cause harm to any person, including especially a minor or crime victim; (C) whether such posting would include lewd or scandalous matters; and (D) the possibility that such papers or documents may ultimately be sealed.

(iii) Nothing in this section shall affect or change existing laws governing service of process, nor shall this section be construed to abrogate existing personal service requirements as set forth in the criminal procedure law.

3. For purposes of this section, the following terms shall have the following meanings:

(a) "Consent of the criminal defense bar" shall mean that consent has been obtained from all provider offices and/or organizations in the county that represented twenty-five percent or more of the persons represented by public defense providers pursuant to section seven hundred twenty-two of the county law, as shown in the most recent annual reports filed pursuant to subdivision one of section seven hundred twenty-two-f of the county law. Such consent, when given, must be expressed in a written document that is provided by a person who is authorized to consent on behalf of the relevant public defender organization, agency or office; and

(b) "Electronic means" shall be as defined in subdivision (f) of rule twenty-one hundred three of the civil practice law and rules; and

(c) The "filing and service of papers in pending criminal actions and proceedings" shall include the filing and service of a notice of appeal pursuant to section 460.10 of this chapter.   * *(Expires 9/1/22,Ch.118,L.2021)*

Title C - GENERAL PRINCIPLES RELATING TO REQUIREMENTS FOR AND EXEMPTIONS FROM CRIMINAL PROSECUTION
ARTICLE 20 - GEOGRAPHICAL JURISDICTION OF OFFENSES

Section
20.10   Geographical jurisdiction of offenses; definitions of terms.
20.20   Geographical jurisdiction of offenses; jurisdiction of state.
20.30   Geographical jurisdiction of offenses; effect of laws of other jurisdictions upon this state's jurisdiction.
20.40   Geographical jurisdiction of offenses; jurisdiction of counties.
20.50   Geographical jurisdiction of offenses; jurisdiction of cities, towns and villages.
20.60   Geographical jurisdiction of offenses; communications and transportation of property between jurisdictions.

§20.10   Geographical jurisdiction of offenses; definitions of terms.
The following definitions are applicable to this article:

1. "This state" means New York State as its boundaries are prescribed in the state law, and the space over it.

2. "County" means any of the sixty-two counties of this state as its boundaries are prescribed by law, and the space over it.

3. "Result of an offense." When a specific consequence, such as the death of the victim in a homicide case, is an element of an offense, the occurrence of such consequence constitutes the "result" of such offense. An offense of which a result is an element is a "result offense."

4. "Particular effect of an offense." When conduct constituting an offense produces consequences which, though not necessarily amounting to a result or element of such offense, have a materially harmful impact upon the governmental processes or community welfare of a particular jurisdiction, or result in the defrauding of persons in such jurisdiction, such conduct and offense have a "particular effect" upon such jurisdiction.

§20.20 Geographical jurisdiction of offenses; jurisdiction of state.

Except as otherwise provided in this section and section 20.30, a person may be convicted in the criminal courts of this state of an offense defined by the laws of this state, committed either by his own conduct or by the conduct of another for which he is legally accountable pursuant to section 20.00 of the penal law, when:

1. Conduct occurred within this state sufficient to establish:
   (a) An element of such offense; or
   (b) An attempt to commit such offense; or
   (c) A conspiracy or criminal solicitation to commit such offense, or otherwise to establish the complicity of at least one of the persons liable therefor; provided that the jurisdiction accorded by this paragraph extends only to conviction of those persons whose conspiratorial or other conduct of complicity occurred within this state; or

2. Even though none of the conduct constituting such offense may have occurred within this state:
   (a) The offense committed was a result offense and the result occurred within this state. If the offense was one of homicide, it is presumed that the result, namely the death of the victim, occurred within this state if the victim's body or a part thereof was found herein; or
   (b) The statute defining the offense is designed to prevent the occurrence of a particular effect in this state and the conduct constituting the offense committed was performed with intent that it would have such effect herein; or
   (c) The offense committed was an attempt to commit a crime within this state; or
   (d) The offense committed was conspiracy to commit a crime within this state and an overt act in furtherance of such conspiracy occurred within this state; or

3. The offense committed was one of omission to perform within this state a duty imposed by the laws of this state. In such case, it is immaterial whether such person was within or outside this state at the time of the omission.

§20.30 Geographical jurisdiction of offenses; effect of laws of other jurisdictions upon this state's jurisdiction.

1. Notwithstanding the provisions of section 20.20, the courts of this state do not have jurisdiction to convict a person of an alleged offense partly committed within this state but consummated in another jurisdiction, or an offense of criminal solicitation, conspiracy or attempt in this state to commit a crime in another jurisdiction, or an offense of criminal facilitation in this state of a felony committed in another jurisdiction, unless the conduct constituting the consummated offense or, as the case may be, the conduct constituting the crime solicited, conspiratorially contemplated or facilitated, constitutes an offense under the laws of such other jurisdiction as well as under the laws of this state.

2. The courts of this state are not deprived of the jurisdiction accorded them by section 20.20 to convict a person of an offense defined by the laws of this state, partly committed in another jurisdiction but consummated in this state, or an offense of attempt or conspiracy in another jurisdiction to

commit in this state a crime defined by the laws of this state, by the circumstance that the conduct constituting the consummated offense or, as the case may be, the crime attempted or conspiratorially contemplated, does not constitute an offense under the laws of such other jurisdiction.

§20.40   Geographical jurisdiction of offenses; jurisdiction of counties.

A person may be convicted in an appropriate criminal court of a particular county, of an offense of which the criminal courts of this state have jurisdiction pursuant to section 20.20, committed either by his or her own conduct or by the conduct of another for which he or she is legally accountable pursuant to section 20.00 of the penal law, when:

1. Conduct occurred within such county sufficient to establish:
   (a) An element of such offense; or
   (b) An attempt or a conspiracy to commit such offense; or

2. Even though none of the conduct constituting such offense may have occurred within such county:
   (a) The offense committed was a result offense and the result occurred in such county; or
   (b) The offense committed was one of homicide and the victim's body or a part thereof was found in such county; or
   (c) Such conduct had, or was likely to have, a particular effect upon such county or a political subdivision or part thereof, and was performed with intent that it would, or with knowledge that it was likely to, have such particular effect therein; or
   (d) The offense committed was attempt, conspiracy or criminal solicitation to commit a crime in such county; or
   (e) The offense committed was criminal facilitation of a felony committed in such county; or

3. The offense committed was one of omission to perform a duty imposed by law, which duty either was required to be or could properly have been performed in such county. In such case, it is immaterial whether such person was within or outside such county at the time of the omission; or

4. Jurisdiction of such offense is accorded to the courts of such county pursuant to any of the following rules:
   (a) An offense of abandonment of a child or non-support of a child may be prosecuted in (i) any county in which such child resided during the period of abandonment or non-support, or (ii) any county in which such person resided during such period, or (iii) any county in which such person was present during such period, provided that he was arrested for such offense in such county or the criminal action therefor was commenced while he was present therein.
   (b) An offense of bigamy may be prosecuted either in the county in which such offense was committed or in (i) any county in which bigamous cohabitation subsequently occurred, or (ii) any county in which such person was present after the commission of the offense, provided that he was arrested for such offense in such county or the criminal action therefor was commenced while he was present therein.
   (c) An offense committed within five hundred yards of the boundary of a particular county, and in an adjoining county of this state, may be prosecuted in either such county.
   (d) An offense committed anywhere on the Hudson river southward of the northern boundary of New York City, or anywhere on New York bay between Staten Island and Long Island, may be prosecuted in any of the five counties of New York City.
   (e) An offense committed upon any bridge or in any tunnel having terminals in different counties may be prosecuted in any terminal county.

(f) An offense committed on board a railroad train, aircraft or omnibus operating as a common carrier may be prosecuted in any county through or over which such common carrier passed during the particular trip, or in any county in which such trip terminated or was scheduled to terminate.

(g) An offense committed in a private vehicle during a trip thereof extending through more than one county may be prosecuted in any county through which such vehicle passed in the course of such trip.

(h) An offense committed on board a vessel navigating or lying in any river, canal or lake flowing through or situated within this state, may be prosecuted in any county bordering upon such body of water, or in which it is located, or through which it passes; and if such offense was committed upon a vessel operating as a common carrier, it may be prosecuted in any county bordering upon any body of water upon which such vessel navigated or passed during the particular trip.

(i) An offense committed in the Atlantic Ocean within two nautical miles from the shore at high water mark may be prosecuted in an appropriate court of the county the shore line of which is closest to the point where the offense was committed. A crime committed more than two nautical miles from the shore but within the boundary of this state may be prosecuted in the supreme court of the county the shore line of which is closest to the point where the crime was committed.

(j) An offense of forgery may be prosecuted in any county in which the defendant, or another for whose conduct the defendant is legally accountable pursuant to section 20.00 of the penal law, possessed the instrument.

(k) An offense of offering of a false instrument for filing, or of larceny by means of a false pretense therein, may be prosecuted (i) in any county in which such instrument was executed, in whole or in part, or (ii) in any county in which any of the goods or services for which payment or reimbursement is sought by means of such instrument were purported to have been provided.

(l) An offense of identity theft or unlawful possession of personal identifying information and all criminal acts committed as part of the same criminal transaction as defined in subdivision two of section 40.10 of this chapter may be prosecuted (i) in any county in which part of the offense took place regardless of whether the defendant was actually present in such county, or (ii) in the county in which the person who suffers financial loss resided at the time of the commission of the offense, or (iii) in the county where the person whose personal identifying information was used in the commission of the offense resided at the time of the commission of the offense. The law enforcement agency of any such county shall take a police report of the matter and provide the complainant with a copy of such report at no charge.

(m) An offense under the tax law or the penal law of filing a false or fraudulent return, report, document, declaration, statement, or filing, or of tax evasion, fraud, or larceny resulting from the filing of a false or fraudulent return, report, document, declaration, or filing in connection with the payment of taxes to the state or a political subdivision of the state, may be prosecuted in any county in which an underlying transaction reflected, reported or required to be reflected or reported, in whole or part, on such return, report, document, declaration, statement, or filing occurred.

(n) (i) An organized retail theft crime, where the defendant knows that such crime is a part of a coordinated plan, scheme or venture of organized retail theft crimes committed by two or more persons, may be prosecuted in any county in which such defendant committed at least one such organized retail theft crime; provided, however, that the county of prosecution is contiguous to another county in which one or more of such other organized retail theft crimes was committed. Multiple organized retail theft crimes committed by the same defendant may be joined in one indictment if authorized and appropriate in accordance with the provisions of section 200.20 of this chapter, provided, however, that notwithstanding section 200.40 of this chapter, no more than one defendant may be charged in the same indictment or prosecuted as part of the same trial under this paragraph. For purposes of this paragraph, the five counties that comprise New York city shall be deemed contiguous with each other.

(ii) For purposes of this paragraph, "organized retail theft crime" shall mean the crime of larceny, including by trick, fraud, embezzlement, stealing or false pretenses, of retail merchandise in quantities that would not normally be purchased for personal use or consumption, for the purposes of reselling, trading, or otherwise reentering such retail merchandise in commerce.   *(Eff.11/1/16,Ch.63,L.2016)*

§20.50   Geographical jurisdiction of offenses; jurisdiction of cities, towns and villages.

1. The principles prescribed in section 20.40, governing geographical jurisdiction over offenses as between counties of this state, are, where appropriate, applicable to the determination of geographical jurisdiction over offenses as between cities, towns and villages within a particular county unless a different determination is required by the provisions of some other express provision of statute.

2. Where an offense prosecutable in a local criminal court is committed in a city other than New York City, or in a town or village, but within one hundred yards of any other such political subdivision, it may be prosecuted in either such political subdivision.

§20.60   Geographical jurisdiction of offenses; communications and transportation of property between jurisdictions.

For purposes of this article:

1. An oral or written statement made by a person in one jurisdiction to a person in another jurisdiction by means of telecommunication, mail or any

other method of communication is deemed to be made in each such jurisdiction.

2. A person who causes property to be transported from one jurisdiction to another by means of mail, common carrier or any other method is deemed to have personally transported it in each jurisdiction, and if delivery is made in the second jurisdiction he is deemed to have personally made such delivery therein.

3. A person who causes by any means the use of a computer or computer service in one jurisdiction from another jurisdiction is deemed to have personally used the computer or computer service in each jurisdiction.

ARTICLE 30 - TIMELINESS OF PROSECUTIONS AND SPEEDY TRIAL
Section
30.10 Timeliness of prosecutions; periods of limitation.
30.20 Speedy trial; in general.
30.30 Speedy trial; time limitations.

§30.10 Timeliness of prosecutions; periods of limitation.
1. A criminal action must be commenced within the period of limitation prescribed in the ensuing subdivisions of this section.

2. Except as otherwise provided in subdivision three:

(a) A prosecution for a class A felony, or rape in the first degree as defined in section 130.35 of the penal law, or a crime defined or formerly defined in section 130.50 of the penal law, or aggravated sexual abuse in the first degree as defined in section 130.70 of the penal law, or course of sexual conduct against a child in the first degree as defined in section 130.75 of the penal law, or incest in the first degree as defined in section 255.27 of the penal law may be commenced at any time;
(Eff.9/18/19,Ch.315,L.2019)

(a-1) A prosecution for rape in the second degree as defined in subdivision two of section 130.30 of the penal law, or criminal sexual act in the second degree as defined in subdivision two of section 130.45 of the penal law, or incest in the second degree as defined in section 255.26 of the penal law (where the crime committed is rape in the second degree as defined in subdivision two of section 130.30 of the penal law or criminal sexual act in the second degree as defined in subdivision two of section 130.45) must be commenced within twenty years after the commission thereof or within ten years from when the offense is first reported to law enforcement, whichever occurs earlier; *(Eff.9/18/19,Ch.315,L.2019)*

(a-2) A prosecution for rape in the third degree as defined in subdivision one or three of section 130.25 of the penal law, or criminal sexual act in the third degree as defined in subdivision one or three of section 130.40 of the penal law must be commenced within ten years after the commission thereof; *(Eff.9/18/19,Ch.315,L.2019)*

(b) A prosecution for any other felony must be commenced within five years after the commission thereof;

(c) A prosecution for a misdemeanor must be commenced within two years after the commission thereof;

(d) A prosecution for a petty offense must be commenced within one year after the commission thereof.

3. Notwithstanding the provisions of subdivision two, the periods of limitation for the commencement of criminal actions are extended as follows in the indicated circumstances:

(a) A prosecution for larceny committed by a person in violation of a fiduciary duty may be commenced within one year after the facts constituting such offense are discovered or, in the exercise of reasonable diligence, should have been discovered by the aggrieved party or by a person under a legal duty to represent him who is not himself implicated in the commission of the offense.

(b) A prosecution for any offense involving misconduct in public office by a public servant including, without limitation, an offense defined in article four hundred ninety-six of the penal law, may be commenced against a public servant, or any other person acting in concert with such public servant at any time during such public servant's service in such office or within five years after the termination of such service; provided however, that in no event shall the period of limitation be extended by more than five years beyond the period otherwise applicable under subdivision two of this section.

(c) A prosecution for any crime set forth in title twenty-seven or article seventy-one of the environmental conservation law may be commenced within four years after the facts constituting such crime are discovered or, in the exercise of reasonable diligence, should have been discovered by a public servant who has the responsibility to enforce the provisions of said title and article.

(d) A prosecution for any misdemeanor set forth in the tax law or chapter forty-six of the administrative code of the city of New York must be commenced within three years after the commission thereof.

(e) A prosecution for course of sexual conduct against a child in the second degree as defined in section 130.80 of the penal law may be commenced within five years of the commission of the most recent act of sexual conduct.

(f) For purposes of a prosecution involving a sexual offense as defined in article one hundred thirty of the penal law, other than a sexual offense delineated in paragraph (a) of subdivision two of this section, committed against a child less than eighteen years of age, incest in the first, second or third degree as defined in sections 255.27, 255.26 and 255.25 of the penal law committed against a child less than eighteen years of age, or use of a child in a sexual performance as defined in section 263.05 of the penal law, the period of limitation shall not begin to run until the child has reached the age of twenty-three or the offense is reported to a law enforcement agency or statewide central register of child abuse and maltreatment, whichever occurs earlier.   *(Eff.2/14/19,Ch.11,L.2019)*

(g) A prosecution for any felony defined in article four hundred ninety of the penal law must be commenced within eight years after the commission thereof provided, however, that in a prosecution for a felony defined in article four hundred ninety of the penal law, if the commission of such felony offense resulted in, or created a foreseeable risk of, death or serious physical injury to another person, the prosecution may be commenced at any time; provided, however, that nothing in this paragraph shall be deemed to shorten or otherwise lessen the period, defined in any other applicable law, in which a prosecution for a felony designated in this paragraph may be commenced.

4. In calculating the time limitation applicable to commencement of a criminal action, the following periods shall not be included:

(a) Any period following the commission of the offense during which (i) the defendant was continuously outside this state or (ii) the whereabouts of the defendant were continuously unknown and continuously unascertainable by the exercise of reasonable diligence. However, in no event shall the period of limitation be extended by more than five years beyond the period otherwise applicable under subdivision two.

(b) When a prosecution for an offense is lawfully commenced within the prescribed period of limitation therefor, and when an accusatory instrument upon which such prosecution is based is subsequently dismissed by an authorized court under directions or circumstances permitting the lodging of another charge for the same offense or an offense based on the same conduct, the period extending from the commencement of the thus defeated prosecution to the dismissal of the accusatory instrument does not constitute a part of the period of limitation applicable to commencement of prosecution by a new charge.

§30.20   Speedy trial; in general.

1. After a criminal action is commenced, the defendant is entitled to a speedy trial.

2. Insofar as is practicable, the trial of a criminal action must be given preference over civil cases; and the trial of a criminal action where the defendant has been committed to the custody of the sheriff during the pendency of the criminal action must be given preference over other criminal actions.

§30.30   Speedy trial; time limitations.

1. Except as otherwise provided in subdivision three of this section, a motion made pursuant to paragraph (e) of subdivision one of section 170.30 or paragraph (g) of subdivision one of section 210.20 of this chapter must be granted where the people are not ready for trial within:

(a) six months of the commencement of a criminal action wherein a defendant is accused of one or more offenses, at least one of which is a felony;

(b) ninety days of the commencement of a criminal action wherein a defendant is accused of one or more offenses, at least one of which is a misdemeanor punishable by a sentence of imprisonment of more than three months and none of which is a felony;

(c) sixty days of the commencement of a criminal action wherein the defendant is accused of one or more offenses, at least one of which is a misdemeanor punishable by a sentence of imprisonment of not more than three months and none of which is a crime punishable by a sentence of imprisonment of more than three months; or

(d) thirty days of the commencement of a criminal action wherein the defendant is accused of one or more offenses, at least one of which is a violation and none of which is a crime.

(e) for the purposes of this subdivision, the term offense shall include vehicle and traffic law infractions.

2. Except as provided in subdivision three of this section, where a defendant has been committed to the custody of the sheriff or the office of children and family services in a criminal action he or she must be released on bail or on his or her own recognizance, upon such conditions as may be just and reasonable, if the people are not ready for trial in that criminal action within:

(a) ninety days from the commencement of his or her commitment to the custody of the sheriff or the office of children and family services in a criminal action wherein the defendant is accused of one or more offenses, at least one of which is a felony;

(b) thirty days from the commencement of his or her commitment to the custody of the sheriff or the office of children and family services in a criminal action wherein the defendant is accused of one or more offenses, at least one of which is a misdemeanor punishable by a sentence of imprisonment of more than three months and none of which is a felony;

(c) fifteen days from the commencement of his or her commitment to the custody of the sheriff or the office of children and family services in a criminal action wherein the defendant is accused of one or more offenses, at least one of which is a misdemeanor punishable by a sentence of imprisonment of not more than three months and none of which is a crime punishable by a sentence of imprisonment of more than three months; or

(d) five days from the commencement of his or her commitment to the custody of the sheriff or the office of children and family services in a criminal action wherein the defendant is accused of one or more offenses, at least one of which is a violation and none of which is a crime.

(e) for the purposes of this subdivision, the term offense shall include vehicle and traffic law infractions.

3. (a) Subdivisions one and two of this section do not apply to a criminal action wherein the defendant is accused of an offense defined in sections 125.10, 125.15, 125.20, 125.25, 125.26 and 125.27 of the penal law.

(b) A motion made pursuant to subdivisions one or two of this section upon expiration of the specified period may be denied where the people are not ready for trial if the people were ready for trial prior to the expiration of the specified period and their present unreadiness is due to some exceptional fact or circumstance, including, but not limited to, the sudden unavailability of evidence material to the people's case, when the district attorney has exercised due diligence to obtain such evidence and there are reasonable grounds to believe that such evidence will become available in a reasonable period.

(c) A motion made pursuant to subdivision two of this section shall not:

(i) apply to any defendant who is serving a term of imprisonment for another offense;

(ii) require the release from custody of any defendant who is also being held in custody pending trial of another criminal charge as to which the applicable period has not yet elapsed;

(iii) prevent the redetention of or otherwise apply to any defendant who, after being released from custody pursuant to this section or otherwise, is charged with another crime or violates the conditions on which he has been released, by failing to appear at a judicial proceeding at which his presence is required or otherwise.

4. In computing the time within which the people must be ready for trial pursuant to subdivisions one and two of this section, the following periods must be excluded:

(a) a reasonable period of delay resulting from other proceedings concerning the defendant, including but not limited to: proceedings for the determination of competency and the period during which defendant is incompetent to stand trial; demand to produce; request for a bill of particulars; pre-trial motions; appeals; trial of other charges; and the period during which such matters are under consideration by the court; or

(b) the period of delay resulting from a continuance granted by the court at the request of, or with the consent of, the defendant or his or her counsel.

The court may grant such a continuance only if it is satisfied that postponement is in the interest of justice, taking into account the public interest in the prompt dispositions of criminal charges. A defendant without counsel must not be deemed to have consented to a continuance unless he or she has been advised by the court of his or her rights under these rules and the effect of his consent, which must be done on the record in open court; or

(c) (i) the period of delay resulting from the absence or unavailability of the defendant. A defendant must be considered absent whenever his location is unknown and he is attempting to avoid apprehension or prosecution, or his location cannot be determined by due diligence. A defendant must be considered unavailable whenever his location is known but his presence for trial cannot be obtained by due diligence; or

(ii) where the defendant has either escaped from custody or has failed to appear when required after having previously been released on bail or on his own recognizance, and provided the defendant is not in custody on another matter, the period extending from the day the court issues a bench warrant pursuant to section 530.70 of this chapter because of the defendant's failure to appear in court when required, to the day the defendant subsequently appears in the court pursuant to a bench warrant or voluntarily or otherwise; or

(d) a reasonable period of delay when the defendant is joined for trial with a co-defendant as to whom the time for trial pursuant to this section has not run and good cause is not shown for granting a severance; or

(e) the period of delay resulting from detention of the defendant in another jurisdiction provided the district attorney is aware of such detention and has been diligent and has made reasonable efforts to obtain the presence of the defendant for trial; or

(f) the period during which the defendant is without counsel through no fault of the court; except when the defendant is proceeding as his own attorney with the permission of the court; or

(g) other periods of delay occasioned by exceptional circumstances, including but not limited to, the period of delay resulting from a continuance granted at the request of a district attorney if (i) the continuance is granted because of the unavailability of evidence material to the people's case, when the district attorney has exercised due diligence to obtain such evidence and there are reasonable grounds to believe that such evidence will become available in a reasonable period; or (ii) the continuance is granted to allow the district attorney additional time to prepare the people's case and additional time is justified by the exceptional circumstances of the case. Any such exclusion when a statement of unreadiness has followed a statement of readiness made by the people must be evaluated by the court after inquiry on the record as to the reasons for the people's unreadiness and shall only be approved upon a showing of sufficient supporting facts; or

(h) the period during which an action has been adjourned in contemplation of dismissal pursuant to sections 170.55, 170.56 and 215.10 of this chapter; or

(i) the period prior to the defendant's actual appearance for arraignment in a situation in which the defendant has been directed to appear by the district attorney pursuant to subdivision three of section 120.20 or subdivision three of section 210.10 of this chapter; or

(j) the period during which a family offense is before a family court until such time as an accusatory instrument or indictment is filed against the defendant alleging a crime constituting a family offense, as such term is defined in section 530.11 of this chapter.

5. Whenever pursuant to this section a prosecutor states or otherwise provides notice that the people are ready for trial, the court shall make inquiry on the record as to their actual readiness. If, after conducting its inquiry, the court determines that the people are not ready to proceed to trial, the prosecutor's statement or notice of readiness shall not be valid for purposes of this section. Any statement of trial readiness must be accompanied or preceded by a certification of good faith compliance with the disclosure requirements of section 245.20 of this chapter and the defense shall be afforded an opportunity to be heard on the record as to whether the disclosure requirements have been met. This subdivision shall not apply to cases where the defense has waived disclosure requirements.

5-a. Upon a local criminal court accusatory instrument, a statement of readiness shall not be valid unless the prosecuting attorney certifies that all counts charged in the accusatory instrument meet the requirements of sections 100.15 and 100.40 of this chapter and those counts not meeting the requirements of sections 100.15 and 100.40 of this chapter have been dismissed.

6. An order finally denying a motion to dismiss pursuant to subdivision one of this section shall be reviewable upon an appeal from an ensuing judgment of conviction notwithstanding the fact that such judgment is entered upon a plea of guilty.

7. For purposes of this section, (a) where the defendant is to be tried following the withdrawal of the plea of guilty or is to be retried following a mistrial, an order for a new trial or an appeal or collateral attack, the criminal action and the commitment to the custody of the sheriff or the office of children and family services, if any, must be deemed to have commenced on the date the withdrawal of the plea of guilty or the date the order occasioning a retrial becomes final;

(b) where a defendant has been served with an appearance ticket, the criminal action must be deemed to have commenced on the date the defendant first appears in a local criminal court in response to the ticket;

(c) where a criminal action is commenced by the filing of a felony complaint, and thereafter, in the course of the same criminal action either the felony complaint is replaced with or converted to an information, prosecutor's information or misdemeanor complaint pursuant to article one hundred eighty of this chapter or a prosecutor's information is filed pursuant to section 190.70 of this chapter, the period applicable for the purposes of subdivision one must be the period applicable to the charges in the new accusatory instrument, calculated from the date of the filing of such new accusatory instrument; provided, however, that when the aggregate of such period and the period of time, excluding the periods provided in subdivision four, already elapsed from the date of the filing of the felony complaint to the date of the filing of the new accusatory instrument exceeds six months, the period applicable to the charges in the felony complaint must remain applicable and continue as if the new accusatory instrument had not been filed;

(d) where a criminal action is commenced by the filing of a felony complaint, and thereafter, in the course of the same criminal action either the felony complaint is replaced with or converted to an information, prosecutor's information or misdemeanor complaint pursuant to article one hundred eighty of this chapter or a prosecutor's information is filed pursuant to section 190.70 of this chapter, the period applicable for the purposes of subdivision two of this section must be the period applicable to the charges in the new accusatory instrument, calculated from the date of the filing of such new accusatory instrument; provided, however, that when the aggregate of such period and the period of time, excluding the periods provided in subdivision four of this section, already elapsed from the date of the filing of the felony complaint to the date of the filing of the new accusatory instrument exceeds ninety days, the period applicable to the charges in the felony complaint must remain applicable and continue as if the new accusatory instrument had not been filed.

(e) where a count of an indictment is reduced to charge only a misdemeanor or petty offense and a reduced indictment or a prosecutor's information is filed pursuant to subdivisions one-a and six of section 210.20 of this chapter, the period applicable for the purposes of subdivision one of this section must be the period applicable to the charges in the new accusatory instrument, calculated from the date of the filing of such new accusatory instrument; provided, however, that when the aggregate of such period and the period of time, excluding the periods provided in subdivision four of this section, already elapsed from the date of the filing of the indictment to the date of the filing of the new accusatory instrument exceeds six months, the period applicable to the charges in the indictment must remain applicable and continue as if the new accusatory instrument had not been filed;

(f) where a count of an indictment is reduced to charge only a misdemeanor or petty offense and a reduced indictment or a prosecutor's information is filed pursuant to subdivisions one-a and six of section 210.20 of this chapter, the period applicable for the purposes of subdivision two of this section must be the period applicable to the charges in the new accusatory instrument, calculated from the date of the filing of such new accusatory instrument; provided, however, that when the aggregate of such period and the period of time, excluding the periods provided in subdivision four of this section, already elapsed from the date of the filing of the indictment to the date of the filing of the new accusatory instrument exceeds ninety days, the period applicable to the charges in the indictment must remain applicable and continue as if the new accusatory instrument had not been filed.

8. The procedural rules prescribed in subdivisions one through seven of section 210.45 of this chapter with respect to a motion to dismiss an indictment are not applicable to a motion made pursuant to subdivision two of this section. If, upon oral argument, a time period is in dispute, the court must promptly conduct a hearing in which the people must prove that the time period is excludable. *(Eff. 1/1/20, Ch.59, L.2019)*

ARTICLE 40 - EXEMPTION FROM PROSECUTION
BY REASON OF PREVIOUS PROSECUTION

Section
40.10   Previous prosecution; definitions of terms.
40.20   Previous prosecution; when a bar to second prosecution.
40.30   Previous prosecution; what constitutes.
40.40   Separate prosecution of jointly prosecutable offenses; when barred.
40.50   Previous prosecution; enterprise corruption.
40.51   Previous prosecution; presidential reprieve, pardon or other form of clemency.

§40.10   Previous prosecution; definitions of terms.
The following definitions are applicable to this article:
1. "Offense." An "offense" is committed whenever any conduct is performed which violates a statutory provision defining an offense; and when the same conduct or criminal transaction violates two or more such statutory provisions each such violation constitutes a separate and distinct offense. The same conduct or criminal transaction also establishes separate and distinct offenses when, though violating only one statutory provision, it results in death, injury, loss or other consequences to two or more victims, and such result is an element of the offense as defined. In such case, as many offenses are committed as there are victims.
2. "Criminal transaction" means conduct which establishes at least one offense, and which is comprised of two or more or a group of acts either (a) so closely related and connected in point of time and circumstance of commission as to constitute a single criminal incident, or (b) so closely related in criminal purpose or objective as to constitute elements or integral parts of a single criminal venture.

§40.20   Previous prosecution; when a bar to second prosecution.
1. A person may not be twice prosecuted for the same offense.
2. A person may not be separately prosecuted for two offenses based upon the same act or criminal transaction unless:
(a) The offenses as defined have substantially different elements and the acts establishing one offense are in the main clearly distinguishable from those establishing the other; or
(b) Each of the offenses as defined contains an element which is not an element of the other, and the statutory provisions defining such offenses are designed to prevent very different kinds of harm or evil; or
(c) One of such offenses consists of criminal possession of contraband matter and the other offense is one involving the use of such contraband matter, other than a sale thereof; or
(d) One of the offenses is assault or some other offense resulting in physical injury to a person, and the other offense is one of homicide based upon the death of such person from the same physical injury, and such death occurs after a prosecution for the assault or other non-homicide offense; or
(e) Each offense involves death, injury, loss or other consequence to a different victim; or
(f) One of the offenses consists of a violation of a statutory provision of another jurisdiction, which offense has been prosecuted in such other jurisdiction and has there been terminated by a court order expressly founded upon insufficiency of evidence to establish some element of such offense which is not an element of the other offense, defined by the laws of this state; or

(g) The present prosecution is for a consummated result offense, as defined in subdivision three of section 20.10, which occurred in this state and the offense was the result of a conspiracy, facilitation or solicitation prosecuted in another state.

(h) One of such offenses is enterprise corruption in violation of section 460.20 of the penal law, racketeering in violation of federal law or any comparable offense pursuant to the law of another state and a separate or subsequent prosecution is not barred by section 40.50 of this article.

(i) One of the offenses consists of a violation of 18 U.S.C. 371, where the object of the conspiracy is to attempt in any manner to evade or defeat any federal income tax or the payment thereof, or a violation of 26 U.S.C. 7201, 26 U.S.C. 7202, 26 U.S.C. 7203, 26 U.S.C. 7204, 26 U.S.C. 7205, 26 U.S.C. 7206 or 26 U.S.C. 7212(A), where the purpose is to evade or defeat any federal income tax or the payment thereof, and the other offense is committed for the purpose of evading or defeating any New York state or New York city income taxes and is defined in article one hundred fifty-five of the penal law, article one hundred seventy of the penal law, article one hundred seventy-five of the penal law, article thirty-seven of the tax law or chapter forty of title eleven of the administrative code of the city of New York.

§40.30   Previous prosecution; what constitutes.

1. Except as otherwise provided in this section, a person "is prosecuted" for an offense, within the meaning of section 40.20, when he is charged therewith by an accusatory instrument filed in a court of this state or of any jurisdiction within the United States, and when the action either:

(a) Terminates in a conviction upon a plea of guilty; or

(b) Proceeds to the trial stage and a jury has been impaneled and sworn or, in the case of a trial by the court without a jury, a witness is sworn.

2. Despite the occurrence of proceedings specified in subdivision one, a person is not deemed to have been prosecuted for an offense, within the meaning of section 40.20, when:

(a) Such prosecution occurred in a court which lacked jurisdiction over the defendant or the offense; or

(b) Such prosecution was for a lesser offense than could have been charged under the facts of the case, and the prosecution was procured by the defendant, without the knowledge of the appropriate prosecutor, for the purpose of avoiding prosecution for a greater offense.

3. Despite the occurrence of proceedings specified in subdivision one, if such proceedings are subsequently nullified by a court order which restores the action to its pre-pleading status or which directs a new trial of the same accusatory instrument, the nullified proceedings do not bar further prosecution of such offense under the same accusatory instrument.

4. Despite the occurrence of proceedings specified in subdivision one, if such proceedings are subsequently nullified by a court order which dismisses the accusatory instrument but authorizes the people to obtain a new accusatory instrument charging the same offense or an offense based upon the same conduct, the nullified proceedings do not bar further prosecution of such offense under any new accusatory instrument obtained pursuant to such court order or authorization.

§40.40   Separate prosecution of jointly prosecutable offenses; when barred.

1. Where two or more offenses are joinable in a single accusatory instrument against a person by reason of being based upon the same criminal transaction, pursuant to paragraph (a) of subdivision two of section 200.20, such person may not, under circumstances prescribed in this section, be separately prosecuted for such offenses even though such separate prosecutions are not otherwise barred by any other section of this article.

2. When (a) one of two or more joinable offenses of the kind specified in subdivision one is charged in an accusatory instrument, and (b) another is not charged therein, or in any other accusatory instrument filed in the same court, despite possession by the people of evidence legally sufficient to support a conviction of the defendant for such uncharged offense, and (c) either a trial of the existing accusatory instrument is commenced or the action thereon is disposed of by a plea of guilty, any subsequent prosecution for the uncharged offense is thereby barred.

3. When (a) two or more of such offenses are charged in separate accusatory instruments filed in the same court, and (b) an application by the defendant for consolidation thereof for trial purposes, pursuant to subdivision five of section 200.20 or section 100.45, is improperly denied, the commencement of a trial of one such accusatory instrument bars any subsequent prosecution upon any of the other accusatory instruments with respect to any such offense.

§40.50   Previous prosecution; enterprise corruption.

1. The following definitions are applicable to this section:

(a) A criminal act or offense is "specifically included" when a count of an accusatory instrument charging a person with enterprise corruption alleges a pattern of criminal activity and the act or offense is alleged to be a criminal act within such pattern.

(b) A criminal act is "a part of" a pattern of criminal activity alleged in a count of enterprise corruption when it is committed prior to commencement of the criminal action in which enterprise corruption is charged and was committed in furtherance of the same common scheme or plan or with intent to participate in or further the affairs of the same criminal enterprise to which the crimes specifically included in the pattern are connected.

(c) A person "is prosecuted" for an offense when he is prosecuted for it within the meaning of section 40.30 of this article or when an indictment or a count of an indictment charging that offense is dismissed pursuant to section 210.20 of this chapter without authorization to submit the charge to the same or another grand jury, or the indictment or the count of the indictment charging that offense is dismissed following the granting of a motion to suppress pursuant to article 710 of this chapter, unless an appeal from the order granting the motion to dismiss or suppress is pending.

(d) An offense was "not prosecutable" in an accusatory instrument in which a person was charged with enterprise corruption when there was no geographical jurisdiction of that offense in the county where the accusatory instrument was filed, or when the offense was prosecutable in the county and was not barred from prosecution by section 40.20 or 40.40 of this article or by any other provision of law but the prosecutor filing the accusatory instrument was not empowered by law to prosecute the offense.

2. A person who has been previously prosecuted for an offense may not be subsequently prosecuted for enterprise corruption based upon a pattern of criminal activity in which that prior offense, or another offense based upon the same act or criminal transaction, is specifically included unless:

(a) he was convicted of that prior offense; and

(b) the subsequent pattern of criminal activity in which he participated includes at least one criminal act for which he was not previously prosecuted, which was a felony, and which occurred after that prior conviction.

3. A person who has been previously prosecuted for enterprise corruption may not be subsequently prosecuted for an offense specifically included in the pattern of criminal activity upon which it was based, or another offense based upon the same act or criminal transaction, unless the offense is a class A felony and was not prosecutable in the accusatory instrument in which the person was charged with enterprise corruption.

4. A person may not be separately prosecuted for enterprise corruption and for an offense specifically included in the pattern of criminal activity upon which it is based or another offense based upon the same act or transaction, unless the offense is a class A felony and is not prosecutable in the accusatory instrument in which the person is charged with enterprise corruption.

5. A person who has been previously prosecuted for enterprise corruption may not be subsequently prosecuted for an offense which, while not specifically included in the pattern of criminal activity on which the prior charge of enterprise corruption was based, was nonetheless a part of that pattern, unless the offense was a class A or B felony and either the offense was not prosecutable in the accusatory instrument in which the person was charged with enterprise corruption or the people show, by clear and convincing evidence, that the prosecutor did not possess evidence legally sufficient to support a conviction of that offense at the time of the earlier prosecution and evidence of that offense was not presented as part of the case in chief in the earlier prosecution.

6. A person who has been previously prosecuted for enterprise corruption may not be subsequently prosecuted for enterprise corruption based upon a pattern of criminal activity that specifically includes a criminal act that was also specifically included in the pattern upon which the prior charge of enterprise corruption was based.

7. A person may not be separately prosecuted for enterprise corruption in two accusatory instruments based upon a pattern of criminal activity, alleged in either instrument, that specifically includes a criminal act that is also specifically included in the pattern upon which the other charge of enterprise corruption is based.

8. When a person is charged in an accusatory instrument with both one or more counts of enterprise corruption and with another offense or offenses specifically included in or otherwise a part of the pattern or patterns of criminal activity upon which the charge or charges of enterprise corruption is or are based, and the court orders that any of the counts be tried separately pursuant to subdivision one of section 200.40 of this chapter, this section shall not apply and subsequent prosecution of the remaining counts or offenses shall not be barred.

9. A person who has been previously prosecuted for racketeering pursuant to federal law, or any comparable offense pursuant to the law of another state may not be subsequently prosecuted for enterprise corruption based upon a pattern of criminal activity that specifically includes a criminal act that was also specifically included in the pattern of racketeering activity upon which the prior charge of racketeering was based provided, however, that this section shall not be construed to prohibit the subsequent prosecution of any other offense specifically included in or otherwise a part of a pattern of racketeering activity alleged in any such prior prosecution for racketeering or other comparable offense.

§40.51   Previous prosecution: presidential reprieve, pardon or other form of clemency.

When a person has been granted a reprieve, pardon or other form of clemency for an offense pursuant to the authority granted in section two of article two of the United States constitution, a separate or subsequent prosecution of an offense is not barred under this article when the people demonstrate, by clear and convincing evidence, that:

1. (a) such person served in or was employed by the executive branch of the government of the United States on the executive staff of the president, in the executive office of the president, or in an acting or confirmed capacity in a position subject to confirmation by the United States senate, at a time when the president granting such reprieve, pardon or other form of clemency served as president or vice-president of the United States; or (b) such person was directly or indirectly employed by, or acted as an agent of, the election, transition or re-election campaign of the president granting such reprieve, pardon or other form of clemency or any for-profit or not-for-profit entity owned or controlled by the president granting such reprieve, pardon or other form of clemency; or

2. such person was, at the time the president granted such reprieve, pardon or other form of clemency, related by consanguinity or affinity within the sixth degree to the president granting such reprieve, pardon or other form of clemency; or

3. such person bears accessorial liability, as defined in section 20.00 of the penal law, or conspiratorial liability, within the meaning of article one hundred five of the penal law, for such offense with one or more persons described in subdivision one or two of this section; or

4. the president who granted such reprieve, pardon or other form of clemency to such person (a) was thereby aided in avoiding potential prosecution or conviction; (b) knowingly obtained a benefit from such offense; or (c) knowingly obtained a tangible, material benefit from or on behalf of such person; or

5. such person possessed or possesses information material to the determination of any criminal or civil investigation, enforcement action or prosecution of the president granting such reprieve, pardon or other form of clemency, or of one or more persons described in subdivision one, two or three of this section.   *(Eff.10/16/19,Ch.374,L.2019)*

ARTICLE 50 - COMPULSION OF EVIDENCE BY OFFER OF IMMUNITY

Section

50.10 Compulsion of evidence by offer of immunity; definitions of terms.

50.20 Compulsion of evidence by offer of immunity.

50.30 Authority to confer immunity in criminal proceedings; court a competent authority.

§50.10 Compulsion of evidence by offer of immunity; definitions of terms.
The following definitions are applicable to this article:

1. "Immunity." A person who has been a witness in a legal proceeding, and who cannot, except as otherwise provided in this subdivision, be convicted of any offense or subjected to any penalty or forfeiture for or on account of any transaction, matter or thing concerning which he gave evidence therein, possesses "immunity" from any such conviction, penalty or forfeiture. A person who possesses such immunity may nevertheless be convicted of perjury as a result of having given false testimony in such legal proceeding, and may be convicted of or adjudged in contempt as a result of having contumaciously refused to give evidence therein.

2. "Legal proceeding" means a proceeding in or before any court or grand jury, or before any body, agency or person authorized by law to conduct the same and to administer the oath or to cause it to be administered.

3. "Give evidence" means to testify or produce physical evidence.

§50.20 Compulsion of evidence by offer of immunity.
1. Any witness in a legal proceeding, other than a grand jury proceeding, may refuse to give evidence requested of him on the ground that it may tend to incriminate him and he may not, except as provided in subdivision two, be compelled to give such evidence.

2. Such a witness may be compelled to give evidence in such a proceeding notwithstanding an assertion of his privilege against self-incrimination if:

(a) The proceeding is one in which, by express provision of statute, a person conducting or connected therewith is declared a competent authority to confer immunity upon witnesses therein; and

(b) Such competent authority (i) orders such witness to give the requested evidence notwithstanding his assertion of his privilege against self-incrimination, and (ii) advises him that upon so doing he will receive immunity.

3. A witness who is ordered to give evidence pursuant to subdivision two and who complies with such order receives immunity. Such witness is not deprived of such immunity because such competent authority did not comply with statutory provisions requiring notice to a specified public servant of intention to confer immunity.

4. A witness who, without asserting his privilege against self-incrimination, gives evidence in a legal proceeding other than a grand jury proceeding does not receive immunity.

5. The rules governing the circumstances in which witnesses may be compelled to give evidence and in which they receive immunity therefor in a grand jury proceeding are prescribed in section 190.40.

§50.30   Authority to confer immunity in criminal proceedings; court a competent authority.

In any criminal proceeding, other than a grand jury proceeding, the court is a competent authority to confer immunity in accordance with the provisions of section 50.20 but only when expressly requested by the district attorney to do so.

TITLE D - RULES OF EVIDENCE, STANDARDS OF PROOF AND RELATED MATTERS

ARTICLE 60 - RULES OF EVIDENCE AND RELATED MATTERS

Section
60.10 Rules of evidence; in general.
60.15 Rules of evidence; what witnesses may be called.
60.20 Rules of evidence; testimonial capacity; evidence given by children.
60.22 Rules of evidence; corroboration of accomplice testimony.
60.25 Rules of evidence; identification by means of previous recognition, in absence of present identification.
60.30 Rules of evidence; identification by means of previous recognition, in addition to present identification.
60.35 Rules of evidence; impeachment of own witness by proof of prior contradictory statement.
60.40 Rules of evidence; proof of previous conviction; when allowed.
60.42 Rules of evidence; admissibility of evidence of victim's sexual conduct in sex offense cases.
60.43 Rules of evidence; admissibility of evidence of victim's sexual conduct in non-sex offense cases.
60.44 Use of anatomically correct dolls.
60.45 Rules of evidence; admissibility of statements of defendants.
60.46 Rules of evidence, family offense proceedings in family court.
60.47 Possession of condoms; receipt into evidence.
60.48 Rules of evidence; admissibility of evidence of victim's manner of dress in sex offense cases.
60.49 Possession of opioid antagonists; receipt into evidence.
60.50 Rules of evidence; statements of defendants; corroboration.
60.55 Rules of evidence; psychiatric testimony in certain cases.
60.60 Rules of evidence; certificates concerning judgments of conviction and fingerprints.
60.70 Rules of evidence; dangerous drugs destroyed pursuant to court order.
60.75 Rules of evidence; chemical test evidence.
60.76 Rules of evidence; rape crisis counselor evidence in certain cases.

§60.10   Rules of evidence; in general.
Unless otherwise provided by statute or by judicially established rules of evidence applicable to criminal cases, the rules of evidence applicable to civil cases are, where appropriate, also applicable to criminal proceedings.

§60.15   Rules of evidence; what witnesses may be called.
1. Unless otherwise expressly provided, in any criminal proceeding involving a defendant in which evidence is or may be received, both the people and the defendant may as a matter of right call and examine witnesses, and each party may cross-examine every witness called by the other party.
2. A defendant may testify in his own behalf, but his failure to do so is not a factor from which any inference unfavorable to him may be drawn.

§60.20   Rules of evidence; testimonial capacity; evidence given by children.
1. Any person may be a witness in a criminal proceeding unless the court finds that, by reason of infancy or mental disease or defect, he does not possess sufficient intelligence or capacity to justify the reception of his evidence.
2. Every witness more than nine years old may testify only under oath unless the court is satisfied that such witness cannot, as a result of mental disease or defect, understand the nature of an oath. A witness less than nine years old may not testify under oath unless the court is satisfied that he or she understands the nature of an oath. If under either of the above provisions, a witness is deemed to be ineligible to testify under oath, the

witness may nevertheless be permitted to give unsworn evidence if the court is satisfied that the witness possesses sufficient intelligence and capacity to justify the reception thereof. A witness understands the nature of an oath if he or she appreciates the difference between truth and falsehood, the necessity for telling the truth, and the fact that a witness who testifies falsely may be punished.

3. A defendant may not be convicted of an offense solely upon unsworn evidence given pursuant to subdivision two.

§60.22 Rules of evidence; corroboration of accomplice testimony.

1. A defendant may not be convicted of any offense upon the testimony of an accomplice unsupported by corroborative evidence tending to connect the defendant with the commission of such offense.

2. An "accomplice" means a witness in a criminal action who, according to evidence adduced in such action, may reasonably be considered to have participated in:

(a) The offense charged; or

(b) An offense based upon the same or some of the same facts or conduct which constitute the offense charged.

3. A witness who is an accomplice as defined in subdivision two is no less such because a prosecution or conviction of himself would be barred or precluded by some defense or exemption, such as infancy, immunity or previous prosecution, amounting to a collateral impediment to such a prosecution or conviction, not affecting the conclusion that such witness engaged in the conduct constituting the offense with the mental state required for the commission thereof.

§60.25 Rules of evidence; identification by means of previous recognition, in absence of present identification.

1. In any criminal proceeding in which the defendant's commission of an offense is in issue, testimony as provided in subdivision two may be given by a witness when:

(a) Such witness testifies that:

(i) He or she observed the person claimed by the people to be the defendant either at the time and place of the commission of the offense or upon some other occasion relevant to the case; and

(ii) On a subsequent occasion he or she observed, under circumstances consistent with such rights as an accused person may derive under the constitution of this state or of the United States, a person or, where the observation is made pursuant to a blind or blinded procedure as defined in paragraph (c) of this subdivision, a pictorial, photographic, electronic, filmed or video recorded reproduction of a person whom he or she recognized as the same person whom he or she had observed on the first or incriminating occasion; and

(iii) He or she is unable at the proceeding to state, on the basis of present recollection, whether or not the defendant is the person in question; and

(b) It is established that the defendant is in fact the person whom the witness observed and recognized or whose pictorial, photographic, electronic, filmed or video recorded reproduction the witness observed and recognized on the second occasion. Such fact may be established by testimony of another person or persons to whom the witness promptly declared his or her recognition on such occasion and by such pictorial, photographic, electronic, filmed or video recorded reproduction.

(c) For purposes of this section, a "blind or blinded procedure" is one in which the witness identifies a person in an array of pictorial, photographic, electronic, filmed or video recorded reproductions under circumstances where, at the time the identification is made, the public servant administering such procedure: (i) does not know which person in the array is the suspect, or (ii) does not know where the suspect is in the array viewed by the witness. The failure of a public servant to follow such a procedure shall be assessed solely for purposes of this article and shall result in the preclusion of testimony regarding the identification procedure as evidence in chief, but shall not constitute a legal basis to suppress evidence made pursuant to subdivision six of section 710.20 of this chapter. This article neither limits nor expands subdivision six of section 710.20 of this chapter.

2. Under circumstances prescribed in subdivision one of this section, such witness may testify at the criminal proceeding that the person whom he or she observed and recognized or whose pictorial, photographic, electronic, filmed or video recorded reproduction he or she observed and recognized on the second occasion is the same person whom he or she observed on the first or incriminating occasion. Such testimony, together with the evidence that the defendant is in fact the person whom the witness observed and recognized or whose pictorial, photographic, electronic, filmed or video recorded reproduction he or she observed and recognized on the second occasion, constitutes evidence in chief.

§60.30   Rules of evidence; identification by means of previous recognition, in addition to present identification.

In any criminal proceeding in which the defendant's commission of an offense is in issue, a witness who testifies that (a) he or she observed the person claimed by the people to be the defendant either at the time and place of the commission of the offense or upon some other occasion relevant to the case, and (b) on the basis of present recollection, the defendant is the person in question and (c) on a subsequent occasion he or she observed the defendant, or where the observation is made pursuant to a blind or blinded procedure, as defined in paragraph (c) of subdivision one of section 60.25 of this article, a pictorial, photographic, electronic, filmed or video recorded reproduction of the defendant, under circumstances consistent with such rights as an accused person may derive under the constitution of this state or of the United States, and then also recognized him or her or the pictorial, photographic, electronic, filmed or video recorded reproduction of him or her as the same person whom he or she had observed on the first or incriminating occasion, may, in addition to making an identification of the defendant at the criminal proceeding on the basis of present recollection as the person whom he or she observed on the first or incriminating occasion, also describe his or her previous recognition of the defendant and testify that the person whom he or she observed or whose pictorial, photographic, electronic, filmed or video recorded reproduction he or she observed on such second occasion is the same person whom he or she had observed on the first or incriminating occasion. Such testimony and such pictorial, photographic, electronic, filmed or video recorded reproduction constitutes evidence in chief.

§60.35   Rules of evidence; impeachment of own witness by proof of prior contradictory statement.

1. When, upon examination by the party who called him, a witness in a criminal proceeding gives testimony upon a material issue of the case which tends to disprove the position of such party, such party may introduce

evidence that such witness has previously made either a written statement signed by him or an oral statement under oath contradictory to such testimony.

2. Evidence concerning a prior contradictory statement introduced pursuant to subdivision one may be received only for the purpose of impeaching the credibility of the witness with respect to his testimony upon the subject, and does not constitute evidence in chief. Upon receiving such evidence at a jury trial, the court must so instruct the jury.

3. When a witness has made a prior signed or sworn statement contradictory to his testimony in a criminal proceeding upon a material issue of the case, but his testimony does not tend to disprove the position of the party who called him and elicited such testimony, evidence that the witness made such prior statement is not admissible, and such party may not use such prior statement for the purpose of refreshing the recollection of the witness in a manner that discloses its contents to the trier of the facts.

§60.40   Rules of evidence; proof of previous conviction; when allowed.

1. If in the course of a criminal proceeding, any witness, including a defendant, is properly asked whether he was previously convicted of a specified offense and answers in the negative or in an equivocal manner, the party adverse to the one who called him may independently prove such conviction. If in response to proper inquiry whether he has ever been convicted of any offense the witness answers in the negative or in an equivocal manner, the adverse party may independently prove any previous conviction of the witness.

2. If a defendant in a criminal proceeding, through the testimony of a witness called by him, offers evidence of his good character, the people may independently prove any previous conviction of the defendant for an offense the commission of which would tend to negate any character trait or quality attributed to the defendant in such witness' testimony.

3. Subject to the limitations prescribed in section 200.60, the people may prove that a defendant has been previously convicted of an offense when the fact of such previous conviction constitutes an element of the offense charged, or proof thereof is otherwise essential to the establishment of a legally sufficient case.

§60.42   Rules of evidence; admissibility of evidence of victim's sexual conduct in sex offense cases.

Evidence of a victim's sexual conduct shall not be admissible in a prosecution for an offense or an attempt to commit an offense defined in article one hundred thirty or in section 230.34 of the penal law unless such evidence: *(Eff.4/12/19,Ch.55,L.2019)*

1. proves or tends to prove specific instances of the victim's prior sexual conduct with the accused; or

2. proves or tends to prove that the victim has been convicted of an offense under section 230.00 of the penal law within three years prior to the sex offense which is the subject of the prosecution; or

3. rebuts evidence introduced by the people of the victim's failure to engage in sexual intercourse, oral sexual conduct, anal sexual conduct or sexual contact during a given period of time; or

4. rebuts evidence introduced by the people which proves or tends to prove that the accused is the cause of pregnancy or disease of the victim, or the source of semen found in the victim; or

5. is determined by the court after an offer of proof by the accused outside the hearing of the jury, or such hearing as the court may require, and a

statement by the court of its findings of fact essential to its determination, to be relevant and admissible in the interests of justice.

§60.43   Rules of evidence; admissibility of evidence of victim's sexual conduct in non-sex offense cases.

Evidence of the victim's sexual conduct, including the past sexual conduct of a deceased victim, may not be admitted in a prosecution for any offense, attempt to commit an offense or conspiracy to commit an offense defined in the penal law unless such evidence is determined by the court to be relevant and admissible in the interests of justice after an offer of proof by the proponent of such evidence outside the hearing of the jury, or such hearing as the court may require, and a statement by the court of its findings of fact essential to its determination.

§60.44   Use of anatomically correct dolls.

Any person who is less than sixteen years old may in the discretion of the court and where helpful and appropriate, use an anatomically correct doll in testifying in a criminal proceeding based upon conduct prohibited by article one hundred thirty, article two hundred sixty or section 255.25, 255.26 or 255.27 of the penal law.

§60.45   Rules of evidence; admissibility of statements of defendants.

1. Evidence of a written or oral confession, admission, or other statement made by a defendant with respect to his participation or lack of participation in the offense charged, may not be received in evidence against him in a criminal proceeding if such statement was involuntarily made.

2. A confession, admission or other statement is "involuntarily made" by a defendant when it is obtained from him:

(a) By any person by the use or threatened use of physical force upon the defendant or another person, or by means of any other improper conduct or undue pressure which impaired the defendant's physical or mental condition to the extent of undermining his ability to make a choice whether or not to make a statement; or

(b) By a public servant engaged in law enforcement activity or by a person then acting under his direction or in cooperation with him:

(i) by means of any promise or statement of fact, which promise or statement creates a substantial risk that the defendant might falsely incriminate himself; or

(ii) in violation of such rights as the defendant may derive from the constitution of this state or of the United States.

3. (a) Where a person is subject to custodial interrogation by a public servant at a detention facility, the entire custodial interrogation, including the giving of any required advice of the rights of the individual being questioned, and the waiver of any rights by the individual, shall be recorded by an appropriate video recording device if the interrogation involves a class A-1 felony, except one defined in article two hundred twenty of the penal law; felony offenses defined in section 130.95 and 130.96 of the penal law; or a felony offense defined in article one hundred twenty-five or one hundred

thirty of such law that is defined as a class B violent felony offense in section 70.02 of the penal law. For purposes of this paragraph, the term "detention facility" shall mean a police station, correctional facility, holding facility for prisoners, prosecutor's office or other facility where persons are held in detention in connection with criminal charges that have been or may be filed against them.

(b) No confession, admission or other statement shall be subject to a motion to suppress pursuant to subdivision three of section 710.20 of this chapter based solely upon the failure to video record such interrogation in a detention facility as defined in paragraph (a) of this subdivision. However, where the people offer into evidence a confession, admission or other statement made by a person in custody with respect to his or her participation or lack of participation in an offense specified in paragraph (a) of this subdivision, that has not been video recorded, the court shall consider the failure to record as a factor, but not as the sole factor, in accordance with paragraph (c) of this subdivision in determining whether such confession, admission or other statement shall be admissible.

(c) Notwithstanding the requirement of paragraph (a) of this subdivision, upon a showing of good cause by the prosecutor, the custodial interrogation need not be recorded. Good cause shall include, but not be limited to:

(i) If electronic recording equipment malfunctions.

(ii) If electronic recording equipment is not available because it was otherwise being used.

(iii) If statements are made in response to questions that are routinely asked during arrest processing.

(iv) If the statement is spontaneously made by the suspect and not in response to police questioning.

(v) If the statement is made during an interrogation that is conducted when the interviewer is unaware that a qualifying offense has occurred.

(vi) If the statement is made at a location other than the "interview room" because the suspect cannot be brought to such room, e.g., the suspect is in a hospital or the suspect is out of state and that state is not governed by a law requiring the recordation of an interrogation.

(vii) If the statement is made after a suspect has refused to participate in the interrogation if it is recorded, and appropriate effort to document such refusal is made.

(viii) If such statement is not recorded as a result of an inadvertent error or oversight, not the result of any intentional conduct by law enforcement personnel.

(ix) If it is law enforcement's reasonable belief that such recording would jeopardize the safety of any person or reveal the identity of a confidential informant.

(x) If such statement is made at a location not equipped with a video recording device and the reason for using that location is not to subvert the intent of the law. For purposes of this section, the term "location" shall include those locations specified in paragraph (b) of subdivision four of section 305.2 of the family court act.

(d) In the event the court finds that the people have not shown good cause for the non-recording of the confession, admission, or other statement, but determines that a non-recorded confession, admission or other statement is nevertheless admissible because it was voluntarily made then, upon request of the defendant, the court must instruct the jury that the people's failure to record the defendant's confession, admission or other statement as required by this section may be weighed as a factor, but not as the sole factor, in determining whether such confession, admission or other statement was voluntarily made, or was made at all.

(e) Video recording as required by this section shall be conducted in accordance with standards established by rule of the division of criminal justice services.

§60.46 Rules of evidence, family offense proceedings in family court.

Evidence of a written or oral admission or any testimony given by either party, or evidence derived therefrom, in a proceeding under article eight of the family court act without the benefit of counsel in such proceedings may not be received into evidence in a criminal proceeding except for the purposes of impeachment unless such party waives the right to counsel on the record. Nothing herein shall be deemed to prohibit any testimony or exhibits received into evidence in a criminal proceeding, or any orders, decisions or judgments arising from such proceeding from being received into evidence in any proceeding under article eight of the family court act.

§60.47 Possession of condoms; receipt into evidence.

Evidence that a person was in possession of one or more condoms may not be admitted at any trial, hearing, or other proceeding in a prosecution for section 230.00 of the penal law for the purpose of establishing probable cause for an arrest or proving any person's commission or attempted commission of such offense. *(Eff.2/2/21,Ch.23,L.2021)*

§60.48 Rules of evidence; admissibility of evidence of victim's manner of dress in sex offense cases.

Evidence of the manner in which the victim was dressed at the time of the commission of an offense may not be admitted in a prosecution for any offense, or an attempt to commit an offense, defined in article one hundred thirty of the penal law, unless such evidence is determined by the court to be relevant and admissible in the interests of justice, after an offer of proof by the proponent of such evidence outside the hearing of the jury, or such hearing as the court may require, and a statement by the court of its findings of fact essential to its determination.

§60.49 Possession of opioid antagonists; receipt into evidence.

1. Evidence that a person was in possession of an opioid antagonist may not be admitted at any trial, hearing or other proceeding in a prosecution for any offense under sections 220.03, 220.06, 220.09, 220.16, 220.18, or 220.21 of the penal law for the purpose of establishing probable cause for an arrest or proving any person's commission of such offense.

2. For the purposes of this section, opioid antagonist is defined as a drug approved by the Food and Drug Administration that, when administered, negates or neutralizes in whole or in part the pharmacological effects of an opioid in the body and shall be limited to naloxone and other medications approved by the department of health for such purpose.

(Eff. 12/6/21, Ch. 431, L. 2021)

§60.50   Rules of evidence; statements of defendants; corroboration.
A person may not be convicted of any offense solely upon evidence of a confession or admission made by him without additional proof that the offense charged has been committed.

§60.55   Rules of evidence; psychiatric testimony in certain cases.
1. When, in connection with the affirmative defense of lack of criminal responsibility by reason of mental disease or defect, a psychiatrist or licensed psychologist testifies at a trial concerning the defendant's mental condition at the time of the conduct charged to constitute a crime, he must be permitted to make a statement as to the nature of any examination of the defendant, the diagnosis of the mental condition of the defendant and his opinion as to the extent, if any, to which the capacity of the defendant to know or appreciate the nature and consequence of such conduct, or its wrongfulness, was impaired as a result of mental disease or defect at that time.

The psychiatrist or licensed psychologist must be permitted to make any explanation reasonably serving to clarify his diagnosis and opinion, and may be cross-examined as to any matter bearing on his competency or credibility or the validity of his diagnosis or opinion.

2. Any statement made by the defendant to a psychiatrist or licensed psychologist during his examination of the defendant shall be inadmissible in evidence on any issue other than that of the affirmative defense of lack of criminal responsibility, by reason of mental disease or defect. The statement shall, however, be admissible upon the issue of the affirmative defense of lack of criminal responsibility by reason of mental disease or defect, whether or not it would otherwise be deemed a privileged communication. Upon receiving the statement in evidence, the court must instruct the jury that the statement is to be considered only on the issue of such affirmative defense and may not be considered by it in its determination of whether the defendant committed the act constituting the crime charged.

§60.60   Rules of evidence; certificates concerning judgments of conviction and fingerprints.
1. A certificate issued by a criminal court, or the clerk thereof, certifying that a judgment of conviction against a designated defendant has been entered in such court, constitutes presumptive evidence of the facts stated in such certificate.

2. A report of a public servant charged with the custody of official fingerprint records which contains a certification that the fingerprints of a designated person who has previously been convicted of an offense are

identical with those of a defendant in a criminal action, constitutes presumptive evidence of the fact that such defendant has previously been convicted of such offense.

§60.70   Rules of evidence; dangerous drugs destroyed pursuant to court order.

The destruction of dangerous drugs pursuant to the provisions of article seven hundred fifteen hereof shall not preclude the admission on trial or in a proceeding in connection therewith of testimony or evidence where such testimony or evidence would otherwise have been admissible if such drugs had not been destroyed.

§60.75   Rules of evidence; chemical test evidence.

In any prosecution where two or more offenses against the same defendant are properly joined in one indictment or charged in two accusatory instruments properly consolidated for trial purposes and where one such offense charges a violation of any subdivision of section eleven hundred ninety-two of the vehicle and traffic law, chemical test evidence properly admissible as evidence of intoxication under subdivision one of section eleven hundred ninety-five of such law shall also, if relevant, be received in evidence with regard to the remaining charges in the indictments.

§60.76   Rules of evidence; rape crisis counselor evidence in certain cases.

Where disclosure of a communication which would have been privileged pursuant to section forty-five hundred ten of the civil practice law and rules is sought on the grounds that the privilege has been waived or that disclosure is required pursuant to the constitution of this state or the United States, the party seeking disclosure must file a written motion supported by an affidavit containing specific factual allegations providing grounds that disclosure is required. Upon the filing of such motion and affidavit, the court shall conduct an in camera review of the communication outside the presence of the jury and of counsel for all parties in order to determine whether disclosure of any portion of the communication is required.

ARTICLE 65 - USE OF CLOSED-CIRCUIT TELEVISION FOR CERTAIN CHILD WITNESSES

(Effective until 9/1/23, Ch.55, L.2021)

Section
65.00   Definitions.
65.10   Closed-circuit television; general rule; declaration of vulnerability.
65.20   Closed-circuit television; procedure for application and grounds for determination.
65.30   Closed-circuit television; special testimonial procedures.

This page intentionally left blank.

§65.00 Definitions.

As used in this article:

1. "Child witness" means a person fourteen years old or less who is or will be called to testify in a criminal proceeding, other than a grand jury proceeding, concerning an offense defined in article one hundred thirty of the penal law or section 255.25, 255.26 or 255.27 of such law which is the subject of such criminal proceeding.

2. "Vulnerable child witness" means a child witness whom a court has declared to be vulnerable.

3. "Testimonial room" means any room, separate and apart from the courtroom, which is furnished comfortably and less formally than a courtroom and from which the testimony of a vulnerable child witness can be transmitted to the courtroom by means of live, two-way closed-circuit television.

4. "Live, two-way closed-circuit television" means a simultaneous transmission, by closed-circuit television, or other electronic means, between the courtroom and the testimonial room in accordance with the provisions of section 65.30.

5. "Operator" means the individual authorized by the court to operate the closed-circuit television equipment used in accordance with the provisions of this article.

6. A person occupies "a position of authority with respect to a child" when he or she is a parent, guardian or other person responsible for the custody or care of the child at the relevant time or is any other person who maintains an ongoing personal relationship with such parent, guardian or other person responsible for custody or care, which relationship involves his or her living, or his or her frequent and repeated presence, in the same household or premises as the child.

§65.10 Closed-circuit television; general rule; declaration of vulnerability.

1. A child witness shall be declared vulnerable when the court, in accordance with the provisions of section 65.20, determines by clear and convincing evidence that it is likely that such child witness will suffer serious mental or emotional harm if required to testify at a criminal proceeding without the use of live, two-way closed-circuit television and that the use of such live, two-way closed-circuit television will diminish the likelihood or extent of, such harm.

2. When the court declares a child witness to be vulnerable, it shall, except as provided in subdivision four of section 65.30, authorize the taking of the testimony of the vulnerable child witness from the testimonial room by means of live, two-way closed-circuit television. Under no circumstances shall the provisions of this article be construed to authorize a closed-circuit television system by which events in the courtroom are not transmitted to the testimonial room during the testimony of the vulnerable child witness.

3. Nothing herein shall be contrued* to preclude the court from exercising its power to close the courtroom or from exercising any authority it otherwise may have to protect the well-being of a witness and the rights of the defendant. *(So in original.)*

§65.20 Closed-circuit television; procedure for application and grounds for determination.

1. Prior to the commencement of a criminal proceeding; other than a grand jury proceeding, either party may apply to the court for an order declaring that a child witness is vulnerable.

2. A child witness should be declared vulnerable when the court, in accordance with the provisions of this section, determines by clear and convincing evidence that the child witness would suffer serious mental or emotional harm that would substantially impair the child witness' ability to

communicate with the finder of fact without the use of live, two-way closed-circuit television.

3. A motion pursuant to subdivision one of this section must be made in writing at least eight days before the commencement of trial or other criminal proceeding upon reasonable notice to the other party and with an opportunity to be heard.

4. The motion papers must state the basis for the motion and must contain sworn allegations of fact which, if true, would support a determination by the court that the child witness is vulnerable. Such allegations may be based upon the personal knowledge of the deponent or upon information and belief, provided that, in the latter event, the sources of such information and the grounds for such belief are stated.

5. The answering papers may admit or deny any of the alleged facts and may, in addition, contain sworn allegations of fact relevant to the motion, including the rights of the defendant, the need to protect the child witness and the integrity of the truth-finding function of the trier of fact.

6. Unless all material facts alleged in support of the motion made pursuant to subdivision one of this section are conceded, the court shall, in addition to examining the papers and hearing oral argument, conduct an appropriate hearing for the purpose of making findings of fact essential to the determination of the motion. Except as provided in subdivision six of this section, it may subpoena or call and examine witnesses, who must either testify under oath or be permitted to give unsworn testimony pursuant to subdivision two of section 60.20 and must authorize the attorneys for the parties to do the same.

7. Notwithstanding any other provision of law, the child witness who is alleged to be vulnerable may not be compelled to testify at such hearing or to submit to any psychological or psychiatric examination. The failure of the child witness to testify at such hearing shall not be a ground for denying a motion made pursuant to subdivision one of this section. Prior statements made by the child witness relating to any allegations of conduct constituting an offense defined in article one hundred thirty of the penal law or incest as defined in section 255.25, 255.26 or 255.27 of such law or to any allegation of words or conduct constituting an attempt to prevent, impede or deter the child witness from cooperating in the investigation or prosecution of the offense shall be admissible at such hearing, provided, however, that a declaration that a child witness is vulnerable may not be based solely upon such prior statements.

8. (a) Notwithstanding any of the provisions of article forty-five of the civil practice law and rules, any physician, psychologist, nurse or social worker who has treated a child witness may testify at a hearing conducted pursuant to subdivision five of this section concerning the treatment of such child witness as such treatment relates to the issue presented at the hearing, provided that any otherwise applicable statutory privileges concerning communications between the child witness and such physician, psychologist, nurse or social worker in connection with such treatment shall not be deemed waived by such testimony alone, except to the limited extent of permitting the court alone to examine in camera reports, records or documents, if any, prepared by such physician, psychologist, nurse or social worker. If upon such examination the court determines that such reports, records or documents, or any one or portion thereof, contain information material and relevant to the issue of whether the child witness is a vulnerable child witness, the court shall disclose such information to both the attorney for the defendant and the district attorney.

(b) At any time after a motion has been made pursuant to subdivision one of this section, upon the demand of the other party the moving party must furnish the demanding party with a copy of any and all of such records, reports or other documents in the possession of such other party and must, in addition, supply the court with a copy of all such reports, records or other documents which are the subject of the demand. At any time after a demand has been made pursuant to this paragraph, the moving party may demand that property of the same kind or character in possession of the party that originally made such demand be furnished to the moving party and, if so furnished, be supplied, in addition, to the court.

9. (a) Prior to the commencement of the hearing conducted pursuant to subdivision six of this section, the district attorney shall, subject to a protective order, comply with the provisions of subdivision one of section 245.20 of this chapter as they concern any witness whom the district attorney intends to call at the hearing and the child witness.

(b) Before a defendant calls a witness at such hearing, he or she must, subject to a protective order, comply with the provisions of subdivision four of section 245.20 of this chapter as they concern all the witnesses the defendant intends to call at such hearing. *(Eff. 1/1/20, Ch. 59, L. 2019)*

10. The court may consider, in determining whether there are factors which would cause the child witness to suffer serious mental or emotional harm, a finding that any one or more of the following circumstances have been established by clear and convincing evidence:

(a) The manner of the commission of the offense of which the defendant is accused was particularly heinous or was characterized by aggravating circumstances.

(b) The child witness is particularly young or otherwise particularly subject to psychological harm on account of a physical or mental condition which existed before the alleged commission of the offense.

(c) At the time of the alleged offense, the defendant occupied a position of authority with respect to the child witness.

(d) The offense or offenses charged were part of an ongoing course of conduct committed by the defendant against the child witness over an extended period of time.

(e) A deadly weapon or dangerous instrument was allegedly used during the commission of the crime.

(f) The defendant has inflicted serious physical injury upon the child witness.

(g) A threat, express or implied, of physical violence to the child witness or a third person if the child witness were to report the incident to any person or communicate information to or cooperate with a court, grand jury, prosecutor, police officer or peace officer concerning the incident has been made by or on behalf of the defendant.

(h) A threat, express or implied, of the incarceration of a parent or guardian of the child witness, the removal of the child witness from the family or the dissolution of the family of the child witness if the child witness were to report the incident to any person or communicate information to or cooperate with a court, grand jury, prosecutor, police officer or peace officer concerning the incident has been made by or on behalf of the defendant.

(i) A witness other than the child witness has received a threat of physical violence directed at such witness or to a third person by or on behalf of the defendant.

(j) The defendant, at the time of the inquiry, (i) is living in the same household with the child witness, (ii) has ready access to the child witness or (iii) is providing substantial financial support for the child witness.

(k) The child witness has previously been the victim of an offense defined in article one hundred thirty of the penal law or incest as defined in section 255.25, 255.26 or 255.27 of such law.

(l) According to expert testimony, the child witness would be particularly suceptible* to psychological harm if required to testify in open court or in the physical presence of the defendant. *(So in original.)*

11. Irrespective of whether a motion was made pursuant to subdivision one of this section, the court, at the request of either party or on its own motion, may decide that a child witness may be vulnerable based on its own observations that a child witness who has been called to testify at a criminal proceeding is suffering severe mental or emotional harm and therefore is physically or mentally unable to testify or to continue to testify in open court or in the physical presence of the defendant and that the use of live, two-way closed-circuit television is necessary to enable the child witness to testify. If the court so decides, it must conduct the same hearing that subdivision five of this section requires when a motion is made pursuant to subdivision one of this section, and it must make findings of fact pursuant to subdivisions nine and eleven of this section, before determining that the child witness is vulnerable.

12. In deciding whether a child witness is vulnerable, the court shall make findings of fact which reflect the causal relationship between the existence of any one or more of the factors set forth in subdivision nine of this section or other relevant factors which the court finds are established and the determination that the child witness is vulnerable. If the court is satisfied that the child witness is vulnerable and that, under the facts and circumstances of the particular case, the defendant's constitutional rights to an impartial jury or of confrontation will not be impaired, it may enter an order granting the application for the use of live, two-way closed-circuit television.

13. When the court has determined that a child witness is a vulnerable child witness, it shall make a specific finding as to whether placing the defendant and the child witness in the same room during the testimony of the child witness will contribute to the likelihood that the child witness will suffer severe mental or emotional harm. If the court finds that placing the defendant and the child witness in the same room during the testimony of the child witness will contribute to the likelihood that the child witness will suffer severe mental or emotional harm, the order entered pursuant to subdivision eleven of this section shall direct that the defendant remain in the courtroom during the testimony of the vulnerable child witness.

§65.30   Closed-circuit television; special testimonial procedures.

1. When the court has entered an order pursuant to section 65.20, the testimony of the vulnerable child witness shall be taken in the testimonial room and the image and voice of the vulnerable child witness, as well as the image of all other persons other than the operator present in the testimonial room, shall be transmitted live by means of closed-circuit television to the courtroom. The courtroom shall be equipped with monitors sufficient to permit the judge, jury, defendant and attorneys to observe the demeanor of the vulnerable child witness during his or her testimony. Unless the courtroom has been closed pursuant to court order, the public shall also be permitted to hear the testimony and view the image of the vulnerable child witness.

2. In all instances, the image of the jury shall be simultaneously transmitted to the vulnerable child witness in the testimonial room. If the court order issued pursuant to section 65.20 specifies that the vulnerable child witness shall testify outside the physical presence of the defendant, the image of the defendant and the image and voice of the person examining the vulnerable child witness shall also be simultaneously transmitted to the vulnerable child witness in the testimonial room.

3. The operator shall place herself or himself and the closed-circuit television equipment in a position that permits the entire testimony of the vulnerable child witness to be transmitted to the courtroom but limits the ability of the vulnerable child witness to see or hear the operator or the equipment.

4. Notwithstanding any provision of this article, if the court in a particular case involving a vulnerable child witness determines that there is no live, two-way closed-circuit television equipment available in the court or another court in the county or which can be transported to the court from another county or that such equipment, if available, is technologically inadequate to protect the constitutional rights of the defendant, it shall not permit the use of the closed-circuit television procedures authorized by this article.

5. If the order of the court entered pursuant to section 65.20 requires that the defendant remain in the courtroom, the attorney for the defendant and the district attorney shall also remain in the courtroom unless the court is satisfied that their presence in the testimonial room will not impede full and private communication between the defendant and his or her attorney and will not encourage the jury to draw an inference adverse to the interest of the defendant.

6. Upon request of the defendant, the court shall instruct the jury that they are to draw no inference from the use of live, two-way closed-circuit television in the examination of the vulnerable child witness.

7. The vulnerable child witness shall testify under oath except as specified in subdivision two of section 60.20. The examination and cross-examination of the vulnerable child witness shall, in all other respects, be conducted in the same manner as if the vulnerable child witness had testified in the courtroom.

8. When the testimony of the vulnerable child witness is transmitted from the testimonial room into the courtroom, the court stenographer shall record the textimony* in the same manner as if the vulnerable child witness had testified in the courtroom.   *(So in original.)

ARTICLE 70 - STANDARDS OF PROOF

Section
70.10   Standards of proof; definitions of terms.
70.20   Standards of proof for conviction.

§70.10   Standards of proof; definitions of terms.

The following definitions are applicable to this chapter:

1. "Legally sufficient evidence" means competent evidence which, if accepted as true, would establish every element of an offense charged and the defendant's commission thereof; except that such evidence is not legally sufficient when corroboration required by law is absent.

2. "Reasonable cause to believe that a person has committed an offense" exists when evidence or information which appears reliable discloses facts or circumstances which are collectively of such weight and persuasiveness as to convince a person of ordinary intelligence, judgment and experience that it is reasonably likely that such offense was committed and that such person committed it. Except as otherwise provided in this chapter, such apparently reliable evidence may include or consist of hearsay.

§70.20   Standards of proof for conviction.

No conviction of an offense by verdict is valid unless based upon trial evidence which is legally sufficient and which establishes beyond a reasonable doubt every element of such offense and the defendant's commission thereof.

This page intentionally left blank.

ARTICLE 95 - PRE-CRIMINAL PROCEEDING SETTLEMENTS

Section
95.00   Pre-criminal proceeding settlement.

*§95.00 Pre-criminal proceeding settlement.

When a county district attorney of a county located in a city of one million or more recovers monies before the filing of an accusatory instrument as defined in subdivision one of section 1.20 of this chapter, after injured parties have been appropriately compensated, the district attorney's office shall retain a percentage of the remaining such monies in recognition that such monies were recovered as a result of investigations undertaken by such office. For each recovery the total amount of such monies to be retained by the county district attorney's office shall equal ten percent of the first twenty-five million dollars received by such office, plus seven and one-half percent of such monies received by such office in excess of twenty-five million dollars but less than fifty million dollars, plus five percent of any such monies received by such office in excess of fifty million dollars but less than one hundred million dollars, plus one percent of such monies received by such office in excess of one hundred million dollars. The remainder of such monies shall be paid by the district attorney's office to the state and to the county in equal amounts within thirty days of receipt, where disposition of such monies is not otherwise prescribed by law. Monies distributed to a county district attorney's office pursuant to this section shall be used to enhance law enforcement efforts within the state of New York. On December first of each year, every district attorney shall provide the governor, temporary president of the senate and speaker of the assembly with an annual report detailing the total amount of monies received as described herein by his or her office, a description of how and where such funds, and an itemization of funds received in the previous ten years, were distributed by his or her office but shall not include a description of the distribution of monies where the disclosure of such information would interfere with a law enforcement investigation or a judicial proceeding, and the current total balance of monies held on deposit for state sanctioned deferred prosecution agreements. The report shall include a detailed description of any entity to which funds are distributed, including but not limited to, whether it is a profit or not-for-profit entity, where it is located, and the intended use of the monies distributed, and shall state the law enforcement purpose.   *(Expires 3/31/23,Ch.55,L.2021)*

PART TWO - THE PRINCIPAL PROCEEDINGS
TITLE H - PRELIMINARY PROCEEDINGS
IN LOCAL CRIMINAL COURT

ARTICLE 100 - COMMENCEMENT OF ACTION IN LOCAL CRIMINAL COURT OR YOUTH PART OF A SUPERIOR COURT--ACCUSATORY INSTRUMENTS

Section
100.05 Commencement of action; in general.
100.07 Commencement of action; effect of family court proceeding.
100.10 Local criminal court and youth part of the superior court accusatory instruments; definitions thereof.
100.15 Information, misdemeanor complaint and felony complaint; form and content.
100.20 Supporting deposition; definition, form and content.
100.25 Simplified information; form and content; defendant's right to supporting deposition; notice requirement.
100.30 Information, misdemeanor complaint, felony complaint, supporting deposition and proof of service of supporting deposition; verification.
100.35 Prosecutor's information; form and content.
100.40 Local criminal court and youth part of the superior court accusatory instruments; sufficiency on face.
100.45 Information, prosecutor's information, misdemeanor complaint; severance, consolidation, amendment, bill of particulars.
100.50 Superseding informations and prosecutor's informations.
100.55 Local criminal court accusatory instruments; in what courts filed.
100.60 Youth part of the superior court accusatory instruments; in what courts filed.

§100.05 Commencement of action; in general.

A criminal action is commenced by the filing of an accusatory instrument with a criminal court, or, in the case of a juvenile offender or adolescent offender, other than an adolescent offender charged with only a violation or traffic infraction, the youth part of the superior court, and if more than one such instrument is filed in the course of the same criminal action, such action commences when the first of such instruments is filed. The only way in which a criminal action can be commenced in a superior court, other than a criminal action against a juvenile offender or adolescent offender is by the filing therewith by a grand jury of an indictment against a defendant who has never been held by a local criminal court for the action of such grand jury with respect to any charge contained in such indictment. Otherwise, a criminal action can be commenced only in a local criminal court, by the filing therewith of a local criminal court accusatory instrument, namely:

1. An information; or
2. A simplified information; or
3. A prosecutor's information; or
4. A misdemeanor complaint; or
5. A felony complaint.

§100.07 Commencement of action; effect of family court proceeding.
A criminal court shall have concurrent jurisdiction over cognizable family offenses, as defined in subdivision one of section 530.11 of this chapter and in subdivision one of section eight hundred twelve of the family court act, notwithstanding the fact that a family court has or may be exercising jurisdiction over a petition under article eight of the family court act containing substantially the same allegations as are set forth in the accusatory instrument or indictment.

§100.10   *Local criminal court *and youth part of the superior court* accusatory instruments; definitions thereof.
(Material in Italics takes Eff.10/1/18; provided however, that when the applicability of such provisions are based on the conviction of a crime or an act committed by a person who was seventeen years of age at the time of such offense such provisions shall take effect 10/1/19, Ch.59,L.2017)
1. An "information" is a verified written accusation by a person, filed with a local criminal court, charging one or more other persons with the commission of one or more offenses, none of which is a felony. It may serve as a basis both for the commencement of a criminal action and for the prosecution thereof in a local criminal court.
2. (a) A "simplified traffic information" is a written accusation by a police officer, or other public servant authorized by law to issue same, filed with a local criminal court, which charges a person with the commission of one or more traffic infractions and/or misdemeanors relating to traffic, and which, being in a brief or simplified form prescribed by the commissioner of motor vehicles, designates the offense or offenses charged but contains no factual allegations of an evidentiary nature supporting such charge or charges. It serves as a basis for commencement of a criminal action for such traffic offenses, alternative to the charging thereof by a regular information, and, under circumstances prescribed in section 100.25, it may serve, either in whole or in part, as a basis for prosecution of such charges.
(b) A "simplified parks information" is a written accusation by a police officer or other public servant authorized by law to issue same, filed with a local criminal court, which charges a person with the commission of one or more offenses, other than a felony, for which a uniform simplified parks information may be issued pursuant to the parks and recreation law and navigation law, and which being in a brief or simplified form prescribed by the commissioner of parks and recreation, designates the offense or offenses charged but contains no factual allegations of an evidentiary nature supporting such charge or charges. It serves as a basis for commencement of a criminal action for such offenses, alternative to the charging thereof by a regular information, and, under circumstances parescribed* in section 100.25, it may serve, either in whole or in part, as a basis for prosecution of such charges.   * (So in original. Probably should read "prescribed".)
(c) A "simplified environmental conservation information" is written accusation by a police officer or other public servant authorized by law to issue same, filed with a local criminal court, which charges a person with the commission of one or more offenses, other than a felony, for which a uniform simplified environmental conservation information may be issued pursuant to the environmental conservation law, and which being in a brief or simplified form prescribed by the commissioner of environmental conservation, designates the offense or offenses charged but contains no factual allegations of an evidentiary nature supporting such charge or charges. It serves as a basis for commencement of a criminal action for such offenses, alternative to the charging thereof by a regular information,

and, under circumstances prescribed in section 100.25, it may serve, either in whole or in part, as a basis for prosecution of such charges.

3. A "prosecutor's information" is a written accusation by a district attorney, filed with a local criminal court, either (a) at the direction of a grand jury pursuant to section 190.70, or (b) at the direction of a local criminal court pursuant to section 180.50 or 180.70, or (c) at the district attorney's own instance pursuant to subdivision two of section 100.50, or (d) at the direction of a superior court pursuant to subdivision one-a of section 210.20, charging one or more persons with the commission of one or more offenses, none of which is a felony. It serves as a basis for the prosecution of a criminal action, but it commences a criminal action only where it results from a grand jury direction issued in a case not previously commenced in a local criminal court.

4. A "misdemeanor complaint" is a verified written accusation by a person, filed with a local criminal court, charging one or more other persons with the commission of one or more offenses, at least one of which is a misdemeanor and none of which is a felony. It serves as a basis for the commencement of a criminal action, but it may serve as a basis for prosecution thereof only where a defendant has waived prosecution by information pursuant to subdivision three of section 170.65.

* 5. A "felony complaint" is a verified written accusation by a person, filed with a local criminal court, *or youth part of the superior court,* charging one or more other persons with the commission of one or more felonies. It serves as a basis for the commencement of a criminal action, but not as a basis for prosecution thereof.
*(Material in Italics takes Eff.10/1/18; provided however, that when the applicability of such provisions are based on the conviction of a crime or an act committed by a person who was seventeen years of age at the time of such offense such provisions shall take effect 10/1/19, Ch.59,L.2017)

§100.15 Information, misdemeanor complaint and felony complaint; form and content.

1. An information, a misdemeanor complaint and a felony complaint must each specify the name of the court with which it is filed and the title of the action, and must be subscribed and verified by a person known as the "complainant." The complainant may be any person having knowledge, whether personal or upon information and belief, of the commission of the offense or offenses charged. Each instrument must contain an accusatory part and a factual part. The complainant's verification of the instrument is deemed to apply only to the factual part thereof and not to the accusatory part.

2. The accusatory part of each such instrument must designate the offense or offenses charged. As in the case of an indictment, and subject to the rules of joinder applicable to indictments, two or more offenses may be charged in separate counts. Also as in the case of an indictment, such instrument may charge two or more defendants provided that all such defendants are jointly charged with every offense alleged therein.

3. The factual part of such instrument must contain a statement of the complainant alleging facts of an evidentiary character supporting or tending to support the charges. Where more than one offense is charged, the factual part should consist of a single factual account applicable to all the counts of the accusatory part. The factual allegations may be based either upon personal knowledge of the complainant or upon information and belief. Nothing contained in this section, however, limits or affects the requirement, prescribed in subdivision one of section 100.40, that in order for an

information or a count thereof to be sufficient on its face, every element of the offense charged and the defendant's commission thereof must be supported by non-hearsay allegations of such information and/or any supporting depositions.

4. Where a felony complaint charges a violent felony offense defined in section 70.02 of the penal law and such offense is an armed felony as defined in subdivision forty-one of section 1.20,

(a) the accusatory part of the instrument must designate the offense as an armed felony, and (b) the factual part of the instrument must allege facts of an evidentiary character supporting or tending to support such designation.

§100.20 Supporting deposition; definition, form and content.

A supporting deposition is a written instrument accompanying or filed in connection with an information, a simplified information, a misdemeanor complaint or a felony complaint, subscribed and verified by a person other than the complainant of such accusatory instrument, and containing factual allegations of an evidentiary character, based either upon personal knowledge or upon information and belief, which supplement those of the accusatory instrument and support or tend to support the charge or charges contained therein.

§100.25 Simplified information; form and content; defendant's right to supporting deposition; notice requirement.

1. A simplified information must be substantially in the form prescribed by the commissioner of motor vehicles, the commissioner of parks and recreation, or the commissioner of environmental conservation, as the case may be.

2. A defendant charged by a simplified information is, upon a timely request, entitled as a matter of right to have filed with the court and served upon him, or if he is represented by an attorney, upon his attorney, a supporting deposition of the complainant police officer or public servant, containing allegations of fact, based either upon personal knowledge or upon information and belief, providing reasonable cause to believe that the defendant committed the offense or offenses charged. To be timely, such a request must, except as otherwise provided herein and in subdivision three of this section, be made before entry of a plea of guilty to the charge specified and before commencement of a trial thereon, but not later than thirty days after the date the defendant is directed to appear in court as such date appears upon the simplified information and upon the appearance ticket issued pursuant thereto. If the defendant's request is mailed to the court, the request must be mailed within such thirty day period. Upon such a request, the court must order the complainant police officer or public servant to serve a copy of such supporting deposition upon the defendant or his attorney, within thirty days of the date such request is received by the court, or at least five days before trial, whichever is earlier, and to file such supporting deposition with the court together with proof of service thereof. Notwithstanding any provision to the contrary, where a defendant is issued an appearance ticket in conjunction with the offense charged in the simplified information and the appearance ticket fails to conform with the requirements of subdivision two of section 150.10, a request is timely when made not later than thirty days after (a) entry of the defendant's plea of not guilty when he or she has been arraigned in person, or (b) written notice to

the defendant of his or her right to receive a supporting deposition when a plea of not guilty has been submitted by mail.

3. When at least one of the offenses charged in a simplified information is a misdemeanor, the court may, upon motion of the defendant, for good cause shown and consistent with the interest of justice, permit the defendant to request a supporting deposition beyond the thirty day request period set forth in subdivision two of this section provided, however, that no motion may be brought under this subdivision after ninety days has elapsed from the date the defendant is directed to appear in court as such date appears upon the simplified information and upon the appearance ticket issued pursuant thereto.

4. Notwithstanding any provision of law to the contrary, where a person is charged by a simplified information and is served with an appearance ticket as defined in section 150.10, such appearance ticket shall contain the following language: "NOTICE: YOU ARE ENTITLED TO RECEIVE A SUPPORTING DEPOSITION FURTHER EXPLAINING THE CHARGES PROVIDED YOU REQUEST SUCH SUPPORTING DEPOSITION WITHIN THIRTY DAYS FROM THE DATE YOU ARE DIRECTED TO APPEAR IN COURT AS SET FORTH ON THIS APPEARANCE TICKET. DO YOU REQUEST A SUPPORTING DEPOSITION? [ ] YES [ ] NO"

§100.30 Information, misdemeanor complaint, felony complaint, supporting deposition and proof of service of supporting deposition; verification.

1. An information, a misdemeanor complaint, a felony complaint, a supporting deposition, and proof of service of a supporting deposition may be verified in any of the following manners:

(a) Such instrument may be sworn to before the court with which it is filed.

(b) Such instrument may be sworn to before a desk officer in charge at a police station or police headquarters or any of his superior officers.

(c) Where such instrument is filed by any public servant following the issuance and service of an appearance ticket, and where by express provision of law another designated public servant is authorized to administer the oath with respect to such instrument, it may be sworn to before such public servant.

(d) Such instrument may bear a form notice that false statements made therein are punishable as a class A misdemeanor pursuant to section 210.45 of the penal law, and such form notice together with the subscription of the deponent constitute a verification of the instrument.

(e) Such instrument may be sworn to before a notary public.

2. An instrument specified in subdivision one may be verified in any manner prescribed therein unless in a particular case the court expressly directs verification in a particular manner prescribed in said subdivision one.

§100.35 Prosecutor's information; form and content.

A prosecutor's information must contain the name of the local criminal court with which it is filed and the title of the action, and must be subscribed by the district attorney by whom it is filed. Otherwise it should be in the form prescribed for an indictment, pursuant to section 200.50, and must, in one or more counts, allege the offense or offenses charged and a plain and concise statement of the conduct constituting each such offense. The rules prescribed in sections 200.20 and 200.40 governing joinder of different offenses and defendants in a single indictment are also applicable to a prosecutor's information.

§100.40 *Local criminal court **and youth part of the superior court** accusatory instruments; sufficiency on face.*

(Material in Italics takes Eff.10/1/18; provided however, that when the applicability of such provisions are based on the conviction of a crime or an act committed by a person who was seventeen years of age at the time of such offense such provisions shall take effect 10/1/19, Ch.59,L.2017)

1. An information, or a count thereof, is sufficient on its face when:

(a) It substantially conforms to the requirements prescribed in section 100.15; and

(b) The allegations of the factual part of the information, together with those of any supporting depositions which may accompany it, provide reasonable cause to believe that the defendant committed the offense charged in the accusatory part of the information; and

(c) Non-hearsay allegations of the factual part of the information and/or of any supporting depositions establish, if true, every element of the offense charged and the defendant's commission thereof.

2. A simplified information is sufficient on its face when, as provided by subdivision one of section 100.25, it substantially conforms to the requirement therefor prescribed by or pursuant to law; provided that when the filing of a supporting deposition is ordered by the court pursuant to subdivision two of said section 100.25, a failure of the complainant police officer or public servant to comply with such order within the time provided by subdivision two of said section 100.25 renders the simplified information insufficient on its face.

3. A prosecutor's information, or a count thereof, is sufficient on its face when it substantially conforms to the requirements prescribed in section 100.35.

4. A misdemeanor complaint or a felony complaint, or a count thereof, is sufficient on its face when:

(a) It substantially conforms to the requirements prescribed in section 100.15; and

(b) The allegations of the factual part of such accusatory instrument and/or any supporting depositions which may accompany it, provide reasonable cause to believe that the defendant committed the offense charged in the accusatory part of such instrument.

§100.45 Information, prosecutor's information, misdemeanor complaint; severance, consolidation, amendment, bill of particulars.

1. Where appropriate, the provisions of sections 200.20 and 200.40 and paragraph (n) of subdivision four of section 20.40 of this chapter, governing severance of counts of an indictment and severance of defendants for trial purposes, and governing consolidation of indictments for trial purposes, apply to informations, to prosecutor's informations and to misdemeanor complaints.

2. The provisions of section 200.70 governing amendment of indictments apply to prosecutor's informations.

3. At any time before the entry of a plea of guilty to or the commencement of a trial of an information, the court may, upon application of the people and with notice to the defendant and opportunity to be heard, order the amendment of the accusatory part of such information by addition of a count charging an offense supported by the allegations of the factual part of such information and/or any supporting depositions which may accompany it. In such case, the defendant must be accorded any reasonable adjournment necessitated by the amendment.

4. The provisions of section 200.95, governing bills of particulars with respect to indictments, apply to informations, to misdemeanor complaints and to prosecutor's informations.

§100.50   Superseding informations and prosecutor's informations.
1. If at any time before entry of a plea of guilty to or commencement of a trial of an information or a prosecutor's information, another information or, as the case may be, another prosecutor's information is filed with the same local criminal court charging the defendant with an offense charged in the first instrument, the first such instrument is, with respect to such offense, superseded by the second and, upon the defendant's arraignment upon the latter, the count of the first instrument charging such offense must be dismissed by the court. The first instrument is not, however, superseded with respect to any count contained therein which charges an offense not charged in the second instrument.
2. At any time before entry of a plea of guilty to or commencement of a trial of an information, the district attorney may file with the local criminal court a prosecutor's information charging any offenses supported, pursuant to the standards prescribed in subdivision one of section 100.40, by the allegations of the factual part of the original information and/or any supporting depositions which may accompany it. In such case, the original information is superseded by the prosecutor's information and, upon the defendant's arraignment upon the latter, is deemed dismissed.
3. A misdemeanor complaint must or may be replaced and superseded by an information pursuant to the provisions of section 170.65.

§100.55   Local criminal court accusatory instruments; in what courts filed.
1. Any local criminal court accusatory instrument may be filed with a district court of a particular county when an offense charged therein was allegedly committed in such county or that part thereof over which such court has jurisdiction.
2. Any local criminal court accusatory instrument may be filed with the New York City criminal court when an offense charged therein was allegedly committed in New York City.
3. Any local criminal court accusatory instrument may be filed with a city court of a particular city when an offense charged therein was allegedly committed in such city.
4. An information, a simplified information, a prosecutor's information or a misdemeanor complaint may be filed with a town court of a particular town when an offense charged therein was allegedly committed anywhere in such town other than in a village thereof having a village court.
5. An information, a simplified information, a prosecutor's information or a misdemeanor complaint may be filed with a village court of a particular village when an offense charged therein was allegedly committed in such village.
6. A felony complaint may be filed with any town court or village court of a particular county when a felony charged therein was allegedly committed in some town of such county. Such court need not be that of the town or village in which such felony was allegedly committed.
7. An information, a simplified information, a misdemeanor complaint or a felony complaint may be filed with a judge of a superior court sitting as a local criminal court when an offense charged therein was allegedly committed in a county in which such judge is then present and in which he

either resides or is currently holding, or has been assigned to hold, a term of a superior court.

8. Where it is otherwise expressly provided by law that a particular kind of accusatory instrument may under given circumstances be filed with a local criminal court other than one authorized by this section, nothing contained in this section precludes the filing of such accusatory instrument accordingly.

9. In any case where each of two or more local criminal courts is authorized as a proper court with which to file an accusatory instrument, such an instrument may, in the absence of an express provision of law to the contrary, be filed with any one of such courts but not with more than one.

10. For purposes of this section, an offense is "committed in" a particular county, city, town, village or other specified political subdivision or area, not only when it is in fact committed therein but also when it is, for other reasons specified in sections 20.40 and 20.50, prosecutable in the criminal courts having geographical jurisdiction over such political subdivision or area.

11. Notwithstanding any provision of law to the contrary, a local criminal court accusatory instrument may be filed with a local criminal court while it is operating an off-hours arraignment part designated in accordance with paragraph (w) of subdivision one of section two hundred twelve of the judiciary law provided that an offense charged therein was allegedly committed in the county in which the local criminal court is located.

*§100.60   Youth part of the superior court accusatory instruments; in what courts filed.
 Any youth part of the superior court accusatory instrument may be filed with the youth part of the superior court of a particular county when an offense charged therein was allegedly committed in such county or that part thereof over which such court has jurisdiction.
*(Eff.10/1/18; provided however, that when the applicability of such provisions are based on the conviction of a crime or an act committed by a person who was seventeen years of age at the time of such offense such provisions shall take effect 10/1/19, Ch.59,L.2017)

ARTICLE 110 - *REQUIRING DEFENDANT'S APPEARANCE IN LOCAL CRIMINAL COURT *OR YOUTH PART OF SUPERIOR COURT* FOR ARRAIGNMENT
*(Material in Italics takes Eff.10/1/18; provided however, that when the applicability of such provisions are based on the conviction of a crime or an act committed by a person who was seventeen years of age at the time of such offense such provisions shall take effect 10/1/19, Ch.59,L.2017)

Section
110.10 Methods of requiring defendant's appearance in local criminal court or youth part of the superior court for arraignment; in general.
110.20 Local criminal court or youth part of the superior court accusatory instruments; notice thereof to district attorney.

*§110.10   Methods of requiring defendant's appearance in local criminal court *or youth part of the superior court* for arraignment; in general.
 1. After a criminal action has been commenced in a local criminal court *or youth part of the superior court* by the filing of an accusatory instrument therewith, a defendant who has not been arraigned in the action and has not come under the control of the court may under certain circumstances be compelled or required to appear for arraignment upon such accusatory instrument by:
    (a) The issuance and execution of a warrant of arrest, as provided in article one hundred twenty; or
    (b) The issuance and service upon him of a summons, as provided in article one hundred thirty; or

(c) Procedures provided in articles five hundred sixty, five hundred seventy, five hundred eighty, five hundred ninety and six hundred for securing attendance of defendants in criminal actions who are not at liberty within the state.

2. Although no criminal action against a person has been commenced in any court, he may under certain circumstances be compelled or required to appear in a local criminal court *or youth part of a superior court* for arraignment upon an accusatory instrument to be filed therewith at or before the time of his appearance by:

(a) An arrest made without a warrant, as provided in article one hundred forty; or

(b) The issuance and service upon him of an appearance ticket, as provided in article one hundred fifty.
(Material in Italics takes Eff.10/1/18; provided however, that when the applicability of such provisions are based on the conviction of a crime or an act committed by a person who was seventeen years of age at the time of such offense such provisions shall take effect 10/1/19, Ch.59,L.2017)

*§110.20   Local criminal court *or youth part of the superior court* accusatory instruments; notice thereof to district attorney.

When a criminal action in which a crime is charged is commenced in a local criminal court, *or youth part of the superior court* other than the criminal court of the city of New York, a copy of the accusatory instrument shall be promptly transmitted to the appropriate district attorney upon or prior to the arraignment of the defendant on the accusatory instrument. If a police officer or a peace officer is the complainant or the filer of a simplified information, or has arrested the defendant or brought him before the local criminal court *or youth part of the superior court* on behalf of an arresting person pursuant to subdivision one of section 140.20, such officer or his agency shall transmit the copy of the accusatory instrument to the appropriate district attorney. In all other cases, the clerk of the court in which the defendant is arraigned shall so transmit it.
(Material in Italics takes Eff.10/1/18; provided however, that when the applicability of such provisions are based on the conviction of a crime or an act committed by a person who was seventeen years of age at the time of such offense such provisions shall take effect 10/1/19, Ch.59,L.2017)

ARTICLE 120 - WARRANT OF ARREST

Section
120.10 Warrant of arrest; definition, function, form and content.
120.20 Warrant of arrest; when issuable.
120.30 Warrant of arrest; by what courts issuable and in what courts returnable.
120.40 Warrant of arrest; attaching accusatory instrument to warrant of town court, village court or city court.
120.50 Warrant of arrest; to what police officers addressed.
120.55 Warrant of arrest; defendant under parole or probation supervision.
120.60 Warrant of arrest; what police officers may execute.
120.70 Warrant of arrest; where executable.
120.80 Warrant of arrest; when and how executed.
120.90 Warrant of arrest; procedure after arrest.

§120.10   Warrant of arrest; definition, function, form and content.

1. A warrant of arrest is a process issued by a local criminal court directing a police officer to arrest a defendant designated in an accusatory instrument filed with such court and to bring him before such court in connection with such instrument. The sole function of a warrant of arrest is to achieve a defendant's court appearance in a criminal action for the purpose of arraignment upon the accusatory instrument by which such action was commenced.

2. A warrant of arrest must be subscribed by the issuing judge and must state or contain (a) the name of the issuing court, and (b) the date of

issuance of the warrant, and (c) the name or title of an offense charged in the underlying accusatory instrument, and (d) the name of the defendant to be arrested or, if such be unknown, any name or description by which he can be identified with reasonable certainty, and (e) the police officer or officers to whom the warrant is addressed, and (f) a direction that such officer arrest the defendant and bring him before the issuing court.

3. A warrant of arrest may be addressed to a classification of police officers, or to two or more classifications thereof, as well as to a designated individual police officer or officers. Multiple copies of such a warrant may be issued.

§120.20 Warrant of arrest; when issuable.

*1. When a criminal action has been commenced in a local criminal court *or youth part of the superior court* by the filing therewith of an accusatory instrument, other than a simplified traffic information, against a defendant who has not been arraigned upon such accusatory instrument and has not come under the control of the court with respect thereto:

(Material in Italics takes Eff.10/1/18; provided however, that when the applicability of such provisions are based on the conviction of a crime or an act committed by a person who was seventeen years of age at the time of such offense such provisions shall take effect 10/1/19, Ch.59,L.2017)

(a) such court may, if such accusatory instrument is sufficient on its face, issue a warrant for such defendant's arrest; or

(b) if such accusatory instrument is not sufficient on its face as prescribed in section 100.40, and if the court is satisfied that on the basis of the available facts or evidence it would be impossible to draw and file an accusatory instrument that is sufficient on its face, the court must dismiss the accusatory instrument.

2. Even though such accusatory instrument is sufficient on its face, the court may refuse to issue a warrant of arrest based thereon until it has further satisfied itself, by inquiry or examination of witnesses, that there is reasonable cause to believe that the defendant committed an offense charged. Upon such inquiry or examination, the court may examine, under oath or otherwise, any available person whom it believes may possess knowledge concerning the subject matter of the charge.

3. Notwithstanding the provisions of subdivision one, if a summons may be issued in lieu of a warrant of arrest pursuant to section 130.20, and if the court is satisfied that the defendant will respond thereto, it may not issue a warrant of arrest. Upon the request of the district attorney, in lieu of a warrant of arrest or summons, the court may instead authorize the district attorney to direct the defendant to appear for arraignment on a designated date if it is satisfied that the defendant will so appear.

*§120.30 Warrant of arrest; by what courts issuable and in what courts returnable.

1. A warrant of arrest may be issued only by the local criminal court *or youth part of the superior court* with which the underlying accusatory instrument has been filed, and it may be made returnable in such issuing court only.

2. The particular local criminal court or courts *or youth part of the superior court* with which any particular local criminal court *or youth part of the superior court* accusatory instrument may be filed for the purpose of obtaining a warrant of arrest are determined, generally, by the provisions of section 100.55 *or 100.60 of this title.* If, however, a particular accusatory

instrument may pursuant to said section 100.55 be filed with a particular town court and such town court is not available at the time such instrument is sought to be filed and a warrant obtained, such accusatory instrument may be filed with the town court of any adjoining town of the same county. If such instrument may be filed pursuant to said section 100.55 with a particular village court and such village court is not available at the time, it may be filed with the town court of the town embracing such village, or if such town court is not available either, with the town court of any adjoining town of the same county.

(Material in Italics takes Eff.10/1/18; provided however, that when the applicability of such provisions are based on the conviction of a crime or an act committed by a person who was seventeen years of age at the time of such offense such provisions shall take effect 10/1/19, Ch.59,L.2017)

§120.40 Warrant of arrest; attaching accusatory instrument to warrant of town court, village court or city court.

A town court, village court or city court which issues a warrant of arrest may attach thereto a duplicate copy of the underlying accusatory instrument. If one or more duplicate copies of the warrant are issued, such court may attach as many copies of such accusatory instrument to copies of such warrant as it chooses. In any case where, pursuant to subdivision five of section 120.90, a defendant arrested upon such a warrant of arrest is brought before a local criminal court other than the town court, village court or city court in which the warrant is returnable, a copy of the accusatory instrument constitutes a valid basis for arraignment, as provided in subdivision one of section 170.15.

§120.50 Warrant of arrest; to what police officers and peace officers appointed by the state university addressed.

A warrant of arrest may be addressed to any police officer or classification of police officers whose geographical area of employment embraces either the place where the offense charged was allegedly committed or the locality of the court by which the warrant is issued.

§120.55 Warrant of arrest; defendant under parole or probation supervision.

If the defendant named within a warrant of arrest issued by a local criminal court *or youth part of the superior court* pursuant to the provisions of this article, or by a superior court issued pursuant to subdivision three of section 210.10 of this chapter, is under the supervision of the state department of corrections and community supervision or a local or state probation department, then a warrant for his or her arrest may be executed by a parole officer or probation officer, when authorized by his or her probation director, within his or her geographical area of employment. The execution of the warrant by a parole officer or probation officer shall be upon the same conditions and conducted in the same manner as provided for execution of a warrant by a police officer.

(Material in Italics takes Eff.10/1/18; provided however, that when the applicability of such provisions are based on the conviction of a crime or an act committed by a person who was seventeen years of age at the time of such offense such provisions shall take effect 10/1/19, Ch.59,L.2017)

§120.60 Warrant of arrest; what police officers may execute.

1. A warrant of arrest may be executed by (a) any police officer to whom it is addressed, or (b) any other police officer delegated to execute it under circumstances prescribed in subdivisions two and three.

2. A police officer to whom a warrant of arrest is addressed may delegate another officer to whom it is not addressed to execute such warrant as his agent when:

(a) He has reasonable cause to believe that the defendant is in a particular county other than the one in which the warrant is returnable; and

(b) The warrant is, pursuant to section 120.70, executable in such other county without endorsement by a local criminal court thereof; and

(c) The geographical area of employment of the delegated police officer embraces the locality where the arrest is to be made.

3. Under circumstances specified in subdivision two, the police officer to whom the warrant is addressed may inform the delegated officer, by telecommunication, mail or any other means, of the issuance of the warrant, of the offense charged in the underlying accusatory instrument and of all other pertinent details, and may request him to act as his agent in arresting the defendant pursuant to such warrant. Upon such request, the delegated police officer is to the same extent as the delegating officer, authorized to make such arrest pursuant to the warrant within the geographical area of such delegated officer's employment. Upon so arresting the defendant, he must proceed as provided in subdivisions two and four of section 120.90.

§120.70 Warrant of arrest; where executable.

*1. A warrant of arrest issued by a district court, by the New York City criminal court, *the youth part of a superior court* or by a superior court judge sitting as a local criminal court may be executed anywhere in the state.

2. A warrant of arrest issued by a city court, a town court or a village court may be executed:

(a) In the county of issuance or in any adjoining county; or

(b) Anywhere else in the state upon the written endorsement thereon of a local criminal court of the county in which the arrest is to be made. When so endorsed, the warrant is deemed the process of the endorsing court as well as that of the issuing court.

(Material in Italics takes Eff.10/1/18; provided however, that when the applicability of such provisions are based on the conviction of a crime or an act committed by a person who was seventeen years of age at the time of such offense such provisions shall take effect 10/1/19, Ch.59,L.2017)

§120.80 Warrant of arrest; when and how executed.

1. A warrant of arrest may be executed on any day of the week and at any hour of the day or night.

2. Unless encountering physical resistance, flight or other factors rendering normal procedure impractical, the arresting police officer must inform the defendant that a warrant for his arrest for the offense designated therein has been issued. Upon request of the defendant, the officer must show him the warrant if he has it in his possession. The officer need not have the warrant in his possession, and, if he has not, he must show it to the defendant upon request as soon after the arrest as possible.

3. In order to effect the arrest, the police officer may use such physical force as is justifiable pursuant to section 35.30 of the penal law.

4. In order to effect the arrest, the police officer may, under circumstances and in the manner prescribed in this subdivision, enter any premises in which he reasonably believes the defendant to be present; provided, however, that where the premises in which the officer reasonably believes the defendant to be present is the dwelling of a third party who is not the subject of the arrest warrant, the officer shall proceed in the manner specified in article 690 of this chapter. Before such entry, he must give, or

make reasonable effort to give, notice of his authority and purpose to an occupant thereof, unless there is reasonable cause to believe that the giving of such notice will:

(a) Result in the defendant escaping or attempting to escape; or

(b) Endanger the life or safety of the officer or another person; or

(c) Result in the destruction, damaging or secretion of material evidence.

5. If the officer is authorized to enter premises without giving notice of his authority and purpose, or if after giving such notice he is not admitted, he may enter such premises, and by a breaking if necessary.

§120.90 Warrant of arrest; procedure after arrest.

*1. Upon arresting a defendant for any offense pursuant to a warrant of arrest in the county in which the warrant is returnable or in any adjoining county, or upon so arresting him or her for a felony in any other county, a police officer, if he or she be one to whom the warrant is addressed, must without unnecessary delay bring the defendant before the local criminal court *or youth part of the superior court* in which such warrant is returnable, provided that, where a local criminal court *or youth part of the superior court* in the county in which the warrant is returnable hereunder is operating an off-hours arraignment part designated in accordance with paragraph (w) of subdivision one of section two hundred twelve of the judiciary law at the time of defendant's return, such police officer may bring the defendant before such local criminal court *or youth part of the superior court.*

2. Upon arresting a defendant for any offense pursuant to a warrant of arrest in a county adjoining the county in which the warrant is returnable, or upon so arresting him for a felony in any other county, a police officer, if he be one delegated to execute the warrant pursuant to section 120.60, must without unnecessary delay deliver the defendant or cause him to be delivered to the custody of the officer by whom he was so delegated, and the latter must then proceed as provided in subdivision one.

3. Upon arresting a defendant for an offense other than a felony pursuant to a warrant of arrest in a county other than the one in which the warrant is returnable or one adjoining it, a police officer, if he be one to whom the warrant is addressed, must inform the defendant that he has a right to appear before a local criminal court of the county of arrest for the purpose of being released on his own recognizance or having bail fixed. If the defendant does not desire to avail himself of such right, the officer must request him to endorse such fact upon the warrant, and upon such endorsement the officer must without unnecessary delay bring him before the court in which the warrant is returnable. If the defendant does desire to avail himself of such right, or if he refuses to make the aforementioned endorsement, the officer must without unnecessary delay bring him before a local criminal court of the county of arrest. Such court must release the defendant on his own recognizance or fix bail for his appearance on a specified date in the court in which the warrant is returnable. If the defendant is in default of bail, the officer must without unnecessary delay bring him before the court in which the warrant is returnable.

4. Upon arresting a defendant for an offense other than a felony pursuant to a warrant of arrest in a county other than the one in which the warrant is returnable or one adjoining it, a police officer, if he be one delegated to execute the warrant pursuant to section 120.60, may hold the defendant in custody in the county of arrest for a period not exceeding two hours for the purpose of delivering him to the custody of the officer by whom he was

delegated to execute such warrant. If the delegating officer receives custody of the defendant during such period, he must proceed as provided in subdivision three. Otherwise, the delegated officer must inform the defendant that he has a right to appear before a local criminal court for the purpose of being released on his own recognizance or having bail fixed. If the defendant does not desire to avail himself of such right, the officer must request him to make, sign and deliver to him a written statement of such fact, and if the defendant does so, the officer must retain custody of him but must without unnecessary delay deliver him or cause him to be delivered to the custody of the delegating police officer. If the defendant does desire to avail himself of such right, or if he refuses to make and deliver the aforementioned statement, the delegated or arresting officer must without unnecessary delay bring him before a local criminal court of the county of arrest and must submit to such court a written statement reciting the material facts concerning the issuance of the warrant, the offense involved, and all other essential matters relating thereto. Upon the submission of such statement, such court must release the defendant on his own recognizance or fix bail for his appearance on a specified date in the court in which the warrant is returnable. If the defendant is in default of bail, the officer must retain custody of him but must without unnecessary delay deliver him or cause him to be delivered to the custody of the delegating officer. Upon receiving such custody, the latter must without unnecessary delay bring the defendant before the court in which the warrant is returnable.

5. Whenever a police officer is required pursuant to this section to bring an arrested defendant before a town court in which a warrant of arrest is returnable, and if such town court is not available at the time, such officer must, if a copy of the underlying accusatory instrument has been attached to the warrant pursuant to section 120.40, instead bring such defendant before any village court embraced, in whole or in part, by such town, or any local criminal court of an adjoining town or city of the same county or any village court embraced, in whole or in part, by such adjoining town. When the court in which the warrant is returnable is a village court which is not available at the time, the officer must in such circumstances bring the defendant before the town court of the town embracing such village or any other village court within such town or, if such town court or village court is not available either, before the local criminal court of any town or city of the same county which adjoins such embracing town or, before the local criminal court of any village embraced in whole or in part by such adjoining town. When the court in which the warrant is returnable is a city court which is not available at the time, the officer must in such circumstances bring the defendant before the local criminal court of any adjoining town or village embraced in whole or in part by such adjoining town of the same county.

*5-a. Whenever a police officer is required, pursuant to this section, to bring an arrested defendant before a youth part of a superior court in which a warrant of arrest is returnable, and if such court is not in session, such officer must bring such defendant before the most accessible magistrate designated by the appellate division of the supreme court in the applicable department to act as a youth part.

*6. Before bringing a defendant arrested pursuant to a warrant before the local criminal court or youth part of a superior court in which such warrant is returnable, a police officer must without unnecessary delay perform all fingerprinting and other preliminary police duties required in the particular case. In any case in which the defendant is not brought by a police officer before such court but, following his arrest in another county for an offense specified in subdivision one of section 160.10, is released by a local criminal court of such other county on his own recognizance or on bail for his appearance on a specified date before the local criminal court before which the warrant is returnable, the latter court must, upon arraignment of the defendant before it, direct that he be fingerprinted by the appropriate officer or agency, and that he appear at an appropriate designated time and place for such purpose.

*7. Upon arresting a juvenile offender *or adolescent offender*, the police officer shall immediately notify the parent or other person legally responsible for his care or the person with whom he is domiciled, that the juvenile offender *or adolescent offender* has been arrested, and the location of the facility where he is being detained.

8. Upon arresting a defendant, other than a juvenile offender, for any offense pursuant to a warrant of arrest, a police officer shall, upon the defendant's request, permit the defendant to communicate by telephone provided by the law enforcement facility where the defendant is held to a phone number located anywhere in the United States or Puerto Rico, for the purposes of obtaining counsel and informing a relative or friend that he or she has been arrested, unless granting the call will compromise an ongoing investigation or the prosecution of the defendant.

(Material in Italics takes Eff.10/1/18; provided however, that when the applicability of such provisions are based on the conviction of a crime or an act committed by a person who was seventeen years of age at the time of such offense such provisions shall take effect 10/1/19, Ch.59,L.2017)

ARTICLE 130 - THE SUMMONS

Section
130.10 Summons; definition, function, form and content.
130.20 Summons; by what courts issuable and in what courts returnable.
130.30 Summons; when issuable.
130.40 Summons; service.
130.50 Summons; defendant's failure to appear.
130.60 Summons; fingerprinting of defendant.

§130.10 Summons; definition, function, form and content.

*1. A summons is a process issued by a local criminal court directing a defendant designated in an information, a prosecutor's information, a felony complaint or a misdemeanor complaint filed with such court, *or a youth part of a superior court directing a defendant designated in a felony complaint,* or by a superior court directing a defendant designated in an indictment filed with such court, to appear before it at a designated future time in connection with such accusatory instrument. The sole function of a summons is to achieve a defendant's court appearance in a criminal action for the purpose of arraignment upon the accusatory instrument by which such action was commenced.

2. A summons must be subscribed by the issuing judge and must state or contain (a) the name of the issuing court, and (b) the name of the defendant to whom it is addressed, and (c) the name or title of an offense charged in the underlying accusatory instrument, and (d) the date of issuance of the summons, and (e) the date and time when it is returnable, and (f) a direction that the defendant appear before the issuing court at such time.

(Material in Italics takes Eff.10/1/18; provided however, that when the applicability of such provisions are based on the conviction of a crime or an act committed by a person who was seventeen years of age at the time of such offense such provisions shall take effect 10/1/19, Ch.59,L.2017)

§130.20 Summons; by what courts issuable and in what courts returnable.
A summons may be issued only by the local criminal court or superior court with which the accusatory instrument underlying it has been filed, and it may be made returnable in such issuing court only.

§130.30 Summons; when issuable.
A local criminal court *or youth part of the superior court* may issue a summons in any case in which, pursuant to section 120.20, it is authorized to issue a warrant of arrest based upon an information, a prosecutor's information, a felony complaint or a misdemeanor complaint. If such information, prosecutor's information, felony complaint or misdemeanor complaint is not sufficient on its face as prescribed in section 100.40, and if the court is satisfied that on the basis of the available facts or evidence it would be impossible to draw and file an authorized accusatory instrument that is sufficient on its face, the court must dismiss the accusatory instrument. A superior court may issue a summons in any case in which, pursuant to section 210.10, it is authorized to issue a warrant of arrest based upon an indictment.
(Material in Italics takes Eff.10/1/18; provided however, that when the applicability of such provisions are based on the conviction of a crime or an act committed by a person who was seventeen years of age at the time of such offense such provisions shall take effect 10/1/19, Ch.59,L.2017)

§130.40 Summons; service.
1. A summons may be served by a police officer, or by a complainant at least eighteen years old or by any other person at least eighteen years old designated by the court.
2. A summons may be served anywhere in the county of issuance or anywhere in an adjoining county.

§130.50 Summons; defendant's failure to appear.
If after the service of a summons the defendant does not appear in the designated local criminal court or superior court at the time such summons is returnable, the court may issue a warrant of arrest.

§130.60 Summons; fingerprinting of defendant.
1. Upon the arraignment of a defendant whose court attendance has been secured by the issuance and service of a summons, based upon an indictment, a prosecutor's information or upon an information, felony complaint or misdemeanor complaint filed by a complainant who is a police officer, the court must, if an offense charged in the accusatory instrument is one specified in subdivision one of section 160.10, direct that the defendant be fingerprinted by the appropriate police officer or agency, and that he or she appear at an appropriate designated time and place for such purpose.
2. Upon the arraignment of a defendant whose court attendance has been secured by the issuance and service of a summons based upon an information or misdemeanor complaint filed by a complainant who is not a police officer, and who has not previously been fingerprinted, the court may, if it finds reasonable cause to believe that the defendant has committed an offense specified in subdivision one of section 160.10, direct that the defendant be fingerprinted by the appropriate police officer or agency and that he appear at an appropriate designated time and place for such purpose. A defendant whose court appearance has been secured by the issuance and service of a criminal summons based upon a misdemeanor complaint or information filed by a complainant who is not a police officer, must be directed by the court, upon conviction of the defendant, to be

fingerprinted by the appropriate police officer or agency and the court must also direct that the defendant appear at an appropriate designated time and place forsuch purpose, if the defendant is convicted of any offense specified in subdivision one of section 160.10.

ARTICLE 140 - ARREST WITHOUT A WARRANT

Section
140.05 Arrest without a warrant; in general.
140.10 Arrest without a warrant; by police officer; when and where authorized.
140.15 Arrest without a warrant; when and how made by police officer.
140.20 Arrest without a warrant; procedure after arrest by police officer.
140.25 Arrest without a warrant; by peace officer.
140.27 Arrest without a warrant; when and how made; procedure after arrest by peace officer.
140.30 Arrest without a warrant; by any person; when and where authorized.
140.35 Arrest without a warrant; by person acting other than as a police officer or a peace officer; when and how made.
140.40 Arrest without a warrant; by person acting other than as a police officer or a peace officer; procedure after arrest.
140.45 Arrest without a warrant; dismissal of insufficient local criminal court accusatory instrument.
140.50 Temporary questioning of persons in public places; search for weapons.
140.55 Arrest without a warrant; by peace officers of other states for offense committed outside state; uniform close pursuit act.

§140.05   Arrest without a warrant; in general.

A person who has committed or is believed to have committed an offense and who is at liberty within the state may, under circumstances prescribed in this article, be arrested for such offense although no warrant of arrest therefor has been issued and although no criminal action therefor has yet been commenced in any criminal court.

§140.10   Arrest without a warrant; by police officer; when and where authorized.

1. Subject to the provisions of subdivision two, a police officer may arrest a person for:

(a) Any offense when he or she has reasonable cause to believe that such person has committed such offense in his or her presence; and

(b) A crime when he or she has reasonable cause to believe that such person has committed such crime, whether in his or her presence or otherwise.

2. A police officer may arrest a person for a petty offense, pursuant to subdivision one, only when:

(a) Such offense was committed or believed by him or her to have been committed within the geographical area of such police officer's employment or within one hundred yards of such geographical area; and

(b) Such arrest is made in the county in which such offense was committed or believed to have been committed or in an adjoining county; except that the police officer may follow such person in continuous close pursuit, commencing either in the county in which the offense was or is believed to have been committed or in an adjoining county, in and through any county of the state, and may arrest him or her in any county in which he or she apprehends him or her.

3. A police officer may arrest a person for a crime, pursuant to subdivision one, whether or not such crime was committed within the geographical area of such police officer's employment, and he or she may make such arrest within the state, regardless of the situs of the commission of the crime. In addition, he or she may, if necessary, pursue such person outside the state

and may arrest him or her in any state the laws of which contain provisions equivalent to those of section 140.55.

*4. Notwithstanding any other provisions of this section, a police officer shall arrest a person, and shall not attempt to reconcile the parties or mediate, where such officer has reasonable cause to believe that:

(a) a felony, other than subdivision three, four, nine or ten of section 155.30 of the penal law, has been committed by such person against a member of the same family or household, as member of the same family or household is defined in subdivision one of section 530.11 of this chapter; or

(b) a duly served order of protection or special order of conditions issued pursuant to subparagraph (i) or (ii) of paragraph (o) of subdivision one of section 330.20 of this chapter is in effect, or an order of which the respondent or defendant has actual knowledge because he or she was present in court when such order was issued, where the order appears to have been issued by a court of competent jurisdiction of this or another state, territorial or tribal jurisdiction; and

(i) Such order directs that the respondent or defendant stay away from persons on whose behalf the order of protection or special order of conditions has been issued and the respondent or defendant committed an act or acts in violation of such "stay away" provision of such order; or

(ii) The respondent or defendant commits a family offense as defined in subdivision one of section eight hundred twelve of the family court act or subdivision one of section 530.11 of this chapter in violation of such order of protection or special order of conditions.

The provisions of this subdivision shall apply only to orders of protection issued pursuant to sections two hundred forty and two hundred fifty-two of the domestic relations law, articles four, five, six and eight of the family court act and section 530.12 of this chapter, special orders of conditions issued pursuant to subparagraph (i) or (ii) of paragraph (o) of subdivision one of section 330.20 of this chapter insofar as they involve a victim or victims of domestic violence as defined by subdivision one of section four hundred fifty-nine-a of the social services law or a designated witness or witnesses to such domestic violence, and to orders of protection issued by courts of competent jurisdiction in another state, territorial or tribal jurisdiction. In determining whether reasonable cause exists to make an arrest for a violation of an order issued by a court of another state, territorial or tribal jurisdiction, the officer shall consider, among other factors, whether the order, if available, appears to be valid on its face or whether a record of the order exists on the statewide registry of orders of protection and warrants established pursuant to section two hundred twenty-one-a of the executive law or the protection order file maintained by the national crime information center; provided, however, that entry of the order of protection or special order of conditions into the statewide registry or the national protection order file shall not be required for enforcement of the order. When a special order of conditions is in effect and a defendant or respondent has been taken into custody pursuant to this paragraph, nothing contained in this paragraph shall restrict or impair a police officer from acting pursuant to section 9.41 of the mental hygiene law; or

(c) a misdemeanor constituting a family offense, as described in subdivision one of section 530.11 of this chapter and section eight hundred twelve of the family court act, has been committed by such person against such family or household member, unless the victim requests otherwise. The officer shall neither inquire as to whether the victim seeks an arrest of such person nor threaten the arrest of any person for the purpose of discouraging requests for police intervention. Notwithstanding the foregoing, when an officer has reasonable cause to believe that more than one family or household member has committed such a misdemeanor, the officer is not required to arrest each such person. In such circumstances, the officer shall attempt to identify and arrest the primary physical aggressor after considering: (i) the comparative extent of any injuries inflicted by and between the parties; (ii) whether any such person is threatening or has threatened future harm against another party or another family or household member; (iii) whether any such person has a prior history of domestic violence that the officer can reasonably ascertain; and (iv) whether any such person acted defensively to protect himself or herself from injury. The officer shall evaluate each complaint separately to determine who is the primary physical aggressor and shall not base the decision to arrest or not to arrest on the willingness of a person to testify or otherwise participate in a judicial proceeding.

The protected party in whose favor the order of protection or temporary order of protection is issued may not be held to violate an order issued in his or her favor nor may such protected party be arrested for violating such order.

Nothing contained in this subdivision shall be deemed to (a) require the arrest of any person when the officer reasonably believes the person's conduct is justifiable under article thirty-five of title C of the penal law; or (b) restrict or impair the authority of any municipality, political subdivision, or the division of state police from promulgating rules, regulations and policies requiring the arrest of persons in additional circumstances where domestic violence has allegedly occurred.

No cause of action for damages shall arise in favor of any person by reason of any arrest made by a police officer pursuant to this subdivision, except as provided in sections seventeen and eighteen of the public officers law and sections fifty-k, fifty-l, fifty-m and fifty-n of the general municipal law, as appropriate.   * (Repealed 9/1/23, Ch.55,L.2021)

5. Upon investigating a report of a crime or offense between members of the same family or household as such terms are defined in section 530.11 of this chapter and section eight hundred twelve of the family court act, a law enforcement officer shall prepare, file, and translate, in accordance with section two hundred fourteen-b or eight hundred forty of the executive law, a

written report of the incident, on a form promulgated pursuant to section eight hundred thirty-seven of the executive law, including statements made by the victim and by any witnesses, and make any additional reports required by local law enforcement policy or regulations. Such report shall be prepared and filed, whether or not an arrest is made as a result of the officers' investigation, and shall be retained by the law enforcement agency for a period of not less than four years. Where the reported incident involved an offense committed against a person who is sixty-five years of age or older a copy of the report required by this subdivision shall be sent to the New York state committee for the coordination of police services to elderly persons established pursuant to section eight hundred forty-four-b of the executive law. Where the reported incident involved an offense committed by an individual known by the law enforcement officer to be under probation or parole supervision, he or she shall transmit a copy of the report as soon as practicable to the supervising probation department or the department of corrections and community supervision.

6. (a) A police officer who responds to a report of a family offense as defined in section 530.11 of this chapter and section eight hundred twelve of the family court act may take temporary custody of any firearm, rifle, electronic dart gun, electronic stun gun, disguised gun, imitation weapon, shotgun, antique firearm, black powder rifle, black powder shotgun, or muzzle-loading firearm that is in plain sight or is discovered pursuant to a consensual or other lawful search, and shall take temporary custody of any such weapon that is in the possession of any person arrested for the commission of such family offense or suspected of its commission. An officer who takes custody of any weapon pursuant to this paragraph shall also take custody of any license to carry, possess, repair, and dispose of such weapon issued to the person arrested or suspected of such family offense. The officer shall deliver such weapon and/or license to the appropriate law enforcement officer as provided in subparagraph (f) of paragraph one of subdivision a of section 265.20 of the penal law.

(b) Upon taking custody of weapons or a license described in paragraph (a) of this subdivision, the responding officer shall give the owner or person in possession of such weapons or license a receipt describing such weapons and/or license and indicating any identification or serial number on such weapons. Such receipt shall indicate where the weapons and/or license can be recovered and describe the process for recovery provided in paragraph (e) of this subdivision.

(c) Not less than forty-eight hours after effecting such seizure, and in the absence of (i) an order of protection, an extreme risk protection order, or other court order prohibiting the owner from possessing such a weapon and/or license, or (ii) a pending criminal charge or conviction which prohibits such owner from possessing such a weapon and/or license, and upon a written finding that there is no legal impediment to the owner's possession of such a weapon and/or license, the court or, if no court is involved, licensing authority or custodian of the weapon shall direct return of a weapon not otherwise disposed of in accordance with subdivision one of section 400.05 of the penal law and/or such license taken into custody pursuant to this section.

(d) If any other person demonstrates that such person is the lawful owner of any weapon taken into custody pursuant to this section, and provided that the court or, if no court is involved, licensing authority or custodian of the weapon has made a written finding that there is no legal impediment to the person's possession of such a weapon, such court, licensing authority or custodian of the weapon, as the case may be, shall direct that such weapon be returned to such lawful owner.

(e) All weapons in the possession of a law enforcement official pursuant to this section shall be subject to the provisions of applicable law, including but not limited to subdivision six of section 400.05 of the penal law; provided, however, that any such weapon shall be retained and not disposed of by the law enforcement agency for at least two years unless legally transferred by the owner to an individual permitted by law to own and possess such weapon.

§140.15 Arrest without a warrant; when and how made by police officer.

1. A police officer may arrest a person for an offense, pursuant to section 140.10, at any hour of any day or night.

2. The arresting police officer must inform such person of his authority and purpose and of the reason for such arrest unless he encounters physical resistance, flight or other factors rendering such procedure impractical.

3. In order to effect such an arrest, such police officer may use such physical force as is justifiable pursuant to section 35.30 of the penal law.

4. In order to effect such an arrest, a police officer may enter premises in which he reasonably believes such person to be present, under the same circumstances and in the same manner as would be authorized, by the provisions of subdivisions four and five of section 120.80, if he were attempting to make such arrest pursuant to a warrant of arrest.

§140.20 Arrest without a warrant; procedure after arrest by police officer.

1. Upon arresting a person without a warrant, a police officer, after performing without unnecessary delay all recording, fingerprinting and other preliminary police duties required in the particular case, must except as otherwise provided in this section, without unnecessary delay bring the arrested person or cause him to be brought before a local criminal court and file therewith an appropriate accusatory instrument charging him with the offense or offenses in question. The arrested person must be brought to the particular local criminal court, or to one of them if there be more than one, designated in section 100.55 as an appropriate court for commencement of the particular action; except that:

(a) If the arrest is for an offense other than a class A, B, C or D felony or a violation of section 130.25, 130.40, 205.10, 205.17, 205.19 or 215.56 of the penal law committed in a town, but not in a village thereof having a village court, and the town court of such town is not available at the time, the arrested person may be brought before the local criminal court of any village within such town or, any adjoining town, village embraced in whole or in part by such adjoining town, or city of the same county; and

(b) If the arrest is for an offense other than a class A, B, C or D felony or a violation of section 130.25, 130.40, 205.10, 205.17, 205.19 or 215.56 of the penal law committed in a village having a village court and such court is not available at the time, the arrested person may be brought before the town court of the town embracing such village or any other village court within such town, or, if such town or village court is not available either, before the local criminal court of any adjoining town, village embraced in whole or in part by such adjoining town, or city of the same county; and

(c) If the arrest is for an offense committed in a city, and the city court thereof is not available at the time, the arrested person may be brought before the local criminal court of any adjoining town or village, or village court embraced by an adjoining town, within the same county as such city; and

(d) If the arrest is for a traffic infraction or for a misdemeanor relating to traffic, the police officer may, instead of bringing the arrested person before the local criminal court of the political subdivision or locality in which the offense was allegedly committed, bring him or her before the local criminal court of the same county nearest available by highway travel to the point of arrest; and

(e) Notwithstanding any other provision of this section, where a local criminal court in the county in which the defendant is arrested is operating an off-hours arraignment part designated in accordance with paragraph (w) of subdivision one of section two hundred twelve of the judiciary law at the time of defendant's arrest, the arrested person may be brought before such local criminal court.

2. If the arrest is for an offense other than a class A, B, C or D felony or a violation of section 130.25, 130.40, 205.10, 205.17, 205.19 or 215.56 of the penal law, the arrested person need not be brought before a local criminal court as provided in subdivision one, and the procedure may instead be as follows:

(a) A police officer may issue and serve an appearance ticket upon the arrested person and release him from custody, as prescribed in subdivision two of section 150.20; or

(b) The desk officer in charge at a police station, county jail or police headquarters, or any of his superior officers, may, in such place fix pre-arraignment bail and, upon deposit thereof, issue and serve an appearance ticket upon the arrested person and release him from custody, as prescribed in section 150.30.

3. If (a) the arrest is for an offense other than a class A, B, C or D felony or a violation of section 130.25, 130.40, 205.10, 205.17, 205.19 or 215.56 of the penal law, and (b) owing to unavailability of a local criminal court the arresting police officer is unable to bring the arrested person before such a court with reasonable promptness, either an appearance ticket must be served unconditionally upon the arrested person or pre-arraignment bail must be fixed, as prescribed in subdivision two. If pre-arraignment bail is fixed but not posted, such arrested person may be temporarily held in custody but must be brought before a local criminal court without unnecessary delay. Nothing contained in this subdivision requires a police officer to serve an appearance ticket upon an arrested person or release him from custody at a time when such person appears to be under the influence of alcohol, narcotics or other drug to the degree that he may endanger himself or other persons.

4. If after arresting a person, for any offense, a police officer upon further investigation or inquiry determines or is satisfied that there is not reasonable cause to believe that the arrested person committed such offense or any other offense based upon the conduct in question, he need not follow any of the procedures prescribed in subdivisions one, two and three, but must immediately release such person from custody.

5. Before service of an appearance ticket upon an arrested person pursuant to subdivision two or three, the issuing police officer must, if the offense designated in such appearance ticket is one of those specified in subdivision one of section 160.10, cause such person to be fingerprinted in the same manner as would be required were no appearance ticket to be issued or served.

*6. Upon arresting a juvenile offender or a person sixteen or commencing October first, two thousand nineteen, seventeen years of age without a warrant, the police officer shall immediately notify the parent or other person legally responsible for his or her care or the person with whom he or she is domiciled, that such offender or person has been arrested, and the location of the facility where he or she is being detained. If the officer determines that it is necessary to question a juvenile offender or such person, the officer must take him or her to a facility designated by the chief administrator of the courts as a suitable place for the questioning of children or, upon the consent of a parent or other person legally responsible for the care of the juvenile or such person, to his or her residence and there question him or her for a reasonable period of time. A juvenile or such person shall not be questioned pursuant to this section unless he or she and a person required to be notified pursuant to this subdivision, if present, have been advised:

(a) of the juvenile offender's or such person's right to remain silent;

(b) that the statements made by him or her may be used in a court of law;

(c) of his or her right to have an attorney present at such questioning; and

(d) of his or her right to have an attorney provided for him or her without charge if he or she is unable to afford counsel.

In determining the suitability of questioning and determining the reasonable period of time for questioning such a juvenile offender or person, his or her age, the presence or absence of his or her parents or other persons legally responsible for his or her care and notification pursuant to this subdivision shall be included among relevant considerations.

7. Upon arresting a person, other than a juvenile offender, for any offense without a warrant, a police officer shall, upon the arrested person's request, permit him or her to communicate by telephone provided by the law enforcement facility where the defendant is held to a phone number located in the United States or Puerto Rico, for the purposes of obtaining counsel and informing a relative or friend that he or she has been arrested, unless granting the call will compromise an ongoing investigation or the prosecution of the defendant.

*8. If the arrest is for a juvenile offender or adolescent offender other than an arrest for a violation or a traffic infraction, such offender shall be brought before the youth part of the superior court. If the youth part is not in session, such offender shall be brought before the most accessible magistrate designated by the appellate division of the supreme court in the applicable department to act as a youth part.

*(Eff.10/1/18; provided however, that when the applicability of such provisions are based on the conviction of a crime or an act committed by a person who was seventeen years of age at the time of such offense such provisions shall take effect 10/1/19, Ch.59,L.2017)

§140.25 Arrest without a warrant; by peace officer.

1. A peace officer, acting pursuant to his special duties, may arrest a person for:

(a) Any offense when he has reasonable cause to believe that such person has committed such offense in his presence; and

(b) A crime when he has reasonable cause to believe that such person has committed such crime, whether in his presence or otherwise.

2. A peace officer acts "pursuant to his special duties" in making an arrest only when the arrest is for:

(a) An offense defined by a statute which such peace officer, by reason of the specialized nature of his particular employment or by express provision of law, is required or authorized to enforce; or

(b) An offense committed or reasonably believed by him to have been committed in such manner or place as to render arrest of the offender by such peace officer under the particular circumstances an integral part of his specialized duties.

3. A peace officer, whether or not he is acting pursuant to his special duties, may arrest a person for an offense committed or believed by him to have been committed within the geographical area of such peace officer's employment, as follows:

(a) He may arrest such person for any offense when such person has in fact committed such offense in his presence; and

(b) He may arrest such person for a felony when he has reasonable cause to believe that such person has committed such felony, whether in his presence or otherwise.

4. A peace officer, when outside the geographical area of his employ-ment, may, anywhere in the state, arrest a person for a felony when he has reasonable cause to believe that such person has there committed such felony in his presence, provided that such arrest is made during or immediately after the allegedly criminal conduct or during the alleged perpetrator's immediate flight therefrom.

5. For the purposes of this section, the "geographical area of employment" of a peace officer is as follows:

(a) The "geographical area of employment" of any peace officer employed as such by any agency of the state consists of the entire state;

(b) The "geographical area of employment" of any peace officer employed as such by an agency of a county, city, town or village consists of (i) such county, city, town or village, as the case may be, and (ii) any other place where he is, at a particular time, acting in the course of his particular duties or employment;

(c) The "geographical area of employment" of any peace officer employed as such by any private organization consists of any place in the state where he is, at a particular time, acting in the course of his particular duties or employment.

§140.27 Arrest without a warrant; when and how made; procedure after arrest by peace officer.

1. The rules governing the manner in which a peace officer may make an arrest, pursuant to section 140.25, are the same as those governing arrests by police officers, as prescribed in section 140.15.

*2. Upon arresting a person without a warrant, a peace officer, except as otherwise provided in subdivision three *or three-a*, must without unneces-sary delay bring him or cause him to be brought before a local criminal court, as provided in section 100.55 and subdivision one of section 140.20, and must without unnecessary delay file or cause to be filed therewith an appropriate accusatory instrument. If the offense which is the subject of the arrest is one of those specified in subdivision one of section 160.10, the arrested person must be fingerprinted and photographed as therein provided. In order to execute the required post-arrest functions, such arresting peace officer may perform such functions himself or he may enlist the aid of a police officer for the performance thereof in the manner provided in subdivision one of section 140.20.

3. If (a) the arrest is for an offense other than a class A, B, C or D felony or a violation of section 130.25, 130.40, 205.10, 205.17, 205.19 or 215.56 of the penal law and (b) owing to unavailability of a local criminal court such peace officer is unable to bring or cause the arrested person to be brought before such a court with reasonable promptness, the arrested person must be brought to an appropriate police station, county jail or police head-quarters where he must be dealt with in the manner prescribed in subdivi-sion three of section 140.20, as if he had been arrested by a police officer.

3-a. If the arrest is for a juvenile offender or adolescent offender other than an arrest for violations or traffic infractions, such offender shall be brought before the youth part of the superior court. If the youth part is not in session, such offender shall be brought before the most accessible magistrate designated by the appellate division of the supreme court in the applicable department to act as a youth part.

(Material in Italics Eff.10/1/18; provided however, that when the applicability of such provisions are based on the conviction of a crime or an act committed by a person who was seventeen years of age at the time of such offense such provisions shall take effect 10/1/19, Ch.59,L.2017)

4. If the arrest is for an offense other than a class A, B, C or D felony or a violation of section 130.25, 130.40, 205.10, 205.17, 205.19 or 215.56 of the

penal law, the arrested person need not be brought before a local criminal court as provided in subdivision two, and the procedure may instead be as follows:

(a) The arresting peace officer, where he is specially authorized by law to issue and serve an appearance ticket, may issue and serve an appearance ticket upon the arrested person and release him from custody; or

(b) The arresting peace officer, where he is not specially authorized by law to issue and serve an appearance ticket, may enlist the aid of a police officer and request that such officer issue and serve an appearance ticket upon the arrested person, and upon such issuance and service the latter must be released from custody.

*5. Upon arresting a juvenile offender without a warrant, the peace officer shall immediately notify the parent or other person legally responsible for his care or the person with whom he is domiciled, that the juvenile offender has been arrested, and the location of the facility where he is being detained.

(Eff. Until 10/1/18,Ch.59,L.2017)

* 5. Upon arresting a juvenile offender or a person sixteen or commencing October first, two thousand nineteen, seventeen years of age without a warrant, the peace officer shall immediately notify the parent or other person legally responsible for his or her care or the person with whom he or she is domiciled, that such offender or person has been arrested, and the location of the facility where he or she is being detained. If the officer determines that it is necessary to question a juvenile offender or such person, the officer must take him or her to a facility designated by the chief administrator of the courts as a suitable place for the questioning of children or, upon the consent of a parent or other person legally responsible for the care of a juvenile offender or such person, to his or her residence and there question him or her for a reasonable period of time. A juvenile offender or such person shall not be questioned pursuant to this section unless the juvenile offender or such person and a person required to be notified pursuant to this subdivision, if present, have been advised:

(a) of his or her right to remain silent;

(b) that the statements made by the juvenile offender or such person may be used in a court of law;

(c) of his or her right to have an attorney present at such questioning; and

(d) of his or her right to have an attorney provided for him or her without charge if he or she is unable to afford counsel.

In determining the suitability of questioning and determining the reasonable period of time for questioning such a juvenile offender or such person, his or her age, the presence or absence of his or her parents or other persons legally responsible for his or her care and notification pursuant to this subdivision shall be included among relevant considerations.

(Eff.10/1/18; provided however, that when the applicability of such provisions are based on the conviction of a crime or an act committed by a person who was seventeen years of age at the time of such offense such provisions shall take effect 10/1/19, Ch.59,L.2017)

§140.30 Arrest without a warrant; by any person; when and where authorized.

1. Subject to the provisions of subdivision two, any person may arrest another person (a) for a felony when the latter has in fact committed such felony, and (b) for any offense when the latter has in fact committed such offense in his presence.

2. Such an arrest, if for a felony, may be made anywhere in the state. If the arrest is for an offense other than a felony, it may be made only in the county in which such offense was committed.

§140.35 Arrest without a warrant; by person acting other than as a police officer or a peace officer; when and how made.

1. A person may arrest another person for an offense pursuant to section 140.30 at any hour of any day or night.

2. Such person must inform the person whom he is arresting of the reason for such arrest unless he encounters physical resistance, flight or other factors rendering such procedure impractical.

3. In order to effect such an arrest, such person may use such physical force as is justifiable pursuant to subdivision four of section 35.30 of the penal law.

§140.40 Arrest without a warrant; by person acting other than as a police officer or a peace officer; procedure after arrest.

1. A person making an arrest pursuant to section 140.30 must without unnecessary delay deliver or attempt to deliver the person arrested to the custody of an appropriate police officer, as defined in subdivision five. For such purpose, he may solicit the aid of any police officer and the latter, if he is not himself an appropriate police officer, must assist in delivering the arrested person to an appropriate officer. If the arrest is for a felony, the appropriate police officer must, upon receiving custody of the arrested person, perform all recording, fingerprinting and other preliminary police duties required in the particular case. In any case, the appropriate police officer, upon receiving custody of the arrested person, except as otherwise provided in subdivisions two and three, must bring him, on behalf of the arresting person, before an appropriate local criminal court, as defined in subdivision five, and the arresting person must without unnecessary delay file an appropriate accusatory instrument with such court.

2. If (a) the arrest is for an offense other than a class A, B, C or D felony or a violation of section 130.25, 130.40, 205.10, 205.17, 205.19 or 215.56 of the penal law and (b) owing to unavailability of a local criminal court the appropriate police officer having custody of the arrested person is unable to bring him before such a court with reasonable promptness, the arrested person must be dealt with in the manner prescribed in subdivision three of section 140.20, as if he had been arrested by a police officer.

3. If the arrest is for an offense other than a class A, B, C or D felony or a violation of section 130.25, 130.40, 205.10, 205.17, 205.19 or 215.56 of the penal law, the arrested person need not be brought before a local criminal court, as provided in subdivision one, and the procedure may instead be as follows:

(a) An appropriate police officer may issue and serve an appearance ticket upon the arrested person and release him from custody, as prescribed in subdivision two of section 150.20; or

(b) The desk officer in charge at the appropriate police officer's station, county jail or police headquarters, or any of his superior officers, may, in such place, fix pre-arraignment bail and, upon deposit thereof, issue and serve an appearance ticket upon the arrested person and release him from custody, as prescribed in section 150.30.

4. Notwithstanding any other provision of this section, a police officer is not required to take an arrested person into custody or to take any other action prescribed in this section on behalf of the arresting person if he has reasonable cause to believe that the arrested person did not commit the alleged offense or that the arrest was otherwise unauthorized.

*5. If a police officer takes an arrested juvenile offender into custody, the police officer shall immediately notify the parent or other person legally responsible for his care or the person with whom he is domiciled, that the juvenile offender has been arrested, and the location of the facility where he is being detained. *(Eff. Until 10/1/18,Ch.59,L.2017)

*5. If a police officer takes an arrested juvenile offender or a person sixteen or commencing October first, two thousand nineteen, seventeen years of age into custody, the police officer shall immediately notify the parent or other person legally responsible for his or her care or the person with whom he or she is domiciled, that such offender or person has been arrested, and the location of the facility where he or she is being detained. If the officer determines that it is necessary to question a juvenile offender or such person the officer must take him or her to a facility designated by the chief administrator of the courts as a suitable place for the questioning of children or, upon the consent of a parent or other person legally responsible for the care of the juvenile offender or such person, to his or her residence and there question him or her for a reasonable period of time. A juvenile offender or such person shall not be questioned pursuant to this section unless he or she and a person required to be notified pursuant to this subdivision, if present, have been advised:

(a) of his or her right to remain silent;

(b) that the statements made by the juvenile offender or such person may be used in a court of law;

(c) of his or her right to have an attorney present at such questioning; and

(d) of his or her right to have an attorney provided for him or her without charge if he or she is unable to afford counsel.

In determining the suitability of questioning and determining the reasonable period of time for questioning such a juvenile offender or such person, his or her age, the presence or absence of his or her parents or other persons legally responsible for his or her care and notification pursuant to this subdivision shall be included among relevant considerations.

6. As used in this section:

(a) An "appropriate police officer" means one who would himself be authorized to make the arrest in question as a police officer pursuant to section 140.10;

(b) An "appropriate local criminal court" means one with which an accusatory instrument charging the offense in question may properly be filed pursuant to the provisions of section 100.55.

*(Eff.10/1/18; provided however, that when the applicability of such provisions are based on the conviction of a crime or an act committed by a person who was seventeen years of age at the time of such offense such provisions shall take effect 10/1/19, Ch.59,L.2017)

§140.45 Arrest without a warrant; dismissal of insufficient local criminal court accusatory instrument.

If a local criminal court accusatory instrument filed with a local criminal court pursuant to section 140.20, 140.25 or 140.40 is not sufficient on its face, as prescribed in section 100.40, and if the court is satisfied that on the basis of the available facts or evidence it would be impossible to draw and file an accusatory instrument which is sufficient on its face, it must dismiss such accusatory instrument and discharge the defendant.

§140.50 Temporary questioning of persons in public places; search for weapons.

1. In addition to the authority provided by this article for making an arrest without a warrant, a police officer may stop a person in a public place located within the geographical area of such officer's employment when he reasonably suspects that such person is committing, has committed or is about to commit either (a) a felony or (b) a misdemeanor defined in the

penal law, and may demand of him his name, address and an explanation of his conduct.

2. Any person who is a peace officer and who provides security services for any court of the unified court system may stop a person in or about the courthouse to which he is assigned when he reasonably suspects that such person is committing, has committed or is about to commit either (a) a felony or (b) a misdemeanor defined in the penal law, and may demand of him his name, address and an explanation of his conduct.

3. When upon stopping a person under circumstances prescribed in subdivisions one and two a police officer or court officer, as the case may be, reasonably suspects that he is in danger of physical injury, he may search such person for a deadly weapon or any instrument, article or substance readily capable of causing serious physical injury and of a sort not ordinarily carried in public places by law-abiding persons. If he finds such a weapon or instrument, or any other property possession of which he reasonably believes may constitute the commission of a crime, he may take it and keep it until the completion of the questioning, at which time he shall either return it, if lawfully possessed, or arrest such person.

4. In cities with a population of one million or more, information that establishes the personal identity of an individual who has been stopped, questioned and/or frisked by a police officer or peace officer, such as the name, address or social security number of such person, shall not be recorded in a computerized or electronic database if that individual is released without further legal action; provided, however, that this subdivision shall not prohibit police officers or peace officers from including in a computerized or electronic database generic characteristics of an individual, such as race and gender, who has been stopped, questioned and/or frisked by a police officer or peace officer.

§140.55 Arrest without a warrant; by peace officers of other states for offense committed outside state; uniform close pursuit act.

1. As used in this section, the word "state" shall include the District of Columbia.

2. Any peace officer of another state of the United States, who enters this state in close pursuit and continues within this state in such close pursuit of a person in order to arrest him, shall have the same authority to arrest and hold in custody such person on the ground that he has committed a crime in another state which is a crime under the laws of the state of New York, as police officers of this state have to arrest and hold in custody a person on the ground that he has committed a crime in this state.

3. If an arrest is made in this state by an officer of another state in accordance with the provisions of subdivision two, he shall without unnecessary delay take the person arrested before a local criminal court which shall conduct a hearing for the sole purpose of determining if the arrest was in accordance with the provisions of subdivision two, and not of determining the guilt or innocence of the arrested person. If such court determines that the arrest was in accordance with such subdivision, it shall commit the person arrested to the custody of the officer making the arrest, who shall without unnecessary delay take him to the state from which he fled. If such court determines that the arrest was unlawful, it shall discharge the person arrested.

4. This section shall not be construed so as to make unlawful any arrest in this state which would otherwise be lawful.

5. Upon the taking effect of this section it shall be the duty of the secretary of state to certify a copy of this section to the executive department of each of the states of the United States.

6. This section shall apply only to peace officers of a state which by its laws has made similar provision for the arrest and custody of persons closely pursued within the territory thereof.

7. If any part of this section is for any reason declared void, it is declared to be the intent of this section that such invalidity shall not affect the validity of the remaining portions of this section.

8. This section may be cited as the uniform act on close pursuit.

ARTICLE 150 - THE APPEARANCE TICKET

Section
150.10 Appearance ticket; definition, form and content.
150.20 Appearance ticket; when and by whom issuable.
150.30 Appearance ticket; issuance and service thereof after arrest upon posting of pre-arraignment bail.
150.40 Appearance ticket; where returnable; how and where served.
150.50 Appearance ticket; filing a local criminal court accusatory instrument; dismissal of insufficient instrument.
150.60 Appearance ticket; defendant's failure to appear.
150.70 Appearance ticket; fingerprinting of defendant.
150.75 Appearance ticket; certain cases.
150.80 Court appearance reminders.

§150.10 Appearance ticket; definition, form and content.

1. An appearance ticket is a written notice issued and subscribed by a police officer or other public servant authorized by state law or local law enacted pursuant to the provisions of the municipal home rule law to issue the same, directing a designated person to appear in a designated local criminal court at a designated future time in connection with his alleged commission of a designated offense. A notice conforming to such definition constitutes an appearance ticket regardless of whether it is referred to in some other provision of law as a summons or by any other name or title.

2. When an appearance ticket as defined in subdivision one of this section is issued to a person in conjunction with an offense charged in a simplified information, said appearance ticket shall contain the language, set forth in subdivision four of section 100.25, notifying the defendant of his right to receive a supporting deposition.

3. Before issuing an appearance ticket a police officer or other public servant must inform the arrestee that they may provide their contact information for the purposes of receiving a court notification to remind them of their court appearance date from the court or a certified pretrial services agency. Such contact information may include one or more phone numbers, a residential address or address at which the arrestee receives mail, or an email address. The contact information shall be recorded and be transmitted to the local criminal court as required by section 150.80 of this article.

(Eff. 1/1/20, Ch. 59, L. 2019)

§150.20 Appearance ticket; when and by whom issuable.

1. (a) Whenever a police officer is authorized pursuant to section 140.10 of this title to arrest a person without a warrant for an offense other than a class A, B, C or D felony or a violation of section 130.25, 130.40, 205.10, 205.17, 205.19 or 215.56 of the penal law, he shall, except as set out in paragraph (b) of this subdivision, subject to the provisions of subdivisions three and four of section 150.40 of this title, instead issue to and serve upon such person an appearance ticket.

(b) An officer is not required to issue an appearance ticket if:

(i) the person has one or more outstanding local criminal court or superior court warrants;

(ii) the person has failed to appear in court proceedings in the last two years;

(iii) the person has been given a reasonable opportunity to make their verifiable identity and a method of contact known, and has been unable or unwilling to do so, so that a custodial arrest is necessary to subject the individual to the jurisdiction of the court. For the purposes of this section, an officer may rely on various factors to determine a person's identity, including but not limited to personal knowledge of such person, such person's self-identification, or photographic identification. There is no requirement that a person present photographic identification in order to be issued an appearance ticket in lieu of arrest where the person's identity is otherwise verifiable; however, if offered by such person, an officer shall accept as evidence of identity the following: a valid driver's license or non-driver identification card issued by the commissioner of motor vehicles, the federal government, any United States territory, commonwealth or possession, the District of Columbia, a state government or municipal government within the United States or a provincial government of the dominion of Canada; a valid passport issued by the United States government or any other country; an identification card issued by the armed forces of the United States; a public benefit card, as defined in paragraph (a) of subdivision one of section 158.00 of the penal law;

(iv) the person is charged with a crime between members of the same family or household, as defined in subdivision one of section 530.11 of this chapter;

(v) the person is charged with a crime defined in article 130 of the penal law;

(vi) it reasonably appears the person should be brought before the court for consideration of issuance of an order of protection, pursuant to section 530.13 of this chapter, based on the facts of the crime or offense that the officer has reasonable cause to believe occurred;

(vii) the person is charged with a crime for which the court may suspend or revoke his or her driver license;

(viii) it reasonably appears to the officer, based on the observed behavior of the individual in the present contact with the officer and facts regarding the person's condition that indicates a sign of distress to such a degree that the person would face harm without immediate medical or mental health care, that bringing the person before the court would be in such person's interest in addressing that need; provided, however, that before making the arrest, the officer shall make all reasonable efforts to assist the person in securing appropriate services. *(Eff. 1/1/20, Ch.59, L.2019)*

2. (a) Whenever a police officer has arrested a person without a warrant for an offense other than a class A, B, C or D felony or a violation of section 130.25, 130.40, 205.10, 205.17, 205.19 or 215.56 of the penal law pursuant to section 140.10, or (b) whenever a peace officer, who is not authorized by law to issue an appearance ticket, has arrested a person for an offense other than a class A, B, C or D felony or a violation of section 130.25, 130.40, 205.10, 205.17, 205.19 or 215.56 of the penal law pursuant to section 140.25, and has requested a police officer to issue and serve upon such arrested person an appearance ticket pursuant to subdivision four of section 140.27, or (c) whenever a person has been arrested for an offense other than a class A, B, C or D felony or a violation of section 130.25, 130.40, 205.10, 205.17, 205.19 or 215.56 of the penal law and has been delivered to the custody of an appropriate police officer pursuant to section 140.40, such police officer may, instead of bringing such person before a local criminal court and promptly filing or causing the arresting peace officer or arresting person to file a local criminal court accusatory instrument therewith, issue to and serve upon such person an appearance ticket. The

issuance and service of an appearance ticket under such circumstances may be conditioned upon a deposit of pre-arraignment bail, as provided in section 150.30.

3. A public servant other than a police officer, who is specially authorized by state law or local law enacted pursuant to the provisions of the municipal home rule law to issue and serve appearance tickets with respect to designated offenses other than class A, B, C or D felonies or violations of section 130.25, 130.40, 205.10, 205.17, 205.19 or 215.56 of the penal law, may in such cases issue and serve upon a person an appearance ticket when he has reasonable cause to believe that such person has committed a crime, or has committed a petty offense in his presence.

§150.40 Appearance ticket; where returnable; how and where served.

1. An appearance ticket must be made returnable at a date as soon as possible, but in no event later than twenty days from the date of issuance; or at the next scheduled session of the appropriate local criminal court if such session is scheduled to occur more than twenty days from the date of issuance; or at a later date, with the court's permission due to enrollment in a pre-arraignment diversion program. The appearance ticket shall be made returnable in a local criminal court designated in section 100.55 of this title as one with which an information for the offense in question may be filed.

(Eff. 7/2/20, Ch. 56, L. 2020)

2. An appearance ticket, other than one issued for a traffic infraction relating to parking, must be served personally, except that an appearance ticket issued for the violation of a local zoning ordinance or local zoning law, or of a building or sanitation code may be served in any manner authorized for service under section three hundred eight of the civil practice law and rules.

3. An appearance ticket may be served anywhere in the county in which the designated offense was allegedly committed or in any adjoining county, and may be served elsewhere as prescribed in subdivision four.

4. A police officer may, for the purpose of serving an appearance ticket upon a person, follow him in continuous close pursuit, commencing either in the county in which the alleged offense was committed or in an adjoining county, in and through any county of the state, and may serve such appearance ticket upon him in any county in which he overtakes him.

§150.50 Appearance ticket; filing a local criminal court accusatory instrument; dismissal of insufficient instrument.

1. A police officer or other public servant who has issued and served an appearance ticket must, at or before the time such appearance ticket is returnable, file or cause to be filed with the local criminal court in which it is returnable a local criminal court accusatory instrument charging the person named in such appearance ticket with the offense specified therein; provided, however, that no separate accusatory instrument shall be required

to be filed for an appearance ticket issued for a parking infraction which conforms to the requirements set forth in paragraph (b) of subdivision one of section 1.20 of this chapter. Nothing herein contained shall authorize the use of a simplified information when not authorized by law.

(Eff.11/8/19,Ch.450,L.2019)

2. If such accusatory instrument is not sufficient on its face, as prescribed in section 100.40, and if the court is satisfied that on the basis of the available facts or evidence it would be impossible to draw and file an accusatory instrument which is sufficient on its face, it must dismiss such accusatory instrument.

§150.60 Appearance ticket; defendant's failure to appear.

If after the service of an appearance ticket and the filing of a local criminal court accusatory instrument charging the offense designated therein, the defendant does not appear in the designated local criminal court at the time such appearance ticket is returnable, the court may issue a summons or a warrant of arrest based upon the local criminal court accusatory instrument filed.

§150.70 Appearance ticket; fingerprinting of defendant.

Upon the arraignment of a defendant who has not been arrested and whose court attendance has been secured by the issuance and service of an appearance ticket pursuant to subdivision one of section 150.20, the court must, if an offense charged in the accusatory instrument is one specified in subdivision one of section 160.10, direct that the defendant be fingerprinted by the appropriate police officer or agency, and that he appear at an appropriate designated time and place for such purpose.

§150.75 Appearance ticket; certain cases.

1. The provision of this section shall apply in any case wherein the defendant is alleged to have committed an offense defined in section 221.05 of the penal law, and no other offense is alleged, notwithstanding any provision of this chapter or any other law to the contrary.

2. Whenever the defendant is arrested without a warrant, an appearance ticket shall promptly be issued and served upon him, as provided in this article. The issuance and service of the appearance ticket may be made conditional upon the posting of pre-arraignment bail as provided in section 150.30 of this chapter but only if the appropriate police officer (a) is unable to ascertain the defendant's identity or residence address; or (b) reasonably suspects that the identification or residence address given by the defendant is not accurate; or (c) reasonably suspects that the defendant does not reside within the state. No warrant of arrest shall be issued unless the defendant has failed to appear in court as required by the terms of the appearance ticket or by the court.

§150.80 Court appearance reminders.

1. A police officer or other public servant who has issued and served an appearance ticket must, within twenty-four hours of issuance, file or cause to be filed with the local criminal court the appearance ticket and any contact information made available pursuant to subdivision three of section 150.10 of this article.

2. Upon receipt of the appearance ticket and any contact information made available pursuant to subdivision three of section 150.10 of this article, the local criminal court shall issue a court appearance reminder and notify the arrestee of their court appearances by text message, telephone call, electronic mail, or first class mail. The local criminal court may partner with a certified pretrial services agency or agencies in that county to provide such notification and shall include a copy of the appearance ticket.

3. A local criminal court is not required to issue a court appearance reminder if the appearance ticket requires the arrestee's appearance within seventy-two hours of its issuance, or no contact information has been provided.   *(Eff. 1/1/20, Ch. 59, L. 2019)*

ARTICLE 160 - FINGERPRINTING AND PHOTOGRAPHING OF DEFENDANT AFTER ARREST - CRIMINAL IDENTIFICATION RECORDS AND STATISTICS

Section
160.10   Fingerprinting; duties of police with respect thereto.
160.20   Fingerprinting; forwarding of fingerprints.
160.30   Fingerprinting; duties of division of criminal justice services.
160.40   Fingerprinting; transmission of report received by police.
160.45   Polygraph tests; prohibition against.
160.50   Order upon termination of criminal action in favor of the accused.
160.55   Order upon termination of criminal action by conviction for noncriminal offense; entry of waiver; administrative findings.
160.58   Conditional sealing of certain controlled substance, marihuana or specified offense convictions.
160.59   Sealing of certain convictions.
160.60   Effect of termination of criminal actions in favor of the accused.

§160.10   Fingerprinting; duties of police with respect thereto.

1. Following an arrest, or following the arraignment upon a local criminal court accusatory instrument of a defendant whose court attendance has been secured by a summons or an appearance ticket under circumstances described in sections 130.60 and 150.70, the arresting or other appropriate police officer or agency must take or cause to be taken fingerprints of the arrested person or defendant if an offense which is the subject of the arrest or which is charged in the accusatory instrument filed is:

   (a) A felony; or
   (b) A misdemeanor defined in the penal law; or
   (c) A misdemeanor defined outside the penal law which would constitute a felony if such person had a previous judgment of conviction for a crime.   *(Eff. 2/2/21, Ch. 23, L. 2021)*

2. In addition, a police officer who makes an arrest for any offense, either with or without a warrant, may take or cause to be taken the fingerprints of the arrested person if such police officer:

   (a) Is unable to ascertain such person's identity; or
   (b) Reasonably suspects that the identification given by such person is not accurate; or
   (c) Reasonably suspects that such person is being sought by law enforcement officials for the commission of some other offense.

3. Whenever fingerprints are required to be taken pursuant to subdivision one or permitted to be taken pursuant to subdivision two, the photograph and palmprints of the arrested person or the defendant, as the case may be, may also be taken.

4. The taking of fingerprints as prescribed in this section and the submission of available information concerning the arrested person or the defendant and the facts and circumstances of the crime charged must be in accordance with the standards established by the commissioner of the division of criminal justice services.

§160.20   Fingerprinting; forwarding of fingerprints.

Upon the taking of fingerprints of an arrested person or defendant as prescribed in section 160.10, the appropriate police officer or agency must without unnecessary delay forward two copies of such fingerprints to the division of criminal justice services.

§160.30   Fingerprinting; duties of division of criminal justice services.

1. Upon receiving fingerprints from a police officer or agency pursuant to section 160.20 of this chapter, the division of criminal justice services must, except as provided in subdivision two of this section, classify them and

search its records for information concerning a previous record of the defendant, including any adjudication as a juvenile delinquent pursuant to article three of the family court act, or as a youthful offender pursuant to article seven hundred twenty of this chapter, and promptly transmit to such forwarding police officer or agency a report containing all information on file with respect to such defendant's previous record, if any, or stating that the defendant has no previous record according to its files. Such a report, if certified, constitutes presumptive evidence of the facts so certified.

2. If the fingerprints so received are not sufficiently legible to permit accurate and complete classification, they must be returned to the forwarding police officer or agency with an explanation of the defects and a request that the defendant's fingerprints be retaken if possible.

§160.40 Fingerprinting; transmission of report received by police.

1. Upon receipt of a report of the division of criminal justice services as provided in section 160.30, the recipient police officer or agency must promptly transmit such report or a copy thereof to the district attorney of the county and two copies thereof to the court in which the action is pending.

2. Upon receipt of such report the court shall furnish a copy thereof to counsel for the defendant or, if the defendant is not represented by counsel, to the defendant.

§160.45 Polygraph tests; prohibition against.

1. No district attorney, police officer or employee of any law enforcement agency shall request or require any victim of a sexual assault crime to submit to any polygraph test or psychological stress evaluator examination.

2. As used in this section, "victim of a sexual assault crime" means any person alleged to have sustained an offense under article one hundred thirty or section 255.25, 255.26 or 255.27 of the penal law.

§160.50 Order upon termination of criminal action in favor of the accused.

1. Upon the termination of a criminal action or proceeding against a person in favor of such person, as defined in subdivision three of this section, unless the district attorney upon motion with not less than five days notice to such person or his or her attorney demonstrates to the satisfaction of the court that the interests of justice require otherwise, or the court on its own motion with not less than five days notice to such person or his or her attorney determines that the interests of justice require otherwise and states the reasons for such determination on the record, the record of such action or proceeding shall be sealed and the clerk of the court wherein such criminal action or proceeding was terminated shall immediately notify the commissioner of the division of criminal justice services and the heads of all appropriate police departments and other law enforcement agencies that the action has been terminated in favor of the accused, and unless the court has directed otherwise, that the record of such action or proceeding shall be sealed. Upon receipt of notification of such termination and sealing:

(a) every photograph of such person and photographic plate or proof, and all palmprints and fingerprints taken or made of such person pursuant to the provisions of this article in regard to the action or proceeding terminated, except a dismissal pursuant to section 170.56 or 210.46 of this chapter, and all duplicates and copies thereof, except a digital fingerprint image where authorized pursuant to paragraph (e) of this subdivision, shall forthwith be, at the discretion of the recipient agency, either destroyed or returned to such person, or to the attorney who represented such person at the time of the termination of the action or proceeding, at the address given by such person or attorney during the action or proceeding, by the division of criminal justice services and by any police department or law enforcement agency having any such photograph, photographic plate or proof, palmprint or fingerprints in its possession or under its control;

(b) any police department or law enforcement agency, including the division of criminal justice services, which transmitted or otherwise forwarded to any agency of the United States or of any other state or of any other jurisdiction outside the state of New York copies of any such photographs, photographic plates or proofs, palmprints and fingerprints, including those relating to actions or proceedings which were dismissed pursuant to section 170.56 or 210.46 of this chapter, shall forthwith formally request in writing that all such copies be destroyed or returned to the police department or law enforcement agency which transmitted or forwarded them, and, if returned, such department or agency shall, at its discretion, either destroy or return them as provided herein, except that those relating to dismissals pursuant to section 170.56 or 210.46 of this chapter shall not be destroyed or returned by such department or agency;

(c) all official records and papers, including judgments and orders of a court but not including published court decisions or opinions or records and briefs on appeal, relating to the arrest or prosecution, including all duplicates and copies thereof, on file with the division of criminal justice services, any court, police agency, or prosecutor's office shall be sealed and not made available to any person or public or private agency;

(d) such records shall be made available to the person accused or to such person's designated agent, and shall be made available to (i) a prosecutor in any proceeding in which the accused has moved for an order pursuant to section 170.56 or 210.46 of this chapter, or (ii) a law enforcement agency upon ex parte motion in any superior court, or in any district court, city court or the criminal court of the city of New York provided that such court sealed the record, if such agency demonstrates to the satisfaction of the court that justice requires that such records be made available to it, or (iii) any state or local officer or agency with responsibility for the issuance of licenses to possess guns, when the accused has made application for such a license, or (iv) the New York state department of corrections and community supervision when the accused is on parole supervision as a result of conditional release or a parole release granted by the New York state board of parole, and the arrest which is the subject of the inquiry is one which occurred while the accused was under such supervision, or (v) any prospective employer of a police officer or peace officer as those terms are defined in subdivisions thirty-three and thirty-four of section 1.20 of this chapter, in relation to an application for employment as a police officer or peace officer; provided, however, that every person who is an applicant for the position of police officer or peace officer shall be furnished with a copy of all records obtained under this paragraph and afforded an opportunity to make an explanation thereto, or (vi) the probation department responsible for supervision of the accused when the arrest which is the subject of the inquiry is one which occurred while the accused was under such supervision; and

(e) where fingerprints subject to the provisions of this section have been received by the division of criminal justice services and have been filed by the division as digital images, such images may be retained, provided that a fingerprint card of the individual is on file with the division which was not sealed pursuant to this section or section 160.55 of this article.

2. A report of the termination of the action or proceeding in favor of the accused shall be sufficient notice of sealing to the commissioner of the division of criminal justice services unless the report also indicates that the court directed that the record not be sealed in the interests of justice. Where the court has determined pursuant to subdivision one of this section that sealing is not in the interest of justice, the clerk of the court shall include

notification of that determination in any report to such division of the disposition of the action or proceeding.

3. For the purposes of subdivision one of this section, a criminal action or proceeding against a person shall be considered terminated in favor of such person where:

(a) an order dismissing the entire accusatory instrument against such person pursuant to article four hundred seventy was entered; or

(b) an order to dismiss the entire accusatory instrument against such person pursuant to section 170.30, 170.50, 170.55, 170.56, 180.70, 210.20, 210.46 or 210.47 of this chapter was entered or deemed entered, or an order terminating the prosecution against such person was entered pursuant to section 180.85 of this chapter, and the people have not appealed from such order or the determination of an appeal or appeals by the people from such order has been against the people; or

(c) a verdict of complete acquittal was made pursuant to section 330.10 of this chapter; or

(d) a trial order of dismissal of the entire accusatory instrument against such person pursuant to section 290.10 or 360.40 of this chapter was entered and the people have not appealed from such order or the determination of an appeal or appeals by the people from such order has been against the people; or

(e) an order setting aside a verdict pursuant to section 330.30 or 370.10 of this chapter was entered and the people have not appealed from such order or the determination of an appeal or appeals by the people from such order has been against the people and no new trial has been ordered; or

(f) an order vacating a judgment pursuant to section 440.10 of this chapter was entered and the people have not appealed from such order or the determination of an appeal or appeals by the people from such order has been against the people, and no new trial has been ordered; or

(g) an order of discharge pursuant to article seventy of the civil practice law and rules was entered on a ground which invalidates the conviction and the people have not appealed from such order or the determination of an appeal or appeals by the people from such order has been against the people; or

(h) where all charges against such person are dismissed pursuant to section 190.75 of this chapter. In such event, the clerk of the court which empaneled the grand jury shall serve a certification of such disposition upon the division of criminal justice services and upon the appropriate police department or law enforcement agency which upon receipt thereof, shall comply with the provisions of paragraphs (a), (b), (c) and (d) of subdivision one of this section in the same manner as is required thereunder with respect to an order of a court entered pursuant to said subdivision one; or

(i) prior to the filing of an accusatory instrument in a local criminal court against such person, the prosecutor elects not to prosecute such person. In such event, the prosecutor shall serve a certification of such disposition upon the division of criminal justice services and upon the appropriate police department or law enforcement agency which, upon receipt thereof, shall comply with the provisions of paragraphs (a), (b), (c) and (d) of subdivision one of this section in the same manner as is required thereunder with respect to an order of a court entered pursuant to said subdivision one.

(j) following the arrest of such person, the arresting police agency, prior to the filing of an accusatory instrument in a local criminal court but subsequent to the forwarding of a copy of the fingerprints of such person to the division of criminal justice services, elects not to proceed further. In such event, the head of the arresting police agency shall serve a certification of such disposition upon the division of criminal justice services which, upon receipt thereof, shall comply with the provisions of paragraphs (a), (b), (c) and (d) of subdivision one of this section in the same manner as is required thereunder with respect to an order of a court entered pursuant to said subdivision one.

(k) (i) The conviction was for a violation of article two hundred twenty or section 240.36 of the penal law prior to the effective date of article two hundred twenty-one of the penal law, and the sole controlled substance involved was marihuana and the conviction was only for a misdemeanor and/or violation; or

(ii) the conviction is for an offense defined in section 221.05 or 221.10 of the penal law prior to the effective date of chapter one hundred thirty-two of the laws of two thousand nineteen; or

(iii) the conviction is for an offense defined in former section 221.05 221.10, 221.15, 221.20, 221.35, or 221.40 of the penal law; or

(iv) the conviction was for an offense defined in section 240.37 of the penal law; or

(v) the conviction was for a violation of section 220.03 or 220.06 of the penal law prior to the effective date of the chapter of the laws of two thousand twenty-one that amended this paragraph, and the sole controlled substance involved was concentrated cannabis; or

(vi) the conviction was for an offense defined in section 222.10, 222.15, 222.25 or 222.45 of the penal law.

No defendant shall be required or permitted to waive eligibility for sealing or expungement pursuant to this section as part of a plea of guilty, sentence or any agreement related to a conviction for a violation of section 222.10, 222.15, 222.25 or 222.45 of the penal law and any such waiver shall be deemed void and wholly unenforceable.

(Eff.2/2/21,Ch.23 & 3/31/21,Ch.92,L.2021)

(*l*) An order dismissing an action pursuant to section 215.40 of this chapter was entered.

4. A person in whose favor a criminal action or proceeding was terminated, as defined in paragraph (a) through (h) of subdivision two of this section, prior to the effective date of this section, may upon motion apply to the court in which such termination occurred, upon not less than twenty days notice to the district attorney, for an order granting to such person the relief set forth in subdivision one of this section, and such order shall be granted unless the district attorney demonstrates to the satisfaction of the court that the interests of justice require otherwise. A person in whose favor a criminal action or proceeding was terminated, as defined in paragraph (i) or (j) of subdivision two of this section, prior to the effective date of this section, may apply to the appropriate prosecutor or police agency for a certification as described in said paragraph (i) or (j) granting to such person the relief set forth therein, and such certification shall be granted by such prosecutor or police agency.

5. (a) Expungement of certain marihuana-related records. A conviction for an offense described in paragraph (k) of subdivision three of this section shall, on and after the effective date of this paragraph, in accordance with the provisions of this paragraph, be vacated and dismissed, and all records of such conviction or convictions and related to such conviction or convictions shall be expunged, as described in subdivision forty-five of section 1.20 of this chapter, and the matter shall be considered terminated in favor of the accused and deemed a nullity, having been rendered by this paragraph legally invalid. All such records for an offense described in this paragraph where the conviction was entered on or before the effective date of the chapter of the laws of 2019 that amended this paragraph shall be expunged promptly and, in any event, no later than one year after such effective date.

(b) Duties of certain state officials and law enforcement agencies. Commencing upon the effective date of this paragraph:

(i) the chief administrator of the courts shall promptly notify the commissioner of the division of criminal justice services and the heads of all appropriate police departments, district attorney's offices and other law enforcement agencies of all convictions that have been vacated and dismissed pursuant to paragraph (a) of this subdivision and that all records related to such convictions shall be expunged and the matter shall be considered terminated in favor of the accused and deemed a nullity, having been rendered legally invalid. Upon receipt of notification of such vacatur, dismissal and expungement, all records relating to such conviction or convictions, or the criminal action or proceeding, as the case may be, shall be marked as expunged by conspicuously indicating on the face of the record and on each page or at the beginning of the digitized file of the record that the record has been designated as expunged. Upon the written request of the individual whose case has been expunged or their designated agent, such records shall be destroyed. Such records and papers shall not be made available to any person, except the individual whose case has been expunged or such person's designated agent; and

(ii) where automatic vacatur, dismissal, and expungement, including record destruction if requested, is required by this subdivision but any record of the court system in this state has not yet been updated to reflect same (A) notwithstanding any other provision of law except as provided in paragraph (d) of subdivision one of this section and paragraph (e) of subdivision four of section eight hundred thirty-seven of the executive law: (1) when the division of criminal justice services conducts a search of its criminal history records, maintained pursuant to subdivision six of section eight hundred thirty-seven of the executive law, and returns a report thereon, all references to a conviction for an offense described in paragraph (k) of subdivision three of this section shall be excluded from such report; and (2) the chief administrator of the courts shall develop and promulgate rules as may be necessary to ensure that no written or electronic report of a criminal history record search conducted by the office of court administration contains information relating to a conviction for an offense described in paragraph (k) of subdivision three of this section; and (B) where court records relevant to such matter cannot be located or have been destroyed, and a person or the person's attorney presents to an appropriate court employee a fingerprint record of the New York state division of criminal justice services, or a copy of a court disposition record or other relevant court record, which indicates that a criminal action or proceeding against such person was terminated by conviction of an offense described in paragraph (k) of subdivision three of this section, then promptly, and in any event within thirty days after such notice to such court employee, the chief administrator of the courts or his or her designee shall assure that such vacatur, dismissal, and expungement, including record destruction if requested, have been completed in accordance with subparagraph (i) of this paragraph.

(c) Vacatur, dismissal and expungement as set forth in this subdivision is without prejudice to any person or such person's attorney seeking further relief pursuant to article four hundred forty of this chapter or any other law. Nothing in this section is intended or shall be interpreted to diminish or abrogate any right or remedy otherwise available to any person.

(d) The office of court administration, in conjunction with the division of criminal justice services, shall develop an affirmative information campaign and widely disseminate to the public, through its website, public service announcements and other means, in multiple languages and through multiple outlets, information concerning the expungement, vacatur and resentencing of marihuana convictions established by the chapter of the laws of two thousand nineteen that added this paragraph, including, but not limited to, the automatic expungement of certain past convictions, the means by which an individual may file a motion for vacatur, dismissal and expungement of certain past convictions, and the impact of such changes on such person's criminal history records.

§160.55 Order upon termination of criminal action by conviction for noncriminal offense; entry of waiver; administrative findings.

1. Regardless of the class of offense for which a person is initially charged, upon the termination of a criminal action or proceeding against a person by the conviction of such person of a traffic infraction or a violation,

other than the violation of operating a motor vehicle while ability impaired as described in subdivision one of section eleven hundred ninety-two of the vehicle and traffic law, unless the district attorney upon motion with not less than five days' notice to such person or his or her attorney demonstrates to the satisfaction of the court that the interests of justice require otherwise, or the court on its own motion with not less than five days' notice to such person or his or her attorney determines that the interests of justice require otherwise and states the reasons for such determination on the record, the clerk of the court wherein such criminal action or proceeding was terminated shall immediately notify the commissioner of the division of criminal justice services and the heads of all appropriate police departments and other law enforcement agencies that the action has been terminated by such conviction. Upon receipt of notification of such termination:

(Eff.2/2/21,Ch.23,L.2021)

(a) every photograph of such person and photographic plate or proof, and all palmprints and fingerprints taken or made of such person pursuant to the provisions of this article in regard to the action or proceeding terminated, and all duplicates and copies thereof, except a digital fingerprint image where authorized pursuant to paragraph (e) of this subdivision, except for the palmprints and fingerprints concerning a disposition of harassment in the second degree as defined in section 240.26 of the penal law, committed against a member of the same family or household as the defendant, as defined in subdivision one of section 530.11 of this chapter, and determined pursuant to subdivision eight-a of section 170.10 of this title, shall forthwith be, at the discretion of the recipient agency, either destroyed or returned to such person, or to the attorney who represented such person at the time of the termination of the action or proceeding, at the address given by such person or attorney during the action or proceeding, by the division of criminal justice services and by any police department or law enforcement agency having any such photograph, photographic plate or proof, palmprints or fingerprints in its possession or under its control;

(b) any police department or law enforcement agency, including the division of criminal justice services, which transmitted or otherwise forwarded to any agency of the United States or of any other state or of any other jurisdiction outside the state of New York copies of any such photographs, photographic plates or proofs, palmprints and fingerprints, shall forthwith formally request in writing that all such copies be destroyed or returned to the police department or law enforcement agency which transmitted or forwarded them, and upon such return such department or agency shall, at its discretion, either destroy or return them as provided herein;

(c) all official records and papers relating to the arrest or prosecution, including all duplicates and copies thereof, on file with the division of criminal justice services, police agency, or prosecutor's office shall be sealed and not made available to any person or public or private agency;

(d) the records referred to in paragraph (c) of this subdivision shall be made available to the person accused or to such person's designated agent, and shall be made available to (i) a prosecutor in any proceeding in which the accused has moved for an order pursuant to section 170.56 or 210.46 of this chapter, or (ii) a law enforcement agency upon ex parte motion in any superior court, or in any district court, city court or the criminal court of the city of New York provided that such court sealed the record, if such agency demonstrates to the satisfaction of the court that justice requires that such records be made available to it, or (iii) any state or local officer or agency with responsibility for the issuance of licenses to possess guns, when the accused has made application for such a license, or (iv) the New York state department of corrections and community supervision when the accused is under parole supervision as a result of conditional release or parole release granted by the New York state board of parole and the arrest which is the subject of the inquiry is one which occurred while the accused was under such supervision, or (v) the probation department responsible for supervision of the accused when the arrest which is the subject of the inquiry is one which occurred while the accused was under such supervision, or (vi) a police agency, probation department, sheriff's office, district attorney's office, department of correction of any municipality and parole department, for law enforcement purposes, upon arrest in instances in which the individual stands convicted of harassment in the second degree, as defined in section 240.26 of the penal law, committed against a member of the same family or household as the defendant, as defined in subdivision one of section 530.11 of this chapter, and determined pursuant to subdivision eight-a of section 170.10 of this title; and

(e) where fingerprints subject to the provisions of this section have been received by the division of criminal justice services and have been filed by the division as digital images, such images may be retained, provided that a fingerprint card of the individual is on file with the division which was not sealed pursuant to this section or section 160.50 of this article.

2. A report of the termination of the action or proceeding by conviction of a traffic violation or a violation other than the violation of operating a motor vehicle while ability impaired as described in subdivision one of section eleven hundred ninety-two of the vehicle and traffic law, shall be sufficient notice of sealing to the commissioner of the division of criminal justice services unless the report also indicates that the court directed that the record not be sealed in the interests of justice. Where the court has determined pursuant to subdivision one of this section that sealing is not in the interests of justice, the clerk of the court shall include notification of that determination in any report to such division of the disposition of the action or proceeding. When the defendant has been found guilty of a violation of harassment in the second degree and it was determined pursuant to subdivision eight-a of section 170.10 of this title that such violation was committed against a member of the same family or household as the defendant, the clerk of the court shall include notification of that determination in any report to such division of the disposition of the action or proceeding for purposes of paragraph (a) and subparagraph (vi) of paragraph (d) of subdivision one of this section.   *(Eff.2/2/21,Ch.23,L.2021)*

3. A person against whom a criminal action or proceeding was terminated by such person's conviction of a traffic infraction or violation other than the violation of operating a motor vehicle while ability impaired as described in subdivision one of section eleven hundred ninety-two of the vehicle and traffic law, prior to the effective date of this section, may upon motion apply to the court in which such termination occurred, upon not less than twenty days notice to the district attorney, for an order granting to such person the relief set forth in subdivision one of this section, and such order shall be granted unless the district attorney demonstrates to the satisfaction of the court that the interests of justice require otherwise.   *(Eff.2/2/21,Ch.23,L.2021)*

4. This section shall not apply to an action terminated in a manner described in paragraph (k) of subdivision two of section 160.50 of this chapter.

5. (a) When a criminal action or proceeding is terminated against a person by the entry of a waiver of a hearing pursuant to paragraph (c) of subdivision ten of section eleven hundred ninety-two of the vehicle and traffic law or section forty-nine-b of the navigation law, the record of the criminal action shall be sealed in accordance with this subdivision. Upon the entry of such waiver, the court or the clerk of the court shall immediately notify the commissioner of the division of criminal justice services and the heads of all appropriate police departments and other law enforcement agencies that a waiver has been entered and that the record of the action shall be sealed when the person reaches the age of twenty-one or three years from the date of commission of the offense, whichever is the greater period of time. At the expiration of such period, the commissioner of the

division of criminal justice services and the heads of all appropriate police departments and other law enforcement agencies shall take the actions required by paragraphs (a), (b) and (c) of subdivision one of section 160.50 of this article.

(b) Where a person under the age of twenty-one is referred by the police to the department of motor vehicles for action pursuant to section eleven hundred ninety-two-a or eleven hundred ninety-four-a of the vehicle and traffic law, or section forty-nine-b of the navigation law and a finding in favor of the motorist or operator is rendered, the commissioner of the department of motor vehicles shall, as soon as practicable, but not later than three years from the date of commission of the offense or when such person reaches the age of twenty-one, whichever is the greater period of time, notify the commissioner of the division of criminal justice services and the heads of all appropriate police departments and other law enforcement agencies that such finding in favor of the motorist or operator was rendered. Upon receipt of such notification, the commissioner of the division of criminal justice services and the heads of such police departments and other law enforcement agencies shall take the actions required by paragraphs (a), (b) and (c) of subdivision one of section 160.50 of this article.

(c) Where a person under the age of twenty-one is referred by the police to the department of motor vehicles for action pursuant to section eleven hundred ninety-two-a or eleven hundred ninety-four-a of the vehicle and traffic law, or section forty-nine-b of the navigation law, and no notification is received by the commissioner of the division of criminal justice services and the heads of all appropriate police departments and other law enforcement agencies pursuant to paragraph (b) of this subdivision, such commissioner of the division of criminal justice services and such heads of police departments and other law enforcement agencies shall, after three years from the date of commission of the offense or when the person reaches the age of twenty-one, whichever is the greater period of time, take the actions required by paragraphs (a), (b) and (c) of subdivision one of section 160.50 of this article.

§160.58 Conditional sealing of certain controlled substance, marihuana or specified offense convictions.

1. A defendant convicted of any offense defined in article two hundred twenty or two hundred twenty-one of the penal law or a specified offense defined in subdivision five of section 410.91 of this chapter who has successfully completed a judicial diversion program under article two hundred sixteen of this chapter, or one of the programs heretofore known as drug treatment alternative to prison or another judicially sanctioned drug treatment program of similar duration, requirements and level of supervision, and has completed the sentence imposed for the offense or offenses, is eligible to have such offense or offenses sealed pursuant to this section.

2. The court that sentenced the defendant to a judicially sanctioned drug treatment program may on its own motion, or on the defendant's motion, order that all official records and papers relating to the arrest, prosecution and conviction which resulted in the defendant's participation in the judicially sanctioned drug treatment program be conditionally sealed. In such case, the court may also conditionally seal the arrest, prosecution and conviction records for no more than three of the defendant's prior eligible misdemeanors, which for purposes of this subdivision shall be limited to misdemeanor offenses defined in article two hundred twenty or two hundred twenty-one of the penal law. The court may only seal the records of the defendant's arrests, prosecutions and convictions when:

(a) the sentencing court has requested and received from the division of criminal justice services or the Federal Bureau of Investigation a fingerprint based criminal history record of the defendant, including any sealed or suppressed information. The division of criminal justice services shall also include a criminal history report, if any, from the Federal Bureau of Investigation regarding any criminal history information that occurred in other jurisdictions. The division is hereby authorized to receive such information from the Federal Bureau of Investigation for this purpose. The parties shall be permitted to examine these records;

    (b) the defendant or court has identified the misdemeanor conviction or convictions for which relief may be granted;

    (c) the court has received documentation that the sentences imposed on the eligible misdemeanor convictions have been completed, or if no such documentation is reasonably available, a sworn affidavit that the sentences imposed on the prior misdemeanors have been completed; and

    (d) the court has notified the district attorney of each jurisdiction in which the defendant has been convicted of an offense with respect to which sealing is sought, and the court or courts of record for such offenses, that the court is considering sealing the records of the defendant's eligible misdemeanor convictions. Both the district attorney and the court shall be given a reasonable opportunity, which shall not be less than thirty days, in which to comment and submit materials to aid the court in making such a determination.

    3. At the request of the defendant or the district attorney of a county in which the defendant committed a crime that is the subject of the sealing application, the court may conduct a hearing to consider and review any relevant evidence offered by either party that would aid the court in its decision whether to seal the records of the defendant's arrests, prosecutions and convictions. In making such a determination, the court shall consider any relevant factors, including but not limited to: (i) the circumstances and seriousness of the offense or offenses that resulted in the conviction or convictions; (ii) the character of the defendant, including his or her completion of the judicially sanctioned treatment program as described in subdivision one of this section; (iii) the defendant's criminal history; and (iv) the impact of sealing the defendant's records upon his or her rehabilitation and his or her successful and productive reentry and reintegration into society, and on public safety.

    4. When a court orders sealing pursuant to this section, all official records and papers relating to the arrests, prosecutions, and convictions, including all duplicates and copies thereof, on file with the division of criminal justice services or any court shall be sealed and not made available to any person or public or private agency; provided, however, the division shall retain any fingerprints, palmprints and photographs, or digital images of the same.

    5. When the court orders sealing pursuant to this section, the clerk of such court shall immediately notify the commissioner of the division of criminal justice services, and any court that sentenced the defendant for an offense which has been conditionally sealed, regarding the records that shall be sealed pursuant to this section.

    6. Records sealed pursuant to this subdivision shall be made available to:

    (a) the defendant or the defendant's designated agent;

    (b) qualified agencies, as defined in subdivision nine of section eight hundred thirty-five of the executive law, and federal and state law enforcement agencies, when acting within the scope of their law enforcement duties; or

    (c) any state or local officer or agency with responsibility for the issuance of licenses to possess guns, when the person has made application for such a license; or

    (d) any prospective employer of a police officer or peace officer as those terms are defined in subdivisions thirty-three and thirty-four of section 1.20 of this chapter, in relation to an application for employment as a police officer or peace officer; provided, however, that every person who is an applicant for the position of police officer or peace officer shall be furnished with a copy of all records obtained under this paragraph and afforded an opportunity to make an explanation thereto.

7. The court shall not seal the defendant's record pursuant to this section while any charged offense is pending.

8. If, subsequent to the sealing of records pursuant to this subdivision, the person who is the subject of such records is arrested for or formally charged with any misdemeanor or felony offense, such records shall be unsealed immediately and remain unsealed; provided, however, that if such new misdemeanor or felony arrest results in a termination in favor of the accused as defined in subdivision three of section 160.50 of this article or by conviction for a non criminal offense as described in section 160.55 of this article, such unsealed records shall be conditionally sealed pursuant to this section.

§160.59 Sealing of certain convictions.

1. Definitions: As used in this section, the following terms shall have the following meanings:

(a) "Eligible offense" shall mean any crime defined in the laws of this state other than a sex offense defined in article one hundred thirty of the penal law, an offense defined in article two hundred sixty-three of the penal law, a felony offense defined in article one hundred twenty-five of the penal law, a violent felony offense defined in section 70.02 of the penal law, a class A felony offense defined in the penal law, a felony offense defined in article one hundred five of the penal law where the underlying offense is not an eligible offense, an attempt to commit an offense that is not an eligible offense if the attempt is a felony, or an offense for which registration as a sex offender is required pursuant to article six-C of the correction law. For the purposes of this section, where the defendant is convicted of more than one eligible offense, committed as part of the same criminal transaction as defined in subdivision two of section 40.10 of this chapter, those offenses shall be considered one eligible offense.

(b) "Sentencing judge" shall mean the judge who pronounced sentence upon the conviction under consideration, or if that judge is no longer sitting in a court in the jurisdiction in which the conviction was obtained, any other judge who is sitting in the criminal court where the judgment of conviction was entered.

1-a. The chief administrator of the courts shall, pursuant to section 10.40 of this chapter, prescribe a form application which may be used by a defendant to apply for sealing pursuant to this section. Such form application shall include all the essential elements required by this section to be included in an application for sealing. Nothing in this subdivision shall be read to require a defendant to use such form application to apply for sealing.

2. (a) A defendant who has been convicted of up to two eligible offenses but not more than one felony offense may apply to the court in which he or she was convicted of the most serious offense to have such conviction or convictions sealed. If all offenses are offenses with the same classification, the application shall be made to the court in which the defendant was last convicted.

(b) An application shall contain (i) a copy of a certificate of disposition or other similar documentation for any offense for which the defendant has been convicted, or an explanation of why such certificate or other documentation is not available; (ii) a sworn statement of the defendant as to whether he or she has filed, or then intends to file, any application for sealing of any other eligible offense; (iii) a copy of any other such application that has been filed; (iv) a sworn statement as to the conviction or convictions for which relief is being sought; and (v) a sworn statement of the reason or reasons why the court should, in its discretion, grant such sealing, along with any supporting documentation.

(c) A copy of any application for such sealing shall be served upon the district attorney of the county in which the conviction, or, if more than one, the convictions, was or were obtained. The district attorney shall notify the court within forty-five days if he or she objects to the application for sealing.

(d) When such application is filed with the court, it shall be assigned to the sentencing judge unless more than one application is filed in which case the application shall be assigned to the county court or the supreme court of the county in which the criminal court is located, who shall request and receive from the division of criminal justice services a fingerprint based criminal history record of the defendant, including any sealed or suppressed records. The division of criminal justice services also shall include a criminal history report, if any, from the federal bureau of investigation regarding any criminal history information that occurred in other jurisdictions. The division is hereby authorized to receive such information from the federal bureau of investigation for this purpose, and to make such information available to the court, which may make this information available to the district attorney and the defendant.

3. The sentencing judge, or county or supreme court shall summarily deny the defendant's application when:

(a) the defendant is required to register as a sex offender pursuant to article six-C of the correction law; or

(b) the defendant has previously obtained sealing of the maximum number of convictions allowable under section 160.58 of the criminal procedure law; or

(c) the defendant has previously obtained sealing of the maximum number of convictions allowable under subdivision four of this section; or

(d) the time period specified in subdivision five of this section has not yet been satisfied; or

(e) the defendant has an undisposed arrest or charge pending; or

(f) the defendant was convicted of any crime after the date of the entry of judgement of the last conviction for which sealing is sought; or

(g) the defendant has failed to provide the court with the required sworn statement of the reasons why the court should grant the relief requested; or

(h) the defendant has been convicted of two or more felonies or more than two crimes.

4. Provided that the application is not summarily denied for the reasons set forth in subdivision three of this section, a defendant who stands convicted of up to two eligible offenses, may obtain sealing of no more than two eligible offenses but not more than one felony offense.

5. Any eligible offense may be sealed only after at least ten years have passed since the imposition of the sentence on the defendant's latest conviction or, if the defendant was sentenced to a period of incarceration, including a period of incarceration imposed in conjunction with a sentence of probation, the defendant's latest release from incarceration. In calculating the ten year period under this subdivision, any period of time the defendant spent incarcerated after the conviction for which the application for sealing is sought, shall be excluded and such ten year period shall be extended by a period or periods equal to the time served under such incarceration.

6. Upon determining that the application is not subject to mandatory denial pursuant to subdivision three of this section and that the application is opposed by the district attorney, the sentencing judge or county or supreme court shall conduct a hearing on the application in order to consider any evidence offered by either party that would aid the sentencing judge in his or her decision whether to seal the records of the defendant's convictions. No hearing is required if the district attorney does not oppose the application.

7. In considering any such application, the sentencing judge or county or supreme court shall consider any relevant factors, including but not limited to:

(a) the amount of time that has elapsed since the defendant's last conviction;

(b) the circumstances and seriousness of the offense for which the defendant is seeking relief, including whether the arrest charge was not an eligible offense;

(c) the circumstances and seriousness of any other offenses for which the defendant stands convicted;

(d) the character of the defendant, including any measures that the defendant has taken toward rehabilitation, such as participating in treatment programs, work, or schooling, and participating in community service or other volunteer programs;

(e) any statements made by the victim of the offense for which the defendant is seeking relief;

(f) the impact of sealing the defendant's record upon his or her rehabilitation and upon his or her successful and productive reentry and reintegration into society; and

(g) the impact of sealing the defendant's record on public safety and upon the public's confidence in and respect for the law.

8. When a sentencing judge or county or supreme court orders sealing pursuant to this section, all official records and papers relating to the arrests, prosecutions, and convictions, including all duplicates and copies thereof, on file with the division of criminal justice services or any court shall be sealed and not made available to any person or public or private agency except as provided for in subdivision nine of this section; provided, however, the division shall retain any fingerprints, palmprints and photographs, or digital images of the same. The clerk of such court shall immediately notify the commissioner of the division of criminal justice services regarding the records that shall be sealed pursuant to this section. The clerk also shall notify any court in which the defendant has stated, pursuant to paragraph (b) of subdivision two of this section, that he or she has filed or intends to file an application for sealing of any other eligible offense.

9. Records sealed pursuant to this section shall be made available to:

(a) the defendant or the defendant's designated agent;

(b) qualified agencies, as defined in subdivision nine of section eight hundred thirty-five of the executive law, and federal and state law enforcement agencies, when acting within the scope of their law enforcement duties; or

(c) any state or local officer or agency with responsibility for the issuance of licenses to possess guns, when the person has made application for such a license; or

(d) any prospective employer of a police officer or peace officer as those terms are defined in subdivisions thirty-three and thirty-four of section 1.20 of this chapter, in relation to an application for employment as a police officer or peace officer; provided, however, that every person who is an applicant for the position of police officer or peace officer shall be furnished with a copy of all records obtained under this paragraph and afforded an opportunity to make an explanation thereto; or

(e) the criminal justice information services division of the federal bureau of investigation, for the purposes of responding to queries to the national instant criminal background check system regarding attempts to purchase or otherwise take possession of firearms, as defined in 18 USC 921 (a) (3).

10. A conviction which is sealed pursuant to this section is included within the definition of a conviction for the purposes of any criminal proceeding in which the fact of a prior conviction would enhance a penalty or is an element of the offense charged.

11. No defendant shall be required or permitted to waive eligibility for sealing pursuant to this section as part of a plea of guilty, sentence or any agreement related to a conviction for an eligible offense and any such waiver shall be deemed void and wholly unenforceable.

§160.60   Effect of termination of criminal actions in favor of the accused.

Upon the termination of a criminal action or proceeding against a person in favor of such person, as defined in subdivision two of section 160.50 of this chapter, the arrest and prosecution shall be deemed a nullity and the accused shall be restored, in contemplation of law, to the status he occupied before the arrest and prosecution. The arrest or prosecution shall not operate as a disqualification of any person so accused to pursue or engage in any lawful activity, occupation, profession, or calling. Except where specifically required or permitted by statute or upon specific authorization of a superior court, no such person shall be required to divulge information pertaining to the arrest or prosecution.

ARTICLE 170
PROCEEDINGS UPON INFORMATION, SIMPLIFIED TRAFFIC INFORMATION, PROSECUTOR'S INFORMATION AND MISDEMEANOR COMPLAINT FROM ARRAIGNMENT TO PLEA

Section
170.10   Arraignment upon information, simplified traffic information, prosecutor's information or misdemeanor complaint; defendant's presence, defendant's rights, court's instructions and bail matters.
170.15   Removal of action from one local criminal court to another.
170.20   Divestiture of jurisdiction by indictment; removal of case to superior court at district attorney's instance.
170.25   Divestiture of jurisdiction by indictment; removal of case to superior court at defendant's instance.
170.30   Motion to dismiss information, simplified information, prosecutor's information or misdemeanor complaint.
170.35   Motion to dismiss information, simplified information, prosecutor's information or misdemeanor complaint; as defective.
170.40   Motion to dismiss information, simplified traffic information, prosecutor's information or misdemeanor complaint; in furtherance of justice.
170.45   Motion to dismiss information, simplified traffic information, prosecutor's information or misdemeanor complaint; procedure.
170.50   Motion in superior court to dismiss prosecutor's information.
170.55   Adjournment in contemplation of dismissal.
170.56   Adjournment in contemplation of dismissal in cases involving marihuana.
170.60   Requirement of plea to information, simplified information or prosecutor's information.
170.65   Replacement of misdemeanor complaint by information and waiver thereof.
170.70   Release of defendant upon failure to replace misdemeanor complaint by information.
170.80   Proceedings regarding certain prostitution charges; certain persons aged sixteen or seventeen.

§170.10   Arraignment upon information, simplified traffic information, prosecutor's information or misdemeanor complaint; defendant's presence, defendant's rights, court's instructions and bail matters.

1. Following the filing with a local criminal court of an information, a simplified information, a prosecutor's information or a misdemeanor complaint, the defendant must be arraigned thereon. The defendant must appear personally at such arraignment except under the following circumstances:

(a) In any case where a simplified information is filed and a procedure is provided by law which is applicable to all offenses charged in such simplified information and, if followed, would dispense with an arraignment or personal appearance of the defendant, nothing contained in this section affects the validity of such procedure or requires such personal appearance;

(b) In any case in which the defendant's appearance is required by a summons or an appearance ticket, the court in its discretion may, for good cause shown, permit the defendant to appear by counsel instead of in person.

2. Upon any arraignment at which the defendant is personally present, the court must immediately inform him, or cause him to be informed in its presence, of the charge or charges against him and must furnish him with a copy of the accusatory instrument.

3. The defendant has the right to the aid of counsel at the arraignment and at every subsequent stage of the action. If he appears upon such arraignment without counsel, he has the following rights:

(a) To an adjournment for the purpose of obtaining counsel; and

(b) To communicate, free of charge, by letter or by telephone provided by the law enforcement facility where the defendant is held to a phone number located in the United States, or Puerto Rico, for the purposes of obtaining counsel and informing a relative or friend that he or she has been charged with an offense; and

(c) To have counsel assigned by the court if he is financially unable to obtain the same; except that this paragraph does not apply where the accusatory instrument charges a traffic infraction or infractions only.

4. Except as provided in subdivision five, the court must inform the defendant:

(a) Of his rights as prescribed in subdivision three; and the court must not only accord him opportunity to exercise such rights but must itself take such affirmative action as is necessary to effectuate them; and

(b) Where a traffic infraction or a misdemeanor relating to traffic is charged, that a judgment of conviction for such offense would in addition to subjecting the defendant to the sentence provided therefor render his license to drive a motor vehicle and his certificate of registration subject to suspension and revocation as prescribed by law and that a plea of guilty to such offense constitutes a conviction thereof to the same extent as a verdict of guilty after trial; and

(c) Where the accusatory instrument is a simplified traffic information, that the defendant has a right to have a supporting deposition filed, as provided in section 100.25; and

(d) Where the accusatory instrument is a misdemeanor complaint, that the defendant may not be prosecuted thereon or required to enter a plea thereto unless he consents to the same, and that in the absence of such consent such misdemeanor complaint will for prosecution purposes have to be replaced and superseded by an information; and

(e) Where an information, a simplified information, a prosecutor's information, a misdemeanor complaint, a felony complaint or an indictment charges harassment in the second degree, as defined in section 240.26 of the penal law, if there is a judgment of conviction for such offense and such offense is determined to have been committed against a member of the same family or household as the defendant, as defined in subdivision one of section 530.11 of this chapter, the record of such conviction shall be accessible for law enforcement purposes and not sealed, as specified in paragraph (a) and subparagraph (vi) of paragraph (d) of subdivision one of section 160.55 of this title; and

5. In any case in which a defendant has appeared for arraignment in response to a summons or an appearance ticket, a printed statement upon such process of any court instruction required by the provisions of subdivision four, other than those specified in paragraphs (d) and (e) thereof, constitutes compliance with such provisions with respect to the instruction so printed.

6. If a defendant charged with a traffic infraction or infractions only desires to proceed without the aid of counsel, the court must permit him to do so. In all other cases, the court must permit the defendant to proceed without the aid of counsel if it is satisfied that he made such decision with knowledge of the significance thereof, but if it is not so satisfied it may not proceed until

the defendant is provided with counsel, either of his own choosing or by assignment. Regardless of the kind or nature of the charges, a defendant who proceeds at the arraignment without counsel does not waive his right to counsel, and the court must inform him that he continues to have such right as well as all the rights specified in subdivision three which are necessary to effectuate it, and that he may exercise such rights at any stage of the action.

7. Upon the arraignment, the court, unless it intends to make a final disposition of the action immediately thereafter, must, as provided in subdivision one of section 530.20, issue a securing order either releasing the defendant on his own recognizance or fixing bail for his future appearance in the action; except that where a defendant appears by counsel pursuant to paragraph (b) of subdivision one of this section, the court must release the defendant on his own recognizance.

8. Notwithstanding any other provision of law to the contrary, a local criminal court may not, at arraignment or within thirty days of arraignment on a simplified traffic information charging a violation of subdivision two, two-a, three, four or four-a of section eleven hundred ninety-two of the vehicle and traffic law and upon which a notation has been made pursuant to subdivision twelve of section eleven hundred ninety-two of the vehicle and traffic law, accept a plea of guilty to a violation of any subdivision of section eleven hundred ninety-two of the vehicle and traffic law, nor to any other traffic infraction arising out of the same incident, nor to any other traffic infraction, violation or misdemeanor where the court is aware that such offense was charged pursuant to an accident involving death or serious physical injury, except upon written consent of the district attorney.

8-a. (a) Where an information, a simplified information, a prosecutor's information, a misdemeanor complaint, a felony complaint or an indictment charges harassment in the second degree as defined in section 240.26 of the penal law, the people may serve upon the defendant and file with the court a notice alleging that such offense was committed against a member of the same family or household as the defendant, as defined in subdivision one of section 530.11 of this chapter. Such notice must be served within fifteen days after arraignment on an information, a simplified information, a prosecutor's information, a misdemeanor complaint, a felony complaint or an indictment for such charge and before trial. Such notice must include the name of the person alleged to be a member of the same family or household as the defendant and specify the specific family or household relationship as defined in subdivision one of section 530.11 of this chapter.

(b) If a defendant, charged with harassment in the second degree as defined in section 240.26 of the penal law stipulates, or admits in the course of a plea disposition, that the person against whom the charged offense is alleged to have been committed is a member of the same family or household as the defendant, as defined in subdivision one of section 530.11 of this chapter, such allegation shall be deemed established for purposes of paragraph (a) and subparagraph (vi) of paragraph (d) of subdivision one of section 160.55 of this title. If the defendant denies such allegation, the people may, by proof beyond a reasonable doubt, prove as part of their case that the alleged victim of such offense was a member of the same family or household as the defendant. In such circumstances, the trier of fact shall make its determination with respect to such allegation orally on the record or in writing.

9. Nothing contained in this section applies to the arraignment of corporate defendants, which is governed generally by the provisions of article six hundred.

10. Notwithstanding any contrary provision of this section, when an off-hours arraignment part designated in accordance with paragraph (w) of subdivision one of section two hundred twelve of the judiciary law is in operation in the county in which the court is located, the court must adjourn the proceedings before it, and direct that the proceedings be continued in such off-hours part when the defendant has appeared before the court without counsel and no counsel is otherwise available at the time of such appearance to aid the defendant, unless the defendant desires to proceed without the aid of counsel and the court is satisfied, pursuant to subdivision six of this section, that the defendant made such decision with knowledge of the significance thereof.

§170.15 Removal of action from one local criminal court to another.

Under circumstances prescribed in this section, a criminal action based upon an information, a simplified information, a prosecutor's information or a misdemeanor complaint may be removed from one local criminal court to another:

1. When a defendant arrested by a police officer for an offense other than a felony, allegedly committed in a city or town, has, owing to special circumstances and pursuant to law, not been brought before the particular local criminal court which by reason of the situs of such offense has trial jurisdiction thereof, but, instead, before a local criminal court which does not have trial jurisdiction thereof, and therein stands charged with such offense by information, simplified information or misdemeanor complaint, such local criminal court must arraign him upon such accusatory instrument. If the defendant desires to enter a plea of guilty thereto immediately following such arraignment, such local criminal court must permit him to do so and must thereafter conduct the action to judgment. Otherwise, it must remit the action, together with all pertinent papers and documents, to the local criminal court which has trial jurisdiction of the action, and the latter court must then conduct such action to judgment or other final disposition.

2. When a defendant arrested by a police officer for an offense other than a felony has been brought before a superior court judge sitting as a local criminal court for arraignment upon an information, simplified information or misdemeanor complaint charging such offense, such judge must, as a local criminal court, arraign the defendant upon such accusatory instrument. Such judge must then remit the action, together with all pertinent papers and documents, to a local criminal court having trial jurisdiction thereof. The latter court must then conduct such action to judgment or other final disposition.

3. At any time within the period provided by section 255.20, where a defendant is arraigned upon an information, a simplified information, a prosecutor's information or a misdemeanor complaint pending in a city court, town court or a village court having trial jurisdiction thereof, a judge of the county court of the county in which such city court, town court or village court is located may, upon motion of the defendant or the people, order that

the action be transferred for disposition from the court in which the matter is pending to another designated local criminal court of the county, upon the ground that disposition thereof within a reasonable time in the court from which removal is sought is unlikely owing to:

(a) Death, disability or other incapacity or disqualification of all of the judges of such court; or

(b) Inability of such court to form a jury in a case, in which the defendant is entitled to and has requested a jury trial.

4. Notwithstanding any provision of this section to the contrary, in any county outside a city having a population of one million or more, upon or after arraignment of a defendant on an information, a simplified information, a prosecutor's information or a misdemeanor complaint pending in a local criminal court, such court may, upon motion of the defendant and after giving the district attorney an opportunity to be heard, order that the action be removed from the court in which the matter is pending to another local criminal court in the same county which has been designated a court formed to address a matter of special concern based upon the status of the defendant or the victim, commonly known as a "problem solving court," including, but not limited to, drug court, domestic violence court, youth court, mental health court, and veterans court, by the chief administrator of the courts, and such problem solving court may then conduct such action to judgment or other final disposition; provided, however, that an order of removal issued under this subdivision shall not take effect until five days after the date the order is issued unless, prior to such effective date, the problem solving court notifies the court that issued the order that:

(a) it will not accept the action, in which event the order shall not take effect, or

(b) it will accept the action on a date prior to such effective date, in which event the order shall take effect upon such prior date.

Upon providing notification pursuant to paragraph (a) or (b) of this subdivision, the problem solving court shall promptly give notice to the defendant, his or her counsel and the district attorney.

5. (a) Notwithstanding any provision of this section to the contrary, in any county outside a city having a population of one million or more, upon or after arraignment of a defendant on an information, a simplified information, a prosecutor's information or a misdemeanor complaint pending in a local criminal court, such court may, upon motion of the defendant and after giving the district attorney an opportunity to be heard, order that the action be removed from the court in which the matter is pending to another local criminal court in the same county, or with consent of the district attorney and the district attorney of the adjoining county to another court in such adjoining county, that has been designated as a human trafficking court or veterans treatment court by the chief administrator of the courts, and such human trafficking court or veterans treatment court may then conduct such action to judgment or other final deposition; provided, however, that no court may order removal pursuant to this subdivision to a veterans treatment court of a family offense charge described in subdivision one of section 530.11 of this chapter where the accused and the person alleged to be the victim of such offense charged are members of the same family or household as defined in

such subdivision one of section 530.11; and provided further that an order of removal issued under this subdivision shall not take effect until five days after the date the order is issued unless, prior to such effective date, the human trafficking court or veterans treatment court notifies the court that issued the order that:

i. it will not accept the action, in which event the order shall not take effect; or

ii. it will accept the action on a date prior to such effective date, in which event the order shall take effect upon such prior date.

(b) Upon providing notification pursuant to subparagraph i or ii of paragraph (a) of this subdivision, the human trafficking court or veterans treatment court shall promptly give notice to the defendant, his or her counsel, and the district attorney. *(Eff.4/28/21,Ch.91,L.2021)*

§170.20 Divestiture of jurisdiction by indictment; removal of case to superior court at a district attorney's instance.

1. If at any time before entry of a plea of guilty to or commencement of a trial of a local criminal court accusatory instrument containing a charge of misdemeanor, an indictment charging the defendant with such misdemeanor is filed in a superior court, the local criminal court is thereby divested of jurisdiction of such misdemeanor charge and all proceedings therein with respect thereto are terminated.

2. At any time before entry of a plea of guilty to or commencement of a trial of an accusatory instrument specified in subdivision one, the district attorney may apply for an adjournment of the proceedings in the local criminal court upon the ground that he intends to present the misdemeanor charge in question to a grand jury with a view to prosecuting it by indictment in a superior court. In such case, the local criminal court must adjourn the proceedings to a date which affords the district attorney reasonable opportunity to pursue such action, and may subsequently grant such further adjournments for that purpose as are reasonable under the circumstances. Following the granting of such adjournment or adjournments, the proceedings must be as follows:

(a) If such charge is presented to a grand jury within the designated period and either an indictment or a dismissal of such charge results, the local criminal court is thereby divested of jurisdiction of such charge, and all proceedings in the local criminal court with respect thereto are terminated.

(b) If the misdemeanor charge is not presented to a grand jury within the designated period, the proceedings in the local criminal court must continue.

This page intentionally left blank.

§170.25 Divestiture of jurisdiction by indictment; removal of case to superior court at defendant's instance.

1. At any time before entry of a plea of guilty to or commencement of a trial of a local criminal court accusatory instrument containing a charge of misdemeanor, a superior court having jurisdiction to prosecute such misdemeanor charge by indictment may, upon motion of the defendant made upon notice to the district attorney, showing good cause to believe that the interests of justice so require, order that such charge be prosecuted by indictment and that the district attorney present it to the grand jury for such purpose.

2. Such order stays the proceedings in the local criminal court pending submission of the charge to the grand jury. Upon the subsequent filing of an indictment in the superior court, the proceedings in the local criminal court terminate and the defendant must be required to appear for arraignment upon the indictment in the manner prescribed in subdivisions one and two of section 210.10. Upon the subsequent filing of a grand jury dismissal of the charge, the proceedings in the local criminal court terminate and the superior court must, if the defendant is not at liberty on his own recognizance, discharge him from custody or exonerate his bail, as the case may be.

3. At any time before entry of a plea of guilty to or commencement of a trial of or within thirty days of arraignment on an accusatory instrument specified in subdivision one, whichever occurs first, the defendant may apply to the local criminal court for an adjournment of the proceedings therein upon the ground that he intends to make a motion in a superior court, pursuant to subdivision one, for an order that the misdemeanor charge be prosecuted by indictment. In such case, the local criminal court must adjourn the proceedings to a date which affords the defendant reasonable opportunity to pursue such action, and may subsequently grant such further adjournments for that purpose as are reasonable under the circumstances. Following the granting of such adjournment or adjournments, the proceedings must be as follows:

(a) If a motion in a superior court is not made by the defendant within the designated period, the proceedings in the local criminal court must continue.

(b) If a motion in a superior court is made by the defendant within the designated period, such motion stays the proceedings in the local criminal court until the entry of an order determining such motion.

(c) If the superior court enters an order granting the motion, such order stays the proceedings in the local criminal court as provided in subdivision two; and upon a subsequent indictment or dismissal of such charge by the grand jury, the proceedings in the local criminal court terminate as provided in subdivision two.

(d) If the superior court enters an order denying the motion, the proceedings in the local criminal court must continue.

4. Upon application of a defendant who on the basis of an order issued by a superior court pursuant to subdivision one is awaiting grand jury action, and who, at the time of such order or subsequent thereto, has been committed to the custody of the sheriff pending grand jury action, and who has been confined in such custody for a period of more than forty-five days without the occurrence of any grand jury action or disposition, the superior court which issued such order must release him on his own recognizance unless:

(a) The lack of a grand jury disposition during such period of confinement was due to the defendant's request, action or condition, or occurred with his consent; or

(b) The people have shown good cause why such order of release should not be issued. Such good cause must consist of some compelling fact or circumstance which precluded grand jury action within the prescribed period or rendered the same against the interest of justice.

§170.30 Motion to dismiss information, simplified information, prosecutor's information or misdemeanor complaint.

1. After arraignment upon an information, a simplified information, a prosecutor's information or a misdemeanor complaint, the local criminal court may, upon motion of the defendant, dismiss such instrument or any count thereof upon the ground that:

(a) It is defective, within the meaning of section 170.35; or

(b) The defendant has received immunity from prosecution for the offense charged, pursuant to sections 50.20 or 190.40; or

(c) The prosecution is barred by reason of a previous prosecution, pursuant to section 40.20; or

(d) The prosecution is untimely, pursuant to section 30.10; or

(e) The defendant has been denied the right to a speedy trial; or

(f) There exists some other jurisdictional or legal impediment to conviction of the defendant for the offense charged; or

(g) Dismissal is required in furtherance of justice, within the meaning of section 170.40.

2. A motion pursuant to this section, except a motion pursuant to paragraph (e) of subdivision one, should be made within the period provided by section 255.20. A motion made pursuant to paragraph (e) of subdivision one should be made prior to the commencement of trial or entry of a plea of guilty.

3. Upon the motion, a defendant who is in a position adequately to raise more than one ground in support thereof should raise every such ground upon which he intends to challenge the accusatory instrument. A subsequent motion based upon such a ground not so raised may be summarily denied, although the court, in the interest of justice and for good cause shown, may in its discretion entertain and dispose of such a motion on the merits notwithstanding.

4. After arraignment upon an information, a simplified information, a prosecutor's information or misdemeanor complaint on a charge of prostitution pursuant to section 230.00 of the penal law the local criminal court may dismiss such charge in its discretion in the interest of justice on the ground that a defendant participated in services provided to him or her.

(Eff. 2/2/21, Ch. 23, L. 2021)

§170.35 Motion to dismiss information, simplified information, prosecutor's information or misdemeanor complaint; as defective.

1. An information, a simplified information, a prosecutor's information or a misdemeanor complaint, or a count thereof, is defective within the meaning of paragraph (a) of subdivision one of section 170.30 when:

(a) It is not sufficient on its face pursuant to the requirement of section 100.40; provided that such an instrument or count may not be dismissed as defective, but must instead be amended, where the defect or irregularity is of a kind that may be cured by amendment and where the people move to so amend; or

(b) The allegations demonstrate that the court does not have jurisdiction of the offense charged; or

(c) The statute defining the offense charged is unconstitutional or otherwise invalid.

2. An information is also defective when it is filed in replacement of a misdemeanor complaint pursuant to section 170.65 but without satisfying the requirements stated therein.

3. A prosecutor's information is also defective when:

(a) It is filed at the direction of a grand jury, pursuant to section 190.70, and the offense or offenses charged are not among those authorized by such grand jury direction; or

(b) It is filed by the district attorney at his own instance, pursuant to subdivision two of section 100.50, and the factual allegations of the original information underlying it and any supporting depositions are not legally sufficient to support the charge in the prosecutor's information.

§170.40 Motion to dismiss information, simplified traffic information, prosecutor's information or misdemeanor complaint; in furtherance of justice.

1. An information, a simplified traffic information, a prosecutor's information or a misdemeanor complaint, or any count thereof, may be dismissed in the interest of justice, as provided in paragraph (g) of subdivision one of section 170.30 when, even though there may be no basis for dismissal as a matter of law upon any ground specified in paragraphs (a) through (f) of said subdivision one of section 170.30, such dismissal is required as a matter of judicial discretion by the existence of some compelling factor, consideration or circumstance clearly demonstrating that conviction or prosecution of the defendant upon such accusatory instrument or count would constitute or result in injustice. In determining whether such compelling factor, consideration, or circumstance exists, the court must, to the extent applicable, examine and consider, individually and collectively, the following:

(a) the seriousness and circumstances of the offense;

(b) the extent of harm caused by the offense;

(c) the evidence of guilt, whether admissible or inadmissible at trial;

(d) the history, character and condition of the defendant;

(e) any exceptionally serious misconduct of law enforcement personnel in the investigation, arrest and prosecution of the defendant;

(f) the purpose and effect of imposing upon the defendant a sentence authorized for the offense;

(g) the impact of a dismissal on the safety or welfare of the community;

(h) the impact of a dismissal upon the confidence of the public in the criminal justice system;

(i) where the court deems it appropriate, the attitude of the complainant or victim with respect to the motion;

(j) any other relevant fact indicating that a judgment of conviction would serve no useful purpose.

2. An order dismissing an accusatory instrument specified in subdivision one in the interest of justice may be issued upon motion of the people or of the court itself as well as upon that of the defendant. Upon issuing such an order, the court must set forth its reasons therefor upon the record.

§170.45 Motion to dismiss information, simplified traffic information, prosecutor's information or misdemeanor complaint; procedure.

The procedural rules prescribed in section 210.45 with respect to the making, consideration and disposition of a motion to dismiss an indictment are also applicable to a motion to dismiss an information, a simplified traffic information, a prosecutor's information or a misdemeanor complaint.

§170.50 Motion in superior court to dismiss prosecutor's information.

1. At any time after arraignment in a local criminal court upon a prosecutor's information filed at the direction of a grand jury and before entry of a plea of guilty thereto or commencement of a trial thereof, the local

criminal court wherein the prosecutor's information is filed may, upon motion of the defendant, dismiss such prosecutor's information or a count thereof upon the ground that:

(a) The evidence before the grand jury was not legally sufficient to support the charge; or

(b) The grand jury proceeding resulting in the filing of such prosecutor's information was defective.

2. The criteria and procedures for consideration and disposition of such motion are the same as those prescribed in sections 210.30 and 210.35, governing consideration and disposition of a motion to dismiss an indictment on the ground of insufficiency of grand jury evidence or of a defective grand jury proceeding; and, where appropriate, the general procedural rules prescribed in section 210.45 for consideration and disposition of a motion to dismiss an indictment are also applicable.

3. Upon dismissing a prosecutor's information or a count thereof pursuant to this section, the court may, upon application of the people, in its discretion authorize the people to resubmit the charge or charges to the same or another grand jury. In the absence of such authorization, such charge or charges may not be resubmitted to a grand jury. The rules prescribed in subdivisions eight and nine of section 210.45 concerning the discharge of a defendant from custody or exoneration of bail in the absence of an authorization to resubmit an indictment to a grand jury, and concerning the issuance of a securing order and the effective period thereof where such an authorization is issued, apply equally where a prosecutor's information is dismissed pursuant to this section.

§170.55   Adjournment in contemplation of dismissal.

1. Upon or after arraignment in a local criminal court upon an information, a simplified information, a prosecutor's information or a misdemeanor complaint, and before entry of a plea of guilty thereto or commencement of a trial thereof, the court may, upon motion of the people or the defendant and with the consent of the other party, or upon the court's own motion with the consent of both the people and the defendant, order that the action be "adjourned in contemplation of dismissal," as prescribed in subdivision two.

2. An adjournment in contemplation of dismissal is an adjournment of the action without date ordered with a view to ultimate dismissal of the accusatory instrument in furtherance of justice. Upon issuing such an order, the court must release the defendant on his own recognizance. Upon application of the people, made at any time not more than six months, or in the case of a family offense as defined in subdivision one of section 530.11 of this chapter, one year, after the issuance of such order, the court may restore the case to the calendar upon a determination that dismissal of the accusatory instrument would not be in furtherance of justice, and the action must thereupon proceed. If the case is not so restored within such six months or one year period, the accusatory instrument is, at the expiration of such period, deemed to have been dismissed by the court in furtherance of justice.

3. In conjunction with an adjournment in contemplation of dismissal the court may issue a temporary order of protection pursuant to section 530.12 or 530.13 of this chapter, requiring the defendant to observe certain specified conditions of conduct.

4. Where the local criminal court information, simplified information, prosecutor's information, or misdemeanor complaint charges a crime or violation between spouses or between parent and child, or between members of the same family or household, as the term "members of the same family or household" is defined in subdivision one of section 530.11 of this chapter, the court may as a condition of an adjournment in contemplation of dismissal order, require that the defendant participate in an educational program addressing the issues of spousal abuse and family violence.

5. The court may grant an adjournment in contemplation of dismissal on condition that the defendant participate in dispute resolution and comply with any award or settlement resulting therefrom.

6. The court may as a condition of an adjournment in contemplation of dismissal order, require the defendant to perform services for a public or not-for-profit corporation, association, institution or agency. Such condition may only be imposed where the defendant has consented to the amount and conditions of such service. The court may not impose such conditions in excess of the length of the adjournment.

6-a. The court may, as a condition of an authorized adjournment in contemplation of dismissal, where the defendant has been charged with an offense and the elements of such offense meet the criteria of an "eligible offense" and such person qualified as an "eligible person" as such terms are defined in section four hundred fifty-eight-l of the social services law, require the defendant to participate in an education reform program in accordance with section four hundred fifty-eight-l of the social services law.

7. The court may, as a condition of an adjournment in contemplation of dismissal order, where a defendant is under twenty-one years of age and is charged with (a) a misdemeanor or misdemeanors other than section eleven hundred ninety-two of the vehicle and traffic law, in which the record indicates the consumption of alcohol by the defendant may have been a contributing factor, or (b) a violation of paragraph (a) of subdivision one of section sixty-five-b of the alcoholic beverage control law, require the defendant to attend an alcohol awareness program established pursuant to subdivision (a) of section 19.07 of the mental hygiene law.

8. The granting of an adjournment in contemplation of dismissal shall not be deemed to be a conviction or an admission of guilt. No person shall suffer any disability or forfeiture as a result of such an order. Upon the dismissal of the accusatory instrument pursuant to this section, the arrest and prosecution shall be deemed a nullity and the defendant shall be restored, in contemplation of law, to the status he occupied before his arrest and prosecution.

9. Notwithstanding any other provision of this section, a court may not issue an order adjourning an action in contemplation of dismissal if the offense is for a violation of the vehicle and traffic law related to the operation of a motor vehicle (except one related to parking, stopping or standing), or a violation of a local law, rule or ordinance related to the operation of a motor vehicle (except one related to parking, stopping or standing), if such offense was committed by the holder of a commercial learner's permit or a commercial driver's license or was committed in a commercial motor vehicle, as defined in subdivision four of section five hundred one-a of the vehicle and traffic law.

§170.56 Adjournment in contemplation of dismissal in cases involving marihuana.

1. Upon or after arraignment in a local criminal court upon an information, a prosecutor's information or a misdemeanor complaint, where the sole remaining count or counts charge a violation or violations of section 222.10, 222.15, 222.25, 222.30, 222.45 or 222.50 of the penal law, or upon summons for a nuisance offense under section sixty-five-c of the alcoholic beverage control law and before the entry of a plea of guilty thereto or commencement of a trial thereof, the court, upon motion of a defendant, may order that all proceedings be suspended and the action adjourned in contemplation of dismissal, or upon a finding that adjournment would not be necessary or appropriate and the setting forth in the record of the reasons for such findings, may dismiss in furtherance of justice the accusatory instrument; provided, however, that the court may not order such adjournment in contemplation of dismissal or dismiss the accusatory instrument if: (a) the defendant has previously been granted such adjournment in contemplation of dismissal, or (b) the defendant has previously been granted a dismissal under this section, or (c) the defendant

has previously been convicted of any offense involving controlled substances, or (d) the defendant has previously been convicted of a crime and the district attorney does not consent or (e) the defendant has previously been adjudicated a youthful offender on the basis of any act or acts involving controlled substances and the district attorney does not consent. Notwithstanding the limitations set forth in this subdivision, the court may order that all proceedings be suspended and the action adjourned in contemplation of dismissal based upon a finding of exceptional circumstances. For purposes of this subdivision, exceptional circumstances exist when, regardless of the ultimate disposition of the case, the entry of a plea of guilty is likely to result in severe or ongoing consequences, including, but not limited to, potential or actual immigration consequences.

(Eff.3/31/21,Ch.92,L.2021)

2. Upon ordering the action adjourned in contemplation of dismissal, the court must set and specify such conditions for the adjournment as may be appropriate, and such conditions may include placing the defendant under the supervision of any public or private agency. At any time prior to dismissal the court may modify the conditions or extend or reduce the term of the adjournment, except that the total period of adjournment shall not exceed twelve months. Upon violation of any condition fixed by the court, the court may revoke its order and restore the case to the calendar and the prosecution thereupon must proceed. If the case is not so restored to the calendar during the period fixed by the court, the accusatory instrument is, at the expiration of such period, deemed to have been dismissed in the furtherance of justice.

3. Upon or after dismissal of such charges against a defendant not previously convicted of a crime, the court shall order that all official records and papers, relating to the defendant's arrest and prosecution, whether on file with the court, a police agency, or the New York state division of criminal justice services, be sealed and, except as otherwise provided in paragraph (d) of subdivision one of section 160.50 of this chapter, not made available to any person or public or private agency; except, such records shall be made available under order of a court for the purpose of determining whether, in subsequent proceedings, such person qualifies under this section for a dismissal or adjournment in contemplation of dismissal of the accusatory instrument.

4. Upon the granting of an order pursuant to subdivision three, the arrest and prosecution shall be deemed a nullity and the defendant shall be restored, in contemplation of law, to the status he occupied before his arrest and prosecution.

§170.60 Requirement of plea to information, simplified information or prosecutor's information.

Unless an information, a simplified information or a prosecutor's information is dismissed or the criminal action thereon terminated or abated pursuant to a provision of this article or some other provision of law, the defendant must be required to enter a plea thereto.

§170.65 Replacement of misdemeanor complaint by information and waiver thereof.

1. A defendant against whom a misdemeanor complaint is pending is not required to enter a plea thereto. For purposes of prosecution, such instrument must, except as provided in subdivision three, be replaced by an information, and the defendant must be arraigned thereon. If the misdemeanor complaint is supplemented by a supporting deposition and such instruments taken together satisfy the requirements for a valid information, such misdemeanor complaint is deemed to have been converted to and to constitute a replacing information.

2. An information which replaces a misdemeanor complaint need not charge the same offense or offenses, but at least one count thereof must charge the commission by the defendant of an offense based upon conduct which was the subject of the misdemeanor complaint. In addition, the information may, subject to the rules of joinder, charge any other offense which the factual allegations thereof or of any supporting depositions accompanying it are legally sufficient to support, even though such offense is not based upon conduct which was the subject of the misdemeanor complaint.

3. A defendant who has been arraigned upon a misdemeanor complaint may waive prosecution by information and consent to be prosecuted upon the misdemeanor complaint. In such case, the defendant must be required, either upon the date of the waiver or subsequent thereto, to enter a plea to the misdemeanor complaint.

§170.70 Release of defendant upon failure to replace misdemeanor complaint by information.

Upon application of a defendant against whom a misdemeanor complaint is pending in a local criminal court, and who, either at the time of his arraignment thereon or subsequent thereto, has been committed to the custody of the sheriff pending disposition of the action, and who has been confined in such custody for a period of more than five days, not including Sunday, without any information having been filed in replacement of such misdemeanor complaint, the criminal court must release the defendant on his own recognizance unless:

1. The defendant has waived prosecution by information and consented to be prosecuted upon the misdemeanor complaint, pursuant to subdivision three of section 170.65; or

2. The court is satisfied that there is good cause why such order of release should not be issued. Such good cause must consist of some compelling fact or circumstance which precluded replacement of the misdemeanor complaint by an information or a prosecutor's information within the prescribed period.

§170.80 Proceedings regarding certain prostitution charges; certain persons aged sixteen or seventeen.

1. Notwithstanding any other provision of law, at any time at or after arraignment on a charge of prostitution pursuant to section 230.00 of the penal law, after consultation with counsel, a knowing and voluntary plea of guilty has been entered to such charge, any judge or justice hearing any stage of such case may, upon consent of the defendant after consultation with counsel: *(Eff.2/2/21,Ch.23,L.2021)*

(a) conditionally convert such charge in accordance with subdivision three of this section and retain it as a person in need of supervision proceeding for all purposes, and shall make such proceeding fully subject to the provisions and grant any relief available under article seven of the family court act; and/or

(b) order the provision of any of the specialized services enumerated in title eight-A of article six of the social services law, as may be reasonably available.

2. In the event of a conviction by plea or verdict to such charge or charges of prostitution or loitering for the purposes of prostitution as described in subdivision one of this section, the court must find that the person is a youthful offender for the purpose of such charge and proceed in accordance with article seven hundred twenty of this chapter, provided, however, that the available sentence shall be the sentence that may be imposed for a violation as defined in subdivision three of section 10.00 of the penal law. In

such case, the records of the investigation and proceedings relating to such charge shall be sealed in accordance with section 720.35 of this chapter.

3. (a) When a charge of prostitution or loitering for the purposes of prostitution has been conditionally converted to a person in need of supervision proceeding pursuant to subdivision one of this section, the defendant shall be deemed a "sexually exploited child" as defined in subdivision one of section four hundred forty-seven-a of the social services law and therefore shall not be considered an adult for purposes related to the charges in the person in need of supervision proceeding. Sections seven hundred eighty-one, seven hundred eighty-two, seven hundred eighty-two-a, seven hundred eighty-three and seven hundred eighty-four of the family court act shall apply to any proceeding conditionally converted under this section.

(b) The court after hearing from the parties shall state the condition or conditions of such conversion, which may include the individual's participation in specialized services provided pursuant to title eight-A of article six of the social services law and other appropriate services available to persons in need of supervision in accordance with article seven of the family court act.

(c)(i) The court may, upon written application by the people at any time during the pendency of the person in need of supervision proceeding or during any disposition thereof, but in no event later than the individual's eighteenth birthday, restore the accusatory instrument if the court is satisfied by competent proof that the individual, without just cause, is not in substantial compliance with the condition or conditions of the conversion.

(ii) Notice of such an application to restore an accusatory instrument shall be served on the person and his or her counsel by the court. The notice shall include a statement setting forth a reasonable description of why the person is not in substantial compliance with the condition or conditions of the conversion and a date upon which such person shall appear before the court. The court shall afford the person the right to counsel and the right to be heard. Upon such appearance, the court must advise the person of the contents of the notice and the consequences of a finding of failure to substantially comply with the conditions of conversion. At the time of such appearance the court must ask the person whether he or she wishes to make any statement with respect to such alleged failure to substantially comply. In determining whether such person has failed to substantially comply with the terms of the conversion, the court shall conduct a hearing at which time such person may cross-examine witnesses and present evidence on his or her own behalf. Any findings the court shall make, shall be made on the court record. If the court finds that such person did not substantially comply, it may restore the accusatory instrument pursuant to subparagraph (i) of this paragraph, modify the terms of conversion in accordance with this section or otherwise continue such terms as in its discretion it deems just and proper.

(iii) If such accusatory instrument is restored pursuant to subparagraph (i) of this paragraph, the proceeding shall continue in accordance with subdivision two of this section. If the individual does not comply with services or does not return to court, the individual shall be returned in accordance with the provisions of article seven of the family court act.

4. At the conclusion of a person in need of supervision proceeding pursuant to this section, all records of the investigation and proceedings relating to such proceedings, including records created before the charge was conditionally converted, shall be sealed in accordance with section 720.35 of this chapter.

ARTICLE 180 - PROCEEDINGS UPON FELONY COMPLAINT FROM ARRAIGNMENT THEREON THROUGH DISPOSITION THEREOF

Section
180.10   Proceedings upon felony complaint; arraignment; defendant's rights, court's instructions and bail matters.
180.20   Proceedings upon felony complaint; removal of action from one local criminal court to another.
180.30   Proceedings upon felony complaint; waiver of hearing; action to be taken.
180.40   Proceedings upon felony complaint; application in superior court following hearing or waiver of hearing.
180.50   Proceedings upon felony complaint; reduction of charge.
180.60   Proceedings upon felony complaint; the hearing; conduct thereof.
180.70   Proceedings upon felony complaint; disposition of felony complaint after hearing.
180.75   Proceedings upon felony complaint; juvenile offender.
180.80   Proceedings upon felony complaint; release of defendant from custody upon failure of timely disposition.
180.85   Termination of prosecution.

§180.10   Proceedings upon felony complaint; arraignment; defendant's rights, court's instructions and bail matters.

1. Upon the defendant's arraignment before a local criminal court upon a felony complaint, the court must immediately inform him, or cause him to be informed in its presence, of the charge or charges against him and that the primary purpose of the proceedings upon such felony complaint is to determine whether the defendant is to be held for the action of a grand jury with respect to the charges contained therein. The court must furnish the defendant with a copy of the felony complaint.

2. The defendant has a right to a prompt hearing upon the issue of whether there is sufficient evidence to warrant the court in holding him for the action of a grand jury, but he may waive such right.

3. The defendant has a right to the aid of counsel at the arraignment and at every subsequent stage of the action, and, if he appears upon such arraignment without counsel, has the following rights:

(a) To an adjournment for the purpose of obtaining counsel; and

(b) To communicate, free of charge, by letter or by telephone provided by the law enforcement facility where the defendant is held to a phone number located in the United States or Puerto Rico, for the purpose of obtaining counsel and informing a relative or friend that he or she has been charged with an offense; and

(c) To have counsel assigned by the court in any case where he is financially unable to obtain the same.

4. The court must inform the defendant of all rights specified in subdivisions two and three. The court must accord the defendant opportunity to exercise such rights and must itself take such affirmative action as is necessary to effectuate them.

5. If the defendant desires to proceed without the aid of counsel, the court must permit him to do so if it is satisfied that he made such decision with knowledge of the significance thereof, but if it is not so satisfied it may not proceed until the defendant is provided with counsel, either of his own choosing or by assignment. A defendant who proceeds at the arraignment without counsel does not waive his right to counsel, and the court must inform him that he continues to have such right as well as all the rights specified in subdivision three which are necessary to effectuate it, and that he may exercise such rights at any stage of the action.

6. Upon the arraignment, the court, unless it intends immediately thereafter to dismiss the felony complaint and terminate the action, must issue a securing order which, as provided in subdivision two of section 530.20, either releases the defendant on his own recognizance or fixes bail or commits him to the custody of the sheriff for his future appearance in such action.

7. Notwithstanding any contrary provision of this section, when an off-hours arraignment part designated in accordance with paragraph (w) of subdivision one of section two hundred twelve of the judiciary law is in operation in the county in which the court is located, the court must adjourn the proceedings before it, and direct that the proceedings be continued in such off-hours part when the defendant has appeared before the court without counsel and no counsel is otherwise available at the time of such appearance to aid the defendant.

§180.20 Proceedings upon felony complaint; removal of action from one local criminal court to another.

Under circumstances prescribed in this section, a criminal action based upon a pending felony complaint may be removed from one local criminal court to another:

1. When a defendant arrested by a police officer for a felony allegedly committed in a town has not been brought before the town court of the town, or as the case may be before the village court of the village, in which the felony charged was allegedly committed, but, instead, to another local criminal court of the county and there stands charged with such offense by felony complaint, such latter court must arraign him upon such felony complaint. Such court must then either:

(a) Dispose of the felony complaint pursuant to this article. If such disposition results in a reduction of the felony charge and the filing of an information or prosecutor's information charging a misdemeanor or a petty offense pursuant to section 180.50 or subdivision two or three of section 180.70, such court must conduct the action to judgment or other final disposition; or

(b) Remit the action upon the felony complaint, together with all pertinent papers and documents, to the town court of the town, or as the case may be to the village court of the village, in which the felony charged was allegedly committed. In such case, the latter court must dispose of the felony complaint pursuant to this article.

1-a. When a defendant arrested by a police officer for a felony allegedly committed in a city has not been brought before the city court of such city but, instead, to the local criminal court of an adjoining town or village of the same county and there stands charged with such offense by felony complaint, such latter court must arraign him upon such felony complaint. Such court must then either:

(a) Dispose of the felony complaint pursuant to this article. If such disposition results in a reduction of the felony charge and the filing of an information or prosecutor's information charging a misdemeanor or a petty offense pursuant to section 180.50 or subdivision two or three of section 180.70 of this article, such court must conduct the action to judgment or other final disposition; or

(b) Remit the action upon the felony complaint, together with all pertinent papers and documents, to the city court of the city in which the felony charged was allegedly committed. In such case, the latter court must dispose of the felony complaint pursuant to this article.

2. When a defendant arrested by a police officer for a felony has been brought before a superior court judge sitting as a local criminal court for arraignment upon a felony complaint charging such felony, such judge must, as a local criminal court, arraign the defendant upon such felony complaint. Such court must then either:

(a) Dispose of the felony complaint pursuant to this article. If however, such disposition results in a reduction of the charge and the filing of an information or prosecutor's information charging a misdemeanor or a petty offense, such judge, after arraigning the defendant upon such accusatory instrument, must remit the action, together with all pertinent papers and documents, to a local criminal court having trial jurisdiction of the offense charged, and the latter court must then conduct the action to judgment or other final disposition; or

(b) Remit the action upon the felony complaint, together with all pertinent papers and documents, to a local criminal court having geographical jurisdiction over the area in which the felony charged was allegedly committed. In such case, such latter court must dispose of the felony complaint pursuant to this article.

3. Notwithstanding any provision of this section to the contrary, in any county outside a city having a population of one million or more, upon or after arraignment of a defendant on a felony complaint pending in a local criminal court having preliminary jurisdiction thereof, such court may, upon motion of the defendant and with the consent of the district attorney, order that the action be removed from the court in which the matter is pending to another local criminal court in the same county which has been designated a drug court by the chief administrator of the courts, and such drug court may then dispose of such felony complaint pursuant to this article; provided, however, that an order of removal issued under this subdivision shall not take effect until five days after the date the order is issued unless, prior to such effective date, the drug court notifies the court that issued the order that:

(a) it will not accept the action, in which event the order shall not take effect, or

(b) it will accept the action on a date prior to such effective date, in which event the order shall take effect upon such prior date.

Upon providing notification pursuant to paragraph (a) or (b) of this subdivision, the drug court shall promptly give notice to the defendant, his or her counsel and the district attorney.

4. (a) Notwithstanding any provision of this section to the contrary, in any county outside a city having a population of one million or more, upon or after arraignment of a defendant on a felony complaint pending in a local criminal court having preliminary jurisdiction thereof, such court may, upon motion of the defendant and after giving the district attorney an opportunity to be heard, order that the action be removed from the court in which the matter is pending to another local criminal court in the same county, or with consent of the district attorney and the district attorney of the adjoining county to another court in such adjoining county, that has been designated as a human trafficking court or veterans treatment court by the chief administrator of the courts, and such human trafficking court or veterans treatment court may then conduct such action to judgment or other final disposition; provided, however, that no court may order removal pursuant to this subdivision to a veterans treatment court of a family offense charge described in subdivision one of section 530.11 of this chapter where the accused and the person alleged to be the victim of such offense charged are members of the same family or household as defined in such subdivision one of section 530.11; and provided further an order of removal issued under this subdivision shall not take effect until five days after the date the order is issued unless, prior to such effective date, the human trafficking court or veterans treatment court notifies the court that issued the order that:

i. it will not accept the action, in which event the order shall not take effect; or

ii. it will accept the action on a date prior to such effective date, in which event the order shall take effect upon such prior date.

(b) Upon providing notification pursuant to subparagraph i or ii of paragraph (a) of this subdivision, the human trafficking court or veterans treatment court shall promptly give notice to the defendant, his or her counsel and the district attorney.   *(Eff.4/28/21,Ch.91,L.2021)*

§180.30 Proceedings upon felony complaint; waiver of hearing; action to be taken.

If the defendant waives a hearing upon the felony complaint, the court must either:

1. Order that the defendant be held for the action of a grand jury of the appropriate superior court with respect to the charge or charges contained in the felony complaint. In such case, the court must promptly transmit to such superior court the order, the felony complaint, the supporting depositions and all other pertinent documents. Until such papers are received by the superior court, the action is deemed to be still pending in the local criminal court; or

2. Make inquiry, pursuant to section 180.50, for the purpose of determining whether the felony complaint should be dismissed and an information, a prosecutor's information or a misdemeanor complaint filed with the court in lieu thereof.

§180.40 Proceedings upon felony complaint; application in superior court following hearing or waiver of hearing.

Where the local criminal court has held a defendant for the action of a grand jury, the district attorney may, at any time before such matter is submitted to the grand jury, apply, ex parte, to the appropriate superior court for an order directing that the felony complaint and other papers transmitted to such court pursuant to subdivision one of section 180.30 be returned to the local criminal court for reconsideration of the action to be taken. The superior court may issue such an order if it is satisfied that the felony complaint is defective or that such action is required in the interest of justice.

§180.50 Proceedings upon felony complaint; reduction of charge.

1. Whether or not the defendant waives a hearing upon the felony complaint, the local criminal court may, upon consent of the district attorney, make inquiry for the purpose of determining whether (a) the available facts and evidence relating to the conduct underlying the felony complaint provide a basis for charging the defendant with an offense other than a felony, and (b) if so, whether the charge should, in the manner prescribed in subdivision three, be reduced from one for a felony to one for a non-felony offense. Upon such inquiry, the court may question any person who it believes may possess information relevant to the matter, including the defendant if he wishes to be questioned.

2. If after such inquiry the court is satisfied that there is reasonable cause to believe that the defendant committed an offense other than a felony, it may order the indicated reduction as follows:

(a) If there is not reasonable cause to believe that the defendant committed a felony in addition to the non-felony offense in question, the court may as a matter of right order a reduction of the charge to one for the non-felony offense;

(b) If there is reasonable cause to believe that the defendant committed a felony in addition to the non-felony offense, the court may order a reduction of the charge to one for the non-felony offense only if (i) it is satisfied that such reduction is in the interest of justice, and (ii) the district attorney consents thereto; provided, however, that the court may not order such reduction where there is reasonable cause to believe that the defendant committed a class A felony, other than those defined in article two hundred twenty of the penal law, or any armed felony as defined in subdivision forty-one of section 1.20.

3. A charge is "reduced" from a felony to a non-felony offense, within the meaning of this section, by replacing the felony complaint with, or converting it to, another local criminal court accusatory instrument, as follows:

(a) If the factual allegations of the felony complaint and/or any supporting depositions are legally sufficient to support the charge that the defendant committed the non-felony offense in question, the court may:

(i) Direct the district attorney to file with the court a prosecutor's information charging the defendant with such non-felony offense; or

(ii) Request the complainant of the felony complaint to file with the court an information charging the defendant with such non-felony offense. If such an information is filed, any supporting deposition supporting or accompanying the felony complaint is deemed also to support or accompany the replacing information; or

(iii) Convert the felony complaint, or a copy thereof, into an information by notations upon or attached thereto which make the necessary and appropriate changes in the title of the instrument and in the names of the offense or offenses charged. In case of such conversion, any supporting deposition supporting or accompanying the felony complaint is deemed also to support or accompany the information to which it has been converted;

(b) If the non-felony offense in question is a misdemeanor, and if the factual allegations of the felony complaint together with those of any supporting depositions, though providing reasonable cause to believe that the defendant committed such misdemeanor are not legally sufficient to support such misdemeanor charge, the court may cause such felony complaint to be replaced by or converted to a misdemeanor complaint charging the misdemeanor in question, in the manner prescribed in subparagraphs two and three of paragraph (a) of this subdivision.

(c) An information, a prosecutor's information or a misdemeanor complaint filed pursuant to this section may, pursuant to the ordinary rules of joinder, charge two or more offenses, and it may jointly charge with each offense any two or more defendants originally so charged in the felony complaint;

(d) Upon the filing of an information, a prosecutor's information or a misdemeanor complaint pursuant to this section, the court must dismiss the felony complaint from which such accusatory instrument is derived. It must then arraign the defendant upon the new accusatory instrument and inform him of his rights in connection therewith in the manner provided in section 170.10.

4. Upon making any finding other than that specified in subdivision two, the court must conduct a hearing upon the felony complaint, unless the defendant has waived the same. In the case of such waiver the court must order that the defendant be held for the action of a grand jury.

§180.60 Proceedings upon felony complaint; the hearing; conduct thereof.
A hearing upon a felony complaint must be conducted as follows:

1. The district attorney must conduct such hearing on behalf of the people.

2. The defendant may as a matter of right be present at such hearing.

3. The court must read to the defendant the felony complaint and any supporting depositions unless the defendant waives such reading.

4. Each witness, whether called by the people or by the defendant, must, unless he would be authorized to give unsworn evidence at a trial, testify under oath. Each witness, including any defendant testifying in his own behalf, may be cross-examined.

5. The people must call and examine witnesses and offer evidence in support of the charge.

6. The defendant may, as a matter of right, testify in his own behalf.

7. Upon request of the defendant, the court may, as a matter of discretion, permit him to call and examine other witnesses or to produce other evidence in his behalf.

8. Upon such a hearing, only non-hearsay evidence is admissible to demonstrate reasonable cause to believe that the defendant committed a felony; except that reports of experts and technicians in professional and scientific fields and sworn statements of the kinds specified in subdivisions two and three of section 190.30 are admissible to the same extent as in a grand jury proceeding, unless the court determines, upon application of the defendant, that such hearsay evidence is, under the particular circumstances of the case, not sufficiently reliable, in which case the court shall require that the witness testify in person and be subject to cross-examination.

9. The court may, upon application of the defendant, exclude the public from the hearing and direct that no disclosure be made of the proceedings.

10. Such hearing should be completed at one session. In the interest of justice, however, it may be adjourned by the court but, in the absence of a showing of good cause therefor, no such adjournment may be for more than one day.

§180.65 *Hearing upon felony complaint; emergency provision during disaster emergency. *(Repealed 4/30/21)*

§180.70 Proceedings upon felony complaint; disposition of felony complaint after hearing.

At the conclusion of a hearing, the court must dispose of the felony complaint as follows:

1. If there is reasonable cause to believe that the defendant committed a felony, the court must, except as provided in subdivision three, order that the defendant be held for the action of a grand jury of the appropriate superior court, and it must promptly transmit to such superior court the order, the felony complaint, the supporting depositions and all other pertinent documents. Until such papers are received by the superior court, the action is deemed to be still pending in the local criminal court.

2. If there is not reasonable cause to believe that the defendant committed a felony but there is reasonable cause to believe that he committed an offense other than a felony, the court may, by means of procedures prescribed in subdivision three of section 180.50, reduce the charge to one for such non-felony offense.

3. If there is reasonable cause to believe that the defendant committed a felony in addition to a non-felony offense, the court may, instead of ordering the defendant held for the action of a grand jury as provided in subdivision one, reduce the charge to one for such non-felony offense as provided in subdivision two, if (a) it is satisfied that such reduction is in the interest of justice, and (b) the district attorney consents thereto; provided, however, that the court may not order such reduction where there is reasonable cause to believe the defendant committed a class A felony, other than those defined in article two hundred twenty of the penal law, or any armed felony as defined in subdivision forty-one of section 1.20.

4. If there is not reasonable cause to believe that the defendant committed any offense, the court must dismiss the felony complaint and discharge the defendant from custody if he is in custody, or, if he is at liberty on bail, it must exonerate the bail.

§180.75 Proceedings upon felony complaint; juvenile offender.

1. When a juvenile offender or adolescent offender is arraigned before the youth part of a superior court or the most accessible magistrate designated by the appellate division of the supreme court in the applicable department to act as a youth part, the provisions of article seven hundred twenty-two of this chapter shall apply in lieu of the provisions of sections 180.30, 180.50 and 180.70 of this article.

§180.80 Proceedings upon felony complaint; release of defendant from custody upon failure of timely disposition.

Upon application of a defendant against whom a felony complaint has been filed with a local criminal court or the youth part of a superior court, and who, since the time of his arrest or subsequent thereto, has been held in custody pending disposition of such felony complaint, and who has been confined in such custody for a period of more than one hundred twenty hours or, in the event that a Saturday, Sunday or legal holiday occurs during such custody, one hundred forty-four hours, without either a disposition of the felony complaint or commencement of a hearing thereon, the court must release him on his own recognizance unless:

1. The failure to dispose of the felony complaint or to commence a hearing thereon during such period of confinement was due to the defendant's request, action or condition, or occurred with his consent; or

2. Prior to the application:

(a) The district attorney files with the court a written certification that an indictment has been voted; or

(b) An indictment or a direction to file a prosecutor's information charging an offense based upon conduct alleged in the felony complaint was filed by a grand jury; or

3. The court is satisfied that the people have shown good cause why such order of release should not be issued. Such good cause must consist of some compelling fact or circumstance which precluded disposition of the felony complaint within the prescribed period or rendered such action against the interest of justice.

§180.85 Termination of prosecution.

1. After arraignment of a defendant upon a felony complaint, other than a felony complaint charging an offense defined in section 125.10, 125.15, 125.20, 125.25, 125.26 or 125.27 of the penal law, either party or the local criminal court or superior court before which the action is pending, on its own motion, may move in accordance with the provisions of this section for an order terminating prosecution of the charges contained in such felony complaint on consent of the parties.

2. A motion to terminate a prosecution pursuant to this section may only be made where the count or counts of the felony complaint have not been presented to a grand jury or otherwise disposed of in accordance with this chapter. Such motion shall be filed in writing with the local criminal court or superior court in which the felony complaint is pending not earlier than twelve months following the date of arraignment on such felony complaint. Upon the filing of such motion, the court shall fix a return date and provide the parties with at least thirty days' written notice of the motion and return date.

3. Where, upon motion to terminate a prosecution pursuant to this section, both parties consent to such termination, the court, on the return date of such motion, shall enter an order terminating such prosecution. For purposes of this subdivision, a party that is given written notice of a motion to terminate a prosecution shall be deemed to consent to such termination unless, prior to the return date of such motion, such party files a notice of

opposition thereto with the court. Except as otherwise provided in subdivision four, where such a notice of opposition is filed, the court, on the return date of the motion, shall enter an order denying the motion to terminate the prosecution.

4. Notwithstanding any other provision of this section, where the people file a notice of opposition pursuant to subdivision three, the court, on the return date of the motion, may defer disposition of such motion for a period of forty-five days. In such event, if the count or counts of such felony complaint are presented to a grand jury or otherwise disposed of within such period, the court, upon the expiration thereof, shall enter an order denying the motion to terminate the prosecution. If such count or counts are not presented to a grand jury or otherwise disposed of within such period, the court, upon the expiration thereof, shall enter an order terminating the prosecution unless, within the forty-five day period, the people, on at least five days' written notice to the defendant, show good cause for their failure to present or otherwise dispose of such count or counts. If such good cause is shown, the court, upon expiration of the forty-five day period, shall enter an order denying the motion to terminate the prosecution.

5. Notwithstanding any other provision of law, the defendant's appearance in court on the return date of the motion or on any other date shall not be required as a prerequisite to entry of an order under this section.

6. The period from the filing of a motion pursuant to this section until entry of an order disposing of such motion shall not, by reason of such motion, be considered a period of delay for purposes of subdivision four of section 30.30, nor shall such period, by reason of such motion, be excluded in computing the time within which the people must be ready for trial pursuant to such section 30.30.

7. Where a prosecution is terminated pursuant to this section, nothing contained herein shall preclude the people from subsequently filing an indictment charging the same count or count provided such filing is in accordance with the provisions of this section, article thirty and any other relevant provisions of this chapter. Where the people indicate their intention to seek an indictment following the entry of an order terminating a prosecution pursuant to this section, the court shall, notwithstanding any provision of section 160.50 to the contrary, stay sealing under that section for a reasonable period not to exceed thirty days to permit the people an opportunity to pursue such indictment.

8. Where an order denying a party's motion to terminate a prosecution is entered pursuant to this section, such party may not file a subsequent motion to terminate the prosecution pursuant to this section for at least six months from the date on which such order is entered.

9. Notwithstanding any other provision of this section, where a motion to terminate a prosecution is filed with a local criminal court pursuant to subdivision two, and, prior to the determination thereof, such court is divested of jurisdiction by the filing of an indictment charging the offense or offenses contained in the felony complaint, such motion shall be deemed to have been denied as of the date of such divestiture.

10. The chief administrator of the courts, in consultation with the director of the division of criminal justice services and representatives of appropriate prosecutorial and criminal defense organizations in the state, shall adopt forms for the motion to terminate a prosecution authorized by subdivision one and for the notice of opposition specified in subdivision three.

*ARTICLE 182 - ALTERNATE METHOD OF COURT APPEARANCE
*(Expires 9/1/23,Ch.55,L.2021)

Section
182.10   **Definition of terms.**
182.20   **Electronic appearance; general rule.**
182.30   **Electronic appearance; conditions and limitations.**
182.40   **Approval by the chief administrator of the courts.**

§182.10 Definition of terms.
As used in this article:

1. "Independent audio-visual system" means an electronic system for the transmission and receiving of audio and visual signals, encompassing encoded signals, frequency domain multiplexing or other suitable means to preclude the unauthorized reception and decoding of the signals by commercially available television receivers, channel converters, or other available receiving devices.

2. "Electronic appearance" means an appearance in which various participants, including the defendant, are not present in the court, but in which, by means of an independent audio-visual system, (a) all of the participants are simultaneously able to see and hear reproductions of the voices and images of the judge, counsel, defendant, police officer, and any other appropriate participant, and (b) counsel is present with the defendant, or if the defendant waives the presence of counsel on the record, the defendant and his or her counsel are able to see and hear each other and engage in private conversation.

§182.20 Electronic appearance; general rule.
1. Notwithstanding any other provision of law and except as provided in section 182.30 of this article, the court, in its discretion, may dispense with the personal appearance of the defendant, except an appearance at a hearing or trial, and conduct an electronic appearance in connection with a criminal action pending in Albany, Bronx, Broome, Erie, Kings, New York, Niagara, Oneida, Onondaga, Ontario, Orange, Putnam, Queens, Richmond, St. Lawrence, Tompkins, Chautauqua, Cattaraugus, Clinton, Essex, Montgomery, Rensselaer, Warren, Westchester, Suffolk, Herkimer or Franklin county, provided that the chief administrator of the courts has authorized the use of electronic appearance and the defendant, after consultation with counsel, consents on the record. Such consent shall be required at the commencement of each electronic appearance to such electronic appearance.

2. If, for any reason, the court determines on its own motion or on the motion of any party that the conduct of an electronic appearance may impair the legal rights of the defendant, it shall not permit the electronic appearance to proceed. If, for any other articulated reason, either party requests at any time during the electronic appearance that such appearance be terminated, the court shall grant such request and adjourn the proceeding to a date certain. Upon the adjourned date the proceeding shall be recommenced from the point at which the request for termination of the

electronic appearance had been granted.

3. The electronic appearance shall be conducted in accordance with rules issued by the chief administrator of the courts.

4. When the defendant makes an electronic appearance, the court stenographer shall record any statements in the same manner as if the defendant had made a personal appearance. No electronic recording of any electronic appearance may be made, viewed or inspected except as may be authorized by the rules issued by the chief administrator of the courts.

§182.30 Electronic appearance; conditions and limitations.

The following conditions and limitations apply to all electronic appearances:

1. The defendant may not enter a plea of guilty to, or be sentenced upon a conviction of, a felony.

2. The defendant may not enter a plea of not responsible by reason of mental disease or defect.

3. The defendant may not be committed to the state department of mental hygiene pursuant to article seven hundred thirty of this chapter.

4. The defendant may not enter a plea of guilty to a misdemeanor conditioned upon a promise of incarceration unless such incarceration will be imposed only in the event that the defendant fails to comply with a term or condition imposed under the original sentence.

5. A defendant who has been convicted of a misdemeanor may not be sentenced to a period of incarceration which exceeds the time the defendant has already served when sentence is imposed.

§182.40 Approval by the chief administrator of the courts.

1. The appropriate administrative judge shall submit to the chief administrator of the courts a written proposal for the use of electronic appearance in his or her jurisdiction. If the chief administrator of the courts approves the proposal, installation of an independent audio-visual system may begin.

2. Upon completion of the installation of an independent audio-visual system, the commission on cable television shall inspect, test, and examine the independent audio-visual system and certify to the chief administrator of the courts whether the system complies with the definition of an independent audio-visual system and is technically suitable for the conducting of electronic appearances as intended.

3. The chief administrator of the courts shall issue rules governing the use of electronic appearances.

TITLE I - PRELIMINARY PROCEEDINGS IN SUPERIOR COURT
ARTICLE 190 - THE GRAND JURY AND ITS PROCEEDINGS

Section
190.05   Grand jury; definition and general functions.
190.10   Grand jury; for what courts drawn.
190.15   Grand jury; duration of term and discharge.
190.20   Grand jury; formation, organization and other matters preliminary to assumption of duties.
190.25   Grand jury; proceedings and operation in general.
190.30   Grand jury; rules of evidence.
190.32   Videotaped examination; definitions, application, order and procedure.
190.35   Grand jury; definitions of terms.
190.40   Grand jury; witnesses, compulsion of evidence and immunity.
190.45   Grand jury; waiver of immunity.
190.50   Grand jury; who may call witnesses; defendant as witness.
190.52   Grand jury; attorney for witness.

©1993 Looseleaf Law Publications, Inc.
    All Rights Reserved. Printed in U.S.A.

190.55   Grand jury; matters to be heard and examined; duties and authority of
          district attorney.
190.60   Grand jury; action to be taken.
190.65   Grand jury; when indictment is authorized.
190.70   Grand jury; direction to file prosecutor's information and related matters.
190.71   Grand jury; direction to file request for removal to family court.
190.75   Grand jury; dismissal of charge.
190.80   Grand jury; release of defendant upon failure of timely grand jury action.
190.85   Grand jury; grand jury reports.
190.90   Grand jury; appeal from order concerning grand jury reports.

§190.05 Grand jury; definition and general functions.

A grand jury is a body consisting of not less than sixteen nor more than twenty-three persons, impaneled by a superior court and constituting a part of such court, the functions of which are to hear and examine evidence concerning offenses and concerning misconduct, nonfeasance and neglect in public office, whether criminal or otherwise, and to take action with respect to such evidence as provided in section 190.60.

§190.10 Grand jury; for what courts drawn.

The appellate division of each judicial department shall adopt rules governing the number and the terms for which grand juries shall be drawn and impaneled by the superior courts within its department; provided, however, that a grand jury may be drawn and impaneled for any extraordinary term of the supreme court upon the order of a justice assigned to hold such term.

§190.15 Grand jury; duration of term and discharge.

1. A term of a superior court for which a grand jury has been impaneled remains in existence at least until and including the opening date of the next term of such court for which a grand jury has been designated. Upon such date, or within five days preceding it, the court may, upon declaration of both the grand jury and the district attorney that such grand jury has not yet completed or will be unable to complete certain business before it, extend the term of court and the existence of such grand jury to a specified future date, and may subsequently order further extensions for such purpose.

2. At any time when a grand jury is in recess and no other appropriate grand jury is in existence in the county, the court may, upon application of the district attorney or of a defendant held by a local criminal court for the action of a grand jury, order such grand jury reconvened for the purpose of dealing with a matter requiring grand jury action.

§190.20 Grand jury; formation, organization and other matters preliminary to assumption of duties.

1. The mode of selecting grand jurors and of drawing and impaneling grand juries is governed by the judiciary law.

2. Neither the grand jury panel nor any individual grand juror may be challenged, but the court may:

(a) At any time before a grand jury is sworn, discharge the panel and summon another panel if it finds that the original panel does not substantially conform to the requirements of the judiciary law; or

(b) At any time after a grand juror is drawn, refuse to swear him, or discharge him after he has been sworn, upon a finding that he is disqualified from service pursuant to the judiciary law, or incapable of performing his duties because of bias or prejudice, or guilty of misconduct in the performance of his duties such as to impair the proper functioning of the grand jury.

3. After a grand jury has been impaneled, the court must appoint one of the grand jurors as foreman and another to act as foreman during any absence or disability of the foreman. At some time before commencement of their duties, the grand jurors must appoint one of their number as secretary to keep records material to the conduct of the grand jury's business.

4. The grand jurors must be sworn by the court. The oath may be in any form or language which requires the grand jurors to perform their duties faithfully.

5. After a grand jury has been sworn, the court must deliver or cause to be delivered to each grand juror a printed copy of all the provisions of this article, and the court may, in addition, give the grand jurors any oral and written instructions relating to the proper performance of their duties as it deems necessary or appropriate.

6. If two or more grand juries are impaneled at the same court term, the court may thereafter, for good cause, transfer grand jurors from one panel to another, and any grand juror so transferred is deemed to have been sworn as a member of the panel to which he has been transferred.

§190.25 Grand jury; proceedings and operation in general.

1. Proceedings of a grand jury are not valid unless at least sixteen of its members are present. The finding of an indictment, a direction to file a prosecutor's information, a decision to submit a grand jury report and every other affirmative official action or decision requires the concurrence of at least twelve members thereof.

2. The foreman or any other grand juror may administer an oath to any witness appearing before the grand jury.

3. Except as provided in subdivision three-a of this section, during the deliberations and voting of a grand jury, only the grand jurors may be present in the grand jury room. During its other proceedings, the following persons, in addition to witnesses, may, as the occasion requires, also be present:

(a) The district attorney;

(b) A clerk or other public servant authorized to assist the grand jury in the administrative conduct of its proceedings;

(c) A stenographer authorized to record the proceedings of the grand jury;

(d) An interpreter. Upon request of the grand jury, the prosecutor must provide an interpreter to interpret the testimony of any witness who does not speak the English language well enough to be readily understood. Such interpreter must, if he has not previously taken the constitutional oath of office, first take an oath before the grand jury that he will faithfully interpret the testimony of the witness and that he will keep secret all matters before such grand jury within his knowledge;

(e) A public servant holding a witness in custody. When a person held in official custody is a witness before a grand jury, a public servant assigned to guard him during his grand jury appearance may accompany him in the grand jury room. Such public servant must, if he has not previously taken the constitutional oath of office, first take an oath before the grand jury that he will keep secret all matters before it within his knowledge.

(f) An attorney representing a witness pursuant to section 190.52 of this chapter while that witness is present.

(g) An operator, as that term is defined in section 190.32 of this chapter, while the videotaped examination of either a special witness or a child witness is being played.

(h) A social worker, rape crisis counselor, psychologist or other professional providing emotional support to a child witness twelve years old or younger, or a social worker or informal caregiver, as provided in subdivision two of section two hundred six of the elder law, for a vulnerable elderly person as provided in subdivision three of section 260.31 of the penal law, who is called to give evidence in a grand jury proceeding

concerning a crime defined in article one hundred twenty-one, article one
hundred thirty, article two hundred sixty, section 120.10, 125.10, 125.15,
125.20, 125.25, 125.26, 125.27, 255.25, 255.26 or 255.27 of the penal law
provided that the district attorney consents. Such support person shall not
provide the witness with an answer to any question or otherwise participate
in such proceeding and shall first take an oath before the grand jury that he
or she will keep secret all matters before such grand jury within his or her
knowledge.

3-a. Upon the request of a deaf or hearing-impaired grand juror, the
prosecutor shall provide a sign language interpreter for such juror. Such
interpreter shall be present during all proceedings of the grand jury which
the deaf or hearing-impaired grand juror attends, including deliberation and
voting. The interpreter shall, if he or she has not previously taken the
constitutional oath of office, first take an oath before the grand jury that he
or she will faithfully interpret the testimony of the witnesses and the
statements of the prosecutor, judge and grand jurors; keep secret all
matters before such grand jury within his or her knowledge; and not seek to
influence the deliberations and voting of such grand jury.

4. (a) Grand jury proceedings are secret, and no grand juror, or other
person specified in subdivision three of this section or section 215.70 of the
penal law, may, except in the lawful discharge of his duties or upon written
order of the court, disclose the nature or substance of any grand jury
testimony, evidence, or any decision, result or other matter attending a
grand jury proceeding. For the purpose of assisting the grand jury in
conducting its investigation, evidence obtained by a grand jury may be
independently examined by the district attorney, members of his staff, police
officers specifically assigned to the investigation, and such other persons as
the court may specifically authorize. Such evidence may not be disclosed to
other persons without a court order. Nothing contained herein shall prohibit
a witness from disclosing his own testimony.

(b) When a district attorney obtains evidence during a grand jury
proceeding which provides reasonable cause to suspect that a child has
been abused or maltreated, as those terms are defined by section ten
hundred twelve of the family court act, he must apply to the court
supervising the grand jury for an order permitting disclosure of such
evidence to the state central register of child abuse and maltreatment. A
district attorney need not apply to the court for such order if he has
previously made or caused a report to be made to the state central register
of child abuse and maltreatment pursuant to section four hundred thirteen of
the social services law and the evidence obtained during the grand jury
proceeding, or substantially similar information, was included in such report.
The district attorney's application to the court shall be made ex parte and in
camera. The court must grant the application and permit the district attorney
to disclose the evidence to the state central register of child abuse and
maltreatment unless the court finds that such disclosure would jeopardize
the life or safety of any person or interfere with a continuing grand jury
proceeding.

5. The grand jury is the exclusive judge of the facts with respect to any
matter before it.

6. The legal advisors of the grand jury are the court and the district
attorney, and the grand jury may not seek or receive legal advice from any
other source. Where necessary or appropriate, the court or the district
attorney, or both, must instruct the grand jury concerning the law with
respect to its duties or any matter before it, and such instructions must be
recorded in the minutes.

§190.30 Grand jury; rules of evidence.

1. Except as otherwise provided in this section, the provisions of article
sixty, governing rules of evidence and related matters with respect to
criminal proceedings in general, are, where appropriate, applicable to grand

jury proceedings.

2. A report or a copy of a report made by a public servant or by a person employed by a public servant or agency who is a physicist, chemist, coroner or medical examiner, firearms identification expert, examiner of questioned documents, fingerprint technician, or an expert or technician in some comparable scientific or professional field, concerning the results of an examination, comparison or test performed by him in connection with a case which is the subject of a grand jury proceeding, may, when certified by such person as a report made by him or as a true copy thereof, be received in such grand jury proceeding as evidence of the facts stated therein.

2-a. When the electronic transmission of a certified report, or certified copy thereof, of the kind described in subdivision two or three-a of this section or a sworn statement or copy thereof, of the kind described in subdivision three of this section results in a written document, such written document may be received in such grand jury proceeding provided that: (a) a transmittal memorandum completed by the person sending the report contains a certification that the report has not been altered and a description of the report specifying the number of pages; and (b) the person who receives the electronically transmitted document certifies that such document and transmittal memorandum were so received; and (c) a certified report or a certified copy or sworn statement or sworn copy thereof is filed with the court within twenty days following arraignment upon the indictment; and (d) where such written document is a sworn statement or sworn copy thereof of the kind described in subdivision three of this section, such sworn statement or sworn copy thereof is also provided to the defendant or his counsel within twenty days following arraignment upon the indictment.

3. A written or oral statement, under oath, by a person attesting to one or more of the following matters may be received in such grand jury proceeding as evidence of the facts stated therein:

(a) that person's ownership or lawful custody of, or license to occupy, premises, as defined in section 140.00 of the penal law, and of the defendant's lack of license or privilege to enter or remain thereupon;

(b) that person's ownership of, or possessory right in, property, the nature and monetary amount of any damage thereto and the defendant's lack of right to damage or tamper with the property;

(c) that person's ownership or lawful custody of, or license to possess property, as defined in section 155.00 of the penal law, including an automobile or other vehicle, its value and the defendant's lack of superior or equal right to possession thereof;

(d) that person's ownership of a vehicle and the absence of his consent to the defendant's taking, operating, exercising control over or using it;

(e) that person's qualifications as a dealer or other expert in appraising or evaluating a particular type of property, his expert opinion as to the value of a certain item or items of property of that type, and the basis for his opinion;

(f) that person's identity as an ostensible maker, drafter, drawer, endorser or other signator of a written instrument and its falsity within the meaning of section 170.00 of the penal law;

(g) that person's ownership of, or possessory right in, a credit card account number or debit card account number, and the defendant's lack of superior or equal right to use or possession thereof.

Provided, however, that no such statement shall be admitted when an adversarial examination of such person has been previously ordered pursuant to subdivision 8 of section 180.60, unless a transcript of such examination is admitted.

3-a. A sex offender registration form, sex offender registration continuation/supplemental form, sex offender registry address verification form, sex offender change of address form or a copy of such form maintained by the division of criminal justice services concerning an individual who is the subject of a grand jury proceeding, may, when certified by a person designated by the commissioner of the division of criminal justice services as the person to certify such records, as a true copy thereof, be received in such grand jury proceeding as evidence of the facts stated therein.

4. An examination of a child witness or a special witness by the district attorney videotaped pursuant to section 190.32 of this chapter may be received in evidence in such grand jury proceeding as the testimony of such witness.

5. Nothing in subdivisions two, three or four of this section shall be construed to limit the power of the grand jury to cause any person to be called as a witness pursuant to subdivision three of section 190.50.

6. Wherever it is provided in article sixty that the court in a criminal proceeding must rule upon the competency of a witness to testify or upon the admissibility of evidence, such ruling may in an equivalent situation in a grand jury proceeding, be made by the district attorney.

7. Wherever it is provided in article sixty that a court presiding at a jury trial must instruct the jury with respect to the significance, legal effect or evaluation of evidence, the district attorney, in an equivalent situation in a grand jury proceeding, may so instruct the grand jury.

8. (a) A business record may be received in such grand jury proceedings as evidence of the following facts and similar facts stated therein:

(i) a person's use of, subscription to and charges and payments for communication equipment and services including but not limited to equipment or services provided by telephone companies and internet service providers, but not including recorded conversations or images communicated thereby; and

(ii) financial transactions, and a person's ownership or possessory interest in any account, at a bank, insurance company, brokerage, exchange or banking organization as defined in section two of the banking law.

(b) Any business record offered for consideration by a grand jury pursuant to paragraph (a) of this subdivision must be accompanied by a written statement, under oath, that (i) contains a list or description of the records it accompanies, (ii) attests in substance that the person making the statement is a duly authorized custodian of the records or other employee or agent of the business who is familiar with such records, and (iii) attests in substance that such records were made in the regular course of business and that it was the regular course of such business to make such records at the time of the recorded act, transaction, occurrence or event, or within a reasonable time thereafter. Such written statement may also include a statement identifying the name and job description of the person making the statement, specifying the matters set forth in subparagraph (ii) of this paragraph and attesting that the business has made a diligent search and does not possess a particular record or records addressing a matter set forth in paragraph (a) of this subdivision, and such statement may be received at grand jury proceedings as evidence of the fact that the business does not possess such record or records. When records of a business are accompanied by more than one sworn written statement of its employees or agents, such statements may be considered together in determining the admissibility of the records under this subdivision. For the purpose of this subdivision, the term "business records" does not include any records prepared by law enforcement agencies or prepared by any entity in anticipation of litigation.

(c) Any business record offered to a grand jury pursuant to paragraph (a) of this subdivision that includes material beyond that described in such paragraph (a) shall be redacted to exclude such additional material, or received subject to a limiting instruction that the grand jury shall not consider such additional material in support of any criminal charge.

(d) No such records shall be admitted when an adversarial examination of such a records custodian or other employee of such business who was familiar with such records has been previously ordered pursuant to subdivision eight of section 180.60 of this chapter, unless a transcript of such examination is admitted.

(e) Nothing in this subdivision shall affect the admissibility of business records in the grand jury on any basis other than that set forth in this subdivision.

§190.32 Videotaped examination; definitions, application, order and procedure.

1. Definitions. As used in this section:

(a) "Child witness" means a person twelve years old or less whom the people intend to call as witness in a grand jury proceeding to give evidence concerning any crime defined in article one hundred thirty or two hundred sixty or section 255.25, 255.26 or 255.27 of the penal law of which the person was a victim.

(b) "Special witness" means a person whom the people intend to call as a witness in a grand jury proceeding and who is either:

(i) Unable to attend and testify in person in the grand jury proceeding because the person is either physically ill or incapacitated; or

(ii) More than twelve years old and who is likely to suffer very severe emotional or mental stress if required to testify in person concerning any crime defined in article one hundred thirty or two hundred sixty or section 255.25, 255.26 or 255.27 of the penal law to which the person was a witness or of which the person was a victim.

(c) "Operator" means a person employed by the district attorney who operates the video camera to record the examination of a child witness or of a special witness.

2. In lieu of requiring a witness who is a child witness to appear in person and give evidence in a grand jury proceeding, the district attorney may cause the examination of such witness to be videotaped in accordance with the provisions of subdivision five of this section.

3. Whenever the district attorney has reason to believe that a witness is a special witness, he may make an ex parte application to the court for an order authorizing the videotaping of an examination of such special witness and the subsequent introduction in evidence in a grand jury proceeding of that videotape in lieu of the live testimony of such special witness. The application must be in writing, must state the grounds of the application and must contain sworn allegations of fact, whether of the district attorney or another person or persons, supporting such grounds. Such allegations may be based upon personal knowledge of the deponent or upon information and belief, provided, that in the latter event, the sources of such information and the grounds for such belief are stated.

4. If the court is satisfied that a witness is a special witness, it shall issue an order authorizing the videotaping of such special witness in accordance

with the provisions of subdivision five of this section. The court order and
the application and all supporting papers shall not be disclosed to any
person except upon further court order.

5. The videotaping of an examination either of a child witness or a special
witness shall proceed as follows:

(a) An examination of a child witness or a special witness which is to be
videotaped pursuant to this section may be conducted anywhere and at any
time provided that the operator begins the videotape by recording a
statement by the district attorney of the date, time and place of the
examination. In addition, the district attorney shall identify himself, the
operator and all other persons present.

(b) An accurate clock with a sweep second hand shall be placed next to
or behind the witness in such position as to enable the operator to videotape
the clock and the witness together during the entire examination. In the
alternative, a date and time generator shall be used to superimpose the day,
hour, minute and second over the video portion of the recording during the
entire examination.

(c) A social worker, rape crisis counselor, psychologist or other
professional providing emotional support to a child witness or to a special
witness, as defined in subparagraph (ii) of paragraph (b) of subdivision one
of this section, or any of those persons enumerated in paragraphs (a), (b),
(c), (d), (e), (f) and (g) of subdivision three of section 190.25 may be present
during the videotaping except that a doctor, nurse or other medical assistant
also may be present if required by the attendant circumstances. Each
person present, except the witness, must, if he has not previously taken a
constitutional oath of office or an oath that he will keep secret all matters
before a grand jury, must take an oath on the record that he will keep secret
the videotaped examination.

(d) The district attorney shall state for the record the name of the
witness, and the caption and the grand jury number, if any, of the case. If
the witness to be examined is a child witness, the date of the witness' birth
must be recorded. If the witness to be examined is a special witness, the
date of the order authorizing the videotaped examination and the name of
the justice who issued the order shall be recorded.

(e) If the witness will give sworn testimony, the administration of the
oath must be recorded. If the witness will give unsworn testimony, a
statement that the testimony is not under oath must be recorded.

(f) If the examination requires the use of more than one tape, the
operator shall record a statement of the district attorney at the end of each
tape declaring that such tape has ended and referring to the succeeding
tape. At the beginning of such succeeding tape, the operator shall record a
statement of the district attorney identifying himself, the witness being
examined and the number of tapes which have been used to record the
examination of such witness. At the conclusion of the examination the
operator shall record a statement of the district attorney certifying that the
recording has been completed, the number of tapes on which the recording
has been made and that such tapes constitute a complete and accurate
record of the examination of the witness.

(g) A videotape of an examination conducted pursuant to this section
shall not be edited unless upon further order of the court.

6. When the videotape is introduced in evidence and played in the grand jury, the grand jury stenographer shall record the examination in the same manner as if the witness had testified in person.

7. Custody of the videotape shall be maintained in the same manner as custody of the grand jury minutes.

§190.35 Grand jury; definitions of terms.

The term definitions contained in section 50.10 are applicable to sections 190.40, 190.45 and 190.50.

§190.40 Grand jury; witnesses, compulsion of evidence and immunity.

1. Every witness in a grand jury proceeding must give any evidence legally requested of him regardless of any protest or belief on his part that it may tend to incriminate him.

2. A witness who gives evidence in a grand jury proceeding receives immunity unless:

(a) He has effectively waived such immunity pursuant to section 190.45; or

(b) Such evidence is not responsive to any inquiry and is gratuitously given or volunteered by the witness with knowledge that it is not responsive.

(c) The evidence given by the witness consists only of books, papers, records or other physical evidence of an enterprise, as defined in subdivision one of section 175.00 of the penal law, the production of which is required by a subpoena duces tecum, and the witness does not possess a privilege against self-incrimination with respect to the production of such evidence. Any further evidence given by the witness entitles the witness to immunity except as provided in subparagraphs (a) and (b) of this subdivision.

§190.45 Grand jury; waiver of immunity.

1. A waiver of immunity is a written instrument subscribed by a person who is or is about to become a witness in a grand jury proceeding, stipulating that he waives his privilege against self-incrimination and any possible or prospective immunity to which he would otherwise become entitled, pursuant to section 190.40, as a result of giving evidence in such proceeding.

2. A waiver of immunity is not effective unless and until it is sworn to before the grand jury conducting the proceeding in which the subscriber has been called as a witness.

3. A person who is called by the people as a witness in a grand jury proceeding and requested by the district attorney to subscribe and swear to a waiver of immunity before giving evidence has a right to confer with counsel before deciding whether he will comply with such request, and, if he desires to avail himself of such right, he must be accorded a reasonable time in which to obtain and confer with counsel for such purpose. The district attorney must inform the witness of all such rights before obtaining his execution of such a waiver of immunity. Any waiver obtained, subscribed or sworn to in violation of the provisions of this subdivision is invalid and ineffective.

4. If a grand jury witness subscribes and swears to a waiver of immunity upon a written agreement with the district attorney that the interrogation will be limited to certain specified subjects, matters or areas of conduct, and if after the commencement of his testimony he is interrogated and testifies concerning another subject, matter or area of conduct not included in such written agreement, he received immunity with respect to any further testimony which he may give concerning such other subject, matter or area of conduct and the waiver of immunity is to that extent ineffective.

§190.50 Grand jury; who may call witnesses; defendant as witness.

1. Except as provided in this section, no person has a right to call a witness or appear as a witness in a grand jury proceeding.

2. The people may call as a witness in a grand jury proceeding any person believed by the district attorney to possess relevant information or knowledge.

3. The grand jury may cause to be called as a witness any person believed by it to possess relevant information or knowledge. If the grand jury desires to hear any such witness who was not called by the people, it may direct the district attorney to issue and serve a subpoena upon such witness, and the district attorney must comply with such direction. At any time after such a direction, however, or at any time after the service of a subpoena pursuant to such a direction and before the return date thereof, the people may apply to the court which impaneled the grand jury for an order vacating or modifying such direction or subpoena on the ground that such is in the public interest. Upon such application, the court may in its discretion vacate the direction or subpoena, attach reasonable conditions thereto, or make other appropriate qualification thereof.

4. Notwithstanding the provisions of subdivision three, the district attorney may demand that any witness thus called at the instance of the grand jury

sign a waiver of immunity pursuant to section 190.45 before being sworn, and upon such demand no oath may be administered to such witness unless and until he complies therewith.

5. Although not called as a witness by the people or at the instance of the grand jury, a person has a right to be a witness in a grand jury proceeding under the circumstances prescribed in this subdivision:

(a) When a criminal charge against a person is being or is about to be or has been submitted to a grand jury, such person has a right to appear before such grand jury as a witness in his own behalf if, prior to the filing of any indictment or any direction to file a prosecutor's information in the matter, he serves upon the district attorney of the county a written notice making such request and stating an address to which communications may be sent. The district attorney is not obliged to inform such a person that such a grand jury proceeding against him is pending, in progress or about to occur unless such person is a defendant who has been arraigned in a local criminal court upon a currently undisposed of felony complaint charging an offense which is a subject of the prospective or pending grand jury proceeding. In such case, the district attorney must notify the defendant or his attorney of the prospective or pending grand jury proceeding and accord the defendant a reasonable time to exercise his right to appear as a witness therein;

(b) Upon service upon the district attorney of a notice requesting appearance before a grand jury pursuant to paragraph (a), the district attorney must notify the foreman of the grand jury of such request, and must subsequently serve upon the applicant, at the address specified by him, a notice that he will be heard by the grand jury at a given time and place. Upon appearing at such time and place, and upon signing and submitting to the grand jury a waiver of immunity pursuant to section 190.45, such person must be permitted to testify before the grand jury and to give any relevant and competent evidence concerning the case under consideration. Upon giving such evidence, he is subject to examination by the people.

(c) Any indictment or direction to file a prosecutor's information obtained or filed in violation of the provisions of paragraph (a) or (b) is invalid and, upon a motion made pursuant to section 170.50 or section 210.20, must be dismissed; provided that a motion based upon such ground must be made not more than five days after the defendant has been arraigned upon the indictment or, as the case may be, upon the prosecutor's information resulting from the grand jury's direction to file the same. If the contention is not so asserted in timely fashion, it is waived and the indictment or prosecutor's information may not thereafter be challenged on such ground.

6. A defendant or person against whom a criminal charge is being or is about to be brought in a grand jury proceeding may request the grand jury, either orally or in writing, to cause a person designated by him to be called as a witness in such proceeding. The grand jury may as a matter of discretion grant such request and cause such witness to be called pursuant to subdivision three.

7. Where a subpoena is made pursuant to this section, all papers and proceedings relating to the subpoena and any motion to quash, fix conditions, modify or compel compliance shall be kept secret and not disclosed to the public by any public officer or public employee or any other

individual described in section 215.70 of the penal law. This subdivision shall not apply where the person subpoenaed and the prosecutor waive the provisions of this subdivision.

This subdivision shall not prevent the publication of decisions and orders made in connection with such proceedings or motions, provided the caption and content of the decision are written or altered by the court to reasonably preclude identification of the person subpoenaed.

§190.52 Grand jury; attorney for witness.

1. Any person who appears as a witness and has signed a waiver of immunity in a grand jury proceeding, has a right to an attorney as provided in this section. Such a witness may appear with a retained attorney, or if he is financially unable to obtain counsel, an attorney who shall be assigned by the superior court which impaneled the grand jury. Such assigned attorney shall be assigned pursuant to the same plan and in the same manner as counsel are provided to persons charged with crime pursuant to section seven hundred twenty-two of the county law.

2. The attorney for such witness may be present with the witness in the grand jury room. The attorney may advise the witness, but may not otherwise take any part in the proceeding.

3. The superior court which impaneled the grand jury shall have the same power to remove an attorney from the grand jury room as such court has with respect to an attorney in a courtroom.

§190.55 Grand jury; matters to be heard and examined; duties and authority of district attorney.

1. A grand jury may hear and examine evidence concerning the alleged commission of any offense prosecutable in the courts of the county, and concerning any misconduct, nonfeasance or neglect in public office by a public servant, whether criminal or otherwise.

2. District attorneys are required or authorized to submit evidence to grand juries under the following circumstances:

(a) A district attorney must submit to a grand jury evidence concerning a felony allegedly committed by a defendant who, on the basis of a felony complaint filed with a local criminal court of the county, has been held for the action of a grand jury of such county, except where indictment has been waived by the defendant pursuant to article one hundred ninety-five.

(b) A district attorney must submit to a grand jury evidence concerning a misdemeanor allegedly committed by a defendant who has been charged therewith by a local criminal court accusatory instrument, in any case where a superior court of the county has, pursuant to subdivision one of section 170.25, ordered that such misdemeanor charge be prosecuted by indictment in a superior court.

(c) A district attorney may submit to a grand jury any available evidence concerning an offense prosecutable in the courts of the county, or concerning misconduct, nonfeasance or neglect in public office by a public servant, whether criminal or otherwise.

§190.60 Grand jury; action to be taken.
After hearing and examining evidence as prescribed in section 190.55, a grand jury may:
1. Indict a person for an offense, as provided in section 190.65;
2. Direct the district attorney to file a prosecutor's information with a local criminal court, as provided in section 190.70;
3. Direct the district attorney to file a request for removal to the family court, as provided in section 190.71 of this article.
4. Dismiss the charge before it, as provided in section 190.75;
5. Submit a grand jury report, as provided in section 190.85.

§190.65 Grand jury; when indictment is authorized.
1. Subject to the rules prescribing the kinds of offenses which may be charged in an indictment, a grand jury may indict a person for an offense when (a) the evidence before it is legally sufficient to establish that such person committed such offense provided, however, such evidence is not legally sufficient when corroboration that would be required, as a matter of law, to sustain a conviction for such offense is absent, and (b) competent and admissible evidence before it provides reasonable cause to believe that such person committed such offense.
2. The offense or offenses for which a grand jury may indict a person in any particular case are not limited to that or those which may have been designated, at the commencement of the grand jury proceeding, to be the subject of the inquiry; and even in a case submitted to it upon a court order, pursuant to the provisions of section 170.25, directing that a misdemeanor charge pending in a local criminal court be prosecuted by indictment, the grand jury may indict the defendant for a felony if the evidence so warrants.
3. Upon voting to indict a person, a grand jury must, through its foreman or acting foreman, file an indictment with the court by which it was impaneled.

§190.70 Grand jury; direction to file prosecutor's information and related matters.
1. Except in a case submitted to it pursuant to the provisions of section 170.25, a grand jury may direct the district attorney to file in a local criminal court a prosecutor's information charging a person with an offense other than a felony when (a) the evidence before it is legally sufficient to establish that such person committed such offense, and (b) competent and admissible evidence before it provides reasonable cause to believe that such person committed such offense. In such case, the grand jury must, through its foreman or acting foreman, file such direction with the court by which it was impaneled.
2. Such direction must be signed by the foreman or acting foreman. It must contain a plain and concise statement of the conduct constituting the offense to be charged, equivalent in content and precision to the factual statement required to be contained in an indictment pursuant to subdivision seven of section 200.50. Subject to the rules prescribed in sections 200.20 and 200.40 governing joinder in a single indictment of multiple offenses and multiple defendants, such grand jury direction may, where appropriate, specify multiple offenses of less than felony grade and multiple defendants, and may direct that the prospective prosecutor's information charge a single defendant with multiple offenses, or multiple defendants jointly with either a single offense or multiple offenses.
3. Upon the filing of such grand jury direction, the court must, unless such direction is insufficient on its face, issue an order approving such direction and ordering the district attorney to file such a prosecutor's information in a

designated local criminal court having trial jurisdiction of the offense or offenses in question.

§190.71 Grand jury; direction to file request for removal to family court.

(a) Except as provided in subdivision six of section 200.20 of this chapter, a grand jury may not indict (i) a person thirteen years of age for any conduct or crime other than conduct constituting a crime defined in subdivisions one and two of section 125.25 (murder in the second degree) or such conduct as a sexually motivated felony, where authorized pursuant to section 130.91 of the penal law; (ii) a person fourteen or fifteen years of age for any conduct or crime other than conduct constituting a crime defined in subdivisions one and two of section 125.25 (murder in the second degree) and in subdivision three of such section provided that the underlying crime for the murder charge is one for which such person is criminally responsible; 135.25 (kidnapping in the first degree); 150.20 (arson in the first degree); subdivisions one and two of section 120.10 (assault in the first degree); 125.20 (manslaughter in the first degree); subdivisions one and two of section 130.35 (rape in the first degree); subdivisions one and two of section 130.50 (criminal sexual act in the first degree); 130.70 (aggravated sexual abuse in the first degree); 140.30 (burglary in the first degree); subdivision one of section 140.25 (burglary in the second degree); 150.15 (arson in the second degree); 160.15 (robbery in the first degree); subdivision two of section 160.10 (robbery in the second degree) of the penal law; subdivision four of section 265.02 of the penal law, where such firearm is possessed on school grounds, as that phrase is defined in subdivision fourteen of section 220.00 of the penal law; or section 265.03 of the penal law, where such machine gun or such firearm is possessed on school grounds, as that phrase is defined in subdivision fourteen of section 220.00 of the penal law; or defined in the penal law as an attempt to commit murder in the second degree or kidnapping in the first degree, or such conduct as a sexually motivated felony, where authorized pursuant to section 130.91 of the penal law.

*(b) A grand jury may vote to file a request to remove a charge to the family court if it finds that a person thirteen, fourteen or fifteen years of age did an act which, if done by a person over the age of sixteen, would constitute a crime provided (1) such act is one for which it may not indict; (2) it does not indict such person for a crime; and (3) the evidence before it is legally sufficient to establish that such person did such act and competent and admissible evidence before it provides reasonable cause to believe that such person did such act.   *(Eff. Until 10/1/18,Ch.59,L.2017)

*(b) A grand jury may vote to file a request to remove a charge to the family court if it finds that a person sixteen, or commencing October first, two thousand nineteen, seventeen years of age or younger did an act which, if done by a person over the age of sixteen, or commencing October first, two thousand nineteen, seventeen, would constitute a crime provided (1) such act is one for which it may not indict; (2) it does not indict such person for a crime; and (3) the evidence before it is legally sufficient to establish that such person did such act and competent and admissible evidence before it provides reasonable cause to believe that such person did such act.
*(Eff.10/1/18; provided however, that when the applicability of such provisions are based on the conviction of a crime or an act committed by a person who was seventeen years of age at the time of such offense such provisions shall take effect 10/1/19, Ch.59,L.2017)

(c) Upon voting to remove a charge to the family court pursuant to subdivision (b) of this section, the grand jury must, through its foreman or acting foreman, file a request to transfer such charge to the family court. Such request shall be filed with the court by which it was impaneled. It must (1) allege that a person named therein did any act which, if done by a person over the age of sixteen, would constitute a crime; (2) specify the act and the time and place of its commission; and (3) be signed by the foreman or the acting foreman.

(d) Upon the filing of such grand jury request, the court must, unless such request is improper or insufficient on its face, issue an order approving such request and direct that the charge be removed to the family court in accordance with the provisions of article seven hundred twenty-five of this chapter.

§190.75 Grand jury; dismissal of charge.

1. If upon a charge that a designated person committed a crime, either (a) the evidence before the grand jury is not legally sufficient to establish that such person committed such crime or any other offense, or (b) the grand jury is not satisfied that there is reasonable cause to believe that such person committed such crime or any other offense, it must dismiss the charge. In such case, the grand jury must, through its foreman or acting foreman, file its finding of dismissal with the court by which it was impaneled.

2. If the defendant was previously held for the action of the grand jury by a local criminal court, the superior court to which such dismissal is presented must order the defendant released from custody if he is in the custody of the sheriff, or, if he is at liberty on bail, it must exonerate the bail.

3. When a charge has been so dismissed, it may not again be submitted to a grand jury unless the court in its discretion authorizes or directs the people to resubmit such charge to the same or another grand jury. If in such case the charge is again dismissed, it may not again be submitted to a grand jury.

4. Whenever all charges against a designated person have been so dismissed, the district attorney must within ninety days of the filing of the finding of such dismissal, notify that person of the dismissal by regular mail to his last known address unless resubmission has been permitted pursuant to subdivision three of this section or an order of postponement of such service is obtained upon a showing of good cause and exigent circumstances.

§190.80 Grand jury; release of defendant upon failure of timely grand jury action.

*Upon application of a defendant who on the basis of a felony complaint has been held by a local criminal court for the action of a grand jury, and who, at the time of such order or subsequent thereto, has been committed to the custody of the sheriff pending such grand jury action, and who has been confined in such custody for a period of more than forty-five days, or, in the case of a juvenile offender *or adolescent offender*, thirty days, without the occurrence of any grand jury action or disposition pursuant to subdivision one, two or three of section 190.60, the superior court by which such grand jury was or is to be impaneled must release him on his own recognizance unless:

(Material in Italics takes Eff.10/1/18; provided however, that when the applicability of such provisions are based on the conviction of a crime or an act committed by a person who was seventeen years of age at the time of such offense such provisions shall take effect 10/1/19, Ch.59,L.2017)

(a) The lack of a grand jury disposition during such period of confinement was due to the defendant's request, action or condition, or occurred with his consent; or

(b) The people have shown good cause why such order of release should not be issued. Such good cause must consist of some compelling fact or circumstance which precluded grand jury action within the prescribed period or rendered the same against the interest of justice.

§190.85 Grand jury; grand jury reports.
1. The grand jury may submit to the court by which it was impaneled, a report:
(a) Concerning misconduct, non-feasance or neglect in public office by a public servant as the basis for a recommendation of removal or disciplinary action; or
(b) Stating that after investigation of a public servant it finds no misconduct, non-feasance or neglect in office by him provided that such public servant has requested the submission of such report; or
(c) Proposing recommendations for legislative, executive or administrative action in the public interest based upon stated findings.
2. The court to which such report is submitted shall examine it and the minutes of the grand jury and, except as otherwise provided in subdivision four, shall make an order accepting and filing such report as a public record only if the court is satisfied that it complies with the provisions of subdivision one and that:
(a) The report is based upon facts revealed in the course of an investigation authorized by section 190.55 and is supported by the preponderance of the credible and legally admissible evidence; and
(b) When the report is submitted pursuant to paragraph (a) of subdivision one, that each person named therein was afforded an opportunity to testify before the grand jury prior to the filing of such report, and when the report is submitted pursuant to paragraph (b) or (c) of subdivision one, it is not critical of an identified or identifiable person.
3. The order accepting a report pursuant to paragraph (a) of subdivision one, and the report itself, must be sealed by the court and may not be filed as a public record, or be subject to subpoena or otherwise be made public until at least thirty-one days after a copy of the order and the report are served upon each public servant named therein, or if an appeal is taken pursuant to section 190.90, until the affirmance of the order accepting the report, or until reversal of the order sealing the report, or until dismissal of the appeal of the named public servant by the appellate division, whichever occurs later. Such public servant may file with the clerk of the court an answer to such report, not later than twenty days after service of the order and report upon him. Such an answer shall plainly and concisely state the facts and law constituting the defense of the public servant to the charges in said report, and, except for those parts of the answer which the court may determine to be scandalously or prejudicially and unnecessarily inserted therein, shall become an appendix to the report. Upon the expiration of the time set forth in this subdivision, the district attorney shall deliver a true copy of such report, and the appendix if any, for appropriate action, to each public servant or body having removal or disciplinary authority over each public servant named therein.
4. Upon the submission of a report pursuant to subdivision one, if the court finds that the filing of such report as a public record, may prejudice fair consideration of a pending criminal matter, it must order such report sealed and such report may not be subject to subpoena or public inspection during the pendency of such criminal matter, except upon order of the court.
5. Whenever the court to which a report is submitted pursuant to paragraph (a) of subdivision one is not satisfied that the report complies with the provisions of subdivision two, it may direct that additional testimony be taken before the same grand jury, or it must make an order sealing such report, and the report may not be filed as a public record, or be subject to subpoena or otherwise be made public.

§190.90 Grand jury; appeal from order concerning grand jury reports.

1. When a court makes an order accepting a report of a grand jury pursuant to paragraph (a) of subdivision one of section 190.85, any public servant named therein may appeal the order; and when a court makes an order sealing a report of a grand jury pursuant to subdivision five of section 190.85, the district attorney or other attorney designated by the grand jury may appeal the order.

2. When a court makes an order sealing a report of a grand jury pursuant to subdivision five of section 190.85, the district attorney or other attorney designated by the grand jury may, within ten days after service of a copy of the order and report upon each public servant named in the report, appeal the order to the appellate division of the department in which the order was made, by filing in duplicate a notice of appeal from the order with the clerk of the court in which the order was made and by serving a copy of such notice of appeal upon each such public servant. Notwithstanding any contrary provision of section 190.85, a true copy of the report of the grand jury shall be served, together with such notice of appeal, upon each such public servant.

3. The mode of and time for perfecting an appeal pursuant to this section, and the mode of and procedure for the argument thereof, are determined by the rules of the appellate division of the department in which the appeal is brought. Such rules shall prescribe the matters referred to in subdivision one of section 460.70 and in section 460.80, except that such appeal is a preferred cause and the appellate division of each department shall promulgate rules to effectuate such preference.

4. The record and all other presentations on appeal shall remain sealed, except that upon reversal of the order sealing the report or dismissal of the appeal of the named public servant by the appellate division, the report of the grand jury, with the appendix, if any, shall be filed as a public record as provided in subdivision three of section 190.85.

5. The procedure provided for in this section shall be the exclusive manner of reviewing an order made pursuant to section 190.85 and the appellate division of the supreme court shall be the sole court having jurisdiction of such an appeal. The order of the appellate division finally determining such appeal shall not be subject to review in any other court or proceeding.

6. The grand jury in an appeal pursuant to this section shall be represented by the district attorney unless the report relates to him or his office, in which event the grand jury may designate another attorney.

ARTICLE 195 - WAIVER OF INDICTMENT

Section
195.10   Waiver of indictment; in general.
195.20   Waiver of indictment; written instrument.
195.30   Waiver of indictment; approval of waiver by the court.
195.40   Waiver of indictment; filing of superior court information.

§195.10 Waiver of indictment; in general.

1. A defendant may waive indictment and consent to be prosecuted by superior court information when:

(a) a local criminal court has held the defendant for the action of a grand jury; and

(b) the defendant is not charged with a class A felony punishable by death or life imprisonment; and

(c) the district attorney consents to the waiver.

2. A defendant may waive indictment pursuant to subdivision one in either:

(a) the local criminal court in which the order was issued holding the defendant for action of a grand jury, at the time such order is issued; or

(b) the appropriate superior court, at any time prior to the filing of an indictment by the grand jury.

§195.20 Waiver of indictment; written instrument.

A waiver of indictment shall be evidenced by a written instrument, which shall contain the name of the court in which it is executed, the title of the action, and the name, date and approximate time and place of each offense to be charged in the superior court information to be filed by the district attorney pursuant to section 195.40. The offenses named may include any offense for which the defendant was held for action of a grand jury and any offense or offenses properly joinable therewith pursuant to sections 200.20 and 200.40. The written waiver shall also contain a statement by the defendant that he is aware that:

(a) under the constitution of the state of New York he has the right to be prosecuted by indictment filed by a grand jury;

(b) he waives such right and consents to be prosecuted by superior court information to be filed by the district attorney;

(c) the superior court information to be filed by the district attorney will charge the offenses named in the written waiver; and

(d) the superior court information to be filed by the district attorney will have the same force and effect as an indictment filed by a grand jury.

The written waiver shall be signed by the defendant in open court in the presence of his attorney. The consent of the district attorney shall be endorsed thereon.

§195.30 Waiver of indictment; approval of waiver by the court.

The court shall determine whether the waiver of indictment complies with the provisions of sections 195.10 and 195.20. If satisfied that the waiver complies with such provisions, the court shall approve the waiver and execute a written order to that effect. When the waiver is approved by a local criminal court, the local criminal court shall promptly transmit to the appropriate superior court the written waiver and order approving the waiver, along with all other documents pertinent to the action. Until such papers are received by the superior court, the action is deemed to be pending in the local criminal court.

§195.40 Waiver of indictment; filing of superior court information.

When indictment is waived in a superior court the district attorney shall file a superior court information in such court at the time the waiver is executed. When indictment is waived in a local criminal court the district attorney shall file a superior court information in the appropriate superior court within ten days of the execution of the court order approving the waiver. Upon application of a defendant whose waiver of indictment has been approved by the court, and who, at the time of such approval or subsequent thereto, has been committed to the custody of the sheriff pending disposition of the action, and who has been confined in such custody for a period of more than ten days from the date of approval without the filing by the district attorney of a superior court information, the superior court must release him on his own recognizance unless:

(a) The failure of the district attorney to file a superior court information during such period of confinement was due to defendant's request, action or condition or occurred with his consent; or

(b) The people have shown good cause why such order of release should not be issued. Such good cause must consist of some compelling fact or circumstance which precluded the filing of the superior court information within the prescribed period.

ARTICLE 200 - INDICTMENT AND RELATED INSTRUMENTS

Section
200.10   Indictment; definition.
200.15   Superior court information; definition.
200.20   Indictment; what offenses may be charged; joinder of offenses and
          consolidation of indictments.
200.30   Indictment; duplicitous counts prohibited.
200.40   Indictment; joinder of defendants and consolidation of indictments against
          different defendants.
200.50   Indictment; form and content.
200.60   Indictment; allegations of previous convictions prohibited.
200.61   Indictment; special information for operators of for-hire vehicles.
200.62   Indictment; special information for child sexual assault offender.
200.63   Indictment; special information for aggravated family offense.
200.65   Indictment; special information for enterprise corruption and criminal
          possession or use of a biological weapon or chemical weapon.
200.70   Indictment; amendment of.
200.80   Indictment; superseding indictments.
200.95   Indictment; bill of particulars.

§200.10 Indictment; definition.

An indictment is a written accusation by a grand jury, filed with a superior court, charging a person, or two or more persons jointly, with the commission of a crime, or with the commission of two or more offenses at least one of which is a crime. Except as used in Article 190, the term indictment shall include a superior court information.

§200.15 Superior court information; definition.

A superior court information is a written accusation by a district attorney filed in a superior court pursuant to article one hundred ninety-five, charging a person, or two or more persons jointly, with the commission of a crime, or with the commission of two or more offenses, at least one of which is a crime. A superior court information may include any offense for which the defendant was held for action of a grand jury and any offense or offenses properly joinable therewith pursuant to sections 200.20 and 200.40, but shall not include an offense not named in the written waiver of indictment executed pursuant to section 195.20. A superior court information has the same force and effect as an indictment and all procedures and provisions of law applicable to indictments are also applicable to superior court informations, except where otherwise expressly provided.

§200.20 Indictment; what offenses may be charged; joinder of offenses and consolidation of indictments.

1. An indictment must charge at least one crime and may, in addition, charge in separate counts one or more other offenses, including petty

offenses, provided that all such offenses are joinable pursuant to the principles prescribed in subdivision two.

2. Two offenses are "joinable" when:

(a) They are based upon the same act or upon the same criminal transaction, as that term is defined in subdivision two of section 40.10; or

(b) Even though based upon different criminal transactions, such offenses, or the criminal transactions underlying them, are of such nature that either proof of the first offense would be material and admissible as evidence in chief upon a trial of the second, or proof of the second would be material and admissible as evidence in chief upon a trial of the first; or

(c) Even though based upon different criminal transactions, and even though not joinable pursuant to paragraph (b), such offenses are defined by the same or similar statutory provisions and consequently are the same or similar in law; or

(d) Though not directly joinable with each other pursuant to paragraph (a), (b) or (c), each is so joinable with a third offense contained in the indictment. In such case, each of the three offenses may properly be joined not only with each of the other two but also with any further offense joinable with either of the other two, and the chain of joinder may be further extended accordingly.

3. In any case where two or more offenses or groups of offenses charged in an indictment are based upon different criminal transactions, and where their joinability rests solely upon the fact that such offenses, or as the case may be at least one offense of each group, are the same or similar in law, as prescribed in paragraph (c) of subdivision two, the court, in the interest of justice and for good cause shown, may upon application of either a defendant or the people, in its discretion, order that any such offenses be tried separately from the other or others thereof. Good cause shall include but not be limited to situations where there is:

(a) Substantially more proof on one or more such joinable offenses than on others and there is a substantial likelihood that the jury would be unable to consider separately the proof as it relates to each offense.

(b) A convincing showing that a defendant has both important testimony to give concerning one count and a genuine need to refrain from testifying on the other, which satisfies the court that the risk of prejudice is substantial.

(i) Good cause, under this paragraph (b), may be established in writing or upon oral representation of counsel on the record. Any written or oral representation may be based upon information and belief, provided the sources of such information and the grounds of such belief are set forth.

(ii) Upon the request of counsel, any written or recorded showing concerning the defendant's genuine need to refrain from testifying shall be ex parte and in camera. The in camera showing shall be sealed but a court for good cause may order unsealing. Any statements made by counsel in the course of an application under this paragraph (b) may not be offered against the defendant in any criminal action for impeachment purposes or otherwise.

4. When two or more indictments against the same defendant or defendants charge different offenses of a kind that are joinable in a single indictment pursuant to subdivision two, the court may, upon application of either

the people or a defendant, order that such indictments be consolidated and treated as a single indictment for trial purposes. If such indictments, in addition to charging offenses which are so joinable charge other offenses which are not so joinable, they may nevertheless be consolidated for the limited purpose of jointly trying the joinable offenses. In such case, such indictments remain in existence with respect to any nonjoinable offenses and may be prosecuted accordingly. Nothing herein precludes the consolidation of an indictment with a superior court information.

5. A court's determination of an application for consolidation pursuant to subdivision four is discretionary; except that where an application by the defendant seeks consolidation with respect to offenses which are, pursuant to paragraph (a) of subdivision two, of a kind that are joinable in a single indictment by reason of being based upon the same act or criminal transaction, the court must order such consolidation unless good cause to the contrary be shown.

*6. Where an indictment charges at least one offense against a defendant who was under the age of sixteen at the time of the commission of the crime and who did not lack criminal responsibility for such crime by reason of infancy, the indictment may, in addition, charge in separate counts one or more other offenses for which such person would not have been criminally responsible by reason of infancy, if: *(Eff.Until 10/1/18,Ch.59,L.2017)

**6. Where an indictment charges at least one offense against a defendant who was under the age of seventeen, or commencing October first, two thousand nineteen, eighteen at the time of the commission of the crime and who did not lack criminal responsibility for such crime by reason of infancy, the indictment may, in addition, charge in separate counts one or more other offenses for which such person would not have been criminally responsible by reason of infancy, if:

*(a) the offense for which the defendant is criminally responsible and the one or more other offenses for which he would not have been criminally responsible by reason of infancy are based upon the same act or upon the same criminal transaction, as that term is defined in subdivision two of section 40.10 of this chapter; or   *(Eff.Until 10/1/18,Ch.59,L.2017)

**(a) the offense for which the defendant is criminally responsible and the one or more other offenses for which he *or she* would not have been criminally responsible by reason of infancy are based upon the same act or upon the same criminal transaction, as that term is defined in subdivision two of section 40.10 of this chapter; or

(b) the offenses are of such nature that either proof of the first offense would be material and admissible as evidence in chief upon a trial of the second, or proof of the second would be material and admissible as evidence in chief upon a trial of the first.

**(Eff.10/1/18; provided however, that when the applicability of such provisions are based on the conviction of a crime or an act committed by a person who was seventeen years of age at the time of such offense such provisions shall take effect 10/1/19, Ch.59,L.2017)*

§200.30 Indictment; duplicitous counts prohibited.

1. Each count of an indictment may charge one offense only.

2. For purpose of this section, a statutory provision which defines the offense named in the title thereof by providing, in different subdivisions or paragraphs, different ways in which such named offense may be committed, defines a separate offense in each such subdivision or paragraph, and a count of an indictment charging such named offense which, without specifying or clearly indicating the particular subdivision or paragraph of the statutory provision, alleges facts which would support a conviction under more than one such subdivision or paragraph, charges more than one offense.

§200.40 Indictment; joinder of defendants and consolidation of indictments against different defendants.

1. Two or more defendants may be jointly charged in a single indictment provided that:

(a) all such defendants are jointly charged with every offense alleged therein; or

(b) all the offenses charged are based upon a common scheme or plan; or

(c) all the offenses charged are based upon the same criminal transaction as that term is defined in subdivision two of section 40.10; or

(d) if the indictment includes a count charging enterprise corruption:

(i) all the defendants are jointly charged with every count of enterprise corruption alleged therein; and

(ii) every offense, other than a count alleging enterprise corruption, is a criminal act specifically included in the pattern of criminal activity on which the charge or charges of enterprise corruption is or are based; and

(iii) each such defendant could have been jointly charged with at least one of the other defendants, absent an enterprise corruption count, under the provisions of paragraph (a), (b) or (c) of this subdivision, in an accusatory instrument charging at least one such specifically included criminal act. For purposes of this subparagraph, joinder shall not be precluded on the ground that a specifically included criminal act which is necessary to permit joinder is not currently prosecutable, when standing alone, by reason of previous prosecution or lack of geographical jurisdiction.

Even in such case, the court, upon motion of a defendant or the people made within the period provided by section 255.20, may for good cause shown order in its discretion that any defendant be tried separately from the other or from one or more or all of the others. Good cause shall include, but not be limited to, a finding that a defendant or the people will be unduly prejudiced by a joint trial or, in the case of a prosecution involving a charge of enterprise corruption, a finding that proof of one or more criminal acts alleged to have been committed by one defendant but not one or more of the others creates a likelihood that the jury may not be able to consider separately the proof as it relates to each defendant, or in such a case, given the scope of the pattern of criminal activity charged against all the defendants, a particular defendant's comparatively minor role in it creates a likelihood of prejudice to him. Upon such a finding of prejudice, the court may order counts to be tried separately, grant a severance of defendants or provide whatever other relief justice requires.

2. When two or more defendants are charged in separate indictments with an offense or offenses but could have been so charged in a single indictment under subdivision one above, the court may, upon application of the people, order that such indictments be consolidated and the charges be heard in a single trial. If such indictments also charge offenses not properly the subject of a single indictment under subdivision one above, those offenses shall not be consolidated, but shall remain in existence and may be separately prosecuted., Nothing herein precludes the consolidation of an indictment with a superior court information.

§200.50　Indictment; form and content.
An indictment must contain:

1. The name of the superior court in which it is filed; and

2. The title of the action and, where the defendant is a juvenile offender, a statement in the title that the defendant is charged as a juvenile offender; and

3. A separate accusation or count addressed to each offense charged, if there be more than one; and

4. A statement in each count that the grand jury, or, where the accusatory instrument is a superior court information, the district attorney, accuses the defendant or defendants of a designated offense, provided that in any prosecution under article four hundred eighty-five of the penal law, the designated offense shall be the specified offense, as defined in subdivision three of section 485.05 of the penal law, followed by the phrase "as a hate crime", and provided further that in any prosecution under section 490.25 of the penal law, the designated offense shall be the specified offense, as

defined in subdivision three of section 490.05 of the penal law, followed by the phrase "as a crime of terrorism"; and provided further that in any prosecution under section 130.91 of the penal law, the designated offense shall be the specified offense, as defined in subdivision two of section 130.91 of the penal law, followed by the phrase "as a sexually motivated felony"; and provided further that in any prosecution under section 496.06 of the penal law, the designated offense shall be the specified offense, as defined in subdivision two of such section, followed by the phrase "as a public corruption crime"; and

5. A statement in each count that the offense charged therein was committed in a designated county; and

6. A statement in each count that the offense charged therein was committed on, or on or about, a designated date, or during a designated period of time; and

7. A plain and concise factual statement in each count which, without allegations of an evidentiary nature,

(a) asserts facts supporting every element of the offense charged and the defendant's or defendants' commission thereof with sufficient precision to clearly apprise the defendant or defendants of the conduct which is the subject of the accusation; and

(b) in the case of any armed felony, as defined in subdivision forty-one of section 1.20, states that such offense is an armed felony and specifies the particular implement the defendant or defendants possessed, were armed with, used or displayed or, in the case of an implement displayed, specifies what the implement appeared to be; and

(c) in the case of any hate crime, as defined in section 485.05 of the penal law, specifies, as applicable, that the defendant or defendants intentionally selected the person against whom the offense was committed or intended to be committed; or intentionally committed the act or acts constituting the offense, in whole or in substantial part because of a belief or perception regarding the race, color, national origin, ancestry, gender, gender identity or expression, religion, religious practice, age, disability or sexual orientation of a person; and *(Eff.11/1/19,Ch.8,L.2019)*

(d) in the case of a crime of terrorism, as defined in section 490.25 of the penal law, specifies, as applicable, that the defendant or defendants acted with intent to intimidate or coerce a civilian population, influence the policy of a unit of government by intimidation or coercion, or affect the conduct of a unit of government by murder, assassination or kidnapping; and

(e) in the case of a sexually motivated felony, as defined in section 130.91 of the penal law, asserts facts supporting the allegation that the offense was sexually motivated; and

8. The signature of the foreman or acting foreman of the grand jury, except where the indictment has been ordered reduced pursuant to subdivision one-a of section 210.20 of this chapter or the accusatory instrument is a superior court information; and

9. The signature of the district attorney.

§200.60 Indictment; allegations of previous convictions prohibited.

1. When the fact that the defendant has been previously convicted of an offense raises an offense of lower grade to one of higher grade and thereby becomes an element of the latter, an indictment for such higher offense may not allege such previous conviction. If a reference to previous conviction is contained in the statutory name or title of such an offense, such name or title may not be used in the indictment, but an improvised name or title must be used which, by means of the phrase "as a felony" or in some other manner, labels and distinguishes the offense without reference to a previous conviction. This subdivision does not apply to an indictment or a count thereof that charges escape in the second degree pursuant to subdivision

two of section 205.10 of the penal law, or escape in the first degree pursuant to section 205.15 thereof.

2. An indictment for such an offense must be accompanied by a special information, filed by the district attorney with the court, charging that the defendant was previously convicted of a specified offense. Except as provided in subdivision three, the people may not refer to such special information during the trial nor adduce any evidence concerning the previous conviction alleged therein.

3. After commencement of the trial and before the close of the people's case, the court, in the absence of the jury, must arraign the defendant upon such special information, and must advise him that he may admit the previous conviction alleged, deny it or remain mute. Depending upon the defendant's response, the trial of the indictment must then proceed as follows:

(a) If the defendant admits the previous conviction, that element of the offense charged in the indictment is deemed established, no evidence in support thereof may be adduced by the people, and the court must submit the case to the jury without reference thereto and as if the fact of such previous conviction were not an element of the offense. The court may not submit to the jury any lesser included offense which is distinguished from the offense charged solely by the fact that a previous conviction is not an element thereof.

(b) If the defendant denies the previous conviction or remains mute, the people may prove that element of the offense charged before the jury as a part of their case. In any prosecution under subparagraph (ix) of paragraph (a) of subdivision one of section 125.27 of the penal law, if the defendant denies the previous murder conviction or remains mute, the people may prove that element of the offense only after the jury has first found the defendant guilty of intentionally causing the death of a person as charged in the indictment, in which case the court shall then permit the people and the defendant to offer evidence and argument consistent with the relevant provisions of section 260.30 of this chapter with respect to the previous murder conviction.

4. Nothing contained in this section precludes the people from proving a prior conviction before a grand jury or relieves them from the obligation or necessity of so doing in order to submit a legally sufficient case.

§200.61 Indictment; special information for operators of for-hire vehicles.
1. The provisions of this section shall govern the procedures for determining whether a defendant is eligible to receive the sentence set forth in subdivision one of section 60.07 of the penal law upon conviction of a specified offense as defined in subdivision two of such section 60.07.

2. To receive the sentence set forth in subdivision one of section 60.07 of the penal law, an indictment for such specified offense must be accompanied by a special information, filed by the district attorney with the court, alleging that the victim of such offense was operating a for-hire vehicle in the course of providing for-hire vehicle services at the time of the commission of such offense.

3. Prior to the commencement of the trial, the court, in the absence of the jury, must arraign the defendant upon such special information, and must advise him that he may admit that the alleged victim of such offense was operating a for-hire vehicle in the course of providing for-hire vehicle services at the time of the alleged commission of such offense, deny such allegation or remain mute. Depending upon the defendant's response, the trial of the indictment must proceed as follows:

(a) If the defendant admits that the alleged victim of such specified offense charged was operating a for-hire vehicle in the course of providing for-hire vehicle services at the time of the commission of such alleged offense, such allegation, and only such allegation, shall be deemed established for purposes of eligibility, if the defendant is convicted of the underlying specified offense, for a sentence pursuant to subdivision one of section 60.07 of the penal law.

(b) If the defendant denies such allegation or remains mute, the people may, by proof beyond a reasonable doubt, prove as part of their case before the jury or, where the defendant has waived a jury trial, the court, that the alleged victim of such offense was operating a for-hire vehicle in the course of providing for-hire vehicle services at the time of the commission of the offense.

4. Where a jury, pursuant to paragraph (b) of subdivision three of this section, is charged with determining whether the alleged victim of such specified offense was operating a for-hire vehicle in the course of providing for-hire vehicle services, such jury shall consider and render its verdict on such matter only if it convicts the defendant of such specified offense or specified offenses charged.

5. For purposes of this section, the terms "for-hire vehicle", "for-hire vehicle services" and "specified offense" shall have the meanings set forth in section 60.07 of the penal law.

§200.62 Indictment; special information for child sexual assault offender.

1. Whenever a person is charged with the commission or attempted commission of an offense defined in article one hundred thirty of the penal law which constitutes a felony and it appears that the victim of such offense was less than fifteen years old, an indictment for such offense may be accompanied by a special information, filed by the district attorney with the court, alleging that the victim was less than fifteen years old at the time of the commission of the offense; provided, however, that such an information need not be filed when the age of the victim is an element of the offense.

2. Prior to trial, or after the commencement of the trial but before the close of the people's case, the court, in the absence of the jury, must arraign the defendant upon such information and advise him or her that he or she may admit such allegation, deny it or remain mute. Depending upon the defendant's response, the trial of the indictment must proceed as follows:

(a) If the defendant admits that the alleged victim was less than fifteen years old at the time of the commission or attempted commission of the offense, that allegation shall be deemed established for all subsequent purposes, including sentencing pursuant to section 70.07 of the penal law.

(b) If the defendant denies such allegation or remains mute, the people may, by proof beyond a reasonable doubt, prove before the jury or, where the defendant has waived a jury trial, the court, that the alleged victim was less than fifteen years old at the time of the commission or attempted commission of the offense.

(c) Nothing in this subdivision shall prevent the people, in a trial before the court or a jury, from making reference to and introducing evidence of the victim's age.

3. Where a jury, pursuant to paragraph (b) of subdivision two of this section, makes the determination of whether the alleged victim of the offense was less than fifteen years old, such jury shall consider and render its verdict on such issue only after rendering its verdict with regard to the offense.

4. A determination pursuant to this section that the victim was less than fifteen years old at the time of the commission of the offense shall be binding in any future proceeding in which the issue may arise unless the underlying conviction or determination is vacated or reversed.

§200.63 Indictment; special information for aggravated family offense.

1. Whenever a person is charged with the commission or attempted commission of an aggravated family offense as defined in section 240.75 of

the penal law, an indictment or information for such offense shall be accompanied by a special information, filed by the district attorney with the court, alleging that the defendant was previously convicted of a specified offense as defined in subdivision two of section 240.75 of the penal law, that at the time of the previous offense the defendant and the person against whom the offense was committed were members of the same family or household as defined in subdivision one of section 530.11 of this chapter, and that such previous conviction took place within the time period specified in subdivision one of section 240.75 of the penal law. Except as provided herein, the people may not refer to such special information during trial nor adduce any evidence concerning the allegations therein.

2. Prior to the commencement of the trial, the court, in the absence of the jury, must arraign the defendant upon such information and advise him or her that he or she may admit each such allegation, deny any such allegation or remain mute with respect to any such allegation. Depending upon the defendant's response, the trial of the indictment or information must then proceed as follows:

(a)(i) If the previous conviction is for an aggravated family offense as defined in section 240.75 of the penal law, and the defendant admits the previous conviction or that it took place within the time period specified in subdivision one of section 240.75 of the penal law, such admitted allegation or allegations shall be deemed established for the purposes of the present prosecution, including sentencing pursuant to section 70.00 of the penal law. The court must submit the case to the jury as if such admitted allegation or allegations were not elements of the offense.

(ii) If the defendant denies the previous conviction or remains mute with respect to it, the people may prove, beyond a reasonable doubt, that element of the offense before the jury as a part of their case.

(iii) If the defendant denies that the previous conviction took place within the time period specified in subdivision one of section 240.75 of the penal law, or remains mute with respect to that matter, the people may prove, beyond a reasonable doubt, before the jury as part of their case, that the previous conviction took place within the time period specified.

(b)(i) If the previous conviction is for a specified offense as defined in subdivision two of section 240.75 of the penal law, other than an aggravated family offense, and the defendant admits such previous conviction, that it took place within the time period specified in subdivision one of section 240.75 of the penal law, or that the defendant and the person against whom the offense was committed were members of the same family or household as defined in subdivision one of section 530.11 of this chapter, such admitted allegation or allegations shall be deemed established for the purposes of the present prosecution, including sentencing pursuant to section 70.00 of the penal law. The court must submit the case to the jury as if the admitted allegation or allegations were not elements of the offense.

(ii) If the defendant denies the previous conviction or remains mute with respect to it, the people may prove, beyond a reasonable doubt, that element of the offense before the jury as a part of their case.

(iii) If the defendant denies that the previous conviction took place within the time period specified in subdivision one of section 240.75 of the penal law, or remains mute with respect to that matter, the people may prove, beyond a reasonable doubt, before the jury as part of their case, that the previous conviction took place within the time period specified.

(iv) If the defendant denies that the defendant and the person against whom the previous offense was committed were members of the same family or household as defined in subdivision one of section 530.11 of this chapter, or remains mute with respect to that matter, the people may prove, beyond a reasonable doubt, that element of the offense before the jury as a part of their case.

§200.65 Indictment; special information for enterprise corruption and criminal possession or use of a biological weapon or chemical weapon.

When filing an indictment which charges enterprise corruption in violation of article four hundred sixty of the penal law, criminal possession of a chemical weapon or biological weapon in violation of section 490.37, 490.40, or 490.45 of the penal law, or criminal use of a chemical weapon or biological weapon in violation of section 490.47, 490.50, or 490.55 of the penal law, the district attorney must submit a statement to the court attesting that he or she has reviewed the substance of the evidence presented to the grand jury and concurs in the judgment that the charge is consistent with legislative findings in article four hundred sixty or four hundred ninety of the penal law, as applicable. For purposes of this section only, "district attorney" means the district attorney of the county, the attorney general, or the deputy attorney general in charge of the organized crime task force, or where such person is actually absent or disabled, the person authorized to act in his or her stead.

§200.70 Indictment; amendment of.

1. At any time before or during trial, the court may, upon application of the people and with notice to the defendant and opportunity to be heard, order the amendment of an indictment with respect to defects, errors or variances from the proof relating to matters of form, time, place, names of persons and the like, when such an amendment does not change the theory or theories of the prosecution as reflected in the evidence before the grand jury which filed such indictment, or otherwise tend to prejudice the defendant on the merits. Where the accusatory instrument is a superior court information, such an amendment may be made when it does not tend to prejudice the defendant on the merits. Upon permitting such an amendment, the court must, upon application of the defendant, order any adjournment of the proceedings which may, by reason of such amendment, be necessary to accord the defendant adequate opportunity to prepare his defense.

2. An indictment may not be amended in any respect which changes the theory or theories of the prosecution as reflected in the evidence before the grand jury which filed it; nor may an indictment or superior court information be amended for the purpose of curing:

(a) A failure thereof to charge or state an offense; or
(b) Legal insufficiency of the factual allegations; or
(c) A misjoinder of offenses; or
(d) A misjoinder of defendants.

§200.80 Indictment; superseding indictments.

If at any time before entry of a plea of guilty to an indictment or commencement of a trial thereof another indictment is filed in the same court charging the defendant with an offense charged in the first indictment, the first indictment is, with respect to such offense, superseded by the second and, upon the defendant's arraignment upon the second indictment, the count of the first indictment charging such offense must be dismissed by the court. The first indictment is not, however, superseded with respect to any count contained therein which charges an offense not charged in the second indictment. Nothing herein precludes the filing of a superseding indictment when the first accusatory instrument is a superior court information.

§200.95 Indictment; bill of particulars.

1. Definitions. (a) "Bill of particulars" is a written statement by the prosecutor specifying, as required by this section, items of factual information which are not recited in the indictment and which pertain to the offense charged and including the substance of each defendant's conduct encompassed by the charge which the people intend to prove at trial on their direct case, and whether the people intend to prove that the defendant acted as principal or accomplice or both, and items of factual information which are not recited in a special forfeiture information or prosecutor's forfeiture information containing one or more forfeiture counts and which pertain to the substance of each defendant's conduct giving rise to the forfeiture claim, the approximate value of property for which forfeiture is sought, the nature and extent of the defendant's interest in such property, and the extent of the defendant's gain, if any, from the offense charged. However, the prosecutor shall not be required to include in the bill of particulars matters of evidence relating to how the people intend to prove the elements of the offense charged or how the people intend to prove any item of factual information included in the bill of particulars.

(b) "Request for a bill of particulars" is a written request served by defendant upon the people, without leave of the court, requesting a bill of particulars, specifying the items of factual information desired, and alleging that defendant cannot adequately prepare or conduct his defense without the information requested.

2. Bill of particulars upon request. Upon a timely request for a bill of particulars by a defendant against whom an indictment is pending, the prosecutor shall within fifteen days of the service of the request or as soon thereafter as is practicable, serve upon the defendant or his attorney, and file with the court, the bill of particulars, except to the extent the prosecutor shall have refused to comply with the request pursuant to subdivision four of this section.

3. Timeliness of request. A request for a bill of particulars shall be timely if made within thirty days after arraignment and before the commencement of trial. If the defendant is not represented by counsel, and has requested an adjournment to obtain counsel or to have counsel assigned, the thirty day period shall commence, for the purposes of a request for a bill of particulars by the defendant, on the date counsel initially appears on his behalf. However, the court may direct compliance with a request for a bill of particulars that, for good cause shown, could not have been made within the time specified.

4. Request refused. The prosecutor may refuse to comply with the request for a bill of particulars or any portion of the request for a bill of particulars to the extent he reasonably believes that the item of factual information requested is not authorized to be included in a bill of particulars, or that such information is not necessary to enable the defendant adequately to prepare or conduct his defense, or that a protective order would be warranted or that the demand is untimely. Such refusal shall be made in a writing, which shall set forth the grounds of such belief as fully as possible, consistent with the reason for the refusal. Within fifteen days of the request or as soon thereafter as practicable, the refusal shall be served upon the defendant and a copy shall be filed with the court.

5. Court ordered bill of particulars. Where a prosecutor has timely served a written refusal pursuant to subdivision four of this section and upon motion, made in writing, of a defendant, who has made a request for a bill of particulars and whose request has not been complied with in whole or in part, the court must, to the extent a protective order is not warranted,

92A

§200.95

order the prosecutor to comply with the request if it is satisfied that the items of factual information requested are authorized to be included in a bill of particulars, and that such information is necessary to enable the defendant adequately to prepare or conduct his defense and, if the request was untimely, a finding of good cause for the delay. Where a prosecutor has not timely served a written refusal pursuant to subdivision four of this section the court must, unless it is satisfied that the people have shown good cause why such an order should not be issued, issue an order requiring the prosecutor to comply or providing for any other order authorized by section 245.80 of this part.   *(Eff.1/1/20,Ch.59,L.2019)*

6. Motion procedure. A motion for a bill of particulars shall be made as prescribed in section 255.20. Upon an order granting a motion pursuant to this section, the prosecutor must file with the court a bill of particulars, reciting every item of information designated in the order, and serve a copy thereof upon the defendant. Pending such filing and service, the proceedings are stayed.

7. Protective order. (a) The court in which the criminal action is pending may, upon motion of the prosecutor, or of any affected person, or upon determination of a motion of defendant for a court ordered bill of particulars, or upon its own initiative, issue a protective order denying, limiting, conditioning, delaying or regulating the bill of particulars for good cause, including constitutional limitations, danger to the integrity of physical evidence or a substantial risk of physical harm, intimidation, economic reprisal, bribery or unjustified annoyance or embarrassment to any person or an adverse effect upon the legitimate needs of law enforcement, including the protection of the confidentiality of informants, or any other factor or set of factors which outweighs the need for the bill of particulars.

(b) An order limiting, conditioning, delaying or regulating the bill of particulars may, among other things, require that any material copied or derived therefrom be maintained in the exclusive possession of the attorney for the defendant and be used for the exclusive purpose of preparing for the defense of the criminal action.

8. Amendment. At any time before commencement of trial, the prosecutor may, without leave of the court, serve upon defendant and file with the court an amended bill of particulars. At any time during trial, upon application of the prosecutor and with notice to the defendant and an opportunity for him to be heard, the court must, upon finding that no undue prejudice will accrue to defendant and that the prosecutor has acted in good faith, permit the prosecutor to amend the bill of particulars. Upon any amendment of the bill of particulars, the court must, upon application of defendant, order an adjournment of the proceedings or any other action it deems appropriate which may, by reason of the amendment, be necessary to accord the defendant an adequate opportunity to defend.

ARTICLE 210 - PROCEEDINGS IN SUPERIOR COURT FROM FILING OF INDICTMENT TO PLEA

Section
210.05   Indictment and superior court information exclusive methods of prosecution.
210.10   Requirement of and methods of securing defendant's appearance for arraignment upon indictment.
210.15   Arraignment upon indictment; defendant's rights, court's instructions and bail matters.
210.16   Requirement of HIV related testing in certain cases.
210.20   Motion to dismiss or reduce indictment.
210.25   Motion to dismiss indictment; as defective.
210.30   Motion to dismiss or reduce indictment on ground of insufficiency of grand jury evidence; motion to inspect grand jury minutes.
210.35   Motion to dismiss indictment; defective grand jury proceeding.
210.40   Motion to dismiss indictment; in furtherance of justice.
210.43   Motion to remove juvenile offender to family court.
210.45   Motion to dismiss indictment; procedure.
210.46   Adjournment in contemplation of dismissal in marihuana cases in a superior court.

Section (Cont'd.)

210.47   **Adjournment in contemplation of dismissal in misdemeanor cases in superior court.**

210.50   **Requirement of plea.**

§210.05 Indictment and superior court information exclusive methods of prosecution.

The only methods of prosecuting an offense in a superior court are by an indictment filed therewith by a grand jury or by a superior court information filed therewith by a district attorney.

§210.10 Requirement of and methods of securing defendant's appearance for arraignment upon indictment.

After an indictment has been filed with a superior court, the defendant must be arraigned thereon. He must appear personally at such arraignment, and his appearance may be secured as follows:

1. If the defendant was previously held by a local criminal court for the action of the grand jury, and if he is confined in the custody of the sheriff pursuant to a previous court order issued in the same criminal action, the superior court must direct the sheriff to produce the defendant for arraignment on a specified date and the sheriff must comply with such direction. The court must give at least two days notice of the time and place of the arraignment to an attorney, if any, who has previously filed a notice of appearance on behalf of the defendant with such superior court, or if no such notice of appearance has been filed, to an attorney, if any who filed a notice of appearance in behalf of the defendant with the local criminal court.

2. If a felony complaint against the defendant was pending in a local criminal court or if the defendant was previously held by a local criminal court for the action of the grand jury, and if the defendant is at liberty on his or her own recognizance or on bail pursuant to a previous court order issued in the same criminal action, the superior court must, upon at least two days notice to the defendant and his or her surety, to any person other than the defendant who posted cash bail and to any attorney who would be entitled to notice under circumstances prescribed in subdivision one, direct the defendant to appear before the superior court for arraignment on a specified date. If the defendant fails to appear on such date, the court may issue a bench warrant and, in addition, may forfeit the bail, if any. Upon taking the defendant into custody pursuant to such bench warrant, the executing police officer must without unnecessary delay bring the defendant before such superior court for arraignment. If such superior court is not available, the executing police officer may bring the defendant to the local correctional facility of the county in which such superior court sits, to be detained there until not later than the commencement of the next session of such court occurring on the next business day.

3. If the defendant has not previously been held by a local criminal court for the action of the grand jury and the filing of the indictment constituted the commencement of the criminal action, the superior court must order the indictment to be filed as a sealed instrument until the defendant is produced or appears for arraignment, and must issue a superior court warrant of arrest. Upon the request of the district attorney, in lieu of a superior court warrant of arrest, the court may issue a summons if it is satisfied that the defendant will respond thereto. Upon the request of the district attorney, in lieu of a warrant of arrest or summons, the court may instead authorize the district attorney to direct the defendant to appear for arraignment on a designated date if it is satisfied that the defendant will so appear. A superior court warrant of arrest is executable anywhere in the state. Such warrant may be addressed to any police officer whose geographical area of employment embraces either the place where the offense charged was allegedly committed or the locality of the court by which the warrant is issued. It must be executed in the same manner as an ordinary warrant of arrest, as pro-

vided in section 120.80, and following the arrest the executing police officer must without unnecessary delay perform all recording, fingerprinting, photographing and other preliminary police duties required in the particular case, and bring the defendant before the superior court. If such superior court is not available, the executing police officer may bring the defendant to the local correctional facility of the county in which such superior court sits, to be detained there until not later than the commencement of the next session of such court occurring on the next business day.

4. A superior court warrant of arrest may be executed by (a) any police officer to whom it is addressed or (b) any other police officer delegated to execute it under circumstances prescribed in subdivisions five and six.

5. The issuing court may authorize the delegation of such warrant. Where the issuing court has so authorized, a police officer to whom a superior court warrant of arrest is addressed may delegate another police officer to whom it is not addressed to execute such warrant as his agent when:

(a) He has reasonable cause to believe that the defendant is in a particular county other than the one in which the warrant is returnable; and

(b) The geographical area of employment of the delegated police officer embraces the locality where the arrest is to be made.

6. Under circumstances specified in subdivision five, the police officer to whom the warrant is addressed may inform the delegated officer, by telecommunication, mail or any other means, of the issuance of the warrant, of the offense charged in the underlying accusatory instrument and of all other pertinent details, and may request such officer to act as his or her agent in arresting the defendant pursuant to such warrant. Upon such request, the delegated police officer is to the same extent as the delegating officer, authorized to make such arrest pursuant to the warrant within the geographical area of such delegated officer's employment. Upon so arresting the defendant, he or she must without unnecessary delay deliver the defendant or cause the defendant to be delivered to the custody of the police officer by whom he or she was so delegated, and the latter must then without unnecessary delay bring the defendant before a court in which such warrant is returnable. If such court is not available, the delegating officer may bring the defendant to the local correctional facility of the county in which such court sits, to be detained there until not later than the commencement of the next session of such court occurring on the next business day.

§210.15 Arraignment upon indictment; defendant's rights, court's instructions and bail matters.

1. Upon the defendant's arraignment before a superior court upon an indictment, the court must immediately inform him, or cause him to be informed in its presence, of the charge or charges against him, and the district attorney must cause him to be furnished with a copy of the indictment.

2. The defendant has a right to the aid of counsel at the arraignment and at every subsequent stage of the action, and, if he appears upon such arraignment without counsel, has the following rights:

(a) To an adjournment for the purpose of obtaining counsel; and

(b) To communicate, free of charge, by letter or by telephone provided by the law enforcement facility where the defendant is held to a phone number located in the United States or Puerto Rico, for the purposes of obtaining counsel and informing a relative or friend that he or she has been charged with an offense; and

(c) To have counsel assigned by the court in any case where he is financially unable to obtain the same.

3. The court must inform the defendant of all rights specified in subdivision two. The court must accord the defendant opportunity to exercise such rights and must itself take such affirmative action as is necessary to effectuate them.

4. *(Repealed.)*

5. If the defendant desires to proceed without the aid of counsel, the court must permit him to do so if it is satisfied that he made such decision with knowledge of the significance thereof, but if it is not so satisfied it may not proceed until the defendant is provided with counsel, either of his own choosing or by assignment. A defendant who proceeds at the arraignment without counsel does not waive his right to counsel, and the court must inform him that he continues to have such right as well as all the rights specified in subdivision two which are necessary to effectuate it, and that he may exercise such rights at any stage of the action.

6. Upon the arraignment, the court, unless it intends to make a final disposition of the action immediately thereafter, must, as provided in section 530.40, issue a securing order, releasing the defendant on his own recognizance or fixing bail or committing him to the custody of the sheriff for his future appearance in such action.

§210.16 Requirement of HIV related testing in certain cases.

1. (a) In a case where an indictment or a superior court information has been filed with a superior court which charges the defendant with a felony offense enumerated in any section of article one hundred thirty of the penal law where an act of "sexual intercourse", "oral sexual conduct" or "anal sexual conduct," as those terms are defined in section 130.00 of the penal law, is required as an essential element for the commission thereof, the court shall, upon a request of the victim within six months of the date of the crimes charged, order that the defendant submit to human immunodeficiency virus (HIV) related testing. Testing of a defendant shall be ordered when the result would provide medical benefit to the victim or a psychological benefit to the victim. Medical benefit shall be found when the following elements are satisfied: (i) a decision is pending about beginning, continuing, or discontinuing a medical intervention for the victim; and (ii) the result of an HIV test of the accused could affect that decision, and could provide relevant information beyond that which would be provided by an HIV test of the victim. If testing the defendant would provide medical benefit to the victim or a psychological benefit to the victim, then the testing is to be conducted by a state, county, or local public health officer designated by the order. Test results, which shall not be disclosed to the court, shall be communicated to the defendant and the victim named in the order in accordance with the provisions of section twenty-seven hundred eighty-five-a of the public health law.

(b) For the purposes of this section, the terms "victim" and "applicant" mean the person with whom the defendant is charged to have engaged in an act of "sexual intercourse", "oral sexual conduct" or "anal sexual conduct", as those terms are defined in section 130.00 of the penal law, where such conduct with such victim was the basis for charging the defendant with an offense specified in paragraph (a) of this subdivision.

2. Any request made by the victim pursuant to this section must be in writing, filed with the court within six months of the date of the crimes charged, and provided by the court to the defendant or his or her counsel. The request must be filed with the court prior to or within forty-eight hours after the indictment or superior court information has been filed with the superior court; provided however that, for good cause shown, the court may permit such request to be filed at a later stage of the action within six months of the date of the crimes charged.

3. At any stage in the action within six months of the date of the crimes charged, prior to the final disposition of the indictment or superior court information and while the defendant is charged with an offense specified in paragraph (a) of subdivision one of this section, the victim may request that the defendant submit to a follow-up HIV related test. Such request must be in writing, filed with the court and provided by the court to the defendant or his or her counsel. Upon a finding that the follow-up HIV related test is

medically appropriate the court must order that the defendant submit to such test. The court shall not make such finding of medical appropriateness unless the follow-up HIV related test is to be administered a sufficient time after the charged offense to be consistent with guidelines that may be issued by the commissioner of health. There shall be no more than one follow-up HIV related test absent a showing of extraordinary circumstances.

4. Any requests, related papers and orders made or filed pursuant to this section, together with any papers or proceedings related thereto, shall be sealed by the court and not made available for any purpose, except as may be necessary for the conduct of judicial proceedings directly related to the provisions of this section. All proceedings on such requests shall be held in camera.

5. The application for an order to compel a defendant to undergo an HIV related test may be made by the victim but, if the victim is an infant or incompetent person, the application may also be made by a representative as defined in section twelve hundred one of the civil practice law and rules. The application must state that: (a) the applicant was the victim of the offense enumerated in paragraph (a) of subdivision one of this section of which the defendant is charged; and (b) the applicant has been offered pre-HIV test counseling and post-HIV test counseling by a public health officer in accordance with article twenty-seven-F of the public health law and has been advised, in accordance with any guidelines that may be issued by the commissioner of health, of (i) the limitations on the information to be obtained through an HIV test on the proposed subject; (ii) current scientific assessments of the risk of transmission of HIV from the exposure he or she may have experienced; and (iii) the need for the applicant to undergo HIV related testing to definitively determine his or her HIV status.

6. The court shall conduct a hearing only if necessary to determine if the applicant is the victim of the offense of which the defendant is charged or to determine whether a follow-up test is medically appropriate. The court ordered test must be performed within forty-eight hours of the date on which the court ordered the test, provided, however, that whenever the defendant is not tested within the period prescribed by the court, the court must again order that the defendant undergo an HIV related test. The defendant shall be advised of information as to HIV testing and medical treatment in accordance with any guidelines that may be issued by the commissioner of health.

7. (a) Test results shall be disclosed subject to the following limitations, which shall be specified in any order issued pursuant to this section:
(i) disclosure of confidential HIV related information shall be limited to that information which is necessary to fulfill the purpose for which the order is granted; and
(ii) disclosure of confidential HIV related information shall be made to the defendant upon his or her request, and disclosure to a person other than the defendant shall be limited to the person making the application; redisclosure shall be permitted only to the victim, the victim's immediate family, guardian, physicians, attorneys, medical or mental health providers and to his or her past and future contacts to whom there was or is a reasonable risk of HIV transmission and shall not be permitted to any other person or the court.
(b) Unless inconsistent with this section, the court's order shall direct compliance with and conform to the provisions of article twenty-seven-F of the public health law. Such order shall include measures to protect against disclosure to others of the identity and HIV status of the applicant and of the person tested and may include such other measures as the court deems necessary to protect confidential information.

8. Any failure to comply with the provisions of this section or section twenty-seven hundred eighty-five-a of the public health law shall not impair or affect the validity of any proceeding upon the indictment or superior court information.

9. No information obtained as a result of a consent, hearing or court order for testing issued pursuant to this section nor any information derived

therefrom may be used as evidence in any criminal or civil proceeding against the defendant which relates to events that were the basis for charging the defendant with an offense enumerated in paragraph (a) of subdivision one of this section, provided however that nothing in this section shall prevent prosecution of a witness testifying in any court hearing held pursuant to this section for perjury pursuant to article two hundred ten of the penal law.

§210.20 Motion to dismiss or reduce indictment.

1. After arraignment upon an indictment, the superior court may, upon motion of the defendant, dismiss such indictment or any count thereof upon the ground that:

(a) Such indictment or count is defective, within the meaning of section 210.25; or

(b) The evidence before the grand jury was not legally sufficient to establish the offense charged or any lesser included offense; or

(c) The grand jury proceeding was defective, within the meaning of section 210.35; or

(d) The defendant has immunity with respect to the offense charged, pursuant to section 50.20 or 190.40; or

(e) The prosecution is barred by reason of a previous prosecution, pursuant to section 40.20; or

(f) The prosecution is untimely, pursuant to section 30.10; or

(g) The defendant has been denied the right to a speedy trial; or

(h) There exists some other jurisdictional or legal impediment to conviction of the defendant for the offense charged; or

(i) Dismissal is required in the interest of justice, pursuant to section 210.40.

1-a. After arraignment upon an indictment, if the superior court, upon motion of the defendant pursuant to this subdivision or paragraph b of subdivision one of this section challenging the legal sufficiency of the evidence before the grand jury, finds that the evidence before the grand jury was not legally sufficient to establish the commission by the defendant of the offense charged in any count contained within the indictment, but was legally sufficient to establish the commission of a lesser included offense, it shall order the count or counts of the indictment with respect to which the finding is made reduced to allege the most serious lesser included offense with respect to which the evidence before the grand jury was sufficient, except that where the most serious lesser included offense thus found is a petty offense, and the court does not find evidence of the commission of any crime in any other count of the indictment, it shall order the indictment dismissed and a prosecutor's information charging the petty offense filed in the appropriate local criminal court. The motion to dismiss or reduce any count of an indictment based on legal insufficiency to establish the offense charged shall be made in accordance with the procedure set forth in subdivisions one through seven of section 210.45, provided however, the court shall state on the record the basis for its determination. Upon entering an order pursuant to this subdivision, the court shall consider the appropriateness of any securing order issued pursuant to article 510 of this chapter.

2. A motion pursuant to this section, except a motion pursuant to paragraph (g) of subdivision one, should be made within the period provided in section 255.20. A motion made pursuant to paragraph (g) of subdivision one must be made prior to the commencement of trial or entry of a plea of guilty.

3. Upon the motion, a defendant who is in a position adequately to raise more than one ground in support thereof should raise every such ground upon which he intends to challenge the indictment. A subsequent motion based upon any such ground not so raised may be summarily denied, although the court, in the interest of justice and for good cause shown,

may in its discretion entertain and dispose of such a motion on the merits notwithstanding.

4. Upon dismissing an indictment or a count thereof upon any of the grounds specified in paragraphs (a), (b), (c) and (i) of subdivision one, or, upon dismissing a superior court information or a count thereof upon any of the grounds specified in paragraphs (a) or (i) of subdivision one, the court may, upon application of the people, in its discretion authorize the people to submit the charge or charges to the same or another grand jury. When the dismissal is based upon some other ground, such authorization may not be granted. In the absence of authorization to submit or resubmit, the order of dismissal constitutes a bar to any further prosecution of such charge or charges, by indictment or otherwise, in any criminal court within the county.

5. If the court dismisses one or more counts of an indictment, against a defendant who was under the age of sixteen at the time of the commission of the crime and who did not lack criminal responsibility for such crime by reason of infancy, and one or more other counts of the indictment having been joined in the indictment solely with the dismissed count pursuant to subdivision six of section 200.20 is not dismissed, the court must direct that such count be removed to the family court in accordance with article seven hundred twenty-five of this chapter.

6. The effectiveness of an order reducing a count or counts of an indictment or dismissing an indictment and directing the filing of a prosecutor's information or dismissing a count or counts of an indictment charging murder in the first degree shall be stayed for thirty days following the entry of such order unless such stay is otherwise waived by the people. On or before the conclusion of such thirty-day period, the people shall exercise one of the following options:

(a) Accept the court's order by filing a reduced indictment, by dismissing the indictment and filing a prosecutor's information, or by filing an indictment containing any count or counts remaining after dismissal of the count or counts charging murder in the first degree, as appropriate;

(b) Resubmit the subject count or counts to the same or a different grand jury within thirty days of the entry of the order or such additional time as the court may permit upon a showing of good cause; provided, however, that if in such case an order is again entered with respect to such count or counts pursuant to subdivision one or one-a of this section, such count or counts may not again be submitted to a grand jury. Where the people exercise this option, the effectiveness of the order further shall be stayed pending a determination by the grand jury and the filing of a new indictment, if voted, charging the resubmitted count or counts;

(c) Appeal the order pursuant to subdivision one or one-a of section 450.20. Where the people exercise this option, the effectiveness of the order further shall be stayed in accordance with the provisions of subdivision two of section 460.40.

If the people fail to exercise one of the foregoing options, the court's order shall take effect and the people shall comply with paragraph (a) of this subdivision.

§210.25 Motion to dismiss indictment; as defective.

An indictment or a count thereof is defective within the meaning of paragraph (a) of subdivision one of section 210.20 when:

1. It does not substantially conform to the requirements stated in article two hundred; provided that an indictment may not be dismissed as

defective, but must instead be amended, where the defect or irregularity is of a kind that may be cured by amendment, pursuant to section 200.70, and where the people move to so amend;

  2. The allegations demonstrate that the court does not have jurisdiction of the offense charged; or

  3. The statute defining the offense charged is unconstitutional or otherwise invalid.

§210.30 Motion to dismiss or reduce indictment on ground of insufficiency of grand jury evidence; motion to inspect grand jury minutes.

  1. A motion to dismiss an indictment or a count thereof pursuant to paragraph (b) of subdivision one of section 210.20 or a motion to reduce a count or counts of an indictment pursuant to subdivision one-a of section 210.20 must be preceded or accompanied by a motion to inspect the grand jury minutes, as prescribed in subdivision two of this section.

  2. A motion to inspect grand jury minutes is a motion by a defendant requesting an examination by the court and the defendant of the stenographic minutes of a grand jury proceeding resulting in an indictment for the purpose of determining whether the evidence before the grand jury was legally sufficient to support the charges or a charge contained in such indictment.

  3. Unless good cause exists to deny the motion to inspect the grand jury minutes, the court must grant the motion. It must then proceed to examine the minutes and to determine the motion to dismiss or reduce the indictment. If the court, after examining the minutes, finds that release of the minutes, or certain portions thereof, to the parties is necessary to assist the court in making its determination on the motion, it may release the minutes or such portions thereof to the parties. Provided, however, such release shall be limited to that grand jury testimony which is relevant to a determination of whether the evidence before the grand jury was legally sufficient to support a charge or charges contained in such indictment. Prior to such release the district attorney shall be given an opportunity to present argument to the court that the release of the minutes, or any portion thereof, would not be in the public interest. For purposes of this section, the minutes shall include any materials submitted to the grand jury pursuant to subdivision eight of section 190.30 of this chapter.

  4. If the court determines that there is not reasonable cause to believe that the evidence before the grand jury may have been legally insufficient, it may in its discretion either (a) deny both the motion to inspect and the motion to dismiss or reduce, or (b) grant the motion to inspect notwithstanding and proceed to examine the minutes and to determine the motion to dismiss or reduce.

  5. In any case, the court must place on the record its ruling upon the motion to inspect.

  6. The validity of an order denying any motion made pursuant to this section is not reviewable upon an appeal from an ensuing judgment of conviction based upon legally sufficient trial evidence.

  *7. Notwithstanding any other provision of law, where the indictment is filed against a juvenile offender *or adolescent offender,* the court shall dismiss the indictment or count thereof where the evidence before the grand jury was not legally sufficient to establish the offense charged or any lesser included offense for which the defendant is criminally responsible. Upon such dismissal, unless the court shall authorize the people to resubmit the

charge to a subsequent grand jury, and upon a finding that there was
sufficient evidence to believe defendant is a juvenile delinquent as defined
in subdivision (a) of section seven hundred twelve of the family court act
and upon specifying the act or acts it found sufficient evidence to believe
defendant committed, the court may direct that such matter be removed to
family court in accordance with the provisions of article seven hundred
twenty-five of this chapter.
*(Material in Italics takes Eff.10/1/18; provided however, that when the applicability of
such provisions are based on the conviction of a crime or an act committed by a
person who was seventeen years of age at the time of such offense such provisions
shall take effect 10/1/19, Ch.59,L.2017)*

§210.35 Motion to dismiss indictment; defective grand jury proceeding.
A grand jury proceeding is defective within the meaning of paragraph (c)
of subdivision one of section 210.20 when:
1. The grand jury was illegally constituted; or
2. The proceeding is conducted before fewer than sixteen grand jurors; or
3. Fewer than twelve grand jurors concur in the finding of the indictment;
or
4. The defendant is not accorded an opportunity to appear and testify
before the grand jury in accordance with the provisions of section 190.50; or
5. The proceeding otherwise fails to conform to the requirements of article
one hundred ninety to such degree that the integrity thereof is impaired and
prejudice to the defendant may result.

§210.40 Motion to dismiss indictment; in furtherance of justice.
1. An indictment or any count thereof may be dismissed in furtherance of
justice, as provided in paragraph (i) of subdivision one of section 210.20,
when, even though there may be no basis for dismissal as a matter of law
upon any ground specified in paragraphs (a) through (h) of said subdivision
one of section 210.20, such dismissal is required as a matter of judicial
discretion by the existence of some compelling factor, consideration or
circumstance clearly demonstrating that conviction or prosecution of the
defendant upon such indictment or count would constitute or result in
injustice. In determining whether such compelling factor, consideration, or
circumstance exists, the court must, to the extent applicable, examined and
consider, individually and collectively, the following:
(a) the seriousness and circumstances of the offense;
(b) the extent of harm caused by the offense;
(c) the evidence of guilt, whether admissible or inadmissible at trial;
(d) the history, character and condition of the defendant;
(e) any exceptionally serious misconduct of law enforcement personnel
in the investigation, arrest and prosecution of the defendant;
(f) the purpose and effect of imposing upon the defendant a sentence
authorized for the offense;
(g) the impact of a dismissal upon the confidence of the public in the
criminal justice system;
(h) the impact of a dismissal on the safety or welfare of the community;
(i) where the court deems it appropriate, the attitude of the complainant
or victim with respect to the motion.
(j) any other relevant fact indicating that a judgment of conviction would
serve no useful purpose.
2. In addition to the grounds specified in subdivision one of this section, a
count alleging enterprise corruption in violation of article four hundred sixty

of the penal law may be dismissed in the interest of justice where prosecution of that count is inconsistent with the stated legislative findings in said article. Upon a motion pursuant to this section, the court must inspect the evidence before the grand jury and such other evidence or information as it may deem proper.

3. An order dismissing an indictment in the interest of justice may be issued upon motion of the people or of the court itself as well as upon that of the defendant. Upon issuing such an order, the court must set forth its reasons therefor upon the record.

*§210.43 Motion to remove juvenile offender to family court.

1. After a motion by a juvenile offender, pursuant to subdivision five of section 180.75 of this chapter, or after arraignment of a juvenile offender upon an indictment, the superior court may, on motion of any party or on its own motion:

(a) except as otherwise provided by paragraph (b), order removal of the action to the family court pursuant to the provisions of article seven hundred twenty-five of this chapter, if, after consideration of the factors set forth in subdivision two of this section, the court determines that to do so would be in the interests of justice; or

(b) with the consent of the district attorney, order removal of an action involving an indictment charging a juvenile offender with murder in the second degree as defined in section 125.25 of the penal law; rape in the first degree, as defined in subdivision one of section 130.35 of the penal law; criminal sexual act in the first degree, as defined in subdivision one of section 130.50 of the penal law; or an armed felony as defined in paragraph (a) of subdivision forty-one of section 1.20, to the family court pursuant to the provisions of article seven hundred twenty-five of this chapter if the court finds one or more of the following factors: (i) mitigating circumstances that bear directly upon the manner in which the crime was committed; (ii) where the defendant was not the sole participant in the crime, the defendant's participation was relatively minor although not so minor as to constitute a defense to the prosecution; or (iii) possible deficiencies in the proof of the crime, and, after consideration of the factors set forth in subdivision two of this section, the court determined that removal of the action to the family court would be in the interests of justice.

2. In making its determination pursuant to subdivision one of this section the court shall, to the extent applicable, examine individually and collectively, the following:

(a) the seriousness and circumstances of the offense;

(b) the extent of harm caused by the offense;

(c) the evidence of guilt, whether admissible or inadmissible at trial;

(d) the history, character and condition of the defendant;

(e) the purpose and effect of imposing upon the defendant a sentence authorized for the offense;

(f) the impact of a removal of the case to the family court on the safety or welfare of the community;

(g) the impact of a removal of the case to the family court upon the confidence of the public in the criminal justice system;

(h) where the court deems it appropriate, the attitude of the complainant or victim with respect to the motion; and

(i) any other relevant fact indicating that a judgment of conviction in the criminal court would serve no useful purpose.

3. The procedure for bringing on a motion pursuant to subdivision one of this section, shall accord with the procedure prescribed in subdivisions one and two of section 210.45 of this article. After all papers of both parties have been filed and after all documentary evidence, if any, has been submitted, the court must consider the same for the purpose of determining whether the motion is determinable on the motion papers submitted and, if not, may make such inquiry as it deems necessary for the purpose of making a determination.

4. For the purpose of making a determination pursuant to this section, any evidence which is not legally privileged may be introduced. If the defendant testifies, his testimony may not be introduced against him in any future proceeding, except to impeach his testimony at such future proceeding as inconsistent prior testimony.

5. a. If the court orders removal of the action to family court, it shall state on the record the factor or factors upon which its determination is based, and, the court shall give its reasons for removal in detail and not in conclusory terms.

b. The district attorney shall state upon the record the reasons for his consent to removal of the action to the family court. The reasons shall be stated in detail and not in conclusory terms.

(Repealed, Eff.10/1/18; provided however, that when the applicability of such provisions are based on the conviction of a crime or an act committed by a person who was seventeen years of age at the time of such offense such provisions shall take effect 10/1/19, Ch.59,L.2017)

§210.45 Motion to dismiss indictment; procedure.

1. A motion to dismiss an indictment pursuant to section 210.20 must be made in writing and upon reasonable notice to the people. If the motion is based upon the existence or occurrence of facts, the motion papers must contain sworn allegations thereof, whether by the defendant or by another person or persons. Such sworn allegations may be based upon personal knowledge of the affiant or upon information and belief, provided that in the latter event

This page intentionally left blank.

the affiant must state the sources of such information and the grounds of such belief. The defendant may further submit documentary evidence supporting or tending to support the allegations of the moving papers.

2. The people may file with the court, and in such case must serve a copy thereof upon the defendant or his counsel, an answer denying or admitting any or all of the allegations of the moving papers, and may further submit documentary evidence refuting or tending to refute such allegations.

3. After all papers of both parties have been filed, and after all documentary evidence, if any, has been submitted, the court must consider the same for the purpose of determining whether the motion is determinable without a hearing to resolve questions of fact.

4. The court must grant the motion without conducting a hearing if:

(a) The moving papers allege a ground constituting legal basis for the motion pursuant to subdivision one of section 210.20; and

(b) Such ground, if based upon the existence or occurrence of facts, is supported by sworn allegations of all facts essential to support the motion; and

(c) The sworn allegations of fact essential to support the motion are either conceded by the people to be true or are conclusively substantiated by unquestionable documentary proof.

5. The court may deny the motion without conducting a hearing if:

(a) The moving papers do not allege any ground constituting legal basis for the motion pursuant to subdivision one of section 210.20; or

(b) The motion is based upon the existence or occurrence of facts, and the moving papers do not contain sworn allegations supporting all the essential facts; or

(c) An allegation of fact essential to support the motion is conclusively refuted by unquestionable documentary proof.

6. If the court does not determine the motion pursuant to subdivision four or five, it must conduct a hearing and make findings of fact essential to the determination thereof. The defendant has a right to be present in person at such hearing but may waive such right.

7. Upon such a hearing, the defendant has the burden of proving by a preponderance of the evidence every fact essential to support the motion.

8. When the court dismisses the entire indictment without authorizing resubmission of the charge or charges to a grand jury, it must order that the defendant be discharged from custody if he is in the custody of the sheriff, or if he is at liberty on bail it must exonerate the bail.

9. When the court dismisses the entire indictment but authorizes resubmission of the charge or charges to a grand jury, such authorization is, for purposes of this subdivision, deemed to constitute an order holding the defendant for the action of a grand jury with respect to such charge or charges. Such order must be accompanied by a securing order either releasing the defendant on his own recognizance or fixing bail or committing him to the custody of the sheriff pending resubmission of the case to the grand jury and the grand jury's disposition thereof. Such securing order remains in effect until the first to occur of any of the following:

(a) A statement to the court by the people that they do not intend to resubmit the case to a grand jury;

(b) Arraignment of the defendant upon an indictment or prosecutor's information filed as a result of resubmission of the case to a grand jury.

Upon such arraignment, the arraigning court must issue a new securing order;

(c) The filing with the court of a grand jury dismissal of the case following resubmission thereof;

(d) The expiration of a period of forty-five days from the date of issuance of the order; provided that such period may, for good cause shown, be extended by the court to a designated subsequent date if such be necessary to accord the people reasonable opportunity to resubmit the case to a grand jury.

Upon the termination of the effectiveness of the securing order pursuant to paragraph (a), (c) or (d), the court must immediately order that the defendant be discharged from custody if he is in the custody of the sheriff, or if he is at liberty on bail it must exonerate the bail. Although expiration of the period of time specified in paragraph (d) without any resubmission or grand jury disposition of the case terminates the effectiveness of the securing order, it does not terminate the effectiveness of the order authorizing resubmission.

§210.46 Adjournment in contemplation of dismissal in marihuana cases in a superior court.

Upon or after arraignment in a superior court upon an indictment where the sole remaining count or counts charge a violation or violations of section 221.05, 221.10, 221.15, 221.35 or 221.40 of the penal law and before the entry of a plea of guilty thereto or commencement of a trial thereof, the court, upon motion of a defendant, may order that all proceedings be suspended and the action adjourned in contemplation of dismissal or may dismiss the indictment in furtherance of justice, in accordance with the provisions of section 170.56 of this chapter.

§210.47 Adjournment in contemplation of dismissal in misdemeanor cases in superior court.

Upon or after the arraignment in a superior court upon an indictment where the sole remaining count or counts charge a misdemeanor offense, and before the entry of a plea of guilty thereto or commencement of a trial thereof, the court, upon motion of the people or the defendant and with the consent of the other party, or upon the court's own motion with the consent of both the people and the defendant, may order that all proceedings be suspended and the action adjourned in contemplation of dismissal, in accordance with the provisions of section 170.55 of this chapter.

§210.50 Requirement of plea.

Unless an indictment is dismissed or the criminal action thereon terminated or abated pursuant to the provisions of this article or some other provision of law, the defendant must be required to enter a plea thereto.

ARTICLE 215 - ADJOURNMENT IN CONTEMPLATION OF DISMISSAL FOR PURPOSES OF REFERRING SELECTED FELONIES TO DISPUTE RESOLUTION

Section
215.10   Referral of selected felonies to dispute resolution.
215.20   Victim; definition.
215.30   Adjournment in contemplation of dismissal; restoration to calendar; dismissal of action.
215.40   Dismissal of action; effect thereof; records.

§215.10 Referral of selected felonies to dispute resolution.

Upon or after arraignment in a local criminal court upon a felony complaint, or upon or after arraignment in a superior court upon an indictment or superior court information, and before final disposition thereof, the court, with the consent of the people and of the defendant, and with reasonable notice to the victim and an opportunity for the victim to be heard, may order that the action be adjourned in contemplation of dismissal, for the purpose of referring the action to a community dispute center established pursuant to article twenty-one-A of the judiciary law. Provided, however, that the court may not order any action adjourned in contemplation of dismissal if the defendant is charged therein with: (i) a class A felony, or (ii) a violent felony offense as defined in section 70.02 of the penal law, or (iii) any drug offense as defined in article two hundred twenty of the penal law, or (iv) a felony upon the conviction of which defendant must be sentenced as a second felony offender, a second violent felony offender, or a persistent violent felony offender pursuant to sections 70.06, 70.04 and 70.08 of the penal law, or a felony upon the conviction of which defendant may be sentenced as a persistent felony offender pursuant to section 70.10 of such law.

§215.20 Victim; definition.

For purposes of section 215.10 of this article, "victim" means any person alleged to have sustained physical or financial injury to person or property as a direct result of the crime or crimes charged in a felony complaint, superior court information, or indictment.

§215.30 Adjournment in contemplation of dismissal; restoration to calendar; dismissal of action.

Upon issuing an order adjourning an action in contemplation of dismissal pursuant to section 215.10 of this article, the court must release the defendant on his own recognizance and refer the action to a dispute resolution center established pursuant to article twenty-one-A of the judiciary law. No later than forty-five days after an action has been referred to a dispute resolution center, such center must advise the district attorney as to whether the charges against defendant have been resolved. Thereafter, if defendant has agreed to pay a fine, restitution or reparation, the district attorney must be advised every thirty days as to the status of such fine, restitution or reparation. Upon application of the people, made at any time not more than six months after the issuance of an order adjourning an action in contemplation of dismissal, the court may restore the action to the calendar upon a determination that dismissal of the accusatory instrument would not be in furtherance of justice, and the action must thereupon proceed. Notwithstanding the foregoing, where defendant has agreed to pay a fine, restitution, or reparation, but has not paid such fine, restitution or reparation, upon application of the people, made at any time not more than one year after the issuance of an order adjourning an action in contemplation of dismissal, the court may restore the action to the calendar upon a determination that defendant has failed to pay such fine, restitution, or reparation, and the action must thereupon proceed.

§215.40 Dismissal of action; effect thereof; records.

If an action has not been restored to the calendar within six months, or where the defendant has agreed to pay a fine, restitution or reparation but has not paid such fine, restitution or reparation, within one year, of the issuance of an order adjourning the action in contemplation of dismissal, the accusatory instrument shall be deemed to have been dismissed by the court in furtherance of justice at the expiration of such six month or one year period, as the case may be. Upon dismissal of an action, the arrest and prosecution shall be deemed a nullity, and defendant shall be restored to the status he or she occupied before his or her arrest and prosecution. All papers and records relating to an action that has been dismissed pursuant to this section shall be subject to the sealing provisions of section 160.50 of this chapter.

ARTICLE 216
JUDICIAL DIVERSION PROGRAM FOR
CERTAIN FELONY OFFENDERS

Section
216.00   **Definitions.**
216.05   **Judicial diversion program; court procedures.**

§216.00 Definitions.

The following definitions are applicable to this article:

1. *"Eligible defendant" means any person who stands charged in an indictment or a superior court information with a class B, C, D or E felony offense defined in article one hundred seventy-nine, two hundred twenty or two hundred twenty-two of the penal law, an offense defined in sections 105.10 and 105.13 of the penal law provided that the underlying crime for the conspiracy charge is a class B, C, D or E felony offense defined in article one hundred seventy-nine, two hundred twenty or two hundred twenty-two of the penal law, auto stripping in the second degree as defined in section 165.10 of the penal law, auto stripping in the first degree as defined in section 165.11 of the penal law, identity theft in the second degree as defined in section 190.79 of the penal law, identity theft in the first degree as defined in section 190.80 of the penal law, or any other specified offense as defined in subdivision five of section 410.91 of this chapter, provided, however, a defendant is not an "eligible defendant" if he or she:

(Repealed 7/5/28, Ch.92,L.2021)(Eff.10/7/21,Ch.435,L.2021)

(a) within the preceding ten years, excluding any time during which the offender was incarcerated for any reason between the time of commission of the previous felony and the time of commission of the present felony, has previously been convicted of: (i) a violent felony offense as defined in section 70.02 of the penal law or (ii) any other offense for which a merit time allowance is not available pursuant to subparagraph (ii) of paragraph (d) of subdivision one of section eight hundred three of the correction law, or (iii) a class A felony offense defined in article two hundred twenty of the penal law; or

(b) has previously been adjudicated a second violent felony offender pursuant to section 70.04 of the penal law or a persistent violent felony offender pursuant to section 70.08 of the penal law.

A defendant who also stands charged with a violent felony offense as defined in section 70.02 of the penal law or an offense for which merit time allowance is not available pursuant to subparagraph (ii) of paragraph (d) of subdivision one of section eight hundred three of the correction law for which the court must, upon the defendant's conviction thereof, sentence the defendant to incarceration in state prison is not an eligible defendant while such charges are pending. A defendant who is excluded from the judicial diversion program pursuant to this paragraph or paragraph (a) or (b) of this subdivision may become an eligible defendant upon the prosecutor's consent.

2. "Alcohol and substance use evaluation" means a written assessment and report by a court-approved entity or licensed health care professional experienced in the treatment of alcohol and substance use disorder, or by an addiction and substance abuse counselor credentialed by the office of addiction services and supports pursuant to section 19.07 of the mental hygiene law, which shall include:

(a) an evaluation as to whether the defendant has a history of alcohol or substance use disorder, as such terms are defined in the diagnostic and statistical manual of mental disorders, fifth edition, and a co-occurring mental disorder or mental illness and the relationship between such use and mental disorder or mental illness, if any;

(b) a recommendation as to whether the defendant's alcohol or substance use, if any, could be effectively addressed by judicial diversion in accordance with this article;

(c) a recommendation as to the treatment modality, level of care and length of any proposed treatment to effectively address the defendant's alcohol or substance use and any co-occurring mental disorder or illness; and

(d) any other information, factor, circumstance, or recommendation deemed relevant by the assessing entity or specifically requested by the court. *(Eff.10/7/21,Ch.435,L.2021)*

§216.05 Judicial diversion program; court procedures.

1. At any time after the arraignment of an eligible defendant, but prior to the entry of a plea of guilty or the commencement of trial, the court at the request of the eligible defendant, may order an alcohol and substance use evaluation. An eligible defendant may decline to participate in such an evaluation at any time. The defendant shall provide a written authorization, in compliance with the requirements of any applicable state or federal laws, rules or regulations authorizing disclosure of the results of the assessment to the defendant's attorney, the prosecutor, the local probation department, the court, authorized court personnel and other individuals specified in such authorization for the sole purpose of determining whether the defendant should be offered judicial diversion for treatment for substance use, alcohol use and any co-occurring mental disorder or mental illness.

2. Upon receipt of the completed alcohol and substance use evaluation report, the court shall provide a copy of the report to the eligible defendant and the prosecutor.

3. (a) Upon receipt of the evaluation report either party may request a hearing on the issue of whether the eligible defendant should be offered alcohol or substance use treatment pursuant to this article. At such a proceeding, which shall be held as soon as practicable so as to facilitate early intervention in the event that the defendant is found to need alcohol or substance use treatment, the court may consider oral and written arguments, may take testimony from witnesses offered by either party, and may consider any relevant evidence including, but not limited to, evidence that:

(i) the defendant had within the preceding ten years (excluding any time during which the offender was incarcerated for any reason between the time of the acts that led to the youthful offender adjudication and the time of commission of the present offense) been adjudicated a youthful offender for: (A) a violent felony offense as defined in section 70.02 of the penal law; or (B) any offense for which a merit time allowance is not available pursuant to subparagraph (ii) of paragraph (d) of subdivision one of section eight hundred three of the correction law; and

(ii) in the case of a felony offense defined in subdivision five of section 410.91 of this chapter, or section 165.10, 165.11, 190.79 or 190.80 of the penal law, any statement of or submitted by the victim, as defined in paragraph (a) of subdivision two of section 380.50 of this chapter.

(b) Upon completion of such a proceeding, the court shall consider and make findings of fact with respect to whether:

(i) the defendant is an eligible defendant as defined in subdivision one of section 216.00 of this article;

(ii) the defendant has a history of alcohol or substance use;

(iii) such alcohol or substance use is a contributing factor to the defendant's criminal behavior;

(iv) the defendant's participation in judicial diversion could effectively address such use; and

(v) institutional confinement of the defendant is or may not be necessary for the protection of the public.

4. When an authorized court determines, pursuant to paragraph (b) of subdivision three of this section, that an eligible defendant should be offered alcohol or substance use treatment, or when the parties and the court agree to an eligible defendant's participation in alcohol or substance use treatment, an eligible defendant may be allowed to participate in the judicial diversion program offered by this article. Prior to the court's issuing an order granting judicial diversion, the eligible defendant shall be required to enter a plea of guilty to the charge or charges; provided, however, that no such guilty plea shall be required when:

(a) the people and the court consent to the entry of such an order without a plea of guilty; or

(b) based on a finding of exceptional circumstances, the court determines that a plea of guilty shall not be required. For purposes of this subdivision, exceptional circumstances exist when, regardless of the ultimate disposition of the case, the entry of a plea of guilty is likely to result in severe collateral consequences.

5. The defendant shall agree on the record or in writing to abide by the release conditions set by the court, which, shall include: participation in a specified period of alcohol or substance use treatment at a specified program or programs identified by the court, which may include periods of detoxification, residential or outpatient treatment, or both, as determined after taking into account the views of the health care professional who conducted the alcohol and substance use evaluation and any health care professionals responsible for providing such treatment or monitoring the defendant's progress in such treatment; and may include: (i) periodic court appearances, which may include periodic urinalysis; (ii) a requirement that the defendant refrain from engaging in criminal behaviors; (iii) if the defendant needs treatment for opioid use, that he or she may participate in and receive medically prescribed drug treatments under the care of a health care professional licensed or certified under title eight of the education law, acting within his or her lawful scope of practice, provided that no court shall require the use of any specified type or brand of drug during the course of medically prescribed drug treatments.

6. Upon an eligible defendant's agreement to abide by the conditions set by the court, the court shall issue a securing order providing for bail or release on the defendant's own recognizance and conditioning any release upon the agreed upon conditions. The period of alcohol or substance use treatment shall begin as specified by the court and as soon as practicable after the defendant's release, taking into account the availability of treatment, so as to facilitate early intervention with respect to the defendant's substance use or condition and the effectiveness of the treatment program. In the event that a treatment program is not immediately available or becomes unavailable during the course of the defendant's participation in the judicial diversion program, the court may release the defendant pursuant to the securing order.

7. When participating in judicial diversion treatment pursuant to this article, any resident of this state who is covered under a private health insurance policy or contract issued for delivery in this state pursuant to article thirty-two, forty-three or forty-seven of the insurance law or article forty-four of the public health law, or who is covered by a self-funded plan which provides coverage for the diagnosis and treatment of chemical abuse and chemical dependence however defined in such policy; shall first seek

reimbursement for such treatment in accordance with the provisions of such policy or contract.

8. During the period of a defendant's participation in the judicial diversion program, the court shall retain jurisdiction of the defendant, provided, however, that the court may allow such defendant to (i) reside in another jurisdiction, or (ii) participate in alcohol and substance use treatment and other programs in the jurisdiction where the defendant resides or in any other jurisdiction, while participating in a judicial diversion program under conditions set by the court and agreed to by the defendant pursuant to subdivisions five and six of this section. The court may require the defendant to appear in court at any time to enable the court to monitor the defendant's progress in alcohol or substance use treatment. The court shall provide notice, reasonable under the circumstances, to the people, the treatment provider, the defendant and the defendant's counsel whenever it orders or otherwise requires the appearance of the defendant in court. Failure to appear as required without reasonable cause therefor shall constitute a violation of the conditions of the court's agreement with the defendant.

9. (a) If at any time during the defendant's participation in the judicial diversion program, the court has reasonable grounds to believe that the defendant has violated a release condition in an important respect or has willfully failed to appear before the court as requested, the court except as provided in subdivision two of section 510.50 of this chapter regarding a failure to appear, shall direct the defendant to appear or issue a bench warrant to a police officer or an appropriate peace officer directing him or her to take the defendant into custody and bring the defendant before the court without unnecessary delay; provided, however, that under no circumstances shall a defendant who requires treatment for opioid use be deemed to have violated a release condition on the basis of his or her participation in medically prescribed drug treatments under the care of a health care professional licensed or certified under title eight of the education law, acting within his or her lawful scope of practice. The relevant provisions of section 530.60 of this chapter relating to issuance of securing orders shall apply to such proceedings under this subdivision.

(b) In determining whether a defendant violated a condition of his or her release under the judicial diversion program, the court may conduct a summary hearing consistent with due process and sufficient to satisfy the court that the defendant has, in fact, violated the condition.

(c) If the court determines that the defendant has violated a condition of his or her release under the judicial diversion program, the court may modify the conditions thereof, reconsider the order of recognizance or bail pursuant to subdivision two of section 510.30 of this chapter, or terminate the defendant's participation in the judicial diversion program; and when applicable proceed with the defendant's sentencing in accordance with the agreement. Notwithstanding any provision of law to the contrary, the court may impose any sentence authorized for the crime of conviction in accordance with the plea agreement, or any lesser sentence authorized to be imposed on a felony drug offender pursuant to paragraph (b) or (c) of subdivision two of section 70.70 of the penal law taking into account the length of time the defendant spent in residential treatment and how best to continue treatment while the defendant is serving that sentence. In determining what action to take for a violation of a release condition, the court shall consider all relevant circumstances, including the views of the prosecutor, the defense and the alcohol or substance use treatment provider, and the extent to which persons who ultimately successfully complete a drug treatment regimen sometimes relapse by not abstaining from alcohol or substance use or by failing to comply fully with all requirements imposed by a treatment program. The court shall also consider using a system of graduated and appropriate responses or sanctions designed to address such inappropriate behaviors, protect public safety and facilitate, where possible, successful completion of the alcohol or substance use treatment program.

(d) Nothing in this subdivision shall be construed as preventing a court from terminating a defendant's participation in the judicial diversion program for violating a release condition when such a termination is necessary to preserve public safety. Nor shall anything in this subdivision be construed as precluding the prosecution of a defendant for the commission of a different offense while participating in the judicial diversion program.

(e) A defendant may at any time advise the court that he or she wishes to terminate participation in the judicial diversion program, at which time the court shall proceed with the case and, where applicable, shall impose sentence in accordance with the plea agreement. Notwithstanding any provision of law to the contrary, the court may impose any sentence authorized for the crime of conviction in accordance with the plea agreement, or any lesser sentence authorized to be imposed on a felony drug offender pursuant to paragraph (b) or (c) of subdivision two of section 70.70 of the penal law taking into account the length of time the defendant spent in residential treatment and how best to continue treatment while the defendant is serving that sentence.

10. Upon the court's determination that the defendant has successfully completed the required period of alcohol or substance use treatment and has otherwise satisfied the conditions required for successful completion of the judicial diversion program, the court shall comply with the terms and conditions it set for final disposition when it accepted the defendant's agreement to participate in the judicial diversion program. Such disposition may include, but is not limited to: (a) requiring the defendant to undergo a period of interim probation supervision and, upon the defendant's successful completion of the interim probation supervision term, notwithstanding the provision of any other law, permitting the defendant to withdraw his or her guilty plea and dismissing the indictment; or (b) requiring the defendant to undergo a period of interim probation supervision and, upon successful completion of the interim probation supervision term, notwithstanding the provision of any other law, permitting the defendant to withdraw his or her guilty plea, enter a guilty plea to a misdemeanor offense and sentencing the defendant as promised in the plea agreement, which may include a period of probation supervision pursuant to section 65.00 of the penal law; or (c) allowing the defendant to withdraw his or her guilty plea and dismissing the indictment.

11. Nothing in this article shall be construed as restricting or prohibiting courts or district attorneys from using other lawful procedures or models for placing appropriate persons into alcohol or substance use treatment.

(Eff.10/7/21,Ch.435,L.2021)

TITLE J - PROSECUTION OF INDICTMENTS
IN SUPERIOR COURTS - PLEA TO SENTENCE

ARTICLE 220 - THE PLEA

Section
220.10   Plea; kinds of pleas.
220.15   Plea; plea of not responsible by reason of mental disease or defect.
220.20   Plea; meaning of lesser included offense for plea purposes.
220.30   Plea; plea of guilty to part of indictment; plea covering other indictments.
220.35   Hearing on predicate felony conviction.
220.40   Plea; plea of not guilty; meaning.
220.50   Plea; entry of plea.
220.51   Notice before entry of plea or trial involving a public official.
220.60   Plea; change of plea.

§220.10 Plea; kinds of pleas.

The only kinds of pleas which may be entered to an indictment are those specified in this section:

1. The defendant may as a matter of right enter a plea of "not guilty" to the indictment.

2. Except as provided in subdivision five, the defendant may as a matter of right enter a plea of "guilty" to the entire indictment.

3. Except as provided in subdivision five, where the indictment charges but one crime, the defendant may, with both the permission of the court and the consent of the people, enter a plea of guilty of a lesser included offense.

4. Except as provided in subdivision five, where the indictment charges two or more offenses in separate counts, the defendant may, with both the permission of the court and the consent of the people, enter a plea of:

    (a) Guilty of one or more but not all of the offenses charged; or

    (b) Guilty of a lesser included offense with respect to any or all of the offenses charged; or

    (c) Guilty of any combination of offenses charged and lesser offenses included within other offenses charged.

5. (a)(i) Where the indictment charges one of the class A felonies defined in article two hundred twenty of the penal law or the attempt to commit any such class A felony, then any plea of guilty entered pursuant to subdivision three or four of this section must be or must include at least a plea of guilty of a class B felony.

    (ii) *(Repealed, Eff.12/27/04,Ch.738,L.2004)*

    (iii) Where the indictment charges one of the class B felonies defined in article two hundred twenty of the penal law then any plea of guilty entered pursuant to subdivision three or four must be or must include at least a plea of guilty of a class D felony.

    (b) Where the indictment charges any class B felony, other than a class B felony defined in article two hundred twenty of the penal law or a class B violent felony offense as defined in subdivision one of section 70.02 of the penal law, then any plea of guilty entered pursuant to subdivision three or four must be or must include at least a plea of guilty of a felony.

    (c) Where the indictment charges a felony, other than a class A felony or class B felony defined in article two hundred twenty of the penal law or class B or class C violent felony offense as defined in subdivision one of section 70.02 of the penal law, and it appears that the defendant has previously been subjected to a predicate felony conviction as defined in penal law section 70.06 then any plea of guilty entered pursuant to subdivision three or four must be or must include at least a plea of guilty of a felony.

    (d) Where the indictment charges a class A felony, other than those defined in article two hundred twenty of the penal law, or charges a class B or class C violent felony offense as defined in subdivision one of section 70.02 of the penal law, then a plea of guilty entered pursuant to subdivision three or four must be as follows:

        (i) Where the indictment charges a class A felony offense or a class B violent felony offense which is also an armed felony offense then a plea of guilty must include at least a plea of guilty to a class C violent felony offense;

        (ii) Except as provided in subparagraph (i) of this paragraph, where the indictment charges a class B violent felony offense or a class C violent felony offense, then a plea of guilty must include at least a plea of guilty to a class D violent felony offense;

(iii) Where the indictment charges the class D violent felony offense of criminal possession of a weapon in the third degree as defined in subdivision four of section 265.02 of the penal law, and the defendant has not been previously convicted of a class A misdemeanor defined in the penal law in the five years preceding the commission of the offense, then a plea of guilty must be either to the class E violent felony offense of attempted criminal possession of a weapon in the third degree or to the class A misdemeanor of criminal possession of a weapon in the fourth degree as defined in subdivision one of section 265.01 of the penal law;

(iv) Where the indictment charges the class D violent felony offenses of criminal possession of a weapon in the third degree as defined in subdivision four of section 265.02 of the penal law and the provisions of subparagraph (iii) of this paragraph do not apply, or subdivision five, seven or eight of section 265.02 of the penal law, then a plea of guilty must include at least a plea of guilty to a class E violent felony offense.

(e) A defendant may not enter a plea of guilty to the crime of murder in the first degree as defined in section 125.27 of the penal law; provided, however, that a defendant may enter such a plea with both the permission of the court and the consent of the people when the agreed upon sentence is either life imprisonment without parole or a term of imprisonment for the class A-I felony of murder in the first degree other than a sentence of life imprisonment without parole.

(f) The provisions of this subdivision shall apply irrespective of whether the defendant is thereby precluded from entering a plea of guilty of any lesser included offense.

(g) Where the defendant is a juvenile offender, the provisions of paragraphs (a), (b), (c) and (d) of this subdivision shall not apply and any plea entered pursuant to subdivision three or four of this section, must be as follows:

(i) If the indictment charges a person fourteen or fifteen years old with the crime of murder in the second degree any plea of guilty entered pursuant to subdivision three or four must be a plea of guilty of a crime for which the defendant is criminally responsible;

(ii) If the indictment does not charge a crime specified in subparagraph (i) of this paragraph, then any plea of guilty entered pursuant to subdivision three or four of this section must be a plea of guilty of a crime for which the defendant is criminally responsible unless a plea of guilty is accepted pursuant to subparagraph (iii) of this paragraph;

(iii) Where the indictment does not charge a crime specified in subparagraph (i) of this paragraph, the district attorney may recommend removal of the action to the family court. Upon making such recommendation the district attorney shall submit a subscribed memorandum setting forth: (1) a recommendation that the interests of justice would best be served by removal of the action to the family court; and (2) if the indictment charges a thirteen year old with the crime of murder in the second degree, or a fourteen or fifteen year old with the crimes of rape in the first degree as defined in subdivision one of section 130.35 of the penal law, or criminal sexual act in the first degree as defined in subdivision one of section 130.50 of the penal law, or an armed felony as defined in paragraph (a) of subdivision forty-one of section 1.20 of this chapter specific factors, one or more of which reasonably supports the recommendation, showing, (i) mitigating circumstances that bear directly upon the manner in which the crime was committed, or (ii) where the defendant was not the sole participant in the crime, that the defendant's participation was relatively minor although not so minor as to constitute a defense to the prosecution, or (iii) possible deficiencies in proof of the crime, or (iv) where the juvenile offender has no previous adjudications of having committed a designated felony act, as defined in subdivision eight of section 301.2 of the family court act, regardless of the age of the offender at the time of commission of the act, that the criminal act was not part of a pattern of criminal behavior and, in view of the history of the offender, is not likely to be repeated.

If the court is of the opinion based on specific factors set forth in the district attorney's memorandum that the interests of justice would best be served by removal of the action to the family court, a plea of guilty of a crime or act for which the defendant is not criminally responsible may be entered pursuant to subdivision three or four of this section, except that a thirteen year old charged with the crime of murder in the second degree may only plead to a designated felony act, as defined in subdivision eight of section 301.2 of the family court act.

Upon accepting any such plea, the court must specify upon the record the portion or portions of the district attorney's statement the court is relying upon as the basis of its opinion and that it believes the interests of justice would best be served by removal of the proceeding to the family court. Such plea shall then be deemed to be a juvenile delinquency fact determination and the court upon entry thereof must direct that the action be removed to the family court in accordance with the provisions of article seven hundred twenty-five of this chapter.

(g-1) Where a defendant is an adolescent offender, the provisions of paragraphs (a), (b), (c) and (d) of this subdivision shall not apply. Where the plea is to an offense constituting a misdemeanor, the plea shall be deemed replaced by an order of fact-finding in a juvenile delinquency proceeding, pursuant to section 346.1 of the family court act, and the action shall be removed to the family court in accordance with article seven hundred twenty-five of this chapter. Where the plea is to an offense constituting a felony, the court may remove the action to the family court in accordance with section 722.23 and article seven hundred twenty-five of this chapter.
(Eff.12/29/21,Ch.809,L.2021)

(h) Where the indictment charges the class E felony offense of aggravated harassment of an employee by an incarcerated individual as defined in section 240.32 of the penal law, then a plea of guilty must include at least a plea of guilty to a class E felony. *(Eff.8/2/21,Ch.322,L.2021)*

6. The defendant may, with both the permission of the court and consent of the people, enter a plea of not responsible by reason of mental disease or defect to the indictment in the manner prescribed in section 220.15 of this chapter.

§220.15 Plea; plea of not responsible by reason of mental disease or defect.

1. The defendant may, with both the permission of the court and consent of the people, enter a plea of not responsible by reason of mental disease or defect to the entire indictment. The district attorney must state to the court either orally on the record or in a writing filed with the court that the people consent to the entry of such plea and that the people are satisfied

that the affirmative defense of lack of criminal responsibility by reason of mental disease or defect would be proven by the defendant at a trial by a preponderance of the evidence. The district attorney must further state to the court in detail the evidence available to the people with respect to the offense or offenses charged in the indictment, including all psychiatric evidence available or known to the people. If necessary, the court may conduct a hearing before accepting such plea. The district attorney must further state to the court the reasons for recommending such plea. The reasons shall be stated in detail and not in conclusory terms.

2. Counsel for the defendant must state that in his opinion defendant has the capacity to understand the proceedings and to assist in his own defense and that the defendant understands the consequences of a plea of not responsible by reason of mental disease or defect. Counsel for the defendant must further state whether in his opinion defendant has any viable defense to the offense or offenses charged in the indictment other than the affirmative defense of lack of criminal responsibility by reason of mental disease or defect. Counsel for the defendant must further state in detail the psychiatric evidence available to the defendant with respect to such latter affirmative defense.

3. Before accepting a plea of not responsible by reason of mental disease or defect, the court must address the defendant in open court and determine that he understands each of the following:

(a) The nature of the charge to which the plea is offered, and the consequences of such plea;

(b) That he has the right to plead not guilty or to persist in that plea if it has already been entered;

(c) That he has the right to be tried by a jury, the right to the assistance of counsel, the right to confront and cross-examine witnesses against him, and the right not to be compelled to incriminate himself;

(d) That if he pleads not responsible by reason of mental disease or defect there will be no trial with respect to the charges contained in the indictment, so that by offering such plea he waives the right to such trial;

(e) That if he pleads not responsible by reason of mental disease or defect the court will ask him questions about the offense or offenses charged in the indictment and that he will thereby waive his right not to be compelled to incriminate himself; and

(f) That the acceptance of a plea of not responsible by reason of mental disease or defect is the equivalent of a verdict of not responsible by reason of mental disease or defect after trial.

4. The court shall not accept a plea of not responsible by reason of mental disease or defect without first determining that there is a factual basis for such plea. The court must address the defendant personally in open court and determine that the plea is voluntary, knowingly made, and not the result of force, threats, or promises. The court must inquire whether the defendant's willingness to plead results from prior discussions between the district attorney and counsel for the defendant. The court must be satisfied that the defendant

understands the proceedings against him, has sufficient capacity to assist in his own defense and understands the consequences of a plea of not responsible by reason of mental disease or defect. The court may make such inquiry as it deems necessary or appropriate for the purpose of making the determinations required by this section.

5. Before accepting a plea of not responsible by reason of mental disease or defect, the court must find and state each of the following on the record in detail and not in conclusory terms:

(a) That it is satisfied that each element of the offense or offenses charged in the indictment would be established beyond a reasonable doubt at a trial;

(b) That the affirmative defense of lack of criminal responsibility by reason of mental disease or defect would be proven by the defendant at a trial by a preponderance of the evidence;

(c) That the defendant has the capacity to understand the proceedings against him and to assist in his own defense;

(d) That such plea by the defendant is knowingly and voluntarily made and that there is a factual basis for the plea;

(e) That the acceptance of such plea is required in the interest of the public in the effective administration of justice.

6. When a plea of not responsible by reason of mental disease or defect is accepted by the court and recorded upon the minutes, the provisions of section 330.20 of this chapter shall govern all subsequent proceedings against the defendant.

§220.20 Plea; meaning of lesser included offense for plea purposes.

1. A "lesser included offense," within the meaning of subdivisions four and five of section 220.10 relating to the entry of a plea of guilty to an offense of lesser grade than one charged in a count of an indictment, means not only a "lesser included offense" as that term is defined in subdivision thirty-seven of section 1.20, but also one which is deemed to be such pursuant to the following rules:

(a) Where the only culpable mental state required for the crime charged is that the proscribed conduct be performed intentionally, any lesser offense consisting of reckless or criminally negligent, instead of intentional, performance of the same conduct is deemed to constitute a lesser included offense;

(b) Where the only culpable mental state required for the crime charged is that the proscribed conduct be performed recklessly, any lesser offense consisting of criminally negligent, instead of reckless, performance of the same conduct is deemed to constitute a lesser included offense;

(c) Where according to the allegations of a count a defendant's participation in the crime charged consisted in whole or in part of solicitation of another person to engage in the proscribed conduct, the offense of criminal solicitation, in any appropriate degree, is, with respect to such defendant, deemed to constitute a lesser included offense;

(d) Where according to the allegations of a count a defendant's participation in the crime charged consisted in whole or in part of conspiratorial agreement or conduct with another person to engage in the proscribed conduct, the crime of conspiracy, in any appropriate degree, is, with respect to such defendant, deemed to constitute a lesser included offense;

(e) Where according to the allegations of a count charging a felony a defendant's participation in such felony consisted in whole or in part of providing another person with means or opportunity for engaging in the proscribed conduct, the crime of criminal facilitation, in any appropriate degree, is, with respect to such defendant, deemed to constitute a lesser included offense;

(f) Where the crime charged is assault or attempted assault, in any degree, allegedly committed by intentionally causing or attempting to cause physical injury to a person by the immediate use of physical force against him, or where the crime charged is menacing, as defined in section 120.15 of the penal law, the offense of harassment, as defined in subdivision one of section 240.25 of the penal law, is deemed to constitute a lesser included offense;

(g) Where the crime charged is murder in the second degree as defined in subdivision three of section 125.25 of the penal law, allegedly committed in the course of the commission or attempted commission of a designated one of the underlying felonies enumerated in said subdivision, or during immediate flight therefrom, such designated underlying felony or attempted felony is deemed to constitute a lesser included offense. If such designated underlying felony is alleged to be robbery, burglary, kidnapping, or arson, without specification of the degree thereof, or an attempt to commit the same, a plea of guilty may be entered to the lowest degree thereof only, or as the case may be to attempted commission of such felony in its lowest degree, unless the allegations of the count clearly indicate the existence of all the elements of a higher degree;

(h) Where the crime charged is criminal sale of a controlled substance, any offense of criminal sale or possession of a controlled substance, in any degree, is deemed to constitute a lesser included offense.

(i) Where the crime charged is criminal possession of a controlled substance, any offense of criminal possession of a controlled substance, in any degree, is deemed to constitute a lesser included offense.

(j) Where the offense charged is unlawful disposal of hazardous wastes in violation of section 27-0914 of the environmental conservation law, any offense of unlawful disposal or possession of hazardous wastes as set forth in sections 71-2707, 71-2709, 71-2711 and 71-2713 of such law, in any degree, is deemed to constitute a lesser included offense;

(k) Where the offense charged is unlawful possession of hazardous wastes in violation of section 27-0914 of the environmental conservation law, any offense of unlawful possession of hazardous wastes as set forth in sections 71-2707 and 71-2709 of such law, in any degree, is deemed to constitute a lesser included offense.

2. An offense is deemed to be a lesser included offense with respect to a crime charged in an indictment, pursuant to the provisions of subdivision one, only for purposes of conviction upon a plea of guilty and not for purposes of conviction by verdict. For the latter purpose, an offense constitutes a lesser included one only when it conforms to the definition of that term contained in subdivision thirty-seven of section 1.20.

§220.30 Plea; plea of guilty to part of indictment; plea covering other indictments.

1. A plea of guilty not embracing the entire indictment, entered pursuant to the provisions of subdivision four or five of section 220.10, is a "plea of guilty to part of the indictment."

2. The entry and acceptance of a plea of guilty to part of the indictment constitutes a disposition of the entire indictment.

3. (a) (i) Except as provided in paragraph (b), or in paragraph (c) dealing with juvenile offenders, a plea of guilty, whether to the entire indictment or to part of the indictment, may, with both the permission of the court and the consent of the people, be entered and accepted upon the condition that it constitutes a complete disposition of one or more other indictments against the defendant then pending.

(ii) If the other indictment or indictments are pending in a different court or courts, they shall not be disposed of under this subdivision unless the other courts and the appropriate prosecutors also transmit their written permission and consent as provided in subdivision four of section 220.50 of this article; in such case the court in which the plea is entered shall so notify the other courts which, upon such notice, shall dismiss the appropriate indictments pending therein.

(b) (i) A plea of guilty, whether to the entire indictment or to part of the indictment for any crime other than a class A felony, may not be accepted on the condition that it constitutes a complete disposition of one or more other indictments against the defendant wherein is charged a class A-I felony as defined in article two hundred twenty of the penal law or the attempt to commit any such class A-I felony, except that an eligible youth, as defined in subdivision two of section 720.10, may plea to a class B felony, upon consent of the district attorney, for purposes of adjudication as a youthful offender.

(ii) Where it appears that the defendant has previously been subjected to a predicate felony conviction as defined in paragraph (b) of subdivision (1) of section 70.06 of the penal law, a plea of guilty, whether to the entire indictment or to part of the indictment, of any offense other than a felony may not be accepted on the condition that it constitutes a complete disposition of one or more other indictments against the defendant wherein is charged a felony, other than a class A felony or a class B or class C violent felony offense as defined in subdivision one of section 70.02 of the penal law.

(iii) A plea of guilty, whether to the entire indictment or part of the indictment for any crime other than a class A felony or a class B or class C violent felony offense as defined in subdivision one of section 70.02 of the penal law, may not be accepted on the condition that it constitutes a complete disposition of one or more other indictments against the defendant wherein is charged a class A felony, other than those defined in article two hundred twenty of the penal law, or a class B violent felony offense which is also an armed felony offense.

(iv) Except as provided in subparagraph (iii) of this paragraph, a plea of guilty, whether to the entire indictment or part of the indictment, for any crime other than a class A felony or a class B, C, or D violent felony offense as defined in subdivision one of section 70.02 of the penal law, may not be accepted on the condition that it constitutes a complete disposition of one or more other indictments against the defendant wherein is charged a class B or class C violent felony offense as defined in subdivision one of section 70.02 of the penal law.

(v) A plea of guilty, whether to the entire indictment or part of the indictment, for any crime other than a violent felony offense as defined in section 70.02 of the penal law, may not be accepted on the condition that it constitutes a complete disposition of one or more other indictments against the defendant wherein is charged the class D violent felony offenses of criminal possession of a weapon in the third degree as defined in subdivision four, five, seven or eight of section 265.02 of the penal law; provided, however, a plea of guilty, whether to the entire indictment or part of the indictment, for the class A misdemeanor of criminal possession of a weapon in the fourth degree as defined in subdivision one of section 265.01 of the penal law may be accepted on the condition that it constitutes a complete disposition of one or more other indictments against the defendant wherein is charged the class D violent felony offense of criminal possession of a weapon in the third degree as defined in subdivision four of section 265.02 of the penal law when the defendant has not been previously convicted of a class A misdemeanor defined in the penal law in the five years preceding the commission of the offense.

(vi) A plea of guilty, whether to the entire indictment or to part of the indictment for any crime other than a felony, may not be accepted on the condition that it constitutes a complete disposition of one or more other indictments against the defendant wherein is charged a class B felony other than a class B violent felony offense as defined in subdivision one of section 70.02 of the penal law.

(vii) A defendant may not enter a plea of guilty to the crime of murder in the first degree as defined in section 125.27 of the penal law; provided, however, that a defendant may enter such a plea with both the permission of the court and the consent of the people when the agreed upon sentence is either life imprisonment without parole or a term of imprisonment for the class A-I felony of murder in the first degree other than a sentence of life imprisonment without parole.

(viii) A plea of guilty, whether to the entire indictment or to part of the indictment for any crime other than a class A or class B felony may not be accepted on condition that it constitutes a complete disposition of one or more other indictments against the defendant wherein is charged a class A-II felony defined in article two hundred twenty of the penal law or the attempt to commit any such felony.

(ix) A plea of guilty, whether to the entire indictment or to part of the indictment for any crime other than a class B, a class C, or a class D felony, may not be accepted on condition that it constitutes a complete disposition of one or more other indictments against the defendant wherein is charged a class B felony defined in article two hundred twenty of the penal law.

(c) Where the defendant is a juvenile offender, a plea of guilty, whether to the entire indictment or to part of the indictment, of any offense other than one for which the defendant is criminally responsible may not be accepted on the condition that it constitutes a complete disposition of one or more other indictments against the defendant.

§220.35 Hearing on predicate felony conviction.

In any case where the defendant offers to enter a plea of guilty of a misdemeanor to constitute a disposition of the entire indictment or to constitute a complete disposition of one or more other indictments, or both, and the permission of the court and the consent of the people must be withheld solely upon the ground that it appears the defendant has previously been subjected to a predicate felony conviction as defined in paragraph (b) of subdivision one of section 70.06 of the penal law the court, if the defendant does not admit such predicate felony conviction, may conduct the hearing required by section 400.21 for the purpose of determining whether the plea may be entered or must be rejected. The finding upon any such hearing shall also be binding upon the defendant for the purpose of sentence.

§220.40 Plea; plea of not guilty; meaning.

A plea of not guilty constitutes a denial of every allegation of the indictment.

§220.50 Plea; entry of plea.

1. A plea to an indictment, other than one against a corporation, must be entered orally by the defendant in person; except that a plea to an indictment which does not charge a felony may, with the permission of the court, be entered by counsel upon submission by him of written authorization of the defendant.

2. A plea to an indictment against a corporation must be entered by counsel.

3. If a defendant who is required to enter a plea to an indictment refuses to do so or remains mute, the court must enter a plea of not guilty to the indictment in his behalf.

4. Where the permission of the court and the consent of the people are a prerequisite to the entry of a plea of guilty, the court and the prosecutor must either orally on the record or in a writing filed with the indictment state their reason for granting permission or consenting, as the case may be, to entry of the plea of guilty.

5. When a sentence is agreed upon by the prosecutor and a defendant as a predicate to entry of a plea of guilty, the court or the prosecutor must orally on the record, or in writing filed with the court, state the sentence agreed upon as a condition of such plea.

6. Where the defendant consents to a plea of guilty to the indictment, or part of the indictment, or consents to be prosecuted by superior court information as set forth in section 195.20 of this chapter, and if the defendant and prosecutor agree that as a condition of the plea or the superior court information certain property shall be forfeited by the defendant, the description and present estimated monetary value of the property shall be stated in court by the prosecutor at the time of plea. Within thirty days of the acceptance of the plea or superior court information by the court, the prosecutor shall send to the commissioner of the division of criminal justice services a document containing the name of the defendant, the description and present estimated monetary value of the property, any other demographic data as required by the division of criminal justice services and the date the plea or superior court information was accepted. Any property forfeited by the defendant as a condition to a plea of guilty to an indictment, or a part thereof, or to a superior court information, shall be

disposed of in accordance with the provisions of section thirteen hundred forty-nine of the civil practice law and rules.

* 7. Prior to accepting a defendant's plea of guilty to a count or counts of an indictment or a superior court information charging a felony offense, the court must advise the defendant on the record, that if the defendant is not a citizen of the United States, the defendant's plea of guilty and the court's acceptance thereof may result in the defendant's deportation, exclusion from admission to the United States or denial of naturalization pursuant to the laws of the United States. Where the plea of guilty is to a count or counts of an indictment charging a felony offense other than a violent felony offense as defined in section 70.02 of the penal law or an A-I felony offense other than an A-I felony as defined in article two hundred twenty of the penal law, the court must also, prior to accepting such plea, advise the defendant that, if the defendant is not a citizen of the United States and is or becomes the subject of a final order of deportation issued by the United States Immigration and Naturalization Service, the defendant may be paroled to the custody of the Immigration and Naturalization Service for deportation purposes at any time subsequent to the commencement of any indeterminate or determinate prison sentence imposed as a result of the defendant's plea. The failure to advise the defendant pursuant to this subdivision shall not be deemed to affect the voluntariness of a plea of guilty or the validity of a conviction, nor shall it afford a defendant any rights in a subsequent proceeding relating to such defendant's deportation, exclusion or denial of naturalization.   *(Repealed 9/1/23, Ch.55, L.2021)

*8. Prior to accepting a defendant's plea of guilty to a count or counts of an indictment or a superior court information charging a felony offense, the court must advise the defendant on the record that conviction will result in loss of the right to vote while the defendant is serving a felony sentence in a correctional facility and that the right to vote will be restored upon the defendant's release.   (Eff.9/1/21, Ch.103, L.2021)

§220.51 Notice before entry of plea or trial involving a public official.

Prior to trial, and before accepting a defendant's plea to a count or counts of an indictment or a superior court information charging a felony offense, the court must individually advise the defendant, on the record, that if at the time of the alleged felony crime the defendant was a public official, as defined in subdivision six of section one hundred fifty-six of the retirement and social security law, the defendant's plea of guilty and the court's acceptance thereof or conviction after trial may result in proceedings for the reduction or revocation of such defendant's pension pursuant to article three-B of the retirement and social security law.

§220.60 Plea; change of plea.

1. A defendant who has entered a plea of not guilty to an indictment may as a matter of right withdraw such plea at any time before rendition of a verdict and enter a plea of guilty to the entire indictment pursuant to subdivision two, but subject to the limitation in subdivision five of section 220.10.

2. A defendant who has entered a plea of not guilty to an indictment may, with both the permission of the court and the consent of the people, withdraw such plea at any time before the rendition of a verdict and enter:

(a) a plea of guilty to part of the indictment pursuant to subdivision three or four but subject to the limitation in subdivision five of section 220.10, or

(b) a plea of not responsible by reason of mental disease or defect to the indictment pursuant to section 220.15 of this chapter.

3. At any time before the imposition of sentence, the court in its discretion may permit a defendant who has entered a plea of guilty to the entire indictment or to part of the indictment, or a plea of not responsible by reason of mental disease or defect, to withdraw such plea, and in such event the entire indictment, as it existed at the time of such plea, is restored.

4. When a special information has been filed pursuant to section 200.61 or 200.62 of this chapter, a defendant may enter a plea of guilty to the count or counts of the indictment to which the special information applies without admitting the allegations of the special information. Whenever a defendant enters a plea of guilty to the count of counts of the indictment to which the special information applies without admitting the allegations of the special information, the court must, unless the people consent otherwise, conduct a hearing in accordance with paragraph (b) of subdivision two of section 200.62 or paragraph (b) of subdivision three of section 200.61 of this chapter, whichever is applicable.

ARTICLE 230 - REMOVAL OF ACTION

Section
230.10   Removal of action; from supreme court to county court and from county court to supreme court; at instance of court.
230.11   Removal of action to certain courts within a county.
230.20   Removal of action; removal from county court to supreme court and change of venue; upon motion of party.
230.21   Removal of action to certain courts in an adjoining county.
230.30   Removal of action; stay of trial pending motion therefor.
230.40   Removal of action; determinations and rulings before and after removal; by which courts made.

§230.10   Removal of action; from supreme court to county court and from county court to supreme court; at instance of court.

Upon order of an appropriate court or judge, made at its or his own instance pursuant to rules established by the appellate division of the appropriate department, (a) an indictment filed with the supreme court at a term held in a particular county outside of New York City may, prior to entry of a plea of guilty thereto or commencement of a trial thereof, be removed to the county court of such county, and (b) an indictment filed in a county court may similarly be removed to the supreme court at a term held or to be held in the same county. Each of the appellate divisions of the second, third and fourth departments may establish rules authorizing such removals with respect to the superior courts within its department, and prescribing the courts or judges who may order such removals and other procedural matters involved therein.

§230.11 Removal of action to certain courts within a county.

1. In any county outside a city having a population of one million or more, upon or after arraignment of a defendant on an indictment pending in a superior court having jurisdiction thereof, such court may, upon motion of the defendant and after giving the district attorney an opportunity to be heard, order that the action be removed from the court in which the matter is pending to another court in the same county that has been designated as a human trafficking court or veterans treatment court by the chief administrator of the courts, and such human trafficking court or veterans treatment court may then conduct such action to judgment or other final disposition; provided, however, that no court may order removal pursuant to this section to a veterans treatment court of a family offense charge described in subdivision one of section 530.11 of this chapter where the accused and the person alleged to be the victim of such offense charged are members of the same family or household as defined in such subdivision one of section 530.11; and provided further that an order of removal issued under this subdivision shall not take effect until five days after the date the order is issued unless, prior to such effective date, the human trafficking court or veterans treatment court notifies the court that issued the order that:

(a) it will not accept the action, in which event the order shall not take effect; or

(b) it will accept the action on a date prior to such effective date, in which event the order shall take effect upon such prior date.

2. Upon providing notification pursuant to paragraph (a) or (b) of subdivision one of this section, the human trafficking court or veterans treatment court shall promptly give notice to the defendant, his or her counsel and the district attorney.   *(Eff.4/28/21,Ch.91,L.2021)*

§230.20 Removal of action; removal from county court to supreme court and change of venue; upon motion of party.

1. At any time within the period provided by section 255.20, the appellate division of the department embracing the county, upon motion of either the defendant or the people, may, for good cause shown, order that the indictment and action be removed from the county court to the supreme court at a term held or to be held in the same county.

2. At any time within the period provided by section 255.20, the appellate division of the department embracing the county in which the superior court is located may, upon motion of either the defendant or the people demonstrating reasonable cause to believe that a fair and impartial trial cannot be had in such county, order either:

(a) that the indictment and action be removed from such superior court to a designated superior court of or located in another county; or

(b) that the commissioner of jurors of such county, in consultation with the appropriate administrative judge of the judicial district in which the county is located, expand the pool of jurors to encompass prospective jurors from the jury lists of counties that are within the judicial district in which, and that are geographically contiguous with the county in which, such superior court is located.

In making such determination the appellate division shall consider, among other factors, the hardship on potential jurors and the potential depletion of a county's qualified juror list that may result from an order expanding the jury pool. An order of removal under paragraph (a) herein must, if the defendant is in custody at the time, include a provision for transfer of custody by the sheriff or other appropriate public servant of the county of confinement to the sheriff or other appropriate public servant of the county to which the action has been removed. If the order is issued upon motion of the people, the appellate division may impose such conditions as it deems equitable and appropriate to insure that the removal does not subject the defendant to an unreasonable burden in making his defense. Any additional cost to the people incurred in complying with the order must be borne by the county from which the action originated.

3. Any motion made pursuant to this section must be based upon papers stating the grounds therefor, and must be made within the period provided by section 255.20 and upon five days notice thereof together with service of the moving papers upon, as the case may be, (a) the district attorney or (b) either the defendant or his counsel. In any case, the motion must be made returnable either during the appellate division term during which such moving papers are served or during the next term thereof.

4. If the appellate division grants the motion and orders a removal of the action, a certified copy of such order must be filed with the clerk of the superior court in which the indictment is pending. Such clerk must thereupon transmit such instrument, together with the pertinent papers and proceedings of the action, including all undertakings for appearances of the defendant and of the witnesses, or a certified copy or copies of the same, to the term of the superior court to which the action has been removed. Such latter court must then proceed to conduct the action to judgment or other final disposition.

§230.21 Removal of action to certain courts in an adjoining county.

1. In any county outside a city having a population of one million or more, the court may, upon motion of the defendant and with consent of the district attorney and the district attorney of the adjoining county that has a superior court designated a human trafficking court or veterans treatment court by the chief administrator of the courts, order that the indictment and action be removed from the court in which the matter is pending to such human trafficking court or veterans treatment court, whereupon such court may then conduct such action to judgment or other final disposition; provided, however, that no court may order removal to a veterans treatment court of a family offense charge described in subdivision one of section 530.11 of this chapter pursuant to this section where the accused and the person alleged to be the victim of such offense charged are members of the same family or household as defined in such subdivision one of section 530.11; and provided further that an order of removal issued under this subdivision shall not take effect until five days after the date the order is issued unless, prior

to such effective date, the human trafficking court or veterans treatment court notifies the court that issued the order that:

(a) it will not accept the action, in which event the order shall not take effect, or

(b) it will accept the action on a date prior to such effective date, in which event the order shall take effect upon such prior date.

2. Upon providing notification pursuant to paragraph (a) or (b) of subdivision one of this section, the human trafficking court or veterans treatment court shall promptly give notice to the defendant, his or her counsel and the district attorney of both counties.   *(Eff. 4/28/21, Ch.91, L.2021)*

§230.30 Removal of action; stay of trial pending motion therefor.

1. At any time when a timely motion for removal of an action from the county court to the supreme court or for a change of venue may be made pursuant to section 230.20, a justice holding a term of the supreme court in the district in which the indictment is pending, or a justice of the appellate division of the department in which the indictment is pending, upon application of either the defendant or the people, may, in his discretion and for good cause shown, order that the trial of such indictment be stayed for a designated period, not to exceed thirty days from the issuance of such order, to allow the applicant party to make a motion in the appropriate court for removal of the action from a county court to the supreme court or for a change of venue.

2. Such an order may be issued only upon an application made in writing and after reasonable notice and opportunity to be heard has been accorded the other party.

3. Upon issuing the order, the supreme court justice or appellate division justice must cause the order to be filed with the clerk of the court in which the indictment is pending. Thereafter, no further proceedings may be had in such court until a motion for removal or change of venue, as the case may be, if made within the designated period, has been determined, or until such designated period has expired without any such motion having been made.

4. When such an application for a stay has been made to and denied by a justice of the supreme court or a justice of the appellate division, a second such application may not be made to any other such justice.

§230.40 Removal of action; determinations and rulings before and after removal; by which courts made.

Upon any removal of an indictment and action from one superior court to another pursuant to the provisions of this article, determinations and rulings with respect to the action made before such removal are not thereby rendered invalid. All subsequent determinations and rulings must be made by the court to which the action is removed; and such latter court is deemed to have control of the grand jury minutes underlying the indictment for the purpose of determining post-removal motions addressed to the legal sufficiency of the grand jury evidence or the validity of the grand jury proceeding.

ARTICLE 245 - DISCOVERY

Section
245.10   Timing of discovery.
245.20   Automatic discovery.
245.25   Disclosure prior to certain guilty pleas.
245.30   Court orders for preservation, access or discovery.
245.35   Court ordered procedures to facilitate compliance.
245.40   Non-testimonial evidence from the defendant.
245.45   DNA comparison order.
245.50   Certificates of compliance; readiness for trial.
245.55   Flow of information.
245.60   Continuing duty to disclose.
245.65   Work product.
245.70   Protective orders.
245.75   Waiver of discovery by defendant.
245.80   Remedies or sanctions for non-compliance.
245.85   Admissibility of discovery.

§245.10 Timing of discovery.

1.(a) Subject to subparagraph (iv) of this paragraph, the prosecution shall perform its initial discovery obligations under subdivision one of section 245.20 of this article as soon as practicable but not later than the time periods specified in subparagraphs (i) and (ii) of this paragraph, as applicable. Portions of materials claimed to be non-discoverable may be withheld pending a determination and ruling of the court under section 245.70 of this article; but the defendant shall be notified in writing that information has not been disclosed under a particular subdivision of such section, and the discoverable portions of such materials shall be disclosed to the extent practicable. When the discoverable materials, including video footage from body-worn cameras, surveillance cameras, or dashboard cameras, are exceptionally voluminous or, despite diligent, good faith efforts, are otherwise not in the actual possession of the prosecution, the time period in this paragraph may be stayed by up to an additional thirty calendar days without need for a motion pursuant to subdivision two of section 245.70 of this article.

(i) When a defendant is in custody during the pendency of the criminal case, the prosecution shall perform its initial discovery obligations within twenty calendar days after the defendant's arraignment on an indictment, superior court information, prosecutor's information, information, simplified information, misdemeanor complaint or felony complaint.

(ii) When the defendant is not in custody during the pendency of the criminal case, the prosecution shall perform its initial discovery obligations within thirty-five calendar days after the defendant's arraignment on an indictment, superior court information, prosecutor's information, information, simplified information, misdemeanor complaint or felony complaint.

(iii) Notwithstanding the timelines contained in the opening paragraph of this paragraph, the prosecutor's discovery obligation under subdivision one of section 245.20 of this article shall be performed as soon as practicable, but not later than fifteen days before the trial of a simplified information charging a traffic infraction under the vehicle and traffic law, or by an information charging one or more petty offenses as defined by the municipal code of a village, town, city, or county, that do not carry a statutorily authorized sentence of imprisonment, and where the defendant stands charged before the court with no crime or offense, provided however that nothing in this subparagraph shall prevent a defendant from filing a motion for disclosure of such items and information under subdivision one of such section 245.20 of this article at an earlier date.

(iv)(A) Portions of materials claimed to be non-discoverable may be withheld pending a determination and ruling of the court under section 245.70 of this article; but the defendant shall be notified in writing that information has not been disclosed under a particular subdivision of such section, and the discoverable portions of such materials shall be disclosed to the extent practicable. Information related to or evidencing the identity of a 911 caller, the victim or witness of an offense defined under article one hundred thirty or sections 230.34 and 230.34-a of the penal law, or any other victim or witness of a crime where the defendant has substantiated affiliation with a criminal enterprise as defined in subdivision three of section 460.10 of the penal law may be withheld, provided, however, the defendant may move the court for disclosure.

(B) When the discoverable materials are exceptionally voluminous or, despite diligent, good faith efforts, are otherwise not in the actual possession of the prosecution, the time period in this paragraph may be extended pursuant to a motion pursuant to subdivision two of section 245.70 of this article. For purposes of this article, voluminous materials may include, but are not limited to, video footage from body worn cameras, surveillance cameras or dashboard cameras.   *(Eff.5/3/20,Ch.56,L.2020)*

(b) The prosecution shall perform its supplemental discovery obligations under subdivision three of section 245.20 of this article as soon as practicable but not later than fifteen calendar days prior to the first scheduled trial date.

(c) The prosecution shall disclose statements of the defendant as described in paragraph (a) of subdivision one of section 245.20 of this article to any defendant who has been arraigned in a local criminal court upon a currently undisposed of felony complaint charging an offense which is a subject of a prospective or pending grand jury proceeding, no later than forty-eight hours before the time scheduled for the defendant to testify at a grand jury proceeding pursuant to subdivision five of section 190.50 of this part.

2. Defendant's performance of obligations. The defendant shall perform his or her discovery obligations under subdivision four of section 245.20 of this article not later than thirty calendar days after being served with the prosecution's certificate of compliance pursuant to subdivision one of section 245.50 of this article, except that portions of materials claimed to be non-discoverable may be withheld pending a determination and ruling of the court under section 245.70 of this article; but the prosecution must be notified in writing that information has not been disclosed under a particular section.

§245.20 Automatic discovery.

1. Initial discovery for the defendant. The prosecution shall disclose to the defendant, and permit the defendant to discover, inspect, copy, photograph and test, all items and information that relate to the subject matter of the case and are in the possession, custody or control of the prosecution or persons under the prosecution's direction or control, including but not limited to:

(a) All written or recorded statements, and the substance of all oral statements, made by the defendant or a co-defendant to a public servant engaged in law enforcement activity or to a person then acting under his or her direction or in cooperation with him or her.

(b) All transcripts of the testimony of a person who has testified before a grand jury, including but not limited to the defendant or a co-defendant. If in the exercise of reasonable diligence, and due to the limited availability of transcription resources, a transcript is unavailable for disclosure within the time period specified in subdivision one of section 245.10 of this article, such time period may be stayed by up to an additional thirty calendar days without need for a motion pursuant to subdivision two of section 245.70 of this article; except that such disclosure shall be made as soon as practicable and not later than thirty calendar days before the first scheduled trial date, unless an order is obtained pursuant to section 245.70 of this article. When the court is required to review grand jury transcripts, the prosecution shall disclose such transcripts to the court expeditiously upon receipt by the prosecutor, notwithstanding the otherwise-applicable time periods for disclosure in this article.

(c) The names and adequate contact information for all persons other than law enforcement personnel whom the prosecutor knows to have evidence or information relevant to any offense charged or to any potential defense thereto, including a designation by the prosecutor as to which of those persons may be called as witnesses. Nothing in this paragraph shall require the disclosure of physical addresses; provided, however, upon a motion and good cause shown the court may direct the disclosure of a physical address. Information under this subdivision relating to the identity of a 911 caller, the victim or witness of an offense defined under article one hundred thirty or section 230.34 or 230.34-a of the penal law, any other victim or witness of a crime where the defendant has substantiated affiliation with a criminal enterprise as defined in subdivision three of section 460.10 of the penal law, or a confidential informant may be withheld, and redacted from discovery materials, without need for a motion pursuant to section 245.70 of this article; but the prosecution shall notify the defendant in writing that such information has not been disclosed, unless the court rules otherwise for good cause shown.   *(Eff.5/3/20,Ch.56,L.2020)*

(d) The name and work affiliation of all law enforcement personnel whom the prosecutor knows to have evidence or information relevant to any offense charged or to any potential defense thereto, including a designation by the prosecutor as to which of those persons may be called as witnesses. Information under this subdivision relating to undercover personnel may be withheld, and redacted from discovery materials, without need for a motion pursuant to section 245.70 of this article; but the prosecution shall notify the defendant in writing that such information has not been disclosed, unless the court rules otherwise for good cause shown.

(e) All statements, written or recorded or summarized in any writing or recording, made by persons who have evidence or information relevant to any offense charged or to any potential defense thereto, including all police reports, notes of police and other investigators, and law enforcement agency reports. This provision also includes statements, written or recorded or summarized in any writing or recording, by persons to be called as witnesses at pre-trial hearings.

(f) Expert opinion evidence, including the name, business address, current curriculum vitae, a list of publications, and a list of proficiency tests and results administered or taken within the past ten years of each expert witness whom the prosecutor intends to call as a witness at trial or a pre-trial hearing, and all reports prepared by the expert that pertain to the case, or if no report is prepared, a written statement of the facts and opinions to which the expert is expected to testify and a summary of the grounds for each opinion. This paragraph does not alter or in any way affect the procedures, obligations or rights set forth in section 250.10 of this title. If in the exercise of reasonable diligence this information is unavailable for disclosure within the time period specified in subdivision one of section

245.10 of this article, that period shall be stayed without need for a motion pursuant to subdivision two of section 245.70 of this article; except that the prosecution shall notify the defendant in writing that such information has not been disclosed, and such disclosure shall be made as soon as practicable and not later than sixty calendar days before the first scheduled trial date, unless an order is obtained pursuant to section 245.70 of this article. When the prosecution's expert witness is being called in response to disclosure of an expert witness by the defendant, the court shall alter a scheduled trial date, if necessary, to allow the prosecution thirty calendar days to make the disclosure and the defendant thirty calendar days to prepare and respond to the new materials.   *(Eff.5/3/20,Ch.56,L.2020)*

(g) All tapes or other electronic recordings, including all electronic recordings of 911 telephone calls made or received in connection with the alleged criminal incident, and a designation by the prosecutor as to which of the recordings under this paragraph the prosecution intends to introduce at trial or a pre-trial hearing. If the discoverable materials under this paragraph exceed ten hours in total length, the prosecution may disclose only the recordings that it intends to introduce at trial or a pre-trial hearing, along with a list of the source and approximate quantity of other recordings and their general subject matter if known, and the defendant shall have the right upon request to obtain recordings not previously disclosed. The prosecution shall disclose the requested materials as soon as practicable and not less than fifteen calendar days after the defendant's request, unless an order is obtained pursuant to section 245.70 of this article. The prosecution may withhold the names and identifying information of any person who contacted 911 without the need for a protective order pursuant to section 245.70 of this article, provided, however, the defendant may move the court for disclosure. If the prosecution intends to call such person as a witness at a trial or hearing, the prosecution must disclose the name and contact information of such witness no later than fifteen days before such trial or hearing, or as soon as practicable.   *(Eff.5/3/20,Ch.56,L.2020)*

(h) All photographs and drawings made or completed by a public servant engaged in law enforcement activity, or which were made by a person whom the prosecutor intends to call as a witness at trial or a pre-trial hearing, or which relate to the subject matter of the case.

(i) All photographs, photocopies and reproductions made by or at the direction of law enforcement personnel of any property prior to its release pursuant to section 450.10 of the penal law.

(j) All reports, documents, records, data, calculations or writings, including but not limited to preliminary tests and screening results and bench notes and analyses performed or stored electronically, concerning physical or mental examinations, or scientific tests or experiments or comparisons, relating to the criminal action or proceeding which were made by or at the request or direction of a public servant engaged in law enforcement activity, or which were made by a person whom the prosecutor intends to call as a witness at trial or a pre-trial hearing, or which the prosecution intends to introduce at trial or a pre-trial hearing. Information under this paragraph also includes, but is not limited to, laboratory information management system records relating to such materials, any preliminary or final findings of non-conformance with accreditation, industry or governmental standards or laboratory protocols, and any conflicting analyses or results by laboratory personnel regardless of the laboratory's final analysis or results. If the prosecution submitted one or more items for testing to, or received results from, a forensic science laboratory or similar entity not under the prosecution's direction or control, the court on motion of a party shall issue subpoenas or orders to such laboratory or entity to cause materials under this paragraph to be made available for disclosure. The prosecution shall not be required to provide information related to the results of physical or mental examinations, or scientific tests or experiments or comparisons, unless and until such examinations, tests, experiments, or comparisons have been completed. *(Eff.5/3/20,Ch.56,L.2020)*

(k) All evidence and information, including that which is known to police or other law enforcement agencies acting on the government's behalf in the case, that tends to: (i) negate the defendant's guilt as to a charged offense; (ii) reduce the degree of or mitigate the defendant's culpability as to a charged offense; (iii) support a potential defense to a charged offense; (iv) impeach the credibility of a testifying prosecution witness; (v) undermine evidence of the defendant's identity as a perpetrator of a charged offense; (vi) provide a basis for a motion to suppress evidence; or (vii) mitigate punishment. Information under this subdivision shall be disclosed whether or not such information is recorded in tangible form and irrespective of whether the prosecutor credits the information. The prosecutor shall disclose the information expeditiously upon its receipt and shall not delay disclosure if it is obtained earlier than the time period for disclosure in subdivision one of section 245.10 of this article.

(*l*) A summary of all promises, rewards and inducements made to, or in favor of, persons who may be called as witnesses, as well as requests for consideration by persons who may be called as witnesses and copies of all documents relevant to a promise, reward or inducement.

(m) A list of all tangible objects obtained from, or allegedly possessed by, the defendant or a co-defendant. The list shall include a designation by the prosecutor as to which objects were physically or constructively possessed by the defendant and were recovered during a search or seizure by a public servant or an agent thereof, and which tangible objects were recovered by a public servant or an agent thereof after allegedly being abandoned by the defendant. If the prosecution intends to prove the defendant's possession of any tangible objects by means of a statutory presumption of possession, it shall designate such intention as to each such object. If reasonably practicable, the prosecution shall also designate the location from which each tangible object was recovered. There is also a right to inspect, copy, photograph and test the listed tangible objects.

(n) Whether a search warrant has been executed and all documents relating thereto, including but not limited to the warrant, the warrant application, supporting affidavits, a police inventory of all property seized under the warrant, and a transcript of all testimony or other oral communications offered in support of the warrant application.

(o) All tangible property that relates to the subject matter of the case, along with a designation of which items the prosecution intends to introduce in its case-in-chief at trial or a pre-trial hearing. If in the exercise of reasonable diligence the prosecutor has not formed an intention within the time period specified in subdivision one of section 245.10 of this article that an item under this subdivision will be introduced at trial or a pre-trial hearing, the prosecution shall notify the defendant in writing, and the time period in which to designate items as exhibits shall be stayed without need for a motion pursuant to subdivision two of section 245.70 of this article; but the disclosure shall be made as soon as practicable and subject to the continuing duty to disclose in section 245.60 of this article.

(p) A complete record of judgments of conviction for all defendants and all persons designated as potential prosecution witnesses pursuant to paragraph (c) of this subdivision, other than those witnesses who are experts.

(q) When it is known to the prosecution, the existence of any pending criminal action against all persons designated as potential prosecution witnesses pursuant to paragraph (c) of this subdivision.

(r) The approximate date, time and place of the offense or offenses charged and of the defendant's seizure and arrest.

(s) In any prosecution alleging a violation of the vehicle and traffic law, where the defendant is charged by indictment, superior court information, prosecutor's information, information, or simplified information, all records of calibration, certification, inspection, repair or maintenance of machines and instruments utilized to perform any scientific tests and experiments, including but not limited to any test of a person's breath, blood, urine or saliva, for the period of six months prior and six months after such test was conducted, including the records of gas chromatography related to the certification of all reference standards and the certification certificate, if any, held by the operator of the machine or instrument. The time period required by subdivision one of section 245.10 of this article shall not apply to the disclosure of records created six months after a test was conducted, but such disclosure shall be made as soon as practicable and in any event, the earlier of fifteen days following receipt, or fifteen days before the first scheduled trial date.

(t) In any prosecution alleging a violation of section 156.05 or 156.10 of the penal law, the time, place and manner such violation occurred.

(u) (i) A copy of all electronically created or stored information seized or obtained by or on behalf of law enforcement from: (A) the defendant as described in subparagraph (ii) of this paragraph; or (B) a source other than the defendant which relates to the subject matter of the case.

(ii) If the electronically created or stored information originates from a device, account, or other electronically stored source that the prosecution believes the defendant owned, maintained, or had lawful access to and is within the possession, custody or control of the prosecution or persons under the prosecution's direction or control, the prosecution shall provide a complete copy of the electronically created or stored information from the device or account or other source.

(iii) If possession of such electronically created or stored information would be a crime under New York state or federal law, the prosecution shall make those portions of the electronically created or stored information that are not criminal to possess available as specified under this paragraph and shall afford counsel for the defendant access to inspect contraband portions at a supervised location that provides regular and reasonable hours for such access, such as a prosecutor's office, police station, or court.

(iv) This paragraph shall not be construed to alter or in any way affect the right to be free from unreasonable searches and seizures or such other rights a suspect or defendant may derive from the state constitution or the United States constitution. If in the exercise of reasonable diligence the information under this paragraph is not available for disclosure within the time period required by subdivision one of section 245.10 of this article, that period shall be stayed without need for a motion pursuant to subdivision two of section 245.70 of this article, except that the prosecution shall notify the defendant in writing that such information has not been disclosed, and such disclosure shall be made as soon as practicable and not later than forty-five calendar days before the first scheduled trial date, unless an order is obtained pursuant to section 245.70 of this article.

2. Duties of the prosecution. The prosecutor shall make a diligent, good faith effort to ascertain the existence of material or information discoverable under subdivision one of this section and to cause such material or information to be made available for discovery where it exists but is not within the prosecutor's possession, custody or control; provided that the prosecutor shall not be required to obtain by subpoena duces tecum material or information which the defendant may thereby obtain. For purposes of subdivision one of this section, all items and information related to the prosecution of a charge in the possession of any New York state or local police or law enforcement agency shall be deemed to be in the possession of the prosecution. The prosecution shall also identify any laboratory having contact with evidence related to the prosecution of a charge. This subdivision shall not require the prosecutor to ascertain the existence of witnesses not known to the police or another law enforcement agency, or the written or recorded statements thereof, under paragraph (c) or (e) of subdivision one of this section.

3. Supplemental discovery for the defendant. The prosecution shall disclose to the defendant a list of all misconduct and criminal acts of the defendant not charged in the indictment, superior court information, prosecutor's information, information, or simplified information, which the prosecution intends to use at trial for purposes of (a) impeaching the credibility of the defendant, or (b) as substantive proof of any material issue in the case. In addition the prosecution shall designate whether it intends to use each listed act for impeachment and/or as substantive proof.

4. Reciprocal discovery for the prosecution. (a) The defendant shall, subject to constitutional limitations, disclose to the prosecution, and permit the prosecution to discover, inspect, copy or photograph, any material and relevant evidence within the defendant's or counsel for the defendant's possession or control that is discoverable under paragraphs (f), (g), (h), (j), (l) and (o) of subdivision one of this section, which the defendant intends to introduce at trial or a pre-trial hearing, and the names, addresses, birth dates, and all statements, written or recorded or summarized in any writing or recording, of those persons other than the defendant whom the defendant intends to call as witnesses at trial or a pre-trial hearing.

(b) Disclosure of the name, address, birth date, and all statements, written or recorded or summarized in any writing or recording, of a person whom the defendant intends to call as a witness for the sole purpose of impeaching a prosecution witness is not required until after the prosecution witness has testified at trial.

(c) If in the exercise of reasonable diligence the reciprocally discoverable information under paragraph (f) or (o) of subdivision one of this section is unavailable for disclosure within the time period specified in subdivision two of section 245.10 of this article, such time period shall be stayed without need for a motion pursuant to subdivision two of section 245.70 of this article; but the disclosure shall be made as soon as practicable and subject to the continuing duty to disclose in section 245.60 of this article.

5. Stay of automatic discovery; remedies and sanctions. Section 245.10 and subdivisions one, two, three and four of this section shall have the force and effect of a court order, and failure to provide discovery pursuant to such section or subdivision may result in application of any remedies or sanctions permitted for non-compliance with a court order under section 245.80 of this article. However, if in the judgment of either party good cause exists for declining to make any of the disclosures set forth above, such party may move for a protective order pursuant to section 245.70 of this article and

production of the item shall be stayed pending a ruling by the court. The opposing party shall be notified in writing that information has not been disclosed under a particular section. When some parts of material or information are discoverable but in the judgment of a party good cause exists for declining to disclose other parts, the discoverable parts shall be disclosed and the disclosing party shall give notice in writing that non-discoverable parts have been withheld.

6. Redactions permitted. Either party may redact social security numbers and tax numbers from disclosures under this article.

7. Presumption of openness. There shall be a presumption in favor of disclosure when interpreting sections 245.10 and 245.25, and subdivision one of section 245.20, of this article.

§245.25 Disclosure prior to certain guilty pleas.

1. Pre-indictment guilty pleas. Upon a felony complaint, where the prosecution has made a pre-indictment guilty plea offer requiring a plea to a crime, the prosecutor must disclose to the defense, and permit the defense to discover, inspect, copy, photograph and test, all items and information that would be discoverable prior to trial under subdivision one of section 245.20 of this article and are in the possession, custody or control of the prosecution. The prosecution shall disclose the discoverable items and information not less than three calendar days prior to the expiration date of any guilty plea offer by the prosecution or any deadline imposed by the court for acceptance of the guilty plea offer. If the prosecution does not comply with the requirements of this subdivision, then, on a defendant's motion alleging a violation of this subdivision, the court must consider the impact of any violation on the defendant's decision to accept or reject a plea offer. If the court finds that such violation materially affected the defendant's decision, and if the prosecution declines to reinstate the lapsed or withdrawn plea offer, the court - as a presumptive minimum sanction - must preclude the admission at trial of any evidence not disclosed as required under this subdivision. The court may take other appropriate action as necessary to address the non-compliance. The rights under this subdivision do not apply to items or information that are the subject of a protective order under section 245.70 of this article; but if such information tends to be exculpatory, the court shall reconsider the protective order. A defendant may waive his or her rights under this subdivision; but a guilty plea offer may not be conditioned on such waiver.

2. Other guilty pleas. Upon an indictment, superior court information, prosecutor's information, information, simplified information, or misdemeanor complaint, where the prosecution has made a guilty plea offer requiring a plea to a crime, the prosecutor must disclose to the defense, and permit the defense to discover, inspect, copy, photograph and test, all items and information that would be discoverable prior to trial under subdivision one of section 245.20 of this article and are within the possession, custody or control of the prosecution. The prosecution shall disclose the discoverable items and information not less than seven calendar days prior to the expiration date of any guilty plea offer by the prosecution or any deadline imposed by the court for acceptance of the guilty plea offer. If the prosecution does not comply with the requirements of this subdivision, then, on a defendant's motion alleging a violation of this subdivision, the court must consider the impact of any violation on the defendant's decision to accept or reject a plea offer. If the court finds that such violation materially affected the defendant's decision, and if the prosecution declines to reinstate the lapsed or withdrawn plea offer, the court - as a presumptive

minimum sanction - must preclude the admission at trial of any evidence not disclosed as required under this subdivision. The court may take other appropriate action as necessary to address the non-compliance. The rights under this subdivision do not apply to items or information that are the subject of a protective order under section 245.70 of this article; but if such information tends to be exculpatory, the court shall reconsider the protective order. A defendant may waive his or her rights under this subdivision; but a guilty plea offer may not be conditioned on such waiver. Notwithstanding the timelines contained in the opening paragraph of paragraph (a) of subdivision one of section 245.10 of this article, the prosecutor's discovery obligation under subdivision one of section 245.20 of this article shall be performed as soon as practicable, but not later than fifteen days before the trial of a simplified information charging a traffic infraction under the vehicle and traffic law, or by an information charging one or more petty offenses as defined by the municipal code of a village, town, city, or county, that do not carry a statutorily authorized sentence of imprisonment, and where the defendant stands charged before the court with no crime or offense, provided however that nothing in this subdivision shall prevent a defendant from filing a motion for disclosure of such items and information under subdivision one of such section 245.20 of this article at an earlier date.

(Eff.5/3/20,Ch.56,L.2020)

3. Repleader. Nothing in this section shall prevent the waiver of discovery from being a condition of a repleader, where the defendant's original conviction is vacated on agreement between the parties pursuant to section 440.10 of this part. *(Eff.5/3/20,Ch.56,L.2020)*

§245.30 Court orders for preservation, access or discovery.

1. Order to preserve evidence. At any time, a party may move for a court order to any individual, agency or other entity in possession, custody or control of items which relate to the subject matter of the case or are otherwise relevant, requiring that such items be preserved for a specified period of time. The court shall hear and rule upon such motions expeditiously. The court may modify or vacate such an order upon a showing that preservation of particular evidence will create significant hardship to such individual, agency or entity, on condition that the probative value of that evidence is preserved by a specified alternative means.

2. Order to grant access to premises. Without prejudice to its ability to issue a subpoena pursuant to this chapter and after an accusatory instrument has been filed, the defendant may move, upon notice to the prosecution and any impacted individual, agency, or entity, for a court order to access a crime scene or other premises relevant to the subject matter of the case, requiring that counsel for the defendant be granted reasonable access to inspect, photograph, or measure such crime scene or premises, and that the condition of the crime scene or premises remain unchanged in the interim. The court shall consider defendant's expressed need for access to the premises including the risk that defendant will be deprived of evidence or information relevant to the case, the position of any individual or entity with possessory or ownership rights to the premises, the nature of the privacy interest and any perceived or actual hardship of the individual or entity with possessory or ownership rights, and the position of the prosecution with respect to any application for access to the premises. The court may deny access to the premises when the probative value of access to such location has been or will be preserved by specified alternative means. If the court grants access to the premises, the individual or entity with ownership or possessory rights to the premises may request law

enforcement presence at the premises while defense counsel or a
representative thereof is present.

3. Discretionary discovery by order of the court. The court in its discretion
may, upon a showing by the defendant that the request is reasonable and
that the defendant is unable without undue hardship to obtain the
substantial equivalent by other means, order the prosecution, or any
individual, agency or other entity subject to the jurisdiction of the court, to
make available for disclosure to the defendant any material or information
which relates to the subject matter of the case and is reasonably likely to be
material. A motion under this subdivision must be on notice to any person or
entity affected by the order. The court may, on its own, upon request of any
person or entity affected by the order, modify or vacate the order if
compliance would be unreasonable or will create significant hardship. For
good cause shown, the court may permit a party seeking or opposing a
discretionary order of discovery under this subdivision, or another affected
person or entity, to submit papers or testify on the record ex parte or in
camera. For good cause shown, any such papers and a transcript of such
testimony may be sealed and shall constitute a part of the record on appeal.

§245.35 Court ordered procedures to facilitate compliance.

To facilitate compliance with this article, and to reduce or streamline
litigation of any disputes about discovery, the court in its discretion may
issue an order:

1. Requiring that the prosecutor and counsel for the defendant diligently
confer to attempt to reach an accommodation as to any dispute concerning
discovery prior to seeking a ruling from the court;

2. Requiring a discovery compliance conference at a specified time prior
to trial between the prosecutor, counsel for all defendants, and the court or
its staff;

3. Requiring the prosecution to file an additional certificate of compliance
that states that the prosecutor and/or an appropriate named agent has
made reasonable inquiries of all police officers and other persons who have
participated in investigating or evaluating the case about the existence of
any favorable evidence or information within paragraph (k) of subdivision
one of section 245.20 of this article, including such evidence or information
that was not reduced to writing or otherwise memorialized or preserved as
evidence, and has disclosed any such information to the defendant; and/or

4. Requiring other measures or proceedings designed to carry into effect
the goals of this article.

§245.40 Non-testimonial evidence from the defendant.

1. Availability. After the filing of an accusatory instrument, and subject to
constitutional limitations, the court may, upon motion of the prosecution
showing probable cause to believe the defendant has committed the crime,
a clear indication that relevant material evidence will be found, and that the
method used to secure such evidence is safe and reliable, require a
defendant to provide non-testimonial evidence, including to:

(a) Appear in a lineup;
(b) Speak for identification by a witness or potential witness;
(c) Be fingerprinted;
(d) Pose for photographs not involving reenactment of an event;
(e) Permit the taking of samples of the defendant's blood, hair, and
other materials of the defendant's body that involves no unreasonable
intrusion thereof;
(f) Provide specimens of the defendant's handwriting; and

(g) Submit to a reasonable physical or medical inspection of the defendant's body.

2. Limitations. This section shall not be construed to alter or in any way affect the issuance of a similar court order, as may be authorized by law, before the filing of an accusatory instrument, consistent with such rights as the defendant may derive from the state constitution or the United States constitution. This section shall not be construed to alter or in any way affect the administration of a chemical test where otherwise authorized. An order pursuant to this section may be denied, limited or conditioned as provided in section 245.70 of this article.

§245.45 DNA comparison order.

Where property in the prosecution's possession, custody, or control consists of a deoxyribonucleic acid ("DNA") profile obtained from probative biological material gathered in connection with the investigation of the crime, or the defendant, or the prosecution of the defendant, and the defendant establishes (a) that such profile complies with federal bureau of investigation or state requirements, whichever are applicable and as such requirements are applied to law enforcement agencies seeking a keyboard search or similar comparison, and (b) that the data meets state DNA index system or national DNA index system criteria as such criteria are applied to law enforcement agencies seeking such a keyboard search or similar comparison, the court may, upon motion of a defendant against whom an indictment, superior court information, prosecutor's information, information, or simplified information is pending, order an entity that has access to the combined DNA index system or its successor system to compare such DNA profile against DNA databanks by keyboard searches, or a similar method that does not involve uploading, upon notice to both parties and the entity required to perform the search, upon a showing by the defendant that such a comparison is material to the presentation of his or her defense and that the request is reasonable. For purposes of this section, a "keyboard search" shall mean a search of a DNA profile against the databank in which the profile that is searched is not uploaded to or maintained in the databank.

§245.50 Certificates of compliance; readiness for trial.

1. By the prosecution. When the prosecution has provided the discovery required by subdivision one of section 245.20 of this article, except for discovery that is lost or destroyed as provided by paragraph (b) of subdivision one of section 245.80 of this article and except for any items or information that are the subject of an order pursuant to section 245.70 of this article, it shall serve upon the defendant and file with the court a certificate of compliance. The certificate of compliance shall state that, after exercising due diligence and making reasonable inquiries to ascertain the existence of material and information subject to discovery, the prosecutor has disclosed and made available all known material and information subject to discovery. It shall also identify the items provided. If additional discovery is subsequently provided prior to trial pursuant to section 245.60 of this article, a supplemental certificate shall be served upon the defendant and filed with the court identifying the additional material and information provided. No adverse consequence to the prosecution or the prosecutor shall result from the filing of a certificate of compliance in good faith and reasonable under the circumstances; but the court may grant a remedy or sanction for a discovery violation as provided in section 245.80 of this article.

2. By the defendant. When the defendant has provided all discovery required by subdivision four of section 245.20 of this article, except for any items or information that are the subject of an order pursuant to section 245.70 of this article, counsel for the defendant shall serve upon the prosecution and file with the court a certificate of compliance. The certificate shall state that, after exercising due diligence and making reasonable inquiries to ascertain the existence of material and information subject to discovery, counsel for the defendant has disclosed and made available all known material and information subject to discovery. It shall also identify the items provided. If additional discovery is subsequently provided prior to trial pursuant to section 245.60 of this article, a supplemental certificate shall be served upon the prosecution and filed with the court identifying the additional material and information provided. No adverse consequence to the defendant or counsel for the defendant shall result from the filing of a certificate of compliance in good faith; but the court may grant a remedy or sanction for a discovery violation as provided in section 245.80 of this article.

3. Trial readiness. Notwithstanding the provisions of any other law, absent an individualized finding of special circumstances in the instant case by the court before which the charge is pending, the prosecution shall not be deemed ready for trial for purposes of section 30.30 of this chapter until it has filed a proper certificate pursuant to subdivision one of this section. A court may deem the prosecution ready for trial pursuant to section 30.30 of this chapter where information that might be considered discoverable under this article cannot be disclosed because it has been lost, destroyed, or otherwise unavailable as provided by paragraph (b) of subdivision one of section 245.80 of this article, despite diligent and good faith efforts, reasonable under the circumstances. Provided, however, that the court may grant a remedy or sanction for a discovery violation as provided by section 245.80 of this article.

4. Challenges to, or questions related to a certificate of compliance shall be addressed by motion.   *(Eff.5/3/20,Ch.56,L.2020)*

§245.55 Flow of information.

1. Sufficient communication for compliance. The district attorney and the assistant responsible for the case, or, if the matter is not being prosecuted by the district attorney, the prosecuting agency and its assigned representative, shall endeavor to ensure that a flow of information is maintained between the police and other investigative personnel and his or her office sufficient to place within his or her possession or control all material and information pertinent to the defendant and the offense or offenses charged, including, but not limited to, any evidence or information discoverable under paragraph (k) of subdivision one of section 245.20 of this article.

2. Provision of law enforcement agency files. Absent a court order or a requirement that defense counsel obtain a security clearance mandated by law or authorized government regulation, upon request by the prosecution, each New York state and local law enforcement agency shall make available to the prosecution a complete copy of its complete records and files related to the investigation of the case or the prosecution of the defendant for compliance with this article.

3. 911 telephone call and police radio transmission electronic recordings, police worn body camera recordings and other police recordings. (a) Whenever an electronic recording of a 911 telephone call or a police radio transmission or video or audio footage from a police body-worn camera or

other police recording was made or received in connection with the investigation of an apparent criminal incident, the arresting officer or lead detective shall expeditiously notify the prosecution in writing upon the filing of an accusatory instrument of the existence of all such known recordings. The prosecution shall expeditiously take whatever reasonable steps are necessary to ensure that all known electronic recordings of 911 telephone calls, police radio transmissions and video and audio footage and other police recordings made or available in connection with the case are preserved. Upon the defendant's timely request and designation of a specific electronic recording of a 911 telephone call, the prosecution shall also expeditiously take whatever reasonable steps are necessary to ensure that it is preserved.

(b) If the prosecution fails to disclose such an electronic recording to the defendant pursuant to paragraph (e), (g) or (k) of subdivision one of section 245.20 of this article due to a failure to comply with this obligation by police officers or other law enforcement or prosecution personnel, the court upon motion of the defendant shall impose an appropriate remedy or sanction pursuant to section 245.80 of this article.

§245.60 Continuing duty to disclose.

If either the prosecution or the defendant subsequently learns of additional material or information which it would have been under a duty to disclose pursuant to any provisions of this article had it known of it at the time of a previous discovery obligation or discovery order, it shall expeditiously notify the other party and disclose the additional material and information as required for initial discovery under this article. This section also requires expeditious disclosure by the prosecution of material or information that became relevant to the case or discoverable based on reciprocal discovery received from the defendant pursuant to subdivision four of section 245.20 of this article.

§245.65 Work product.

This article does not authorize discovery by a party of those portions of records, reports, correspondence, memoranda, or internal documents of the adverse party which are only the legal research, opinions, theories or conclusions of the adverse party or its attorney or the attorney's agents, or of statements of a defendant, written or recorded or summarized in any writing or recording, made to the attorney for the defendant or the attorney's agents.

§245.70 Protective orders.

1. Any discovery subject to protective order. Upon a showing of good cause by either party, the court may at any time order that discovery or inspection of any kind of material or information under this article be denied, restricted, conditioned or deferred, or make such other order as is appropriate, including, for 911 calls, allowing the disclosure of a transcript of an audio recording in lieu of the recording. The court may impose as a condition on discovery to a defendant that the material or information to be discovered be available only to counsel for the defendant; or, alternatively, that counsel for the defendant, and persons employed by the attorney or appointed by the court to assist in the preparation of a defendant's case, may not disclose physical copies of the discoverable documents to a defendant or to anyone else, provided that the prosecution affords the defendant access to inspect redacted copies of the discoverable documents at a supervised location that provides regular and reasonable hours for such

access, such as a prosecutor's office, police station, facility of detention, or court. Should the court impose as a condition that some material or information be available only to counsel for the defendant, the court shall inform the defendant on the record that his or her attorney is not permitted by law to disclose such material or information to the defendant. The court may permit a party seeking or opposing a protective order under this section, or another affected person, to submit papers or testify on the record ex parte or in camera. Any such papers and a transcript of such testimony may be sealed and shall constitute a part of the record on appeal. This section does not alter the allocation of the burden of proof with regard to matters at issue, including privilege. *(Eff.5/3/20,Ch.56,L.2020)*

2. **Modification of time periods for discovery.** Upon motion of a party in an individual case, the court may alter the time periods for discovery imposed by this article upon a showing of good cause.

3. **Prompt hearing.** Upon request for a protective order, unless the defendant voluntarily consents to the people's request for a protective order, the court shall conduct an appropriate hearing within three business days to determine whether good cause has been shown and when practicable shall render a decision expeditiously. Any materials submitted and a transcript of the proceeding may be sealed and shall constitute a part of the record on appeal. When the defendant is charged with a violent felony offense as defined in section 70.02 of the penal law, or any class A felony other than those defined in article two hundred twenty of the penal law, the court may, at the prosecutor's request, for good cause shown, conduct such hearing in camera and outside the presence of the defendant, provided however that this shall not affect the rights of the court to receive testimony or papers ex-parte or in camera as provided in subdivision one of this section.
(Eff.5/3/20,Ch.56,L.2020)

4. **Showing of good cause.** In determining good cause under this section the court may consider: constitutional rights or limitations; danger to the integrity of physical evidence or the safety of a witness; risk of intimidation, economic reprisal, bribery, harassment or unjustified annoyance or embarrassment to any person, and the nature, severity and likelihood of that risk; a risk of an adverse effect upon the legitimate needs of law enforcement, including the protection of the confidentiality of informants, and the nature, severity and likelihood of that risk; the nature and circumstances of the factual allegations in the case; whether the defendant has a history of witness intimidation or tampering and the nature of that history; the nature of the stated reasons in support of a protective order; the nature of the witness identifying information that is sought to be addressed by a protective order, including the option of employing adequate alternative contact information; danger to any person stemming from factors such as a defendant's substantiated affiliation with a criminal enterprise as defined in subdivision three of section 460.10 of the penal law; and other similar factors found to outweigh the usefulness of the discovery.

5. **Successor counsel or pro se defendant.** In cases in which the attorney-client relationship is terminated prior to trial for any reason, any material or information disclosed subject to a condition that it be available only to counsel for the defendant, or limited in dissemination by protective order or otherwise, shall be provided only to successor counsel for the defendant under the same condition or conditions or be returned to the prosecution, unless the court rules otherwise for good cause shown or the prosecutor gives written consent. Any work product derived from such material or information shall not be provided to the defendant, unless the court rules otherwise or the prosecutor gives written consent. If the

defendant is acting as his or her own attorney, the court may regulate the time, place and manner of access to any discoverable material or information; and it may as appropriate appoint persons to assist the defendant in the investigation or preparation of the case. Upon motion or application of a defendant acting as his or her own attorney, the court may at any time modify or vacate any condition or restriction relating to access to discoverable material or information, for good cause shown.

6. Expedited review of adverse ruling. (a) A party that has unsuccessfully sought, or unsuccessfully opposed the granting of, a protective order under this section relating to the name, address, contact information or statements of a person may obtain expedited review of that ruling by an individual justice of the intermediate appellate court to which an appeal from a judgment of conviction in the case would be taken.

(b) Such review shall be sought within two business days of the adverse or partially adverse ruling, by order to show cause filed with the intermediate appellate court. The order to show cause shall in addition be timely served on the lower court and on the opposing party, and shall be accompanied by a sworn affirmation stating in good faith (i) that the ruling affects substantial interests, and (ii) that diligent efforts to reach an accommodation of the underlying discovery dispute with opposing counsel failed or that no accommodation was feasible; except that service on the opposing party, and a statement regarding efforts to reach an accommodation, are unnecessary where the opposing party was not made aware of the application for a protective order and good cause is shown for omitting service of the order to show cause on the opposing party. The lower court's order subject to review shall be stayed until the appellate justice renders a determination.

(c) The assignment of the individual appellate justice, and the mode of and procedure for the review, shall be determined by rules of the individual appellate courts. The appellate justice may consider any relevant and reliable information bearing on the issue, and may dispense with written briefs other than supporting and opposing materials previously submitted to the lower court. The appellate justice may dispense with the issuance of a written opinion in rendering his or her decision, and when practicable shall render decision and order expeditiously. Such review, decision and order shall not affect the right of a defendant, in a subsequent appeal from a judgment of conviction, to claim as error the ruling reviewed.

7. Compliance with protective order. Any protective order issued under this article is a mandate of the court for purposes of the offense of criminal contempt in subdivision three of section 215.50 of the penal law.

§245.75 Waiver of discovery by defendant.

1. A defendant who does not seek discovery from the prosecution under this article shall so notify the prosecution and the court at the defendant's arraignment on an indictment, superior court information, prosecutor's information, information, or simplified information, or expeditiously thereafter but before receiving discovery from the prosecution pursuant to subdivision one of section 245.20 of this article, and the defendant need not provide discovery to the prosecution pursuant to subdivision four of section 245.20 and section 245.60 of this article. A waiver shall be in writing, signed for the individual case by the counsel for the defendant and filed with the court. The court shall inquire of the defendant on the record to ensure that the defendant understands his or her right to discovery and right to waive discovery. Such a waiver does not alter or in any way affect the procedures, obligations or rights set forth in sections 250.10, 250.20 and 250.30 of this

title, or otherwise established or required by law. The prosecution may not condition a guilty plea offer on the defense's execution of a waiver under this section. Counsel for the defendant may advise his or her client about the defendant's right to discovery and right to waive discovery; such advice shall not constitute a condition of a guilty plea.

2. Nothing in this section shall prevent the waiver of discovery from being a condition of the repleader, where the defendant's original conviction is vacated on agreement between the parties pursuant to section 440.10 of this part.   *(Eff.5/3/20,Ch.56,L.2020)*

§245.80 Remedies or sanctions for non-compliance.

1. Need for remedy or sanction. (a) When material or information is discoverable under this article but is disclosed belatedly, the court shall impose an appropriate remedy or sanction if the party entitled to disclosure shows that it was prejudiced. Regardless of a showing of prejudice the party entitled to disclosure shall be given reasonable time to prepare and respond to the new material.

(b) When material or information is discoverable under this article but cannot be disclosed because it has been lost or destroyed, the court shall impose an appropriate remedy or sanction if the party entitled to disclosure shows that the lost or destroyed material may have contained some information relevant to a contested issue. The appropriate remedy or sanction is that which is proportionate to the potential ways in which the lost or destroyed material reasonably could have been helpful to the party entitled to disclosure.

2. Available remedies or sanctions. For failure to comply with any discovery order imposed or issued pursuant to this article, the court may make a further order for discovery, grant a continuance, order that a hearing be reopened, order that a witness be called or recalled, instruct the jury that it may draw an adverse inference regarding the non-compliance, preclude or strike a witness's testimony or a portion of a witness's testimony, admit or exclude evidence, order a mistrial, order the dismissal of all or some of the charges, or make such other order as it deems just under the circumstances; except that any sanction against the defendant shall comport with the defendant's constitutional right to present a defense, and precluding a defense witness from testifying shall be permissible only upon a finding that the defendant's failure to comply with the discovery obligation or order was willful and motivated by a desire to obtain a tactical advantage.

3. Consequences of non-disclosure of statement of testifying prosecution witness. The failure of the prosecutor or any agent of the prosecutor to disclose any written or recorded statement made by a prosecution witness which relates to the subject matter of the witness's testimony shall not constitute grounds for any court to order a new pre-trial hearing or set aside a conviction, or reverse, modify or vacate a judgment of conviction, in the absence of a showing by the defendant that there is a reasonable possibility that the non-disclosure materially contributed to the result of the trial or other proceeding; provided, however, that nothing in this section shall affect or limit any right the defendant may have to a reopened pre-trial hearing when such statements were disclosed before the close of evidence at trial.

§245.85 Admissibility of discovery.

The fact that a party has indicated during the discovery process an intention to offer specified evidence or to call a specified witness is not admissible in evidence or grounds for adverse comment at a hearing or a trial.

ARTICLE 250 - PRE-TRIAL NOTICES OF DEFENSES

Section
250.10 Notice of intent to proffer psychiatric evidence; examination of defendant upon application of prosecutor.
250.20 Notice of alibi.
250.30 Notice of defenses in offenses involving computers.
250.40 Notice of intent to seek death penalty.

§250.10 Notice of intent to proffer psychiatric evidence; examination of defendant upon application of prosecutor.

1. As used in this section, the term "psychiatric evidence" means:

(a) Evidence of mental disease or defect to be offered by the defendant in connection with the affirmative defense of lack of criminal responsibility by reason of mental disease or defect.

(b) Evidence of mental disease or defect to be offered by the defendant in connection with the affirmative defense of extreme emotional disturbance as defined in paragraph (a) of subdivision one of section 125.25 of the penal law and paragraph (a) of subdivision two of section 125.27 of the penal law.

(c) Evidence of mental disease or defect to be offered by the defendant in connection with any other defense not specified in the preceding paragraphs.

2. Psychiatric evidence is not admissible upon a trial unless the defendant serves upon the people and files with the court a written notice of his intention to present psychiatric evidence. Such notice must be served and filed before trial and not more than thirty days after entry of the plea of not guilty to the indictment. In the interest of justice and for good cause shown, however, the court may permit such service and filing to be made at any later time prior to the close of the evidence.

3. When a defendant, pursuant to subdivision two of this section, serves notice of intent to present psychiatric evidence, the district attorney may apply to the court, upon notice to the defendant, for an order directing that the defendant submit to an examination by a psychiatrist or licensed psychologist as defined in article one hundred fifty-three of the education law designated by the district attorney. If the application is granted, the psychiatrist or psychologist designated to conduct the examination must notify the district attorney and counsel for the defendant of the time and place of the examination. Defendant has a right to have his counsel present at such examination. The district attorney may also be present. The role of each counsel at such examination is that of an observer, and neither counsel shall be permitted to take an active role at the examination.

4. After the conclusion of the examination, the psychiatrist or psychologist must promptly prepare a written report of his findings and evaluation. A copy of such report must be made available to the district attorney and to the counsel for the defendant. No transcript or recording of the examination is required, but if one is made, it shall be made available to both parties prior to the trial.

5. If the court finds that the defendant has willfully refused to cooperate fully in the examination ordered pursuant to subdivision three of this section it may preclude introduction of testimony by a psychiatrist or psychologist concerning mental disease or defect of the defendant at trial. Where, however, the defendant has other proof of his affirmative defense, and the court has found that the defendant did not submit to or cooperate fully in the examination ordered by the court, this other evidence, if otherwise competent, shall be admissible. In such case, the court must instruct the jury that the defendant did not submit to or cooperate fully in the pretrial

psychiatric examination ordered by the court pursuant to subdivision three of this section and that such failure may be considered in determining the merits of the affirmative defense.

§250.20 Notice of alibi.

1. At any time, not more than twenty days after arraignment, the people may serve upon the defendant or his counsel, and file a copy thereof with the court, a demand that if the defendant intends to offer a trial defense that at the time of the commission of the crime charged he was at some place or places other than the scene of the crime, and to call witnesses in support of such defense, he must, within eight days of service of such demand, serve upon the people, and file a copy thereof with the court, a "notice of alibi," reciting (a) the place or places where the defendant claims to have been at the time in question, and (b) the names, the residential addresses, the places of employment and the addresses thereof of every such alibi witness upon whom he intends to rely. For good cause shown, the court may extend the period for service of the notice.

2. Within a reasonable time after receipt of the defendant's witness list but not later than ten days before trial, the people must serve upon the defendant or his counsel, and file a copy thereof with the court, a list of the witnesses the people propose to offer in rebuttal to discredit the defendant's alibi at the trial together with the residential addresses, the places of employment and the addresses thereof of any such rebuttal witnesses. A witness who will testify that the defendant was at the scene of the crime is not such an alibi rebuttal witness. For good cause shown, the court may extend the period for service of the list of witnesses by the people.

3. If at the trial the defendant calls such an alibi witness without having served the demanded notice of alibi, or if having served such a notice he calls a witness not specified therein, the court may exclude any testimony of such witness relating to the alibi defense. The court may in its discretion receive such testimony, but before doing so, it must, upon application of the people, grant an adjournment not in excess of three days.

4. Similarly, if the people fail to serve and file a list of any rebuttal witnesses, the provisions of subdivision three, above, shall reciprocally apply.

5. Both the defendant and the people shall be under a continuing duty to promptly disclose the names and addresses of additional witnesses which come to the attention of either party subsequent to filing their witness lists as provided in this section.

§250.30 Notice of defenses in offenses involving computers.

1. In any prosecution in which the defendant seeks to invoke any of the defenses specified in section 156.50 of the penal law, the defendant must within forty-five days after arraignment and not less than twenty days before

the commencement of the trial serve upon the people and file with the court a written notice of his intention to present such defense. For good cause shown, the court may extend the period for service of the notice.

2. The notice served must specify the subdivision or subdivisions upon which the defendant relies and must also state the reasonable grounds that led the defendant to believe that he had the authorization required by the statute or the right required by the statute to engage in such conduct. 3. If at the trial the defendant seeks to invoke any of the defenses specified in section 156.50 of the penal law without having served the notice as required, or seeks to invoke a subdivision or a ground not specified in the notice, the court may exclude any testimony or evidence in regard to the defense, or any subdivision or ground, not noticed. The court may in its discretion, for good cause shown, receive such testimony or evidence, but before doing so, it may, upon application of the people, grant an adjournment.

§250.40 Notice of intent to seek death penalty.

1. A sentence of death may not be imposed upon a defendant convicted of murder in the first degree unless, pursuant to subdivision two of this section, the people file with the court and serve upon the defendant a notice of intent to seek the death penalty.

2. In any prosecution in which the people seek a sentence of death, the people shall, within one hundred twenty days of the defendant's arraignment upon an indictment charging the defendant with murder in the first degree, serve upon the defendant and file with the court in which the indictment is pending a written notice of intention to seek the death penalty. For good cause shown the court may extend the period for service and filing of the notice.

3. Notwithstanding any other provisions of law, where the people file a notice of intent to seek the death penalty pursuant to this section the defendant shall be entitled to an additional sixty days for the purpose of filing new motions or supplementing pending motions.

4. A notice of intent to seek the death penalty may be withdrawn at any time by a written notice of withdrawal filed with the court and served upon the defendant. Once withdrawn the notice of intent to seek the death penalty may not be refiled.

ARTICLE 255 - PRE-TRIAL MOTIONS
Section
255.10 Definitions.
255.20 Pre-trial motions; procedure.

§255.10 Definitions.

1.* "Pre-trial motion" as used in this article means any motion by a defendant which seeks an order of the court:

(a) dismissing or reducing an indictment pursuant to article 210 or removing an action to the family court pursuant to article 722; or

(b) dismissing an information, prosecutor's information, simplified information or misdemeanor complaint pursuant to article 170; or

(c) granting discovery pursuant to article 245; or
(Eff. 1/20/20, Ch. 59, L. 2019)

(d) granting a bill of particulars pursuant to sections 100.45 of 200.90; or

(e) removing the action pursuant to sections 170.15, 230.20 or 230.30; or

(f) suppressing the use at trial of any evidence pursuant to article 710;
or

(g) granting separate trials pursuant to article 100 or 200.

(So in original. No subdivision 2 enacted.)

§255.20 Pre-trial motions; procedure.

1. Except as otherwise expressly provided by law, whether the defendant is represented by counsel or elects to proceed pro se, all pre-trial motions shall be served or filed within forty-five days after arraignment and before commencement of trial, or within such additional time as the court may fix upon application of the defendant made prior to entry of judgment. In an action in which either (a) material or information has been disclosed pursuant to paragraph (m) or (n) of subdivision one of section 245.20 of this title, (b) an eavesdropping warrant and application have been furnished pursuant to section 700.70 of this chapter, or (c) a notice of intention to introduce evidence has been served pursuant to section 710.30 of this chapter, such period shall be extended until forty-five days after the last date of such service. If the defendant is not represented by counsel and has requested an adjournment to obtain counsel or to have counsel assigned, such forty-five day period shall commence on the date counsel initially appears on defendant's behalf.   *(Eff.1/20/20,Ch.59,L.2019)*

2. All pre-trial motions, with supporting affidavits, affirmations, exhibits and memoranda of law, whenever practicable, shall be included within the same set of motion papers, and shall be made returnable on the same date, unless the defendant shows that it would be prejudicial to the defense were a single judge to consider all the pre-trial motions. Where one motion seeks to provide the basis for making another motion, it shall be deemed impracticable to include both motions in the same set of motion papers pursuant to this subdivision.

3. Notwithstanding the provisions of subdivisions one and two hereof, the court must entertain and decide on its merits, at any time before the end of the trial, any appropriate pre-trial motion based upon grounds of which the defendant could not, with due diligence, have been previously aware, or which for other good cause, could not reasonably have been raised within the period specified in subdivision one of this section or included within the single set of motion papers as required by subdivision two. Any other pre-trial motion made after the forty-five day period may be summarily denied, but the court, in the interest of justice, and for good cause shown, may, in its discretion, at any time before sentence, entertain and dispose of the motion on the merits.

4. Any pre-trial motion, whether made before or after expiration of the period specified in subdivision one of this section, may be referred by the court to a judicial hearing officer who shall entertain it in the same manner as a court. In the discharge of this responsibility, the judicial hearing officer shall have the same powers as a judge of the court making the assignment, except that the judicial hearing officer shall not determine the motion but shall file a report with the court setting forth findings of fact and conclusions of law. The rules of evidence shall be applicable at any hearing conducted hereunder by a judicial hearing officer. A transcript of any testimony taken, together with the exhibits or copies thereof, shall be filed with the report. The court shall determine the motion on the motion papers, affidavits and other documents submitted by the parties thereto, the record of the hearing before the judicial hearing officer, and the judicial hearing officer's report.

ARTICLE 260 - JURY TRIAL--GENERALLY

Section
260.10 Jury trial; requirement thereof.
260.20 Jury trial; defendant's presence at trial.
260.30 Jury trial; in what order to proceed.

§260.10 Jury trial; requirement thereof.
Except as otherwise provided in section 320.10, every trial of an indictment must be a jury trial.

§260.20 Jury trial; defendant's presence at trial.
A defendant must be personally present during the trial of an indictment; provided, however, that a defendant who conducts himself in so disorderly and disruptive a manner that his trial cannot be carried on with him in the courtroom may be removed from the courtroom if, after he has been warned by the court that he will be removed if he continues such conduct, he continues to engage in such conduct.

§260.30 Jury trial; in what order to proceed.
The order of a jury trial, in general, is as follows:
1. The jury must be selected and sworn.
2. The court must deliver preliminary instructions to the jury.
3. The people must deliver an opening address to the jury.
4. The defendant may deliver an opening address to the jury.
5. The people must offer evidence in support of the indictment.
6. The defendant may offer evidence in his defense.
7. The people may offer evidence in rebuttal of the defense evidence, and the defendant may then offer evidence in rebuttal of the people's rebuttal evidence. The court may in its discretion permit the parties to offer further rebuttal or surrebuttal evidence in this pattern. In the interest of justice, the court may permit either party to offer evidence upon rebuttal which is not technically of a rebuttal nature but more properly a part of the offering party's original case.
8. At the conclusion of the evidence, the defendant may deliver a summation to the jury.
9. The people may then deliver a summation to the jury.
10. The court must then deliver a charge to the jury.
11. The jury must then retire to deliberate and, if possible, render a verdict.

ARTICLE 270 - JURY TRIAL--FORMATION AND CONDUCT OF JURY

Section
270.05 Trial jury; formation in general.
270.10 Trial jury; challenge to the panel.
270.15 Trial jury; examination of prospective jurors; challenges generally.
270.16 Capital cases; individual questioning for racial bias.
270.20 Trial jury; challenge for cause of an individual juror.
270.25 Trial jury; peremptory challenge of an individual juror.
270.30 Trial jury; alternate jurors.
270.35 Trial jury; discharge of juror; replacement by alternate juror.
270.40 Trial jury; preliminary instructions by court.
270.45 Trial jury; when separation permitted.
270.50 Trial jury; viewing of premises.
270.55 Sentencing jury in capital cases.

§270.05 Trial jury; formation in general.

1. A trial jury consists of twelve jurors, but "alternate jurors" may be selected and sworn pursuant to section 270.30.

2. The panel from which the jury is drawn is formed and selected as prescribed in the judiciary law. The first twelve members of the panel returned for the term who appear as their names are drawn and called, and who are not excluded as prescribed by this article, must be sworn and thereupon constitute the trial jury.

§270.10 Trial jury; challenge to the panel.

1. A challenge to the panel is an objection made to the entire panel of prospective trial jurors returned for the term and may be taken to such panel or to any additional panel that may be ordered by the court. Such a challenge may be made only by the defendant and only on the ground that there has been such a departure from the requirements of the judiciary law in the drawing or return of the panel as to result in substantial prejudice to the defendant.

2. A challenge to the panel must be made before the selection of the jury commences and, if it is not, such challenge is deemed to have been waived. Such challenge must be made in writing setting forth the facts constituting the ground of challenge. If such facts are denied by the people, witnesses may be called and examined by either party. All issues of fact and law arising on the challenge must be tried and determined by the court. If a challenge to the panel is allowed, the court must discharge that panel and order another panel of prospective trial jurors returned for the term.

§270.15 Trial jury; examination of prospective jurors; challenges generally.

1. (a) If no challenge to the panel is made as prescribed by section 270.10, or if such challenge is made and disallowed, the court shall direct that the names of not less than twelve members of the panel be drawn and called as prescribed by the judiciary law. Such persons shall take their places in the jury box and shall be immediately sworn to answer truthfully questions asked them relative to their qualifications to serve as jurors in the action. In its discretion, the court may require prospective jurors to complete a questionnaire concerning their ability to serve as fair and impartial jurors, including but not limited to place of birth, current address, education, occupation, prior jury service, knowledge of, relationship to, or contact with the court, any party, witness or attorney in the action and any other fact relevant to his or her service on the jury. An official form for such questionnaire shall be developed by the chief administrator of the courts in consultation with the administrative board of the courts. A copy of questionnaires completed by the members of the panel shall be given to the court and each attorney prior to examination of prospective jurors.

(b) The court shall initiate the examination of prospective jurors by identifying the parties and their respective counsel and briefly outlining the nature of case to all the prospective jurors. The court shall then put to the members of the panel who have been sworn pursuant to this subdivision and to any prospective jurors subsequently sworn, questions affecting their qualifications to serve as jurors in the action.

(c) The court shall permit both parties, commencing with the people, to examine the prospective jurors, individually or collectively, regarding their qualifications to serve as jurors. Each party shall be afforded a fair opportunity to question the prospective jurors as to any unexplored matter affecting their qualifications, but the court shall not permit questioning that is repetitious or irrelevant, or questions as to a juror's knowledge of rules of law. If necessary to prevent improper questioning as to any matter, the court shall personally examine the prospective jurors as to that matter. The scope of such examination shall be within the discretion of the court. After the parties have concluded their examinations of the prospective jurors, the court may ask such further questions as it deems proper regarding the qualifications of such prospective jurors.

1-a. The court may for good cause shown, upon motion of either party or any affected person or upon its own initiative, issue a protective order for a stated period regulating disclosure of the business or residential address of any prospective or sworn juror to any person or persons, other than to counsel for either party. Such good cause shall exist where the court determines that there is a likelihood of bribery, jury tampering or of physical injury or harassment of the juror.

2. Upon the completion of such examination by both parties, each, commencing with the people, may challenge a prospective juror for cause, as prescribed by section 270.20. If such challenge is allowed, the prospective juror must be excluded from service. After both parties have had an opportunity to challenge for cause, the court must permit them to peremptorily challenge any remaining prospective juror, as prescribed by section 270.25, and such juror must be excluded from service. The people must exercise their peremptory challenges first and may not, after the defendant has exercised his peremptory challenges, make such a challenge to any remaining prospective juror who is then in the jury box. If either party so requests, challenges for cause must be made and determined, and peremptory challenges must be made, within the courtroom but outside of the hearing of the prospective jurors in such manner as not to disclose which party made the challenge. The prospective jurors who are not excluded from service must retain their place in the jury box and must be immediately sworn as trial jurors. They must be sworn to try the action in a just and impartial manner, to the best of their judgment, and to render a verdict according to the law and the evidence.

3. The court may thereupon direct that the persons excluded be replaced in the jury box by an equal number from the panel or, in its discretion, direct that all sworn jurors be removed from the jury box and that the jury box be occupied by such additional number of persons from the panel as the court shall direct. In the court's discretion, sworn jurors who are removed from the jury box as provided herein may be seated elsewhere in the courtroom separate and apart from the unsworn members of the panel or may be removed to the jury room or be allowed to leave the courthouse. The process of jury selection as prescribed herein shall continue until twelve persons are selected and sworn as trial jurors. The juror whose name was first drawn and called must be designated by the court as the foreperson, and no special oath need be administered to him or her. If before twelve jurors are sworn, a juror already sworn becomes unable to serve by reason of illness or other incapacity, the court must discharge him or her and the

selection of the trial jury must be completed in the manner prescribed in this section.

4. A challenge for cause of a prospective juror which is not made before he is sworn as a trial juror shall be deemed to have been waived, except that such a challenge based upon a ground not known to the challenging party at that time may be made at any time before a witness is sworn at the trial. If such challenge is allowed by the court, the juror shall be discharged and the selection of the trial jury shall be completed in the manner prescribed in this section, except that if alternate jurors have been sworn, the alternate juror whose name was first drawn and called shall take the place of the juror so discharged.

§270.16 Capital cases; individual questioning for racial bias.

1. In any case in which the crime charged may be punishable by death, the court shall, upon motion of either party, permit the parties, commencing with the people, to examine the prospective jurors individually and outside the presence of the other prospective jurors regarding their qualifications to serve as jurors. Each party shall be afforded a fair opportunity to question a prospective juror as to any unexplored matter affecting his or her qualifications, including without limitation the possibility of racial bias on the part of the prospective juror, but the court shall not permit questioning that is repetitious or irrelevant, or questions as to a prospective juror's knowledge of rules of law. If necessary to prevent improper questioning as to any matter, the court shall personally examine the prospective jurors as to that matter. The scope of such examination shall be within the discretion of the court. After the parties have concluded their examinations of a prospective juror, the court may ask such further questions as it deems proper regarding the qualifications of the prospective juror.

2. The proceedings provided for in this section shall be conducted on the record; provided, however, that upon motion of either party, and for good cause shown, the court may direct that all or a portion of the record of such proceedings be sealed.

§270.20 Trial jury; challenge for cause of an individual juror.

1. A challenge for cause is an objection to a prospective juror and may be made only on the ground that:

(a) He does not have the qualifications required by the judiciary law; or

(b) He has a state of mind that is likely to preclude him from rendering an impartial verdict based upon the evidence adduced at the trial; or

(c) He is related within the sixth degree by consanguinity or affinity to the defendant, or to the person allegedly injured by the crime charged, or to a prospective witness at the trial, or to counsel for the people or for the defendant; or that he is or was a party adverse to any such person in a civil action; or that he has complained against or been accused by any such person in a criminal action; or that he bears some other relationship to any such person of such nature that it is likely to preclude him from rendering an impartial verdict; or

(d) He was a witness at a preliminary examination or before the grand jury or is to be a witness at the trial; or

(e) He served on the grand jury which found the indictment in issue or served on a trial jury in a prior civil or criminal action involving the same incident charged in such indictment; or

(f) The crime charged may be punishable by death and the prospective juror entertains such conscientious opinions either against or in favor of such punishment as to preclude such juror from rendering an impartial verdict or from properly exercising the discretion conferred upon such juror by law in the determination of a sentence pursuant to section 400.27.

2. All issues of fact or law arising on the challenge must be tried and determined by the court. If the challenge is allowed, the court must exclude the person challenged from service. An erroneous ruling by the court allowing a challenge for cause by the people does not constitute reversible error unless the people have exhausted their peremptory challenges at the time or exhaust them before the selection of the jury is complete. An erroneous ruling by the court denying a challenge for cause by the defendant does not constitute reversible error unless the defendant has exhausted his peremptory challenges at the time or, if he has not, he peremptorily challenges such prospective juror and his peremptory challenges are exhausted before the selection of the jury is complete.

§270.25 Trial jury; peremptory challenge of an individual juror.

1. A peremptory challenge is an objection to a prospective juror for which no reason need be assigned. Upon any peremptory challenge, the court must exclude the person challenged from service.

2. Each party must be allowed the following number of peremptory challenges:

(a) Twenty for the regular jurors if the highest crime charged is a class A felony, and two for each alternate juror to be selected.

(b) Fifteen for the regular jurors if the highest crime charged is a class B or class C felony, and two for each alternate juror to be selected.

(c) Ten for the regular jurors in all other cases, and two for each alternate juror to be selected.

3. When two or more defendants are tried jointly, the number of peremptory challenges prescribed in subdivision two is not multiplied by the number of defendants, but such defendants are to be treated as a single party. In any such case, a peremptory challenge by one or more defendants must be allowed if a majority of the defendants join in such challenge. Otherwise, it must be disallowed.

§270.30 Trial jury; alternate jurors.

1. Immediately after the last trial juror is sworn, the court may in its discretion direct the selection of one or more, but not more than six additional jurors to be known as "alternate jurors", except that, in a prosecution under section 125.27 of the penal law, the court may, in its discretion, direct the selection of as many alternate jurors as the court determines to be appropriate. Alternate jurors must be drawn in the same manner, must have the same qualifications, must be subject to the same examination and challenges for cause and must take the same oath as the regular jurors. After the jury has retired to deliberate, the court must either (1) with the consent of the defendant and the people, discharge the alternate jurors or (2) direct the alternate jurors not to discuss the case and must further direct that they be kept separate and apart from the regular jurors.

2. In any prosecution in which the people seek a sentence of death, the court shall not discharge the alternate jurors when the jury retires to deliberate upon its verdict and the alternate jurors, in the discretion of the court, may be continuously kept together under the supervision of an appropriate public servant or servants until such time as the jury returns its verdict. If the jury returns a verdict of guilty to a charge for which the death penalty may be imposed, the alternate jurors shall not be discharged and shall remain available for service during any separate sentencing proceeding which may be conducted pursuant to section 400.27.

§270.35 Trial jury; discharge of juror; replacement by alternate juror.

1. If at any time after the trial jury has been sworn and before the rendition of its verdict, a juror is unable to continue serving by reason of illness or other incapacity, or for any other reason is unavailable for continued service, or the court finds, from facts unknown at the time of the selection of

the jury, that a juror is grossly unqualified to serve in the case or has engaged in misconduct of a substantial nature, but not warranting the declaration of a mistrial, the court must discharge such juror. If an alternate juror or jurors are available for service, the court must order that the discharged juror be replaced by the alternate juror whose name was first drawn and called, provided, however, that if the trial jury has begun its deliberations, the defendant must consent to such replacement. Such consent must be in writing and must be signed by the defendant in person in open court in the presence of the court. If the discharged juror was the foreperson, the court shall designate as the new foreperson the juror whose name was second drawn and called. If no alternate juror is available, the court must declare a mistrial pursuant to subdivision three of section 280.10.

2. (a) In determining pursuant to this section whether a juror is unable to continue serving by reason of illness or other incapacity, or is for any other reason unavailable for continued service, the court shall make a reasonably thorough inquiry concerning such illness, incapacity or unavailability, and shall attempt to ascertain when such juror will be appearing in court. If such juror fails to appear, or if the court determines that there is no reasonable likelihood such juror will be appearing, in court within two hours of the time set by the court for the trial to resume, the court may presume such juror is unavailable for continued service and may discharge such juror. Nothing contained in this paragraph shall affect the court's discretion, under this or any other provision of law, to discharge a juror who repeatedly fails to appear in court in a timely fashion.

(b) The court shall afford the parties an opportunity to be heard before discharging a juror. If the court discharges a juror pursuant to this subdivision, it shall place on the record the facts and reasons for its determination that such juror is ill, incapacitated or unavailable for continued service.

(c) Nothing contained in this subdivision shall affect the requirements of subdivision one of this section pertaining to the discharge of a juror where the trial jury has begun its deliberations.

§270.40 Trial jury; preliminary instructions by court.

After the jury has been sworn and before the people's opening address, the court must instruct the jury generally concerning its basic functions, duties and conduct. Such instructions must include among other matters, admonitions that the jurors may not converse among themselves or with anyone else upon any subject connected with the trial; that they may not read or listen to any accounts or discussions of the case reported by newspapers or other news media; that they may not visit or view the premises or place where the offense or offenses charged were allegedly committed or any other premises or place involved in the case; that prior to discharge, they may not request, accept, agree to accept, or discuss with any person receiving or accepting, any payment or benefit in consideration for supplying any information concerning the trial; and that they must promptly report to the court any incident within their knowledge involving an attempt by any person improperly to influence any member of the jury.

§270.45 Trial jury; when separation permitted.

During the period extending from the time the jurors are sworn to the time they retire to deliberate upon their verdict, the court may in its discretion either permit them to separate during recesses and adjournments or direct that they be continuously kept together during such periods under the supervision of an appropriate public servant or servants. In the latter case, such public servant or servants may not speak to or communicate with any juror concerning any subject connected with the trial nor permit any other person to do so, and must return the jury to the court room at the next designated trial session.

§270.50 Trial jury; viewing of premises.

1. When the court is of the opinion that a viewing or observation by the jury of the premises or place where an offense on trial was allegedly committed, or of any other premises or place involved in the case, will be helpful to the jury in determining any material factual issue, it may in its discretion, at any time before the commencement of the summations, order that the jury be conducted to such premises or place for such purpose in accordance with the provisions of this section.

2. In such case, the jury must be kept together throughout under the supervision of an appropriate public servant or servants appointed by the court, and the court itself must be present throughout. The prosecutor, the defendant and counsel for the defendant may as a matter of right be present throughout, but such right may be waived.

3. The purpose of such an inspection is solely to permit visual observation by the jury of the premises or place in question, and neither the court, the parties, counsel nor the jurors may engage in discussion or argumentation concerning the significance or implications of anything under observation or concerning any issue in the case.

§270.55 Sentencing jury in capital cases.

During the period extending from when a jury returns a verdict of guilty upon a count of an indictment charging murder in the first degree as defined by section 125.27 of the penal law until a jury retires to deliberate on the sentence pursuant to section 400.27, the court may in its discretion either permit the jurors to separate during recesses and adjournments or direct that they be continuously kept together during such periods under the supervision of an appropriate public servant or servants. In the latter case, such public servant or servants may not speak to or communicate with any juror concerning any subject connected with the sentencing proceeding nor permit any other person to do so, and must return the jury to the court room at the next designated session. Unless otherwise provided for in section 400.27, the provisions of sections 270.35, 270.40 and 270.50 shall govern the sentencing proceeding provided for in section 400.27.

ARTICLE 280 - JURY TRIAL - MOTION FOR A MISTRIAL

Section
280.10 Motion for mistrial.
280.20 Motion for mistrial; status of indictment upon new trial.

§280.10 Motion for mistrial.

At any time during the trial, the court must declare a mistrial and order a new trial of the indictment under the following circumstances:

1. Upon motion of the defendant, when there occurs during the trial an error or legal defect in the proceedings, or conduct inside or outside the courtroom, which is prejudicial to the defendant and deprives him of a fair trial. When such an error, defect or conduct occurs during a joint trial of two or more defendants and a mistrial motion is made by one or more but not by all, the court must declare a mistrial only as to the defendant or defendants making or joining in the motion, and the trial of the other defendant or defendants must proceed;

2. Upon motion of the people, when there occurs during the trial, either inside or outside the courtroom, gross misconduct by the defendant or some person acting on his behalf, or by a juror, resulting in substantial and irreparable prejudice to the people's case. When such misconduct occurs during a joint trial of two or more defendants, and when the court is satisfied that it did not result in substantial prejudice to the people's case as against a particular defendant and that such defendant was in no way responsible for the misconduct, it may not declare a mistrial with respect to such defendant but must proceed with the trial as to him;

3. Upon motion of either party or upon the court's own motion, when it is physically impossible to proceed with the trial in conformity with law.

§280.20   Motion for mistrial; status of indictment upon new trial.

Upon a new trial resulting from an order declaring a mistrial, the indictment is deemed to contain all the counts which it contained at the time the previous trial was commenced, regardless of whether any count was thereafter dismissed by the court prior to the mistrial order.

ARTICLE 290 - JURY TRIAL--TRIAL ORDER OF DISMISSAL

Section
290.10 Trial order of dismissal.

§290.10   Trial order of dismissal.

1. At the conclusion of the people's case or at the conclusion of all the evidence, the court may, except as provided in subdivision two, upon motion of the defendant, (a) issue a "trial order of dismissal," dismissing any count of an indictment upon the ground that the trial evidence is not legally sufficient to establish the offense charged therein or any lesser included offense, or (b) reserve decision on the motion until after the verdict has been rendered and accepted by the court. Where the court has reserved decision and the jury thereafter renders a verdict of guilty, the court shall proceed to determine the motion upon such evidence as it would have been authorized to consider upon the motion had the court not reserved decision. If the court determines that such motion should have been granted upon the ground specified in paragraph (a) herein, it shall enter an order both setting aside the verdict and dismissing any count of the indictment upon such ground. If the jury is discharged before rendition of a verdict the court shall proceed to determine the motion as set forth in this paragraph.

2. Despite the lack of legally sufficient trial evidence in support of a count of an indictment as described in subdivision one, issuance of a trial order of dismissal is not authorized and constitutes error when the trial evidence would have been legally sufficient had the court not erroneously excluded admissible evidence offered by the people.

3. When the court excludes trial evidence offered by the people under such circumstances that the substance or content thereof does not appear in the record, the people may, in anticipation of a possible subsequent trial order of dismissal emanating from the allegedly improper exclusion and erroneously issued in violation of subdivision two, and in anticipation of a possible appeal therefrom pursuant to subdivision two of section 450.20, place upon the record, out of the presence of the jury, an "offer of proof" summarizing the substance or content of such excluded evidence. Upon the subsequent issuance of a trial order of dismissal and an appeal therefrom, such offer of proof constitutes a part of the record on appeal and has the effect and significance prescribed in subdivision two of section 450.40. In the absence of such an order and an appeal therefrom, such offer of proof is not deemed a part of the record and does not constitute such for purposes of an ensuing appeal by the defendant from a judgment of conviction.

4. Upon issuing a trial order of dismissal which dismisses the entire indictment, the court must immediately discharge the defendant from custody if he is in custody of the sheriff or, if he is at liberty on bail, it must exonerate the bail.

ARTICLE 300 - JURY TRIAL - COURT'S CHARGE
AND INSTRUCTIONS TO JURY

Section
300.10 Court's charge; in general.
300.30 Court's charge; submission of indictment to jury; definitions of terms.
300.40 Court's charge; submission of indictment to jury; counts to be submitted.
300.50 Court's charge; submission of lesser included offenses.

§300.10 Court's charge; in general.

1. At the conclusion of the summations, the court must deliver a charge to the jury.

2. In its charge, the court must state the fundamental legal principles applicable to criminal cases in general. Such principles include, but are not limited to, the presumption of the defendant's innocence, the requirement that guilt be proved beyond a reasonable doubt and that the jury may not, in determining the issue of guilt or innocence, consider or speculate concerning matters relating to sentence or punishment., Upon request of a defendant who did not testify in his own behalf, but not otherwise, the court must state that the fact that he did not testify is not a factor from which any inference unfavorable to the defendant may be drawn. The court must also state the material legal principles applicable to the particular case, and, so far as practicable, explain the application of the law to the facts, but it need not marshal or refer to the evidence to any greater extent than is necessary for such explanation.

3. Where a defendant has raised the affirmative defense of lack of criminal responsibility by reason of mental disease or defect, as defined in section 40.15 of the penal law, the court must, without elaboration, instruct the jury as follows: "A jury during its deliberations must never consider or speculate concerning matters relating to the consequences of its verdict. However, because of the lack of common knowledge regarding the consequences of a verdict of not responsible by reason of mental disease or defect, I charge you that if this verdict is rendered by you there will be hearings as to the defendant's present mental condition and, where appropriate, involuntary commitment proceedings."

4. The court must specifically designate and submit, in accordance with the provisions of sections 300.30 and 300.40, those counts and offenses contained and charged in the indictment which the jury are to consider. Such determination must be made, and the parties informed thereof, prior to the summations. In its charge, the court must define each offense so submitted and, except as otherwise expressly provided, it must instruct the jury to render a verdict separately and specifically upon each count submitted to it, and with respect to each defendant if there be more than one, and must require that the verdict upon each such count be one of the following:

(a) "Guilty" of the offense submitted, if there be but one; or

(b) Where appropriate, "guilty" of a specified one of two or more offenses submitted under the same count in the alternative pursuant to section 300.40; or

(c) "Not guilty"; or

(d) Where appropriate, "not responsible by reason of mental disease or defect."

5. Both before and after the court's charge, the parties may submit requests to charge, either orally or in writing, and the court must rule promptly upon each request. A failure to rule upon a request is deemed a denial thereof.

6. In a prosecution involving a charge of enterprise corruption, as defined in article four hundred sixty of the penal law, the court must specifically designate and separately submit for jury consideration those criminal acts which are contained and charged in the indictment and which are supported by legally sufficient trial evidence. Every criminal act which is not so supported shall be dismissed and stricken from the indictment. If legally sufficient trial evidence exists to support a lesser included offense which is also a criminal act within the meaning of subdivision one of section 460.10 of the penal law, such lesser offense shall be substituted. Such determination must be made and the parties informed thereof, prior to the summations. In its charge, the court must define each criminal act so submitted and, as when it may or must do so pursuant to sections 300.40 and 300.50 of this article, any lesser included offense that is also a criminal act within the meaning of subdivision one of section 460.10 of the penal law. It must instruct the jury to render a verdict separately and specifically upon each criminal act (and where necessary, any submitted lesser included offense) submitted to it with respect to each defendant. It must further explain to the jury that they may not consider a charge of enterprise corruption against any defendant until they have separately and unanimously agreed that the defendant has committed each of at least three criminal acts alleged as part of the pattern of criminal activity, including any submitted lesser included offenses.

§300.30 Court's charge; submission of indictment to jury; definitions of terms.
The following definitions are applicable to this article:

1. "Submission of a count" of an indictment means submission of the offense charged therein, or of a lesser included offense, or submission in the alternative of both the offense charged and a lesser included offense or offenses. When the court "submits a count," it must, at the least, submit the offense charged therein if such is supported by legally sufficient trial evidence, or if it is not, the greatest lesser included offense which is supported by legally sufficient trial evidence.

2. "Consecutive counts" means two or more counts of an indictment upon which consecutive sentences may be imposed in case of conviction thereon.

3. "Concurrent counts" means two or more counts of an indictment upon which concurrent sentences only may be imposed in case of conviction thereon.

4. "Inclusory concurrent counts." Concurrent counts are "inclusory" when the offense charged in one is greater than any of those charged in the others and when the latter are all lesser offenses included within the greater. All other kinds of concurrent counts are "non-inclusory.

5. "Inconsistent counts." Two counts are "inconsistent" when guilty of the offense charged in one necessarily negates guilt of the offense charged in the other.

§300.40 Court's charge; submission of indictment to jury; counts to be submitted.

The court may submit to the jury only those counts of an indictment remaining therein at the time of its charge which are supported by legally sufficient trial evidence, and every count not so supported should be dismissed by a trial order of dismissal. The court's determination as to which of the sufficient counts are to be submitted must be in accordance with the following rules:

1. If the indictment contains but one count, the court must submit such count.

2. If a multiple count indictment contains consecutive counts only, the court must submit every count thereof.

3. If a multiple count indictment contains concurrent counts of murder in the first degree, the court must submit every such count. In any other case, if a multiple count indictment contains concurrent counts only, the court must submit at least one such count, and may submit more than one as follows:

(a) With respect to non-inclusory concurrent counts, the court may in its discretion submit one or more or all thereof;

(b) With respect to inclusory concurrent counts, the court must submit the greatest or inclusive count and may or must, under circumstances prescribed in section 300.50, also submit, but in the alternative only, one or more of the lesser included counts. A verdict of guilty upon the greatest count submitted is deemed a dismissal of every lesser count submitted, but not an acquittal thereon. A verdict of guilty upon a lesser count is deemed an acquittal upon every greater count submitted.

4. If a multiple count indictment contains two or more groups of counts, with the counts within each group being concurrent as to each other but consecutive as to those of the other group or groups, the court must submit at least one count of each group, in the manner prescribed in subdivision three. If an indictment contains one or more of such groups of concurrent counts, and also one or more other counts each of which is consecutive as to every other count of the indictment, the court must submit each individual consecutive count and at least one count of each group of concurrent counts.

5. If an indictment contains two inconsistent counts, the court must submit at least one thereof. If a verdict of guilty upon either would be supported by legally sufficient trial evidence, the court may submit both counts in the alternative and authorize the jury to convict upon one or the other depending upon its findings of fact. In such case, the court must direct the jury that if it renders a verdict of guilty upon one such count it must render a verdict of not guilty upon the other. If the court is satisfied that a conviction upon one such count, though supported by legally sufficient trial evidence, would be against the weight of the evidence while a conviction upon the other would not, it may in its discretion submit the latter count only.

6. Notwithstanding any other provision of this section, the court is not required to submit any particular count to the jury when:

(a) The people consent that it not be submitted; except that nothing contained in this paragraph limits the right accorded a defendant by section 300.50 to the submission, in certain situations, of counts charging lesser included offenses; or

(b) The number of counts or the complexity of the indictment requires selectivity of counts by the court in order to avoid placing an unduly heavy burden upon the jury in its consideration of the case. In such case, the court may submit to the jury a portion of the counts which are representative of the people's case.

7. Every count not submitted to the jury is deemed to have been dismissed by the court. Where the court, over objection of the people, refuses to submit a count which is consecutive as to every count actually submitted, such count is deemed to have been dismissed by a trial order of dismissal even though no such order was expressly made by the court.

§300.50 Court's charge; submission of lesser included offenses.

1. In submitting a count of an indictment to the jury, the court in its discretion may, in addition to submitting the greatest offense which it is required to submit, submit in the alternative any lesser included offense if there is a reasonable view of the evidence which would support a finding that the defendant committed such lesser offense but did not commit the greater. If there is no reasonable view of the evidence which would support such a finding, the court may not submit such lesser offense. Any error respecting such submission, however, is waived by the defendant unless he objects thereto before the jury retires to deliberate.

2. If the court is authorized by subdivision one to submit a lesser included offense and is requested by either party to do so, it must do so. In the absence of such a request, the court's failure to submit such offense does not constitute error.

3. The principles prescribed in subdivisions one and two apply equally where the lesser included offense is specifically charged in another count of the indictment.

4. Whenever the court submits two or more offenses in the alternative pursuant to this section, it must instruct the jury that it may render a verdict of guilty with respect to any one of such offenses, depending upon its findings of fact, but that it may not render a verdict of guilty with respect to more than one. A verdict of guilty of any such offense is not deemed an acquittal of any lesser offense submitted, but is deemed an acquittal of every greater offense submitted.

5. Where the indictment charges a crime committed by the defendant while he was under the age of sixteen but a lesser included offense would be one for which the defendant is not criminally responsible by reason of infancy, such lessor included offense may nevertheless be submitted to the jury in the same manner as an offense for which the defendant would be criminally responsible notwithstanding the fact that a verdict of guilty would not result in a criminal conviction.

6. For purposes of this section, the offenses of rape in the third degree as defined in subdivision three of section 130.25 of the penal law and criminal sexual act in the third degree as defined in subdivision three of section 130.40 of the penal law, are not lesser included offenses of rape in the first degree, criminal sexual act in the first degree or any other offense. Notwithstanding the foregoing, either such offense may be submitted as a lesser included offense of the applicable first degree offense when (i) there is a reasonable view of the evidence which would support a finding that the defendant committed such lesser offense but did not commit the greater offense, and (ii) both parties consent to its submission.

ARTICLE 310 - JURY TRIAL--DELIBERATION AND VERDICT OF JURY

Section
310.10 Jury deliberation; requirement of; where conducted.
310.20 Jury deliberation; use of exhibits and other material.
310.30 Jury deliberation; request for information.
310.40 Verdict; rendition thereof.
310.50 Verdict; form; reconsideration of defective verdict.
310.60 Discharge of jury before rendition of verdict and effect thereof.
310.70 Rendition of partial verdict and effect thereof.
310.80 Recording and checking of verdict and polling of jury.
310.85 Verdict of guilty where defendant not criminally responsible.

§310.10 Jury deliberation; requirement of; where conducted.

1. Following the court's charge, except as otherwise provided by subdivision two of this section, the jury must retire to deliberate upon its verdict in a place outside the courtroom. It must be provided with suitable accommodations therefor and must, except as otherwise provided in subdivision two of this section, be continuously kept together under the supervision of a court officer or court officers. In the event such court officer or court officers are not available, the jury shall be under the supervision of an appropriate public servant or public servants. Except when so authorized by the court or when performing administerial duties with respect to the jurors, such court officers or public servants, as the case may be, may not speak to or communicate with them or permit any other person to do so.

2. At any time after the jury has been charged or commenced its deliberations, and after notice to the parties and affording such parties an opportunity to be heard on the record outside of the presence of the jury, the court may declare the deliberations to be in recess and may thereupon direct the jury to suspend its deliberations and to separate for a reasonable period of time to be specified by the court, not lasting beyond close of business on the second day following such recess or, for good cause shown, beyond close of business on the third day following recess of jury deliberations unless the defendant consents to a longer period of suspension and separation. For the purposes of this section, where a day referred to in this subdivision falls on a Saturday, Sunday or holiday, such day shall mean the next day thereafter during which the courthouse is open for the conduct of trials. Before each recess, the court must admonish the jury as provided in section 270.40 of this title and direct it not to resume its deliberations until all twelve jurors have reassembled in the designated place at the termination of the declared recess. *(Eff.11/25/19,Ch.569,L.2019)*

§310.20 Jury deliberation; use of exhibits and other material.

Upon retiring to deliberate, the jurors may take with them:

1. Any exhibits received in evidence at the trial which the court, after according the parties an opportunity to be heard upon the matter, in its discretion permits them to take;

2. A written list prepared by the court containing the offenses submitted to the jury by the court in its charge and the possible verdicts thereon. Whenever the court submits two or more counts charging offenses set forth in the same article of the law, the court may set forth the dates, names of

complainants or specific statutory language, without defining the terms, by which the counts may be distinguished; provided, however, that the court shall instruct the jury in its charge that the sole purpose of the notations is to distinguish between the counts; and

3. A written list prepared by the court containing the names of every witness whose testimony has been presented during the trial, if the jury requests such a list and the court, in its discretion, determines that such a list will assist the jury.

§310.30 Jury deliberation; request for information.

At any time during its deliberation, the jury may request the court for further instruction or information with respect to the law, with respect to the content or substance of any trial evidence, or with respect to any other matter pertinent to the jury's consideration of the case. Upon such a request, the court must direct that the jury be returned to the courtroom and, after notice to both the people and counsel for the defendant, and in the presence of the defendant, must give such requested information or instruction as the court deems proper. With the consent of the parties and upon the request of the jury for further instruction with respect to a statute, the court may also give to the jury copies of the text of any statute which, in its discretion, the court deems proper.

§310.40 Verdict; rendition thereof.

1. The verdict must be rendered and announced by the foreperson of the jury in the courtroom in the presence of the court, a prosecutor, the defendant's counsel and the defendant; provided, however, that where the foreperson refuses or is unable to render and announce the verdict, the court may designate another member of the jury to do so.

2. Before rendering and announcing the verdict, the foreperson of the jury, or such other member of the jury as may be designated by the court pursuant to subdivision one, must be asked whether the jury has agreed upon a verdict and must answer in the affirmative.

§310.50 Verdict; form; reconsideration of defective verdict.

1. The form of the verdict must be in accordance with the court's instructions, as prescribed in article three hundred.

2. If the jury renders a verdict which in form is not in accordance with the court's instructions or which is otherwise legally defective, the court must explain the defect or error and must direct the jury to reconsider such verdict, to resume its deliberation for such purpose, and to render a proper verdict. If the jury persists in rendering a defective or improper verdict, the court may in its discretion either order that the verdict in its entirety as to any defendant be recorded as an acquittal, or discharge the jury and authorize the people to retry the indictment or a specified count or counts thereof as to such defendant; provided that if it is clear that the jury intended to find a defendant not guilty upon any particular count, the court must order that the verdict be recorded as an acquittal of such defendant upon

such count.

3. If the court accepts a verdict which is defective or incomplete by reason of the jury's failure to render a verdict upon every count upon which it was instructed to do so, such verdict is deemed to constitute an acquittal upon every such count improperly ignored in the verdict.

4. In a prosecution involving a charge of enterprise corruption in violation of article four hundred sixty of the penal law, the jury must separately and specifically render a special verdict with regard to each criminal act and any lesser included offense submitted for its consideration as a part of a pattern of criminal activity in addition to its verdict on the charge of enterprise corruption. In the absence of a unanimous special verdict of guilty with regard to each of at least three criminal acts and/or lesser included offenses submitted for its consideration and legally sufficient to constitute a person's participation in a pattern of criminal activity within the meaning of subdivision four of section 460.10 of the penal law, the court must order that the verdict on the count charging enterprise corruption be recorded as an acquittal.

§310.60 Discharge of jury before rendition of verdict and effect thereof.

1. A deliberating jury may be discharged by the court without having rendered a verdict only when:

(a) The jury has deliberated for an extensive period of time without agreeing upon a verdict with respect to any of the charges submitted and the court is satisfied that any such agreement is unlikely within a reasonable time; or

(b) The court, the defendant and the people all consent to such discharge; or

(c) a mistrial is declared pursuant to section 280.10

2. When the jury is so discharged, the defendant or defendants may be retried upon the indictment. Upon such retrial the indictment is deemed to contain all counts which it contained, except those which were dismissed or were deemed to have resulted in an acquittal pursuant to subdivision one of section 290.10.

§310.70 Rendition of partial verdict and effect thereof.

1. If a deliberating jury declares that it has reached a verdict with respect to one or more but not all of the offenses submitted to it, or with respect to one or more but not all of the defendants, the court must proceed as follows:

(a) If the possibility of ultimate agreement with respect to the other submitted offenses or defendants is so small and the circumstances are such that if they were the only matters under consideration the court would be authorized to discharge the jury pursuant to paragraph (a) of subdivision one of section 310.60, the court must terminate the deliberation and order the jury to render a partial verdict with respect to those offenses and defendants upon which or with respect to whom it has reached a verdict;

(b) If the court is satisfied that there is a reasonable possibility of ultimate agreement upon any of the unresolved offenses with respect to any defendant, it may either:

(i) Order the jury to render its verdict with respect to those offenses and defendants upon which or with respect to whom it has reached agreement and resume its deliberation upon the remainder; or

(ii) Refuse to accept a partial verdict at the time and order the jury to resume its deliberation upon the entire case.

2. Following the rendition of a partial verdict pursuant to subdivision one, a defendant may be retried for any submitted offense upon which the jury was unable to agree unless:

(a) A verdict of conviction thereon would have been inconsistent with a verdict, of either conviction or acquittal, actually rendered with respect to some other offense, or

(b) The submitted offense which was the subject of the disagreement, and some other submitted offense of higher or equal grade which was the subject of a verdict of conviction, were so related that consecutive sentences thereon could not have been imposed upon a defendant convicted of both such offenses.

3. As used in this section, a "submitted offense" means any offense submitted by the court to the jury, whether it be one which was expressly charged in a count of the indictment or a lesser included offense thereof submitted pursuant to section 300.50.

§310.80 Recording and checking of verdict and polling of jury.

After a verdict has been rendered, it must be recorded on the minutes and read to the jury, and the jurors must be collectively asked whether such is their verdict. Even though no juror makes any declaration in the negative, the jury must, if either party makes such an application, be polled and each juror separately asked whether the verdict announced by the foreman is in all respects his verdict. If upon either the collective or the separate inquiry any juror answers in the negative, the court must refuse to accept the verdict and must direct the jury to resume its deliberation. If no disagreement is expressed, the jury must be discharged from the case, except as otherwise provided in section 400.27.

§310.85 Verdict of guilty where defendant not criminally responsible.

1. Where a verdict of guilty is rendered with respect to a crime, but the defendant is not criminally responsible for such crime by reason of infancy, the court shall proceed as provided in this section.

2. If a verdict of guilty also is rendered with respect to a crime for which the defendant is criminally responsible, or if the defendant is awaiting sentence upon another criminal conviction or is under a sentence of imprisonment on another criminal conviction, the verdict rendered with respect to a crime for which he is not criminally responsible must be set aside and shall be deemed a nullity.

3. In any case where the verdict is not set aside pursuant to subdivision two of this section, the court must order that the verdict be deemed vacated and replaced by a juvenile delinquency fact determination. Upon so ordering, the court must direct that the action be removed to the family court in accordance with the provisions of article seven hundred twenty-five of this chapter.

ARTICLE 320 - WAIVER OF JURY TRIAL AND CONDUCT OF NON-JURY TRIAL

Section
320.10 Non-jury trial; when authorized.
320.20 Non-jury trial; nature and conduct thereof.

§320.10 Non-jury trial; when authorized.

1. Except where the indictment charges the crime of murder in the first degree, the defendant, subject to the provisions of subdivision two, may at any time before trial waive a jury trial and consent to a trial without a jury in the superior court in which the indictment is pending.

2. Such waiver must be in writing and must be signed by the defendant in person in open court in the presence of the court, and with the approval of the court. The court must approve the execution and submission of such waiver unless it determines that it is tendered as a stratagem to procure an otherwise impermissible procedural advantage or that the defendant is not fully aware of the consequences of the choice he is making. If the court disapproves the waiver, it must state upon the record its reasons for such disapproval.

§320.20 Non-jury trial; nature and conduct thereof.

1. A non-jury trial of an indictment must be conducted by one judge of the superior court in which the indictment is pending.

2. The court, in addition to determining all questions of law, is the execlusive* trier of all issues of fact and must render a verdict. *(So in original.)*

3. The order of the trial must be as follows:

(a) The court must permit the parties to deliver opening addresses in the order provided for a trial by jury pursuant to section 260.30.

(b) The order in which evidence must or may be offered by the respective parties is the same as that applicable to a jury trial of an indictment as prescribed in subdivisions five, six and seven of section 260.30.

(c) The court must permit the parties to deliver summations in the order provided for a trial by jury pursuant to section 260.30.

(d) The court must then consider the case and render a verdict.

4. The provisions governing motion practice and general procedure with respect to a jury trial are, wherever appropriate, applicable to a non-jury trial.

5. Before considering a multiple count indictment for the purpose of rendering a verdict thereon, and before the summations if there be any, the court must designate and state upon the record the counts upon which it will render a verdict and the particular defendant or defendants, if there be more than one, with respect to whom it will render a verdict upon any particular count. In determining what counts, offenses and defendants must be considered by it and covered by its verdict, and the form of the verdict in general, the court must be governed, so far as appropriate and practicable,

by the provisions of article three hundred governing the court's submission of counts and offenses to a jury upon a jury trial.

ARTICLE 330 - PROCEEDINGS FROM VERDICT TO SENTENCE

Section
330.10 Disposition of defendant after verdict of acquittal.
330.20 Procedure following verdict or plea of not responsible by reason of mental disease or defect.
330.25 Removal after verdict.
330.30 Motion to set aside verdict; grounds for.
330.40 Motion to set aside verdict; procedure.
330.50 Motion to set aside verdict; order granting motion.

§330.10 Disposition of defendant after verdict of acquittal.

1. Upon a verdict of complete acquittal, the court must immediately discharge the defendant if he is in the custody of the sheriff, or, if he is at liberty on bail, it must exonerate the bail.

2. Upon a verdict of not responsible by reason of mental disease or defect, the provisions of section 330.20 of this chapter shall govern all subsequent proceedings against the defendant.

§330.20 Procedure following verdict or plea of not responsible by reason of mental disease or defect.

1. Definition of terms. As used in this section, the following terms shall have the following meanings:

(a) "Commissioner" means the state commissioner of mental health or the state commissioner of the office for people with developmental disabilities. *(Eff.12/16/19,Ch.672,L.2019)*

(b) "Secure facility" means a facility within the state office of mental health or the state office for people with developmental disabilities which is staffed with personnel adequately trained in security methods and is so equipped as to minimize the risk or danger of escapes, and which has been so specifically designated by the commissioner. *(Eff.12/16/19,Ch.672,L.2019)*

(c) "Dangerous mental disorder" means: (i) that a defendant currently suffers from a "mental illness" as that term is defined in subdivision twenty of section 1.03 of the mental hygiene law, and (ii) that because of such condition he currently constitutes a physical danger to himself or others.

(d) "Mentally ill" means that a defendant currently suffers from a mental illness for which care and treatment as a patient, in the in-patient services of a psychiatric center under the jurisdiction of the state office of mental health, is essential to such defendant's welfare and that his judgment is so impaired that he is unable to understand the need for such care and treatment; and, where a defendant is mentally retarded, the term "mentally ill" shall also mean, for purposes of this section, that the defendant is in need of care and treatment as a resident in the in-patient services of a developmental center or other residential facility for the mentally retarded and developmentally disabled under the jurisdiction of the state office for people with developmental disabilities. *(Eff.12/16/19,Ch.672,L.2019)*

(e) "Examination order" means an order directed to the commissioner requiring that a defendant submit to a psychiatric examination to determine whether the defendant has a dangerous mental disorder, or if he does not have dangerous mental disorder, whether he is mentally ill.

(f) "Commitment order" or "recommitment order" means an order committing a defendant to the custody of the commissioner for confinement in a secure facility for care and treatment for six months from the date of the order.

(g) "First retention order" means an order which is effective at the expiration of the period prescribed in a commitment order for a recommitment order, authorizing continued custody of a defendant by the commissioner for a period not to exceed one year.

(h) "Second retention order" means an order which is effective at the expiration of the period prescribed in a first retention order, authorizing continued custody of a defendant by the commissioner for a period not to exceed two years.

(i) "Subsequent retention order" means an order which is effective at the expiration of the period prescribed in a second retention order or a prior subsequent retention order authorizing continued custody of a defendant by the commissioner for a period not to exceed two years.

(j) "Retention order" means a first retention order, a second retention order or a subsequent retention order.

(k) "Furlough order" means an order directing the commissioner to allow a defendant in confinement pursuant to a commitment order, recommitment order or retention order to temporarily leave the facility for a period not exceeding fourteen days, either with or without the constant supervision of one or more employees of the facility.

(*l*) "Transfer order" means an order directing the commissioner to transfer a defendant from a secure facility to a non-secure facility under the jurisdiction of the commissioner or to any non-secure facility designated by the commissioner.

(m) "Release order" means an order directing the commissioner to terminate a defendant's in-patient status without terminating the commissioner's responsibility for the defendant.

(n) "Discharge order" means an order terminating an order of conditions or unconditionally discharging a defendant from supervision under the provisions of this section.

(o) "Order of conditions" means an order directing a defendant to comply with this prescribed treatment plan, or any other condition which the court determines to be reasonably necessary or appropriate, and, in addition, where a defendant is in custody of the commissioner, not to leave the facility without authorization. In addition to such conditions, when determined to be reasonably necessary or appropriate, an order of conditions may be accompanied by a special order of conditions set forth in a separate document requiring that the defendant: (i) stay away from the home, school, business or place of employment of the victim or victims, or of any witness designated by the court, of such offense; or (ii) refrain from harassing, intimidating, threatening or otherwise interfering with the victim or victims of the offense and such members of the family or household of such victim or victims as shall be specifically named by the court in such special order. An order of conditions or special order of conditions shall be valid for five years from the date of its issuance, except that, for good cause shown, the court may extend the period for an additional five years.

(p) "District attorney" means the office which prosecuted the criminal action resulting in the verdict or plea of not responsible by reason of mental disease or defect.

(q) "Qualified psychiatrist" means a physician who (i) is a diplomate of the American board of psychiatry and neurology or is eligible to be certified by that board; or (ii) is certified by the American osteopathic board of neurology and psychiatry or is eligible to be certified by that board.

(r) "Licensed psychologist" means a person who is registered as a psychologist under article one hundred fifty-three of the education law.

(s) "Psychiatric examiner" means a qualified psychiatrist or a licensed psychologist who has been designated by the commissioner to examine a defendant pursuant to this section, and such designee need not be an employee of the department of mental hygiene.

2. Examination order; psychiatric examiners. Upon entry of a verdict of not responsible by reason of mental disease or defect, or upon the acceptance of a plea of not responsible by reason of mental disease or defect, the court must immediately issue an examination order. Upon receipt of such order, the commissioner must designate two qualified psychiatric examiners to conduct the examination to examine the defendant. In conducting their examination, the psychiatric examiners may employ any method which is accepted by the medical profession for the examination of persons alleged to be suffering from a dangerous mental disorder or to be mentally ill or retarded. The court may authorize a psychiatrist or psychologist retained by a defendant to be present at such examination. The clerk of the court must promptly forward a copy of the examination order to the mental hygiene legal service and such service may thereafter participate in all subsequent proceedings under this section.

In all subsequent proceedings under this section, prior to the issuance of a special order of conditions, the court shall consider whether any order of protection had been issued prior to a verdict of not responsible by reason of mental disease or defect in the case, or prior to the acceptance of a plea of not responsible by reason of mental disease or defect in the case.

2-a. Firearm, rifle or shotgun surrender order. Upon entry of a verdict of not responsible by reason of mental disease or defect, or upon the acceptance of a plea of not responsible by reason of mental disease or defect, or upon a finding that the defendant is an incapacitated person pursuant to article seven hundred thirty of this chapter, the court shall revoke the defendant's firearm license, if any, inquire of the defendant as to the existence and location of any firearm, rifle or shotgun owned or possessed by such defendant and direct the surrender of such firearm, rifle or shotgun pursuant to subparagraph (f) of paragraph one of subdivision a of section 265.20 and subdivision six of section 400.05 of the penal law.

3. Examination order; place of examination. Upon issuing an examination order, the court must, except as otherwise provided in this subdivision, direct that the defendant be committed to a secure facility designated by the commissioner as the place for such psychiatric examination. The sheriff must hold the defendant in custody pending such designation by the commissioner, and when notified of the designation, the sheriff must promptly deliver the defendant to such secure facility. When the defendant is not in custody at the time of such verdict or plea, because he was previously released on bail or on his own recognizance, the court, in its discretion,

may direct that such examination be conducted on an out-patient basis, and at such time and place as the commissioner shall designate. If, however, the commissioner informs the court that confinement of the defendant is necessary for an effective examination, the court must direct that the defendant be confined in a facility designated by the commissioner until the examination is completed.

4. Examination order, duration. Confinement in a secure facility pursuant to an examination order shall be for a period not exceeding thirty days, except that, upon application of the commissioner, the court may authorize confinement for an additional period not exceeding thirty days when a longer period is necessary to complete the examination. If the initial hearing required by subdivision six of this section has not commenced prior to the termination of such examination period, the commissioner shall retain custody of the defendant in such secure facility until custody is transferred to the sheriff in the manner prescribed in subdivision six of this section. During the period of such confinement, the physician in charge of the facility may administer or cause to be administered to the defendant such emergency psychiatric, medical or other therapeutic treatment as in his judgment should be administered. If the court has directed that the examination be conducted on an out-patient basis, the examination shall be completed within thirty days after the defendant has first reported to the place designated by the commissioner, except that, upon application of the commissioner, the court may extend such period for a reasonable time if a longer period is necessary to complete the examination.

5. Examination order; reports. After he has completed his examination of the defendant, each psychiatric examiner must promptly prepare a report of his findings and evaluation concerning the defendant's mental condition, and submit such report to the commissioner. If the psychiatric examiners differ in their opinion as to whether the defendant is mentally ill or is suffering from a dangerous mental disorder, the commissioner must designate another psychiatric examiner to examine the defendant. Upon receipt of the examination reports, the commissioner must submit them to the court that issued the examination order. If the court is not satisfied with the findings of these psychiatric examiners, the court may designate one or more additional psychiatric examiners pursuant to subdivision fifteen of this section. The court must furnish a copy of the reports to the district attorney, counsel for the defendant and the mental hygiene legal service.

6. Initial hearing; commitment order. After the examination reports are submitted, the court must, within ten days of the receipt of such reports, conduct an initial hearing to determine the defendant's present mental condition. If the defendant is in the custody of the commissioner pursuant to an examination order, the court must direct the sheriff to obtain custody of the defendant from the commissioner and to confine the defendant pending further order of the court, except that the court may direct the sheriff to confine the defendant in an institution located near the place where the court sits if that institution has been designated by the commissioner as suitable for the temporary and secure detention of mentally disabled persons. At such initial hearing, the district attorney must establish to the satisfaction of the court that the defendant has a dangerous mental disorder or is mentally ill. If the court finds that the defendant has a dangerous mental disorder, it must issue a commitment order. If the court finds that the defendant does not have a dangerous mental disorder but is mentally ill, the provisions of subdivision seven of this section shall apply.

7. Initial hearing civil commitment and order of conditions. If, at the conclusion of the initial hearing conducted pursuant to subdivision six of this section, the court finds that the defendant is mentally ill but does not have a dangerous mental disorder, the provisions of articles nine or fifteen of the mental hygiene law shall apply at that stage of the proceedings and at all subsequent proceedings. Having found that the defendant is mentally ill, the court must issue an order of conditions and an order committing the defendant to the custody of the commissioner. The latter order shall be deemed an order made pursuant to the mental hygiene law and not pursuant to this section, and further retention, conditional release or discharge of such defendant shall be in accordance with the provisions of the mental hygiene law. If, at the conclusion of the initial hearing, the court finds that the defendant does not have a dangerous mental disorder and is not mentally ill, the court must discharge the defendant either unconditionally or subject to an order of conditions.

7-a. Whenever the court issues a special order of conditions pursuant to this section, the commissioner shall make reasonable efforts to notify the victim or victims or the designated witness or witnesses that a special order of conditions containing such provisions has been issued, unless such victim or witness has requested that such notice should not be provided.

8. First retention order. When a defendant is in the custody of the commissioner pursuant to a commitment order, the commissioner must, at least thirty days prior to the expiration of the period prescribed in the order, apply to the court that issued the order, or to a superior court in the county where the secure facility is located, for a first retention order or a release order. The commissioner must give written notice of the application to the district attorney, the defendant, counsel for the defendant, and the mental hygiene legal service. Upon receipt of such application, the court may, on its own motion, conduct a hearing to determine whether the defendant has a dangerous mental disorder, and it must conduct such hearing if a demand therefor is made by the district attorney, the defendant, counsel for the defendant, or the mental hygiene legal service within ten days from the date that notice of the application was given to them. If such a hearing is held on an application for retention, the commissioner must establish to the satisfaction of the court that the defendant has a dangerous mental disorder or is mentally ill. The district attorney shall be entitled to appear and present evidence at such hearing. If such a hearing is held on an application for release, the district attorney must establish to the satisfaction of the court that the defendant has a dangerous mental disorder or is mentally ill. If the court finds that the defendant has a dangerous mental disorder it must issue a first retention order. If the court finds that the defendant is mentally ill but does not have a dangerous mental disorder, it must issue a first retention order and, pursuant to subdivision eleven of this section, a transfer order and an order of conditions. If the court finds that the defendant does not have a dangerous mental disorder and is not mentally ill, it must issue a release order and an order of conditions pursuant to subdivision twelve of this section.

9. Second and subsequent retention orders. When a defendant is in the custody of the commissioner pursuant to a first retention order, the commissioner must, at least thirty days prior to the expiration of the period prescribed in the order, apply to the court that issued the order, or to a superior court in the county where the facility is located, for a second retention order or a release order. The commissioner must give written notice of

the application to the district attorney, the defendant, counsel for the defendant, and the mental hygiene legal service. Upon receipt of such application, the court may, on its own motion, conduct a hearing to determine whether the defendant has a dangerous mental disorder, and it must conduct such hearing if a demand therefor is made by the district attorney, the defendant, counsel for the defendant, or the mental hygiene legal service within ten days from the date that notice of the application was given to them. If such a hearing is held on an application for retention, the commissioner must establish to the satisfaction of the court that the defendant has a dangerous mental disorder or is mentally ill. The district attorney shall be entitled to appear and present evidence at such hearing. If such a hearing is held on an application for release, the district attorney must establish to the satisfaction of the court that the defendant has a dangerous mental disorder or is mentally ill. If the court finds that the defendant has a dangerous mental disorder it must issue a second retention order. If the court finds that the defendant is mentally ill but does not have a dangerous mental disorder, it must issue a second retention order and, pursuant to subdivision eleven of this section, a transfer order and an order of conditions. If the court finds that the defendant does not have a dangerous mental disorder and is not mentally ill, it must issue a release order and an order of conditions pursuant to subdivision twelve of this section. When a defendant is in the custody of the commissioner prior to the expiration of the period prescribed in a second retention order, the procedures set forth in this subdivision for the issuance of a second retention order shall govern the application for and the issuance of any subsequent retention order.

10. Furlough order. The commissioner may apply for a furlough order, pursuant to this subdivision, when a defendant is in his custody pursuant to a commitment order, recommitment order, or retention order and the commissioner is of the view that, consistent with the public safety and welfare of the community and the defendant, the clinical condition of the defendant warrants a granting of the privileges authorized by a furlough order. The application for a furlough order may be made to the court that issued the commitment order, or to a superior court in the county where the secure facility is located. The commissioner must give ten days written notice to the district attorney, the defendant, counsel for the defendant, and the mental hygiene legal service. Upon receipt of such application, the court may, on its own motion, conduct a hearing to determine whether the application should be granted, and must conduct such hearing if a demand therefor is made by the district attorney. If the court finds that the issuance of a furlough order is consistent with the public safety and welfare of the community and the defendant, and that the clinical condition of the defendant warrants a granting of the privileges authorized by a furlough order, the court must grant the application and issue a furlough order containing any terms and conditions that the court deems necessary or appropriate. If the defendant fails to return to the secure facility at the time specified in the furlough order, then, for purposes of subdivision nineteen of this section, he shall be deemed to have escaped.

11. Transfer order and order of conditions. The commissioner may apply for a transfer order, pursuant to this subdivision, when a defendant is in his custody pursuant to a retention order or a recommitment order, and the commissioner is of the view that the defendant does not have a dangerous mental disorder or that, consistent with the public safety and welfare of the

community and the defendant, the clinical condition of the defendant warrants his transfer from a secure facility to a non-secure facility under the jurisdiction of the commissioner or to any non-secure facility designated by the commissioner. The application for a transfer order may be made to the court that issued the order under which the defendant is then in custody, or to a superior court in the county where the secure facility is located. The commissioner must give ten days written notice to the district attorney, the defendant, counsel for the defendant, and the mental hygiene legal service. Upon receipt of such application, the court may, on its own motion, conduct a hearing to determine whether the application should be granted, and must conduct such hearing if the demand therefor is made by the district attorney. At such hearing, the district attorney must establish to the satisfaction of the court that the defendant has a dangerous mental disorder or that the issuance of a transfer order is inconsistent with the public safety and welfare of the community. The court must grant the application and issue a transfer order if the court finds that the defendant does not have a dangerous mental disorder, or if the court finds that the issuance of a transfer order is consistent with the public safety and welfare of the community and the defendant and that the clinical condition of the defendant, warrants his transfer from a secure facility to a non-secure facility. A court must also issue a transfer order when, in connection with an application for a first retention order pursuant to subdivision eight of this section or a second or subsequent retention order pursuant to subdivision nine of this section, it finds that a defendant is mentally ill but does not have a dangerous mental disorder. Whenever a court issues a transfer order it must also issue an order of conditions.

12. Release order and order of conditions. The commissioner may apply for a release order, pursuant to this subdivision, when a defendant is in his custody pursuant to a retention order or recommitment order, and the commissioner is of the view that the defendant no longer has a dangerous mental disorder and is no longer mentally ill. The application for a release order may be made to the court that issued the order under which the defendant is then in custody, or to a superior court in the county where the facility is located. The application must contain a description of the defendant's current mental condition, the past course of treatment, a history of the defendant's conduct subsequent to his commitment, a written service plan for continued treatment which shall include the information specified in subdivision (g) of section 29.15 of the mental hygiene law, and a detailed statement of the extent to which supervision of the defendant after release is proposed. The commissioner must give ten days written notice to the district attorney, the defendant, counsel for the defendant, and the mental hygiene legal service. Upon receipt of such application, the court must promptly conduct a hearing to determine the defendant's present mental condition. At such hearing, the district attorney must establish to the satisfaction of the court that the defendant has a dangerous mental disorder or is mentally ill. If the court finds that the defendant has a dangerous mental disorder, it must deny the application for a release order. If the court finds that the defendant does not have a dangerous mental disorder but is mentally ill, it must issue a transfer order pursuant to subdivision eleven of this section if the defendant is then confined in a secure facility. If the court finds that the defendant does not have a dangerous mental disorder and is not mentally ill, it must grant the application and issue a release order.

A court must also issue a release order when, in connection with an application for a first retention order pursuant to subdivision eight of this section or a second or subsequent retention order pursuant to subdivision nine of this section, it finds that the defendant does not have a dangerous mental disorder and is not mentally ill. Whenever a court issues a release order it must also issue an order of conditions. If the court has previously issued a transfer order and an order of conditions, it must issue a new order of conditions upon issuing a release order. The order of conditions issued in conjunction with a release order shall incorporate a written service plan prepared by a psychiatrist familiar with the defendant's case history and approved by the court, and shall contain any conditions that the court determines to be reasonably necessary or appropriate. It shall be the responsibility of the commissioner to determine that such defendant is receiving the services specified in the written service plan and is complying with any conditions specified in such plan and the order of conditions.

13. Discharge order. The commissioner may apply for a discharge order, pursuant to this subdivision, when a defendant has been continuously on an out-patient status for three years or more pursuant to a release order, and the commissioner is of the view that the defendant no longer has a dangerous mental disorder and is no longer mentally ill and that the issuance of a discharge order is consistent with the public safety and welfare of the community and the defendant. The application for a discharge order may be made to the court that issued the release order, or to a superior court in the county where the defendant is then residing. The commissioner must give ten days written notice to the district attorney, the defendant, counsel for the defendant, and the mental hygiene legal service. Upon receipt of such application, the court may, on its own motion, conduct a hearing to determine whether the application should be granted, and must conduct such hearing if a demand therefor is made by the district attorney. The court must grant the application and issue a discharge order if the court finds that the defendant has been continuously on an out-patient status for three years or more, that he does not have a dangerous mental disorder and is not mentally ill, and that the issuance of the discharge order is consistent with the public safety and welfare of the community and the defendant.

14. Recommitment order. At any time during the period covered by an order of conditions an application may be made by the commissioner or the district attorney to the court that issued such order, or to a superior court in the county where the defendant is then residing, for a recommitment order when the applicant is of the view that the defendant has a dangerous mental disorder. The applicant must give written notice of the application to the defendant, counsel for the defendant, and the mental hygiene legal service, and if the applicant is the commissioner he must give such notice to the district attorney or if the applicant is the district attorney he must give such notice to the commissioner. Upon receipt of such application the court must order the defendant to appear before it for a hearing to determine if the defendant has a dangerous mental disorder. Such order may be in the form of a written notice, specifying the time and place of appearance, served personally upon the defendant, or mailed to his last known address, as the court may direct. If the defendant fails to appear in court as directed, the court may issue a warrant to an appropriate peace officer directing him to take the defendant into custody and bring him before the court. In such circumstance, the court may direct that the defendant be confined in an appropriate institution located near the place where the court sits. The court must conduct a hearing to determine whether the defendant has a

dangerous mental disorder. At such hearing, the applicant, whether he be the commissioner or the district attorney must establish to the satisfaction of the court that the defendant has a dangerous mental disorder. If the applicant is the commissioner, the district attorney shall be entitled to appear and present evidence at such hearing; if the applicant is the district attorney, the commissioner shall be entitled to appear and present evidence at such hearing. If the court finds that the defendant has a dangerous mental disorder, it must issue a recommitment order. When a defendant is in the custody of the commissioner pursuant to a recommitment order, the procedures set forth in subdivisions eight and nine of this section for the issuance of retention orders shall govern the application for and the issuance of a first retention order, a second retention order, and subsequent retention orders.

15. Designation of psychiatric examiners. If, at any hearing conducted under this section to determine the defendant's present mental condition, the court is not satisfied with the findings of the psychiatric examiners, the court may direct the commissioner to designate one or more additional psychiatric examiners to conduct an examination of the defendant and submit a report of their findings. In addition, the court may on its own motion, or upon request of a party, may designate one or more psychiatric examiners to examine the defendant and submit a report of their findings. The district attorney may apply to the court for an order directing that the defendant submit to an examination by a psychiatric examiner designated by the district attorney, and such psychiatric examiner may testify at the hearing.

16. Rehearing and review. Any defendant who is in the custody of the commissioner pursuant to a commitment order, a retention order, or a recommitment order, if dissatisfied with such order, may, within thirty days after the making of such order, obtain a rehearing and review of the proceedings and of such order in accordance with the provisions of section 9.35 or 15.35 of the mental hygiene law.

17. Rights of defendants. Subject to the limitations and provisions of this section, a defendant committed to the custody of the commissioner pursuant to this section shall have the rights granted to patients under the mental hygiene law.

18. Notwithstanding any other provision of law, no person confined by reason of a commitment order, recommitment order or retention order to a secure facility may be discharged or released unless the commissioner shall deliver written notice, at least four days excluding Saturdays, Sundays and holidays, in advance of such discharge or release to all of the following:

(a) the district attorney.

(b) the police department having jurisdiction of the area to which the defendant is to be discharged or released.

(c) any other person the court may designate.

The notices required by this subdivision shall be given by the facility staff physician who was treating the defendant or, if unavailable, by the defendant's treatment team leader, but if neither is immediately available, notice must be given by some other member of the clinical staff of the facility. Such notice must be given by any means reasonably calculated to give prompt actual notice.

19. Escape from custody; notice requirements. If a defendant is in the custody of the commissioner pursuant to an order issued under this section, and such defendant escapes from custody, immediate notice of such escape shall be given by the department facility staff to: (a) the district

attorney, (b) the superintendent of state police, (c) the sheriff of the county where the escape occurred, (d) the police department having jurisdiction of the area where the escape occurred, (e) any person the facility staff believes to be in danger, and (f) any law enforcement agency and any person the facility staff believes would be able to apprise such endangered person that the defendant has escaped from the facility. Such notice shall be given as soon as the facility staff know that the defendant has escaped from the facility and shall include such information as will adequately identify the defendant and the person or persons believed to be in danger and the nature of the danger. The notices required by this subdivision shall be given by the facility staff physician who was treating the defendant or, if unavailable, by the defendant's treatment team leader, but if neither is immediately available, notice must be given by some other member of the clinical staff of the facility. Such notice must be given by any means reasonably calculated to give prompt actual notice. The defendant may be apprehended, restrained, transported to, and returned to the facility from which he escaped by any peace officer, and it shall be the duty of the officer to assist any representative of the commissioner to take the defendant into custody upon the request of such representative.

20. Required affidavit. No application may be made by the commissioner under this section without an accompanying affidavit from at least one psychiatric examiner supportive of relief requested in the application, which affidavit shall be served on all parties entitled to receive the notice of application. Such affidavit shall set forth the defendant's clinical diagnosis, a detailed analysis of his or her mental condition which caused the psychiatric examiner to formulate an opinion, and the opinion of the psychiatric examiner with respect to the defendant. Any application submitted without the required affidavit shall be dismissed by the court.

21. Appeals. (a) A party to proceedings conducted in accordance with the provisions of this section may take an appeal to an intermediate appellate court by permission of the intermediate appellate court as follows:

(i) the commissioner may appeal from any release order, retention order, transfer order, discharge order, order of conditions, or recommitment order, for which he has not applied;

(ii) a defendant, or the mental hygiene legal service on his or her behalf, may appeal from any commitment order, retention order, recommitment order, or, if the defendant has obtained a rehearing and review of any such order pursuant to subdivision sixteen of this section, from an order, not otherwise appealable as of right, issued in accordance with the provisions of section 9.35 or 15.35 of the mental hygiene law authorizing continued retention under the original order, provided, however, that a defendant who takes an appeal from a commitment order, retention order, or recommitment order may not subsequently obtain a rehearing and review of such order pursuant to subdivision sixteen of this section;

(iii) the district attorney may appeal from any release order, transfer order, discharge order, order of conditions, furlough order, or order denying an application for a recommitment order which he opposed.

(b) An aggrieved party may appeal from a final order of the intermediate appellate court to the court of appeals by permission of the intermediate appellate court granted before application to the court of appeals, or by permission of the court of appeals upon refusal by the intermediate appellate court or upon direct application.

(c) An appeal taken under this subdivision shall be deemed civil in nature, and shall be governed by the laws and rules applicable to civil appeals; provided, however, that a stay of the order appealed from must be obtained in accordance with the provisions of paragraph (d) hereof.

(d) The court from or to which an appeal is taken may stay all proceedings to enforce the order appealed from pending an appeal or determination on a motion for permission to appeal, or may grant a limited stay, except that only the court to which an appeal is taken may vacate, limit, or modify a stay previously granted. If the order appealed from is affirmed or modified, the stay shall continue for five days after service upon the appellant of the order of affirmance or modification with notice of its entry in the court to which the appeal was taken. If a motion is made for permission to appeal from such an order, before the expiration of the five days, the stay, or any other stay granted pending determination of the motion for permission to appeal, shall:

(i) if the motion is granted, continue until five days after the appeal is determined; or

(ii) if the motion is denied, continue until five days after the movant is served with the order of denial with notice of its entry.

22. Any special order of conditions issued pursuant to subparagraph (i) or (ii) of paragraph (o) of subdivision one of this section shall bear in a conspicuous manner the term "special order of conditions" and a copy shall be filed by the clerk of the court with the sheriff's office in the county in which anyone intended to be protected by such special order resides, or, if anyone intended to be protected by such special order resides within a city, with the police department of such city. The absence of language specifying that the order is a "special order of conditions" shall not affect the validity of such order. A copy of such special order of conditions may from time to time be filed by the clerk of the court with any other police department or sheriff's office having jurisdiction of the residence, work place, or school of anyone intended to be protected by such special order. A copy of such special order may also be filed by anyone intended to be protected by such provisions at the appropriate police department or sheriff's office having jurisdiction. Any subsequent amendment or revocation of such special order may be filed in the same manner as provided in this subdivision. Such special order of conditions shall plainly state the date that the order expires.

§330.25 Removal after verdict.

*1. Where a defendant is a juvenile offender *or an adolescent offender* who does not stand convicted of murder in the second degree, upon motion and with the consent of the district attorney, the action may be removed to the family court in the interests of justice pursuant to article seven hundred twenty-five of this chapter notwithstanding the verdict.
(Material in Italics takes Eff.10/1/18; provided however, that when the applicability of such provisions are based on the conviction of a crime or an act committed by a person who was seventeen years of age at the time of such offense such provisions shall take effect 10/1/19, Ch.59,L.2017

*2. If the district attorney consents to the motion for removal pursuant to this section, he shall file a subscribed memorandum with the court setting forth (1) a recommendation that the interests of justice would best be served by removal of the action to the family court; and (2) if the conviction is of an offense set forth in paragraph (b) of subdivision one of section 210.43 of this chapter, specific factors, one or more of which reasonably support the recommendation, showing, (i) mitigating circumstances that bear directly upon the manner in which the crime was committed, or (ii) where the defendant was not the sole participant in the crime, that the defendant's participation was relatively minor although not so minor as to constitute a defense to prosecution, or (iii) where the juvenile offender has no previous adjudications of having committed a designated felony act, as defined in subdivision eight of section 301.2 of the family court act, regardless of the age of the offender at the time of commission of the act, that the criminal act was not part of a pattern of criminal behavior and, in view of the history of the offender, is not likely to be repeated.   *(Eff. Until 10/1/18,Ch.59,L.2017)

*2. If the district attorney consents to the motion for removal pursuant to this section, he shall file a subscribed memorandum with the court setting forth (1) a recommendation that the interests of justice would best be served by removal of the action to the family court; and (2) if the conviction is of an offense set forth in paragraph (b) of subdivision one of section 722.22 of this chapter, specific factors, one or more of which reasonably support the recommendation, showing, (i) mitigating circumstances that bear directly upon the manner in which the crime was committed, or (ii) where the defendant was not the sole participant in the crime, that the defendant's participation was relatively minor although not so minor as to constitute a defense to prosecution, or (iii) where the juvenile offender has no previous adjudications of having committed a designated felony act, as defined in subdivision eight of section 301.2 of the family court act, regardless of the age of the offender at the time of commission of the act, that the criminal act was not part of a pattern of criminal behavior and, in view of the history of the offender, is not likely to be repeated.

*(Eff.10/1/18; provided however, that when the applicability of such provisions are based on the conviction of a crime or an act committed by a person who was seventeen years of age at the time of such offense such provisions shall take effect 10/1/19, Ch.59,L.2017)

3. If the court is of the opinion, based upon the specific factors set forth in the district attorney's memorandum, that the interests of justice would best be served by removal of the action to the family court, the verdict shall be set aside and a plea of guilty of a crime or act for which the defendant is not criminally responsible may be entered pursuant to subdivision three or four of section 220.10 of this chapter. Upon accepting any such plea, the court must specify upon the record the portion or portions of the district attorney's statement the court is relying upon as the basis of its opinion and that it believes the interests of justice would best be served by removal of the proceeding to the family court. Such plea shall then be deemed to be a juvenile delinquency fact determination and the court upon entry thereof must direct that the action be removed to the family court in accordance with the provisions of article seven hundred twenty-five of this chapter.

§330.30 Motion to set aside verdict; grounds for.

At any time after rendition of a verdict of guilty and before sentence, the court may, upon motion of the defendant, set aside or modify the verdict or any part thereof upon the following grounds:

1. Any ground appearing in the record which, if raised upon an appeal from a prospective judgment of conviction, would require a reversal or modification of the judgment as a matter of law by an appellate court.

2. That during the trial there occurred, out of the presence of the court, improper conduct by a juror, or improper conduct by another person in

relation to a juror, which may have affected a substantial right of the defendant and which was not known to the defendant prior to the rendition of the verdict; or

3. That new evidence has been discovered since the trial which could not have been produced by the defendant at the trial even with due diligence on his part and which is of such character as to create a probability that had such evidence been received at the trial the verdict would have been more favorable to the defendant.

§330.40 Motion to set aside verdict; procedure.

1. A motion to set aside a verdict based upon a ground specified in subdivision one of section 330.30 need not be in writing, but the people must be given reasonable notice thereof and an opportunity to appear in opposition thereto.

2. A motion to set aside a verdict based upon a ground specified in subdivisions two and three of section 330.30 must be made and determined as follows:

(a) The motion must be in writing and upon reasonable notice to the people. The moving papers must contain sworn allegations, whether by the defendant or by another person or persons, of the occurrence or existence of all facts essential to support the motion. Such sworn allegations may be based upon personal knowledge of the affiant or upon information and belief, provided that in the latter event the affiant must state the sources of such information and the grounds of such belief;

(b) The people may file with the court, and in such case must serve a copy thereof upon the defendant or his counsel, an answer denying or admitting any or all of the allegations of the moving papers;

(c) After all papers of both parties have been filed, the court must consider the same and, if the motion is determinable pursuant to paragraphs (d) or (e), must or may, as therein provided, determine the motion without holding a hearing to resolve questions of fact;

(d) The court must grant the motion if:

(i) The moving papers allege a ground constituting legal basis for the motion; and

(ii) Such papers contain sworn allegations of all facts essential to support such ground; and

(iii) All the essential facts are conceded by the people to be true.

(e) The court may deny the motion if:

(i) The moving papers do not allege any ground constituting legal basis for the motion; or

(ii) The moving papers do not contain sworn allegations of all facts essential to support the motion.

(f) If the court does not determine the motion pursuant to paragraphs (d) or (e), it must conduct a hearing and make findings of fact essential to the termination thereof;

(g) Upon such a hearing, the defendant has the burden of proving by a preponderance of the evidence every fact essential to support the motion.

§330.50 Motion to set aside verdict; order granting motion.

1. Upon setting aside or modifying a verdict or a part thereof upon a ground specified in subdivision one of section 330.30, the court must take the same action as the appropriate appellate court would be required to take upon reversing or modifying a judgment upon the particular ground in issue.

2. Upon setting aside a verdict upon a ground specified in subdivision two of section 330.30, the court must order a new trial.

3. Upon setting aside a verdict upon a ground specified in subdivision three of section 330.30, the court must, except as otherwise provided in this subdivision, order a new trial. If a verdict is set aside upon the ground that had the newly discovered evidence in question been received at the trial the verdict probably would have been more favorable to the defendant in that the conviction probably would have been for a lesser offense than the one contained in the verdict, the court may either (a) set aside such verdict or (b) with the consent of the people modify such verdict by reducing it to one of conviction of such lesser offense.

4. Upon a new trial resulting from an order setting aside a verdict, the indictment is deemed to contain all the counts and to charge all the offenses

which it contained and charged at the time the previous trial was commenced, regardless of whether any count was dismissed by the court in the course of such trial, except those upon or of which the defendant was acquitted or is deemed to have been acquitted.

TITLE K - PROSECUTION OF INFORMATIONS IN LOCAL CRIMINAL COURTS-PLEA TO SENTENCE

ARTICLE 340 - PRE-TRAIL PROCEEDINGS

Section
340.10 Definition of terms.
340.20 The plea.
340.30 Pre-trial discovery and notices of defenses.
340.40 Modes of trial.
340.50 Defendant's presence at trial.

§340.10   Definitions of terms.

The following definitions are applicable to this title:

1. "Information," in addition to its meaning as defined in subdivision one of section 100.10, includes (a) a simplified information and (b) a prosecutor's information and (c) a misdemeanor complaint upon which the defendant, by a waiver executed pursuant to subdivision three of section 170.65, has consented to be prosecuted.

2. "Single judge trial" means a trial in a local criminal court conducted by one judge sitting without a jury.

3. "Jury trial" means a trial in a local criminal court conducted by one judge sitting with a jury.

§340.20   The plea.

1. Except as provided in subdivisions two and three, the provisions of article two hundred twenty, governing the kinds of pleas to indictments which may be entered and related matters, are, to the extent that they can be so applied, applicable to pleas to informations, and changes of pleas thereto, in local criminal courts.

2. A plea to an information, other than one against a corporation, must be entered in the following manner:

(a) Subject to the provisions of paragraph (b), a plea to an information must be entered orally by the defendant in person unless the court permits entry thereof by counsel upon the filing by him of a written and subscribed statement by the defendant declaring that he waives his right to plead to the information in person and authorizing his attorney to enter a plea on his behalf as set forth in the authorization.

(b) If the only offense or offenses charged are traffic infractions, the procedure provided in sections eighteen hundred five, eighteen hundred six and eighteen hundred seven of the vehicle and traffic law, relating to pleas in such cases, is, when appropriate, applicable and controlling.

3. A plea to an information against a corporation must be entered by counsel.

4. When a sentence is agreed upon by the prosecutor and a defendant as a predicate to entry of a plea of guilty, the court or the prosecutor must orally on the record, or in writing filed with the court, state the sentence agreed upon as a condition of such plea.

§340.30 Pre-trial discovery and notices of defenses.

The provisions of article two hundred forty-five of this part, concerning pre-trial discovery by a defendant under indictment in a superior court, and article two hundred fifty of this part, concerning pre-trial notice to the people by a defendant under indictment in a superior court who intends to advance a trial defense of mental disease or defect or of alibi, apply to a prosecution of an information in a local criminal court.

§340.40 Modes of trial.

1. Except as otherwise provided in this section, a trial of an information in a local criminal court must be a single judge trial.

2. In any local criminal court a defendant who has entered a plea of not guilty to an information which charges a misdemeanor must be accorded a jury trial, conducted pursuant to article three hundred sixty. The defendant may at any time before trial waive a jury trial in the manner prescribed in subdivision two of section 320.10 of this chapter, and consent to a single judge trial.

3. A defendant entitled to a jury trial pursuant to subdivision two of this section, shall be so entitled even though the information also charges an offense for which he is otherwise not entitled to a jury trial. In such case, the defendant is not entitled both to a jury trial and a separate single judge trial and the court may not order separate trials.

4. Notwithstanding any other provision of law, in any local criminal court the trial of a person who is an eligible youth within the meaning of the youthful offender procedure set forth in article seven hundred twenty of this chapter and who has not prior to commencement of the trial been convicted of a crime or adjudicated a youthful offender must be a single judge trial.

(Eff.7/1/22,Ch.806,L.2021)

§340.50 Defendant's presence at trial.

1. Except as provided in subdivision two or three, a defendant must be personally present during the trial.

2. On motion of a defendant represented by counsel, the court may, in the absence of an objection by the people, issue an order dispensing with the requirement that the defendant be personally present at trial. Such an order may be made only upon the filing of a written and subscribed statement by the defendant declaring that he waives his right to be personally present at the trial and authorizing his attorney to conduct his defense.

3. A defendant who conducts himself in so disorderly and disruptive a manner that his trial cannot be carried on with him in the courtroom may be removed from the courtroom if, after he has been warned by the court that he will be removed if he continues such conduct, he continues to engage in such conduct.

ARTICLE 350 - NON-JURY TRIALS

Section
350.10 Conduct of single judge trial.
350.20 Trial by judicial hearing officer.

§350.10 Conduct of single judge trial.

1. A single judge trial of an information in a local criminal court must be conducted pursuant to this section.

2. The court, in addition to determining all questions of law, is the exclusive trier of all issues of fact and must render a verdict.

3. The order of the trial must be as follows:

(a) The court may in its discretion permit the parties to deliver opening addresses. If the court grants such permission to one party, it must grant it to the other also. If both parties deliver opening addresses, the people's address must be delivered first.

(b) The order in which evidence must or may be offered by the respective parties is the same as that applicable to a jury trial of an indictment as prescribed in subdivisions five, six and seven of section 260.30.

(c) The court may in its discretion permit the parties to deliver summations. If the court grants such permission to one party, it must grant permission to the other also. If both parties deliver summations, the defendant's summation must be delivered first.

(d) The court must then consider the case and render a verdict.

4. The provisions governing motion practice and general procedure with respect to a jury trial of an indictment are, wherever appropriate, applicable to a non-jury trial of an information.

5. If the information contains more than one count, the court must render a verdict upon each count not previously dismissed or must otherwise state upon the record its disposition of each such count. A verdict which does not so dispose of each count constitutes a verdict of not guilty with respect to each undisposed of count.

6. In rendering a verdict of guilty upon a count charging a misdemeanor, the court may find the defendant guilty of such misdemeanor if it is established by legally sufficient trial evidence, or guilty of any lesser included offense which is established by legally sufficient trial evidence.

§350.20 Trial by judicial hearing officer.

1. Notwithstanding any provision of section 350.10 of this article, in any case where a single judge trial of an information in a local criminal court is authorized or required, the court may, upon agreement of the parties, assign a judicial hearing officer to conduct the trial. Where such assignment is made, the judicial hearing officer shall entertain the case in the same manner as a court and shall:

(a) determine all questions of law;

(b) act as the exclusive trier of all issues of fact; and

(c) render a verdict.

2. In the discharge of this responsibility, the judicial hearing officer shall have the same powers as a judge of the court in which the proceeding is pending. The rules of evidence shall be applicable at a trial conducted by a judicial hearing officer.

3. Any action taken by a judicial hearing officer in the conduct of a trial shall be deemed the action of the court in which the proceeding is pending.

4. This section shall not apply where the single judge trial is of an information at least one count of which charges a class A misdemeanor.

5. Notwithstanding the provisions of subdivision one of this section, for all proceedings before the district court of Nassau county the administrative judge of Nassau county may, and for all proceedings before the district court of Suffolk county, the administrative judge of Suffolk county may, without the consent of the parties, assign matters involving traffic and parking infractions except those described in paragraphs (a), (b), (c), (d), (e) and (f) of subdivision two of section three hundred seventy-one of the general municipal law to a judicial hearing officer in accordance with the provisions of section sixteen hundred ninety of the vehicle and traffic law and for all proceedings before the Buffalo city court the administrative judge of the eighth judicial district may, without the consent of the parties, assign matters involving traffic infractions except those described in paragraphs (a), (b), (c), (d), (e), (f) and (g) of subdivision two-a of section three hundred seventy-one of the general municipal law to a judicial hearing officer in accordance with the provisions of section sixteen hundred ninety of the vehicle and traffic law and for all proceedings before the Rochester city court the administrative judge of the seventh judicial district may, without the consent of the parties, assign matters involving traffic infractions except those described in paragraphs (a), (b), (c), (d), (e), (f) and (g) of subdivision two-b of section three hundred seventy-one of the general municipal law to a judicial hearing officer in accordance with the provisions of section sixteen hundred ninety of the vehicle and traffic law.   *(Eff.4/21/18,Ch.157,L.2017)*

ARTICLE 360 - JURY TRIAL

Section
360.05 Jury trial; order of trial.
360.10 Trial jury; formation in general.
360.15 Trial jury; challenge to the panel.
360.20 Trial jury; examination of prospective jurors; challenges generally.
360.25 Trial jury; challenge for cause of an individual juror.
360.30 Trial jury; peremptory challenge of an individaul* juror.
360.35 Trial jury; alternate juror.
360.40 Trial jury; conduct of jury trial in general.
360.45 Court's charge and instructions; in general.
360.50 Court's submission of information to jury; counts and offenses to be submitted.
360.55 Deliberation and verdict of jury.
                              (So in original, probably should read "individual")

§360.05 Jury trial; order of trial.

The provisions of section 260.30, governing the order of proceedings of a jury trial of an indictment in a superior court, are applicable to a jury trial of an information in a local criminal court.

§360.10 Trial jury; formation in general.

1. A trial jury consists of six jurors, but "alternate jurors" may be selected and sworn pursuant to section 360.35.

2. The panel from which the jury is drawn is formed and selected as prescribed in the uniform district court act, uniform city court act, and uniform justice court act. In the New York city criminal court the panel from which the jury is drawn is formed and selected in the same manner as is prescribed for the formation and selection of a panel in the supreme court in counties within cities having a population of one million or more.

§360.15 Trial jury; challenge to the panel.

1. A challenge to the panel is an objection made to the entire panel of prospective trial jurors returned for the trial of the action and may be taken to such panel or to any additional panel that may be ordered by the court. Such a challenge may be made only by the defendant and only on the ground that there has been such a departure from the requirements of the appropriate law in the drawing or return of the panel as to result in substantial prejudice to the defendant.

2. A challenge to the panel must be made before the selection of the jury commences, and, if it is not, such challenge is deemed to have been waived. Such challenge must be made in writing setting forth the facts constituting the ground of challenge. If such facts are denied by the people, witnesses may be called and examined by either party. All issues of fact and questions of law arising on the challenge must be tried and determined by the court. If a challenge to the panel is allowed, the court must discharge that panel and order the return of another panel of prospective trial jurors.

§360.20 Trial jury; examination of prospective jurors; challenges generally.

If no challenge to the panel is made as prescribed by section 360.15, or if such challenge is made and disallowed, the court must direct that the names of not less than six members of the panel be drawn and called. Such persons must take their places in the jury box and must be immediately sworn to answer truthfully questions asked them relative to their qualifications to serve as jurors in the action. The procedural rules prescribed in section 270.15 with respect to the examination of the prospective jurors and to challenges are also applicable to the selection of a trial jury in a local criminal court.

§360.25 Trial jury; challenge for cause of an individual juror.

1. A challenge for cause is an objection to a prospective member of the jury and may be made only on the ground that:

(a) He does not have the qualifications required by the judiciary law; or

(b) He has a state of mind that is likely to preclude him from rendering an impartial verdict based upon the evidence adduced at the trial; or

(c) He is related within the sixth degree by consanguinity or affinity to the defendant, or to the person allegedly injured by the crime charged, or to a prospective witness at the trial, or to counsel for the people or for the defendant; or that he is or was a party adverse to any such person in a civil action; or that he has complained against or been accused by any such person in a criminal action; or that he bears some other relationship to any such person of such nature that it is likely to preclude him from rendering an impartial verdict; or

(d) He is to be a witness at the trial; or where a prosecutor's information was filed at the direction of a grand jury, he was a witness before the grand jury or at the preliminary hearing; or

(e) He or she served on a trial jury in a prior civil or criminal action involving the same incident charged; or where a prosecutor's information was filed at the direction of a grand jury, he or she served on the grand jury which directed such filing.

2. All issues of fact or questions of law arising on the challenge must be tried and determined by the court. The provisions of subdivision two of section 270.20 with respect to challenges are also applicable to the selection of a trial jury in a local criminal court.

§360.30   Trial jury; peremptory challenge of an individaul* juror.

1. A peremptory challenge is an objection to a prospective juror for which no reason need be assigned. Upon any peremptory challenge, the court must exclude the person challenged from service.

2. Each party must be allowed three peremptory challenges. When two or more defendants are tried jointly, such challenges are not multiplied by the number of defendants, but such defendants are to be treated as a single party. In any such case, a peremptory challenge by one or more defendants must be allowed if a majority of the defendants join in such challenge. Otherwise, it must be disallowed.* *(So in original. Probably should read "individual.")*

§360.35   Trial jury; alternate juror.

1. Immediately after the last trial juror is sworn, the court may in its discretion direct the selection of either one or two additional jurors to be known as "alternate jurors." The alternate jurors must be drawn in the same manner, must have the same qualifications, must be subject to the same examination and challenges for cause and must take the same oath as the regular jurors. Whether or not a party has used its peremptory challenge in the selection of the trial jury, one peremptory challenge is authorized in the selection of the alternate jurors.

2. The provisions of section 270.35 with respect to alternate jurors are also applicable to a trial jury in a local criminal court.

§360.40   Trial jury; conduct of jury trial in general.

A jury trial of an information must be conducted generally in the same manner as a jury trial of an indictment, and the rules governing preliminary instructions by the court, supervision of the jury, motion practice and other procedural matters involved in the conduct of a jury trial of an indictment are, where appropriate, applicable to the conduct of a jury trial of an information.

§360.45   Court's charge and instructions; in general.

The general principles, prescribed in section 300.10, governing the court's charge to the jury and requests to charge upon a trial of an indictment, are applicable to a jury trial of an information in a local criminal court.

§360.50 Court's submission of information to jury; counts and offenses to be submitted.

1. The term definitions contained in section 300.30 are applicable to this section, except that the word "information" is to be substituted for the word "indictment" wherever the latter appears in said section 300.30.

2. The court may submit to the jury only those counts of an information remaining therein at the time of its charge which are supported by legally sufficient trial evidence, and every count not so supported should be dismissed by a trial order of dismissal. If the trial evidence is not legally sufficient to establish a misdemeanor charged in a particular count which the court would otherwise be required to submit pursuant to this section, but is legally sufficient to establish a lesser included offense, the court may submit such lesser included offense and, upon the people's request, must do so. In submitting a count charging a misdemeanor established by legally sufficient trial evidence, the court in its discretion may, in addition to submitting such misdemeanor, submit in the alternative any lesser included offense if there is a reasonable view of the evidence which would support a finding that the defendant committed such lesser offense but did not commit the misdemeanor charged.

3. If the information contains but one count, the court must submit such count.

4. If a multiple count information contains consecutive counts only, the court must submit every count thereof.

5. In any case where the information may be more complex by reason of concurrent counts or inconsistent counts or other factors indicated in subdivisions three, four and five of section 300.40, relating to multiple count indictments, the court, in its submission of such information to the jury, should, so far as practicable, be guided by the provisions of the said subdivisions of said section 300.40.

6. Notwithstanding any other provision of this section, the court is not required to submit to the jury any particular count of a multiple count information if the people consent that it not be submitted.

7. Every count not submitted to the jury is deemed to have been dismissed by the court. Where the court, over objection of the people, refuses to submit a count which is consecutive as to every count actually submitted, such count is deemed to have been dismissed by a trial order of dismissal even though no such order was expressly made by the court.

§360.55 Deliberation and verdict of jury.

The provisions of article three hundred ten, governing the deliberation and verdict of a jury upon a jury trial of an indictment in a superior court, are applicable to a jury trial of an information in a local criminal court.

ARTICLE 370 - PROCEEDINGS FROM VERDICT TO SENTENCE

Section
370.10 Proceedings from verdict to sentence.
370.15 Procedure for determining whether certain misdemeanor crimes are serious
offenses under the penal law.
370.25 Procedure for the surrender of firearms, rifles and shotguns upon judgment of
conviction for a felony or a serious offense.

§370.10 Proceedings from verdict to sentence.

The provisions of article three hundred thirty, governing the proceedings from verdict to sentence in an action prosecuted by indictment in a superior court, are applicable to a prosecution by information in a local criminal court; provided, however, where a judicial hearing officer has conducted the trial pursuant to section 350.20 of this chapter, all references to a court therein shall be deemed references to such judicial hearing officer.

§370.15 Procedure for determining whether certain misdemeanor crimes are serious offenses under the penal law.

1. When a defendant has been charged with assault in the third degree, menacing in the third degree, menacing in the second degree, criminal obstruction of breathing or blood circulation, unlawful imprisonment in the second degree, coercion in the third degree, criminal tampering in the third degree, criminal contempt in the second degree, harassment in the first degree, aggravated harassment in the second degree, criminal trespass in the third degree, criminal trespass in the second degree, arson in the fifth degree, or attempt to commit any of the above-listed offenses, the people shall, at arraignment or no later than forty-five days after arraignment, serve on the defendant and file with the court a notice alleging that the defendant and the person alleged to be the victim of such crime were members of the same family or household as defined in subdivision one of section 530.11 of this chapter.   *(Deemed eff.4/1/20,Ch.55,L.2020)*

2. Such notice shall include the name of the person alleged to be the victim of such crime and shall specify the nature of the alleged relationship as set forth in subdivision one of section 530.11 of this chapter. Upon conviction of such offense, the court shall advise the defendant that he or she is entitled to a hearing solely on the allegation contained in the notice and, if necessary, an adjournment of the sentencing proceeding in order to prepare for such hearing, and that if such allegation is sustained, that determination and conviction will be reported to the division of criminal justice services. If such allegation is sustained, the court shall report the determination and conviction to the division of criminal justice services within three business days.   *(Deemed eff.4/1/20,Ch.55,L.2020)*

3. After having been advised by the court as provided in subdivision two of this section, the defendant may stipulate or admit, orally on the record or in writing, that he or she is related or situated to the victim of such crime in the manner described in subdivision one of this section. In such case, such

relationship shall be deemed established. If the defendant denies that he or she is related or situated to the victim of the crime as alleged in the notice served by the people, or stands mute with respect to such allegation, then the people shall bear the burden to prove beyond a reasonable doubt that the defendant is related or situated to the victim in the manner alleged in the notice. The court may consider reliable hearsay evidence submitted by either party provided that it is relevant to the determination of the allegation. Facts previously proven at trial or elicited at the time of entry of a plea of guilty shall be deemed established beyond a reasonable doubt and shall not be relitigated. At the conclusion of the hearing, or upon such a stipulation or admission, as applicable, the court shall make a specific written determination with respect to such allegation.

§370.25 Procedure for the surrender of firearms, rifles and shotguns upon judgment of conviction for a felony or a serious offense.

1. Upon judgment of conviction for a felony or a serious offense, the court shall inquire of the defendant as to the existence of all firearms, rifles and shotguns he or she owns or possesses. The court shall order the immediate surrender, pursuant to subparagraph (f) of paragraph one of subdivision a of section 265.20 of the penal law and subdivision six of section 400.05 of the penal law, of any or all firearms, rifles and shotguns owned or possessed by the defendant.

2. The court ordering the surrender of any firearms, rifles or shotguns as provided in this section shall immediately notify the duly constituted police authorities of the locality of such action and the division of state police at its office in the city of Albany. The court shall direct the authority receiving such surrendered firearms, rifles and shotguns to immediately notify the court of such surrender.

3. The disposition of any firearms, rifles or shotguns surrendered pursuant to this section shall be in accordance with the provisions of subdivision six of section 400.05 of the penal law.

4. The provisions of this section shall not be deemed to limit, restrict or otherwise impair the authority of the court to order and direct the surrender of any or all firearms, rifles and shotguns owned or possessed by a defendant pursuant to any other provision of law.

TITLE L - SENTENCE
ARTICLE 380 - SENTENCING IN GENERAL

Section
380.10   Applicability.
380.20   Sentence required.
380.30   Time for pronouncing sentence.
380.40   Defendant's presence at sentencing.
380.50   Statements at time of sentence.
380.55   Application for poor person relief on appeal.
380.60   Authority for the execution of sentence.
380.65   Sentence and commitment and order of protection to accompany defendant sentenced to imprisonment.
380.70   Minutes of sentence.
380.80   Reporting sentence to social services.
380.85   Reporting sentences to office of professional medical conduct; licensed physician, physician assistant, or specialist assistant.
380.90   Reporting sentences to schools.
380.95   Reporting convictions of certain school employees.
380.95   Reporting convictions of certain school employees.
380.96   Obligation of sentencing court pursuant to article four hundred of the penal law.
380.97   Notification to division of criminal justice services of certain misdemeanor convictions.

§380.10 Applicability.

1. In general. The procedure prescribed by this title applies to sentencing for every offense, whether defined within or outside of the penal law; provided, however, where a judicial hearing officer has conducted the trial pursuant to section 350.20 of this chapter, all references to a court herein shall be deemed references to such judicial hearing officer.

2. Exception. Whenever a different or inconsistent procedure is provided by any other law in relation to sentencing for a non-criminal offense defined therein, such different or inconsistent procedure applies thereto.

§380.20 Sentence required.

The court must pronounce sentence in every case where a conviction is entered. If an accusatory instrument contains multiple counts and a conviction is entered on more than one count the court must pronounce sentence on each count.

§380.30 Time for pronouncing sentence.

1. In general. Sentence must be pronounced without unreasonable delay.

2. Court to fix time. Upon entering a conviction the court must:

(a) Fix a date for pronouncing sentence; or

(b) Fix a date for one of the pre-sentence proceedings specified in article four hundred; or

(c) Pronounce sentence on the date the conviction is entered in accordance with the provisions of subdivision three.

3. Sentence on date of conviction. The court may sentence the defendant at the time the conviction is entered if:

(a) A pre-sentence report or a fingerprint report is not required; or

(b) Where any such report is required, the report has been received. Provided, however, that the court may not pronounce sentence at such time without inquiring as to whether an adjournment is desired by the defendant. Where an adjournment is requested, the defendant must state the purpose thereof and the court may, in its discretion, allow a reasonable time.

4. Time for pre-sentence proceedings. The court may conduct one or more of the pre-sentence proceedings specified in article four hundred at any time before sentence is pronounced. Notice of any such proceeding issued after the date for pronouncing sentence has been fixed automatically adjourns the date for pronouncing sentence. In such case the court must fix a date for pronouncing sentence at the conclusion of such proceeding.

§380.40 Defendant's presence at sentencing.

1. In general. The defendant must be personally present at the time sentence is pronounced.

2. Exception. Where sentence is to be pronounced for a misdemeanor or for a petty offense, the court may, on motion of the defendant, dispense with the requirement that the defendant be personally present. Any such motion must be accompanied by a waiver, signed and acknowledged by the defendant, reciting the maximum sentence that may be imposed for the offense and stating that the defendant waives the right to be personally present at the time sentence is pronounced.

3. Corporations. Sentence may be pronounced against a corporation in the absence of counsel if counsel fails to appear on the date of sentence after reasonable notice thereof.

§380.50 Statements at time of sentence.

1. At the time of pronouncing sentence, the court must accord the prosecutor an opportunity to make a statement with respect to any matter relevant to the question of sentence. The court must then accord counsel for the defendant an opportunity to speak on behalf of the defendant. The defendant also has the right to make a statement personally in his or her own behalf, and before pronouncing sentence the court must ask the defendant whether he or she wishes to make such a statement.

2. (a) For purposes of this section "victim" shall mean:

(1) the victim as indicated in the accusatory instrument; or

(2) if such victim is unable or unwilling to express himself or herself before the court or a person so mentally or physically disabled as to make it impracticable to appear in court in person or the victim is deceased, a member of the family of such victim, or the legal guardian or representative of the legal guardian of the victim where such guardian or representative has personal knowledge of and a relationship with the victim, unless the court finds that it would be inappropriate for such person to make a statement on behalf of the victim.

(b) If the defendant is being sentenced for a felony the court, if requested at least ten days prior to the sentencing date, shall accord the victim the right to make a statement with regard to any matter relevant to the question of sentence. The court shall notify the defendant no less than seven days prior to sentencing of the victim's intent to make a statement at sentencing. If the defendant does not receive timely notice pursuant to this subdivision, the defendant may request a reasonable adjournment.

(c) Any statement by the victim must precede any statement by counsel to the defendant or the defendant made pursuant to subdivision one of this section. The defendant shall have the right to rebut any statement made by the victim.

(d) Where the people and the defendant have agreed to a disposition which includes a sentence acceptable to the court, and the court intends to impose such sentence, any rebuttal by the defendant shall be limited to an oral presentation made at the time of sentencing.

(e) Where (1) the defendant has been found guilty after trial or there is no agreement between the people and the defendant as to a proposed sentence or the court, after the statement by the victim, chooses not to impose the proposed sentence agreed to by the parties; (2) the statement by the victim includes allegations about the crime that were not fully explored during the proceedings or that materially vary from or contradict the evidence at trial; and (3) the court determines that the allegations are relevant to the issue of sentencing, then the court shall afford the defendant the following rights:

(A) a reasonable adjournment of the sentencing to allow the defendant to present information to rebut the allegations by the victim; and

(B) allow the defendant to present written questions to the court that the defendant desires the court to put to the victim. The court may, in its discretion, decline to put any or all of the questions to the victim. Where the court declines to put any or all of the questions to the victim it shall state its reasons therefor on the record.

(f) If the victim does not appear to make a statement at the time of sentencing, the right to make a statement is waived. The failure of the victim to make a statement shall not be cause for delaying the proceedings against the defendant nor shall it affect the validity of a conviction, judgment or order.

3. The court may, either before or after receiving such statements, summarize the factors it considers relevant for the purpose of sentence and afford an opportunity to the defendant or his or her counsel to comment thereon.

4. Regardless of whether the victim requests to make a statement with regard to the defendant's sentence, where the defendant is committed to the custody of the department of corrections and community supervision upon a sentence of imprisonment for conviction of a violent felony offense as defined in section 70.02 of the penal law or a felony defined in article one hundred twenty-five of such law, or a sex offense as defined in subdivision (p) of section 10.03 of the mental hygiene law, within sixty days of the imposition of sentence the prosecutor shall provide the victim with a form, prepared and distributed by the commissioner of the department of corrections and community supervision, on which the victim may indicate a demand to be informed of the escape, absconding, discharge, parole, conditional release, release to post-release supervision, transfer to the

custody of the office of mental health pursuant to article ten of the mental hygiene law, or release from confinement under article ten of the mental hygiene law of the person so imprisoned. If the victim submits a completed form to the prosecutor, it shall be the duty of the prosecutor to mail promptly such form to the department of corrections and community supervision.

5. Following the receipt of such form from the prosecutor, it shall be the duty of the department of corrections and community supervision or, where the person is committed to the custody of the office of mental health, at the time such person is discharged, paroled, conditionally released, released to post-release supervision, or released from confinement under article ten of the mental hygiene law, to notify the victim of such occurrence by certified mail or with the prior consent of the victim either by regular mail or by electronic transmission using the contact information provided by the victim. In the event such person escapes or absconds from a facility under the jurisdiction of the department of corrections and community supervision, it shall be the duty of such department to notify immediately the victim of such occurrence using the contact information provided by the victim in the most reasonable and expedient possible manner. In the event such escapee or absconder is subsequently taken into custody by the department of corrections and community supervision, it shall be the duty of such department to notify the victim of such occurrence by certified or regular mail or by electronic transmission using the contact information provided by the victim within forty-eight hours of regaining such custody. In the case of a person who escapes or absconds from confinement under article ten of the mental hygiene law, the office of mental health shall notify the victim or victims in accordance with the procedures set forth in subdivision (g) of section 10.10 of the mental hygiene law. In no case shall the state be held liable for failure to provide any notice required by this subdivision.

(Eff. 7/31/21, Ch.210, L.2021)

6. Regardless of whether the victim requests to make a statement with regard to the defendant's sentence, where the defendant is sentenced for a violent felony offense as defined in section 70.02 of the penal law or a felony defined in article one hundred twenty-five of such law or any of the following provisions of such law sections 130.25, 130.30, 130.40, 130.45, 255.25, 255.26, 255.27, article two hundred sixty-three, 135.10, 135.25, 230.05, 230.06, 230.11, 230.12, 230.13, subdivision two of section 230.30 or 230.32, the prosecutor shall, within sixty days of the imposition of sentence, provide the victim with a form, prepared and distributed by the commissioner of the division of criminal justice services, in consultation with the director of the office of victim services, on which the victim may indicate a demand to be informed of any petition to change the name of such defendant. Such forms shall be maintained by such prosecutor. Upon receipt of a notice of a petition to change the name of any such defendant, pursuant to subdivision two of section sixty-two of the civil rights law, the prosecutor shall promptly notify the victim at the most current address or telephone number provided by such victim in the most reasonable and expedient possible manner of the time and place such petition will be presented to the court.

§380.55 Application for poor person relief on appeal.

1. Where counsel has been assigned to represent a defendant in a criminal action on the ground that the defendant is financially unable to retain counsel, the court may in its discretion at the time of sentencing entertain an application to grant the defendant poor person relief on appeal. As part of an application for such relief, assigned counsel must represent that the defendant continues to be eligible for assignment of counsel and that granting the application will expedite the appeal. If the court grants the application, it shall file a written order and shall provide a copy of the order to the appropriate appellate court. The denial of an application shall not preclude the defendant from making a de novo application for poor person relief to the appropriate appellate court.

2. Where counsel has been assigned to represent a defendant in a criminal action on the ground that the defendant is financially unable to retain counsel, the appellate court shall presume the defendant eligible for assignment of counsel on appeal without further proof of eligibility, and, thereby, issue an order assigning such counsel, if counsel provides a sworn representation that the defendant continues to be eligible for assignment of counsel.   *(Eff. 1/14/22, Ch.616, L.2021)*

§380.60   Authority for the execution of sentence.

Except where a sentence of death is pronounced, a sentence and commitment or certificate of conviction showing the sentence pronounced by the court, or a certified copy thereof, constitutes the authority for execution of the sentence and serves as the order of commitment, and no other warrant, order of commitment or authority is necessary to justify or to require execution of the sentence.

§380.65   Sentence and commitment and order of protection to accompany defendant sentenced to imprisonment.

A sentence and commitment or certificate of conviction, specifying the section, and to the extent applicable, the subdivision, paragraph and subparagraph of the penal law or other statute under which the defendant was convicted, or a certified copy thereof, and a copy of any order of protection or temporary order of protection issued against the defendant at the time of sentencing, must be delivered to the person in charge of the correctional facility or office of children and family services facility to which the defendant is committed at the time the defendant is delivered thereto. A sentence and commitment or certificate of conviction is not defective by reason of a failure to comply with the provisions of this section.

*§380.70   Minutes of sentence.

In any case where a person receives an indeterminate or determinate sentence of imprisonment, a certified copy of the stenographic minutes of the sentencing proceeding must be delivered by the court to the person in charge of the institution to which the defendant has been delivered within thirty days from the date such sentence was imposed.

*(Amendments deemed repealed 9/1/23, Ch.55, L.2021)

§380.80 Reporting sentence to social services.

Whenever a person receives a sentence of imprisonment, the court that has sentenced such person shall deliver the certificate of conviction and provide notification of the sentence imposed to the commissioner of social services who, in turn, shall deliver the certificate of conviction and provide notification of the sentence imposed to the appropriate local commissioner of social services.

§380.85 Reporting sentences to office of professional medical conduct; licensed physician, physician assistant, or specialist assistant.

Whenever a person who is a licensed physician, physician assistant, or specialist assistant or a physician who is practicing under a limited permit or as a medical resident is sentenced for a crime, the court that has sentenced such person shall deliver a copy of the certificate of conviction and provide notification of the conviction and sentence to the office of professional medical conduct.

§380.90 Reporting sentences to schools.

1. "Designated educational official" shall mean (a) an employee or representative of a school district who is designated by the school district or (b) an employee or representative of a charter school or private elementary or secondary school who is designated by such school to receive records pursuant to this section and to coordinate the student's participation in programs which may exist in the school district or community, including: non-violent conflict resolution programs, peer mediation programs and youth courts, extended day programs and other school violence prevention and intervention programs.

2. Whenever a person under the age of nineteen who is enrolled as a student in a public or private elementary or secondary school is sentenced for a crime, the court that has sentenced such person shall provide notification of the conviction and sentence to the designated educational official of the school in which such person is enrolled as a student. Such notification shall be used by the designated educational official only for purposes related to the execution of the student's educational plan, where applicable, successful school adjustment and reentry into the community. Such notification shall be kept separate and apart from such student's school records and shall be accessible only by the designated educational official. Such notification shall not be part of such student's permanent school record and shall not be appended to or included in any documentation regarding such student and shall be destroyed at such time as such student is no longer enrolled in the school district. At no time shall such notification be used for any purpose other than those specified in this subdivision.

*§380.95 Reporting convictions of certain school employees.

Upon conviction of a teacher, as defined in subparagraph three of paragraph b of subdivision seven-a of section three hundred five of the education law, of a sex offense or sex offenses defined in subparagraph two of paragraph b of subdivision seven-a of section three hundred five of the education law, the district attorney or other prosecuting authority who obtained such conviction shall provide notice of such conviction to the commissioner of education identifying the sex offense or sex offenses of which the teacher has been convicted, the name and address of such offender and other identifying information prescribed by the commissioner of education, including the offender's date of birth and social security number, to the extent consistent with federal and state laws governing personal privacy and confidentiality of information. Such district attorney or other prosecuting authority shall include in such notice the name and business address of the offender's counsel of record in the criminal proceeding.

* (There are 2 § 380.95's)

*§380.95   Reporting convictions of certain school employees.
  Upon conviction of a school administrator or supervisor, as defined in subparagraph three of paragraph b of subdivision seven-b of section three hundred five of the education law, of an offense defined in subparagraph two of paragraph b of subdivision seven-b of section three hundred five of the education law, the district attorney or other prosecuting authority who obtained such conviction shall provide notice of such conviction to the commissioner of education identifying the offense of which the school administrator or supervisor has been convicted, the name and address of such offender and other identifying information prescribed by the commissioner of education, including the offender's date of birth and social security number, to the extent consistent with federal and state laws governing personal privacy and confidentiality of information. Such district attorney or other prosecuting authority shall include in such notice the name and business address of the offender's counsel of record in the criminal proceeding.

* (There are 2 § 380.95's)

§380.96   Obligation of sentencing court pursuant to article four hundred of the penal law.
  Upon judgment of conviction of any offense which would require the seizure of firearms, shotguns or rifles from an individual so convicted, and the revocation of any license or registration issued pursuant to article four hundred of the penal law, the judge pronouncing sentence shall demand surrender of any such license or registration and all firearms, shotguns and rifles. The failure to so demand surrender shall not effect the validity of any revocation pursuant to article four hundred of the penal law.

§380.97   Notification to division of criminal justice services of certain misdemeanor convictions.
  Upon judgment of conviction of assault in the third degree, menacing in the third degree, menacing in the second degree, criminal obstruction of breathing or blood circulation, unlawful imprisonment in the second degree, coercion in the third degree, criminal tampering in the third degree, criminal contempt in the second degree, harassment in the first degree, or aggravated harassment in the second degree, criminal trespass in the third degree, criminal trespass in the second degree, arson in the fifth degree, or attempt to commit any of the above-listed offenses, when the defendant and victim have been determined, pursuant to section 370.15 of this part, to be members of the same family or household as defined in subdivision one of section 530.11 of this chapter, the clerk of the court shall include notification and a copy of the written determination in a report of such conviction to the division of criminal justice services to enable the division to report such determination to the Federal Bureau of Investigation and assist the bureau

in identifying persons prohibited from purchasing and possessing a firearm or other weapon due to conviction of an offense specified in paragraph c of subdivision seventeen of section 265.00 of the penal law.

(Eff.6/11/18,Ch.60,L.2018)

ARTICLE 390 - PRE-SENTENCE REPORTS

Section
390.10 Requirement of fingerprint report.
390.15 Requirement of HIV related testing in certain cases.
390.20 Requirement of pre-sentence report.
390.30 Scope of pre-sentence investigation and report.
390.40 Defendant's or prosecutor's pre-sentence memorandum.
390.50 Confidentiality of pre-sentence reports and memoranda.
390.60 Copy of reports to accompany defendant sentenced to imprisonment.

§390.10 Requirement of fingerprint report.

In any case where the defendant is convicted of an offense specified in subdivision one of section 160.10, the court may not pronounce sentence until it has received a fingerprint report from the division of criminal justice services or a police department report with respect to the defendant's prior arrest record. For such purpose, the court may use the original fingerprint report obtained after the arrest or arraignment of the defendant, or it may direct that a new report be prepared and transmitted to it.

§390.15 Requirement of HIV related testing in certain cases.

1. (a) In any case where the defendant is convicted of a felony offense enumerated in any section of article one hundred thirty of the penal law, or any subdivision of section 130.20 of such law, where an act of "sexual intercourse", "oral sexual conduct" or "anal sexual conduct," as those terms are defined in section 130.00 of the penal law, is required as an essential element for the commission thereof, the court must, upon a request of the victim, order that the defendant submit to human immunodeficiency (HIV) related testing. The testing is to be conducted by a state, county, or local public health officer designated by the order. Test results, which shall not be disclosed to the court, shall be communicated to the defendant and the victim named in the order in accordance with the provisions of section twenty-seven hundred eighty-five-a of the public health law, but such results and disclosure need not be completed prior to the imposition of sentence.

(b) For the purposes of this section, the terms "defendant", "conviction" and "sentence" mean and include, respectively, an "eligible youth," a "youthful offender finding" and a "youthful offender sentence" as those terms are defined in section 720.10 of this chapter. The term "victim" means the person with whom the defendant engaged in an act of "sexual intercourse", "oral sexual conduct" or "anal sexual conduct", as those terms are defined in section 130.00 of the penal law, where such conduct with such victim was the basis for the defendant's conviction of an offense specified in paragraph (a) of this subdivision.

2. Any request made by the victim pursuant to this section must be in writing, filed with the court and provided by the court to the defendant or his or her counsel. The request must be filed with the court prior to or within ten days after entry of the defendant's conviction; provided that, for good cause shown, the court may permit such request to be filed at any time before sentence is imposed.

3. Any requests, related papers and orders made or filed pursuant to this section, together with any papers or proceedings related thereto, shall be sealed by the court and not made available for any purpose, except as may be necessary for the conduct of judicial proceedings directly related to the provisions of this section. All proceedings on such requests shall be held in camera.

4. The application for an order to compel a convicted person to undergo an HIV related test may be made by the victim but, if the victim is an infant or incompetent person, the application may also be made by a representative as defined in section twelve hundred one of the civil practice law and rules. The application must state that (a) the applicant was the victim of the offense enumerated in paragraph (a) of subdivision one of this section of which the defendant stands convicted; and (b) the applicant has been offered counseling by a public health officer and been advised of (i) the limitations on the information to be obtained through an HIV test on the proposed subject; (ii) current scientific assessments of the risk of transmission of HIV from the exposure he or she may have experienced, and (iii) the need for the applicant to undergo HIV related testing to definitively determine his or her HIV status.

5. The court shall conduct a hearing only if necessary to determine if the applicant is the victim of the offense of which the defendant was convicted. The court ordered test must be performed within fifteen days of the date on which the court ordered the test, provided, however, that whenever the defendant is not tested within the period prescribed by the court, the court must again order that the defendant undergo an HIV related test.

6. (a) Test results shall be disclosed subject to the following limitations, which shall be specified in any order issued pursuant to this section:

(i) disclosure of confidential HIV related information shall be limited to that information which is necessary to fulfill the purpose for which the order is granted;

(ii) disclosure of confidential HIV related information shall be limited to the person making the application; redisclosure shall be permitted only to the victim, the victim's immediate family, guardian, physicians, attorneys, medical or mental health providers and to his or her past and future contacts to whom there was or is a reasonable risk of HIV transmission and shall not be permitted to any other person or the court.

(b) Unless inconsistent with this section, the court's order shall direct compliance with and conform to the provisions of article twenty-seven-F of the public health law. Such order shall include measures to protect against disclosure to others of the identity and HIV status of the applicant and of the person tested and may include such other measures as the court deems necessary to protect confidential information.

7. Any failure to comply with the provisions of this section or section twenty-seven hundred eighty-five-a of the public health law shall not impair or affect the validity of any sentence imposed by the court.

8. No information obtained as a result of a consent, hearing or court order for testing issued pursuant to this section nor any information derived therefrom may be used as evidence in any criminal or civil proceeding against the defendant which relates to events that were the basis for the defendant's conviction, provided however that nothing herein shall prevent prosecution of a witness testifying in any court hearing held pursuant to this section for perjury pursuant to article two hundred ten of the penal law.

§390.20 Requirement of pre-sentence report.

1. Requirement for felonies. In any case where a person is convicted of a felony, the court must order a pre-sentence investigation of the defendant and it may not pronounce sentence until it has received a written report of such investigation.

2. Requirement for misdemeanors. Where a person is convicted of a misdemeanor a pre-sentence report is not required, but the court may not pronounce any of the following sentences unless it has ordered a pre-sentence investigation of the defendant and has received a written report thereof:

(a) A sentence of probation except where the provisions of subparagraph (ii) of paragraph (a) of subdivision four of this section apply;

(b) A sentence of imprisonment for a term in excess of one hundred eighty days;

(c) Consecutive sentences of imprisonment with terms aggregating more than ninety days.

3. Permissible in any case. For purposes of sentence, the court may, in its discretion, order a pre-sentence investigation and report in any case, irrespective of whether such investigation and report is required by subdivision one or two.

4. Waiver. (a) Notwithstanding the provisions of subdivision one or two of this section, a pre-sentence investigation of the defendant and a written report thereon may be waived by the mutual consent of the parties and with consent of the judge, stated on the record or in writing, whenever:

(i) A sentence of imprisonment has been agreed upon by the parties and will be satisfied by the time served, or

(ii) A sentence of probation or conditional discharge has been agreed upon by the parties and will be imposed, or

(iii) A report has been prepared in the preceding twelve months, or

(iv) A sentence of probation is revoked.

*Provided, however, a pre-sentence investigation of the defendant and a written report thereon shall not be waived if an indeterminate or determinate sentence of imprisonment is to be imposed.

(Eff. Until 9/1/23,Ch.55,L.2021)

*Provided, however, a pre-sentence investigation of the defendant and a written report thereon shall not be waived if an indeterminate sentence of imprisonment is to be imposed.   *(Eff.9/1/23,Ch.55,L.2021)*

(b) Whenever a pre-sentence investigation and report has been waived pursuant to subparagraph (i), (ii) or (iii) of paragraph (a) of this subdivision and the court determines that such information would be relevant to the court disposition, a victim impact statement shall be provided in accordance with this section.

5. Negotiated sentence of imprisonment. In any city having a population of one million or more and notwithstanding the provisions of subdivision one or two of this section, a pre-sentence investigation and written report thereon shall not be required where a negotiated sentence of imprisonment for a term of three hundred sixty-five days or less has been mutually agreed upon by the parties with consent of the judge, as a result of a conviction or revocation of a sentence of probation.

§390.30 Scope of pre-sentence investigation and report.

1. The investigation. The pre-sentence investigation consists of the gathering of information with respect to the circumstances attending the commission of the offense, the defendant's history of delinquency or criminality, and the defendant's social history, employment history, family situation, economic status, education, and personal habits. Such investigation may also include any other matter which the agency conducting the investigation deems relevant to the question of sentence, and must include any matter the court directs to be included.

2. Physical and mental examinations. Whenever information is available with respect to the defendant's physical and mental condition, the pre-sentence investigation must include the gathering of such information. In the case of a felony or a class A misdemeanor, or in any case where a person under the age of twenty-one is convicted of a crime, the court may order that the defendant undergo a thorough physical or mental examination in a designated facility and may further order that the defendant remain in such facility for such purpose for a period not exceeding thirty days.

3. The report and victim impact statement. (a) The report of the pre-sentence investigation must contain an analysis of as much of the information gathered in the investigation as the agency that conducted the investigation deems relevant to the question of sentence. The report must also include any other imformation* that the court directs to be included and the material required by paragraph (b) of this subdivision which shall be considered part of the report.   *(So in original.)

(b) The report shall also contain a victim impact statement, unless it appears that such information would be of no relevance to the recommendation or court disposition, which shall include an analysis of the victim's version of the offense, the extent of injury or economic loss and the actual out-of-pocket loss to the victim and the views of the victim relating to disposition including the amount of restitution and reparation sought by the victim after the victim has been informed of the right to seek restitution and reparation, subject to the availability of such information. In the case of a homicide or where the victim is unable to assist in the preparation of the victim impact statement, the information may be acquired from the victim's family. The victim impact statement shall be made available to the victim by the prosecutor pursuant to subdivision two of section 390.50 of this article. Nothing contained in this section shall be interpreted to require that a victim supply information for the preparation of this report.

4. Abbreviated investigation and short form report. In lieu of the procedure set forth in subdivisions one, two and three of this section, where the conviction is of a misdemeanor the scope of the pre-sentence investigation may be abbreviated and a short form report may be made. The use of abbreviated investigations and short form reports, the matters to be covered therein and the form of the reports shall be in accordance with the general rules regulating methods and procedures in the administration of probation as adopted from time to time by the commissioner of the division of criminal justice services pursuant to the provisions of article twelve of the executive law. No such rule, however, shall be construed so as to relieve the agency conducting the investigation of the duty of investigating and reporting upon:

(a) the extent of the injury or economic loss and the actual out-of-pocket loss to the victim including the amount of restitution and reparation sought by the victim, after the victim has been informed of the right to seek restitution and reparation, or

(b) any matter relevant to the question of sentence that the court directs to be included in particular cases.

5. Information to be forwarded to the state office of probation and correctional alternatives. Investigating agencies under this article shall be responsible for the collection, and transmission to the state office of probation and correctional alternatives, of data on the number of victim impact statements prepared. Such information shall be transmitted annually to the office of victim services and included in the office's biennial report pursuant to subdivision twenty-one of section six hundred twenty-three of the executive law.

6. Interim probation supervision. (a) In any case where the court determines that a defendant is eligible for a sentence of probation, the court, after consultation with the prosecutor and upon the consent of the defendant, may adjourn the sentencing to a specified date and order that

the defendant be placed on interim probation supervision. In no event may the sentencing be adjourned for a period exceeding one year from the date the conviction is entered, except that upon good cause shown, the court may, upon the defendant's consent, extend the period for an additional one year where the defendant has agreed to and is still participating in a treatment program in connection with a court designated a treatment court by the chief administrator of the courts. When ordering that the defendant be placed on interim probation supervision, the court shall impose all of the conditions relating to supervision specified in subdivision three of section 65.10 of the penal law and the court may impose any or all of the conditions relating to conduct and rehabilitation specified in subdivisions two, four, five and five-a of section 65.10 of such law. The defendant must receive a written copy of any such conditions at the time he or she is placed on interim probation supervision. The defendant's record of compliance with such conditions, as well as any other relevant information, shall be included in the presentence report, or updated presentence report, prepared pursuant to this section, and the court must consider such record and information when pronouncing sentence. If a defendant satisfactorily completes a term of interim probation supervision, he or she shall receive credit for the time served under the period of interim probation supervision toward any probation sentence that is subsequently imposed in that case.

(Eff.11/12/19,Ch.279,L.2019)

(b) In its discretion, the supervising probation department may utilize the provisions of sections 410.20, 410.30, 410.40, 410.50, 410.60 and 410.92 of this title, where applicable.

§390.40 Defendant's or prosecutor's pre-sentence memorandum.

1. Either the defendant or prosecutor may, at any time prior to the pronouncement of sentence, file with the court a written memorandum setting forth any information he may deem pertinent to the question of sentence. Such memorandum may include information with respect to any of the matters described in section 390.30. The defendant may annex written statements by others in support of facts alleged in the memorandum.

2. The memorandum of the prosecutor shall be served on the defendant's attorney at least ten days prior to the date fixed for sentence.

3. The act of seeking health care for someone who is experiencing a drug or alcohol overdose or other life threatening medical emergency shall be considered by the court when presented as a mitigating factor in any criminal prosecution for a controlled substance, marihuana, drug paraphernalia, or alcohol related offense.

§390.50 Confidentiality of pre-sentence reports and memoranda.

1. In general. Any pre-sentence report or memorandum submitted to the court pursuant to this article and any medical, psychiatric or social agency report or other information gathered for the court by a probation department, or submitted directly to the court, in connection with the question of sentence is confidential and may not be made available to any person or public or private agency except where specifically required or permitted by statute or upon specific authorization of the court. For purposes of this section, any report, memorandum or other information forwarded to a probation department within this state from a probation agency outside this state is governed by the same rules of confidentiality. Any person, public or private agency receiving such material must retain it under the same conditions of confidentiality as apply to the probation department that made it available.

2. Pre-sentence report; disclosure, victim access to impact statements; general principles. (a) Not less than one court day prior to sentencing, unless such time requirement is waived by the parties, the pre-sentence

report or memorandum shall be made available by the court for examination and for copying by the defendant's attorney, the defendant himself, if he has no attorney, and the prosecutor. In its discretion, the court may except from disclosure a part or parts of the report or memoranda which are not relevant to a proper sentence, or a diagnostic opinion which might seriously disrupt a program of rehabilitation, or sources of information which have been obtained on a promise of confidentiality, or any other portion thereof, disclosure of which would not be in the interest of justice. In all cases where a part or parts of the report or memoranda are not disclosed, the court shall state for the record that a part or parts of the report or memoranda have been excepted and the reasons for its action. The action of the court excepting information from disclosure shall be subject to appellate review. The pre-sentence report shall be made available by the court for examination and copying in connection with any appeal in the case, including an appeal under this subdivision. Upon written request, the court shall make a copy of the presentence report, other than a part or parts of the report redacted by the court pursuant to this paragraph, available to the defendant for use before the parole board for release consideration or an appeal of a parole board determination or an application for resentencing pursuant to section 440.46 or 440.47 of this chapter. In his or her written request to the court the defendant shall affirm that he or she anticipates an appearance before the parole board or intends to file an administrative appeal of a parole board determination or meets the eligibility criteria for and intends to file a motion for resentencing pursuant to 440.46 of this chapter or has received notification from the court which received his or her request to apply for resentencing pursuant to section 440.47 of this chapter confirming that he or she is eligible to submit an application for resentencing pursuant to section 440.47 of this chapter. The court shall respond to the defendant's written request within twenty days from receipt of the defendant's written request.   *(Eff.8/12/19,Ch.31,L.2019)*

(b) The victim impact statement prepared pursuant to subdivision three of section 390.30 of this article shall be made available by the prosecutor prior to sentencing to the victim or victim's family in accordance with his responsibilities under subdivision one of section 60.27 of the penal law and sections six hundred forty-one and six hundred forty-two of the executive law. The district attorney shall also give at least twenty-one days notice to the victim or victim's family of the date of sentencing and of the rights of the victim pursuant to subdivision two of section 380.50 of this chapter, including the victim or victim's family's obligation to inform the court of its intention, at least ten days prior to the sentencing date, to make a statement at sentencing. If the victim has not received timely notice pursuant to this paragraph, the court may proceed with sentencing if it determines that the victim and the defendant have received reasonable notice or may adjourn sentencing for no more than seven days in order to afford such reasonable notice. Failure to give notice shall not affect the validity of any sentence imposed.

3. Public agencies within this state. A probation department must make available a copy of its pre-sentence report and any medical, psychiatric or social agency report submitted to it in connection with its pre-sentence investigation or its supervision of a defendant, to any court, or to the probation department of any court, within this state that subsequently has jurisdiction over such defendant for the purpose of pronouncing or reviewing sentence and to any state agency to which the defendant is subsequently committed or certified or under whose care and custody or jurisdiction the defendant subsequently is placed upon the official request of such court or agency therefor. In any such case, the court or agency receiving such material must retain it under the same conditions of confidentiality as apply

to the probation department that made it available, except that an agency with jurisdiction as that term is defined in subdivision (a) of section 10.03 of the mental hygiene law shall make such material available to the commissioner of mental health, attorney general, case review panel, or psychiatric examiners described in article ten of the mental hygiene law when such persons or entities request such material in the exercise of their statutory functions, powers, and duties under article ten of the mental hygiene law.

4. Public agencies outside this state. Upon official request of any probation, parole or public institutional agency outside this state, a probation department may make any information in its files available to such agency. Any such release of information shall be conditioned upon the agreement of the receiving agency to retain it under the same conditions of confidentiality as apply to the probation department that made it available.

5. Division of criminal justice services. Nothing contained in this section may be construed to prevent the voluntary submission by a probation department of data in its files to the division of criminal justice services.

6. Professional licensing agencies. Probation departments shall provide a copy of presentence reports prepared in the case of individuals who are known to be licensed pursuant to title eight of the education law to the state department of health if the licensee is a physician, a specialist's assistant or a physician's assistant, and to the state education department with respect to all other such licensees. Such reports shall be accumulated and forwarded every three months, shall be in writing, may be submitted in a hard copy or electronically, and shall contain the following information:

   (a) the name of the licensee and the profession in which licensure is held,

   (b) the date of the conviction and the nature thereof,

   (c) the index or other identifying file number.

In any such case, the state department receiving such material must retain it under the same conditions of confidentiality as apply to the probation department that made it available.

§390.60 Copy of reports to accompany defendant sentenced to imprisonment.

1. Cases where copy of report is required. Whenever a person is sentenced to a term of imprisonment, a copy of any pre-sentence report prepared, a copy of any pre-sentence memorandum filed by the defendant and a copy of any medical, psychiatric or social agency report submitted to the court or to the probation department in connection with the question of sentence must be delivered to the person in charge of the correctional or division for youth facility to which the defendant is committed at the time the defendant is delivered thereto. When a person is committed to any hospital operated by the office of mental health or referred to any program established pursuant to section four hundred one of the correction law, from a correctional facility or division for youth facility, the person in charge of the correctional facility or division for youth facility shall ensure that a copy of any pre-sentence report concerning such person, a copy of any pre-sentence memorandum filed by such person, and a copy of any medical, psychiatric or social agency report submitted to the court or to the probation department in connection with the question of sentence is provided to such hospital or program.

2. Effect of failure to deliver required report. A commitment is not void by reason of failure to comply with the provisions of subdivision one, but the person in charge of the correctional facility to which the defendant has been delivered in execution of the sentence is authorized to refuse to accept custody of such person until the required report is delivered.

ARTICLE 400 - PRE-SENTENCE PROCEEDINGS

Section
400.10 Pre-sentence conference.
400.15 Procedure for determining whether defendant is a second violent felony
         offender.
400.16 Procedure for determining whether defendant is a persistent violent felony
         offender.
400.19 Procedure for determining whether defendant is a second child sexual assault
         felony offender.
400.20 Procedure for determining whether defendant should be sentenced as a
         persistent felony offender.
400.21 Procedure for determining whether defendant is a second felony offender or a
         second felony drug offender.
400.22 Evidence of imprisonment.
400.27 Procedure for determining sentence upon conviction for the offense of murder in
         the first degree.
400.30 Procedure for determining the amount of a fine based upon the defendant's gain
         from the offense.
400.40 Procedure for determining prior convictions for the purpose of sentence in
         certain cases.

§400.10 Pre-sentence conference.

1. Authorization and purpose. Before pronouncing sentence, the court, in its discretion, may hold one or more pre-sentence conferences in open court or in chambers in order to (a) resolve any discrepancies between the pre-sentence report, or other information the court has received, and the defendant's or prosecutor's pre-sentence memorandum submitted pursuant to section 390.40 or (b) assist the court in its consideration of any matter relevant to the sentence to be pronounced.

2. Attendance. Such conference may be held with the prosecutor and defense counsel in the absence of the defendant, or the court may direct that the defendant attend. The court may also direct that any person who has furnished or who can furnish information to the court concerning sentence attend. Reasonable notice of the conference must be given to the prosecutor and the defense counsel, who must be afforded an opportunity to participate therein.

3. Procedure at conference. The court may advise the persons present at the conference of the factual contents of any report or memorandum it has received and afford any of the participants an opportunity to controvert or to comment upon any fact. The court may also conduct a summary hearing at the conference on any matter relevant to sentence and may take testimony under oath. In the discretion of the court, all or any part of the proceedings at the conference may be recorded by a court stenographer and the transcript made part of the presentence report.

4. Pre-sentence conditions. After conviction and prior to sentencing the court may adjourn sentencing to a subsequent date and order the defendant to comply with any of the conditions contained in paragraphs (a) through (f) and paragraph (l) of subdivision two of section 65.10 of the penal law. In imposing sentence, the court shall take into consideration the defendant's record of compliance with pre-sentence conditions ordered by the court.

§400.15 Procedure for determining whether defendant is a second violent felony offender.

1. Applicability. The provisions of this section govern the procedure that must be followed in any case where it appears that a defendant who stands convicted of a violent felony offense as defined in subdivision one of section 70.02 of the penal law has previously been subject to a predicate violent

felony conviction as defined in paragraph (b) of subdivision one of section 70.04 of the penal law and may be a second violent felony offender.

2. Statement to be filed. When information available to the court or to the people prior to sentencing for a violent felony offense indicates that the defendant may have previously been subjected to a predicate violent felony conviction, a statement must be filed by the prosecutor before sentence is imposed setting forth the date and place of each alleged predicate violent felony conviction. Where the provisions of subparagraph (v) of paragraph (c) of subdivision one of section 70.04 of the penal law apply, such statement also shall set forth the date of commencement and the date of termination as well as the place of imprisonment for each period of incarceration to be used for tolling of the ten year limitation set forth in subparagraph (iv) of paragraph (b) of such subdivision.

3. Preliminary examination. The defendant must be given a copy of such statement and the court must ask him whether he wishes to controvert any allegation made therein. If the defendant wishes to controvert any allegation in the statement, he must specify the particular allegation or allegations he wishes to controvert. Uncontroverted allegations in the statement shall be deemed to have been admitted by the defendant.

4. Cases where further hearing is not required. Where the uncontroverted allegations in the statement are sufficient to support a finding that the defendant has been subjected to a predicate violent felony conviction the court must enter such finding and when imposing sentence must sentence the defendant in accordance with the provisions of section 70.04 of the penal law.

5. Cases where further hearing is required. Where the defendant controverts an allegation in the statement and the uncontroverted allegations in such statement are not sufficient to support a finding that the defendant has been subjected to a predicate violent felony conviction the court must proceed to hold a hearing.

6. Time for hearing. In any case where a copy of the statement was not received by the defendant at least two days prior to the preliminary examination, the court must upon request of the defendant grant an adjournment of at least two days before proceeding with the hearing.

7. Manner of conducting hearing.

(a) A hearing pursuant to this section must be before the court without jury. The burden of proof is upon the people and a finding that the defendant has been subjected to a predicate violent felony conviction must be based upon proof beyond a reasonable doubt by evidence admissible under the rules applicable to a trial of the issue of guilt.

(b) A previous conviction in this or any other jurisdiction which was obtained in violation of the rights of the defendant under the applicable provisions of the constitution of the United States must not be counted in determining whether the defendant has been subjected to a predicate violent felony conviction. The defendant may, at any time during the course of the hearing hereunder controvert an allegation with respect to such conviction in the statement on the grounds that the conviction was unconstitutionally obtained. Failure to challenge the previous conviction in the manner provided herein constitutes a waiver on the part of the defendant of any allegation of unconstitutionality unless good cause be shown for such failure to make timely challenge.

(c) At the conclusion of the hearing the court must make a finding as to whether or not the defendant has been subjected to a predicate violent felony conviction.

8. Subsequent use of predicate violent felony conviction finding. Where a finding has been entered pursuant to this section, such finding shall be binding upon the defendant in any future proceeding in which the issue may arise.

§400.16 Procedure for determining whether defendant is a persistent violent felony offender.

1. Applicability. The provisions of this section govern the procedure that must be followed in any case where it appears that a defendant who stands convicted of a violent felony offense as defined in subdivision one of section 70.02 of the penal law has previously been subjected to two or more predicate violent felony convictions as defined in paragraph (b) of subdivision one of section 70.04, and may be a persistent violent felony offender as defined in section 70.08 of the penal law.

2. Statement; preliminary examination; hearing; subsequent use of predicate violent felony conviction finding. The requirements set forth in subdivisions two, three, four, five, six, seven and eight of section 400.15 with respect to the statement to be filed, preliminary examination, hearing and subsequent use of a predicate violent felony conviction finding in the case of a second violent felony offender, shall also apply to a determination of whether a defendant has been subjected to two or more violent predicate felony convictions and is a persistent violent felony offender.

§400.19 Procedure for determining whether defendant is a second child sexual assault felony offender.

1. Applicability. The provisions of this section govern the procedure that must be followed in any case where it appears that a defendant who stands convicted of a felony offense for a sexual assault upon a child as defined in section 70.07 of the penal law has previously been convicted of a predicate felony for a sexual assault upon a child.

2. Statement to be filed. When information available to the people prior to the trial of a felony offense for a sexual assault against a child indicates that the defendant may have previously been subjected to a predicate felony conviction for a sexual assault against a child, a statement may be filed by the prosecutor at any time before trial commences setting forth the date and place of each alleged predicate felony conviction for a sexual assault against a child and a statement whether the defendant was eighteen years of age or older at the time of the commission of the predicate felony. Where the provisions of subparagraph (v) of paragraph (b) of subdivision one of section 70.06 of the penal law apply, such statement also shall set forth the date of commencement and the date of termination as well as the place of imprisonment for each period of incarceration to be used for tolling of the ten year limitation set forth in subparagraph (iv) of paragraph (b) of such subdivision.

3. Preliminary examination. The defendant must be given a copy of such statement and the court must ask him whether he wishes to controvert any allegation made therein. If the defendant wishes to controvert any allegation in the statement, he must specify the particular allegation or allegations he wishes to controvert. Uncontroverted allegations in the statement shall be deemed to have been admitted by the defendant.

4. Cases where further hearing is not required. Where the uncontroverted allegations in the statement are sufficient to support a finding that the defendant has been subjected to a predicate felony conviction for a sexual assault upon a child and that the defendant was 18 years of age or older at the time of the commission of the predicate felony, the court must enter such finding and when imposing sentence must sentence the defendant in accordance with the provisions of section 70.07 of the penal law.

5. Cases where further hearing is required. Where the defendant controverts an allegation in the statement, the court must proceed to hold a hearing.

6. Manner of conducting hearing. (a) A hearing pursuant to this section must be before the court without jury. The burden of proof is upon the people and a finding that the defendant has been subjected to a predicate felony conviction for a sexual assault against a child as defined in subdivision two of section 70.07 of the penal law and that the defendant was 18 years of age or older at the time of the commission of the predicate felony must be based upon proof beyond a reasonable doubt by evidence admissible under the rules applicable to a trial of the issue of guilt.

(b) Regardless of whether the age of the victim is an element of the alleged predicate felony offense, where the defendant controverts an allegation that the victim of an alleged sexual assault upon a child was less than fifteen years old, the people may prove that the child was less than fifteen years old by any evidence admissible under the rules applicable to a trial of the issue of guilt. For purposes of determining whether a child was less than fifteen years old, the people shall not be required to prove that the defendant knew the child was less than fifteen years old at the time of the alleged sexual assault.

(c) A previous conviction in this or any other jurisdiction which was obtained in violation of the rights of the defendant under the applicable provisions of the constitution of the United States must not be counted in determining whether the defendant has been subjected to a predicate felony conviction for a sexual assault upon a child. The defendant may, at any time during the course of the hearing hereunder, controvert an allegation with respect to such conviction in the statement on the grounds that the conviction was unconstitutionally obtained. Failure to challenge the previous conviction in the manner provided herein constitutes a waiver on the part of the defendant of any allegation of unconstitutionality unless good cause be shown for such failure to make timely challenge.

(d) At the conclusion of the hearing the court must make a finding as to whether or not the defendant has been subjected to a predicate felony conviction for a sexual assault against a child as defined in subdivision two of section 70.07 of the penal law and whether the defendant was 18 years of age or older at the time of the commission of the predicate felony.

7. Subsequent use of predicate felony conviction finding. Where a finding has been entered pursuant to this section, such finding shall be binding in any future proceeding in which the issue may arise.

§400.20 Procedure for determining whether defendant should be sentenced as a persistent felony offender.

1. Applicability. The provisions of this section govern the procedure that must be followed in order to impose the persistent felony offender sentence authorized by subdivision two of section 70.10 of the penal law. Such sentence may not be imposed unless, based upon evidence in the record of a hearing held pursuant to this section, the court (a) has found that the defendant is a persistent felony offender as defined in subdivision one of section 70.10 of the penal law, and (b) is of the opinion that the history and character of the defendant and the nature and circumstances of his criminal conduct are such that extended incarceration and lifetime supervision of the defendant are warranted to best serve the public interest.

2. Authorization for hearing. When information available to the court prior to sentencing indicates that the defendant is a persistent felony offender, and when, in the opinion of the court, the available information shows that a persistent felony offender sentence may be warranted, the

court may order a hearing to determine (a) whether the defendant is in fact a persistent felony offender, and (b) if so, whether a persistent felony offender sentence should be imposed.

3. Order directing a hearing. An order directing a hearing to determine whether the defendant should be sentenced as a persistent felony offender must be filed with the clerk of the court and must specify a date for the hearing not less than twenty days from the date the order is filed. The court must annex to and file with the order a statement setting forth the following:

(a) The dates and places of the previous convictions which render the defendant a persistent felony offender as defined in subdivision one of section 70.10 of the penal law; and

(b) The factors in the defendant's background and prior criminal conduct which the court deems relevant for the purpose of sentencing the defendant as a persistent felony offender.

4. Notice of hearing. Upon receipt of the order and statement of the court, the clerk of the court must sent a notice of hearing to the defendant, his counsel and the district attorney. Such notice must specify the time and place of the hearing and the fact that the purpose of the hearing is to determine whether or not the defendant should be sentenced as a persistent felony offender. Each notice required to be sent hereunder must be accompanied by a copy of the statement of the court.

5. Burden and standard of proof; evidence. Upon any hearing held pursuant to this section the burden of proof is upon the people. A finding that the defendant is a persistent felony offender, as defined in subdivision one of section 70.10 of the penal law, must be based upon proof beyond a reasonable doubt by evidence admissible under the rules applicable to the trial of the issue of guilt. Matters pertaining to the defendant's history and character and the nature and circumstances of his criminal conduct may be established by any relevant evidence, not legally privileged, regardless of admissibility under the exclusionary rules of evidence, and the standard of proof with respect to such matters shall be a preponderance of the evidence.

6. Constitutionality of prior convictions. A previous conviction in this or any other jurisdiction which was obtained in violation of the rights of the defendant under the applicable provisions of the Constitution of the United States may not be counted in determining whether the defendant is a persistent felony offender. The defendant may, at any time during the course of the hearing hereunder controvert an allegation with respect to such conviction in the statement of the court on the grounds that the conviction was unconstitutionally obtained. Failure to challenge the previous conviction in the manner provided herein constitutes a waiver on the part of the defendant of any allegation of unconstitutionality unless good cause be shown for such failure to make timely challenge.

7. Preliminary examination. When the defendant appears for the hearing the court must ask him whether he wishes to controvert any allegation made in the statement prepared by the court, and whether he wishes to present evidence on the issue of whether he is a persistent felony offender or on the question of his background and criminal conduct. If the defendant wishes to controvert any allegation in the statement of the court, he must specify the particular allegation or allegations he wishes to controvert. If he wishes to present evidence in his own behalf, he must specify the nature of such evidence. Uncontroverted allegations in the statement of the court are deemed evidence in the record.

8. Cases where further hearing is not required. Where the uncontroverted allegations in the statement of the court are sufficient to support a finding that the defendant is a persistent felony offender and the court is satisfied that (a) the uncontroverted allegations with respect to the defendant's background and the nature of his prior criminal conduct warrant sentencing the defendant as a persistent felony offender, and (b) the defendant either has no

relevant evidence to present or the facts which could be established through the evidence offered by the defendant would not affect the court's decision, the court may enter a finding that the defendant is a persistent felony offender and sentence him in accordance with the provisions of subdivision two of section 70.10 of the penal law.

9. Cases where further hearing is required. Where the defendant controverts an allegation in the statement of the court and the uncontroverted allegations in such statement are not sufficient to support a finding that the defendant is a persistent felony offender as defined in subdivision one of section 70.10 of the penal law, or where the uncontroverted allegations with respect to the defendant's history and the nature of his prior criminal conduct do not warrant sentencing him as a persistent felony offender, or where the defendant has offered to present evidence to establish facts that would affect the court's decision on the question of whether a persistent felony offender sentence is warranted, the court may fix a date for a further hearing. Such hearing shall be before the court without a jury and either party may introduce evidence with respect to the controverted allegations or any other matter relevant to the issue of whether or not the defendant should be sentenced as a persistent felony offender. At the conclusion of the hearing the court must make a finding as to whether or not the defendant is a persistent felony offender and, upon a finding that he is such, must then make such findings of fact as it deems relevant to the question of whether a persistent felony offender sentence is warranted. If the court both finds that the defendant is a persistent felony offender and is of the opinion that a persistent felony offender sentence is warranted, it may sentence the defendant in accordance with the provisions of subdivision two of section 70.10 of the penal law.

10. Termination of hearing. At any time during the pendency of a hearing pursuant to this section, the court may, in its discretion, terminate the hearing without making any finding. In such case, unless the court recommences the proceedings and makes the necessary findings, the defendant may not be sentenced as a persistent felony offender.

§400.21 Procedure for determining whether defendant is a second felony offender or a second felony drug offender.

1. Applicability. The provisions of this section govern the procedure that must be followed in any case where it appears that a defendant who stands convicted of a felony has previously been convicted of a predicate felony and may be a second felony offender as defined in section 70.06 of the penal law or a second felony drug offender as defined in either paragraph (b) of subdivision one of section 70.70 of the penal law, or paragraph (b) of subdivision one of section 70.71 of the penal law.

2. Statement to be filed. When information available to the court or to the people prior to sentencing for a felony indicates that the defendant may have previously been subjected to a predicate felony conviction, a statement must be filed by the prosecutor before sentence is imposed setting forth the date and place of each alleged predicate felony conviction and whether the predicate felony conviction was a violent felony as that term is defined in subdivision one of section 70.02 of the penal law, or in any other jurisdiction of an offense which includes all of the essential elements of any such felony for which a sentence to a term of imprisonment in excess of one year or death was authorized and is authorized in this state regardless of whether such sentence was imposed. Where the provisions of subparagraph (v) of paragraph (b) of subdivision one of section 70.06 of the penal law apply, such statement also shall set forth the date of commencement and the date of termination as well as the state or local incarcerating agency for each period of incarceration to be used for tolling of the ten year limitation set forth in subparagraph (iv) of paragraph (b) of such subdivision.

3. Preliminary examination. The defendant must be given a copy of such statement and the court must ask him or her whether he or she wishes to controvert any allegation made therein. If the defendant wishes to controvert any allegation in the statement, he must specify the particular allegation or allegations he wishes to controvert. Uncontroverted allegations in the statement shall be deemed to have been admitted by the defendant.

4. Cases where further hearing is not required. Where the uncontroverted allegations in the statement are sufficient to support a finding that the defendant has been subjected to a predicate felony conviction the court must enter such finding, including a finding that the predicate felony conviction was of a violent felony as that term is defined in subdivision one of section 70.02 of the penal law, or in any other jurisdiction of an offense which includes all of the essential elements of any such felony for which a sentence to a term of imprisonment in excess of one year or death was authorized and is authorized in this state regardless of whether such sentence was imposed, and when imposing sentence must sentence the defendant in accordance with the applicable provisions of section 70.06, 70.70 or 70.71 of the penal law.

5. Cases where further hearing is required. Where the defendant controverts an allegation in the statement and the uncontroverted allegations in such statement are not sufficient to support a finding that the defendant has been subjected to such a predicate felony conviction the court must proceed to hold a hearing.

6. Time for hearing. In any case where a copy of the statement was not received by the defendant at least two days prior to the preliminary examination, the court must upon the request of the defendant grant an adjournment of at least two days before proceeding with the hearing.

7. Manner of conducting hearing. (a) A hearing pursuant to this section must be before the court without jury. The burden of proof is upon the people and a finding that the defendant has been subjected to such a predicate felony conviction must be based upon proof beyond a reasonable doubt by evidence admissible under the rules applicable to a trial of the issue of guilt.

(b) A previous conviction in this or any other jurisdiction which was obtained in violation of the rights of the defendant under the applicable provisions of the constitution of the United States must not be counted in determining whether the defendant has been subjected to such a predicate felony conviction. The defendant may, at any time during the course of the hearing hereunder controvert an allegation with respect to such conviction in the statement on the grounds that the conviction was unconstitutionally obtained. Failure to challenge the previous conviction in the manner provided herein constitutes a waiver on the part of the defendant of any allegation of unconstitutionality unless good cause be shown for such failure to make timely challenge.

(c) At the conclusion of the hearing the court must make a finding as to whether or not the defendant has been subjected to a predicate felony conviction, including a finding as to whether or not the predicate felony conviction was of a violent felony as that term is defined in subdivision one of section 70.02 of the penal law, or in any other jurisdiction of an offense which includes all of the essential elements of any such felony for which a sentence to a term of imprisonment in excess of one year or death was authorized and is authorized in this state regardless of whether such sentence was imposed.

8. Subsequent use of predicate felony conviction finding. Where a finding has been entered pursuant to this section, such finding shall be binding upon that defendant in any future proceeding in which the issue may arise.

§400.22 Evidence of imprisonment.

The certificate of the commissioner of correction or of the warden or other chief officer of any prison, or of the superintendent or other chief officer of any penitentiary under the seal of his office containing name of person, a statement of the court in which conviction was had, the date and term of sentence, length of time imprisoned, and date of discharge from prison or penitentiary, shall be prima facie evidence of the imprisonment and discharge of any person under the conviction stated and set forth in such certificate for the purposes of any proceeding under section 400.20.

§400.27 Procedure for determining sentence upon conviction for the offense of murder in the first degree.

1. Upon the conviction of a defendant for the offense of murder in the first degree as defined by section 125.27 of the penal law, the court shall promptly conduct a separate sentencing proceeding to determine whether the defendant shall be sentenced to death or to life imprisonment without parole pursuant to subdivision five of section 70.00 of the penal law. Nothing in this section shall be deemed to preclude the people at any time from determining that the death penalty shall not be sought in a particular case, in which case the separate sentencing proceeding shall not be conducted and the court may sentence such defendant to life imprisonment without parole or to a sentence of imprisonment for the class A-I felony of murder in the first degree other than a sentence of life imprisonment without parole.

2. The separate sentencing proceeding provided for by this section shall be conducted before the court sitting with the jury that found the defendant guilty. The court may discharge the jury and impanel another jury only in extraordinary circumstances and upon a showing of good cause, which may include, but is not limited to, a finding of prejudice to either party. If a new jury is impaneled, it shall be formed in accordance with the procedures in article two hundred seventy of this chapter. Before proceeding with the jury that found the defendant guilty, the court shall determine whether any juror has a state of mind that is likely to preclude the juror from rendering an impartial decision based upon the evidence adduced during the proceeding. In making such determination the court shall personally examine each juror individually outside the presence of the other jurors. The scope of the examination shall be within the discretion of the court and may include questions supplied by the parties as the court deems proper. The proceedings provided for in this subdivision shall be conducted on the record; provided, however, that upon motion of either party, and for good cause shown, the court may direct that all or a portion of the record of such proceedings be sealed. In the event the court determines that a juror has such a state of mind, the court shall discharge the juror and replace the juror with the alternate juror whose name was first drawn and called. If no alternate juror is available, the court must discharge the jury and impanel another jury in accordance with article two hundred seventy of this chapter.

3. For the purposes of a proceeding under this section each subparagraph of paragraph (a) of subdivision one of section 125.27 of the penal law shall be deemed to define an aggravating factor. Except as provided in subdivision seven of this section, at a sentencing proceeding pursuant to this section the only aggravating factors that the jury may consider are those proven beyond a reasonable doubt at trial, and no other aggravating factors may be considered. Whether a sentencing proceeding is conducted before the jury that found the defendant guilty or before another jury, the aggravating factor or factors proved at trial shall be deemed established beyond a reasonable doubt at the separate sentencing

proceeding and shall not be relitigated. Where the jury is to determine sentences for concurrent counts of murder in the first degree, the aggravating factor included in each count shall be deemed to be an aggravating factor for the purpose of the jury's consideration in determining the sentence to be imposed on each such count.

4. The court on its own motion or on motion of either party, in the interest of justice or to avoid prejudice to either party, may delay the commencement of the separate sentencing proceeding.

5. Notwithstanding the provisions of article three hundred ninety of this chapter, where a defendant is found guilty of murder in the first degree, no pre-sentence investigation shall be conducted; provided, however, that where the court is to impose a sentence of imprisonment, a pre-sentence investigation shall be conducted and a pre-sentence report shall be prepared in accordance with the provisions of such article.

6. At the sentencing proceeding the people shall not relitigate the existence of aggravating factors proved at the trial or otherwise present evidence, except, subject to the rules governing admission of evidence in the trial of a criminal action, in rebuttal of the defendant's evidence. However, when the sentencing proceeding is conducted before a newly impaneled jury, the people may present evidence to the extent reasonably necessary to inform the jury of the nature and circumstances of the count or counts of murder in the first degree for which the defendant was convicted in sufficient detail to permit the jury to determine the weight to be accorded the aggravating factor or factors established at trial. Whenever the people present such evidence, the court must instruct the jury in its charge that any facts elicited by the people that are not essential to the verdict of guilty on such count or counts shall not be deemed established beyond a reasonable doubt. Subject to the rules governing the admission of evidence in the trial of a criminal action, the defendant may present any evidence relevant to any mitigating factor set forth in subdivision nine of this section; provided, however, the defendant shall not be precluded from the admission of reliable hearsay evidence. The burden of establishing any of the mitigating factors set forth in subdivision nine of this section shall be on the defendant, and must be proven by a preponderance of the evidence. The people shall not offer evidence or argument relating to any mitigating factor except in rebuttal of evidence offered by the defendant.

7. (a) The people may present evidence at the sentencing proceeding to prove that in the ten year period prior to the commission of the crime of murder in the first degree for which the defendant was convicted, the defendant has previously been convicted of two or more offenses committed on different occasions; provided, that each such offense shall be either (i) a class A felony offense other than one defined in article two hundred twenty of the penal law, a class B violent felony offense specified in paragraph (a) of subdivision of one of section 70.02 of the penal law, or a felony offense under the penal law a necessary element of which involves either the use or attempted use or threatened use of a deadly weapon or the intentional infliction of or the attempted intentional infliction of serious physical injury or death, or (ii) an offense under the laws of another state or of the United States punishable by a term of imprisonment of more than one year a necessary element of which involves either the use or attempted use or threatened use of a deadly weapon or the intentional infliction of or the attempted intentional inflic-

tion of serious physical injury or death. For the purpose of this paragraph, the term "deadly weapon" shall have the meaning set forth in subdivision twelve of section 10.00 of the penal law. In calculating the ten year period under this paragraph, any period of time during which the defendant was incarcerated for any reason between the time of commission of any of the prior felony offenses and the time of commission of the crime of murder in the first degree shall be excluded and such ten year period shall be extended by a period or periods equal to the time served under such incarceration. The defendant's conviction of two or more such offenses shall, if proven at the sentencing proceeding, constitute an aggravating factor.

(b) In order to be deemed established, an aggravating factor set forth in this subdivision must be proven by the people beyond a reasonable doubt and the jury must unanimously find such factor to have been so proven. The defendant may present evidence relating to an aggravating factor defined in this subdivision and either party may offer evidence in rebuttal. Any evidence presented by either party relating to such factor shall be subject to the rules governing admission of evidence in the trial of a criminal action.

(c) Whenever the people intend to offer evidence of an aggravating factor set forth in this subdivision, the people must within a reasonable time prior to trial file with the court and serve upon the defendant a notice of intention to offer such evidence. Whenever the people intend to offer evidence of the aggravating factor set forth in paragraph (a) of this subdivision, the people shall file with the notice of intention to offer such evidence a statement setting forth the date and place of each of the alleged offenses in paragraph (a) of this subdivision. The provisions of section 400.15 of this chapter, except for subdivisions one and two thereof, shall be followed.

8. Consistent with the provisions of this section, the people and the defendant shall be given fair opportunity to rebut any evidence received at the separate sentencing proceeding.

9. Mitigating factors shall include the following:

(a) The defendant has no significant history of prior criminal convictions involving the use of violence against another person;

(b) The defendant was mentally retarded at the time of the crime, or the defendant's mental capacity was impaired or his ability to conform his conduct to the requirements of law was impaired but not so impaired in either case as to constitute a defense to prosecution;

(c) The defendant was under duress or under the domination of another person, although not such duress or domination as to constitute a defense to prosecution;

(d) The defendant was criminally liable for the present offense of murder committed by another, but his participation in the offense was relatively minor although not so minor as to constitute a defense to prosecution;

(e) The murder was committed while the defendant was mentally or emotionally disturbed or under the influence of alcohol or any drug, although not to such an extent as to constitute a defense to prosecution; or

(f) Any other circumstance concerning the crime, the defendant's state of mind or condition at the time of the crime, or the defendant's character, background or record that would be relevant to mitigation or punishment for the crime.

10. At the conclusion of all the evidence, the people and the defendant may present argument in summation for or against the sentence sought by the people. The people may deliver the first summation and the defendant may then deliver the last summation. Thereafter, the court shall deliver a charge to the jury on any matters appropriate in the circumstances. In its charge, the court must instruct the jury that with respect to each count of murder in the first degree the jury should consider whether or not a sentence of death should be imposed and whether or not a sentence of life imprisonment without parole should be imposed, and that the jury must be unanimous with respect to either sentence. The court must also instruct the jury that in the event the jury fails to reach unanimous agreement with respect to the sentence, the court will sentence the defendant to a term of imprisonment with a minimum term of between twenty and twenty-five years and a maximum term of life. Following the court's charge, the jury shall retire to consider the sentence to be imposed. Unless inconsistent with the provisions of this section, the provisions of sections 310.10, 310.20 and 310.30 shall govern the deliberations of the jury.

11. (a) The jury may not direct imposition of a sentence of death unless it unanimously finds beyond a reasonable doubt that the aggravating factor or factors substantially out weigh the mitigating factor or factors established, if any, and unanimously determines that the penalty of death should be imposed. Any member or members of the jury who find a mitigating factor to have been proven by the defendant by a preponderance of the evidence may consider such factor established regardless of the number of jurors who concur that the factor has been established.

(b) If the jury directs imposition of either a sentence of death or life imprisonment without parole, it shall specify on the record those mitigating and aggravating factors considered and those mitigating factors established by the defendant, if any.

(c) With respect to a count or concurrent counts of murder in the first degree, the court may direct the jury to cease deliberation with respect to the sentence or sentences to be imposed if the jury has deliberated for an extensive period of time without reaching unanimous agreement on the sentence or sentences to be imposed and the court is satisfied that any such agreement is unlikely within a reasonable time. The provisions of this paragraph shall apply with respect to consecutive counts of murder in the first degree. In the event the jury is unable to reach unanimous agreement, the court must sentence the defendant in accordance with subdivisions one through three of section 70.00 of the penal law with respect to any count or counts of murder in the first degree upon which the jury failed to reach unanimous agreement as to the sentence to be imposed.

(d) If the jury unanimously determines that a sentence of death should be imposed, the court must thereupon impose a sentence of death. Thereafter, however, the court may, upon written motion of the defendant, set aside the sentence of death upon any of the grounds set forth in section 330.30. The procedures set forth in sections 330.40 and 330.50, as applied to separate sentencing proceedings under this section, shall govern the motion and the court upon granting the motion shall, except as may otherwise be required by subdivision one of section 330.50, direct a new sentencing proceeding pursuant to this section. Upon granting the motion upon any of the grounds set forth in section 330.30 and setting aside the sentence, the court must afford the people a reasonable period of time, which shall not be less than ten days, to determine whether to take an appeal from the order setting aside the sentence of death. The taking of an appeal by the people stays the effectiveness of that portion of the court's order that directs a new sentencing proceeding.

(e) If the jury unanimously determines that a sentence of life imprisonment without parole should be imposed the court must thereupon impose a sentence of life imprisonment without parole.

(f) Where a sentence has been unanimously determined by the jury it must be recorded on the minutes and read to the jury, and the jurors must be collectively asked whether such is their sentence. Even though no juror makes any declaration in the negative, the jury must, if either party makes such an application, be polled and each juror separately asked whether the sentence announced by the foreman is in all respects his or her sentence. If, upon either the collective or the separate inquiry, any juror answers in the negative, the court must refuse to accept the sentence and must direct the jury to resume its deliberation. If no disagreement is expressed, the jury must be discharged from the case.

12. (a) Upon the conviction of a defendant for the offense of murder in the first degree as defined in section 125.27 of the penal law, the court shall, upon oral or written motion of the defendant based upon a showing that there is reasonable cause to believe that the defendant is mentally retarded, promptly conduct a hearing without a jury to determine whether the defendant is mentally retarded. Upon the consent of both parties, such a hearing, or a portion thereof, may be conducted by the court contemporaneously with the separate sentencing proceeding in the presence of the sentencing jury, which in no event shall be the trier of fact with respect to the hearing. At such hearing the defendant has the burden of proof by a preponderance of the evidence that he or she is mentally retarded. The court shall defer rendering any finding pursuant to this subdivision as to whether the defendant is mentally retarded until a sentence is imposed pursuant to this section.

(b) In the event the defendant is sentenced pursuant to this section to life imprisonment without parole or to a term of imprisonment for the class A-I felony of murder in the first degree other than a sentence of life imprisonment without parole, the court shall not render a finding with respect to whether the defendant is mentally retarded.

(c) In the event the defendant is sentenced pursuant to this section to death, the court shall thereupon render a finding with respect to whether the defendant is mentally retarded. If the court finds the defendant is mentally retarded, the court shall set aside the sentence of death and sentence the defendant either to life imprisonment without parole or to a term of imprisonment for the class A-I felony of murder in the first degree other than a sentence of life imprisonment without parole. If the court finds the defendant is not mentally retarded, then such sentence of death shall not be set aside pursuant to this subdivision.

(d) In the event that a defendant is convicted of murder in the first degree pursuant to subparagraph (iii) of paragraph (a) of subdivision one of section 125.27 of the penal law, and the killing occurred while the defendant was confined or under custody in a state correctional facility or local correctional institution, and a sentence of death is imposed, such sentence may not be set aside pursuant to this subdivision upon the ground that the defendant is mentally retarded. Nothing in this paragraph or paragraph (a) of this subdivision shall preclude a defendant from presenting mitigating evidence of mental retardation at the separate sentencing proceeding.

(e) The foregoing provisions of this subdivision notwithstanding, at a reasonable time prior to the commencement of trial the defendant may, upon a written motion alleging reasonable cause to believe the defendant is mentally retarded, apply for an order directing that a mental retardation hearing be conducted prior to trial. If, upon review of the defendant's motion and any response thereto, the court finds reasonable cause to believe the defendant is mentally retarded, it shall promptly conduct a hearing without a jury to determine whether the defendant is mentally retarded. In the event the court finds after the hearing that the defendant is not mentally retarded, the court must, prior to commencement of trial, enter an order so stating, but nothing in this paragraph shall preclude a defendant from presenting mitigating evidence of mental retardation at a separate sentencing proceeding. In the event the court finds after the hearing that the defendant, based upon a preponderance of the evidence, is mentally retarded, the court must, prior to commencement of trial, enter an order so stating. Unless the order is reversed on an appeal by the people or unless the provisions of paragraph (d) of this subdivision apply, a separate sentencing proceeding under this section shall not be conducted if the defendant is thereafter convicted of murder in the first degree. In the event a separate sentencing proceeding is not conducted, the court, upon conviction of a defendant for the crime of murder in the first degree, shall sentence the defendant to life imprisonment without parole or to a sentence of imprisonment for the class A-I felony of murder in the first degree other than a sentence of life imprisonment without parole, Whenever a mental retardation hearing is held and a finding is rendered pursuant to this paragraph, the court may not conduct a hearing pursuant to paragraph (a) of this subdivision. For purposes of this subdivision and paragraph (b) of subdivision nine of this section, "mental retardation" means significantly subaverage general intellectual functioning existing concurrently with deficits in adaptive behavior which were manifested before the age of eighteen.

(f) In the event the court enters an order pursuant to paragraph (e) of this subdivision finding that the defendant is mentally retarded, the people may appeal as of right from the order pursuant to subdivision ten of section 450.20 of this chapter. Upon entering such an order the court must afford the people a reasonable period of time, which shall not be less than ten days, to determine whether to take an appeal from the order finding that the defendant is mentally retarded. The taking of an appeal by the people stays the effectiveness of the court's order and any order fixing a date for trial. Within six months of the effective date of this subdivision, the court of appeals shall adopt rules to ensure that appeals pursuant to this paragraph are expeditiously perfected, reviewed and determined so that pre-trial delays are minimized. Prior to adoption of the rules, the court of appeals shall issue proposed rules and receive written comments thereon from interested parties.

13. (a) As used in this subdivision, the term "psychiatric evidence" means evidence of mental disease, defect or condition in connection with either a mitigating factor defined in this section or a mental retardation hearing pursuant to this section to be offered by a psychiatrist, psychologist or other person who has received training, or education, or

has experience relating to the identification, diagnosis, treatment or evaluation of mental disease, mental defect or mental condition.

(b) When either party intends to offer psychiatric evidence, the party must, within a reasonable time prior to trial, serve upon the other party and file with the court a written notice of intention to present psychiatric evidence. The notice shall include a brief but detailed statement specifying the witness, nature and type of psychiatric evidence sought to be introduced. If either party fails to serve and file written notice, no psychiatric evidence is admissible unless the party failing to file thereafter serves and files such notice and the court affords the other party an adjournment for a reasonable period. If a party fails to give timely notice, the court in its discretion may impose upon offending counsel a reasonable monetary sanction for an intentional failure but may not in any event preclude the psychiatric evidence. In the event a monetary sanction is imposed, the offending counsel shall be personally liable therefor, and shall not receive reimbursement of any kind from any source in order to pay the cost of such monetary sanction. Nothing contained herein shall preclude the court from entering an order directing a party to provide timely notice.

(c) When a defendant serves notice purusant to this subdivision, the district attorney may make application, upon notice to the defendant, for an order directing that the defendant submit to an examination by a psychiatrist, licensed psychologist, or licensed clinical social worker designated by the district attorney, for the purpose of rebutting evidence offered by the defendant with respect to a mental disease, defect, or condition in connection with either a mitigating factor defined in this section, including whether the defendant was acting under duress, was mentally or emotionally disturbed or mentally retarded, or was under the influence of alcohol or any drug. If the application is granted, the district attorney shall schedule a time and place for the examination, which shall be recorded. Counsel for the people and the defendant shall have the right to be present at the examination. A transcript of the examination shall be made available to the defendant and the district attorney promptly after its conclusion. The district attorney shall promptly serve on the defendant a written copy of the findings and evaluation of the examiner. If the court finds that the defendant has wilfully refused to cooperate fully in an examination pursuant to this paragraph, it shall, upon request of the district attorney, instruct the jury that the defendant did not submit to or cooperate fully in such psychiatric examination. When a defendant is subjected to an examination pursuant to an order issued in accordance with this subdivision, any statement made by the defendant for the purpose of the examination shall be inadmissible in evidence against him in any criminal action or proceeding on any issue other than that of whether a mitigating factor has been established or whether the defendant is mentally retarded, but such statement is admissible upon such an issue whether or not it would otherwise be deemed a privileged communication.

14. (a) At a reasonable time prior to the sentencing proceeding or a mental retardation hearing:

(i) the prosecutor shall, unless previously disclosed and subject to a protective order, make available to the defendant the statements and information specified in subdivision one of section 245.20 of this part and make available for inspection, photographing, copying or testing the property specified in subdivision one of section 245.20; and

(ii) the defendant shall, unless previously disclosed and subject to a protective order, make available to the prosecution the statements and information specified in subdivision four of section 245.20 and make available for inspection, photographing, copying or testing, subject to constitutional limitations, the reports, documents and other property specified in section 245.20 of this part.

(b) Where a party refuses to make disclosure pursuant to this section, the provisions of section 245.70, 245.75 and/or 245.80 of this part shall apply.

(c) If, after complying with the provisions of this section or an order pursuant thereto, a party finds either before or during a sentencing proceeding or mental retardation hearing, additional material subject to discovery or covered by court order, the party shall promptly make disclosure or apply for a protective order.

(d) If the court finds that a party has failed to comply with any of the provisions of this section, the court may employ any of the remedies or sanctions specified in subdivision one of section 245.80 of this part.

(Eff.1/1/20,Ch.59,L.2019)

15. The court of appeals shall formulate and adopt rules for the development of forms for use by the jury in recording its findings and determinations of sentence.

§400.30 Procedure for determining the amount of a fine based upon the defendant's gain from the offense.

1. Order directing a hearing. In any case where the court is of the opinion that the sentence should consist of or include a fine and that, pursuant to article eighty of the penal law, the amount of the fine should be based upon the defendant's gain from the commission of the offense, the court may order a hearing to determine the amount of such gain. The order must be filed with the clerk of the court and must specify a date for the hearing not less than ten days after the filing of the order.

2. Notice of hearing. Upon receipt of the order, the clerk of the court must send a notice of the hearing to the defendant, his counsel and the district attorney. Such notice must specify the time and place of the hearing and the fact that the purpose thereof is to determine the amount of the defendant's gain from the commission of the offense so that an appropriate fine can be imposed.

3. Hearing. When the defendant appears for the hearing the court must ask him whether he wishes to make any statement with respect to the amount of his gain from the commission of the offense. If the defendant does make a statement, the court may accept such statement and base its finding thereon. Where the defendant does not make a statement, or where the court does not accept the defendant's statement, it may proceed with the hearing.

4. Burden and standard of proof; evidence. At any hearing held pursuant to this section the burden of proof rests upon the people. A finding as to the amount of the defendant's gain from the commission of the offense must be based upon a preponderance of the evidence. Any relevant evidence, not legally privileged, may be received regardless of its admissibility under the exclusionary rules of evidence.

5. Termination of hearing. At any time during the pendency of a hearing pursuant to this section the court may, in its discretion, terminate the hearing without making any finding.

§400.40 Procedure for determining prior convictions for the purpose of sentence in certain cases.

1. Applicability. Where a conviction is entered for an unclassified misdemeanor or for a traffic infraction and the authorized sentence depends upon whether the defendant has a previous judgment of conviction for an offense, or where a conviction is entered for a violation defined outside the penal law and the amount of the fine authorized by the law defining such violation depends upon whether the defendant has a previous judgment of conviction for an offense, such issue is determined as provided in this section.

2. Statement to be filed. If it appears that the defendant has a previous judgment of conviction and if the court is required, or in its discretion desires, to impose a sentence that would not be authorized in the absence of such previous judgment, a statement must be filed after conviction and before sentence setting forth the date and place of the previous judgment or judgments and the court must conduct a hearing to determine whether the defendant is the same person mentioned in the record of such judgment or judgments. In any case where an increased sentence is mandatory, the statement may be filed by the court or by the prosecutor. In any case where an increased sentence is discretionary, the statement may be filed only by the court.

3. Preliminary examination. The defendant must be given a copy of such statement and the court must ask him whether he admits or denies such prior judgment or judgments. If the defendant denies the same or remains mute, the court may proceed with the hearing and, where the increased sentence is mandatory, it must impose such.

4. Time for hearing. In any case where a copy of the statement was not received by the defendant at least two days prior to the preliminary examination, the court must upon request of the defendant grant an adjournment of at least two days before proceeding with the hearing.

5. Manner of conducting hearing. A hearing pursuant to this section must be before the court without a jury. The burden of proof is upon the people and a finding that the defendant has been convicted of any offense alleged in the statement must be based upon proof beyond a reasonable doubt by evidence admissible under the rules applicable to trial of the issue of guilt.

ARTICLE 410 - SENTENCES OF PROBATION, CONDITIONAL DISCHARGE AND PAROLE SUPERVISION

(Article Heading Expires 9/1/23, Ch.55, L.2021)

Section
410.10   Specification of conditions of the sentence.
410.20   Modification or enlargement of conditions.
410.30   Declaration of delinquency.
410.40   Notice to appear, warrant.
410.50   Custody and supervision of probationers.
410.60   Appearance before court.
410.70   Hearing on violation.
410.80   Transfer of supervision of probationers.
410.90   Termination of sentence.
410.90-a Superior court; youth part.
410.91   Sentence of parole supervision.

§410.10 Specification of conditions of the sentence.

1. When the court pronounces a sentence of probation or of conditional discharge it must specify as part of the sentence the conditions to be complied with. Where the sentence is one of probation, the defendant must be given a written copy of the conditions at the time sentence is imposed. In any case where the defendant is given a written copy of the conditions, a

copy thereof must be filed with and become part of the record of the case, and it is not necessary to specify the conditions orally.

2. Commission of an additional offense, other than a traffic infraction, after imposition of a sentence of probation or of conditional discharge, and prior to expiration or termination of the period of the sentence, constitutes a ground for revocation of such sentence irrespective of whether such fact is specified as a condition of the sentence.

3. When the court pronounces a sentence of probation or conditional discharge for a specified crime defined in paragraph (e) of subdivision one of section six hundred thirty-two-a of the executive law, in addition to specifying the conditions of the sentence, the court shall provide written notice to such defendant concerning any requirement to report to the office of victim services funds of a convicted person as defined in section six hundred thirty-two-a of the executive law, the procedures for such reporting and any potential penalty for a failure to comply.

4. When the court pronounces a sentence of probation or conditional discharge, the court shall provide that the performance of bona fide work for an employer, including travel time to and from bona fide work, regardless if such work or related travel time is performed during curfew times set by conditions of probation, parole, presumptive release, conditional release, release to post-release supervision or any other type of supervised release, shall not be considered a violation of such sentence of probation or conditional discharge. For purposes of this section, bona fide work is work performed as an employee for an employer, as defined in section two of the labor law.   *(Eff.10/22/21,Ch.487,L.2021)*

§410.20 Modification or enlargement of conditions.

1. The court may modify or enlarge the conditions of a sentence of probation or of conditional discharge at any time prior to the expiration or termination of the period of the sentence. Such action may not, however, be taken unless the defendant is personally present, except that the defendant need not be present if the modification consists solely of the elimination or relaxation of one or more conditions. Whenever the defendant has not been present, the court shall notify the defendant in writing within twenty days of such modification specifying the nature of the elimination or relaxation of such condition or conditions and the effective date thereof. In any such case the modification or enlargement may be specified in the same manner as the conditions originally imposed and becomes part of the sentence.

2. The procedure set forth in this section applies to the imposition of an additional period of conditional discharge as authorized by subdivision three of section 65.05 of the penal law.

§410.30 Declaration of delinquency.

If at any time during the period of a sentence of probation or of conditional discharge the court has reasonable cause to believe that the defendant has violated a condition of the sentence, it may declare the defendant delinquent and file a written declaration of delinquency. When the court receives a request for a declaration of delinquency by a probation officer, it shall make a decision on such request within seventy-two hours of its receipt of the request. Upon filing a written declaration of delinquency, the court must promptly take reasonable and appropriate action to cause the defendant to appear before it for the purpose of enabling the court to make a final determination with respect to the alleged delinquency in accordance with section 410.70 of this article.

§410.40 Notice to appear, warrant.

1. Notice to appear. The court may at any time order that a person who is under a sentence of probation or of conditional discharge appear before it. Such order may be in the form of a written notice, specifying the time and place of appearance, mailed to or served personally upon the defendant as the court may direct. In the absence of a warrant issued pursuant to subdivision two of this section, where a probation officer has submitted a violation petition and report, the court shall promptly consider such petition and, where the court issues a notice to appear, the court shall direct that the defendant appear within ten business days of the court's order. When the order is in the form of such a notice, failure to appear as ordered without reasonable cause therefor constitutes a violation of the conditions of the sentence irrespective of whether such requirement is specified as a condition thereof.

2. Warrant. *(a)* Where the probation officer has requested that a probation warrant be issued, the court shall, within seventy-two hours of its receipt of the request, issue or deny the warrant or take any other lawful action including issuance of a notice to appear pursuant to subdivision one of this section. If at any time during the period of a sentence of probation or of conditional discharge the court has reasonable grounds to believe that the defendant has violated a condition of the sentence, the court may issue a warrant to a police officer or to an appropriate peace officer directing him or her to take the defendant into custody and bring the defendant before the court without unnecessary delay; provided, however, if the court in which the warrant is returnable is a superior court, and such court is not available, and the warrant is addressed to a police officer or appropriate probation officer certified as a peace officer, such executing officer mayunless otherwise specified under paragraph (b) of this subdivision, bring the defendant to the local correctional facility of the county in which such court sits, to be detained there until not later than the commencement of the next session of such court occurring on the next business day; or if the court in which the warrant is returnable is a local criminal court, and such court is not available, and the warrant is addressed to a police officer or appropriate probation officer certified as a peace officer, such executing officer must without unnecessary delay bring the defendant before an alternate local criminal court, as provided in subdivision five of section 120.90 of this chapter. A court which issues such a warrant may attach thereto a summary of the basis for the warrant. In any case where a defendant arrested upon the warrant is brought before a local criminal court other than the court in which the warrant is returnable, such local criminal court shall consider such summary before issuing a securing order with respect to the defendant.

(b) If the court in which the warrant is returnable is a superior court, and such court is not available, and the warrant is addressed to a police officer or appropriate probation officer certified as a peace officer, such executing officer shall, where a defendant is sixteen years of age or younger who allegedly commits an offense or a violation of his or her probation or conditional discharge imposed for an offense on or after October first, two thousand eighteen, or where a defendant is seventeen years of age or younger who allegedly commits an offense or a violation of his or her probation or conditional discharge imposed for an offense on or after

October first, two thousand nineteen, bring the defendant without unnecessary delay before the youth part, provided, however that if the youth part is not in session, the defendant shall be brought before the most accessible magistrate designated by the appellate division.

§410.50　Custody and supervision of probationers.

1. Custody. A person who is under a sentence of probation is in the legal custody of the court that imposed it pending expiration or termination of the period of the sentence.

2. Supervision. The probation department serving the court that imposed a sentence of probation has the duty of supervising the defendant during the period of such legal custody.

3. Search order. If at any time during the period of probation the court has reasonable cause to believe that the defendant has violated a condition of the sentence, it may issue a search order. Such order must be directed to a probation officer and may authorize such officer to search the person of the defendant and/or any premises in which he resides or any real or personal property which he owns or which is in his possession.

4. Taking custody without warrant. When a probation officer has reasonable cause to believe that a person under his supervision pursuant to a sentence of probation has violated a condition of the sentence, such officer may, without a warrant, take the probationer into custody and search his person.

5. Assistance by police officer. In executing a search order, or in taking a person into custody, pursuant to this section, a probation officer may be assisted by a police officer.

§410.60　Appearance before court.

A person who has been taken into custody pursuant to section 410.40 or section 410.50 of this article for violation of a condition of a sentence of probation or a sentence of conditional discharge must forthwith be brought before the court that imposed the sentence. Where a violation of probation petition and report has been filed and the person has not been taken into custody nor has a warrant been issued, an initial court appearance shall occur within ten business days of the court's issuance of a notice to appear. If the court has reasonable cause to believe that such person has violated a condition of the sentence, it may commit such person to the custody of the sheriff, fix bail, release such person under non-monetary conditions or release such person on such person's own recognizance for future appearance at a hearing to be held in accordance with section 410.70 of this article. If the court does not have reasonable cause to believe that such person has violated a condition of the sentence, it must direct that such person be released.　　　　　　　　　　*(Eff. 1/1/20, Ch. 59, L. 2019)*

§410.70 Hearing on violation.

1. In general. The court may not revoke a sentence of probation or a sentence of conditional discharge, or extend a period of probation, unless (a) the court has found that the defendant has violated a condition of the sentence and (b) the defendant has had an opportunity to be heard pursuant to this section. The defendant is entitled to a hearing in accordance with this section promptly after the court has filed a declaration of delinquency or has committed him or has fixed bail pursuant to this article.

2. Statement; preliminary examination. The court must file or cause to be filed with the clerk of the court a statement setting forth the condition or conditions of the sentence violated and a reasonable description of the time, place and manner in which the violation occurred. The defendant must appear before the court within ten business days of the court's issuance of the notice to appear and the court must advise him of the contents of the statement and furnish him with a copy thereof. At the time of such appearance the court must ask the defendant whether he wishes to make any statement with respect to the violation. If the defendant makes a statement, the court may accept it and base its decision thereon. If the court does not accept it, or if the defendant does not make a statement, the court must proceed with the hearing. Provided, however, that upon request, the court must grant a reasonable adjournment to the defendant to enable him to prepare for the hearing.

3. Manner of conducting hearing. The hearing must be a summary one by the court without a jury and the court may receive any relevant evidence not legally privileged. The defendant may cross-examine witnesses and may present evidence on his own behalf. A finding that the defendant has violated a condition of his sentence must be based upon a preponderance of the evidence.

4. Counsel. The defendant is entitled to counsel at all stages of any proceeding under this section and the court must advise him of such right at the outset of the proceeding.

5. Revocation; modification; continuation. At the conclusion of the hearing the court may revoke, continue or modify the sentence of probation or conditional discharge. Where the court revokes the sentence, it must impose sentence as specified in subdivisions three and four of section 60.01 of the penal law. Where the court continues or modifies the sentence, it must vacate the declaration of delinquency and direct that the defendant be released. If the alleged violation is sustained and the court continues or modifies the sentence, it may extend the sentence up to the period of interruption specified in subdivision two of section 65.15 of the penal law, but any time spent in custody in any correctional institution pursuant to section 410.60 of this article shall be credited against the term of the sentence. Provided further, where the alleged violation is sustained and the court continues or modifies the sentence, the court may also extend the remaining period of probation up to the maximum term authorized by section 65.00 of the penal law. Provided, however, a defendant shall receive credit for the time during which he or she was supervised under the original probation sentence prior to any declaration of delinquency and for any time spent in custody pursuant to this article for an alleged violation of probation.

§410.80 Transfer of supervision of probationers.

1. Authority to transfer supervision. Where a probationer at the time of sentencing or an interim probationer at the time of the imposition of the period of interim probation supervision resides in another jurisdiction within the state, the sentencing court shall transfer supervision to the appropriate probation department in such other jurisdiction. Where, after a probation sentence or interim probation supervision is pronounced, a probationer or interim probationer desires to reside in another jurisdiction within the state that is not served by the sentencing court, such court, in its discretion, may approve a change in residency and, upon approval, shall transfer supervision to the appropriate probation department serving the county of the probationer's proposed new residence. Any transfer under this subdivision must be in accordance with rules adopted by the commissioner of the division of criminal justice services.

2. Transfer of powers. (a) Upon completion of transfer of probation as authorized pursuant to subdivision one, the probation department in the receiving jurisdiction shall assume all powers and duties of the probation department in the jurisdiction of the sentencing court. Upon completion of transfer, the appropriate court within the jurisdiction of the receiving probation department shall assume all powers and duties of the sentencing court and shall have sole jurisdiction in the case including jurisdiction over matters specified in article twenty-three of the correction law. Further, the sentencing court shall immediately forward its entire case record to the receiving court.

(i) In transfers involving a defendant sentenced to probation upon conviction of a felony, the receiving court served by the probation department to which supervision is transferred shall be the superior court within the jurisdiction of the probation department.

(ii) In transfers involving a defendant sentenced to probation upon conviction of a misdemeanor, the receiving court served by the probation department to which supervision is transferred shall be the appropriate criminal court within the jurisdiction of the probation department. The sending probation department shall consult with the probation department to which supervision will be transferred to determine the appropriate criminal court to receive the case.

(b) Where a transfer is authorized for a defendant on interim probation supervision pursuant to subdivision one of this section, the sentencing court shall retain jurisdiction during the period of interim probation. The probation department in the receiving jurisdiction shall assume all powers and duties of the original probation department in the jurisdiction of the sentencing court.

3. Interstate compact. Nothing contained in this section affects or limits the provisions of section two hundred fifty-nine-mm of the executive law relating to out-of-state probation supervision.

4. Federal transfer of custody and supervision. Notwithstanding the provisions of any other law, the court served by the probation department may consent to the transfer of custody and supervision of a probationer to the United States Department of Justice pursuant to the Witness Security Act of nineteen hundred eighty-four.

§410.90 Termination of sentence.

1. The court may at any time terminate either a period of probation, other than a period of lifetime probation, for conviction to a crime or a period of conditional discharge for an offense.

2. The court may terminate a period of probation for a person who is subject to lifetime probation and who has been on unrevoked probation for at least five consecutive years.

3. (a) The court shall grant a request for termination of a sentence of probation under this section when, having regard to the conduct and condition of the probationer, the court is of the opinion that:

(i) the probationer is no longer in need of such guidance, training or other assistance which would otherwise be administered through probation supervision;

(ii) the probationer has diligently complied with the terms and conditions of the sentence of probation; and

(iii) the termination of the sentence of probation is not adverse to the protection of the public.

No such termination shall be granted unless the court is satisfied that the probationer, who is otherwise financially able to comply with an order of restitution or reparation, has made a good faith effort to comply therewith.

(b) The court shall grant a request for termination of sentence of conditional discharge under this section when, having regard to the conduct and condition of the defendant, the court is of the opinion that:

(i) the defendant has diligently complied with the terms and conditions of the sentence of conditional discharge; and

(ii) termination of the sentence of conditional discharge is not adverse to protection of the public.

§410.90-a Superior court; youth part.

Notwithstanding any other provisions of this article, all proceedings relating to a juvenile offender or adolescent offender shall be heard in the youth part of the superior court having jurisdiction and any intrastate transfers under this article shall be between courts designated as a youth part pursuant to article seven hundred twenty-two of this chapter.

*§410.91 Sentence of parole supervision.

1. A sentence of parole supervision is an indeterminate sentence of imprisonment, or a determinate sentence of imprisonment imposed pursuant to paragraphs (b) and (d) of subdivision three of section 70.70 of the penal law, which may be imposed upon an eligible defendant, as defined in subdivision two of this section. If an indeterminate sentence, such sentence shall have a minimum term and a maximum term within the ranges specified by subdivisions three and four of section 70.06 of the penal law. If a determinate sentence, such sentence shall have a term within the ranges specified by subparagraphs (iii) and (iv) of paragraph (b) of subdivision three of section 70.70 of the penal law. Provided, however, if the court directs that the sentence be executed as a sentence of parole supervision, it shall remand the defendant for immediate delivery to a reception center operated by the state department of corrections and community supervision, in accordance with section 430.20 of this chapter and section six hundred one of the correction law, for a period not to exceed ten days. An individual who receives such a sentence shall be placed under the immediate supervision of the department of corrections and community supervision and must comply with the conditions of parole, which shall

include an initial placement in a drug treatment campus for a period of ninety days at which time the defendant shall be released therefrom.

2. A defendant is an "eligible defendant" for purposes of a sentence of parole supervision when such defendant is a felony offender convicted of a specified offense or offenses as defined in subdivision five of this section, who stands convicted of no other felony offense, who has not previously been convicted of either a violent felony offense as defined in section 70.02 of the penal law, a class A felony offense or a class B felony offense other than a class B felony offense defined in article two hundred twenty of the penal law, and is not subject to an undischarged term of imprisonment.

3. When an indeterminate or determinate sentence of imprisonment is imposed upon an eligible defendant for a specified offense, as defined in subdivision five of this section, the court may direct that such sentence be executed as a sentence of parole supervision if the court finds (i) that the defendant has a history of controlled substance dependence that is a significant contributing factor to such defendant's criminal conduct; (ii) that such defendant's controlled substance dependence could be appropriately addressed by a sentence of parole supervision; and (iii) that imposition of such a sentence would not have an adverse effect on public safety or public confidence in the integrity of the criminal justice system.

4. *(Repealed.)*

**5. For the purposes of this section, a "specified offense" is an offense defined by any of the following provisions of the penal law: burglary in the third degree as defined in section 140.20, criminal mischief in the third degree as defined in section 145.05, criminal mischief in the second degree as defined in section 145.10, grand larceny in the fourth degree as defined in subdivision one, two, three, four, five, six, eight, nine or ten of section 155.30, grand larceny in the third degree as defined in section 155.35 (except where the property consists of one or more firearms, rifles or shotguns), unauthorized use of a vehicle in the second degree as defined in section 165.06, criminal possession of stolen property in the fourth degree as defined in subdivision one, two, three, five or six of section 165.45, criminal possession of stolen property in the third degree as defined in section 165.50 (except where the property consists of one or more firearms, rifles or shotguns), forgery in the second degree as defined in section 170.10, criminal possession of a forged instrument in the second degree as defined in section 170.25, unlawfully using slugs in the first degree as defined in section 170.60, criminal diversion of medical marihuana in the first degree as defined in section 179.10 or an attempt to commit any of the aforementioned offenses if such attempt constitutes a felony offense; or a class B felony offense defined in article two hundred twenty where a sentence is imposed pursuant to paragraph (a) of subdivision two of section 70.70 of the penal law; or any class C, class D or class E controlled substance or marihuana felony offense as defined in article two hundred twenty or two hundred twenty-one.   ** *(Repealed 7/5/28, Ch.92,L.2021)*

6. Upon delivery of the defendant to the reception center, he or she shall be given a copy of the conditions of parole by a representative of the department of corrections and community supervision and shall acknowledge receipt of a copy of the conditions in writing. The conditions shall be established in accordance with article twelve-B of the executive law and the rules and regulations of the board of parole. Thereafter and while the parolee is participating in the intensive drug treatment program provided at the drug treatment campus, the department of corrections and community supervision shall assess the parolee's special needs and shall develop an intensive program of parole supervision that will address the parolee's substance abuse history and which shall include periodic urinalysis testing.

Unless inappropriate, such program shall include the provision of treatment services by a community-based substance abuse service provider which has a contract with the department of corrections and community supervision.

7. Upon completion of the drug treatment program at the drug treatment campus, a parolee will be furnished with money, clothing and transportation in a manner consistent with section one hundred twenty-five of the correction law to permit the parolee's travel from the drug treatment campus to the county in which the parolee's supervision will continue.

8. If the parole officer having charge of a person sentenced to parole supervision pursuant to this section has reasonable cause to believe that such person has violated the conditions of his or her parole, the procedures of subdivision three of section two hundred fifty-nine-i of the executive law shall apply to the issuance of a warrant and the conduct of further proceedings; provided, however, that a parole violation warrant issued for a violation committed while the parolee is being supervised at a drug treatment campus shall constitute authority for the immediate placement of the parolee into a correctional facility operated by the department of corrections and community supervision, which to the extent practicable shall be reasonably proximate to the place at which the violation occurred, to hold in temporary detention pending completion of the procedures required by subdivision three of section two hundred fifty-nine-i of the executive law.

(Amendments deemed repealed 9/1/23,Ch.55,L.2021)

ARTICLE 420 - FINES, RESTITUTION AND REPARATION
Section
420.05 Payment of fines, mandatory surcharges and fees by credit card.
420.10 Collection of fines, restitution or reparation.
420.20 Collection of fines, restitution or reparation imposed upon corporations.
420.30 Remission of fines, restitution or reparation.
420.35 Mandatory surcharge and crime victim assistance fee; applicability to sentences mandating payment of fines.
420.40 Deferral of a mandatory surcharge; financial hardship hearings.
420.45 Post-trial motion relating to certain instruments affecting residential real property.

§420.05 Payment of fines, mandatory surcharges and fees by credit card.

When the court imposes a fine, mandatory surcharge or fee upon an individual who stands convicted of any offense, such individual may pay such fine, mandatory surcharge or fee by credit card or similar device. In such event, notwithstanding any other provision of law, he or she also may be required to pay a reasonable administrative fee. The amount of such administrative fee and the time and manner of its payment shall be in accordance with the system established by the chief administrator of the courts pursuant to paragraph (j) of subdivision two of section two hundred twelve of the judiciary law.

§420.10 Collection of fines, restitution or reparation.

1. Alternative methods of payment. When the court imposes a fine upon an individual, it shall designate the official other than the district attorney to whom payment is to be remitted. When the court imposes restitution or reparation and requires that the defendant pay a designated surcharge thereon pursuant to the provisions of subdivision eight of section 60.27 of the penal law, it shall designate the official or organization other than the district attorney, selected pursuant to subdivision eight of this section, to whom payment is to be remitted. (a) The court may direct:

(i) That the defendant pay the entire amount at the time sentence is pronounced;

(ii) That the defendant pay the entire amount at some later date; or

(iii) That the defendant pay a specified portion at designated periodic intervals.

(b) When the court imposes both (i) a fine and (ii) restitution or reparation and such designated surcharge upon an individual and imposes a schedule of payments, the court shall also direct that payment of restitution or reparation and such designated surcharge take priority over the payment of the fine.

(c) Where the defendant is sentenced to a period of probation as well as a fine, restitution or reparation and such designated surcharge, the court may direct that payment of the fine, restitution or reparation and such designated surcharge be a condition of the sentence.

(d) When a court requires that restitution or reparation and such designated surcharge be made it must direct that notice be given to a person or persons to whom it is to be paid of the conditions under which it is to be remitted; the name and address of the public official or organization to whom it is to be remitted for payment and the amount thereof; and the availability of civil proceedings for collection under subdivision six of this section. An official or organization designated to receive payment under this subdivision must report to the court any failure to comply with the order and shall cooperate with the district attorney pursuant to his responsibilities under subdivision six of this section.

(e) Where cash bail has been posted by the defendant as the principal and is not forfeited or assigned, the court at its discretion may order that bail be applied toward payment of any order of restitution or reparation or fine. If the court so orders, the bail proceeds shall be applied to payment first of the restitution or reparation and then of the fine.

2. Death of victim. In the event that the individual to whom restitution or reparation is to be made dies prior to completion of said restitution or reparation, the remaining payments shall be made to the estate of the deceased.

3. Imprisonment for failure to pay. Where the court imposes a fine, restitution or reparation, the sentence may provide that if the defendant fails to pay the fine, restitution or reparation in accordance with the direction of the court, the defendant must be imprisoned until the fine, restitution or reparation is satisfied. Such provision may be added at the time sentence is pronounced or at any later date while the fine, restitution or reparation or any part thereof remains unpaid; provided, however, that if the provision is added at a time subsequent to the pronouncement of sentence the defendant must be personally present when it is added. In any case where the defendant fails to pay a fine, restitution or reparation as directed the court may issue a warrant directing a peace officer, acting pursuant to his special duties, or a police officer, to take him into custody and bring him before the court; provided, however, if the court in which the warrant is returnable is a city, town or village court, and such court is not available, and the warrant is addressed to a police officer, such executing police officer must without unnecessary delay bring the defendant before an alternate local criminal court, as provided in subdivision five of section 120.90 of this chapter; or if the court in which the warrant is returnable is a superior court, and such court is not available, and the warrant is addressed to a police officer, such executing police officer may bring the defendant to the local correctional facility of the county in which such court sits, to be detained there until not later than the commencement of the next session of such court occurring on the next business day. Such warrant may also be delegated in the same manner as a warrant pursuant to section 530.70 of this chapter. Where a sentence provides that the defendant be imprisoned for failure to pay a fine, the court shall advise the defendant that if he is unable to pay such fine, he has a right, at any time, to apply to the court to be resentenced as provided in subdivision five of this section.

4. Period of imprisonment. When the court directs that the defendant be imprisoned until the fine, restitution or reparation be satisfied, it must specify a maximum period of imprisonment subject to the following limits:

(a) Where the fine, restitution or reparation is imposed for a felony, the period may not exceed one year;

(b) Where the fine, restitution or reparation is imposed for a misdemeanor, the period may not exceed one-third of the maximum authorized term of imprisonment;

(c) Where the fine, restitution or reparation is imposed for a petty offense, the period may not exceed fifteen days; and

(d) Where a sentence of imprisonment as well as a fine, restitution or reparation is imposed, the aggregate of the period and the term of the sentence may not exceed the maximum authorized term of imprisonment.

(e) Jail time and good behavior time shall be credited against the full period of imprisonment, if served, as provided in section 70.30 of the penal law for definite sentences.

5. Application for resentence. In any case where the defendant is unable to pay a fine, restitution or reparation imposed by the court, he may at any time apply to the court for resentence. In such case, if the court is satisfied that the defendant is unable to pay the fine, restitution or reparation it must:

(a) Adjust the terms of payment; or

(b) Lower the amount of the fine, restitution or reparation; or

(c) Where the sentence consists of probation or imprisonment and a fine, restitution or reparation, revoke the portion of the sentence imposing the fine, restitution or reparation; or

(d) Revoke the entire sentence imposed and resentence the defendant. Upon such resentence the court may impose any sentence it originally could have imposed, except that the amount of any fine, restitution or reparation imposed may not be in excess of the amount the defendant is able to pay.

In any case where the defendant applies for resentencing with respect to any condition of the sentence relating to restitution or reparation the court must order that notice of such application and a reasonable opportunity to be heard be given to the person or persons given notice pursuant to subdivision one of this section. If the court grants the defendant's application by changing the original order for restitution or reparation in any manner, the court must place the reasons therefor on the record.

For the purposes of this subdivision, the court shall not determine that the defendant is unable to pay the fine, restitution or reparation ordered solely because of such defendant's incarceration but shall consider all the defendant's sources of income including, but not limited to, moneys in the possession of an incarcerated individual at the time of his or her admission into such facility, funds earned by him or her in a work release program as defined in subdivision four of section one hundred fifty of the correction law, funds earned by him or her as provided for in section one hundred eighty-seven of the correction law and any other funds received by him or her or on his or her behalf and deposited with the superintendent or the municipal official of the facility where the person is confined.

(Eff.8/2/21,Ch.322,L.2021)

6. Civil proceeding for collection. (a) A fine, restitution or reparation imposed or directed by the court shall be imposed or directed by a written order of the court containing the amount thereof required to be paid by the defendant. The court's order also shall direct the district attorney to file a certified copy of such order with the county clerk of the county in which the court is situate except where the court which issues such order is the supreme court in which case the order itself shall be filed by the clerk of the court acting in his or her capacity as the county clerk of the county in which the court is situate. Such order shall be entered by the county clerk in the

same manner as a judgment in a civil action in accordance with subdivision (a) of rule five thousand sixteen of the civil practice law and rules. Even if the defendant was imprisoned for failure to pay such fine, restitution or reparation, or has served the period of imprisonment imposed, such order after entry thereof pursuant to this subdivision may be collected in the same manner as a judgment in a civil action by the victim, as defined in paragraph (b) of subdivision four of section 60.27 of the penal law, to whom restitution or reparation was ordered to be paid, the estate of such person or the district attorney. The entered order shall be deemed to constitute a judgment-roll as defined in section five thousand seventeen of the civil practice law and rules and immediately after entry of the order, the county clerk shall docket the entered order as a money judgment pursuant to section five thousand eighteen of such law and rules. Wherever appropriate, the district attorney shall file a transcript of the docket of the judgment with the clerk of any other county of the state. Such a restitution or reparation order, when docketed shall be a first lien upon all real property in which the defendant thereafter acquires an interest, having preference over all other liens, security interests, and encumbrances whatsoever, except:

(i) a lien or interest running to the benefit of the government of the United States or the state of New York, or any political subdivision or public benefit corporation thereof; or

(ii) a purchase money interest in any property.

(b) The district attorney may, in his or her discretion, and must, upon order of the court, institute proceedings to collect such fine, restitution or reparation.

7. Undisbursed restitution payments. Where a court requires that restitution or reparation be made by a defendant, the official or organization to whom payments are to be remitted pursuant to subdivision one of this section may place such payments in an interest-bearing account. The interest accrued and any undisbursed payments shall be designated for the payment of restitution orders that have remained unsatisfied for the longest period of time. For the purposes of this subdivision, the term "undisbursed restitution payments" shall mean those payments which have been remitted by a defendant but not disbursed to the intended beneficiary and such payment has gone unclaimed for a period of one year and the location of the intended beneficiary cannot be ascertained by such official or organization after using reasonable efforts.

8. Designation of restitution agency. (a) The chief elected official in each county, and in the city of New York the mayor, shall designate an official or organization other than the district attorney to be responsible for the collection and administration of restitution and reparation payments under provisions of the penal law and this chapter. This official or organization shall be eligible for the designated surcharge provided for by subdivision eight of section 60.27 of the penal law.

(b) The restitution agency, as designated by paragraph (a) of this subdivision, shall be responsible for the collection of data on a monthly basis regarding the numbers of restitution and reparation orders issued, the numbers of satisfied restitution and reparation orders and information concerning the types of crimes for which such orders were required. A probation department designated as the restitution agency shall then forward such information to the office of probation and correctional alternatives within the first ten days following the end of each month. In all other cases the restitution agency shall report to the division of criminal justice services directly. The division of criminal justice services shall compile and review all such information and make recommendations to promote the use of restitution and encourage its enforcement.

§420.20 Collection of fines, restitution or reparation imposed upon corporations.

Where a corporation is sentenced to pay a fine, restitution or reparation, the fine, restitution or reparation must be paid at the time sentence is imposed. If the fine, restitution or reparation is not so paid, it may be collected in the same manner as a judgment in a civil action, and if execution issued upon such judgment be returned unsatisfied an action may be brought in the name of the people of the state of New York to procure a judgment sequestering the property of the corporation, as provided by the business corporation law. It is the duty of the attorney general in all criminal proceedings prosecuted by him, and, in all other proceedings, the county attorney for counties outside the city of New York, and, in the city of New York the corporation counsel of the city of New York, to institute proceedings to collect such fine, restitution or reparation.

§420.30 Remission of fines, restitution or reparation.

1. Applicability. The procedure specified in this section governs remission of fines, restitution or reparation in all cases not covered by subdivision four of section 420.10.

2. Procedure. (a) Any superior court which has imposed a fine, restitution or reparation for any offense may, in its discretion, on five days notice to the district attorney of the county in which such fine, restitution or reparation was imposed and to each person otherwise required to be given notice of restitution or reparation pursuant to subdivision one of section 420.10, remit such fine, restitution or reparation or any portion thereof. In case of a fine, restitution or reparation imposed by a local criminal court for any offense, a superior court holding a term in the county in which the fine, restitution or reparation was imposed may, upon like notice, remit such fine, restitution or reparation or any portion thereof.

(b) The court shall give each person given notice a reasonable opportunity to be heard on the question of remitting an order of restitution or reparation. If the court remits such restitution or reparation, or any part thereof, the reasons therefor shall be placed upon the record.

3. Restrictions. Except as provided for in subdivision two-a of section 420.35 of this article, in no event shall a mandatory surcharge, sex offender registration fee, DNA databank fee or crime victim assistance fee be remitted.

§420.35 Mandatory surcharge and crime victim assistance fee; applicability to sentences mandating payment of fines.

1. The provisions of section 420.10 of this article governing the collection of fines and the provisions of section 420.40 of this article governing deferral of mandatory surcharges, sex offender registration fees, DNA databank fees and financial hardship hearings and the provisions of section 430.20 of this

chapter governing the commitment of a defendant for failure to pay a fine shall be applicable to a mandatory surcharge, sex offender registration fee, DNA databank fee and a crime victim assistance fee imposed pursuant to subdivision one of section 60.35 of the penal law, subdivision twenty-a of section three hundred eighty-five of the vehicle and traffic law, subdivision nineteen-a of section four hundred one of the vehicle and traffic law, or a mandatory surcharge imposed pursuant to section eighteen hundred nine of the vehicle and traffic law or section 27.12 of the parks, recreation and historic preservation law. When the court directs that the defendant be imprisoned until the mandatory surcharge, sex offender registration fee or DNA databank fee is satisfied, it must specify a maximum period of imprisonment not to exceed fifteen days; provided, however, a court may not direct that a defendant be imprisoned until the mandatory surcharge, sex offender registration fee, or DNA databank fee is satisfied or otherwise for failure to pay the mandatory surcharge, sex offender registration fee or DNA databank fee unless the court makes a contemporaneous finding on the record, after according defendant notice and an opportunity to be heard, that the payment of the mandatory surcharge, sex offender registration fee or DNA databank fee upon defendant will not work an unreasonable hardship upon him or her or his or her immediate family.

2. Except as provided in this subdivision or subdivision two-a of this section, under no circumstances shall the mandatory surcharge, sex offender registration fee, DNA databank fee or the crime victim assistance fee be waived. A court shall waive any mandatory surcharge, DNA databank fee and crime victim assistance fee when: (i) the defendant is convicted of prostitution under section 230.00 of the penal law; (ii) the defendant is convicted of a violation in the event such conviction is in lieu of a plea to or conviction for prostitution under section 230.00 of the penal law; (iii) the court finds that a defendant is a victim of sex trafficking under section 230.34 of the penal law or a victim of trafficking in persons under the trafficking victims protection act (United States Code, Title 22, Chapter 78); or (iv) the court finds that the defendant is a victim of sex trafficking of a child under section 230.34-a of the penal law.   *(Eff. 2/2/21, Ch.23, L.2021)*

2-a. A court may waive any mandatory surcharge, additional surcharge, town or village surcharge, the crime victim assistance fee, DNA databank fee, sex offender registration fee and/or supplemental sex offender victim fee when the court finds that the defendant was under the age of twenty-one at the time the offense was committed and:

(a) the imposition of such surcharge or fee would work an unreasonable hardship on the defendant, his or her immediate family, or any other person who is dependent on such defendant for financial support; or

(b) after considering the goal of promoting successful and productive reentry and reintegration as set forth in subdivision six of section 1.05 of the penal law, the imposition of such surcharge or fee would adversely impact the defendant's reintegration into society; or

(c) the interests of justice.   *(Eff.8/24/20,Ch.144,L.2020)*

3. It shall be the duty of a court of record or administrative tribunal to report to the division of criminal justice services on the disposition and collection of mandatory surcharges, sex offender registration fees or DNA databank fees and crime victim assistance fees. Such report shall include, for all cases, whether the surcharge, sex offender registration fee, DNA databank fee or crime victim assistance fee levied pursuant to subdivision one of section 60.35 of the penal law or section eighteen hundred nine of the vehicle and traffic law has been imposed pursuant to law, collected, or is to be collected by probation or corrections or other officials. The form, manner and frequency of such reports shall be determined by the commissioner of the division of criminal justice services after consultation with the chief administrator of the courts and the commissioner of the department of motor vehicles.

§420.40 Deferral of a mandatory surcharge; financial hardship hearings.

1. Applicability. The procedure specified in this section governs the deferral of the obligation to pay all or part of a mandatory surcharge, sex offender registration fee or DNA databank fee imposed pursuant to subdivision one of section 60.35 of the penal law and financial hardship hearings relating to mandatory surcharges.

2. On an appearance date set forth in a summons issued pursuant to subdivision three of section 60.35 of the penal law, section eighteen hundred nine of the vehicle and traffic law or section 27.12 of the parks, recreation and historic preservation law, a person upon whom a mandatory surcharge, sex offender registration fee or DNA databank fee was levied shall have an opportunity to present on the record credible and verifiable information establishing that the mandatory surcharge, sex offender registration fee or DNA databank fee should be deferred, in whole or in part, because, due to the indigence of such person the payment of said surcharge, sex offender registration fee or DNA databank fee would work an unreasonable hardship on the person or his or her immediate family.

3. In assessing such information the superior court shall be mindful of the mandatory nature of the surcharge, sex offender registration fee and DNA databank fee, and the important criminal justice and victim services sustained by such fees.

4. Where a court determines that it will defer part or all of a mandatory surcharge, sex offender registration fee or DNA databank fee imposed pursuant to subdivision one of section 60.35 of the penal law, a statement of such finding and of the facts upon which it is based shall be made part of the record.

5. A court which defers a person's obligation to pay a mandatory surcharge, sex offender registration fee or DNA databank fee imposed pursuant to subdivision one of section 60.35 of the penal law shall do so in a

written order. Such order shall not excuse the person from the obligation to pay the surcharge, sex offender registration fee or DNA databank fee. Rather, the court's order shall direct the filing of a certified copy of the order with the county clerk of the county in which the court is situate except where the court which issues such order is the supreme court in which case the order itself shall be filed by the clerk of the court acting in his or her capacity as the county clerk of the county in which the court is situate. Such order shall be entered by the county clerk in the same manner as a judgment in a civil action in accordance with subdivision (a) of rule five thousand sixteen of the civil practice law and rules. The order shall direct that any unpaid balance of the mandatory surcharge, sex offender registration fee or DNA databank fee may be collected in the same manner as a civil judgment. The entered order shall be deemed to constitute a judgment-roll as defined in section five thousand seventeen of the civil practice law and rules and immediately after entry of the order, the county clerk shall docket the entered order as a money judgment pursuant to section five thousand eighteen of such law and rules.

§420.45 Post-trial motion relating to certain instruments affecting residential real property.

1. When a defendant has been convicted after a trial or pled guilty to violating either section 175.30 or 175.35 of the penal law in connection to an instrument that is material to the transfer or purchase of residential real property, the district attorney may file a motion in the supreme court in the county where the property that is subject to the instrument is located on behalf of the victim to void the instrument that is the subject of such criminal information or indictment. Such motion must be in writing and provide reasonable notice to all persons who have an interest in the property affected by such instrument. The motion papers must state the county or borough, if in the city of New York, and block, lot, street address of such property, and a description of such property. The motion papers must state the grounds of the motion, must contain sworn allegations of fact supporting such grounds, and include a copy of the guilty disposition attached to the document.

2. Within ten days after filing a motion pursuant to subdivision one of this section, the district attorney shall record a copy of the notice of motion in the office of the clerk of the county in which the property is situated. The notice shall be indexed by the clerk in the manner prescribed by subdivision (c) of rule sixty-five hundred eleven of the civil practice law and rules for a notice of pendency of action and shall have the same effect as such notice.

3. The supreme court must conduct a hearing and make findings of fact essential to the determination whether to declare the instrument described in subdivision one of this section void ab initio. All persons providing factual information at such hearing must testify under oath. There will be a rebuttable presumption that where a party is convicted after a trial in criminal court or a guilty plea to either section 175.30 or section 175.35 of

the penal law in connection with an instrument that is material to the transfer or sale of residential real property, that such instrument is void ab initio.

4. Upon the defendant's conviction of or guilty plea to section 175.30 or section 175.35 of the penal law as described in subdivision one of this section, and after conducting a hearing pursuant to subdivision three of this section, a court shall make a determination and if appropriate shall order that the instrument described in subdivision one of this section be declared void ab initio or grant other appropriate relief to the victim. The order of the court shall describe the nature of the false statement or false information contained in such instrument. A copy of such instrument shall be attached to the order of the court.

5. If the order relates to an instrument that has been filed with, registered, or recorded in a public office, the district attorney shall record a certified copy of such order in the office of the recording officer of the county in which such property is situated, in the same manner as a conveyance duly acknowledged or proved and certified so as to entitle it to be recorded. Such recording officer shall record the same in his or her said office.

6. For purposes of this section, "all persons who have an interest in the property affected by such instrument" shall mean all parties who have recorded an instrument affecting the real property that is the subject of the instrument described in subdivision one of this section, including any party or entity that may have liens of interest on the property, and any current residents of the property, as of the date of the filing of the criminal information or indictment.

7. Nothing in this section shall be deemed to inhibit or prevent a party's right to appeal such order.

ARTICLE 430 - SENTENCES OF IMPRISONMENT

Section
430.10 Sentence of imprisonment not to be changed after commencement.
430.20 Commitment of defendant.
430.30 Duty to deliver defendant.

§430.10 Sentence of imprisonment not to be changed after commencement.

Except as otherwise specifically authorized by law, when the court has imposed a sentence of imprisonment and such sentence is in accordance with law, such sentence may not be changed, suspended or interrupted once the term or period of the sentence has commenced.

§430.20 Commitment of defendant.

1. In general. When a sentence of imprisonment is pronounced, or when th sentence consists of a fine and the court has directed that the defendant be imprisoned until it is satisfied, the defendant must forthwith be committed to the custody of the appropriate public servant and detained until the sentence is complied with.

* 2. Indeterminate and determinate sentences. In the case of an indeterminate or determinate sentence of imprisonment, commitment must be to the custody of the state department of corrections and community supervision as provided in subdivision one of section 70.20 of the penal law. The order of commitment must direct that the defendant be delivered to an institution designated by the commissioner of corrections and community supervision in accordance with the provisions of the correction law.

(Amendments deemed repealed 9/1/23,Ch.55,L.2021)

3. Definite and intermittent sentences. In the case of a definite or intermittent sentence of imprisonment, commitment must be as follows:

(a) In counties contained within New York City or in any county that has a county department of correction, commitment must be to the custody of the department of correction of such city or county;

(b) In any other case, commitment must be to the county jail, workhouse or penitentiary, or to a penitentiary outside the county and the order of commitment must specify the institution to which the defendant is to be delivered.

*4. Certain resentences. When a sentence of imprisonment that has been imposed on a defendant is vacated and a new sentence is imposed on such defendant for the same offense, or for an offense based upon the same act, if the term of the new definite or determinate sentence or the maximum term of the new indeterminate sentence so imposed is less than or equal to that of the vacated sentence:

(a) where the time served by the defendant on the vacated sentence is equal to or greater than the term or maximum term of the new sentence, the new sentence shall be deemed to be served in its entirety and the defendant shall not be committed to a correctional facility pursuant to said sentence; and

(b) where the defendant was under the supervision of a local conditional release commission or the department of corrections and community supervision at the time the sentence was vacated, then the commitment shall direct that said conditional release or parole be recommenced, and the defendant shall not be committed to a correctional facility pursuant to said sentence, except as a result of revocation of parole or of conditional release; and

(c) where the defendant was not under the supervision of the department of corrections and community supervision at the time the indeterminate or determinate sentence was vacated, but would immediately be eligible for conditional release from the new indeterminate or determinate sentence, the court shall ascertain from the department of corrections and community supervision whether the defendant has earned a sufficient amount of good time under the vacated sentence so as to require the conditional release of the defendant under the new sentence; in the event the defendant has earned a sufficient amount of good time, the court shall stay execution of sentence until the defendant surrenders at a correctional facility pursuant to the direction of the department of corrections and community supervision, which shall occur no later than sixty days after imposition of sentence; upon said stay of execution, the court clerk shall immediately mail to the commissioner of corrections and community supervision a certified copy of the commitment reflecting said stay of execution and the name, mailing address and telephone number of the defendant's legal representative; in the event the defendant fails to surrender as directed by the department of corrections and community supervision, the department shall notify the court which shall thereafter remand the defendant to custody pursuant to section 430.30 of this article; and

(d) upon the resentence of a defendant as described in this subdivision, the court clerk shall immediately mail a certified copy of the commitment to the commissioner of corrections and community supervision if the vacated sentence or the new sentence is an indeterminate or determinate sentence and no mailing is required by paragraph (c) of this subdivision; additionally, the court clerk shall immediately mail a certified copy of the new commitment to the head of the appropriate local correctional facility if the vacated sentence or the new sentence is a definite sentence.

(Amendments deemed repealed 9/1/23, Ch.55, L.2021)

5. Commitment for failure to pay fine. Where the sentence consists of a fine and the court has directed that the defendant be imprisoned until it is satisfied, commitment must be as follows:

(a) If the sentence also includes a term of imprisonment, commitment must be to the same institution as is designated for service of the term of imprisonment, and the period of commitment commences (i) when the term of imprisonment is satisfied, or (ii) with the approval of the state board of parole, when the defendant becomes eligible for parole, or (iii) when the defendant becomes eligible for conditional release, whichever occurs first; provided, however, that the court may direct that the period of imprisonment for the fine run concurrently with the term of imprisonment; and

(b) In any other case, commitment must be to the agency or institution that would be designated in the case of a definite sentence.

§430.30 Duty to deliver defendant.

In counties contained within New York City and in counties that have a commissioner of correction who is responsible for detention of defendants in criminal actions, it is the duty of the commissioner of correction of such city or county to deliver the defendant forthwith to the proper institution in accordance with the commitment. In all other counties it is the duty of the sheriff to deliver the defendant forthwith to the proper institution in accordance with the commitment.

TITLE M - PROCEEDINGS AFTER JUDGMENT
ARTICLE 440 - POST-JUDGMENT MOTIONS

Section
440.10   Motion to vacate judgment.
440.20   Motion to set aside sentence; by defendant.
440.30   Motion to vacate judgment and to set aside sentence; procedure.
440.40   Motion to set aside sentence; by people.
440.46   Motion for resentence; certain controlled substance offenders.
440.46-a   Motion for resentence; persons convicted of certain marihuana offenses.
440.47   Motion for resentence;domestic violence cases.
440.50   Notice to crime victims of case disposition.
440.55   Notice to education department where a licensed professional has been
            convicted of a felony.
440.60   Notification of invalid sentences of probation.
440.65   Notice to child protective agency of conviction for certain crimes against a
            child.
440.70   Notice to the secretary of state when false financing statement filed.

§440.10 Motion to vacate judgment.

1. At any time after the entry of a judgment, the court in which it was entered may, upon motion of the defendant, vacate such judgment upon the ground that:

(a) The court did not have jurisdiction of the action or of the person of the defendant; or

(b) The judgment was procured by duress, misrepresentation or fraud on the part of the court or a prosecutor or a person acting for or in behalf of a court or a prosecutor; or

(c) Material evidence adduced at a trial resulting in the judgment was false and was, prior to the entry of the judgment, known by the prosecutor or by the court to be false; or

(d) Material evidence adduced by the people at a trial resulting in the judgment was procured in violation of the defendant's rights under the constitution of this state or of the United States; or

(e) During the proceedings resulting in the judgment, the defendant, by reason of mental disease or defect, was incapable of understanding or participating in such proceedings; or

(f) Improper and prejudicial conduct not appearing in the record occurred during a trial resulting in the judgment which conduct, if it had appeared in the record, would have required a reversal of the judgment upon an appeal therefrom; or

(g) New evidence has been discovered since the entry of a judgment based upon a verdict of guilty after trial, which could not have been produced by the defendant at the trial even with due diligence on his part and which is of such character as to create a probability that had such evidence been received at the trial the verdict would have been more favorable to the defendant; provided that a motion based upon such ground must be made with due diligence after the discovery of such alleged new evidence; or

(g-1) Forensic DNA testing of evidence performed since the entry of a judgment, (1) in the case of a defendant convicted after a guilty plea, the court has determined that the defendant has demonstrated a substantial probability that the defendant was actually innocent of the offense of which he or she was convicted, or (2) in the case of a defendant convicted after a trial, the court has determined that there exists a reasonable probability that the verdict would have been more favorable to the defendant.

(h) The judgment was obtained in violation of a right of the defendant under the constitution of this state or of the United States; or

(i) The judgment is a conviction where the defendant's participation in the offense was a result of having been a victim of sex trafficking under section 230.34 of the penal law, sex trafficking of a child under section 230.34-a of the penal law, labor trafficking under section 135.35 of the penal law, aggravated labor trafficking under section 135.37 of the penal law, compelling prostitution under section 230.33 of the penal law, or trafficking in persons under the Trafficking Victims Protection Act (United States Code, title 22, chapter 78); provided that *(Eff.11/16/21,Ch.629,L.2021)*

(i) official documentation of the defendant's status as a victim of sex trafficking, labor trafficking, aggravated labor trafficking, compelling prostitution, or trafficking in persons at the time of the offense from a federal, state or local government agency shall create a presumption that the defendant's participation in the offense was a result of having been a victim of sex trafficking, labor trafficking, aggravated labor trafficking, compelling prostitution or trafficking in persons, but shall not be required for granting a motion under this paragraph; *(Eff.11/16/21,Ch.629,L.2021)*

(ii) a motion under this paragraph, and all pertinent papers and documents, shall be confidential and may not be made available to any person or public or private entity except where specifically authorized by the court; and *(Eff.1/15/22,Ch.629,L.2021)*

(iii) when a motion is filed under this paragraph, the court may, upon the consent of the petitioner and all of the state and local prosecutorial agencies that prosecuted each matter, consolidate into one proceeding a motion to vacate judgments imposed by distinct or multiple criminal courts; or *(Eff.11/16/21,Ch.629,L.2021)*

(j) The judgment is a conviction for a class A or unclassified misdemeanor entered prior to the effective date of this paragraph and satisfies the ground prescribed in paragraph (h) of this subdivision. There shall be a rebuttable presumption that a conviction by plea to such an offense was not knowing, voluntary and intelligent, based on ongoing collateral consequences, including potential or actual immigration consequences, and there shall be a rebuttable presumption that a conviction by verdict constitutes cruel and unusual punishment under section five of article one of the state constitution based on such consequences; or

(k) The judgment occurred prior to the effective date of the laws of two thousand twenty-one that amended this paragraph and is a conviction for an offense as defined in subparagraphs (i), (ii), (iii) or (iv) of paragraph (k) of subdivision three of section 160.50 of this part, in which case the court shall presume that a conviction by plea for the aforementioned offenses was not knowing, voluntary and intelligent if it has severe or ongoing consequences, including but not limited to potential or actual immigration consequences, and shall presume that a conviction by verdict for the aforementioned offenses constitutes cruel and unusual punishment under section five of article one of the state constitution, based on those consequences. The people may rebut these presumptions. *(Eff.3/31/21,Ch.92,L.2021)*

2. Notwithstanding the provisions of subdivision one, the court must deny a motion to vacate a judgment when:

(a) The ground or issue raised upon the motion was previously determined on the merits upon an appeal from the judgment, unless since the time of such appellate determination there has been a retroactively effective change in the law controlling such issue; or

(b) The judgment is, at the time of the motion, appealable or pending on appeal, and sufficient facts appear on the record with respect to the ground or issue raised upon the motion to permit adequate review thereof upon such an appeal unless the issue raised upon such motion is ineffective assistance of counsel. This paragraph shall not apply to a motion under paragraph (i) of subdivision one of this section; or *(Eff.10/25/21,Ch.501,L.2021)*

(c) Although sufficient facts appear on the record of the proceedings underlying the judgment to have permitted, upon appeal from such judgment, adequate review of the ground or issue raised upon the motion, no such appellate review or determination occurred owing to the defendant's unjustifiable failure to take or perfect an appeal during the prescribed period or to his or her unjustifiable failure to raise such ground or issue upon an appeal actually perfected by him or her unless the issue raised upon such motion is ineffective assistance of counsel; or   *(Eff.10/25/21,Ch.501,L.2021)*

(d) The ground or issue raised relates solely to the validity of the sentence and not to the validity of the conviction.

3. Notwithstanding the provisions of subdivision one, the court may deny a motion to vacate a judgment when:

(a) Although facts in support of the ground or issue raised upon the motion could with due diligence by the defendant have readily been made to appear on the record in a manner providing adequate basis for review of such ground or issue upon an appeal from the judgment, the defendant unjustifiably failed to adduce such matter prior to sentence and the ground or issue in question was not subsequently determined upon appeal. This paragraph does not apply to a motion based upon deprivation of the right to counsel at the trial or upon failure of the trial court to advise the defendant of such right, or to a motion under paragraph (i) of subdivision one of this section; or

(b) The ground or issue raised upon the motion was previously determined on the merits upon a prior motion or proceeding in a court of this state, other than an appeal from the judgment, or upon a motion or proceeding in a federal court; unless since the time of such determination there has been a retroactively effective change in the law controlling such issue; or

(c) Upon a previous motion made pursuant to this section, the defendant was in a position adequately to raise the ground or issue underlying the present motion but did not do so.

Although the court may deny the motion under any of the circumstances specified in this subdivision, in the interest of justice and for good cause shown it may in its discretion grant the motion if it is otherwise meritorious and vacate the judgment.

4. If the court grants the motion, it must, except as provided in subdivision five or six of this section, vacate the judgment, and must dismiss the accusatory instrument, or order a new trial, or take such other action as is appropriate in the circumstances.

5. Upon granting the motion upon the ground, as prescribed in paragraph (g) of subdivision one, that newly discovered evidence creates a probability that had such evidence been received at the trial the verdict would have been more favorable to the defendant in that the conviction would have been for a lesser offense than the one contained in the verdict, the court may either:

(a) Vacate the judgment and order a new trial; or

(b) With the consent of the people, modify the judgment by reducing it to one of conviction for such lesser offense. In such case, the court must re-sentence the defendant accordingly.

6. If the court grants a motion under paragraph (i) or paragraph (k) of subdivision one of this section, it must vacate the judgment and dismiss the accusatory instrument, and may take such additional action as is appropriate in the circumstances. In the case of a motion granted under paragraph (i) of subdivision one of this section, the court must vacate the judgment on the merits because the defendant's participation in the offense was a result of having been a victim of trafficking. *(Eff.11/16/21,Ch.629,L.2021)*

7. Upon a new trial resulting from an order vacating a judgment pursuant to this section, the indictment is deemed to contain all the counts and to charge all the offenses which it contained and charged at the time the previous trial was commenced, regardless of whether any count was dismissed by the court in the course of such trial, except (a) those upon or

of which the defendant was acquitted or deemed to have been acquitted, and (b) those dismissed by the order vacating the judgment, and (c) those previously dismissed by an appellate court upon an appeal from the judgment, or by any court upon a previous post-judgment motion.

8. Upon an order which vacates a judgment based upon a plea of guilty to an accusatory instrument or a part thereof, but which does not dismiss the entire accusatory instrument, the criminal action is, in the absence of an express direction to the contrary, restored to its prepleading status and the accusatory instrument is deemed to contain all the counts and to charge all the offenses which it contained and charged at the time of the entry of the plea, except those subsequently dismissed under circumstances specified in paragraphs (b) and (c) of subdivision six. Where the plea of guilty was entered and accepted, pursuant to subdivision three of section 220.30, upon the condition that it constituted a complete disposition not only of the accusatory instrument underlying the judgment vacated but also of one or more other accusatory instruments against the defendant then pending in the same court, the order of vacation completely restores such other accusatory instruments; and such is the case even though such order dismisses the main accusatory instrument underlying the judgment.

9. Upon granting of a motion pursuant to paragraph (j) of subdivision one of this section, the court may either:

(a) With the consent of the people, vacate the judgment or modify the judgment by reducing it to one of conviction for a lesser offense; or

(b) Vacate the judgment and order a new trial wherein the defendant enters a plea to the same offense in order to permit the court to resentence the defendant in accordance with the amendatory provisions of subdivision one-a of section 70.15 of the penal law.   *(Eff.4/12/19,Ch.55,L.2019)*

§440.20 Motion to set aside sentence; by defendant.

1. At any time after the entry of a judgment, the court in which the judgment was entered may, upon motion of the defendant, set aside the sentence upon the ground that it was unauthorized, illegally imposed or otherwise invalid as a matter of law. Where the judgment includes a sentence of death, the court may also set aside the sentence upon any of the grounds set forth in paragraph (b), (c), (f), (g) or (h) or subdivision one of section 440.10 as applied to a separate sentencing proceeding under section 400.27, provided, however, that to the extent the ground or grounds asserted include one or more of the aforesaid paragraphs of subdivision one of section 440.10, the court must also apply subdivisions two and three of section 440.10, other than paragraph (d) of subdivision two of such section, in determining the motion. In the event the court enters an order granting a motion to set aside a sentence of death under this section, the court must either direct a new sentencing proceeding in accordance with section 400.27 or, to the extent that the defendant cannot be resentenced to death consistent with the laws of this state or the constitution of this state or of the United States, resentence the defendant to life imprisonment without parole or to a sentence of imprisonment for the class A-I felony of murder in the first degree other than a sentence of life imprisonment without parole. Upon granting the motion upon any of the grounds set forth in the aforesaid paragraphs of subdivision one of section 440.10 and setting aside the sentence, the court must afford the people a reasonable period of time, which shall not be less than ten days, to determine whether to take an appeal from the order setting aside the sentence of death. The taking of an appeal by the people stays the effectiveness of that portion of the court's order that directs a new sentencing proceeding.

2. Notwithstanding the provisions of subdivision one, the court must deny such a motion when the ground or issue raised thereupon was previously

determined on the merits upon an appeal from the judgment or sentence,
unless since the time of such appellate determination there has been a
retroactively effective change in the law controlling such issue.

3. Notwithstanding the provisions of subdivision one, the court may deny
such a motion when the ground or issue raised thereupon was previously
determined on the merits upon a prior motion or proceeding in a court of this
state, other than an appeal from the judgment, or upon a prior motion or
proceeding in a federal court, unless since the time of such determination
there has been a retroactively effective change in the law controlling such
issue. Despite such determination, however, the court in the interest of
justice and for good cause shown, may in its discretion grant the motion if it
is otherwise meritorious.

4. An order setting aside a sentence pursuant to this section does not
affect the validity or status of the underlying conviction, and after entering
such an order the court must resentence the defendant in accordance with
the law.

§440.30 **Motion to vacate judgment and to set aside sentence; procedure.**
1. (a) A motion to vacate a judgment pursuant to section 440.10 of this
article and a motion to set aside a sentence pursuant to section 440.20 of
this article must be made in writing and upon reasonable notice to the
people. Upon the motion, a defendant who is in a position adequately to
raise more than one ground should raise every such ground upon which he
or she intends to challenge the judgment or sentence. If the motion is based
upon the existence or occurrence of facts, the motion papers must contain
sworn allegations thereof, whether by the defendant or by another person or
persons. Such sworn allegations may be based upon personal knowledge of
the affiant or upon information and belief, provided that in the latter event
the affiant must state the sources of such information and the grounds of
such belief. The defendant may further submit documentary evidence or
information supporting or tending to support the allegations of the moving
papers. The people may file with the court, and in such case must serve a
copy thereof upon the defendant or his or her counsel, if any, an answer
denying or admitting any or all of the allegations of the motion papers, and
may further submit documentary evidence or information refuting or tending
to refute such allegations. After all papers of both parties have been filed,
and after all documentary evidence or information, if any, has been
submitted, the court must consider the same for the purpose of ascertaining
whether the motion is determinable without a hearing to resolve questions of
fact.

(b) In conjunction with the filing or consideration of a motion to vacate a
judgment pursuant to section 440.10 of this article by a defendant convicted
after a trial, in cases where the court has ordered an evidentiary hearing
upon such motion, the court may order that the people produce or make
available for inspection property in its possession, custody, or control that
was secured in connection with the investigation or prosecution of the
defendant upon credible allegations by the defendant and a finding by the
court that such property, if obtained, would be probative to the determination
of defendant's actual innocence, and that the request is reasonable. The
court shall deny or limit such a request upon a finding that such a request, if
granted, would threaten the integrity or chain of custody of property or the
integrity of the processes or functions of a laboratory conducting DNA
testing, pose a risk of harm, intimidation, embarrassment, reprisal, or other
substantially negative consequences to any person, undermine the proper
functions of law enforcement including the confidentiality of informants, or
on the basis of any other factor identified by the court in the interests of

justice or public safety. The court shall further ensure that any property produced pursuant to this paragraph is subject to a protective order, where appropriate. The court shall deny any request made pursuant to this paragraph where: *(Eff.1/1/20,Ch.59,L.2019)*

(i) (1) the defendant's motion pursuant to section 440.10 of this article does not seek to demonstrate his or her actual innocence of the offense or offenses of which he or she was convicted that are the subject of the motion, or (2) the defendant has not presented credible allegations and the court has not found that such property, if obtained, would be probative to the determination of the defendant's actual innocence and that the request is reasonable;

(ii) the defendant has made his or her motion after five years from the date of the judgment of conviction; provided, however, that this limitation period shall be tolled for five years if the defendant is in custody in connection with the conviction that is the subject of his or her motion, and provided further that, notwithstanding such limitation periods, the court may consider the motion if the defendant has shown: (A) that he or she has been pursuing his or her rights diligently and that some extraordinary circumstance prevented the timely filing of the motion; (B) that the facts upon which the motion is predicated were unknown to the defendant or his or her attorney and could not have been ascertained by the exercise of due diligence prior to the expiration of the statute of limitations; or (C) considering all circumstances of the case including but not limited to evidence of the defendant's guilt, the impact of granting or denying such motion upon public confidence in the criminal justice system, or upon the safety or welfare of the community, and the defendant's diligence in seeking to obtain the requested property or related relief, the interests of justice would be served by considering the motion;

(iii) the defendant is challenging a judgment convicting him or her of an offense that is not a felony defined in section 10.00 of the penal law; or

(iv) upon a finding by the court that the property requested in this motion would be available through other means through reasonable efforts by the defendant to obtain such property.

1-a. (a) (1) Where the defendant's motion requests the performance of a forensic DNA test on specified evidence, and upon the court's determination that any evidence containing deoxyribonucleic acid ("DNA") was secured in connection with the trial resulting in the judgment, the court shall grant the application for forensic DNA testing of such evidence upon its determination that if a DNA test had been conducted on such evidence, and if the results had been admitted in the trial resulting in the judgment, there exists a reasonable probability that the verdict would have been more favorable to the defendant.

(2) Where the defendant's motion for forensic DNA testing of specified evidence is made following a plea of guilty and entry of judgment thereon convicting him or her of: (A) a homicide offense defined in article one hundred twenty-five of the penal law, any felony sex offense defined in article one hundred thirty of the penal law, a violent felony offense as defined in paragraph (a) of subdivision one of section 70.02 of the penal law, or (B) any other felony offense to which he or she pled guilty after being charged in an indictment or information in superior court with one or more of the offenses listed in clause (A) of this subparagraph, then the court shall grant such a motion upon its determination that evidence containing DNA was secured in connection with the investigation or prosecution of the defendant, and if a DNA test had been conducted on such evidence and the results had been known to the parties prior to the entry of the defendant's plea and judgment thereon, there exists a substantial probability that the

evidence would have established the defendant's actual innocence of the offense or offenses that are the subject of the defendant's motion; provided, however, that:

(i) the court shall consider whether the defendant had the opportunity to request such testing prior to entering a guilty plea, and, where it finds that the defendant had such opportunity and unjustifiably failed to do so, the court may deny such motion; and

(ii) a court shall deny the defendant's motion for forensic DNA testing where the defendant has made his or her motion more than five years after entry of the judgment of conviction; except that the limitation period may be tolled if the defendant has shown: (A) that he or she has been pursuing his or her rights diligently and that some extraordinary circumstance prevented the timely filing of the motion for forensic DNA testing; (B) that the facts upon which the motion is predicated were unknown to the defendant or his or her attorney and could not have been ascertained by the exercise of due diligence prior to the expiration of this statute of limitations; or (C) considering all circumstances of the case including but not limited to evidence of the defendant's guilt, the impact of granting or denying such motion upon public confidence in the criminal justice system, or upon the safety or welfare of the community, and the defendant's diligence in seeking to obtain the requested property or related relief, the interests of justice would be served by tolling such limitation period.

(b) In conjunction with the filing of a motion under this subdivision, the court may direct the people to provide the defendant with information in the possession of the people concerning the current physical location of the specified evidence and if the specified evidence no longer exists or the physical location of the specified evidence is unknown, a representation to that effect and information and documentary evidence in the possession of the people concerning the last known physical location of such specified evidence. If there is a finding by the court that the specified evidence no longer exists or the physical location of such specified evidence is unknown, such information in and of itself shall not be a factor from which any inference unfavorable to the people may be drawn by the court in deciding a motion under this section. The court, on motion of the defendant, may also issue a subpoena duces tecum directing a public or private hospital, laboratory or other entity to produce such specified evidence in its possession and/or information and documentary evidence in its possession concerning the location and status of such specified evidence.

(c) In response to a motion under this paragraph, upon notice to the parties and to the entity required to perform the search the court may order an entity that has access to the combined DNA index system ("CODIS") or its successor system to compare a DNA profile obtained from probative biological material gathered in connection with the investigation or prosecution of the defendant against DNA databanks by keyboard searches, or a similar method that does not involve uploading, upon a court's determination that (1) such profile complies with federal bureau of investigation or state requirements, whichever are applicable and as such requirements are applied to law enforcement agencies seeking such a comparison, and that the data meet state DNA index system and/or national DNA index system criteria as such criteria are applied to law enforcement agencies seeking such a comparison and (2) if such comparison had been conducted, and if the results had been admitted in the trial resulting in the judgment, a reasonable probability exists that the verdict would have been more favorable to the defendant, or in a case involving a plea of guilty, if the results had been available to the defendant prior to the plea, a reasonable probability exists that the conviction would not have resulted. For purposes of this subdivision, a "keyboard search" shall mean a search of a DNA profile against the databank in which the profile that is searched is not uploaded to or maintained in the databank.

2. If it appears by conceded or uncontradicted allegations of the moving papers or of the answer, or by unquestionable documentary proof, that there are circumstances which require denial thereof pursuant to subdivision two of section 440.10 or subdivision two of section 440.20, the court must summarily deny the motion. If it appears that there are circumstances authorizing, though not requiring, denial thereof pursuant to subdivision three of section 440.10 or subdivision three of section 440.20, the court may in its discretion either (a) summarily deny the motion, or (b) proceed to consider the merits thereof.

3. Upon considering the merits of the motion, the court must grant it without conducting a hearing and vacate the judgment or set aside the sentence, as the case may be, if:

(a) The moving papers allege a ground constituting legal basis for the motion; and

(b) Such ground, if based upon the existence or occurrence of facts, is supported by sworn allegations thereof; and

(c) The sworn allegations of fact essential to support the motion are either conceded by the people to be true or are conclusively substantiated by unquestionable documentary proof.

4. Upon considering the merits of the motion, the court may deny it without conducting a hearing if:

(a) The moving papers do not allege any ground constituting legal basis for the motion; or

(b) The motion is based upon the existence or occurrence of facts and the moving papers do not contain sworn allegations substantiating or tending to substantiate all the essential facts, as required by subdivision one; or

(c) An allegation of fact essential to support the motion is conclusively refuted by unquestionable documentary proof; or

(d) An allegation of fact essential to support the motion (i) is contradicted by a court record or other official document, or is made solely by the defendant and is unsupported by any other affidavit or evidence, and (ii) under these and all the other circumstances attending the case, there is no reasonable possibility that such allegation is true.

5. If the court does not determine the motion pursuant to subdivisions two, three or four, it must conduct a hearing and make findings of fact essential to the determination thereof. The defendant has a right to be present at such hearing but may waive such right in writing. If he does not so waive it and if he is confined in a prison or other institution of this state, the court must cause him to be produced at such hearing.

6. At such a hearing, the defendant has the burden of proving by a preponderance of the evidence every fact essential to support the motion.

7. Regardless of whether a hearing was conducted, the court, upon determining the motion, must set forth on the record its findings of fact, its conclusions of law and the reasons for its determination.

§440.40 Motion to set aside sentence; by people.

1. At any time not more than one year after the entry of a judgment, the court in which it was entered may, upon motion of the people, set aside the sentence upon the ground that it was invalid as a matter of law.

2. Notwithstanding the provisions of subdivision one, the court must summarily deny the motion when the ground or issue raised thereupon was previously determined on the merits upon an appeal from the judgment or

sentence, unless since the time of such appellate determination there has been a retroactively effective change in the law controlling such issue.

3. Notwithstanding the provisions of subdivision one, the court may summarily deny such a motion when the ground or issue raised thereupon was previously determined on the merits upon a prior motion or proceeding in a court of this state, other than an appeal from the judgment or sentence, unless since the time of such determination there has been a retroactively effective change in the law controlling such issue. Despite such circumstance, however, the court, in the interests of justice and for good cause shown, may in its discretion grant the motion if it is otherwise meritorious.

4. The motion must be made upon reasonable notice to the defendant and to the attorney if any who appeared for him in the last proceeding which occurred in connection with the judgment or sentence, and the defendant must be given adequate opportunity to appear in opposition to the motion. The defendant has a right to be present at such proceeding but may waive such right in writing. If he does not so waive it and if he is confined in a prison or other institution of this state, the court must cause him to be produced at the proceeding upon the motion.

5. An order setting aside a sentence pursuant to this section does not affect the validity or status of the underlying conviction, and after entering such an order the court must resentence the defendant in accordance with the law.

6. Upon a resentence imposed pursuant to subdivision five, the terms of which are more severe than those of the original sentence, the defendant's time for taking an appeal from the judgment is automatically extended in the manner prescribed in subdivision four of section 450.30.

§440.46 Motion for resentence; certain controlled substance offenders.

1. Any person in the custody of the department of corrections and community supervision convicted of a class B felony offense defined in article two hundred twenty of the penal law which was committed prior to January thirteenth, two thousand five, who is serving an indeterminate sentence with a maximum term of more than three years, may, except as provided in subdivision five of this section, upon notice to the appropriate district attorney, apply to be resentenced to a determinate sentence in accordance with sections 60.04 and 70.70 of the penal law in the court which imposed the sentence.

2. As part of any such application, the defendant may also move to be resentenced to a determinate sentence in accordance with section 70.70 of the penal law for any one or more class C, D, or E felony offenses defined in article two hundred twenty or two hundred twenty-one of the penal law, the sentence or sentences for which were imposed by the sentencing court at the same time or were included in the same order of commitment as such class B felony.

3. The provisions of section twenty-three of chapter seven hundred thirty-eight of the laws of two thousand four shall govern the proceedings on and determination of a motion brought pursuant to this section; provided, however that the court's consideration of the institutional record of confinement of such person shall include but not be limited to such person's participation in or willingness to participate in treatment or other programming while incarcerated and such person's disciplinary history. The fact that a person may have been unable to participate in treatment or other programming while incarcerated despite such person's willingness to do so shall not be considered a negative factor in determining a motion pursuant to this section.

4. Subdivision one of section seven hundred seventeen and subdivision four of section seven hundred twenty-two of the county law, and the related provisions of article eighteen-A of such law, shall apply to the preparation of and proceedings on motions pursuant to this section, including any appeals.

5. The provisions of this section shall not apply to any person who is serving a sentence on a conviction for or has a predicate felony conviction for an exclusion offense. For purposes of this subdivision, an "exclusion offense" is:

(a) a crime for which the person was previously convicted within the preceding ten years, excluding any time during which the offender was incarcerated for any reason between the time of commission of the previous felony and the time of commission of the present felony, which was: (i) a violent felony offense as defined in section 70.02 of the penal law; or (ii) any other offense for which a merit time allowance is not available pursuant to subparagraph (ii) of paragraph (d) of subdivision one of section eight hundred three of the correction law; or

(b) a second violent felony offense pursuant to section 70.04 of the penal law or a persistent violent felony offense pursuant to section 70.08 of the penal law for which the person has previously been adjudicated.

§440.46-a   Motion for resentence; persons convicted of certain marihuana offenses.

1. When a person is serving a sentence for a conviction in this state, whether by trial verdict or guilty plea, under former article two hundred twenty-one of the penal law, and such persons' conduct as alleged in the accusatory instrument and/or shown by the guilty plea or trial verdict would not have been a crime under article two hundred twenty-two of the penal law, had such article two hundred twenty-two rather than former article two hundred twenty-one of the penal law been in effect at the time of such conduct, then the chief administrative judge of the state of New York shall, in accordance with this section, automatically vacate, dismiss and expunge such conviction in accordance with section 160.50 of this chapter, and the office of court administration shall immediately notify the state division of criminal justice services, state department of corrections and community supervision and the appropriate local correctional facility which shall immediately effectuate the appropriate relief. Such notification to the division of criminal justice services shall also direct that such agency notify all relevant police and law enforcement agencies of their duty to destroy and/or mark records related to such case in accordance with section 160.50 of this chapter. Nothing in this section shall prevent a person who believes his or her sentence is required by this section to be vacated, dismissed and/or expunged from filing a petition with the court to effectuate all appropriate relief.

2. (a) When a person is serving or has completed serving a sentence for a conviction in this state, whether by trial verdict or guilty plea, under former article two hundred twenty-one of the penal law, and such person's conduct as alleged in the accusatory instrument and/or shown by the guilty plea or trial verdict, or shown by other information: (i) would not have been a crime under article two hundred twenty-two of the penal law, had such article two hundred twenty-two rather than former article two hundred twenty-one of the penal law been in effect at the time of such conduct; or (ii) under such circumstances such person would have been guilty of a lesser or potentially less onerous offense under such article two hundred twenty-two than such former article two hundred twenty-one of the penal law; then such person

may petition the court of conviction pursuant to this article for vacatur of such conviction.

(b) (i) Upon receiving a served and filed motion under paragraph (a) of this subdivision, the court shall presume that any conviction by plea was not knowing, voluntary and intelligent and that any conviction by verdict and any accompanying sentence constitutes cruel and unusual punishment under the state constitution if either has severe or ongoing consequences, including but not limited to potential or actual immigration consequences; and the court shall further presume that the movant satisfies the criteria in such paragraph (a) and thereupon make such finding and grant the motion to vacate such conviction on such grounds in a written order unless the party opposing the motion proves, by clear and convincing evidence, that the movant does not satisfy the criteria to bring such motion. (ii) If the petition meets the criteria in subparagraph (i) of paragraph (a) of this subdivision, the court after affording the parties an opportunity to be heard and present evidence, may substitute, unless it is not in the interests of justice to do so, a conviction for an appropriate lesser offense under article two hundred twenty-two of the penal law.

(c) In the event of any vacatur and/or substitution pursuant to this subdivision, the office of court administration shall immediately notify the state division of criminal justice services concerning such determination. Such notification to the division of criminal justice services shall also direct that such agency notify all relevant police and law enforcement agencies of their duty to destroy and/or mark records related to such case in accordance with section 160.50 of this chapter or, where conviction for a crime is substituted pursuant to this subdivision, update such agencies' records accordingly.

3. Under no circumstances may substitution under this section result in the imposition of a term of imprisonment or sentencing term, obligation or condition that is in any way either harsher than the original sentence or harsher than the sentence authorized for any substituted lesser offense.

4. (a) If the judge who originally sentenced the movant for such offense is not reasonably available, then the presiding judge for such court shall designate another judge authorized to act in the appropriate jurisdiction to determine the petition or application.

(b) Unless requested by the movant, no hearing is necessary to grant an application filed under subdivision two of this section.

(c) When a felony conviction is vacated pursuant to this section and a lesser offense that is a misdemeanor or violation is substituted for such conviction, such lesser offense shall be considered a misdemeanor or violation, as the case may be, for all purposes. When a misdemeanor conviction is vacated pursuant to this section and a lesser offense that is a violation is substituted for such conviction, such lesser offense shall be considered a violation for all purposes.

(d) Nothing in this section is intended to or shall diminish or abrogate any rights or remedies otherwise available to a defendant, petitioner or applicant. Relief under this section is available notwithstanding that the judgment was for a violation of former sections 221.05, 221.10, 221.15, 221.20, 221.35 or 221.40 of the penal law in effect prior to the effective date of this paragraph and that the underlying action or proceeding has already been vacated, dismissed and expunged.

(e) Nothing in this and related sections of law is intended to diminish or abrogate the finality of judgments in any case not falling within the purview of this section.

(f) The provisions of this section shall be available, used and applied in parallel fashion by the family court and the criminal courts to juvenile delinquency adjudications, adolescent offender adjudications and youthful offender adjudications.

(g) The chief administrator of the courts shall promulgate all necessary rules and make available all necessary forms to enable the filing of the petitions and applications provided in this section no later than sixty days following the effective date of this section. All sentences eligible for automatic vacatur, dismissal and expungement pursuant to subdivision one of this section shall be identified and the required entities notified within one year of the effective date of this section. *(Eff.3/31/21,Ch.92,L.2021)*

§440.47 Motion for resentence; domestic violence cases.

1. (a) Notwithstanding any contrary provision of law, any person confined in an institution operated by the department of correction and community supervision serving a sentence with a minimum or determinate term of eight years or more for an offense committed prior to the effective date of this section and eligible for an alternative sentence pursuant to section 60.12 of the penal law may, on or after such effective date, submit to the judge or justice who imposed the original sentence upon such person a request to apply for resentencing in accordance with section 60.12 of the penal law. Such person must include in his or her request documentation proving that she or he is confined in an institution operated by the department of corrections and community supervision serving a sentence with a minimum or determinate term of eight years or more for an offense committed prior to the effective date of this section and that she or he is serving such sentence for any offense eligible for an alternative sentence under section 60.12 of the penal law.

(b) If, at the time of such person's request to apply for resentencing pursuant to this section, the original sentencing judge or justice is a judge or justice of a court of competent jurisdiction, but such court is not the court in which the original sentence was imposed, then the request shall be randomly assigned to another judge or justice of the court in which the original sentence was imposed. If the original sentencing judge is no longer a judge or justice of a court of competent jurisdiction, then the request shall be randomly assigned to another judge or justice of the court.

(c) If the court finds that such person has met the requirements to apply for resentencing in paragraph (a) of this subdivision, the court shall notify such person that he or she may submit an application for resentencing. Upon such notification, the person may request that the court assign him or her an attorney for the preparation of and proceedings on the application for resentencing pursuant to this section. The attorney shall be assigned in accordance with the provisions of subdivision one of section seven hundred seventeen and subdivision four of section seven hundred twenty-two of the county law and the related provisions of article eighteen-A of such law.

(d) If the court finds that such person has not met the requirements to apply for resentencing in paragraph (a) of subdivision one of this section, the court shall notify such person and dismiss his or her request without prejudice.

2. (a) Upon the court's receipt of an application for resentencing, the court shall promptly notify the appropriate district attorney and provide such district attorney with a copy of the application.

(b) If the judge or justice that received the application is not the original sentencing judge or justice, the application may be referred to the original sentencing judge or justice provided that he or she is a judge or justice of a court of competent jurisdiction and that the applicant and the district attorney agree that the application should be referred.

(c) An application for resentencing pursuant to this section must include at least two pieces of evidence corroborating the applicant's claim that he or she was, at the time of the offense, a victim of domestic violence subjected to substantial physical, sexual or psychological abuse inflicted by a member of the same family or household as the applicant as such term is defined in subdivision one of section 530.11 of this chapter.

At least one piece of evidence must be either a court record, pre-sentence report, social services record, hospital record, sworn statement from a witness to the domestic violence, law enforcement record, domestic incident report, or order of protection. Other evidence may include, but shall not be limited to, local and state department of corrections records, a showing based in part on documentation prepared at or near the time of the commission of the offense or the prosecution thereof tending to support the person's claim, or when there is verification of consultation with a licensed medical or mental health care provider, employee of a court acting within the scope of his or her employment, member of the clergy, attorney, social worker, or rape crisis counselor as defined in section forty-five hundred ten of the civil practice law and rules, or other advocate acting on behalf of an agency that assists victims of domestic violence for the purpose of assisting such person with domestic violence victim counseling or support.

(d) If the court finds that the applicant has not complied with the provisions of paragraph (c) of this subdivision, the court shall dismiss the application without prejudice.

(e) If the court finds that the applicant has complied with the provisions of paragraph (c) of this subdivision, the court shall conduct a hearing to aid in making its determination of whether the applicant should be resentenced in accordance with section 60.12 of the penal law. At such hearing the court shall determine any controverted issue of fact relevant to the issue of sentencing. Reliable hearsay shall be admissible at such hearings.

The court may consider any fact or circumstances relevant to the imposition of a new sentence which are submitted by the applicant or the district attorney and may, in addition, consider the institutional record of confinement of such person, but shall not order a new pre-sentence investigation and report or entertain any matter challenging the underlying basis of the subject conviction. The court's consideration of the institutional record of confinement of such applicant shall include, but not be limited to, such applicant's participation in or willingness to participate in programming such as domestic violence, parenting and substance abuse treatment while incarcerated and such applicant's disciplinary history. The fact that the applicant may have been unable to participate in treatment or other programming while incarcerated despite such applicant's willingness to do so shall not be considered a negative factor in determining a motion pursuant to this section.

(f) If the court determines that the applicant should not be resentenced in accordance with section 60.12 of the penal law, the court shall inform such applicant of its decision and shall enter an order to that effect. Any order issued by a court pursuant to this section must include written findings of fact and the reasons for such order.

(g) If the court determines that the applicant should be resentenced in accordance with section 60.12 of the penal law, the court shall notify the applicant that, unless he or she withdraws the application or appeals from such order, the court will enter an order vacating the sentence originally imposed and imposing the new sentence to be imposed as authorized by section 60.12 of the penal law. Any order issued by a court pursuant to this section must include written findings of fact and the reasons for such order.

3. An appeal may be taken as of right in accordance with applicable provisions of this chapter: (a) from an order denying resentencing; or (b) from a new sentence imposed under this provision and may be based on the grounds that (i) the term of the new sentence is harsh or excessive; or (ii) that the term of the new sentence is unauthorized as a matter of law. An appeal in accordance with the applicable provisions of this chapter may also be taken as of right by the applicant from an order specifying and informing such applicant of the term of the determinate sentence the court would impose upon resentencing on the ground that the term of the proposed sentence is harsh or excessive; upon remand to the sentencing court following such appeal the applicant shall be given an opportunity to withdraw an application for resentencing before any resentence is imposed. The applicant may request that the court assign him or her an attorney for the preparation of and proceedings on any appeals regarding his or her application for resentencing pursuant to this section. The attorney shall be assigned in accordance with the provisions of subdivision one of section seven hundred seventeen and subdivision four of section seven hundred twenty-two of the county law and the related provisions of article eighteen-A of such law.

4. In calculating the new term to be served by the applicant pursuant to section 60.12 of the penal law, such applicant shall be credited for any jail time credited towards the subject conviction as well as any period of incarceration credited toward the sentence originally imposed.

§440.50 Notice to crime victims of case disposition.

1. Upon the request of a victim of a crime, or in any event in all cases in which the final disposition includes a conviction of a violent felony offense as defined in section 70.02 of the penal law, a felony defined in article one hundred twenty-five of such law, or a felony defined in article one hundred thirty of such law, the district attorney shall, within sixty days of the final disposition of the case, inform the victim by letter of such final disposition. If such final disposition results in the commitment of the defendant to the custody of the department of corrections and community supervision for an indeterminate sentence, the notice provided to the crime victim shall also inform the victim of his or her right to submit a written, audiotaped, or videotaped victim impact statement to the department of corrections and community supervision or to meet personally with a member of the state board of parole at a time and place separate from the personal interview between a member or members of the board and the incarcerated individual and make such a statement, subject to procedures and limitations contained in rules of the board, both pursuant to subdivision two of section two hundred fifty-nine-i of the executive law. A copy of such letter shall be provided to the board of parole. The right of the victim under this subdivision to submit a written victim impact statement or to meet personally with a member of the state board of parole applies to each personal interview

between a member or members of the board and the incarcerated
individual.   *(Eff.8/2/21,Ch.322,L.2021)*

2. As used in this section, "victim" means any person alleged or found,
upon the record, to have sustained physical or financial injury to person or
property as a direct result of the crime charged or a person alleged or found
to have sustained, upon the record, an offense under article one hundred
thirty of the penal law, or in the case of a homicide or minor child, the
victim's family.

3. As used in this section, "final disposition" means an ultimate
termination of the case at the trial level including, but not limited to,
dismissal, acquittal, or imposition of sentence by the court, or a decision by
the district attorney, for whatever reason, to not file the case.

§440.55 Notice to education department where a licensed professional has been convicted of a felony.

The district attorney shall give written notification to the department of
education upon the conviction of a felony of any person holding a license
pursuant to title eight of the education law. In addition, the district attorney
shall give written notification to the department upon the vacatur or reversal
of any felony conviction of any such person.

§440.60 Notification of invalid sentences of probation.

Whenever it shall appear to the satisfaction of the appropriate director of
the probation department that a person sentenced pursuant to article sixty
of the penal law has received a sentence which is invalid as a matter of law,
it shall become his duty to notify the district attorney of the county in which
such person was convicted. Upon such notification, the district attorney shall
immediately investigate the matter and if such sentence of probation is in
fact invalid as a matter of law, the district attorney shall immediately move to
set aside such sentence pursuant to section 440.40 of this chapter.

§440.65 Notice to child protective agency of conviction for certain crimes against a child.

Upon conviction of any person for a crime under article one hundred
twenty, article one hundred twenty-five, article one hundred thirty, article two
hundred sixty or article two hundred sixty-three of the penal law committed
against a child under the age of eighteen by a person legally responsible for
such child, as defined in subdivision three of section four hundred twelve of
the social services law, the district attorney serving the jurisdiction in which
such conviction is entered shall notify the local child protective services
agency of such conviction including the name of the defendant, the name of
the child, the court case number and the name of the prosecutor who
appeared for the people.

§440.70 Notice to the secretary of state when false financing statement filed.

Upon conviction of any person for a crime where the defendant
intentionally filed or caused to be filed a financing statement pursuant to
article nine of the uniform commercial code on form UCC1 that falsely
claims that a person is indebted or obligated to such defendant, the court
wherein such conviction is entered, or the clerk thereof, shall issue and
cause to be filed a certificate with the New York secretary of state: (a)
certifying that a judgment of conviction has been entered in such court
against the defendant who was listed as the secured party in such form; and
(b) specifying the date and location of the filing, any filing or indexing
number assigned to such filing, the debtor named in such statement, and a
description of the collateral encumbered by the instrument.

ARTICLE 450 - APPEALS--IN WHAT CASES AUTHORIZED AND TO WHAT COURTS TAKEN

Section
450.10 Appeal by defendant to intermediate appellate court; in what cases authorized as of right.
450.15 Appeal by defendant to intermediate appellate court; in what cases authorized by permission.
450.20 Appeal by people to intermediate appellate court; in what cases authorized.
450.30 Appeal from sentence.
450.40 Appeal by people from trial order of dismissal.
450.50 Appeal by people from order suppressing evidence; filing of statement in appellate court.
450.55 Appeal by people from order reducing a count of an indictment or directing the filing of a prosecutor's information.
450.60 Appeal to intermediate appellate court; to what court taken.
450.70 Appeal by defendant directly to court of appeals; in what cases authorized.
450.80 Appeal by people directly to court of appeals; in what cases authorized.
450.90 Appeal to court of appeals from order of intermediate appellate court; in what cases authorized.

§450.10 Appeal by defendant to intermediate appellate court; in what cases authorized as of right.

An appeal to an intermediate appellate court may be taken as of right by the defendant from the following judgment, sentence and order of a criminal court:

1. A judgment other than one including a sentence of death, unless the appeal is based solely upon the ground that a sentence was harsh or excessive when such sentence was predicated upon entry of a plea of guilty and the sentence imposed did not exceed that which was agreed to by the defendant as a condition of the plea and set forth on the record or filed with the court as required by subdivision five of section 220.50 or subdivision four of section 340.20;

2. A sentence other than one of death, as prescribed in subdivision one of section 450.30, unless the appeal is based solely upon the ground that a sentence was harsh or excessive when such sentence was predicated upon entry of a plea of guilty and the sentence imposed did not exceed that which was agreed to by the defendant as a condition of the plea and set forth in the record or filed with the court as required by subdivision five of section 220.50 or subdivision four of section 340.20;

3. A sentence including an order of criminal forfeiture entered pursuant to section 460.30 of the penal law with respect to such forfeiture order.

4. An order, entered pursuant to section 440.40, setting aside a sentence other than one of death, upon motion of the People.

5. An order denying a motion, made pursuant to subdivision one-a of section 440.30, for forensic DNA testing of evidence.

§450.15 Appeal by defendant to intermediate appellate court; in what cases authorized by permission.

If an appeal by defendant is not authorized as of right pursuant to section 450.10, the defendant may appeal from the following orders of a criminal court, provided that a certificate granting leave to appeal is issued pursuant to section 460.15:

1. An order denying a motion, made pursuant to section 440.10, to vacate a judgment other than one including a sentence of death;

2. An order denying a motion by the defendant made pursuant to section 440.20, to set aside a sentence other than one of death;

3. A sentence which is not otherwise appealable as of right pursuant to subdivision one or two of section 450.10.

§450.20 Appeal by people to intermediate appellate court; in what cases authorized.

An appeal to an intermediate appellate court may be taken as of right by the people from the following sentence and orders of a criminal court;

1. An order dismissing an accusatory instrument or a count thereof, entered pursuant to section 170.30, 170.50 or 210.20, or an order terminating a prosecution pursuant to subdivision four of section 180.85;

1-a. An order reducing a count or counts of an indictment or dismissing an indictment and directing the filing of a prosecutor's information, entered pursuant to subdivision one-a of section 210.20;

2. An order setting aside a verdict and dismissing an accusatory instrument or a count thereof, entered pursuant to paragraph (b) of subdivision one of section 290.10 or 360.40;

3. An order setting aside a verdict, entered pursuant to section 330.30 or 370.10;

4. A sentence other than one of death, as prescribed in subdivision two and three of section 450.30;

5. An order, entered pursuant to section 440.10, vacating a judgment other than one including a sentence of death;

6. An order, entered pursuant to section 440.20, setting aside a sentence other than one of death;

7. An order denying a motion by the people, made pursuant to section 440.40, to set aside a sentence other than one of death;

8. An order suppressing evidence, entered before trial pursuant to section 710.20; provided that the people file a statement in the appellate court pursuant to section 450.50.

9. An order entered pursuant to section 460.30 of the penal law setting aside or modifying a verdict of forfeiture.

10. An order, entered pursuant to paragraph (e) of subdivision twelve of section 400.27, finding that the defendant is mentally retarded.

11. An order granting a motion, made pursuant to subdivision one-a of section 440.30, for forensic DNA testing of evidence.

§450.30 Appeal from sentence.

1. An appeal by the defendant from a sentence, as authorized by subdivision two of section 450.10, may be based upon the ground that such sentence either was (a) invalid as a matter of law, or (b) harsh or excessive. A sentence is invalid as a matter of law not only when the terms thereof are unauthorized but also when it is based upon an erroneous determination that the defendant had a previous valid conviction for an offense or, in the case of a resentence following a revocation of a sentence of probation or conditional discharge, upon an improper revocation of such original sentence. An appeal by the defendant from a sentence, as authorized by subdivision three of section 450.15, may be based upon the ground that such sentence was harsh or excessive.

2. An appeal by the people from a sentence, as authorized by subdivision four of section 450.20, may be based only upon the ground that such sentence was invalid as a matter of law.

3. An appeal from a sentence, within the meaning of this section and sections 450.10 and 450.20, means an appeal from either the sentence originally imposed or from a resentence following an order vacating the original sentence. For purposes of appeal, the judgment consists of the conviction and the original sentence only, and when a resentence occurs more than thirty days after the original sentence, a defendant who has not previously filed a notice of appeal from the judgment may not appeal from the judgment, but only from the resentence.

4. When as a result of a successful appeal by the people from a sentence, the defendant receives a resentence the terms of which are more severe than those of the original or reversed sentence, the defendant, if he has not taken an appeal from the judgment, may, even though the period for doing so as prescribed in section 460.10 has expired, take such an appeal by filing and serving a notice of appeal, or an affidavit of errors as the case may be, within thirty days after imposition of the resentence. Upon such an appeal, only the conviction is reviewable; and any appellate challenge to the resentence must be made upon a separate appeal therefrom.

§450.40 Appeal by people from trial order of dismissal.

1. An appeal by the people from a trial order of dismissal, as authorized by subdivision two of section 450.20, may, as indicated by section 290.10, be based either (a) upon the ground that the evidence adduced at the trial was legally sufficient to support the count or counts of the accusatory instrument dismissed by the order, or (b) upon the ground that, though not legally sufficient, such evidence would have been legally sufficient had the court not erroneously excluded admissible evidence offered by the people.

2. If the appeal is based upon the ground specified in paragraph (b) of subdivision one, and if the appellate court determines that the evidence unsuccessfully offered by the people was improperly excluded, and if at the trial the people made on* offer of proof with respect thereto pursuant to subdivision three of section 290.10, the appellate court, in making its determination whether the people's evidence would have been legally sufficient had it not been for the improper exclusion, must treat the excluded evidentiary matter as it is summarized in the offer of proof as evidence constituting a part of the people's case. * *(So in original.Probably should read "an".)*

§450.50 Appeal by people from order suppressing evidence; filing of statement in appellate court.

1. In taking an appeal, pursuant to subdivision eight of section 450.20, to an intermediate appellate court from an order of a criminal court suppressing evidence, the people must file, in addition to a notice of appeal or, as the case may be, an affidavit of errors, a statement asserting that the deprivation of the use of the evidence ordered suppressed has rendered the sum of the proof available to the people with respect to a criminal charge which has been filed in the court either (a) insufficient as a matter of law, or (b) so weak in its entirety that any reasonable possibility of prosecuting such charge to a conviction has been effectively destroyed.

2. The taking of an appeal by the people, pursuant to subdivision eight of section 450.20, from an order suppressing evidence constitutes a bar to the prosecution of the accusatory instrument involving the evidence ordered

suppressed, unless and until such suppression order is reversed upon appeal and vacated.

§450.55 Appeal by people from order reducing a count of an indictment or directing the filing of a prosecutor's information.

In taking an appeal to an intermediate appellate court pursuant to subdivision one-a of section 450.20, the people shall file a notice of appeal. Upon request of either party, the hearing and determination of such appeal shall be conducted in an expeditious manner. The chief administrator of the courts, with the advice and consent of the administrative board of the courts, shall adopt rules for the expeditious briefing, hearing and determination of such appeals.

§450.60 Appeal to intermediate appellate court; to what court taken.

The particular intermediate appellate courts to which appeals authorized by sections 450.10 and 450.20 must be taken are as follows:

1. An appeal from a judgment, sentence or order of the supreme court must be taken to the appellate division of the department in which such judgment, sentence or order was entered.

2. An appeal from a judgment, sentence or order of a county court must be taken to the appellate division of the department in which such judgment, sentence or order was entered.

3. An appeal from a judgment, sentence or order of a local criminal court located outside of New York City must, except as otherwise provided in this subdivision, be taken to the county court of the county in which such judgment, sentence or order was entered.

If the appellate division of the second, third or fourth department has established an appellate term of the supreme court for its department, it may direct that appeals from such judgments, sentences and orders of such local criminal courts, or of particular classifications of such local criminal courts, be taken to such appellate term of the supreme court instead of to the county court; and in such case an appeal must be so taken.

4. An appeal from a judgment, sentence or order of the New York City criminal court must be taken, if such judgment, sentence or order was entered at a term of such court held in New York or Bronx county, to the appellate division of the first department, and, if entered at a term of such court held in Kings, Queens or Richmond county, to the appellate division of the second department; except that if the appellate division of either such department has established an appellate term of the supreme court for its department, it may direct that all such appeals be taken thereto; and in such case such an appeal must be so taken.

§450.70 Appeal by defendant directly to court of appeals; in what cases authorized.

An appeal directly to the court of appeals may be taken as of right by the defendant from the following judgment and orders of a superior court:

1. A judgment including a sentence of death;

2. An order denying a motion, made pursuant to section 440.10, to vacate a judgment including a sentence of death;

3. An order denying a motion, made pursuant to section 440.20, to set aside a sentence of death;

4. An order denying a motion, made pursuant to paragraph (d) of subdivision eleven of section 400.27, to set aside a sentence of death.

§450.80 Appeal by people directly to court of appeals; in what cases authorized.

An appeal directly to the court of appeals may be taken as of right by the people from the following orders of a superior court:

1. An order, entered pursuant to section 440.10, vacating a judgment including a sentence of death;

2. An order, entered pursuant to section 440.20, setting aside a sentence of death;

3. An order, entered pursuant to paragraph (d) of subdivision eleven of section 400.27, setting aside a sentence of death;

4. An order, entered pursuant to subdivision twelve of section 400.27, setting aside a sentence of death.

§450.90 Appeal to court of appeals from order of intermediate appellate court; in what cases authorized.

1. Provided that a certificate granting leave to appeal is issued pursuant to section 460.20, an appeal may, except as provided in subdivision two, be taken to the court of appeals by either the defendant or the people from any adverse or partially adverse order of an intermediate appellate court entered upon an appeal taken to such intermediate appellate court pursuant to section 450.10, 450.15, or 450.20, or from an order granting or denying a motion to set aside an order of an intermediate appellate court on the ground of ineffective assistance or wrongful deprivation of appellate counsel, or by either the defendant or the people from any adverse or partially adverse order of an intermediate appellate court entered upon an appeal taken to such intermediate appellate court from an order entered pursuant to section 440.46 or section 440.47 of this chapter. An order of an intermediate appellate court is adverse to the party who was the appellant in such court when it affirms the judgment, sentence or order appealed from, and is adverse to the party who was the respondent in such court when it reverses the judgment, sentence or order appealed from. An appellate court order which modifies a judgment or order appealed from is partially adverse to each party. *(Eff.8/12/19,Ch.31,L.2019)*

2. An appeal to the court of appeals from an order of an intermediate appellate court reversing or modifying a judgment, sentence or order of a criminal court may be taken only if:

(a) The court of appeals determines that the intermediate appellate court's determination of reversal or modification was on the law alone or upon the law and such facts which, but for the determination of law, would not have led to reversal or modification; or

(b) The appeal is based upon a contention that corrective action, as that term is defined in section 470.10, taken or directed by the intermediate appellate court was illegal.

ARTICLE 460 - APPEALS--TAKING AND PERFECTION THEREOF AND STAYS DURING PENDENCY THEREOF

Section
460.10 Appeal; how taken.
460.15 Certificate granting leave to appeal to intermediate appellate court.
460.20 Certificate granting leave to appeal to court of appeals.
460.30 Extension of time for taking appeal.
460.40 Effect of taking of appeal upon judgment or order of courts below; when stayed.
460.50 Stay of judgment pending appeal to intermediate appellate court.
460.60 Stay of judgment pending appeal to court of appeals from intermediate appellate court.
460.70 Appeal; how perfected.
460.80 Appeal; argument and submission thereof.
460.90 Filing of papers on appeal to the appellate division by electronic means.

§460.10 Appeal; how taken.

1. Except as provided in subdivisions two and three, an appeal taken as of right to an intermediate appellate court or directly to the court of appeals from a judgment, sentence or order of a criminal court is taken as follows:

(a) A party seeking to appeal from a judgment or a sentence or an order and sentence included within such judgment, or from a resentence, or from an order of a criminal court not included in a judgment, must, within thirty days after imposition of the sentence or, as the case may be, within thirty days after service upon such party of a copy of an order not included in a judgment, file with the clerk of the criminal court in which such sentence was imposed or in which such order was entered a written notice of appeal, in duplicate, stating that such party appeals therefrom to a designated appellate court.

(b) If the defendant is the appellant, he must, within such thirty day period, serve a copy of such notice of appeal upon the district attorney of the county embracing the criminal court in which the judgment or order being appealed was entered. If the appeal is directly to the court of appeals, the district attorney, following such service upon him, must immediately give written notice thereof to the public servant having custody of the defendant.

(c) If the people are the appellant, they must, within such thirty day period, serve a copy of such notice of appeal upon the defendant or upon the attorney who last appeared for him in the court in which the order being appealed was entered.

(d) Upon filing and service of the notice of appeal as prescribed in paragraphs (a), (b) and (c), the appeal is deemed to have been taken.

(e) Following the filing with him of the notice of appeal in duplicate, the clerk of the court in which the judgment, sentence or order being appealed was entered or imposed, must endorse upon such instruments the filing date and must transmit the duplicate notice of appeal to the clerk of the court to which the appeal is being taken.

2. An appeal taken as of right to a county court or to an appellate term of the supreme court from a judgment, sentence or order of a local criminal court in a case in which the underlying proceedings were recorded by a court stenographer is taken in the manner provided in subdivision one; except that where no clerk is employed by such local criminal court the appellant must file the notice of appeal with the judge of such court, and must further file a copy thereof with the clerk of the appellate court to which the appeal is being taken.

3. An appeal taken as of right to a county court or to an appellate term of the supreme court from a judgment, sentence or order of a local criminal court in a case in which the underlying proceedings were not recorded by a court stenographer is taken as follows:

(a) Within thirty days after entry or imposition in such local criminal court of the judgment, sentence or order being appealed, the appellant must file with such court either (i) an affidavit of errors, setting forth alleged errors or defects in the proceedings which are the subjects of the appeal, or (ii) a notice of appeal. Where a notice of appeal is filed, the appellant must serve a copy thereof upon the respondent in the manner provided in paragraphs (b) and (c) of subdivision one, and, within sixty days after the appellant receives a transcript of the electronically recorded proceedings, must file with such court an affidavit of errors.

(b) Not more than three days after the filing of the affidavit of errors, the appellant must serve a copy thereof upon the respondent or the respondent's counsel or authorized representative. If the defendant is the appellant, such service must be upon the district attorney of the county in which the local criminal court is located. If the people are the appellant, such service must be upon the defendant or upon the attorney who appeared for him in the proceedings in the local criminal court.

(c) Upon filing and service of the affidavit of errors as prescribed in paragraphs (a) and (b), the appeal is deemed to have been taken.

(d) Within ten days after the appellant's filing of the affidavit of errors with the local criminal court, such court must file with the clerk of the appellate court to which the appeal has been taken both the affidavit of errors and the court's return, and must deliver a copy of such return to each party or a representative thereof as indicated in paragraph (b). The court's return must set forth or summarize evidence, facts or occurrences in or adduced at the proceedings resulting in the judgment, sentence or order, which constitute the factual foundation for the contentions alleged in the affidavit of errors.

(e) If the local criminal court does not file such return within the prescribed period, or if it files a defective return, the appellate court, upon application of the appellant, must order such local criminal court to file a return or an amended return, as the case may be, within a designated time which such appellate court deems reasonable.

4. An appeal by a defendant to an intermediate appellate court by permission, pursuant to section 450.15, is taken as follows:

(a) Within thirty days after service upon the defendant of a copy of the order sought to be appealed, the defendant must make application, pursuant to section 460.15, for a certificate granting leave to appeal to the intermediate appellate court.

(b) If such application is granted and such certificate is issued, the defendant, within fifteen days after issuance thereof, must file with the criminal court in which the order sought to be appealed was rendered the certificate granting leave to appeal together with a written notice of appeal, or if the appeal is from a local criminal court in a case in which the underlying proceedings were not recorded by a court stenographer, either (i) an affidavit of errors, or (ii) a notice of appeal. In all other respects the appeal shall be taken as provided in subdivisions one, two and three.

5. An appeal to the court of appeals from an order of an intermediate appellate court is taken as follows:

(a) Within thirty days after service upon the appellant of a copy of the order sought to be appealed, the appellant must make application, pursuant to section 460.20, for a certificate granting leave to appeal to the court of appeals. The appellate division of each judicial department shall adopt rules governing the procedures for service of a copy of such order.

(b) If such application is granted, the issuance of the certificate granting leave to appeal shall constitute the taking of the appeal.

6. Where a notice of appeal, an affidavit of errors, an application for leave to appeal to an intermediate appellate court, or an application for leave to appeal to the court of appeals is premature or contains an inaccurate description of the judgment, sentence or order being or sought to be appealed, the appellate court, in its discretion, may, in the interest of justice, treat such instrument as valid. Where an appellant files a notice of appeal within the prescribed period but, through mistake, inadvertence or excusable neglect, omits to serve a copy thereof upon the respondent within the prescribed period, the appellate court to which the appeal is sought to be taken may, in its discretion and for good cause shown, permit such service to be made within a designated period of time, and upon such service the appeal is deemed to be taken.

§460.15 Certificate granting leave to appeal to intermediate appellate court.

1. A certificate granting leave to appeal to an intermediate appellate court is an order of one judge or justice of the intermediate appellate court to

which the appeal is sought to be taken granting such permission and certifying that the case involves questions of law or fact which ought to be reviewed by the intermediate appellate court.

2. An application for such a certificate must be made in a manner determined by the rules of the appellate division of the department in which such intermediate appellate court is located. Not more than one application may be made for such a certificate.

§460.20 Certificate granting leave to appeal to court of appeals.

1. A certificate granting leave to appeal to the court of appeals from an order of an intermediate appellate court is an order of a judge granting such permission and certifying that the case involves a question of law which ought to be reviewed by the court of appeals.

2. Such certificate may be issued by the following judges in the indicated situations:

(a) Where the appeal sought is from an order of the appellate division, the certificate may be issued by (i) a judge of the court of appeals or (ii) a justice of the appellate division of the department which entered the order sought to be appealed.

(b) Where the appeal sought is from an order of an intermediate appellate court other than the appellate division, the certificate may be issued only by a judge of the court of appeals.

3. An application for such a certificate must be made in the following manner:

(a) An application to a justice of the appellate division must be made upon reasonable notice to the respondent;

(b) An application seeking such a certificate from a judge of the court of appeals must be made to the chief judge of such court by submission thereof, either in writing or first orally and then in writing, to the clerk of the court of appeals. The chief judge must then designate a judge of such court to determine the application. The clerk must then notify the respondent of the application and must inform both parties of such designation.

4. A justice of the appellate division to whom such an application has been made, or a judge of the court of appeals designated to determine such an application, may in his discretion determine it upon such papers as he may request the parties to submit, or upon oral argument, or upon both.

5. Every judge or justice acting pursuant to this section shall file with the clerk of the court of appeals, immediately upon issuance, a copy of every certificate granting or denying leave to appeal.

§460.30 Extension of time for taking appeal.

1. Upon motion to an intermediate appellate court of a defendant who desires to take an appeal to such court from a judgment, sentence or order of a criminal court but has failed to file a notice of appeal, an application for leave to appeal, or, as the case may be, an affidavit of errors, with such criminal court within the prescribed period, or upon motion to the court of appeals of a defendant who desires to take an appeal to such court from an order of a superior court or of an intermediate appellate court, but has failed to make an application for a certificate granting leave to appeal to the court of appeals, or has failed to file a notice of appeal with the intermediate appellate court, within the prescribed period, such intermediate appellate court or the court of appeals, as the case may be, may order that the time for the taking of such appeal or applying for leave to appeal be extended to a date not more than thirty days subsequent to the determination of such motion, upon the ground that the failure to so file or make application in timely fashion resulted from (a) improper conduct of a public servant or improper conduct, death or disability of the defendant's attorney, or

(b) inability of the defendant and his attorney to have communicated, in person or by mail, concerning whether an appeal should be taken, prior to the expiration of the time within which to take an appeal due to defendant's incarceration in an institution and through no lack of due diligence or fault of the attorney or defendant. Such motion must be made with due diligence after the time for the taking of such appeal has expired, and in any case not more than one year thereafter.

2. The motion must be in writing and upon reasonable notice to the people and with opportunity to be heard. The motion papers must contain sworn allegations of facts claimed to establish the improper conduct, inability to communicate, or other facts essential to support the motion, and the people may file papers in opposition thereto. After all papers have been filed, the court must consider the same for the purpose of ascertaining whether the motion is determinable without a hearing to resolve issues of fact.

3. If the motion papers allege facts constituting a legal basis for the motion, and if the essential allegations are either conclusively substantiated by unquestionable documentary proof or are conceded by the people to be true, the court must grant the motion.

4. If the motion papers do not allege facts constituting a legal basis for the motion, or if an essential allegation is conclusively refuted by unquestionable documentary proof, the court may deny the motion.

5. If the court does not determine the motion pursuant to subdivision three or four, it must order the criminal court which entered or imposed the judgment, sentence or order sought to be appealed to conduct a hearing and to make and report findings of fact essential to the determination of such motion. Upon receipt of such report, the intermediate appellate court or the court of appeals, as the case may be, must determine the motion.

6. An order of an intermediate appellate court granting or denying a motion made pursuant to this section is appealable to the court of appeals if (a) such order states that the determination was made upon the law alone, and (b) a judge of the court of appeals, pursuant to procedure provided in section 460.20, of this chapter, issues a certificate granting leave to the appellant to appeal to the court of appeals.

§460.40 Effect of taking of appeal upon judgment or order of courts below; when stayed.

1. The taking of an appeal by the defendant directly to the court of appeals, pursuant to subdivision one of section 450.70, from a superior court judgment including a sentence of death stays the execution of such sentence. Except as provided in subdivision two of this section, in no other case does the taking of an appeal, by either party, in and of itself stay the execution of any judgment, sentence or order of either a criminal court or an intermediate appellate court.

2. The taking of an appeal by the people to an intermediate appellate court pursuant to subdivision one-a of section 450.20, from an order reducing a count or counts of an indictment or dismissing an indictment and directing the filing of a prosecutor's information, stays the effect of such order. In addition, the taking of an appeal by the people to an intermediate appellate court pursuant to subdivision one of section 450.20, from an order dismissing a count or counts of an indictment charging murder in the first degree, stays the effect of such order.

3. Within six months of the effective date of this subdivision, the court of appeals shall adopt rules to ensure that a defendant is granted a stay of the execution of any death warrant issued pursuant to article twenty-two-B of the correction law to allow the defendant an opportunity to prepare and

timely file an initial motion pursuant to section 440.10 or 440.20 seeking to set aside a sentence of death or vacate a judgment including a sentence of death and to allow the motion and any appeal from the denial thereof to be timely determined. The rules shall provide that in the event a defendant seeks to file any subsequent motion with respect to the judgment or sentence following a final determination of the defendant's initial motion pursuant to section 440.10 or 440.20, a motion for a stay of the execution of the death warrant may only be granted for good cause shown. The people and the defendant shall have a right to appeal to the court of appeals from orders granting or denying such stay motions and any rules adopted pursuant to this subdivision shall provide that the court of appeals may affirm such orders, reverse them or modify them upon such terms as the court deems appropriate and shall provide for the expeditious perfection and determination of such appeals. Prior to adoption of the rules, the court of appeals shall issue proposed rules and receive written comments thereon from interested parties.

§460.50 Stay of judgment pending appeal to intermediate appellate court.

1. Upon application of a defendant who has taken an appeal to an intermediate appellate court from a judgment or from a sentence of a criminal court, a judge designated in subdivision two may issue an order both (a) staying or suspending the execution of the judgment pending the determination of the appeal, and (b) either releasing the defendant on his own recognizance or fixing bail pursuant to the provisions of article five hundred thirty. That phase of the order staying or suspending execution of the judgment does not become effective unless and until the defendant is released, either on his own recognizance or upon the posting of bail.

2. An order as prescribed in subdivision one may be issued by the following judges in the indicated situations:

(a) If the appeal is to the appellate division from a judgment or a sentence of either the supreme court or the New York City criminal court, such order may be issued by (i) a justice of the appellate division of the department in which the judgment was entered, or (ii) a justice of the supreme court of the judicial district embracing the county in which the judgment was entered:

(b) If the appeal is to the appellate division from a judgment or a sentence of a county court, such order may be issued by (i) a justice of such appellate division, or (ii) a justice of the supreme court of the judicial district embracing the county in which the judgment was entered, or (iii) a judge of such county court;

(c) If the appeal is to an appellate term of the supreme court from a judgment or sentence of the New York City criminal court, such order may be issued by a justice of the supreme court of the judicial district embracing the county in which the judgment was entered;

(d) With respect to appeals to county courts from judgments or sentences of local criminal courts, and with respect to appeals to appellate terms of the supreme court from judgments or sentences of any criminal courts located outside of New York City, the judges who may issue such orders in any particular situation are determined by rules of the appellate division of the department embracing the appellate court to which the appeal has been taken.

3. An application for an order specified in this section must be made upon reasonable notice to the people, and the people must be accorded adequate opportunity to appear in opposition thereto. Not more than one application may be made pursuant to this section.

4. Notwithstanding the provisions of subdivision one, if within one hundred twenty days after the issuance of such an order the appeal has not been brought to argument in or submitted to the intermediate appellate court, the operation of such order terminates and the defendant must surrender himself to the criminal court in which the judgment was entered in order that execution of the judgment be commenced or resumed; except that this subdivision does not apply where the intermediate appellate court has (a) extended the time for argument or submission of the appeal to a date beyond the specified period of one hundred twenty days, and (b) upon application of the defendant, expressly ordered that the operation of the order continue until the date of the determination of the appeal or some other designated future date or occurrence.

5. Where the defendant is at liberty during the pendency of an appeal as a result of an order issued pursuant to this section, the intermediate appellate court, upon affirmance of the judgment, must by appropriate certificate remit the case to the criminal court in which such judgment was entered. The criminal court must, upon at least two days notice to the defendant, his surety and his attorney, promptly direct the defendant to surrender himself to the criminal court in order that execution of the judgment be commenced or resumed, and if necessary the criminal court may issue a bench warrant to secure his appearance.

6. Upon application of a defendant who has been granted a certificate granting leave to appeal pursuant to section 460.15 of this chapter, and in accordance with the procedures set forth in subdivisions three, four and five of this section, the intermediate appellate court may issue an order both (a) staying or suspending the execution of the judgment pending the determination of the appeal, and (b) either releasing the defendant on his own recognizance or fixing bail pursuant to the provisions of article five hundred thirty. That phase of the order staying or suspending execution of the judgment does not become effective unless and until the defendant is released, either on his own recognizance or upon the posting of bail.

§460.60   Stay of judgment pending appeal to court of appeals from intermediate appellate court.

1. (a) A judge who, pursuant to section 460.20 of this chapter, has received an application for a certificate granting a defendant leave to appeal to the court of appeals from an order of an intermediate appellate court affirming or modifying a judgment including a sentence of imprisonment, a sentence of imprisonment, or an order appealed pursuant to section 450.15 of this chapter, of a criminal court, may, upon application of such defendant-appellant issue an order both (i) staying or suspending the execution of the judgment pending the determination of the application for leave to appeal, and, if that application is granted, staying or suspending the execution of the judgment pending the determination of the appeal, and (ii) either releasing the defendant on his own recognizance or continuing bail as previously determined or fixing bail pursuant to the provisions of article five hundred thirty. Such an order is effective immediately and that phase of the order staying or suspending execution of the judgment does not become effective unless and until the defendant is released, either on his own recognizance or upon the posting of bail.

(b) If the application for leave to appeal is denied, the stay or suspension pending the application automatically terminates upon the signing of the certificate denying leave. Upon such termination, the certificate denying leave must be sent to the criminal court in which the original judgment was entered, and the latter must proceed in the manner provided in subdivision five of section 460.50 of this chapter.

2. An application pursuant to subdivision one must be made upon reasonable notice to the people, and the people must be accorded adequate opportunity to appear in opposition thereto. Such an application may be made immediately after the entry of the order sought to be appealed

or at any subsequent time during the pendency of the appeal. Not more than one application may be made pursuant to this section.

3. Notwithstanding the provisions of subdivision one, if within one hundred twenty days after the issuance of a certificate granting leave to appeal, the appeal or prospective appeal has not been brought to argument in or submitted to the court of appeals, the operation of an order issued pursuant to subdivision one of this section terminates and the defendant must surrender himself to the criminal court in which the original judgment was entered in order that execution of such judgment be commenced or resumed; except that this subdivision does not apply where the court of appeals has (a) extended the time for argument or submission of the appeal to a date beyond the specified period of one hundred twenty days and (b) upon application of the defendant expressly ordered that the operation of such order continue until the date of the determination of the appeal or some other designated future date or occurrence.

4. Where the defendant is at liberty during the pendency of an appeal as a result of an order issued pursuant to this section, the court of appeals upon affirmance of the judgment or order, must, by appropriate certificate, remit the case to the criminal court in which the judgment was entered, and the latter must proceed in the manner provided in subdivision five of section 460.50 of this chapter.

§460.70 Appeal; how perfected.

1. Except as provided in subdivision two, the mode of and time for perfecting an appeal which has been taken to an intermediate appellate court from a judgment, sentence or order of a criminal court are determined by rules of the appellate division of the department in which such appellate court is located. Among the matters to be determined by such court rules are the times when the appeal must be noticed for and brought to argument, the content and form of the records and briefs to be served and filed, and the time when such records and briefs must be served and filed.

When an appeal is taken by a defendant pursuant to section 450.10, a transcript shall be prepared and settled and shall be filed with the criminal court by the court reporter. Electronically recorded proceedings that were not recorded by a stenographer shall be transcribed and filed with the court as directed by the chief administrator of the courts. The expense for such transcript and any reproduced copies of such transcript shall be paid by the defendant. Where the defendant is granted permission to proceed as a poor person by the appellate court, the court reporter shall promptly make and file with the criminal court a transcript of the stenographic minutes of such proceedings as the appellate court shall direct. The expense of transcripts and any reproduced copies of transcripts prepared for poor persons under this section shall be a state charge payable out of funds appropriated to the office of court administration for that purpose. The appellate court shall where such is necessary for perfection of the appeal, order that the criminal court furnish a reproduced copy of such transcript to the defendant or his counsel.   *(Eff.10/20/17,Ch.195,L.2017)*

2. An appeal which has been taken to a county court or to an appellate term of the supreme court from a judgment, sentence or order of a local criminal court pursuant to subdivision three of section 460.10 is perfected as follows:

(a) After the local criminal court has, pursuant to paragraph (d) of subdivision three of section 460.10, filed its return with the clerk of the appellate court and delivered a copy thereof to the appellant, the appellant must file with such clerk, and serve a copy thereof upon the respondent, a notice of argument, noticing the appeal for argument at the term of such appellate court immediately following the term being held at the time of the appellant's receipt of the return. Upon motion of the appellant, however, such appellate court may for good cause shown enlarge the time to a subsequent term, in which case the appellant must notice the appeal for argument at such subsequent term;

(b) The appellant must further comply with all court rules applicable to the mode of perfecting such appeals;

(c) If the appellant does not file a notice of argument as provided in paragraph (a) or does not comply with all applicable court rules as provided in paragraph (b), the appellate court may, either upon motion of the respondent or upon its own motion dismiss the appeal.

3. The mode of and time for perfecting any appeal which has been taken to the court of appeals are determined by the rules of the court of appeals. Among the matters to be determined by such court rules are the times when the appeal must be noticed for and brought to argument, the content, form and number of the records and briefs and copies thereof to be served and filed, and the times when such records and briefs must be served and filed.

When an appeal is taken by a defendant pursuant to section 450.70, the defendant shall cause to be prepared and printed or otherwise duplicated pursuant to rules of the court of appeals the record on appeal and the required number of copies thereof. If the defendant is granted permission to appeal as a poor person, the expense thereof shall be a state charge payable out of funds appropriated to the office of court administration for that purpose.

§460.80 Appeal; argument and submission thereof.

The mode of and procedure for arguing or otherwise litigating appeals in criminal cases are determined by rules of the individual appellate courts. Among the matters to be determined by such court rules are the circumstances in which oral argument is required and those in which the case may be submitted by either or both parties without oral argument; the consequences or effect of failure to present oral argument when such is required; the amount of time for oral argument allowed to each party; and the number of counsel entitled to be heard.

*§460.90   Filing of papers on appeal to the appellate division by electronic means.

Notwithstanding any other provision of law, the appellate division in each judicial department may promulgate rules authorizing a program in the use of electronic means for the taking and perfection of appeals in accordance with the provisions of section twenty-one hundred twelve of the civil practice law and rules. Provided however, such rules shall not require an unrepresented party or any attorney who furnishes a certification specified in subparagraph (i) or (ii) of paragraph (c) of subdivision two of section 10.40 of this chapter to take or perfect an appeal by electronic means. Provided further, however, before promulgating any such rules, the appellate division in each judicial department shall consult with the chief administrator of the courts and shall provide an opportunity for review and comment by all those who are or would be affected including district attorneys; representatives of the office of indigent legal services; not-for-profit legal service providers; public defenders; statewide and local specialty bar associations whose membership devotes a significant portion of their practice to assigned criminal cases pursuant to subparagraph (i) of paragraph (a) of subdivision three of section seven hundred twenty-two of the county law; institutional providers of criminal defense services and other members of the criminal defense bar; representatives of victims' rights organizations; unaffiliated attorneys who regularly appear in proceedings that are or would be affected by such electronic filing program; interested members of the criminal justice community; and any other persons in whose county a program has been implemented in any of the courts therein as deemed to be appropriate by any appellate division. To the extent practicable, rules promulgated by the appellate division in each judicial department pursuant to this section shall be uniform. For purposes of this section, "electronic means" shall be as defined in subdivision (f) of rule twenty-one hundred three of such law and rules. *(Expires 9/1/22, Ch.118,L.2021)*

ARTICLE 470 - APPEALS--DETERMINATION THEREOF

Section
470.05 Determination of appeals; general criteria.
470.10 Determination of appeals; definitions of terms.
470.15 Determination of appeals by intermediate appellate courts; scope of review.
470.20 Determination of appeals by intermediate appellate courts; corrective action upon reversal or modification.
470.25 Determination of appeals by intermediate appellate courts; form and content of order.
470.30 Determination by court of appeals of appeals taken directly thereto from judgments and orders of criminal courts.
470.35 Determination by court of appeals of appeals from orders of intermediate appellate courts; scope of review.
470.40 Determination by court of appeals of appeals from intermediate appellate courts; corrective action upon reversal or modification.
470.45 Remission of case by appellate court to criminal court upon reversal or modification of judgment; action by criminal court.
470.50 Reargument of appeal; motion and criteria for.
470.55 Status of accusatory instrument upon order of new trial or restoration of action to pre-pleading status.
470.60 Dismissal of appeal.

§470.05 Determination of appeals; general criteria.

1. An appellate court must determine an appeal without regard to technical errors or defects which do not affect the substantial rights of the parties.

2. For purposes of appeal, a question of law with respect to a ruling or instruction of a criminal court during a trial or proceeding is presented when a protest thereto was registered, by the party claiming error, at the time of such ruling or instruction or at any subsequent time when the court had an opportunity of effectively changing the same. Such protest need not be in the form of an "exception" but is sufficient if the party made his position with respect to the ruling or instruction known to the court, or if in reponse* to a protest by a party, the court expressly decided the question raised on appeal. In addition, a party who without success has either expressly or impliedly sought or requested a particular ruling or instruction, is deemed to have thereby protested the court's ultimate disposition of the matter or failure to rule or instruct accordingly sufficiently to raise a question of law with respect to such disposition or failure regardless of whether any actual protest thereto was registered. * *(So in original. Probably should read "response".)*

§470.10 Determination of appeals; definitions of terms.

The following definitions are applicable to this article:

1. "Reversal" by an appellate court of a judgment, sentence or order of another court means the vacating of such judgment, sentence or order.

2. "Modification" by an appellate court of a judgment or order of another court means the vacating of a part thereof and affirmance of the remainder.

3. "Corrective action" means affirmative action taken or directed by an appellate court upon reversing or modifying a judgment, sentence or order of another court, which disposes of or continues the case in a manner consonant with the determinations and principles underlying the reversal or modification.

§470.15 Determination of appeals by intermediate appellate courts; scope of review.

1. Upon an appeal to an intermediate appellate court from a judgment, sentence or order of a criminal court, such intermediate appellate court may consider and determine any question of law or issue of fact involving error or defect in the criminal court proceedings which may have adversely affected the appellant.

2. Upon such an appeal, the intermediate appellate court must either affirm or reverse or modify the criminal court judgment, sentence or order. The ways in which it may modify a judgment include, but are not limited to, the following:

(a) Upon a determination that the trial evidence adduced in support of a verdict is not legally sufficient to establish the defendant's guilt of an offense of which he was convicted but is legally sufficient to establish his guilt of a lesser included offense, the court may modify the judgment by changing it to one of conviction for the lesser offense;

(b) Upon a determination that the trial evidence is not legally sufficient to establish the defendant's guilt of all the offenses of which he was convicted but is legally sufficient to establish his guilt of one or more of such offenses, the court may modify the judgment by reversing it with respect to the unsupported counts and otherwise affirming it;

(c) Upon a determination that a sentence imposed upon a valid conviction is illegal or unduly harsh or severe, the court may modify the judgment by reversing it with respect to the sentence and by otherwise affirming it.

3. A reversal or a modification of a judgment, sentence or order must be based upon a determination made:

(a) Upon the law; or

(b) Upon the facts; or

(c) As a matter of discretion in the interest of justice; or

(d) Upon any two or all three of the bases specified in paragraphs (a), (b) and (c).

4. The kinds of determinations of reversal or modification deemed to be upon the law include, but are not limited to, the following:

(a) That a ruling or instruction of the court, duly protested by the defendant, as prescribed in subdivision two of section 470.05, at a trial resulting in a judgment, deprived the defendant of a fair trial;

(b) That evidence adduced at a trial resulting in a judgment was not legally sufficient to establish the defendant's guilt of an offense of which he was convicted;

(c) That a sentence was unauthorized, illegally imposed or otherwise invalid as a matter of law.

5. The kinds of determinations of reversal or modification deemed to be on the facts include, but are not limited to, a determination that a verdict of conviction resulting in a judgment was, in whole or in part, against the weight of the evidence.

6. The kinds of determinations of reversal or modification deemed to be made as a matter of discretion in the interest of justice include, but are not limited to, the following:

(a) That an error or defect occurring at a trial resulting in a judgment, which error or defect was not duly protested at trial as prescribed in subdivision two of section 470.05 so as to present a question of law, deprived the defendant of a fair trial;

(b) That a sentence, though legal, was unduly harsh or severe.

§470.20 Determination of appeals by intermediate appellate courts; corrective action upon reversal or modification.

Upon reversing or modifying a judgment, sentence or order of a criminal court, an intermediate appellate court must take or direct such corrective action as is necessary and appropriate both to rectify any injustice to the appellant resulting from the error or defect which is the subject of the reversal or modification and to protect the rights of the respondent. The particular corrective action to be taken or directed is governed in part by the following rules:

1. Upon a reversal of a judgment after trial for error or defect which resulted in prejudice to the defendant or deprived him of a fair trial, the court must, whether such reversal be on the law or as a matter of discretion in the interest of justice, order a new trial of the accusatory instrument and remit the case to the criminal court for such action.

2. Upon a reversal of a judgment after trial for legal insufficiency of trial evidence, the court must dismiss the accusatory instrument.

3. Upon a modification of a judgment after trial for legal insufficiency of trial evidence with respect to one or more but not all of the offenses of which the defendant was convicted, the court must dismiss the count or counts of the accusatory instrument determined to be legally unsupported and must otherwise affirm the judgment. In such case, it must either reduce the total sentence to that imposed by the criminal court upon the counts with respect to which the judgment is affirmed or remit the case to the criminal court for re-sentence upon such counts; provided that nothing contained in this paragraph precludes further sentence reduction in the exercise of the appellate court's discretion pursuant to subdivision six.

4. Upon a modification of a judgment after trial which reduces a conviction of a crime to one for a lesser included offense, the court must remit the case to the criminal court with a direction that the latter sentence the defendant accordingly.

5. Upon a reversal or modification of a judgment after trial upon the ground that the verdict, either in its entirety or with respect to a particular count or counts, is against the weight of the trial evidence, the court must dismiss the accusatory instrument or any reversed count.

6. Upon modifying a judgment or reversing a sentence as a matter of discretion in the interest of justice upon the ground that the sentence is unduly harsh or severe, the court must itself impose some legally authorized lesser sentence.

§470.25 Determination of appeals by intermediate appellate courts; form and content of order.

1. An order of an intermediate appellate court which affirms a judgment, sentence or order of a criminal court need only state such affirmance.

2. An order of an intermediate appellate court which reverses or modifies a judgment, sentence or order of a criminal court must contain the following:

(a) A statement of whether the determination was upon the law or upon the facts or as a matter of discretion in the interest of justice, or upon any specified two or all three of such bases; and

(b) If the decision is rendered without opinion, a brief statement of the specific grounds of the reversal or modification; and

(c) A statement of the corrective action taken or directed by the court; and

(d) If the determination is exclusively upon the law, a statement of whether or not the facts upon which the criminal court's judgment, sentence or order is based have been considered and determined to have been established. In the absence of such a statement, it is presumed that the intermediate appellate court did not consider or make any determination with respect to such facts.

§470.30 Determination by court of appeals of appeals taken directly thereto from judgments and orders of criminal courts.

1. Wherever appropriate, the rules set forth in sections 470.15 and 470.20, governing the consideration and determination by intermediate appellate courts of appeals thereto from judgments and orders of criminal courts, and prescribing their scope of review and the corrective action to be taken by them upon reversal or modification, apply equally to the consideration and determination by the court of appeals of appeals taken directly thereto, pursuant to sections 450.70 and 450.80, from judgments and orders of superior criminal courts.

2. Whenever a sentence of death is imposed, the judgment and sentence shall be reviewed on the record by the court of appeals. Review by the court of appeals pursuant to subdivision one of section 450.70 may not be waived.

3. With regard to sentence, the court shall, in addition to exercising the powers and scope of review granted under subdivision one of this section, determine:

(a) whether the sentence of death was imposed under the influence of passion, prejudice, or any other arbitrary or legally impermissible factor including whether the imposition of the verdict or sentence was based upon the race of the defendant or a victim of the crime for which the defendant was convicted;

(b) whether the sentence of death is excessive or disproportionate to the penalty imposed in similar cases considering both the crime and the defendant. In conducting such review the court, upon request of the defendant, in addition to any other determination, shall review whether the sentence of death is excessive or disproportionate to the penalty imposed in similar cases by virtue of the race of the defendant or a victim of the crime for which the defendant was convicted; and

(c) whether the decision to impose the sentence of death was against the weight of evidence.

4. The court shall include in its decision: (a) the aggravating and mitigating factors established in the record on appeal; and (b) those similar cases it took into consideration.

5. In addition to exercising any other corrective action pursuant to subdivision one of this section, the court, with regard to review of a sentence of death, shall be authorized to:

(a) affirm the sentence of death; or

(b) set the sentence aside and remand the case for resentencing pursuant to the procedures set forth in section 400.27 for a determination as to whether the defendant shall be sentenced to death, life imprisonment without parole or to a term of imprisonment for the class A-I felony of murder in the first degree other than a sentence of life imprisonment without parole; or

(c) set the sentence aside and remand the case for resentencing by the court for a determination as to whether the defendant shall be sentenced to life imprisonment without parole or to a term of imprisonment for the class A-I felony of murder in the first degree other than a sentence of life imprisonment without parole.

§470.35 Determination by court of appeals of appeals from orders of intermediate appellate courts; scope of review.

1. Upon an appeal to the court of appeals from an order of an intermediate appellate court affirming a judgment, sentence or order of a criminal court, the court of appeals may consider and determine not only questions of law which were raised or considered upon the appeal to the intermediate appellate court, but also any question of law involving alleged

error or defect in the criminal court proceedings resulting in the original criminal court judgment, sentence or order, regardless of whether such question was raised, considered or determined upon the appeal to the intermediate appellate court.

2. Upon an appeal to the court of appeals from an order of an intermediate appellate court reversing or modifying a judgment, sentence or order of a criminal court, the court of appeals may consider and determine:

(a) Any question of law which was determined by the intermediate appellate court and which, as so determined, constituted a basis for such court's order of reversal or modification; and

(b) Any other question of law involving alleged or possible error or defect in the criminal court proceedings resulting in the original judgment, sentence or order which may have adversely affected the party who was appellant in the intermediate appellate court and who is respondent in the court of appeals. The court of appeals is not precluded from considering and determining such a question by the circumstance that it was not considered or determined by the intermediate appellate court, or that it did not constitute a basis for such court's reversal or modification, or that the party who may have been adversely affected thereby is the respondent rather than the appellant in the court of appeals; and the court of appeals, even though rejecting the intermediate appellate court's reasons for its order of reversal or modification, may affirm or modify such order upon the basis of such other questions; and

(c) Any question concerning the legality of the corrective action taken by the intermediate appellate court.

3. Upon such an appeal, the court must affirm, reverse or modify the intermediate appellate court order.

§470.40 Determination by court of appeals of appeals from intermediate appellate courts; corrective action upon reversal or modification.

1. Upon reversing or modifying an order of an intermediate appellate court affirming a criminal court judgment, sentence or order, the court of appeals must take or direct such corrective action as the intermediate appellate court would, pursuant to section 470.20, have been required or authorized to take or direct had it reversed or modified the criminal court judgment, sentence or order upon the same ground or grounds.

2. Upon reversing an order of an intermediate appellate court reversing or modifying a criminal court judgment, sentence or order upon the ground that questions of law were erroneously determined by the intermediate appellate court in favor of the party appellant therein, the court of appeals must take or direct corrective action as follows:

(a) If the facts underlying the original criminal court judgment, sentence or order were considered and determined to have been established by the intermediate appellate court, the court of appeals must reinstate and affirm the original criminal court judgment, sentence or order and remit the case to such criminal court for whatever further proceedings may be necessary to complete the action or proceedings therein; provided, however, that where such facts were applied to an erroneous determination of law, the court of appeals may remit the case to the intermediate appellate court for a further determination of the facts;

(b) If the facts underlying the original criminal court judgment, sentence or order were not, or are presumed not to have been, considered and deter-mined by the intermediate appellate court, the court of appeals must remit the case to such intermediate appellate court for determination of the facts.

3. Upon modifying an intermediate appellate court order reversing or modifying a criminal court judgment or order, upon the ground that corrective

action taken or directed by the intermediate appellate court was illegal, the court of appeals must either (a) itself take or direct the appropriate corrective action or (b) remit the case to the intermediate appellate court for appropriate corrective action by the latter.

§470.45 Remission of case by appellate court to criminal court upon reversal or modification of judgment; action by criminal court.

Upon reversing or modifying a judgment and directing corrective action, an appellate court must remit the case to the criminal court in which the judgment was entered. Such criminal court must execute the direction of the appellate court and must, depending upon the nature of such direction, either discharge the defendant from custody, exonerate his bail or issue a securing order.

§470.50 Reargument of appeal; motion and criteria for.

1. After its determination of an appeal taken pursuant to article four hundred fifty, an appellate court, in the interest of justice and for good cause shown, may in its discretion, upon motion of a party adversely affected by its determination, or upon its own motion, order a reargument or reconsideration of the appeal. Upon such an order the court may either direct further oral argument by the parties or confine its reconsideration to re-examination of the issues as previously argued or submitted upon the appeal proper. Upon ordering a reargument or reconsideration of an appeal, the court must again determine the appeal pursuant to the provisions of this article.

2. The court of appeals may promulgate rules limiting the time within which a motion for reargument of appeals determined by such court may be made, and the appellate division of each department may similarly promulgate such rules with respect to appeals determined by such appellate division and appeals determined by the other intermediate appellate courts located within such department. In the absence of any such rule of limitation, a motion for reargument may be made at any time.

§470.55 Status of accusatory instrument upon order of new trial or restoration of action to pre-pleading status.

1. Upon a new trial of an accusatory instrument resulting from an appellate court order reversing a judgment and ordering such new trial, such accusatory instrument is deemed to contain all the counts and to charge all the offenses which it contained and charged at the time the previous trial was commenced, regardless of whether any count was dismissed by the court in the course of such trial, except (a) those upon or of which the defendant was acquitted or deemed to have been acquitted, and (b) those dismissed upon appeal or upon some other post-judgment order.

2. Upon an appellate court order which reverses a judgment based upon a plea of guilty to an accusatory instrument or a part thereof, but which does not dismiss the entire accusatory instrument, the criminal action is, in the absence of express appellate court direction to the contrary, restored to its pre-pleading status and the accusatory instrument is deemed to contain all the counts and to charge all the offenses which it contained and charged at the time of the entry of the plea, except those dismissed upon appeal or upon some other post-judgment order. Where the plea of guilty was entered and accepted, pursuant to subdivision three of section 220.30, upon the condition that it constituted a complete disposition and dismissal not only of the accusatory instrument underlying the judgment reversed but also of one

or more other accusatory instruments against the defendant then pending in the same court, the appellate court order of reversal completely restores such other accusatory instruments; and such is the case even where the order of reversal dismisses the entire accusatory instrument underlying the judgment reversed.

§470.60 Dismissal of appeal.

1. At any time after an appeal has been taken and before determination thereof, the appellate court in which such appeal is pending may, upon motion of the respondent or upon its own motion, dismiss such appeal upon the ground of mootness, lack of jurisdiction to determine it, failure of timely prosecution or perfection thereof, or other substantial defect, irregularity or failure of action by the appellant with respect to the prosecution or perfection of such appeal.

2. Such motion must be made upon reasonable notice to the appellant and with opportunity to be heard. If the people are the appellant, such notice must be served upon the appropriate district attorney either personally or by ordinary mail. If the appellant is a defendant, such notice must be served upon him by ordinary mail at his last known place of resident or, if he is imprisoned, at the institution in which he is confined, and similar notice must be served upon the attorney, if any, who last appeared for him. Upon determination of the motion, a copy of the order entered thereon must similarly be served.

3. Provided that a certificate granting leave to appeal is issued pursuant to this subdivision, an appeal may be taken, in the manner prescribed in subdivision four of section 460.10, to the court of appeals from an order of an intermediate appellate court dismissing an appeal thereto. Such appeal may be based either upon the ground that the dismissal was invalid as a matter of law or upon the ground that it constituted an abuse of discretion. A certificate granting leave to appeal from such an order of dismissal may be issued only by a judge of the court of appeals upon an application made in the manner prescribed in paragraph (b) of subdivision three of section 460.20. Upon such an appeal, the court of appeals must either affirm or reverse the intermediate appellate court order.

PART THREE - SPECIAL PROCEEDINGS AND MISCELLANEOUS PROCEDURES

TITLE P - PROCEDURES FOR SECURING ATTENDANCE AT CRIMINAL ACTIONS AND PROCEEDINGS OF DEFENDANTS AND WITNESSES UNDER CONTROL OF COURT - RECOGNIZANCE, BAIL AND COMMITMENT

ARTICLE 500 - RECOGNIZANCE, BAIL AND COMMITMENT--DEFINITIONS OF TERMS

Section
500.10 Recognizance, bail and commitment; definitions of terms.

§500.10 Recognizance, bail and commitment; definitions of terms.

As used in this title, and in this chapter generally, the following terms have the following meanings:

1. "Principal" means a defendant in a criminal action or proceeding, or a person adjudged a material witness therein, or any other person so involved therein that the principal may by law be compelled to appear before a court

for the purpose of having such court exercise control over the principal's person to secure the principal's future attendance at the action or proceeding when required, and who in fact either is before the court for such purpose or has been before it and been subjected to such control.

2. "Release on own recognizance." A court releases a principal on the principal's own recognizance when, having acquired control over the principal's person, it permits the principal to be at liberty during the pendency of the criminal action or proceeding involved upon condition that the principal will appear thereat whenever the principal's attendance may be required and will at all times render the principal amenable to the orders and processes of the court.

3. "Fix bail." A court fixes bail when, having acquired control over the person of a principal, it designates a sum of money and stipulates that, if bail in such amount is posted on behalf of the principal and approved, it will permit him to be at liberty during the pendency of the criminal action or proceeding involved.

3-a. "Release under non-monetary conditions." A court releases a principal under non-monetary conditions when, having acquired control over a person, it authorizes the person to be at liberty during the pendency of the criminal action or proceeding involved under conditions ordered by the court, which shall be the least restrictive conditions that will reasonably assure the principal's return to court and reasonably assure the principal's compliance with court conditions. A principal shall not be required to pay for any part of the cost of release on non-monetary conditions. Such conditions may include, among other conditions reasonable under the circumstances:

(a) that the principal be in contact with a pretrial services agency serving principals in that county;

(b) that the principal abide by reasonable, specified restrictions on travel that are reasonably related to an actual risk of flight from the jurisdiction, or that the principal surrender his or her passport;

(c) that the principal refrain from possessing a firearm, destructive device or other dangerous weapon;

(d) that, when it is shown pursuant to subdivision four of section 510.45 of this title that no other realistic non-monetary condition or set of non-monetary conditions will suffice to reasonably assure the person's return to court, the person be placed in reasonable pretrial supervision with a pretrial services agency serving principals in that county;

(e) that the principal refrain from associating with certain persons who are connected with the instant charge, including, when appropriate, specified victims, witnesses, or co-defendants;

(f) that the principal be referred to a pretrial services agency for placement in mandatory programming, including counseling, treatment, and intimate partner violence intervention programs. Where applicable, the court may direct the principal be removed to a hospital pursuant to section 9.43 of the mental hygiene law;

(g) that the principal make diligent efforts to maintain employment, housing, or enrollment in school or educational programming;

(h) that the principal obey an order of protection issued by the court, including an order issued pursuant to section 530.11 of this title;

(i) that the principal obey conditions set by the court addressed to the safety of a victim of a family offense as defined in section 530.11 of this title including conditions that may be requested by or on behalf of the victim; and

(j) that, when it is shown pursuant to paragraph (a) of subdivision four of section 510.40 of this title that no other realistic non-monetary condition or set of non-monetary conditions will suffice to reasonably assure the principal's return to court, the principal's location be monitored with an approved electronic monitoring device, in accordance with such subdivision four of section 510.40 of this title.   *(Eff.7/2/20,Ch.56,L.2020)*

3-b. Subdivision three-a of this section presents a non-exclusive list of conditions that may be considered and imposed by law, singularly or in combination, when reasonable under the circumstances of the defendant, the case, and the situation of the defendant. The court need not necessarily order one or more specific conditions first before ordering one or more or additional conditions.   *(Eff.7/2/20,Ch.56,L.2020)*

4. "Commit to the custody of the sheriff." A court commits a principal to the custody of the sheriff when, having acquired control over the principal's person, it orders that the principal be confined in the custody of the sheriff during the pendency of the criminal action or proceeding involved.

5. "Securing order" means an order of a court committing a principal to the custody of the sheriff or fixing bail, where authorized, or releasing the principal on the principal's own recognizance or releasing the principal under non-monetary conditions.

6. "Order of recognizance or bail" means a securing order releasing a principal on the principal's own recognizance or under non-monetary conditions or, where authorized, fixing bail.

7. "Application for recognizance or bail" means an application by a principal that the court, instead of committing the principal to or retaining the principal in the custody of the sheriff, either release the principal on the principal's own recognizance, release under non-monetary conditions, or, where authorized, fix bail.

8. "Post bail" means to deposit bail in the amount and form fixed by the court, with the court or with some other authorized public servant or agency.

9. "Bail" means cash bail, a bail bond or money paid with a credit card.

10. "Cash bail" means a sum of money, in the amount designated in an order fixing bail, posted by a principal or by another person on his behalf with a court or other authorized public servant or agency, upon the condition that such money will become forfeit to the people of the state of New York if the principal does not comply with the directions of a court requiring his attendance at the criminal action or proceeding involved or does not otherwise render himself amenable to the orders and processes of the court.

11. "Obligor" means a person who executes a bail bond on behalf of a principal and thereby assumes the undertaking described therein. The principal himself may be an obligor.

12. "Surety" means an obligor who is not a principal.

13. "Bail bond" means a written undertaking, executed by one or more obligors, that the principal designated in such instrument will, while at liberty as a result of an order fixing bail and of the posting of the bail bond in satisfaction thereof, appear in a designated criminal action or proceeding when his attendance is required and otherwise render himself amenable to the orders and processes of the court, and that in the event that he fails to do so the obligor or obligors will pay to the people of the state of New York a specified sum of money, in the amount designated in the order fixing bail.

14. "Appearance bond" means a bail bond in which the only obligor is the principal.

15. "Surety bond" means a bail bond in which the obligor or obligors consist of one or more sureties or of one or more sureties and the principal.

16. "Insurance company bail bond" means a surety bond, executed in the form prescribed by the superintendent of financial services, in which the

surety-obligor is a corporation licensed by the superintendent of financial services to engage in the business of executing bail bonds.

17. "Secured bail bond" means a bail bond secured by either:

(a) Personal property which is not exempt from execution and which, over and above all liabilities and encumbrances, has a value equal to or greater than the total amount of the undertaking; or

(b) Real property having a value of at least twice the total amount of the undertaking. For purposes of this paragraph, value of real property is determined by either:

(i) dividing the last assessed value of such property by the last given equalization rate or in a special assessing unit, as defined in article eighteen of the real property tax law, the appropriate class ratio established pursuant to section twelve hundred two of such law of the assessing municipality wherein the property is situated and by deducting from the resulting figure the total amount of any liens or other encumbrances upon such property; or

(ii) the value of the property as indicated in a certified appraisal report submitted by a state certified general real estate appraiser duly licensed by the department of state as provided in section one hundred sixty-j of the executive law, and by deducting from the appraised value the total amount of any liens or other encumbrances upon such property. A lien report issued by a title insurance company licensed under article sixty-four of the insurance law, that guarantees the correctness of a lien search conducted by it, shall be presumptive proof of liens upon the property.

18. "Partially secured bail bond" means a bail bond secured only by a deposit of a sum of money not exceeding ten percent of the total amount of the undertaking.

19. "Unsecured bail bond" means a bail bond, other than an insurance company bail bond, not secured by any deposit of or lien upon property.

20. "Court" includes, where appropriate, a judge authorized to act as described in a particular statute, though not as a court.

21. "Qualifies for electronic monitoring," for purposes of subdivision four of section 510.40 of this title, means a person charged with a felony, a misdemeanor crime of domestic violence, a misdemeanor defined in article one hundred thirty of the penal law, a crime and the circumstances of paragraph (b) of subdivision two of section 530.60 of this title apply, or any misdemeanor where the defendant stands previously convicted, within the past five years, of a violent felony offense as defined in section 70.02 of the penal law. For the purposes of this subdivision, in calculating such five year period, any period of time during which the defendant was incarcerated for any reason between the time of the commission of any such previous crime and the time of commission of the present crime shall be excluded and such five year period shall be extended by a period or periods equal to the time served under such incarceration.

22. "Misdemeanor crime of domestic violence," for purposes of subdivision twenty-one of this section, means a misdemeanor under the penal law provisions and circumstances described in subdivision one of section 530.11 of this title.

ARTICLE 510 - RECOGNIZANCE, BAIL AND COMMITMENT-DETERMINATION OF APPLICATION FOR RECOGNIZANCE OR BAIL, ISSUANCE OF SECURING ORDERS, AND RELATED MATTERS

Section
510.10 Securing order; when required; alternatives available; standard to be applied.
510.15 Commitment of principal under seventeen or eighteen.
510.20 Application for a change in securing order.
510.30 Application for securing order; rules of law and criteria controlling determination.
510.40 Court notification to principal of conditions of release and of alleged violations of conditions of release.
510.43 Court appearances: additional notifications.
510.45 Pretrial services agencies.
510.50 Enforcement of securing order.

§510.10 Securing order; when required; alternatives available; standard to be applied.

1. When a principal, whose future court attendance at a criminal action or proceeding is or may be required, comes under the control of a court, such court shall, in accordance with this title, by a securing order release the principal on the principal's own recognizance, release the principal under non-monetary conditions, or, where authorized, fix bail or commit the principal to the custody of the sheriff. In all such cases, except where another type of securing order is shown to be required by law, the court shall release the principal pending trial on the principal's own recognizance, unless it is demonstrated and the court makes an individualized determination that the principal poses a risk of flight to avoid prosecution. If such a finding is made, the court must select the least restrictive alternative and condition or conditions that will reasonably assure the principal's return to court. The court shall explain its choice of release, release with conditions, bail or remand on the record or in writing.

2. A principal is entitled to representation by counsel under this chapter in preparing an application for release, when a securing order is being considered and when a securing order is being reviewed for modification, revocation or termination. If the principal is financially unable to obtain counsel, counsel shall be assigned to the principal.

3. In cases other than as described in subdivision four of this section the court shall release the principal pending trial on the principal's own recognizance, unless the court finds on the record or in writing that release on the principal's own recognizance will not reasonably assure the principal's return to court. In such instances, the court shall release the principal under non-monetary conditions, selecting the least restrictive alternative and conditions that will reasonably assure the principal's return to court. The court shall explain its choice of alternative and conditions on the record or in writing.

4. Where the principal stands charged with a qualifying offense, the court, unless otherwise prohibited by law, may in its discretion release the principal pending trial on the principal's own recognizance or under non-monetary conditions, fix bail, or, where the defendant is charged with a qualifying offense which is a felony, the court may commit the principal to the custody of the sheriff. A principal stands charged with a qualifying offense for the purposes of this subdivision when he or she stands charged with:

(a) a felony enumerated in section 70.02 of the penal law, other than robbery in the second degree as defined in subdivision one of section

160.10 of the penal law, provided, however, that burglary in the second degree as defined in subdivision two of section 140.25 of the penal law shall be a qualifying offense only where the defendant is charged with entering the living area of the dwelling;

(b) a crime involving witness intimidation under section 215.15 of the penal law;

(c) a crime involving witness tampering under section 215.11, 215.12 or 215.13 of the penal law;

(d) a class A felony defined in the penal law, provided that for class A felonies under article two hundred twenty of the penal law, only class A-I felonies shall be a qualifying offense;

(e) a sex trafficking offense defined in section 230.34 or 230.34-a of the penal law, or a felony sex offense defined in section 70.80 of the penal law, or a crime involving incest as defined in section 255.25, 255.26 or 255.27 of such law, or a misdemeanor defined in article one hundred thirty of such law;

(f) conspiracy in the second degree as defined in section 105.15 of the penal law, where the underlying allegation of such charge is that the defendant conspired to commit a class A felony defined in article one hundred twenty-five of the penal law;

(g) money laundering in support of terrorism in the first degree as defined in section 470.24 of the penal law; money laundering in support of terrorism in the second degree as defined in section 470.23 of the penal law; money laundering in support of terrorism in the third degree as defined in section 470.22 of the penal law; money laundering in support of terrorism in the fourth degree as defined in section 470.21 of the penal law; or a felony crime of terrorism as defined in article four hundred ninety of the penal law, other than the crime defined in section 490.20 of such law;

(h) criminal contempt in the second degree as defined in subdivision three of section 215.50 of the penal law, criminal contempt in the first degree as defined in subdivision (b), (c) or (d) of section 215.51 of the penal law or aggravated criminal contempt as defined in section 215.52 of the penal law, and the underlying allegation of such charge of criminal contempt in the second degree, criminal contempt in the first degree or aggravated criminal contempt is that the defendant violated a duly served order of protection where the protected party is a member of the defendant's same family or household as defined in subdivision one of section 530.11 of this title;

(i) facilitating a sexual performance by a child with a controlled substance or alcohol as defined in section 263.30 of the penal law, use of a child in a sexual performance as defined in section 263.05 of the penal law or luring a child as defined in subdivision one of section 120.70 of the penal law, promoting an obscene sexual performance by a child as defined in section 263.10 of the penal law or promoting a sexual performance by a child as defined in section 263.15 of the penal law;

(j) any crime that is alleged to have caused the death of another person;

(k) criminal obstruction of breathing or blood circulation as defined in section 121.11 of the penal law, strangulation in the second degree as defined in section 121.12 of the penal law or unlawful imprisonment in the first degree as defined in section 135.10 of the penal law, and is alleged to have committed the offense against a member of the defendant's same family or household as defined in subdivision one of section 530.11 of this title;

(*l*) aggravated vehicular assault as defined in section 120.04-a of the penal law or vehicular assault in the first degree as defined in section 120.04 of the penal law;

(m) assault in the third degree as defined in section 120.00 of the penal law or arson in the third degree as defined in section 150.10 of the penal law, when such crime is charged as a hate crime as defined in section 485.05 of the penal law;

(n) aggravated assault upon a person less than eleven years old as defined in section 120.12 of the penal law or criminal possession of a weapon on school grounds as defined in section 265.01-a of the penal law;

(o) grand larceny in the first degree as defined in section 155.42 of the penal law, enterprise corruption as defined in section 460.20 of the penal law, or money laundering in the first degree as defined in section 470.20 of the penal law;

(p) failure to register as a sex offender pursuant to section one hundred sixty-eight-t of the correction law or endangering the welfare of a child as defined in subdivision one of section 260.10 of the penal law, where the defendant is required to maintain registration under article six-C of the correction law and designated a level three offender pursuant to subdivision six of section one hundred sixty-eight-l of the correction law;

(q) a crime involving bail jumping under section 215.55, 215.56 or 215.57 of the penal law, or a crime involving escaping from custody under section 205.05, 205.10 or 205.15 of the penal law;

(r) any felony offense committed by the principal while serving a sentence of probation or while released to post release supervision;

(s) a felony, where the defendant qualifies for sentencing on such charge as a persistent felony offender pursuant to section 70.10 of the penal law; or

(t) any felony or class A misdemeanor involving harm to an identifiable person or property, where such charge arose from conduct occurring while the defendant was released on his or her own recognizance or released under conditions for a separate felony or class A misdemeanor involving harm to an identifiable person or property, provided, however, that the prosecutor must show reasonable cause to believe that the defendant committed the instant crime and any underlying crime. For the purposes of this subparagraph, any of the underlying crimes need not be a qualifying offense as defined in this subdivision.   *(Eff. 7/2/20, Ch. 56, L. 2020)*

5. Notwithstanding the provisions of subdivisions three and four of this section, with respect to any charge for which bail or remand is not ordered, and for which the court would not or could not otherwise require bail or remand, a defendant may, at any time, request that the court set bail in a nominal amount requested by the defendant in the form specified in paragraph (a) of subdivision one of section 520.10 of this title; if the court is satisfied that the request is voluntary, the court shall set such bail in such amount.

6. When a securing order is revoked or otherwise terminated in the course of an uncompleted action or proceeding but the principal's future court attendance still is or may be required and the principal is still under the control of a court, a new securing order must be issued. When the court revokes or otherwise terminates a securing order which committed the principal to the custody of the sheriff, the court shall give written notification to the sheriff of such revocation or termination of the securing order.

§510.15 Commitment of principal under seventeen or eighteen.

1. When a principal who is under the age of sixteen is committed to the custody of the sheriff the court must direct that the principal be taken to and lodged in a place certified by the office of children and family services as a juvenile detention facility for the reception of children. When a principal who (a) commencing October first, two thousand eighteen, is sixteen years of age; or (b) commencing October first, two thousand nineteen, is sixteen or seventeen years of age, is committed to the custody of the sheriff, the court must direct that the principal be taken to and lodged in a place certified by the office of children and family services in conjunction with the state commission of correction as a specialized secure juvenile detention facility for older youth. Where such a direction is made the sheriff shall deliver the principal in accordance therewith and such person shall although lodged and cared for in a juvenile detention facility continue to be deemed to be in the custody of the sheriff. No principal under the age specified to whom the provisions of this section may apply shall be detained in any prison, jail, lockup, or other place used for adults convicted of a crime or under arrest and charged with the commission of a crime without the approval of the office of children and family services which shall consult with the commission of correction if the principal is sixteen years of age or older in the case of each principal and the statement of its reasons therefor; nor shall a principal under the age specified who is charged solely with a violation as defined in subdivision three of section 10.00 of the penal law be subject to detention. The sheriff shall not be liable for any acts done to or by such principal resulting from negligence in the detention of and care for such principal, when the principal is not in the actual custody of the sheriff.

(Eff. 12/29/21, Ch. 813, L. 2021)

2. Except upon consent of the defendant or for good cause shown, in any case in which a new securing order is issued for a principal previously committed to the custody of the sheriff pursuant to this section, such order shall further direct the sheriff to deliver the principal from a juvenile detention facility to the person or place specified in the order.

§510.20 Application for a change in securing order.

1. Upon any occasion when a court has issued a securing order with respect to a principal and the principal is confined in the custody of the sheriff as a result of the securing order or a previously issued securing order, the principal may make an application for recognizance, release under non-monetary conditions or bail.

2. (a) The principal is entitled to representation by counsel in the making and presentation of such application. If the principal is financially unable to obtain counsel, counsel shall be assigned to the principal.

(b) Upon such application, the principal must be accorded an opportunity to be heard, present evidence and to contend that an order of recognizance, release under non-monetary conditions or, where authorized, bail must or should issue, that the court should release the principal on the principal's own recognizance or under non-monetary conditions rather than fix bail, and that if bail is authorized and fixed it should be in a suggested amount and form.

§510.30 Application for securing order; rules of law and criteria controlling determination.

1. With respect to any principal, the court in all cases, unless otherwise provided by law, must impose the least restrictive kind and degree of control

or restriction that is necessary to secure the principal's return to court when required. In determining that matter, the court must, on the basis of available information, consider and take into account information about the principal that is relevant to the principal's return to court, including:

(a) The principal's activities and history;

(b) If the principal is a defendant, the charges facing the principal;

(c) The principal's criminal conviction record if any;

(d) The principal's record of previous adjudication as a juvenile delinquent, as retained pursuant to section 354.2 of the family court act, or, of pending cases where fingerprints are retained pursuant to section 306.1 of such act, or a youthful offender, if any;

(e) The principal's previous record with respect to flight to avoid criminal prosecution;

(f) If monetary bail is authorized, according to the restrictions set forth in this title, the principal's individual financial circumstances, and, in cases where bail is authorized, the principal's ability to post bail without posing undue hardship, as well as his or her ability to obtain a secured, unsecured, or partially secured bond;

(g) Where the principal is charged with a crime or crimes against a member or members of the same family or household as that term is defined in subdivision one of section 530.11 of this title, the following factors:

(i) any violation by the principal of an order of protection issued by any court for the protection of a member or members of the same family or household as that term is defined in subdivision one of section 530.11 of this title, whether or not such order of protection is currently in effect; and

(ii) the principal's history of use or possession of a firearm; and

(h) If the principal is a defendant, in the case of an application for a securing order pending appeal, the merit or lack of merit of the appeal.

2. Where the principal is a defendant-appellant in a pending appeal from a judgment of conviction, the court must also consider the likelihood of ultimate reversal of the judgment. A determination that the appeal is palpably without merit alone justifies, but does not require, a denial of the application, regardless of any determination made with respect to the factors specified in subdivision one of this section.

3. When bail or recognizance is ordered, the court shall inform the principal, if the principal is a defendant charged with the commission of a felony, that the release is conditional and that the court may revoke the order of release and may be authorized to commit the principal to the custody of the sheriff in accordance with the provisions of subdivision two of section 530.60 of this chapter if the principal commits a subsequent felony while at liberty upon such order.

§510.40 Court notification to principal of conditions of release and of alleged violations of conditions of release.

1. Upon ordering that a principal be released on the principal's own recognizance, or released under non-monetary conditions, or, if bail has been fixed, upon the posting of bail, the court must direct the principal to appear in the criminal action or proceeding involved whenever the principal's attendance may be required and to be at all times amenable to the orders and processes of the court. If such principal is in the custody of the sheriff or at liberty upon bail at the time of the order, the court must direct that the principal be discharged from such custody or, as the case may be, that the principal's bail be exonerated.

2. Upon the issuance of an order fixing bail, where authorized, and upon the posting thereof, the court must examine the bail to determine whether it complies with the order. If it does, the court must, in the absence of some factor or circumstance which in law requires or authorizes disapproval thereof, approve the bail and must issue a certificate of release, authorizing the principal to be at liberty, and, if the principal is in the custody of the sheriff at the time, directing the sheriff to discharge the principal therefrom. If the bail fixed is not posted, or is not approved after being posted, the court must order that the principal be committed to the custody of the sheriff. In the event of any such non-approval, the court shall explain promptly in writing the reasons therefor.

3. Non-monetary conditions of release shall be individualized and established in writing by the court. At future court appearances, the court shall consider a lessening of conditions or modification of conditions to a less burdensome form based on the principal's compliance with such conditions of release. In the event of alleged non-compliance with the conditions of release in an important respect, pursuant to this subdivision, additional conditions may be imposed by the court, on the record or in writing, only after notice of the facts and circumstances of such alleged non-compliance, reasonable under the circumstances, affording the principal and the principal's attorney and the people an opportunity to present relevant, admissible evidence, relevant witnesses and to cross-examine witnesses, and a finding by clear and convincing evidence that the principal violated a condition of release in an important respect. Following such a finding, in determining whether to impose additional conditions for non-compliance, the court shall consider and may select conditions consistent with the court's obligation to impose the least restrictive condition or conditions that will reasonably assure the defendant's return to court. The court shall explain on the record or in writing the reasons for its determination and for any changes to the conditions imposed.

4. (a) Electronic monitoring of a principal's location may be ordered only if the court finds, after notice, an opportunity to be heard and an individualized determination explained on the record or in writing, that the defendant qualifies for electronic monitoring in accordance with subdivision twenty-one of section 500.10 of this title, and no other realistic non-monetary condition or set of non-monetary conditions will suffice to reasonably assure a principal's return to court.

(b) The specific method of electronic monitoring of the principal's location must be approved by the court. It must be the least restrictive procedure and method that will reasonably assure the principal's return to court, and unobtrusive to the greatest extent practicable.

(c) Electronic monitoring of the location of a principal may be conducted only by a public entity under the supervision and control of a county or municipality or a non-profit entity under contract to the county, municipality or the state. A county or municipality shall be authorized to enter into a contract with another county or municipality in the state to monitor principals under non-monetary conditions of release in its county, but counties, municipalities and the state shall not contract with any private for-profit entity for such purposes. Counties, municipalities and the state may contract with a private for-profit entity to supply electronic monitoring devices or other items, provided that any interaction with persons under electronic monitoring or the data produced by such monitoring shall be conducted solely by employees of a county, municipality, the state, or a non-profit entity under contract with such county, municipality or the state.

(d) Electronic monitoring of a principal's location may be for a maximum period of sixty days, and may be renewed for such period, after notice, an opportunity to be heard and a de novo, individualized determination in accordance with this subdivision, which shall be explained on the record or in writing.

A defendant subject to electronic location monitoring under this subdivision shall be considered held or confined in custody for purposes of section 180.80 of this chapter and shall be considered committed to the custody of the sheriff for purposes of section 170.70 of the chapter, as applicable.

5. If a principal is released under non-monetary conditions, the court shall, on the record and in an individualized written document provided to the principal, notify the principal, in plain language and a manner sufficiently clear and specific:

(a) of any conditions to which the principal is subject, to serve as a guide for the principal's conduct; and

(b) that the possible consequences for violation of such a condition may include revocation of the securing order and the ordering of a more restrictive securing order.

§510.43 Court appearances: additional notifications.

1. The court or, upon direction of the court, a certified pretrial services agency, shall notify all principals released under non-monetary conditions and on recognizance of all court appearances in advance by text message, telephone call, electronic mail or first class mail. The chief administrator of the courts shall, pursuant to subdivision one of section 10.40 of this chapter, develop a form which shall be offered to the principal at court appearances. On such form, which upon completion shall be retained in the court file, the principal may select one such preferred manner of notice.

2. Such form may request the information necessary for the defendant to be provided with notice in accordance with such single, selected manner of notice. After notice of such consequence, a defendant who intentionally declines to provide the information necessary for the defendant to be provided with such notice pursuant to this section shall forfeit the opportunity to receive such notice until such information is timely provided. Any failure by the court or certified pretrial services agency to provide notice of a scheduled court appearance in the manner provided in this section shall not in and of itself constitute grounds or authorization for the defendant to fail to appear for such scheduled court appearance.

§510.45 Pretrial services agencies.

1. The office of court administration shall certify and regularly review for recertification one or more pretrial services agencies in each county to monitor principals released under non-monetary conditions. Such office shall maintain a listing on its public website identifying by county each pretrial services agency so certified in the state.

2. Every such agency shall be a public entity under the supervision and control of a county or municipality or a non-profit entity under contract to the county, municipality or the state. A county or municipality shall be authorized to enter into a contract with another county or municipality in the state to monitor principals under non-monetary conditions of release in its county, but counties, municipalities and the state shall not contract with any private for-profit entity for such purposes.

3. (a) Any questionnaire, instrument or tool used with a principal in the process of considering or determining the principal's possible release on recognizance, release under non-monetary conditions or on bail, or used with a principal in the process of considering or determining a condition or conditions of release or monitoring by a pretrial services agency, shall be promptly made available to the principal and the principal's counsel upon written request. Any such blank form questionnaire, instrument or tool regularly used in the county for such purpose or a related purpose shall be made available to any person promptly upon request.

(b) Any such questionnaire, instrument or tool used to inform determinations on release or conditions of release shall be:

(i) designed and implemented in a way that ensures the results are free from discrimination on the basis of race, national origin, sex, or any other protected class; and

(ii) empirically validated and regularly revalidated, with such validation and revalidation studies and all underlying data, except personal identifying information for any defendant, publicly available upon request.

4. Supervision by a pre-trial services agency may be ordered as a non-monetary condition pursuant to this title only if the court finds, after notice, an opportunity to be heard and an individualized determination explained on the record or in writing, that no other realistic non-monetary condition or set of non-monetary conditions will suffice to reasonably assure the principal's return to court.

5. Each pretrial service agency certified by the office of court administration pursuant to this section shall at the end of each year prepare and file with such office an annual report, which the office shall compile, publish on its website and make available upon request to members of the public. Such reports shall not include any personal identifying information for any individual defendants. Each such report, in addition to other relevant information, shall set forth, disaggregated by each county served:

(a) the number of defendants supervised by the agency;

(b) the length of time (in months) each such person was supervised by the agency prior to acquittal, dismissal, release on recognizance, revocation of release on conditions, and sentencing;

(c) the race, ethnicity, age and sex of each person supervised;

(d) the crimes with which each person supervised was charged;

(e) the number of persons supervised for whom release conditions were modified by the court, describing generally for each person or group of persons the type and nature of the condition or conditions added or removed;

(f) the number of persons supervised for whom release under conditions was revoked by the court, and the basis for such revocations; and

(g) the court disposition in each supervised case, including sentencing information.   *(Eff. 1/1/20, Ch. 59, L. 2019)*

§510.50 Enforcement of securing order.

1. When the attendance of a principal confined in the custody of the sheriff is required at the criminal action or proceeding at a particular time and place, the court may compel such attendance by directing the sheriff to produce the principal at such time and place. If the principal is at liberty on the principal's own recognizance or non-monetary conditions or on bail, the principal's attendance may be achieved or compelled by various methods, including notification and the issuance of a bench warrant, prescribed by law in provisions governing such matters with respect to the particular kind of action or proceeding involved.

2. Except when the principal is charged with a new crime while at liberty, absent relevant, credible evidence demonstrating that a principal's failure to appear for a scheduled court appearance was willful, the court, prior to issuing a bench warrant for a failure to appear for a scheduled court appearance, shall provide at least forty-eight hours notice to the principal or the principal's counsel that the principal is required to appear, in order to give the principal an opportunity to appear voluntarily.

(Eff. 1/1/20, Ch.59, L.2019)

ARTICLE 520 - BAIL AND BAIL BONDS

Section
520.10 Bail and bail bonds; fixing of bail and authorized forms thereof.
520.15 Bail and bail bonds; posting of cash bail.
520.20 Bail and bail bonds; posting of bail bond and justifying affidavits; form and
        contents thereof.
520.30 Bail and bail bonds; examination as to sufficiency.
520.40 Transfer of cash bail from local criminal court to superior court.

§520.10 Bail and bail bonds; fixing of bail and authorized forms thereof.

1. The only authorized forms of bail are the following:
   (a) Cash bail.
   (b) An insurance company bail bond.
   (c) A secured surety bond.
   (d) A secured appearance bond.
   (e) A partially secured surety bond.
   (f) A partially secured appearance bond.
   (g) An unsecured surety bond.
   (h) An unsecured appearance bond.
   (i) Credit card or similar device; provided, however, that notwithstanding any other provision of law, any person posting bail by credit card or similar device also may be required to pay a reasonable administrative fee. The amount of such administrative fee and the time and manner of its payment shall be in accordance with the system established pursuant to subdivision four of section 150.30 of this chapter or paragraph (j) of subdivision two of section two hundred twelve of the judiciary law, as appropriate.

2. The methods of fixing bail are as follows:
   (a) A court may designate the amount of the bail without designating the form or forms in which it may be posted. In such case, the bail may be posted in either of the forms specified in paragraphs (g) and (h) of subdivision one;
   (b) The court shall direct that the bail be posted in any one of three or more of the forms specified in subdivision one of this section, designated in the alternative, and may designate different amounts varying with the forms, except that one of the forms shall be either an unsecured or partially secured surety bond, as selected by the court.   *(Eff. 1/1/20, Ch.59, L.2019)*

§520.15 Bail and bail bonds; posting of cash bail.

1. Where a court has fixed bail pursuant to subdivision two of section 520.10, at any time after the principal has been committed to the custody of the sheriff pending the posting thereof, cash bail in the amount designated in the order fixing bail may be posted even though such bail was not specified in such order. Cash bail may be deposited with (a) the county treasurer of the county in which the criminal action or proceeding is pending or, in the city of New York with the commissioner of finance, or (b) the court which issued such order, or (c) the sheriff in whose custody the principal has been committed. Upon proof of the deposit of the designated amount the principal must be forthwith released from custody.

2. The person posting cash bail must complete and sign a form which states (a) the name, residential address and occupation of each person posting cash bail; and (b) the title of the criminal action or proceeding involved; and (c) the offense or offenses which are the subjects of the action or proceeding involved, and the status of such action or proceeding; and (d) the name of the principal and the nature of his involvement in or connection with such action or proceeding; and (e) that the person or persons posting cash bail undertake that the principal will appear in such action or proceeding whenever required and will at all times render himself amenable to the orders and processes of the court; and (f) the date of the principal's next appearance in court; and (g) and acknowledgment that the cash bail will be forfeited if the principal does not comply with any requirement or order of process to appear in court; and (h) the amount of money posted as cash bail.

3. Money posted as cash bail is and shall remain the property of the person posting it unless forfeited to the court.

§520.20 Bail and bail bonds; posting of bail bond and justifying affidavits; form and contents thereof.

1. (a) Except as provided in paragraph (b) when a bail bond is to be posted in satisfaction of bail, the obligor or obligors must submit to the court a bail bond in the amount fixed, executed in the form prescribed in subdivision two, accompanied by a justifying affidavit of each obligor, executed in the form prescribed in subdivision four.

(b) When a bail bond is to be posted in satisfaction of bail fixed for a defendant charged by information or simplified information or prosecutor's information with one or more traffic infractions and no other offense, the defendant may submit to the court, with the consent of the court, an insurance company bail bond covering the amount fixed, executed in a form prescribed by the superintendent of financial services.

2. Except as provided in paragraph (b) of subdivision one, a bail bond must be subscribed and sworn to by each obligor and must state:

(a) The name, residential address and occupation of each obligor; and

(b)The title of the criminal action or proceeding involved; and

(c) The offense or offenses which are the subjects of the action or proceeding involved, and the status of such action or proceeding; and

(d) The name of the principal and the nature of his involvement in or connection with such action or proceeding; and

(e) That the obligor, or the obligors jointly and severally, undertake that the principal will appear in such action or proceeding whenever required and will at all times render himself amenable to the orders and processes of the court; and

(f) That in the event that the principal does not comply with any such requirement, order or process, such obligor or obligors will pay to the people of the state of New York a designated sum of money fixed by the court.

3. A bail bond posted in the course of a criminal action is effective and binding upon the obligor or obligors until the imposition of sentence or other termination of the action, regardless of whether the action is dismissed in the local criminal court after an indictment on the same charge or charges by a superior court, and regardless of whether such action is partially conducted or prosecuted in a court or courts other than the one in which the action was pending when such bond was posted, unless prior to such termination such order of bail is vacated or revoked or the principal is surrendered, or unless the terms of such bond expressly limit its effectiveness to a lesser period; provided, however, the effectiveness of such bond may only be limited to a lesser period if the obligor or obligors submit notice of the limitation to the court and the district attorney not less than fourteen days before the effectiveness ends.

4. A justifying affidavit must be subscribed and sworn to by the obligor affiant and must state his name, residential address and occupation. Depending upon the kind of bail bond which it justifies, such affidavit must contain further statements as follows:

(a) An affidavit justifying an insurance company bail bond must state:

(i) The amount of the premium paid to the obligor; and

(ii) All security and all promises of indemnity received by the surety-obligor in connection with its execution of the bond, and the name, occupation and residential and business addresses of every persons who has given any such indemnifying security or promise.

An action by the surety-obligor against an indemnitor, seeking retention of security deposited by the latter with the former or enforcement of any indemnity agreement of a kind described in this subparagraph, will not lie except with respect to agreements and security specified in the justifying affidavit.

(b) An affidavit justifying a secured bail bond must state every item of personal property deposited and of real property pledged as security, the value of each such item, and the nature and amount of every lien or encumbrance thereon.

(c) An affidavit justifying a partially secured bail bond or an unsecured bail bond must state the place and nature of the obligor-affiant's business or employment, the length of time he has been engaged therein, his income during the past year, and his average income over the past five years.

§520.30 Bail and bail bonds; examination as to sufficiency.

1. Following the posting of a bail bond and the justifying affidavit or affidavits or the posting of cash bail, the court may conduct an inquiry for the purpose of determining the reliability of the obligors or person posting cash bail, the value and sufficiency of any security offered, and whether any feature of the undertaking contravenes public policy; provided that before undertaking an inquiry, of a person posting cash bail the court, after application of the district attorney, must have had reasonable cause to believe that the person posting cash bail is not in rightful possession of money posted as cash bail or that such money constitutes the fruits of criminal or unlawful conduct. The court may inquiry into any matter stated or required to be stated in the justifying affidavits, and may also inquire into other matters appropriate to the determination, which include but are not limited to the following:

(a) The background, character and reputation of any obligor, and, in the case of an insurance company bail bond, the qualifications of the surety-obligor and its executing agent; and

(b) The source of any money or property deposited by any obligor as security, and whether any such money or property constitutes the fruits of criminal or unlawful conduct; and

(c) The source of any money or property delivered or agreed to be delivered to any obligor as indemnification on the bond, and whether any such money or property constitutes the fruits of criminal or unlawful conduct; and

(d) The background, character and reputation of any person who has indemnified or agreed to indemnify an obligor upon the bond; and whether any such indemnitor, not being licensed by the superintendent of financial services in accordance with the insurance law, has within a period of one month prior to such indemnity transaction given indemnification or security for like purpose in more than two cases not arising out of the same transaction; and

(e) The source of any money posted as cash bail, and whether any such money constitutes the fruits of criminal or unlawful conduct; and

(f) The background, character and reputation of the person posting cash bail.

2. Upon such inquiry, the court may examine, under oath or otherwise, the obligors and any other persons who may possess material information. The district attorney has a right to attend such inquiry, to call witnesses and to examine any witness in the proceeding. The court may, upon application of the district attorney, adjourn the proceeding for a reasonable period to allow him to investigate the matter.

3. At the conclusion of the inquiry, the court must issue an order either approving or disapproving the bail.

§520.40 Transfer of cash bail from local criminal court to superior court.

When a local criminal court acquires control over the person of an accused and such court designates the amount of bail that the accused may post and such bail is posted in cash and subsequently the accused is arraigned in superior court where bail is fixed by such court, the accused may request that the cash bail posted in the local criminal court be transferred to the superior court. Notice of such request must be given to the person who posted cash bail. Upon such a request the superior court shall make an order directing the local criminal court to transfer the cash bail that it holds to the superior court for use in the superior court. If there is an overage, the superior court shall order it be paid over to the person who posted the cash bail in the local criminal court. If there is a deficiency, the accused shall post additional bail as directed by the superior court.

ARTICLE 530 - ORDERS OF RECOGNIZANCE OR BAIL WITH RESPECT TO DEFENDANTS IN CRIMINAL ACTIONS AND PROCEEDINGS - WHEN AND BY WHAT COURTS AUTHORIZED

Section
530.10 Order of recognizance release under non-monetary conditions or bail; in general.
530.11 Procedures for family offense matters.
530.12 Protection for victims of family offenses.
530.13 Protection of victims of crimes, other than family offenses.
530.14 Suspension and revocation of a license to carry, possess, repair or dispose of a firearm or firearms pursuant to section 400.00 of the penal law and ineligibility for such a license; order to surrender firearms; order to seize firearms.
530.20 Securing order by local criminal court when action is pending therein.
530.30 Order of recognizance, release under non-monetary conditions or bail; by superior court judge when action is pending in local criminal court.
530.40 Order of recognizance, release under non-monetary conditions or bail; by superior court when action is pending therein.
530.45 Order of recognizance or bail; after conviction and before sentence.
530.50 Order of recognizance or bail; during pendency of appeal.
530.60 Certain modifications of a securing order.
530.70 Order of recognizance or bail; bench warrant.
530.80 Order of recognizance or bail; surrender of defendant.

§530.10 Order of recognizance release under non-monetary conditions or bail; in general.

Under circumstances prescribed in this article, a court, upon application of a defendant charged with or convicted of an offense, is required to issue a securing order for such defendant during the pendency of either:

1. A criminal action based upon such charge; or

2. An appeal taken by the defendant from a judgment of conviction or a sentence or from an order of an intermediate appellate court affirming or modifying a judgment of conviction or a sentence.

§530.11 Procedures for family offense matters.

1. Jurisdiction.The family court and the criminal courts shall have concurrent jurisdiction over any proceeding concerning acts which would constitute disorderly conduct, unlawful dissemination or publication of an intimate image, harassment in the first degree, harassment in the second degree, aggravated harassment in the second degree, sexual misconduct, forcible touching, sexual abuse in the third degree, sexual abuse in the second degree as set forth in subdivision one of section 130.60 of the penal law, stalking in the first degree, stalking in the second degree, stalking in the third degree, stalking in the fourth degree, criminal mischief, menacing in the second degree, menacing in the third degree, reckless endangerment, strangulation in the first degree, strangulation in the second degree, criminal obstruction of breathing or blood circulation, assault in the second degree, assault in the third degree, an attempted assault, identity theft in the first degree, identity theft in the second degree, identity theft in the third degree, grand larceny in the fourth degree, grand larceny in the third degree, coercion in the second degree or coercion in the third degree as set forth in subdivisions one, two and three of section 135.60 of the penal law between spouses or former spouses, or between parent and child or between members of the same family or household except that if the respondent would not be criminally responsible by reason of age pursuant to section 30.00 of the penal law, then the family court shall have exclusive jurisdiction over such proceeding. Notwithstanding a complainant's election to proceed in family court, the criminal court shall not be divested of jurisdiction to hear a family offense proceeding pursuant to this section. For purposes of this section, "disorderly conduct" includes disorderly conduct not in a public place. For purposes of this section, "members of the same

family or household" with respect to a proceeding in the criminal courts shall mean the following: *(Eff.9/21/19,Ch.109,L.2019)*

    (a) persons related by consanguinity or affinity;

    (b) persons legally married to one another;

    (c) persons formerly married to one another regardless of whether they still reside in the same household;

    (d) persons who have a child in common, regardless of whether such persons have been married or have lived together at any time; and

    (e) persons who are not related by consanguinity or affinity and who are or have been in an intimate relationship regardless of whether such persons have lived together at any time. Factors the court may consider in determining whether a relationship is an "intimate relationship" include but are not limited to: the nature or type of relationship, regardless of whether the relationship is sexual in nature; the frequency of interaction between the persons; and the duration of the relationship. Neither a casual acquaintance nor ordinary fraternization between two individuals in business or social contexts shall be deemed to constitute an "intimate relationship".

    2. Information to petitioner or complainant. The chief administrator of the courts shall designate the appropriate probation officers, warrant officers, sheriffs, police officers, district attorneys or any other law enforcement officials, to inform any petitioner or complainant bringing a proceeding under this section before such proceeding is commenced, of the procedures available for the institution of family offense proceedings, including but not limited to the following:

    (a) That there is concurrent jurisdiction with respect to family offenses in both family court and the criminal courts;

    (b) That a family court proceeding is a civil proceeding and is for the purpose of attempting to stop the violence, end family disruption and obtain protection. That referrals for counseling, or counseling services, are available through probation for this purpose;

    (c) That a proceeding in the criminal courts is for the purpose of prosecution of the offender and can result in a criminal conviction of the offender;

    (d) That a proceeding or action subject to the provisions of this section is initiated at the time of the filing of an accusatory instrument or family court petition, not at the time of arrest, or request for arrest, if any;

    (e) *(Repealed.)*

    (f) That an arrest may precede the commencement of a family court or a criminal court proceeding, but an arrest is not a requirement for commencing either proceeding.

    (g) *(Repealed.)*

    (h) At such time as the complainant first appears before the court on a complaint or information, the court shall advise the complainant that the complainant may: continue with the proceeding in criminal court; or have the allegations contained therein heard in a family court proceeding; or proceed concurrently in both criminal and family court. Notwithstanding a complainant's election to proceed in family court, the criminal court shall not be divested of jurisdiction to hear a family offense proceeding pursuant to this section;

    (i) Nothing herein shall be deemed to limit or restrict complainant's rights to proceed directly and without court referral in either a criminal or family court, or both, as provided for in section one hundred fifteen of the family court act and section 100.07 of this chapter;

    2-a. Upon the filing of an accusatory instrument charging a crime or violation described in subdivision one of this section between members of the same family or household, as such terms are defined in this section, or as soon as the complainant first appears before the court, whichever is sooner, the court shall advise the complainant of the right to proceed in both the criminal and family courts, pursuant to section 100.07 of this chapter.

3. Official responsibility. No official or other person designated pursuant to subdivision two of this section shall discourage or prevent any person who wishes to file a petition or sign a complaint from having access to any court for that purpose.

4. When a person is arrested for an alleged family offense or an alleged violation of an order of protection or temporary order of protection or arrested pursuant to a warrant issued by the supreme or family court, and the supreme or family court, as applicable, is not in session, such person shall be brought before a local criminal court in the county of arrest or in the county in which such warrant is returnable pursuant to article one hundred twenty of this chapter. Such local criminal court may issue any order authorized under subdivision eleven of section 530.12 of this article, section one hundred fifty-four-d or one hundred fifty-five of the family court act or subdivision three-b of section two hundred forty or subdivision two-a of section two hundred fifty-two of the domestic relations law, in addition to discharging other arraignment responsibilities as set forth in this chapter. In making such order, the local criminal court shall consider de novo the recommendation and securing order, if any, made by the supreme or family court as indicated on the warrant or certificate of warrant. Unless the petitioner or complainant requests otherwise, the court, in addition to scheduling further criminal proceedings, if any, regarding such alleged family offense or violation allegation, shall make such matter returnable in the supreme or family court, as applicable, on the next day such court is in session.   *(Eff.1/1/20,Ch.59,L.2019)*

5. Filing and enforcement of out-of-state orders of protection. A valid order of protection or temporary order of protection issued by a court of competent jurisdiction in another state, territorial or tribal jurisdiction shall be accorded full faith and credit and enforced as if it were issued by a court within the state for as long as the order remains in effect in the issuing jurisdiction in accordance with sections two thousand two hundred sixty-five and two thousand two hundred sixty-six of title eighteen of the United States Code.

(a) An order issued by a court of competent jurisdiction in another state, territorial or tribal jurisdiction shall be deemed valid if:

(i) the issuing court had personal jurisdiction over the parties and over the subject matter under the law of the issuing jurisdiction;

(ii) the person against whom the order was issued had reasonable notice and an opportunity to be heard prior to issuance of the order; provided, however, that if the order was a temporary order of protection issued in the absence of such person, that notice had been given and that an opportunity to be heard had been provided within a reasonable period of time after the issuance of the order; and

(iii) in the case of orders of protection or temporary orders of protection issued against both a petitioner, plaintiff or complainant and respondent or defendant, the order or portion thereof sought to be enforced was supported by: (A) a pleading requesting such order, including, but not limited to, a petition, cross-petition or counterclaim; and (B) a judicial finding that the requesting party is entitled to the issuance of the order which may result from a judicial finding of fact, judicial acceptance of an admission by the party against whom the order was issued or judicial finding that the party against whom the order was issued had given knowing, intelligent and voluntary consent to its issuance.

(b) Notwithstanding the provisions of article fifty-four of the civil practice law and rules, an order of protection or temporary order of protection issued by a court of competent jurisdiction in another state, territorial or tribal jurisdiction, accompanied by a sworn affidavit that upon information and belief such order is in effect as written and has not been vacated or modified, may be filed without fee with the clerk of the court, who shall transmit information regarding such order to the statewide registry of orders of protection and warrants established pursuant to section two hundred twenty-one-a of the executive law; provided, however, that such filing and registry entry shall not be required for enforcement of the order.

6. Notice. Every police officer, peace officer or district attorney investigating a family offense under this article shall advise the victim of the availability of a shelter or other services in the community, and shall immediately give the victim written notice of the legal rights and remedies available to a victim of a family offense under the relevant provisions of this chapter and the family court act. Such notice shall be prepared, at minimum, in plain English, Spanish, Chinese and Russian and if necessary, shall be delivered orally, and shall include but not be limited to the information contained in the following statement:

"Are you the victim of domestic violence? If you need help now, you can call 911 for the police to come to you. You can also call a domestic violence hotline. You can have a confidential talk with an advocate at the hotline about help you can get in your community including: where you can get treatment for injuries, where you can get shelter, where you can get support, and what you can do to be safe. The New York State 24-hour Domestic & Sexual Violence Hotline number is (insert the statewide multilingual 800 number). They can give you information in many languages. If you are deaf or hard of hearing, call 711.

This is what the police can do:

They can help you and your children find a safe place such as a family or friend's house or a shelter in your community.

You can ask the officer to take you or help you and your children get to a safe place in your community.

They can help connect you to a local domestic violence program.

They can help you get to a hospital or clinic for medical care.

They can help you get your personal belongings.

They must complete a report discussing the incident. They will give you a copy of this police report before they leave the scene. It is free.

They may, and sometimes must, arrest the person who harmed you if you are the victim of a crime. The person arrested could be released at any time, so it is important to plan for your safety.

If you have been abused or threatened, this is what you can ask the police or district attorney to do:

File a criminal complaint against the person who harmed you.

Ask the criminal court to issue an order of protection for you and your child if the district attorney files a criminal case with the court.

Give you information about filing a family offense petition in your local family court.

You also have the right to ask the family court for an order of protection for you and your children.

This is what you can ask the family court to do:

To have your family offense petition filed the same day you go to court.

To have your request heard in court the same day you file or the next day court is open.

Only a judge can issue an order of protection. The judge does that as part of a criminal or family court case against the person who harmed you. An order of protection in family court or in criminal court can say:

That the other person have no contact or communication with you by mail, phone, computer or through other people.

That the other person stay away from you and your children, your home, job or school.

That the other person not assault, harass, threaten, strangle, or commit another family offense against you or your children.

That the other person turn in their firearms and firearms licenses, and not get any more firearms.

That you have temporary custody of your children.

That the other person pay temporary child support.

That the other person not harm your pets or service animals.

If the family court is closed because it is night, a weekend, or a holiday, you can go to a criminal court to ask for an order of protection.

If you do not speak English or cannot speak it well, you can ask the police, the district attorney, or the criminal or family court to get you an interpreter who speaks your language. The interpreter can help you explain what happened.

You can get the forms you need to ask for an order of protection at your local family court (insert addresses and contact information for courts). You can also get them online: www.NYCourts.gov/forms.

You do not need a lawyer to ask for an order of protection.

You have a right to get a lawyer in the family court. If the family court finds that you cannot afford to pay for a lawyer, it must get you one for free.

If you file a complaint or family court petition, you will be asked to swear to its truthfulness because it is a crime to file a legal document that you know is false."

The division of criminal justice services in consultation with the state office for the prevention of domestic violence shall prepare the form of such written notice consistent with provisions of this section and distribute copies thereof to the appropriate law enforcement officials pursuant to subdivision nine of section eight hundred forty-one of the executive law.

Additionally, copies of such notice shall be provided to the chief administrator of the courts to be distributed to victims of family offenses through the criminal court at such time as such persons first come before the court and to the state department of health for distribution to all hospitals defined under article twenty-eight of the public health law. No cause of action for damages shall arise in favor of any person by reason of any failure to comply with the provisions of this subdivision except upon a showing of gross negligence or willful misconduct. *(Eff.3/15/20,Ch.663,L.2019)*

7. Rules of court regarding concurrent jurisdiction. The chief administrator of the courts, pursuant to paragraph (e) of subdivision two of section two hundred twelve of the judiciary law, shall promulgate rules to facilitate record sharing and other communication between the criminal and family courts, subject to applicable provisions of this chapter and the family court act pertaining to the confidentiality, expungement and sealing of records, when such courts exercise concurrent jurisdiction over family offense proceedings.

§530.12 Protection for victims of family offenses.

1. When a criminal action is pending involving a complaint charging any crime or violation between spouses, former spouses, parent and child, or between members of the same family or household, as members of the same family or household are defined in subdivision one of section 530.11 of this article, the court, in addition to any other powers conferred upon it by this chapter may issue a temporary order of protection in conjunction with any securing order committing the defendant to the custody of the sheriff or as a condition of any order of recognizance or bail or an adjournment in contemplation of dismissal.

(a) In addition to any other conditions, such an order may require the defendant: (1) to stay away from the home, school, business or place of employment of the family or household member or of any designated witness, provided that the court shall make a determination, and shall state such determination in a written decision or on the record, whether to impose a condition pursuant to this paragraph, provided further, however, that failure to make such a determination shall not affect the validity of such temporary order of protection. In making such determination, the court shall consider, but shall not be limited to consideration of, whether the temporary order of protection is likely to achieve its purpose in the absence of such a condition, conduct subject to prior orders of protection, prior incidents of abuse, past or present injury, threats, drug or alcohol abuse, and access to weapons;

(2) to permit a parent, or a person entitled to visitation by a court order or a separation agreement, to visit the child at stated periods;

(3) to refrain from committing a family offense, as defined in subdivision one of section 530.11 of this article, or any criminal offense against the child or against the family or household member or against any person to whom custody of the child is awarded, or from harassing, intimidating or threatening such persons;

(4) to refrain from acts of commission or omission that create an unreasonable risk to the health, safety and welfare of a child, family or household member's life or health;

(5) to permit a designated party to enter the residence during a specified period of time in order to remove personal belongings not in issue in this proceeding or in any other proceeding or action under this chapter, the family court act or the domestic relations law;

(6) (A) to refrain from intentionally injuring or killing, without justification, any companion animal the defendant knows to be owned, possessed, leased, kept or held by the victim or a minor child residing in the household.

(B) "Companion animal", as used in this section, shall have the same meaning as in subdivision five of section three hundred fifty of the agriculture and markets law;

(7) (A) to promptly return specified identification documents to the protected party, in whose favor the order of protection or temporary order of protection is issued; provided, however, that such order may: (i) include any appropriate provision designed to ensure that any such document is available for use as evidence in this proceeding, and available if necessary for legitimate use by the party against whom such order is issued; and (ii) specify the manner in which such return shall be accomplished.

(B) For purposes of this subparagraph, "identification document" shall mean any of the following: (i) exclusively in the name of the protected party: birth certificate, passport, social security card, health insurance or other benefits card, a card or document used to access bank, credit or other financial accounts or records, tax returns, any driver's license, and immigration documents including but not limited to a United States permanent resident card and employment authorization document; and (ii) upon motion and after notice and an opportunity to be heard, any of the following, including those that may reflect joint use or ownership, that the court determines are necessary and are appropriately transferred to the protected party: any card or document used to access bank, credit or other financial accounts or records, tax returns, and any other identifying cards and documents;

(8) (A) to refrain from remotely controlling any connected devices affecting the home, vehicle or property of the person protected by the order.

(B) For purposes of this subparagraph, "connected device" shall mean any device, or other physical object that is capable of connecting to the internet, directly or indirectly, and that is assigned an internet protocol address or bluetooth address. *(Eff.11/11/20,Ch.261,L.2020)*

(b) The court may issue an order, pursuant to section two hundred twenty-seven-c of the real property law, authorizing the party for whose benefit any order of protection has been issued to terminate a lease or rental agreement pursuant to section two hundred twenty-seven-c of the real property law.

2. Notwithstanding any other provision of law, a temporary order of protection issued or continued by a family court pursuant to section eight hundred thirteen of the family court act shall continue in effect, absent action by the appropriate criminal court pursuant to subdivision three of this section, until the defendant is arraigned upon an accusatory instrument filed pursuant to section eight hundred thirteen of the family court act in such criminal court.

3. The court may issue a temporary order of protection ex parte upon the filing of an accusatory instrument and for good cause shown. When a family court order of protection is modified, the criminal court shall forward a copy of such modified order to the family court issuing the original order of protection; provided, however, that where a copy of the modified order is transmitted to the family court by facsimile or other electronic means, the original copy of such modified order and accompanying affidavit shall be forwarded immediately thereafter.

3-a. Emergency powers when family court not in session; issuance of temporary orders of protection. Upon the request of the petitioner, a local criminal court may on an ex parte basis issue a temporary order of protection pending a hearing in family court, provided that a sworn affidavit, verified in accordance with subdivision one of section 100.30 of this chapter, is submitted: (i) alleging that the family court is not in session; (ii) alleging that a family offense, as defined in subdivision one of section eight hundred twelve of the family court act and subdivision one of section 530.11 of this article, has been committed; (iii) alleging that a family offense petition has been filed or will be filed in family court on the next day the court is in session; and (iv) showing good cause. Upon appearance in a local criminal court, the petitioner shall be advised that he or she may continue with the proceeding either in family court or upon the filing of a local criminal court accusatory instrument in criminal court or both. Upon issuance of a temporary order of protection where petitioner requests that it be returnable in family court, the local criminal court shall transfer the matter forthwith to the family court and shall make the matter returnable in family court on the next day the family court is in session, or as soon thereafter as practicable, but in no event more than four calendar days after issuance of the order. The local criminal court, upon issuing a temporary order of protection returnable in family court pursuant to this subdivision, shall immediately forward, in a manner designed to insure arrival before the return date set in the order, a copy of the temporary order of protection and sworn affidavit to the family court and shall provide a copy of such temporary order of protection to the petitioner; provided, however, that where a copy of the temporary order of protection and affidavit are transmitted to the family court by facsimile or other electronic means, the original order and affidavit shall be forwarded to the family court immediately thereafter. Any temporary order of protection issued pursuant to this subdivision shall be issued to the respondent, and copies shall be filed as required in subdivisions six and eight of this section for orders of protection issued pursuant to this section. Any temporary order of protection issued pursuant to this subdivision shall plainly state the date that such order expires which, in the case of an order returnable in family court, shall be not more than four calendar days after its issuance, unless sooner vacated or modified by the family court. A petitioner requesting a temporary order of protection returnable in family court pursuant to this subdivision in a case in which a family court petition has not been filed shall be informed that such temporary order of protection shall expire as provided for herein, unless the petitioner files a petition pursuant to subdivision one of section eight hundred twenty-one of the family court act on or before the return date in family court and the family court issues a temporary order of protection or order of protection as authorized under article eight of the family court act. Nothing in this subdivision shall limit or restrict the petitioner's right to proceed directly and without court referral in either a criminal or family court, or both, as provided for in section one hundred fifteen of the family court act and section 100.07 of this chapter.

3-b. Emergency powers when family court not in session; modifications of orders of protection or temporary orders of protection. Upon the request of the petitioner, a local criminal court may on an ex parte basis modify a temporary order of protection or order of protection which has been issued under article four, five, six or eight of the family court act pending a hearing in family court, provided that a sworn affidavit verified in accordance with subdivision one of section 100.30 of this chapter is submitted: (i) alleging that the family court is not in session and (ii) showing good cause, including a showing that the existing order is insufficient for the purposes of protection of the petitioner, the petitioner's child or children or other members of the petitioner's family or household. The local criminal court shall make the matter regarding the modification of the order returnable in family court on the next day the family court is in session, or as soon thereafter as practicable, but in no event more than four calendar days after issuance of the modified order. The court shall immediately forward a copy of the modified order, if any, and sworn affidavit to the family court and shall provide a copy of such modified order, if any, and affidavit to the petitioner; provided, however, that where copies of such modified order and affidavit are transmitted to the family court by facsimile or other electronic means, the original copies of such modified order and affidavit shall be forwarded to the family court immediately thereafter. Any modified temporary order of protection or order of protection issued pursuant to this subdivision shall be issued to the respondent and copies shall be filed as required in subdivisions six and eight of this section for orders of protection issued pursuant to this section.

4. The court may issue or extend a temporary order of protection ex parte or on notice simultaneously with the issuance of a warrant for the arrest of defendant. Such temporary order of protection may continue in effect until the day the defendant subsequently appears in court pursuant to such warrant or voluntarily or otherwise.

5. * Upon sentencing on a conviction for any crime or violation between spouses, between a parent and child, or between members of the same family or household as defined in subdivision one of section 530.11 of this article, the court may in addition to any other disposition, including a conditional discharge or youthful offender adjudication, enter an order of protection. Where a temporary order of protection was issued, the court shall state on the record the reasons for issuing or not issuing an order of protection. The duration of such an order shall be fixed by the court and: (A) in the case of a felony conviction, shall not exceed the greater of: (i) eight years from the date of such sentencing, except where the sentence is or includes a sentence of probation on a conviction for a felony sexual assault, as provided in subparagraph (iii) of paragraph (a) of subdivision three of section 65.00 of the penal law, in which case, ten years from the date of

such sentencing, or (ii) eight years from the date of the expiration of the maximum term of an indeterminate or the term of a determinate sentence of imprisonment actually imposed; or (B) in the case of a conviction for a class A misdemeanor, shall not exceed the greater of: (i) five years from the date of such sentencing, except where the sentence is or includes a sentence of probation on a conviction for a misdemeanor sexual assault, as provided in subparagraph (ii) of paragraph (b) of subdivision three of section 65.00 of the penal law, in which case, six years from the date of such sentencing, or (ii) five years from the date of the expiration of the maximum term of a definite or intermittent term actually imposed; or (C) in the case of a conviction for any other offense, shall not exceed the greater of: (i) two years from the date of sentencing, or (ii) two years from the date of the expiration of the maximum term of a definite or intermittent term actually imposed. For purposes of determining the duration of an order of protection entered pursuant to this subdivision, a conviction shall be deemed to include a conviction that has been replaced by a youthful offender adjudication. In addition to any other conditions, such an order may require the defendant: *(Deemed repealed 9/1/23,Ch.55,L.2021)

5. * Upon sentencing on a conviction for any crime or violation between spouses, between a parent and child, or between members of the same family or household as defined in subdivision one of section 530.11 of this article, the court may in addition to any other disposition, including a conditional discharge or youthful offender adjudication, enter an order of protection. Where a temporary order of protection was issued, the court shall state on the record the reasons for issuing or not issuing an order of protection. The duration of such an order shall be fixed by the court and, in the case of a felony conviction, shall not exceed the greater of: (i) five years from the date of such sentencing, or (ii) three years from the date of the expiration of the maximum term of an indeterminate sentence of imprisonment actually imposed; or in the case of a conviction for a class A misdemeanor, shall not exceed three years from the date of such sentencing; or in the case of a conviction for any other offense, shall not exceed one year from the date of sentencing. For purposes of determining the duration of an order of protection entered pursuant to this subdivision, a conviction shall be deemed to include a conviction that has been replaced by a youthful offender adjudication. In addition to any other conditions, such an order may require the defendant: *(Eff. Upon repeal of subdivision 5. Above)

(a) to stay away from the home, school, business or place of employment of the family or household member, the other spouse or the child, or of any witness designated by the court, provided that the court shall make a determination, and shall state such determination in a written decision or on the record, whether to impose a condition pursuant to this paragraph, provided further, however, that failure to make such a determination shall not affect the validity of such order of protection. In making such determination, the court shall consider, but shall not be limited to consideration of, whether the order of protection is likely to achieve its purpose in the absence of such a condition, conduct subject to prior orders of protection, prior incidents of abuse, extent of past or present injury, threats, drug or alcohol abuse, and access to weapons;

(b) to permit a parent, or a person entitled to visitation by a court order or a separation agreement, to visit the child at stated periods;

(c) to refrain from committing a family offense, as defined in subdivision one of section 530.11 of this article, or any criminal offense against the child or against the family or household member or against any person to whom custody of the child is awarded, or from harassing, intimidating or threatening such persons;

(d) to refrain from acts of commission or omission that create an unreasonable risk to the health, safety and welfare of a child, family or household member's life or health;

(e) to permit a designated party to enter the residence during a specified period of time in order to remove personal belongings not in issue in this proceeding or in any other proceeding or action under this chapter, the family court act or the domestic relations law; or

(f) (i) to refrain from remotely controlling any connected devices affecting the home, vehicle or property of the person protected by the order.

(ii) For purposes of this paragraph, "connected device" shall mean any device, or other physical object that is capable of connecting to the internet, directly or indirectly, and that is assigned an internet protocol address or bluetooth address. *(Eff.11/11/20,Ch.261,L.2020)*

6. An order of protection or a temporary order of protection issued pursuant to subdivision one, two, three, four or five of this section shall bear in a conspicuous manner the term "order of protection" or "temporary order of protection" as the case may be and a copy shall be filed by the clerk of the court with the sheriff's office in the county in which the complainant resides, or, if the complainant resides within a city, with the police department of such city. The order of protection or temporary order of protection shall also contain the following notice: "This order of protection will remain in effect even if the protected party has, or consents to have, contact or communication with the party against whom the order is issued. This order of protection can only be modified or terminated by the court. The protected party cannot be held to violate this order nor be arrested for violating this order.". The absence of such language shall not affect the validity of such order. A copy of such order of protection or temporary order of protection may from time to time be filed by the clerk of the court with any other police department or sheriff's office having jurisdiction of the residence, work place, and school of anyone intended to be protected by such order. A copy of the order may also be filed by the complainant at the appropriate police department or sheriff's office having jurisdiction. Any subsequent amendment or revocation of such order shall be filed in the same manner as herein provided.

Such order of protection shall plainly state the date that such order expires.

6-a. The court shall inquire as to the existence of any other orders of protection between the defendant and the person or persons for whom the order of protection is sought.

7. A family offense subject to the provisions of this section which occurs subsequent to the issuance of an order of protection under this chapter shall be deemed a new offense for which the complainant may seek to file a new accusatory instrument and may file a family court petition under article eight of the family court act as provided for in section 100.07 of this chapter.

8. In any proceeding in which an order of protection or temporary order of protection or a warrant has been issued under this section, the clerk of the court shall issue to the complainant and defendant and defense counsel and to any other person affected by the order a copy of the order of protection or temporary order of protection and ensure that a copy of the order of protection or temporary order of protection be transmitted to the local correctional facility where the individual is or will be detained, the state or local correctional facility where the individual is or will be imprisoned, and the supervising probation department or department of corrections and community supervision where the individual is under probation or parole supervision. The presentation of a copy of such order or a warrant to any

peace officer acting pursuant to his or her special duties or police officer shall constitute authority for him or her to arrest a person who has violated the terms of such order and bring such person before the court and, otherwise, so far as lies within his or her power, to aid in securing the protection such order was intended to afford. The protected party in whose favor the order of protection or temporary order of protection is issued may not be held to violate an order issued in his or her favor nor may such protected party be arrested for violating such order.

9. If no warrant, order or temporary order of protection has been issued by the court, and an act alleged to be a family offense as defined in section 530.11 of this chapter is the basis of the arrest, the magistrate shall permit the complainant to file a petition, information or accusatory instrument and for reasonable cause shown, shall thereupon hold such respondent or defendant, admit to, fix or accept bail, or parole him or her for hearing before the family court or appropriate criminal court as the complainant shall choose in accordance with the provisions of section 530.11 of this chapter.

10. Punishment for contempt based on a violation of an order of protection or temporary order of protection shall not affect the original criminal action, nor reduce or diminish a sentence upon conviction for the original crime or violation alleged therein or for a lesser included offense thereof.

11. If a defendant is brought before the court for failure to obey any lawful order issued under this section, or an order of protection issued by a court of competent jurisdiction in another state, territorial or tribal jurisdiction, and if, after hearing, the court is satisfied by competent proof that the defendant has willfully failed to obey any such order, the court may:

(a) revoke an order of recognizance or release under non-monetary conditions or revoke an order of bail or order forfeiture of such bail and commit the defendant to custody; or

(b) restore the case to the calendar when there has been an adjournment in contemplation of dismissal and commit the defendant to custody; or

(c) revoke a conditional discharge in accordance with section 410.70 of this chapter and impose probation supervision or impose a sentence of imprisonment in accordance with the penal law based on the original conviction; or

(d) revoke probation in accordance with section 410.70 of this chapter and impose a sentence of imprisonment in accordance with the penal law based on the original conviction. In addition, if the act which constitutes the violation of the order of protection or temporary order of protection is a crime or a violation the defendant may be charged with and tried for that crime or violation.

12. The chief administrator of the courts shall promulgate appropriate uniform temporary orders of protection and orders of protection forms to be used throughout the state. Such forms shall be promulgated and developed in a manner to ensure the compatability of such forms with the statewide computerized registry established pursuant to section two hundred twenty-one-a of the executive law.

13. Notwithstanding the foregoing provisions, an order of protection, or temporary order of protection when applicable, may be entered against a former spouse and persons who have a child in common, regardless of whether such persons have been married or have lived together at any time, or against a member of the same family or household as defined in subdivision one of section 530.11 of this article.

14. The people shall make reasonable efforts to notify the complainant alleging a crime constituting a family offense when the people have decided to decline prosecution of such crime, to dismiss the criminal charges against the

defendant or to enter into a plea agreement. The people shall advise the complainant of the right to file a petition in the family court pursuant to section 100.07 of this chapter and section one hundred fifteen of the family court act.

In any case where allegations of criminal conduct are transferred from the family court to the criminal court pursuant to paragraph (ii) of subdivision (b) of section eight hundred forty-six of the family court act, the people shall advise the family court making the transfer of any decision to file an accusatory instrument against the family court respondent and shall notify such court of the disposition of such instrument and the sentence, if any, imposed upon such respondent.

Release of a defendant from custody shall not be delayed because of the requirements of this subdivision.

15. Any motion to vacate or modify an order of protection or temporary order of protection shall be on notice to the non-moving party, except as provided in subdivision three-b of this section.

§530.13 Protection of victims of crimes, other than family offenses.

1. When any criminal action is pending, and the court has not issued a temporary order of protection pursuant to section 530.12 of this article, the court, in addition to the other powers conferred upon it by this chapter, may for good cause shown issue a temporary order of protection in conjunction with any securing order or an adjournment in contemplation of dismissal. In addition to any other conditions, such an order may require that the defendant:

(a) stay away from the home, school, business or place of employment of the victims of, or designated witnesses to, the alleged offense;

(b) refrain from harassing, intimidating, threatening or otherwise interfering with the victims of the alleged offense and such members of the family or household of such victims or designated witnesses as shall be specifically named by the court in such order;

(c) 1. to refrain from intentionally injuring or killing, without justification, any companion animal the defendant knows to be owned, possessed, leased, kept or held by such victim or victims or a minor child residing in such victim's or victims' household.

2. "Companion animal", as used in this section, shall have the same meaning as in subdivision five of section three hundred fifty of the agriculture and markets law;

(d) 1. to refrain from remotely controlling any connected devices affecting the home, vehicle or property of the person protected by the order.

2. For purposes of this paragraph, "connected device" shall mean any device, or other physical object that is capable of connecting to the internet, directly or indirectly, and that is assigned an internet protocol address or bluetooth address.

In addition to the foregoing provisions, the court may issue an order, pursuant to section two hundred twenty-seven-c of the real property law, authorizing the party for whose benefit any order of protection has been issued to terminate a lease or rental agreement pursuant to section two hundred twenty-seven-c of the real property law.

2. The court may issue a temporary order of protection under this section ex parte upon the filing of an accusatory instrument and for good cause shown.

3. The court may issue or extend a temporary order of protection under this section ex parte simultaneously with the issuance of a warrant for the arrest of the defendant. Such temporary order of protection may continue in

effect until the day the defendant subsequently appears in court pursuant to such warrant or voluntarily or otherwise.

4. * Upon sentencing on a conviction for any offense, where the court has not issued an order of protection pursuant to section 530.12 of this article, the court may, in addition to any other disposition, including a conditional discharge or youthful offender adjudication, enter an order of protection. Where a temporary order of protection was issued, the court shall state on the record the reasons for issuing or not issuing an order of protection. The duration of such an order shall be fixed by the court and; (A) in the case of a felony conviction, shall not exceed the greater of: (i) eight years from the date of such sentencing, except where the sentence is or includes a sentence of probation on a conviction for a felony sexual assault, as provided in subparagraph (iii) of paragraph (a) of subdivision three of section 65.00 of the penal law, in which case, ten years from the date of such sentencing, or (ii) eight years from the date of the expiration of the maximum term of an indeterminate or the term of a determinate sentence of imprisonment actually imposed; or (B) in the case of a conviction for a class A misdemeanor, shall not exceed the greater of: (i) five years from the date of such sentencing, except where the sentence is or includes a sentence of probation on a conviction for a misdemeanor sexual assault, as provided in subparagraph (ii) of paragraph (b) of subdivision three of section 65.00 of the penal law, in which case, six years from the date of such sentencing or (ii) five years from the date of the expiration of the maximum term of a definite or intermittent term actually imposed; or (C) in the case of a conviction for any other offense, shall not exceed the greater of: (i) two years from the date of sentencing, or (ii) two years from the date of the expiration of the maximum term of a definite or intermittent term actually imposed. For purposes of determining the duration of an order of protection entered pursuant to this subdivision, a conviction shall be deemed to include a conviction that has been replaced by a youthful offender adjudication. In addition to any other conditions such an order may require that the defendant: *(Deemed repealed 9/1/23,Ch.55,L.2021)

*Upon sentencing on a conviction for any offense, where the court has not issued an order of protection pursuant to section 530.12 of this article, the court may, in addition to any other disposition, including a conditional discharge or youthful offender adjudication, enter an order of protection. Where a temporary order of protection was issued, the court shall state on the record the reasons for issuing or not issuing an order of protection. The duration of such an order shall be fixed by the court and, in the case of a felony conviction, shall not exceed the greater of: (i) five years from the date of such sentencing, or (ii) three years from the date of the expiration of the maximum term of an indeterminate sentence of imprisonment actually imposed; or in the case of a conviction for a class A misdemeanor, shall not exceed three years from the date of such sentencing; or in the case of a conviction for any other offense, shall not exceed one year from the date of sentencing. For purposes of determining the duration of an order of protection entered pursuant to this subdivision, a conviction shall be deemed to include a conviction that has been replaced by a youthful offender adjudication. In addition to any other conditions such an order may require that the defendant: *(Eff. Upon repeal of subdivision 4 above)

(a) stay away from the home, school, business or place of employment of the victim or victims, or of any witness designated by the court, of such offense;

(b) refrain from harassing, intimidating, threatening or otherwise interfering with the victim or victims of the offense and such members of the family or household of such victim or victims as shall be specifically named by the court in such order;

(c) 1. to refrain from intentionally injuring or killing, without justification, any companion animal the defendant knows to be owned, possessed, leased, kept or held by such victim or victims or a minor child residing in such victim's or victims' household.

2. "Companion animal", as used in this section, shall have the same meaning as in subdivision five of section three hundred fifty of the agriculture and markets law;

(d) 1. to refrain from remotely controlling any connected devices affecting the home, vehicle or property of the person protected by the order.

2. For purposes of this paragraph, "connected device" shall mean any device, or other physical object that is capable of connecting to the internet, directly or indirectly, and that is assigned an internet protocol address or bluetooth address.   (*Eff. 11/11/20, Ch.261, L.2020*)

5. The court shall inquire as to the existence of any other orders of protection between the defendant and the person or persons for whom the order of protection is sought. An order of protection issued under this section shall plainly state the date that such order expires. Orders of protection issued to protect victims of domestic violence, as defined in section four hundred fifty-nine-a of the social services law, shall be on uniform statewide forms that shall be promulgated by the chief administrator of the courts in a manner to ensure the compatibility of such forms with the statewide registry of orders of protection and warrants established pursuant to section two hundred twenty-one-a of the executive law. A copy of an order of protection or a temporary order of protection issued pursuant to subdivision one, two, three, or four of this section shall be filed by the clerk of the court with the sheriff's office in the county in which such victim or victims reside, or, if the victim or victims reside within a city, with the police department of such city. A copy of such order of protection or temporary order of protection may from time to time be filed by the clerk of the court with any other police department or sheriff's office having jurisdiction of the residence, work place, and school of anyone intended to be protected by such order. A copy of the order may also be filed by the victim or victims at the appropriate police department or sheriff's office having jurisdiction. Any subsequent amendment or revocation of such order shall be filed in the same manner as herein provided.

6. In any proceeding in which an order of protection or temporary order of protection or a warrant has been issued under this section, the clerk of the court shall issue to the victim and the defendant and defense counsel and to any other person affected by the order, a copy of the order of protection or temporary order of protection and ensure that a copy of the order of protection or temporary order of protection be transmitted to the local correctional facility where the individual is or will be detained, the state or local correctional facility where the individual is or will be imprisoned, and the supervising probation department or department of corrections and community supervision where the individual is under probation or parole supervision. The presentation of a copy of such order or a warrant to any police officer or peace officer acting pursuant to his or her special duties shall constitute authority for him or her to arrest a person who has violated the terms of such order and bring such person before the court and, otherwise, so far as lies within his or her power, to aid in securing the protection such order was intended to afford.

7. Punishment for contempt based upon a violation of an order or protection or temporary order of protection issued under this section shall

not affect a pending criminal action, nor reduce or diminish a sentence upon conviction for any other crimes or offenses.

8. If a defendant is brought before the court for failure to obey any lawful order issued under this section and if, after hearing, the court is satisfied by competent proof that the defendant has willfully failed to obey any such order, the court may:

(a) revoke an order of recognizance, release under non-monetary conditions or bail and commit the defendant to custody; or

(b) restore the case to the calendar when there has been an adjournment in contemplation of dismissal and commit the defendant to custody or impose or increase bail pending a trial of the original crime or violation; or

(c) revoke a conditional discharge in accordance with section 410.70 of this chapter and impose probation supervision or impose a sentence of imprisonment in accordance with the penal law based on the original conviction; or

(d) revoke probation in accordance with section 410.70 of this chapter and impose a sentence of imprisonment in accordance with the penal law based on the original conviction. In addition, if the act which constitutes the violation of the order of protection or temporary order of protection is a crime or a violation the defendant may be charged with and tried for that crime or violation.

9. The chief administrator of the courts shall promulgate appropriate uniform temporary order of protection and order of protection forms to be used throughout the state.

§530.14 Suspension and revocation of a license to carry, possess, repair or dispose of a firearm or firearms pursuant to section 400.00 of the penal law and ineligibility for such a license; order to surrender firearms; order to seize firearms.   *(Eff.11/1/20,Ch.261,L.2020)*

1. Suspension of firearms license and ineligibility for such a license upon issuance of temporary order of protection. Whenever a temporary order of protection is issued pursuant to subdivision one of section 530.12 or subdivision one of section 530.13 of this article:

(a) the court shall suspend any such existing license possessed by the defendant, order the defendant ineligible for such a license and order the immediate surrender of any or all firearms, rifles and shotguns owned or possessed where the court receives information that gives the court good cause to believe that (i) the defendant has a prior conviction of any violent felony offense as defined in section 70.02 of the penal law; (ii) the defendant has previously been found to have willfully failed to obey a prior order of protection and such willful failure involved (A) the infliction of physical injury, as defined in subdivision nine of section 10.00 of the penal law, (B) the use or threatened use of a deadly weapon or dangerous instrument as those terms are defined in subdivisions twelve and thirteen of section 10.00 of the penal law, or (C) behavior constituting any violent felony offense as defined in section 70.02 of the penal law; or (iii) the defendant has a prior conviction for stalking in the first degree as defined in section 120.60 of the penal law, stalking in the second degree as defined in section 120.55 of the penal law, stalking in the third degree as defined in section 120.50 of the penal law or stalking in the fourth degree as defined in section 120.45 of such law;

(Eff.11/1/20,Ch.261,L.2020)

(b) the court shall where the court finds a substantial risk that the defendant may use or threaten to use a firearm, rifle or shotgun unlawfully against the person or persons for whose protection the temporary order of protection is issued, suspend any such existing license possessed by the defendant, order the defendant ineligible for such a license and order the immediate surrender pursuant to subparagraph (f) of paragraph one of subdivision a of section 265.20 and subdivision six of section 400.05 of the penal law, of any or all firearms, rifles and shotguns owned or possessed; and *(Eff.11/1/20,Ch.261,L.2020)*

(c) the court may where the defendant willfully refuses to surrender such firearm, rifle or shotgun pursuant to paragraphs (a) and (b) of this subdivision, or for other good cause shown, order the immediate seizure of such firearm, rifle or shotgun, and search therefor, pursuant to an order issued in accordance with article six hundred ninety of this part, consistent with such rights as the defendant may derive from this article or the constitution of this state or the United States. *(Eff.11/1/20,Ch.55,L.2020)*

2. Revocation or suspension of firearms license and ineligibility for such a license upon issuance of an order of protection. Whenever an order of protection is issued pursuant to subdivision five of section 530.12 or subdivision four of section 530.13 of this article:

(a) the court shall revoke any such existing license possessed by the defendant, order the defendant ineligible for such a license and order the immediate surrender of any or all firearms, rifles and shotguns owned or possessed where such action is required by section 400.00 of the penal law; *(Eff.11/1/20,Ch.55,L.2020)*

(b) the court shall where the court finds a substantial risk that the defendant may use or threaten to use a firearm, rifle or shotgun unlawfully against the person or persons for whose protection the order of protection is issued, (i) revoke any such existing license possessed by the defendant, order the defendant ineligible for such a license and order the immediate surrender of any or all firearms, rifles and shotguns owned or possessed or (ii) suspend or continue to suspend any such existing license possessed by the defendant, order the defendant ineligible for such a license and order the immediate surrender pursuant to subparagraph (f) of paragraph one of subdivision a of section 265.20 and subdivision six of section 400.05 of the penal law, of any or all firearms, rifles and shotguns owned or possessed; and *(Eff.11/1/20,Ch.55,L.2020)*

(c) the court may where the defendant willfully refuses to surrender such firearm, rifle or shotgun pursuant to paragraphs (a) and (b) of this subdivision, or for other good cause shown, order the immediate seizure of such firearm, rifle or shotgun, and search therefor, pursuant to an order issued in accordance with article six hundred ninety of this part, consistent with such rights as the defendant may derive from this article or the constitution of this state or the United States. *(Eff.11/1/20,Ch.55,L.2020)*

3. Revocation or suspension of firearms license and ineligibility for such a license upon a finding of a willful failure to obey an order of protection. Whenever a defendant has been found pursuant to subdivision eleven of section 530.12 or subdivision eight of section 530.13 of this article to have willfully failed to obey an order of protection issued by a court of competent jurisdiction in this state or another state, territorial or tribal jurisdiction, in addition to any other remedies available pursuant to subdivision eleven of section 530.12 or subdivision eight of section 530.13 of this article:

(a) the court shall revoke any such existing license possessed by the defendant, order the defendant ineligible for such a license and order the immediate surrender of any or all firearms, rifles and shotguns owned or possessed where the willful failure to obey such order involved (i) the infliction of physical injury, as defined in subdivision nine of section 10.00 of the penal law, (ii) the use or threatened use of a deadly weapon or dangerous instrument as those terms are defined in subdivisions twelve and thirteen of section 10.00 of the penal law, (iii) behavior constituting any violent felony offense as defined in section 70.02 of the penal law; or (iv) behavior constituting stalking in the first degree as defined in section 120.60 of the penal law, stalking in the second degree as defined in section 120.55 of the penal law, stalking in the third degree as defined in section 120.50 of the penal law or stalking in the fourth degree as defined in section 120.45 of such law;   *(Eff.11/1/20,Ch.55,L.2020)*

(b) the court shall where the court finds a substantial risk that the defendant may use or threaten to use a firearm, rifle or shotgun unlawfully against the person or persons for whose protection the order of protection was issued, (i) revoke any such existing license possessed by the defendant, order the defendant ineligible for such a license and order the immediate surrender pursuant to subparagraph (f) of paragraph one of subdivision a of section 265.20 and subdivision six of section 400.05 of the penal law, of any or all firearms, rifles and shotguns owned or possessed or (ii) suspend any such existing license possessed by the defendant, order the defendant ineligible for such a license and order the immediate surrender pursuant to subparagraph (f) of paragraph one of subdivision a of section 265.20 and subdivision six of section 400.05 of the penal law, of any or all firearms, rifles and shotguns owned or possessed; and

(Eff.11/1/20,Ch.55,L.2020)

(c) the court may where the defendant willfully refuses to surrender such firearm, rifle or shotgun pursuant to paragraphs (a) and (b) of this subdivision, or for other good cause shown, order the immediate seizure of such firearm, rifle or shotgun, and search therefor, pursuant to an order issued in accordance with article six hundred ninety of this part, consistent with such rights as the defendant may derive from this article or the constitution of this state or the United States.   *(Eff.11/1/20,Ch.55,L.2020)*

4. Suspension. Any suspension order issued pursuant to this section shall remain in effect for the duration of the temporary order of protection or order of protection, unless modified or vacated by the court.

5. Surrender. (a) Where an order to surrender one or more firearms, rifles and shotguns has been issued, the temporary order of protection or order of protection shall specify the place where such weapons shall be surrendered, shall specify a date and time by which the surrender shall be completed and, to the extent possible, shall describe such weapons to be surrendered, and shall direct the authority receiving such surrendered weapons to immediately notify the court of such surrender.

(b) The prompt surrender of one or more firearms, rifles or shotguns pursuant to a court order issued pursuant to this section shall be considered a voluntary surrender for purposes of subparagraph (f) of paragraph one of subdivision a of section 265.20 of the penal law. The disposition of any such weapons, including weapons ordered to be seized pursuant to this section and section eight hundred forty-two-a of the family court act, shall be in accordance with the provisions of subdivision six of section 400.05 of the penal law; provided, however, that upon termination of any suspension order issued pursuant to this section or section eight hundred forty-two-a of the family court act, upon written application of the subject of the order, with notice and opportunity to be heard to the district attorney, the county attorney, the protected party, and every licensing officer responsible for issuance of a firearms license to the subject of the order pursuant to article four hundred of the penal law, and upon a written finding that there is no legal impediment to the subject's possession of a surrendered firearm, rifle or shotgun, any court of record exercising criminal jurisdiction may order the return of a firearm, rifle or shotgun not otherwise disposed of in accordance with subdivision six of section 400.05 of the penal law. When issuing such order in connection with any firearm subject to a license requirement under article four hundred of the penal law, if the licensing officer informs the court that he or she will seek to revoke the license, the order shall be stayed by the court until the conclusion of any license revocation proceeding.

(Eff.11/1/20,Ch.55,L.2020)

(c) The provisions of this section shall not be deemed to limit, restrict or otherwise impair the authority of the court to order and direct the surrender of any or all firearms, rifles and shotguns owned or possessed by a defendant pursuant to sections 530.12 or 530.13 of this article.

(d) If any other person demonstrates that such person is the lawful owner of any weapon taken into custody pursuant to this section or section eight hundred forty-two-a of the family court act, and provided that the court has made a written finding that there is no legal impediment to the person's possession of such a weapon, such court shall direct that such weapon be returned to such lawful owner. *(Eff.11/1/20,Ch.55,L.2020)*

6. Notice. (a) Where an order requiring surrender, revocation, suspension, seizure or ineligibility has been issued pursuant to this section, any temporary order of protection or order of protection issued shall state that such firearm license has been suspended or revoked or that the defendant is ineligible for such license, as the case may be, and that the defendant is prohibited from possessing any firearm, rifle or shotgun.

(b) The court revoking or suspending the license, ordering the defendant ineligible for such a license, or ordering the surrender or seizure of any firearm, rifle or shotgun shall immediately notify the duly constituted police authorities of the locality concerning such action and, in the case of orders of protection and temporary orders of protection issued pursuant to section 530.12 of this article, shall immediately notify the statewide registry of orders of protection.

(c) The court revoking or suspending the license or ordering the defendant ineligible for such a license shall give written notice thereof without unnecessary delay to the division of state police at its office in the city of Albany.

(d) Where an order of revocation, suspension, ineligibility, surrender or seizure is modified or vacated, the court shall immediately notify the statewide registry of orders of protection and the duly constituted police authorities of the locality concerning such action and shall give written notice thereof without unnecessary delay to the division of state police at its office in the city of Albany. *(Eff.11/1/20,Ch.55,L.2020)*

7. Hearing. The defendant shall have the right to a hearing before the court regarding any revocation, suspension, ineligibility, surrender or seizure order issued pursuant to this section, provided that nothing in this subdivision shall preclude the court from issuing any such order prior to a hearing. Where the court has issued such an order prior to a hearing, it shall commence such hearing within fourteen days of the date such order was issued. *(Eff.11/1/20,Ch.55,L.2020)*

8. Nothing in this section shall delay or otherwise interfere with the issuance of a temporary order of protection or the timely arraignment of a defendant in custody.

§530.20 Securing order by local criminal court when action is pending therein.

When a criminal action is pending in a local criminal court, such court, upon application of a defendant, shall proceed as follows:

1. (a) In cases other than as described in paragraph (b) of this subdivision the court shall release the principal pending trial on the principal's own

recognizance, unless the court finds on the record or in writing that release on the principal's own recognizance will not reasonably assure the principal's return to court. In such instances, the court shall release the principal under non-monetary conditions, selecting the least restrictive alternative and conditions that will reasonably assure the principal's return to court. The court shall explain its choice of alternative and conditions on the record or in writing.

(b) Where the principal stands charged with a qualifying offense, the court, unless otherwise prohibited by law, may in its discretion release the principal pending trial on the principal's own recognizance or under non-monetary conditions, fix bail, or, where the defendant is charged with a qualifying offense which is a felony, the court may commit the principal to the custody of the sheriff. The court shall explain its choice of release, release with conditions, bail or remand on the record or in writing. A principal stands charged with a qualifying offense when he or she stands charged with:

(i) a felony enumerated in section 70.02 of the penal law, other than robbery in the second degree as defined in subdivision one of section 160.10 of the penal law, provided, however, that burglary in the second degree as defined in subdivision two of section 140.25 of the penal law shall be a qualifying offense only where the defendant is charged with entering the living area of the dwelling;

(ii) a crime involving witness intimidation under section 215.15 of the penal law;

(iii) a crime involving witness tampering under section 215.11, 215.12 or 215.13 of the penal law;

(iv) a class A felony defined in the penal law, provided, that for class A felonies under article two hundred twenty of such law, only class A-I felonies shall be a qualifying offense;

(v) a sex trafficking offense defined in section 230.34 or 230.34-a of the penal law, or a felony sex offense defined in section 70.80 of the penal law or a crime involving incest as defined in section 255.25, 255.26 or 255.27 of such law, or a misdemeanor defined in article one hundred thirty of such law;

(vi) conspiracy in the second degree as defined in section 105.15 of the penal law, where the underlying allegation of such charge is that the defendant conspired to commit a class A felony defined in article one hundred twenty-five of the penal law;

(vii) money laundering in support of terrorism in the first degree as defined in section 470.24 of the penal law; money laundering in support of terrorism in the second degree as defined in section 470.23 of the penal law; money laundering in support of terrorism in the third degree as defined in section 470.22 of the penal law; money laundering in support of terrorism in the fourth degree as defined in section 470.21 of the penal law; or a felony crime of terrorism as defined in article four hundred ninety of the penal law, other than the crime defined in section 490.20 of such law;

(viii) criminal contempt in the second degree as defined in subdivision three of section 215.50 of the penal law, criminal contempt in the first degree as defined in subdivision (b), (c) or (d) of section 215.51 of the penal law or aggravated criminal contempt as defined in section 215.52 of the penal law, and the underlying allegation of such charge of criminal contempt in the second degree, criminal contempt in the first degree or aggravated criminal contempt is that the defendant violated a duly served order of protection where the protected party is a member of the defendant's same family or household as defined in subdivision one of section 530.11 of this article;

(ix) facilitating a sexual performance by a child with a controlled substance or alcohol as defined in section 263.30 of the penal law, use of a child in a sexual performance as defined in section 263.05 of the penal law or luring a child as defined in subdivision one of section 120.70 of the penal law, promoting an obscene sexual performance by a child as defined in section 263.10 of the penal law or promoting a sexual performance by a child as defined in section 263.15 of the penal law;

(x) any crime that is alleged to have caused the death of another person;

(xi) criminal obstruction of breathing or blood circulation as defined in section 121.11 of the penal law, strangulation in the second degree as defined in section 121.12 of the penal law or unlawful imprisonment in the first degree as defined in section 135.10 of the penal law, and is alleged to have committed the offense against a member of the defendant's same family or household as defined in subdivision one of section 530.11 of this article;

(xii) aggravated vehicular assault as defined in section 120.04-a of the penal law or vehicular assault in the first degree as defined in section 120.04 of the penal law;

(xiii) assault in the third degree as defined in section 120.00 of the penal law or arson in the third degree as defined in section 150.10 of the penal law, when such crime is charged as a hate crime as defined in section 485.05 of the penal law;

(xiv) aggravated assault upon a person less than eleven years old as defined in section 120.12 of the penal law or criminal possession of a weapon on school grounds as defined in section 265.01-a of the penal law;

(xv) grand larceny in the first degree as defined in section 155.42 of the penal law, enterprise corruption as defined in section 460.20 of the penal law, or money laundering in the first degree as defined in section 470.20 of the penal law;

(xvi) failure to register as a sex offender pursuant to section one hundred sixty-eight-t of the correction law or endangering the welfare of a child as defined in subdivision one of section 260.10 of the penal law, where the defendant is required to maintain registration under article six-C of the correction law and designated a level three offender pursuant to subdivision six of section one hundred sixty-eight-l of the correction law;

(xvii) a crime involving bail jumping under section 215.55, 215.56 or 215.57 of the penal law, or a crime involving escaping from custody under section 205.05, 205.10 or 205.15 of the penal law;

(xviii) any felony offense committed by the principal while serving a sentence of probation or while released to post release supervision;

(xix) a felony, where the defendant qualifies for sentencing on such charge as a persistent felony offender pursuant to section 70.10 of the penal law; or

(xx) any felony or class A misdemeanor involving harm to an identifiable person or property, where such charge arose from conduct occurring while the defendant was released on his or her own recognizance or released under conditions for a separate felony or class A misdemeanor involving harm to an identifiable person or property, provided, however, that the prosecutor must show reasonable cause to believe that the defendant committed the instant crime and any underlying crime. For the purposes of this subparagraph, any of the underlying crimes need not be a qualifying offense as defined in this subdivision.   *(Eff. 7/2/20, Ch.56, L.2020)*

(d) Notwithstanding the provisions of paragraphs (a) and (b) of this subdivision, with respect to any charge for which bail or remand is not ordered, and for which the court would not or could not otherwise require bail or remand, a defendant may, at any time, request that the court set bail in a nominal amount requested by the defendant in the form specified in paragraph (a) of subdivision one of section 520.10 of this title; if the court is satisfied that the request is voluntary, the court shall set such bail in such amount.

2. When the defendant is charged, by felony complaint, with a felony, the court may, in its discretion, order recognizance, release under non-monetary conditions, or, where authorized, bail or commit the defendant to the custody of the sheriff except as otherwise provided in subdivision one of this section or this subdivision:

(a) A city court, a town court or a village court may not order recognizance or bail when (i) the defendant is charged with a class A felony, or (ii) the defendant has two previous felony convictions;

(b) No local criminal court may order recognizance, release under non-monetary conditions or bail with respect to a defendant charged with a felony unless and until:

(i) The district attorney has been heard in the matter or, after knowledge or notice of the application and reasonable opportunity to be heard, has failed to appear at the proceeding or has otherwise waived his right to do so; and

(ii) The court and counsel for the defendant have been furnished with a report of the division of criminal justice services concerning the defendant's criminal record, if any, or with a police department report with respect to the defendant's prior arrest and conviction record, if any. If neither report is available, the court, with the consent of the district attorney, may dispense with this requirement; provided, however, that in an emergency, including but not limited to a substantial impairment in the ability of such division or police department to timely furnish such report, such consent shall not be required if, for reasons stated on the record, the court deems it unnecessary. When the court has been furnished with any such report or record, it shall furnish a copy thereof to counsel for the defendant or, if the defendant is not represented by counsel, to the defendant.

§530.30 Order of recognizance, release under non-monetary conditions or bail; by superior court judge when action is pending in local criminal court.

1. When a criminal action is pending in a local criminal court, other than one consisting of a superior court judge sitting as such, a judge of a superior court holding a term thereof in the county, upon application of a defendant, may order recognizance, release under non-monetary conditions or, where authorized, bail when such local criminal court:

(a) Lacks authority to issue such an order, pursuant to the relevant provisions of section 530.20 of this article; or

(b) Has denied an application for recognizance, release under non-monetary conditions or bail; or

(c) Has fixed bail, where authorized, which is excessive; or

(d) Has set a securing order of release under non-monetary conditions which are more restrictive than necessary to reasonably assure the defendant's return to court.

In such case, such superior court judge may vacate the order of such local criminal court and release the defendant on recognizance or under non-monetary conditions, or where authorized, fix bail in a lesser amount or in a less burdensome form, whichever are the least restrictive alternative and conditions that will reasonably assure the defendant's return to court. The court shall explain its choice of alternative and conditions on the record or in writing.

2. Notwithstanding the provisions of subdivision one of this section, when the defendant is charged with a felony in a local criminal court, a superior court judge may not order recognizance, release under non-monetary conditions or, where authorized, bail unless and until the district attorney has had an opportunity to be heard in the matter and such judge and counsel for the defendant have been furnished with a report as described in subparagraph (ii) of paragraph (b) of subdivision two of section 530.20 of this article.

3. Not more than one application may be made pursuant to this section.

§530.40 Order of recognizance, release under non-monetary conditions or bail; by superior court when action is pending therein.

When a criminal action is pending in a superior court, such court, upon application of a defendant, must or may order recognizance or bail as follows:

1. When the defendant is charged with an offense or offenses of less than felony grade only, the court must, unless otherwise provided by law, order recognizance or release under non-monetary conditions in accordance with this section.

2. When the defendant is charged with a felony, the court may, unless otherwise provided by law in its discretion, order recognizance, release under non-monetary conditions or, where authorized, bail. In any such case in which an indictment (a) has resulted from an order of a local criminal court holding the defendant for the action of the grand jury, or (b) was filed at a time when a felony complaint charging the same conduct was pending in a local criminal court, and in which such local criminal court or a superior court judge has issued an order of recognizance, release under non-monetary conditions or, where authorized, bail which is still effective, the superior court's order may be in the form of a direction continuing the effectiveness of the previous order.

3. In cases other than as described in subdivision four of this section the court shall release the principal pending trial on the principal's own recognizance, unless the court finds on the record or in writing that release

on the principal's own recognizance will not reasonably assure the principal's return to court. In such instances, the court shall release the principal under non-monetary conditions, selecting the least restrictive alternative and conditions that will reasonably assure the principal's return to court. The court shall explain its choice of alternative and conditions on the record or in writing.

4. Where the principal stands charged with a qualifying offense, the court, unless otherwise prohibited by law, may in its discretion release the principal pending trial on the principal's own recognizance or under non-monetary conditions, fix bail, or, where the defendant is charged with a qualifying offense which is a felony, the court may commit the principal to the custody of the sheriff. The court shall explain its choice of release, release with conditions, bail or remand on the record or in writing. A principal stands charged with a qualifying offense for the purposes of this subdivision when he or she stands charged with:

(a) a felony enumerated in section 70.02 of the penal law, other than robbery in the second degree as defined in subdivision one of section 160.10 of the penal law, provided, however, that burglary in the second degree as defined in subdivision two of section 140.25 of the penal law shall be a qualifying offense only where the defendant is charged with entering the living area of the dwelling;

(b) a crime involving witness intimidation under section 215.15 of the penal law;

(c) a crime involving witness tampering under section 215.11, 215.12 or 215.13 of the penal law;

(d) a class A felony defined in the penal law, provided that for class A felonies under article two hundred twenty of such law, only class A-I felonies shall be a qualifying offense;

(e) a sex trafficking offense defined in section 230.34 or 230.34-a of the penal law, or a felony sex offense defined in section 70.80 of the penal law or a crime involving incest as defined in section 255.25, 255.26 or 255.27 of such law, or a misdemeanor defined in article one hundred thirty of such law;

(f) conspiracy in the second degree as defined in section 105.15 of the penal law, where the underlying allegation of such charge is that the defendant conspired to commit a class A felony defined in article one hundred twenty-five of the penal law;

(g) money laundering in support of terrorism in the first degree as defined in section 470.24 of the penal law; money laundering in support of terrorism in the second degree as defined in section 470.23 of the penal law; money laundering in support of terrorism in the third degree as defined in section 470.22 of the penal law; money laundering in support of terrorism in the fourth degree as defined in section 470.21 of the penal law; or a felony crime of terrorism as defined in article four hundred ninety of the penal law, other than the crime defined in section 490.20 of such law;

(h) criminal contempt in the second degree as defined in subdivision three of section 215.50 of the penal law, criminal contempt in the first degree as defined in subdivision (b), (c) or (d) of section 215.51 of the penal law or aggravated criminal contempt as defined in section 215.52 of the penal law, and the underlying allegation of such charge of criminal contempt in the second degree, criminal contempt in the first degree or aggravated criminal contempt is that the defendant violated a duly served order of protection where the protected party is a member of the defendant's same family or household as defined in subdivision one of section 530.11 of this article;

(i) facilitating a sexual performance by a child with a controlled substance or alcohol as defined in section 263.30 of the penal law, use of a child in a sexual performance as defined in section 263.05 of the penal law or luring a child as defined in subdivision one of section 120.70 of the penal law, promoting an obscene sexual performance by a child as defined in section 263.10 of the penal law or promoting a sexual performance by a child as defined in section 263.15 of the penal law;

(j) any crime that is alleged to have caused the death of another person;

(k) criminal obstruction of breathing or blood circulation as defined in section 121.11 of the penal law, strangulation in the second degree as defined in section 121.12 of the penal law or unlawful imprisonment in the first degree as defined in section 135.10 of the penal law, and is alleged to have committed the offense against a member of the defendant's same family or household as defined in subdivision one of section 530.11 of this article;

(*l*) aggravated vehicular assault as defined in section 120.04-a of the penal law or vehicular assault in the first degree as defined in section 120.04 of the penal law;

(m) assault in the third degree as defined in section 120.00 of the penal law or arson in the third degree as defined in section 150.10 of the penal law, when such crime is charged as a hate crime as defined in section 485.05 of the penal law;

(n) aggravated assault upon a person less than eleven years old as defined in section 120.12 of the penal law or criminal possession of a weapon on school grounds as defined in section 265.01-a of the penal law;

(o) grand larceny in the first degree as defined in section 155.42 of the penal law, enterprise corruption as defined in section 460.20 of the penal law, or money laundering in the first degree as defined in section 470.20 of the penal law;

(p) failure to register as a sex offender pursuant to section one hundred sixty-eight-t of the correction law or endangering the welfare of a child as defined in subdivision one of section 260.10 of the penal law, where the defendant is required to maintain registration under article six-C of the correction law and designated a level three offender pursuant to subdivision six of section one hundred sixty-eight-l of the correction law;

(q) a crime involving bail jumping under section 215.55, 215.56 or 215.57 of the penal law, or a crime involving escaping from custody under section 205.05, 205.10 or 205.15 of the penal law;

(r) any felony offense committed by the principal while serving a sentence of probation or while released to post release supervision;

(s) a felony, where the defendant qualifies for sentencing on such charge as a persistent felony offender pursuant to section 70.10 of the penal law; or

(t) any felony or class A misdemeanor involving harm to an identifiable person or property, where such charge arose from conduct occurring while the defendant was released on his or her own recognizance or released under conditions for a separate felony or class A misdemeanor involving harm to an identifiable person or property, provided, however, that the prosecutor must show reasonable cause to believe that the defendant committed the instant crime and any underlying crime. For the purposes of this subparagraph, any of the underlying crimes need not be a qualifying offense as defined in this subdivision. *(Eff.7/2/20,Ch.56,L.2020)*

5. Notwithstanding the provisions of subdivisions three and four of this section, with respect to any charge for which bail or remand is not ordered,

and for which the court would not or could not otherwise require bail or remand, a defendant may, at any time, request that the court set bail in a nominal amount requested by the defendant in the form specified in paragraph (a) of subdivision one of section 520.10 of this title; if the court is satisfied that the request is voluntary, the court shall set such bail in such amount.

6. Notwithstanding the provisions of subdivisions two, three and four of this section, a superior court may not order recognizance, release under non-monetary conditions or, where authorized, bail, or permit a defendant to remain at liberty pursuant to an existing order, after the defendant has been convicted of either: (a) a class A felony or (b) any class B or class C felony as defined in article one hundred thirty of the penal law committed or attempted to be committed by a person eighteen years of age or older against a person less than eighteen years of age. In either case the court must commit or remand the defendant to the custody of the sheriff.

7. Notwithstanding the provisions of subdivisions two, three and four of this section, a superior court may not order recognizance, release under non-monetary conditions or, where authorized, bail when the defendant is charged with a felony unless and until the district attorney has had an opportunity to be heard in the matter and such court and counsel for the defendant have been furnished with a report as described in subparagraph (ii) of paragraph (b) of subdivision two of section 530.20 of this article.

§530.45 Order of recognizance or bail; after conviction and before sentence.
1. When the defendant is at liberty in the course of a criminal action as a result of a prior order of recognizance, release under non-monetary conditions or bail and the court revokes such order and then, where authorized, fixes no bail or fixes bail in a greater amount or in a more burdensome form than was previously fixed and remands or commits defendant to the custody of the sheriff, or issues a more restrictive securing order, a judge designated in subdivision two of this section, upon application of the defendant following conviction of an offense other than a class A felony or a class B or class C felony offense as defined in article one hundred thirty of the penal law committed or attempted to be committed by a person eighteen years of age or older against a person less than eighteen years of age, and before sentencing, may issue a securing order and release the defendant on the defendant's own recognizance, release the defendant under non-monetary conditions, or, where authorized, fix bail or fix bail in a lesser amount or in a less burdensome form, or issue a less restrictive securing order, than fixed by the court in which the conviction was entered.

2. An order as prescribed in subdivision one may be issued by the following judges in the indicated situations:
(a) If the criminal action was pending in supreme court or county court, such order may be issued by a justice of the appellate division of the department in which the conviction was entered.
(b) If the criminal action was pending in a local criminal court, such order may be issued by a judge of a superior court holding a term thereof in the county in which the conviction was entered.

2-a. Notwithstanding the provisions of subdivision four of section 510.10, paragraph (b) of subdivision one of section 530.20 and subdivision four of section 530.40 of this title, when a defendant charged with an offense that is not such a qualifying offense is convicted, whether by guilty plea or verdict, in such criminal action or proceeding of an offense that is not a qualifying offense, the court may, in accordance with law, issue a securing order:

releasing the defendant on the defendant's own recognizance or under non-monetary conditions where authorized, fix bail, or remand the defendant to the custody of the sheriff where authorized. *(Eff. 7/2/20, Ch.56, L.2020)*

3. An application for an order specified in this section must be made upon reasonable notice to the people, and the people must be accorded adequate opportunity to appear in opposition thereto. Not more than one application may be made pursuant to this section. Defendant must allege in his application that he intends to take an appeal to an intermediate appellate court immediately after sentence is pronounced.

4. Notwithstanding the provisions of subdivision one, if within thirty days after sentence the defendant has not taken an appeal to an intermediate appellate court from the judgment or sentence, the operation of such order terminates and the defendant must surrender himself to the criminal court in which the judgment was entered in order that execution of the judgment be commenced.

5. Notwithstanding the provisions of subdivision one, if within one hundred twenty days after the filing of the notice of appeal such appeal has not been brought to argument in or submitted to the intermediate appellate court, the operation of such order terminates and the defendant must surrender himself to the criminal court in which the judgment was entered in order that execution of the judgment be commenced or resumed; except that this subdivision does not apply where the intermediate appellate court has (a) extended the time for argument or submission of the appeal to a date beyond the specified period of one hundred twenty days, and (b) upon application of the defendant, expressly ordered that the operation of the order continue until the date of the determination of the appeal or some other designated future date or occurrence.

6. Where the defendant is at liberty during the pendency of an appeal as a result of an order issued pursuant to this section, the intermediate appellate court, upon affirmance of the judgment, must by appropriate certificate remit the case to the criminal court in which such judgment was entered. The criminal court must, upon at least two days notice to the defendant, his surety and his attorney, promptly direct the defendant to surrender himself to the criminal court in order that execution of the judgment be commenced or resumed, and if necessary the criminal court may issue a bench warrant to secure his appearance.

§530.50 Order of recognizance or bail; during pendency of appeal.

1. A judge who is otherwise authorized pursuant to section 460.50 or section 460.60 to issue an order of recognizance or bail pending the determination of an appeal, may do so unless the defendant received a class A felony sentence or a sentence for any class B or class C felony offense defined in article one hundred thirty of the penal law committed or attempted to be committed by a person eighteen years of age or older against a person less than eighteen years of age.

2. Notwithstanding the provisions of subdivision four of section 510.10, paragraph (b) of subdivision one of section 530.20 and subdivision four of section 530.40 of this title, when a defendant charged with an offense that is not such a qualifying offense applies, pending determination of an appeal, for an order of recognizance or release on non-monetary conditions, where authorized, or fixing bail, a judge identified in subdivision two of section 460.50 or paragraph (a) of subdivision one of section 460.60 of this chapter may, in accordance with law, and except as otherwise provided by law, issue a securing order: releasing the defendant on the defendant's own recognizance or under non-monetary conditions where authorized, fixing

bail, or remanding the defendant to the custody of the sheriff where
authorized. *(Eff. 7/2/20, Ch. 56, L. 2020)*

§530.60 Certain modifications of a securing order.

1. Whenever in the course of a criminal action or proceeding a defendant
is at liberty as a result of an order of recognizance, release under
non-monetary conditions or bail issued pursuant to this chapter, and the
court considers it necessary to review such order, whether due to a motion
by the people or otherwise, the court may, and except as provided in
subdivision two of section 510.50 of this title concerning a failure to appear
in court, by a bench warrant if necessary, require the defendant to appear
before the court. Upon such appearance, the court, for good cause shown,
may revoke the order of recognizance, release under non-monetary
conditions, or bail. If the defendant is entitled to recognizance, release
under non-monetary conditions, or bail as a matter of right, the court must
issue another such order. If the defendant is not, the court may either issue
such an order or commit the defendant to the custody of the sheriff in
accordance with this section.

Where the defendant is committed to the custody of the sheriff and is held
on a felony complaint, a new period as provided in section 180.80 of this
chapter shall commence to run from the time of the defendant's commitment
under this subdivision.

2. (a) Whenever in the course of a criminal action or proceeding a
defendant charged with the commission of a felony is at liberty as a result of
an order of recognizance, release under non-monetary conditions or bail
issued pursuant to this article it shall be grounds for revoking such order
that the court finds reasonable cause to believe the defendant committed
one or more specified class A or violent felony offenses or intimidated a
victim or witness in violation of section 215.15, 215.16 or 215.17 of the
penal law while at liberty.

(b) Except as provided in paragraph (a) of this subdivision or any other
law, whenever in the course of a criminal action or proceeding a defendant
charged with the commission of an offense is at liberty as a result of an
order of recognizance, release under non-monetary conditions or bail issued
pursuant to this article it shall be grounds for revoking such order and fixing
bail in such criminal action or proceeding when the court has found, by clear
and convincing evidence, that the defendant:

(i) persistently and willfully failed to appear after notice of scheduled
appearances in the case before the court; or

(ii) violated an order of protection in the manner prohibited by
subdivision (b), (c) or (d) of section 215.51 of the penal law while at liberty;
or

(iii) stands charged in such criminal action or proceeding with a
misdemeanor or violation and, after being so charged, intimidated a victim
or witness in violation of section 215.15, 215.16 or 215.17 of the penal law
or tampered with a witness in violation of section 215.11, 215.12 or 215.13
of the penal law, law while at liberty; or

(iv) stands charged in such action or proceeding with a felony and,
after being so charged, committed a felony while at liberty.

(c) Before revoking an order of recognizance, release under
non-monetary conditions, or bail pursuant to this subdivision, the court must
hold a hearing and shall receive any relevant, admissible evidence not
legally privileged. The defendant may cross-examine witnesses and may
present relevant, admissible evidence on his own behalf. Such hearing may
be consolidated with, and conducted at the same time as, a felony hearing

conducted pursuant to article one hundred eighty of this chapter. A transcript of testimony taken before the grand jury upon presentation of the subsequent offense shall be admissible as evidence during the hearing. The district attorney may move to introduce grand jury testimony of a witness in lieu of that witness' appearance at the hearing.

(d) Revocation of an order of recognizance, release under non-monetary conditions or bail and a new securing order fixing bail or commitment, as specified in this paragraph and pursuant to this subdivision shall be for the following periods:

(i) Under paragraph (a) of this subdivision, revocation of the order of recognizance, release under non-monetary conditions or, as the case may be, bail, and a new securing order fixing bail or committing the defendant to the custody of the sheriff shall be as follows:

(A) For a period not to exceed ninety days exclusive of any periods of adjournment requested by the defendant; or

(B) Until the charges contained within the accusatory instrument have been reduced or dismissed such that no count remains which charges the defendant with commission of a felony; or

(C) Until reduction or dismissal of the charges contained within the accusatory instrument charging the subsequent offense such that no count remains which charges the defendant with commission of a class A or violent felony offense.

Upon expiration of any of the three periods specified within this subparagraph, whichever is shortest, the court may grant or deny release upon an order of bail or recognizance in accordance with the provisions of this article. Upon conviction to an offense the provisions of article five hundred thirty of this chapter shall apply; and

(ii) Under paragraph (b) of this subdivision, revocation of the order of recognizance, release under non-monetary conditions or, as the case may be, bail shall result in the issuance of a new securing order which may, if otherwise authorized by law, permit the principal's release on recognizance or release under non-monetary conditions, but shall also render the defendant eligible for an order fixing bail provided, however, that in accordance with the principles in this title the court must select the least restrictive alternative and condition or conditions that will reasonably assure the principal's return to court. Nothing in this subparagraph shall be interpreted as shortening the period of detention, or requiring or authorizing any less restrictive form of a securing order, which may be imposed pursuant to any other law.

(e) Notwithstanding the provisions of paragraph (a) or (b) of this subdivision a defendant, against whom a felony complaint has been filed which charges the defendant with commission of a class A or violent felony offense or violation of section 215.15, 215.16 or 215.17 of the penal law committed while he was at liberty as specified therein, may be committed to the custody of the sheriff pending a revocation hearing for a period not to exceed seventy-two hours. An additional period not to exceed seventy-two hours may be granted by the court upon application of the district attorney upon a showing of good cause or where the failure to commence the

This page intentionaly left blank.

hearing was due to the defendant's request or occurred with his consent. Such good cause must consist of some compelling fact or circumstance which precluded conducting the hearing within the initial prescribed period.

(Eff.1/1/20,Ch.59,L.2019)

§530.70   Order of recognizance or bail; bench warrant.

1. A bench warrant issued by a superior court, by a district court, by the New York City criminal court or by a superior court judge sitting as a local criminal court may be executed anywhere in the state. A bench warrant issued by a city court, a town court or a village court may be executed in the county of issuance or any adjoining county; and it may be executed anywhere else in the state upon the written endorsement thereon of a local criminal court of the county in which the defendant is to be taken into custody. When so endorsed, the warrant is deemed the process of the endorsing court as well as that of the issuing court.

2. A bench warrant may be addressed to: (a) any police officer whose geographical area of employment embraces either the place where the offense charged was allegedly committed or the locality of the court by which the warrant is issued; or (b) any uniformed court officer for a court in the city of New York, the county of Nassau, the county of Suffolk or the county of Westchester or for any other court that is part of the unified court system of the state for execution in the building wherein such court officer is employed or in the immediate vicinity thereof. A bench warrant must be executed in the same manner as a warrant of arrest, as provided in section 120.80, and following the arrest, such executing police officer or court officer must without unnecessary delay bring the defendant before the court in which it is returnable; provided, however, if the court in which the bench warrant is returnable is a city, town or village court, and such court is not available, and the bench warrant is addressed to a police officer, such executing police officer must without unnecessary delay bring the defendant before an alternate local criminal court, as provided in subdivision five of section 120.90; or if the court in which the bench warrant is returnable is a superior court, and such court is not available, and the bench warrant is addressed to a police officer, such executing police officer may bring the defendant to the local correctional facility of the county in which such court sits, to be detained there until not later than the commencement of the next session of such court occurring on the next business day.

2-a. A court which issues a bench warrant may attach thereto a summary of the basis for the warrant. In any case where, pursuant to subdivision two of this section, a defendant arrested upon a bench warrant is brought before a local criminal court other than the court in which the warrant is returnable, such local criminal court shall consider such summary before issuing a securing order with respect to the defendant.

3. A bench warrant may be executed by (a) any officer to whom it is addressed, or (b) any other police officer delegated to execute it under circumstances prescribed in subdivisions four and five.

4. The issuing court may authorize the delegation of such warrant. Where the issuing court has so authorized, a police officer to whom a bench warrant is addressed may delegate another police officer to whom it is not addressed to execute such warrant as his or her agent when:

(a) He or she has reasonable cause to believe that the defendant is in a particular county other than the one in which the warrant is returnable; and

(b) The geographical area of employment of the delegated police officer embraces the locality where the arrest is to be made.

5. Under circumstances specified in subdivision four, the police officer to whom the bench warrant is addressed may inform the delegated officer, by telecommunication, mail or any other means, of the issuance of the warrant, of the offense charged in the underlying accusatory instrument and of all other pertinent details, and may request him or her to act as his or her agent in arresting the defendant pursuant to such bench warrant. Upon such request, the delegated police officer is to the same extent as the delegating officer, authorized to make such arrest pursuant to the bench warrant within the geographical area of such delegated officer's employment. Upon so arresting the defendant, he or she must without unnecessary delay deliver the defendant or cause him or her to be delivered to the custody of the police officer by whom he or she was so delegated, and the latter must then without unnecessary delay bring the defendant before the court in which such bench warrant is returnable.

6. A bench warrant may be executed by an officer of the state department of corrections and community supervision or a probation officer when the person named within the warrant is under the supervision of the department of corrections and community supervision or a department of probation and the probation officer is authorized by his or her probation director, as the case may be. The warrant must be executed upon the same conditions and in the same manner as is otherwise provided for execution by a police officer.

§530.80 Order of recognizance or bail; surrender of defendant.

1. At any time before the forfeiture of a bail bond, an obligor may surrender the defendant in his exoneration, or the defendant may surrender himself, to the court in which his case is pending or to the sheriff to whose custody he was committed at the time of giving bail, in the following manner:

(a) A certified copy of the bail bond must be delivered to the sheriff, who must detain the defendant in his custody thereon, as upon a commitment. The sheriff must acknowledge the surrender by a certificate in writing, and must forthwith notify the court in which the case is pending that such surrender has been made.

(b) Upon the bail bond and the certificate of the sheriff, or upon the surrender to the court in which the case is pending, such court must, upon five days notice to the district attorney, order that the bail be exonerated. On filing such order, the bail is exonerated accordingly.

2. For the purpose of surrendering the defendant, an obligor or the person who posted cash bail for the defendant may take him into custody at any place within the state, or he may, by a written authority indorsed on a certified copy of the bail bond, empower any person over twenty years of age to do so.

3. At any time before the forfeiture of cash bail, the defendant may surrender himself or the person who posted bail for the defendant may surrender the defendant in the manner prescribed in subdivision one. In such case, the court must order a return of the money to the person who posted it, upon producing a certificate of the sheriff showing the surrender, and upon a notice of five days to the district attorney.

ARTICLE 540 - FORFEITURE OF BAIL AND REMISSION THEREOF
Section
540.10 Forfeiture of bail; generally.
540.20 Forfeiture of bail; certain local criminal courts.
540.30 Remission of forfeiture.

§540.10 Forfeiture of bail; generally.

1. If, without sufficient excuse, a principal does not appear when required or does not render himself amenable to the orders and processes of the criminal court wherein bail has been posted, the court must enter such facts upon its minutes and the bail bond or the cash bail, as the case may be, is thereupon forfeited.

2. If the principal appears at any time before the final adjournment of the court, and satisfactorily excuses his neglect, the court may direct the forfeiture to be discharged upon such terms as are just. If the forfeiture is not so discharged and the forfeited bail consisted of a bail bond, the district attorney, within one hundred twenty days after the adjournment of the court at which such bond was directed to be forfeited, must proceed against the obligor or obligors who executed such bond, in the manner prescribed in subdivision three. If the forfeited bail consisted of cash bail, the county treasurer with whom it is deposited shall give written notice of the forfeiture to the person who posted cash bail for the defendant may at any time after the final adjournment of the court or forty-five days after notice of forfeiture required herein has been given, whichever comes later, apply the money deposited to the use of the county.

3. A bail bond or cash bail, upon being forfeited, together with a certified copy of the order of the court forfeiting the same, must be filed by the district attorney in the office of the clerk of the county wherein such order was issued. Such clerk must docket the same in the book kept by him for docketing of judgments and enter therein a judgment against the obligor or obligors who executed such bail bond for the amount of the penalty of said bond or against the person who posted the cash bail for the amount of the cash bail, and the bond and the certified copy of the order of the court forfeiting the bond or the cash bail constitutes the judgment roll. Such judgment constitutes a lien on the real estate of the obligor or obligors who executed such bail bond from the time of the entry of the judgment. An execution may be issued to collect the amount of said bail bond in the same form and with the same effect as upon a judgment recovered in an action in said county upon a debt in favor of the people of the state of New York against such obligor or obligors.

§540.20 Forfeiture of bail; certain local criminal courts.

Notwithstanding the provisions of section 540.10, when bail has been posted in a city court, town court or village court in connection with a local criminal court accusatory instrument, other than a felony complaint, and thereafter such bail is forfeited, the following rules are applicable:

1. If such bail consists of a bail bond, the financial officer of such city, town or village must promptly commence an action for the recovery of the sum of money specified in such bond, and upon collection thereof shall pay the same over to the treasurer or financial officer of the city, the supervisor of the town or the treasurer of the village. Any amount recovered in such action, unless otherwise provided by law, shall be the property of the city, town or village in which the offense charged is alleged to have been committed.

This page intentionally left blank

2. If such bail consists of cash bail, the local criminal court must:

(a) If it is a city court, pay the forfeited bail to the treasurer or other financial officer of the city. Such forfeited bail, unless otherwise provided by law, is the property of such city.

(b) If it is a town court or a village court, pay the forfeited bail to the state comptroller on or before the tenth day of the month next succeeding such forfeiture. Such forfeited bail, unless otherwise provided by law, is the property of the town or village in which the offense charged is alleged to have been committed; provided, however, that when (i) a single amount of bail is posted for more than a single offense charged, and (ii) the town or village justice court does not attribute a specific amount of bail to each offense, and (iii) forfeited bail for at least two of the offenses would be the property of different governmental entities, the entire amount of forfeited bail shall be the property of the town or village in which the offenses charged are alleged to have been committed, except that, when forfeited bail for at least one of the offenses would be the property of the state, the entire amount of forfeited bail shall be the property of the state.

§540.30 Remission of forfeiture.

1. After the forfeiture of a bail bond or cash bail, as provided in section 540.10, an application for remission of such forfeiture may be made to a court as follows:

(a) If the forfeiture has been ordered by a superior court, the application must be made in such court;

(b) If the forfeiture has been ordered by a local criminal court, the application must be made to a superior court in the county, except that if the local criminal court which ordered the forfeiture was a district court, the application may alternatively be made to that district court.

2. The application must be made within one year after the forfeiture of the bail is declared upon at least five days notice to the district attorney and service of copies of the affidavits and papers upon which the application is founded. The court may grant the application and remit the forfeiture or any part thereof, upon such terms are just. The application may be granted only upon payment of the costs and expenses incurred in the proceedings for the enforcement of the forfeiture.

TITLE Q - PROCEDURES FOR SECURING ATTENDANCE AT CRIMINAL ACTIONS AND PROCEEDINGS OF DEFENDANTS NOT SECURABLE BY CONVENTIONAL MEANS-AND RELATED MATTERS

ARTICLE 550 - SECURING ATTENDANCE OF DEFENDANTS - IN GENERAL

Section
550.10 Securing attendance of defendants; in general.

§550.10 Securing attendance of defendants; in general.

Depending upon the status of a criminal action pending against a defendant, the geographical location of the defendant at the time and other factors, his attendance thereat for purposes of arraignment or prosecution may be secured by the following methods:

1. If the defendant has never been arraigned in the action, and if he is at liberty within the state, his attendance may, under given circumstances, be secured by a warrant of arrest, as prescribed in article one hundred twenty, a superior court warrant of arrest, as prescribed in subdivision three of section 210.10, or a summons, as prescribed in article one hundred thirty.

2. If the defendant has been arraigned in the action and, by virtue of a securing order, is either in the custody of the sheriff or at liberty within the state on his own recognizance or on bail, his attendance may be secured as follows:

(a) If the defendant is confined in the custody of the sheriff, the court may direct the sheriff to produce him;

(b) If the defendant is at liberty within the state as a result of an order releasing him on his own recognizance or on bail, the court may secure his attendance by notification or by the issuance of a bench warrant.

3. If the defendant's attendance cannot be secured by methods described in subdivisions one and two, either because he is outside the state or because he is confined in an institution within the state as a result of an order issued in some other action, proceeding or matter, his attendance may, under indicated circumstances, be secured by procedures prescribed in the ensuing articles of this title.

ARTICLE 560 - SECURING ATTENDANCE OF DEFENDANTS CONFINED IN INSTITUTIONS WITHIN THE STATE

Section
560.10 Securing attendance of defendants confined in institutions within the state.

§560.10 Securing attendance of defendants confined in institutions within the state.

1. When a criminal action is pending against a defendant who is confined in an institution within the state pursuant to a court order issued in a different action, proceeding or matter, the following courts and judges may, under the indicated circumstances, order that the defendant be produced in the court in which the criminal action is pending for purposes of arraignment or prosecution therein:

(a) If the action is pending in a superior court or with a superior court judge sitting as a local criminal court, or in a district court or the New York City criminal court, such court may, upon application of the district attorney, order the production therein of a defendant confined in any institution within the state.

(b) If the action is pending in a city court or a town court or a village court, such court may, upon application of the district attorney, order production therein of a defendant confined in a county jail of such county. Production therein of a defendant confined in any other institution in the state may, upon application of the district attorney, be ordered by a judge of a superior court holding a term thereof in the county in which the action is pending.

2. An application by a district attorney, pursuant to subdivision one, for production of a defendant confined in an institution located in another county in connection with a criminal action or proceeding pending in such other county, must be made upon reasonable notice to the district attorney of such other county and to the attorney representing such defendant in or in connection with the action or proceeding pending therein, and the court or judge must accord them reasonable opportunity to be heard in the matter. If such court or judge determines that production of the defendant would result in an unreasonable interference with the conduct of the action in such other county, it must deny the application. If an order of production is issued, a justice of the appellate division, of either the department embracing the county of issuance thereof or of the department embracing the county of the defendant's confinement, upon application of the district attorney of the county of confinement or of the attorney representing the defendant in or in connection with the action pending therein, may for good cause shown vacate such order of production.

ARTICLE 570 - SECURING ATTENDANCE OF DEFENDANTS WHO ARE OUTSIDE THE STATE BUT WITHIN THE UNITED STATES--RENDITION TO OTHER JURISDICTIONS OF DEFENDANTS WITHIN THE STATE - UNIFORM CRIMINAL EXTRADITION ACT

Section
570.02 Short title.
570.04 Definitions.
570.06 Fugitives from justice; duty of governor.
570.08 Demand; form.
570.10 Investigation by governor.
570.12 Extradition of persons imprisoned or awaiting trial in another state.
570.14 Extradition of persons who left the demanding state under compulsion.
570.16 Extradition of persons not present in demanding state at time of commission of crime.
570.18 Issuance of warrant of arrest by governor; recitals therein.
570.20 Execution of warrant; manner and place thereof.
570.22 Authority of arresting officer.
570.24 Rights of accused person; application for writ of habeas corpus.
570.26 Noncompliance with preceding section; penalties for violation.
570.28 Confinement of the accused in jail when necessary.
570.30 Confinement of extradited persons passing through this state.
570.32 Arrest of accused before making of requisition.
570.34 Arrest of accused without warrant therefor.
570.36 Commitment to await requisition; bail.
570.38 Bail; in what cases; conditions of bond.
570.40 Extension of time of commitment; adjournment.
570.42 Bail; when forfeited.
570.44 Persons under criminal prosecution in this state at time of requisition.
570.46 Guilt or innocence of accused; when inquired into.
570.48 Alias warrant of arrest.
570.50 Written waiver of extradition proceedings.
570.52 Fugitives from this state; duty of governor.
570.54 Application for issuance of requisition; by whom made; contents.
570.56 Expense of extradition.
570.58 Immunity from service of process in certain civil actions.
570.60 No immunity from other criminal prosecution while in this state.
570.62 Non-waiver by this state.
570.64 Interpretation.
570.66 Constitutionality.

§570.02 Short title.

This article may be cited and referred to as the uniform criminal extradition act.

§570.04 Definitions.

As used in this article, the following terms have the following meanings:

1. "Governor" includes any person performing the functions of governor by authority of the law of this state.

2. "Executive authority" includes the governor, and any person performing the functions of governor in a state other than this state.

3. "State," when referring to a state other than this state, includes any other state or territory, organized or unorganized, of the United States of America.

§570.06 Fugitives from justice; duty of governor.

Subject to the provisions of this article, the provisions of the constitution of the United States controlling, and any and all acts of congress enacted in pursuance thereof, it is the duty of the governor of this state to have arrested and delivered up to the executive authority of any other state of the United States any person charged in that state with treason, felony, or other crime, who has fled from justice and is found in this state.

§570.08 Demand; form.

No demand for the extradition of a person charged with crime in another state shall be recognized by the governor unless in writing alleging that the accused was present in the demanding state at the time of the commission of the alleged crime, and that thereafter he fled from the state, except in cases arising under section 570.14 or 570.16, and accompanied by a copy of an indictment found or by information supported by an affidavit in the state having jurisdiction of the crime, or by a copy of an affidavit made before a magistrate there, together with a copy of any warrant which was issued thereon, or by a copy of a judgment of conviction or of a sentence imposed in execution thereof, together with a statement by the executive authority of the demanding state that the person claimed has escaped from confinement or has broken the terms of his bail, probation or parole. The indictment, information or affidavit made before the magistrate must substantially charge the person demanded with having committed a crime under the law of that state; and the copy of the indictment, information, affidavit, judgment of conviction or sentence must be authenticated by the executive authority making the demand.

§570.10 Investigation by governor.

When a demand shall be made upon the governor of this state by the executive authority of another state for the surrender of a person so charged with crime, the governor may call upon the attorney general or any district attorney in this state to investigate or assist in investigating the demand, and to report to him the situation and circumstances of the person so demanded, and whether he ought to be surrendered.

§570.12 Extradition of persons imprisoned or awaiting trial in another state.

When it is desired to have returned to this state a person charged in this state with a crime and such person is imprisoned or is held under criminal proceedings then pending against him in another state, the governor of this state may agree with the executive authority of such other state for the extradition of such person before the conclusion of his term of sentence in such other state, upon condition that such person be returned to such other state at the expense of this state as soon as the prosecution in this state is terminated.

§570.14 Extradition of persons who left the demanding state under compulsion.

The governor of this state may also surrender, on demand of the executive authority of any other state, any person in this state who is charged in the manner provided in section 570.08 with having violated the laws of the state whose executive authority is making the demand, even though such person left the demanding state involuntarily.

§570.16 Extradition of persons not present in demanding state at time of commission of crime.

The governor of this state may also surrender, on demand of the executive authority of any other state, any person in this state charged in such other state in the manner provided in section 570.08 with committing an act in this state or in a third state, intentionally resulting in a crime in the state whose executive authority is making the demand, when the acts for which extradition is sought would be punishable by the laws of this state, if the consequences claimed to have resulted therefrom in the demanding state had taken effect in this state; and the provisions of this article not otherwise inconsistent, shall apply to such cases, even though the accused was not in that state at the time of the commission of the crime, and has not fled therefrom; provided, however, that the governor of this state may, in his discretion, make any such surrender conditional upon agreement by the executive authority of the demanding state, that the person so surrendered will be held to answer no criminal charges of any nature except those set forth in the requisition upon which such person is so surrendered, at least until such person has been given reasonable opportunity to return to this state after his acquittal, if he shall be acquitted, or if he shall be convicted, after he shall be released from confinement. Nothing in this section shall apply to the crime of libel.

§570.18 Issuance of warrant of arrest by governor; recitals therein.

If the governor decides that the demand should be complied with, he shall sign a warrant of arrest, which shall be sealed with the state seal, and be directed to any police officer or other person whom he may think fit to entrust with the execution thereof. The warrant must substantially recite the facts necessary to the validity of its issuance.

§570.20 Execution of warrant; manner and place thereof.

Such warrant shall authorize the police officer or other person to whom directed to arrest the accused at any time and any place where he may be found within the state and to command the aid of all police officers or other persons in the execution of the warrant, and to deliver the accused, subject to the provisions of this article to the duly authorized agent of the demanding state.

§570.22 Authority of arresting officer.

Every such police officer or other person empowered to make the arrest, shall have the same authority, in arresting the accused to command assistance therein, as police officers have by law in the execution of any criminal process directed to them, with like penalties against those who refuse their assistance.

§570.24 Rights of accused person; application for writ of habeas corpus.

No person arrested upon such warrant shall be delivered over to the agent whom the executive authority demanding him shall have appointed to receive him unless he shall first be taken forthwith before a justice or judge of a court of record in this state, who shall inform him of the demand made for his surrender and of the crime with which he is charged, and that he has the right to demand and procure legal counsel; and if the prisoner or his counsel shall state that he or they desire to test the legality of his arrest, the justice or judge of such court of record shall fix a reasonable time to be allowed within which to apply for a writ of habeas corpus. When such writ is applied for, notice thereof, and of the time and place of hearing thereon, shall be given to the district attorney of the county in which the arrest is made and in which the accused is in custody, and to the said agent of the demanding state.

§570.26 Noncompliance with preceding section; penalties for violation.

Any officer who shall deliver to the agent for extradition of the demanding state a person in his custody under the governor's warrant, in disobedience of the preceding section, shall be guilty of a felony.

§570.28 Confinement of the accused in jail when necessary.

The officer or persons executing the governor's warrant of arrest, or the agent of the demanding state to whom the prisoner may have been delivered may, when necessary, confine the prisoner in the jail of any county or city through which he may pass; and the keeper of such jail must receive and safely keep the prisoner until the officer or person having charge of him is ready to proceed on his route, such officer or person, however, being chargeable with the expense of keeping.

§570.30 Confinement of extradited persons passing through this state.

The officer or agent of a demanding state to whom a prisoner may have been delivered following extradition proceedings in another state, or to whom a prisoner may have been delivered after waiving extradition in such other state, and who is passing through this state with such a prisoner for the purpose of immediately returning such prisoner to the demanding state may, when necessary, confine the prisoner in the jail of any county or city through which he may pass; and the keeper of such jail must receive and safely keep the prisoner until the officer or agent having charge of him is ready to proceed on his route, such officer or agent, however, being chargeable with the expense of keeping, provided, however, that such officer or agent shall produce and show to the keeper of such jail satisfactory written evidence of the fact that he is actually transporting such prisoner to the demanding state after a requisition by the executive authority of such demanding state or waiver thereof. Such person shall not be entitled to demand a new requisition while in this state.

§570.32 Arrest of accused before making of requisition.

Whenever any person within this state shall be charged on the oath of any credible person before any local criminal court of this state with the commission of any crime in any other state and, except in cases arising under section 570.14 or 570.16, with having fled from justice, or, with having been convicted of a crime in that state and having escaped from confinement, or having broken the terms of his bail, probation or parole, or, whenever complaint shall have been made before any local criminal court in this state setting forth on the affidavit of any credible person in another state that a crime has been committed in such other state and that the accused has been charged in such other state with the commission of the crime, and, except in cases arising under section 570.14 or 570.16, has fled from justice, or with having been convicted of a crime in that state and having escaped from confinement or having broken the terms of his bail, probation or parole and is believed to be in this state, the local criminal court shall issue a warrant directed to any police officer directing him to apprehend the person named therein, wherever he may be found in this state, and to bring him before the same or any other local criminal court which may be available in or convenient of access to the place where the arrest may be made, to answer the charge or complaint and affidavit, and a certified copy of the sworn charge or complaint and affidavit upon which the warrant is issued shall be attached to such warrant.

§570.34 Arrest of accused without warrant therefor.

The arrest of a person in this state may be lawfully made also by any police officer or a private person, without a warrant, upon reasonable information that the accused stands charged in the courts of another state with a crime punishable by death or imprisonment for a term exceeding one year; but when so arrested the accused must be taken before a local criminal court with all practicable speed and complaint must be made against him under oath setting forth the ground for the arrest as in the preceding section; and, thereafter, his answers shall be heard as if he had been arrested on a warrant.

§570.36 Commitment to await requisition; bail.

If from the examination before the local criminal court it appears that the person held is the person charged with having committed the crime alleged, and, except in cases arising under section 570.14 or 570.16, that he has fled from justice, the local criminal court must, by a warrant reciting the accusation, commit him to the county jail for such a time not exceeding thirty days and specified in the warrant, as will enable the arrest of the accused to be made under a warrant of the governor on a requisition of the executive authority of the state having jurisdiction of the offense, unless the accused gives bail as provided in the next section, or until he shall be legally discharged.

§570.38 Bail; in what cases; conditions of bond.

Unless the offense with which the prisoner is charged is shown to be an offense punishable by death or life imprisonment under the laws of the state in which it was committed, a justice of the supreme court or county judge in this state may admit the person arrested to bail by bond or undertaking, with sufficient sureties, and in such sum as he deems proper, conditioned for his appearance before him at a time specified in such bond or undertaking but not later than thirty days after the examination referred to in section 570.36 and for his surrender, to be arrested upon the warrant of the governor of this state.

§570.40 Extension of time of commitment; adjournment.

If the accused is not arrested under warrant of the governor by the expiration of the time specified in the warrant, bond or undertaking, a local criminal court may discharge him or may recommit him for a further period of sixty days, or for further periods not to exceed in the aggregate sixty days, or a supreme court justice or county judge may again take bail for his appearance and surrender, as provided in section 570.38 but within a period not to exceed sixty days after the date of such new bond or undertaking.

§570.42 Bail; when forfeited.

If the prisoner is admitted to bail, and fails to appear and surrender himself according to the conditions of his bond or undertaking, the justice of the supreme court or county judge, by proper order, shall declare the bond forfeited and order his immediate arrest without warrant if he be within this state. Recovery may be had on such bond or undertaking in the name of the state as in the case of other bonds or undertakings given by the accused in criminal proceedings within this state.

§570.44 Persons under criminal prosecution in this state at time of requisition.

If a criminal prosecution has been instituted against such person under the laws of this state and is still pending, the governor, in his discretion, may either surrender him on demand of the executive authority of another state or hold him until he has been tried and discharged or convicted and punished in this state.

§570.46 Guilt or innocence of accused; when inquired into.

The guilt or innocence of the accused as to the crime with which he is charged may not be inquired into by the governor, or in any proceeding after the demand for extradition accompanied by a charge of crime in legal form as above provided shall have been presented to the governor, except as it may be involved in identifying the person held as the person charged with the crime.

§570.48 Alias warrant of arrest.

The governor may recall his warrant of arrest or may issue another warrant whenever he deems proper.

§570.50 Written waiver of extradition proceedings.

Any person arrested in this state charged with having committed any crime in another state or alleged to have escaped from confinement, or broken the terms of his bail, probation or parole, may waive the issuance and service of the warrant provided for in sections 570.18 and 570.20 and all other procedure incidental to extradition proceedings by executing or subscribing in the presence of a judge of any court of record within this state a writing which states that he consents to return to the demanding state, provided, however, that before such waiver shall be executed or subscribed by such person it shall be the duty of such judge to inform such person of his rights to the issuance and service of a warrant of extradition and to obtain a writ of habeas corpus as provided for in section 570.24.

If and when such consent has been duly executed and it shall forthwith be forwarded to the office of the secretary of state of this state and filed therein. The judge shall direct the officer having such person in custody to deliver forthwith such person to the duly accredited agent or agents of the demanding state, and shall deliver or cause to be delivered to such agent or agents a copy of such consent. Provided, however, that nothing in this section shall be deemed to limit the rights of the accused person to return voluntarily and without formality to the demanding state, nor shall this waiver procedure be deemed to be an exclusive procedure or to limit the powers, rights or duties of the officers of the demanding state or of this state.

§570.52 Fugitives from this state; duty of governor.

Whenever the governor of this state shall demand a person charged with crime or with escaping from confining or breaking the terms of his bail, probation or parole in this state from the executive authority of any other state, or from the chief justice or an associate justice of the supreme court of the District of Columbia authorized to receive such demand under the laws of the United States, he shall issue a warrant under the seal of this state to some agent commanding him to receive the person so charged, if delivered to him, and convey him to the proper officer of the county in this state in which the offense was committed.

§570.54 Application for issuance of requisition; by whom made; contents.

1. When the return to this state of a person charged with crime in this state is required, the district attorney of the county in which the offense was committed, or, if the offense is one which is cognizable by him or her, the attorney general shall present to the governor his or her written application for a requisition for the return of the person charged, in which application shall be stated the name of the person so charged, the crime charged against him or her, the approximate time, place and circumstances of its commission, the state in which he or she is believed to be, including the location of the accused therein at the time the application is made and certifying that, in the opinion of the said district attorney or attorney general the ends of justice require the arrest and return of the accused to this state for trial and that the proceeding is not instituted to enforce a private claim.

2. When there is required the return to this state of a person who has been convicted of a crime in this state and has escaped from confinement or broken the terms of his or her bail, probation or parole, the district attorney of the county in which the offense was committed, the warden of the institution or sheriff of the county, from which escape was made, or the commissioner of the state department of corrections and community supervision or his or her designee shall present to the governor a written application for a requisition for the return of such person, in which application shall be stated the name of the person, the crime of which he or she was convicted, the circumstances of his or her escape from confinement or of the breach of the terms of his or her bail, probation or parole, the state in which he or she is believed to be, including the location of the person therein at the time the application is made.

3. The application shall be verified by affidavit, shall be executed in duplicate and shall be accompanied by two certified copies of the accusatory instrument stating the offense with which the accused is charged, or of the judgment of conviction or of the sentence. The district attorney, attorney general, warden, sheriff or the commissioner of the state department of corrections and community supervision or his or her designee may also attach such further affidavits and other documents in duplicate as he or she shall deem proper to be submitted with such application. One copy of the application, with the action of the governor indicated by endorsement thereon, and one of the certified copies of the accusatory instrument, or of the judgment of conviction or the sentence shall be filed in the office of the secretary of state to remain of record in that office. The other copies of all papers shall be forwarded with the governor's requisition.

§570.56 Expense of extradition.

The expenses of extradition must be borne by the county from which the pplication for a requisition comes or, where the application is made by the attorney general, by the county in which the offense was committed. In the case of extradition of a person who has been convicted of a crime in this state and has escaped from a state prison or reformatory, the expense of extradition shall be borne by the department of corrections and community supervision. Where a person has broken the terms of his or her parole from a state prison or reformatory, the expense of extradition shall be borne by the state department of corrections and community supervision. Where a person has broken the terms of his or her bail or probation, the expense of extradition shall be borne by the county. Where a person has been convicted but not yet confined to a prison, or has been sentenced for a felony to a county jail or penitentiary and escapes, the expenses of extradition shall be charged to the county from whose custody the escape is effected. Nothing in this section shall preclude a county or the department of corrections and community supervision, as the case may be, from collecting the expenses involved in extradition from the person who was extradited.

§570.58 Immunity from service of process in certain civil actions.

A person brought into this state on or after waiver of extradition based on a criminal charge shall not be subject to service of personal process in civil actions arising out of the same facts as the criminal proceeding to answer which he is being or has been returned until he has been convicted in the criminal proceeding, or if acquitted, until he has had reasonable opportunity to return to the state from which he was extradicted.*

(So in original. probably should read "extradited".)

§570.60 No immunity from other criminal prosecution while in this state.

After a person has been brought back to this state by extradition proceedings, he may be tried in this state for other offenses which he may be charged with having committed here as well as that specified in the requisition for his extradition.

§570.62 Non-waiver by this state.

Nothing in this article contained shall be deemed to constitute a waiver by this state of its right, power or privilege to try such demanded person for offenses committed within this state, or of its right, power or privilege to regain custody of such person by extradition proceedings or otherwise for the purpose of trial, sentence or punishment for any offense committed within this state, nor shall any proceedings had under this article which result in, or fail to result in, extradition be deemed a waiver by this state of any of its rights, privileges or jurisdiction in any way whatsoever.

§570.64 Interpretation.

The provisions of this article shall be so interpreted and construed as to effectuate its general purposes to make uniform the law of those states which enact it.

§570.66 Constitutionality.

If any part of this article is for any reason declared void, such invalidity shall not affect the validity of the remaining portions thereof.

ARTICLE 580 - SECURING ATTENDANCE OF DEFENDANTS CONFINED AS PRISONERS IN INSTITUTIONS OF OTHER JURISDICTIONS OF THE UNITED STATES--RENDITION TO OTHER JURISDICTIONS OF PERSONS CONFINED AS PRISONERS IN THIS STATE--AGREEMENT ON DETAINERS

Section
580.10 Securing attendance of defendants confined as prisoners in institutions of other jurisdictions of the United States; methods.
580.20 Agreement on detainers.
580.30 Securing attendance of defendants confined in federal prisons.

§580.10 Securing attendance of defendants confined as prisoners in institutions of other jurisdictions of the United States; methods.

The attendance in a criminal action pending in a court of this state of a defendant confined as a prisoner in an institution of another jurisdiction of the United States may, under prescribed circumstances, be secured pursuant to:

1. Section 570.12 of article five hundred seventy, known as the uniform criminal extradition act; or

2. Section 580.20, known as the agreement on detainers; or

3. Section 580.30.

§580.20 Agreement on detainers.

The agreement on detainers is hereby enacted into law and entered into by this state with all other jurisdictions legally joining therein in the form substantially as follows:

TEXT OF THE AGREEMENT ON DETAINERS
The contracting states solemnly agree that:

ARTICLE I

The party states find that charges outstanding against a prisoner, detainers based on untried indictments, informations or complaints, and difficulties in securing speedy trial of persons already incarcerated in other jurisdictions, produce uncertainties which obstruct programs of prisoner treatment and rehabilitation. Accordingly, it is the policy of the party states and the purpose of this agreement to encourage the expeditious and orderly disposition of such charges and determination of the proper status of any and all detainers based on untried indictments, informations or complaints. The party states also find that proceedings with reference to such charges and detainers, when emanating from another jurisdiction, cannot properly be had in the absence of cooperative procedures. It is the further purpose of this agreement to provide such cooperative procedures.

ARTICLE II

As used in this agreement:

(a) "State" shall mean a state of the United States; the United States of America; a territory or possession of the United States; the District of Columbia; the Commonwealth of Puerto Rico.

(b) "Sending state" shall mean a state in which a prisoner is incarcerated at the time that he initiates a request for final disposition pursuant to Article

III hereof or at the time that a request for custody or availability is initiated pursuant to Article IV hereof.

(c) "Receiving state" shall mean the state in which trial is to be had on an indictment, information or complaint pursuant to Article III or Article IV hereof.

ARTICLE III

(a) Whenever a person has entered upon a term of imprisonment in a penal or correctional institution of a party state, and whenever during the continuance of the term of imprisonment there is pending in any other party state any untried indictment, information or complaint on the basis of which a detainer has been lodged against the prisoner, he shall be brought to trial within one hundred eighty days after he shall have caused to be delivered to the prosecuting officer and the appropriate court of the prosecuting officer's jurisdiction written notice of the place of his imprisonment and his request for a final disposition to be made of the indictment, information or complaint; provided that for good cause shown in open court, the prisoner or his counsel being present, the court having jurisdiction of the matter may grant any necessary or reasonable continuance. The request of the prisoner shall be accompanied by a certificate of the appropriate official having custody of the prisoner, stating the term of commitment under which the prisoner is being held, the time already served, the time remaining to be served on the sentence, the amount of good time earned, the time of parole eligibility of the prisoner, and any decisions of the state parole agency relating to the prisoner.

(b) The written notice and request for final disposition referred to in paragraph (a) hereof shall be given or sent by the prisoner to the warden, commissioner of correction or other official having custody of him, who shall promptly forward it together with the certificate to the appropriate prosecuting official and court by registered or certified mail, return receipt requested.

(c) The warden, commissioner of correction or other official having custody of the prisoner shall promptly inform him of the source and contents of any detainer lodged against him and shall also inform him of his right to make a request for final disposition of the indictment, information or complaint on which the detainer is based.

(d) Any request for final disposition made by a prisoner pursuant to paragraph (a) hereof shall operate as a request for final disposition of all untried indictments, informations or complaints on the basis of which detainers have been lodged against the prisoner from the state to whose prosecuting official the request for final disposition is specifically directed. The warden, commissioner of correction or other official having custody of the prisoner shall forthwith notify all appropriate prosecuting officers and courts in the several jurisdictions within the state to which the prisoner's request for final disposition is being sent of the proceeding being initiated by the prisoner. Any notification sent pursuant to this paragraph shall be accompanied by copies of the prisoner's written notice, request, and the certificate. If trial is not had on any indictment, information or complaint contemplated hereby prior to the return of the prisoner to the original place of imprisonment, such indictment, information or complaint shall not be of any further force or effect, and the court shall enter an order dismissing the same with prejudice.

(e) Any request for final disposition made by a prisoner pursuant to paragraph (a) hereof shall also be deemed to be a waiver of extradition with respect to any charge or proceeding contemplated thereby or included therein by reason of paragraph (d) hereof, and a waiver of extradition to the receiving state to serve any sentence there imposed upon him, after completion of his term of imprisonment in the sending state. The request for final disposition shall also constitute a consent by the prisoner to the production of his body in any court where his presence may be required in order to effectuate the purposes of this agreement and a further consent voluntarily to be returned to the original place of imprisonment in accordance with the provisions of this agreement. Nothing in this paragraph shall prevent the imposition of a concurrent sentence if otherwise permitted by law.

(f) Escape from custody by the prisoner subsequent to his execution of the request for final disposition referred to in paragraph (a) hereof shall void the request.

ARTICLE IV

(a) The appropriate officer of the jurisdiction in which an untried indictment, information or complaint is pending shall be entitled to have a prisoner against whom he has lodged a detainer and who is serving a term of imprisonment in any party state made available in accordance with Article V (a) hereof upon presentation of a written request for temporary custody or availability to the appropriate authorities of the state in which the prisoner is incarcerated; provided that the court having jurisdiction of such indictment, information or complaint shall have duly approved, recorded and transmitted the request; and provided further that there shall be a period of thirty days after receipt by the appropriate authorities before the request be honored, within which period the governor of the sending state may disapprove the request for temporary custody or availability, either upon his own motion or upon motion of the prisoner.

(b) Upon receipt of the officer's written request as provided in paragraph (a) hereof, the appropriate authorities having the prisoner in custody shall furnish the officer with a certificate stating the term of commitment under which the prisoner is being held, the time already served, the time remaining to be served on the sentence, the amount of good time earned, the time of parole eligibility of the prisoner, and any decisions of the state parole agency relating to the prisoner. Said authorities simultaneously shall furnish all other officers and appropriate courts in the receiving state who have lodged detainers against the prisoner with similar certificates and with notices informing them of the request for custody or availability and of the reasons therefor.

(c) In respect of any proceeding made possible by this Article, trial shall be commenced within one hundred twenty days of the arrival of the prisoner in the receiving state, but for good cause shown in open court, the prisoner or his counsel being present, the court having jurisdiction of the matter may grant any necessary or reasonable continuance.

(d) Nothing contained in this Article shall be construed to deprive any prisoner of any right which he may have to contest the legality of his delivery as provided in paragraph (a) hereof but such delivery may not be opposed or denied on the ground that the executive authority of the sending state has not affirmatively consented to or ordered such delivery.

(e) If trial is not had on any indictment, information or complaint contemplated hereby prior to the prisoner's being returned to the original place of imprisonment pursuant to Article V (e) hereof, such indictment, information or complaint shall not be of any further force or effect, and the court shall enter an order dismissing the same with prejudice.

ARTICLE V

(a) In response to a request made under Article III or Article IV hereof, the appropriate authority in a sending state shall offer to deliver temporary custody of such prisoner to the appropriate authority in the state where such indictment, information or complaint is pending against such person in order that speedy and efficient prosecution may be had. If the request for final disposition is made by the prisoner, the offer of temporary custody shall accompany the written notice provided for in Article III of this agreement. In the case of a federal prisoner, the appropriate authority in receiving state shall be entitled to temporary custody as provided by this agreement or to the prisoner's presence in federal custody at the place for trial, whichever custodial arrangement may be approved by the custodian.

(b) The officer or other representative of a state accepting an offer of temporary custody shall present the following upon demand:

(1) Proper identification and evidence of his authority to act for the state into whose temporary custody the prisoner is to be given.

(2) A duly certified copy of the indictment, information or complaint on the basis of which the detainer has been lodged and on the basis of which the request for temporary custody of the prisoner has been made.

(c) If the appropriate authority shall refuse or fail to accept temporary custody of said person, or in the event that an action on the indictment, information or complaint on the basis of which the detainer has been lodged is not brought to trial within the period provided in Article III or Article IV hereof, the appropriate court of the jurisdiction where the indictment, information or complaint has been pending shall enter an order dismissing the same with prejudice, and any detainer based thereon shall cease to be of any force or effect.

(d) The temporary custody referred to in this agreement shall be only for the purpose of permitting prosecution on the charge or charges contained in one or more untried indictments, informations or complaints which form the basis of the detainer or detainers or for prosecution on any other charge or charges arising out of the same transaction. Except for his attendance at court and while being transported to or from any place at which his presence may be required, the prisoner shall be held in a suitable jail or other facility regularly used for persons awaiting prosecution.

(e) At the earliest practicable time consonant with the purposes of this agreement, the prisoner shall be returned to the sending state.

(f) During the continuance of temporary custody or while the prisoner is otherwise being made available for trial as required by this agreement, time being served on the sentence shall continue to run but good time shall be earned by the prisoner only if, and to the extent that, the law and practice of the jurisdiction which imposed the sentence may allow.

(g) For all purposes other than that for which temporary custody as provided in this agreement is exercised, the prisoner shall be deemed to remain in the custody of and subject to the jurisdiction of the sending state and any escape from temporary custody may be dealt with in the same manner as an escape from the original place of imprisonment or in any other manner permitted by law.

(h) From the time that a party state receives custody of a prisoner pursuant to this agreement until such prisoner is returned to the territory and custody of the sending state, the state in which the one or more untried indictments, informations or complaints are pending or in which trial is being had shall be responsible for the prisoner and shall also pay all costs of transporting, caring for, keeping and returning the prisoner. The provisions of this paragraph shall govern unless the states concerned shall have entered into a supplementary agreement providing for a different allocation of costs and responsibilities as between or among themselves. Nothing herein contained shall be construed to alter or affect any internal relationship among the departments, agencies and officers of and in the government of a party state, or between a party state and its subdivisions, as to the payment of costs, or responsibilities therefor.

ARTICLE VI

(a) In determining the duration and expiration dates of the time periods provided in Articles III and IV of this agreement, the running of said time periods shall be tolled whenever and for as long as the prisoner is unable to stand trial, as determined by the court having jurisdiction of the matter.

(b) No provision of this agreement, and no remedy made available by this agreement, shall apply to any person who is adjudged to be mentally ill.

ARTICLE VII

Each state party to this agreement shall designate an officer who, acting jointly with like officers of other party states, shall promulgate rules and regulations to carry out more effectively the terms and provisions of this agreement, and who shall provide, within and without the state, information necessary to the effective operation of this agreement.

ARTICLE VIII

This agreement shall enter into full force and effect as to a party state when such state has enacted the same into law. A state party to this agreement may withdraw herefrom by enacting a statute repealing the same. However, the withdrawal of any state shall not affect the status of any proceedings already initiated by incarcerated individuals or by state officers at the time such withdrawal takes effect, nor shall it affect their rights in respect thereof.   *(Eff.8/2/21,Ch.322,L.2021)*

ARTICLE IX

1. This agreement shall be liberally construed so as to effectuate its purposes. The provisions of this agreement shall be severable and if any phrase, clause, sentence or provision of this agreement is declared to be

contrary to the constitution of any party state or of the United States or the applicability thereof to any government, agency, person or circumstance is held invalid, the validity of the remainder of this agreement and the applicability thereof to any government, agency, person or circumstance shall not be affected thereby. If this agreement shall be held contrary to the constitution of any state party hereto, the agreement shall remain in full force and effect as to the remaining states and in full force and effect as to the state affected as to all severable matters.

2. The phrase "appropriate court" as used in the agreement on detainers shall, with reference to the courts of this state, mean any court with criminal jurisdiction.

3. All courts, departments, agencies, officers and employees of this state and its political subdivisions are hereby directed to enforce the agreement on detainers and to cooperate with one another and with other party states in enforcing the agreement and effectuating its purposes.

4. Escape from custody while in another state pursuant to the agreement on detainers shall constitute an offense against the laws of this state to the same extent and degree as an escape from the institution in which the prisoner was confined immediately prior to having been sent to another state pursuant to the provisions of the agreement on detainers and shall be punishable in the same manner as an escape from said institution.

5. It shall be lawful and mandatory upon the warden or other official in charge of a penal or correctional institution in this state to give over the person of any incarcerated individual thereof whenever so required by the operation of the agreement on detainers.   *(Eff.8/2/21,Ch.322,L.2021)*

6. The governor is hereby authorized and empowered to designate an administrator who shall perform the duties and functions and exercise the powers conferred upon such person by Article VII of the agreement on detainers.

7. In order to implement Article IV (a) of the agreement on detainers, and in furtherance of its purposes, the appropriate authorities having custody of the prisoner shall, promptly upon receipt of the officer's written request, notify the prisoner and the governor in writing that a request for temporary custody has been made and such notification shall describe the source and contents of said request. The authorities having custody of the prisoner shall also advise him in writing of his rights to counsel, to make representations to the governor within thirty days, and to contest the legality of his delivery.

§580.30 Securing attendance of defendants confined in federal prisons.

1. A defendant against whom a criminal action is pending in a court of record of this state, and who is confined in a federal prison or custody either within or outside the state, may, with the consent of the attorney general of the United States, be produced in such court for the purpose of criminal prosecution, pursuant to the provisions of:

(a) Section four thousand eighty-five of title eighteen of the United States Code; or

(b) Subdivision two of this section.

2. When such a defendant is in federal custody as specified in subdivision one, a superior court, at a term held in the county in which the criminal action against him is pending, may, upon application of the district attorney of such county, issue a certificate, known as a writ of habeas corpus ad prosequendum,

addressed to the attorney general of the United States, certifying that such defendant has been charged by the particular accusatory instrument filed against him in the specified court with the offense or offenses alleged therein, and that attendance of the defendant in such court for the purpose of criminal prosecution thereon is necessary in the interest of justice, and requesting the attorney general of the United States to cause such defendant to be produced in such court, under custody of a federal public servant, upon a designated date and for a period of time necessary to complete the prosecution. Upon issuing such a certificate, the court may deliver it, or cause or authorize it to be delivered, together with a certified copy of the accusatory instrument upon which it is based, to the attorney general of the United States or to his representative authorized to entertain the request.

ARTICLE 590 - SECURING ATTENDANCE OF DEFENDANTS WHO ARE OUTSIDE THE UNITED STATES

Section
590.10 Securing attendance of defendants who are outside the United States.

§590.10 Securing attendance of defendants who are outside the United States.

1. When a criminal action for an offense committed in this state is pending in a criminal court of this state against a defendant who is in a foreign country with which the United States has an extradition treaty, and when the accusatory instrument charges an offense which is declared in such treaty to be an extraditable one, the district attorney of the county in which such offense was allegedly committed may make an application to the Governor, requesting him to make an application to the President of the United States to institute extradition proceedings for the return of the defendant to this country and state for the purpose of prosecution of such action. The district attorney's application must comply with rules, regulations and guidelines established by the Governor for such applications and must be accompanied by all the accusatory instruments, affidavits and other documents required by such rules, regulations and guidelines.

2. Upon receipt of the district attorney's application, the Governor, if satisfied that the defendant is in the foreign country in question, that the offense charged is an extraditable one pursuant to the treaty in question, and that there are no factors or impediments which in law preclude such an extradition, may in his discretion make an application, addressed to the secretary of state of the United States, requesting that the President of the United States institute extradition proceedings for the return of the defendant from such foreign country. The Governor's application must comply with rules, regulations and guidelines established by the secretary of state for such applications and must be accompanied by all accusatory instruments, affidavits and other documents required by such rules, regulations and guidelines.

3. If the Governor's application is granted and the extradition is achieved or attempted, all expenses incurred therein must be borne by the county from which the application emanated.

4. The provisions of this section apply equally to extradition or attempted extradition of a person who is a fugitive following the entry of a judgment of conviction against him in a criminal court of this state.

ARTICLE 600 - SECURING ATTENDANCE OF CORPORATE DEFENDANTS AND RELATED MATTERS

Section
600.10 Corporate defendants; securing attendance.
600.20 Corporate defendants; prosecution thereof.

§600.10 Corporate defendants; securing attendance.

1. The court attendance of a corporation for purposes of commencing or prosecuting a criminal action against it may be accomplished by the issuance and service of a summons or an appearance ticket if such action has been or is about to be commenced in a local criminal court, and by a corporate summons if such action has been commenced in a superior court. Such process must be served upon the corporation by delivery thereof to an officer, director, managing or general agent, or cashier or assistant cashier of such corporation or to any other agent of such corporation authorized by appointment or by law to receive service of process.

2. A "corporate summons" is a process issued by a superior court directing a corporate defendant designated in an indictment to appear before it at a designated future time in connection with such indictment. A corporate summons must be generally in the form of a summons as prescribed in subdivision two of section 130.10. A corporate summons may be served by a public servant designated by the issuing court, and may be served anywhere in the state.

§600.20 Corporate defendants; prosecution thereof.

At all stages of a criminal action, from the commencement thereof through sentence, a corporate defendant must appear by counsel. Upon failure of appearance at the time such defendant is required to enter a plea to the accusatory instrument, the court may enter a plea of guilty and impose sentence.

TITLE R - PROCEDURES FOR SECURING ATTENDANCE OF WITNESSES IN CRIMINAL ACTIONS

ARTICLE 610 - SECURING ATTENDANCE OF WITNESSES BY SUBPOENA

Section
610.10 Securing attendance of witnesses by subpoena; in general.
610.20 Securing attendance of witnesses by subpoena; when and by whom subpoena may be issued.
610.25 Securing attendance of witness by subpoena; possession of physical evidence.
610.30 Securing attendance of witnesses by subpoena; where subpoena may be served.
610.40 Securing attendance of witnesses by subpoena; how and by whom subpoena may be served.
610.50 Securing attendance of witness by subpoena; fees.

§610.10 Securing attendance of witnesses by subpoena; in general.

1. Under circumstances prescribed in this article, a person at liberty within the state may be required to attend a criminal court action or proceeding as a witness by the issuance and service upon him of a subpoena.

2. A "subpoena" is a process of a court directing the person to whom it is addressed to attend and appear as a witness in a designated action or proceeding in such court, on a designated date and any recessed or adjourned date of the action or proceeding. If the witness is given reasonable notice of such recess or adjournment, no further process is required to compel his attendance on the adjourned date.

3. As used in this article, "subpoena" includes a "subpoena duces tecum." A subpoena duces tecum is a subpoena requiring the witness to bring with him and produce specified physical evidence.

§610.20 Securing attendance of witnesses by subpoena; when and by whom subpoena may be issued.

1. Any criminal court may issue a subpoena for the attendance of a witness in any criminal action or proceeding in such court.

2. A district attorney, or other prosecutor where appropriate, as an officer of a criminal court in which he is conducting the prosecution of a criminal action or proceeding, may issue a subpoena of such court, subscribed by himself, for the attendance in such court or a grand jury thereof of any witness whom the people are entitled to call in such action or proceeding.

3. An attorney for a defendant in a criminal action or proceeding, as an officer of a criminal court, may issue a subpoena of such court, subscribed by himself, for the attendance in such court of any witness whom the defendant is entitled to call in such action or proceeding. An attorney for a defendant may not issue a subpoena duces tecum of the court directed to any department, bureau or agency of the state or of a political subdivision thereof, or to any officer or representative thereof, unless the subpoena is indorsed by the court and provides at least three days for the production of the requested materials. In the case of an emergency, the court may by order dispense with the three-day production period. *(Eff.1/1/20,Ch.59,L.2019)*

4. The showing required to sustain any subpoena under this section is that the testimony or evidence sought is reasonably likely to be relevant and material to the proceedings, and the subpoena is not overbroad or unreasonably burdensome. *(Eff.1/1/20,Ch.59,L.2019)*

§610.25 Securing attendance of witness by subpoena; possession of physical evidence.

1. Where a subpoena duces tecum is issued on reasonable notice to the person subpoenaed, the court or grand jury shall have the right to possession of the subpoenaed evidence. Such evidence may be retained by the court, grand jury or district attorney on behalf of the grand jury.

2. The possession shall be for a period of time, and on terms and conditions, as may reasonably be required for the action or proceeding. The reasonableness of such possession, time, terms, and conditions shall be determined with consideration for, among other things, (a) the good cause shown by the party issuing the subpoena or in whose behalf the subpoena is issued, (b) the rights and legitimate needs of the person subpoenaed and (c) the feasibility and appropriateness of making copies of the evidence. The cost of reproduction and transportation incident thereto shall be borne by the person or party issuing the subpoena unless the court determines otherwise in the interest of justice. Nothing in this article shall be deemed to

prohibit the designation of a return date for a subpoena duces tecum prior to trial. Where physical evidence specified to be produced will be sought to be retained in custody, notice of such fact shall be given the subpoenaed party. In any case where the court receives or retains evidence prior to trial, it may, as may otherwise be authorized by law, grant the issuing party a reasonable opportunity to inspect such evidence.

§610.30 Securing attendance of witnesses by subpoena; where subpoena may be served.

1. A subpoena of any criminal court, issued pursuant to section 610.20, may be served anywhere in the county of issuance or anywhere in adjoining county.

2. A subpoena of a superior court or of a superior court judge sitting as a local criminal court, issued pursuant to section 610.20, may be served anywhere in the state.

3. A subpoena of a district court or of the New York City criminal court, issued pursuant to section 610.20, may be served anywhere in the state; provided that, if such subpoena is issued by a prosecutor or by an attorney for a defendant, it may be served in a county other than the county of issuance or an adjoining county only if such court, upon application of such prosecutor or attorney, endorses upon such subpoena an order for the attendance of the witness.

4. A subpoena of a city court or a town court or a village court, issued pursuant to section 610.20, may be served in a county other than the one of issuance or an adjoining county if a judge of a superior court, upon application of the issuing court or the district attorney or an attorney for the defendant, endorses upon such subpoena an order for the attendance of the witness.

§610.40 Securing attendance of witnesses by subpoena; how and by whom subpoena may be served.

A subpoena may be served by any person more than eighteen years old. Service must be made in the manner provided by the civil practice law and rules for the service of subpoenas in civil cases.

§610.50 Securing attendance of witness by subpoena; fees.

1. A witness subpoenaed by the people in a criminal action is entitled to the same fees and mileage as a witness in a civil action, payable by the treasurer of the county upon the certificate of the court or the clerk thereof, stating the number of days the witness actually attended and the number of miles traveled by him in order to attend. In any such action, the court may, by order, direct the county treasurer to pay to such witness a further reasonable sum for expenses, to be specified in the order, and the county treasurer, upon the production of the order or a certified copy thereof, must pay the witness the sum specified therein out of the county treasury. Such certificates shall only be issued by the court or the clerk thereof, upon the production of the affidavit of the witness, stating that he attended as such either on subpoena or request of the district attorney, the number of miles necessarily traveled and the duration of attendance. An officer in any state department who attends as a witness under this section in his official capacity, or in consequence of any official action taken by him, and who receives a fixed sum in lieu of expenses, or who is entitled to receive the actual expenses incurred by him in the discharge of his official duties, is not entitled to the compensation herein provided.

2. A witness subpoenaed by the defendant in a criminal action is not entitled as of right to witness and mileage fees, but the court may in its discretion, by order, direct the county treasurer to pay to such a witness a reasonable sum for expenses, to be specified in the order. Upon the production of the order or a certified copy thereof, the county treasurer must pay the witness the sum specified therein, out of the county treasury.

ARTICLE 620 - SECURING ATTENDANCE OF WITNESSES BY MATERIAL WITNESS ORDER

Section
620.10 Material witness order; defined.
620.20 Material witness order; when authorized; by what courts issuable; duration thereof.
620.30 Material witness order; commencement of proceeding by application; procurement of appearance of prospective witness.
620.40 Material witness order; arraignment.
620.50 Material witness order; hearing, determination and execution of order.
620.60 Material witness order; vacation, modification and amendment thereof.
620.70 Material witness order; compelling attendance of witness who fails to appear.
620.80 Material witness order; witness fee.

§620.10 Material witness order; defined.

A material witness order is a court order (a) adjudging a person a material witness in a pending criminal action and (b) fixing bail to secure his future attendance thereat.

§620.20 Material witness order; when authorized; by what courts issuable; duration thereof.

1. A material witness order may be issued upon the ground that there is reasonable cause to believe that a person whom the people or the defendant desire to call as a witness in a pending criminal action:

(a) Possesses information material to the determination of such action; and

(b) Will not be amenable or responsive to a subpoena at a time when his attendance will be sought.

2. A material witness order may be issued only when:

(a) An indictment has been filed in a superior court and is currently pending therein; or

(b) A grand jury proceeding has been commenced and is currently pending; or

(c) A felony complaint has been filed with a local criminal court and is currently pending therein.

3. The following courts may issue material witness orders under the indicated circumstances:

(a) When an indictment has been filed, or a grand jury proceeding has been commenced, or a defendant has been held by a local criminal court for the action of a grand jury, a material witness order may be issued only by the superior court in which such indictment is pending or by which such grand jury has been or is to be impaneled;

(b) When a felony complaint is currently pending in a district court or in the New York City criminal court or before a superior court judge sitting as a local criminal court, a material witness order may be issued either by such court or by the superior court which would have jurisdiction of the case upon a holding of the defendant for the action of the grand jury;

(c) When a felony complaint is currently pending in a city court or a town court or a village court, a material witness order may be issued only by the superior court which would have jurisdiction of the case upon a holding of the defendant for the action of the grand jury.

4. Unless vacated pursuant to section 620.60, a material witness order remains in effect during the following periods of time under the indicated circumstances:

(a) An order issued by a superior court under the circumstances prescribed in paragraph (a) of subdivision three remains in effect during the pendency of the criminal action in such superior court;

(b) An order issued by a district court or the New York City criminal court or a superior court judge sitting as a local criminal court, under circumstances prescribed in paragraph (b) of subdivision three, remains in effect (i) until the disposition of the felony complaint pending in such court, and (ii) if the defendant is held for the action of a grand jury, during the pendency of the grand jury proceeding, and (iii) if an indictment results, for a period of ten days following the filing of such indictment, and (iv) if within such ten day period such order is indorsed by the superior court in which the indictment is pending, during the pendency of the action in such superior court. Upon such indorsement, the order is deemed to be that of the superior court.

(c) An order issued by a superior court under circumstances prescribed in paragraph (c) of subdivision three remains in effect (i) until the disposition of the felony complaint pending in the city, town or village court, and (ii) if the defendant is held for the action of the grand jury, during the pendency of the action in the superior court.

§620.30 Material witness order; commencement of proceeding by application; procurement of appearance of prospective witness.

1. A proceeding to adjudge a person a material witness must be commenced by application to the appropriate court, made in writing and subscribed and sworn to by the applicant, demonstrating reasonable cause to believe the existence of facts, as specified in subdivision one of section 620.20, warranting the adjudication of such person as a material witness.

2. If the court is satisfied that the application is well founded, the prospective witness may be compelled to appear in response thereto as follows:

(a) The court may issue an order directing him to appear therein at a designated time in order that a determination may be made whether he should be adjudged a material witness, and upon personal service of such order or a copy thereof within the state, he must so appear.

(b) If in addition to the allegations specified in subdivision one, the application contains further allegations demonstrating to the satisfaction of the court reasonable cause to believe that (i) the witness would be unlikely to respond to such an order, or (ii) after previously having been served with such an order, he did not respond thereto, the court may issue a warrant addressed to a police officer, directing such officer to take such prospective witness into custody within the state and to bring him before the court forthwith in order that a proceeding may be conducted to determine whether he is to be adjudged a material witness.

§620.40 Material witness order; arraignment.

1. When the prospective witness appears before the court, the court must inform him of the nature and purpose of the proceeding, and that he is entitled to a prompt hearing upon the issue of whether he should be adjudged a material witness. The prospective witness possesses all the rights, and is entitled to all the court instructions, with respect to right to counsel, opportunity to obtain counsel and assignment of counsel in case of financial inability to retain such, which, pursuant to subdivisions three through five of section 180.10, accrue to a defendant arraigned upon a felony complaint in a local criminal court.

2. If the proceeding is adjourned at the prospective witness' instance, for the purpose of obtaining counsel or otherwise, the court must order him to appear upon the adjourned date. The court may further fix bail to secure his appearance upon such date or until the proceeding is completed and, upon default thereof, may commit him to the custody of the sheriff for such period.

§620.50 Material witness order; hearing, determination and execution of order.

1. The hearing upon the application must be conducted as follows:

(a) The applicant has the burden of proving by a preponderance of the evidence all facts essential to support a material witness order, and any testimony so adduced must be given under oath;

(b) The prospective witness may testify under oath or may make an unsworn statement;

(c) The prospective witness may call witnesses in his behalf, and the court must cause process to be issued for any such witness whom he reasonably wishes to call, and any testimony so adduced must be given under oath;

(d) Upon the hearing, evidence tending to demonstrate that the prospective witness does or does not possess information material to the criminal action in issue, or that he will or will not be amenable or respond to a subpoena at the time his attendance will be sought, is admissible even though it consists of hearsay.

2. If the court is satisfied after such hearing that there is reasonable cause to believe that the prospective witness (a) possesses information material to the pending action or proceeding, and (b) will not be amenable or respond to a subpoena at a time when his attendance will be sought, it may issue a material witness order, adjudging him a material witness and fixing bail to secure his future attendance.

3. A material witness order must be executed as follows:

(a) If the bail is posted and approved by the court, the witness must, as provided in subdivision two of section 510.40 of this part, be released and be permitted to remain at liberty; provided that, where the bail is posted by a person other than the witness himself, he may not be so released except upon his signed written consent thereto;

(b) If the bail is not posted, or if though posted it is not approved by the court, the witness must, as provided in subdivision two of section 510.40 of this part, be committed to the custody of the sheriff.

(Eff.1/1/20,Ch.59,L.2019)

§620.60 Material witness order; vacation, modification and amendment thereof.

1. At any time after a material witness order has been issued the court must, upon application of such witness, with notice to the party upon whose application the order was issued, and with opportunity to be heard, make inquiry whether by reason of new or changed facts or circumstances the material witness order is no longer necessary or warranted, or, if it is, whether the original bail currently appears excessive. Upon making any such determination, the court must vacate the order. If its determination is that the order is no longer necessary or warranted, it must, as the situation requires, either discharge the witness from custody or exonerate the bail. If its determination is that the bail is excessive, it must issue a new order fixing bail in a lesser amount or on less burdensome terms.

2. At any time when a witness is at liberty upon bail pursuant to a material witness order, the court may, upon application of the party upon whose application the order was issued, with notice to the witness if possible and to his attorney if any and opportunity to be heard, make inquiry whether, by reason of new or changed facts or circumstances, the original bail is no longer sufficient to secure the future attendance of the witness at the pending action. Upon making such a determination, the court must vacate the order and issue a new order fixing bail in a greater amount or on terms more likely to secure the future attendance of the witness.

§620.70 Material witness order; compelling attendance of witness who fails to appear.

If a witness at liberty on bail pursuant to a material witness order cannot be found or notified at the time his appearance as a witness is required, or if after notification he fails to appear in such action or proceeding as required, the court may issue a warrant, addressed to a police officer, directing such officer to take such witness into custody anywhere within the state and to bring him to the court forthwith.

§620.80 Material witness order; witness fee.

A witness held in the custody of the sheriff as a result of a material witness order must be paid the sum of three dollars per day for each day of confinement in such custody. Such compensation is a county charge and is payable upon release of such material witness from custody or, in the discretion of the court, at any designated times or intervals during the confinement as the court may deem appropriate.

ARTICLE 630 - SECURING ATTENDANCE AS WITNESSES
OF PERSONS CONFINED IN INSTITUTIONS WITHIN THE STATE

Section
630.10 Securing attendance of witnesses confined in institutions within the state; in
        general.
630.20 Securing attendance of witnesses confined in institutions within the state; when
        and by what courts order may be issued.

§630.10 Securing attendance of witnesses confined in institutions within the state; in general.

Under the circumstances prescribed in this article, a person confined in an institution within this state pursuant to a court order may, upon application of a party to a criminal action or proceeding, demonstrating reasonable cause to believe that such person possesses information material thereto, be produced by court order and compelled to attend such action or proceeding as a witness.

§630.20 Securing attendance of witnesses confined in institutions within the state; when and by what courts order may be issued.

The following courts and judges may, under the indicated circumstances, order production as witnesses of persons confined by court order in institutions within the state.

1. If the criminal action or proceeding is one pending in a superior court or with a superior court judge sitting as a local criminal court, such court may, except as provided in subdivision four, order the production as a witness therein of a person confined in any institution in the state.

2. If the criminal action or proceeding is one pending in a district court or the New York City criminal court, such court may order the production as a witness therein of a person confined in any institution within the state other than a state prison. Production therein of a prospective witness confined in a state prison may, except as provided in subdivision four, be ordered, upon application of the party desiring to call him, by a judge of a superior court holding a term thereof in the county in which the action or proceeding is pending.

3. If the criminal action or proceeding is one pending in a city court or a town court or a village court, such court may order the production as a witness therein of a person confined in a county jail of such county. Production therein of a prospective witness confined in any other institution within the state may, except as provided in subdivision four, be ordered, upon application of the party desiring to call him, by a judge of a superior court holding a term thereof in the county in which the action or proceeding is pending.

4. Regardless of the court in which the criminal action or proceeding is pending, production as a witness therein of a prisoner who has been sentenced to death may be ordered, upon application of the party desiring to call him, only by a justice of the appellate division of the department in which the action or proceeding is pending. The application for such order, if made by the defendant, must be upon notice to the district attorney of the county in which the action or proceeding is pending, and an application made by either party must be based upon a showing that the prisoner's attendance is clearly necessary in the interests of justice. Upon issuing such an order, the appellate division justice may fix and include therein any terms or conditions which he deems appropriate for execution thereof.

ARTICLE 640 - SECURING ATTENDANCE AS WITNESSES OF PERSONS AT LIBERTY OUTSIDE THE STATE--RENDITION TO OTHER JURISDICTIONS OF WITNESSES AT LIBERTY WITHIN THE STATE - UNIFORM ACT TO SECURE ATTENDANCE OF WITNESSES FROM WITHOUT THE STATE IN CRIMINAL CASES

Section
640.10   Securing attendance of witnesses from within and without the state in criminal proceedings.

§640.10   Securing attendance of witnesses from within and without the state in criminal proceedings.

1. As used in this section the following words shall have the following meanings unless the context requires otherwise.

"Witness" shall include a person whose testimony is desired in any proceeding or investigation by a grand jury or in a criminal action, prosecution or proceeding.

"State" shall include any territory of the United States and the District of Columbia.

"Subpoena" shall include a summons in any state where a summons is used in lieu of a subpoena.

2. Subpoenaing witness in this state to testify in another state. If a judge of a court of record in any state which by its laws has made provision for commanding persons within that state to attend and testify in this state certifies under the seal of such court that there is a criminal prosecution pending in such court, or that a grand jury investigation has commenced or is about to commence, that a person being within this state is a material witness in such prosecution, or grand jury investigation, and that his presence will be required for a specified number of days, upon presentation of such certificate to a justice of the supreme court or a county judge in the county in which such person is, such justice or judge shall fix a time and place for a hearing, and shall make an order directing the witness to appear at a time and place certain for the hearing.

If at such hearing the justice or judge determines that the witness is material and necessary, that it will not cause undue hardship to the witness to be compelled to attend and testify in the prosecution or a grand jury investigation in the other state, and that the laws of the state in which the prosecution is pending, or grand jury investigation has commenced or is about to commence, will give to him protection from arrest and the service of civil and criminal process, he shall issue a subpoena, with a copy of the certificate attached, directing the witness to attend and testify in the court where the prosecution is pending, or where a grand jury investigation has commenced or is about to commence at a time and place specified in the subpoena. In any such hearing the certificate shall be prima facie evidence of all the facts stated therein.

If said certificate recommends that the witness be taken into immediate custody and delivered to an officer of the requesting state to assure his attendance in the requesting state such justice or judge may, in lieu of notification of the hearing, direct that such witness be forthwith brought before him for said hearing; and the justice or judge at the hearing being satisfied of the desirability of such custody and delivery, for which determination the certificate shall be prima facie proof of such desirability may, in lieu of issuing subpoena, order that said witness be forthwith taken into custody and delivered to an officer of the requesting state.

If the witness, who is subpoenaed as above provided, after being paid or tendered by some properly authorized person the sum of ten cents a mile for each mile and five dollars for each day that he is required to travel and attend as a witness fails without good cause to attend and testify as directed in the subpoena, he shall be punished in the manner provided for the punishment of any witness who disobeys a subpoena issued from a court of record in this state.

3. Witness from another state subpoenaed to testify in this state. If a person in any state, which by its laws has made provision for commanding persons within its borders to attend and testify in criminal prosecutions, or grand jury investigations commenced or about to commence, in this state, is a material witness in a prosecution pending in a court of record in this state, or in a grand jury investigation which has commenced or is about to commence, a judge of such court may issue a certificate under the seal of the court stating these facts and specifying the number of days the witness will be required. This certificate shall be presented to a judge of a court of record in the county in which the witness is found.

If said certificate recommends that the witness be taken into immediate custody and delivered to an officer of this state to assure his attendance in this state, such judge may direct that such witness be forthwith brought before him; and the judge being satisfied of the desirability of such custody and delivery, for which determination said certificate shall be prima facie proof, may order that said witness be forthwith taken into custody and delivered to an officer of this state, which order shall be sufficient authority to such officer to take such witness into custody and hold him unless and until he may be released by bail, recognizance, or order of the judge issuing the certificate.

If the witness is summoned to attend and testify in this state he shall be tendered the sum of ten cents a mile for each mile and five dollars for each day that he is required to travel and attend as a witness. Such fees shall be a proper charge upon the county in which such criminal prosecution or grand jury investigation is pending. A witness who has appeared in accordance with the provisions of the subpoena shall not be required to remain within this state a longer period of time than the period mentioned in the certificate, unless otherwise ordered by the court. If such witness fails without good cause to attend and testify as directed in this subpoena, he shall be punished in the manner provided for the punishment of any witness who disobeys a subpoena issued from a court of record in this state.

4. Exemption from arrest and service of process. If a person comes into this state in obedience to a subpoena directing him to attend and testify in this state he shall not while in this state pursuant to such subpoena or order be subject to arrest or the service of process, civil or criminal, in connection with matters which arose before his entrance into this state under the subpoena.

If a person passes through this state while going to another state in obedience to a subpoena or order to attend and testify in that state or while returning therefrom, he shall not while so passing through this state be subject to arrest or the service of process, civil or criminal, in connection with matters which arose before his entrance into this state under the subpoena or order.

5. Uniformity of interpretation. This section shall be so interpreted and construed as to effectuate its general purpose to make uniform the law of the states which enact it.

6. Short title. This section may be cited as "Uniform act to secure the attendance of witnesses from without the state in criminal cases."

7. Constitutionality. If any part of this section is for any reason declared void, such invalidity shall not affect the validity of the remaining portions thereof.

ARTICLE 650 - SECURING ATTENDANCE AS WITNESSES OF PRISONERS CONFINED IN INSTITUTIONS OF OTHER JURISDICTIONS OF THE UNITED STATES -- RENDITION TO OTHER JURISDICTIONS OF PRISONERS CONFINED IN INSTITUTIONS WITHIN THE STATE

Section
650.10 Securing attendance of prisoner in this state as witness in proceeding without the state.
650.20 Securing attendance of prisoner outside the state as witness in criminal action in the state.
650.30 Securing attendance of prisoner in federal institution as witness in criminal action in the state.

§650.10 Securing attendance of prisoner in this state as witness in proceeding without the state.

If a judge of a court of record in any other state, which by its laws has made provision for commanding a prisoner within that state to attend and testify in this state, certifies under the seal of that court that there is a criminal prosecution pending in such court or that a grand jury investigation has commenced, and that a person confined in a New York state correctional institution or prison within the department of correction, other than a person confined as criminally mentally ill, or as a defective delinquent, or confined in the death house awaiting execution, is a material witness in such prosecution or investigation and that his presence is required for a specified number of days, upon presentment of such certificate to a judge of a superior court in the county where the person is confined, upon notice to the attorney general, such judge, shall fix a time and place for a hearing and shall make an order directed to the person having custody of the prisoner requiring that such prisoner be produced at the hearing.

If at such hearing the judge determines that the prisoner is a material and necessary witness in the requesting state, the judge shall issue an order directing that the prisoner attend in the court where the prosecution or investigation is pending, upon such terms and conditions as the judge prescribes, including among other things, provision for the return of the prisoner at the conclusion of his testimony, proper safeguards on his custody, and proper financial reimbursement or other payment by the demanding jurisdiction for all expenses incurred in the production and return of the prisoner.

221

§650.30

The attorney general is authorized as agent for the state of New York, when in his judgment it is necessary, to enter into such agreements with the appropriate authorities of the demanding jurisdiction as he determines necessary to ensure proper compliance with the order of the court.

§650.20 Securing attendance of prisoner outside the state as witness in criminal action in the state.

1. When (a) a criminal action is pending in a court of record of this state, or a grand jury proceeding has been commenced, and (b) there is reasonable cause to believe that a person confined in a correctional institution or prison of another state, other than a person awaiting execution of a sentence of death or one confined as mentally ill or as a defective delinquent, possesses information material to such criminal action or proceeding, and (c) the attendance of such person as a witness in such action or proceeding is desired by a party thereto, and (d) the state in which such person is confined possesses a statute equivalent to section 650.10, the court in which such action or proceeding is pending may issue a certificate under the seal of such court, certifying all such facts and that the attendance of such person as a witness in such court is required for a specified number of days.

2. Such certificate may be issued upon application, of either the people or a defendant, demonstrating all the facts specified in subdivision one.

3. Upon issuing such a certificate, the court may deliver it, or cause or authorize it to be delivered, to a judge or a court of such other state who or which, pursuant to the laws thereof, is authorized to initiate or undertake legal action for the delivery of such prisoners to this state as witnesses.

§650.30 Securing attendance of prisoner in federal institution as witness in criminal action in the state.

1. When (a) a criminal action is pending in a court of record of this state by reason of the filing therewith of an accusatory instrument, or a grand jury proceeding has been commenced, and (b) there is reasonable cause to believe that a person confined in a federal prison or other federal custody, either within or outside this state, possesses information material to such criminal action or proceeding, and (c) the attendance of such person as a witness in such action or proceeding is desired by a party thereto, a superior court, at a term held in the county in which such action or proceeding is pending, may issue a certificate, known as a writ of habeas corpus ad testificandum, addressed to the attorney general of the United States, certifying all such facts and requesting the attorney general of the United States to cause the attendance of such person as a witness in such court for a specified number of days under custody of a federal public servant.

2. Such a certificate may be issued upon application of either the people or a defendant, demonstrating all the facts specified in subdivision one.

3. Upon issuing such certificate, the court may deliver it, or cause or authorize it to be delivered, to the attorney general of the United States or to his representative authorized to entertain the request.

TITLE S - PROCEDURES FOR SECURING TESTIMONY FOR FUTURE USE, AND FOR USING TESTIMONY GIVEN IN A PRIOR PROCEEDING

ARTICLE 660 - SECURING TESTIMONY FOR USE IN A SUBSEQUENT PROCEEDING - EXAMINATION OF WITNESSES CONDITIONALLY

Section
660.10 Examination of witnesses conditionally; in general.
660.20 Examination of witnesses conditionally; grounds for order.
660.30 Examination of witnesses conditionally; when and to what courts application
       may be made.
660.40 Examination of witnesses conditionally; application and notice.
660.50 Examination of witnesses conditionally; determination of application.
660.60 Examination of witnesses conditionally; the examination proceeding.

§660.10 Examination of witnesses conditionally; in general.

After a defendant has been arraigned upon an accusatory instrument, and under circumstances prescribed in this article, a criminal court may, upon application of either the people or a defendant, order that a witness or prospective witness in the action be examined conditionally under oath in order that such testimony may be received into evidence at subsequent proceedings in or related to the action.

§660.20 Examination of witnesses conditionally; grounds for order.

An order directing examination of a witness conditionally must be based upon the ground that there is reasonable cause to believe that such witness:

1. Possesses information material to the criminal action or proceeding in issue; and

2. Will not be amenable or responsive to legal process or available as a witness at a time when his testimony will be sought, either because he is:

(a) About to leave the state and not return for as substantial period of time; or

(b) Physically ill or incapacitated.

§660.30 Examination of witnesses conditionally; when and to what courts application may be made.

1. An application to examine a witness conditionally may be made at any time after the defendant has been arraigned upon an accusatory instrument and before termination of the action, or of a proceeding therein or related thereto, in which the witness's testimony is sought.

2. Such application must be made to and determined by the following courts under the indicated circumstances:

(a) If the action is pending in a local criminal court as a result of an accusatory instrument filed therewith, the application must be made to and determined by such local criminal court;

(b) If the defendant has been held by a local criminal court for the action of a grand jury on the basis of a felony complaint, or if an indictment has been filed against him, the application must be made to and determined by the superior court by which the grand jury was or is to be impaneled or in which the indictment is pending. If the superior court by which the grand jury is to be impaneled is the supreme court, the motion may, in the alternative be made in the county court of the county in which the action is pending.

§660.40 Examination of witnesses conditionally; application and notice.

1. An application to examine a witness conditionally must be made in writing, must be subscribed and sworn to, and must contain:

(a) The title of the action, the offense or offenses charged, the nature and status of the action, and the name and residential address of the witness sought to be examined; and

(b) A statement that there is reasonable cause to believe that grounds for such an examination, as specified in section 660.20, exist, together with allegations of fact supporting such statement. Such allegations of fact may be those of the applicant, or those of another person in an accompanying deposition, or of both. They may be based either upon personal knowledge of the deponent or upon information and belief, provided that in the latter event the sources of such information and the grounds of such belief are stated.

2. The application may also contain a request that the examination, in addition to its being recorded in the same manner as would be required were the witness testifying at trial, also be recorded by videotape or other photographic method approved by and subject to standards and administrative policies promulgated pursuant to section twenty-eight of article six of the constitution.

3. A copy of the application, with reasonable notice and opportunity to be heard, must be served upon the other party to the action. If the defendant is the applicant, such service must be upon the district attorney. If the people are the applicant, such service must be upon the defendant and upon his attorney if any. The respondent party may file and serve a sworn written answer to the application.

§660.50 Examination of witnesses conditionally; determination of application.

1. Before ruling upon the application, the court may, in addition to examining the papers and hearing oral argument, make any inquiry it deems appropriate for the purpose of making findings of fact essential to the determination. For such purpose, it may examine witnesses, under oath or otherwise, subpoena or call witnesses and authorize the attorneys for the parties to do so.

2. If the court is satisfied that grounds for the application exist, it must order an examination of the witness conditionally at a designated time and place. Such examination must be conducted by the same court; except that, if it is to be held in another county, it may be conducted by a designated superior court of such other county.

3. The court must order that the examination be recorded in the same manner as would be required were the witness testifying at trial, and the court may, in addition, order that the examination also be recorded by videotape or other photographic method approved by and subject to standards and administrative policies promulgated pursuant to section twenty-eight of article six of the constitution.

4. Upon ordering the examination, the court must direct the party securing the order of examination to serve a copy of the order upon the respondent party and, if a defendant be such, upon his attorney also, and must either issue a subpoena for the witness' attendance thereat or authorize the applicant party's attorney to do so.

§660.60 Examination of witnesses conditionally; the examination proceeding.

1. The examination proceeding must be conducted in the same manner as would be required were the witness testifying at a trial, and must be recorded in such fashion as the court has directed pursuant to subdivision

three of section 660.50 of this chapter. The witness must testify under oath. The applicant party must first examine the witness and the respondent party may then cross-examine him, with each party entitled to register objections and to receive rulings of the court thereon.

2. Upon conclusion of the examination, a transcript and any videotape or photographic recording thereof must be certified and filed with the court which ordered the examination.

ARTICLE 670 - USE IN A CRIMINAL PROCEEDING OF TESTIMONY GIVEN IN A PREVIOUS PROCEEDING

Section
670.10 Use in a criminal proceeding of testimony given in a previous proceeding; when authorized.
670.20 Use in a criminal proceeding of testimony given in a previous proceeding; procedure.

§670.10 Use in a criminal proceeding of testimony given in a previous proceeding; when authorized.

1. Under circumstances prescribed in this article, testimony given by a witness at (a) a trial of an accusatory instrument, or (b) a hearing upon a felony complaint conducted pursuant to section 180.60, or (c) an examination of such witness conditionally, conducted pursuant to article six hundred sixty, may, where otherwise admissible, be received into evidence at a subsequent proceeding in or relating to the action involved when at the time of such subsequent proceeding the witness is unable to attend the same by reason of death, illness or incapacity, or cannot with due diligence be found, or is outside the state or in federal custody and cannot with due diligence be brought before the court. Upon being received into evidence, such testimony may be read and any videotape or photographic recording thereof played. Where any recording is received into evidence, the stenographic transcript of that examination shall also be received.

2. The subsequent proceedings at which such testimony may be received in evidence consist of:

(a) Any proceeding constituting a part of a criminal action based upon the charge or charges which were pending against the defendant at the time of the witness's testimony and to which such testimony related; and

(b) Any post-judgment proceeding in which a judgment of conviction upon a charge specified in paragraph (a) is challenged.

§670.20 Use in a criminal proceeding of testimony given in a previous proceeding; procedure.

1. In any criminal action or proceeding other than a grand jury proceeding, a party thereto who desires to offer in evidence testimony of a witness given in a previous action or proceeding as provided in section 670.10, must so move, either in writing or orally in open court, and must submit to the court, and serve a copy thereof upon the adverse party, an authenticated transcript of the testimony and any videotape or photographic recording thereof sought to be introduced. Such moving party must further state facts showing that personal attendance of the witness in question is precluded by some factor specified in subdivision one of section 670.10. In determining the motion, the court, with opportunity for both parties to be heard, must make inquiry and conduct a hearing to determine whether personal attendance of the witness is so precluded. If the court determines that such is the case and grants the motion, the moving party may introduce the transcript in evidence and read into evidence the testimony contained therein. In such case, the adverse party may register any objection or protest thereto that he would be entitled to register were the witness testifying in person, and the court must rule thereon.

2. Without obtaining any court order or authorization, a district attorney may introduce in evidence in a grand jury proceeding testimony of a witness given in a previous action or proceeding specified in subdivision one of section 670.10, provided that a foundation for such evidence is laid by other evidence demonstrating that personal attendance of such witness is precluded by some factor specified in subdivision one of section 670.10.

ARTICLE 680 - SECURING TESTIMONY OUTSIDE THE STATE FOR USE IN PROCEEDING WITHIN THE STATE-EXAMINATION OF WITNESSES ON COMMISSION

Section
680.10 Examination of witnesses on commission; in general.
680.20 Examination of witnesses on commission; when commission issuable; form and content of application.
680.30 Examination of witnesses on commission; application by people for examination of witnesses.
680.40 Examination of witnesses on commission; when commission issuable upon application of people.
680.50 Examination of witnesses on commission; interrogatories.
680.60 Examination of witnesses on commission; form and content of the commission.
680.70 Examination of witnesses on commission; the examination.
680.80 Examination of witnesses on commission; use at trial of transcript of examination.

§680.10 Examination of witnesses on commission; in general.
1. Under circumstances prescribed in this article, testimony material to a trial or pending trial of an accusatory instrument which charges a crime, may be taken by "examination on a commission" outside the state and received in evidence at such trial.
2. A "commission" is a process issued by a superior court designating one or more persons as commissioners and authorizing them to conduct a recorded examination of a witness or witnesses under oath, primarily on the basis of interrogatories annexed to the commission, and to remit to the issuing court the transcript of such examination.

§680.20 Examination of witnesses on commission; when commission issuable; form and content of application.
1. Upon a pre-trial application of a defendant who has pleaded not guilty to an indictment or other accusatory instrument which charges a crime, the superior court in which such indictment is pending, or a superior court in the county in which such other accusatory instrument is pending, may issue a commission for examination of a designated person as a witness in the action, at a designated place outside this state, if it is satisfied that (a) such person possesses information material to the action which in the interest of justice should be disclosed at the trial, and (b) resides outside the state.
2. The application and moving papers must be in writing and must be subscribed and sworn to by the defendant or his attorney. A copy thereof must be served on the district attorney, with reasonable notice and opportunity to be heard. The moving papers must allege:
    (a) The offense or offenses charged; and
    (b) The status of the action; and
    (c) The name of the prospective witness; and

(d) A statement that such prospective witness resides outside the state, and his address in the jurisdiction in which the examination sought is to occ ur; and

(e) A statement that he possesses information material to the action which in the interest of justice should be disclosed at the trial, together with a brief summary of the facts supporting such statement.

3. An application for issuance of a commission may request examination pursuant thereto of more than one person residing in the particular jurisdiction. In such case, it must contain allegations specified in subdivision two with respect to each such person, and the court must make separate rulings as to each.

§680.30 Examination of witnesses on commission; application by people for examination of witnesses.

1. Upon granting the defendant's application for issuance of a commission, the court may, upon application of the people, determine that the commission shall also authorize examination of a person or persons designated by the people, who reside in the jurisdiction in which the examination proceeding is to occur, if it is satisfied that such person or persons possess material information, reside outside the state and otherwise meet the standards for examination of witnesses on a commission as prescribed in subdivision one of section 680.20.

2. Such application and the moving papers must be in writing, must be subscribed and sworn to by the district attorney, and copies thereof must be served upon the defendant and his attorney, with reasonable notice and opportunity to be heard. The moving papers must contain all of the allegations required upon a defendant's application, as specified in subdivision two of section 680.20.

§680.40 Examination of witnesses on commission; when commission issuable upon application of people.

When a commission has been issued upon application of a defendant pursuant to section 680.20, the court may, upon application of the people, issue another commission for examination, either in the same or another jurisdiction, of a person designated by the people, under the same conditions as prescribed in said section 680.20. In such case, the court may, upon application of the defendant, determine, in the manner provided in section 680.30, that such commission shall also authorize examination of a person or persons designated by the defendant.

§680.50 Examination of witnesses on commission; interrogatories.

1. Following an order for the issuance of a commission and the court's designation of the witnesses to be examined thereon, each party must prepare interrogatories or questions to be asked of each witness who is to be exam- ined upon his or its request, and must submit the same to the court and serve a copy thereof upon the other party. Following such submission and service, such other party may in the same manner submit and serve cross-interroga-

tories or questions, to be asked of the witness following his examination upon the direct inquiry.

2. After all such interrogatories and cross-interrogatories have been submitted and served, the court may examine them and, with opportunity for counsel to be heard, exclude and strike any question which it considers irrelevant, incompetent or otherwise improper or violative of the rules of evidence which prevail at a criminal trial.

§680.60 Examination of witnesses on commission; form and content of the commission.

1. The commission must be subscribed by the court and must contain:

(a) The name and address of each witness to be examined; and

(b) The name, or a descriptive title, of a commissioner or commissioners who, pursuant to subdivision two, are authorized to conduct the examination; and

(c) A statement authorizing such commissioner or commissioners to administer the oath to witnesses; and

(d) A direction that, upon completion of such examination, such commissioner or commissioners cause it to be transcribed and remit to the court the transcript, the commission, the interrogatories and all other pertinent instruments and documents.

2. The following persons may be designated commissioners:

(a) If the examination is to occur within the United States or any territory thereof, any attorney authorized to practice law in the specified jurisdiction or any person authorized to administer oaths therein;

(b) If the examination is to occur in a foreign country, any diplomatic or consular agent or representative of the United States employed in such capacity in such country, or any commissioned officer of the armed forces.

3. The court must cause the commission to be delivered to a commissioner designated therein, together with a copy of this article.

§680.70 Examination of witnesses on commission; the examination.

The examination on the commission must be conducted as follows:

1. Each witness must testify under oath, and the examination must be recorded and transcribed.

2. Each witness must first be asked all the questions contained in the interrogatories submitted by the party requesting his examination. He must then be asked all the questions contained in the cross-interrogatories, if any, submitted by the other party.

3. The defendant has a right to be represented by counsel at the examination, and the district attorney also has a right to be present, but both such rights may be waived. Upon the conclusion of the questioning of a witness upon the written interrogatories, he may be further examined by the attorney or representative of the party who requested his examination, and may then be cross-examined by the attorney or representative of the adverse party. Each such attorney or representative may register objections to the authority or qualifications of the commissioner, to the manner in which the examination is conducted, and to the admissibility of evidence, and all such objections must be recorded and transcribed.

4. Documentary or other physical evidence may be produced and submitted by a witness. Such evidence must be subscribed or otherwise identified by the witness, and certified by a commissioner and annexed to the transcript of the examination as a part of the record.

5. After the examination is transcribed, the commissioner or commissioners must subscribe and certify the transcript as an accurate record of the proceedings, and must then remit such transcript and all other pertinent instruments, documents and evidence to the court which issued the commission, in accordance with the directions thereof.

§680.80 Examination of witnesses on commission; use at trial of transcript of examination.

1. When the transcript and record of the examination on commission are received by the superior court which issued the commission, they must be filed therewith if such court be the trial court, and, if not, transmitted to the trial court. A copy of the transcript must be delivered by the trial court to each party.

2. Upon the trial of the action, either party may, subject to the provisions of subdivision three, introduce and read into evidence the transcript or that portion thereof containing the testimony of a witness examined on the commission.

3. At any time prior to the introduction of such evidence, the trial court may examine the transcript and, upon according both parties opportunity to be heard and to register objections, may exclude and strike therefrom irrelevant, incompetent or otherwise inadmissible testimony. While the transcript or any portion thereof is being read into evidence at the trial by a party, the other party may register any objection or protest thereto that he would be entitled to register were the witness testifying in person, regardless of whether such protest has previously been raised and passed upon by the court, and the court must rule thereon.

TITLE T - PROCEDURES FOR SECURING EVIDENCE BY MEANS OF COURT ORDER AND FOR SUPPRESSING EVIDENCE UNLAWFULLY OR IMPROPERLY OBTAINED
ARTICLE 690 - SEARCH WARRANTS

Section
690.05 Search warrants; in general; definition.
690.10 Search warrants; property subject to seizure thereunder.
690.15 Search warrants; what and who are subject to search thereunder.
690.20 Search warrants; where executable.
690.25 Search warrants; to whom addressable and by whom executable.
690.30 Search warrants; when executable.
690.35 Search warrants; the application.
690.36 Search warrants; special provisions governing oral applications therefor.
690.40 Search warrants; determination of application.
690.45 Search warrants; form and content.
690.50 Search warrants; execution thereof.
690.55 Search warrants; disposition of seized property.

§690.05 Search warrants; in general; definition.

1. Under circumstances prescribed in this article, a local criminal court may, upon application of a police officer, a district attorney or other public servant acting in the course of his official duties, issue a search warrant.

2. A search warrant is a court order and process directing a police officer to conduct:

(a) a search of designated premises, or of a designated vehicle, or of a designated person, for the purpose of seizing designated property or kinds of property, and to deliver any property so obtained to the court which issued the warrant; or

(b) a search of a designated premises for the purpose of searching for and arresting a person who is the subject of: (i) a warrant of arrest issued pursuant to this chapter, a superior court warrant of arrest issued pursuant to this chapter, or a bench warrant for a felony issued pursuant to this chapter, where the designated premises is the dwelling of a third party who is not the subject of the arrest warrant; or (ii) a warrant of arrest issued by any other state or federal court for an offense which would constitute a felony under the laws of this state, where the designated premises is the dwelling of a third party who is not the subject of the arrest warrant.

§690.10 Search warrants; property subject to seizure thereunder.

Personal property is subject to seizure pursuant to a search warrant if there is reasonable cause to believe that it:

1. Is stolen; or
2. Is unlawfully possessed; or
3. Has been used, or is possessed for the purpose of being used, to commit or conceal the commission of an offense against the laws of this state or another state, provided however, that if such offense was against the laws of another state, the court shall only issue a warrant if the conduct comprising such offense would, if occurring in this state, constitute a felony against the laws of this state; or
4. Constitutes evidence or tends to demonstrate that an offense was committed in this state or another state, or that a particular person participated in the commission of an offense in this state or another state, provided however, that if such offense was against the laws of another state, the court shall only issue a warrant if the conduct comprising such offense would, if occurring in this state, constitute a felony against the laws of this state.

§690.15 Search warrants; what and who are subject to search thereunder.

1. A search warrant must direct a search of one or more of the following:
    (a) A designated or described place or premises;
    (b) A designated or described vehicle, as that term is defined in section 10.00 of the penal law;
    (c) A designated or described person.
2. A search warrant which directs a search of a designated or described place, premises or vehicle, may also direct a search of any person present thereat or therein.

§690.20 Search warrants; where executable.

1. A search warrant issued by a district court, the New York city criminal court or a superior court judge sitting as a local criminal court may be executed pursuant to its terms anywhere in the state.
2. A search warrant issued by a city court, a town court or a village court may be executed pursuant to its terms only in the county of issuance or an adjoining county.

§690.25 Search warrants; to whom addressable and by whom executable.

1. A search warrant must be addressed to a police officer whose geographical area of employment embraces or is embraced or partially embraced by the county of issuance. The warrant need not be addressed to a specific police officer but may be addressed to any police officer of a designated classification, or to any police officer of any classification employed or having general jurisdiction to act as a police officer in the county.
2. A police officer to whom a search warrant is addressed, as provided in subdivision one, may execute it pursuant to its terms anywhere in the county of issuance or an adjoining county, and he may execute it pursuant to its terms in any other county of the state in which it is executable if (a) his geographical area of employment embraces the entire county of issuance or (b) he is a member of the police department or force of a city located in such county of issuance.

§690.30 Search warrants; when executable.

1. A search warrant must be executed not more than ten days after the date of issuance and it must thereafter be returned to the court without unnecessary delay.

2. A search warrant may be executed on any day of the week. It may be executed only between the hours of 6:00 A.M. and 9:00 P.M., unless the warrant expressly authorizes execution thereof at any time of the day or night, as provided in subdivision five of section 690.45.

§690.35 Search warrants; the application.

1. An application for a search warrant may be in writing or oral. If in writing, it must be made, subscribed and sworn to by a public servant specified in subdivision one of section 690.05. If oral, it must be made by such a public servant and sworn to and recorded in the manner provided in section 690.36.

2. The application shall be made to:

(a) A local criminal court, as defined in section 10.10 of this chapter, having preliminary jurisdiction over the underlying offense, or geographical jurisdiction over the location to be searched when the search is to be made for personal property of a kind or character described in section 690.10 of this article except that:

(i) if a town court has such jurisdiction but is not available to issue the search warrant, the warrant may be issued by the local criminal court of any village within such town or, any adjoining town, village embraced in whole or in part by such adjoining town, or city of the same county;

(ii) if a village court has such jurisdiction but is not available to issue the search warrant, the warrant may be issued by the town court of the town embracing such village or any other village court within such town, or, if such town or village court is not available either, before the local criminal court of any adjoining town, village embraced in whole or in part by such adjoining town, or city of the same county; and

(iii) if a city court has such jurisdiction but is not available to issue the search warrant, the warrant may be issued by the local criminal court of any adjoining town or village, or village court embraced by an adjoining town, within the same county as such city.

(b) A local criminal court, as defined in section 10.10 of this chapter, with geographical jurisdiction over the location where the premises to be searched is located, or which issued the underlying arrest warrant, when the search warrant is sought pursuant to paragraph (b) of subdivision two of section 690.05 of this article, for the purpose of arresting a wanted person.

Any search warrant issued pursuant to this section shall be subject to the territorial limitations provided by section 690.20 of this article.

3. The application must contain:

(a) The name of the court and the name and title of the applicant; and

(b) A statement that there is reasonable cause to believe that property of a kind or character described in section 690.10 may be found in or upon a designated or described place, vehicle or person, or, in the case of an application for a search warrant as defined in paragraph (b) of subdivision two of section 690.05, a statement that there is reasonable cause to believe that the person who is the subject of the warrant of arrest may be found in the designated premises; and

(c) Allegations of fact supporting such statement. Such allegations of fact may be based upon personal knowledge of the applicant or upon information and belief, provided that in the latter event the sources of such information and the grounds of such belief are stated. The applicant may also submit depositions of other persons containing allegations of fact supporting or tending to support those contained in the application; and

(d) A request that the court issue a search warrant directing a search for and seizure of the property or person in question; and

(e) In the case of an application for a search warrant as defined in paragraph (b) of subdivision two of section 690.05, a copy of the warrant of arrest and the underlying accusatory instrument.

4. The application may also contain:

(a) A request that the search warrant be made executable at any time of the day or night, upon the ground that there is reasonable cause to believe that (i) it cannot be executed between the hours of 6:00 A.M. and 9:00 P.M., or (ii) the property sought will be removed or destroyed if not seized forthwith, or (iii) in the case of an application for a search warrant as defined in paragraph (b) of subdivision two of section 690.05, the person sought is likely to flee or commit another crime, or may endanger the safety of the executing police officers or another person if not seized forthwith or between the hours of 9:00 P.M. and 6:00 A.M.; and

(b) A request that the search warrant authorize the executing police officer to enter premises to be searched without giving notice of his authority and purpose, upon the ground that there is reasonable cause to believe that (i) the property sought may be easily and quickly destroyed or disposed of, or (ii) the giving of such notice may endanger the life or safety of the executing officer or another person, or (iii) in the case of an application for a search warrant as defined in paragraph (b) of subdivision two of section 690.05 for the purpose of searching for and arresting a person who is the subject of a warrant for a felony, the person sought is likely to commit another felony, or may endanger the life or safety of the executing officer or another person.

Any request made pursuant to this subdivision must be accompanied and supported by allegations of fact of a kind prescribed in paragraph (c) of subdivision two.

§690.36 Search warrants; special provisions governing oral applications therefor.

1. An oral application for a search warrant may be communicated to a judge by telephone, radio or other means of electronic communication.

2. Where an oral application for a search warrant is made, the applicant therefor must identify himself and the purpose of his communication. After being sworn as provided in subdivision three of this section, the applicant must also make the statement required by paragraph (b) of subdivision two of section 690.35 and provide the same allegations of fact required by paragraph (c) of such subdivision; provided, however, persons, properly identified, other than the applicant may also provide some or all of such allegations of fact directly to the court. Where appropriate, the applicant may also make a request specified in subdivision three of section 690.35.

3. Upon being advised that an oral application for a search warrant is being made, a judge shall place under oath the applicant and any other person providing information in support of the application. Such oath or oaths and all of the remaining communication must be recorded, either by means of a voice recording device or verbatim stenographic or verbatim longhand notes. If a voice recording device is used or a stenographic record made, the judge must have the record transcribed, certify to the accuracy of the transcription and file the original record and transcription with the court

within twenty-four hours of the issuance of a warrant. If longhand notes are taken, the judge shall subscribe a copy and file it with the court within twenty-four hours of the issuance of a warrant.

§690.40 Search warrants; determination of application.

1. In determining an application for a search warrant the court may examine, under oath, any person whom it believes may possess pertinent information. Any such examination must be either recorded or summarized on the record by the court.

2. If the court is satisfied that there is reasonable cause to believe that property of a kind or character referred to in section 690.10, and described in the application, may be found in or upon the place, premises, vehicle or person designated or described in the application, or, in the case of an application for a search warrant as defined in paragraph (b) of subdivision two of section 690.05, that there is reasonable cause to believe that the person who is the subject of a warrant of arrest, a superior court warrant of arrest, or a bench warrant for a felony may be found at the premises designated in the application, it may grant the application and issue a search warrant directing a search of the said place, premises, vehicle or person and a seizure of the described property or the described person. If the court is further satisfied that grounds, described in subdivision four of section 690.35, exist for authorizing the search to be made at any hour of the day or night, or without giving notice of the police officer's authority and purpose, it may make the search warrant executable accordingly.

3. When a judge determines to issue a search warrant based upon an oral application, the applicant therefor shall prepare the warrant in accordance with section 690.45 and shall read it, verbatim, to the judge.

§690.45 Search warrants; form and content.

A search warrant must contain:

1. The name of the issuing court and, except where the search warrant has been obtained on oral application, the subscription of the issuing judge; and

2. Where the search warrant has been obtained on an oral application, it shall so indicate and shall state the name of the issuing judge and the time and date on which such judge directed its issuance.

3. The name, department or classification of the police officer to whom it is addressed; and

4. A description of the property which is the subject of the search, or, in the case of a search warrant as defined in paragraph (b) of subdivision two of section 690.05, a description of the person to be searched for; and

5. A designation or description of the place, premises or person to be searched, by means of address, ownership, name or any other means essential to identification with certainty; and

6. A direction that the warrant be executed between the hours of 6:00 A.M. and 9:00 P.M., or, where the court has specially so determined, an authorization for execution thereof at any time of the day or night; and

7. An authorization, where the court has specially so determined, that the executing police officer enter the premises to be searched without giving notice of his authority and purpose; and

8. A direction that the warrant and any property seized pursuant thereto be returned and delivered to the court without unnecessary delay; and

9. In the case of a search warrant as defined in paragraph (b) of subdivi-

sion two of section 690.05, a copy of the warrant of arrest and the underlying accusatory instrument.

§690.50 Search warrants; execution thereof.

1. In executing a search warrant directing a search of premises or a vehicle, a police officer must, except as provided in subdivision two, give, or make reasonable effort to give, notice of his authority and purpose to an occupant thereof before entry and show him the warrant or a copy thereof upon request. If he is not thereafter admitted he may forcibly enter such premises or vehicle and may use against any person resisting his entry or search thereof as much physical force, other than deadly physical force, as is necessary to execute the warrant; and he may use deadly physical force if he reasonably believes such to be necessary to defend himself or a third person from what he reasonably believes to be the use or imminent use of deadly physical force.

2. In executing a search warrant directing a search of premises or a vehicle, a police officer need not give notice to anyone of his authority and purpose, as prescribed in subdivision one, but may promptly enter the same if:

(a) Such premises or vehicle are at the time unoccupied or reasonably believed by the officer to be unoccupied; or

(b) The search warrant expressly authorizes entry without notice.

3. In executing a search warrant directing or authorizing a search of a person, a police officer must give, or make reasonable effort to give, such person notice of his authority and purpose and show him the warrant or a copy thereof upon request. If such person, or another, thereafter resists or refuses to permit the search, the officer may use as much physical force, other than deadly physical force, as is necessary to execute the warrant; and he may use deadly physical force if he reasonably believes such to be necessary to defend himself or a third person from what he reasonably believes to be the use or imminent use of deadly physical force.

4. Upon seizing property pursuant to a search warrant, a police officer must write and subscribe a receipt itemizing the property taken and containing the name of the court by which the warrant was issued. If property is taken from a person, such receipt must be given to such person. If property is taken from premises or a vehicle, such receipt must be given to the owner, tenant or other person in possession thereof if he is present; or if he is not, the officer must leave such a receipt in the premises or vehicle from which the property was taken.

5. Upon seizing property pursuant to a search warrant, a police officer must without unnecessary delay return to the court the warrant and the property, and must file therewith a written inventory of such property, subscribed and sworn to by such officer.

6. Upon arresting a person during a search for him or her pursuant to a search warrant as defined in paragraph (b) of subdivision two of section 690.05, a police officer shall comply with the terms of the warrant of arrest, superior court warrant of arrest, or bench warrant for a felony, and shall proceed in the manner directed by this chapter. Upon arresting such person, the police officer shall also, without unnecessary delay, file a written statement with the court which issued the search warrant, subscribed and sworn to by such officer, setting forth that the person has been arrested and duly brought before the appropriate court, return to the court the warrant and the property seized in the course of its execution, and file therewith a written inventory of any such property, subscribed and sworn to by such officer.

§690.55 Search warrants; disposition of seized property.

1. Upon receiving property seized pursuant to a search warrant, the court must either:

(a) Retain it in the custody of the court pending further disposition thereof pursuant to subdivision two or some other provision of law; or

(b) Direct that it be held in the custody of the person who applied for the warrant, or of the police officer who executed it, or of the governmental or official agency or department by which either such public servant is employed, upon condition that upon order of such court such property be returned thereto or delivered to another court.

2. A local criminal court which retains custody of such property must, upon request of another criminal court in which a criminal action involving or relating to such property is pending, cause it to be delivered thereto.

ARTICLE 700 - EAVESDROPPING AND VIDEO SURVEILLANCE WARRANTS

Section
700.05 Eavesdropping and video surveillance warrants; definitions of terms.
700.10 Eavesdropping and video surveillance warrants; in general.
700.15 Eavesdropping and video surveillance warrants; when issuable.
700.20 Eavesdropping and video surveillance warrants; application.
700.21 Temporary authorization for eavesdropping or video surveillance in emergency situations.
700.25 Eavesdropping warrants; determination of application.
700.30 Eavesdropping and video surveillance warrants; form and content.
700.35 Eavesdropping and video surveillance warrants; manner and time of execution.
700.40 Eavesdropping and video surveillance warrants; order of extension.
700.50 Eavesdropping and video surveillance warrants; progress reports and notice.
700.55 Eavesdropping and video surveillance warrants; custody of warrants, applications and recordings.
700.60 Eavesdropping warrants; reports to the administrative office of the United States courts.
700.65 Eavesdropping and video surveillance warrants; disclosure and use of information; order of amendment.
700.70 Eavesdropping warrants; notice before use of evidence.

§700.05 Eavesdropping and video surveillance warrants; definitions of terms.

As used in this article, the following terms have the following meanings:

1. "Eavesdropping" means "wiretapping", "mechanical overhearing of conversation," or the "intercepting or accessing of an electronic communication", as those terms are defined in section 250.00 of the penal law, but does not include the use of a pen register or trap and trace device when authorized pursuant to article 705 of this chapter.

2. "Eavesdropping warrant" means an order of a justice authorizing or approving eavesdropping.

3. "Intercepted communication" means (a) a telephonic or telegraphic communication which was intentionally overheard or recorded by a person other than the sender or receiver thereof, without the consent of the sender or receiver, by means of any instrument, device or equipment, or (b) a conversation or discussion which was intentionally overheard or recorded, without the consent of at least one party thereto, by a person not present thereat, by means of any instrument, device or equipment; or (c) an electronic communication which was intentionally intercepted or accessed, as that term is defined in section 250.00 of the penal law. The term "contents," when used with respect to a communication, includes any information concerning the identity of the parties to such communications, and the existence, substance, purport, or meaning of that communication. The term "communication" includes conversation and discussion.

3-a. "Telephonic communication", "electronic communication", and "intentionally intercepted or accessed" have the meanings given to those terms by subdivisions three, five, and six respectively, of section 250.00 of the penal law.

4. "Justice," except as otherwise provided herein, means any justice of an appellate division of the judicial department in which the eavesdropping warrant is to be executed, or any justice of the supreme court of the judicial district in which the eavesdropping warrant is to be executed, or any county court judge of the county in which the eavesdropping warrant is to be executed. When the eavesdropping warrant is to authorize the interception of oral communications occurring in a vehicle or wire communications occurring over a telephone located in a vehicle, "justice" means any justice of the supreme court of the judicial department or any county court judge of the county in which the eavesdropping device is to be installed or connected or of any judicial department or county in which communications are expected to be intercepted. When such a justice issues such an eavesdropping warrant, such warrant may be executed and such oral or wire communications may be intercepted anywhere in the state.

5. "Applicant" means a district attorney or the attorney general or if authorized by the attorney general, the deputy attorney general in charge of the organized crime task force. If a district attorney or the attorney general is actually absent or disabled, the term "applicant" includes that person designated to act for him and perform his official function in and during his actual absence or disability.

6. "Law enforcement officer" means any public servant who is empowered by law to conduct an investigation of or to make an arrest for a designated offense, and any attorney authorized by law to prosecute or participate in the prosecution of a designated offense.

7. "Exigent circumstances" means conditions requiring the preservation of secrecy, and whereby there is a reasonable likelihood that a continuing investigation would be thwarted by alerting any of the persons subject to surveillance to the fact that such surveillance had occurred.

8. "Designated offense" means any one or more of the following crimes:

(a) A conspiracy to commit any offense enumerated in the following paragraphs of this subdivision, or an attempt to commit any felony enumerated in the following paragraphs of this subdivision which attempt would itself constitute a felony;

(b) Any of the following felonies: assault in the second degree as defined in section 120.05 of the penal law, assault in the first degree as defined in section 120.10 of the penal law, reckless endangerment in the first degree as defined in section 120.25 of the penal law, promoting a suicide attempt as defined in section 120.30 of the penal law, strangulation in the second degree as defined in section 121.12 of the penal law, strangulation in the first degree as defined in section 121.13 of the penal law, criminally negligent homicide as defined in section 125.10 of the penal law, manslaughter in the second degree as defined in section 125.15 of the penal law, manslaughter in the first degree as defined in section 125.20 of the penal law, murder in the second degree as defined in section 125.25 of the penal law, murder in the first degree as defined in section 125.27 of the penal law, rape in the third degree as defined in section 130.25 of the penal law, rape in the second degree as defined in section 130.30 of the penal law, rape in the first degree as defined in section 130.35 of the penal law, criminal sexual act in the third degree as defined in section 130.40 of the penal law, criminal sexual act in the second degree as defined in section 130.45 of the penal law, criminal sexual act in the first degree as defined in section 130.50 of the penal law, sexual abuse in the first degree as defined in section 130.65 of the penal law, unlawful imprisonment in the first degree as defined in section 135.10 of the penal law, kidnapping in the second degree as defined in section 135.20 of the penal law, kidnapping in the first degree as defined in section 135.25 of the penal law, labor trafficking as defined in section 135.35 of the penal law, aggravated labor trafficking as defined in section 135.37 of the penal law, custodial interference in the first degree as defined in section 135.50 of the penal law, coercion in the first degree as defined in section 135.65 of the penal law, criminal trespass in the first degree as defined in section 140.17 of the penal law, burglary in the third degree as defined in section 140.20 of the penal law, burglary in the second degree as defined in section 140.25 of the penal law, burglary in the first degree as defined in section 140.30 of the penal law, criminal mischief in the third degree as defined in section 145.05 of the penal law, criminal mischief in the second degree as defined in section 145.10 of the penal law, criminal mischief in the first degree as defined in section 145.12 of the penal law, criminal tampering in the first degree as defined in section 145.20 of the penal law, arson in the fourth degree as defined in section 150.05 of the penal law, arson in the third degree as defined in section 150.10 of the penal law, arson in the second degree as defined in section 150.15 of the penal law, arson in the first degree as defined in section 150.20 of the penal law, grand larceny in the fourth degree as defined in section 155.30 of the penal law, grand larceny in the third degree as defined in section 155.35 of the penal law, grand larceny in the second degree as defined in section 155.40 of the penal law, grand larceny in the first degree as defined in section 155.42 of the penal law, health care fraud in the fourth degree as defined in section 177.10 of the penal law, health care fraud in the third degree as defined in section 177.15 of the penal law, health care fraud in the second degree as defined in section 177.20 of the penal law, health care fraud in the first degree as defined in section 177.25 of the penal law, robbery in the third degree as defined in section 160.05 of the penal law, robbery in the second degree as defined in section 160.10 of the penal law, robbery in the first degree as defined in section 160.15 of the penal law, unlawful use of secret scientific material as defined in section 165.07 of the penal law, criminal possession of stolen property in the fourth degree as defined in section 165.45 of the penal law, criminal possession of stolen property in the third degree as defined in section 165.50 of the penal law, criminal possession of stolen property in the second degree as defined by section 165.52 of the penal law, criminal possession of stolen property in the first degree as defined by section 165.54 of the penal law, trademark counterfeiting in the second degree as defined in section 165.72 of the penal law, trademark counterfeiting in the first degree as defined in section 165.73 of the penal law, forgery in the second degree as defined in section 170.10 of the penal law, forgery in the first degree as defined in section 170.15 of the penal law, criminal possession of a forged instrument in the second degree as defined in section 170.25 of the penal law, criminal possession of a forged instrument in the first degree as defined in section 170.30 of the penal law, criminal possession of forgery devices as defined in section 170.40 of the penal law, falsifying business records in the first degree as defined in section 175.10 of the penal law, tampering with public records in the first degree as defined in section 175.25 of the penal law, offering a false instrument for filing in the first degree as defined in section 175.35 of the penal law, issuing a false certificate as defined in section 175.40 of the penal law, criminal diversion of prescription medications and prescriptions in the second degree as defined in section 178.20 of the penal law, criminal diversion of prescription medications and prescriptions in the first degree as defined in section 178.25 of the penal law, residential mortgage fraud in the fourth degree as defined in section 187.10 of the penal law, residential mortgage fraud in the third degree as defined in section 187.15 of the penal law, residential mortgage fraud in the second degree as defined in section 187.20 of the penal law, residential mortgage fraud in the first degree as defined in section 187.25 of the penal law, escape in the second degree as defined in section 205.10 of the penal law, escape in the first degree as defined in section 205.15 of the penal law, absconding from temporary release in the first degree as defined in section 205.17 of the penal law, promoting prison contraband in the first degree as defined in section 205.25 of the penal law, hindering prosecution in the second degree as defined in section 205.60 of the penal law, hindering prosecution in the first degree as defined in section 205.65 of the penal law, sex trafficking as defined in section 230.34 of the penal law, sex trafficking of a child as defined in section 230.34-a of the penal law, criminal possession of a weapon in the third degree as defined in subdivisions two, three and five of section 265.02 of the penal law, criminal possession of a weapon in the second degree as defined in section 265.03 of the penal law, criminal possession of a weapon in the first degree as defined in section 265.04 of the penal law, manufacture, transport, disposition and defacement of weapons and dangerous instruments and appliances defined as felonies in subdivisions one, two, and three of section 265.10 of the penal law, sections 265.11, 265.12 and 265.13 of the penal law, or prohibited use of weapons as defined in subdivision two of section 265.35 of the penal law, relating to firearms and other dangerous weapons, criminal manufacture, sale or transport of an undetectable firearm, rifle or shotgun as defined in section 265.50 of the penal law, or failure to disclose the origin of a recording in the first degree as defined in section 275.40 of the penal law;

  (c) Criminal possession of a controlled substance in the seventh degree as defined in section 220.03 of the penal law, criminal possession of a controlled substance in the fifth degree as defined in section 220.06 of the penal law, criminal possession of a controlled substance in the fourth degree as defined in section 220.09 of the penal law, criminal possession of a controlled substance in the third degree as defined in section 220.16 of the penal law, criminal possession of a controlled substance in the second degree as defined in section 220.18 of the penal law, criminal possession of a controlled substance in the first degree as defined in section 220.21 of the penal law, criminal sale of a controlled substance in the fifth degree as defined in section 220.31 of the penal law, criminal sale of a controlled substance in the fourth degree as defined in section 220.34 of the penal law, criminal sale of a controlled substance in the third degree as defined in section 220.39 of the penal law, criminal sale of a controlled substance in the second degree as defined in section 220.41 of the penal law, criminal sale of a controlled substance in the first degree as defined in section 220.43 of the penal law, criminally possessing a hypodermic instrument as defined in section 220.45 of the penal law, criminal sale of a prescription for a controlled substance or a controlled substance by a practitioner or pharmacist as defined in section 220.65 of the penal law, criminal possession of methamphetamine manufacturing material in the second degree as defined in section 220.70 of the penal law, criminal possession of methamphetamine manufacturing material in the first degree as defined in section 220.71 of the penal law, criminal possession of precursors of methamphetamine as defined in section 220.72 of the penal law, unlawful manufacture of methamphetamine in the third degree as defined in section 220.73 of the penal law, unlawful manufacture of methamphetamine in the second degree as defined in section 220.74 of the penal law, unlawful manufacture of methamphetamine in the first degree as defined in section 220.75 of the penal law, unlawful disposal of methamphetamine laboratory material as defined in section 220.76 of the penal law, operating as a major trafficker as defined in section 220.77 of the penal law, promoting gambling in the second degree as defined in section 225.05 of the penal law, promoting gambling in the first degree as defined in section 225.10 of the penal law, possession of gambling records in the second degree as defined in section 225.15 of the penal law, possession of gambling records in the first degree as defined in section 225.20 of the penal law, and possession of a gambling device as defined in section 225.30 of the penal law;

(Eff.3/31/21,Ch.92,L.2021)

(d) Commercial bribing, commercial bribe receiving, bribing a labor official, bribe receiving by a labor official, sports bribing and sports bribe receiving, as defined in article one hundred eighty of the penal law;

(e) Criminal usury, as defined in article one hundred ninety of the penal law;

(f) Bribery in the third degree, bribery in the second degree, bribery in the first degree, bribe receiving in the third degree, bribe receiving in the second degree, bribe receiving in the first degree, bribe giving for public office, bribe receiving for public office and corrupt use of position or authority, as defined in article two hundred of the penal law;

(g) Bribing a witness, bribe receiving by a witness, bribing a juror and bribe receiving by a juror, as defined in article two hundred fifteen of the penal law;

(h) Promoting prostitution in the first degree, as defined in section 230.32 of the penal law, promoting prostitution in the second degree, as defined by subdivision one of section 230.30 of the penal law, promoting prostitution in the third degree, as defined in section 230.25 of the penal law;

(i) Riot in the first degree and criminal anarchy, as defined in article two hundred forty of the penal law;

(j) Eavesdropping, as defined in article two hundred fifty of the penal law;

(k) Any of the acts designated as felonies in subdivisions two and four of section four hundred eighty-one of the tax law, which section relates to penalties under the tax on cigarettes imposed by article twenty of such law, and any of the acts designated as felonies in subdivision c of section 11-1317 of the administrative code of the city of New York, which section relates to penalties under the cigarette tax imposed by chapter thirteen of title eleven of such code.

(l) Scheme to defraud in the first degree as defined in article one hundred ninety of the penal law.

(m) Any of the acts designated as felonies in section three hundred fifty-two-c of the general business law.

(n) Any of the acts designated as felonies in title twenty-seven of article seventy-one of the environmental conservation law.

(o) Money laundering in the first degree, as defined in section 470.20 of the penal law, money laundering in the second degree as defined in section 470.15 of the penal law, money laundering in the third degree as defined in section 470.10 of such law, and money laundering in the fourth degree as defined in section 470.05 of such law, where the property involved represents or is represented to be the proceeds of specified criminal conduct which itself constitutes a designated offense within the meaning of this subdivision.

(p) Stalking in the second degree as defined in section 120.55 of the penal law, and stalking in the first degree as defined in section 120.60 of the penal law.

*(q) Soliciting or providing support for an act of terrorism in the second degree as defined in section 490.10 of the penal law, soliciting or providing support for an act of terrorism in the first degree as defined in section 490.15 of the penal law, making a terroristic threat as defined in section 490.20 of the penal law, crime of terrorism as defined in section 490.25 of the penal law, domestic act of terrorism motivated by hate in the second degree as defined in section 490.27 of the penal law, domestic act of terrorism motivated by hate in the first degree as defined in section 490.28 of the penal law, hindering prosecution of terrorism in the second degree as defined in section 490.30 of the penal law, hindering prosecution of terrorism in the first degree as defined in section 490.35 of the penal law, criminal possession of a chemical weapon or biological weapon in the third degree as defined in section 490.37 of the penal law, criminal possession of a chemical weapon or biological weapon in the second degree as defined in section 490.40 of the penal law, criminal possession of a chemical weapon or biological weapon in the first degree as defined in section 490.45 of the penal law, criminal use of a chemical weapon or biological weapon in the third degree as defined in section 490.47 of the penal law, criminal use of a chemical weapon or biological weapon in the second degree as defined in section 490.50 of the penal law, and criminal use of a chemical weapon or biological weapon in the first degree as defined in section 490.55 of the penal law.   *(Eff. 11/1/20, Ch. 55, L. 2020)

(r) Falsely reporting an incident in the second degree as defined in section 240.55 of the penal law, falsely reporting an incident in the first degree as defined in section 240.60 of the penal law, placing a false bomb in the second degree as defined in section 240.61 of the penal law, placing a false bomb in the first degree as defined in section 240.62 of the penal law, and placing a false bomb in a sports stadium or arena, mass transportation facility or enclosed shopping mall as defined in section 240.63 of the penal law.

(s) Identity theft in the second degree, as defined in section 190.79 of the penal law, identity theft in the first degree, as defined in section 190.80 of the penal law, unlawful possession of personal identification information in the second degree, as defined in section 190.82 of the penal law, and unlawful possession of personal identification information in the first degree, as defined in section 190.83 of the penal law.

(t) Menacing a police officer or peace officer as defined in section 120.18 of the penal law; aggravated criminally negligent homicide as defined in section 125.11 of the penal law; aggravated manslaughter in the second degree as defined in section 125.21 of the penal law; aggravated manslaughter in the first degree as defined in section 125.22 of the penal law; aggravated murder as defined in section 125.26 of the penal law.

(u) Any felony defined in article four hundred ninety-six of the penal law.

(v) Any of the acts designated as felonies in section three hundred fifty-one of the agriculture and markets law.

9. "Video surveillance" means the intentional visual observation by law enforcement of a person by means of a television camera or other electronic device that is part of a television transmitting apparatus, whether or not such observation is recorded on film or video tape, without the consent of that person or another person thereat and under circumstances in which such observation in the absence of a video surveillance warrant infringes upon such person's reasonable expectation of privacy under the constitution of this state or of the United States.

10. "Video surveillance warrant" means an order of a justice authorizing or approving video surveillance.

§700.10 Eavesdropping and video surveillance warrants; in general.

1. Under circumstances prescribed in this article, a justice may issue an eavesdropping warrant or a video surveillance warrant upon ex parte application of an applicant who is authorized by law to investigate, prosecute or participate in the prosecution of the particular designated offense which is the subject of the application.

2. No eavesdropping or video surveillance warrant may authorize or approve the interception of any communication or the conducting of any video surveillance for any period longer than is necessary to achieve the objective of the authorization, or in any event longer than thirty days. Such thirty day period shall begin on the date designated in the warrant as the

effective date, which date may be no later than ten days after the warrant is issued.

§700.15 Eavesdropping and video surveillance warrants; when issuable.

An eavesdropping or video surveillance warrant may issue only:

1. Upon an appropriate application made in conformity with this article; and

2. Upon probable cause to believe that a particularly described person is committing, has committed, or is about to commit a particular designated offense; and

3. Upon probable cause to believe that particular communications concerning such offense will be obtained through eavesdropping, or upon probable cause to believe that particular observations concerning such offense will be obtained through video surveillance; and

4. Upon a showing that normal investigative procedures have been tried and have failed, or reasonably appear to be unlikely to succeed if tried, or to be too dangerous to employ; and

5. Upon probable cause to believe that the facilities from which, or the place where, the communications are to be intercepted or the video surveillance is to be conducted, are being used, or are about to be used, in connection with the commission of such offense, or are leased to, listed in the name of, or commonly used by such person.

§700.20 Eavesdropping and video surveillance warrants; application.

1. An ex parte application for an eavesdropping or video surveillance warrant must be made to a justice in writing, except as provided in section 700.21 of this article, and must be subscribed and sworn to by an applicant.

2. The application must contain:

(a) The identity of the applicant and a statement of the applicant's authority to make such application; and

(b) A full and complete statement of the facts and circumstances relied upon by the applicant, to justify his belief that an eavesdropping or video surveillance warrant should be issued, including (i) a statement of facts establishing probable cause to believe that a particular designated offense has been, is being, or is about to be committed, (ii) a particular description of the nature and location of the facilities from which or the place where the communication is to be intercepted or the video surveillance is to be conducted, (iii) a particular description of the type of the communications sought to be intercepted or of the observations sought to be made, and (iv) the identity of the person, if known, committing such designated offense and whose communications are to be intercepted or who is to be the subject of the video surveillance; and

(c) A statement that such communications or observations are not otherwise legally privileged; and

(d) A full and complete statement of facts establishing that normal investigative procedures have been tried and have failed or reasonably appear to be unlikely to succeed if tried or to be too dangerous to employ, to obtain the evidence sought; and

(e) A statement of the period of time for which the eavesdropping or video surveillance is required to be maintained. If the nature of the investigation is such that the authorization for eavesdropping or video surveillance should not automatically terminate when the described type of communication has been first obtained or when the described type of observation has been first made, a particular description of facts establishing probable cause to believe that additional communications or observations of the same type will occur thereafter; and

(f) A full and complete statement of the facts concerning all previous applications, known to the applicant, for an eavesdropping or video surveillance warrant involving any of the same persons, facilities or places specified in the application, and the action taken by the justice on each such application.

3. Allegations of fact in the application may be based either upon the personal knowledge of the applicant or upon information and belief. If the applicant personally knows the facts alleged, it must be so stated. If the facts stated in the application are derived in whole or part from the statements of persons other than the applicant, the sources of such facts must be either disclosed or described, and the application must contain facts establishing the existence and reliability of the informants or the reliability of the information supplied by them. The application must also state, so far as possible, the basis of the informant's knowledge or belief. Affidavits of persons other than the applicant may be submitted in conjunction with the application if they tend to support any fact or conclusion alleged therein. Such accompanying affidavits may be based either on personal knowledge of the affiant, or information and belief with the source thereof and the reason therefor specified.

§700.21 Temporary authorization for eavesdropping or video surveillance in emergency situations.

1. In an emergency situation where imminent danger of death or serious physical injury exists and, under the circumstances, it is impractical for the applicant to prepare a written application without risk of such death or injury occurring, an application for an eavesdropping or video surveillance warrant need not be in writing but may be communicated to a justice by telephone, radio or other means of electronic communication.

2. Where an oral application for an eavesdropping or video surveillance warrant is made, the applicant therefor must identify himself and the purpose of his communication or observation, after being sworn as provided in subdivision three of this section. The application must meet the requirements of section 700.20 of this article and provide the same allegations of fact required by that section.

3. Upon being advised that an oral application for an eavesdropping or video surveillance warrant is being made, a justice shall place under oath the applicant and any other person providing information in support of the application. Such oath or oaths and all of the remaining communication must be recorded, either by means of a voice recording device or verbatim stenographic or verbatim longhand notes. If a voice recording device is used or a stenographic record made, the justice must have the record transcribed, certify to the accuracy of the transcription and file the original record and transcription with the court within twenty-four hours of the issuance of a warrant. If longhand notes are taken, the justice shall subscribe a copy and file it with the court within twenty-four hours of the issuance of a warrant.

4. Upon oral application, the court may, where it finds that an emergency situation exists and that the requirements of section 700.15 of this article have been satisfied, issue a temporary eavesdropping or video surveillance warrant authorizing eavesdropping or video surveillance for a period not to exceed twenty-four hours. Such eavesdropping or video surveillance warrant shall be executed in the manner prescribed by this article. The twenty-four hour period may not be extended nor may a temporary warrant be renewed except by written application in conformity with the requirements of this article.

§700.25 Eavesdropping warrants; determination of application.

1. If the application conforms to section 700.20, the justice may require the applicant to furnish additional testimony or documentary evidence in support of the application. He may examine, under oath, any person for the purpose of determining whether grounds exist for the issuance of the warrant pursuant to section 700.15. Any such examination must be either recorded or summarized in writing.

2. If the justice determines on the basis of the facts submitted by the applicant that grounds exist for the issuance of an eavesdropping warrant pursuant to section 700.15, the justice may grant the application and

issue an eavesdropping warrant, in accordance with section 700.30.

3. If the application does not conform to section 700.20, or if the justice is not satisfied that grounds exist for the issuance of an eavesdropping warrant, the application must be denied.

§700.30 Eavesdropping and video surveillance warrants; form and content.

An eavesdropping or video surveillance warrant must contain:

1. The name of the applicant, date of issuance, and the subscription and title of the issuing justice; and

2. The identity of the person, if known, whose communications are to be intercepted or who is to be the subject of video surveillance; and

3. The nature and location of the communications facilities as to which, or the place where, authority to intercept or conduct video surveillance is granted; and

4. A particular description of the type of communications sought to be intercepted or of the type of observations to be made, and a statement of the particular designated offense to which it relates; and

5. The identity of the law enforcement agency authorized to intercept the communications or conduct the video surveillance; and

6. The period of time during which such interception or observation is authorized, including a statement as to whether or not the interception or video surveillance shall automatically terminate when the described communication has been first obtained or the described observation has been first made; and

7. A provision that the authorization to intercept or conduct video surveillance shall be executed as soon as practicable, shall be conducted in such a way as to minimize the interception of communications or the making of observations not otherwise subject to eavesdropping or video surveillance under this article, and must terminate upon attainment of the authorized objective, or in any event in thirty days; and

8. An express authorization to make secret entry upon a private place or premises to install an eavesdropping or video surveillance device, if such entry is necessary to execute the warrant; and

9. An order authorizing eavesdropping or video surveillance may direct that providers of wire or electronic communication services furnish the applicant information, facilities, or technical assistance necessary to accomplish the interception unobtrusively and with a minimum of interference with the services that the service provider accords the party whose communications are to be intercepted. The order shall not direct the service providers to perform the intercept or use the premises of the service provider for such activity.

§700.35 Eavesdropping and video surveillance warrants; manner and time of execution.

1. An eavesdropping or video surveillance warrant must be executed according to its terms by a law enforcement officer who is a member of the law enforcement agency authorized in the warrant to intercept the communications or conduct the video surveillance.

2. Upon termination of the authorization in the warrant, eavesdropping or video surveillance must cease and as soon as practicable thereafter any device installed for such purpose either must be removed or must be permanently inactivated as soon as practicable by any means approved by the issuing justice. Entry upon a private place or premise for the removal or permanent inactivation of such device is deemed to be authorized by the warrant.

3. The contents of any communication intercepted or of any observation made by any means authorized by this article must, if possible, be recorded on tape or wire or other comparable device. The recording of the contents of any such communication or observation must be done in such way as will protect the recording from editing or other alterations.

4. In the event an intercepted communication is in a code or foreign language, and the services of an expert in that foreign language or code cannot reasonably be obtained during the interception period, where the warrant so authorizes and in a manner specified therein, the minimization required by subdivision seven of section 700.30 of this article may be accomplished as soon as practicable after such interception.

5. A good faith reliance by a provider of a wire or electronic communication service upon the validity of a court order issued pursuant to this article is a complete defense against any civil cause of action or criminal action based solely on a failure to comply with this article.

§700.40 Eavesdropping and video surveillance warrants; order of extension.

At any time prior to the expiration of an eavesdropping or video surveillance warrant, the applicant may apply to the issuing justice, or, if he is unavailable, to another justice, for an order of extension. The period of extension shall be no longer than the justice deems necessary to achieve the purposes for which it was granted and in no event longer than thirty days. The application for an order of extension must conform in all respects to the provisions of section 700.20 and, in addition, must contain a statement setting forth the results thus far obtained from the interception, or a reasonable explanation of the failure to obtain such results. The provisions of sections 700.15 and 700.25 are applicable in the determination of such application. The order of extension must conform in all respects to the provisions of section 700.30. In the execution of such order of extension the provisions of section 700.35 are applicable.

§700.50 Eavesdropping and video surveillance warrants; progress reports and notice.

1. An eavesdropping or video surveillance warrant may require reports to be made to the issuing justice showing what progress has been made toward achievement of the authorized objective and the need for continued eavesdropping or video surveillance. Such reports shall be made at such intervals as the justice may require.

2. Immediately upon the expiration of the period of an eavesdropping or video surveillance warrant, the recordings of communications or observations made pursuant to subdivision three of section 700.35 must be made available to the issuing justice and sealed under his directions.

3. Within a reasonable time, but in no case later than ninety days after termination of an eavesdropping or video surveillance warrant, or expiration of an extension order, except as otherwise provided in subdivision four, written notice of the fact and date of the issuance of the eavesdropping or video surveillance warrant, and of the period of authorized eavesdropping or video surveillance, and of the fact that during such period communications were or were not intercepted or observation were or were not made, must be served upon the person named in the warrant and such other parties to the intercepted communications or subjects of the video surveillance as the justice may determine in his discretion is in the interest of justice. Service reasonably calculated to give affected parties the notice required by this subdivision shall be effected within the time limits provided for herein and in a manner prescribed by the justice. The justice, upon the filing of a motion by any person served with such notice, may in his discretion make available to such person or his counsel for inspection such portions of the intercepted communications or video surveillance, applications and warrants as the justice determines to be in the interest of justice.

4. On a showing of exigent circumstances to the issuing justice, the service of the notice required by subdivision three may be postponed by order of the justice for a reasonable period of time. Renewals of an order of postponement may be obtained on a new showing of exigent circumstances.

§700.55 Eavesdropping and video surveillance warrants; custody of warrants, applications and recordings.

1. Applications made and warrants issued under this article shall be sealed by the justice. Any eavesdropping or video surveillance warrant, together with a copy of papers upon which the application is based, shall be delivered to and retained by the applicant as authority for the eavesdropping or video surveillance authorized therein. A copy of such eavesdropping or video surveillance warrant, together with all the original papers upon which the application was based, must be retained by the justice issuing the same, and, in the event of the denial of an application for such an eavesdropping or video surveillance warrant, a copy of the papers upon which the application was based must be retained by the justice denying the same. Such applications and warrants may be disclosed only upon a showing of good cause before a court and may not be destroyed except on order of the issuing or denying justice, and in any event must be kept for ten years.

2. Custody of the recordings made pursuant to subdivision three of section 700.35 may be wherever the justice orders. They may not be destroyed except upon an order of the justice who issued the warrant and in any event must be kept for ten years. Duplicate recordings may be made for use or disclosure pursuant to the provisions of subdivisions one and two of section 700.65 for investigations.

§700.60 Eavesdropping warrants; reports to the administrative office of the United States courts.

1. Within thirty days after the termination of an eavesdropping warrant or the expiration of an extension order, the issuing or denying justice must submit such report to the administrative office of the United States courts as is required by federal law.

2. In January of each year, the attorney general and each district attorney must submit such report to the administrative office of the United States courts as is required by federal law.

§700.65 Eavesdropping and video surveillance warrants; disclosure and use of information; order of amendment.

1. Any law enforcement officer who, by any means authorized by this article, has obtained knowledge of the contents of any intercepted communication or video surveillance, or evidence derived therefrom, may disclose such contents to another law enforcement officer to the extent that such disclosure is appropriate to the proper performance of the official duties of the officer making or receiving the disclosure.

2. Any law enforcement officer who, by any means authorized by this article, has obtained knowledge of the contents of any intercepted communication or video surveillance, or evidence derived therefrom, may use such contents to the extent such use is appropriate to the proper performance of his official duties.

3. Any person who has received, by any means authorized by this article, any information concerning a communication or video surveillance, or evidence derived therefrom, intercepted or conducted in accordance with the provisions of this article, may disclose the contents of that communication or video surveillance, or such derivative evidence, while giving testimony under oath in any criminal proceeding in any court, in any grand jury proceeding or in any action commenced pursuant to article thirteen-A or thirteen-B of the civil practice law and rules; provided, however, that the presence of the seal provided for by subdivision two of section 700.50, or a satisfactory explanation of the absence thereof, shall be a prerequisite for the use or disclosure of the contents of any communication or video surveillance, or evidence derived therefrom; and provided further, however, that where a criminal court of competent jurisdiction has ordered exclusion or suppression of the contents of an intercepted communication or video surveillance, or evidence derived therefrom, such determination shall

be binding in an action commenced pursuant to article thirteen-A or thirteen-B of the civil practice law and rules.

4. When a law enforcement officer, while engaged in intercepting communications or conducting video surveillance in the manner authorized by this article, intercepts a communication or makes an observation which was not otherwise sought and which constitutes evidence of any crime that has been, is being or is about to be committed, the contents of such communications or observation, and evidence derived therefrom, may be disclosed or used as provided in subdivisions one and two. Such contents and any evidence derived therefrom may be used under subdivision three when a justice amends the eavesdropping or video surveillance warrant to include such contents. The application for such amendment must be made by the applicant as soon as practicable by giving notice to the court of the interception of the communication or the making of the observation and of the contents of such interception or observation; provided that during the period in which the eavesdropping or video surveillance is continuing, such notice must be given within ten days after probable cause exists to believe that a crime not named in the warrant has been, is being, or is about to be committed, or at the time an application for an order of extension is made pursuant to section 700.40 of this article, if such probable cause then exists, whichever is earlier. If the justice finds that such contents were otherwise intercepted in accordance with the provisions of this article, he may grant the application.

§700.70 Eavesdropping warrants; notice before use of evidence.

The contents of any intercepted communication, or evidence derived therefrom, may not be received in evidence or otherwise disclosed upon a trial of a defendant unless the people, within fifteen days after arraignment and before the commencement of the trial, furnish the defendant with a copy of the eavesdropping warrant, and accompanying application, under which interception was authorized or approved. This fifteen day period may be extended by the trial court upon good cause shown if it finds that the defendant will not be prejudiced by the delay in receiving such papers.

ARTICLE 705 - PEN REGISTERS AND TRAP AND TRACE DEVICES

Section
705.00 **Definitions.**
705.05 **Pen register and trap and trace authorizations; in general.**
705.10 **Orders authorizing the use of a pen register or a trap and trace device; when issuable.**
705.15 **Application for an order authorizing the use of a pen register or a trap and trace device.**
705.20 **Orders authorizing the use of a pen register or a trap and trace device; determination of application.**
705.25 **Pen register or trap and trace device orders; time period and extensions.**
705.30 **Nondisclosure of existence of pen register or a trap and trace device.**
705.35 **Assistance in installation and use of a pen register or a trap and trace device.**

§705.00 Definitions.

As used in this article, the following terms have the following meanings:

1. "Pen register" means a device which records or decodes electronic or other impulses which identify the numbers dialed or otherwise transmitted on the telephone line to which such device is attached, but such term does not include any device used by a provider or customer of a wire or electronic communication service for billing, or recording as an incident to billing, for communications services provided by such provider or any device used by a provider or customer of a wire communication service for cost accounting or other like purposes in the ordinary course of its business.

2. "Trap and trace device" means a device which captures the incoming electronic or other impulses which identify the originating number of an instrument or device from which a wire or electronic communication was transmitted.

3. "Applicant" means a district attorney, an assistant district attorney, and when empowered by law to conduct an investigation of or to prosecute or participate in the prosecution of a designated crime, the attorney general, an assistant attorney general, the deputy attorney general in charge of the statewide organized crime task force, or an assistant deputy attorney general of such task force.

4. "Law enforcement agency" means any agency which is empowered by law to conduct an investigation or to make an arrest for a felony, and any agency which is authorized by law to prosecute or participate in the prosecution of a felony.

5. "Designated crime" means any crime included within the definition of a "designated offense" in subdivision eight of section 700.05 of this chapter, any criminal act as defined in subdivision one of section 460.10 of the penal law, bail jumping in the first and second degree as defined in sections 215.57 and 215.56 of such law, or aggravated harassment as defined in subdivisions one and two of section 240.30 of such law.

6. "Justice" means justice as defined in subdivision four of section 700.05 of this chapter.

§705.05 Pen register and trap and trace authorizations; in general.

Under circumstances prescribed in this article, a justice may issue an order authorizing the use of a pen register or a trap and trace device upon ex parte application of an applicant who is authorized by law to investigate, prosecute or participate in the prosecution of the designated crimes which are the subject of the application.

§705.10 Orders authorizing the use of a pen register or a trap and trace device; when issuable.

An author authorizing the use of a pen register or a trap and trace device may issue only:

1. Upon an appropriate application made in conformity with this article; and

2. Upon a determination that an application sets forth specific, articulable facts, warranting the applicant's reasonable suspicion that a designated crime has been, is being, or is about to be committed and demonstrating that the information likely to be obtained by use of a pen register or trap and trace device is or will be relevant to an ongoing criminal investigation of such designated crime.

§705.15 Application for an order authorizing the use of a pen register or a trap and trace device.

1. An ex parte application for an order or an extension of an order authorizing the use of a pen register or a trap and trace device must be made to a justice in writing, and must be subscribed and sworn to by the applicant.

2. The application must contain:

(a) The identity of the applicant and the identity of the law enforcement agency conducting the investigation; and

(b) A statement of facts and circumstances sufficient to justify the applicant's belief that an order authorizing the use of a pen register or a trap and trace device should be issued, including (i) a statement of the specific facts on the basis of which the applicant reasonably suspects that the designated crime has been, is being, or is about to be committed and demonstrating that the information likely to be obtained by use of a pen register or a trap and trace device is or will be relevant to an ongoing criminal investigation of such designated offense, (ii) the identity, if known, of the person to whom is leased or in whose name is listed the telephone line to which the pen register or trap and trace device is to be attached, (iii) the identity, if known, of the person who is the subject of the criminal investigation, (iv) the number and, if known, the physical location of the telephone line to which the pen register or trap and trace device is to be attached and, in the case of a trap and trace device, the geographic limits of the trap and trace order, and (v) a statement of the designated crime or crimes to which the information likely to be obtained by the use of the pen register or trap and trace device relates; and

(c) A statement of the period of time for which the authorization for the use of a pen register or a trap and trace device is required; and

(d) A statement of the facts concerning all previous applications, known to the applicant, for an order authorizing the use of a pen register or a trap and trace device involving any of the same persons or facilities specified in the application, and the action taken by the justice on each such application.

3. Allegations of fact in the application may be based either upon the personal knowledge of the applicant or upon information and belief. If the applicant personally knows the facts alleged, it must be so stated. If the facts stated in the application are derived in whole or in part from the statements of persons other than the applicant, the sources of such facts must be either disclosed or described.

§705.20 Orders authorizing the use of a pen register or a trap and trace device; determination of application.

1. If the justice determines on the basis of the facts submitted by the applicant that grounds exist for the issue of an order authorizing the use of a pen register or a trap and trace device pursuant to section 705.10 of this article, the justice shall grant the application and issue an order authorizing the use of a pen register or a trap and trace device, in accordance with subdivision three of this section.

2. If the application does not conform to section 705.15 of this article, or if the justice is not satisfied that grounds exist for the issuance of an order authorizing the use of a pen register or a trap and trace device, the application must be denied.

3. An order issued under this section must contain:

(a) the name of the applicant, date of issuance, and the subscription and title of the issuing justice; and

(b) the identity, if known, of the person to whom is leased or in whose name is listed the telephone line to which the pen register or trap and trace device is to be attached; and

(c) the identity, if known, of the person who is the subject of the criminal investigation; and

(d) the number and, if known, the physical location of the telephone line to which the pen register or trap and trace device is to be attached and, in the case of a trap and trace device, the geographic limits of the trap and trace order; and

(e) a statement of the designated crime or crimes to which the information likely to be obtained by the pen register or trap and trace device relates.

4. An order issued under this section shall direct, upon the request of the applicant, the furnishing of information, facilities, and technical assistance necessary to accomplish the installation of the pen register or trap and trace device under section 705.25 of this article.

§705.25 Pen register or trap and trace device orders; time period and extensions.

1. An order issued under this section shall authorize the installation and use of a pen register or a trap and trace device for a period not to exceed sixty days.

2. Extensions of such an order may be granted, but only upon an application for an order under section 705.05 of this article and upon the judicial finding required by subdivision one of section 705.10 of this article. The period of extension shall be for a period not to exceed sixty days.

§705.30 Nondisclosure of existence of pen register or a trap and trace device.

An order authorizing or approving the installation and use of a pen register or a trap and trace device shall direct that:

1. the order be sealed until otherwise ordered by the court; and

2. the person owning or leasing the line to which the pen register or a trap and trace device is attached, or who has been ordered by the court to provide assistance to the applicant, not disclose the existence of the pen register or trap and trace device or the existence of the investigation to the listed subscriber, or to any other person, unless or until otherwise ordered by the court.

§705.35 Assistance in installation and use of a pen register or a trap and trace device.

1. Upon the request of an applicant authorized to use a pen register under this article, a provider of a wire or electronic communication service, landlord, custodian, or other person shall furnish such applicant, or his agent, forthwith all information, facilities and technical assistance necessary to accomplish the installation of the pen register unobtrusively and with a minimum of interference with the services that the person so ordered by the court accords the party with respect to whom the installation and use is to take place, if such assistance is directed by a court order as provided in section 705.10 of this article.

2. Upon the request of an applicant authorized to receive the results of a trap and trace device under this article, a provider of a wire or electronic communication service, landlord, custodian, or other person shall install such device forthwith on the appropriate line and shall furnish such applicant forthwith all information, facilities and technical assistance including installation and operation of the device unobtrusively and with a minimum of interference with the services that the person so ordered by the court accords the party with respect to whom the installation and use is to take place, if such installation and assistance is directed by the court order as provided in section 705.10 of this article. Unless otherwise ordered by the court, the results of the trap and trace device shall be furnished to the applicant, or his agent, at reasonable intervals during regular business hours for the duration of the order.

3. A provider of a wire or electronic communication service, landlord, custodian, or other person who furnishes facilities or technical assistance pursuant to this section shall be reasonably compensated for such reasonable expenses incurred in providing such facilities and assistance.

4. No cause of action shall lie in any court against any provider of a wire or electronic communication service, its officers, employees, agents or other specified persons for providing information, facilities or assistance in accordance with the terms of a court order under this article. A good faith reliance by a provider of a wire or electronic communication service upon the validity of a court order issued pursuant to this article is a complete defense against any civil cause of action or criminal action based entirely on a failure to comply with this article.

ARTICLE 710 - MOTION TO SUPPRESS EVIDENCE

Section
710.10 Motion to suppress evidence; definitions of terms.
710.20 Motion to suppress evidence; in general; grounds for.
710.30 Motion to suppress evidence; notice to defendant of intention to offer evidence.
710.40 Motion to suppress evidence; when made and determined.
710.50 Motion to suppress evidence; in what courts made.
710.60 Motion to suppress evidence; procedure.
710.70 Motion to suppress evidence; orders of suppression; effects of orders and of failure to make motion.

§710.10 Motion to suppress evidence; definitions of terms.

As used in this article, the following terms have the following meanings:

1. "Defendant" means a person who has been charged by an accusatory instrument with the commission of an offense.

2. "Evidence" when referring to matter in the possession of or available to a prosecutor, means any tangible property or potential testimony which may be offered in evidence in a criminal action.

3. "Potential testimony" means information or factual knowledge of a person who is or may be available as a witness.

4. "Eavesdropping" means "wiretapping", "mechanical overhearing of a conversation," or "intercepting or accessing of an electronic communication", as those terms are defined in section 250.00 of the penal law.

5. "Aggrieved." An "aggrieved person" includes, but is in no wise limited to, an "aggrieved person" as defined in subdivision two of section forty-five hundred six of the civil practice law and rules.

6. "Video surveillance" has the meaning given to that term by section 700.05 of this chapter.

7. "Pen register" and "trap and trace device" have the meanings given to those terms by subdivisions one and two respectively of section 705.00 of this chapter.

§710.20 Motion to suppress evidence; in general; grounds for.

Upon motion of a defendant who (a) is aggrieved by unlawful or improper acquisition of evidence and has reasonable cause to believe that such may be offered against him in a criminal action, or (b) claims that improper identification testimony may be offered against him in a criminal action, a court may, under circumstances prescribed in this article, order that such evidence be suppressed or excluded upon the ground that it:

1. Consists of tangible property obtained by means of an unlawful search and seizure under circumstances precluding admissibility thereof in a criminal action against such defendant; or

2. Consists of a record or potential testimony reciting or describing declarations, conversations, or other communications overheard, intercepted, accessed, or recorded by means of eavesdropping, or observations made by means of video surveillance, obtained under circumstances precluding admissibility thereof in a criminal action against such defendant; or

3. Consists of a record or potential testimony reciting or describing a statement of such defendant involuntarily made, within the meaning of section 60.45; or

4. Was obtained as a result of other evidence obtained in a manner described in subdivisions one, two and three; or

5. Consists of a chemical test of the defendant's blood administered in violation of the provisions of subdivision three of section eleven hundred ninety-four of the vehicle and traffic law, subdivision eight of section forty-nine-a of the navigation law, subdivision seven of section 25.24 of the parks, recreation and historic preservation law, or any other applicable law; or

*6. Consists of potential testimony regarding an observation of the defendant either at the time or place of the commission of the offense or upon some other occasion relevant to the case, which potential testimony would not be admissible upon the prospective trial of such charge owing to

an improperly made previous identification of the defendant or of a pictorial, photographic, electronic, filmed or video recorded reproduction of the defendant by the prospective witness. A claim that the previous identification of the defendant or of a pictorial, photographic, electronic, filmed or video recorded reproduction of the defendant by a prospective witness did not comply with paragraph (c) of subdivision one of section 60.25 of this chapter or with the protocol promulgated in accordance with subdivision twenty-one of section eight hundred thirty-seven of the executive law shall not constitute a legal basis to suppress evidence pursuant to this subdivision. A claim that a public servant failed to comply with paragraph (c) of subdivision one of section 60.25 of this chapter or of subdivision twenty-one of section eight hundred thirty-seven of the executive law shall neither expand nor limit the rights an accused person may derive under the constitution of this state or of the United States.   *(Eff.7/1/17,Ch.59,L.2017)

7. Consists of information obtained by means of a pen register or trap and trace device installed or used in violation of the provisions of article seven hundred five of this chapter.

§710.30   Motion to suppress evidence; notice to defendant of intention to offer evidence.

*1. Whenever the people intend to offer at a trial (a) evidence of a statement made by a defendant to a public servant, which statement if involuntarily made would render the evidence thereof suppressible upon motion pursuant to subdivision three of section 710.20, or (b) testimony regarding an observation of the defendant either at the time or place of the commission of the offense or upon some other occasion relevant to the case, to be given by a witness who has previously identified him or her or a pictorial, photographic, electronic, filmed or video recorded reproduction of him or her as such, they must serve upon the defendant a notice of such intention, specifying the evidence intended to be offered.

*(Eff.7/1/17,Ch.59,L.2017)

2. Such notice must be served within fifteen days after arraignment and before trial, and upon such service the defendant must be accorded reasonable opportunity to move before trial, pursuant to subdivision one of section 710.40, to suppress the specified evidence. For good cause shown, however, the court may permit the people to serve such notice, thereafter and in such case it must accord the defendant reasonable opportunity thereafter to make a suppression motion.

3. In the absence of service of notice upon a defendant as prescribed in this section, no evidence of a kind specified in subdivision one may be received against him upon trial unless he has, despite the lack of such notice, moved to suppress such evidence and such motion has been denied and the evidence thereby rendered admissible as prescribed in subdivision two of section 710.70.

§710.40   Motion to suppress evidence; when made and determined.

1. A motion to suppress evidence must be made after the commencement of the criminal action in which such evidence is allegedly about to be offered, and, except as otherwise provided in section 710.30 and in subdivision two of this section, it must be made within the period provided in subdivision one of section 255.20.

2. The motion may be made for the first time when, owing to unawareness of facts constituting the basis thereof or to other factors, the defendant did not have reasonable opportunity to make the motion previously, or when the evidence which he seeks to suppress is of a kind specified in section 710.30 and he was not served by the people, as provided in said section 710.30, with a pre-trial notice of intention to offer such evidence at the trial.

3. When the motion is made before trial, the trial may not be commenced until determination of the motion.

4. If after a pre-trial determination and denial of the motion the court is satisfied, upon a showing by the defendant, that additional pertinent facts have been discovered by the defendant which he could not have discovered with reasonable diligence before the determination of the motion, it may

permit him to renew the motion before trial or, if such was not possible owing to the time of the discovery of the alleged new facts, during trial.

§710.50 Motion to suppress evidence; in what courts made.

1. The particular courts in which motions to suppress evidence must be made are as follows:

(a) If an indictment is pending in a superior court, or if the defendant has been held by a local criminal court for the action of a grand jury, the motion must be made in the superior court in which such indictment is pending or which impaneled or will impanel such grand jury. If the superior court which will impanel such grand jury is the supreme court, the motion may, in the alternative, be made in the county court of the county in which the action is pending;

(b) If a currently undetermined felony complaint is pending in a local criminal court, the motion must be made in the superior court which would have trial jurisdiction of the offense or offenses charged were an indictment therefor to result;

(c) If an information, a simplified information, a prosecutor's information or a misdemeanor complaint is pending in a local criminal court, the motion must be made in such court.

2. If after a motion has been made in and determined by a superior court a local criminal court acquires trial jurisdiction of the action by reason of an information, a prosecutor's information or a misdemeanor complaint filed therewith, such superior court's determination is binding upon such local criminal court. If, however, the motion has been made in but not yet determined by the superior court at the time of the filing of such information, prosecutor's information or misdemeanor complaint, the superior court may not determine the motion but must refer it to the local criminal court of trial jurisdiction.

§710.60 Motion to suppress evidence; procedure.

1. A motion to suppress evidence made before trial must be in writing and upon reasonable notice to the people and with opportunity to be heard. The motion papers must state the ground or grounds of the motion and must contain sworn allegations of fact, whether of the defendant or of another person or persons, supporting such grounds. Such allegations may be based upon personal knowledge of the deponent or upon information and belief, provided that in the latter event the sources of such information and the grounds of such belief are stated. The people may file with the court, and in such case must serve a copy thereof upon the defendant or his counsel, an answer denying or admitting any or all of the allegations of the moving papers.

2. The court must summarily grant the motion if:

(a) The motion papers comply with the requirements of subdivision one and the people concede the truth of allegations of fact therein which support the motion; or

(b) The people stipulate that the evidence sought to be suppressed will not be offered in evidence in any criminal action or proceeding against the defendant.

3. The court may summarily deny the motion if:

(a) The motion papers do not allege a ground constituting legal basis for the motion; or

(b) The sworn allegations of fact do not as a matter of law support the ground alleged; except that this paragraph does not apply where the motion is based upon the ground specified in subdivision three or six of section 710.20.

4. If the court does not determine the motion pursuant to subdivisions two or three, it must conduct a hearing and make findings of fact essential to the determination thereof. All persons giving factual information at such hearing must testify under oath, except that unsworn evidence pursuant to subdivision

two of section 60.20 of this chapter may also be received. Upon such hearing, hearsay evidence is admissible to establish any material fact.

5. A motion to suppress evidence made during trial may be in writing and may be litigated and determined on the basis of motion papers as provided in subdivisions one through four, or it may, instead, be made orally in open court. In the latter event, the court must, where necessary, also conduct a hearing as provided in subdivision four, out of the presence of the jury if any, and make findings of fact essential to the determination of the motion.

6. Regardless of whether a hearing was conducted, the court, upon determining the motion, must set forth on the record its findings of fact, its conclusions of law and the reasons for its determination.

§710.70 Motion to suppress evidence; orders of suppression; effects of orders and of failure to make motion.

1. Upon granting a motion to suppress evidence, the court must order that the evidence in question be excluded in the criminal action pending against the defendant. When the order is based upon the ground specified in subdivision one of section 710.20 and excludes tangible property unlawfully taken from the defendant's possession, and when such property is not otherwise subject to lawful retention, the court may, upon request of the defendant, further order that such property be restored to him.

2. An order finally denying a motion to suppress evidence may be reviewed upon an appeal from an ensuing judgment of conviction notwithstanding the fact that such judgment is entered upon a plea of guilty.

3. A motion to suppress evidence made pursuant to this article is the exclusive method of challenging the admissibility of evidence upon the grounds specified in section 710.20, and a defendant who does not make such a motion before or in the course of a criminal action waives his right to judicial determination of any such contention.

Nothing contained in this article, however, precludes a defendant from attempting to establish at a trial that evidence introduced by the people of a pre-trial statement made by him should be disregarded by the jury or other trier of the facts on the ground that such statement was involuntarily made within the meaning of section 60.45. Even though the issue of the admissibility of such evidence was not submitted to the court, or was determined adversely to the defendant upon motion, the defendant may adduce trial evidence and otherwise contend that the statement was involuntarily made. In the case of a jury trial, the court must submit such issue to the jury under instructions to disregard such evidence upon a finding that the statement was involuntarily made.

ARTICLE 715 - DESTRUCTION OF DANGEROUS DRUGS

Section
715.05 Dangerous drugs; definition.
715.10 Pretrial motion to destroy dangerous drugs.
715.20 Proceedings on motion upon notice.
715.30 Orders of the court.
715.40 Affidavit of destruction.
715.50 Analysis of dangerous drugs.

§715.05 Dangerous drugs; definition.

"Dangerous drugs" means any substance listed in schedule I, II, III, IV or V of section thirty-three hundred six of the public health law.

§715.10 Pretrial motion to destroy dangerous drugs.

1. Subject to the limitations in paragraph (b) of subdivision two hereof a district attorney may move in a superior court for an order of destruction of the dangerous drugs in felony cases involving the possession or sale of such drugs.

2. A motion for an order of destruction of dangerous drugs shall be in writing, having attached thereto a copy of the report of analysis and shall be made in the following manner:

(a) Ex parte; where no defendants have been arrested in connection with the seizure of such drugs and a showing is made upon affidavit that the likelihood of any future arrest in connection therewith is nonexistent; or

(b) Upon notice, when a defendant has been arraigned in a superior court upon an indictment charging him with a felony involving the possession or sale of a dangerous drug and the dangerous drugs sought to be destroyed are material to the prosecution of said indictment.

3. When such motion is ex parte, the court may order the destruction of all or part of the subject drugs.

4. When such motion is upon notice, further proceedings shall be had as provided in section 715.20 hereof.

§715.20 Proceedings on motion upon notice.

1. When such motion is on notice, a hearing thereon shall be held by the court before which it is returnable not later than thirty days after the return date and the defendant shall be present at such hearing.

2. A hearing held pursuant to this section shall be conducted and recorded in the same manner as would be required were the witnesses testifying at trial. The district attorney shall establish by competent evidence the nature and quantity of the dangerous drugs which are the subject of the motion. Each party shall have the right to call and cross examine witnesses and to register objections and to receive rulings of the court thereon.

3. If the court finds upon the conclusion of the hearing that neither the prosecution nor the defendant will be prejudiced thereby it may grant the motion and may make such order as it may deem appropriate for the destruction of part or all of such drugs.

4. A defendant may waive such hearing and consent to the granting of the motion and entry of an order of destruction either by sworn affidavit or by personal appearance in court and declaration on the record of such waiver and consent.

§715.30 Orders of the court.

1. In any proceeding brought pursuant to this article, the court may grant or deny any motion made hereunder or the relief requested therein in whole or in part and issue any order thereon as it may deem proper and as the interests of justice may require in order to effectuate the provisions of this article.

2. An order of destruction of a dangerous drug issued by the court pursuant to this article shall state the time within which the provisions of such order are to be complied with. It shall direct the person having custody of the drug to make provision for the destruction thereof in the presence of at least two witnesses, at least one of whom shall be a police officer.

§715.40 Affidavit of destruction.

An affidavit attesting to the date, time, place and manner of destruction of a dangerous drug pursuant to an order therefor and identifying the same by reference to the report of analysis or by other identifying number or system and the order of the court issued thereon, shall be filed with the court by the person who destroyed the drugs and by each of the witnesses required to be present by subdivision two of section 715.30 of this article.

§715.50 Analysis of dangerous drugs.

1. On and after September first, nineteen hundred seventy-three, in every felony case involving the possession or sale of a dangerous drug, the head of the agency charged with custody of such drugs, or his designee,

shall within forty-five days after receipt thereof perform or cause to be performed an analysis of such drugs, such analysis to include qualitative identification; weight and quantity where appropriate.

2. Within ten days after the report of such analysis is received by such agency, the head thereof or his designee shall forward a copy thereof to the appropriate district attorney and inform him of the location where the subject drugs are being held.

3. The failure to have an analysis made or to forward a copy thereof within the time specified in subdivisions one and two of this section shall not be deemed or construed to bar the making or granting of a motion pursuant to this article or to the prosecution of a case involving such drugs.

TITLE U - SPECIAL PROCEEDINGS WHICH REPLACE, SUSPEND OR ABATE CRIMINAL ACTIONS

ARTICLE 720 - YOUTHFUL OFFENDER PROCEDURE

Section
720.10 Youthful offender procedure; definition of terms.
720.15 Youthful offender procedure; sealing of accusatory instrument; privacy of proceedings; preliminary instructions to jury.
720.20 Youthful offender determination; when and how made; procedure thereupon.
720.25 Youthful offender adjudication; certain exemptions.
720.30 Youthful offender adjudication; post-judgment motions and appeal.
720.35 Youthful offender adjudication; effect thereof; records.

§720.10 Youthful offender procedure; definition of terms.

As used in this article, the following terms have the following meanings:

1. "Youth" means a person charged with a crime alleged to have been committed when he was at least sixteen years old and less than nineteen years old or a person charged with being a juvenile offender as defined in subdivision forty-two of section 1.20 of this chapter.

2. "Eligible youth" means a youth who is eligible to be found a youthful offender. Every youth is so eligible unless:

(a) the conviction to be replaced by a youthful offender finding is for (i) a class A-I or class A-II felony, or (ii) an armed felony as defined in subdivision forty-one of section 1.20, except as provided in subdivision three, or (iii) rape in the first degree, criminal sexual act in the first degree, or aggravated sexual abuse, except as provided in subdivision three, or

(b) such youth has previously been convicted and sentenced for a felony, or

(c) such youth has previously been adjudicated a youthful offender following conviction of a felony or has been adjudicated on or after September first, nineteen hundred seventy-eight a juvenile delinquent who committed a designated felony act as defined in the family court act.

3. Notwithstanding the provisions of subdivision two, a youth who has been convicted of an armed felony offense or of rape in the first degree, criminal sexual act in the first degree, or aggravated sexual abuse is an eligible youth if the court determines that one or more of the following factors exist: (i) mitigating circumstances that bear directly upon the manner

in which the crime was committed; or (ii) where the defendant was not the sole participant in the crime, the defendant's participation was relatively minor although not so minor as to constitute a defense to the prosecution. Where the court determines that the eligible youth is a youthful offender, the court shall make a statement on the record of the reasons for its determination, a transcript of which shall be forwarded to the state division of criminal justice services, to be kept in accordance with the provisions of subdivision three of section eight hundred thirty-seven-a of the executive law.

4. "Youthful offender finding" means a finding, substituted for the conviction of an eligible youth, pursuant to a determination that the eligible youth is a youthful offender.

5. "Youthful offender sentence" means the sentence imposed upon a youthful offender finding.

6. "Youthful offender adjudication". A youthful offender adjudication is comprised of a youthful offender finding and the youthful offender sentence imposed thereon and is completed by imposition and entry of the youthful offender sentence.

§720.15 Youthful offender procedure; sealing of accusatory instrument; privacy of proceedings; preliminary instructions to jury.

1. When an accusatory instrument against an apparently eligible youth is filed with a court, it shall be filed as a sealed instrument, though only with respect to the public.

2. When a youth is initially arraigned upon an accusatory instrument, such arraignment and all proceedings in the action thereafter may, in the discretion of the court and with the defendant's consent, be conducted in private.

3. The provisions of subdivisions one and two of this section requiring or authorizing the accusatory instrument filed against a youth to be sealed, and the arraignment and all proceedings in the action to be conducted in private shall not apply in connection with a pending charge of committing any felony offense as defined in the penal law. The provisions of subdivision one requiring the accusatory instrument filed against a youth to be sealed shall not apply where such youth has previously been adjudicated a youthful offender or convicted of a crime.

4. Notwithstanding any provision in this article, a person charged with prostitution as defined in section 230.00 of the penal law regardless of whether such person (i) had prior to commencement of trial or entry of a plea of guilty been convicted of a crime or found a youthful offender, or (ii) subsequent to such conviction for prostitution is convicted of a crime or found a youthful offender, the provisions of subdivisions one and two of this section requiring or authorizing the accusatory instrument filed against a youth to be sealed, and the arraignment and all proceedings in the action to be conducted in private shall apply.   *(Eff.2/2/21,Ch.23,L.2021)*

§720.20 Youthful offender determination; when and how made; procedure thereupon.

1. Upon conviction of an eligible youth, the court must order a presentence investigation of the defendant. After receipt of a written report of the investigation and at the time of pronouncing sentence the court must determine whether or not the eligible youth is a youthful offender. Such determination shall be in accordance with the following criteria:

(a) If in the opinion of the court the interest of justice would be served by relieving the eligible youth from the onus of a criminal record and by not imposing an indeterminate term of imprisonment of more than four years, the court may, in its discretion, find the eligible youth is a youthful offender; and

(b) Where the conviction is had in a local criminal court and the eligible youth had not prior to commencement of trial or entry of a plea of guilty been convicted of a crime or found a youthful offender, the court must find he is a youthful offender.

2. Where an eligible youth is convicted of two or more crimes set forth in separate counts of an accusatory instrument or set forth in two or more accusatory instruments consolidated for trial purposes, the court must not find him a youthful offender with respect to any such conviction pursuant to subdivision one of this section unless it finds him a youthful offender with respect to all such convictions.

3. Upon determining that an eligible youth is a youthful offender, the court must direct that the conviction be deemed vacated and replaced by a youthful offender finding; and the court must sentence the defendant pursuant to section 60.02 of the penal law.

4. Upon determining that an eligible youth is not a youthful offender, the court must order the accusatory instrument unsealed and continue the action to judgment pursuant to the ordinary rules governing criminal prosecutions.

5. (a) An individual who was an eligible youth who was not determined to be a youthful offender by the sentencing court may apply to the sentencing court for a new determination after at least five years have passed since the imposition of the sentence for which such individual was not determined to be a youthful offender, or, if the individual was sentenced to a period of incarceration, including a period of incarceration imposed in conjunction with a sentence of probation, the individual's latest release from incarceration, provided that such individual has not been convicted of any new crime since the imposition of such sentence.

(b) In considering whether such individual should be determined to be a youthful offender pursuant to paragraph (a) of this subdivision, the court shall consider the following factors:

(i) whether relieving the individual from the onus of a criminal record would facilitate rehabilitation and successful reentry and reintegration into society;

(ii) the manner in which the crime was committed;

(iii) the role of the individual in the crime which resulted in the conviction;

(iv) the individual's age at the time of the crime;

(v) the length of time since the crime was committed;

(vi) any mitigating circumstances at the time the crime was committed;

(vii) the individual's criminal record;

(viii) the individual's attitude toward society and respect for the law; and

(ix) evidence of rehabilitation and demonstration of living a productive life including, but not limited to participation in educational and vocational programs, employment history, alcohol and substance abuse treatment, and family and community involvement.

(c) A copy of an application filed under this subdivision shall be served upon the district attorney of the county in which the individual was convicted. The district attorney shall notify the court within forty-five days if he or she objects to the application for sealing. The court may hold a hearing on the application on its own motion or on motion of the district attorney or the individual filing the application. If the district attorney does not file a timely objection, the court shall proceed forthwith.   *(Eff.11/2/21,Ch.552,L.2021)*

§720.25 Youthful offender adjudication; certain exemptions.

Notwithstanding any inconsistent provisions of law:

1. where the court is required to find that a person is a youthful offender pursuant to section 170.80 of this chapter, the fact that such person has previously been convicted of a crime or adjudicated a youthful offender shall not prevent such person from being adjudicated a youthful offender as required by such section; and

2. a youthful offender adjudication pursuant to section 170.80 of this chapter shall not be considered in determining whether a person is an eligible youth, or in determining whether to find a person a youthful offender, in any subsequent youthful offender adjudication.

§720.30 Youthful offender adjudication; post-judgment motions and appeal.

The provisions of this chapter, governing the making and determination of post-judgment motions and the taking and determination of appeals in criminal cases, apply to post-judgment motions and appeals with respect to youthful offender adjudications wherever such provisions can reasonably be so applied.

§720.35 Youthful offender adjudication; effect thereof; records.

1. A youthful offender adjudication is not a judgment of conviction for a crime or any other offense, and does not operate as a disqualification of any person so adjudged to hold public office or public employment or to receive any license granted by public authority but shall be deemed a conviction only for the purposes of transfer of supervision and custody pursuant to section two hundred fifty-nine-m of the executive law. A defendant for whom a youthful offender adjudication was substituted, who was originally charged with prostitution as defined in section 230.00 of the penal law, shall be deemed a "sexually exploited child" as defined in subdivision one of

section four hundred forty-seven-a of the social services law and therefore shall not be considered an adult for purposes related to the charges in the youthful offender proceeding or a proceeding under section 170.80 of this chapter.
(Eff. 2/2/21, Ch. 23, L. 2021)

2. Except where specifically required or permitted by statute or upon specific authorization of the court, all official records and papers, whether on file with the court, a police agency or the division of criminal justice services, relating to a case involving a youth who has been adjudicated a youthful offender, are confidential and may not be made available to any person or public or private agency, other than the designated educational official of the public or private elementary or secondary school in which the youth is enrolled as a student provided that such local educational official shall only have made available a notice of such adjudication and shall not have access to any other official records and papers, such youth or such youth's designated agent (but only where the official records and papers sought are on file with a court and request therefor is made to that court or to a clerk thereof), an institution to which such youth has been committed, the department of corrections and community supervision and a probation department of this state that requires such official records and papers for the purpose of carrying out duties specifically authorized by law; provided, however, that information regarding an order of protection or temporary order of protection issued pursuant to section 530.12 of this chapter or a warrant issued in connection therewith may be maintained on the statewide automated order of protection and warrant registry established pursuant to section two hundred twenty-one-a of the executive law during the period that such order of protection or temporary order of protection is in full force and effect or during which such warrant may be executed. Such confidential information may be made available pursuant to law only for purposes of adjudicating or enforcing such order of protection or temporary order of protection and, where provided to a designated educational official, as defined in section 380.90 of this chapter, for purposes related to the execution of the student's educational plan, where applicable, successful school adjustment and reentry into the community. Such notification shall be kept separate and apart from such student's school records and shall be accessible only by the designated educational official. Such notification shall not be part of such student's permanent school record and shall not be appended to or included in any documentation regarding such student and shall be destroyed at such time as such student is no longer enrolled in the school district. At no time shall such notification be used for any purpose other than those specified in this subdivision.

3. If a youth who has been adjudicated a youthful offender is enrolled as a student in a public or private elementary or secondary school the court that has adjudicated the youth as a youthful offender shall provide notification of such adjudication to the designated educational official of the school in which such youth is enrolled as a student. Such notification shall be used by the designated educational official only for purposes related to the execution of the student's educational plan, where applicable, successful school

This page intentionally eft blank.

adjustment and reentry into the community. Such notification shall be kept separate and apart from such student's school records and shall be accessible only by the designated educational official. Such notification shall not be part of such student's permanent school record and shall not be appended to or included in any documentation regarding such student and shall be destroyed at such time as such student is no longer enrolled in the school district. At no time shall such notification be used for any purpose other than those specified in this subdivision.

4. Notwithstanding subdivision two of this section, whenever a person is adjudicated a youthful offender and the conviction that was vacated and replaced by the youthful offender finding was for a sex offense as that term is defined in article ten of the mental hygiene law, all records pertaining to the youthful offender adjudication shall be included in those records and reports that may be obtained by the commissioner of mental health or the commissioner of developmental disabilities, as appropriate; the case review panel; and the attorney general pursuant to section 10.05 of the mental hygiene law.

ARTICLE 722
PROCEEDINGS AGAINST JUVENILE OFFENDERS
AND ADOLESCENT OFFENDERS; ESTABLISHMENT OF YOUTH
PART AND RELATED PROCEDURES

Section
722.00 Probation case plans.
722.10 Youth part of the superior court established.
722.20 Proceedings upon felony complaint; juvenile offender.
722.21 Proceedings upon felony complaint; adolescent offender.
722.22 Motion to remove juvenile offender to family court.
722.23 Removal of adolescent offenders to family court.
722.24 Applicability of chapter to actions and matters involving juvenile offenders or
        adolescent offenders.

§722.00 Probation case plans.

1. All juvenile offenders and adolescent offenders shall be notified of the availability of services through the local probation department. Such services shall include the ability of the probation department to conduct a risk and needs assessment, utilizing a validated risk assessment tool, in order to help determine suitable and individualized programming and referrals. Participation in such risk and needs assessment shall be voluntary and the adolescent offender or juvenile offender may be accompanied by counsel during any such assessment. Based upon the assessment findings, the probation department shall refer the adolescent offender or juvenile offender to available and appropriate services. *(Eff.10/1/19,Ch.240,L.2019)*

2. Nothing shall preclude the probation department and the adolescent offender or juvenile offender from entering into a voluntary service plan which may include alcohol, substance use and mental health treatment and services. To the extent practicable, such services shall continue through the pendency of the action and shall further continue where such action is removed in accordance with this article.

3. When preparing a pre-sentence investigation report of any such adolescent offender or juvenile offender, the probation department shall incorporate a summary of any assessment findings, referrals and progress with respect to mitigating risk and addressing any identified needs.

4. The probation service shall not transmit or otherwise communicate to the district attorney or the youth part any statement made by the juvenile or

adolescent offender to a probation officer. However, the probation service may make a recommendation regarding the completion of his or her case plan to the youth part and provide such information as it shall deem relevant.

5. No statement made to the probation service may be admitted into evidence at a fact-finding hearing at any time prior to a conviction.

§722.10 Youth part of the superior court established.

1. The chief administrator of the courts is hereby directed to establish, in a superior court in each county of the state, a part of the court to be known as the youth part of the superior court for the county in which such court presides. Judges presiding in the youth part shall be family court judges, as described in article six, section one of the constitution. To aid in their work, such judges shall receive training in specialized areas, including, but not limited to, juvenile justice, adolescent development, custody and care of youths and effective treatment methods for reducing unlawful conduct by youths, and shall be authorized to make appropriate determinations within the power of such superior court with respect to the cases of youths assigned to such part. The youth part shall have exclusive jurisdiction in all proceedings in relation to juvenile offenders and adolescent offenders, except as provided in this article or article seven hundred twenty-five of this chapter.

2. The chief administrator of the courts shall also direct the presiding justice of the appellate division, in each judicial department of the state, to designate judges authorized by law to exercise criminal jurisdiction to serve as accessible magistrates, for the purpose of acting in place of the youth part for certain first appearance proceedings involving youths, as provided by law. When designating such magistrates, the presiding justice shall ensure that all areas of a county are within a reasonable distance of a designated magistrate. A judge authorized to preside as such a magistrate shall have received training in specialized areas, including, but not limited to, juvenile justice, adolescent development, custody and care of youths and effective treatment methods for reducing unlawful conduct by youths.

§722.20 Proceedings upon felony complaint; juvenile offender.

1. When a juvenile offender is arraigned before a youth part, the provisions of this section shall apply. If the youth part is not in session, the defendant shall be brought before the most accessible magistrate designated by the appellate division of the supreme court to act as a youth part for the purpose of making a determination whether such juvenile shall be detained or, with the consent of the district attorney, immediately removed to family court. If the defendant is ordered to be detained, he or she shall be brought before the next session of the youth part. If the defendant is not detained, he or she shall be ordered to appear at the next session of the youth part or the family court.   *(Eff.10/1/18,Ch.240,L.2019)*

2. If the defendant waives a hearing upon the felony complaint, the court must order that the defendant be held for the action of the grand jury with respect to the charge or charges contained in the felony complaint.

3. If there be a hearing, then at the conclusion of the hearing, the youth part court must dispose of the felony complaint as follows:

(a) If there is reasonable cause to believe that the defendant committed a crime for which a person under the age of sixteen is criminally responsible, the court must order that the defendant be held for the action of a grand jury; or

(b) If there is not reasonable cause to believe that the defendant committed a crime for which a person under the age of sixteen is criminally responsible but there is reasonable cause to believe that the defendant is a "juvenile delinquent" as defined in subdivision one of section 301.2 of the family court act, the court must specify the act or acts it found reasonable cause to believe the defendant did and direct that the action be removed to the family court in accordance with the provisions of article seven hundred twenty-five of this title; or

(c) If there is not reasonable cause to believe that the defendant committed any criminal act, the court must dismiss the felony complaint and discharge the defendant from custody if he is in custody, or if he is at liberty on bail, it must exonerate the bail.

4. Notwithstanding the provisions of subdivisions two and three of this section, the court shall, at the request of the district attorney, order removal of an action against a juvenile offender to the family court pursuant to the provisions of article seven hundred twenty-five of this title if, upon consideration of the criteria specified in subdivision two of section 722.22 of this article, it is determined that to do so would be in the interests of justice. Where, however, the felony complaint charges the juvenile offender with murder in the second degree as defined in section 125.25 of the penal law, rape in the first degree as defined in subdivision one of section 130.35 of the penal law, criminal sexual act in the first degree as defined in subdivision one of section 130.50 of the penal law, or an armed felony as defined in paragraph (a) of subdivision forty-one of section 1.20 of this chapter, a determination that such action be removed to the family court shall, in addition, be based upon a finding of one or more of the following factors: (i) mitigating circumstances that bear directly upon the manner in which the crime was committed; or (ii) where the defendant was not the sole participant in the crime, the defendant's participation was relatively minor although not so minor as to constitute a defense to the prosecution; or (iii) possible deficiencies in proof of the crime.

5. Notwithstanding the provisions of subdivision two, three, or four of this section, if a currently undetermined felony complaint against a juvenile offender is pending, and the defendant has not waived a hearing pursuant to subdivision two of this section and a hearing pursuant to subdivision three of this section has not commenced, the defendant may move to remove the action to family court pursuant to 722.22 of this article. The procedural rules of subdivisions one and two of section 210.45 of this chapter are applicable to a motion pursuant to this subdivision. Upon such motion, the court shall proceed and determine the motion as provided in section 722.22 of this article; provided, however, that the exception provisions of paragraph (b) of subdivision one of section 722.22 of this article shall not apply when there is not reasonable cause to believe that the juvenile offender committed one or more of the crimes enumerated therein, and in such event the provisions of paragraph (a) thereof shall apply.

6. (a) If the court orders removal of the action to family court, it shall state on the record the factor or factors upon which its determination is based, and the court shall give its reasons for removal in detail and not in conclusory terms.

(b) The district attorney shall state upon the record the reasons for his consent to removal of the action to the family court where such consent is required. The reasons shall be stated in detail and not in conclusory terms.

(c) For the purpose of making a determination pursuant to subdivision four or five of this section, the court may make such inquiry as it deems necessary. Any evidence which is not legally privileged may be introduced. If the defendant testifies, his testimony may not be introduced against him in any future proceeding, except to impeach his testimony at such future proceeding as inconsistent prior testimony.

(d) Where a motion for removal by the defendant pursuant to subdivision five of this section has been denied, no further motion pursuant to this section or section 722.22 of this article may be made by the juvenile offender with respect to the same offense or offenses.

(e) Except as provided by paragraph (f) of this subdivision, this section shall not be construed to limit the powers of the grand jury.

(f) Where a motion by the defendant pursuant to subdivision five of this section has been granted, there shall be no further proceedings against the juvenile offender in any local or superior criminal court including the youth part of the superior court for the offense or offenses which were the subject of the removal order.

§722.21 Proceedings upon felony complaint; adolescent offender.

1. When an adolescent offender is arraigned before a youth part, the provisions of this section shall apply. If the youth part is not in session, the defendant shall be brought before the most accessible magistrate designated by the appellate division of the supreme court to act as a youth part for the purpose of making a determination whether such adolescent offender shall be detained or, with the consent of the district attorney, immediately removed to family court. If the defendant is ordered to be detained, he or she shall be brought before the next session of the youth part. If the defendant is not detained, he or she shall be ordered to appear at the next session of the youth part, family court or the local probation department.   *(Eff. 10/1/18, Ch. 240, L. 2019)*

2. If the defendant waives a hearing upon the felony complaint, the court must order that the defendant be held for the action of the grand jury with respect to the charge or charges contained in the felony complaint.

3. If there be a hearing, then at the conclusion of the hearing, the youth part court must dispose of the felony complaint as follows:

(a) If there is reasonable cause to believe that the defendant committed a felony, the court must order that the defendant be held for the action of a grand jury; or

(b) If there is not reasonable cause to believe that the defendant committed a felony but there is reasonable cause to believe that the defendant is a "juvenile delinquent" as defined in subdivision one of section 301.2 of the family court act, the court must specify the act or acts it found reasonable cause to believe the defendant did and direct that the action be transferred to the family court in accordance with the provisions of article seven hundred twenty-five of this title, provided, however, notwithstanding any other provision of law, section 308.1 of the family court act shall apply to actions transferred pursuant to this subdivision and such actions shall not be considered removals subject to subdivision thirteen of such section 308.1; or

(c) If there is not reasonable cause to believe that the defendant committed any criminal act, the court must dismiss the felony complaint and discharge the defendant from custody if he is in custody, or if he is at liberty on bail, it must exonerate the bail.

4. Notwithstanding the provisions of subdivisions two and three of this section, where the defendant is charged with a felony, other than a class A felony defined outside article two hundred twenty of the penal law, a violent felony defined in section 70.02 of the penal law or a felony listed in paragraph one or two of section forty-two of section 1.20 of this chapter, except as provided in paragraph (c) of subdivision two of section 722.23 of this article, the court shall, upon notice from the district attorney that he or she will not file a motion to prevent removal pursuant to section 722.23 of this article, order transfer of an action against an adolescent offender to the family court pursuant to the provisions of article seven hundred twenty-five of this title, provided, however, notwithstanding any other provision of law, section 308.1 of the family court act shall apply to actions transferred pursuant to this subdivision and such actions shall not be considered removals subject to subdivision thirteen of such section 308.1.

5. Notwithstanding subdivisions two and three of this section, at the request of the district attorney, the court shall order removal of an action against an adolescent offender charged with an offense listed in paragraph (a) of subdivision two of section 722.23 of this article, to the family court pursuant to the provisions of article seven hundred twenty-five of this title and upon consideration of the criteria specified in subdivision two of section 722.22 of this article, it is determined that to do so would be in the interests of justice. Where, however, the felony complaint charges the adolescent offender with murder in the second degree as defined in section 125.25 of the penal law, rape in the first degree as defined in subdivision one of section 130.35 of the penal law, criminal sexual act in the first degree as defined in subdivision one of section 130.50 of the penal law, or an armed felony as defined in paragraph (a) of subdivision forty-one of section 1.20 of this chapter, a determination that such action be removed to the family court shall, in addition, be based upon a finding of one or more of the following factors: (i) mitigating circumstances that bear directly upon the manner in which the crime was committed; or (ii) where the defendant was not the sole participant in the crime, the defendant's participation was relatively minor although not so minor as to constitute a defense to the prosecution; or (iii) possible deficiencies in proof of the crime.

6. (a) If the court orders removal of the action to family court pursuant to subdivision five of this section, it shall state on the record the factor or factors upon which its determination is based, and the court shall give its reasons for removal in detail and not in conclusory terms.

(b) The district attorney shall state upon the record the reasons for his consent to removal of the action to the family court where such consent is required. The reasons shall be stated in detail and not in conclusory terms.

(c) For the purpose of making a determination pursuant to subdivision five the court may make such inquiry as it deems necessary. Any evidence which is not legally privileged may be introduced. If the defendant testifies, his testimony may not be introduced against him in any future proceeding, except to impeach his testimony at such future proceeding as inconsistent prior testimony.

(d) Except as provided by paragraph (e), this section shall not be construed to limit the powers of the grand jury.

(e) Where an action against a defendant has been removed to the family court pursuant to this section, there shall be no further proceedings against the adolescent offender in any local or superior criminal court including the youth part of the superior court for the offense or offenses which were the subject of the removal order.

§722.22 Motion to remove juvenile offender to family court.

1. After a motion by a juvenile offender, pursuant to subdivision five of section 722.20 of this article, or after arraignment of a juvenile offender upon an indictment, the court may, on motion of any party or on its own motion:

(a) except as otherwise provided by paragraph (b) of this subdivision, order removal of the action to the family court pursuant to the provisions of article seven hundred twenty-five of this title, if, after consideration of the factors set forth in subdivision two of this section, the court determines that to do so would be in the interests of justice; or

(b) with the consent of the district attorney, order removal of an action involving an indictment charging a juvenile offender with murder in the second degree as defined in section 125.25 of the penal law; rape in the first degree, as defined in subdivision one of section 130.35 of the penal law; criminal sexual act in the first degree, as defined in subdivision one of section 130.50 of the penal law; or an armed felony as defined in paragraph (a) of subdivision forty-one of section 1.20 of this chapter, to the family court pursuant to the provisions of article seven hundred twenty-five of this title if the court finds one or more of the following factors: (i) mitigating circumstances that bear directly upon the manner in which the crime was committed; (ii) where the defendant was not the sole participant in the crime, the defendant's participation was relatively minor although not so minor as to constitute a defense to the prosecution; or (iii) possible deficiencies in the proof of the crime, and, after consideration of the factors set forth in subdivision two of this section, the court determined that removal of the action to the family court would be in the interests of justice.

2. In making its determination pursuant to subdivision one of this section the court shall, to the extent applicable, examine individually and collectively, the following:

(a) the seriousness and circumstances of the offense;

(b) the extent of harm caused by the offense;

(c) the evidence of guilt, whether admissible or inadmissible at trial;

(d) the history, character and condition of the defendant;

(e) the purpose and effect of imposing upon the defendant a sentence authorized for the offense;

(f) the impact of a removal of the case to the family court on the safety or welfare of the community;

(g) the impact of a removal of the case to the family court upon the confidence of the public in the criminal justice system;

(h) where the court deems it appropriate, the attitude of the complainant or victim with respect to the motion; and

(i) any other relevant fact indicating that a judgment of conviction in the criminal court would serve no useful purpose.

3. The procedure for bringing on a motion pursuant to subdivision one of this section, shall accord with the procedure prescribed in subdivisions one and two of section 210.45 of this chapter. After all papers of both parties have been filed and after all documentary evidence, if any, has been submitted, the court must consider the same for the purpose of determining whether the motion is determinable on the motion papers submitted and, if not, may make such inquiry as it deems necessary for the purpose of making a determination.

4. For the purpose of making a determination pursuant to this section, any evidence which is not legally privileged may be introduced. If the defendant testifies, his testimony may not be introduced against him in any future proceeding, except to impeach his testimony at such future proceeding as inconsistent prior testimony.

5. a. If the court orders removal of the action to family court, it shall state on the record the factor or factors upon which its determination is based, and, the court shall give its reasons for removal in detail and not in conclusory terms.

b. The district attorney shall state upon the record the reasons for his consent to removal of the action to the family court. The reasons shall be stated in detail and not in conclusory terms.

§722.23 Removal of adolescent offenders to family court.

1. (a) Following the arraignment of a defendant charged with a crime committed when he or she was sixteen, or commencing October first, two thousand nineteen, seventeen years of age, other than any class A felony except for those defined in article two hundred twenty of the penal law, a violent felony defined in section 70.02 of the penal law or a felony listed in paragraph one or two of subdivision forty-two of section 1.20 of this chapter, or an offense set forth in the vehicle and traffic law, the court shall order the removal of the action to the family court in accordance with the applicable provisions of article seven hundred twenty-five of this title unless, within thirty calendar days of such arraignment, the district attorney makes a motion to prevent removal of the action pursuant to this subdivision. If the defendant fails to report to the probation department as directed, the thirty day time period shall be tolled until such time as he or she reports to the probation department.

(b) A motion to prevent removal of an action in youth part shall be made in writing and upon prompt notice to the defendant. The motion shall contain allegations of sworn fact based upon personal knowledge of the affiant, and shall indicate if the district attorney is requesting a hearing. The motion shall be noticed to be heard promptly.

(c) The defendant shall be given an opportunity to reply. The defendant shall be granted any reasonable request for a delay. Either party may request a hearing on the facts alleged in the motion to prevent removal of the action. The hearing shall be held expeditiously.

(d) The court shall deny the motion to prevent removal of the action in youth part unless the court makes a determination upon such motion by the district attorney that extraordinary circumstances exist that should prevent the transfer of the action to family court.

(e) The court shall make a determination in writing or on the record within five days of the conclusion of the hearing or submission by the defense, whichever is later. Such determination shall include findings of fact and to the extent practicable conclusions of law.

(f) For the purposes of this section, there shall be a presumption against custody and case planning services shall be made available to the defendant.

(g) Notwithstanding any other provision of law, section 308.1 of the family court act shall apply to all actions transferred pursuant to this section provided, however, such cases shall not be considered removals subject to subdivision thirteen of such section 308.1.

(h) Nothing in this subdivision shall preclude, and a court may order, the removal of an action to family court where all parties agree or pursuant to this chapter.

2. (a) Upon the arraignment of a defendant charged with a crime committed when he or she was sixteen or, commencing October first, two thousand nineteen, seventeen years of age on a class A felony, other than those defined in article 220 of the penal law, or a violent felony defined in section 70.02 of the penal law, the court shall schedule an appearance no later than six calendar days from such arraignment for the purpose of reviewing the accusatory instrument pursuant to this subdivision. The court shall notify the district attorney and defendant regarding the purpose of such appearance.

(b) Upon such appearance, the court shall review the accusatory instrument and any other relevant facts for the purpose of making a determination pursuant to paragraph (c) of this subdivision. Both parties may be heard and submit information relevant to the determination.

(c) The court shall order the action to proceed in accordance with subdivision one of this section unless, after reviewing the papers and hearing from the parties, the court determines in writing that the district attorney proved by a preponderance of the evidence one or more of the following as set forth in the accusatory instrument:

(i) the defendant caused significant physical injury to a person other than a participant in the offense; or

(ii) the defendant displayed a firearm, shotgun, rifle or deadly weapon as defined in the penal law in furtherance of such offense; or

(iii) the defendant unlawfully engaged in sexual intercourse, oral sexual conduct, anal sexual conduct or sexual contact as defined in section 130.00 of the penal law.

(d) Where the court makes a determination that the action shall not proceed in accordance with subdivision one of this section, such determination shall be made in writing or on the record and shall include findings of fact and to the extent practicable conclusions of law.

(e) Nothing in this subdivision shall preclude, and the court may order, the removal of an action to family court where all parties agree or pursuant to this chapter.

3. Notwithstanding the provisions of any other law, if at any time one or more charges in the accusatory instrument are reduced, such that the elements of the highest remaining charge would be removable pursuant to subdivisions one or two of this section, then the court, sua sponte or in response to a motion pursuant to subdivisions one or two of this section by the defendant, shall promptly notify the parties and direct that the matter

proceed in accordance with subdivision one of this section, provided, however, that in such instance, the district attorney must file any motion to prevent removal within thirty days of effecting or receiving notice of such reduction.

4. A defendant may waive review of the accusatory instrument by the court and the opportunity for removal in accordance with this section, provided that such waiver is made by the defendant knowingly, voluntarily and in open court, in the presence of and with the approval of his or her counsel and the court. An earlier waiver shall not constitute a waiver of review and the opportunity for removal under this section.

§722.24 Applicability of chapter to actions and matters involving juvenile offenders or adolescent offenders.

Except where inconsistent with this article, all provisions of this chapter shall apply to all criminal actions and proceedings, and all appeals and post-judgment motions relating or attached thereto, involving a juvenile offender or adolescent offender.

ARTICLE 725 - REMOVAL OF PROCEEDING AGAINST JUVENILE OFFENDER TO FAMILY COURT

Section
725.00 Applicability.
725.05 Order of removal.
725.10 Removal of action.
725.15 Sealing of records.
725.20 Record of certain actions removed.

§725.00 Applicability.

The provisions of this article apply in any case where a court directs that an action or charge is to be removed to the family court under section 180.75, 190.71, 210.43, 220.10, 310.85 or 330.25 of this chapter.

§725.05 Order of removal.

When a youth part directs that an action or charge is to be removed to the family court the youth part must issue an order of removal in accordance with this section. Such order must be as follows:

1. It must provide that the action or charge is to be removed to the family court of the county in which such action or charge was pending, and it must specify the section pursuant to which the removal is authorized.

2. Where the direction is authorized pursuant to paragraph (b) of subdivision three of sections 722.20 or 722.21 of this title, it must specify the act or acts it found reasonable cause to believe the defendant did.

3. Where the direction is authorized pursuant to subdivision four of section 722.20 or section 722.21 of this title, it must specify the act or acts it found reasonable cause to allege.

4. Where the direction is authorized pursuant to section 190.71 of this chapter, the court shall annex to the order as part thereof a certified copy of the grand jury request.

4-a. Where the direction is authorized pursuant to subdivision seven of section 210.30 of this chapter, it must specify the act or acts for which there was sufficient evidence to believe that defendant did.

5. Where the direction is authorized pursuant to section 220.10, 310.85 or 330.25 of this chapter, it must specify the act or acts for which a plea or verdict of guilty was rendered or accepted and entered.

6. Where a securing order has not been made, the order of removal must provide that the police officer or peace officer who made the arrest or some

other proper officer forthwith and with all reasonable speed take the juvenile to the designated family court or, where that cannot be done, it must provide for release or detention in the same manner as provided for a family court proceeding pursuant to section 320.5 of the family court act.

7. Whether or not a securing order has been made, the order of removal must specify a date certain within ten days from the date of the order of removal for the defendant's appearance in the family court and where the defendant is in detention or in the custody of the sheriff that date must be not later than the next day the family court is in session. Unless the defendant is in detention or is in the custody of the sheriff or unless the order of removal specifies a juvenile or adolescent offense for which the defendant is not eligible for consideration for adjustment under subdivision thirteen of section 308.1 of the family court act, the order of removal shall direct the defendant to appear at the family court intake office of the county department of probation for adjustment consideration; provided, however, that pursuant to subdivision three of section 308.1 of the family court act, the fact that the defendant is in detention or is in the custody of the sheriff shall not preclude the probation service from adjusting the case if the defendant is otherwise eligible for adjustment.   *(Eff.12/29/21,Ch.809,L.2021)*

8. The order of removal must direct that all of the pleadings and proceedings in the action, or a certified copy of same be transferred to the designated family court and be delivered to and filed with the clerk of that court. For the purposes of this subdivision the term "pleadings and proceedings" includes the minutes of any hearing inquiry or trial held in the action, the minutes of any grand jury proceeding and the minutes of any plea accepted and entered.

9. The order of removal must be signed by a judge or justice of the court that directed the removal.

§725.10 Removal of action.

1.Unless the defendant is an adolescent offender who has been directed to appear at the family court intake office of the county department of probation for adjustment consideration in accordance with subdivision seven of section 725.05 of this article, when an order of removal is filed with the family court, a proceeding pursuant to article three of the family court act must be originated. The family court thereupon must assume jurisdiction and proceed to render such judgment as the circumstances require, in the manner and to the extent provided by law.   *(Eff.12/29/21,Ch.809,L.2021)*

2. Upon the filing of an order of removal in a criminal court the criminal action upon which the order is based shall be terminated, and there shall be no further criminal proceedings in any criminal court as defined in section 10.10 of this chapter with respect to the offense or offenses charged in the accusatory instrument which was the subject of removal. All further proceedings including motions and appeals shall be in accordance with laws appertaining to the family court and for this purpose all findings, determinations, verdicts and orders other than the order of removal, shall be deemed to have been made by the family court.

§725.15 Sealing of records.

Except where specifically required or permitted by statute or upon specific authorization of the court that directed removal of an action to the family court all official records and papers of the action up to and including the order of removal, whether on file with the court, a police agency or the division of criminal justice services, are confidential and must not be made available to any person or public or private agency, provided however that availability of copies of any such records and papers on file with the family court shall be governed by provisions that apply to family court records, and further provided that all official records and papers of the action shall be included in those records and reports that may be obtained upon request by the commissioner of mental health or commissioner of the office for people with developmental disabilities, as appropriate; the case review panel; and the attorney general pursuant to section 10.05 of the mental hygiene law.

(Eff.12/16/19,Ch.672,L.2019)

§725.20 Record of certain actions removed.

1. The provisions of this section shall apply in any case where an order of removal to the family court is entered pursuant to a direction authorized by article 722 of this title, or subparagraph (iii) of paragraph (g) of subdivision five of section 220.10 of this chapter, or section 330.25 of this chapter.

2. When such an action is removed the court that directed the removal must cause the following additional records to be filed with the clerk of the county court or in the city of New York with the clerk of the supreme court of the county wherein the action was pending and with the division of criminal justice services:

(a) A certified copy of the order of removal;

(b) Where the direction is one authorized by subparagraph (iii) of paragraph (g) of subdivision five of section 220.10 or section 330.25 of this chapter, a copy of the minutes of the plea of guilty, including the minutes of the memorandum submitted by the district attorney and the court; and

(c) In addition to the records specified in this subdivision, such further statement or submission of additional information pertaining to the proceeding in criminal court in accordance with standards established by the commissioner of the division of criminal justice services, subject to the provisions of subdivision three of this section.

3. It shall be the duty of said clerk to maintain a separate file for copies of orders and minutes filed pursuant to this section. Upon receipt of such orders and minutes the clerk must promptly delete such portions as would identify the defendant, but the clerk shall nevertheless maintain a separate confidential system to enable correlation of the documents so filed with identification of the defendant. After making such deletions the orders and minutes shall be placed within the file and must be available for public inspection. Information permitting correlation of any such record with the identity of any defendant shall not be divulged to any person except upon order of a justice of the supreme court based upon a finding that the public interest or the interests of justice warrant disclosure in a particular cause for a particular case or for a particular purpose or use.

ARTICLE 730 - MENTAL DISEASE OR DEFECT EXCLUDING FITNESS TO PROCEED

Section
730.10 Fitness to proceed; definitions.
730.20 Fitness to proceed; generally.
730.30 Fitness to proceed; order of examination.
730.40 Fitness to proceed; local criminal court accusatory instrument.
730.50 Fitness to proceed; indictment.
730.60 Fitness to proceed; procedure following custody by commissioner.
730.70 Fitness to proceed; procedure following termination of custody by commissioner.

§730.10 Fitness to proceed; definitions.

As used in this article, the following terms have the following meanings:

1. "Incapacitated person" means a defendant who as a result of mental disease or defect lacks capacity to understand the proceedings against him or to assist in his own defense.

2. "Order of examination" means an order issued to an appropriate director by a criminal court wherein a criminal action is pending against a defendant or by a court evaluating the capacity of an alleged violator in a parole revocation proceeding pursuant to subparagraph (xii) of paragraph (f) of subdivision three of section two hundred fifty-nine-i of the executive law, or by a family court pursuant to section 322.1 of the family court act wherein a juvenile delinquency proceeding is pending against a juvenile, directing that such person be examined for the purpose of determining if he is an incapacitated person.

3. "Commissioner" means the state commissioner of mental health or the state commissioner of the office for people with developmental disabilities.
(Eff.12/16/19,Ch.672,L.2019)

4. "Director" means (a) the director of a state hospital operated by the office of mental health or the director of a developmental center operated by the office for people with developmental disabilities, or (b) the director of a hospital operated by any local government of the state that has been certified by the commissioner as having adequate facilities to examine a defendant to determine if he is an incapacitated person, or (c) the director of community mental health services.   *(Eff.12/16/19,Ch.672,L.2019)*

5. "Qualified psychiatrist" means a physician who:

(a) is a diplomate of the American board of psychiatry and neurology or is eligible to be certified by that board; or,

(b) is certified by the American osteopathic board of neurology and psychiatry or is eligible to be certified by that board.

6. "Certified psychologist" means a person who is registered as a certified psychologist under article one hundred fifty-three of the education law.

7. "Psychiatric examiner" means a qualified psychiatrist or a certified psychologist who has been designated by a director to examine a defendant pursuant to an order of examination.

8. "Examination report" means a report made by a psychiatric examiner wherein he sets forth his opinion as to whether the defendant is or is not an incapacitated person, the nature and extent of his examination and, if he finds that the defendant is an incapacitated person, his diagnosis and prognosis and a detailed statement of the reasons for his opinion by making particular reference to those aspects of the proceedings wherein the defendant lacks capacity to understand or to assist in his own defense. The state administrator and the commissioner must jointly adopt the form of the examination report; and the state administrator shall prescribe the number of copies thereof that must be submitted to the court by the director.

9. "Appropriate institution" means: (a) a hospital operated by the office of mental health or a developmental center operated by the office for people with developmental disabilities; or (b) a hospital licensed by the department of health which operates a psychiatric unit licensed by the office of mental health, as determined by the commissioner provided, however, that any such hospital that is not operated by the state shall qualify as an "appropriate institution" only pursuant to the terms of an agreement between the commissioner and the hospital. Nothing in this article shall be construed as requiring a hospital to consent to providing care and treatment to an incapacitated person at such hospital.

§730.20 Fitness to proceed; generally.

1. The appropriate director to whom a criminal court issues an order of examination must be determined in accordance with rules jointly adopted by the judicial conference and the commissioner. Upon receipt of an examination order, the director must designate two qualified psychiatric examiners, of whom he may be one, to examine the defendant to determine if he is an incapacitated person. In conducting their examination, the psychiatric examiners may employ any method which is accepted by the medical profession

for the examination of persons alleged to be mentally ill or mentally defective. The court may authorize a psychiatrist or psychologist retained by the defendant to be present at such examination.

2. When the defendant is not in custody at the time a court issues an order of examination, because he was theretofore released on bail or on his own recognizance, the court may direct that the examination be conducted on an out-patient basis, and at such time and place as the director shall designate. If, however, the director informs the court that hospital confinement of the defendant is necessary for an effective examination, the court may direct that the defendant be confined in a hospital designated by the director until the examination is completed.

3. When the defendant is in custody at the time a court issues an order of examination, the examination must be conducted at the place where the defendant is being held in custody. If, however, the director determines that hospital confinement of the defendant is necessary for an effective examination, the sheriff must deliver the defendant to a hospital designated by the director and hold him in custody therein, under sufficient guard, until the examination is completed.

4. Hospital confinement under subdivisions two and three shall be for a period not exceeding thirty days, except that, upon application of the director, the court may authorize confinement for an additional period not exceeding thirty days if it is satisfied that a longer period is necessary to complete the examination. During the period of hospital confinement, the physician in charge of the hospital may administer or cause to be administered to the defendant such emergency psychiatric, medical or other therapeutic treatment as in his judgment should be administered.

5. Each psychiatric examiner, after he has completed his examination of the defendant, must promptly prepare an examination report and submit it to the director. If the psychiatric examiners are not unanimous in their opinion as to whether the defendant is or is not an incapacitated person, the director must designate another qualified psychiatric examiner to examine the defendant to determine if he is an incapacitated person. Upon receipt of the examination reports, the director must submit them to the court that issued the order of examination. The court must furnish a copy of the reports to counsel for the defendant and to the district attorney.

6. When a defendant is subjected to examination pursuant to an order issued by a criminal court in accordance with this article, any statement made by him for the purpose of the examination or treatment shall be inadmissible in evidence against him in any criminal action on any issue other than that of his mental condition, but such statement is admissible upon that issue whether or not it would otherwise be deemed a privileged communication.

7. A psychiatric examiner is entitled to his reasonable traveling expenses, a fee of fifty dollars for each examination of a defendant and a fee of fifty dollars for each appearance at a court hearing or trial but not exceeding two hundred dollars in fees for examination and testimony in any one case; except that if such psychiatric examiner be an employee of the state of New York he shall be entitled only to reasonable traveling expenses, unless such psychiatric examiner makes the examination or appears at a court hearing or trial outside his hours of state employment in a county in which the director of community mental health services certifies to the fiscal officer thereof that there is a shortage of qualified psychiatrists available to conduct examinations under the criminal procedure law in such county, in which event he shall be entitled to the foregoing fees and reasonable traveling expenses. Such fees and traveling expenses and the costs of sending a defendant to another place of detention or to a hospital for examination, of

This page intentionally left blank.

his maintenance therein and of returning him shall, when approved by the court, be a charge of the county in which the defendant is being tried.

§730.30   Fitness to proceed; order of examination.

1. At any time after a defendant is arraigned upon an accusatory instrument other than a felony complaint and before the imposition of sentence, or at any time after a defendant is arraigned upon a felony complaint and before he is held for the action of the grant jury, the court wherein the criminal action is pending must issue an order of examination when it is of the opinion that the defendant may be an incapacitated person.

2. When the examination reports submitted to the court show that each psychiatric examiner is of the opinion that the defendant is not an incapacitated person, the court may on its own motion, conduct a hearing to determine the issue of capacity, and it must conduct a hearing upon motion therefor by the defendant or by the district attorney. If no motion for a hearing is made, the criminal action against the defendant must proceed. If, following a hearing, the court is satisfied that the defendant is not an incapacitated person, the criminal action against him must proceed; if the court is not so satisfied, it must issue a further order of examination directing that the defendant be examined by different psychiatric examiners designated by the director.

3. When the examination reports submitted to the courts show that each psychiatric examiner is of the opinion that the defendant is an incapacitated person, the court may, on its own motion, conduct a hearing to determine the issue of capacity and it must conduct such hearing upon motion therefor by the defendant or by the district attorney.

4. When the examination reports submitted to the court show that the psychiatric examiners are not unanimous in their opinion as to whether the defendant is or is not an incapacitated person, or when the examination reports submitted to the superior court show that the psychiatric examiners are not unanimous in their opinion as to whether the defendant is or is not a dangerous incapacitated person, the court must conduct a hearing to determine the issue of capacity or dangerousness.

§730.40 Fitness to proceed; local criminal court accusatory instrument.

1. When a local criminal court, following a hearing conducted pursuant to subdivision three or four of section 730.30 of this article, is satisfied that the defendant is not an incapacitated person, the criminal action against him or her must proceed. If it is satisfied that the defendant is an incapacitated person, or if no motion for such a hearing is made, such court must issue a final or temporary order of observation committing him or her to the custody of the commissioner for care and treatment in an appropriate institution for a period not to exceed ninety days from the date of the order, provided, however, that the commissioner may designate an appropriate hospital for placement of a defendant for whom a final order of observation has been issued, where such hospital is licensed by the office of mental health and has agreed to accept, upon referral by the commissioner, defendants subject to final orders of observation issued under this subdivision. When a local criminal court accusatory instrument other than a felony complaint has been filed against the defendant, such court must issue a final order of observation. When a felony complaint has been filed against the defendant, such court must issue a temporary order of observation committing him or her to the custody of the commissioner for care and treatment in an appropriate institution or, upon the consent of the district attorney, committing him or her to the custody of the commissioner for care and treatment on an out-patient basis, for a period not to exceed ninety days

from the date of such order, except that, with the consent of the district attorney, it may issue a final order of observation. Upon the issuance of a final order of observation, the district attorney shall immediately transmit to the commissioner, in a manner intended to protect the confidentiality of the information, a list of names and contact information of persons who may reasonably be expected to be the victim of any assault or any violent felony offense, as defined in the penal law, or any offense listed in section 530.11 of this chapter which would be carried out by the committed person; provided that the person who reasonably may be expected to be a victim does not need to be a member of the same family or household as the committed person.

2. When a local criminal court has issued a final order of observation, it must dismiss the accusatory instrument filed in such court against the defendant and such dismissal constitutes a bar to any further prosecution of the charge or charges contained in such accusatory instrument. When the defendant is in the custody of the commissioner pursuant to a final order of observation, the commissioner or his or her designee, which may include the director of an appropriate institution, immediately upon the discharge of the defendant, must certify to such court that he or she has complied with the notice provisions set forth in paragraph (a) of subdivision six of section 730.60 of this article. When the defendant is in the custody of the commissioner at the expiration of the period prescribed in a temporary order of observation, the proceedings in the local criminal court that issued such order shall terminate for all purposes and the commissioner must promptly certify to such court and to the appropriate district attorney that the defendant was in his or her custody on such expiration date. Upon receipt of such certification, the court must dismiss the felony complaint filed against the defendant.

3. When a local criminal court has issued an order of examination or a temporary order of observation, and when the charge or charges contained in the accusatory instrument are subsequently presented to a grand jury, such grand jury need not hear the defendant pursuant to section 190.50 unless, upon application by defendant to the superior court that impaneled such grand jury, the superior court determines that the defendant is not an incapacitated person.

4. When an indictment is filed against a defendant after a local criminal court has issued an order of examination and before it has issued a final or temporary order of observation, the defendant must be promptly arraigned upon the indictment, and the proceedings in the local criminal court shall thereupon terminate for all purposes. The district attorney must notify the local criminal court of such arraignment, and such court must thereupon dismiss the accusatory instrument filed in such court against the defendant. If the director has submitted the examination reports to the local criminal court, such court must forward them to the superior court in which the indictment was filed. If the director has not submitted such reports to the local criminal court, he must submit them to the superior court in which the indictment was filed.

5. When an indictment is timely filed against the defendant after the issuance of a temporary order of observation or after the expiration of the period prescribed in such order, the superior court in which such indictment is filed must direct the sheriff to take custody of the defendant at the institution in which he is confined and bring him before the court for arraignment upon the indictment. After the defendant is arraigned upon the indictment, such temporary order of observation or any order issued pursuant to the mental hygiene law after the expiration of the period prescribed in the temporary order of observation shall be deemed nullified. Notwithstanding any other provision of law, an indictment filed in a superior court against a defendant for a crime charged in the felony complaint is not timely for the purpose of this subdivision if it is filed more than six months after the expiration of the period prescribed in a temporary order of

observation issued by a local criminal court wherein such felony complaint was pending. An untimely indictment must be dismissed by the superior court unless such court is satisfied that there was good cause for the delay in filing such indictment.

§730.50 Fitness to proceed; indictment.

1. When a superior court, following a hearing conducted pursuant to subdivision three or four of section 730.30 of this article, is satisfied that the defendant is not an incapacitated person, the criminal action against him or her must proceed. If it is satisfied that the defendant is an incapacitated person, or if no motion for such a hearing is made, it must adjudicate him or her an incapacitated person, and must issue a final order of observation or an order of commitment. When the indictment does not charge a felony or when the defendant has been convicted of an offense other than a felony, such court (a) must issue a final order of observation committing the defendant to the custody of the commissioner for care and treatment in an appropriate institution for a period not to exceed ninety days from the date of such order, provided, however, that the commissioner may designate an appropriate hospital for placement of a defendant for whom a final order of observation has been issued, where such hospital is licensed by the office of mental health and has agreed to accept, upon referral by the commissioner, defendants subject to final orders of observation issued under this subdivision, and (b) must dismiss the indictment filed in such court against the defendant, and such dismissal constitutes a bar to any further prosecution of the charge or charges contained in such indictment. Upon the issuance of a final order of observation, the district attorney shall immediately transmit to the commissioner, in a manner intended to protect the confidentiality of the information, a list of names and contact information of persons who may reasonably be expected to be the victim of any assault or any violent felony offense, as defined in the penal law, or any offense listed in section 530.11 of this chapter which would be carried out by the committed person; provided that the person who reasonably may be expected to be a victim does not need to be a member of the same family or household as the committed person. When the indictment charges a felony or when the defendant has been convicted of a felony, it must issue an order of commitment committing the defendant to the custody of the commissioner for care and treatment in an appropriate institution or, upon the consent of the district attorney, committing him or her to the custody of the commissioner for care and treatment on an out-patient basis, for a period not to exceed one year from the date of such order. Upon the issuance of an order of commitment, the court must exonerate the defendant's bail if he or she was previously at liberty on bail; provided, however, that exoneration of bail is not required when a defendant is committed to the custody of the commissioner for care and treatment on an out-patient basis. When the defendant is in the custody of the commissioner pursuant to a final order of observation, the commissioner or his or her designee, which may include the director of an appropriate institution, immediately upon the discharge of the defendant, must certify to such court that he or she has complied with the notice provisions set forth in paragraph (a) of subdivision six of section 730.60 of this article.

2. When a defendant is in the custody of the commissioner immediately prior to the expiration of the period prescribed in a temporary order of commitment and the superintendent of the institution wherein the defendant is confined is of the opinion that the defendant continues to be an incapacitated person, such superintendent must apply to the court that issued such order for an order of retention. Such application must be made within sixty days prior to the expiration of such period on forms that have been jointly adopted by the judicial conference and the commissioner. The

superintendent must give written notice of the application to the defendant and to the mental hygiene legal service. Upon receipt of such application, the court may, on its own motion, conduct a hearing to determine the issue of capacity, and it must conduct such hearing if a demand therefor is made by the defendant or the mental hygiene legal service within ten days from the date that notice of the application was given them. If, at the conclusion of a hearing conducted pursuant to this subdivision, the court is satisfied that the defendant is no longer an incapacitated person, the criminal action against him must proceed. If it is satisfied that the defendant continues to be an incapacitated person, or if no demand for a hearing is made, the court must adjudicate him an incapacitated person and must issue an order of retention which shall authorize continued custody of the defendant by the commissioner for a period not to exceed one year.

3. When a defendant is in the custody of the commissioner immediately prior to the expiration of the period prescribed in the first order of retention, the procedure set forth in subdivision two shall govern the application for and the issuance of any subsequent order of retention, except that any subsequent orders of retention must be for periods not to exceed two years each; provided, however, that the aggregate of the periods prescribed in the temporary order of commitment, the first order of retention and all subsequent orders of retention must not exceed two-thirds of the authorized maximum term of imprisonment for the highest class felony charged in the indictment or for the highest class felony of which he was convicted.

4. When a defendant is in the custody of the commissioner at the expiration of the authorized period prescribed in the last order of retention, the criminal action pending against him in the superior court that issued such order shall terminate for all purposes, and the commissioner must promptly certify to such court and to the appropriate district attorney that the defendant was in his custody on such expiration date. Upon receipt of such certification, the court must dismiss the indictment, and such dismissal constitutes a bar to any further prosecution of the charge or charges contained in such indictment.

5. When, on the effective date of this subdivision, any defendant remains in the custody of the commissioner pursuant to an order issued under former code of criminal procedure section six hundred sixty-two-b, the superintendent or director of the institution where such defendant is confined shall, if he believes that the defendant continues to be an incapacitated person, apply forthwith to a court of record in the county where the institution is located for an order of retention. The procedures for obtaining any order pursuant to this subdivision shall be in accordance with the provisions of subdivisions two, three and four of this section, except that the period of retention pursuant to the first order obtained under this subdivision shall be for not more than one year and any subsequent orders of retention must be for periods not to exceed two years each; provided, however, that the aggregate of the time spent in the custody of the commissioner pursuant to any order issued in accordance with the provisions of former code of criminal procedure section six hundred sixty-two-b and the periods prescribed by the first order obtained under this subdivision and all subsequent orders of retention must not exceed two-thirds of the authorized maximum term of imprisonment for the highest class felony charged in the indictment or the highest class felony of which he was convicted.

§730.60   **Fitness to proceed; procedure following custody by commissioner**.

1. When a local criminal court issues a final or temporary order of observation or an order of commitment, it must forward such order and a

copy of the examination reports and the accusatory instrument to the commissioner, and, if available, a copy of the pre-sentence report. Upon receipt thereof, the commissioner must designate an appropriate institution operated by the department of mental hygiene in which the defendant is to be placed, provided, however, that the commissioner may designate an appropriate hospital for placement of a defendant for whom a final order of observation has been issued, where such hospital is licensed by the office of mental health and has agreed to accept, upon referral by the commissioner, defendants subject to final orders of observation issued under this subdivision. The sheriff must hold the defendant in custody pending such designation by the commissioner, and when notified of the designation, the sheriff must deliver the defendant to the superintendent of such institution. The superintendent must promptly inform the appropriate director of the mental hygiene legal service of the defendant's admission to such institution. If a defendant escapes from the custody of the commissioner, the escape shall interrupt the period prescribed in any order of observation, commitment or retention, and such interruption shall continue until the defendant is returned to the custody of the commissioner.

2. Except as otherwise provided in subdivisions four and five, when a defendant is in the custody of the commissioner pursuant to a temporary order of observation or an order of commitment or an order of retention, the criminal action pending against the defendant in the court that issued such order is suspended until the superintendent of the institution in which the defendant is confined determines that he is no longer an incapacitated person. In that event, the court that issued such order and the appropriate district attorney must be notified, in writing, by the superintendent of his determination. The court must thereupon proceed in accordance with the provisions of subdivision two of section 730.30 of this chapter; provided, however, if the court is satisfied that the defendant remains an incapacitated person, and upon consent of all parties, the court may order the return of the defendant to the institution in which he had been confined for such period of time as was authorized by the prior order of commitment or order of retention. Upon such return, the defendant shall have all rights and privileges accorded by the provisions of this article.

3. When a defendant is in the custody of the commissioner pursuant to an order issued in accordance with this article, the commissioner may transfer him to any appropriate institution operated by the department of mental hygiene, provided, however, that the commissioner may designate an appropriate hospital for placement of a defendant for whom a final order of observation has been issued, where such hospital is licensed by the office of mental health and has agreed to accept, upon referral by the commissioner, defendants subject to final orders of observation issued under this section. The commissioner may discharge a defendant in his custody under a final order of observation at any time prior to the expiration date of such order, or otherwise treat or transfer such defendant in the same manner as if he were a patient not in confinement under a criminal court order.

4. When a defendant is in the custody of the commissioner pursuant to an order of commitment or an order of retention, he may make any motion authorized by this chapter which is susceptible of fair determination without

his personal participation. If the court denies any such motion it must be without prejudice to a renewal thereof after the criminal action against the defendant has been ordered to proceed. If the court enters an order dismissing the indictment and does not direct that the charge or charges be resubmitted to a grand jury, the court must direct that such order of dismissal be served upon the commissioner.

5. When a defendant is in the custody of the commissioner pursuant to an order of commitment or an order of retention, the superior court that issued such order may, upon motion of the defendant, and with the consent of the district attorney, dismiss the indictment when the court is satisfied that (a) the defendant is a resident or citizen of another state or country and that he will be removed thereto upon dismissal of the indictment, or (b) the defendant has been continuously confined in the custody of the commissioner for a period of more than two years. Before granting a motion under this subdivision, the court must be further satisfied that dismissal of the indictment is consistent with the ends of justice and that custody of the defendant by the commissioner pursuant to an order of commitment or an order of retention is not necessary for the protection of the public and that care and treatment can be effectively administered to the defendant without the necessity of such order. If the court enters an order of dismissal under this subdivision, it must set forth in the record the reasons for such action, and must direct that such order of dismissal be served upon the commissioner. The dismissal of an indictment pursuant to this subdivision constitutes a bar to any further prosecution of the charge or charges contained in such indictment.

6. (a) Notwithstanding any other provision of law, no person committed to the custody of the commissioner pursuant to this article, or continuously thereafter retained in such custody, shall be discharged, released on condition or placed in any less secure facility or on any less restrictive status, including, but not limited to vacations, furloughs and temporary passes, unless the commissioner or his or her designee, which may include the director of an appropriate institution, shall deliver written notice, at least four days, excluding Saturdays, Sundays and holidays, in advance of the change of such committed person's facility or status, or in the case of a person committed pursuant to a final order of observation written notice upon discharge of such committed person, to all of the following:

(1) The district attorney of the county from which such person was committed;

(2) The superintendent of state police;

(3) The sheriff of the county where the facility is located;

(4) The police department having jurisdiction of the area where the facility is located;

(5) Any person who may reasonably be expected to be the victim of any assault or any violent felony offense, as defined in the penal law, or any offense listed in section 530.11 of this part which would be carried out by the committed person; provided that the person who reasonably may be expected to be a victim does not need to be a member of the same family or household as the committed person; and

(6) Any other person the court may designate.

Said notice may be given by any means reasonably calculated to give prompt actual notice.

(b) The notice required by this subdivision shall also be given immediately upon the departure of such committed person from the actual custody of the commissioner or an appropriate institution, without proper authorization. Nothing in this subdivision shall be construed to impair any other right or duty regarding any notice or hearing contained in any other provision of law.

(c) Whenever a district attorney has received the notice described in this subdivision, and the defendant is in the custody of the commissioner pursuant to a final order of observation or an order of commitment, he may apply within three days of receipt of such notice to a superior court, for an order directing a hearing to be held to determine whether such committed person is a danger to himself or others. Such hearing shall be held within ten days following the issuance of such order. Such order may provide that there shall be no further change in the committed person's facility or status until the hearing. Upon a finding that the committed person is a danger to himself or others, the court shall issue an order to the commissioner authorizing retention of the committed person in the status existing at the time notice was given hereunder, for a specified period, not to exceed six months. The district attorney and the committed person's attorney shall be entitled to the committed person's clinical records in the commissioner's custody, upon the issuance of an order directing a hearing to be held.

(d) Nothing in this subdivision shall be construed to impair any other right or duty regarding any notice or hearing contained in any other provision of law.

§730.70 Fitness to proceed; procedure following termination of custody by commissioner.

When a defendant is in the custody of the commissioner on the expiration date of a final or temporary order of observation or an order of commitment, or on the expiration date of the last order of retention, or on the date an order dismissing an indictment is served upon the commissioner, the superintendent of the institution in which the defendant is confined may retain him for care and treatment for a period of thirty days from such date.

If the superintendent determines that the defendant is so mentally ill or mentally defective as to require continued care and treatment in an institution, he may, before the expiration of such thirty day period, apply for an order of certification in the manner prescribed in section 31.33 of the mental hygiene law.

This page intentionally left blank.

CRIMINAL PROCEDURE LAW INDEX

Sections

A

Abandonment of child 20.40
Accomplice 60.22, 200.95
Accusatory instrument ... Arts. 100 & 110,
.... 470.55
  defined 1.20
Acquittal .... Arts. 300, 310, 330
Adjournment .... Art. 215; 170.55,.56,
  ... 180.60, 210.46, 215.30, 380.30,
  .... 540.10, 570.40, 620.40
Admission .... Art. 60
Adolescent offender
  defined 1.20
  proceedings against .... Art. 722
  youth part/superior court ..... Art. 100
Affidavits, justifying .... 520.20, .30
Affirmations 255.20
Agencies 390.50
Aggravated family offense 200.63
Aggrieved person, defined 710.10
Aircraft, offense on 20.40
Alias warrant of arrest 570.48
Alibi 250.20, 340.30
Appeals .... Arts. 450, 460, 470
  re: DNA testing .... 450.10, .20
  electronic filing 460.90
Appearance bond, defined 500.10
Appearance ticket .... Art. 150
  defined 1.20
  fingerprinting of defendant 150.70
  reminders 150.80
Applicability of CPL 1.10
  to sentencing 380.10
Armed felony, defined 1.20
Arraignment 110.10, 170.10, 180.10,
  .... 210.10, .15, 620.40
  defined 1.20
Arrest
  assisting person arresting 570.22
  authority of officer 570.22
  close pursuit ...... 140.10, .55, 150.40
  fingerprinting &
    photographing .... Art. 160
  warrant of .... Art. 120
  without a warrant .... Art. 140
Arson 220.20, 700.05
Assault & battery 40.20, 220.20

B

Bail .... Arts. 500 - 540
  bonds .... Art. 520
  forfeiture & remission .... Art. 540
Bench warrant, defined 1.20
Bills of particulars 100.45, 200.95
Blind procedure 60.25
Burden of Proof ...... Art. 460; 210.45,
  .... 330.40, 620.50

C

Capital cases 270.16, 270.55
Capital punishment (appeals) .... Art. 450
Cash bail, defined 500.10
Charge to jury by court .... Art. 300
Chemical test evidence 60.75
Child
  as witness 60.20
  under sixteen, in custody 510.15
  use of closed-circuit
    television .... Art. 65
  vulnerable, defined 65.00
  witness .... Art. 65
    defined 65.00
Child sexual assault offender 200.62
City court, defined 10.10
Close pursuit .... 140.10, .55, 150.40
Closed-circuit television .... Art. 65
Commencement
  criminal action 100.05, 10, 210.10
  defined 1.20
  family court proceeding, effect .. 100.07
  information 100.45
  jury trial, defined 1.20
  local criminal court .... Art. 100
  non-jury trial, defined 1.20
Commitment .... Arts. 500, 510
  to custody of sheriff, defined 1.20
Companion animal .... 530.12, .13
Computers, notice of defenses 250.30
Concurrent counts, defined 300.30
Conditional discharge .... Art. 410
Conditional sealing of specified
  offense convictions 160.58
Confession .... 60.45, .50
Consecutive counts, defined 300.30
Consent
  adjournment 170.55
  discharge of jury 310.60
  extradition proceeding 570.50
  felony, release upon failure of timely
    disposition 180.80
  motion to vacate judgment 440.10
  reduction of charge, felony to
    non-felony 180.50
Consolidation 40.40, 100.45,
  .... 200.20, .40, 720.20
Constables, defined 1.20
Constitutional rights,
  rules of evidence 60.45
Convictions
  accomplice testimony 60.22
  admission by defendant 60.50
  child, evidence by 60.20

I

CRIMINAL PROCEDURE LAW INDEX

Sections

Convictions (Cont.)
conditional sealing of 160.58
confession by defendant 60.50
defined 1.20
immunity from 50.10
sealing of 160.59
standards of proof 70.20
surrender of firearms 370.25
traffic infractions 170.10
Corporate Defendants . . . . Art. 600
Corroboration 60.22,.50,70.10,190.65
Court Appearance; alternate method Art.182
notifications 510.43
Credit card
payment of bail 520.10
payment of fines 420.05
Crimes against children, notice of
conviction 440.65
Criminal action, defined 1.20
termination . . . . 160.50, .60
Criminal courts . . . . Art. 10
defined 1.20
electronic filing 10.40
Criminal proceeding, defined 1.20
Criminal transaction, defined 40.10

D

Dangerous drugs 220.20
destruction of . . . . Art. 715
rules of evidence,
drugs destroyed 60.70
Deadly physical force; executing
search warrant 690.50
Deadly weapons, search for 140.50
Defendants
securing attendant of . . . Arts. 550 - 600
statement of . . . . 60.45, .50
Definitions, terms of general
use . . . . 1.00 - 1.20
Deliberation and verdict in
jury trial . . . . Art. 310
Detainers, agreement on 580.20
Discovery . . . . Art. 245
Dismissal
adjournment 170.55,.56,
. . . . 210.46,215.30
appeals 470.60
arrest without warrant 140.45
grand jury charges 190.75
indictment . . . . . . 200.80, 210.20 - .46,
. . . . 290.10,730.40 - .60
insufficient information 140.45
trial, order of 290.10
District attorney, defined 1.20
DNA testing
appeal . . . . 450.10, .20

Sections

motion to vacate judgment 440.30
Dolls, use of anatomically
correct 60.44
Double jeopardy . . . . Art. 40
Drugs, destruction of . . . . Art. 715
Duplicitous counts, indictment 200.30
Duress 60.45, 440.10

E

Eavesdropping
defined 700.05
warrants . . . . Art. 700
Endangerment, of officer . . 120.80,140.15
Enterprise corruption 40.20,.50;
. . . 200.40,.65;210.40;300.10,310.50
Escape
indictment 200.60
interrupt period prescribed 730.60
murder in course of 220.20
Evidence
compulsion of 50.10,.20; 190.40
condom possession 60.47
given by children 60.20
grand jury 190.30;255.20;
. . . . 350.20;400.20,.30
in chief, defined 1.20
insufficiency 40.20;210.20,.30;
. . . . 170.50;470.20
legally sufficient 70.10
motion to suppress . . . . Art. 710
opioid antagonists, possession . . 60.49
rape crisis counselor 60.76
rules of . . . . Art. 60
victim's sexual conduct 60.42,.43
Examination of witness
conditionally . . . . Art. 660
on commission . . . . Art. 680
Exigent circumstances,
defined 700.05
postponement, due to . . 190.75, 700.50
Experts 180.60, 190.30
Expunge, defined 1.20
Extradition
outside United States Art.590
within United States . . . . Art. 570

F

Family Court, removal of
juvenile offender . . . . . 210.43, Art. 725
Family offenses . . . . Art. 530
adjournment in contemplation
of dismissal 170.55
arrest without warrant 140.10
family court proceeding 100.07
rules of evidence 60.46

Sections

Federal law enforcement officers
powers 2.15
Felony complaint 100.15,.30
arraignment through
defined 1.20
disposition . . . . Art. 180
fingerprint, photograph 160.10
juvenile offender 180.75
pre-sentence reports 390.20
proceedings . . . . Art. 180
Felony offender
judicial diversion program . . . . Art. 216
persistent 400.20
persistent violent 400.16
second violent 400.15
sexual assault on child 400.19
surrender of firearms 370.25
Fines . . . . 400.30, Art. 420
Fingerprint
appearance ticket 150.70
arrest with warrant 120.90
arrest without warrant 140.20
Fingerprinting and
photographing . . . . Art. 160, 130.60
Firearms license, suspension &
revocation 530.14
Fitness to proceed . . . . Article 730
Fix bail, defined 500.10
Force
admissibility of statements
obtained by 60.45
used in effecting
arrest . . . . 120.80,140.15, .35
Foreign countries 590.10, 680.60
Forfeiture of bail . . . . Art. 540
Forgery 20.40, 700.05
Former jeopardy . . . . Art. 40

G

Gambling 700.05
Geographical area of employment,
defined 1.20
Geographical jurisdiction of
offenses . . . . Art. 20
Give evidence, defined 50.10
Grand jury . . . . Art. 190
Guilty plea . . . . Art. 220

H

Habeas corpus 570.24,.50;
. . . . 580.30,650.30
Hearsay 70.10,100.15,180.60,
. . . . 400.27,710.60
HIV testing, required 210.16, 390.15
Homicide, geographical
jurisdiction 20.20,.40

Sections

I

Immunity . . . . Art. 50, 60.22; 170.30;
190.40,.45,.50,.52; 210.20;570.58,.60
Imprisonment
evidence of 400.22
sentences of . . . . Art. 430
Indian Police Officer 1.20
Indictment
amendment of 200.70
defined 1.20
enterprise corruption 200.65
related instruments . . . . Art. 200
to plea, superior court . . . . Art. 210
Informations . . . . Art. 100, 340.10
defined 1.20
Innocence, presumption of 300.10
Intermediate appellate court, defined . 1.20

J

Jail 420.10,570.28,.30
Jeopardy, former, double . . . . Art. 40
Judge, defined 1.20
Judgment
defined 1.20
proceedings after . . Arts. 440, 450, 460
Judicial diversion program . . . . . . Art. 216
Jurisdiction
divestiture of 170.20,.25
geographical . . . . Art. 20
local criminal court 10.30
superior court 10.20
Jurors, alternate . . . . . . Art. 270, 360.10,
. . . . 360.35, 400.27
Jury
courts charge & instruction to . . Art. 300
deliberation & verdict of . . . . . . Art. 310
formation & conduct of . . . . . . Art. 270
Jury trial . . . . Art. 270
conduct of non-jury trial . . . . . . Art. 320
generally . . . . Art. 260
mistrial Art. 280,30.30,270.35.,310.10,.60
trial order for dismissal . . . . Art. 290
waiver of jury trial . . . . Art. 320
Juvenile offender, defined 1.20
arresting 120.90
felony complaint proceedings . . . 180.75
removal to family court Art. 725; 210.43
Juvenile under sixteen, in custody . 510.15

L

Larceny 30.10, 700.05
Law enforcement officer 60.45,
. . . . 160.10,700.05,710.20
Legal proceeding, defined 50.10
Legally sufficient evidence,
defined 70.10

Sections

Lesser included offense, defined 1.20
Local criminal court
  definitions 1.20, 10.10
  jurisdiction 10.30
  preliminary proceedings in Art. 100 - 182
  prosecution of
    informations . . . . Arts.340 - 370

M

Marihuana cases, dismissal 210.46
  motion for resentence 440.46-a
Material witness order . . . . Art. 620
Medical professional, notification
  of sentencing 380.85
Mental disease or defect
  definitions 330.20
  examination 60.55
  exclude fitness to proceed . . . . Art. 730
  notice of 250.10
  procedure following verdict 330.20
Misdemeanor
  certain serious offenses 370.15
  failure to pay fine 420.10
  fingerprints & photographs 160.10
  notification to DCJS 380.97
  relating to traffic 170.10
  stop suspect, public place 140.50
Misdemeanor complaint
  arraignment to plea . . . . Art. 170
  defined 1.20
Mistrial 30.30;270.35,280.10,.20,310.10,.60
  motion for . . . . Art. 280
Modes of trial 340.40
Motion for resentence . . . . . . 440.46 - .47
Motion to suppress evidence . . . . Art. 710
Murder, determining sentence upon
  conviction, 1st degree 400.27

N

Narcotics 140.20, 220.20
New trial 280.10,.20; 330.50,
  . . . . 440.10,470.20,.55
Non-jury trial, defined . . . . Art. 320

O

Oath . . . . Arts. 190,660;
  . . . . 60.20,180.60,400.10,
  . . . . 620.50,690.40,700.25
  defined 1.20
Offender, certain controlled
  substances 160.58, 440.46
Offense, defined 40.10
Oral, search warrants . . . . . . 690.35 - .45

P

Parole
  warrant of arrest 120.55
  sentence of parole supervision . . 410.91
Peace officer . . . . Art. 2
  appearance ticket 150.20
  arrest by without
    warrant 140.25,.27,.35,.40,.55
  defined 1.20
  federal officers 2.15
  notice to appear; warrant 410.40
  persons designated as 2.10
  powers of 2.20
  training requirements 2.30
  warrant of arrest, addressed to120.50,.60
  watershed protection & enforcement
    officers 2.16
Pen registers . . . . Art. 705
Penal law definitions applicable to CPL 1.20
Peremptory challenge of juror 270.25
Persistent felony offender 400.20
Petty offenses
  arrest for 140.10
  defined 1.20
  trial jurisdiction 10.20,.30
Photographing & fingerprinting . . . Art. 160
Plea 170.60, Art.220, 340.20
  defined 1.20
Police officer, defined 1.20
Polygraph tests
  prohibitions 160.45
Post bail 500.10
Post-judgment motions . . . . Art. 440
Pre-criminal proceedings settlement Art. 95
Pre-sentence proceedings . . . . . . Art. 400
Pre-sentence reports . . . . Art. 390
Pre-trial
  motions . . . . Art. 255
  notices of defenses . . . . Art. 250
  proceedings . . . . Art. 340
  service agencies 510.45
Preliminary jurisdiction, defined 1.20
Premises, viewing of 270.50
Presumptions 20.20, 60.60, 160.30,
  . . . . 300.10, 470.25
Principal, defined 500.10
Probation/probationer
  custody and supervision 410.50
  invalid sentences of probation . . 440.60
  transfer of supervision 410.80
  warrant of arrest 120.55
Proceedings
  adolescent offenders . . . . Art. 722
  after judgment . . . . Arts. 440 - 470
  pre-criminal . . . . Art. 95

Sections

Proceedings (Cont.)
   upon felony complaint . . . . Art. 180
   upon information . . . . Art. 170
Proceedings from verdict to sentence
   . . . . Art. 330 & Art. 370
Prosecution, termination of 180.85
Prosecutions, previous . . . . Art. 40
Prosecutions; timeliness of . . . . . Art. 30
Prosecutor, defined 1.20
Prosecutor's information
   defined 1.20
   form and content 100.35
   proceedings upon . . . . Art. 170
   protection for family offense
     matters 530.12,.13
Prostitution, teenage 170.80
Psychiatric evidence 220.15, 250.10,
   . . . . 400.27
Public official, re: plea or trial 220.51
Public places, questioning in 140.50
Pursuit 140.10, 140.55, 150.40

R

Railroads, offenses committed on . . 20.40
Rape crisis counselor evidence 60.76
Reasonable cause, defined 70.10
Recognizance . . . . Arts. 500, 510, 530
Records; criminal identification . . . Art. 160
Relatives and friends,
   communication with170.10,180.10,210.15
Release on own recognizance,
   defined 500.10
Removal of
   action . . . 170.15,180.20,725.10,Art. 230
Rendition
   in regard to verdict . . . . Art. 300
   to other jurisdiction . . . . . Arts. 570,580
Reporting of convictions 380.80-.95
Resistance to arrest . . 120.80,140.15,.35
Restitution, fines and reparation . . Art. 420
Rules of evidence . Art. 60, 190.30,255.20,
   . . . . 350.20,400.20,.30

S

School employees,
   reporting conviction 380.95
Sealing of certain convictions 160.59
Search warrants . . . . Art. 690
Secured bail bond 520.10,.20
   defined 500.10
Securing attendance of
   corporate defendants . . . . Art. 600
   defendants . . . . Arts. 550 - 600
   defendants confined in institutions
     in NYS . . . . Art. 560
   defendants outside NYS but
     in USA . . . . Art. 570

Sections

   defendants outside USA . . . . . Art. 590
   of prisoners in other
     jurisdictions . . . . Arts. 580, 650
   of witnesses . . . . Arts. 610, 620
   of witnesses outside state . . . Art. 640
   persons confined in NYS . . . . Art. 630
Securing order 500.10
Securing testimony Art.660, 670
   from outside state . . . . Art. 680
Sentence, defined 1.20
   reporting to schools 380.90
   reporting to social services 380.80
Sentencing . Arts.380,390,400.410,420,430
   in general . . . . Art. 380
Sex offense, rules of evidence 60.42
Simplified information . . . . Art. 100
   definitions 1.20
   proceedings upon . . . . Art. 170
   single jury trial, defined 340.10
Speedy trial 30.20,.30,170.30,210.20,580.20
Standards of proof . . . . Art. 70
Statements of defendant 60.45,.50
Statute of limitations 30.10
Stay of judgment 460.50,.60
Subpoena duces tecum . . . . 610.10 - .25,
   . . . . 190.40
Subpoena of witness . . . . Art. 610
Summons . . . . Art. 130
   defined 1.20
   fingerprinting 130.60
Superior Court
   defined 1.20,10.10
   information; defined 200.15
   jurisdiction 10.20
   preliminary proceeding . Arts. 190 - 200
   proceedings . . . . Art. 210
   youth part 410.90-a
Superseding indictments 200.80
Superseding informations 100.50
Supporting deposition, defined 100.20
Suppression of evidence . . Arts. 690, 710

T

Testimonial capacity 60.20
Testimonial room, defined 65.00
Testimony given in a previous
   proceeding . . . . Art. 670
Timeliness of prosecution . . . . Art. 30
Town court, defined 10.10
Traffic infraction150.40,170.10,340.20,400.40
Training requirements, peace officers . 2.30
Trains, jurisdiction for;
   offenses thereon 20.40
Trap and trace devices . . . . Art. 705

CRIMINAL PROCEDURE LAW INDEX

Sections

Trial
   jury . . . . Art. 270
   non-jury . . . . Art. 350
   order of dismissal 290.10
Trial, defined 1.20
Trial jurisdiction 10.20,10.30
   defined 1.20

U

Uniform act to secure
   witness attendance . . . . Art. 640
Uniform close pursuit act 140.55
Uniform criminal extradition
   act . . . . Art. 570

V

Vehicles, search of . . . . Art. 690
Verdict . . . Arts. 310, 320,330,350,360,370
   defined 1.20
Vessels, jurisdiction of;
   offenses thereon 20.40
Victim, definition 215.20
Victims
   protection of 530.12,.13
   videotaped examination 190.32
Video surveillance, warrants . . . . Art. 700
   defined 700.05
Videotaped examination 190.32

Sections

Viewing of premises 270.40,.50
Village court, defined 10.10

W

Waiver of indictment . . . . Art. 195
Warrant . . . . Art. 120
   arrest, without . . . . Art. 140
   of arrest, defined 1.20
   eavesdropping . . . . Art. 700
   search . . . . Art. 690
   video surveillance . . . . Art. 700
   wiretapping . . . . Art. 700
   without . . . . Art. 140
Watershed protection &
   enforcement officers 2.16
Witness
   child as a . . . . Art. 65, 60.20
   conditional examination of . . . . Art. 660
   examination on a
     commission . . . . Art. 680
   impeachment of own 60.35
   material witness . . . . Art. 620
   securing attendance of . . Arts.610-650
     by subpoena . . . . Art. 610

Y

Youth part/superior court . . Arts. 100, 722
Youthful offender . . . . Art. 720

SELECTED
LAWS
of
NEW YORK
STATE

Part III

Looseleaf
Law Publications, Inc.

43-08 162nd Street
Flushing, NY 11358
www.LooseleafLaw.com   800-647-5547

Law Changes Through Chapter 834, Laws of 2021
Which Affect The Following:

Section	Subdivision	Change	Chapter	Eff. Date
Correction Law				
803	1.(d)(ii)	Amended	322	8/2/21
803	1.(d)(iv)	Amended	242	7/16/21
803		Amended	322	8/2/21
803		Eff. Extended	55	4/19/21
865	1., 2.	Amended	322	8/2/21
Executive Law				
995	1.	Amended	209	9/1/21
995	7.	Amended	715	12/22/21
Public Health Law				
3302		Amended	92	3/31/21
3306	Sch. I (d)(13) to (31)	Amended	92	3/31/21
3309	3-a (c),(d)	Amended	741	12/22/21
3309	5. & 6.	Amended	741	12/22/21
3309	7.		803	6/27/22
Vehicle & Traffic Law				
510	4-a.	Amended	76	6/29/21
510	4-a.(c)(iv)	Amended	713	12/21/21
510	4-c.	Eff. Extended	55	4/19/21
510	4-e.	Eff. Extended	183	6/29/21
600	1.a., 2.a., 3.	Amended	795	3/22/22
601		Amended	795	3/22/22
1198		Eff. Extended	55	4/19/21

Table of Contents

CORRECTION LAW 1
  ARTICLE 6-C
    SEX OFFENDER REGISTRATION ACT 1
    §168.   Short title 1
    §168-a. Definitions 1
    §168-b. Duties of the division; registration information 5
    §168-c. Sex offender; relocation; notification 8
    §168-d. Duties of the court 9
    §168-e. Discharge of sex offender from correctional facility;
              duties of official in charge 12
    §168-f. Duty to register and to verify 13
    §168-g. Prior convictions; duty to inform and register 15
    §168-h. Duration of registration and verification 16
    §168-i. Registration and verification requirements 16
    §168-j. Notification of local law enforcement agencies of
              change of address 16
    §168-k. Registration for change of address from another state . 17
    §168-*l.* Board of examiners of sex offenders 19
    §168-m. Review 22
    §168-n. Judicial determination 23
    §168-o. Petition for relief or modification 25
    §168-p. Special telephone number 27
    §168-q. Subdirectory; internet posting 29
    §168-r. Immunity from liability 30
    §168-s. Annual report 30
    §168-t. Penalty 30
    §168-u. Unauthorized release of information 30
    §168-v. Prohibition of employment on motor vehicles
              engaged in retail sales of frozen desserts 31
    §168-w. Separability 31
    §803.   Good behavior allowances against indeterminate and
              determinate sentences 31
    §865.   Definitions. 35

EDUCATION LAW 37
  TITLE 8 - THE PROFESSIONS
    ARTICLE 130 - GENERAL PROVISIONS
    SUBARTICLE 4
    UNAUTHORIZED ACTS 37
    §6512. Unauthorized practice a crime 37
    §6513. Unauthorized use of a professional title a crime 37
    §6514. Criminal proceedings 37
  ARTICLE 137
    PHARMACY 38
    §6811. Misdemeanors 38
    §6812. Special provisions 40
    §6813. Seizure 40

§6814.   Records of shipment 42
§6815.   Adulterating, misbranding and substituting 42

EXECUTIVE LAW 47
  ARTICLE 49-B
  COMMISSION ON FORENSIC SCIENCE AND
  ESTABLISHMENT OF DNA IDENTIFICATION INDEX ... 47
  §995.   Definitions 47
  §995-a.   Commission on forensic science 48
  §995-b.   Powers and duties of the commission 49
  §995-c.   State DNA identification index 54
  §995-d.   Confidentiality 57
  §995-e.   Applicability 58
  §995-f.   Penalties 58

GENERAL BUSINESS LAW 59
  ARTICLE 29-A
  UNAUTHORIZED OR IMPROPER USE
  OF CREDIT CARDS AND DEBIT CARDS 59
  §511.   Definitions 59
  §511-a.   Additional definition 60

PUBLIC HEALTH LAW 61
  ARTICLE 33
  CONTROLLED SUBSTANCES 61
  TITLE I
  GENERAL PROVISIONS 61
  §3300.   Short title 61
  §3300-a. Legislative purposes 61
  §3301.   Applicability of this article to actions and matters
            occurring or arising before and after the effective date   61
  §3302.   Definitions of terms of general use in this article 62
  §3304.   Prohibited acts 65
  §3304.   Prohibited acts 66
  §3305.   Exemptions 66
  §3306.   Schedules of controlled substances 67
  §3307.   Exception from schedules 81
  §3308.   Powers and duties of the commissioner 82
  §3309.   Opioid overdose prevention 83
  §3309-a. Prescription pain medication awareness program. ... 86
  TITLE II
  MANUFACTURE AND DISTRIBUTION
  OF CONTROLLED SUBSTANCES 89
  §3310.   Licenses for manufacture or distribution of controlled
            substances 89

VEHICLE & TRAFFIC LAW 91
  ARTICLE 19
    LICENSING OF DRIVERS 91
    §509.   Violations. 91
  ARTICLE 19-A
    SPECIAL REQUIREMENTS FOR BUS DRIVERS 92
    §509-a. Definitions 93
    §509-h. Operation by person not licensed to drive a bus 94
    §509-i. Notification of a conviction resulting from a violation
         of this chapter in this state or a motor vehicle
         conviction in another state and license revocation 94
    §509-j. Compliance required 95
    §509-k. Ill or fatigued operator 97
    §509-l. Drugs, controlled substances and intoxicating liquor .. 97
    §509-m. Duties of the department 97
    §509-n. Exempt carriers; reporting requirements 99
    §509-o. Penalties 100
  ARTICLE 20
    SUSPENSION AND REVOCATION 100
    §510.   Suspension, revocation and reissuance of licenses
         and registrations 100
    §510-a. Suspension and revocation of commercial driver's
         licenses 116
    §510-aa. Downgrade of commercial driver's licenses. 122
    §510-b. Suspension and revocation for violations committed
         during probationary periods 123
    §511.   Operation while license or privilege is suspended or
         revoked; aggravated unlicensed operation 125
    §511-a. Facilitating aggravated unlicensed operation of a
         motor vehicle 128
    §511-b. Seizure and redemption of unlawfully operated
         vehicles 129
    §511-c. Seizure and forfeiture of vehicles used in the
         unlicensed operation of a motor vehicle under
         certain circumstances 131
    §511-d. Aggravated failure to answer appearance tickets or
         pay fines imposed 136
    §512.   Operation while registration or privilege is
         suspended or revoked 137
  ARTICLE 22
    ACCIDENTS AND ACCIDENT REPORTS 137
    §600.   Leaving scene of an incident without reporting 137
    §601.   Leaving scene of injury to certain animals without
         reporting 140
    §602.   Arrest for violations of sections six hundred and six
         hundred one 140
    §603.   Accidents; police authorities and coroners to report .. 141
    §603-a. Accidents; police authorities to investigate 141

§603-b. Accidents; police to indicate serious physical injury
         and death on simplified traffic information or
         summons and compliant 142
ARTICLE 23
   OBEDIENCE TO AND EFFECT OF TRAFFIC LAWS 143
   §1100. Provisions of title refer to vehicles upon highways;
           exceptions 143
   §1101. Required obedience to traffic laws 143
   §1102. Obedience to police officers and flagpersons 143
   §1103. Public officers and employees to obey title;
           exceptions 143
   §1104. Authorized emergency vehicles 144
ARTICLE 30
   SPEED RESTRICTIONS 146
   §1180.   Basic rule and maximum limits 146
   §1180-a. Maximum speed limits 149
   §1180-b. Owner liability for failure of operator to comply
            with certain posted maximum speed limits. 151
   §1180-c. Owner liability for failure of operator to comply
            with certain posted maximum speed limits. 158
   **§1180-d. Owner liability for failure of operator to comply
            with certain posted maximum speed limits.** 158
   §1181.   Minimum speed regulations 165
ARTICLE 31
   ALCOHOL AND DRUG-RELATED OFFENSES
   AND PROCEDURES APPLICABLE THERETO 165
   §1192.   Operating a motor vehicle while under the influence
            of alcohol or drugs 165
   §1192-a. Operating a motor vehicle after having consumed
            alcohol; under the age of twenty-one; per se 170
   §1193.   Sanctions 171
   §1194.   Arrest and testing 188
   §1194-a. Driving after having consumed alcohol; under
            twenty-one; procedure 197
   §1195.   Chemical test evidence 201
   §1196.   Alcohol and drug rehabilitation program 202
   §1197.   Special traffic options program for driving while
            intoxicated 205
   §1198.   Installation and operation of ignition interlock
            devices. 208
   §1198-a. Special procedures and disposition involving
            alcohol and substance abuse assessment
            and treatment 213
ARTICLE 33
   MISCELLANEOUS RULES 217
   §1212. Reckless driving 217

CORRECTION LAW
ARTICLE 6-C
SEX OFFENDER REGISTRATION ACT

Section
168.   Short title.
168-a.   Definitions.
168-b.   Duties of the division; registration information.
168-c.   Sex offender; relocation; notification.
168-d.   Duties of the court.
168-e.   Discharge of sex offender from correctional facility; duties of official in charge.
168-f.   Duty to register and to verify.
168-g.   Prior convictions; duty to inform and register.
168-h.   Duration of registration and verification.
168-i.   Registration and verification requirements.
168-j.   Notification of local law enforcement agencies of change of address.
168-k.   Registration for change of address from another state.
168-l.   Board of examiners of sex offenders.
168-m.   Review.
168-n.   Judicial determination.
168-o.   Petition for relief or modification.
168-p.   Special telephone number.
168-q.   Subdirectory; internet posting.
168-r.   Immunity from liability.
168-s.   Annual report.
168-t.   Penalty.
168-u.   Unauthorized release of information.
168-v.   Prohibition of employment on motor vehicles engaged in retail sales of frozen desserts.
168-w.   Separability.

§168.   Short title.

This article shall be known and may be cited as the "Sex Offender Registration Act".

§168-a.   Definitions.

As used in this article, the following definitions apply:

1. "Sex offender" includes any person who is convicted of any of the offenses set forth in subdivision two or three of this section. Convictions that result from or are connected with the same act, or result from offenses committed at the same time, shall be counted for the purpose of this article as one conviction. Any conviction set aside pursuant to law is not a conviction for purposes of this article.

2. "Sex offense" means:

(a) (i) a conviction of or a conviction for an attempt to commit any of the provisions of sections 120.70, 130.20, 130.25, 130.30, 130.40, 130.45, 130.60, 230.34, 230.34-a, 250.50, 255.25, 255.26 and 255.27 or article two hundred sixty-three of the penal law, or section 135.05, 135.10, 135.20 or 135.25 of such law relating to kidnapping offenses, provided the victim of such kidnapping or related offense is less than seventeen years old and the offender is not the parent of the victim, or section 230.04, where the person patronized is in fact less than seventeen years of age, 230.05, 230.06, 230.11, 230.12, 230.13, subdivision two of section 230.30, section 230.32, 230.33, or 230.34

of the penal law, or section 230.25 of the penal law where the person prostituted is in fact less than seventeen years old, or

(ii) a conviction of or a conviction for an attempt to commit any of the provisions of section 235.22 of the penal law, or

(iii) a conviction of or a conviction for an attempt to commit any provisions of the foregoing sections committed or attempted as a hate crime defined in section 485.05 of the penal law or as a crime of terrorism defined in section 490.25 of such law or as a sexually motivated felony defined in section 130.91 of such law; or

(b) a conviction of or a conviction for an attempt to commit any of the provisions of section 130.52 or 130.55 of the penal law, provided the victim of such offense is less than eighteen years of age; or

(c) a conviction of or a conviction for an attempt to commit any of the provisions of section 130.52 or 130.55 of the penal law regardless of the age of the victim and the offender has previously been convicted of:

(i) a sex offense defined in this article,

(ii) a sexually violent offense defined in this article, or

(iii) any of the provisions of section 130.52 or 130.55 of the penal law, or an attempt thereof; or

(d) a conviction of

(i) an offense in any other jurisdiction which includes all of the essential elements of any such crime provided for in paragraph (a), (b) or (c) of this subdivision or

(ii) a felony in any other jurisdiction for which the offender is required to register as a sex offender in the jurisdiction in which the conviction occurred or,

(iii) any of the provisions of 18 U.S.C. 2251, 18 U.S.C. 2251A, 18 U.S.C. 2252, 18 U.S.C. 2252A, 18 U.S.C. 2260, 18 U.S.C. 2422(b), 18 U.S.C. 2423, or 18 U.S.C. 2425, provided that the elements of such crime of conviction are substantially the same as those which are a part of such offense as of the date on which this subparagraph takes effect.

(e) a conviction of or a conviction for an attempt to commit any of the provisions of subdivision two, three or four of section 250.45 of the penal law, unless upon motion by the defendant, the trial court, having regard to the nature and circumstances of the crime and to the history and character of the defendant, is of the opinion that registration would be unduly harsh and inappropriate.

3. "Sexually violent offense" means:

(a) (i) a conviction of or a conviction for an attempt to commit any of the provisions of sections 130.35, 130.50, 130.65, 130.66, 130.67, 130.70, 130.75, 130.80, 130.95 and 130.96 of the penal law, or

(ii) a conviction of or a conviction for an attempt to commit any of the provisions of sections 130.53, 130.65-a and 130.90 of the penal law, or

(iii) a conviction of or a conviction for an attempt to commit any provisions of the foregoing sections committed or attempted as a hate crime defined in section 485.05 of the penal law or as a crime of terrorism defined in section 490.25 of such law; or

(b) a conviction of an offense in any other jurisdiction which includes all of the essential elements of any such felony provided for in paragraph (a) of this subdivision or conviction of a felony in any other jurisdiction for which the offender is required to register as a sex offender in the jurisdiction in which the conviction occurred.

4. "Law enforcement agency having jurisdiction" means:

(a) (i) the chief law enforcement officer in the village, town or city in which the offender expects to reside upon his or her discharge, probation, parole, release to post-release supervision or upon any form of state or local conditional release; or

(ii) if there be no chief law enforcement officer in such village, town or city, the chief law enforcement officer of the county in which the offender expects to reside; or

(iii) if there be no chief enforcement officer in such village, town, city or county, the division of state police and

(b) in the case of a sex offender who is or expects to be employed by, enrolled in, attending or employed, whether for compensation or not, at an institution of higher education,

(i) the chief law enforcement officer in the village, town or city in which such institution is located; or

(ii) if there be no chief law enforcement officer in such village, town or city, the chief law enforcement officer of the county in which such institution is located; or

(iii) if there be no chief law enforcement officer in such village, town, city or county, the division of state police; and

(iv) if such institution operates or employs a campus law enforcement or security agency, the chief of such agency; and

(c) in the case of a sex offender who expects to reside within a state park or on other land under the jurisdiction of the office of parks, recreation and historic preservation, the state regional park police.

5. "Division" means the division of criminal justice services as defined by section eight hundred thirty-seven of the executive law.

6. "Hospital" means:

(a) a hospital as defined in subdivision two of section four hundred of this chapter and applies to persons committed to such hospital by order of commitment made pursuant to article sixteen of this chapter; or

(b) a secure treatment facility as defined in section 10.03 of the mental hygiene law and applies to persons committed to such facility by an order made pursuant to article ten of the mental hygiene law.

7. (a) "Sexual predator" means a sex offender who has been convicted of a sexually violent offense defined in subdivision three of this section and who suffers from a mental abnormality or personality disorder that makes him or her likely to engage in predatory sexually violent offenses.

(b) "Sexually violent offender" means a sex offender who has been convicted of a sexually violent offense defined in subdivision three of this section.

(c) "Predicate sex offender" means a sex offender who has been convicted of an offense set forth in subdivision two or three of this section when the offender has been previously convicted of an offense set forth in subdivision two or three of this section.

8. "Mental abnormality" means a congenital or acquired condition of a person that affects the emotional or volitional capacity of the person in a manner that predisposes that person to the commission of criminal sexual acts to a degree that makes the person a menace to the health and safety of other persons.

9. "Predatory" means an act directed at a stranger, or a person with whom a relationship has been established or promoted for the primary purpose of victimization.

10. "Board" means the "board of examiners of sex offenders" established pursuant to section one hundred sixty-eight-l of this article.

11. "Local correctional facility" means a local correctional facility as that term is defined in subdivision sixteen of section two of this chapter.

12. Probation means a sentence of probation imposed pursuant to article sixty-five of the penal law and shall include a sentence of imprisonment imposed in conjunction with a sentence of probation.

13. "Institution of higher education" means an institution in the state providing higher education as such term is defined in subdivision eight of section two of the education law.

14. "Nonresident worker" means any person required to register as a sex offender in another jurisdiction who is employed or carries on a vocation in this state, on either a full-time or a part-time basis, with or without compensation, for more than fourteen consecutive days, or for an aggregate period exceeding thirty days in a calendar year.

15. "Nonresident student" means a person required to register as a sex offender in another jurisdiction who is enrolled on a full-time or part-time basis in any public or private educational institution in this state including any secondary school, trade or professional institution or institution of higher education.

16. "Authorized internet entity" means any business, organization or other entity providing or offering a service over the internet which permits persons under eighteen years of age to access, meet, congregate or communicate with other users for the purpose of social networking. This definition shall not include general e-mail services.

17. "Internet access provider" means any business, organization or other entity engaged in the business of providing a computer and communications facility through which a customer may obtain access to the internet, but does not include a business, organization or other entity to the extent that it provides only telecommunications services.

18. "Internet identifiers" means electronic mail addresses and designations used for the purposes of chat, instant messaging, social networking or other similar internet communication.

§168-b. Duties of the division; registration information.

1. The division shall establish and maintain a file of individuals required to register pursuant to the provisions of this article which shall include the following information of each registrant:

. (a) The sex offender's name, all aliases used, date of birth, sex, race, height, weight, eye color, driver's license number, home address and/or expected place of domicile, any internet accounts with internet access providers belonging to such offender and internet identifiers that such offender uses.

(b) A photograph and set of fingerprints. For a sex offender given a level three designation, the division shall, during the period of registration, update such photograph once each year. For a sex offender given a level one or level two designation, the division shall, during the period of registration, update such photograph once every three years. The division shall notify the sex offender by mail of the duty to appear and be photographed at the specified law enforcement agency having jurisdiction. Such notification shall be mailed at least thirty days and not more than sixty days before the photograph is required to be taken pursuant to subdivision two of section one hundred sixty-eight-f of this article.

(c) A description of the offense for which the sex offender was convicted, the date of conviction and the sentence imposed including the type of assigned supervision and the length of time of such supervision.

(d) The name and address of any institution of higher education at which the sex offender is or expects to be enrolled, attending or employed, whether for compensation or not, and whether such offender resides in or will reside in a facility owned or operated by such institution.

(e) If the sex offender has been given a level two or three designation, such offender's employment address and/or expected place of employment.

(f) Any other information deemed pertinent by the division.

2. a. The division is authorized to make the registry available to any regional or national registry of sex offenders for the purpose of sharing information. The division shall accept files from any regional or national registry of sex offenders and shall make such files available when requested pursuant to the provisions of this article.

b. The division shall also make registry information available to:

(i) the department of health, to enable such department to identify persons ineligible to receive reimbursement or coverage for drugs, procedures or supplies pursuant to subdivision seven of section twenty-five hundred ten of the public health law, paragraph (e) of subdivision four of section three hundred sixty-five-a of the social services law, paragraph (e-1) of subdivision one of section three hundred sixty-nine-ee of the social services law, and subdivision one of section two hundred forty-one of the elder law;

(ii) the department of financial services to enable such department to identify persons ineligible to receive reimbursement or coverage for drugs, procedures or supplies pursuant to subsection (b-1) of section four thousand three hundred twenty-two and subsection (d-1) of section four thousand three hundred twenty-six of the insurance law; and

b. The division shall also make registry information available to: (i) the department of health, to enable such department to identify persons ineligible to receive reimbursement or coverage for drugs, procedures or supplies pursuant to subdivision seven of section twenty-five hundred ten of the public health law, paragraph (e) of subdivision four of section three hundred sixty-five-a of the social services law, paragraph (e-1) of subdivision one of section three hundred sixty-nine-ee of the social services law, and subdivision one of section two hundred forty-one of the elder law; (ii) the department of financial services to enable such department to identify persons ineligible to receive reimbursement or coverage for drugs, procedures or supplies pursuant to subsection (b-1) of section four thousand three hundred twenty-two and subsection (d-1) of section four thousand three hundred twenty-six of the insurance law; and (iii) a court, to enable the court to promptly comply with the provisions of paragraph (a-1) of subdivision one of section two hundred forty of the domestic relations law, subdivision (e) of section six hundred fifty-one of the family court act, and subdivision (g) of section 81.19 of the mental hygiene law.

c. The department of health and the department of financial services may disclose to plans providing coverage for drugs, procedures or supplies for the treatment of erectile dysfunction pursuant to section three hundred sixty-nine-ee of the social services law or sections four thousand three hundred twenty-one, four thousand three hundred twenty-two or four thousand three hundred twenty-six of the insurance law registry information that is limited to the names, dates of birth, and social security numbers of persons who are ineligible by law to receive payment or reimbursement for specified drugs, procedures and supplies pursuant to such provisions of law. Every such plan shall identify to the department of health or the department of financial services, in advance of disclosure, each person in its employ who is authorized to receive such information provided, however, that such information may be disclosed by such authorized employee or employees to other personnel who are directly involved in approving or disapproving reimbursement or coverage for such drugs, procedures and supplies for such plan members, and provided further that no person receiving registry information shall redisclose such information except to other personnel who are directly involved in approving or disapproving reimbursement or coverage for such drugs, procedures and supplies.

d. No official, agency, authorized person or entity, whether public or private, shall be subject to any civil or criminal liability for damages for any decision or action made in the ordinary course of business of that official, agency, authorized person or entity pursuant to paragraphs b and c of this subdivision, provided that such official, agency, authorized person or entity acted reasonably and in good faith with respect to such registry information.

e. The division shall require that no information included in the registry shall be made available except in the furtherance of the provisions of this article.

3. The division shall develop a standardized registration form to be made available to the appropriate authorities and promulgate rules and regulations to implement the provisions of this section. Such form shall be written in clear and concise language and shall advise the sex offender of his or her duties and obligations under this article.

4. The division shall mail a nonforwardable verification form to the last reported address of the person for annual verification requirements.

5. The division shall also establish and operate a telephone number as provided for in section one hundred sixty-eight-p of this article.

6. The division shall also establish a subdirectory pursuant to section one hundred sixty-eight-q of this article.

7. The division shall also establish a public awareness campaign to advise the public of the provisions of this article.

8. The division shall charge a fee of ten dollars each time a sex offender registers any change of address or any change of his or her status of enrollment, attendance, employment or residence at any institution of higher education as required by subdivision four of section one hundred sixty-eight-f of this article. The fee shall be paid to the division by the sex offender. The state comptroller is hereby authorized to deposit such fees into the general fund.

9. The division shall, upon the request of any children's camp operator, release to such person any information in the registry relating to a prospective employee of any such person or entity in accordance with the provisions of this article. The division shall promulgate rules and regulations relating to procedures for the release of information in the registry to such persons.

10. The division shall, upon the request of any authorized internet entity, release to such entity internet identifiers that would enable such entity to prescreen or remove sex offenders from its services or, in conformity with state and federal law, advise law enforcement and/or other governmental entities of potential violations of law and/or threats to public safety. Before releasing any information the division shall require an authorized internet entity that requests information from the registry to submit to the division the name, address and telephone number of such entity and the specific legal nature and corporate status of such entity. Except for the purposes specified in this subdivision, an authorized internet entity shall not publish or in any way disclose or redisclose any information provided to it by the division pursuant to this subdivision. The division may charge an authorized internet entity a fee for access to registered internet identifiers requested by such entity pursuant to this subdivision. The division shall promulgate rules and regulations relating to procedures for the release of information in the registry, including but not limited to, the disclosure and redisclosure of such information, and the imposition of any fees.

11. The division shall promptly notify each sex offender whose term of registration and verification would otherwise have expired prior to March thirty-first, two thousand seven of the continuing duty to register and verify under this article.

12. The division shall make registry information regarding level two and three sex offenders available to municipal housing authorities, as established pursuant to article three of the public housing law, to enable such authorities to identify persons ineligible to reside in public housing. The division shall, at least monthly, release to each municipal housing authority information about level two and three sex offenders with a home address and/or expected place of domicile within the corresponding municipality. The division may promulgate rules and regulations relating to procedures for the release of information in the registry to such authorities.

§168-c. Sex offender; relocation; notification.

1. In the case of any sex offender, it shall be the duty of the department, hospital or local correctional facility at least ten calendar days prior to the release or discharge of any sex offender from a correctional facility, hospital or local correctional facility to notify the division of the contemplated release or discharge of such sex offender, informing the division in writing on a form provided by the division indicating the address at which he or she proposes to reside and the name and address of any institution of higher education at which he or she expects to be enrolled, attending or employed, whether for compensation or not, and whether he or she resides in or will reside in a facility owned or operated by such institution. If such sex offender changes his or her place of residence while on parole, such notification of the change of residence shall be sent by the sex offender's parole officer within forty-eight hours to the division on a form provided by the division. If such sex offender changes the status of his or her enrollment, attendance, employment or residence at any institution of higher education while on parole, such notification of the change of status shall be sent by the sex offender's parole officer within forty-eight hours to the division on a form provided by the division.

2. In the case of any sex offender on probation, it shall be the duty of the sex offender's probation officer to notify the division within forty-eight hours of the new place of residence on a form provided by the division. If such sex offender changes the status of his or her enrollment, attendance, employment or residence at any institution of higher education while on probation, such notification of the change of status shall be sent by the sex offender's probation officer within forty-eight hours to the division on a form provided by the division.

3. In the case in which any sex offender escapes from a state or local correctional facility or hospital, the designated official of the facility or hospital where the person was confined shall notify within twenty-four hours the law enforcement agency having had jurisdiction at the time of his or her conviction, informing such law enforcement agency of the name and aliases of the person, and the address at which he or she resided at the time of his or her conviction,

the amount of time remaining to be served, if any, on the full term for which he or she was sentenced, and the nature of the crime for which he or she was sentenced, transmitting at the same time a copy of such sex offender's fingerprints and photograph and a summary of his or her criminal record.

4. The division shall provide general information, in registration materials and annual correspondence, to registrants concerning notification and registration procedures that may apply if the registrant is authorized to relocate and relocates to another state or United States possession, or commences employment or attendance at an education institution in another state or United States possession. Such information shall include addresses and telephone numbers for relevant agencies from which additional information may be obtained.

§168-d. Duties of the court.

1. (a) Except as provided in paragraphs (b) and (c) of this subdivision, upon conviction of any of the offenses set forth in subdivision two or three of section one hundred sixty-eight-a of this article the court shall certify that the person is a sex offender and shall include the certification in the order of commitment, if any, and judgment of conviction, except as provided in paragraph (e) of subdivision two of section one hundred sixty-eight-a of this article. The court shall also advise the sex offender of his or her duties under this article. Failure to include the certification in the order of commitment or the judgment of conviction shall not relieve a sex offender of the obligations imposed by this article.

(b) Where a defendant stands convicted of an offense defined in paragraph (b) of subdivision two of section one hundred sixty-eight-a of this article or where the defendant was convicted of patronizing a person for prostitution in the third degree under section 230.04 of the penal law and the defendant controverts an allegation that the victim of such offense was less than eighteen years of age or, in the case of a conviction under section 230.04 of the penal law, less than seventeen years of age, the court, without a jury, shall, prior to sentencing, conduct a hearing, and the people may prove by clear and convincing evidence that the victim was less than eighteen years old or less than seventeen years old, as applicable, by any evidence admissible under the rules applicable to a trial of the issue of guilt. The court in addition to such admissible evidence may also consider reliable hearsay evidence submitted by either party provided that it is relevant to the determination of the age of the victim. Facts concerning the age of the victim proven at trial or ascertained at the time of entry of a plea of guilty shall be deemed established by clear and convincing evidence and shall not be relitigated. At the conclusion of the hearing, or if the defendant does not controvert an allegation that the victim of the offense was less than eighteen years old or less than seventeen years old, as applicable, the court must make a finding and enter an order setting forth the age of the victim. If the court finds that the victim of such offense was under eighteen years old or under seventeen years old, as applicable, the court shall certify the defendant as a sex offender, the provisions of paragraph (a) of this subdivision shall apply and the defendant shall register with the division in accordance with the provisions of this article.

(c) Where a defendant stands convicted of an offense defined in paragraph (c) of subdivision two of section one hundred sixty-eight-a of this article and the defendant controverts an allegation that the defendant was previously convicted of a sex offense or a sexually violent offense defined in this article or has previously been convicted of or convicted for an attempt to commit any of the provisions of section 130.52 or 130.55 of the penal law, the court, without a jury, shall, prior to sentencing, conduct a hearing, and the people may prove by clear and convincing evidence that the defendant was previously convicted of a sex offense or a sexually violent offense defined in this article or has previously been convicted of or convicted for an attempt to commit any of the provisions of section 130.52 or 130.55 of the penal law, by any evidence admissible under the rules applicable to a trial of the issue of guilt. The court in addition to such admissible evidence may also consider reliable hearsay evidence submitted by either party provided that it is relevant to the determination of whether the defendant was previously convicted of a sex offense or a sexually violent offense defined in this article or has previously been convicted of or convicted for an attempt to commit any of the provisions of section 130.52 or 130.55 of the penal law. At the conclusion of the hearing, or if the defendant does not controvert an allegation that the defendant was previously convicted of a sex offense or a sexually violent offense defined in this article or has previously been convicted of or convicted for an attempt to commit any of the provisions of section 130.52 or 130.55 of the penal law, the court must make a finding and enter an order determining whether the defendant was previously convicted of a sex offense or a sexually violent offense defined in this article or has previously been convicted of or convicted for an attempt to commit any of the provisions of section 130.52 or 130.55 of the penal law. If the court finds that the defendant has such a previous conviction, the court shall certify the defendant as a sex offender, the provisions of paragraph (a) of this subdivision shall apply and the defendant shall register with the division in accordance with the provisions of this article.

2. Any sex offender, who is released on probation or discharged upon payment of a fine, conditional discharge or unconditional discharge shall, prior to such release or discharge, be informed of his or her duty to register under this article by the court in which he or she was convicted. At the time sentence is imposed, such sex offender shall register with the division on a form prepared by the division. The court shall require the sex offender to read and sign such form and to complete the registration portion of such form. The court shall on such form obtain the address where the sex offender expects to reside upon his or her release, and the name and address of any institution of higher education he or she expects to be employed by, enrolled in, attending or employed, whether for compensation or not, and whether he or she expects to reside in a facility owned or operated by such an institution, and shall report such information to the division. The court shall give one copy of the form to the sex offender and shall send two copies to the division which shall forward

the information to the law enforcement agencies having jurisdiction. The court shall also notify the district attorney and the sex offender of the date of the determination proceeding to be held pursuant to subdivision three of this section, which shall be held at least forty-five days after such notice is given. This notice shall include the following statement or a substantially similar statement: "This proceeding is being held to determine whether you will be classified as a level 3 offender (risk of repeat offense is high), a level 2 offender (risk of repeat offense is moderate), or a level 1 offender (risk of repeat offense is low), or whether you will be designated as a sexual predator, a sexually violent offender or a predicate sex offender, which will determine how long you must register as a sex offender and how much information can be provided to the public concerning your registration. If you fail to appear at this proceeding, without sufficient excuse, it shall be held in your absence. Failure to appear may result in a longer period of registration or a higher level of community notification because you are not present to offer evidence or contest evidence offered by the district attorney." The court shall also advise the sex offender that he or she has a right to a hearing prior to the court's determination, that he or she has the right to be represented by counsel at the hearing and that counsel will be appointed if he or she is financially unable to retain counsel. If the sex offender applies for assignment of counsel to represent him or her at the hearing and counsel was not previously assigned to represent the sex offender in the underlying criminal action, the court shall determine whether the offender is financially unable to retain counsel. If such a finding is made, the court shall assign counsel to represent the sex offender pursuant to article eighteen-B of the county law. Where the court orders a sex offender released on probation, such order must include a provision requiring that he or she comply with the requirements of this article. Where such sex offender violates such provision, probation may be immediately revoked in the manner provided by article four hundred ten of the criminal procedure law.

3. For sex offenders released on probation or discharged upon payment of a fine, conditional discharge or unconditional discharge, it shall be the duty of the court applying the guidelines established in subdivision five of section one hundred sixty-eight-l of this article to determine the level of notification pursuant to subdivision six of section one hundred sixty-eight-l of this article and whether such sex offender shall be designated a sexual predator, sexually violent offender, or predicate sex offender as defined in subdivision seven of section one hundred sixty-eight-a of this article. At least fifteen days prior to the determination proceeding, the district attorney shall provide to the court and the sex offender a written statement setting forth the determinations sought by the district attorney together with the reasons for seeking such determinations. The court shall allow the sex offender to appear and be heard. The state shall appear by the district attorney, or his or her designee, who shall bear the burden of proving the facts supporting the determinations sought by clear and convincing evidence. Where there is a dispute between the parties concerning the determinations, the court shall adjourn the hearing as necessary to permit the sex offender or the district attorney to obtain materials relevant

to the determinations from any state or local facility, hospital, institution, office, agency, department or division. Such materials may be obtained by subpoena if not voluntarily provided to the requesting party. In making the determinations, the court shall review any victim's statement and any relevant materials and evidence submitted by the sex offender and the district attorney and the court may consider reliable hearsay evidence submitted by either party provided that it is relevant to the determinations. Facts previously proven at trial or elicited at the time of entry of a plea of guilty shall be deemed established by clear and convincing evidence and shall not be relitigated. The court shall render an order setting forth its determinations and the findings of fact and conclusions of law on which the determinations are based. A copy of the order shall be submitted by the court to the division. Upon application of either party, the court shall seal any portion of the court file or record which contains material that is confidential under any state or federal statute. Either party may appeal as of right from the order pursuant to the provisions of articles fifty-five, fifty-six and fifty-seven of the civil practice law and rules. Where counsel has been assigned to represent the sex offender upon the ground that the sex offender is financially unable to retain counsel, that assignment shall be continued throughout the pendency of the appeal, and the person may appeal as a poor person pursuant to article eighteen-B of the county law.

4. If a sex offender, having been given notice, including the time and place of the determination proceeding in accordance with this section, fails to appear at this proceeding, without sufficient excuse, the court shall conduct the hearing and make the determinations in the manner set forth in subdivision three of this section.

§168-e. Discharge of sex offender from correctional facility; duties of official in charge.

1. Any sex offender, to be discharged, paroled, released to post-release supervision or released from any state or local correctional facility, hospital or institution where he or she was confined or committed, shall at least fifteen calendar days prior to discharge, parole or release, be informed of his or her duty to register under this article, by the facility in which he or she was confined or committed. The facility shall require the sex offender to read and sign such form as may be required by the division stating the duty to register and the procedure for registration has been explained to him or her and to complete the registration portion of such form. The facility shall obtain on such form the address where the sex offender expects to reside upon his or her discharge, parole or release and the name and address of any institution of higher education he or she expects to be employed by, enrolled in, attending or employed, whether for compensation or not, and whether he or she expects to reside in a facility owned or operated by such an institution, and shall report such information to the division. The facility shall give one copy of the form to the sex offender, retain one copy and shall send one copy to the division which shall provide the information to the law enforcement agencies having jurisdiction. The facility shall give the sex offender a form prepared by the

division, to register with the division at least fifteen calendar days prior to release and such form shall be completed, signed by the sex offender and sent to the division by the facility at least ten days prior to the sex offender's release or discharge.

2. The division shall also immediately transmit the conviction data and fingerprints to the Federal Bureau of Investigation if not already obtained.

§168-f. Duty to register and to verify.

1. Any sex offender shall, (a) at least ten calendar days prior to discharge, parole, release to post-release supervision or release from any state or local correctional facility, hospital or institution where he or she was confined or committed, or,

(b) at the time sentence is imposed for any sex offender released on probation or discharged upon payment of a fine, conditional discharge or unconditional discharge, register with the division on a form prepared by the division.

2. For a sex offender required to register under this article on each anniversary of the sex offender's initial registration date during the period in which he is required to register under this section the following applies:

(a) The sex offender shall mail the verification form to the division within ten calendar days after receipt of the form.

(b) The verification form shall be signed by the sex offender, and state that he still resides at the address last reported to the division.

(b-1) If the sex offender has been given a level two or three designation, such offender shall sign the verification form, and state that he or she still is employed at the address last reported to the division.

(b-2) If the sex offender has been given a level three designation, he or she shall personally appear at the law enforcement agency having jurisdiction within twenty days of the first anniversary of the sex offender's initial registration and every year thereafter during the period of registration for the purpose of providing a current photograph of such offender. The law enforcement agency having jurisdiction shall photograph the sex offender and shall promptly forward a copy of such photograph to the division. For purposes of this paragraph, if such sex offender is confined in a state or local correctional facility, the local law enforcement agency having jurisdiction shall be the warden, superintendent, sheriff or other person in charge of the state or local correctional facility.

(b-3) If the sex offender has been given a level one or level two designation, he or she shall personally appear at the law enforcement agency having jurisdiction within twenty days of the third anniversary of the sex offender's initial registration and every three years thereafter during the period of registration for the purpose of providing a current photograph of such offender. The law enforcement agency having jurisdiction shall photograph the sex offender and shall promptly forward a copy of such photograph to the division. For purposes of this paragraph, if such sex offender is confined in a state or local correctional facility, the local law enforcement agency having jurisdiction shall be the warden, superintendent, sheriff or other person in charge of the state or local correctional facility.

(c) If the sex offender fails to mail the signed verification form to the division within ten calendar days after receipt of the form, he or she shall be in violation of this section unless he proves that he or she has not changed his or her residence address.

(c-1) If the sex offender, to whom a notice has been mailed at the last reported address pursuant to paragraph b of subdivision one of section one hundred sixty-eight-b of this article, fails to personally appear at the law enforcement agency having jurisdiction, as provided in paragraph (b-2) or (b-3) of this subdivision, within twenty days of the anniversary of the sex offender's initial registration, or an alternate later date scheduled by the law enforcement agency having jurisdiction, he or she shall be in violation of this section. The duty to personally appear for such updated photograph shall be temporarily suspended during any period in which the sex offender is confined in any hospital or institution, and such sex offender shall personally appear for such updated photograph no later than ninety days after release from such hospital or institution, or an alternate later date scheduled by the law enforcement agency having jurisdiction.

3. The provisions of subdivision two of this section shall be applied to a sex offender required to register under this article except that such sex offender designated as a sexual predator or having been given a level three designation must personally verify his or her address with the local law enforcement agency every ninety calendar days after the date of release or commencement of parole or post-release supervision, or probation, or release on payment of a fine, conditional discharge or unconditional discharge. At such time the law enforcement agency having jurisdiction may take a new photograph of such sex offender if it appears that the offender has had a change in appearance since the most recent photograph taken pursuant to paragraph (b-2) of subdivision two of this section. If such photograph is taken, the law enforcement agency shall promptly forward a copy of such photograph to the division. The duty to personally verify shall be temporarily suspended during any period in which the sex offender is confined to any state or local correctional facility, hospital or institution and shall immediately recommence on the date of the sex offender's release.

4. Any sex offender shall register with the division no later than ten calendar days after any change of address, internet accounts with internet access providers belonging to such offender, internet identifiers that such offender uses, or his or her status of enrollment, attendance, employment or residence at any institution of higher education. A fee of ten dollars, as authorized by subdivision eight of section one hundred sixty-eight-b of this article, shall be submitted by the sex offender each time such offender registers any change of address or any change of his or her status of enrollment, attendance, employment or residence at any institution of higher education. Any failure or omission to submit the required fee shall not affect the acceptance by the division of the change of address or change of status.

5. The duty to register under the provisions of this article shall not be applicable to any sex offender whose conviction was reversed upon appeal or who was pardoned by the governor.

6. Any nonresident worker or nonresident student, as defined in subdivisions fourteen and fifteen of section one hundred sixty-eight-a of this article, shall register his or her current address and the address of his or her place of employment or educational institution attended with the division within ten calendar days after such nonresident worker or nonresident student commences employment or attendance at an educational institution in the state. Any nonresident worker or nonresident student shall notify the division of any change of residence, employment or educational institution address no later than ten days after such change. The division shall notify the law enforcement agency where the nonresident worker is employed or the educational institution is located that a nonresident worker or nonresident student is present in that agency's jurisdiction.

§168-g. Prior convictions; duty to inform and register.

1. The department or office of probation and correctional alternatives in accordance with risk factors pursuant to section one hundred sixty-eight-l of this article shall determine the duration of registration and notification for every sex offender who on the effective date of this article is then on community supervision or probation for an offense provided for in subdivision two or three of section one hundred sixty-eight-a of this article.

2. Every sex offender who on the effective date of this article is then on community supervision or probation for an offense provided for in subdivision two or three of section one hundred sixty-eight-a of this article shall within ten calendar days of such determination register with his parole or probation officer. On each anniversary of the sex offender's initial registration date thereafter, the provisions of section one hundred sixty-eight-f of this article shall apply. Any sex offender who fails or refuses to so comply shall be subject to the same penalties as otherwise provided for in this article which would be imposed upon a sex offender who fails or refuses to so comply with the provisions of this article on or after such effective date.

3. It shall be the duty of the parole or probation officer to inform and register such sex offender according to the requirements imposed by this article. A parole or probation officer shall give one copy of the form to the sex offender and shall, within three calendar days, send two copies electronically or otherwise to the department which shall forward one copy electronically or otherwise to the law enforcement agency having jurisdiction where the sex offender resides upon his or her community supervision, probation, or local conditional release.

4. A petition for relief from this section is permitted to any sex offender required to register while released to community supervision or probation pursuant to section one hundred sixty-eight-o of this article.

§168-h. Duration of registration and verification.

1. The duration of registration and verification for a sex offender who has not been designated a sexual predator, or a sexually violent offender, or a predicate sex offender, and who is classified as a level one risk, or who has not yet received a risk level classification, shall be annually for a period of twenty years from the initial date of registration.

2. The duration of registration and verification for a sex offender who, on or after March eleventh, two thousand two, is designated a sexual predator, or a sexually violent offender, or a predicate sex offender, or who is classified as a level two or level three risk, shall be annually for life. Notwithstanding the foregoing, a sex offender who is classified as a level two risk and who is not designated a sexual predator, a sexually violent offender or a predicate sex offender, may be relieved of the duty to register and verify as provided by subdivision one of section one hundred sixty-eight-o of this article.

3. Any sex offender having been designated a level three risk or a sexual predator shall also personally verify his or her address every ninety calendar days with the local law enforcement agency having jurisdiction where the offender resides.

§168-i. Registration and verification requirements.

Registration and verification as required by this article shall consist of a statement in writing signed by the sex offender giving the information that is required by the division and the division shall enter the information into an appropriate electronic data base or file.

§168-j. Notification of local law enforcement agencies of change of address.

1. Upon receipt of a change of address by a sex offender required to register under this article, but in any event no more than two business days after such receipt, the division shall notify the local law enforcement agency having jurisdiction of the new place of residence and the local law enforcement agency where the sex offender last resided of the new place of residence.

2. Upon receipt of change of address information, the local law enforcement agency having jurisdiction of the new place of residence shall adhere to the notification provisions set forth in subdivision six of section one hundred sixty-eight-l of this article.

3. The division shall, if the sex offender changes residence to another state, notify the appropriate agency within that state of the new place of residence.

4. Upon receipt of a change in the status of the enrollment, attendance, employment or residence at an institution of higher education by a sex offender required to register under this article, but in any event no more than two business days after such receipt, the division shall notify each law enforcement agency having jurisdiction which is affected by such change.

5. Upon receipt of change in the status of the enrollment, attendance, employment or residence at an institution of higher education by a sex offender required to register under this article, each law enforcement agency having

jurisdiction shall adhere to the notification provisions set forth in subdivision six of section one hundred sixty-eight-l of this article.

§168-k. Registration for change of address from another state.

1. A sex offender who has been convicted of an offense which requires registration under paragraph (d) of subdivision two or paragraph (b) of subdivision three of section one hundred sixty-eight-a of this article shall notify the division of the new address no later than ten calendar days after such sex offender establishes residence in this state.

2. The division shall advise the board that the sex offender has established residence in this state. The board shall determine whether the sex offender is required to register with the division. If it is determined that the sex offender is required to register, the division shall notify the sex offender of his or her duty to register under this article and shall require the sex offender to sign a form as may be required by the division acknowledging that the duty to register and the procedure for registration has been explained to the sex offender. The division shall obtain on such form the address where the sex offender expects to reside within the state and the sex offender shall retain one copy of the form and send two copies to the division which shall provide the information to the law enforcement agency having jurisdiction where the sex offender expects to reside within this state. No later than thirty days prior to the board making a recommendation, the sex offender shall be notified that his or her case is under review and that he or she is permitted to submit to the board any information relevant to the review. After reviewing any information obtained, and applying the guidelines established in subdivision five of section one hundred sixty-eight-l of this article, the board shall within sixty calendar days make a recommendation regarding the level of notification pursuant to subdivision six of section one hundred sixty-eight-l of this article and whether such sex offender shall be designated a sexual predator, sexually violent offender, or predicate sex offender as defined in subdivision seven of section one hundred sixty-eight-a of this article. This recommendation shall be confidential and shall not be available for public inspection. It shall be submitted by the board to the county court or supreme court and to the district attorney in the county of residence of the sex offender and to the sex offender. It shall be the duty of the county court or supreme court in the county of residence of the sex offender, applying the guidelines established in subdivision five of section one hundred sixty-eight-l of this article, to determine the level of notification pursuant to subdivision six of section one hundred sixty-eight-l of this article and whether such sex offender shall be designated a sexual predator, sexually violent offender, or predicate sex offender as defined in subdivision seven of section one hundred sixty-eight-a of this article. At least thirty days prior to the determination proceeding, such court shall notify the district attorney and the sex offender, in writing, of the date of the determination proceeding and the court shall also provide the district attorney and sex offender with a copy of the recommendation received from the board and any statement of the reasons for the recommendation received from the board. This notice shall include the

following statement or a substantially similar statement: "This proceeding is being held to determine whether you will be classified as a level 3 offender (risk of repeat offense is high), a level 2 offender (risk of repeat offense is moderate), or a level 1 offender (risk of repeat offense is low), or whether you will be designated as a sexual predator, a sexually violent offender or a predicate sex offender, which will determine how long you must register as a sex offender and how much information can be provided to the public concerning your registration. If you fail to appear at this proceeding, without sufficient excuse, it shall be held in your absence. Failure to appear may result in a longer period of registration or a higher level of community notification because you are not present to offer evidence or contest evidence offered by the district attorney." The court shall also advise the sex offender that he or she has a right to a hearing prior to the court's determination, that he or she has the right to be represented by counsel at the hearing and that counsel will be appointed if he or she is financially unable to retain counsel. A returnable form shall be enclosed in the court's notice to the sex offender on which the sex offender may apply for assignment of counsel. If the sex offender applies for assignment of counsel and the court finds that the offender is financially unable to retain counsel, the court shall assign counsel to represent the sex offender pursuant to article eighteen-B of the county law. If the district attorney seeks a determination that differs from the recommendation submitted by the board, at least ten days prior to the determination proceeding the district attorney shall provide to the court and the sex offender a statement setting forth the determinations sought by the district attorney together with the reasons for seeking such determinations. The court shall allow the sex offender to appear and be heard. The state shall appear by the district attorney, or his or her designee, who shall bear the burden of proving the facts supporting the determinations sought by clear and convincing evidence. It shall be the duty of the court applying the guidelines established in subdivision five of section one hundred sixty-eight-l of this article to determine the level of notification pursuant to subdivision six of section one hundred sixty-eight-l of this article and whether such sex offender shall be designated a sexual predator, sexually violent offender, or predicate sex offender as defined in subdivision seven of section one hundred sixty-eight-a of this article. Where there is a dispute between the parties concerning the determinations, the court shall adjourn the hearing as necessary to permit the sex offender or the district attorney to obtain materials relevant to the determinations from the state board of examiners of sex offenders or any state or local facility, hospital, institution, office, agency, department or division. Such materials may be obtained by subpoena if not voluntarily provided to the requesting party. In making the determinations the court shall review any victim's statement and any relevant materials and evidence submitted by the sex offender and the district attorney and the recommendation and any material submitted by the board, and may consider reliable hearsay evidence submitted by either party, provided that it is relevant to the determinations. If available, facts proven at trial or elicited at the time of a plea of guilty shall be deemed established by clear and convincing evidence and shall not be relitigated. The court shall render an order setting forth its determinations and the findings of fact and conclusions of law on which the determinations are based. A copy of the order shall be submitted by the court to the division. Upon application of either party, the court shall seal any portion of the court file or record which contains material that is confidential under any state or federal statute. Either party may appeal as of right from the order pursuant to the provisions of articles fifty-five, fifty-six and fifty-seven of the civil practice law and rules. Where counsel has been assigned to represent the sex offender upon the ground that the sex offender is financially unable to retain counsel, that assignment shall be continued throughout the pendency of the appeal, and the person may appeal as a poor person pursuant to article eighteen-B of the county law.

3. The division shall undertake an information campaign designed to provide information to officials and appropriate individuals in other states and United States possessions concerning the notification procedures required by this article. Such information campaign shall be ongoing, and shall include, but not be limited to, letters, notice forms and similar materials providing relevant information about this article and the specific procedures required to effect notification. Such materials shall include an address and telephone number which such officials and individuals in other states and United States possessions may use to obtain additional information.

4. If a sex offender, having been given notice, including the time and place of the determination proceeding in accordance with this section, fails to appear at this proceeding, without sufficient excuse, the court shall conduct the hearing and make the determinations in the manner set forth in subdivision two of this section.

§168-*l*. Board of examiners of sex offenders.

1. There shall be a board of examiners of sex offenders which shall possess the powers and duties hereinafter specified. Such board shall consist of five members appointed by the governor. All members shall be employees of the department and shall be experts in the field of the behavior and treatment of sex offenders. The term of office of each member of such board shall be for six years; provided, however, that any member chosen to fill a vacancy occurring otherwise than by expiration of term shall be appointed for the remainder of the unexpired term of the member whom he or she is to succeed. In the event of the inability to act of any member, the governor may appoint some competent informed person to act in his or her stead during the continuance of such disability.

2. The governor shall designate one of the members of the board as chairman to serve in such capacity at the pleasure of the governor or until the member's term of office expires and a successor is designated in accordance with law, whichever first occurs.

3. Any member of the board may be removed by the governor for cause after an opportunity to be heard.

4. Except as otherwise provided by law, a majority of the board shall constitute a quorum for the transaction of all business of the board.

5. The board shall develop guidelines and procedures to assess the risk of a repeat offense by such sex offender and the threat posed to the public safety. Such guidelines shall be based upon, but not limited to, the following:

(a) criminal history factors indicative of high risk of repeat offense, including:

(i) whether the sex offender has a mental abnormality or personality disorder that makes him or her likely to engage in predatory sexually violent offenses;

(ii) whether the sex offender's conduct was found to be characterized by repetitive and compulsive behavior, associated with drugs or alcohol;

(iii) whether the sex offender served the maximum term;

(iv) whether the sex offender committed the felony sex offense against a child;

(v) the age of the sex offender at the time of the commission of the first sex offense;

(b) other criminal history factors to be considered in determining risk, including:

(i) the relationship between such sex offender and the victim;

(ii) whether the offense involved the use of a weapon, violence or infliction of serious bodily injury;

(iii) the number, date and nature of prior offenses;

(c) conditions of release that minimize risk or re-offense, including but not limited to whether the sex offender is under supervision; receiving counseling, therapy or treatment; or residing in a home situation that provides guidance and supervision;

(d) physical conditions that minimize risk of re-offense, including but not limited to advanced age or debilitating illness;

(e) whether psychological or psychiatric profiles indicate a risk of recidivism;

(f) the sex offender's response to treatment;

(g) recent behavior, including behavior while confined;

(h) recent threats or gestures against persons or expressions of intent to commit additional offenses; and

(i) review of any victim impact statement.

6. Applying these guidelines, the board shall within sixty calendar days prior to the discharge, parole, release to post-release supervision or release of a sex offender make a recommendation which shall be confidential and shall not be available for public inspection, to the sentencing court as to whether such sex offender warrants the designation of sexual predator, sexually violent offender, or predicate sex offender as defined in subdivision seven of section one hundred sixty-eight-a of this article. In addition, the guidelines shall be applied by the board to make a recommendation to the sentencing court which shall be confidential and shall not be available for public inspection, providing

for one of the following three levels of notification depending upon the degree of the risk of re-offense by the sex offender.

(a) If the risk of repeat offense is low, a level one designation shall be given to such sex offender. In such case the law enforcement agency or agencies having jurisdiction and the law enforcement agency or agencies having had jurisdiction at the time of his or her conviction shall be notified and may disseminate relevant information which may include a photograph and description of the offender and which may include the name of the sex offender, approximate address based on sex offender's zip code, background information including the offender's crime of conviction, modus of operation, type of victim targeted, the name and address of any institution of higher education at which the sex offender is enrolled, attends, is employed or resides and the description of special conditions imposed on the offender to any entity with vulnerable populations related to the nature of the offense committed by such sex offender. Any entity receiving information on a sex offender may disclose or further disseminate such information at its discretion.

(b) If the risk of repeat offense is moderate, a level two designation shall be given to such sex offender. In such case the law enforcement agency or agencies having jurisdiction and the law enforcement agency or agencies having had jurisdiction at the time of his or her conviction shall be notified and may disseminate relevant information which shall include a photograph and description of the offender and which may include the exact name and any aliases used by the sex offender, exact address, background information including the offender's crime of conviction, mode of operation, type of victim targeted, the name and address of any institution of higher education at which the sex offender is enrolled, attends, is employed or resides and the description of special conditions imposed on the offender to any entity with vulnerable populations related to the nature of the offense committed by such sex offender. Any entity receiving information on a sex offender may disclose or further disseminate such information at its discretion. In addition, in such case, the information described herein shall also be provided in the subdirectory established in this article and notwithstanding any other provision of law, such information shall, upon request, be made available to the public.

Such law enforcement agencies shall compile, maintain and update a listing of vulnerable organizational entities within its jurisdiction. Such listing shall be utilized for notification of such organizations in disseminating such information on level two sex offenders pursuant to this paragraph. Such listing shall include and not be limited to: superintendents of schools or chief school administrators, superintendents of parks, public and private libraries, public and private school bus transportation companies, day care centers, nursery schools, pre-schools, neighborhood watch groups, community centers, civic associations, nursing homes, victim's advocacy groups and places of worship.

(c) If the risk of repeat offense is high and there exists a threat to the public safety a level three designation shall be given to such sex offender. In such case, the law enforcement agency or agencies having jurisdiction and the law enforcement agency or agencies having had jurisdiction at the time of his or her conviction shall be notified and may disseminate relevant information which shall include a photograph and description of the offender and which may include the sex offender's exact name and any aliases used by the offender, exact address, address of the offender's place of employment, background information including the offender's crime of conviction, mode of operation, type of victim targeted, the name and address of any institution of higher education at which the sex offender is enrolled, attends, is employed or resides and the description of special conditions imposed on the offender to any entity with vulnerable populations related to the nature of the offense committed by such sex offender. Any entity receiving information on a sex offender may disclose or further disseminate such information at its discretion. In addition, in such case, the information described herein shall also be provided in the subdirectory established in this article and notwithstanding any other provision of law, such information shall, upon request, be made available to the public. Such law enforcement agencies shall compile, maintain and update a listing of vulnerable organizational entities within its jurisdiction. Such listing shall be utilized for notification of such organizations in disseminating such information on level three sex offenders pursuant to this paragraph. Such listing shall include and not be limited to: superintendents of schools or chief school administrators, superintendents of parks, public and private libraries, public and private school bus transportation companies, day care centers, nursery schools, pre-schools, neighborhood watch groups, community centers, civic associations, nursing homes, victim's advocacy groups and places of worship.

7. Upon request by the court, pursuant to section one hundred sixty-eight-o of this article, the board shall provide an updated report pertaining to the sex offender petitioning for relief of the duty to register or for a modification of his or her level of notification.

8. A failure by a state or local agency or the board to act or by a court to render a determination within the time period specified in this article shall not affect the obligation of the sex offender to register or verify under this article nor shall such failure prevent a court from making a determination regarding the sex offender's level of notification and whether such offender is required by law to be registered for a period of twenty years or for life. Where a court is unable to make a determination prior to the date scheduled for a sex offender's discharge, parole, release to post-release supervision or release, it shall adjourn the hearing until after the offender is discharged, paroled, released to post-release supervision or released, and shall then expeditiously complete the hearing and issue its determination.

§168-m. Review.

Notwithstanding any other provision of law to the contrary, any state or local correctional facility, hospital or institution, district attorney, law enforcement agency, probation department, state board of parole, court or child protective agency shall forward relevant information pertaining to a sex offender to be discharged, paroled, released to post-release supervision or released to the board for review no later than one hundred twenty days prior to the release or discharge and the board shall make recommendations as provided in subdivision six of section one hundred sixty-eight-l of this article within sixty days of receipt of the information. Information may include but may not be limited to all or a portion of the arrest file, prosecutor's file, probation or parole file, child protective file, court file, commitment file, medical file and treatment file pertaining to such person. Such person shall be permitted to submit to the board any information relevant to the review. Upon application of the sex offender or the district attorney, the court shall seal any portion of the board's file pertaining to the sex offender that contains material that is confidential under any state or federal law; provided, however, that in any subsequent proceedings in which the sex offender who is the subject of the sealed record is a party and which requires the board to provide a recommendation to the court pursuant to this article, such sealed record shall be available to the sex offender, the district attorney, the court and the attorney general where the attorney general is a party, or represents a party, in the proceeding.

§168-n. Judicial determination.

1. A determination that an offender is a sexual predator, sexually violent offender, or predicate sex offender as defined in subdivision seven of section one hundred sixty-eight-a of this article shall be made prior to the discharge, parole, release to post-release supervision or release of such offender by the sentencing court applying the guidelines established in subdivision five of section one hundred sixty-eight-l of this article after receiving a recommendation from the board pursuant to section one hundred sixty-eight-l of this article.

2. In addition, applying the guidelines established in subdivision five of section one hundred sixty-eight-l of this article, the sentencing court shall also make a determination with respect to the level of notification, after receiving a recommendation from the board pursuant to section one hundred sixty-eight-l of this article. Both determinations of the sentencing court shall be made thirty calendar days prior to discharge, parole or release.

3. No later than thirty days prior to the board's recommendation, the sex offender shall be notified that his or her case is under review and that he or she is permitted to submit to the board any information relevant to the review. Upon receipt of the board's recommendation, the sentencing court shall determine whether the sex offender was previously found to be eligible for assigned counsel in the underlying case. Where such a finding was previously made, the court shall assign counsel to represent the offender, pursuant to article eighteen-B of the county law. At least twenty days prior to the determination proceeding, the sentencing court shall notify the district attorney, the sex offender and the sex offender's counsel, in writing, of the date of the determination proceeding and shall also provide the district attorney, the sex offender and the sex offender's counsel with a copy of the recommendation received from the board and any statement of the reasons for the recommendation received from the board. This notice shall include the following statement or a substantially similar statement: "This proceeding is being held to determine whether you will be classified as a level 3 offender (risk of repeat offense is high), a level 2 offender (risk of repeat offense is moderate), or a level 1 offender (risk of repeat offense is low), or whether you will be designated as a sexual predator, a sexually violent offender or a

predicate sex offender, which will determine how long you must register as a sex offender and how much information can be provided to the public concerning your registration. If you fail to appear at this proceeding, without sufficient excuse, it shall be held in your absence. Failure to appear may result in a longer period of registration or a higher level of community notification because you are not present to offer evidence or contest evidence offered by the district attorney." The written notice to the sex offender shall also advise the offender that he or she has a right to a hearing prior to the court's determination, and that he or she has the right to be represented by counsel at the hearing. If counsel has been assigned to represent the offender at the determination proceeding, the notice shall also provide the name, address and telephone number of the assigned counsel. Where counsel has not been assigned, the notice shall advise the sex offender that counsel will be appointed if he or she is financially unable to retain counsel, and a returnable form shall be enclosed in the court's notice to the sex offender on which the sex offender may apply for assignment of counsel. If the sex offender applies for assignment of counsel and the court finds that the offender is financially unable to retain counsel, the court shall assign counsel to represent the sex offender pursuant to article eighteen-B of the county law. If the district attorney seeks a determination that differs from the recommendation submitted by the board, at least ten days prior to the determination proceeding the district attorney shall provide to the court and the sex offender a statement setting forth the determinations sought by the district attorney together with the reasons for seeking such determinations. The court shall allow the sex offender to appear and be heard. The state shall appear by the district attorney, or his or her designee, who shall bear the burden of proving the facts supporting the determinations sought by clear and convincing evidence. Where there is a dispute between the parties concerning the determinations, the court shall adjourn the hearing as necessary to permit the sex offender or the district attorney to obtain materials relevant to the determinations from the state board of examiners of sex offenders or any state or local facility, hospital, institution, office, agency, department or division. Such materials may be obtained by subpoena if not voluntarily provided to the requesting party. In making the determinations the court shall review any victim's statement and any relevant materials and evidence submitted by the sex offender and the district attorney and the recommendation and any materials submitted by the board, and may consider reliable hearsay evidence submitted by either party, provided that it is relevant to the determinations. Facts previously proven at trial or elicited at the time of entry of a plea of guilty shall be deemed established by clear and convincing evidence and shall not be relitigated. The court shall render an order setting forth its determinations and the findings of fact and conclusions of law on which the determinations are based. A copy of the order shall be submitted by the court to the division. Upon application of either party, the court shall seal any portion of the court file or record which contains material that is confidential under any state or federal statute. Either party may appeal as of right from the order pursuant to the provisions of articles fifty-five, fifty-six and fifty-seven of the civil practice law and rules. Where counsel has been assigned to represent the sex offender upon the ground that the sex offender is financially unable to retain counsel, that assignment shall be continued throughout the pendency of the appeal, and the person may appeal as a poor person pursuant to article eighteen-B of the county law.

4. Upon determination that the risk of repeat offense and threat to public safety is high, the sentencing court shall also notify the division of such fact for the purposes of section one hundred sixty-eight-q of this article.

5. Upon the reversal of a conviction of a sexual offense defined in paragraphs (a) and (b) of subdivision two or three of section one hundred sixty-eight-a of this article, the appellate court shall remand the case to the lower court for entry of an order directing the expungement of any records required to be kept herein.

6. If a sex offender, having been given notice, including the time and place of the determination proceeding in accordance with this section, fails to appear at this proceeding, without sufficient excuse, the court shall conduct the hearing and make the determinations in the manner set forth in subdivision three of this section.

§168-o. Petition for relief or modification.

1. Any sex offender who is classified as a level two risk, and who has not been designated a sexual predator, or a sexually violent offender, or a predicate sex offender, who is required to register or verify pursuant to this article and who has been registered for a minimum period of thirty years may be relieved of any further duty to register upon the granting of a petition for relief by the sentencing court or by the court which made the determination regarding duration of registration and level of notification. The sex offender shall bear the burden of proving by clear and convincing evidence that his or her risk of repeat offense and threat to public safety is such that registration or verification is no longer necessary. Such petition, if granted, shall not relieve the petitioner of the duty to register pursuant to this article upon conviction of any offense requiring registration in the future. Such a petition shall not be considered more than once every two years. In the event that the sex offender's petition for relief is granted, the district attorney may appeal as of right from the order pursuant to the provisions of articles fifty-five, fifty-six and fifty-seven of the civil practice law and rules. Where counsel has been assigned to represent the sex offender upon the ground that the sex offender is financially unable to retain counsel, that assignment shall be continued throughout the pendency of the appeal, and the person may appeal as a poor person pursuant to article eighteen-B of the county law.

2. Any sex offender required to register or verify pursuant to this article may petition the sentencing court or the court which made the determination regarding the level of notification for an order modifying the level of notification. The petition shall set forth the level of notification sought, together with the reasons for seeking such determination. The sex offender shall bear the burden of proving the facts supporting the requested modification by clear and convincing evidence. Such a petition shall not be considered more than annually. In the event that the sex offender's petition to modify the level of notification is granted, the district attorney may appeal as of right from the order pursuant to the provisions of articles fifty-five, fifty-six and fifty-seven

of the civil practice law and rules. Where counsel has been assigned to represent the sex offender upon the ground that the sex offender is financially unable to retain counsel, that assignment shall be continued throughout the pendency of the appeal, and the person may appeal as a poor person pursuant to article eighteen-B of the county law.

3. The district attorney may file a petition to modify the level of notification for a sex offender with the sentencing court or with the court which made the determination regarding the level of notification, where the sex offender

(a) has been convicted of a new crime, or there has been a determination after a proceeding pursuant to section 410.70 of the criminal procedure law or section two hundred fifty-nine-i of the executive law that the sex offender has violated one or more conditions imposed as part of a sentence of a conditional discharge, probation, parole or post-release supervision for a designated crime, and

(b) the conduct underlying the new crime or the violation is of a nature that indicates an increased risk of a repeat sex offense. The petition shall set forth the level of notification sought, together with the reasons for seeking such determination. The district attorney shall bear the burden of proving the facts supporting the requested modification, by clear and convincing evidence. In the event that the district attorney's petition is granted, the sex offender may appeal as of right from the order, pursuant to the provisions of articles fifty-five, fifty-six and fifty-seven of the civil practice law and rules. Where counsel has been assigned to represent the offender upon the ground that he or she is financially unable to retain counsel, that assignment shall be continued throughout the pendency of the appeal, and the person may proceed as a poor person, pursuant to article eighteen-B of the county law. 4. Upon receipt of a petition submitted pursuant to subdivision one, two or three of this section, the court shall forward a copy of the petition to the board and request an updated recommendation pertaining to the sex offender and shall provide a copy of the petition to the other party. The court shall also advise the sex offender that he or she has the right to be represented by counsel at the hearing and counsel will be appointed if he or she is financially unable to retain counsel. A returnable form shall be enclosed in the court's notice to the sex offender on which the sex offender may apply for assignment of counsel. If the sex offender applies for assignment of counsel and the court finds that the offender is financially unable to retain counsel, the court shall assign counsel to represent the offender, pursuant to article eighteen-B of the county law. Where the petition was filed by a district attorney, at least thirty days prior to making an updated recommendation the board shall notify the sex offender and his or her counsel that the offender's case is under review and he or she is permitted to submit to the board any information relevant to the review. The board's updated recommendation on the sex offender shall be confidential and shall not be available for public inspection. After receiving an updated recommendation from the board concerning a sex offender, the court shall, at least thirty days prior to ruling upon the petition, provide a copy of the updated recommendation to the sex offender, the sex offender's counsel and the district attorney and notify them, in writing, of the date set by the court for a hearing on the petition. After reviewing the recommendation received from the board and any relevant materials and evidence submitted by the sex offender and the district attorney, the court may grant or deny the petition. The court may also consult with the victim prior to making a determination on the petition. The court shall render an order setting forth its determination, and the findings of fact and conclusions of law on which the determination is based. If the petition is granted, it shall be the obligation of the court to submit a copy of its order to the division. Upon application of either party, the court shall seal any portion of the court file or record which contains material that is confidential under any state or federal statute.

§168-p. Special telephone number.

1. Pursuant to section one hundred sixty-eight-b of this article, the division shall also operate a telephone number that members of the public may call free of charge and inquire whether a named individual required to register pursuant to this article is listed. The division shall ascertain whether a named person reasonably appears to be a person so listed and provide the caller with the relevant information according to risk as described in subdivision six of section one hundred sixty-eight-l of this article. The division shall decide whether the named person reasonably appears to be a person listed, based upon information from the caller providing information that shall include

(a) an exact street address, including apartment number, driver's license number or birth date, along with additional information that may include social security number, hair color, eye color, height, weight, distinctive markings, ethnicity; or

(b) any combination of the above listed characteristics if an exact birth date or address is not available. If three of the characteristics provided include ethnicity, hair color, and eye color, other identifying characteristics shall be provided. Any information identifying the victim by name, birth date, address or relation to the person listed by the division shall be excluded by the division.

2. When the telephone number is called, a preamble shall be played which shall provide the following information:

(a) notice that the caller's telephone number will be recorded;

(b) that there is no charge for use of the telephone number;

(c) notice that the caller is required to identify himself or herself to the operator and provide current address and shall be maintained in a written record;

(d) notice that the caller is required to be eighteen years of age or older;

(e) a warning that it is illegal to use information obtained through the telephone number to commit a crime against any person listed or to engage in illegal discrimination or harassment against such person;

(f) notice that the caller is required to have the birth date, driver's license or identification number, or address or other identifying information regarding the person about whom information is sought in order to achieve a positive identification of that person;

(g) a statement that the number is not a crime hotline and that any suspected criminal activity should be reported to local authorities;

(h) a statement that an information package which will include a description of the law and sex abuse and abduction prevention materials is available upon request from the division. Such information package shall include questions and answers regarding the most commonly asked questions about the sex offender registration act, and current sex abuse and abduction prevention material.

2-a. (a) The division shall establish a program allowing non-profit and not-for-profit youth services organizations to pre-register with the division for use of the telephone number. Pre-registration shall include the identification of up to two officials of the organization who may call the telephone number and obtain information on behalf of the organization. A pre-registered certificate issued under this subdivision shall be valid for two years, unless earlier revoked by the division for good cause shown. No fee shall be charged to an applicant for the issuance of a pre-registered certificate pursuant to this subdivision.

(b) An organization granted a pre-registered certificate pursuant to this subdivision may, upon calling the telephone number, inquire whether multiple named individuals are listed on the sex offender registry. Notwithstanding any per call limitation the division may place on calls by private individuals, the division shall allow such pre-registered organizations to inquire about up to twenty prospective coaches, leaders or volunteers in each call to the telephone number.

(c) For purposes of this subdivision, "youth services organization" shall mean a formalized program operated by a corporation pursuant to subparagraph five of paragraph (a) of section one hundred two of the not-for-profit corporation law that functions primarily to:

(a) provide children the opportunity to participate in adult-supervised sporting activities; or

(b) match children or groups of children with adult volunteers for the purpose of providing children with positive role models to enhance their development.

2-b. The division shall maintain a program allowing a transportation network company (TNC), as defined in section one thousand six hundred ninety-one of the vehicle and traffic law, to electronically submit multiple names, and other necessary identifying information as required by the division and in accordance with subdivision one of this section, of applicants applying to be TNC drivers for the purpose of determining whether such applicants are listed on the sex offender registry pursuant to this article. The division shall respond to such inquiry electronically, within four business days, and notify such TNC of any such applicant who is listed on the registry pursuant to this article. A TNC shall pre-register with the division before the electronic submission of names and shall agree in writing that information obtained by a TNC pursuant to this subdivision be used only for the purposes of determining eligibility of an applicant for a TNC permit, pursuant to sections one thousand six hundred ninety-six and one thousand six hundred ninety-nine of the vehicle and traffic law, by designated employees of such TNC and that such information shall not be distributed or disclosed except as specifically authorized by law.

3. Whenever there is reasonable cause to believe that any person or group of persons is engaged in a pattern or practice of misuse of the telephone

number, the attorney general, any district attorney or any person aggrieved by the misuse of the number is authorized to bring a civil action in the appropriate court requesting preventive relief, including an application for a permanent or temporary injunction, restraining order or other order against the person or group of persons responsible for the pattern or practice of misuse. The foregoing remedies shall be independent of any other remedies or procedures that may be available to an aggrieved party under other provisions of law. Such person or group of persons shall be subject to a fine of not less than five hundred dollars and not more than one thousand dollars.

4. The division shall submit to the legislature an annual report on the operation of the telephone number. The annual report shall include, but not be limited to, all of the following:

(a) number of calls received;

(b) a detailed outline of the amount of money expended and the manner in which it was expended for purposes of this section;

(c) number of calls that resulted in an affirmative response and the number of calls that resulted in a negative response with regard to whether a named individual was listed;

(d) number of persons listed; and

(e) a summary of the success of the telephone number program based upon selected factors.

§168-q. Subdirectory; internet posting.

1. The division shall maintain a subdirectory of level two and three sex offenders. The subdirectory shall include the exact address, address of the offender's place of employment and photograph of the sex offender along with the following information, if available: name, physical description, age and distinctive markings. Background information including all of the sex offender's crimes of conviction that require him or her to register pursuant to this article, modus of operation, type of victim targeted, the name and address of any institution of higher education at which the sex offender is enrolled, attends, is employed or resides and a description of special conditions imposed on the sex offender shall also be included. The subdirectory shall have sex offender listings categorized by county and zip code. Such subdirectory shall be made available at all times on the internet via the division homepage. Any person may apply to the division to receive automated e-mail notifications whenever a new or updated subdirectory registration occurs in a geographic area specified by such person. The division shall furnish such service at no charge to such person, who shall request e-mail notification by county and/or zip code on forms developed and provided by the division. E-mail notification is limited to three geographic areas per e-mail account.

2. Any person who uses information disclosed pursuant to this section in violation of the law shall in addition to any other penalty or fine imposed, be subject to a fine of not less than five hundred dollars and not more than one thousand dollars. Unauthorized removal or duplication of the subdirectory from the offices of local, village or city police department shall be punishable by a fine not to exceed one thousand dollars. In addition, the attorney general, any district attorney, or any person aggrieved is authorized to bring a civil action

in the appropriate court requesting preventive relief, including an application for a permanent or temporary injunction, restraining order, or other order against the person or group of persons responsible for such action. The foregoing remedies shall be independent of any other remedies or procedures that may be available to an aggrieved party under other provisions of law.

§168-r. Immunity from liability.

1. No official, employee or agency, whether public or private, shall be subject to any civil or criminal liability for damages for any discretionary decision to release relevant and necessary information pursuant to this section, unless it is shown that such official, employee or agency acted with gross negligence or in bad faith. The immunity provided under this section applies to the release of relevant information to other employees or officials or to the general public.

2. Nothing in this section shall be deemed to impose any civil or criminal liability upon or to give rise to a cause of action against any official, employee or agency, whether public or private, for failing to release information as authorized in this section unless it is shown that such official, employee or agency acted with gross negligence or in bad faith.

§168-s. Annual report.

The division shall on or before February first in each year file a report with the governor, and the legislature detailing the program, compliance with provisions of this article and effectiveness of the provisions of this article, together with any recommendations to further enhance the intent of this article.

§168-t. Penalty.

Any sex offender required to register or to verify pursuant to the provisions of this article who fails to register or verify in the manner and within the time periods provided for in this article shall be guilty of a class E felony upon conviction for the first offense, and upon conviction for a second or subsequent offense shall be guilty of a class D felony. Any sex offender who violates the provisions of section one hundred sixty-eight-v of this article shall be guilty of a class A misdemeanor upon conviction for the first offense, and upon conviction for a second or subsequent offense shall be guilty of a class D felony. Any such failure to register or verify may also be the basis for revocation of parole pursuant to section two hundred fifty-nine-i of the executive law or the basis for revocation of probation pursuant to article four hundred ten of the criminal procedure law.

§168-u. Unauthorized release of information.

The unauthorized release of any information required by this article shall be a class B misdemeanor.

§168-v. Prohibition of employment on motor vehicles engaged in retail sales of frozen desserts.

No person required to maintain registration under this article (sex offender registration act) shall operate, be employed on or dispense goods for sale at retail on a motor vehicle engaged in retail sales of frozen desserts as defined in subdivision thirty-seven of section three hundred seventy-five of the vehicle and traffic law.

§168-w. Separability.

If any section of this article, or part thereof shall be adjudged by a court of competent jurisdiction to be invalid, such judgment shall not affect, impair or invalidate the remainder or any other section or part thereof.

*§803. Good behavior allowances against indeterminate and determinate sentences.

1. (a) Every person confined in an institution of the department or a facility in the department of mental hygiene serving an indeterminate or determinate sentence of imprisonment, except a person serving a sentence with a maximum term of life imprisonment, may receive time allowance against the term or maximum term of his or her sentence imposed by the court. Such allowances may be granted for good behavior and efficient and willing performance of duties assigned or progress and achievement in an assigned treatment program, and may be withheld, forfeited or canceled in whole or in part for bad behavior, violation of institutional rules or failure to perform properly in the duties or program assigned.

(b) A person serving an indeterminate sentence of imprisonment may receive time allowance against the maximum term of his or her sentence not to exceed one-third of the maximum term imposed by the court.

(c) A person serving a determinate sentence of imprisonment may receive time allowance against the term of his or her sentence not to exceed one-seventh of the term imposed by the court.

(d) (i) Except as provided in subparagraph (ii) of this paragraph, every person under the custody of the department or confined in a facility in the department of mental hygiene serving an indeterminate sentence of imprisonment with a minimum period of one year or more or a determinate sentence of imprisonment of one year or more imposed pursuant to section 70.70 or 70.71 of the penal law, may earn a merit time allowance.

(ii) Such merit time allowance shall not be available to any person serving an indeterminate sentence authorized for an A-I felony offense, other than an A-I felony offense defined in article two hundred twenty of the penal law, or any sentence imposed for a violent felony offense as defined in section 70.02 of the penal law, manslaughter in the second degree, vehicular manslaughter in the second degree, vehicular manslaughter in the first degree, criminally negligent homicide, an offense defined in article one hundred thirty of the penal law, incest, or an offense defined in article two hundred sixty-three of the penal law, or aggravated harassment of an employee by an incarcerated individual.   *(Eff.8/2/21,Ch.322,L.2021)*

(iii) The merit time allowance credit against the minimum period of the indeterminate sentence shall be one-sixth of the minimum period imposed by the court except that such credit shall be one-third of the minimum period imposed by the court for an A-I felony offense defined in article two hundred twenty of the penal law. In the case of such a determinate sentence, in addition to the time allowance credit authorized by paragraph (c) of this subdivision, the merit time allowance credited against the term of the determinate sentence pursuant to this paragraph shall be one-seventh of the term imposed by the court.

(iv) Such merit time allowance may be granted when an incarcerated individual successfully participates in the work and treatment program assigned pursuant to section eight hundred five of this article and when such incarcerated individual obtains a general equivalency diploma, an alcohol and substance abuse treatment certificate, a vocational trade certificate following at least six months of vocational programming, at least eighteen credits in a program registered by the state education department from a degree-granting higher education institution or performs at least four hundred hours of service as part of a community work crew.

Such allowance shall be withheld for any serious disciplinary infraction or upon a judicial determination that the person, while an incarcerated individual, commenced or continued a civil action, proceeding or claim that was found to be frivolous as defined in subdivision (c) of section eight thousand three hundred three-a of the civil practice law and rules, or an order of a federal court pursuant to rule 11 of the federal rules of civil procedure imposing sanctions in an action commenced by a person, while an incarcerated individual, against a state agency, officer or employee.   *(Eff.7/16/21,Ch.242,& Eff.8/2/21,Ch.322,L.2021)*

(v) The provisions of this paragraph shall apply to persons in custody serving an indeterminate sentence on the effective date of this paragraph as well as to persons sentenced to an indeterminate sentence on and after the effective date of this paragraph and prior to September first, two thousand five and to persons sentenced to a determinate sentence prior to September first, two thousand eleven for a felony as defined in article two hundred twenty or two hundred twenty-one of the penal law.

2. If a person is serving more than one sentence, the authorized allowances may be granted separately against the term or maximum term of each sentence or, where consecutive sentences are involved, against the aggregate maximum term. Such allowances shall be calculated as follows:

(a) A person serving two or more indeterminate sentences which run concurrently may receive time allowance not to exceed one-third of the indeterminate sentence which has the longest unexpired time to run.

(b) A person serving two or more indeterminate sentences which run consecutively may receive time allowance not to exceed one-third of the aggregate maximum term.

(c) A person serving two or more determinate sentences which run concurrently may receive time allowance not to exceed one-seventh of the determinate sentence which has the longest unexpired time to run.

(d) A person serving two or more determinate sentences which run consecutively may receive time allowance not to exceed one-seventh of the aggregate maximum term.

(e) A person serving one or more indeterminate sentence and one or more determinate sentence which run concurrently may receive time allowance not to exceed one-third of the indeterminate sentence which has the longest unexpired term to run or one-seventh of the determinate sentence which has the longest unexpired time to run, whichever allowance is greater.

(f) A person serving one or more indeterminate sentence and one or more determinate sentence which run consecutively may receive time allowance not to exceed the sum of one-third of the maximum or aggregate maximum of the indeterminate sentence or sentences and one-seventh of the term or aggregate maximum of the determinate sentence or sentences.

2-a. If a person is serving more than one sentence, the authorized merit time allowances may be granted against the period or aggregate minimum period of the indeterminate sentence or sentences, or against the term or aggregate term of the determinate sentence or sentences, or where consecutive determinate and indeterminate sentences are involved, against the aggregate minimum period as calculated pursuant to subparagraph (iv) of paragraph (a) of subdivision one of section 70.40 of the penal law. Such allowances shall be calculated as follows:

(a) A person serving two or more indeterminate sentences which run concurrently may receive a merit time allowance not to exceed one-sixth of the minimum period of the indeterminate sentence imposed for an offense other than an A-I felony offense defined in article two hundred twenty of the penal law, or one-third of the minimum period of the indeterminate sentence imposed for an A-I felony offense defined in article two hundred twenty of the penal law, whichever allowance results in the longest unexpired time to run.

(b) A person serving two or more indeterminate sentences which run consecutively may receive a merit time allowance not to exceed the amount of one-third of the minimum or aggregate minimum period of the sentences imposed for an A-I felony offense defined in article two hundred twenty of the penal law, plus one-sixth of the minimum or aggregate minimum period of the sentences imposed for an offense other than such A-I felony offense.

(c) A person serving two or more determinate sentences for an offense defined in article two hundred twenty or two hundred twenty-one of the penal law which run concurrently may receive a merit time allowance not to exceed one-seventh of the term of the determinate sentence which has the longest unexpired time to run.

(d) A person serving two or more determinate sentences for an offense defined in article two hundred twenty or two hundred twenty-one of the penal law which run consecutively may receive a merit time allowance not to exceed one-seventh of the aggregate term of such determinate sentences.

(e) A person serving one or more indeterminate sentences and one or more determinate sentences for an offense defined in article two hundred twenty or two hundred twenty-one of the penal law which run concurrently may receive a merit time allowance not to exceed one-sixth of the minimum period of the indeterminate sentence imposed for an offense other than an A-I felony offense defined in article two hundred twenty of the penal law, one-third of the minimum period of the indeterminate sentence imposed for an A-I felony offense defined in article two hundred twenty of the penal law, or one-seventh of the term of the determinate sentence, whichever allowance results in the largest unexpired time to run.

(f) A person serving one or more indeterminate sentences and one or more determinate sentences which run consecutively may receive a merit time allowance not to exceed the sum of one-sixth of the minimum or aggregate minimum period of the indeterminate sentence or sentences imposed for an offense other than an A-I felony offense defined in article two hundred twenty of the penal law, one-third of the minimum or aggregate minimum period of the indeterminate sentence or sentences imposed for an A-I felony offense defined in article two hundred twenty of the penal law and one-seventh of the term or aggregate term of the determinate sentence or sentences.

(g) The provisions of this subdivision shall apply to persons in custody serving an indeterminate sentence on the effective date of this subdivision as well as to persons sentenced to an indeterminate sentence on and after the effective date of this subdivision and prior to September first, two thousand five and to persons sentenced to a determinate sentence prior to September first, two thousand eleven for a felony as defined in article two hundred twenty or two hundred twenty-one of the penal law.

**2-b. Notwithstanding the foregoing, if a person is serving more than one indeterminate sentence, at least one of which is imposed for a class A-I felony offense defined in article two hundred twenty of the penal law, the authorized merit time allowance granted pursuant to paragraph (d) of subdivision one of this section shall be calculated as follows:

(a) In the event a person is serving two or more indeterminate sentences with different minimum periods which run concurrently, the merit time allowance shall be based upon the sentence with the longest unexpired minimum period. If the sentence with the longest unexpired minimum period was imposed for a class A-I felony, the merit time credit shall be one-third of such sentence's minimum period; if such sentence was imposed for an offense other than a class A-I felony, such merit time credit shall be one-sixth of such sentence's minimum period. Provided, however, that where the minimum period of any other concurrent indeterminate sentence is greater than such reduced minimum period, the minimum period of such other concurrent indeterminate sentence shall also be reduced but only to the extent that the minimum period of such other concurrent sentence, as so reduced, is equal to the reduced minimum period of such sentence with the longest unexpired minimum period to run.

(b) A person serving two or more indeterminate sentences with the same minimum periods which run concurrently, and no concurrent indeterminate sentence with any greater minimum period, shall have the minimum period of each such sentence reduced in the amount of one-third of such minimum period if all such sentences were imposed for a class A-I felony.

(c) A person serving two or more indeterminate sentences that run consecutively shall have the aggregate minimum period of such sentences reduced in the amount of one-third of such aggregate minimum period of the sentences imposed for a class A-I felony, plus one-sixth of such aggregate minimum period of the sentences imposed for an offense other than a class A-I felony.   **(Repealed, 9/1/23,Ch.55,L.2021)*

3. The commissioner of corrections and community supervision shall promulgate rules and regulations for the granting, withholding, forfeiture, cancellation and restoration of allowances authorized by this section in accordance with the criteria herein specified. Such rules and regulations shall include provisions designating the person or committee in each correctional institution delegated to make discretionary determinations with respect to the allowances, the books and records to be kept, and a procedure for review of the institutional determinations by the commissioner.

4. No person shall have the right to demand or require the allowances authorized by this section. The decision of the commissioner of corrections and community supervision as to the granting, withholding, forfeiture, cancellation or restoration of such allowances shall be final and shall not be reviewable if made in accordance with law.

5. Time allowances granted prior to any release to community supervision shall be forfeited and shall not be restored if the released person is returned to an institution under the jurisdiction of the state department of corrections and community supervision for violation of community supervision or by reason of a conviction for a crime committed while on community supervision. A person who is so returned may, however, subsequently receive time allowances against the remaining portion of his or her term, maximum term or aggregate maximum term pursuant to this section and provided such remaining portion of his or her term, maximum term, or aggregate maximum term is more than one year.

6. Upon commencement of an indeterminate or a determinate sentence the provisions of this section shall be furnished to the person serving the sentence and the meaning of same shall be fully explained to him by a person designated by the commissioner to perform such duty.   *(Eff.Until 9/1/23,Ch.55,L.2021)*

§865.   Definitions.

As used in this article, the following terms mean:

1. "Eligible incarcerated individual" means a person sentenced to an indeterminate term of imprisonment who will become eligible for release on parole within three years or sentenced to a determinate term of imprisonment who will become eligible for conditional release within three years, who has not reached the age of fifty years, who has not previously been convicted of a violent felony as defined in article seventy of the penal law, or a felony in any

other jurisdiction which includes all of the essential elements of any such violent felony, upon which an indeterminate or determinate term of imprisonment was imposed and who was between the ages of sixteen and fifty years at the time of commission of the crime upon which his or her present sentence was based. Notwithstanding the foregoing, no person who is convicted of any of the following crimes shall be deemed eligible to participate in this program: (a) a violent felony offense as defined in article seventy of the penal law; provided, however, that a person who is convicted of burglary in the second degree as defined in subdivision two of section 140.25 of the penal law, or robbery in the second degree as defined in subdivision one of section 160.10 of the penal law, or an attempt thereof, is eligible to participate, (b) an A-I felony offense, (c) any homicide offense as defined in article one hundred twenty-five of the penal law, (d) any felony sex offense as defined in article one hundred thirty of the penal law and (e) any escape or absconding offense as defined in article two hundred five of the penal law. *(Eff.8/2/21,Ch.322,L.2021)*

2. "Shock incarceration program" means a program pursuant to which eligible incarcerated individuals are selected to participate in the program and serve a period of six months in a shock incarceration facility, which shall provide rigorous physical activity, intensive regimentation and discipline and rehabilitation therapy and programming. Such incarcerated individuals may be selected either: (i) at a reception center; or (ii) at a general confinement facility when the otherwise eligible incarcerated individual then becomes eligible for release on parole within three years in the case of an indeterminate term of imprisonment, or then becomes eligible for conditional release within three years in the case of a determinate term of imprisonment. *(Eff.8/2/21,Ch.322,L.2021)*

EDUCATION LAW
TITLE 8 - THE PROFESSIONS
ARTICLE 130 - GENERAL PROVISIONS
SUBARTICLE 4
UNAUTHORIZED ACTS

Section
6512.   Unauthorized practice a crime.
6513.   Unauthorized use of a professional title a crime.
6514.   Criminal proceedings.

Balance of Article not reproduced.

§6512. Unauthorized practice a crime.

1. Anyone not authorized to practice under this title who practices or offers to practice or holds himself out as being able to practice in any profession in which a license is a prerequisite to the practice of the acts, or who practices any profession as an exempt person during the time when his professional license is suspended, revoked or annulled, or who aids or abets an unlicensed person to practice a profession, or who fraudulently sells, files, furnishes, obtains, or who attempts fraudulently to sell, file, furnish or obtain any diploma, license, record or permit purporting to authorize the practice of a profession, shall be guilty of a class E felony.

2. Anyone who knowingly aids or abets three or more unlicensed persons to practice a profession or employs or holds such unlicensed persons out as being able to practice in any profession in which a license is a prerequisite to the practice of the acts, or who knowingly aids or abets three or more persons to practice any profession as exempt persons during the time when the professional licenses of such persons are suspended, revoked or annulled, shall be guilty of a class E felony.

§6513. Unauthorized use of a professional title a crime.

1. Anyone not authorized to use a professional title regulated by this title, and who uses such professional title, shall be guilty of a class A misdemeanor.

2. Anyone who knowingly aids or abets three or more persons not authorized to use a professional title regulated by this title, to use such professional title, or knowingly employs three or more persons not authorized to use a professional title regulated by this title, who use such professional title in the course of such employment, shall be guilty of a class E felony.

§6514. Criminal proceedings.

1. All alleged violations of sections sixty-five hundred twelve or sixty-five hundred thirteen of this article shall be reported to the department which shall cause an investigation to be instituted. All alleged violations of section sixty-five hundred thirty-one of the education law shall be reported to the department of health which shall cause an investigation to be instituted. If the investigation substantiates that violations exist, such violations shall be reported to the attorney general with a request for prosecution.

2. The attorney general shall prosecute such alleged offenses in the name of the state, provided, however, in the event of alleged violations of article one hundred fifty-five of this title, a district attorney may prosecute such alleged offenses in the name of the state provided, however, that any district attorney may prosecute such offenses where they are incidental to a criminal prosecution instituted by him under other statutes.

3. All criminal courts having jurisdiction over misdemeanors are hereby empowered to hear, try and determine alleged violations under this title, which constitute misdemeanors, without indictment and to impose applicable punishment of fines or imprisonments or both. It shall be necessary to prove in any prosecution under this title only a single prohibited act or a single holding out without proving a general course of conduct.

4. A proceeding before a committee on professional conduct shall not be deemed to be a criminal proceeding within the meaning of this section.

ARTICLE 137
PHARMACY

Section
6811.   Misdemeanors.
6812.   Special provisions.
6813.   Seizure.
6814.   Records of shipment.
6815.   Adulterating, misbranding and substituting.

§6811. Misdemeanors.

It shall be a class A misdemeanor for:

1. Any person knowingly or intentionally to prevent or refuse to permit any board member or department representative to enter a pharmacy or any other establishment for the purpose of lawful inspection;

2. Any person whose license has been revoked to refuse to deliver the license;

3. Any pharmacist to display his license or permit it to be displayed in a pharmacy of which he is not the owner or in which he is not employed, or any owner to fail to display in his pharmacy the license of the pharmacist employed in said pharmacy;

4. Any holder of a license to fail to display the license;

5. Any owner of a pharmacy to display or permit to be displayed in his pharmacy the license of any pharmacist not employed in said pharmacy;

6. Any person to carry on, conduct or transact business under a name which contains as a part thereof the words "drugs", "medicines", "drug store", "apothecary", or "pharmacy", or similar terms or combination of terms, or in any manner by advertisement, circular, poster, sign or otherwise describe or refer to the place of business conducted by such person, or describe the type of service or class of products sold by such person, by the terms "drugs", "medicine", "drug store", "apothecary", or "pharmacy", unless the place of business so conducted is a pharmacy licensed by the department;

7. Any person to enter into an agreement with a physician, dentist, podiatrist or veterinarian for the compounding or dispensing of secret formula (coded) prescriptions;

8. *(Repealed, Eff.1/22/19, Ch. 1, L.2019)*

9. Any person to manufacture, sell, deliver for sale, hold for sale or offer for sale of any drug, device or cosmetic that is adulterated or misbranded;

10. Any person to adulterate or misbrand any drug, device or cosmetic;

11. Any person to receive in commerce any drug, device or cosmetic that is adulterated or misbranded, and to deliver or proffer delivery thereof for pay or otherwise;

12. Any person to sell, deliver for sale, hold for sale, or offer for sale any drug, device or cosmetic in violation of this article;

13. Any person to disseminate any false advertisement;

14. Any person to refuse to permit entry or inspection as authorized by this article;

15. Any person to forge, counterfeit, simulate, or falsely represent, or without proper authority using any mark, stamp, tag, label or other identification device authorized or required by rules and regulations promulgated under the provisions of this article;

16. Any person to use for his own advantage, or reveal, other than to the commissioner or his duly authorized representative, or to the courts when relevant in any judicial proceedings under this article, any information acquired under authority of this article or concerning any method or process, which is a trade secret;

17. Any person to alter, mutilate, destroy, obliterate or remove the whole or any part of the labeling of, or the doing of any other act with respect to a drug, device, or cosmetic, if such act is done while such article is held for sale and results in such article being misbranded;

18. Any person to use on the labeling of any drug or in any advertising relating to such drug any representation or suggestion that an application with respect to such drug is effective under section sixty-eight hundred seventeen of this chapter or that such is in compliance with the provisions of such section;

19. Any person to violate any of the provisions of section sixty-eight hundred ten of this article;

20. Any person to violate any of the provisions of section sixty-eight hundred sixteen of this article;

21. Any person, to sell at retail or give away in tablet form bichloride of mercury, mercuric chloride or corrosive sublimate, unless such bichloride of mercury, mercuric chloride or corrosive sublimate, when so sold, or given away, shall conform to the provisions of national formulary XII. Nothing contained in this paragraph shall be construed to prohibit the sale and dispensing of bichloride of mercury in any form, shape, or color, when combined or compounded with one or more other drugs or excipients, for the purposes of internal medication only, or when sold in bulk in powder form, or

to any preparation containing one-tenth of a grain or less of bichloride of mercury;

22. Any pharmacy to fail to properly post the list required by section sixty-eight hundred twenty-six of this article;

23. Any pharmacy to change its current selling price without changing the listed price as provided by section sixty-eight hundred twenty-six of this article;

24. Any person to refuse to permit access to or copying of any record as required by this article; or

25. Any manufacturer to sell or offer for sale any drug not manufactured, prepared or compounded under the personal supervision of a chemist or licensed pharmacist or not labeled with the full name of the manufacturer or seller.

26. Any outsourcing facility to sell or offer to sell any drug that is not both compounded under the personal supervision of a licensed pharmacist and labeled with the full name of the outsourcing facility.

§6812. Special provisions.

1. Where any pharmacy, manufacturer, wholesaler or outsourcing facility registered by the department is damaged by fire the board shall be notified within a period of forty-eight hours, and the board shall have power to impound all drugs for analysis and condemnation, if found unfit for use. Where a pharmacy is discontinued, the owner of its prescription records shall notify the department as to the disposition of said prescription records, and in no case shall records be sold or given away to a person who does not currently possess a registration to operate a pharmacy.

2. Nothing in this article shall be construed as requiring the prosecution or the institution of injunction proceedings for minor violations of this article whenever the public interest will be adequately served by a suitable written notice of warning.

3. The executive secretary of the state board of pharmacy is authorized to conduct examinations and investigations for the purposes of this article through officers and employees of the United States, or through any health, food, or drug officer or employee of any city, county or other political subdivision of this state.

§6813. Seizure.

1. Any drug, device or cosmetic that is adulterated, misbranded or may not be sold under the provisions of this chapter, may be seized on petition or complaint of the board and condemned in the supreme court of any county in which it is found. Seizure shall be made:

    a. by process pursuant to the petition or complaint, or

    b. if the secretary or other officer designated by him has probable cause to believe that the article

(1) is one which may not be sold under the provisions of section sixty-eight hundred seventeen of this chapter, or

(2) is adulterated, or

(3) is so misbranded as to be dangerous to health.

The article shall be seized by order of such officer. The order shall describe the article to be seized, the place where the article is located, and the officer or employee making the seizure. The officer, in lieu of taking actual possession, may affix a tag or other appropriate marking to the article giving notice that the article has been quarantined and warning all persons not to remove or dispose of it by sale or otherwise until permission for removal or disposal is given by the officer or the court. In case of seizures or quarantine, pursuant to such order, the jurisdiction of such court shall attach upon such seizure or quarantine, and a petition or complaint for condemnation shall be filed promptly.

2. The procedure for cases under this section shall conform as much as possible to the procedure for attachment. Any issue of fact joined in any case under this section shall be tried by jury on the demand of either party. The court at any time after seizure and up to the time of trial shall allow by order any party or his agent or attorney to obtain a representative sample of the condemned material, a true copy of the analysis on which the proceeding was based, and the identifying marks or numbers, if any, on the packages from which the samples analyzed were obtained.

3. Any drug, device or cosmetic condemned under this section shall be disposed of by destruction or sale as the court may direct after the decree in accordance with the provisions of this section. The proceeds of the sale, if any, shall be paid into the state treasury after deduction for legal costs and charges. However, the drug, device or cosmetic shall not be sold contrary to the provisions of this article. After entry of the decree, if the owner of the condemned articles pays the costs of the proceeding and posts a sufficient bond as security that the articles will not be disposed of contrary to the provisions of this article, the court may by order direct that the seized articles be delivered to the owner to be destroyed or brought into conformance with this article under supervision of the secretary. The expenses of the supervision shall be borne by the person obtaining the release under bond. Any drug condemned by reason of its being a new drug which may not be sold under this article shall be disposed of by destruction.

4. When the decree of condemnation is entered, court costs and fees, storage and other expense shall be awarded against the person, if any, intervening as claimant of the condemned articles.

5. In any proceeding against the board, or the secretary, or an agent of either, because of seizure, or quarantine, under this section, the board, or the secretary, or such agent shall not be liable if the court finds that there was probable cause for the acts done by them.

§6814. Records of shipment.

For the purpose of enforcing provisions of this article, carriers engaged in commerce, and persons receiving drugs, devices or cosmetics in commerce or holding such articles so received, shall, upon the request of an officer duly assigned by the secretary, permit such officer, at reasonable times, to have access to and to copy all records showing the movement in commerce of any drug, device or cosmetic, or the holding thereof during or after such movement, and the quantity, shipper, and consignee thereof: and it shall be unlawful for any such carrier or person to fail to permit such access to and copying of any such record so requested when such request is accompanied by a statement in writing specifying the nature or kind of drug, device or cosmetic to which such request relates: Provided, that evidence obtained under this section shall not be used in a criminal prosecution of the person from whom obtained: Provided further, that carriers shall not be subject to the other provisions of this article by reason of their receipt, carriage, holding or delivery of drugs, devices or cosmetics in the usual course of business as carriers.

§6815. Adulterating, misbranding and substituting.

1. Adulterated drugs. A drug or device shall be deemed to be adulterated:

a. (1) If it consists in whole or in part of any filthy, putrid, or decomposed substance; or

(2) if it has been prepared, packed, or held under insanitary conditions whereby it may have been contaminated with filth, or whereby it may have been rendered injurious to health; or

(3) if it is a drug and its container is composed, in whole or in part, of any poisonous or deleterious substance which may render the contents injurious to health; or (4) if it is a drug and it bears or contains, for purposes of coloring only, a coal-tar color other than one from a batch that has been certified in accordance with regulations provided in this article.

b. If it purports to be, or is represented as, a drug the name of which is recognized in an official compendium, and its strength differs from, or its quality or purity falls below, the standard set forth in such compendium. Such determination as to strength, quality or purity shall be made in accordance with the tests or methods of assay set forth in such compendium, or, in the absence or inadequacy of such tests or methods of assay, then in accordance with tests or methods of assay prescribed by regulations of the board of pharmacy as promulgated under this article. Deviations from the official assays may be made in the quantities of samples and reagents employed, provided they are in proportion to the quantities stated in the official compendium. No drug defined in an official compendium shall be deemed to be adulterated under this paragraph because

(1) it exceeds the standard of strength therefor set forth in such compendium, if such difference is plainly stated on its label; or

(2) it falls below the standard of strength, quality, or purity therefor set forth in such compendium if such difference is plainly stated on its label, except that this clause shall apply only to such drugs, or classes of drugs, as are

specified in regulations which the board shall promulgate when, as applied to any drug, or class of drugs, the prohibition of such difference is not necessary for the protection of the public health. Whenever a drug is recognized in both the United States pharmacopoeia and the homeopathic pharmacopoeia of the United States, it shall be subject to the requirements of the United States pharmacopoeia unless it is labeled and offered for sale as a homeopathic drug, in which case it shall be subject to the provisions of the homeopathic pharmacopoeia of the United States and not to those of the United States pharmacopoeia.

    c. If it is not subject to the provisions of paragraph b of this subdivision and its strength differs from, or its purity or quality falls below, that which it purports or is represented to possess.

    d. If it is a drug and any substance has been

        (1) mixed or packed therewith so as to reduce its quality or strength or

        (2) substituted wholly or in part therefor.

    e. If it is sold under or by a name not recognized in or according to a formula not given in the United States pharmacopoeia or the national formulary but that is found in some other standard work on pharmacology recognized by the board, and it differs in strength, quality or purity from the strength, quality or purity required, or the formula prescribed in, the standard work.

    2. Misbranded and substituted drugs and devices. A drug or device shall be deemed to be misbranded:

    a. If its labeling is false or misleading in any particular.

    b. If in package form, unless it bears a label containing

        (1) the name and place of business of the manufacturer, packer, or distributor; and

        (2) an accurate statement of the quantity of the contents in terms of weight, measure, or numerical count: Provided, that under clause (2) of this paragraph the board may establish reasonable variations as to quantity and exemptions as to small packages.

    c. If any word, statement, or other information required by or under authority of this article to appear on the label or labeling is not prominently placed thereon with such conspicuousness (as compared with other words, statements, designs, or devices, in the labeling) and in such terms as to render it likely to be read and understood by the ordinary individual under customary conditions of purchase and use.

    d. If it is for use by man and contains any quantity of the narcotic or hypnotic substance alpha eucaine, barbituric acid, beta eucaine, bromal, cannabis, carbromal, chloral, coca, cocaine, codeine, heroin, marihuana, morphine, opium, paraldehyde, peyote, or sulphonmethane; or any chemical derivative of such substance, which derivative has been by the secretary, after investigation, found to be, and by regulations under this article, or by regulations promulgated by the board, designated as, habit forming; unless its label bears the name and quantity, or proportion, of such substance or derivative and in juxtaposition therewith the statement "Warning--May be habit forming."

e. If it is a drug and is not designated solely by a name recognized in an official compendium unless its label bears (1) the common or usual name of the drug, if such there be; and (2) in case it is fabricated from two or more ingredients, the common or usual name of each active ingredient, including the kind and quantity by percentage or amount of any alcohol, and also including, whether active or not, the name and quantity or proportion of any bromides, ether, chloroform, acetanilid, acetphenetidin, amidopyrine, antipyrine, atropine, hyoscine, hyoscyamine, arsenic, digitalis, digitalis glucosides, mercury, ouabain, strophanthin, strychnine, thyroid, or any derivative or preparation of any such substances, contained therein: Provided, that, to the extent that compliance with the requirements of clause (2) of this paragraph is impracticable, exemptions shall be established by regulations promulgated by the board.

f. Unless its labeling bears (1) adequate directions for use; and (2) such adequate warnings against use in those pathological conditions or by children where its use may be dangerous to health, or against unsafe dosage or methods or duration of administration or application, in such manner and form, as are necessary for the protection of users: Provided, that, where any requirement of clause (1) of this paragraph, as applied to any drug or device, is not necessary for the protection of the public health, the board shall promulgate regulations exempting such drug or device from such requirement.

g. If it purports to be a drug the name of which is recognized in an official compendium, unless it is packaged and labeled as prescribed therein: Provided, that, the method of packing may be modified with the consent of the secretary in accordance with regulations promulgated by the board. Whenever a drug is recognized in both the United States pharmacopoeia and the homeopathic pharmacopoeia of the United States, it shall be subject to the requirements of the United States pharmacopoeia with respect to packaging and labeling unless it is labeled and offered for sale as a homeopathic drug, in which case it shall be subject to the provisions of the homeopathic pharmacopoeia of the United States, and not to those of the United States pharmacopoeia.

h. (1) If it is a drug and its container is so made, formed or filled as to be misleading; (2) if it is an imitation of another drug; (3) if it is offered for sale under the name of another drug; or (4) if it bears a copy, counterfeit, or colorable imitation of the trademark, label, container or identifying name or design of another drug.

i. If it is dangerous to health when used in the dosage, or with the frequency or duration prescribed, recommended or suggested in the labeling thereof.

j. Except as required by article thirty-three of the public health law, the labeling provisions of this article shall not apply to the compounding and dispensing of drugs on the written prescription of a physician, a dentist, a podiatrist or a veterinarian, which prescription when filled shall be kept on file for at least five years by the pharmacist or druggist. Such drug shall bear a label containing the name and place of business of the dispenser, the serial number and date of the prescription, directions for use as may be stated in the prescription, name and address of the patient and the name of the physician or other practitioner authorized by law to issue the prescription. In addition, such label shall contain the proprietary or brand name of the drug and, if applicable, the strength of the contents, unless the person issuing the prescription explicitly states on the prescription, in his own handwriting, that the name of the drug and the strength thereof should not appear on the label.

This page intentionally left blank.

EXECUTIVE LAW
ARTICLE 49-B
COMMISSION ON FORENSIC SCIENCE AND
ESTABLISHMENT OF
DNA IDENTIFICATION INDEX

Section
995.   Definitions.
995-a.   Commission on forensic science.
995-b.   Powers and duties of the commission.
995-c.   State DNA identification index.
995-d.   Confidentiality.
995-e.   Applicability.
995-f.   Penalties.

§995. Definitions.

When used in this article, the following words and terms shall have the meanings ascribed to them in this section:

1. For purposes of general forensic analysis the term "forensic laboratory" shall mean any laboratory operated by the state or unit of local government that performs forensic testing on evidence in a criminal investigation or proceeding or for purposes of identification.   *(Eff.9/1/21,Ch.209,L.2021)*

2. For purposes of forensic DNA analysis, the term "forensic DNA laboratory" shall mean any forensic laboratory operated by the state or unit of local government, that performs forensic DNA testing on crime scenes or materials derived from the human body for use as evidence in a criminal proceeding or for purposes of identification and the term "forensic DNA testing" shall mean any test that employs techniques to examine deoxyribonucleic acid (DNA) derived from the human body for the purpose of providing information to resolve issues of identification. Regulation pursuant to this article shall not include DNA testing on materials derived from the human body pursuant to title five of article five of the public health law for the purpose of determining a person's genetic disease or medical condition and shall not include a laboratory operated by the federal government.

3. "DNA testing methodology" means methods and procedures used to extract and analyze DNA material, as well as the methods, procedures, assumptions, and studies used to draw statistical inferences from the test results.

4. "Blind external proficiency testing" means a test sample that is presented to a forensic laboratory for forensic DNA testing through a second agency, and which appears to the analysts to involve routine evidence submitted for forensic DNA testing.

5. "DNA" means deoxyribonucleic acid.

6. "State DNA identification index" means the DNA identification record system for New York state established pursuant to this article.

7. "Designated offender" means a person convicted of any felony defined in any chapter of the laws of the state or any misdemeanor defined in the penal law except: (a) a person convicted of prostitution under section 230.00 of the penal law, or (b) a person whose participation in the offense is determined by

a court to have been a result of having been a victim of sex trafficking under section 230.34 of the penal law, sex trafficking of a child under section 230.34-a of the penal law, or trafficking in persons under the trafficking victims protection act (United States Code, Title 22, Chapter 78).

(Eff.3/31/21,Ch.92 & Eff.12/22/21,Ch.715,L.2021)

8. "DNA record" means DNA identification information prepared by a forensic DNA laboratory and stored in the state DNA identification index for purposes of establishing identification in connection with law enforcement investigations or supporting statistical interpretation of the results of DNA analysis. A DNA record is the objective form of the results of a DNA analysis sample.

9. "DNA subcommittee" shall mean the subcommittee on forensic DNA laboratories and forensic DNA testing established pursuant to subdivision thirteen of section nine hundred ninety-five-b of this article.

10. "Commission" shall mean the commission on forensic science established pursuant to section nine hundred ninety-five-a of this article.

§995-a. Commission on forensic science.

1. There is hereby created in the executive department, the commission on forensic science, which shall consist of the following fourteen members:

(a) the commissioner of the division of criminal justice services who shall be chair of the commission and the commissioner of the department of health or his or her designee, who shall serve as an ex-officio member of the commission;

(b) twelve members appointed by the governor.

2. Of the members appointed by the governor,

(a) one member shall be the chair of the New York state crime laboratory advisory committee;

(b) one member shall be the director of a forensic laboratory located in New York state;

(c) one member shall be the director of the office of forensic services within the division of criminal justice services;

(d) two members shall be a scientist having experience in the areas of laboratory standards or quality assurance regulation and monitoring and shall be appointed upon the recommendation of the commissioner of health;

(e) one member shall be a representative of a law enforcement agency and shall be appointed upon the recommendation of the commissioner of criminal justice services;

(f) one member shall be a representative of prosecution services who shall be appointed upon the recommendation of the commissioner of criminal justice services;

(g) one member shall be a representative of the public criminal defense bar who shall be appointed upon the recommendation of an organization representing public defense services;

(h) one member shall be a representative of the private criminal defense bar who shall be appointed upon the recommendation of an organization of such bar;

(i) two members shall be members-at-large, one of whom shall be appointed upon the recommendation of the temporary president of the senate, and one of whom shall be appointed upon the recommendation of the speaker of the assembly; and

(j) one member, who shall be an attorney or judge with a background in privacy issues and biomedical ethics, shall be appointed upon the recommendation of the chief judge of the court of appeals.

3. Of the members appointed by the governor, each member shall be appointed to serve a three year term. Any member appointed by the governor may be reappointed for additional three year terms.

4. Any member chosen to fill a vacancy created otherwise than by expiration of term shall be appointed by the governor for the unexpired term of the member he or she is to succeed. Any such vacancy shall be filled in the same manner as the original appointment.

5. The commission shall meet at least four times each year and may establish its own rules and procedures concerning the conduct of its meetings and other affairs not inconsistent with law.

6. No member of the commission on forensic science shall be disqualified from holding any public office or employment, nor shall he or she forfeit any such office or employment, by reason of his or her appointment hereunder, and members of the commission shall not be required to take and file oaths of office before serving on the commission.

7. Members of the commission shall receive no compensation for their services but shall be allowed their actual and necessary expenses incurred in the performance of their functions hereunder.

§995-b. Powers and duties of the commission.

1. The commission shall develop minimum standards and a program of accreditation for all forensic laboratories in New York state, including establishing minimum qualifications for forensic laboratory directors and such other personnel as the commission may determine to be necessary and appropriate, and approval of forensic laboratories for the performance of specific forensic methodologies. Nothing in this article shall be deemed to preclude forensic laboratories from performing research and validation studies on new methodologies and technologies which may not yet be approved by the commission at that time. In designing a system of accreditation pursuant to this article, the commission shall evaluate other systems of accreditation.

2. The minimum standards and program of accreditation shall be designed to accomplish the following objectives:

(a) increase and maintain the effectiveness, efficiency, reliability, and accuracy of forensic laboratories, including forensic DNA laboratories;

(b) ensure that forensic analyses, including forensic DNA testing, are performed in accordance with the highest scientific standards practicable;

(c) promote increased cooperation and coordination among forensic laboratories and other agencies in the criminal justice system;

(d) ensure compatibility, to the extent consistent with the provisions of this article and any other applicable provision of law pertaining to privacy or restricting disclosure or redisclosure of information, with other state and federal forensic laboratories to the extent necessary to share and exchange information, data and results of forensic analyses and tests; and

(e) set forth minimum requirements for the quality and maintenance of equipment.

2-a. Any program of forensic laboratory accreditation with respect to a DNA laboratory pursuant to this section shall be under the direction of the DNA subcommittee established pursuant to subdivision thirteen of this section. Such subcommittee shall have the sole authority to grant, deny, review or modify a DNA forensic laboratory accreditation pursuant to this article, provided that such authority shall be effectuated through binding recommendations made by the DNA subcommittee to the commission. In the event the commission disagrees with any of the binding recommendations of the DNA subcommittee made pursuant to this article, the commission may so notify such subcommittee and request such subcommittee to reasonably review such binding recommendations. The DNA subcommittee shall conduct such review and either forward revised binding recommendations to the commission or indicate, with the reasons therefor, that following such review such subcommittee has determined that such binding recommendations shall not be revised.

3. The program of forensic laboratory accreditation shall include, at a minimum, the following requirements:

(a) an initial laboratory inspection, and routine inspections, as necessary, to ensure compliance with accreditation requirements;

(b) routine internal and external proficiency testing of all laboratory personnel involved in forensic analysis, including blind external proficiency testing if the commission, or the DNA subcommittee as the case may be, determines such a blind proficiency testing program to be practicable and appropriate. In determining whether a blind proficiency testing program is practicable and appropriate, the commission, or the DNA subcommittee as the case may be, shall consider such factors as accuracy and reliability of laboratory results, cost-effectiveness, time, allocation of resources, and availability;

(c) quality control and quality assurance protocols, a method validation procedure and a corrective action and remedial program;

(d) annual certification to the commission by the forensic laboratories of their continued compliance with the requirements of the accreditation program which certification, in the case of a forensic DNA laboratory, shall be forwarded to the DNA subcommittee;

(e) the accreditation of a forensic laboratory may be revoked, suspended or otherwise limited, upon a determination by the commission or, in the case of a forensic DNA laboratory, upon the binding recommendation of the DNA subcommittee, that the laboratory or one or more persons in its employ:

(i) is guilty of misrepresentation in obtaining a forensic laboratory accreditation;

(ii) rendered a report on laboratory work actually performed in another forensic laboratory without disclosing the fact that the examination or procedure was performed by such other forensic laboratory;

(iii) showed a pattern of excessive errors in the performance of forensic laboratory examination procedures;

(iv) failed to file any report required to be submitted pursuant to this article or the rules and regulations promulgated pursuant thereto; or

(v) violated in a material respect any provision of this article or the rules and regulations promulgated pursuant thereto; and

(f) no forensic laboratory accreditation shall be revoked, suspended, or otherwise limited without a hearing. The commission shall serve written notice of the alleged violation, together with written notice of the time and place of the hearing, which notice shall be mailed by certified mail to the holder of the forensic laboratory accreditation at the address of such holder at least twenty-one days prior to the date fixed for such hearing. An accredited laboratory may file a written answer to the charges with the commission, not less than five days prior to the hearing.

4. A laboratory director who knowingly operates a laboratory without obtaining the accreditation required by this article, or who, with the intent to mislead or deceive, misrepresents a material fact to the commission or DNA subcommittee, shall be subject to a civil penalty not to exceed seventy-five hundred dollars and such other penalties as are prescribed by the law.

5. The commission and the DNA subcommittee established pursuant to subdivision thirteen of this section may require and receive from any agency of the state or any political subdivision thereof such assistance and data as may be necessary to enable the commission or DNA subcommittee to administer the provisions of this article. The commission or DNA subcommittee may enter into such cooperative arrangements with the division of criminal justice services, the department of health, and any other state agency, each of which is authorized to enter into such cooperative arrangements as shall be necessary or appropriate. Upon request of the commission or DNA subcommittee, any state agency may transfer to the commission such officers and employees as the commission or DNA subcommittee may deem necessary from time to time to assist the commission or DNA subcommittee in carrying out its functions and duties. Officers and employees so transferred shall not lose their civil service status or rights, and shall remain in the negotiating unit, if any, established prior to such transfer.

6. All of the commission's records, reports, assessments, and evaluation with respect to accreditation, implementation of quality assurance standards (including proficiency testing) and monitoring thereof, shall be archived by the commission.

7. The commission and DNA subcommittee may establish, appoint, and set terms of members to as many advisory councils as it deems necessary to provide specialized expertise to the commission with respect to new forensic technologies including DNA testing methodologies.

8. The commission or DNA subcommittee shall designate one or more entities for the performance of proficiency tests required pursuant to the provisions of this article.

9. After reviewing recommendations from the division of criminal justice services, the commission, in consultation with the DNA subcommittee, shall promulgate a policy for the establishment and operation of a DNA identification index consistent with the operational requirements and capabilities of the division of criminal justice services. Such policy shall address the following issues:

(a) the forensic DNA methodology or methodologies to be utilized in compiling the index;

(b) procedures for assuring that the state DNA identification index contains the following safeguards:

(i) that any records maintained as part of such an index are accurate and complete;

(ii) that effective software and hardware designs are instituted with security features to prevent unauthorized access to such records;

(iii) that periodic audits will be conducted to ensure that no illegal disclosures of such records have taken place;

(iv) that access to record information system facilities, systems operating environments, data file contents whether while in use or when stored in a media library is restricted to authorized personnel only;

(v) that operation programs are used that will prohibit inquiry, record updates, or destruction of records from any source other than an authorized source of inquiry, update, or destruction of records;

(vi) that operational programs are used to detect and store for the output of authorized employees only all unauthorized attempts to penetrate the state DNA identification index;

(vii) that adequate and timely procedures exist to insure that any subject of the state DNA identification index has the right of access to and review of records relating to such individual contained in such index for the purpose of ascertaining their accuracy and completeness, including procedures for review of information maintained about such individuals and administrative review (including procedures for administrative appeal) and the necessary documentation to demonstrate that the information is inaccurate or incomplete;

(viii) that access to the index will be granted to an agency authorized by this article to have such access only pursuant to a written use and dissemination agreement, a copy of which is filed with the commission, which agreement sets forth the specific procedures by which such agency shall implement the provisions of subparagraphs (i) through (vii) of this paragraph, as applicable, and which agreement specifically prohibits the redisclosure by such agency of any information obtained from the DNA identification index; and

(ix) such policy shall provide for the mutual exchange, use and storage of DNA records with the system of DNA identification utilized by the federal bureau of investigation provided that the commission determines that such exchange, use and storage are consistent with the provisions of this article and applicable provisions of law.

10. Review, and if necessary, recommend modifications to, a plan for implementation of the DNA identification index submitted by the commissioner of criminal justice services pursuant to section nine hundred ninety-five-c of this article.

11. Upon the recommendation of the DNA subcommittee established pursuant to subdivision thirteen of this section, the commission shall designate one or more approved methodologies for the performance of forensic DNA testing, and shall review and act upon applications by forensic DNA laboratories for approval to perform forensic DNA testing.

12. Promulgate standards for a determination of a match between the DNA records contained in the state DNA identification index and a DNA record of a person submitted for comparison therewith.

13. (a) The commission shall establish a subcommittee on forensic DNA laboratories and forensic DNA testing. The chair of the subcommittee shall be appointed by the chair of the commission. The chair of the subcommittee shall appoint six other members to the subcommittee, one of whom shall represent the discipline of molecular biology and be appointed upon the recommendation of the commissioner of the department of health, one of whom shall represent the discipline of population genetics and be appointed upon the recommendation of the commissioner of the department of health, one of whom shall be representative of the discipline of laboratory standards and quality assurance regulation and monitoring and be appointed upon the recommendation of the commissioner of the department of health, one of whom shall be a forensic scientist and be appointed upon the recommendation of the commissioner of the department of health, one of whom shall be representative of the discipline of population genetics and be appointed upon the recommendation of the commissioner of criminal justice services and one of whom shall be representative of the discipline of forensic science and be appointed upon the recommendation of the commissioner of criminal justice services. Members of the DNA subcommittee shall serve for three year terms and be subject to the conditions of service specified in section nine hundred ninety-five-a of this article.

(b) The DNA subcommittee shall assess and evaluate all DNA methodologies proposed to be used for forensic analysis, and make reports and recommendations to the commission as it deems necessary. The DNA subcommittee shall make binding recommendations for adoption by the commission addressing minimum scientific standards to be utilized in conducting forensic DNA analysis including, but not limited to, examination of specimens, population studies and methods employed to determine probabilities and interpret test results. The DNA subcommittee may require a demonstration by an independent laboratory of any proposed forensic DNA testing methodology proposed to be used by a forensic laboratory.

(c) The DNA subcommittee shall make binding recommendations for adoption by the commission with regard to an accreditation program for laboratories performing forensic DNA testing in accordance with the provisions of the state administrative procedure act. Such recommendations shall include the adoption and implementation of internal and external proficiency testing programs, including, if possible, a blind external proficiency testing program for forensic laboratories performing forensic DNA testing. The DNA subcommittee shall also provide the commission with a list of accepted proficiency testers.

(d) The DNA subcommittee shall be authorized to advise the commission on any other matters regarding the implementation of scientific controls and quality assurance procedures for the performance of forensic DNA testing, or on any other matters referred to it by the commission.

§995-c. State DNA identification index.

1. Following the promulgation of a policy by the commission pursuant to subdivision nine of section nine hundred ninety-five-b of this article, the commissioner of criminal justice services is authorized to promulgate a plan for the establishment of a computerized state DNA identification index within the division of criminal justice services.

2. Following the review and approval of the plan by the DNA subcommittee and the commission and the filing of such plan with the speaker of the assembly and the temporary president of the senate, the commissioner of criminal justice services is hereby authorized to establish a computerized state DNA identification index pursuant to the provisions of this article.

3. (a) Any designated offender subsequent to conviction and sentencing for a crime specified in subdivision seven of section nine hundred ninety-five of this article, shall be required to provide a sample appropriate for DNA testing to determine identification characteristics specific to such person and to be included in a state DNA identification index pursuant to this article.

(b) (i) In the case of a designated offender who is sentenced to a term of imprisonment, such sample shall be collected by the public servant to whose custody the designated offender has been committed.

(ii) In the case of a designated offender who is sentenced to a term of probation, including a sentence of probation imposed in conjunction with a sentence of imprisonment when a sample has not already been taken, such sample shall be collected by the probation department supervising the designated offender.

(iii) In the case of a designated offender whose sentence does not include either a term of imprisonment or a term of probation, outside of the city of New York, the court shall order that a court officer take a sample or that the designated offender report to an office of the sheriff of that county, and when the designated offender does so, such sample shall be collected by the sheriff's office. Within the city of New York, the court shall order that the sample be collected by a court officer.

(iv) Nothing in this paragraph shall prohibit the collection of a DNA sample from a designated offender by any court official, state or local correction official or employee, probation officer, parole officer, police officer, peace officer, other law enforcement official, or designated personnel of the division of criminal justice services who has been notified by the division of criminal justice services that such designated offender has not provided a DNA sample. Upon notification by the division of criminal justice services that a designated offender has not provided a DNA sample, such court official, state or local correction official or employee, probation officer, parole officer, police officer, peace officer or other law enforcement official, or designated personnel of the division of criminal justice services shall collect the DNA sample.

4. The commissioner of the division of criminal justice services, in consultation with the commission, the commissioner of health, the director of the office of probation and correctional alternatives and the department of corrections and community supervision, shall promulgate rules and regulations governing the procedures for notifying designated offenders of the requirements of this section.

5. The sample shall be collected, stored and forwarded to any forensic DNA laboratory which has been authorized by the commission to perform forensic DNA testing and analysis for inclusion in the state DNA identification index. Such laboratory shall promptly perform the requisite testing and analysis, and forward the resulting DNA record only to the state DNA identification index in accordance with the regulations of the division of criminal justice services. Such laboratory shall perform DNA analysis only for those markers having value for law enforcement identification purposes. For the purposes of this article, the term "marker" shall have the meaning generally ascribed to it by members of the scientific community experienced in the use of DNA technology.

6. DNA records contained in the state DNA identification index shall be released only for the following purposes:

(a) to a federal law enforcement agency, or to a state or local law enforcement agency or district attorney's office for law enforcement identification purposes upon submission of a DNA record in connection with the investigation of the commission of one or more crimes or to assist in the recovery or identification of specified human remains, including identification of missing persons, provided that there exists between the division and such agency a written agreement governing the use and dissemination of such DNA records in accordance with the provisions of this article;

(b) for criminal defense purposes, to a defendant or his or her representative, who shall also have access to samples and analyses performed in connection with the case in which such defendant is charged;

(c) after personally identifiable information has been removed by the division, to an entity authorized by the division for the purpose of creating or maintaining a population statistics database or for identification research and protocol development for forensic DNA analysis or quality control purposes.

7. Requests for DNA records must be in writing, or in a form prescribed by the division authorized by the requesting party, and, other than a request pursuant to paragraph (b) of subdivision six of this section, maintained on file at the state DNA identification index in accordance with rules and regulations promulgated by the commissioner of the division of criminal justice services.

8. The defendant, including the representative of a defendant, in a criminal action or proceeding shall have access to information in the state DNA identification index relating to the number of requests previously made for a comparison search and the name and identity of any requesting party.

9. (a) Upon receipt of notification of a reversal or a vacatur of a conviction, or of the granting of a pardon pursuant to article two-A of this chapter, of an individual whose DNA record has been stored in the state DNA identification index in accordance with this article by the division of criminal justice services, the DNA record shall be expunged from the state DNA identification index, and such individual may apply to the court in which the judgment of conviction was originally entered for an order directing the expungement of any DNA record and any samples, analyses, or other documents relating to the DNA testing of such individual in connection with the investigation or prosecution of the crime which resulted in the conviction that was reversed or vacated or for which the pardon was granted. A copy of such application shall be served on the district attorney and an order directing expungement may be granted if the court finds that all appeals relating to the conviction have been concluded; that such individual will not be retried, or, if a retrial has occurred, the trier of fact has rendered a verdict of complete acquittal, and that expungement will not adversely affect the investigation or prosecution of some other person or persons for the crime. The division shall, by rule or regulation, prescribe procedures to ensure that the DNA record in the state DNA identification index, and any samples, analyses, or other documents relating to such record, whether in the possession of the division, or any law enforcement or police agency, or any forensic DNA laboratory, including any duplicates or copies thereof, at the discretion of the possessor thereof, are either destroyed or returned to such individual, or to the attorney who represented him or her at the time such reversal, vacatur or pardon, was granted. The commissioner shall also adopt by rule and regulation a procedure for the expungement in other appropriate circumstances of DNA records contained in the index.

(b) As prescribed in this paragraph, if an individual, either voluntarily or pursuant to a warrant or order of a court, has provided a sample for DNA testing in connection with the investigation or prosecution of a crime and (i) no criminal action against the individual relating to such crime was commenced within the period specified by section 30.10 of the criminal procedure law, or (ii) a criminal action was commenced against the individual relating to such crime which resulted in a complete acquittal, or (iii) a criminal action against the individual relating to such crime resulted in a conviction that was subsequently reversed or vacated, or for which the individual was granted a pardon pursuant to article two-A of this chapter, such individual may apply to the supreme court or the court in which the judgment of conviction was originally entered for an order directing the expungement of any DNA record and any samples, analyses, or other documents relating to the DNA testing of such individual in connection with the investigation or prosecution of such crime. A copy of such application shall be served on the district attorney and an order directing expungement may be granted if the court finds that the individual has satisfied the conditions of one of the subparagraphs of this paragraph; that if a judgment of conviction was reversed or vacated, all appeals relating thereto have been concluded and the individual will not be retried, or, if a retrial has occurred, the trier of fact has rendered a verdict of complete acquittal, and that expungement will not adversely affect the investigation or prosecution of some other person or persons for the crime. If an order directing the expungement of any DNA record and any samples, analyses or other documents relating to the DNA testing of such individual is issued, such record and any samples, analyses, or other documents shall, at the discretion of the possessor thereof, be destroyed or returned to such individual or to the attorney who represented him or her in connection with the application for the order of expungement.

§995-d. Confidentiality.

1. All records, findings, reports, and results of DNA testing performed on any person shall be confidential and may not be disclosed or redisclosed without the consent of the subject of such DNA testing. Such records, findings, reports and results shall not be released to insurance companies, employers or potential employers, health providers, employment screening or personnel companies, agencies, or services, private investigation services, and may not be disclosed in response to a subpoena or other compulsory legal process or warrant, or upon request or order of any agency, authority, division, office, corporation, partnership, or any other private or public entity or person, except that nothing contained herein shall prohibit disclosure in response to a subpoena issued on behalf of the subject of such DNA record or on behalf of a party in a civil proceeding where the subject of such DNA record has put such record in issue.

2. Notwithstanding the provisions of subdivision one of this section, records, findings, reports, and results of DNA testing, other than a DNA record maintained in the state DNA identification index, may be disclosed in a criminal proceeding to the court, the prosecution, and the defense pursuant to a written request on a form prescribed by the commissioner of the division of criminal justice services. Notwithstanding the provisions of subdivision one of this section, a DNA record maintained in the state DNA identification index may be disclosed pursuant to section nine hundred ninety-five-c of this article.

§995-e. Applicability.

This article shall not apply to a forensic DNA laboratory operated by any agency of the federal government, or to any forensic DNA test performed by any such federal laboratory.

§995-f. Penalties.

Any person who (a) intentionally discloses a DNA record, or the results of a forensic DNA test or analysis, to an individual or agency other than one authorized to have access to such records pursuant to this article or (b) intentionally uses or receives DNA records, or the results of a forensic DNA test or analysis, for purposes other than those authorized pursuant to this article or (c) any person who knowingly tampers or attempts to tamper with any DNA sample or the collection container without lawful authority shall be guilty of a class E felony.

GENERAL BUSINESS LAW
ARTICLE 29-A
UNAUTHORIZED OR IMPROPER USE
OF CREDIT CARDS AND DEBIT CARDS

Section
511.   Definitions.
511-a.   Additional definition.

§511. Definitions.

In this article, unless the context or subject matter otherwise requires:

1. "Credit card" means and includes any credit card, credit plate, charge plate, courtesy card, or other identification card or device issued by a person to another person which may be used to obtain a cash advance or a loan or credit or to purchase or lease property or services on the credit of the issuer or of the holder;

2. "Person" includes an individual, corporation, partnership or association, two or more persons having a joint or common interest or any other legal or commercial entity;

3. "Issuer" means a person who issues a credit card or a debit card;

4. "Holder" means a person to whom such a credit card or debit card is issued or who has agreed with the issuer to pay obligations arising from the use of a credit card or debit card issued to another person;

5. "Unauthorized use" means use of a credit card or a debit card by a person other than the holder who does not have actual, implied or apparent authority from the holder for such use and from which use the holder receives no benefit;

6. "Seller" means any person who honors credit cards or debit cards which may be used to purchase or lease property or services;

7. "Lender" means any person who honors credit cards which may be used to obtain a cash advance or loan.

8. "Improper use" means unauthorized use of a credit card or a debit card or use of a revoked, cancelled, expired or forged credit card or debit card at the premises of a seller or lender, to obtain a cash advance or loan, or to purchase or lease property or services, or an attempt to do so;

9. "Debit card" means a card, plate or other similar device issued by a person to another person which may be used, without a personal identification number, code or similar identification number, code or similar identification, to purchase or lease property or services. The term does not include a credit card or a check, draft or similar instrument.

10. "Secured credit card" means any credit card for which an issuer takes a pledge of a specifically identified interest-bearing deposit account as provided in section four hundred thirteen of the personal property law.

§511-a. Additional definition.

For purposes of this article "credit card" shall also mean any number assigned to a credit card.

PUBLIC HEALTH LAW
ARTICLE 33
CONTROLLED SUBSTANCES

TITLE I
GENERAL PROVISIONS

Section
3300.   Short title.
3300-a.   Legislative purposes.
3301.   Applicability of this article to actions and matters occurring or arising before and after the effective date.
3302.   Definitions of terms of general use in this article.
3304.   Prohibited acts.
3304*.   Prohibited acts.
3305.   Exemptions.
3306.   Schedules of controlled substances.
3307.   Exception from schedules.
3308.   Powers and duties of the commissioner.
3309.   Opioid overdose prevention.
3309-a.   Prescription pain medication awareness program.

§3300. Short title.

This article shall be known as the New York State Controlled Substances Act.

§3300-a. Legislative purposes.

The purposes of this article are:

1. to combat illegal use of and trade in controlled substances; and

2. to allow legitimate use of controlled substances in health care, including palliative care; veterinary care; research and other uses authorized by this article or other law; under appropriate regulation and subject to this article, title eight of the education law, and other applicable law.

§3301. Applicability of this article to actions and matters occurring or arising before and after the effective date.

Unless otherwise expressly provided, or unless the context otherwise requires:

(a) the provisions of this article shall govern and control the possession, manufacture, dispensing, administering, and distribution of controlled substances with respect to any matter, act or omission, arising or occurring on or after the effective date hereof;

(b) the provisions of this article do not apply to or govern any matter, act, or omission arising or occurring prior to the effective date hereof. Such matters, acts, or omissions must be governed and construed according to provisions of law existing at the time such matter, act or omission arose or occurred in the same manner as if this article had not been enacted.

§3302. Definitions of terms of general use in this article.

Except where different meanings are expressly specified in subsequent provisions of this article, the following terms have the following meanings:

1. "Addict" means a person who habitually uses a controlled substance for a non-legitimate or unlawful use, and who by reason of such use is dependent thereon.

2. "Administer" means the direct application of a controlled substance, whether by injection, inhalation, ingestion, or any other means, to the body of a patient or research subject.

3. "Agent" means an authorized person who acts on behalf of or at the direction of a manufacturer, distributor, or dispenser. No person may be authorized to so act if under title VIII of the education law such person would not be permitted to engage in such conduct. It does not include a common or contract carrier, public warehouseman, or employee of the carrier or warehouseman when acting in the usual and lawful course of the carrier's or warehouseman's business.

4. "Controlled substance" means a substance or substances listed in section thirty-three hundred six of this title.

5. "Commissioner" means commissioner of health of the state of New York.

6. "Deliver" or "delivery" means the actual, constructive or attempted transfer from one person to another of a controlled substance, whether or not there is an agency relationship.

7. "Department" means the department of health of the state of New York.

8. "Dispense" means to deliver a controlled substance to an ultimate user or research subject by lawful means, including by means of the internet, and includes the packaging, labeling, or compounding necessary to prepare the substance for such delivery.

9. "Distribute" means to deliver a controlled substance, including by means of the internet, other than by administering or dispensing.

10. "Distributor" means a person who distributes a controlled substance.

11. "Diversion" means manufacture, possession, delivery or use of a controlled substance by a person or in a manner not specifically authorized by law.

12. "Drug" means

(a) substances recognized as drugs in the official United States Pharmacopoeia, official Homeopathic Pharmacopoeia of the United States, or official National Formulary, or any supplement to any of them;

(b) substances intended for use in the diagnosis, cure, mitigation, treatment, or prevention of disease in man or animals; and

(c) substances (other than food) intended to affect the structure or a function of the body of man or animal. It does not include devices or their components, parts, or accessories.

13. "Federal agency" means the Drug Enforcement Administration, United States Department of Justice, or its successor agency.

14. "Federal controlled substances act" means the Comprehensive Drug Abuse Prevention and Control Act of 1970, Public Law 91-513, and any act or acts amendatory or supplemental thereto or regulations promulgated thereunder.

15. "Federal registration number" means such number assigned by the Federal agency to any person authorized to manufacture, distribute, sell, dispense or administer controlled substances.

16. "Habitual user" means any person who is, or by reason of repeated use of any controlled substance for non-legitimate or unlawful use is in danger of becoming, dependent upon such substance.

17. "Institutional dispenser" means a hospital, veterinary hospital, clinic, dispensary, maternity home, nursing home, mental hospital or similar facility approved and certified by the department as authorized to obtain controlled substances by distribution and to dispense and administer such substances pursuant to the order of a practitioner.

18. "License" means a written authorization issued by the department or the New York state department of education permitting persons to engage in a specified activity with respect to controlled substances.

19. "Manufacture" means the production, preparation, propagation, compounding, cultivation, conversion or processing of a controlled substance, either directly or indirectly or by extraction from substances of natural origin, or independently by means of chemical synthesis, or by a combination of extraction and chemical synthesis, and includes any packaging or repackaging of the substance or labeling or relabeling of its container, except that this term does not include the preparation, compounding, packaging or labeling of a controlled substance:

(a) by a practitioner as an incident to his administering or dispensing of a controlled substance in the course of his professional practice; or

(b) by a practitioner, or by his authorized agent under his supervision, for the purpose of, or as an incident to, research, teaching, or chemical analysis and not for sale; or

(c) by a pharmacist as an incident to his dispensing of a controlled substance in the course of his professional practice.

20. "Narcotic drug" means any of the following, whether produced directly or indirectly by extraction from substances of vegetable origin, or independently by means of chemical synthesis, or by a combination of extraction and chemical synthesis:

(a) opium and opiate, and any salt, compound, derivative, or preparation of opium or opiate;

(b) any salt, compound, isomer, derivative, or preparation thereof which is chemically equivalent or identical with any of the substances referred to in paragraph (a) of this subdivision, but not including the isoquinoline alkaloids of opium;

(c) opium poppy and poppy straw.

21. "Opiate" means any substance having an addiction-forming or addiction-sustaining liability similar to morphine or being capable of conversion into a drug having addiction-forming or addiction-sustaining liability. It

does not include, unless specifically designated as controlled under section thirty-three hundred six of this title, the dextrorotatory isomer of 3-methoxy-n-methylmorphinan and its salts (dextromethorphan). It does include its racemic and levorotatory forms.

22. "Opium poppy" means the plant of the species Papaver somniferum L., except its seeds.

23. "Person" means individual, institution, corporation, government or governmental subdivision or agency, business trust, estate, trust, partnership or association, or any other legal entity.

24. "Pharmacist" means any person licensed by the state department of education to practice pharmacy.

25. "Pharmacy" means any place registered as such by the New York state board of pharmacy and registered with the Federal agency pursuant to the federal controlled substances act.

26. "Poppy straw" means all parts, except the seeds, of the opium poppy, after mowing.

27. "Practitioner" means: A physician, dentist, podiatrist, veterinarian, scientific investigator, or other person licensed, or otherwise permitted to dispense, administer or conduct research with respect to a controlled substance in the course of a licensed professional practice or research licensed pursuant to this article. Such person shall be deemed a "practitioner" only as to such substances, or conduct relating to such substances, as is permitted by his license, permit or otherwise permitted by law.

28. "Prescribe" means a direction or authorization, by prescription, permitting an ultimate user lawfully to obtain controlled substances from any person authorized by law to dispense such substances.

29. "Prescription" shall mean an official New York state prescription, an electronic prescription, an oral prescription or an out-of-state prescription.

30. "Sell" means to sell, exchange, give or dispose of to another, or offer or agree to do the same.

31. "Ultimate user" means a person who lawfully obtains and possesses a controlled substance for his own use or the use by a member of his household or for an animal owned by him or in his custody. It shall also mean and include a person designated, by a practitioner on a prescription, to obtain such substance on behalf of the patient for whom such substance is intended.

32. "Internet" means collectively computer and telecommunications facilities which comprise the worldwide network of networks that employ a set of industry standards and protocols, or any predecessor or successor protocol to such protocol, to exchange information of all kinds. "Internet," as used in this article, also includes other networks, whether private or public, used to transmit information by electronic means.

33. "By means of the internet" means any sale, delivery, distribution, or dispensing of a controlled substance that uses the internet, is initiated by use of the internet or causes the internet to be used.

34. "Online dispenser" means a practitioner, pharmacy, or person in the United States that sells, delivers or dispenses, or offers to sell, deliver, or dispense, a controlled substance by means of the internet.

35. "Electronic prescription" means a prescription issued with an electronic signature and transmitted by electronic means in accordance with regulations of the commissioner and the commissioner of education and consistent with federal requirements. A prescription generated on an electronic system that is printed out or transmitted via facsimile is not considered an electronic prescription and must be manually signed.

36. "Electronic" means of or relating to technology having electrical, digital, magnetic, wireless, optical, electromagnetic or similar capabilities. "Electronic" shall not include facsimile.

37. "Electronic record" means a paperless record that is created, generated, transmitted, communicated, received or stored by means of electronic equipment and includes the preservation, retrieval, use and disposition in accordance with regulations of the commissioner and the commissioner of education and in compliance with federal law and regulations.

38. "Electronic signature" means an electronic sound, symbol, or process, attached to or logically associated with an electronic record and executed or adopted by a person with the intent to sign the record, in accordance with regulations of the commissioner and the commissioner of education.

39. "Registry" or "prescription monitoring program registry" means the prescription monitoring program registry established pursuant to section thirty-three hundred forty-three-a of this article.

40. "Compounding" means the combining, admixing, mixing, diluting, pooling, reconstituting, or otherwise altering of a drug or bulk drug substance to create a drug with respect to an outsourcing facility under section 503B of the federal Food, Drug and Cosmetic Act and further defined in this section.

41. "Outsourcing facility" means a facility that:

(a) is engaged in the compounding of sterile drugs as defined in section sixty-eight hundred two of the education law;

(b) is currently registered as an outsourcing facility pursuant to article one hundred thirty-seven of the education law; and

(c) complies with all applicable requirements of federal and state law, including the Federal Food, Drug and Cosmetic Act.

Notwithstanding any other provision of law to the contrary, when an outsourcing facility distributes or dispenses any drug to any person pursuant to a prescription, such outsourcing facility shall be deemed to be providing pharmacy services and shall be subject to all laws, rules and regulations governing pharmacies and pharmacy services.   *(Eff.3/31/21,Ch.92,L.2021)*

*§3304. Prohibited acts.

1. It shall be unlawful for any person to manufacture, sell, prescribe, distribute, dispense, administer, possess, have under his control, abandon, or transport a controlled substance except as expressly allowed by this article.

2. It shall be unlawful for any person to possess or have under his control an official New York state prescription form except as expressly allowed by this article. *Separately amended -- cannot be put together*

*§3304. Prohibited acts.

a. It shall be unlawful for any person to manufacture, sell, prescribe, distribute, dispense, administer, possess, have under his control, abandon, or transport a controlled substance except as expressly allowed by this article.

b. It shall be unlawful for any physician practicing medicine as defined in section sixty-five hundred twenty-one of the education law to prescribe, dispense or administer any amphetamines or sympathomimetic amine drug or compound thereof, designated as a schedule II controlled substance pursuant to section thirty-three hundred six of this article for the exclusive treatment of obesity, weight control or weight loss. A violation of the provisions of this subdivision shall not be grounds for prosecution under article two hundred twenty of the penal law. *Separately amended -- cannot be put together*

§3305. Exemptions.

1. The provisions of this article restricting the possession and control of controlled substances and official New York state prescription forms shall not apply:

(a) to common carriers or to warehousemen, while engaged in lawfully transporting or storing such substances, or to any employee of the same acting within the scope of his employment; or

(b) to public officers or their employees in the lawful performance of their official duties requiring possession or control of controlled substances; or

(c) to temporary incidental possession by employees or agents of persons lawfully entitled to possession, or by persons whose possession is for the purpose of aiding public officers in performing their official duties.

(d) to a duly authorized agent of an incorporated society for the prevention of cruelty to animals or a municipal animal control facility for the limited purpose of buying, possessing, and dispensing to registered and certified personnel, ketamine hydrochloride to anesthetize animals and/or sodium pentobarbital to euthanize animals, including but not limited to dogs and cats. The department shall, consistent with the public interest, register such duly authorized agent and such agent shall file, on a quarterly basis, a report of purchase, possession, and use of ketamine hydrochloride and/or sodium pentobarbital, which report shall be certified by the society for the prevention of cruelty to animals or municipal animal control facility as to its accuracy and validity. This report shall be in addition to any other record keeping and reporting requirements of state and federal law and regulation. The department shall adopt rules and regulations providing for the registration and certification of any individual who, under the direction of the duly authorized and registered agent of an incorporated society for the prevention of cruelty to animals, or municipal animal control facility, uses ketamine hydrochloride to anesthetize animals and/or sodium pentobarbital to euthanize animals, including but not limited to dogs and cats. The department may also adopt such other rules and regulations as shall provide for the safe and efficient use of ketamine hydrochloride and/or sodium pentobarbital by incorporated societies for the prevention of cruelty to animals and animal control facilities. Nothing in this paragraph shall be deemed to waive any other requirement imposed on incorporated societies for the prevention of cruelty to animals and animal control facilities by state and federal law and regulation.

2. The commissioner may, by regulation, provide for the exemption from all or part of the requirements of this article the possession of substances in schedule III or IV and use thereof as part of an industrial process or manufacture of substances other than drugs. The commissioner may impose such conditions upon the granting of such exemption as may be necessary to protect against diversion or misuse of the controlled substance.

3. The commissioner is hereby authorized and empowered to make any rules, regulations and determinations permitting the following categories of persons to obtain, dispense and administer controlled substances under such conditions and in such manner as he shall prescribe:

(a) a person in the employ of the United States government or of any state, territory, district, county, municipal, or insular government, obtaining, possessing, dispensing and administering controlled substances by reason of his official duties;

(b) a master of a ship or a person in charge of any aircraft upon which no physician is regularly employed, or to a physician or surgeon duly licensed in any state, territory, or the District of Columbia to practice his profession, or to a retired commissioned medical officer of the United States army, navy, or public health service, employed upon such ship or aircraft, for the actual medical needs of persons on board such ship or aircraft when not in port.

(c) a person in a foreign country in compliance with the provisions of this article.

4. The provisions of this article with respect to the payment of fees and costs shall not apply to the state of New York or any political subdivision thereof or any agency or instrumentality of either.

§3306. Schedules of controlled substances.

There are hereby established five schedules of controlled substances, to be known as schedules I, II, III, IV and V respectively. Such schedules shall consist of the following substances by whatever name or chemical designation known:

Schedule I. (a) Schedule I shall consist of the drugs and other substances, by whatever official name, common or usual name, chemical name, or brand name designated, listed in this section.

(b) Opiates. Unless specifically excepted or unless listed in another schedule, any of the following opiates, including their isomers, esters, ethers, salts, and salts of isomers, esters, and ethers, whenever the existence of such isomers, esters, ethers and salts is possible within the specific chemical designation (for purposes of 3-methylfentanyl only, the term isomer includes the optical and geometric isomers):

(1) Acetyl-alpha-methylfentanyl (N-{1-(-methyl-2-phenethyl)-4-pipe-ridinyl} -N-phenylacetamide. (2) Acetylmethadol. (3) Allylprodine. (4) Alpha-cetylmethadol (except levo- alphacetylmethadol also known as levo-alpha-ace-tylmethadol, levomethadylacetate or LAAM). (5) Alphameprodine. (6) Alpha-methadol. (7) Alpha-methylfentanyl (N-{1-(alpha-methyl-beta-phenyl) ethyl-4-piperidyl} propionanilide; 1-(1-methyl-2-phenylethyl)-4-(N-propanilido) pipe-ridine). (8) Alpha-methylthiofentanyl (N-{1-methyl-2)2-thienyl) ethyl-4-piperidinyl} -N-phenylpropanamide). (9) Beta-hydroxyfentanyl (N-{1-2 (2-hy-droxy-2-phenethyl)- 4-piperidinyl} -N-phenylpropanamide). (10) Beta-hy-droxy-3-methylfentanyl (other name: N-{1- (2-hydroxy-2-phenethyl)-3-methyl -4-piperidinyl} -N-phenylpropanamide. (11) Benzethidine. (12) Betacetyl-methadol. (13) Betameprodine. (14) Betamethadol. (15) Betaprodine. (16) Clonitazene. (17) Dextromoramide. (18) Diampromide. (19) Diethylthiam-butene. (20) Difenoxin. (21) Dimenoxadol. (22) Dimepheptanol. (23) Dime-thylthiambutene. (24) Dioxaphetyl butyrate. (25) Dipipanone. (26) Ethyl-methylthiambutene. (27) Etonitazene. (28) Etoxeridine. (29) Furethidine. (30) Hydroxypethidine. (31) Ketobemidone. (32) Levomoramide. (33) Levophena-cylmorphan. (34) 3-Methylfentanyl (N-{3-methyl-1-1- (2- phenylethyl -4-piperi-dyl} -N-phenylpropanamide). (35) 3-Methylthiofentanyl (N-{3-methyl-1-(2-thienyl)ethyl -4-piperidinyl} -N-phenylpropanamide). (36) Morpheridine. (37) MPPP (1-methyl -4-phenyl -4-propionoxypiperidine). (38) Noracy-methadol. (39) Norlevorphanol. (40) Normethadone. (41) Norpipanone. (42) Para-fluorofentanyl (N- (4-fluorophenyl) -N-{1- (2-phenethyl) -4-piperidinyl} -propanamide. (43) PEPAP (1- (-2-phenethyl) -4-phenyl -4-acetoxypiperidine. (44) Phenadoxone. (45) Phenampromide. (46) Phenomorphan. (47) Pheno-peridine. (48) Piritramide. (49) Proheptazine. (50) Properidine. (51) Propiram. (52) Racemoramide. (53) Thiofentanyl (N-phenyl-N-{1- (2-thienyl) ethyl -4-piperidinyl} -propanamide. (54) Tilidine. (55) Trimeperidine, (56) 3,4-dichloro-N-{(1-dimethylamino)cyclohexylmethyl}benzamide. Some trade or other names: AH-7921. (57) N-(1-phenethylpiperidin-4-yl)-N-phenyl-acetamide. Some trade or other names: Acetyl Fentanyl. (58) N-(1-phene-thylpiperidin-4-yl)-N-phenylbutyramide. Other name: Butyryl Fentanyl. (59) N-{1-{2-hydroxy-2-(thiophen-2-yl)ethyl}piperidin-4-yl}-N-phenylpropiona mide. Other name: Beta-Hydroxythiofentanyl. (60) N-(1-phenethylpipe-ridin-4-yl)-N-phenylfuran-2-carboxamide. Other name: Furanyl Fentanyl. (61) 3,4-Dichloro-N-{2-(dimethylamino) cyclohexyl}-N-methylbenzamide. Other name: U-47700. (62) N-(1-phenethylpiperidin-4-yl)-N-phenylacrylamide. Other names: Acryl Fentanyl or Acryloylfentanyl. (63) N-(4-fluoro-phenyl)-N-(1-phenethylpiperidin-4-yl)isobutyramide. Other names: 4-fluoro-isobutyryl fentanyl, para-fluoroisobutyryl fentanyl. (64) N-(2-fluorophenyl) -N-(1-phenethylpiperidin-4-yl)propionamide. Other names: ortho-fluorofen-tanyl or 2-fluorofentanyl. (65) N-(1-phenethylpiperidin-4-yl)-N-phenyltetra-hydrofuran-2-carboxamide. Other name: tetrahydrofuranyl fentanyl. (66) 2-methoxy-N-(1-phenethylpiperidin-4-yl)-N-phenylacetamide. Other name: methoxyacetyl fentanyl. (67) N-(1-phenethylpiperidin-4-yl)-N-phenylcyclo-propanecarboxamide. Other name: cyclopropyl fentanyl. (68) N-(4-fluoro

phenyl)-N-(1-phenethylpiperidin-4-yl)butyramide. Other name: para-fluorobu-tyrylfentanyl. (69) N-(2-fluorophenyl)-2-methoxy-N-(1-phenethylpiperi-din-4-yl)acetamide. Other name: Ocfentanil. (70) 1-cyclohexyl-4-(1,2-dipheny-lethyl)piperazine. Other name: MT-45.

(c) Opium derivatives. Unless specifically excepted or unless listed in another schedule, any of the following opium derivatives, its salts, isomers, and salts of isomers whenever the existence of such salts, isomers, and salts of isomers is possible within the specific chemical designation: (1) Acetorphine. (2) Acetyldihydrocodeine. (3) Benzylmorphine. (4) Codeine methylbromide. (5) Codeine-N-oxide. (6) Cyprenorphine. (7) Desomorphine. (8) Dihydro-morphine. (9) Drotebanol. (10) Etorphine (except hydrochloride salt). (11) Heroin. (12) Hydromorphinol. (13) Methyldesorphine. (14) Methyldihydro-morphine. (15) Morphine methylbromide. (16) Morphine methylsulfonate. (17) Morphine-N-oxide. (18) Myrophine. (19) Nicocodeine. (20) Nicomorphine. (21) Normorphine. (22) Pholcodine. (23) Thebacon.

(d) Hallucinogenic substances. Unless specifically excepted or unless listed in another schedule, any material, compound, mixture, or preparation, which contains any quantity of the following hallucinogenic substances, or which contains any of its salts, isomers, and salts of isomers whenever the existence of such salts, isomers, and salts of isomers is possible within the specific chemical designation (for purposes of this paragraph only, the term "isomer" includes the optical, position and geometric isomers):

(EXPLANATION--Within the following chemical designations, character symbol substitutions were made from the original text: "@" = Greek alpha, "&" = Greek beta, """" = prime mark and "/\" = triangle.)

(1) 4-bromo-2, 5-dimethoxy-amphetamine Some trade or other names: 4-bromo -2, 5-dimethoxy-@-methylphenethylamine; 4-bromo-2, 5-DMA. (2) 2, 5-dimethoxyamphetamine Some trade or other names: 2, 5-dimethoxy-@-methylphenethylamine; 2, 5-DMA. (3) 4-methoxyamphetamine Some trade or other names: 4-methoxy-@-methylphenethylamine; paramethoxyamphetamine, PMA. (4) 5-methoxy-3, 4-methylenedioxy - amphetamine. (5) 4-methyl-2, 5-dimethoxy-amphetamine Some trade and other names: 4-methyl-2, 5-dime-thoxy-@-methylphenethylamine; "DOM"; and "STP". (6) 3, 4-methylenedioxy amphetamine. (7) 3, 4, 5-trimethoxy amphetamine. (8) Bufotenine Some trade and other names: 3-(&-dimethylaminoethyl)-5 hydroxindole; 3-(2-dimethyl-aminoethyl)- 5-indolol; N, N-dimethylserotonin; -5-hydroxy-N, N-dimethyl-tryptamine; mappine. (9) Diethyltryptamine Some trade and other names: N, N-diethyltryptamine; DET. (10) Dimethyltryptamine Some trade or other names: DMT. (11) Ibogane Some trade and other names: 7-ethyl-6, 6&, 7, 8, 9, 10, 12, 13-octahydro-2-methoxy-6, 9-methano-5h-pyrido {1',2':1,2} azepino {5,4-b} indole: tabernanthe iboga. (12) Lysergic acid diethylamide. (13) Mescaline. (14) Parahexyl. Some trade or other names: 3-Hexyl-1-hy-droxy-7,8,9,10-tetra hydro-6,6,9-trimethyl-6H-dibenfo{b,d} pyran. (15) Peyote. Meaning all parts of the plant presently classified botanically as Lophophora williamsii Lemaire, whether growing or not, the seeds thereof, any

extract from any part of such plant, and every compound, manufacture, salts, derivative, mixture, or preparation of such plant, its seeds or extracts. (16) N-ethyl-3-piperidyl benzilate. (17) N-methyl-3-piperidyl benzilate. (18) Psilocybin. (19) Psilocyn. (20) Tetrahydrocannabinols. Synthetic tetrahydrocannabinols not derived from the cannabis plant that are equivalents of the substances contained in the plant, or in the resinous extractives of cannabis, sp. and/or synthetic substances, derivatives, and their isomers with similar chemical structure and pharmacological activity such as the following:

     delta 1 cis or trans tetrahydrocannabinol, and their optical isomers

     delta 6 cis or trans tetrahydrocannabinol, and their optical isomers

     delta 3, 4 cis or trans tetrahydrocannabinol, and its optical isomers

     (since nomenclature of these substances is not internationally standardized, compounds of these structures, regardless of numerical designation of atomic positions covered). Any Federal Food and Drug Administration approved product containing tetrahydrocannabinol shall not be considered a synthetic tetrahydrocannabinol.

(21) Ethylamine analog of phencyclidine. Some trade or other names: N-ethyl-1-phenylcyclohexylamine, (1-phenylcyclohexyl) ethylamine, N-(1-phenylcyclohexyl) ethylamine cyclohexamine, PCE. (22) Pyrrolidine analog of phencyclidine. Some trade or other names 1-(1-phenylcyclohexyl)-pyrrolidine; PCPy, PHP. (23) Thiophene analog of phencyclidine. Some trade or other names: 1-{1-(2-thienyl)-cyclohexyl}-piperidine, 2-thienylanalog of phencyclidine, TPCP, TCP. (24) 3,4-methylenedioxymethamphetamine (MDMA). (25) 3,4-methylendioxy-N-ethylamphetamine (also known as N-ethyl-alpha-methyl-3,4 (methylenedioxy) phenethylamine, N-ethyl MDA, MDE, MDEA. (26) N-hydroxy-3,4-methylenedioxyamphetamine (also known as N-hydroxy-alpha-methyl-3,4 (methylenedioxy) phenethylamine, and N-hydroxy MDA. (27) 1-{1- (2-thienyl) cyclohexyl} pyrrolidine. Some other names: TCPY. (28) Alpha-ethyltryptamine. Some trade or other names: etryptamine; Monase; Alpha-ethyl-1H-indole-3-ethanamine; 3- (2-aminobutyl) indole; Alpha-ET or AET. (29) 2,5-dimethoxy-4-ethylamphetamine. Some trade or other names: DOET. (30) 4-Bromo-2,5-dimethoxyphenethylamine. Some trade or other names: 2-(4-bromo-2,5-dimethoxyphenyl)-1-aminoethane; alpha-desmethyl DOB; 2C-B, Nexus. (31) 2,5-dimethoxy-4-(n)-propylthiophenethylamine (2C-T-7), its optical isomers, salts and salts of isomers. *(33) 2-(4-iodo-2,5-dimethoxyphenyl)-N-(2-methoxybenzyl)ethanamine, also known as 25I-NBOMe; 2C-I-NBOMe; 25I; or Cimbi-5. (34) 2-(4-chloro-2,5-dimethoxyphenyl)-N-(2-methoxybenzyl)ethanamine, also known as 25 CNBOMe; 2C-C-NBOMe; 25C; or Cimbi-82, (35) 2-(4-bromo-2,5-dimethoxyphenyl)-N-(2-methoxy benzyl)ethanamine, also known as, 25 BNBOMe; 2C-B-NBOMe; Cimbi-36; (36) 5-methoxy-N,N-dimethyltryptamine. (37) Alpha-methyltryptamine. Some trade or other names: AMT. (38) 5-methoxy-N,N-diisopropyltryptamine. Some trade or other names: 5-MeO-DIPT.   *(Eff.3/31/21,Ch.92,L.2021)*

---

* As in law, (32) omitted.

(e) Depressants. Unless specifically excepted or unless listed in another schedule, any material, compound, mixture, or preparation which contains any quantity of the following substances having a depressant effect on the central nervous system, including its salts, isomers, and salts of isomers whenever the existence of such salts, isomers, and salts of isomers is possible within the specific chemical designation: (1) Mecloqualone. (2) Methaqualone. (3) Phencyclidine. (4) Gamma hydroxybutyric acid, and salt, hydroxybutyric compound, derivative or preparation of gamma hydroxybutyric acid, including any isomers, esters and ethers and salts of isomers, esters and ethers of gamma hydroxybutyric acid, except gamma-butyrolactone, whenever the existence of such isomers, esters and ethers and salts is possible within the specific chemical. (5) Gamma-butyrolactone, including butyrolactone; butyrolactone gamma; 4-butyrolactone; 2(3H)-furanone dihydro; dihydro-2(3H)-furanone; tetrahydro-2-furanone; 1,2-butanolide; 1,4-butanolide; 4-butanolide; gamma-hydroxybutyric acid lactone; 3-hydroxybutyric acid lactone and 4-hydroxybutanoic acid lactone with Chemical Abstract Service number (96-48-0) when any such substance is intended for human consumption. (6) 1,4 butanediol, including butanediol; butane-1,4-diol; 1,4-butylene glyco; butylene glycol; 1,4-dihydroxybutane; 1,4-tetramethylene glycol; tetramethylene glycol; tetramethylene 1,4-diol with Chemical Abstract Service number (110-63-4) when any such substance is intended for human consumption.

(f) Stimulants. Unless specifically excepted or unless listed in another schedule, any material, compound, mixture, or preparation which contains any quantity of the following substances having a stimulant effect on the central nervous system, including its salts, isomers, and salts of isomers: (1) Fenethylline. (2) N-ethylamphetamine. (3) (+ -)cis-4-methylaminorex ((+ -)cis-4,5-dihydro-4-methyl-5-phenyl-2-oxazolamine). (4) N,N-dimethylamphetamine (also known as N,N-alpha-trimethyl-benzeneethanamine; N,N-alpha- trimethyl-phenethylamine). (5) Methcathinone (some other names: 2-(methylamino) - propiophenone; alpha-(methylamino) propiophenone; 2-(methylamino) -1-phenyl-propan-1-one; alpha-N-methylaminopropiophenone; monomethylpropion; ephedrone, N-methylcathinone, methylcathinone; AL-464; AL-422; AL-463 and UR 1432), its salts, optical isomers and salts of optical isomers. (6) Aminorex. Some other names: aminoxaphen; 2-amino-5-phenyl -2-oxazoline; or 4,5-dihydro-5-phenyl-2-oxazolamine. (7) Cathinone. Some trade or other names: 2-amino-1-phenyl-1-propanone, alpha-aminopropiophenone, 2-aminopropiophenone, and norephedrone. (8) N-benzylpiperazine (some other names: BZP; 1-benzylpiper azine), its optical isomers, salts and salts of isomers. (9) 4-methyl-N-methyl cathinone or 4-Methylmethcathinone, also known as Mephedrone. (10) 3,4-methylenedioxypyrovalerone or Methylenedioxypyrovalerone, also known as MDPV. (11) 3,4-methylenedioxy-N-methylcathinone (some other names: methylone). (12) 4-Methoxymethcathinone. (13) 3-Fluoromethcathinone. (14) 4-Fluoromethcathinone. (15) Ethylpropion (Ethcathinone). (16) 2-(2,5-Dimethoxy-4-ethylphenyl)ethanamine (2C-E). (17) 2-(2,5-Dimethoxy-4-methylphenyl)ethanamine (2C-D). (18) 2-(4-Chloro-2,5-dimethoxyphenyl)ethanamine (2C-C). (19) 2-(4-Iodo-2,5-dimethoxyphenyl)ethanamine (2C-I). (20) 2-{4-(Ethylthio)-2,5-

dimethoxyphenyl}ethanamine (2C-T-2). (21) 2-{4-(Isopropylthio)-2,5-dimethoxyphenyl}ethanamine (2C-T-4). (22) 2-(2,5-Dimethoxyphenyl)ethanamine (2C-H). (23) 2-(2,5-Dimethoxy-4-nitro-phenyl)ethanamine (2C-N). (24) 2-(2,5-Dimethoxy-4-(n)-propylphenyl)ethanamine (2C-P).

(g) Synthetic cannabinoids. Unless specifically excepted or unless listed in another schedule, any material, compound, mixture, or preparation, which contains any quantity of the following synthetic cannabinoid substances, or which contains any of its salts, isomers, and salts of isomers whenever the existence of such salts, isomers, and salts of isomers is possible within the specific chemical designation (for purposes of this paragraph only, the term "isomer" includes the optical, position and geometric isomers):

(1) (1-pentyl-1H-indol-3-yl)(2,2,3,3-tetramethylcyclopropyl) methanone. Some trade or other names: UR-144.

(2) {1-(5-fluro-pentyl)-1H-indol-3-yl}(2,2,3,3-tetramethylcyclopropyl) methanone. Some trade names or other names: 5-fluoro-UR-144, XLR11.

(3) N-(1-adamantyl)-1-pentyl-1H-indazole-3-carboxamide. Some trade or other names: APINACA, AKB48.

(4) quinolin-8-yl 1-pentyl-1H-indole-3-carboxylate. Some trade or other names: PB-22; QUPIC.

(5) quinolin-8-yl 1-(5-fluoropentyl)-1H-indole-3-carboxylate. Some trade or other names: 5-fluoro-PB-22; 5F-PB-22.

(6) N-(1-amino-3-methyl-1-oxobutan-2-yl)-1-(4-fluorobenzyl)-1H-indazole-3-carboxamide. Some trade or other names: AB-FUBINACA.

(7) N-(1-amino-3,3-dimethyl-1-oxobutan-2-yl)-1-pentyl-1H-indazole-3-carboxamide. Some trade or other names: ADB-PINACA.

(8) N-(1-amino-3-methyl-1-oxobutan-2-yl)-1-(cyclohexylmethyl)-1H-indazole-3-carboxamide. Some trade or other names: AB-CHMINACA.

(9) N-(1-amino-3-methyl-1-oxobutan-2-yl)-1-pentyl-1H-indazole-3-carboxamide. Some trade or other names: AB-PINACA.

(10) {1-(5-fluoropentyl)-1H-indazol-3-yl}(naphthalen-1-yl)methanone. Some trade or other names: THJ-2201.

(h)(1) Cannabimimetic agents. Unless specifically exempted or unless listed in another schedule, any material, compound, mixture, or preparation that is not approved by the federal food and drug administration (FDA) which contains any quantity of cannabimimetic agents, or which contains their salts, isomers, and salts of isomers whenever the existence of such salts, isomers, and salts of isomers is possible within the specific chemical designation.

(2) As used in this subdivision, the term "cannabimimetic agents" means any substance that is a cannabinoid receptor type 1 (CB1 receptor) agonist as demonstrated by binding studies and functional assays within any of the following structural classes:

(i) 2-(3-hydroxycyclohexyl)phenol with substitution at the 5-position of the phenolic ring by alkyl or alkenyl, whether or not substituted on the cyclohexyl ring to any extent.

(ii) 3-(1-naphthoyl)indole or 3-(1-naphthylmethane)indole by substitution at the nitrogen atom of the indole ring, whether or not further substituted on the indole ring to any extent, whether or not substituted on the naphthoyl or naphthyl ring to any extent.

(iii) 3-(1-naphthoyl)pyrrole by substitution at the nitrogen atom of the pyrrole ring, whether or not further substituted in the pyrrole ring to any extent, whether or not substituted on the naphthoyl ring to any extent.

(iv) 1-(1-naphthylmethylene)indene by substitution of the 3-position of the indene ring, whether or not further substituted in the indene ring to any extent, whether or not substituted on the naphthyl ring to any extent.

(v) 3-phenylacetylindole or 3-benzoylindole by substitution at the nitrogen atom of the indole ring, whether or not further substituted in the indole ring to any extent, whether or not substituted on the phenyl ring to any extent.

(3) Such term includes:

(i) 5-(1,1-dimethylheptyl)-2-{(1R,3S)-3-hydroxycyclohexyl}-phenol (CP-47,497);

(ii) 5-(1,1-dimethyloctyl)-2-{(1R,3S)-3-hydroxycyclohexyl}-phenol (cannabicyclohexanol or CP-47,497 C8-homolog);

(iii) 1-pentyl-3-(1-naphthoyl)indole (JWH-018 and AM678);

(iv) 1-butyl-3-(1-naphthoyl)indole (JWH-073);

(v) 1-hexyl-3-(1-naphthoyl)indole (JWH-019);

(vi) 1-{2-(4-morpholinyl)ethyl}-3-(1-naphthoyl)indole (JWH-200);

(vii) 1-pentyl-3-(2-methoxyphenylacetyl)indole (JWH-250);

(viii) 1-pentyl-3-{1-(4-methoxynaphthoyl)}indole (JWH-081);

(ix) 1-pentyl-3-(4-methyl-1-naphthoyl)indole (JWH-122);

(x) 1-pentyl-3-(4-chloro-1-naphthoyl)indole (JWH-398);

(xi) 1-(5-fluoropentyl)-3-(1-naphthoyl)indole (AM2201);

(xii) 1-(5-fluoropentyl)-3-(2-iodobenzoyl)indole (AM694);

(xiii) 1-pentyl-3-{(4-methoxy)-benzoyl}indole (SR-19 and RCS-4);

(xiv) 1-cyclohexylethyl-3-(2-methoxyphenylacetyl)indole (SR-18 and RCS-8); and

(xv) 1-pentyl-3-(2-chlorophenylacetyl)indole (JWH-203).

Schedule II. (a) Schedule II shall consist of the drugs and other substances, by whatever official name, common or usual name, chemical name, or brand name designated, listed in this section.

(b) Substances, vegetable origin or chemical synthesis. Unless specifically excepted or unless listed in another schedule, any of the following substances whether produced directly or indirectly by extraction from substances of vegetable origin, or independently by means of chemical synthesis, or by a combination of extraction and chemical synthesis:

(1) Opium and opiate, and any salt, compound, derivative, or preparation of opium or opiate, excluding apomorphine, dextrorphan, nalbuphine, nalmefene, naloxone, and naltrexone, and their respective salts, but including the following: 1. Raw opium. 2. Opium extracts. 3. Opium fluid. 4. Powdered opium. 5. Granulated opium. 6. Tincture of opium. 7. Codeine. 8. Ethylmorphine. 9. Etorphine hydrochloride. 10. Hydrocodone (also known as dihydrocodeinone). 11. Hydro-

morphone. 12. Metopon. 13. Morphine. 14. Oxycodone. 15. Oxymorphone. 16. Thebaine. 17. Dihydroetorphine. 18. Oripavine.

(2) Any salt, compound, derivative, or preparation thereof which is chemically equivalent or identical with any of the substances referred to in this section, except that these substances shall not include the isoquinoline alkaloids of opium.

(3) Opium poppy and poppy straw.

(4) Coca leaves and any salt, compound, derivative, or preparation of coca leaves, and any salt, compound, derivative, or preparation thereof which is chemically equivalent or identical with any of these substances including cocaine and ecgonine, their salts, isomers, and salts of isomers, except that the substances shall not include: (A) decocainized coca leaves or extraction of coca leaves, which extractions do not contain cocaine or ecgonine; or (B) {123I} ioflupane.

(5) Concentrate of poppy straw (the crude extract of poppy straw in either liquid, solid or powder form which contains the phenanthrene alkaloids of the opium poppy).

(b-1) Unless specifically excepted or unless listed in another schedule, any material, compound, mixture, or preparation containing any of the following, or their salts calculated as the free anhydrous base or alkaloid, in limited quantities as set forth below:

(1) Not more than three hundred milligrams of dihydrocodeinone (hydrocodone) per one hundred milliliters or not more than fifteen milligrams per dosage unit, with a fourfold or greater quantity of an isoquinoline alkaloid of opium.

(2) Not more than three hundred milligrams of dihydrocodeinone (hydrocodone) per one hundred milliliters or not more than fifteen milligrams per dosage unit, with one or more active nonnarcotic ingredients in recognized therapeutic amounts.

(c) Opiates. Unless specifically excepted or unless in another schedule any of the following opiates, including its isomers, esters, ethers, salts and salts of isomers, esters and ethers whenever the existence of such isomers, esters, ethers, and salts is possible within the specific chemical designation, dextrorphan and levopropoxyphene excepted: (1) Alfentanil. (2) Alphaprodine. (3) Anileridine. (4) Bezitramide. (5) Bulk dextropropoxyphene (non-dosage forms). (6) Carfentanil. (7) Dihydrocodeine. (8) Diphenoxylate. (9) Fentanyl. (10) Isomethadone. (11) Levo-alphacetylmethadol (also known as levo-alpha-acetylmethadol, levomethadylacetate or LAAM). (12) Levomethorphan. (13) Levorphanol. (14) Metazocine. (15) Methadone. (16) Methadone-intermediate, 4-cyano-2-dimethylamino-4, 4-diphenyl butane. (17) Moramide-intermediate, 2-methyl-3-morpholino-1, 1-diphenylpropane-carboxylic (18) Pethidine (meperidine). (19) Pethidine-intermediate-A, 4-cyano-1-methyl-4-phenylpiperidine. (20) Pethidine-intermediate-B, ethyl-4-phenylpiperidine-4-carboxylate. (21) Pethidine-intermediate-C, 1-methyl-4- phenylpiperidine-4-carboxylic acid. (22) Phenazocine. (23) Piminodine. (24) Racemethorphan. (25) Racemorphan. (26) Sufentanil. (27) Remifentanil. (28) Tapentadol, (29) Thiafentanil.

(d) Stimulants. Unless specifically excepted or unless listed in another schedule, any material, compound, mixture, or preparation which contains any quantity of the following substances having a stimulant effect on the central nervous system, including its salts, isomers, and salts of isomers:

(1) Amphetamine.

(2) Methamphetamine.

(3) Phenmetrazine.

(4) Methylphenidate.

(5) Lisdexamfetamine.

(e) Depressants. Unless specifically excepted or unless listed in another schedule, any material, compound, mixture, or preparation which contains any quantity of the following substances having a depressant effect on the central nervous system, including its salts, isomers, and salts of isomers whenever the existence of such salts, isomers, and salts of isomers is possible within the specific chemical designation: (1) Amobarbital. (2) Glutethimide. (3) Pentobarbital. (4) Secobarbital.

(f) Hallucinogenic substances. Nabilone: Another name for nabilone: (+,-)-trans -3-(1,1-dimethylheptyl)-6, 6a, 7, 8, 10, 10a-hexahydro-1-hydroxy-6, 6-dimethyl-9H-dibenzo{b,d}pyran-9-one.

(g) Immediate precursors. Unless specifically excepted or unless listed in another schedule, any material, compound, mixture or preparation which contains any quantity of the following substances:

(1) Immediate precursor to amphetamine and methamphetamine:

(i) Phenylacetone Some trade or other names: phenyl-2-propanone; P2P; benzyl methyl ketone; methyl benzyl ketone;

(2) Immediate precursors to phencyclidine (PCP):

(i) 1-phenylcyclohexylamine;

(ii) 1-piperidinocyclohexanecarbonitrile (PCC).

(3) Immediate precursor to fentanyl:

(i) 4-anilino-N-phenethyl-4-piperidine (ANPP).

(h) Anabolic steroids. Unless specifically excepted or unless listed in another schedule, "anabolic steroid" shall mean any drug or hormonal substance, chemically and pharmacologically related to testosterone (other than estrogens, progestins, corticosteroids and dehydroepiandrosterone) and includes:

(1) 3{beta}, 17-dihydroxy-5a-androstane.

(2) 3{alpha}, 17{beta}-dihydroxy-5a-androstane.

(3) 5{alpha}-androstan-3,17-dione.

(4) 1-androstenediol (3{beta},17{beta}-dihydroxy-5{alpha}-androst-1-ene).

(5) 1-androstenediol (3{alpha},17{beta}-dihydroxy-5{alpha}-androst-1-ene).

(6) 4-androstenediol (3{beta}, 17{beta}-dihydroxy-androst-4-ene).

(7) 5-androstenediol (3{beta}, 17{beta}-dihydroxy-androst-5-ene).

(8) 1-androstenedione ({5{alpha}}-androst-1-en-3,17-dione).

(9) 4-androstenedione (androst-4-en-3,17-dione).

(10) 5-androstenedione (androst-5-en-3,17-dione).

(11) Bolasterone (7{alpha},17{alpha}-dimethyl-17{beta}-hydroxyandrost-4-en-3-one).

(12) Boldenone (17{beta}-hydroxyandrost-1, 4,-diene-3-one).

(13) Boldione (androsta-1,4-diene-3,17-dione).

(14) Calusterone (7{beta}, 17{alpha}-dimethyl-17{beta}-hydroxyandrost-4-en-3-one).

(15) Clostebol (4-chloro-17{beta}-hydroxyandrost-4-en-3-one).

(16) Dehydrochloromethyltestosterone(4-chloro-17{beta}-hydroxy-17 {alpha} -methyl-androst-1, 4-dien-3-one).

(17) {Delta} 1-dihydrotestosterone (a.k.a. '1-testosterone') (17 {beta}-hydroxy-5{alpha}-androst-1-en-3-one).

(18) 4-dihydrotestosterone (17{beta}-hydroxy-androstan-3-one).

(19) Drostanolone (17{beta}-hydroxy-2{alpha}-methyl-5{alpha}-androstan-3-one).

(20) Ethylestrenol (17{alpha}-ethyl-17{beta}-hydroxyestr-4-ene).

(21) Fluoxymesterone (9-fluoro-17{alpha}-methyl-11{beta}, 17 {beta}-dihydroxyandrost-4-en-3-one).

(22) Formebolone (2-formyl-17{alpha}- methyl-11{alpha}, 17{beta}- dihy droxyandrost-1, 4-dien-3-one).

(23) Furazabol (17{alpha}-methyl-17{beta}-hydroxyandrostano{2, 3-c}-furazan).

(24) 13{beta}-ethyl-17{beta}-hyroxygon-4-en-3-one.

(25) 4-hydroxytestosterone (4, 17{beta}-dihydroxy-androst-4-en-3-one).

(26) 4-hydroxy-19-nortestosterone (4,17{beta}-dihydroxy-estr-4-en-3-one).

(27) desoxymethyltestosterone (17{alpha}-methyl-5{alpha}-androst-2-en-17 {beta}-ol) (a.k.a., madoc).

(28) Mestanolone (17{alpha}-methyl-17{beta}-hydroxy-5-androstan-3-one).

(29) Mesterolone (1{alpha}-methyl-17{beta}-hydroxy-{5{alpha}}-androstan-3-one).

(30) Methandienone (17{alpha}-methyl-17{beta}-hydroxyandrost-1,4-dien-3-one).

(31) Methandriol (17{alpha}-methyl-3{beta}, 17{beta}- dihydrox- yandrost-5-ene).

(32) Methenolone (1-methyl-17{beta}-hydroxy-5{alpha}-androst-1-en-3-one).

(33) 17{alpha}-methyl-3{beta}, 17{beta}-dihydroxy-5a-androstane.

(34) 17{alpha}-methyl-3{alpha}, 17{beta}-dihydroxy-5a-androstane.

(35) 17{alpha}-methyl-3{beta}, 17{beta}-dihydroxyandrost-4-ene.

(36) 17{alpha}-methyl-4-hydroxynandrolone (17{alpha}-methyl-4-hydroxy-17{beta}-hydroxyestr-4-en-3-one).

(37) Methyldienolone (17{alpha}-methyl-17{beta}-hydroxyestra-4,9(10)-dien-3-one).

(38) Methyltrienolone (17{alpha}-methyl-17{beta}-hydroxyestra-4,9-11-trien-3-one).

(39) Methyltestosterone (17{alpha}-methyl-17{beta}- hydroxyandrost-4-en-3-one).

(40) Mibolerone (7{alpha},17{alpha}-dimethyl-17{beta}-hydroxyestr-4-en-3-one).

(41) 17{alpha}-methyl-{Delta} 1-dihydrotestosterone (17b{beta}-hydroxy-17{alpha}-methyl-5{alpha}-androst-1-en-3-one)(a.k.a. '17-{alpha}-methyl-1-testosterone').

(42) Nandrolone (17{beta}-hydroxyestr-4-en-3-one).

(43) 19-nor-4-androstenediol (3{beta},17{beta}-dihydroxyestr-4-ene).

(44) 19-nor-4-androstenediol (3{alpha},17{beta}-dihydroxyestr-4-ene).

(45) 19-nor-5-androstenediol (3{beta},17{beta}-dihydroxyestr-5-ene).

(46) 19-nor-5-androstenediol (3{alpha},17{beta}-dihydroxyestr-5-ene).

(47) 19-nor-4,9(10)-androstadienedione (estra-4,9(10)-diene-3,17-dione).

(48) 19-nor-4-androstenedione (estr-4-en-3,17-dione).

(49) 19-nor-5-androstenedione (estr-5-en-3,17-dione).

(50) Norbolethone (13{beta}, 17{alpha}-diethyl-17{beta}-hydroxygon-4-en-3-one).

(51) Norclostebol (4-chloro-17{beta}-hydroxyestr-4-en-3-one).

(52) Norethandrolone (17{alpha}-ethyl-17{beta}-hydroxyestr-4-en-3-one).

(53) Normethandrolone (17{alpha}-methyl-17{beta}-hydroxyestr-4-en-3-one).

(54) Oxandrolone (17{alpha}-methyl-17{beta}-hydroxy-2-oxa-{5{alpha}}-androstan-3-one).

(55) Oxymesterone (17{alpha}-methyl-4, 17{beta}-dihydroxy-androst-4-en-3-one).

(56) Oxymetholone (17 {alpha}-methyl-2-hydroxymethylene-17 {beta}-hydroxy-{5{alpha}}- androstan-3-one).

(57) Stanozolol (17{alpha}-methyl-17{beta}-hydroxy-{5{alpha}}-androst-2-eno{3, 2-c}-pyrazole).

(58) Stenbolone (17{beta}-hydroxy-2-methyl-{5{alpha}}-androst-1-en-3-one).

(59) Testolactone (13-hydroxy-3-oxo-13, 17-secoandrosta-1, 4-dien-17-oic acid lactone).

(60) Testosterone (17{beta}-hydroxyandrost-4-en-3-one).

(61) Tetrahydrogestrinone (13{beta}, 17{alpha}-diethyl-17{beta}-hydroxy gon-4, 9, 11-trien-3-one).

(62) Trenbolone (17{beta}-hydroxyestr-4, 9, 11-trien-3-one).

(63) Any salt, ester or ether of a drug or substance described or listed in this subdivision.

(i) Subdivision (h) of this section shall not include any substance containing anabolic steroids expressly intended for administration through implants to cattle or other nonhuman species and that are approved by the federal food and drug administration solely for such use. Any individual who knowingly and willfully administers to himself or another person, prescribes, dispenses or distributes such substances for other than implantation to cattle or nonhuman species shall be subject to the same penalties as a practitioner who violates the provisions of this section or any other penalties prescribed by law.

Schedule III. (a) Schedule III shall consist of the drugs and other substances, by whatever official name, common or usual name, chemical name, or brand name designated, listed in this section.

(b) Stimulants. Unless specifically excepted or unless listed in another schedule, any material, compound, mixture, or preparation which contains any quantity of the following substances having a stimulant effect on the central nervous system, including its salts, isomers (whether optical, position, or geometric), and salts of such isomers whenever the existence of such salts, isomers, and salts of isomers is possible within the specific chemical designation: (1) Those compounds, mixtures, or preparations in dosage unit form containing any stimulant substances listed in schedule II which compounds, mixtures, or preparations were listed on August twenty-five, nineteen hundred seventy-one, as excepted compounds under title twenty-one, section 308.32 of the code of federal regulations and any other drug of the quantitive composition shown in that list for those drugs or which is the same except that it contains a lesser quantity of controlled substances. (2) Benzphetamine. (3) Chlorphentermine. (4) Clortermine. (6) Phendimetrazine.

(c) Depressants. Unless specifically excepted or unless listed in another schedule, any material, compound, mixture, or preparation which contains any quantity of the following substances having a depressant effect on the central nervous system, including its salts, isomers, and salts of isomers:

(1) Any compound, mixture or preparation containing: (i) Amobarbital; (ii) Secobarbital; (iii) Pentobarbital; or any salt thereof and one or more other active medicinal ingredients which are not listed in any schedule.

(2) Any suppository dosage form containing:

 (i) Amobarbital;

 (ii) Secobarbital;

 (iii) Pentobarbital; or any salt of any of these drugs and approved by the federal food and drug administration for marketing only as a suppository.

(3) Any substance which contains any quantity of a derivative of barbituric acid or any salt thereof.

(4) Chlorhexadol.

(5) Lysergic acid.

(6) Lysergic acid amide.

(7) Methyprylon.

(8) Sulfondiethylmethane.

(9) Sulfonethylmethane.

(10) Sulfonmethane.

(11) Tiletamine and zolazepam or any salt thereof. Some trade or other names for a tiletamine-zolazepam combination product: Telazol. Some trade or other names for tiletamine: 2-(ethylamino) -2-(2-thienyl) -cyclohexanone. Some trade or other names for zolazepam: 4-(2-fluorophenyl) -6,8-dihydro -1, 3, 8i-trimethylpyrazolo-{3,4-e} {1,4} -diazepin-7(1H)-one, flupyrazapon.

(12) Gamma hydroxybutyric acid, and salt, hydroxybutyric compound, derivative or preparation of gamma hydroxybutyric acid, including any isomers, esters and ethers and salts of isomers, esters and ethers of gamma hydroxybutyric acid, contained in a drug product for which an application has been approved under section 505 of the federal food, drug and cosmetic act.

(13) Ketamine, its salts, isomers and salts of isomers (some other names for ketamine: (±)-2-(2-chlorophenyl)-2-(methylamino)- cyclohexanone).

(14) Embutramide.

(d) Nalorphine.

(e) Narcotic drugs. Unless specifically excepted or unless listed in another schedule, any material, compound, mixture, or preparation containing any of the following narcotic drugs, or their salts calculated as the free anhydrous base or alkaloid, in limited quantities as set forth below:

(1) Not more than 1.8 grams of codeine per one hundred milliliters or not more than ninety milligrams per dosage unit, with an equal or greater quantity of an isoquinoline alkaloid of opium.

(2) Not more than 1.8 grams of codeine per one hundred milliliters or not more than ninety milligrams per dosage unit, with one or more active, nonnarcotic ingredients in recognized therapeutic amounts.

(3) Not more than 1.8 grams of dihydrocodeine per one hundred milliliters or not more than ninety milligrams per dosage unit, with one or more active nonnarcotic ingredients in recognized therapeutic amounts.

(4) Not more than three hundred milligrams of ethylmorphine per one hundred milliliters or not more than fifteen milligrams per dosage unit, with one or more active, nonnarcotic ingredients in recognized therapeutic amounts.

(5) Not more than five hundred milligrams of opium per one hundred milliliters or per one hundred grams or not more than twenty-five milligrams per dosage unit, with one or more active, nonnarcotic ingredients in recognized therapeutic amounts.

(6) Not more than fifty milligrams of morphine per one hundred milliliters or per one hundred grams, with one or more active, nonnarcotic ingredients in recognized therapeutic amounts.

(7) Buprenorphine in any quantities.

(f) Dronabinol synthetic in sesame oil and encapsulated in a soft gelatin capsule in a drug product approved for marketing by the U.S. Food and Drug Administration approved product.

Some other names for dronabinol include: (6aR-trans)-6a, 7, 8, 10a-tetrahydro-6, 6, 9-trimethyl-3-pentyl-6H-dibenzo{b,d} pyran-1-ol, or (-) delta-9-(trans) - tetrahydrocannabinol.

(g) Chorionic gonadotropin.

(1) Unless specifically excepted or unless listed in another schedule any material, compound, mixture, or preparation which contains any amount of chorionic gonadotropin.

(2) Paragraph one of this subdivision shall not include any substance containing chorionic gonadotropin expressly intended for administration through implants or injection to cattle or other nonhuman species and that are approved by the federal food and drug administration solely for such use. Any individual who knowingly and willfully administers to himself or another person, prescribes, dispenses or distributes such substances for other than implantation or injection to cattle or nonhuman species shall be subject to the same penalties as a practitioner who violates the provisions of this section or any other penalties prescribed by law.

Schedule IV. (a) Schedule IV shall consist of the drugs and other substances, by whatever official name, common or usual name, chemical name, or brand name designated, listed in this section.

(b) Narcotic drugs. Unless specifically excepted or unless listed in another schedule, any material, compound, mixture, or preparation containing any of the following narcotic drugs, or their salts calculated as the free anhydrous base or alkaloid, in limited quantities as set forth below:

(1) Not more than one milligram of difenoxin and not less than twenty-five micrograms of atropine sulfate per dosage unit.

(2) Dextropropoxyphene (alpha-(+)-4-dimethylamino-1, 2-diphenyl-3-methyl-2-propionoxybutane).

(c) Depressants. Unless specifically excepted or unless listed in another schedule, any material, compound, mixture, or preparation which contains any quantity of the following substances, including its salts, isomers, and salts of isomers whenever the existence of such salts, isomers, and salts of isomers is possible within the specific chemical designation: (1) Alprazolam. (2) Barbital. (3) Bromazepam. (4) Camazepam. (5) Chloral betaine. (6) Chloral hydrate. (7) Chlordiazepoxide. (8) Clobazam. (9) Clonazepam. (10) Clorazepate. (11) Clotiazepam. (12) Cloxazolam. (13) Delorazepam. (14) Diazepam. (15) Estazolam. (16) Ethchlorvynol. (17) Ethinamate. (18) Ethyl Loflazepate. (19) Fludiazepam. (20) Flunitrazepam. (21) Flurazepam. (22) Halazepam. (23) Haloxazolam. (24) Ketazolam. (25) Loprazolam. (26) Lorazepam. (27) Lormetazepam. (28) Mebutamate. (29) Medazepam. (30) Meprobamate. (31) Methohexital. (32) Methylphenobarbital (mephobarbital). (33) Nimetazepam. (34) Nitrazepam. (35) Nordiazepam. (36) Oxazepam. (37) Oxazolam. (38) Paraldehyde. (39) Petrichoral. (40) Phenobarbital. (41) Pinazepam. (42) Prazepam. (43) Temazepam. (44) Tetrazepam. (45) Triazolam. (46) Midazolam. (47) Quazepam. (48) Zolpidem. (49) Dichloralphenazone. (50) Zaleplon. (51) Zopiclone (eszopiclone). (52) Fospropofol. (53) Carisoprodol.

*(d) Fenfluramine. Any material, compound, mixture, or preparation which contains any quantity of the following substances, including its salts, isomers (whether optical, position, or geometric), and salts of such isomers, whenever the existence of such salts, isomers and salts of isomers is possible:

(1) Fenfluramine.   *Repealed upon the removal of fenfluramine and its salts and isomers from Schedule IV of the federal Controlled Substances Act*

(e) Stimulants. Unless specifically excepted or unless listed in another schedule, any material, compound, mixture, or preparation which contains any quantity of the following substances having a stimulant effect on the central nervous system, including its salts, isomers, and salts of such isomers: (1) Cathine ((+) - norpseudoephedrine). (2) Diethylpropion. (3) Fencamfamin. (4) Fenproporex. (5) Mazindol. (6) Mefenorex. (7) Pemoline (including organometallic complexes and chelates thereof). (8) Phentermine. (9) Pipradrol. (10) SPA ((-))-1-dimethylamino-1, 2-diphenylethane). (11) Modafinil. (12) Sibutramine.

(f) Other substances. Unless specifically excepted or unless listed in another schedule, any material, compound, mixture or preparation which contains any quantity of the following substances, including its salts:

(1) Pentazocine.

(2) Butorphanol (including its optical isomers).

(3) Tramadol in any quantities.

Schedule V. (a) Schedule V shall consist of the drugs and other substances, by whatever official name, common or usual name, chemical name, or brand name designated, listed in this section.

(b) Narcotic drugs containing nonnarcotic active medicinal ingredients. Any compound, mixture, or preparation containing any of the following narcotic drugs, or their salts calculated as the free anhydrous base or alkaloid, in limited quantities as set forth below, which shall include one or more non-narcotic active medicinal ingredients in sufficient proportion to confer upon the compound, mixture, or preparation valuable medicinal qualities other than those possessed by narcotic drugs alone:

(1) Not more than two hundred milligrams of codeine per one hundred milliliters or per one hundred grams.

(2) Not more than one hundred milligrams of dihydrocodeine per one hundred milliliters or per one hundred grams.

(3) Not more than one hundred milligrams of ethylmorphine per one hundred milliliters or per one hundred grams.

(4) Not more than 2.5 milligrams of diphenoxylate and not less than twenty-five micrograms of atropine sulfate per dosage unit.

(5) Not more than one hundred milligrams of opium per one hundred milliliters or per one hundred grams.

(6) Not more than 0.5 milligram of difenoxin and not less than twenty-five micrograms of atropine sulfate per dosage unit.

(c) Stimulants. Unless specifically exempted or excluded or unless listed in another schedule, any material, compound, mixture, or preparation which contains any quantity of the following substances having a stimulant effect on the central nervous system, including its salts, isomers and salts of isomers:

(1) Pyrovalerone.

(d) Depressants. Unless specifically exempted or excluded or unless listed in another schedule, any material, compound, mixture, or preparation which contains any quantity of the following substances having a depressant effect on the central nervous system, including its salts, isomers, and salts of isomers:

(1) Ezogabine {N-{2-amino-4-(4-fluorobenzylamino)-phenyl}-carbamic acid ethyl ester}.

(2) Lacosamide {(R)-2-acetoamido-N-benzyl-3-methoxy-propionamide}.

(3) Pregabalin {(S)-3-(aminomethyl)-5-methylhexanoic acid}.

§3307. Exception from schedules.

1. The commissioner may, by regulation, except any compound, mixture, or preparation containing any depressant substance in paragraph (a) of schedule III or in schedule IV from the application of all or any part of this article if (1) the compound, mixture, or preparation contains one or more active medicinal ingredients not having a depressant effect on the central nervous system, and

(2) such ingredients are included therein in such combinations, quantity, proportion, or concentration as to vitiate the potential for abuse of the substances which do have a depressant effect on the central nervous system.

2. The commissioner may, by regulation, reclassify as a schedule III substance, any compound, mixture or preparation containing any stimulant substance listed in paragraph (c) of schedule II, if (a) the compound, mixture or preparation contains one or more active medicinal ingredients not having a stimulant effect on the central nervous system; and

(b) such ingredients are included therein in such combinations, quantity, proportion or concentration as to vitiate the potential for abuse of the substances which do have a stimulant effect on the central nervous system.

3. The commissioner may, by regulation, except any compound, mixture or preparation containing a narcotic antagonist substance from the application of all or any part of this article if (1) such compound, mixture or preparation has no potential for abuse, and (2) such compound, mixture or preparation has been excepted or exempted from control under the Federal Controlled Substances Act.

4. The commissioner may by regulation exempt or reclassify any compound, mixture or preparation containing any substance listed in subdivision (h) or (j) of Schedule II of section three thousand three hundred six of this article as a Schedule III, IV or V substance if (a) the compound, mixture or preparation contains one or more active medicinal ingredients not found in subdivision (h) or (j) of Schedule II of section three thousand three hundred six of this article; and (b) such ingredients are included therein in such combinations, quantity, proportion or concentration as to substantially reduce the potential for abuse.

5. The commissioner may by regulation or emergency regulation, reclassify any compound, mixture or preparation containing any substance listed in Schedule I of section three thousand three hundred six of this title as a Schedule II, III, IV or V substance, or exempt it from this article, if that same compound, mixture or preparation is redesignated or rescheduled other than under Schedule I under the federal Controlled Substances Act, or deleted as a controlled substance under the federal Controlled Substances Act. If the commissioner acts under this subdivision and does not exempt the compound, mixture or preparation from this article, he or she may only reclassify it to a newly created subdivision in the same numbered schedule or a higher numbered schedule than to which it is redesignated or rescheduled under the federal act.

6. The commissioner shall establish minimum standards for the storage, reporting, ordering and record keeping of controlled substances specified in subdivision (b-1) of schedule II of section thirty-three hundred six of this article by manufacturers and distributors as if such substances were set forth in schedule III of section thirty-three hundred six of this article.

§3308. Powers and duties of the commissioner.

1. The commissioner, and any representative authorized by him, shall have the power to administer oaths, compel the attendance of witnesses and the

production of books, papers and records and to take proof and testimony concerning all matters within the jurisdiction of the department.

2. The commissioner is hereby authorized and empowered to make any rules, regulations and determinations which in his judgment may be necessary or proper to supplement the provisions of this article to effectuate the purposes and intent thereof or to clarify its provisions so as to provide the procedure or details to secure effective and proper enforcement of its provisions.

3. No rule or regulation hereunder shall become effective unless, at least twenty-one days prior to the proposed effective date, persons who have conveyed to the department in writing a request to be notified of proposed changes and additions to the department's rules and regulations under this article have been provided with the text of such proposed rules and regulations and have been given an opportunity to comment in writing thereon.

4. The rules, regulations and determinations, when made and promulgated by the commissioner, shall be the rules, regulations and determinations of the department and, until modified or rescinded, shall have the force and effect of law. It shall be the duty of the department, to enforce all of the provisions of this article and all of the rules, regulations and determinations made thereunder.

5. Notwithstanding any inconsistent provision of this article, the commissioner in consultation with the commissioner of education is hereby authorized to promulgate regulations regarding the prescribing, dispensing, use and transmission of electronic prescriptions, which may be prescribed and dispensed in lieu of an official New York state prescription.

6. The commissioner in consultation with the commissioner of education is hereby authorized to promulgate regulations regarding the dispensing of out-of-state prescriptions.

§3309. Opioid overdose prevention.

1. The commissioner is authorized to establish standards for approval of any opioid overdose prevention program, and opioid antagonist prescribing, dispensing, distribution, possession and administration pursuant to this section which may include, but not be limited to, standards for program directors, appropriate clinical oversight, training, record keeping and reporting.

2. Notwithstanding any inconsistent provisions of section sixty-five hundred twelve of the education law or any other law, the purchase, acquisition, possession or use of an opioid antagonist pursuant to this section shall not constitute the unlawful practice of a profession or other violation under title eight of the education law or this article.

3. (a) As used in this section:

(i) "Opioid antagonist" means a drug approved by the Food and Drug Administration that, when administered, negates or neutralizes in whole or in part the pharmacological effects of an opioid in the body. "Opioid antagonist" shall be limited to naloxone and other medications approved by the department for such purpose.

(ii) "Health care professional" means a person licensed, registered or authorized pursuant to title eight of the education law to prescribe prescription drugs.

(iii) "Pharmacist" means a person licensed or authorized to practice pharmacy pursuant to article one hundred thirty-seven of the education law.

(iv) "Opioid antagonist recipient" or "recipient" means a person at risk of experiencing an opioid-related overdose, or a family member, friend or other person in a position to assist a person experiencing or at risk of experiencing an opioid-related overdose, or an organization registered as an opioid overdose prevention program pursuant to this section or any person or entity or any person employed by the person or entity.

(v) As used in this section, "entity" includes, but is not limited to, a school district, public library, board of cooperative educational services, county vocational education and extension board, charter school, non-public elementary or secondary school, restaurant, bar, retail store, shopping mall, barber shop, beauty parlor, theater, sporting or event center, inn, hotel or motel.

(b)(i) A health care professional may prescribe by a patient-specific or non-patient-specific prescription, dispense or distribute, directly or indirectly, an opioid antagonist to an opioid antagonist recipient.

(ii) A pharmacist may dispense an opioid antagonist, through a patient-specific or non-patient-specific prescription pursuant to this paragraph, to an opioid antagonist recipient.

(iii) An opioid antagonist recipient may possess an opioid antagonist obtained pursuant to this paragraph, may distribute such opioid antagonist to a recipient, and may administer such opioid antagonist to a person the recipient reasonably believes is experiencing an opioid overdose.

(iv) The provisions of this paragraph shall not be deemed to require a prescription for any opioid antagonist that does not otherwise require a prescription; nor shall it be deemed to limit the authority of a health care professional to prescribe, dispense or distribute, or of a pharmacist to dispense, an opioid antagonist under any other provision of law.

(v) Any pharmacy with twenty or more locations in the state, shall either: (1) pursue or maintain a non-patient-specific prescription with an authorized health care professional to dispense an opioid antagonist to a consumer upon request, as authorized by this section; or (2) register with the department as an opioid overdose prevention program.

3-a. Any distribution of opioid antagonists through this program shall include an informational card or sheet. The informational card or sheet shall include, at a minimum, information on:

(a) how to recognize symptoms of an opioid overdose;

(b) steps to take prior to and after an opioid antagonist is administered, including calling first responders;

(c) the number for the toll free office of addiction services and supports HOPE line; *(Eff.12/22/21,Ch.741,L.2021)*

(d) how to access the office of addiction services and supports' website; *(Eff.12/22/21,Ch.741,L.2021)*

(e) the application of good samaritan protections provided in section three thousand-a of this chapter; and

(f) any other information deemed relevant by the commissioner.

The educational card shall be provided in languages other than English as deemed appropriate by the commissioner. The department shall make such informational cards available to the opioid overdose prevention programs.

4. (a) Use of an opioid antagonist pursuant to this section shall be considered first aid or emergency treatment for the purpose of any statute relating to liability.

(b) A recipient, opioid overdose prevention program, person or entity, or any person employed by the person or entity, acting reasonably and in good faith in compliance with this section, shall not be subject to criminal, civil or administrative liability solely by reason of such action.

5. The commissioner shall publish findings on statewide opioid and alcohol overdose data that reviews overdose death rates and other information to ascertain changes in the cause and rates of opioid and alcohol overdoses, including fatal opioid and alcohol overdoses. The report shall be submitted annually, on or before October first, to the governor, the temporary president of the senate, the speaker of the assembly and the chairs of the senate and assembly health committees, and shall be made public on the department's internet website. The report shall include, at a minimum, the following information on a county basis: *(Eff.12/22/21,Ch.741,L.2021)*

(a) information on opioid and alcohol overdoses and opioid and alcohol overdose deaths, including age, gender, ethnicity, and geographic location;
                                                         (Eff.12/22/21,Ch.741,L.2021)

(b) data on emergency room utilization for the treatment of opioid and alcohol overdose;   *(Eff.12/22/21,Ch.741,L.2021)*

(c) data on utilization of pre-hospital services;

(d) data on the dispensing and utilization of opioid antagonists; and

(e) any other information necessary to ascertain the success of the program, areas of the state which are experiencing particularly high rates of overdoses, ways to determine if services, resources and responses in particular areas of the state are having a positive impact on reducing overdoses, and ways to further reduce overdoses.

6. The commissioner shall provide the current information and data specified by each type of drug included in the report required by subdivision five of this section to each county every three months. Such information and data shall be posted on the office of addiction services and supports' website and may be utilized by a county or any combination thereof as it works to address the opioid epidemic.   *(Eff.12/22/21,Ch.741,L.2021)*

*7. With the first prescription to a particular patient of an opioid of each year for use in a setting other than a general hospital or nursing home under article twenty-eight of this chapter or facility under article thirty-one of the mental hygiene law, or when a practitioner is prescribing a controlled substance to a patient under the care of hospice as defined by section four thousand two of this chapter, the prescriber shall prescribe an opioid antagonist when any of the following risk factors are present: (a) a history of substance use disorder;

(b) high dose or cumulative prescriptions that result in ninety morphine milligram equivalents or higher per day; (c) concurrent use of opioids and benzodiazepine or nonbenzodiazepine sedative hypnotics.

(Eff.6/27/22,Ch.803,L.2021)

§3309-a.   Prescription pain medication awareness program.

1. There is hereby established within the department a prescription pain medication awareness program to educate the public and health care practitioners about the risks associated with prescribing and taking controlled substance pain medications.

2. Within the amounts appropriated, the commissioner, in consultation with the commissioner of the office of alcoholism and substance abuse services, shall develop and conduct a public health education media campaign designed to alert youth, parents and the general population about the risks associated with prescription pain medications and the need to properly dispose of any unused medication. In developing this campaign, the commissioner shall consult with and use information provided by the work group established pursuant to subdivision four of this section and other relevant professional organizations. The campaign shall include an internet website providing information for parents, children and health care professionals on the risks associated with taking opioids and resources available to those needing assistance with prescription pain medication addiction. Such website shall also provide information regarding where individuals may properly dispose of controlled substances in their community and include active links to further information and resources. The campaign shall begin no later than September first, two thousand twelve.

3. Course work or training in pain management, palliative care and addiction. (a) Every person licensed under title eight of the education law to treat humans, registered under the federal controlled substances act and in possession of a registration number from the drug enforcement administration, United States Department of Justice or its successor agency, and every medical resident who is prescribing under a facility registration number from the drug enforcement administration, United States Department of Justice or its successor agency, shall, on or before July first, two thousand seventeen and once within each three year period thereafter, complete three hours of course work or training in pain management, palliative care, and addiction approved by the department.

(b) Every person licensed on or after July first, two thousand seventeen under title eight of the education law to treat humans, registered under the federal controlled substances act and in possession of a registration number from the drug enforcement administration, United States Department of Justice or its successor agency, and every medical resident who begins prescribing under a facility registration number from the drug enforcement administration, United States Department of Justice or its successor agency on or after July first, two thousand seventeen, shall complete such course work or training within one year of such registration and once within each three year period thereafter.

(c) The commissioner, in consultation with the department of education and the office of alcoholism and substance abuse services, shall establish standards and review and approve course work or training in pain management, palliative care, and addiction and shall publish information related to such standards, course work or training on the department's website.

(d) Existing course work or training, including course work or training developed by a nationally recognized health care professional, specialty, or provider association, or nationally recognized pain management association, may be considered in implementing this subdivision.

(e) Nothing shall preclude course work or training that meets the requirements of paragraph (c) of this subdivision from counting toward this requirement if taken online.

(f) Course work or training shall include, but not be limited to: state and federal requirements for prescribing controlled substances; pain management; appropriate prescribing; managing acute pain; palliative medicine; prevention, screening and signs of addiction; responses to abuse and addiction; and end of life care.

(g) Each licensed person required by this subdivision to complete course work or training shall document to the department by attestation on a form prescribed by the commissioner that such licensed person has completed the course work or training required by this subdivision. For medical residents who are prescribing under a facility registration number from the drug enforcement administration, United States Department of Justice or its successor agency, such attestation shall be made by the facility.

(h) The department shall institute a procedure for application for an exemption from said requirement. The department may provide an exemption from the course work and training required by this subdivision to any such licensed person who: (i) clearly demonstrates to the department's satisfaction that there would be no need for him or her to complete such course work or training; or (ii) that he or she has completed course work or training deemed by the department to be equivalent to the course work or training approved by the department pursuant to this subdivision.

(i) Nothing herein shall preclude such course work or training in pain management, palliative care, and addiction from counting toward continuing education requirements under title eight of the education law to the extent provided in the regulations of the commissioner of education.

(j) Nothing herein shall preclude such course work or training in pain management, palliative care, and addiction from counting toward continuing education requirements of a nationally accredited medical board to the extent acceptable to such board.

4. Establish a work group, no later than June first, two thousand twelve, which shall be composed of experts in the fields of palliative and chronic care pain management and addiction medicine. Members of the work group shall receive no compensation for their services, but shall be allowed actual and necessary expenses in the performance of their duties pursuant to this section. The work group shall:

(a) Report to the commissioner regarding the development of recommendations and model courses for continuing medical education, refresher courses and other training materials for licensed health care professionals on appropriate use of prescription pain medication. Such recommendations, model courses and other training materials shall be submitted to the commissioner, who shall make such information available for the use in medical education, residency programs, fellowship programs, and for use in continuing medication education programs no later than January first, two thousand thirteen. Such recommendations also shall include recommendations on: (i) educational and continuing medical education requirements for practitioners appropriate to address prescription pain medication awareness among health care professionals; (ii) continuing education requirements for pharmacists related to prescription pain medication awareness; and (iii) continuing education in palliative care as it relates to pain management, for which purpose the work group shall consult the New York state palliative care education and training council;

(b) No later than January first, two thousand thirteen, provide outreach and assistance to health care professional organizations to encourage and facilitate continuing medical education training programs for their members regarding appropriate prescribing practices for the best patient care and the risks associated with over prescribing and under prescribing pain medication;

(c) Provide information to the commissioner for use in the development and continued update of the public awareness campaign, including information, resources, and active web links that should be included on the website; and

(d) Consider other issues deemed relevant by the commissioner, including how to protect and promote the access of patients with a legitimate need for controlled substances, particularly medications needed for pain management by oncology patients, and whether and how to encourage or require the use or substitution of opioid drugs that employ tamper-resistance technology as a mechanism for reducing abuse and diversion of opioid drugs.

5. On or before September first, two thousand twelve, the commissioner, in consultation with the commissioner of the office of alcoholism and substance abuse services, the commissioner of education, and the executive secretary of the state board of pharmacy, shall add to the workgroup such additional members as appropriate so that the workgroup may provide guidance in furtherance of the implementation of the I-STOP act. For such purposes, the workgroup shall include but not be limited to consumer advisory organizations, health care practitioners and providers, oncologists, addiction treatment providers, practitioners with experience in pain management, pharmacists and pharmacies, and representatives of law enforcement agencies.

6. The commissioner shall report to the governor, the temporary president of the senate and the speaker of the assembly no later than March first, two thousand thirteen, and annually thereafter, on the work group's findings. The report shall include information on opioid over-dose deaths, emergency room utilization for the treatment of opioid overdose, the utilization of pre-hospital addiction services and recommendations to reduce opioid addiction and the consequences thereof.

TITLE II
MANUFACTURE AND DISTRIBUTION
OF CONTROLLED SUBSTANCES

Section

3310.   Licenses for manufacture or distribution of controlled substances.

§3310. Licenses for manufacture or distribution of controlled substances.

1. No person shall manufacture or distribute a controlled substance in this state without first having obtained a license to do so from the department.

2. A license issued under this section shall be valid for two years from the date of issue, except that in order to facilitate the renewals of such licenses, the commissioner may upon the initial application for a license, issue some licenses which may remain valid for a period of time greater than two years but not exceeding an additional eleven months.

3. The fee for a license under this section shall be one thousand two hundred dollars; provided however, if the license is issued for a period greater than two years the fee shall be increased, pro rata, for each additional month of validity.

4. Licenses issued under this section shall be effective only for and shall specify:

(a) the name and address of the licensee;

(b) the nature of the controlled substances, either by name or schedule, or both, which may be manufactured or distributed;

(c) whether manufacture or distribution or both such activities are permitted by the license.

5. Upon application of a licensee, a license may be amended to allow the licensee to relocate within the state or to add a manufacturing or distributing activity or to add further substances or schedules to the manufacturing or distribution activity permitted thereunder. The fee for such amendment shall be two hundred fifty dollars.

This page intentionally left blank.

VEHICLE & TRAFFIC LAW
ARTICLE 19
LICENSING OF DRIVERS

Section
509.   Violations.

§509. Violations.

1. Except while operating a motor vehicle during the course of a road test conducted pursuant to the provisions of this article, no person shall operate or drive a motor vehicle upon a public highway of this state or upon any sidewalk or to or from any lot adjacent to a public garage, supermarket, shopping center or car washing establishment or to or from or into a public garage or car washing establishment unless he is duly licensed pursuant to the provisions of this chapter.

1-a. Whenever a license is required to operate a commercial motor vehicle, no person shall operate a commercial motor vehicle without the proper endorsements for the specific vehicle being operated or for the passengers or type of cargo being transported.

2. Whenever a license is required to operate a motor vehicle, no person shall operate a motor vehicle unless he is the holder of a class of license which is valid for the operation of such vehicle.

3. Whenever a permit or license is required to operate a motor vehicle, no person shall operate any motor vehicle in violation of any restriction contained on, or applicable to, the permit or license.

4. No person shall knowingly authorize or permit a motor vehicle owned by him or in his charge to be operated in violation of subdivisions one, two or three of this section.

5. No person shall hold more than one unexpired license issued by the commissioner at any one time. The holding of a license of one class and a learner's permit for another class at the same time shall not be deemed a violation of this subdivision.

6. No licensee shall voluntarily permit any other person to use his license, nor shall any person at any time possess or use any forged, fictitious or illegally obtained license, or use any license belonging to another person.

7. No person shall operate a commercial motor vehicle without being in possession of the appropriate license for the motor vehicle being operated.

7-a. No person shall operate a commercial motor vehicle while knowing or having reason to know that he or she is not medically certified, as required, in accordance with the federal motor carrier safety improvement act of 1999 and Part 383.71(h) of title 49 of the code of federal regulations.

8. No licensee shall fail to notify the commissioner in writing of a change of residence as required by this article.

9. Whenever notice of disability is required to be given to the commissioner as required by this article, no person shall operate any motor vehicle until such notice has been given.

92

10. No person shall hold an unexpired license issued by the commissioner while holding a driver's license issued by any other jurisdiction. This prohibition shall not apply to any license which by its terms is valid only within the jurisdiction of issuance. Nor shall it apply if such person has informed the commissioner of such multiple licenses and the commissioner has determined that it is necessary for such person to hold more than one license to comply with the laws of each of the jurisdictions in which such licenses were issued. The foregoing exceptions shall not be applicable to commercial driver's licenses after December thirty-first, nineteen hundred eighty-nine.

11. A violation of any provision of this section shall be punishable by a fine of not less than seventy-five nor more than three hundred dollars, or by imprisonment for not more than fifteen days, or by both such fine and imprisonment except, if the violation consists of failure to renew a license which was valid within sixty days, the fine shall be not more than forty dollars, and except that a violation of subdivision seven or eight of this section shall be punishable by a fine of not more than seventy-five dollars.

12. A violation of subdivision two of this section involving the operation for hire of any vehicle as a taxicab, livery as defined in section one hundred twenty-one-e of this chapter, coach, limousine, van or wheelchair accessible van or tow truck within the state without the appropriate license therefor, shall be punishable by a fine of not less than two hundred twenty-five dollars nor more than four hundred fifty dollars. A person who operates a vehicle for hire without the appropriate license therefor pursuant to subdivision two of this section after having been convicted of such a violation within the preceding five years shall be punished by a fine of not less than three hundred seventy-five dollars nor more than seven hundred fifty dollars. A person who operates a vehicle for hire without the appropriate license therefor pursuant to subdivision two of this section after having been convicted two or more times of such a violation within the preceding ten years shall be punished by a fine of not less than seven hundred fifty dollars nor more than one thousand five hundred dollars.

ARTICLE 19-A
SPECIAL REQUIREMENTS FOR BUS DRIVERS

Section
509-a.	Definitions.
509-h.	Operation by person not licensed to drive a bus.
509-i.	Notification of a conviction resulting from a violation of this chapter in this state or a motor vehicle conviction in another state and license revocation.
509-j.	Compliance required.
509-k.	Ill or fatigued operator.
509-l.	Drugs, controlled substance and intoxicating liquor.
509-m.	Duties of the department.
509-n.	Exempt carriers; reporting requirements.
509-o.	Penalties.

§509-a. Definitions.

As used in this article the term:

(1) bus shall mean every motor vehicle, owned, leased, rented or otherwise controlled by a motor carrier, which (a) is a school bus as defined in section one hundred forty-two of this chapter or has a seating capacity of more than ten adult passengers in addition to the driver and which is used for the transportation of persons under the age of twenty-one or persons of any age who are mentally or physically disabled to a place of vocational, academic or religious instruction or religious service including nursery schools, day care centers and camps, (b) is required to obtain approval to operate in the state as a common or contract carrier of passengers by motor vehicle from the commissioner of transportation, or the interstate commerce commission, (c) is regulated as a bus line by a city that has adopted an ordinance, local law or charter to regulate or franchise bus line operations pursuant to subdivision four of section eighty of the transportation law, (d) is regulated as a van service or other common carrier of passengers by motor vehicle covered under article seven of the transportation law by a city with a population of over one million pursuant to an ordinance or local law adopted pursuant to subdivision five of section eighty of the transportation law or (e) is operated by a transit authority or municipality and is used to transport persons for hire. Provided, however, that bus shall not mean an authorized emergency vehicle operated in the course of an emergency, or a motor vehicle used in the transportation of agricultural workers to and from their place of employment;

(2) driver or bus driver shall mean every person: (i) who is self-employed and drives a bus for hire or profit; or (ii) who is employed by a motor carrier and operates a bus owned, leased or rented by such employer; or (iii) who as a volunteer drives a bus which is owned, leased or rented by a motor carrier. Provided, however, bus driver shall not include those persons who are engaged in the maintenance, repair or garaging of such buses and in the course of their duties must incidentally drive a bus without passengers, or who, as a volunteer, drive a bus with passengers for less than thirty days each year;

(3) motor carrier shall mean any person, corporation, municipality, or entity, public or private, who directs one or more bus drivers and who operates a bus wholly within or partly within and partly without this state in connection with the business of transporting passengers for hire or in the operation or administration of any business, or place of vocational, academic or religious instruction or religious service for persons under the age of twenty-one or persons of any age who are mentally disabled including nursery schools, day care centers and camps, or public agency, except such out-of-state public or governmental operators who may be exempted from the provisions of this article by the commissioner through regulation promulgated by the commissioner;

(4) intoxicating liquor shall mean and include, alcohol, spirits, liquor, wine, beer and cider having alcoholic content;

(5) drug shall mean any substance listed in section thirty-three hundred six of the public health law not dispensed or consumed pursuant to a lawful prescription;

(6) controlled substance shall mean any substance listed in section thirty-three hundred six of the public health law not dispensed or consumed pursuant to lawful prescription.

(7) accident shall include any accident with another vehicle, object or person, which occurs in this state or elsewhere, in which any person is killed or injured, or in which damage to the property of any one person, including the operator, in excess of one thousand five hundred dollars is sustained, or in which damage in excess of two thousand five hundred dollars is sustained to any bus as defined in section one hundred four of this chapter; provided however that accidents occurring outside this state shall not be recorded on the driver's license record.

§509-h. Operation by person not licensed to drive a bus.

The motor carrier shall not knowingly permit any person to operate a bus carrying passengers unless the driver meets all of the requirements of this article; except that a motor carrier may permit a conditional school bus driver who is not otherwise disqualified under the provisions of this article to operate a bus for a period not to exceed ninety days or a longer period if granted a written extension of such ninety day period by the department pursuant to regulations established by the commissioner. Such regulation shall authorize extension for at least that period of time necessary to review information regarding the prior criminal history of the applicant.

§509-i. Notification of a conviction resulting from a violation of this chapter in this state or a motor vehicle conviction in another state and license revocation.

1. A driver who receives a notice that his or her license, permit or privilege to operate a motor vehicle has been revoked, suspended or withdrawn or who is convicted of a violation of such provisions of this chapter as shall constitute a misdemeanor or a felony in any jurisdiction shall notify the motor carrier that employs such person of the contents of the notice before the end of the business day following the day he or she received it. A driver who fails to notify his or her employer of such suspension, revocation or conviction of a violation of such provisions of this chapter as shall constitute a misdemeanor or a felony shall be subject to a five (5) working day suspension, or a suspension equivalent to the number of working days such driver was not in compliance with this article, whichever is longer.

1-a. A driver who is convicted of a traffic infraction in any jurisdiction shall notify his or her employer within five (5) working days from the date of conviction. A driver who fails to notify his or her employer of such conviction within the five (5) working day period shall be subject to a five (5) working day suspension; provided, however, that a first such infraction occurring on or before September sixteenth, nineteen hundred eighty-six, shall not subject such violator to the said suspension.

1-b. A driver who is involved in an accident of a nature or type set forth in section five hundred nine-a of this article in any jurisdiction shall notify his or her employer within five working days from the date of the accident. A driver who fails to notify his or her employer of such accident within the five working day period shall be subject to a five working day suspension.

2. Any driver who is convicted of an offense listed in section five hundred nine-c of this article that would disqualify such driver from operating a bus shall provide notice of such conviction in writing by the following business day to the motor carrier that employs such person. The motor carrier shall not permit any driver who fails to provide such notice to operate a bus.

3. The commissioner upon receipt of information that a driver's license, permit or privilege to operate a motor vehicle has been revoked, suspended or withdrawn in this state or elsewhere shall notify all motor carriers who have notified the commissioner of the employment of such driver; and may, if requested by a political subdivision which contracts with a motor carrier for the transportation of school children, provide such notice to the political subdivision.

4. In addition to the requirements of subdivision three of this section, the commissioner shall notify the motor carrier of any conviction for any traffic violation or accident resulting from operation of a motor vehicle against a bus driver employed by the motor carrier, shall require payment of the fee necessary to defray the cost of the notification, and shall require all motor carriers to establish an escrow account with the department which shall be used to pay for the costs incurred by the department when it informs the motor carrier of a driver's conviction or accident; and may, if requested by a political subdivision which contracts with a motor carrier for the transportation of school children, provide such notice to the political subdivision.

§509-j. Compliance required.

(a) Every motor carrier, its officers, agents, representatives, and employees responsible for the management, maintenance, operation or driving of motor vehicles, or the hiring, supervising, training, assigning, or dispatching of drivers, shall be instructed in and comply with this article.

(b) Nothing contained herein shall prevent a motor carrier or political subdivision from imposing qualifications that are more stringent than those contained in this article or from disqualifying a person who has been issued a conditional or restricted use license pursuant to the provisions of article twenty-one or twenty-one-A of this chapter.

(c) Every motor carrier shall submit an affidavit to the commissioner attesting to compliance with this article. Such affidavit shall be submitted annually, in a manner prescribed by regulations of the commissioner, and shall include as an attachment thereto a copy of the report required by subdivision seven of section five hundred nine-d of this chapter.

(d) Notwithstanding any provision of any other article of this law, where an affidavit is not submitted pursuant to this section, the commissioner may, in his discretion, suspend the registration of the vehicle or the vehicles or deny registration or renewal to the vehicle or vehicles owned or operated by the motor carrier or suspend the motor carrier's privilege of operation in this state. Such suspension or denial shall only remain in effect as long as the motor carrier fails to submit such affidavit.

(e) The commissioner or any person deputized by the commissioner, may require any motor carrier to pay to the people of this state a civil penalty, if after the motor carrier has had an opportunity to be heard, the commissioner finds that the motor carrier has violated any provision of this article or regulations promulgated therein, or has made any false statement or misrepresentation on any affidavit of compliance filed with the commissioner or with respect to violations of paragraphs (i) and (ii) of subdivision one, paragraphs (a) and (b) of subdivision two, and subdivisions three, four and five of section five hundred nine-d, section five hundred nine-g, section five hundred nine-h and subdivision two of section five hundred nine-l of this article the commissioner may in lieu of or in addition to a civil penalty suspend all of a motor carrier's registrations. Any civil penalty assessed for a first violation shall not be less than five hundred dollars nor greater than two thousand five hundred dollars for each violation, false statement or representation found to have been made or committed, and for a second or subsequent violation, not arising out of the same incident, all of which were committed within a period of eighteen months, shall not be less than five hundred dollars nor greater than five thousand dollars for each violation, false statement or representation found to have been made or committed. If the registrant fails to pay such penalty within twenty days after the mailing of such order, postage prepaid, certified and addressed to the last known place of business of such registrant, unless such order is stayed by an order of a court of competent jurisdiction, the commissioner may revoke the vehicle registrations or out of state registration privilege of operation in the state of such motor carrier or may suspend the same for such periods as the commissioner may determine. Civil penalties assessed under this subdivision shall be paid to the commissioner for deposit into the state treasury, and unpaid civil penalties may be recovered by the commissioner in a civil action in the name of the commissioner.

(f) As an alternative to civil action under subdivision (e) of this section and provided that no proceeding for judicial review shall then be pending and the time for initiation of such proceeding shall have expired, the commissioner may file with the county clerk of the county in which the registrant is located a final order of the commissioner containing the amount of the penalty assessed. The filing of such final order shall have the same force and effect as a judgment duly docketed in the office of a county clerk and may be enforced in the same manner and with the same effect as that provided by law.

(g) Upon the suspension of a vehicle registration pursuant to subdivision (d) or (e) of this section, the commissioner shall have the authority to deny a registration or renewal application to any other person for the same vehicle and may deny a registration or renewal application for any other motor vehicle registered in the name of the applicant where the commissioner has reasonable grounds to believe that such registration or renewal will have the effect of defeating the purposes of this article. Such suspension or denial shall remain in effect only as long as the suspension entered pursuant to subdivision (d) or (e) of this section remains in effect.

§509-k. Ill or fatigued operator.

No driver shall operate a bus and a motor carrier shall not permit a driver to operate a bus while the driver's ability or alertness is so impaired, or so likely to become impaired, through fatigue, illness or any other cause, as to make it unsafe for him to begin or continue to operate the bus. At the request of the driver or the motor carrier such illness, fatigue, or other cause shall be certified by a qualified physician. However, in a case of grave emergency where the hazard to occupants of the bus or other users of the highway would be increased by compliance with this section, the driver may continue to operate the bus to the nearest place at which that hazard is removed.

§509-*l*. Drugs, controlled substances and intoxicating liquor.

1. No person shall:

(a) consume a drug, controlled substance or an intoxicating liquor, regardless of its alcoholic content, or be under the influence of an intoxicating liquor or drug, within six hours before going on duty or operating, or having physical control of a bus, or

(b) consume a drug, controlled substance or an intoxicating liquor, regardless of its alcoholic content while on duty, or operating, or in physical control of a bus, or

(c) possess a drug, controlled substance or an intoxicating liquor, regardless of its alcoholic content while on duty, operating or in physical control of a bus. However, this paragraph does not apply to possession of a drug, controlled substance or an intoxicating liquor which is transported as part of a shipment or personal effects of a passenger or to alcoholic beverages which are in sealed containers.

2. No motor carrier shall require or permit a driver to:

(a) violate any provision of subdivision one of this section; or

(b) be on duty or operate a bus if, by such person's general appearance or by such person's conduct or by other substantiating evidence, such person appears to have consumed a drug, controlled substance or an intoxicating liquor within the preceding six hours, or eight hours when such driver operates a school bus as defined by section one hundred forty-two of this chapter.

§509-m. Duties of the department.

The department of motor vehicles shall:

1. At least once every three years, review the bus driver files of each motor carrier, provided, however, that the commissioner may review such bus driver files at his discretion at any other time during regular business hours. Provided, however, that the commissioner shall review at least annually the bus driver files of each driver employed by a motor carrier who operates an altered motor

vehicle commonly referred to as a "stretch limousine" designed to carry nine or more passengers including the driver pursuant to operating authority issued by the commissioner of transportation, and annually verify whether each such driver holds a valid driver's license valid for the operation of such altered motor vehicle.

2. Establish regulations and forms for the orderly administration of and compliance with this article. Regulations shall also be established which are necessary for implementation of the process for appeal pursuant to subdivision two of section five hundred nine-d of this article.

3. Provide each motor carrier with notice whenever one of the drivers of such motor carrier has received revocation or suspension of a driver's license, learner's permit or privilege to operate.

4. Provide a motor carrier who has complied with the requirements of subdivision four of section five hundred nine-i of this article with information on any employee of the motor carrier regarding a conviction for a violation of this chapter.

5. Upon receipt of the criminal history record report of a school bus driver, notify the motor carrier of disqualification of an applicant or school bus driver which would or could disqualify such driver under the provisions of section five hundred nine-cc of this article. Notification to the carrier shall be without specification of the grounds for disqualification, those grounds to be made available only to the school bus driver or his or her representative.

6. In order to effectuate the provisions of this article, establish procedures, by regulation, to conduct curbside verification of bus driver and motor carrier identity to determine whether or not such motor carrier has notified the commissioner of the bus driver's employment as required by subdivision four of section five hundred nine-d of this article and whether or not such motor carrier has compiled with the provisions of this article and with any regulations promulgated thereunder; provided, however, such verifications shall be conducted so as not to disrupt the flow of traffic or endanger public safety.

7. The commissioner shall prepare and distribute a form for the provision of objective data concerning the driving history of a bus driver who is subject to regulation under this article. Such form shall be completed by current or former employers of such bus drivers upon the request of a prospective or subsequent employer.

8. Maintain and annually update its website to provide information with regard to each motor carrier that operates altered motor vehicles commonly referred to as "stretch limousines" designed to carry nine or more passengers including the driver pursuant to operating authority issued by the commissioner of transportation that includes the motor carrier's name, location and region of operation including place of address, whether such motor carrier is in compliance with this article as required by section five hundred nine-j of this article in relation to the operation of such altered motor vehicles, the number and nature of violations of this article resulting in convictions of such motor carrier in relation to the operation of such altered motor vehicles, the number of miles traveled by such altered motor vehicles operated by such motor carrier in the preceding

twelve months, and, with respect to drivers employed by such motor carrier operating such altered motor vehicles, the total number so employed, the number holding valid licenses which are valid for the operation of such altered motor vehicles, the number which lack licenses valid for such operation, the number disqualified from operating such altered motor vehicles, the number of convictions and accidents involving any such driver employed by such motor carrier during the preceding twelve months, and the number of convictions and accidents per ten thousand miles traveled.

§509-n. Exempt carriers; reporting requirements.

1. A motor carrier subject to the motor carrier regulations of the United States department of transportation will be exempt from all of the annual and biennial requirements of this article, except the annual requirement which mandates that an affidavit of compliance be filed with the commissioner, provided that (i) such motor carrier does not operate in this state a school bus as defined in section one hundred forty-two of this chapter or a bus used for the transportation of persons under the age of twenty-one or persons of any age who are mentally disabled to a place of vocational, academic or religious instruction or religious service including nursery schools, day care centers and camps or (ii) such motor carrier did not operate in the state during the previous calendar year more than one hundred days or more than ten thousand bus vehicle miles. Provided, however, for the purpose of this subdivision a school bus shall not mean a bus operated by a motor carrier subject to the motor carrier regulations of the United States department of transportation, that occasionally transports pupils or persons of any age who are mentally disabled and who are not residents of this state on chaperoned chartered trips in New York state.

2. A motor carrier subject to the motor carrier regulations of the United States department of transportation who is not exempt pursuant to the provisions of subdivision one of this section may apply to the commissioner for a waiver for those bus drivers, other than those drivers who operate a school bus as defined in section one hundred forty-two of this chapter or a bus used for the transportation of persons under the age of twenty-one to a place of vocational, academic or religious instruction or service including schools and camps, who operate a bus in this state less than thirty days each year. Such application shall include a description of a training and qualifying program which has demonstrated the motor carrier's procedures for qualifying bus drivers. Such program shall include an appropriate health and driving record review and such other information as shall be required by the commissioner to satisfy the intent of this article in an effective manner.

3. The annual affidavit of compliance required under subdivision one shall certify to the commissioner that the motor carrier does not employ a bus driver who would operate a bus in New York state and who is disqualified under section five hundred nine-c of this article, and also shall certify the number of days and vehicle miles of bus service that the carrier provided in the state during the previous calendar year. A motor carrier exempted by this section

shall furnish to the commissioner upon request any records concerning drivers required to be kept by the motor carrier regulations of the United States department of transportation within ten days of receipt of such request. Failure of a motor carrier to furnish such records requested within the ten day period shall be a violation of this article.

§509-o. Penalties.

Upon conviction for the violation of any provision of this article the court shall impose a sentence consisting of a fine of not less than one hundred dollars nor more than two hundred fifty dollars.

ARTICLE 20
SUSPENSION AND REVOCATION

Section
510.   Suspension, revocation and reissuance of licenses and registrations.
510-a.   Suspension and revocation of commercial driver's licenses.
510-aa.   Downgrade of commercial driver's licenses.
510-b.   Suspension and revocation for violations committed during probationary periods.
510-c.   Suspension and revocation of learner's permits and driver's licenses for violations committed by holders of class DJ or class MJ learner's permits or licenses.
511.   Operation while license or privilege is suspended or revoked; aggravated unlicensed operation.
511-a.   Facilitating aggravated unlicensed operation of a motor vehicle.
511-b.   Seizure and redemption of unlawfully operated vehicles.
511-c.   Seizure and forfeiture of vehicles used in the unlicensed operation of a motor vehicle under certain circumstances.
511-d.   Aggravated failure to answer appearance tickets or pay fines imposed.
512.   Operation while registration or privilege is suspended or revoked.

§510.   Suspension, revocation and reissuance of licenses and registrations.

1. Who may suspend or revoke. Any magistrate, justice or judge, in a city, in a town, or in a village, any supreme court justice, any county judge, any judge of a district court, the superintendent of state police and the commissioner of motor vehicles or any person deputized by him, shall have power to revoke or suspend the license to drive a motor vehicle or motorcycle of any person, or in the case of an owner, the registration, as provided herein.

A learner's permit, or a license which has expired but is renewable, shall be deemed a license within the meaning of this section.

2. Mandatory revocations and suspensions. a. Mandatory revocations. Such licenses shall be revoked and such registrations may also be revoked where the holder is convicted:

(i) of homicide or assault arising out of the operation of a motor vehicle or motorcycle or criminal negligence in the operation of a motor vehicle or motorcycle resulting in death, whether the conviction was had in this state or elsewhere;

(ii) pursuant to section twenty-three hundred eighty-five of title eighteen of the United States code, of the crime of advocating the overthrow of government, whether the conviction was had in this state or elsewhere;

(iii) of any violation of subdivision two of section six hundred or section three hundred ninety-two or of a local law or ordinance making it unlawful to leave the scene of an accident without reporting;

(iv) of a third or subsequent violation, committed within a period of eighteen months, of any provision of section eleven hundred eighty of this chapter, any ordinance or regulation limiting the speed of motor vehicles and motorcycles or any provision constituted a misdemeanor by this chapter, not included in subparagraphs (i) or (iii) of this paragraph, except violations of subdivision one of section three hundred seventy-five of this chapter or of subdivision one of section four hundred one of this chapter and similar violations under any local law, ordinance or regulation committed by an employed driver if the offense occurred while operating, in the course of his employment, a vehicle not owned by said driver, whether such three or more violations were repetitions of the same offense or were different offenses;

(v) of a violation for the conviction of which any such license is subject to revocation under subdivision two of section five hundred ten-b;

(vi) of a violation of any provision of section eleven hundred eighty-two of this chapter;

(vii) of a second violation of any provision of section eleven hundred eighty-two committed within a period of three years of a previous violation of the aforesaid section shall result in a license revocation of one year;

(viii) of a third violation, committed within a period of three years, of any provision of subdivision a of section eleven hundred seventy-four of this chapter;

(ix) of a violation of section twelve hundred twenty-four of this chapter, other than a violation adjudicated by the environmental control board of a city having a population of one million or more pursuant to subdivision seven of such section, and fails to pay the fine imposed thereon pursuant to subdivision seven of such section;

(x) of a traffic infraction for a subsequent violation of article twenty-six of this chapter and the commission of such violation caused serious physical injury to another person and such subsequent violation occurred within eighteen months of a prior violation of any provision of article twenty-six of this chapter where the commission of such prior violation caused the serious physical injury or death of another person;

(xi) of a traffic infraction for a subsequent violation of article twenty-six of this chapter and the commission of such violation caused the death of another person and such subsequent violation occurred within eighteen months of a prior violation of any provision of article twenty-six of this chapter where the commission of such prior violation caused the serious physical injury or death of another person; or

(xii) of a second or subsequent conviction of a violation of section twelve hundred twenty-five-c or section twelve hundred twenty-five-d of this chapter committed where such person is the holder of a probationary license, as defined in subdivision four of section five hundred one of this title, at the time of the commission of such violation and such second or subsequent violation was committed within six months following the restoration or issuance of such probationary license; or

(xiii) of a second or subsequent conviction of a violation of section twelve hundred twenty-five-c or section twelve hundred twenty-five-d of this chapter committed where such person is the holder of a class DJ or MJ learner's permit or a class DJ or MJ license at the time of the commission of such violation and such second or subsequent violation was committed within six months following the restoration of such permit or license.

b. Mandatory suspensions. Such licenses shall be suspended, and such registrations may also be suspended:

(i) for a period of sixty days where the holder is convicted of a violation for the conviction of which such license is subject to suspension pursuant to subdivision one of section five hundred ten-b;

(ii) when the holder forfeits bail given upon being charged with any of the offenses mentioned in this subdivision, until the holder submits to the jurisdiction of the court in which he forfeited bail; and

(iii) such registrations shall be suspended when necessary to comply with subdivision nine of section one hundred forty or subdivision four of section one hundred forty-five of the transportation law or with an out of service order issued by the United States department of transportation. The commissioner shall have the authority to deny a registration or renewal application to any other person for the same vehicle and may deny a registration or renewal application for any other motor vehicle registered in the name of the applicant where it has been determined that such registrant's intent has been to evade the purposes of this subdivision and where the commissioner has reasonable grounds to believe that such registration or renewal will have the effect of defeating the purposes of this subdivision. Any suspension issued pursuant to this subdivision by reason of an out of service order issued by the United States department of transportation shall remain in effect until such time as the commissioner is notified by the United States department of transportation or the commissioner of transportation that the order resulting in the suspension is no longer in effect.

(iv) For a period of not less than thirty nor greater than one hundred eighty days where the holder is convicted of the crime of assault in the first, second or third degree as defined in article one hundred twenty of the penal law, where such offense was committed against a traffic enforcement agent employed by the city of New York or the city of Buffalo while such agent was enforcing or attempting to enforce the traffic regulations of such city.

(v) *(Repealed)*

(vi) for a period of sixty days where the holder is convicted of a violation of subdivision one of section twelve hundred twenty-b of this chapter within a period of eighteen months of a previous violation of such subdivision.

(vii) for a period of ninety days where the holder is convicted of a violation of subdivision one of section twelve hundred twenty-b of this chapter within a period of eighteen months of two or more previous violations of such subdivision.

(viii) *(Removed Eff. 8/1/20,Ch.58,L.2020)*

(ix) For a period of three months where the holder is sentenced to a license suspension pursuant to paragraph (a) of subdivision five of section sixty-five-b of the alcoholic beverage control law, provided however, that, in accordance with such subdivision five, such suspension shall be only a license suspension.

(x) For a period of six months where the holder is sentenced to a license suspension pursuant to paragraph (b) of subdivision five of section sixty-five-b of the alcoholic beverage control law, provided however, that, in accordance with such subdivision five, such suspension shall be only a license suspension.

(xi) For a period of one year or until the holder reaches the age of twenty-one, whichever is the greater period of time, where the holder is sentenced to a license suspension pursuant to paragraph (c) of subdivision five of section sixty-five-b of the alcoholic beverage control law, provided however, that, in accordance with such subdivision five, such suspension shall be only a license suspension.

(xii) for a period of one year where the holder is convicted of, or receives a youthful offender or juvenile delinquency adjudication in connection with a violation of section 240.62 or subdivision five of section 240.60 of the penal law.

(xiii) for a period of sixty days where the holder is convicted of two or more violations of paragraph two of subdivision (d) or subdivision (f) of section eleven hundred eighty of this chapter.

(xiv) for a period of forty-five days where the holder is convicted of a traffic infraction for a first violation of article twenty-six of this chapter and the commission of such violation caused serious physical injury to another person, except: (A) where the holder is convicted of a traffic infraction for a first violation of section eleven hundred forty-six of this chapter and the commission of such violation caused serious physical injury to another person, the suspension shall be for a period of six months; and (B) where the holder is convicted of a traffic infraction for a second violation of section eleven hundred forty-six of this chapter and the commission of such violation caused serious physical injury to another person, and such person has previously been convicted of a traffic infraction for a violation of section eleven hundred forty-six of this chapter and the commission of such violation caused serious physical injury to another person within five years, the suspension shall be for a period of one year.

(xv) for a period of seventy-five days where the holder is convicted of a traffic infraction for a first violation of article twenty-six of this chapter and the commission of such violation caused the death of another person.

(xvi) for a period of one hundred twenty days where the holder is convicted of a violation of section twelve hundred twenty-five-c or section twelve hundred twenty-five-d of this chapter when such violation was committed while such holder had a probationary license, as defined in subdivision four of section five hundred one of this title.

(xvii) for a period of one hundred twenty days where the holder is convicted of a violation of section twelve hundred twenty-five-c or section twelve hundred twenty-five-d of this chapter when such violation was committed while such holder had a class DJ or MJ learner's permit or a class DJ or MJ license.

c. Application of mandatory revocations and suspensions to non-residents and to unlicensed persons. Whenever a non-resident or a person who is unlicensed is convicted of any violation or receives a youthful offender or juvenile delinquency adjudication in conjunction with a violation of section 240.62 or subdivision five of section 240.60 of the penal law, which would require the revocation or suspension of a license, pursuant to the provisions of this chapter, if the person so convicted or adjudicated was the holder of a license issued by the commissioner, such non-resident's privilege of operating a motor vehicle in this state or such unlicensed person's privilege of obtaining a license issued by the commissioner shall be revoked or suspended, and such non-resident's privilege of operation within this state of any motor vehicle owned by such person or such unlicensed person's privilege of obtaining a registration issued by the commissioner may be suspended as if such non-resident or unlicensed person was the holder of a license issued by the commissioner. The provisions of subdivisions six and seven of this section shall be applicable to any such suspension or revocation.

d. Mandatory suspensions; vehicles over eighteen thousand pounds. A license or privilege shall be suspended by the commissioner for a period of sixty days, where the holder is convicted of a violation of subdivision (g) of section eleven hundred eighty of this chapter, and (i) the recorded or entered speed upon which the conviction was based exceeded the applicable speed limit by more than twenty miles per hour or (ii) the recorded or entered speed upon which the conviction was based exceeded the applicable speed limit by more than ten miles per hour and the vehicle was either (A) in violation of any rules or regulations involving an out-of-service defect relating to brake systems, steering components and/or coupling devices, or (B) transporting flammable gas, radioactive materials or explosives. Whenever a license is suspended pursuant to this paragraph, the commissioner shall immediately issue a restricted license provided the holder of such license is otherwise eligible to receive such restricted license, except that no such restricted license shall be valid for the operation of a vehicle with a GVWR of more than eighteen thousand pounds and further provided that issuing a license to such person does not create a substantial traffic safety hazard.

2-a. Mandatory suspension and revocation of a license and registration in certain cases. (a) Within seven days after conviction for a violation of any local law which prohibits the knowing operation or offering to operate or permitting the operation for hire of any vehicle as a taxicab, livery, as defined in section one hundred twenty-one-e of this chapter, coach, limousine, van or wheelchair accessible van or tow truck within the state without first having obtained an appropriate license therefor from the appropriate licensing authority and appropriate for-hire insurance from the appropriate insurance agency, the taxi and limousine commission or other local body having jurisdiction over such offenses with respect to such vehicles shall provide notice of such conviction to the commissioner in a manner agreed upon between any such local body and the commissioner. Upon receipt of such notice, the commissioner shall suspend the license of such operator and the registration of such vehicle for a period of sixty days.

(b) Within seven days after conviction for a violation of any local law which prohibits the knowing operation or offering to operate or permitting the operation for hire of any vehicle as a taxicab, livery, as defined in section one hundred twenty-one-e of this chapter, coach, limousine, van or wheelchair accessible van or tow truck within the state without first having obtained an appropriate license therefor from the appropriate licensing authority and appropriate for-hire insurance from the appropriate insurance agency where the operator has, within the previous five years, been convicted of any such violation, the taxi and limousine commission or other local body having jurisdiction over such offenses with respect to such vehicles shall provide notice to the commissioner in a manner agreed upon between any such local body and the commissioner. Upon receipt of such notice, the commissioner shall revoke the license of such operator.

(c) Within seven days after conviction for a violation of any local law which prohibits the knowing operation or offering to operate or permitting the operation for hire of any vehicle as a taxicab, livery, as defined in section one hundred twenty-one-e of this chapter, coach, limousine, van or wheelchair accessible van or tow truck within the state without first having obtained an appropriate license therefor from the appropriate licensing authority and appropriate for-hire insurance from the appropriate insurance agency where the registrant has, within the previous five years, been convicted of any such viola-tion, the taxi and limousine commission or other local body having jurisdiction over such offenses with respect to such vehicles shall provide notice to the commissioner in a manner agreed upon between any such local body and the commissioner. Upon receipt of such notice, the commissioner shall revoke the registration of such vehicle, and no new registration shall be issued for at least six months, nor thereafter, except in the discretion of the commissioner.

(d) The provisions of this subdivision shall not apply to any taxicab or livery as defined in section one hundred twenty-one-e of this chapter, coach, limousine, van or wheelchair accessible van or tow truck licensed or permitted for such operation by the appropriate local body of any other municipality, the department of transportation, the metropolitan transportation authority or the interstate commerce commission.

3. Permissive suspensions and revocations. Such licenses and registrations and the privilege of a non-resident of operating a motor vehicle in this state and of operation within this state of any motor vehicle owned by him and the privi-lege of an unlicensed person of obtaining a license issued by the commissioner and of obtaining a registration issued by the commissioner may be suspended or revoked:

a. for any violation of the provisions of this chapter, except section eleven hundred ninety-two, or for any violation of a local ordinance or regulation prohibiting dangerous driving as shall, in the discretion of the officer acting hereunder, justify such revocation or suspension;

b. because of some physical or mental disability of the holder, the court commitment of the holder to an institution under the jurisdiction of the department of mental hygiene or the disability of the holder by reason of intoxication or the use of drugs;

c. because of the conviction of the holder at any time of a felony;

d. for habitual or persistent violation of any of the provisions of this chapter, or of any lawful ordinance, rule or regulation made by local authorities in relation to traffic;

e. for gross negligence in the operation of a motor vehicle or motorcycle or operating a motor vehicle or motorcycle in a manner showing a reckless disregard for life or property of others;

f. for knowingly permitting or suffering any motor vehicle or motorcycle under the direction or control of the holder to be used in aid or furtherance of the commission of any crime;

g. for preventing lawful identification of any motor vehicle or motorcycle under the holder's direction or control, or evading lawful arrest or prosecution while operating such motor vehicle or motorcycle;

h. for wilfully evading lawful prosecution in this state or in another state or jurisdiction for an offense committed therein against the motor vehicle or traffic laws thereof;

i. for habitual or persistent violation of any provisions of this chapter, and/or any lawful ordinance, rule or regulation made by local authorities in relation to traffic, and/or violations committed in a commercial motor vehicle of any law, statute, ordinance, rule or regulation in relation to traffic made by any other state, District of Columbia, Canadian province or local authority of such state, district or province;

j. except as provided in subdivision one herein or section eleven hundred ninety-three of this chapter upon the conviction of a person under eighteen years of age of any crime or in the case of an adjudication of youthful offender under nineteen years of age, such license or registration may be suspended or revoked for a maximum period of one year by the judge or justice sentencing him;

k. for a period of up to ninety days because of the conviction of the holder of the offenses of menacing as defined in section 120.15 of the penal law, where such offense was committed against a traffic enforcement agent employed by the city of New York or the city of Buffalo while such agent was enforcing or attempting to enforce the traffic regulations of such city.

3-a. Opportunity to be heard and temporary suspensions. Where revocation or suspension is permissive, the holder, unless he shall waive such right, shall have an opportunity to be heard except where such revocation or suspension is based solely on a court conviction or convictions or on a court commitment to an institution under the jurisdiction of the department of mental hygiene. A license or registration, or the privilege of a non-resident of operating a motor vehicle in this state or of the operation within this state of any motor vehicle owned by him, may, however, be temporarily suspended without notice, pending any prosecution, investigation or hearing.

4. Administrative action pursuant to interstate compact. a. Such licenses may be suspended where pursuant to any compact or agreement authorized by section five hundred seventeen of this chapter the holder thereof is issued a summons for a moving traffic violation, is not detained or required to furnish bail or collateral and fails to appear in response to such summons. Such suspension shall remain in effect only until such holder submits to the jurisdiction of the court in which such summons is returnable.

b. If notification is received by the commissioner pursuant to any compact or agreement authorized by section five hundred sixteen-b of this article that the holder of a New York license or an unlicensed New York resident has been convicted of an offense set forth in such compact or agreement, such conviction, for the purpose of administrative action which must or may be taken by the commissioner pursuant to the provisions of this section, shall be deemed to be a conviction of an offense committed within this state in accordance with the provisions of such compact or agreement.

4-a. Suspension for failure to answer an appearance ticket.

(a) Upon receipt of a court notification of the failure of a person to appear within sixty days of the return date or new subsequent adjourned date, pursuant to an appearance ticket charging said person with a violation of any of the provisions of this chapter (except one for parking, stopping, or standing), of any violation of the tax law or of the transportation law regulating traffic or of any lawful ordinance or regulation made by a local or public authority, relating to traffic (except one for parking, stopping, or standing) the commissioner or his or her agent may suspend the driver's license or privileges of such person pending receipt of notice from the court that such person has appeared in response to such appearance ticket or has paid or has entered into an installment payment plan to pay the fine associated with a conviction entered as a result of the failure to appear in response to such appearance ticket, or the defendant has been acquitted of the charge that led to the suspension or such charge was otherwise dismissed. Such suspension shall take effect no less than thirty days from the day upon which an initial notice thereof is sent by the commissioner to the person whose driver's license or privileges are to be suspended, provided that the commissioner shall send such person at least two notices thereof, including such initial notice, at least fifteen days apart during such period. Any suspension issued pursuant to this paragraph shall be subject to the provisions of paragraph (j-l) of subdivision two of section five hundred three of this chapter. *(Eff.6/9/21,Ch.76,& Eff.12/21/21,Ch.713,L.2021)*

(b) The provisions of paragraph (a) of this subdivision shall not apply to a registrant who was not operating a vehicle, but who was issued a summons or an appearance ticket for a violation of section three hundred eighty-five, section four hundred one or section five hundred eleven-a of this chapter. Upon the receipt of a court notification of the failure of such person to appear within sixty days of the return date or a new subsequent adjourned date, pursuant to an appearance ticket charging said person with such violation, or the failure of such person to pay a fine imposed by a court, the commissioner or his or her agent may suspend the registration of the vehicle or vehicles involved in such violation or privilege of operation of any motor vehicle owned by the registrant pending receipt of notice from the court that such person has appeared in response to such appearance ticket or has paid such fine. Such suspension shall take effect no less than thirty days from the day upon which notice thereof is sent by the commissioner to the person whose registration or privilege is to be suspended. Any suspension issued pursuant to this paragraph shall be subject to the provisions of paragraph (j-1) of subdivision two of section five hundred three of this chapter.

(c) Upon receipt of notification from a traffic and parking violations agency or a traffic violations agency of the failure of a person to appear within sixty days of the return date or new subsequent adjourned date, pursuant to an appearance ticket charging said person with a violation of:

(i) any of the provisions of this chapter except one for parking, stopping or standing and except those violations described in paragraphs (a), (b), (d), (e) and (f) of subdivision two and in paragraphs (a), (b), (d), (e), (f) and (g) of subdivision two-a and in paragraphs (a), (b), (d), (e), (f) and (g) of subdivision two-b of section three hundred seventy-one of the general municipal law;

(ii) section five hundred two or subdivision (a) of section eighteen hundred fifteen of the tax law;

(iii) section fourteen-f (except paragraph (b) of subdivision four of section fourteen-f), two hundred eleven or two hundred twelve of the transportation law; or

(iv) any lawful ordinance or regulation made by a local or public authority relating to traffic (except one for parking, stopping or standing), the commissioner or his or her agent may suspend the driver's license or privileges of such person pending receipt of notice from the agency that such person has appeared in response to such appearance ticket or has paid or has entered into an installment payment plan to pay the fine associated with a conviction entered as a result of the failure to appear in response to such appearance ticket, or the defendant has been acquitted of the charge that led to the suspension or such charge was otherwise dismissed. Such suspension shall take effect no less than thirty days from the day upon which an initial notice thereof is sent by the commissioner to the person whose driver's license or privileges are to be suspended, provided that the commissioner shall send such person at least two notices thereof, including such initial notice, at least fifteen days apart during such period. Any suspension issued pursuant to this paragraph shall be subject to the provisions of paragraph (j-1) of subdivision two of section five hundred three of this chapter. *(Eff. 6/9/21, Ch. 76, & Eff. 12/21/21, Ch. 713, L. 2021)*

4-b. Suspension of registration for failure to answer or to pay fines with respect to certain violations. Upon receipt of certification from a court or administrative tribunal of appropriate jurisdiction that the owner of a motor vehicle or his representative failed to appear on the return date or dates or any subsequent adjourned date or dates or failed to comply with the rules and regulations of an administrative tribunal following entry of a final decision or decisions in response to twenty-five or more summonses or other process, issued within an eighteen month period charging that such motor vehicle is parked, stopped or standing in violation of any of the provisions of this chapter or of any law, ordinance, rule or regulation made by a local authority, the commissioner shall suspend the registration of such motor vehicle. Such suspension shall take effect no less than thirty days from the date on which notice thereof is sent by the commissioner to the person whose registration is to be suspended and shall remain in effect as long as the summons or summonses remain unanswered, or in the case of an administrative tribunal, the registrant fails to comply with the rules and regulations following the entry of a final decision or decisions.

*4-c. Suspension of registration for failure to answer or to pay fines with respect to parking, stopping and standing violations. Upon receipt of certification from a court or administrative tribunal of appropriate jurisdiction in a city with a population in excess of one hundred thousand persons according to the nineteen hundred eighty United States census that the owner of a motor vehicle or his representative following compliance by such city with the notice provisions of subdivision two of section two hundred thirty-five of this chapter, failed to appear on the return date or dates or any subsequent adjourned date or dates or failed to comply with the rules and regulations of an administrative tribunal following entry of a final decision or decisions, in response to five or more summonses or other process, issued within a twelve month period charging that such motor vehicle is parked, stopped or standing in violation of any of the provisions of this chapter or of any law, ordinance, rule or regulation made by a local authority, the commissioner shall suspend the registration of such motor vehicle. Such suspension shall take effect no less than thirty days from the date on which notice thereof is sent by the commissioner to the person whose registration is to be suspended and shall remain in effect as long as the summons or summonses remain unanswered, or in the case of an administrative tribunal, the registrant fails to comply with the rules and regulations following the entry of a final decision or decisions.   *(Repealed 9/1/23, Ch.55, L.2021)*

4-d. Suspension of registration for failure to answer or pay penalties with respect to certain violations. Upon the receipt of a notification from a court or an administrative tribunal that an owner of a motor vehicle failed to appear on the return date or dates or a new subsequent adjourned date or dates or failed to pay any penalty imposed by a court or failed to comply with the rules and regulations of an administrative tribunal following entry of a final decision or decisions, in response to five or more notices of liability or other process, issued within an eighteen month period charging such owner with a violation of toll collection regulations in accordance with the provisions of section two thousand nine hundred eighty-five of the public authorities law or sections sixteen-a, sixteen-b and sixteen-c of chapter seven hundred seventy-four of the laws of nineteen hundred fifty, the commissioner or his agent shall suspend the registration of the vehicle or vehicles involved in the violation or the privilege of operation of any motor vehicle owned by the registrant. Such suspension shall take effect no less than thirty days from the date on which notice thereof is sent by the commissioner to the person whose registration or privilege is suspended and shall remain in effect until such registrant has appeared in response to such notices of liability or has paid such penalty or in the case of an administrative tribunal, the registrant has complied with the rules and regulations following the entry of a final decision or decisions.

*4-e. Suspension and disqualification for failure to make child support payments or failure to comply with a summons, subpoena or warrant relating to a paternity or child support proceeding. (1) The commissioner, on behalf of the department, shall enter into a written agreement with the commissioner of the office of temporary and disability assistance, on behalf of the office of temporary and disability assistance, which shall set forth the procedures for suspending the driving privileges of individuals who have failed to make payments of child support or combined child and spousal support.

(2) Such agreement shall include:

(i) the procedure under which the office of temporary and disability assistance shall notify the department of an individual's liability for support arrears;

(ii) the procedure under which the department shall be notified by the office of temporary and disability assistance that an individual has satisfied or commenced payment of his or her support arrears; or has made satisfactory payment arrangements thereon and shall have the suspension of his or her driving privileges terminated;

(iii) the procedure for reimbursement of the department and its agents by the office of temporary and disability assistance for the full additional costs of carrying out the procedures authorized by this section, and may include, subject to the approval of the director of the budget, a procedure for reimbursement of necessary additional costs of collecting social security numbers pursuant to section five hundred two of this title;

(iv) provision for the publicizing of sanctions for nonpayment of child support including the potential for the suspension of delinquent support obligors' driving privileges if they fail to pay child support or combined child and spousal support; and

(v) such other matters as the parties to such agreement shall deem necessary to carry out provisions of this section.

(3) Upon receipt of notification from the office of temporary and disability assistance of a person's failure to satisfy support arrears or to make satisfactory payment arrangements thereon pursuant to paragraph (e) of subdivision twelve of section one hundred eleven-b of the social services law or notification from a court issuing an order pursuant to section four hundred fifty-eight-a of the family court act or section two hundred forty-four-b of the domestic relations law, the commissioner or his or her agent shall suspend the license of such person to operate a motor vehicle. In the event such person is unlicensed, such person's privilege of obtaining a license shall be suspended. Such suspension shall take effect no later than fifteen days from the date of the notice thereof to

the person whose license or privilege of obtaining a license is to be suspended, and shall remain in effect until such time as the commissioner is advised that the person has satisfied the support arrears or has made satisfactory payment arrangements thereon pursuant to paragraph (e) of subdivision twelve of section one hundred eleven-b of the social services law or until such time as the court issues an order to terminate such suspension;

(4) From the time the commissioner is notified by the office of temporary and disability assistance of a person's liability for support arrears under this section, the commissioner shall be relieved from all liability to such person which may otherwise arise under this section, and such person shall have no right to commence a court action or proceeding or to any other legal recourse against the commissioner to recover such driving privileges as authorized by this section. In addition, notwithstanding any other provision of law, such person shall have no right to a hearing or appeal pursuant to this chapter with respect to a suspension of driving privileges as authorized by this section. However, nothing herein shall be construed to prohibit such person from proceeding against the support collection unit pursuant to article seventy-eight of the civil practice law and rules.

(5) Any person whose license has been suspended pursuant to subdivision three of this section may apply for the issuance of a restricted use license as provided in section five hundred thirty of this title. *(Repealed 8/31/23,Ch.183,L.2021)*

4-f. Suspension for failure to pay past-due tax liabilities. (1) The commissioner shall enter into a written agreement with the commissioner of taxation and finance, as provided in section one hundred seventy-one-v of the tax law, which shall set forth the procedures for suspending the drivers' licenses of individuals who have failed to satisfy past-due tax liabilities as such terms are defined in such section.

(2) Upon receipt of notification from the department of taxation and finance that an individual has failed to satisfy past-due tax liabilities, or to otherwise make payment arrangements satisfactory to the commissioner of taxation and finance, or has failed to comply with the terms of such payment arrangements more than once within a twelve month period, the commissioner or his or her agent shall suspend the license of such person to operate a motor vehicle. In the event such person is unlicensed, such person's privilege of obtaining a license shall be suspended. Such suspension shall take effect no later than fifteen days from the date of the notice thereof provided to the person whose license or privilege of obtaining a license is to be suspended, and shall remain in effect until such time as the commissioner is advised that the person has satisfied his or her past-due tax liabilities, or has otherwise made payment arrangements satisfactory to the commissioner of taxation and finance.

(3) From the time the commissioner is notified by the department of taxation and finance under this section, the commissioner shall be relieved from all liability to such person which may otherwise arise under this section, and such person shall have no right to commence a court action or proceeding or to any other legal recourse against the commissioner to recover such driving privileges as authorized by this section. In addition, notwithstanding any other

provision of law, such person shall have no right to a hearing or appeal pursuant to this chapter with respect to a suspension of driving privileges as authorized by this section.

(4) Notwithstanding any provision of law to the contrary, the department shall furnish the department of taxation and finance with the information necessary for the proper identification of an individual referred to the department for the purpose of driver's license suspension pursuant to this section and section one hundred seventy-one-v of the tax law. This shall include the individual's name, social security number and any other information the commissioner of motor vehicles deems necessary.

(5) Any person whose driver's license is suspended pursuant to paragraph two of this subdivision may apply for the issuance of a restricted use license as provided in section five hundred thirty of this title.

4-g. Suspension of registration for unlawful solicitation of ground transportation services at an airport. Upon the receipt of a notification from a court or an administrative tribunal that an owner of a motor vehicle was convicted of a second conviction of unlawful solicitation of ground transportation services at an airport in violation of subdivision one of section twelve hundred twenty-b of this chapter both of which were committed within a period of eighteen months, the commissioner or his agent shall suspend the registration of the vehicle involved in the violation for a period of ninety days; upon the receipt of such notification of a third or subsequent conviction for a violation of such subdivision all of which were committed within a period of eighteen months, the commissioner or his agent shall suspend such registration for a period of one hundred eighty days. Such suspension shall take effect no less than thirty days from the date on which notice thereof is sent by the commissioner to the person whose registration or privilege is suspended. The commissioner shall have the authority to deny a registration or renewal application to any other person for the same vehicle, where it has been determined that such registrant's intent has been to evade the purposes of this subdivision and where the commissioner has reasonable grounds to believe that such registration or renewal will have the effect of defeating the purposes of this subdivision.

5. Restoration. A license or registration may be restored by direction of the commissioner but not otherwise. Reversal on appeal, of any conviction because of which any license or registration has been revoked or suspended, shall entitle the holder to restoration thereof forthwith. The privileges of a non-resident may be restored by direction of the commissioner in his discretion but not otherwise.

6. Restrictions. a. Where revocation is mandatory hereunder, no new license shall be issued for at least six months or, in certain cases a longer period as specified in this chapter, nor thereafter, except in the discretion of the commissioner of motor vehicles.

b. Except as otherwise provided in paragraph c of this subdivision, where revocation is mandatory pursuant to subparagraph (iii) of paragraph a of subdivision two of this section, no new commercial driver's license shall be issued for at least one year nor thereafter except in the discretion of the commissioner, except that if such person has previously been found to have refused a chemical test pursuant to section eleven hundred ninety-four of this chapter or has a prior conviction of any of the following offenses: any violation of section eleven hundred ninety-two of this chapter; any violation of subdivision one or two of section six hundred of this chapter; or has a prior conviction of any felony involving the use of a motor vehicle pursuant to paragraph (a) of subdivision one of section five hundred ten-a of this article, then such commercial driver's license revocation shall be permanent.

c. Where revocation is mandatory pursuant to subdivision one of section five hundred ten-a of this chapter or subparagraph (iii) of paragraph a of subdivision two of this section and the violation of subdivision two of section six hundred of this chapter was committed while operating a commercial motor vehicle transporting hazardous materials, no new commercial driver's license shall be issued for at least three years nor thereafter except in the discretion of the commissioner, except that if such person has previously been found to have refused a chemical test pursuant to section eleven hundred ninety-four of this chapter or has a prior conviction of any of the following offenses: any violation of section eleven hundred ninety-two of this chapter; any violation of subdivision one or two of section six hundred of this chapter; or has a prior conviction of any felony involving the use of a motor vehicle pursuant to paragraph (a) of subdivision one of section five hundred ten-a of this article, then such commercial driver's license revocation shall be permanent.

d. The permanent commercial driver's license revocation required by paragraphs b and c of this subdivision may be waived by the commissioner after a period of ten years has expired from such sentence provided:

(i) that during such ten year period such person has not been found to have refused a chemical test pursuant to section eleven hundred ninety-four of this chapter and has not been convicted of any one of the following offenses: any violation of section eleven hundred ninety-two of this chapter; any violation of subdivision one or two of section six hundred of this chapter; or has a prior conviction of any felony involving the use of a motor vehicle pursuant to paragraph (a) of subdivision one of section five hundred ten-a of this article;

(ii) if any of the grounds upon which the permanent commercial driver's license revocation is based involved a finding of refusal to submit to a chemical test pursuant to section eleven hundred ninety-four of this chapter or a conviction of a violation of any subdivision of section eleven hundred ninety-two of this chapter, that such person provides acceptable documentation to the commissioner that such person has voluntarily enrolled in and successfully completed an appropriate rehabilitation program; and

(iii) after such documentation, if required, is accepted, that such person is granted a certificate of relief from disabilities or a certificate of good conduct pursuant to article twenty-three of the correction law by the court in which such person was last penalized.

e. Upon a third finding of refusal and/or conviction of any of the offenses which require a permanent commercial driver's license revocation, such permanent revocation may not be waived by the commissioner under any circumstances.

f. Where revocation is mandatory hereunder, based upon a conviction had outside this state, no new license shall be issued until after sixty days from the date of such revocation, nor thereafter, except in the discretion of the commissioner.

g. Except as provided in paragraph k of this subdivision, where revocation is permissive, no new license or certificate shall be issued by such commissioner to any person until after thirty days from the date of such revocation, nor thereafter, except in the discretion of the commissioner after an investigation or upon a hearing, provided, however, that where the revocation is based upon a failure in a reexamination pursuant to section five hundred six of this chapter, a learner's permit may be issued immediately and provided further, that where revocation is based upon a conviction of a felony, other than a felony relating to the operation of a motor vehicle or motorcycle, a license shall be issued immediately, if the applicant is otherwise qualified and if the application for such license is accompanied by consent in writing issued by the parole or probation authority having jurisdiction over such applicant.

h. The provisions of this subdivision shall not apply to revocations issued pursuant to sections eleven hundred ninety-three and eleven hundred ninety-four of this chapter.

i. and j. *(Repealed, Eff.4/12/19,Ch.55,L.2019).*

k. Where revocation is permissive hereunder, based upon a finding of a violation of section three hundred ninety-two or section three hundred ninety-two-a of this chapter, no new license or certificate shall be issued until after one year from the date of such revocation, nor thereafter, except in the discretion of the commissioner.

l. Where revocation is mandatory pursuant to subparagraph (x) of paragraph a of subdivision two of this section, no new license shall be issued for at least seventy-five days, nor thereafter except in the discretion of the commissioner.

m. Where revocation is mandatory pursuant to subparagraph (xi) of paragraph a of subdivision two of this section, no new license shall be issued for at least one hundred twenty days, nor thereafter except in the discretion of the commissioner.

n. Notwithstanding the provisions of paragraph a of this subdivision, subdivision two of section five hundred ten-b of this article or paragraph (b) of subdivision one of section five hundred ten-c of this article, where revocation is mandatory pursuant to subparagraph (xii) or subparagraph (xiii) of paragraph a of subdivision two of this section, no new license shall be issued for at least one year, nor thereafter except in the discretion of the commissioner.

o. Notwithstanding the provisions of paragraph a of this subdivision, where revocation is mandatory pursuant to subparagraph (iii) of paragraph a of subdivision two of this section involving a violation of section three hundred ninety-two of this chapter in relation to an application for the commercial driver's license or the commercial learner's permit being revoked, no new commercial driver's license or commercial learner's permit shall be issued for at least one year, nor thereafter except in the discretion of the commissioner.

7. Miscellaneous provisions. Except as expressly provided, a court conviction shall not be necessary to sustain a revocation or suspension. Revocation or suspension hereunder shall be deemed an administrative act reviewable by the supreme court as such. Notice of revocation or suspension, as well as any required notice of hearing, where the holder is not present, may be given by mailing the same in writing to him or her at the address contained in his or her license, certificate of registration or at the current address provided by the United States postal service, as the case may be. Proof of such mailing by certified mail to the holder shall be presumptive evidence of the holder's receipt and actual knowledge of such notice. Attendance of witnesses may be compelled by subpoena. Failure of the holder or any other person possessing the license card or number plates, to deliver the same to the suspending or revoking officer is a misdemeanor. Suspending or revoking officers shall place such license cards and number plates in the custody of the commissioner except where the commissioner shall otherwise direct. If any person shall fail to deliver a license card or number plates as provided herein, any police officer, bridge and tunnel officer of the Triborough bridge and tunnel authority, or agent of the commissioner having knowledge of such facts shall have the power to secure possession thereof and return the same to the commissioner, and the commissioner may forthwith direct any police officer, bridge and tunnel officer of the Triborough bridge and tunnel authority, acting pursuant to his or her special duties, or agent of the commissioner to secure possession thereof and to return the same to the commissioner. Failure of the holder or of any person possessing the license card or number plates to deliver to any police officer, bridge and tunnel officer of the Triborough bridge and tunnel authority, or agent of the commissioner who requests the same pursuant to this subdivision shall be a misdemeanor. Notice of revocation or suspension of any license or registration shall be transmitted forthwith by the commissioner to the chief of police of the city or prosecuting officer of the locality in which the person whose license or registration so revoked or suspended resides. In case any license or registration shall expire before the end of any period for which it has been revoked or suspended, and before it shall have been restored as provided in this chapter, then and in that event any renewal thereof may be withheld until the end of such period of suspension or until restoration, as the case may be. The revocation of a learner's permit shall automatically cancel the application for a license of the holder of such permit. No suspension or revocation of a license or registration shall be made because of a judgment of conviction if the suspending or revoking officer is satisfied that the magistrate who pronounced the judgment failed to comply with subdivision one of section eighteen hundred seven of this chapter. In case a suspension or revocation has been made and the commissioner is satisfied that

there was such failure, the commissioner shall restore the license or registration or both as the case may be.

8. Cancellation. Upon receipt of a license which has been surrendered to the licensing authority of any other jurisdiction as a prerequisite to the issuance of a license by such other jurisdiction in accordance with the provisions of the Driver License Compact or any other laws of such jurisdiction, the commissioner shall cancel such license. Provided, however, that such license shall not be cancelled if the licensee is a resident of this state.

9. Railroad vehicle violations. Upon certification by the commissioner of transportation that there has been a violation of section seventy-six-b of the railroad law, the commissioner of motor vehicles may rescind, cancel or suspend the registration of any motor vehicle described in subdivision one of section seventy-six-b of the railroad law and may rescind, cancel, suspend or take possession of the current registration certificate and number plates of any such motor vehicle.

10. Where a youth is determined to be a youthful offender, following a conviction of a violation for which a license suspension or revocation is mandatory or where a youth receives a juvenile delinquency adjudication in conjunction with a violation of section 240.62 or subdivision five of section 240.60 of the penal law, the court shall impose such suspension or revocation as is otherwise required upon conviction and, further, shall notify the commissioner of said suspension or revocation and its finding that said violator is granted youthful offender status as is required pursuant to section five hundred thirteen of this chapter or received a juvenile delinquency adjudication.

11. Notwithstanding any contrary provision of law, the division of criminal justice services is authorized to share with the commissioner such criminal history information in its possession as may be necessary to effect the provisions of this chapter.

§510-a. Suspension and revocation of commercial driver's licenses.

1. Revocation. A commercial driver's license shall be revoked by the commissioner whenever the holder is convicted within or outside of this state (a) of a felony involving the use of a motor vehicle except a felony as described in paragraph (b) of this subdivision; (b) of a felony involving manufacturing, distributing or dispensing a drug as defined in section one hundred fourteen-a of this chapter or possession of any such drug with intent to manufacture, distribute or dispense such drug in which a motor vehicle was used; (c) of a violation of subdivision one or two of section six hundred of this chapter; (d) of operating a commercial motor vehicle when, as a result of prior violations committed while operating a commercial motor vehicle, the driver's commercial driver's license is revoked, suspended, or canceled, or the driver is disqualified from operating a commercial motor vehicle; (e) has been convicted of causing a fatality through the negligent operation of a commercial motor vehicle, including but not limited to the crimes of vehicular manslaughter or criminally negligent homicide; or (f) the commissioner determines that the holder has made a false statement regarding information: (i) required by the

federal motor carrier safety improvement act of 1999 and Subpart J of Part 383 of title 49 of the code of federal regulations relating to a commercial driver's license document in an application for a commercial driver's license; (ii) required by the federal motor carrier safety improvement act of 1999 and Part 383.71 (a) and (g) of title 49 of the code of federal regulations relating to an initial commercial driver's license or existing commercial driver's license holder's self-certification in any of the self-certifications regarding the type of driving engaged or to be engaged in by the holder or regarding the non-applicability to the holder of the physical qualification requirements of the federal motor carrier safety improvement act of 1999 and Part 391 of title 49 of the code of federal regulations relating to qualifications of drivers; or (iii) required by the federal motor carrier safety improvement act of 1999 and Part 383.71(h) of title 49 of the code of federal regulations relating to commercial driver's license requirements in any medical certificate.

    2. Duration of revocation. (a) Except as otherwise provided in paragraph (b) of this subdivision, where revocation of a commercial driver's license is mandatory pursuant to paragraph (a), (c), (d), (e) or (f) of subdivision one of this section no new commercial driver's license shall be issued for at least one year nor thereafter except in the discretion of the commissioner, except that for revocations pursuant to paragraph (a), (c), (d) or (e) of subdivision one of this section, if such person has previously been found to have refused a chemical test pursuant to section eleven hundred ninety-four of this chapter or has a prior conviction of any of the following offenses: any violation of section eleven hundred ninety-two of this chapter, any violation of subdivision one or two of section six hundred of this chapter, or any felony involving the use of a motor vehicle pursuant to paragraph (a) of subdivision one of this section, or has been convicted of operating a commercial motor vehicle when, as a result of prior violations committed while operating a commercial motor vehicle, the driver's commercial driver's license is revoked, suspended, or canceled, or the driver is disqualified from operating a commercial motor vehicle, or has been convicted of causing a fatality through the negligent operation of a commercial motor vehicle, including but not limited to the crimes of vehicular manslaughter or criminally negligent homicide, then such commercial driver's license revocation shall be permanent.

    (b) Where revocation is mandatory pursuant to paragraph (a), (c), (d) or (e) of subdivision one of this section and the commercial motor vehicle was transporting hazardous materials, no new commercial driver's license shall be issued for at least three years nor thereafter except in the discretion of the commissioner, except that if such person has previously been found to have refused a chemical test pursuant to section eleven hundred ninety-four of this chapter or has a prior conviction of any of the following offenses: any violation of section eleven hundred ninety-two of this chapter, any violation of subdivision one or two of section six hundred of this chapter, or any felony involving the use of a motor vehicle pursuant to paragraph (a) of subdivision one of this section, or been convicted of operating a commercial motor vehicle when, as a result of prior violations committed while operating a commercial motor vehicle the driver's commercial driver's license is revoked, suspended, or canceled, or the driver is disqualified from operating a commercial motor vehicle, or has been convicted of causing a fatality through the negligent operation of a commercial motor vehicle, including but not limited to the crimes of vehicular manslaughter or criminally negligent homicide, then such commercial driver's license revocation shall be permanent.

(c) The permanent commercial driver's license revocation required by paragraphs (a) and (b) of this subdivision may be waived by the commissioner after a period of ten years has expired from such sentence provided:

(i) that during such ten year period such person has not been found to have refused a chemical test pursuant to section eleven hundred ninety-four of this chapter and has not been convicted of any one of the following offenses: any violation of section eleven hundred ninety-two of this chapter, any violation of subdivision one or two of section six hundred of this chapter, or any felony involving the use of a motor vehicle pursuant to paragraph (a) of subdivision one of this section, or has been convicted of operating a commercial motor vehicle when, as a result of prior violations committed while operating a commercial motor vehicle, the driver's commercial driver's license is revoked, suspended, or canceled, or the driver is disqualified from operating a commercial motor vehicle; or has been convicted of causing a fatality through the negligent operation of a commercial motor vehicle, including but not limited to the crimes of vehicular manslaughter or criminally negligent homicide;

(ii) if any of the grounds upon which the permanent commercial driver's license revocation is based involved a finding of refusal to submit to a chemical test pursuant to section eleven hundred ninety-four of this chapter or a conviction of a violation of any subdivision of section eleven hundred ninety-two of this chapter, that such person provides acceptable documentation to the commissioner that such person has enrolled in and successfully completed an appropriate rehabilitation program; and

(iii) after such documentation, if required, is accepted, that such person is granted a certificate of relief from disabilities or a certificate of good conduct pursuant to article twenty-three of the correction law by the court in which such person was last penalized.

(d) Upon a third finding of refusal and/or conviction of any of the offenses which require a permanent commercial driver's license revocation, such permanent revocation may not be waived by the commissioner under any circumstances.

(e) Where revocation is mandatory pursuant to paragraph (b) of subdivision one of this section such revocation shall be permanent and may not be waived by the commissioner under any circumstances.

3. Suspension. (a) A commercial driver's license shall be suspended by the commissioner for a period of sixty days where the holder is convicted of two serious traffic violations as defined in subdivision four of this section committed within a three year period, in separate incidents whether such convictions occurred within or outside of this state.

(b) A commercial driver's license shall be suspended by the commissioner for a period of one hundred twenty days where the holder is convicted of three serious traffic violations as defined in subdivision four of this section committed within a three year period, in separate incidents whether such convictions occurred within or outside of this state.

(c) A commercial drivers license shall be suspended by the commissioner for a period of sixty days where the holder is convicted of a violation of subdivision (g) of section eleven hundred eighty of this chapter, and (i) the recorded or entered speed upon which the conviction was based exceeded the applicable speed limit by more than twenty miles per hour or (ii) the recorded or entered speed upon which the conviction was based exceeded the applicable speed limit by more than ten miles per hour and the vehicle was either (A) in violation of any rules or regulations involving an out-of-service defect relating to brake systems, steering components and/or coupling devices, or (B) transporting flammable gas, radioactive materials or explosives.

(d) A commercial driver's license shall be suspended by the commissioner:

(i) for a period of one hundred eighty days where the holder was found to have operated a commercial motor vehicle designed or used to transport property as defined in subparagraphs (i) and (ii) of paragraph (a) of subdivision four of section five hundred one-a of this title, in violation of an out-of-service order as provided for in the rules and regulations of the department of transportation whether such violation was committed within this state or was the same or a similar violation involving an out-of-service order committed outside of this state;

(ii) for a period of two years if, during any ten-year period, the holder is found to have committed two such violations not arising from the same incident whether such violations were committed within or outside of the state;

(iii) for a period of three years if, during any ten-year period, the holder is convicted of three or more such violations not arising from the same incident whether such violations were committed within or outside of the state;

(iv) for a period of one hundred eighty days if the holder is found to have operated a commercial motor vehicle designed or used to transport passengers or property as defined in subparagraphs (iii) and (v) of paragraph (a) of subdivision four of section five hundred one-a of this title, in violation of an out-of-service order, as provided for in the rules and regulations of the department of transportation, while transporting hazardous materials or passengers whether such violation was committed within this state or was the same or a similar violation committed outside of this state;

(v) for a period of three years if, during any ten-year period, the holder is found to have committed two or more violations, not arising from the same incident, of operating a commercial motor vehicle designed or used to transport passengers or property as defined in subparagraphs (iii) and (v) of paragraph (a) of subdivision four of section five hundred one-a of this title, in violation of an out-of-service order, as provided for in the rules and regulations of the department of transportation, while transporting hazardous materials or passengers whether such violation was committed within this state or was the same or a similar violation involving an out-of-service order committed outside of this state.

(e) A commercial driver's license shall be suspended by the commissioner:

(i) for a period of sixty days where the holder is convicted of a violation of section eleven hundred seventy-one or section eleven hundred seventy-six of this chapter whether such violation was committed within this state or was the same or a similar violation involving railroad grade crossings committed outside of this state.

(ii) for a period of one hundred twenty days where the holder is convicted of a second violation of section eleven hundred seventy-one or section eleven hundred seventy-six of this chapter whether such violations were committed within or outside of this state, both of which were committed within a three year period.

(iii) for a period of one year where the holder is convicted of a third violation of section eleven hundred seventy-one or section eleven hundred seventy-six of this chapter whether such violations were committed within or outside of this state, all of which were committed within a three year period.

4. Serious traffic violations. (a) A serious traffic violation shall mean operating a commercial motor vehicle in violation of any provision of this chapter or the laws or ordinances of any other state or locality outside of this state that restricts or prohibits the use of a hand-held mobile telephone or a portable electronic device while operating a commercial motor vehicle or in violation of any provision of this chapter or the laws of any other state, the District of Columbia or any Canadian province which (i) limits the speed of motor vehicles, provided the violation involved fifteen or more miles per hour over the established speed limit; (ii) is defined as reckless driving by state or local law or regulation; (iii) prohibits improper or erratic lane change; (iv) prohibits following too closely; (v) relates to motor vehicle traffic (other than parking, standing or stopping) and which arises in connection with a fatal accident; (vi) operating a commercial motor vehicle without first obtaining a commercial driver's license as required by section five hundred one of this title; (vii) operating a commercial motor vehicle without a commercial driver's license in the driver's possession; or (viii) operating a commercial motor vehicle without the proper class of commercial driver's license and/or endorsement for the specific vehicle being operated or for the passengers or type of cargo being transported.

(b) Whether any specific violation which occurs without this state is a serious violation shall be dependent upon whether the state or province in which the violation occurs, reports such violation to the commissioner as, or deems it to be, a serious traffic violation under the provisions of the federal commercial motor vehicle safety act of nineteen hundred eighty-six, public law 99-570, title XII or the motor carrier safety improvement act of 1999, public law 106-159 and regulations promulgated thereunder.

4-a. Dismissal. The court shall dismiss any charge of operating a commercial motor vehicle without a commercial driver's license in the driver's possession if, between the date the driver is charged with such violation and the appearance date for such violation, the driver supplies the court with proof that he or she held a valid commercial driver's license on the date of such violation. Such driver must also supply such proof to the law enforcement authority that issued the citation, prior to such driver's appearance in court.

5. Limitation of effect of revocation or suspension. Any revocation or suspension of a commercial driver's license issued pursuant to this section shall be applicable only to that portion of the holder's driver's license or privilege which permits the operation of commercial motor vehicles, and the commissioner shall immediately issue a license, other than a commercial driver's license, to such person, provided that such person is otherwise eligible to receive such license and further provided that issuing a license to such person does not create a substantial traffic safety hazard.

6. Application of section to persons not holding a commercial driver's license. Whenever a person who is not the holder of a commercial driver's license issued by the commissioner is convicted of a violation arising out of the operation of a commercial motor vehicle which would require the mandatory revocation or suspension of a commercial driver's license pursuant to this section or clause (i) or (ii) of subparagraph five of paragraph (b) or clause b of subparagraph three of paragraph (e) of subdivision two of section eleven hundred ninety-three, or clause c of subparagraph one of paragraph (d) of subdivision two of section eleven hundred ninety-four of this chapter, the privilege of such person to operate a commercial motor vehicle and/or to obtain a commercial driver's license issued by the commissioner will be suspended or revoked for the same periods of time and subject to the same conditions provided in this section, or clause (i) or (ii) of subparagraph five of paragraph (b) or clause b of subparagraph three of paragraph (e) of subdivision two of section eleven hundred ninety-three, or clause c of subparagraph one of paragraph (d) of subdivision two of section eleven hundred ninety-four of this chapter, which would be applicable to the holder of a commercial driver's license.

7. Other revocation or suspension action not prohibited. The provisions of this section shall not be construed to prevent any person who has the authority to suspend or revoke a license to drive or privilege of operating pursuant to section five hundred ten of this chapter from exercising any such authority based upon a conviction for which suspension or revocation of a commercial driver's license by the commissioner is mandated.

8. Disqualifications based upon record review. (a) Where the commissioner conducts a state record review pursuant to section 384.206 of title 49 of the code of federal regulations and he or she determines that: (i) a person applying for a commercial driver's license was convicted outside of this state of an offense set forth in section 383.51 of title 49 of the code of federal regulations while holding a commercial driver's license issued by another state; and (ii) such other state failed to impose the commercial driver's license disqualification, suspension or revocation set forth in section 383.51 of title 49 of the code of federal regulations for such offense, then the commissioner shall immediately suspend such person's commercial driver's license or privilege of

operating a commercial motor vehicle. Provided, however, that where such licenses would have been subject to revocation upon a conviction for such conduct had it occurred in this state, the commissioner shall revoke such license. Such suspension or revocation shall be for the applicable period of time set forth for a conviction for such offense in such section 383.51 as it existed on the date of the violation.

(b) Any suspension or revocation of a commercial driver's license issued pursuant to paragraph (a) of this subdivision shall be applicable only to that portion of the holder's driver's license or privilege which permits the operation of commercial motor vehicles, and the commissioner shall immediately issue a license, other than a commercial driver's license, to such person provided that such person is otherwise eligible to receive such license and further provided that issuing a license to such person does not create a substantial traffic safety hazard.

9. Application of disqualifications to holders of a commercial learner's permit. Notwithstanding any other provision of law, any provision of this chapter relating to the revocation, suspension, downgrading, disqualification or cancellation of a commercial driver's license shall apply in the same manner to a commercial learner's permit.

10. Consecutive disqualification periods. Notwithstanding any other provision of law, whenever a suspension, revocation or disqualification applicable to a commercial driver's license or commercial learner's permit is required by Part 383.51 of title 49 of the code of federal regulations and thereby imposed pursuant to this section or paragraph b or c of subdivision six of section five hundred ten or section eleven hundred ninety-three or eleven hundred ninety-four of this chapter, such suspension, revocation or disqualification shall take effect upon the expiration of the minimum period of a suspension, revocation or disqualification required by Part 383.51 of title 49 of the code of federal regulations and thereby imposed pursuant to this section or paragraph b or c of subdivision six of section five hundred ten or section eleven hundred ninety-three or eleven hundred ninety-four of this chapter which is currently in effect for such license or permit and arose from a separate incident. Provided, however, that the term or terms of any other suspension, revocation or disqualification applicable to a commercial driver's license or commercial learner's permit shall run concurrently if: (a) such suspension, revocation or disqualification is not required by Part 383.51 of title 49 of the code of federal regulations; or (b) such suspension, revocation or disqualification arose from the same incident.

§510-aa. Downgrade of commercial driver's licenses.

A commercial driver's license shall be downgraded to a non-commercial driver's license by the commissioner within sixty days of the holder's medical certification status becoming "not-certified" based upon the expiration of the holder's medical certification or medical variance documentation required by the federal motor carrier safety improvement act of 1999 and Part 383.71(h) of title 49 of the code of federal regulations, or upon the holder's failure to submit such medical certification or medical variance documentation at such intervals as required by the federal motor carrier safety improvement act of 1999 and Part 383.71(h) of title 49 of the code of federal regulations and in a manner prescribed by the commissioner. A commercial driver's license shall also be downgraded to a non-commercial driver's license by the commissioner within sixty days of the holder's medical certification status becoming "not-certified" based upon receipt of information from the issuing medical examiner or the federal motor carrier safety administration that a medical certification or medical variance was issued in error or rescinded. Such downgrade shall be terminated, and the commercial driver's license restored, upon: (1) the holder's submission of the required valid medical examiner's certificate or medical variance documentation; or (2) the holder's self-certification specifying the type of commercial motor vehicle operation he or she engages, or expects to engage in, and that the holder is therefore not subject to the physical qualification requirements of the federal motor carrier safety improvement act of 1999 and Part 383.71(h) of title 49 of the code of federal regulations. The commissioner shall, upon a holder's status becoming "not-certified", notify the holder of such commercial driver's license by first class mail to the address of such person on file with the department or at the current address provided by the United States postal service of his or her "not-certified" medical certification status and that his or her commercial driver's license will be downgraded to a non-commercial driver's license unless he or she submits a current medical certificate and/or medical variance in accordance with Part 383.71(h) of title 49 of the code of federal regulations or changes his or her self-certification to driving only in excepted or intrastate commerce in accordance with Part 383.71(b)(ii)(B), (C) or (D) of title 49 of the code of federal regulations.

§510-b. Suspension and revocation for violations committed during probationary periods.

1. A license, other than a class DJ or class MJ license, shall be suspended, for a period of sixty days, (i) upon the first conviction of the licensee of a violation, committed during the probationary period provided for in subdivision four of section five hundred one of this title, of any provision of section eleven hundred twenty-nine of this chapter, section eleven hundred eighty of this chapter or any ordinance or regulation limiting the speed of motor vehicles and motorcycles, section eleven hundred eighty-two of this chapter, subdivision one of section eleven hundred ninety-two of this chapter or section twelve hundred twelve of this chapter; or (ii) upon the second conviction of the licensee of a violation, committed during the aforesaid probationary period, of any other provision of this chapter or of any other law, ordinance, order, rule or regulation relating to traffic.

2. A license, other than a class DJ or class MJ license, considered probationary pursuant to subdivision three of this section shall be revoked upon the conviction of the licensee of a violation or violations committed within six months following the restoration or issuance of such license, which conviction

or convictions would result in the suspension of a probationary license pursuant to subdivision one of this section or subparagraph (xvi) of paragraph b of subdivision two of section five hundred ten of this article.

3. Any license, other than a class DJ or class MJ license, which is restored or issued to a person who has had his last valid license suspended or revoked pursuant to the provisions of this section or the provisions of subparagraph (xii) of paragraph a or subparagraph (xvi) of paragraph b of subdivision two of section five hundred ten of this article shall be considered probationary until the expiration of six months following the date of restoration or issuance thereof.

4. The provisions of subdivisions one, five, six and seven of section five hundred ten of this chapter shall apply to any suspension or revocation under this section. However, the provisions of this section shall not operate to prevent a mandatory revocation or suspension for a greater period of time under subdivision two of section five hundred ten of this chapter or section eleven hundred ninety-three of this chapter; nor shall the provisions of this section prevent revocation or suspension under subdivisions two and three of section five hundred ten based upon two or more violations, including the same violation which was the basis for suspension or revocation under this section.

§510-c. Suspension and revocation of learner's permits and driver's licenses for violations committed by holders of class DJ or class MJ learner's permits or licenses.

1. (a) A learner's permit or a driver's license shall be suspended for a period of sixty days:

(i) upon a conviction or finding of a serious traffic violation as defined in subdivision two of this section, when such violation was committed while the holder had a class DJ or class MJ learner's permit or a class DJ or MJ license; or

(ii) upon the second conviction or finding of such permit or license holder of a violation of any other provision of this chapter or any other law, ordinance, order, rule or regulation relating to traffic, and when such violation was committed while such holder had a class DJ or class MJ learner's permit or a class DJ or MJ license.

(b) A learner's permit or a driver's license shall be revoked for a period of sixty days upon the conviction or finding of the permit or license holder of a violation or violations, committed within six months after the restoration of such permit or license suspended pursuant to paragraph (a) of this subdivision, which convictions or findings would result in the suspension of such permit or license pursuant to paragraph (a) of this subdivision.

2. For purposes of this section, the term "serious traffic violation" shall mean operating a motor vehicle in violation of any of the following provisions of this chapter: articles twenty-five and twenty-six; subdivision one of section six hundred; section six hundred one; sections eleven hundred eleven, eleven hundred seventy, eleven hundred seventy-two and eleven hundred seventy-four; subdivisions (a), (b), (c), (d) and (f) of section eleven hundred eighty, provided

that the violation involved ten or more miles per hour over the established limit; section eleven hundred eighty-two; subdivision three-a of section twelve hundred twenty-nine-c for violations involving use of safety belts or seats by a child under the age of sixteen; and section twelve hundred twelve of this chapter.

3. Any suspension or revocation required for a violation of section twelve hundred twenty-five-c or section twelve hundred twenty-five-d of this chapter shall be subject to the provisions of subdivisions two and six of section five hundred ten of this article.

§511. Operation while license or privilege is suspended or revoked; aggravated unlicensed operation.

1. Aggravated unlicensed operation of a motor vehicle in the third degree.

(a) A person is guilty of the offense of aggravated unlicensed operation of a motor vehicle in the third degree when such person operates a motor vehicle upon a public highway while knowing or having reason to know that such person's license or privilege of operating such motor vehicle in this state or privilege of obtaining a license to operate such motor vehicle issued by the commissioner is suspended, revoked or otherwise withdrawn by the commissioner.

(b) Aggravated unlicensed operation of a motor vehicle in the third degree is a misdemeanor. When a person is convicted of this offense, the sentence of the court must be: (i) a fine of not less than two hundred dollars nor more than five hundred dollars; or (ii) a term of imprisonment of not more than thirty days; or (iii) both such fine and imprisonment.

(c) When a person is convicted of this offense with respect to the operation of a motor vehicle with a gross vehicle weight rating of more than eighteen thousand pounds, the sentence of the court must be: (i) a fine of not less than five hundred dollars nor more than fifteen hundred dollars; or (ii) a term of imprisonment of not more than thirty days; or (iii) both such fine and imprisonment.

2. Aggravated unlicensed operation of a motor vehicle in the second degree. (a) A person is guilty of the offense of aggravated unlicensed operation of a motor vehicle in the second degree when such person commits the offense of aggravated unlicensed operation of a motor vehicle in the third degree as defined in subdivision one of this section; and

(i) has previously been convicted of an offense that consists of or includes the elements comprising the offense committed within the immediately preceding eighteen months; or

(ii) the suspension or revocation is based upon a refusal to submit to a chemical test pursuant to section eleven hundred ninety-four of this chapter, a finding of driving after having consumed alcohol in violation of section eleven hundred ninety-two-a of this chapter or upon a conviction for a violation of any of the provisions of section eleven hundred ninety-two of this chapter; or

(iii) the suspension was a mandatory suspension pending prosecution of a charge of a violation of section eleven hundred ninety-two of this chapter ordered pursuant to paragraph (e) of subdivision two of section eleven hundred ninety-three of this chapter or other similar statute; or

(iv) such person has in effect three or more suspensions, imposed on at least three separate dates, for failure to answer, appear or pay a fine, pursuant to subdivision three of section two hundred twenty-six or subdivision four-a of section five hundred ten of this chapter.

(b) Aggravated unlicensed operation of a motor vehicle in the second degree is a misdemeanor. When a person is convicted of this crime under subparagraph (i) of paragraph (a) of this subdivision, the sentence of the court must be:

(i) a fine of not less than five hundred dollars; and

(ii) a term of imprisonment not to exceed one hundred eighty days; or

(iii) where appropriate a sentence of probation as provided in subdivision six of this section; or (iv) a term of imprisonment as a condition of a sentence of probation as provided in the penal law and consistent with this section. When a person is convicted of this crime under subparagraph (ii), (iii) or (iv) of paragraph (a) of this subdivision, the sentence of the court must be: (i) a fine of not less than five hundred dollars nor more than one thousand dollars; and (ii) a term of imprisonment of not less than seven days nor more than one hundred eighty days, or (iii) where appropriate a sentence of probation as provided in subdivision six of this section; or (iv) a term of imprisonment as a condition of a sentence of probation as provided in the penal law and consistent with this section.

3. Aggravated unlicensed operation of a motor vehicle in the first degree.

(a) A person is guilty of the offense of aggravated unlicensed operation of a motor vehicle in the first degree when such person:

(i) commits the offense of aggravated unlicensed operation of a motor vehicle in the second degree as provided in subparagraph (ii), (iii) or (iv) of paragraph (a) of subdivision two of this section and is operating a motor vehicle while under the influence of alcohol or a drug in violation of subdivision one, two, two-a, three, four, four-a or five of section eleven hundred ninety-two of this chapter; or

(ii) commits the offense of aggravated unlicensed operation of a motor vehicle in the third degree as defined in subdivision one of this section; and is operating a motor vehicle while such person has in effect ten or more suspensions, imposed on at least ten separate dates for failure to answer, appear or pay a fine, pursuant to subdivision three of section two hundred twenty-six of this chapter or subdivision four-a of section five hundred ten of this article; or

(iii) commits the offense of aggravated unlicensed operation of a motor vehicle in the third degree as defined in subdivision one of this section; and is operating a motor vehicle while under permanent revocation as set forth in subparagraph twelve of paragraph (b) of subdivision two of section eleven hundred ninety-three of this chapter; or

(iv) operates a motor vehicle upon a public highway while holding a conditional license issued pursuant to paragraph (a) of subdivision seven of section eleven hundred ninety-six of this chapter while under the influence of alcohol or a drug in violation of subdivision one, two, two-a, three, four, four-a or five of section eleven hundred ninety-two of this chapter.

(b) Aggravated unlicensed operation of a motor vehicle in the first degree is a class E felony. When a person is convicted of this crime, the sentence of the court must be: (i) a fine in an amount not less than five hundred dollars nor more than five thousand dollars; and (ii) a term of imprisonment as provided in the penal law, or (iii) where appropriate and a term of imprisonment is not required by the penal law, a sentence of probation as provided in subdivision six of this section, or (iv) a term of imprisonment as a condition of a sentence of probation as provided in the penal law.

4. Defense. In any prosecution under this section or section five hundred eleven-a of this chapter, it is a defense that the person operating the motor vehicle has at the time of the offense a license issued by a foreign country, state, territory or federal district, which license is valid for operation in this state in accordance with the provisions of section two hundred fifty of this chapter.

5. Limitation on pleas. Where an accusatory instrument charges a violation of this section, any plea of guilty entered in satisfaction of such charge must include at least a plea of guilty of one of the offenses defined by this section and no other disposition by plea of guilty to any other charge in satisfaction of such charge shall be authorized; provided, however, that if the district attorney upon reviewing the available evidence determines that the charge of a violation of this section is not warranted, he may set forth upon the record the basis for such determination and consent to a disposition by plea of guilty to another charge in satisfaction of such charge, and the court may accept such plea.

6. Sentence of probation. In any case where a sentence of probation is authorized by this section, the court may in its discretion impose such sentence, provided however, if the court is of the opinion that a program of alcohol or drug treatment may be effective in assisting in prevention of future offenses of a similar nature upon imposing such sentence, the court shall require as a condition of the sentence that the defendant participate in such a program.

7. Exceptions. When a person is convicted of a violation of subdivision one or two of this section, and the suspension was issued pursuant to (a) subdivision four-e of section five hundred ten of this article due to a support arrears, or (b) subdivision four-f of section five hundred ten of the article due to past-due tax liabilities, the mandatory penalties set forth in subdivision one or two of this section shall not be applicable if, on or before the return date or subsequent adjourned date, such person presents proof that such support arrears or past-due tax liabilities have been satisfied as shown by certified check, notice issued by the court ordering the suspension, or notice from a support collection unit or department of taxation and finance as applicable. The sentencing court shall take the satisfaction of arrears or the payment of the past-due tax liabilities into account when imposing a sentence for any such conviction. For licenses suspended for non-payment of past-due tax liabilities, the court shall also take into consideration proof, in the form of a notice from

the department of taxation and finance, that such person has made payment arrangements that are satisfactory to the commissioner of taxation and finance.

§511-a. Facilitating aggravated unlicensed operation of a motor vehicle.
1. A person is guilty of the offense of facilitating aggravated unlicensed operation of a motor vehicle in the third degree when such person consents to the operation upon a public highway of a motor vehicle registered in such person's name knowing or having reason to know that the operator of such vehicle is a person whose license or privilege of operating such motor vehicle in this state or privilege of obtaining a license issued to operate such motor vehicle by the commissioner is suspended, revoked or otherwise withdrawn by the commissioner and the vehicle is operated upon a public highway by such person.

2. Facilitating aggravated unlicensed operation of a motor vehicle in the third degree is a traffic infraction. When a person is convicted thereof the sentence of the court must be: (i) a fine of not less than two hundred dollars nor more than five hundred dollars or (ii) a term of imprisonment of not more than fifteen days, or (iii) both.

3. A person is guilty of facilitating aggravated unlicensed operation of a motor vehicle in the second degree when such person:

(a) commits the offense of facilitating aggravated unlicensed operation of a motor vehicle in the third degree as defined in subdivision one of this section after having been convicted of such offense within the preceding eighteen months; or

(b) consents to the operation upon a public highway of a motor vehicle registered in such person's name knowing or having reason to know that the operator of such vehicle is a person who has in effect three or more suspensions, imposed on at least three separate dates, for failure to answer, appear or pay a fine, pursuant to subdivision three of section two hundred twenty-six or subdivision four-a of section five hundred ten of this chapter; or

(c) commits the crime of facilitating aggravated unlicensed operation of a motor vehicle in the third degree after having been convicted of such an offense two or more times within the preceding five years. For purposes of this subdivision, "motor vehicle" shall mean any vehicle for hire, including a taxicab, livery, as defined in section one hundred twenty-one-e of this chapter, coach, limousine, van or wheelchair accessible van, tow truck, bus or commercial motor vehicle as defined section five hundred nine-a of this chapter. Facilitating aggravated unlicensed operation of a motor vehicle in the second degree is a misdemeanor. When a person is convicted of this crime pursuant to paragraphs (a) or (b) of this subdivision, the sentence of the court must be: (i) a fine of not less than five hundred dollars, nor more than seven hundred fifty dollars; or (ii) a term of imprisonment not to exceed sixty days; or (iii) both a fine and imprisonment; or (iv) where appropriate, a sentence of probation; or (v) a term of imprisonment as a condition of a sentence of probation as provided in the penal law. When a person is convicted of this crime pursuant to paragraph (c) of this subdivision, the sentence of the court must be: (i) a fine of not less than five hundred, nor more than one thousand dollars; or (ii) a term of imprisonment not to exceed one hundred eighty days; or (iii) both a fine and imprisonment; or (iv) where appropriate, a sentence of probation; or (v) a term of imprisonment as a condition of probation as provided in the penal law.

4. A person is guilty of facilitating aggravated unlicensed operation of a motor vehicle in the first degree when such person consents to the operation upon a public highway of a motor vehicle registered in such person's name knowing or having reason to know that the operator of such vehicle is a person who has in effect ten or more suspensions, imposed on at least ten separate dates, for failure to answer, appear or pay a fine, pursuant to subdivision three of section two hundred twenty-six or subdivision four-a of section five hundred ten of this chapter. For purposes of this subdivision, "motor vehicle" shall mean any vehicle for hire, including a taxicab, livery, as defined in section one hundred twenty-one-e of this chapter, coach, limousine, van or wheelchair accessible van, tow truck, bus or commercial motor vehicle as defined in section five hundred nine-a of this chapter. Facilitating aggravated unlicensed operation of a motor vehicle in the first degree is a class E felony. When a person is convicted of this crime, the sentence of the court must be: (i) a fine in an amount not less than one thousand dollars nor more than five thousand dollars; and (ii) a term of imprisonment as provided in the penal law; or (iii) where appropriate, a sentence of probation; or (iv) a term of imprisonment as a condition of a sentence of probation as provided in the penal law.

5. Upon a conviction of a violation of subdivision three or four of this section the commissioner shall revoke the registration of the motor vehicle for which the defendant's consent is given and shall only be restored pursuant to the provisions of subdivision five of section five hundred ten of this article. If such defendant is a corporation, partnership, association or other group, none of its officers, principals, directors or stockholders owning more than ten percent of the outstanding stock of the corporation shall be eligible to register the motor vehicle.

§511-b. Seizure and redemption of unlawfully operated vehicles.

1. Upon making an arrest or upon issuing a summons or an appearance ticket for the crime of aggravated unlicensed operation of a motor vehicle in the first or second degree committed in his presence, an officer shall remove or arrange for the removal of the vehicle to a garage, automobile pound, or other place of safety where it shall remain impounded, subject to the provisions of this section if:

(a) the operator is the registered owner of the vehicle or the vehicle is not properly registered; or

(b) proof of financial security is not produced; or

(c) where a person other than the operator is the registered owner and, such person or another properly licensed and authorized to possess and operate the vehicle is not present. The vehicle shall be entered into the New York state-wide police information network as an impounded vehicle and the impounding police department shall promptly notify the owner and the local authority that the vehicle has been impounded.

2. A motor vehicle so impounded shall be in the custody of the local authority and shall not be released unless:

(a) The person who redeems it has furnished satisfactory evidence of registration and financial security;

(b) Payment has been made for the reasonable costs of removal and storage of the motor vehicle. The registered owner of the vehicle shall be responsible for such payment provided, however, that if he was not the operator at the time of the offense he shall have a cause of action against such operator to recover such costs. Payment prior to release of the vehicle shall not be required in cases where the impounded vehicle was stolen or was rented or leased pursuant to a written agreement for a period of thirty days or less, however the operator of such a vehicle shall be liable for the costs of removal and storage of the vehicle to any entity rendering such service.

(c) Where the motor vehicle was operated by a person who at the time of the offense was the owner thereof,

(i) satisfactory evidence that the registered owner or other person seeking to redeem the vehicle has a license or privilege to operate a motor vehicle in this state, and

(ii) (A) satisfactory evidence that the criminal action founded upon the charge of aggravated unlicensed operation of a motor vehicle has been terminated and that any fine imposed as a result of a conviction thereon has been paid, or (B) a certificate issued by the court in which the criminal action was commenced ordering release of the vehicle prior to the judgment or compliance therewith in the interest of justice, or (C) a certificate issued by the district attorney or other officer authorized to prosecute such charge waiving the requirement that the vehicle be held as security for appearance before and compliance with the judgment of the court.

3. When a vehicle seized and impounded pursuant to this section has been in the custody of the local authority for thirty days, such authority shall make inquiry in the manner prescribed by the commissioner as to the name and address of the owner and any lienholder and upon receipt of such information shall notify the owner and the lienholder, if any, at his last known address by certified mail, return receipt requested, that if the vehicle is not retrieved pursuant to subdivision two of this section within thirty days from the date the notice is given, it will be forfeited. If the vehicle was registered in New York the last known address shall be that address on file with the commissioner. If the vehicle was registered out-of-state or never registered, notification shall be made in the manner prescribed by the commissioner.

4. A motor vehicle that has been seized and not retrieved pursuant to the foregoing provisions of this section shall be forfeited to the local authority upon expiration of the period of the notice set forth in subdivision three of this section provided, however, in computing such period, the period of time during which a criminal prosecution is or was pending against the owner for a violation of this section shall be excluded. A proceeding to decree such for-

feiture and to recover towing and storage costs, if any, to the extent such costs exceed the fair market value of the vehicle may be brought by the local authority in the court in which the criminal action for aggravated unlicensed operation of a motor vehicle was commenced by petition for an order decreeing forfeiture of the motor vehicle accompanied by an affidavit attesting to facts showing that forfeiture is warranted. If the identity and address of the owner and/or lienholder is known to the local authority, ten days notice shall be given to such party, who shall have an opportunity to appear and be heard prior to entry of an order decreeing forfeiture. Where the court is satisfied that forfeiture of a motor vehicle is warranted in accordance with this section, it shall enter an order decreeing forfeiture of such vehicle. Provided, however, that the court at any time prior to entry of such an order may authorize release of the vehicle in accordance with subdivision two of this section upon a showing of good cause for failure to retrieve same prior to commencement of the proceeding to decree forfeiture, but if the court orders release of the motor vehicle as herein provided and the vehicle is not redeemed within ten days from the date of such order, the vehicle shall be deemed to have been abandoned and the court upon application of the local authority must enter an order decreeing its forfeiture.

5. A motor vehicle forfeited in accordance with the provisions of this section shall be and become the property of the local authority, subject however to any lien that was recorded prior to the seizure.

6. For the purposes of this section, the term "local authority" means the municipality in which the motor vehicle was seized; except that if the motor vehicle was seized on property of the New York state thruway authority or property under the jurisdiction of the office of parks, recreation and historic preservation, the department of transportation, or a public authority or commission, the term "local authority" means such authority, office, department, or commission. A county may provide by local law that the county may act as the agent for a local authority under this section.

7. When a vehicle has been seized and impounded pursuant to this section, the local authority or any person having custody of the vehicle shall make the vehicle available or grant access to it to any owner or any person designated or authorized by such owner for the purpose of

(i) taking possession of any personal property found within the vehicle and

(ii) obtaining proof of registration, financial security, title or documentation in support thereof.

§511-c. Seizure and forfeiture of vehicles used in the unlicensed operation of a motor vehicle under certain circumstances.

1. For purposes of this section:

(a) The term "owner" shall mean an owner as defined in section one hundred twenty-eight and in subdivision three of section three hundred eighty-eight of this chapter.

(b) The term "security interest" shall mean a security interest as defined in subdivision (k) of section two thousand one hundred one of this chapter.

(c) The term "termination of the criminal proceeding" shall mean the earliest of (i) thirty-one days following the imposition of sentence; or (ii) the date of acquittal of a person arrested for an offense; or (iii) where leave to file new charges or to resubmit the case to a new grand jury is required and has not been granted, thirty-one days following the dismissal of the last accusatory instrument filed in the case, or, if applicable, upon expiration of the time granted by the court or permitted by statute for filing new charges or resubmitting the case to a new grand jury; or (iv) where leave to file new charges or to resubmit the case to a new grand jury is not required, thirty-one days following the dismissal of the last accusatory instrument filed in the case, or, if applicable, upon expiration of the time granted by the court or permitted by statute for filing new charges or resubmitting the case to a new grand jury; or (v) six months from the issuance of an "adjournment in contemplation of dismissal" order pursuant to section 170.55 of the criminal procedure law, where the case is not restored to the court's calendar within the applicable six-month period; or (vi) the date when, prior to the filing of an accusatory instrument against a person arrested for an offense, the prosecuting authority elects not to prosecute such person.

2. Any motor vehicle which has been or is being used in violation of paragraph (a) of subdivision three of section five hundred eleven of this article may be seized by any peace officer, acting pursuant to his or her special duties, or police officer, and forfeited as hereinafter provided in this section.

3. A vehicle may be seized upon service of a notice of violation upon the owner or operator of a vehicle. The seized motor vehicle shall be delivered by the officer having made the seizure to the custody of the district attorney of the county wherein the seizure was made, except that in the cities of New York, Yonkers, Rochester and Buffalo the seized motor vehicle shall be delivered to the custody of the police department of such cities and such motor vehicle seized by a member or members of the state police shall be delivered to the custody of the superintendent of state police, together with a report of all the facts and circumstances of the seizure. Within one business day after the seizure, notice of such violation and a copy of the notice of violation shall be mailed to the owner of such vehicle at the address for such owner set forth in the records maintained by the department of motor vehicles or, for vehicles not registered in New York state, such equivalent record in such state of registration.

4. (a) The attorney general in seizures by members of the state police, or the district attorney of the county wherein the seizure is made, if elsewhere than in the cities of New York, Yonkers, Rochester or Buffalo, or where the seizure is made in such cities, the corporation counsel of the city shall inquire into the facts of the seizure so reported to him or her. If it appears that there is a basis for the commencement and prosecution of a forfeiture proceeding pursuant to this section, any such forfeiture proceeding shall be commenced in supreme court not later than twenty days after the date of receipt of a written demand by

a person claiming ownership of the motor vehicle accompanied by the documentation required to be presented upon release of the vehicle pursuant to subparagraphs (i), (ii), and (iv) of paragraph (a) of subdivision five of this section.

(b) Where forfeiture proceedings are commenced and prosecuted pursuant to this section, the motor vehicle which is the subject of such proceedings shall remain in the custody of such district attorney, police department or superintendent of state police, as applicable, pending the final determination of such proceedings.

(c) To the extent applicable, the procedures of article thirteen-A of the civil practice law and rules shall govern proceedings and actions under this section.

5. A motor vehicle seized pursuant to this section shall be released when:

(a) (i) Such attorney general, district attorney or corporation counsel has made a determination not to institute forfeiture proceedings pursuant to this section or the time period within which a forfeiture proceeding could have been commenced pursuant to this section has elapsed and no such forfeiture proceeding was commenced or the criminal proceeding has been terminated in favor of the accused, as defined in subdivision three of section 160.50 of the criminal procedure law; and

(ii) The person seeking to claim the motor vehicle has furnished satisfactory evidence of registration and financial security and, if the person was the operator of the vehicle at the time of the violation of paragraph (a) of subdivision three of section five hundred eleven of this article, satisfactory evidence of payment of any fines or penalties imposed in connection therewith; and

(iii) Payment has been made for the reasonable costs of removal and storage of the motor vehicle. The owner of the motor vehicle shall be responsible for such payment provided, however, that if he or she was not the operator at the time of the offense, such person shall have a cause of action against such operator to recover such costs. Payment prior to release of the motor vehicle shall not be required in cases where the seized motor vehicle was stolen or rented or leased pursuant to a written agreement for a period of thirty days or less, however the operator of such a motor vehicle shall be liable for the costs of removal and storage of the motor vehicle to any entity rendering such service; and

(iv) If the motor vehicle is held as evidence, the person seeking to claim the motor vehicle has presented a release from the prosecuting authority providing that the motor vehicle is not needed as evidence.

(b) (i) Pending completion of forfeiture proceedings which have been commenced, the person seeking to claim the motor vehicle has posted a bond in a form satisfactory to such attorney general, district attorney or corporation counsel in an amount that shall not exceed an amount sufficient to cover the maximum fines or civil penalties which may be imposed for the violation underlying the seizure and all reasonable costs for removal and storage of such vehicle; and

(ii) The persons seeking to claim the motor vehicle has furnished satisfactory evidence of registration and financial security.

6. Where a demand for the return of a motor vehicle is not made within ninety days after the termination of the criminal proceeding founded upon the charge of aggravated unlicensed operation of a motor vehicle in the first degree, such motor vehicle shall be deemed to be abandoned. Such vehicle shall be disposed of by the county, cities of New York, Yonkers, Rochester or Buffalo or the state, as applicable, in accordance with section twelve hundred twenty-four of this chapter or as otherwise provided by law.

7. Notice of the institution of the forfeiture proceeding shall be served:

(a) By personal service pursuant to the civil practice law and rules upon all owners of the seized motor vehicle listed in the records maintained by the department, or for vehicles not registered in New York state, in the records maintained by the state of registration; and

(b) By first class mail upon all individuals who have notified such attorney general, district attorney or corporation counsel that they are an owner of the vehicle and upon all persons holding a security interest in such motor vehicle which security interest has been filed with the department pursuant to the provisions of title ten of this chapter, at the address set forth in the records of such department, or for motor vehicles not registered in New York state, all persons holding a security interest in such motor vehicle which security interest has been filed with such state of registration, at the address provided by such state of registration.

8. Any owner who receives notice of the institution of a forfeiture action who claims an interest in the motor vehicle subject to forfeiture shall assert a claim for the recovery of the motor vehicle or satisfaction of the owner's interest in such motor vehicle by intervening in the forfeiture action in accordance with subdivision (a) of section one thousand twelve of the civil practice law and rules. Any person with a security interest in such vehicle who receives notice of the institution of the forfeiture action shall assert a claim for the satisfaction of such person's security interest in such vehicle by intervening in the forfeiture action in accordance with subdivision (a) of section one thousand twelve of the civil practice law and rules. If the action relates to a vehicle in which a person holding a security interest has intervened pursuant to this subdivision, the burden shall be upon the designated official to prove by clear and convincing evidence that such intervenor knew that such vehicle was or would be used for the commission of a violation of subparagraph (ii) of paragraph (a) of subdivision three of section five hundred eleven of the vehicle and traffic law and either (a) knowingly and unlawfully benefitted from such conduct or (b) voluntarily agreed to the use of the vehicle for the commission of such violation by consent freely given. For purposes of this subdivision, such intervenor knowingly and unlawfully benefited from the commission of such violation when he or she derived in exchange for permitting the use of such vehicle by a person or persons committing such specified violation a substantial benefit that would otherwise not have accrued as a result of the

lawful use of such vehicle. "Benefit" means benefit as defined in subdivision seventeen of section 10.00 of the penal law.

9. No motor vehicle shall be forfeited under this section to the extent of the interest of a person who claims an interest in the motor vehicle, where such person pleads and proves that:

(a) The use of such motor vehicle for the conduct that was the basis for a seizure occurred without the knowledge of such person, or if such person had knowledge of such use, without the consent of such person, and that such person did not knowingly obtain such interest in the motor vehicle in order to avoid the forfeiture of such vehicle; or

(b) The conduct that was the basis for such seizure was committed by any person other than such person claiming an interest in the motor vehicle, while such motor vehicle was unlawfully in the possession of a person who acquired possession thereof in violation of the criminal laws of the United States or any state.

10. The court in which a forfeiture action is pending may dismiss said action in the interests of justice upon its own motion or upon an application as provided for herein.

(a) At any time during the pendency of a forfeiture action, the designated official who instituted the action, or a defendant may apply for an order dismissing the complaint and terminating the forfeiture action in the interest of justice.

(b) Such application for the relief provided in paragraph (a) of this subdivision must be made in writing and upon notice to all parties. The court may, in its discretion, direct that notice be given to any other person having an interest in the property.

(c) An application for the relief provided for in paragraph (a) of this subdivision must be brought exclusively in the superior court in which the forfeiture action is pending.

(d) The court may grant the relief provided in paragraph (a) of this subdivision if it finds that such relief is warranted by the existence of some compelling factor, consideration or circumstance demonstrating that forfeiture of the property or any part thereof, would not serve the ends of justice. Among the factors, considerations and circumstances the court may consider, among others, are:

(i) the seriousness and circumstances of the crime to which the property is connected relative to the impact of forfeiture of property upon the person who committed the crime; or

(ii) the adverse impact of a forfeiture of property upon innocent persons.

(e) The court must issue a written decision stating the basis for an order issued pursuant to this subdivision.

11. The district attorney, police department or superintendent of state police having custody of the seized motor vehicle, after such judicial determination of forfeiture, shall, by a public notice of at least twenty days, sell such forfeited motor vehicle at public sale. The net proceeds of any such sale,

after deduction of the lawful expenses incurred, shall be paid into the general fund of the county wherein the seizure was made, provided, however, that the net proceeds of the sale of a motor vehicle seized in the cities of New York, Yonkers, Rochester and Buffalo shall be paid into the respective general funds of such cities, and provided further that the net proceeds of the sale of a motor vehicle seized by the state police shall be paid into the state police seized assets account.

12. In any action commenced pursuant to this section, where the court awards a sum of money to one or more persons in satisfaction of such person's or persons' interest or interests in the forfeited motor vehicle, the total amount awarded to satisfy such interest or interests shall not exceed the amount of the net proceeds of the sale of the forfeited motor vehicle, after deduction of the lawful expenses incurred by the county, cities of New York, Yonkers, Rochester or Buffalo or the state, as applicable, and storage of the motor vehicle between the time of seizure and the date of sale.

13. At any time within two years after the seizure, any person claiming an interest in a motor vehicle which has been forfeited pursuant to this section who was not sent notice of the commencement of the forfeiture action pursuant to subdivision seven of this section, or who did not otherwise receive actual notice of the forfeiture action, may assert in an action commenced before the justice of the supreme court before whom the forfeiture action was held such claim as could have been asserted in the forfeiture action pursuant to this section. The court may grant the relief sought upon such terms and conditions as it deems reasonable and just if the person claiming an interest in the motor vehicle establishes that he or she was not sent notice of the commencement of the forfeiture action and was without actual knowledge of the forfeiture action, and establishes either of the affirmative defenses set forth in subdivision nine of this section.

14. No action under this section for wrongful seizure shall be instituted unless such action is commenced within two years after the time when the motor vehicle was seized.

§511-d. Aggravated failure to answer appearance tickets or pay fines imposed.

1. A person is guilty of the offense of aggravated failure to answer appearance tickets or pay fines imposed when such person has in effect twenty or more suspensions, imposed on at least twenty separate dates, for failure to answer, appear or pay a fine pursuant to subdivision three of section two hundred twenty-six or subdivision four-a of section five hundred ten of this chapter.

2. A person may be prosecuted for a violation of this section in any court of competent jurisdiction in any county: (a) in which more than ten tickets which resulted in suspension for failures to answer, appear or pay fines were issued, or (b) in which the twentieth or any subsequent ticket which resulted in a suspension for failure to answer, appear or pay a fine was issued. The provi-

sions of this subdivision shall not apply to any suspension which has been terminated prior to the defendant's being charged with a violation of this section.

3. Aggravated failure to answer appearance tickets or pay fines imposed is a misdemeanor. When a person is convicted of this crime, the sentence of the court must be: (i) a fine of not less than five hundred dollars; or (ii) a term of imprisonment of not more than one hundred eighty days; or (iii) both such fine and imprisonment.

§512. Operation while registration or privilege is suspended or revoked.

Any person who operates any motor vehicle upon a public highway while the certificate of registration of such motor vehicle or privilege of operation of such motor vehicle in this state or privilege of obtaining a certificate of registration issued by the commissioner is suspended or revoked shall be guilty of a misdemeanor, and upon conviction shall be subject to a fine of not less than fifty dollars nor more than one hundred dollars or by imprisonment for not exceeding thirty days or by both such fine and imprisonment for conviction of a first offense; by a fine of not less than one hundred dollars nor more than two hundred dollars or by imprisonment for not exceeding ninety days or by both such fine and imprisonment for a conviction of a second offense committed within a period of eighteen months; by a fine of not less than two hundred dollars nor more than five hundred dollars or by imprisonment for not exceeding one hundred eighty days or by both such fine and imprisonment for a conviction of a third or subsequent offense committed within a period of eighteen months.

ARTICLE 22
ACCIDENTS AND ACCIDENT REPORTS

Section
600.   Leaving scene of an incident without reporting.
601.   Leaving scene of injury to certain animals without reporting.
602.   Arrest for violations of sections six hundred and six hundred one.
603.   Accidents; police authorities and coroners to report.
603-a.   Accidents; police authorities to investigate.
603-b.   Accidents; police to indicate serious physical injury and death on simplified traffic information.

§600. Leaving scene of an incident without reporting.

1. Property damage. a. Any person operating a motor vehicle who, knowing or having cause to know that damage has been caused to the real property or to the personal property, not including animals, of another, due to an incident involving the motor vehicle operated by such person shall, before leaving the place where the damage occurred, stop, exhibit his or her license and insurance identification card for such vehicle, when such card is required pursuant to articles six and eight of this chapter, and give his or her name, residence, including street and number, insurance carrier and insurance identification information including but not limited to the number and effective dates of said individual's insurance policy, and license number to the party

sustaining the damage, or in case the person sustaining the damage is not present at the place where the damage occurred then he or she shall report the same as soon as physically able to the nearest police station, or judicial officer. In addition to the foregoing, any such person shall also: (i) (A) produce the proof of insurance coverage required pursuant to article forty-four-B of this chapter if such person is a TNC driver operating a TNC vehicle while the incident occurred who was (1) logged on to the TNC's digital network but not engaged in a TNC prearranged trip or (2) was engaged in a TNC prearranged trip; and (B) disclose whether he or she, at the time such incident occurred, was (1) logged on to the TNC's digital network but not engaged in a TNC prearranged trip or (2) was engaged in a TNC prearranged trip, or (ii) (A) produce the proof of insurance coverage required pursuant to article forty of the general business law if such person is a shared vehicle owner or shared vehicle driver operating a shared vehicle during a peer-to-peer car sharing period while the incident occurred; and (B) disclose whether he or she, at the time such incident occurred, was operating a shared vehicle during a peer-to-peer car sharing period. *(Eff.3/22/22,Ch.795,L.2021)*

b. It shall be the duty of any member of a law enforcement agency who is at the scene of the accident to request the said operator or operators of the motor vehicles, when physically capable of doing so, to exchange the information required hereinabove and such member of a law enforcement agency shall assist such operator or operators in making such exchange of information in a reasonable and harmonious manner.

A violation of the provisions of paragraph a of this subdivision shall constitute a traffic infraction punishable by a fine of up to two hundred fifty dollars or a sentence of imprisonment for up to fifteen days or both such fine and imprisonment.

2. Personal injury. a. Any person operating a motor vehicle who, knowing or having cause to know that personal injury has been caused to another person, due to an incident involving the motor vehicle operated by such person shall, before leaving the place where the said personal injury occurred, stop, exhibit his or her license and insurance identification card for such vehicle, when such card is required pursuant to articles six and eight of this chapter, and give his or her name, residence, including street and street number, insurance carrier and insurance identification information including but not limited to the number and effective dates of said individual's insurance policy and license number, to the injured party, if practical, and also to a police officer, or in the event that no police officer is in the vicinity of the place of said injury, then, he or she shall report said incident as soon as physically able to the nearest police station or judicial officer. In addition to the foregoing, any such person shall also: (i) (A) produce the proof of insurance coverage required pursuant to article forty-four-B of this chapter if such person is a TNC driver operating a TNC vehicle at the time of the incident who was (1) logged on to the TNC's digital network but not engaged in a TNC prearranged trip or (2) was engaged in a TNC prearranged trip; and (B) disclose whether he or she, at the time such incident occurred, was (1) logged on to the TNC's digital network but not

engaged in a TNC prearranged trip or (2) was engaged in a TNC prearranged trip, or (ii) (A) produce the proof of insurance coverage required pursuant to article forty of the general business law if such person is a shared vehicle owner or shared vehicle driver operating a shared vehicle during a peer-to-peer car sharing period while the incident occurred; and (B) disclose whether he or she, at the time such incident occurred, was operating a shared vehicle during a peer-to-peer car sharing period. *(Eff.3/22/22,Ch.795,L.2021)*

b. It shall be the duty of any member of a law enforcement agency who is at the scene of the accident to request the said operator or operators of the motor vehicles, when physically capable of doing so, to exchange the information required hereinabove and such member of a law enforcement agency shall assist such operator or operators in making such exchange of information in a reasonable and harmonious manner.

c. A violation of the provisions of paragraph a of this subdivision resulting solely from the failure of an operator to exhibit his or her license and insurance identification card for the vehicle or exchange the information required in such paragraph shall constitute a class B misdemeanor punishable by a fine of not less than two hundred fifty nor more than five hundred dollars in addition to any other penalties provided by law. Any subsequent such violation shall constitute a class A misdemeanor punishable by a fine of not less than five hundred nor more than one thousand dollars in addition to any other penalties provided by law. Any violation of the provisions of paragraph a of this subdivision, other than for the mere failure of an operator to exhibit his or her license and insurance identification card for such vehicle or exchange the information required in such paragraph, shall constitute a class A misdemeanor, punishable by a fine of not less than five hundred dollars nor more than one thousand dollars in addition to any other penalties provided by law. Any such violation committed by a person after such person has previously been convicted of such a violation shall constitute a class E felony, punishable by a fine of not less than one thousand nor more than two thousand five hundred dollars in addition to any other penalties provided by law. Any violation of the provisions of paragraph a of this subdivision, other than for the mere failure of an operator to exhibit his or her license and insurance identification card for such vehicle or exchange the information required in such paragraph, where the personal injury involved (i) results in serious physical injury, as defined in section 10.00 of the penal law, shall constitute a class E felony, punishable by a fine of not less than one thousand nor more than five thousand dollars in addition to any other penalties provided by law, or (ii) results in death shall constitute a class D felony punishable by a fine of not less than two thousand nor more than five thousand dollars in addition to any other penalties provided by law.

3. For the purposes of this article, the terms "TNC", "TNC driver", "TNC vehicle", "TNC prearranged trip" and "digital network" shall have the same meanings as such terms are defined in article forty-four-B of this chapter and the terms "shared vehicle owner", "shared vehicle driver", "shared vehicle" and "peer-to-peer car sharing period" shall have the same meanings as such terms are defined in article forty of the general business law. *(Eff.3/22/22,Ch.795,L.2021)*

§601. Leaving scene of injury to certain animals without reporting.

Any person operating a motor vehicle which shall strike and injure any horse, dog, cat or animal classified as cattle shall stop and endeavor to locate the owner or custodian of such animal or a police, peace or judicial officer of the vicinity, and take any other reasonable and appropriate action so that the animal may have necessary attention, and shall also promptly report the matter to such owner, custodian or officer (or if no one of such has been located, then to a police officer of some other nearby community), exhibiting his or her license and insurance identification card for such vehicle, when such card is required pursuant to articles six and eight of this chapter, giving his or her name and residence, including street and street number, insurance carrier and insurance identification information and license number. In addition to the foregoing, any such person shall also: (i) (A) produce the proof of insurance coverage required pursuant to article forty-four-B of this chapter if such person is a TNC driver operating a TNC vehicle at the time of the incident who was (1) logged on to the TNC's digital network but not engaged in a TNC prearranged trip or (2) was engaged in a TNC prearranged trip; and (B) disclose whether he or she, at the time such incident occurred, was (1) logged on to the TNC's digital network but not engaged in a TNC prearranged trip or (2) was engaged in a TNC prearranged trip, or (ii) (A) produce the proof of insurance coverage required pursuant to article forty of the general business law if such person is a shared vehicle owner or shared vehicle driver operating a shared vehicle during a peer-to-peer car sharing period while the incident occurred; and (B) disclose whether he or she, at the time such incident occurred, was operating a shared vehicle during a peer-to-peer car sharing period. Violation of this section shall be punishable by a fine of not more than one hundred dollars for a first offense and by a fine of not less than fifty nor more than one hundred fifty dollars for a second offense and each subsequent offense; provided, however where the animal that has been struck and injured is a guide dog, hearing dog or service dog, as such terms are defined in section forty-seven-b of the civil rights law which is actually engaged in aiding or guiding a person with a disability, a violation of this section shall be punishable by a fine of not less than fifty nor more than one hundred fifty dollars for a first offense and by a fine of not less than one hundred fifty dollars nor more than three hundred dollars for a second offense and each subsequent offense.

(Eff.3/22/22,Ch.795,L.2021)

§602. Arrest for violations of sections six hundred and six hundred one.

A peace officer, acting pursuant to his special duties, or a police officer may, without a warrant, arrest a person, in case of violation of section six hundred and section six hundred one, which in fact have been committed, though not in his presence, when he has reasonable cause to believe that the violation was committed by such person.

§603. Accidents; police authorities and coroners to report.

1. Every police or judicial officer to whom an accident resulting in injury to a person shall have been reported, pursuant to the foregoing provisions of this chapter, shall immediately investigate the facts, or cause the same to be investigated, and report the matter to the commissioner forthwith; provided, however, that the report of the accident is made to the police officer or judicial officer within five days after such accident. Every coroner, or other official performing like functions, shall likewise make a report to the commissioner with respect to all deaths found to have been the result of motor vehicle or motorcycle accidents. Such report shall include information on the width and length of trucks, tractors, trailers and semitrailers, which are in excess of ninety-five inches in width or thirty-four feet in length and which are involved in such accidents, whether such accident took place in a work area and whether it was being operated with an overweight or overdimension permit. Such report shall distinctly indicate and include information as to whether the inflatable restraint system inflated and deployed. Nothing contained in this subdivision shall be deemed to preclude a police officer from reporting any other accident which, in the judgment of such police officer, would be required to be reported to the commissioner by the operator of a vehicle pursuant to section six hundred five of this article.

2. In addition to the requirements of subdivision one of this section, every police officer or judicial officer to whom an accident shall have been reported involving a commercial vehicle as defined in either subdivision four of section five hundred one-a or subdivision one of section five hundred nine-p of this chapter shall immediately investigate the facts, or cause the same to be investigated and report the matter to the commissioner forthwith, provided that the report of the accident is made to the police officer or judicial officer within five days after such accident, whenever such accident has resulted in (i) a vehicle being towed from the accident scene as the result of incurring disabling damage, (ii) a fatality, or (iii) any individual being transported to a medical facility to receive treatment as the result of physical injury sustained in the accident.

§603-a. Accidents; police authorities to investigate.

1. In addition to the requirements of section six hundred three of this article, whenever a motor vehicle accident results in serious physical injury or death to a person, and such accident either is discovered by a police officer, or reported to a police officer within five days after such accident occurred, the police shall conduct an investigation of such accident.

(a) Such investigation shall be conducted for the purposes of making a determination of the following: the facts and circumstances of the accident; the type or types of vehicles involved, including passenger motor vehicles, commercial motor vehicles, motorcycles, limited use motorcycles, off-highway motorcycles, and/or bicycles; whether pedestrians were involved; the contributing factor or factors; whether it can be determined if a violation or violations of this chapter occurred, and if so, the specific provisions of this chapter which were violated and by whom; and, the cause of such accident, where such cause can be determined.

(b) When present at the scene of such accident, the investigating officer shall also request that all operators of motor vehicles involved in such accident submit to field testing as defined in section eleven hundred ninety-four of this chapter provided there are reasonable grounds to believe such motor vehicle operator committed a serious traffic violation in the same accident. The results of such field testing or refusal of such testing shall be included in the police investigation report. For the purposes of this section, "serious traffic violation" shall mean operating a motor vehicle in violation of any of the following provisions of this chapter: articles twenty-three, twenty-four, twenty-five, twenty-six, twenty-eight, twenty-nine and thirty and sections five hundred eleven, six hundred and twelve hundred twelve.

(c) The police shall forward a copy of the investigation report to the commissioner within five business days of the completion of such report.

2. For purposes of this section, the following terms shall have the following meanings:

(a) "commercial motor vehicle" shall have the same meaning as such term is defined in either subdivision four of section five hundred one-a or subdivision one of section five hundred nine-p of this chapter; and

(b) "serious physical injury" shall have the same meaning as such term is defined in section 10.00 of the penal law.

§603-b. Accidents; police to indicate serious physical injury and death on simplified traffic information or summons and compliant*.

In addition to the requirements of section six hundred three of this article and subdivision twelve of section eleven hundred ninety-two of this chapter, in every case where a law enforcement officer is required to report pursuant to section six hundred three of this article and a person is charged with a violation of this chapter arising out of such accident, the law enforcement officer alleging such charge shall make a clear notation in the "Description of Violation" section of a simplified traffic information, or in an area provided on a summons and complaint pursuant to subdivision one of section two hundred twenty-six of this chapter, if, arising out of the same accident, someone other than the person charged was killed or suffered serious physical injury as defined in section 10.00 of the penal law; such notation shall be in the form of a "D" if someone other than the person charged was killed and such notation shall be in the form of a "S.P.I." if someone other than the person charged suffered serious physical injury; provided however, that the failure to make such notation shall in no way affect a charge for a violation of this chapter.

---

*So in original. Probably should be "complaint."

ARTICLE 23
OBEDIENCE TO AND EFFECT OF TRAFFIC LAWS

Section
1100.   Provisions of title refer to vehicles upon highways; exceptions.
1101.   Required obedience to traffic laws.
1102.   Obedience to police officers and flagpersons.
1103.   Public officers and employees to obey title; exceptions.
1104.   Authorized emergency vehicles.
1105.   Traffic laws apply to persons riding animals or driving animal-drawn vehicles.

§1100. Provisions of title refer to vehicles upon highways; exceptions.

(a) The provisions of this title apply upon public highways, private roads open to public motor vehicle traffic and any other parking lot, except where a different place is specifically referred to in a given section.

(b) The provisions of this title relating to obedience to stop signs, flashing signals, yield signs, traffic-control signals and other traffic-control devices, and to one-way, stopping, standing, parking and turning regulations shall apply to a parking lot only when the legislative body of any city, village or town has adopted a local law, ordinance, rule or regulation ordering such signs, signals, devices, or regulations.

(c) Notwithstanding the provisions of subdivision (b) of this section, the provisions of subparagraph e of paragraph two of subdivision (a) of section twelve hundred two and section twelve hundred three-c of this chapter shall also apply to any area which has been designated as a place for parking for handicapped persons pursuant to such section.

(d) The provisions of this title shall apply upon roadways, streets, and highways located within the boundaries of any federal military installations over which the federal government has proprietary jurisdiction if written request therefor is made by the commanding officer of such installation of the chief executive officer or officers of the political subdivision or subdivisions in which such installation is located and if the commanding officer of such installation shall post at the gates of such installation a notice informing all motorists entering such installation of such enforcement.

§1101. Required obedience to traffic laws.

It is unlawful and, unless otherwise declared in this title with respect to particular offenses, it is a traffic infraction for any person to do any act forbidden or fail to perform any act required in this title.

§1102. Obedience to police officers and flagpersons.

No person shall fail or refuse to comply with any lawful order or direction of any police officer or flagperson or other person duly empowered to regulate traffic.

§1103. Public officers and employees to obey title; exceptions.

(a) The provisions of this title applicable to the drivers of vehicles upon the highways shall apply to drivers of all vehicles owned or operated by the

United States, this state, or any county, city, town, district, or any other political subdivision of the state, except as provided in this section and subject to such specific exceptions as are set forth in this title with reference to authorized emergency vehicles.

(b) Unless specifically made applicable, the provisions of this title, except the provisions of sections eleven hundred ninety-two through eleven hundred ninety-six of this chapter, shall not apply to persons, teams, motor vehicles, and other equipment while actually engaged in work on a highway nor shall the provisions of subsection (a) of section twelve hundred two apply to hazard vehicles while actually engaged in hazardous operation on or adjacent to a highway but shall apply to such persons and vehicles when traveling to or from such hazardous operation. The foregoing provisions of this subdivision shall not relieve any person, or team or any operator of a motor vehicle or other equipment while actually engaged in work on a highway from the duty to proceed at all times during all phases of such work with due regard for the safety of all persons nor shall the foregoing provisions protect such persons or teams or such operators of motor vehicles or other equipment from the consequences of their reckless disregard for the safety of others.

§1104. Authorized emergency vehicles.

(a) The driver of an authorized emergency vehicle, when involved in an emergency operation, may exercise the privileges set forth in this section, but subject to the conditions herein stated.

(b) The driver of an authorized emergency vehicle may:

1. Stop, stand or park irrespective of the provisions of this title;

2. Proceed past a steady red signal, a flashing red signal or a stop sign, but only after slowing down as may be necessary for safe operation;

3. Exceed the maximum speed limits so long as he does not endanger life or property;

4. Disregard regulations governing directions of movement or turning in specified directions.

(c) Except for an authorized emergency vehicle operated as a police vehicle or bicycle, the exemptions herein granted to an authorized emergency vehicle shall apply only when audible signals are sounded from any said vehicle while in motion by bell, horn, siren, electronic device or exhaust whistle as may be reasonably necessary, and when the vehicle is equipped with at least one lighted lamp so that from any direction, under normal atmospheric conditions from a distance of five hundred feet from such vehicle, at least one red light will be displayed and visible.

(d) An authorized emergency vehicle operated as a police, sheriff or deputy sheriff vehicle may exceed the maximum speed limits for the purpose of calibrating such vehicles' speedometer. Notwithstanding any other law, rule or regulation to the contrary, a police, sheriff or deputy sheriff bicycle operated as an authorized emergency vehicle shall not be prohibited from using any sidewalk, highway, street or roadway during an emergency operation.

(e) The foregoing provisions shall not relieve the driver of an authorized emergency vehicle from the duty to drive with due regard for the safety of all persons, nor shall such provisions protect the driver from the consequences of his reckless disregard for the safety of others.

(f) Notwithstanding any other law, rule or regulation to the contrary, an ambulance operated in the course of an emergency shall not be prohibited from using any highway, street or roadway; provided, however, that an authority having jurisdiction over any such highway, street or roadway may specifically prohibit travel thereon by ambulances if such authority shall deem such travel to be extremely hazardous and would endanger patients being transported thereby.

§1105. Traffic laws apply to persons riding animals or driving animal-drawn vehicles.

Every person riding an animal or driving an animal-drawn vehicle upon a roadway shall be granted all of the rights and shall be subject to all of the duties applicable to the driver of a vehicle by this title, except those provisions of this title which by their very nature can have no application.

ARTICLE 30
SPEED RESTRICTIONS

Section
1180.   **Basic rule and maximum limits.**
1180-a.   **Maximum speed limits.**
1180-b.   **Owner liability for failure of operator to comply with certain posted maximum speed limits.**
1180-c.   *(Repealed, L. 2014)*
1180-d.   **Owner liability for failure of operator to comply with certain posted maximum speed limits.**
1181.   **Minimum speed regulations.**

§1180. Basic rule and maximum limits.

(a) No person shall drive a vehicle at a speed greater than is reasonable and prudent under the conditions and having regard to the actual and potential hazards then existing.

(b) Except as provided in subdivision (g) of this section and except when a special hazard exists that requires lower speed for compliance with subdivision (a) of this section or when maximum speed limits have been established as hereinafter authorized, no person shall drive a vehicle at a speed in excess of fifty-five miles per hour.

(c) Except as provided in subdivision (g) of this section, whenever maximum school speed limits have been established on a highway adjacent to a school as authorized in section sixteen hundred twenty, sixteen hundred twenty-two, sixteen hundred thirty, sixteen hundred forty-three or sixteen hundred sixty-two-a, no person shall drive in excess of such maximum school speed limits during:

(1) school days at times indicated on the school zone speed limit sign, provided, however, that such times shall be between the hours of seven o'clock A.M. and six o'clock P.M. or alternative times within such hours; or

(2) a period when the beacons attached to the school zone speed limit sign are flashing and such sign is equipped with a notice that indicates that the school zone speed limit is in effect when such beacons are flashing, provided, however, that such beacons shall only flash during student activities at the school and up to thirty minutes immediately before and up to thirty minutes immediately after such student activities.

(d) 1. Except as provided in subdivision (g) of this section, whenever maximum speed limits, other than school speed limits, have been established as authorized in sections sixteen hundred twenty, sixteen hundred twenty-two, sixteen hundred twenty-three, sixteen hundred twenty-seven, sixteen hundred thirty, sixteen hundred forty-three, sixteen hundred forty-four, sixteen hundred fifty-two, sixteen hundred sixty-two-a, sixteen hundred sixty-three, and sixteen hundred seventy, no person shall drive in excess of such maximum speed limits at any time.

2. Except as provided in subdivision (g) of this section, whenever maximum speed limits, other than school speed limits, have been established with respect to any restricted highway as authorized in section sixteen hundred

twenty-five, no person shall drive in excess of such maximum speed limits at any time.

(e) The driver of every vehicle shall, consistent with the requirements of subdivision (a) of this section, drive at an appropriate reduced speed when approaching and crossing an intersection or railway grade crossing, when approaching and going around a curve, when approaching a hill crest, when approaching and passing by an emergency situation involving any authorized emergency vehicle which is parked, stopped or standing on a highway and which is displaying one or more red or combination red and white lights pursuant to the provisions of paragraph two of subdivision forty-one of section three hundred seventy-five of this chapter, when traveling upon any narrow or winding roadway, and when any special hazard exists with respect to pedestrians, or other traffic by reason of weather or highway conditions, including, but not limited to a highway construction or maintenance work area, or when approaching a hazard vehicle which is parked, stopped or standing on the shoulder or on any portion of such highway and such hazard vehicle is displaying one or more amber lights pursuant to the provisions of paragraph three of subdivision forty-one of section three hundred seventy-five of this chapter.

(f) Except as provided in subdivision (g) of this section and except when a special hazard exists that requires lower speed for compliance with subdivision (a) or (e) of this section or when a lower maximum speed limit has been established, no person shall drive a vehicle through a highway construction or maintenance work area at a speed in excess of the posted work area speed limit. The agency having jurisdiction over the affected street or highway may establish work area speed limits which are less than the normally posted speed limits; provided, however, that such normally posted speed limit may exceed the work area speed limit by no more than twenty miles per hour; and provided further that no such work area speed limit may be established at less than twenty-five miles per hour.

(g) (i) No person who uses a radar or laser detector in a vehicle with a gross vehicle weight rating of more than eighteen thousand pounds, or a commercial motor vehicle with a gross vehicle weight rating of more than ten thousand pounds, shall drive at a speed in excess of fifty-five miles per hour or, if a maximum speed limit other than fifty-five miles per hour as hereinbefore authorized has been established, at a speed in excess of such speed limit. The presence in any such vehicle of either:

(1) a radar or laser detector connected to a power source and in an operable condition; or

(2) a concealed radar or laser detector where a part of such detector is securely affixed to some part of the vehicle outside of the cab, in a manner which renders the detector not readily observable, is presumptive evidence of its use by any person operating such vehicle. Either such presumption shall be rebutted by any credible and reliable evidence which tends to show that such radar or laser detector was not in use.

(ii) The provisions of this section shall not be construed as authorizing the seizure or forfeiture of a radar or laser detector, unless otherwise provided by law.

(h) Upon a conviction for a violation of subdivision (b), (c), (d), (f) or (g) of this section, the court shall record the speed upon which the conviction was based on the certificate required to be filed with the commissioner pursuant to section five hundred fourteen of this chapter, or if the conviction occurs in an administrative tribunal established pursuant to article two-A of this chapter, the speed upon which the conviction was based shall be entered in the department's records.

1. Every person convicted of a violation of subdivision (b) or paragraph one of subdivision (d) of this section shall be punished as follows:

(i) Where the court or tribunal records or enters that the speed upon which the conviction was based exceeded the applicable speed limit by not more than ten miles per hour, by a fine of not less than forty-five nor more than one hundred fifty dollars;

(ii) Where the court or tribunal records or enters that the speed upon which the conviction was based exceeded the applicable speed limit by more than ten miles per hour but not more than thirty miles per hour, by a fine of not less than ninety nor more than three hundred dollars or by imprisonment for not more than fifteen days or by both such fine and imprisonment;

(iii) Where the court or tribunal records or enters that the speed upon which the conviction was based exceeded the applicable speed limit by more than thirty miles per hour, by a fine of not less than one hundred eighty nor more than six hundred dollars, or by imprisonment for not more than thirty days, or by both such fine and imprisonment.

2. Every person convicted of a violation of subdivision (a) or (e) of this section shall be punished by a fine of not less than forty-five nor more than one hundred fifty dollars, or by imprisonment for not more than fifteen days, or by both such fine and imprisonment.

3. Every person convicted of a violation of paragraph two of subdivision (d), subdivision (f) or (g) of this section shall be punished as follows:

(i) Where the court or tribunal records or enters that the speed upon which the conviction was based exceeded the applicable speed limit by not more than ten miles per hour, by a fine of not less than ninety nor more than one hundred fifty dollars;

(ii) Where the court or tribunal records or enters that the speed upon which the conviction was based exceeded the applicable speed limit by more than ten miles per hour, but not more than thirty miles per hour, by a fine of not less than one hundred eighty nor more than three hundred dollars or by imprisonment for not more than thirty days, or by both such fine and imprisonment, provided, however, that where the vehicle is either (A) in violation of any rules or regulations involving an out-of-service defect relating to brake systems, steering components and/or coupling devices, or (B) transporting flammable gas, radioactive materials or explosives, the fine shall be three hundred dollars or imprisonment for not more than thirty days, or both such fine and imprisonment;

(iii) Where the court or tribunal records or enters that the speed upon which the conviction was based exceeded the applicable speed limit by more than thirty miles per hour, by a fine of not less than three hundred sixty nor more than six hundred dollars or by imprisonment for not more than thirty days or by both such fine and imprisonment, provided, however, that where the vehicle is either (A) in violation of any rules or regulations involving an out-of-service defect relating to brake systems, steering components and/or coupling devices, or (B) transporting flammable gas, radioactive materials or explosives, the fine shall be six hundred dollars or imprisonment for not more than thirty days, or both such fine and imprisonment.

4. Every person convicted of a violation of subdivision (c) of this section when such violation occurs in a school speed zone during a school day between the hours of seven o'clock A.M. and six o'clock P.M., shall be punished as follows:

(i) Where the court or tribunal records or enters that the speed upon which the conviction was based exceeded the applicable speed limit by not more than ten miles per hour, by a fine of not less than ninety nor more than three hundred dollars;

(ii) Where the court or tribunal records or enters that the speed upon which the conviction was based exceeded the applicable speed limit by more than ten miles per hour but not more than thirty miles per hour, by a fine of not less than one hundred eighty nor more than six hundred dollars or by imprisonment for not more than fifteen days or by both such fine and imprisonment;

(iii) Where the court or tribunal records or enters that the speed upon which the conviction was based exceeded the applicable speed limit by more than thirty miles per hour, by a fine of not less than three hundred sixty nor more than one thousand two hundred dollars, or by imprisonment for not more than thirty days, or by both such fine and imprisonment.

5. Notwithstanding the foregoing provisions of this subdivision, the maximum fine provided herein for the violation for which the person is sentenced may be increased by an additional one hundred fifty dollars if the conviction is for a second violation of any subdivision of this section where both violations were committed within an eighteen month period, and the maximum fine provided herein for the violation for which the person is sentenced may be increased by an additional three hundred seventy-five dollars if the conviction is for a third or subsequent violation of any subdivision of this section where all such violations were committed within an eighteen month period. Where an additional fine is provided by this paragraph, a sentence of imprisonment for not more than thirty days may be imposed in place of or in addition to any fine imposed.

§1180-a. Maximum speed limits.

1. Notwithstanding any other provision of law, no city, village, town, county, public authority, division, office or department of the state shall

maintain or create (a) any speed limit in excess of fifty-five miles per hour on any road, highway, parkway or bridge or (b) any speed limit on any other portion of a public highway, which is not uniformly applicable to all types of motor vehicles using such portion of highway, if on November first, nineteen hundred seventy-three, such portion of highway had a speed limit which was uniformly applicable to all types of motor vehicles using it; provided however, a lower speed limit may be established for any vehicle operating under a special permit because of any weight or dimension of such vehicle, including any load thereon, and (c) provided further, paragraph (b) of this subdivision shall not apply to any portion of a highway during such time that the condition of the highway, weather, an accident, or other condition creates a temporary hazard to the safety of traffic on such portion of a highway. However, the commissioner of the department of transportation may establish a maximum speed limit of not more than sixty-five miles per hour on any state roadway which meets department criteria for such maximum speed.

2. Notwithstanding the provisions of paragraphs (a) and (b) of subdivision one of this section, upon The Governor Thomas E. Dewey Thruway as such term is defined in section three hundred fifty-six of the public authorities law, the New York state thruway authority may establish a maximum speed limit of not more than sixty-five miles per hour provided that such maximum allowable speed limit is established in accordance with all applicable rules and regulations.

3. Notwithstanding the provisions of paragraphs (a) and (b) of subdivision one of this section, upon (a) the southern tier expressway from a point east of the town of Lowman, in the county of Chemung, thence generally westerly to the Pennsylvania border and from the Chemung interchange to New York touring route twenty-six, (b) interstate route eighty-one from the Pennsylvania border in Broome county to the interchange with New York state touring route twelve in Jefferson county, (c) the Adirondack northway portion of interstate route eighty-seven from the interchange with Crescent Road in Saratoga county to the province of Quebec, (d) interstate route eighty-eight from the interchange with New York state touring route three hundred sixty-nine in Broome county to the interchange with interstate route ninety in Schenectady county, (e) interstate route three hundred ninety, known as the Genesee Expressway, from the interchange with the southern tier expressway in Steuben county to the interchange with interstate route four hundred ninety in Monroe county, (f) interstate route four hundred ninety from interstate ninety exit forty-five in Ontario county to the city of Rochester in Monroe county and from interstate ninety exit forty-seven in Genesee county to the city of Rochester in Monroe county, (g) interstate route five hundred ninety from the interchange with interstate route three hundred ninety in Monroe county to the interchange with interstate route four hundred ninety in Monroe county, (h) route seventeen from the interchange with New York touring route three hundred ninety-four to the Pennsylvania border, (i) interstate route four hundred eighty-one from the southerly interchange with interstate route eighty-one in Onondaga county to the northerly interchange with interstate route eighty-one in Onondaga county,

(j) New York state touring route four hundred eighty-one from the northerly interchange with interstate route eighty-one in Onondaga county to the city of Fulton in Oswego county, (k) interstate ninety from exit eight, in the county of Rensselaer, thence generally easterly to the interchange with the Berkshire section of The Governor Thomas E. Dewey Thruway, (l) interstate route six hundred ninety, from the city of Syracuse and town of Geddes border, thence generally westerly to the interchange with the New York state thruway, (m) New York state touring route six hundred ninety, from the interchange with the New York state thruway, thence generally westerly to its intersection with New York state touring route forty-eight in the town of Lysander, (n) New York state touring route six hundred ninety-five, from the interchange with interstate route six hundred ninety approximately 2.3 miles to the interchange with New York state touring route five, (o) New York state touring route five from the interchange with New York state touring route six hundred ninety-five approximately 5.0 miles to the interchange with New York state touring route one hundred seventy-four in the town of Camillus, and (p) route five hundred thirty-one from the interchange with interstate route four hundred ninety in Monroe county to the interchange with route thirty-six in Monroe county, and (q) United States route two hundred nineteen, from the interchange with Armor Duelles Road in the town of Orchard Park, thence generally southerly to the interchange with New York state route thirty-nine in the town of Concord, the commissioner of the department of transportation may establish a maximum speed limit of not more than sixty-five miles per hour provided that such maximum allowable speed limit is established in accordance with all applicable rules and regulations.

*§1180-b.   Owner liability for failure of operator to comply with certain posted maximum speed limits.

(a) 1. Notwithstanding any other provision of law, the city of New York is hereby authorized to establish a demonstration program imposing monetary liability on the owner of a vehicle for failure of an operator thereof to comply with posted maximum speed limits in a school speed zone within such city (i) when a school speed limit is in effect as provided in paragraphs one and two of subdivision (c) of section eleven hundred eighty of this article or (ii) when other speed limits are in effect as provided in subdivision (b), (d), (f) or (g) of section eleven hundred eighty of this article weekdays between the hours of six o'clock A.M. and ten o'clock P.M. Such demonstration program shall empower the city of New York to install photo speed violation monitoring systems within no more than seven hundred fifty school speed zones within such city at any one time and to operate such systems within such zones (iii) when a school speed limit is in effect as provided in paragraphs one and two of subdivision (c) of section eleven hundred eighty of this article or (iv) when other speed limits are in effect as provided in subdivision (b), (d), (f) or (g) of section eleven hundred eighty of this article weekdays between the hours of six o'clock A.M. and ten o'clock P.M. In selecting a school speed zone in which to install and operate a photo speed violation monitoring system, the city of New York shall consider criteria including, but not limited to, the speed data, crash history, and the roadway geometry applicable to such school speed zone. Such city shall prioritize the placement of photo speed violation monitoring systems in school speed zones based upon speed data or the crash history of a school speed zone. A photo speed violation monitoring system shall not be installed or operated on a controlled-access highway exit ramp or within three hundred feet along a highway that continues from the end of a controlled-access highway exit ramp.

2. No photo speed violation monitoring system shall be used in a school speed zone unless (i) on the day it is to be used it has successfully passed a self-test of its functions; and (ii) it has undergone an annual calibration check performed pursuant to paragraph four of this subdivision. The city shall install signs giving notice to approaching motor vehicle operators that a photo speed violation monitoring system is in use, in conformance with standards established in the MUTCD.

3. Operators of photo speed violation monitoring systems shall have completed training in the procedures for setting up, testing, and operating such systems. Each such operator shall complete and sign a daily set-up log for each such system that he or she operates that (i) states the date and time when, and the location where, the system was set up that day, and (ii) states that such operator successfully performed, and the system passed, the self-tests of such system before producing a recorded image that day. The city shall retain each such daily log until the later of the date on which the photo speed violation monitoring system to which it applies has been permanently removed from use or the final resolution of all cases involving notices of liability issued based on photographs, microphotographs, video or other recorded images produced by such system.

4. Each photo speed violation monitoring system shall undergo an annual calibration check performed by an independent calibration laboratory which shall issue a signed certificate of calibration. The city shall keep each such annual certificate of calibration on file until the final resolution of all cases involving a notice of liability issued during such year which were based on photographs, microphotographs, videotape or other recorded images produced by such photo speed violation monitoring system.

5. (i) Such demonstration program shall utilize necessary technologies to ensure, to the extent practicable, that photographs, microphotographs, videotape or other recorded images produced by such photo speed violation monitoring systems shall not include images that identify the driver, the passengers, or the contents of the vehicle. Provided, however, that no notice of liability issued pursuant to this section shall be dismissed solely because such a photograph, microphotograph, videotape or other recorded image allows for the identification of the driver, the passengers, or the contents of vehicles where the city shows that it made reasonable efforts to comply with the provisions of this paragraph in such case.

(ii) Photographs, microphotographs, videotape or any other recorded image from a photo speed violation monitoring system shall be for the exclusive use of the city for the purpose of the adjudication of liability imposed pursuant to this section and of the owner receiving a notice of liability pursuant to this section, and shall be destroyed by the city upon the final resolution of the notice of liability to which such photographs, microphotographs, videotape or other recorded images relate, or one year following the date of issuance of such notice of liability, whichever is later. Notwithstanding the provisions of any other law, rule or regulation to the contrary, photographs, microphotographs, videotape or any other recorded image from a photo speed violation monitoring system shall not be open to the public, nor subject to civil or criminal process or discovery, nor used by any court or administrative or adjudicatory body in any action or proceeding therein except that which is necessary for the adjudication of a notice of liability issued pursuant to this section, and no public entity or employee, officer or agent thereof shall disclose such information, except that such photographs, microphotographs, videotape or any other recorded images from such systems:

(A) shall be available for inspection and copying and use by the motor vehicle owner and operator for so long as such photographs, microphotographs, videotape or other recorded images are required to be maintained or are maintained by such public entity, employee, officer or agent; and

(B) (1) shall be furnished when described in a search warrant issued by a court authorized to issue such a search warrant pursuant to article six hundred ninety of the criminal procedure law or a federal court authorized to issue such a search warrant under federal law, where such search warrant states that there is reasonable cause to believe such information constitutes evidence of, or tends to demonstrate that, a misdemeanor or felony offense was committed in this state or another state, or that a particular person participated in the commission of a misdemeanor or felony offense in this state or another state, provided, however, that if such offense was against the laws of another state, the court shall only issue a warrant if the conduct comprising such offense would, if occurring in this state, constitute a misdemeanor or felony against the laws of this state; and

(2) shall be furnished in response to a subpoena duces tecum signed by a judge of competent jurisdiction and issued pursuant to article six hundred ten of the criminal procedure law or a judge or magistrate of a federal court authorized to issue such a subpoena duces tecum under federal law, where the judge finds and the subpoena states that there is reasonable cause to believe such information is relevant and material to the prosecution, or the defense, or the investigation by an authorized law enforcement official, of the alleged commission of a misdemeanor or felony in this state or another state, provided, however, that if such offense was against the laws of another state, such judge or magistrate shall only issue such subpoena if the conduct comprising such offense would, if occurring in this state, constitute a misdemeanor or felony in this state; and

(3) may, if lawfully obtained pursuant to this clause and clause (A) of this subparagraph and otherwise admissible, be used in such criminal action or proceeding.

(b) If the city of New York establishes a demonstration program pursuant to subdivision (a) of this section, the owner of a vehicle shall be liable for a penalty imposed pursuant to this section if such vehicle was used or operated with the permission of the owner, express or implied, within a school speed zone in violation of subdivision (c) or during the times authorized pursuant to subdivision (a) of this section in violation of subdivision (b), (d), (f) or (g) of section eleven hundred eighty of this article, such vehicle was traveling at a speed of more than ten miles per hour above the posted speed limit in effect within such school speed zone, and such violation is evidenced by information obtained from a photo speed violation monitoring system; provided however that no owner of a vehicle shall be liable for a penalty imposed pursuant to this section where the operator of such vehicle has been convicted of the underlying violation of subdivision (b), (c), (d), (f) or (g) of section eleven hundred eighty of this article.

(c) For purposes of this section, the following terms shall have the following meanings:

1. "manual on uniform traffic control devices" or "MUTCD" shall mean the manual and specifications for a uniform system of traffic control devices maintained by the commissioner of transportation pursuant to section sixteen hundred eighty of this chapter;

2. "owner" shall have the meaning provided in article two-B of this chapter.

3. "photo speed violation monitoring system" shall mean a vehicle sensor installed to work in conjunction with a speed measuring device which automatically produces two or more photographs, two or more microphotographs, a videotape or other recorded images of each vehicle at the time it is used or operated in a school speed zone in violation of subdivision (b), (c), (d), (f) or (g) of section eleven hundred eighty of this article in accordance with the provisions of this section; and

4. "school speed zone" shall mean a radial distance not to exceed one thousand three hundred twenty feet from a school building, entrance, or exit.

(d) A certificate, sworn to or affirmed by a technician employed by the city of New York, or a facsimile thereof, based upon inspection of photographs, microphotographs, videotape or other recorded images produced by a photo speed violation monitoring system, shall be prima facie evidence of the facts contained therein. Any photographs, microphotographs, videotape or other recorded images evidencing such a violation shall include at least two date and time stamped images of the rear of the motor vehicle that include the same stationary object near the motor vehicle and shall be available for inspection reasonably in advance of and at any proceeding to adjudicate the liability for such violation pursuant to this section.

(e) An owner liable for a violation of subdivision (b), (c), (d), (f) or (g) of section eleven hundred eighty of this article pursuant to a demonstration program established pursuant to this section shall be liable for monetary penalties in accordance with a schedule of fines and penalties to be promulgated by the parking violations bureau of the city of New York. The liability of the owner pursuant to this section shall not exceed fifty dollars for each violation; provided, however, that such parking violations bureau may provide for an additional penalty not in excess of twenty-five dollars for each violation for the failure to respond to a notice of liability within the prescribed time period.

(f) An imposition of liability under the demonstration program established pursuant to this section shall not be deemed a conviction as an operator and shall not be made part of the operating record of the person upon whom such liability is imposed nor shall it be used for insurance purposes in the provision of motor vehicle insurance coverage.

(g) 1. A notice of liability shall be sent by first class mail to each person alleged to be liable as an owner for a violation of subdivision (b), (c), (d), (f) or (g) of section eleven hundred eighty of this article pursuant to this section, within fourteen business days if such owner is a resident of this state and within forty-five business days if such owner is a non-resident. Personal delivery on the owner shall not be required. A manual or automatic record of mailing prepared in the ordinary course of business shall be prima facie evidence of the facts contained therein.

2. A notice of liability shall contain the name and address of the person alleged to be liable as an owner for a violation of subdivision (b), (c), (d), (f) or (g) of section eleven hundred eighty of this article pursuant to this section, the registration number of the vehicle involved in such violation, the location where such violation took place, the date and time of such violation, the identification number of the camera which recorded the violation or other document locator number, at least two date and time stamped images of the rear of the motor vehicle that include the same stationary object near the motor vehicle, and the certificate charging the liability.

3. The notice of liability shall contain information advising the person charged of the manner and the time in which he or she may contest the liability alleged in the notice. Such notice of liability shall also contain a prominent warning to advise the person charged that failure to contest in the manner and time provided shall be deemed an admission of liability and that a default judgment may be entered thereon.

4. The notice of liability shall be prepared and mailed by the city of New York, or by any other entity authorized by the city to prepare and mail such notice of liability.

(h) Adjudication of the liability imposed upon owners of this section shall be by the New York city parking violations bureau.

(i) If an owner receives a notice of liability pursuant to this section for any time period during which the vehicle or the number plate or plates of such vehicle was reported to the police department as having been stolen, it shall be a valid defense to an allegation of liability for a violation of subdivision (b), (c), (d), (f) or (g) of section eleven hundred eighty of this article pursuant to this section that the vehicle or the number plate or plates of such vehicle had been reported to the police as stolen prior to the time the violation occurred and had not been recovered by such time. For purposes of asserting the defense provided by this subdivision, it shall be sufficient that a certified copy of the police report on the stolen vehicle or number plate or plates of such vehicle be sent by first class mail to the New York city parking violations bureau, or by any other entity authorized by the city to prepare and mail such notice of liability.

(j) Adjudication of the liability imposed upon owners of this section shall be by the New York city parking violations bureau.

(k) 1. An owner who is a lessor of a vehicle to which a notice of liability was issued pursuant to subdivision (g) of this section shall not be liable for the violation of subdivision (b), (c), (d), (f) or (g) of section eleven hundred eighty of this article pursuant to this section, provided that:

(i) prior to the violation, the lessor has filed with such parking violations bureau in accordance with the provisions of section two hundred thirty-nine of this chapter; and

(ii) within thirty-seven days after receiving notice from such bureau of the date and time of a liability, together with the other information contained in the original notice of liability, the lessor submits to such bureau the correct name and address of the lessee of the vehicle identified in the notice of liability at the time of such violation, together with such other additional information contained in the rental, lease or other contract document, as may be reasonably required by such bureau pursuant to regulations that may be promulgated for such purpose.

2. Failure to comply with subparagraph (ii) of paragraph (a) of this subdivision shall render the owner liable for the penalty prescribed in this section.

3. Where the lessor complies with the provisions of paragraph (a) of this subdivision, the lessee of such vehicle on the date of such violation shall be deemed to be the owner of such vehicle for purposes of this section, shall be subject to liability for such violation pursuant to this section and shall be sent a notice of liability pursuant to subdivision nine of this section.

(*l*) 1. If the owner liable for a violation of subdivision (c) or (d) of section eleven hundred eighty of this article pursuant to this section was not the operator of the vehicle at the time of the violation, the owner may maintain an action for indemnification against the operator.

2. Notwithstanding any other provision of this section, no owner of a vehicle shall be subject to a monetary fine imposed pursuant to this section if the operator of such vehicle was operating such vehicle without the consent of the owner at the time such operator operated such vehicle in violation of subdivision (b), (c), (d), (f) or (g) of section eleven hundred eighty of this article. For purposes of this subdivision there shall be a presumption that the operator of such vehicle was operating such vehicle with the consent of the owner at the time of such operator operated such vehicle in violation of subdivision (b), (c), (d), (f) or (g) of section eleven hundred eighty of this article.

(m) Nothing in this section shall be construed to limit the liability of an operator of a vehicle for any violation of subdivision (c) or (d) of section eleven hundred eighty of this article.

(n) (n) If the city adopts a demonstration program pursuant to subdivision (a) of this section it shall conduct a study and submit an annual report on the results of the use of photo devices to the governor, the temporary president of the senate and the speaker of the assembly on or before June first, two thousand twenty and on the same date in each succeeding year in which the demonstration program is operable. Such report shall include:

1. the locations where and dates when photo speed violation monitoring systems were used;

2. the aggregate number, type and severity of crashes, fatalities, injuries and property damage reported within all school speed zones within the city, to the extent the information is maintained by the department of motor vehicles of this state;

3. the aggregate number, type and severity of crashes, fatalities, injuries and property damage reported within school speed zones where photo speed violation monitoring systems were used, to the extent the information is maintained by the department of motor vehicles of this state;

4. the number of violations recorded within all school speed zones within the city, in the aggregate on a daily, weekly and monthly basis;

5. the number of violations recorded within each school speed zone where a photo speed violation monitoring system is used, in the aggregate on a daily, weekly and monthly basis;

6. the number of violations recorded within all school speed zones within the city that were:

(i) more than ten but not more than twenty miles per hour over the posted speed limit;

(ii) more than twenty but not more than thirty miles per hour over the posted speed limit;

(iii) more than thirty but not more than forty miles per hour over the posted speed limit; and

(iv) more than forty miles per hour over the posted speed limit;

7. the number of violations recorded within each school speed zone where a photo speed violation monitoring system is used that were:

(i) more than ten but not more than twenty miles per hour over the posted speed limit;

(ii) more than twenty but not more than thirty miles per hour over the posted speed limit;

(iii) more than thirty but not more than forty miles per hour over the posted speed limit; and

(iv) more than forty miles per hour over the posted speed limit;

8. the total number of notices of liability issued for violations recorded by such systems;

9. the number of fines and total amount of fines paid after the first notice of liability issued for violations recorded by such systems;

10. the number of violations adjudicated and the results of such adjudications including breakdowns of dispositions made for violations recorded by such systems;

11. the total amount of revenue realized by the city in connection with the program;

12. the expenses incurred by the city in connection with the program;

13. the quality of the adjudication process and its results;

14. the total amount of revenue expended on traffic and pedestrian safety within the city of New York; and

15. the effectiveness and adequacy of the hours of operation for such program to determine the impact on speeding violations and prevention of crashes.

(o) It shall be a defense to any prosecution for a violation of subdivision (b), (c), (d), (f) or (g) of section eleven hundred eighty of this article pursuant to this section that such photo speed violation monitoring system was malfunctioning at the time of the alleged violation.   *(Repealed, 7/1/22,Ch.30,L.2019)

§1180-c.   **Owner liability for failure of operator to comply with certain posted maximum speed limits.**   (Repealed, L.2014)

*§1180-d.   **Owner liability for failure of operator to comply with certain posted maximum speed limits.**

(a) 1. Notwithstanding any other provision of law, the city of Buffalo is hereby authorized to establish a demonstration program imposing monetary liability on the owner of a vehicle for failure of an operator thereof to comply with posted maximum speed limits in a school speed zone within the city (i) when a school speed limit is in effect as provided in paragraphs one and two of subdivision (c) of section eleven hundred eighty of this article or (ii) when other speed limits are in effect as provided in subdivision (b), (d), (f) or (g) of section eleven hundred eighty of this article during the following times: (A) on school days during school hours and one hour before and one hour after the school day, and (B) a period during student activities at the school and up to thirty minutes immediately before and up to thirty minutes immediately after such student activities. Such demonstration program shall empower the city to install photo speed violation monitoring systems within no more than twenty school speed zones within the city at any one time and to operate such systems within such zones (iii) when a school speed limit is in effect as provided in paragraphs one and two of subdivision (c) of section eleven hundred eighty of this article or (iv) when other speed limits are in effect as provided in subdivision (b), (d), (f) or (g) of section eleven hundred eighty of this article during the following times: (A) on school days during school hours and one hour before and one hour after the school day, and (B) a period during student activities at the school and up to thirty minutes immediately before and up to thirty minutes immediately after such student activities. In selecting a school speed zone in which to install and operate a photo speed violation monitoring system, the city shall consider criteria including, but not limited to the speed data, crash history, and the roadway geometry applicable to such school speed zone.

2. No photo speed violation monitoring system shall be used in a school speed zone unless (i) on the day it is to be used it has successfully passed a self-test of its functions; and (ii) it has undergone an annual calibration check performed pursuant to paragraph four of this subdivision. The city shall install signs giving notice that a photo speed violation monitoring system is in use to be mounted on advance warning signs notifying motor vehicle operators of such upcoming school speed zone and/or on speed limit signs applicable within such school speed zone, in conformance with standards established in the MUTCD.

3. Operators of photo speed violation monitoring systems shall have completed training in the procedures for setting up, testing, and operating such systems. Each such operator shall complete and sign a daily set-up log for each such system that he or she operates that (i) states the date and time when, and the location where, the system was set up that day, and (ii) states that such operator successfully performed, and the system passed, the self-tests of such system before producing a recorded image that day. The city shall retain each such daily log until the later of the date on which the photo speed violation monitoring system to which it applies has been permanently removed from use or the final resolution of all cases involving notices of liability issued based on photographs, microphotographs, video or other recorded images produced by such system.

4. Each photo speed violation monitoring system shall undergo an annual calibration check performed by an independent calibration laboratory which shall issue a signed certificate of calibration. The city shall keep each such annual certificate of calibration on file until the final resolution of all cases involving a notice of liability issued during such year which were based on photographs, microphotographs, videotape or other recorded images produced by such photo speed violation monitoring system.

5. (i) Such demonstration program shall utilize necessary technologies to ensure, to the extent practicable, that photographs, microphotographs, videotape or other recorded images produced by such photo speed violation monitoring systems shall not include images that identify the driver, the passengers, or the contents of the vehicle. Provided, however, that no notice of liability issued pursuant to this section shall be dismissed solely because such a photograph, microphotograph, videotape or other recorded image allows for the identification of the driver, the passengers, or the contents of vehicles where the city shows that it made reasonable efforts to comply with the provisions of this paragraph in such case.

(ii) Photographs, microphotographs, videotape or any other recorded image from a photo speed violation monitoring system shall be for the exclusive use of the city for the purpose of the adjudication of liability imposed pursuant to this section and of the owner receiving a notice of liability pursuant to this section, and shall be destroyed by the city upon the final resolution of the notice of liability to which such photographs, microphotographs, videotape or other recorded images relate, or one year following the date of issuance of such notice of liability, whichever is later. Notwithstanding the provisions of any other law, rule or regulation to the contrary, photographs, micro-photographs, videotape or any other recorded image from a photo speed violation monitoring system shall not be open to the public, nor subject to civil or criminal process or discovery, nor used by any court or administrative or adjudicatory body in any action or proceeding therein except that which is necessary for the adjudication of a notice of liability issued pursuant to this section, and no public entity or employee, officer or agent thereof shall disclose such information, except that such photographs, microphotographs, videotape or any other recorded images from such systems:

(A) shall be available for inspection and copying and use by the motor vehicle owner and operator for so long as such photographs, microphotographs, videotape or other recorded images are required to be maintained or are maintained by such public entity, employee, officer or agent; and

(B) (1) shall be furnished when described in a search warrant issued by a court authorized to issue such a search warrant pursuant to article six hundred ninety of the criminal procedure law or a federal court authorized to issue such a search warrant under federal law, where such search warrant states that there is reasonable cause to believe such information constitutes evidence of, or tends to demonstrate that, a misdemeanor or felony offense was committed in this state or another state, or that a particular person participated in the commission of a misdemeanor or felony offense in this state or another state, provided, however, that if such offense was against the laws of another state, the court shall only issue a warrant if the conduct comprising such offense would, if occurring in this state, constitute a misdemeanor or felony against the laws of this state; and

(2) shall be furnished in response to a subpoena duces tecum signed by a judge of competent jurisdiction and issued pursuant to article six hundred ten of the criminal procedure law or a judge or magistrate of a federal court authorized to issue such a subpoena duces tecum under federal law, where the judge finds and the subpoena states that there is reasonable cause to believe such information is relevant and material to the prosecution, or the defense, or the investigation by an authorized law enforcement official, of the alleged commission of a misdemeanor or felony in this state or another state, provided, however, that if such offense was against the laws of another state, such judge or magistrate shall only issue such subpoena if the conduct comprising such offense would, if occurring in this state, constitute a misdemeanor or felony in this state; and

(3) may, if lawfully obtained pursuant to this clause and clause (A) of this subparagraph and otherwise admissible, be used in such criminal action or proceeding.

(b) If the city of Buffalo establishes a demonstration program pursuant to subdivision (a) of this section, the owner of a vehicle shall be liable for a penalty imposed pursuant to this section if such vehicle was used or operated with the permission of the owner, express or implied, within a school speed zone in violation of subdivision (c) or during the times authorized pursuant to subdivision (a) of this section in violation of subdivision (b), (d), (f) or (g) of section eleven hundred eighty of this article, such vehicle was traveling at a speed of more than ten miles per hour above the posted speed limit in effect within such school speed zone, and such violation is evidenced by information obtained from a photo speed violation monitoring system; provided however that no owner of a vehicle shall be liable for a penalty imposed pursuant to this section where the operator of such vehicle has been convicted of the underlying violation of subdivision (b), (c), (d), (f) or (g) of section eleven hundred eighty of this article.

(c) For purposes of this section, the following terms shall have the following meanings:

1. "manual on uniform traffic control devices" or "MUTCD" shall mean the manual and specifications for a uniform system of traffic control devices maintained by the commissioner of transportation pursuant to section sixteen hundred eighty of this chapter;

2. "owner" shall have the meaning provided in article two-B of this chapter;

3. "photo speed violation monitoring system" shall mean a vehicle sensor installed to work in conjunction with a speed measuring device which automatically produces two or more photographs, two or more microphotographs, a videotape or other recorded images of each vehicle at the time it is used or operated in a school speed zone in violation of subdivision (b), (c), (d), (f) or (g) of section eleven hundred eighty of this article in accordance with the provisions of this section; and

4. "school speed zone" shall mean a distance not to exceed one thousand three hundred twenty feet on a highway passing a school building, entrance or exit of a school abutting on the highway.

(d) A certificate, sworn to or affirmed by a technician employed by the city of Buffalo, or a facsimile thereof, based upon inspection of photographs, microphotographs, videotape or other recorded images produced by a photo speed violation monitoring system, shall be prima facie evidence of the facts contained therein. Any photographs, microphotographs, videotape or other recorded images evidencing such a violation shall include at least two date and time stamped images of the rear of the motor vehicle that include the same stationary object near the motor vehicle and shall be available for inspection reasonably in advance of and at any proceeding to adjudicate the liability for such violation pursuant to this section.

(e) An owner liable for a violation of subdivision (b), (c), (d), (f) or (g) of section eleven hundred eighty of this article pursuant to a demonstration program established pursuant to this section shall be liable for monetary penalties in accordance with a schedule of fines and penalties to be promulgated by the parking violations bureau of the city of Buffalo. The liability of the owner pursuant to this section shall not exceed fifty dollars for each violation; provided, however, that such parking violations bureau may provide for an additional penalty not in excess of twenty-five dollars for each violation for the failure to respond to a notice of liability within the prescribed time period.

(f) An imposition of liability under the demonstration program established pursuant to this section shall not be deemed a conviction as an operator and shall not be made part of the operating record of the person upon whom such liability is imposed nor shall it be used for insurance purposes in the provision of motor vehicle insurance coverage.

(g) 1. A notice of liability shall be sent by first class mail to each person alleged to be liable as an owner for a violation of subdivision (b), (c), (d), (f) or (g) of section eleven hundred eighty of this article pursuant to this section, within fourteen business days if such owner is a resident of this state and within forty-five business days if such owner is a non-resident. Personal delivery on the owner shall not be required. A manual or automatic record of mailing prepared in the ordinary course of business shall be prima facie evidence of the facts contained therein.

2. A notice of liability shall contain the name and address of the person alleged to be liable as an owner for a violation of subdivision (b), (c), (d), (f) or (g) of section eleven hundred eighty of this article pursuant to this section, the registration number of the vehicle involved in such violation, the location where such violation took place, the date and time of such violation, the identification number of the camera which recorded the violation or other document locator number, at least two date and time stamped images of the rear of the motor vehicle that include the same stationary object near the motor vehicle, and the certificate charging the liability.

3. The notice of liability shall contain information advising the person charged of the manner and the time in which he or she may contest the liability alleged in the notice. Such notice of liability shall also contain a prominent warning to advise the person charged that failure to contest in the manner and time provided shall be deemed an admission of liability and that a default judgment may be entered thereon.

4. The notice of liability shall be prepared and mailed by the city of Buffalo, or by any other entity authorized by the city to prepare and mail such notice of liability.

(h) Adjudication of the liability imposed upon owners of this section shall be by the city of Buffalo parking violations bureau.

(i) If an owner receives a notice of liability pursuant to this section for any time period during which the vehicle or the number plate or plates of such vehicle was reported to the police department as having been stolen, it shall be a valid defense to an allegation of liability for a violation of subdivision (b), (c), (d), (f) or (g) of section eleven hundred eighty of this article pursuant to this section that the vehicle or the number plate or plates of such vehicle had been reported to the police as stolen prior to the time the violation occurred and had not been recovered by such time. For purposes of asserting the defense provided by this subdivision, it shall be sufficient that a certified copy of the police report on the stolen vehicle or number plate or plates of such vehicle be sent by first class mail to the city of Buffalo parking violations bureau or by any other entity authorized by the city to prepare and mail such notice of liability.

(j) Adjudication of the liability imposed upon owners of this section shall be by the city of Buffalo parking violations bureau.

(k) 1. An owner who is a lessor of a vehicle to which a notice of liability was issued pursuant to subdivision (g) of this section shall not be liable for the violation of subdivision (b), (c), (d), (f) or (g) of section eleven hundred eighty of this article pursuant to this section, provided that:

(i) prior to the violation, the lessor has filed with such parking violations bureau in accordance with the provisions of section two hundred thirty-nine of this chapter; and

(ii) within thirty-seven days after receiving notice from such division of the date and time of a liability, together with the other information contained in the original notice of liability, the lessor submits to such division the correct name and address of the lessee of the vehicle identified in the notice of liability at the time of such violation, together with such other additional information contained in the rental, lease or other contract document, as may be reasonably required by such division pursuant to regulations that may be promulgated for such purpose.

2. Failure to comply with subparagraph (ii) of paragraph one of this subdivision shall render the owner liable for the penalty prescribed in this section.

3. Where the lessor complies with the provisions of paragraph one of this subdivision, the lessee of such vehicle on the date of such violation shall be deemed to be the owner of such vehicle for purposes of this section, shall be subject to liability for such violation pursuant to this section and shall be sent a notice of liability pursuant to subdivision (i) of this section.

(*l*) 1. If the owner liable for a violation of subdivision (c) or (d) of section eleven hundred eighty of this article pursuant to this section was not the operator of the vehicle at the time of the violation, the owner may maintain an action for indemnification against the operator.

2. Notwithstanding any other provision of this section, no owner of a vehicle shall be subject to a monetary fine imposed pursuant to this section if the operator of such vehicle was operating such vehicle without the consent of the owner at the time such operator operated such vehicle in violation of subdivision (b), (c), (d), (f) or (g) of section eleven hundred eighty of this article. For purposes of this subdivision there shall be a presumption that the operator of such vehicle was operating such vehicle with the consent of the owner at the time of such operator operated such vehicle in violation of subdivision (b), (c), (d), (f) or (g) of section eleven hundred eighty of this article.

(m) Nothing in this section shall be construed to limit the liability of an operator of a vehicle for any violation of subdivision (c) or (d) of section eleven hundred eighty of this article.

(n) If the city adopts a demonstration program pursuant to subdivision (a) of this section it shall conduct a study and submit a report on the results of the use of photo devices to the governor, the temporary president of the senate and the speaker of the assembly. Such report shall include:

1. the locations where and dates when photo speed violation monitoring systems were used;

2. the aggregate number, type and severity of crashes, fatalities, injuries and property damage reported within all school speed zones within the city, to the extent the information is maintained by the department of motor vehicles of this state;

3. the aggregate number, type and severity of crashes, fatalities, injuries and property damage reported within school speed zones where photo speed violation monitoring systems were used, to the extent the information is maintained by the department of motor vehicles of this state;

4. the number of violations recorded within all school speed zones within the city, in the aggregate on a daily, weekly and monthly basis;

5. the number of violations recorded within each school speed zone where a photo speed violation monitoring system is used, in the aggregate on a daily, weekly and monthly basis;

6. the number of violations recorded within all school speed zones within the city that were:

(i) more than ten but not more than twenty miles per hour over the posted speed limit;

(ii) more than twenty but not more than thirty miles per hour over the posted speed limit;

(iii) more than thirty but not more than forty miles per hour over the posted speed limit; and

(iv) more than forty miles per hour over the posted speed limit;

7. the number of violations recorded within each school speed zone where a photo speed violation monitoring system is used that were:

(i) more than ten but not more than twenty miles per hour over the posted speed limit;

(ii) more than twenty but not more than thirty miles per hour over the posted speed limit;

(iii) more than thirty but not more than forty miles per hour over the posted speed limit; and

(iv) more than forty miles per hour over the posted speed limit;

8. the total number of notices of liability issued for violations recorded by such systems;

9. the number of fines and total amount of fines paid after the first notice of liability issued for violations recorded by such systems;

10. the number of violations adjudicated and the results of such adjudications including breakdowns of dispositions made for violations recorded by such systems;

11. the total amount of revenue realized by the city in connection with the program;

12. the expenses incurred by the city in connection with the program; and

13. the quality of the adjudication process and its results.

(o) It shall be a defense to any prosecution for a violation of subdivision (b), (c), (d), (f) or (g) of section eleven hundred eighty of this article pursuant to this section that such photo speed violation monitoring system was malfunctioning at the time of the alleged violation.   *(Repealed 9/6/24)

§1181.   Minimum speed regulations.

(a) No person shall drive a motor vehicle at such a slow speed as to impede the normal and reasonable movement of traffic except when reduced speed is necessary for safe operation or in compliance with law.

(b) Whenever a minimum speed limit has been established as authorized in sections sixteen hundred twenty or sixteen hundred forty-two, no person shall drive at a speed less than such minimum speed limit except when entering upon or preparing to exit from the highway upon which such a minimum speed limit has been established, when preparing to stop, or when necessary for safe operation or in compliance with law.

ARTICLE 31
ALCOHOL AND DRUG-RELATED OFFENSES
AND PROCEDURES APPLICABLE THERETO

Section
1192.   Operating a motor vehicle while under the influence of alcohol or drugs.
1192-a.   Operating a motor vehicle after having consumed alcohol; under the age of twenty-one; per se.
1193.   Sanctions.
1194.   Arrest and testing.
1194-a.   Driving after having consumed alcohol; under twenty-one; procedure.
1195.   Chemical test evidence.
1196.   Alcohol and drug rehabilitation program.
1197.   Special traffic options program for driving while intoxicated.
1198.   Ignition interlock device program.
1198-a.   Special procedures and disposition involving alcohol and substance abuse assessment and treatment.
1199.   Driver responsibility assessment.

§1192.   Operating a motor vehicle while under the influence of alcohol or drugs.

1. Driving while ability impaired. No person shall operate a motor vehicle while the person's ability to operate such motor vehicle is impaired by the consumption of alcohol.

2. Driving while intoxicated; per se. No person shall operate a motor vehicle while such person has .08 of one per centum or more by weight of alcohol in the person's blood as shown by chemical analysis of such person's blood, breath, urine or saliva, made pursuant to the provisions of section eleven hundred ninety-four of this article.

2-a. Aggravated driving while intoxicated.

(a) Per se. No person shall operate a motor vehicle while such person has .18 of one per centum or more by weight of alcohol in such person's blood as shown by chemical analysis of such person's blood, breath, urine or saliva made pursuant to the provisions of section eleven hundred ninety-four of this article.

(b) With a child. No person shall operate a motor vehicle in violation of subdivision two, three, four or four-a of this section while a child who is fifteen years of age or less is a passenger in such motor vehicle.

3. Driving while intoxicated. No person shall operate a motor vehicle while in an intoxicated condition.

4. Driving while ability impaired by drugs. No person shall operate a motor vehicle while the person's ability to operate such a motor vehicle is impaired by the use of a drug as defined in this chapter.

4-a. Driving while ability impaired by the combined influence of drugs or of alcohol and any drug or drugs. No person shall operate a motor vehicle while the person's ability to operate such motor vehicle is impaired by the combined influence of drugs or of alcohol and any drug or drugs.

5. Commercial motor vehicles: per se - level I. Notwithstanding the provisions of section eleven hundred ninety-five of this article, no person shall operate a commercial motor vehicle while such person has .04 of one per centum or more but not more than .06 of one per centum by weight of alcohol in the person's blood as shown by chemical analysis of such person's blood, breath, urine or saliva, made pursuant to the provisions of section eleven hundred ninety-four of this article; provided, however, nothing contained in this subdivision shall prohibit the imposition of a charge of a violation of subdivision one of this section, or of section eleven hundred ninety-two-a of this article where a person under the age of twenty-one operates a commercial motor vehicle where a chemical analysis of such person's blood, breath, urine, or saliva, made pursuant to the provisions of section eleven hundred ninety-four of this article, indicates that such operator has .02 of one per centum or more but less than .04 of one per centum by weight of alcohol in such operator's blood.

6. Commercial motor vehicles; per se - level II. Notwithstanding the provisions of section eleven hundred ninety-five of this article, no person shall operate a commercial motor vehicle while such person has more than .06 of one per centum but less than .08 of one per centum by weight of alcohol in the person's blood as shown by chemical analysis of such person's blood, breath, urine or saliva, made pursuant to the provisions of section eleven hundred ninety-four of this article; provided, however, nothing contained in this subdivision shall prohibit the imposition of a charge of a violation of subdivision one of this section.

7. Where applicable. The provisions of this section shall apply upon public highways, private roads open to motor vehicle traffic and any other parking lot. For the purposes of this section "parking lot" shall mean any area or areas of private property, including a driveway, near or contiguous to and provided in connection with premises and used as a means of access to and egress from a public highway to such premises and having a capacity for the parking of four

or more motor vehicles. The provisions of this section shall not apply to any area or areas of private property comprising all or part of property on which is situated a one or two family residence.

8. Effect of prior out-of-state conviction. A prior out-of-state conviction for operating a motor vehicle while under the influence of alcohol or drugs shall be deemed to be a prior conviction of a violation of this section for purposes of determining penalties imposed under this section or for purposes of any administrative action required to be taken pursuant to subdivision two of section eleven hundred ninety-three of this article; provided, however, that such conduct, had it occurred in this state, would have constituted a misdemeanor or felony violation of any of the provisions of this section. Provided, however, that if such conduct, had it occurred in this state, would have constituted a violation of any provisions of this section which are not misdemeanor or felony offenses, then such conduct shall be deemed to be a prior conviction of a violation of subdivision one of this section for purposes of determining penalties imposed under this section or for purposes of any administrative action required to be taken pursuant to subdivision two of section eleven hundred ninety-three of this article.

8-a. Effect of prior finding of having consumed alcohol. A prior finding that a person under the age of twenty-one has operated a motor vehicle after having consumed alcohol pursuant to section eleven hundred ninety-four-a of this article shall have the same effect as a prior conviction of a violation of subdivision one of this section solely for the purpose of determining the length of any license suspension or revocation required to be imposed under any provision of this article, provided that the subsequent offense is committed prior to the expiration of the retention period for such prior offense or offenses set forth in paragraph (k) of subdivision one of section two hundred one of this chapter.

9. Conviction of a different charge. A driver may be convicted of a violation of subdivision one, two or three of this section, notwithstanding that the charge laid before the court alleged a violation of subdivision two or three of this section, and regardless of whether or not such conviction is based on a plea of guilty.

10. Plea bargain limitations. (a) (i) In any case wherein the charge laid before the court alleges a violation of subdivision two, three, four or four-a of this section, any plea of guilty thereafter entered in satisfaction of such charge must include at least a plea of guilty to the violation of the provisions of one of the subdivisions of this section, other than subdivision five or six, and no other disposition by plea of guilty to any other charge in satisfaction of such charge shall be authorized; provided, however, if the district attorney, upon reviewing the available evidence, determines that the charge of a violation of this section is not warranted, such district attorney may consent, and the court may allow a disposition by plea of guilty to another charge in satisfaction of such charge; provided, however, in all such cases, the court shall set forth upon the record the basis for such disposition.

(ii) In any case wherein the charge laid before the court alleges a violation of subdivision two, three, four or four-a of this section, no plea of guilty to subdivision one of this section shall be accepted by the court unless such plea includes as a condition thereof the requirement that the defendant attend and complete the alcohol and drug rehabilitation program established pursuant to section eleven hundred ninety-six of this article, including any assessment and treatment required thereby; provided, however, that such requirement may be waived by the court upon application of the district attorney or the defendant demonstrating that the defendant, as a condition of the plea, has been required to enter into and complete an alcohol or drug treatment program prescribed pursuant to an alcohol or substance abuse screening or assessment conducted pursuant to section eleven hundred ninety-eight-a of this article or for other good cause shown. The provisions of this subparagraph shall apply, notwithstanding any bars to participation in the alcohol and drug rehabilitation program set forth in section eleven hundred ninety-six of this article; provided, however, that nothing in this paragraph shall authorize the issuance of a conditional license unless otherwise authorized by law.

(iii) In any case wherein the charge laid before the court alleges a violation of subdivision one of this section and the operator was under the age of twenty-one at the time of such violation, any plea of guilty thereafter entered in satisfaction of such charge must include at least a plea of guilty to the violation of such subdivision; provided, however, such charge may instead be satisfied as provided in paragraph (c) of this subdivision, and, provided further that, if the district attorney, upon reviewing the available evidence, determines that the charge of a violation of subdivision one of this section is not warranted, such district attorney may consent, and the court may allow a disposition by plea of guilty to another charge in satisfaction of such charge; provided, however, in all such cases, the court shall set forth upon the record the basis for such disposition.

(b) In any case wherein the charge laid before the court alleges a violation of subdivision one or six of this section while operating a commercial motor vehicle, any plea of guilty thereafter entered in satisfaction of such charge must include at least a plea of guilty to the violation of the provisions of one of the subdivisions of this section and no other disposition by plea of guilty to any other charge in satisfaction of such charge shall be authorized; provided, however, if the district attorney upon reviewing the available evidence determines that the charge of a violation of this section is not warranted, he may consent, and the court may allow, a disposition by plea of guilty to another charge is satisfaction of such charge.

(c) Except as provided in paragraph (b) of this subdivision, in any case wherein the charge laid before the court alleges a violation of subdivision one of this section by a person who was under the age of twenty-one at the time of commission of the offense, the court, with the consent of both parties, may allow the satisfaction of such charge by the defendant's agreement to be subject to action by the commissioner pursuant to section eleven hundred ninety-four-a of this article. In any such case, the defendant shall waive the right to a hearing under section eleven hundred ninety-four-a of this article and such waiver shall have the same force and effect as a finding of a violation of section eleven hundred ninety-two-a of this article entered after a hearing conducted pursuant to such section eleven hundred ninety-four-a. The defendant shall execute such waiver in open court, and, if represented by counsel, in the presence of his attorney, on a form to be provided by the commissioner, which shall be forwarded by the court to the commissioner within ninety-six hours. To be valid, such form shall, at a minimum, contain clear and conspicuous language advising the defendant that a duly executed waiver: (i) has the same force and effect as a guilty finding following a hearing pursuant to section eleven hundred ninety-four-a of this article; (ii) shall subject the defendant to the imposition of sanctions pursuant to such section eleven hundred ninety-four-a; and (iii) may subject the defendant to increased sanctions upon a subsequent violation of this section or section eleven hundred ninety-two-a of this article. Upon receipt of a duly executed waiver pursuant to this paragraph, the commissioner shall take such administrative action and impose such sanctions as may be required by section eleven hundred ninety-four-a of this article.

(d) In any case wherein the charge laid before the court alleges a violation of subdivision two-a of this section, any plea of guilty thereafter entered in satisfaction of such charge must include at least a plea of guilty to the violation of the provisions of subdivision two, two-a or three of this section, and no other disposition by plea of guilty to any other charge in satisfaction of such charge shall be authorized; provided, however, if the district attorney, upon reviewing the available evidence, determines that the charge of a violation of this section is not warranted, such district attorney may consent and the court may allow a disposition by plea of guilty to another charge in satisfaction of such charge, provided, however, in all such cases, the court shall set forth upon the record the basis for such disposition. Provided, further, however, that no such plea shall be accepted by the court unless such plea includes as a condition thereof the requirement that the defendant attend and complete the alcohol and drug rehabilitation program established pursuant to section eleven hundred ninety-six of this article, including any assessment and treatment required thereby; provided, however, that such requirement may be waived by the court upon application of the district attorney or the defendant demonstrating that the defendant, as a condition of the plea, has been required to enter into and complete an alcohol or drug treatment program prescribed pursuant to an alcohol or substance abuse screening or assessment conducted pursuant to section eleven hundred ninety-eight-a of this article or for other good cause shown. The provisions of this paragraph shall apply, notwithstanding any bars to participation in the alcohol and drug rehabilitation program set forth in section eleven hundred ninety-six of this article; provided, however, that nothing in this paragraph shall authorize the issuance of a conditional license unless otherwise authorized by law.

11. No person other than an operator of a commercial motor vehicle may be charged with or convicted of a violation of subdivision five or six of this section.

12. Driving while intoxicated or while ability impaired by drugs--serious physical injury or death or child in the vehicle. (a) In every case where a person is charged with a violation of subdivision two, two-a, three, four or four-a of this section, the law enforcement officer alleging such charge shall make a clear notation in the "Description of Violation" section of a simplified traffic information (I) if, arising out of the same incident, someone other than the person charged was killed or suffered serious physical injury as defined in section 10.00 of the penal law; such notation shall be in the form of a "D" if someone other than the person charged was killed and such notation shall be in the form of a "S.P.I." if someone other than the person charged suffered serious physical injury; and (ii) if a child aged fifteen years or less was present in the vehicle of the person charged with a violation of subdivision two, two-a, three, four or four-a of this section; such notation shall be in the form of "C.I.V.". Provided, however, that the failure to make such notations shall in no way affect a charge for a violation of subdivision two, two-a, three, four or four-a of this section.

(b) Where a law enforcement officer alleges a violation of paragraph (b) of subdivision two-a of this section and the operator of the vehicle is a parent, guardian, or custodian of, or other person legally responsible for, a child aged fifteen years or less who is a passenger in such vehicle, then the officer shall report or cause a report to be made, if applicable, in accordance with title six of article six of the social services law.

§1192-a.   **Operating a motor vehicle after having consumed alcohol; under the age of twenty-one; per se.**

No person under the age of twenty-one shall operate a motor vehicle after having consumed alcohol as defined in this section. For purposes of this section, a person under the age of twenty-one is deemed to have consumed alcohol only if such person has .02 of one per centum or more but not more than .07 of one per centum by weight of alcohol in the person's blood, as shown by chemical analysis of such person's blood, breath, urine or saliva, made pursuant to the provisions of section eleven hundred ninety-four of this article. Any person who operates a motor vehicle in violation of this section, and who is not charged with a violation of any subdivision of section eleven hundred ninety-two of this article arising out of the same incident shall be referred to the department for action in accordance with the provisions of section eleven hundred ninety-four-a of this article. Except as otherwise provided in subdivision five of section eleven hundred ninety-two of this article, this section shall not apply to a person who operates a commercial motor vehicle. Notwithstanding any provision of law to the contrary, a finding that a person under the age of twenty-one operated a motor vehicle after having consumed alcohol in violation of this section is not a judgment of conviction for a crime or any other offense.

§1193. Sanctions.

1. Criminal penalties. (a) Driving while ability impaired. A violation of subdivision one of section eleven hundred ninety-two of this article shall be a traffic infraction and shall be punishable by a fine of not less than three hundred dollars nor more than five hundred dollars or by imprisonment in a penitentiary or county jail for not more than fifteen days, or by both such fine and imprisonment. A person who operates a vehicle in violation of such subdivision after having been convicted of a violation of any subdivision of section eleven hundred ninety-two of this article within the preceding five years shall be punished by a fine of not less than five hundred dollars nor more than seven hundred fifty dollars, or by imprisonment of not more than thirty days in a penitentiary or county jail or by both such fine and imprisonment. A person who operates a vehicle in violation of such subdivision after having been convicted two or more times of a violation of any subdivision of section eleven hundred ninety-two of this article within the preceding ten years shall be guilty of a misdemeanor, and shall be punished by a fine of not less than seven hundred fifty dollars nor more than fifteen hundred dollars, or by imprisonment of not more than one hundred eighty days in a penitentiary or county jail or by both such fine and imprisonment.

(b) Driving while intoxicated or while ability impaired by drugs or while ability impaired by the combined influence of drugs or of alcohol and any drug or drugs; aggravated driving while intoxicated; misdemeanor offenses. (i) A violation of subdivision two, three, four or four-a of section eleven hundred ninety-two of this article shall be a misdemeanor and shall be punishable by a fine of not less than five hundred dollars nor more than one thousand dollars, or by imprisonment in a penitentiary or county jail for not more than one year, or by both such fine and imprisonment. A violation of paragraph (a) of subdivision two-a of section eleven hundred ninety-two of this article shall be a misdemeanor and shall be punishable by a fine of not less than one thousand dollars nor more than two thousand five hundred dollars or by imprisonment in a penitentiary or county jail for not more than one year, or by both such fine and imprisonment.

(ii) In addition to the imposition of any fine or period of imprisonment set forth in this paragraph, the court shall also sentence such person convicted of, or adjudicated a youthful offender for, a violation of subdivision two, two-a or three of section eleven hundred ninety-two of this article to a term of probation or conditional discharge, as a condition of which it shall order such person to install and maintain, in accordance with the provisions of section eleven hundred ninety-eight of this article, an ignition interlock device in any motor vehicle owned or operated by such person during the term of such probation or conditional discharge imposed for such violation of section eleven hundred ninety-two of this article and in no event for a period of less than twelve months; provided, however, that such period of interlock restriction shall terminate upon submission of proof that such person installed and maintained an ignition interlock device for at least six months, unless the court ordered such person to install and maintain an ignition interlock device for a longer period as authorized by this subparagraph and specified in such order. The period of interlock restriction shall commence from the earlier of the date of sentencing, or the date that an ignition interlock device was installed in advance of sentencing. Provided, however, the court may not authorize the operation of a motor vehicle by any person whose license or privilege to operate a motor vehicle has been revoked pursuant to the provisions of this section.

(c) Felony offenses. (i) A person who operates a vehicle (A) in violation of subdivision two, two-a, three, four or four-a of section eleven hundred ninety-two of this article after having been convicted of a violation of subdivision two, two-a, three, four or four-a of such section or of vehicular assault in the second or first degree, as defined, respectively, in sections 120.03 and 120.04 and aggravated vehicular assault as defined in section 120.04-a of the penal law or of vehicular manslaughter in the second or first degree, as defined, respectively, in sections 125.12 and 125.13 and aggravated vehicular homicide as defined in section 125.14 of such law, within the preceding ten years, or (B) in violation of paragraph (b) of subdivision two-a of section eleven hundred ninety-two of this article shall be guilty of a class E felony, and shall be punished by a fine of not less than one thousand dollars nor more than five thousand dollars or by a period of imprisonment as provided in the penal law, or by both such fine and imprisonment.

(ii) A person who operates a vehicle in violation of subdivision two, two-a, three, four or four-a of section eleven hundred ninety-two of this article after having been convicted of a violation of subdivision two, two-a, three, four or four-a of such section or of vehicular assault in the second or first degree, as defined, respectively, in sections 120.03 and 120.04 and aggravated vehicular assault as defined in section 120.04-a of the penal law or of vehicular manslaughter in the second or first degree, as defined, respectively, in sections 125.12 and 125.13 and aggravated vehicular homicide as defined in section 125.14 of such law, twice within the preceding ten years, shall be guilty of a class D felony, and shall be punished by a fine of not less than two thousand dollars nor more than ten thousand dollars or by a period of imprisonment as provided in the penal law, or by both such fine and imprisonment.

(ii-a) A person who operates a vehicle in violation of subdivision two, two-a, three, four or four-a of section eleven hundred ninety-two of this article after having been convicted of a violation of subdivision two, two-a, three, four or four-a of such section or of vehicular assault in the second or first degree, as defined, respectively, in sections 120.03 and 120.04 and aggravated vehicular assault as defined in section 120.04-a of the penal law or of vehicular manslaughter in the second or first degree, as defined, respectively, in sections 125.12 and 125.13 and aggravated vehicular homicide as defined in section 125.14 of such law, three or more times within the preceding fifteen years, shall be guilty of a class D felony, and shall be punished by a fine of not less than two thousand dollars nor more than ten thousand dollars or by a period of imprisonment as provided in the penal law, or by both such fine and imprisonment.

(iii) In addition to the imposition of any fine or period of imprisonment set forth in this paragraph, the court shall also sentence such person convicted of, or adjudicated a youthful offender for, a violation of subdivision two, two-a or three of section eleven hundred ninety-two of this article to a period of probation or conditional discharge, as a condition of which it shall order such person to install and maintain, in accordance with the provisions of section eleven hundred ninety-eight of this article, an ignition interlock device in any motor vehicle owned or operated by such person during the term of such probation or conditional discharge imposed for such violation of section eleven hundred ninety-two of this article and in no event for a period of less than twelve months; provided, however, that such period of interlock restriction shall terminate upon submission of proof that such person installed and maintained an ignition interlock device for at least six months, unless the court ordered such person to install and maintain a ignition interlock device for a longer period as authorized by this subparagraph and specified in such order. The period of interlock restriction shall commence from the earlier of the date of sentencing, or the date that an ignition interlock device was installed in advance of sentencing. Provided, however, the court may not authorize the operation of a motor vehicle by any person whose license or privilege to operate a motor vehicle has been revoked pursuant to the provisions of this section.

(d) Alcohol or drug related offenses; special vehicles.

(1) Except as provided in subparagraph four of this paragraph, a violation of subdivision one, two, three, four or four-a of section eleven hundred ninety-two of this article wherein the violator is operating a taxicab as defined in section one hundred forty-eight-a of this chapter, or livery as defined in section one hundred twenty-one-e of this chapter, and such taxicab or livery is carrying a passenger for compensation, or a truck with a GVWR of more than eighteen thousand pounds but not more than twenty-six thousand pounds and which is not a commercial motor vehicle shall be a misdemeanor punishable by a fine of not less than five hundred dollars nor more than fifteen hundred dollars or by a period of imprisonment as provided in the penal law, or by both such fine and imprisonment. A violation of subdivision two-a of section eleven hundred ninety-two of this article wherein the violator is operating a taxicab as defined in section one hundred forty-eight-a of this chapter, or livery as defined in section one hundred twenty-one-e of this chapter, and such taxicab or livery is carrying a passenger for compensation, or a truck with a GVWR of more than eighteen thousand pounds but not more than twenty-six thousand pounds and which is not a commercial motor vehicle shall be a class E felony punishable by a fine of not less than one thousand dollars nor more than five thousand dollars or by a period of imprisonment as provided in the penal law, or by both such fine and imprisonment.

(1-a) A violation of subdivision one of section eleven hundred ninety-two of this article wherein the violator is operating a school bus as defined in section one hundred forty-two of this chapter and such school bus is carrying at least one student passenger shall be a misdemeanor punishable by a fine of not less than five hundred dollars nor more than fifteen hundred dollars or by a period of imprisonment as provided in the penal law, or by both such fine and imprisonment.

(2) A violation of subdivision five of section eleven hundred ninety-two of this article shall be a traffic infraction punishable as provided in paragraph (a) of this subdivision. Except as provided in subparagraph three or five of this paragraph, a violation of subdivision one, two, three, four, four-a or six of section eleven hundred ninety-two of this article wherein the violator is operating a commercial motor vehicle, or any motor vehicle registered or registerable under schedule F of subdivision seven of section four hundred one of this chapter shall be a misdemeanor. A violation of subdivision one, two, three, four or four-a of section eleven hundred ninety-two of this article shall be punishable by a fine of not less than five hundred dollars nor more than fifteen hundred dollars or by a period of imprisonment as provided in the penal law, or by both such fine and imprisonment. A violation of subdivision six of section eleven hundred ninety-two of this article shall be punishable by a fine of not less than five hundred dollars nor more than fifteen hundred dollars or by a period of imprisonment not to exceed one hundred eighty days, or by both such fine and imprisonment. A person who operates any such vehicle in violation of such subdivision six after having been convicted of a violation of subdivision one, two, two-a, three, four, four-a or six of section eleven hundred ninety-two of this article within the preceding five years shall be punishable by a fine of not less than five hundred dollars nor more than fifteen hundred dollars or by a period of imprisonment as provided in the penal law, or by both such fine and imprisonment. A violation of subdivision two-a of section eleven hundred ninety-two of this article wherein the violator is operating a commercial motor vehicle, or any motor vehicle registered or registerable under schedule F of subdivision seven of section four hundred one of this chapter shall be a class E felony punishable by a fine of not less than one thousand dollars nor more than five thousand dollars or by a period of imprisonment as provided in the penal law, or by both such fine and imprisonment.

(3) A violation of subdivision one of section eleven hundred ninety-two of this article wherein the violator is operating a motor vehicle with a gross vehicle weight rating of more than eighteen thousand pounds which contains flammable gas, radioactive materials or explosives shall be a misdemeanor punishable by a fine of not less than five hundred dollars nor more than fifteen hundred dollars or by a period of imprisonment as provided in the penal law, or by both such fine and imprisonment.

(4) (i) A person who operates a vehicle in violation of subdivision one, two, two-a, three, four or four-a of section eleven hundred ninety-two of this article and which is punishable as provided in subparagraph one, one-a, two or three of this paragraph after having been convicted of a violation of any such subdivision of section eleven hundred ninety-two of this article and penalized under subparagraph one, one-a, two or three of this paragraph within the preceding ten years, shall be guilty of a class E felony, which shall be punishable by a fine of not less than one thousand dollars nor more than five

thousand dollars, or by a period of imprisonment as provided in the penal law, or by both such fine and imprisonment. A person who operates a vehicle in violation of subdivision six of section eleven hundred ninety-two of this article after having been convicted of two or more violations of subdivisions one, two, two-a, three, four, four-a or six of section eleven hundred ninety-two of this article within the preceding five years, any one of which was a misdemeanor, shall be guilty of a class E felony, which shall be punishable by a fine of not less than one thousand dollars nor more than five thousand dollars, or by a period of imprisonment as provided in the penal law, or by both such fine and imprisonment. In addition, any person sentenced pursuant to this subparagraph shall be subject to the disqualification provided in subparagraph three of paragraph (e) of subdivision two of this section.

(ii) A person who operates a vehicle in violation of subdivision one, two, two-a, three, four or four-a of section eleven hundred ninety-two of this article and which is punishable as provided in subparagraph one, one-a, two or three of this paragraph after having been convicted of a violation of any such subdivision of section eleven hundred ninety-two of this article and penalized under subparagraph one, one-a, two or three of this paragraph twice within the preceding ten years, shall be guilty of a class D felony, which shall be punishable by a fine of not less than two thousand dollars nor more than ten thousand dollars, or by a period of imprisonment as provided in the penal law, or by both such fine and imprisonment. A person who operates a vehicle in violation of subdivision six of section eleven hundred ninety-two of this article after having been convicted of three or more violations of subdivisions one, two, two-a, three, four, four-a or six of section eleven hundred ninety-two of this article within the preceding five years, any one of which was a misdemeanor, shall be guilty of a class D felony, which shall be punishable by a fine of not less than two thousand dollars nor more than ten thousand dollars, or by a period of imprisonment as provided in the penal law, or by both such fine and imprisonment. In addition, any person sentenced pursuant to this subparagraph shall be subject to the disqualification provided in subparagraph three of paragraph (e) of subdivision two of this section.

(4-a) A violation of subdivision two, three, four or four-a of section eleven hundred ninety-two of this article wherein the violator is operating a school bus as defined in section one hundred forty-two of this chapter and such school bus is carrying at least one student passenger shall be a class E felony punishable by a fine of not less than one thousand dollars nor more than five thousand dollars, or by a period of imprisonment as provided in the penal law, or by both such fine and imprisonment. A violation of subdivision two-a of section eleven hundred ninety-two of this article wherein the violator is operating a school bus as defined in section one hundred forty-two of this chapter and such school bus is carrying at least one student passenger shall be a class D felony punishable by a fine of not less than two thousand dollars nor more than ten thousand dollars, or by a period of imprisonment as provided in the penal law, or by both such fine and imprisonment.

(5) A violation of subdivision two, three, four or four-a of section eleven hundred ninety-two of this article wherein the violator is operating a motor vehicle with a gross vehicle weight rating of more than eighteen thousand pounds which contains flammable gas, radioactive materials or explosives, shall be a class E felony punishable by a fine of not less than one thousand dollars and such other penalties as provided for in the penal law; provided, however, that a conviction for such violation shall not be considered a predicate felony pursuant to section 70.06 of such law, or a previous felony conviction pursuant to section 70.10 of such law. A violation of subdivision two-a of section eleven hundred ninety-two of this article wherein the violator is operating a motor vehicle with a gross vehicle weight rating of more than eighteen thousand pounds which contains flammable gas, radioactive materials or explosives, shall be a class D felony punishable by a fine of not less than two thousand nor more than ten thousand dollars and such other penalties as provided for in the penal law; provided, however, that a conviction for such violation shall not be considered a predicate felony pursuant to section 70.06 of such law, or a previous felony conviction pursuant to section 70.10 of such law.

(6) The sentences required to be imposed by subparagraph one, one-a, two, three, four, four-a or five of this paragraph shall be imposed notwithstanding any contrary provision of this chapter or the penal law.

(7) Nothing contained in this paragraph shall prohibit the imposition of a charge of any other felony set forth in this or any other provision of law for any acts arising out of the same incident.

(e) Certain sentences prohibited. Notwithstanding any provisions of the penal law, no judge or magistrate shall impose a sentence of unconditional discharge for a violation of any subdivision of section eleven hundred ninety-two of this article nor shall a judge or magistrate impose a sentence of conditional discharge or probation unless such conditional discharge or probation is accompanied by a sentence of a fine as provided in this subdivision.

(f) Where the court imposes a sentence for a violation of section eleven hundred ninety-two of this article, the court may require the defendant, as a part of or as a condition of such sentence, to attend a single session conducted by a victims impact program. For purposes of this section, "victims impact program" means a program operated by a county, a city with a population of one million or more, by a not-for-profit organization authorized by any such county or city, or a combination thereof, in which presentations are made concerning the impact of operating a motor vehicle while under the influence of alcohol or drugs to one or more persons who have been convicted of such offenses. A description of any such program shall be filed with the commissioner and with the coordinator of the special traffic options program for driving while intoxicated established pursuant to section eleven hundred ninety-seven of this article, and shall be made available to the court upon request. Nothing contained herein shall be construed to require any governmental entity to create such a victim impact program.

(g) The division of probation and correctional alternatives shall promulgate regulations governing the monitoring of compliance by persons ordered to install and maintain ignition interlock devices to provide standards for monitoring by departments of probation, and options for monitoring of compliance by such persons, that counties may adopt as an alternative to monitoring by a department of probation.

1-a. Additional penalties. (a) Except as provided for in paragraph (b) of this subdivision, a person who operates a vehicle in violation of subdivision two or three of section eleven hundred ninety-two of this article after having been convicted of a violation of subdivision two or three of such section within the preceding five years shall, in addition to any other penalties which may be imposed pursuant to subdivision one of this section, be sentenced to a term of imprisonment of five days or, as an alternative to such imprisonment, be required to perform thirty days of service for a public or not-for-profit corporation, association, institution or agency as set forth in paragraph (h) of subdivision two of section 65.10 of the penal law as a condition of sentencing for such violation. Notwithstanding the provisions of this paragraph, a sentence of a term of imprisonment of five days or more pursuant to the provisions of subdivision one of this section shall be deemed to be in compliance with this subdivision.

(b) A person who operates a vehicle in violation of subdivision two or three of section eleven hundred ninety-two of this article after having been convicted on two or more occasions of a violation of any of such subdivisions within the preceding five years shall, in addition to any other penalties which may be imposed pursuant to subdivision one of this section, be sentenced to a term of imprisonment of ten days or, as an alternative to such imprisonment, be required to perform sixty days of service for a public or not-for-profit corporation, association, institution or agency as set forth in paragraph (h) of subdivision two of section 65.10 of the penal law as a condition of sentencing for such violation. Notwithstanding the provisions of this paragraph, a sentence of a term of imprisonment of ten days or more pursuant to the provisions of subdivision one of this section shall be deemed to be in compliance with this subdivision.

(c) A court sentencing a person pursuant to paragraph (a) or (b) of this subdivision shall: (i) order the installation of an ignition interlock device approved pursuant to section eleven hundred ninety-eight of this article in any motor vehicle owned or operated by the person so sentenced. Such devices shall remain installed during any period of license revocation required to be imposed pursuant to paragraph (b) of subdivision two of this section, and, upon the termination of such revocation period, for an additional period as determined by the court; and (ii) order that such person receive an assessment of the degree of their alcohol or substance abuse and dependency pursuant to the provisions of section eleven hundred ninety-eight-a of this article. Where such assessment indicates the need for treatment, such court is authorized to impose treatment as a condition of such sentence except that such court shall impose treatment as a condition of a sentence of probation or conditional discharge pursuant to the provisions of subdivision three of section eleven hundred ninety-eight-a of this article. Any person ordered to install an ignition interlock device pursuant to this paragraph shall be subject to the provisions of subdivisions four, five, seven, eight and nine of section eleven hundred ninety-eight of this article.

(d) Confidentiality of records. The provisions of subdivision six of section eleven hundred ninety-eight-a of this article shall apply to the records and content of all assessments and treatment conducted pursuant to this subdivision.

2. License sanctions. (a) Suspensions. Except as otherwise provided in this subdivision, a license shall be suspended and a registration may be suspended for the following periods:

(1) Driving while ability impaired. Ninety days, where the holder is convicted of a violation of subdivision one of section eleven hundred ninety-two of this article;

(2) Persons under the age of twenty-one; driving after having consumed alcohol. Six months, where the holder has been found to have operated a motor vehicle after having consumed alcohol in violation of section eleven hundred ninety-two-a of this article where such person was under the age of twenty-one at the time of commission of such violation.

(b) Revocations. A license shall be revoked and a registration may be revoked for the following minimum periods:

(1) Driving while ability impaired; prior offense. Six months, where the holder is convicted of a violation of subdivision one of section eleven hundred ninety-two of this article committed within five years of a conviction for a violation of any subdivision of section eleven hundred ninety-two of this article.

(1-a) Driving while ability impaired; misdemeanor offense. Six months, where the holder is convicted of a violation of subdivision one of section eleven hundred ninety-two of this article committed within ten years of two previous convictions for a violation of any subdivision of section eleven hundred ninety-two of this article.

(2) Driving while intoxicated or while ability impaired by drugs or while ability impaired by the combined influence of drugs or of alcohol and any drug or drugs; aggravated driving while intoxicated. Six months, where the holder is convicted of a violation of subdivision two, three, four or four-a of section eleven hundred ninety-two of this article. One year where the holder is convicted of a violation of subdivision two-a of section eleven hundred ninety-two of this article.

(3) Driving while intoxicated or while ability impaired by drugs or while ability impaired by the combined influence of drugs or of alcohol and any drug or drugs; aggravated driving while intoxicated; prior offense. One year, where the holder is convicted of a violation of subdivision two, three, four or four-a of section eleven hundred ninety-two of this article committed within ten years of a conviction for a violation of subdivision two, three, four or four-a of section eleven hundred ninety-two of this article. Eighteen months, where the holder is convicted of a violation of subdivision two-a of section eleven hundred ninety-two of this article committed within ten years of a conviction for a violation of subdivision two, two-a, three, four or four-a of

section eleven hundred ninety-two of this article; or where the holder is convicted of a violation of subdivision two, three, four or four-a of section eleven hundred ninety-two of this article committed within ten years of a conviction for a violation of subdivision two-a of section eleven hundred ninety-two of this article.

(4) Special vehicles other than school buses. One year, where the holder is convicted of a violation of any subdivision of section eleven hundred ninety-two of this article and is sentenced pursuant to subparagraph one of paragraph (d) of subdivision one of this section.

(4-a) School buses. (A) One year, where the holder is convicted of a violation of any subdivision of section eleven hundred ninety-two of this article, such violation was committed while the holder was driving a school bus, and the holder is sentenced pursuant to subparagraph one, one-a or four-a of paragraph (d) of subdivision one of this section.

(B) Three years where the holder is convicted of a violation of any subdivision of section eleven hundred ninety-two of this article, such violation was committed while the holder was driving a school bus, and the holder is sentenced pursuant to subparagraph four of paragraph (d) of subdivision one of this section.

(C) Notwithstanding the provisions of the opening paragraph of this paragraph (b), the commissioner shall not revoke the registration of a school bus driven in violation of section eleven hundred ninety-two of this article.

(5) Holder of a commercial driver's license. (i) Except as otherwise provided in this subparagraph, one year where the holder of a commercial driver's license is convicted of a violation of any subdivision of section eleven hundred ninety-two of this article or if such holder is convicted of an offense consisting of operating a motor vehicle under the influence of alcohol or drugs where such conviction was had outside of this state.

(ii) Three years, where the holder is convicted of a violation of any subdivision of section eleven hundred ninety-two of this article, such violation was committed while the holder was operating a commercial motor vehicle transporting hazardous materials or if such holder is convicted of an offense consisting of operating a motor vehicle under the influence of alcohol or drugs where such conviction was had outside of this state.

(6) Persons under the age of twenty-one. One year, where the holder is convicted of or adjudicated a youthful offender for a violation of any subdivision of section eleven hundred ninety-two of this article, or is convicted of or receives a youthful offender or other juvenile adjudication for an offense consisting of operating a motor vehicle under the influence of intoxicating liquor where the conviction, or youthful offender or other juvenile adjudication was had outside this state, where such person was under the age of twenty-one at the time of commission of such violation.

(7) Persons under the age of twenty-one; prior offense or finding. One year or until the holder reaches the age of twenty-one, whichever is the greater period of time, where the holder has been found to have operated a motor vehicle after having consumed alcohol in violation of section eleven hundred

ninety-two-a of this article, or is convicted of, or adjudicated a youthful offender for, a violation of any subdivision of section eleven hundred ninety-two of this article, or is convicted of or receives a youthful offender or juvenile adjudication for an offense consisting of operating a motor vehicle under the influence of intoxicating liquor where the conviction, or youthful offender or other juvenile adjudication was had outside this state, where such person was under the age of twenty-one at the time of commission of such violation and has previously been found to have operated a motor vehicle after having consumed alcohol in violation of section eleven hundred ninety-two-a of this article, or has previously been convicted of, or adjudicated a youthful offender for, any violation of section eleven hundred ninety-two of this article not arising out of the same incident, or has previously been convicted of or received a youthful offender or juvenile adjudication for an offense consisting of operating a motor vehicle under the influence of intoxicating liquor when the conviction, or youthful offender or other juvenile adjudication was had outside this state and not arising out of the same.

(8) Out-of-state offenses. Except as provided in subparagraph six or seven of this paragraph: (i) ninety days, where the holder is convicted of an offense consisting of operating a motor vehicle under the influence of intoxicating liquor where the conviction was had outside this state and (ii) six months, where the holder is convicted of, or receives a youthful offender or other juvenile adjudication, which would have been a misdemeanor or felony if committed by an adult, in connection with, an offense consisting of operating a motor vehicle under the influence of or while impaired by the use of drugs where the conviction or youthful offender or other juvenile adjudication was had outside this state.

(9) Effect of rehabilitation program. No period of revocation arising out of subparagraph four, five, six or seven of this paragraph may be set aside by the commissioner for the reason that such person was a participant in the alcohol and drug rehabilitation program set forth in section eleven hundred ninety-six of this chapter.

(10) Action required by commissioner. Where a court fails to impose, or incorrectly imposes, a suspension or revocation required by this subdivision, the commissioner shall, upon receipt of a certificate of conviction filed pursuant to section five hundred fourteen of this chapter, impose such mandated suspension or revocation, which shall supersede any such order which the court may have imposed.

(11) Limitation of certain mandatory revocations. Where revocation is mandatory pursuant to subparagraph five of this paragraph for a conviction of a violation of subdivision five of section eleven hundred ninety-two of this article, such revocation shall be issued only by the commissioner and shall be applicable only to that portion of the holder's driver's license or privilege which permits the operation of commercial motor vehicles, and the commissioner shall immediately issue a license, other than a commercial driver's license, to such person provided that such person is otherwise eligible

to receive such license and further provided that issuing a license to such person does not create a substantial traffic safety hazard.

(12) Permanent revocation. (a) Notwithstanding any other provision of this chapter to the contrary, whenever a revocation is imposed upon a person for the refusal to submit to a chemical test pursuant to the provisions of section eleven hundred ninety-four of this article or conviction for any violation of section eleven hundred ninety-two of this article for which a sentence of imprisonment may be imposed, and such person has: (i) within the previous four years been twice convicted of any provisions of section eleven hundred ninety-two of this article or a violation of the penal law for which a violation of such section eleven hundred ninety-two is an essential element and at least one such conviction was for a crime, or has twice been found to have refused to submit to a chemical test pursuant to section eleven hundred ninety-four of this article, or has any combination of two such convictions and findings of refusal not arising out of the same incident; or (ii) within the previous eight years been convicted three times of any provision of section eleven hundred ninety-two of this article for which a sentence of imprisonment may be imposed or a violation of the penal law for which a violation of such section eleven hundred ninety-two is an essential element and at least two such convictions were for crimes, or has been found, on three separate occasions, to have refused to submit to a chemical test pursuant to section eleven hundred ninety-four of this article, or has any combination of such convictions and findings of refusal not arising out of the same incident, such revocation shall be permanent.

(b) The permanent driver's license revocation required by clause (a) of this subparagraph shall be waived by the commissioner after a period of five years has expired since the imposition of such permanent revocation, provided that during such five-year period such person has not been found to have refused a chemical test pursuant to section eleven hundred ninety-four of this article while operating a motor vehicle and has not been convicted of a violation of any subdivision of section eleven hundred ninety-two of this article or section five hundred eleven of this chapter or a violation of the penal law for which a violation of any subdivision of such section eleven hundred ninety-two is an essential element and either: (i) that such person provides acceptable documentation to the commissioner that such person has voluntarily enrolled in and successfully completed an appropriate rehabilitation program; or (ii) that such person is granted a certificate of relief from disabilities as provided for in section seven hundred one of the correction law by the court in which such person was last sentenced. Provided, however, that the commissioner may, on a case by case basis, refuse to restore a license which otherwise would be restored pursuant to this item, in the interest of the public safety and welfare.

(c) For revocations imposed pursuant to clause (a) of this subparagraph, the commissioner may adopt rules to permit conditional or restricted operation of a motor vehicle by any such person after a mandatory revocation period of not less than three years subject to such criteria, terms and conditions as established by the commissioner.

(d) Upon (i) a finding of refusal after having been convicted three times within four years of a violation of any subdivision of section eleven hundred ninety-two of this article or of the penal law for which a violation of any subdivision of such section eleven hundred ninety-two is an essential element or any combination of three such convictions not arising out of the same incident within four years or (ii) a fourth conviction of any subdivision of section eleven hundred ninety-two of this article after having been convicted of any such subdivision of such section eleven hundred ninety-two or of the penal law for which a violation of any of such subdivisions of such section eleven hundred ninety-two is an essential element or any combination of three such convictions not arising out of the same incident within four years or (iii) a finding of refusal after having been convicted four times within eight years of a violation of any subdivision of section eleven hundred ninety-two of this article or of the penal law for which a violation of any of such subdivisions of such section eleven hundred ninety-two is an essential element or any combination of four such convictions not arising out of the same incident within eight years or (iv) a fifth conviction of any subdivision of section eleven hundred ninety-two of this article after having been convicted of such subdivision or of the penal law for which a violation of any of such subdivisions of such section eleven hundred ninety-two is an essential element or any combination of four such convictions not arising out of the same incident within eight years, such revocation shall be permanent.

(e) The permanent driver's license revocation required by clause (d) of this subparagraph may be waived by the commissioner after a period of eight years has expired since the imposition of such permanent revocation provided:

(i) that during such eight-year period such person has not been found to have refused a chemical test pursuant to section eleven hundred ninety-four of this article while operating a motor vehicle and has not been convicted of a violation of any subdivision of section eleven hundred ninety-two of this article or section five hundred eleven of this chapter or a violation of the penal law for which a violation of any such subdivisions of such section eleven hundred ninety-two is an essential element; and

(ii) that such person provides acceptable documentation to the commissioner that such person has voluntarily enrolled in and successfully completed an appropriate rehabilitation program; and

(iii) after such documentation is accepted, that such person is granted a certificate of relief from disabilities as provided for in section seven hundred one of the correction law by the court in which such person was last sentenced.

Notwithstanding the provisions of this clause, nothing contained in this clause shall be deemed to require the commissioner to restore a license to an applicant who otherwise has complied with the requirements of this item, in the interest of the public safety and welfare.

(f) Nothing contained in this subparagraph shall be deemed to reduce a license revocation period imposed pursuant to any other provision of law.

(c) Reissuance of licenses; restrictions. (1) Except as otherwise provided in this paragraph, where a license is revoked pursuant to paragraph (b) of this subdivision, no new license shall be issued after the expiration of the minimum period specified in such paragraph, except in the discretion of the commissioner.

(2) Where a license is revoked pursuant to subparagraph two, three or eight of paragraph (b) of this subdivision for a violation of subdivision four of section eleven hundred ninety-two of this article, and where the individual does not have a driver's license or the individual's license was suspended at the time of conviction or youthful offender or other juvenile adjudication, the commissioner shall not issue a new license nor restore the former license for a period of six months after such individual would otherwise have become eligible to obtain a new license or to have the former license restored; provided, however, that during such delay period the commissioner may issue a restricted use license pursuant to section five hundred thirty of this chapter.

(3) In no event shall a new license be issued where a person has been twice convicted of a violation of subdivision three, four or four-a of section eleven hundred ninety-two of this article or of driving while intoxicated or of driving while ability is impaired by the use of a drug or of driving while ability is impaired by the combined influence of drugs or of alcohol and any drug or drugs where physical injury, as defined in section 10.00 of the penal law, has resulted from such offense in each instance.

(d) Suspension or revocation; sentencing. (1) Notwithstanding anything to the contrary contained in a certificate of relief from disabilities issued pursuant to article twenty-three of the correction law, where a suspension or revocation, other than a revocation required to be issued by the commissioner, is mandatory pursuant to paragraph (a) or (b) of this subdivision, the magistrate, justice or judge shall issue an order suspending or revoking such license upon sentencing, and the license holder shall surrender such license to the court. Except as hereinafter provided, such suspension or revocation shall take effect immediately.

(2) Except where the license holder has been charged with a violation of article one hundred twenty or one hundred twenty-five of the penal law arising out of the same incident or convicted of such violation or a violation of any subdivision of section eleven hundred ninety-two of this article within the preceding five years, the judge, justice or magistrate may issue an order making said license suspension or revocation take effect twenty days after the date of sentencing. The license holder shall be given a copy of said order permitting the continuation of driving privileges for twenty days after sentencing, if granted by the court. The court shall forward to the commissioner the certificates required in sections five hundred thirteen and five hundred fourteen of this chapter, along with a copy of any order issued pursuant to this paragraph and the license, within ninety-six hours of sentencing.

(e) Special provisions. (1) Suspension pending prosecution; procedure. a. Without notice, pending any prosecution, the court shall suspend such license, where the holder has been charged with a violation of subdivision two, two-a, three, four or four-a of section eleven hundred ninety-two of this article and either (i) a violation of a felony under article one hundred twenty or one hundred twenty-five of the penal law arising out of the same incident, or (ii) has been convicted of any violation under section eleven hundred ninety-two of this article within the preceding five years.

b. The suspension under the preceding clause shall occur no later than twenty days after the holder's first appearance before the court on the charges or at the conclusion of all proceedings required for the arraignment. In order for the court to impose such suspension it must find that the accusatory instrument conforms to the requirements of section 100.40 of the criminal procedure law and there exists reasonable cause to believe that the holder operated a motor vehicle in violation of subdivision two, two-a, three, four or four-a of section eleven hundred ninety-two of this article and either (i) the person had been convicted of any violation under such section eleven hundred ninety-two of this article within the preceding five years; or (ii) that the holder committed a violation of a felony under article one hundred twenty or one hundred twenty-five of the penal law. At such time the holder shall be entitled to an opportunity to make a statement regarding the enumerated issues and to present evidence tending to rebut the court's findings. Where such suspension is imposed upon a pending charge of a violation of a felony under article one hundred twenty or one hundred twenty-five of the penal law and the holder has requested a hearing pursuant to article one hundred eighty of the criminal procedure law, the court shall conduct such hearing. If upon completion of the hearing, the court fails to find that there is reasonable cause to believe that the holder committed a felony under article one hundred twenty or one hundred twenty-five of the penal law and the holder has not been previously convicted of any violation of section eleven hundred ninety-two of this article within the preceding five years the court shall promptly notify the commissioner and direct restoration of such license to the license holder unless such license is suspended or revoked pursuant to any other provision of this chapter.

(2) Bail forfeiture. A license shall be suspended where the holder forfeits bail upon a charge of a violation of any subdivision of section eleven hundred ninety-two of this article. Such suspension shall not be terminated until the holder submits to the jurisdiction of the court in which the bail was forfeited.

(3) Permanent disqualification from operating certain motor vehicles.

a. Except as otherwise provided herein, in addition to any revocation set forth in subparagraph four or five of paragraph (b) of this subdivision, any person sentenced pursuant to subparagraph three of paragraph (d) of subdivision one of this section shall be permanently disqualified from operating any vehicle set forth in such paragraph. In addition, the commissioner shall not issue such person a license valid for the operation of any vehicle set forth therein by such person. The commissioner may waive such disqualification and prohibition hereinbefore provided after a period of five years has expired from such sentencing provided:

(i) that during such five year period such person has not violated any of the provisions of section eleven hundred ninety-two of this article or any alcohol or drug related traffic offense in this state or in any jurisdiction outside this state;

(ii) that such person provides acceptable documentation to the commissioner that such person is not in need of alcohol or drug treatment or has satisfactorily completed a prescribed course of such treatment; and

(iii) after such documentation is accepted, that such person is granted a certificate of relief from disabilities as provided for in section seven hundred one of the correction law by the court in which such person was last penalized pursuant to paragraph (d) of subdivision one of this section.

b. Any person who holds a commercial driver's license and is convicted of a violation of any subdivision of section eleven hundred ninety-two of this article who has had a prior finding of refusal to submit to a chemical test pursuant to section eleven hundred ninety-four of this article or has had a prior conviction of any of the following offenses: any violation of section eleven hundred ninety-two of this article; any violation of subdivision one or two of section six hundred of this chapter; or has a prior conviction of any felony involving the use of a motor vehicle pursuant to paragraph (a) of subdivision one of section five hundred ten-a of this chapter, shall be permanently disqualified from operating a commercial motor vehicle. The commissioner may waive such disqualification and prohibition hereinbefore provided after a period of ten years has expired from such sentence provided:

(i) that during such ten year period such person has not been found to have refused a chemical test pursuant to section eleven hundred ninety-four of this article while operating a motor vehicle and has not been convicted of any one of the following offenses while operating a motor vehicle: any violation of section eleven hundred ninety-two of this article; any violation of subdivision one or two of section six hundred of this chapter; or has a prior conviction of any felony involving the use of a motor vehicle pursuant to paragraph (a) of subdivision one of section five hundred ten-a of this chapter;

(ii) that such person provides acceptable documentation to the commissioner that such person is not in need of alcohol or drug treatment or has satisfactorily completed a prescribed course of such treatment; and

(iii) after such documentation is accepted, that such person is granted a certificate of relief from disabilities as provided for in section seven hundred one of the correction law by the court in which such person was last penalized pursuant to paragraph (d) of subdivision one of this section.

c. Upon a third finding of refusal and/or conviction of any of the offenses which require a permanent commercial driver's license revocation, such permanent revocation may not be waived by the commissioner under any circumstances.

(4) Youthful offenders. Where a youth is determined to be a youthful offender, following a conviction of a violation of section eleven hundred ninety-two of this article for which a license suspension or revocation is mandatory, the court shall impose such suspension or revocation as is otherwise required upon conviction and, further, shall notify the commissioner of said suspension or revocation and its finding that said violator is granted youthful offender status as is required pursuant to section five hundred thirteen of this chapter.

(5) Probation. When a license to operate a motor vehicle has been revoked pursuant to this chapter, and the holder has been sentenced to a period of probation pursuant to section 65.00 of the penal law for a violation of any provision of this chapter, or any other provision of the laws of this state, and a condition of such probation is that the holder thereof not operate a motor vehicle or not apply for a license to operate a motor vehicle during the period of such condition of probation, the commissioner may not restore such license until the period of the condition of probation has expired.

(6) Application for new license. Where a license has been revoked pursuant to paragraph (b) of this subdivision, or where the holder is subject to a condition of probation as provided in subparagraph five of this paragraph, application for a new license may be made within forty-five days prior to the expiration of such minimum period of revocation or condition of probation, whichever expires last.

(7) Suspension pending prosecution; excessive blood alcohol content.

a. Except as provided in clause a-1 of this subparagraph, a court shall suspend a driver's license, pending prosecution, of any person charged with a violation of subdivision two, two-a, three or four-a of section eleven hundred ninety-two of this article who, at the time of arrest, is alleged to have had .08 of one percent or more by weight of alcohol in such driver's blood as shown by chemical analysis of blood, breath, urine or saliva, made pursuant to subdivision two or three of section eleven hundred ninety-four of this article.

a-1. A court shall suspend a class DJ or MJ learner's permit or a class DJ or MJ driver's license, pending prosecution, of any person who has been charged with a violation of subdivision one, two, two-a and/or three of section eleven hundred ninety-two of this article.

b. The suspension occurring under clause a of this subparagraph shall occur no later than at the conclusion of all proceedings required for the arraignment and the suspension occurring under clause a-1 of this subparagraph shall occur immediately after the holder's first appearance before the court on the charge which shall, whenever possible, be the next regularly scheduled session of the court after the arrest or at the conclusion of all proceedings required for the arraignment; provided, however, that if the results of any test administered pursuant to section eleven hundred ninety-four of this article are not available within such time period, the complainant police officer or other public servant shall transmit such results to the court at the time they become available, and the court shall, as soon as practicable following the receipt of such results and in compliance with the requirements of this subparagraph, suspend such license. In order for the court to impose such suspension it must find that the accusatory instrument conforms to the requirements of section 100.40 of the criminal procedure law and there exists reasonable cause to believe either that (a) the holder operated a motor vehicle while such holder had .08 of one percent or more by weight of alcohol in his or her blood as was shown by chemical analysis of such person's blood, breath, urine or saliva, made pursuant to the provisions of section eleven hundred ninety-four of this article or (b) the person was the holder of a class DJ or MJ learner's permit or a class DJ or MJ driver's license and operated a motor vehicle while such holder was in violation of subdivision one, two and/or three of section eleven hundred ninety-two of this article. At the time of such license suspension the holder shall be entitled to an opportunity to make a statement regarding these two issues and to present evidence tending to rebut the court's findings.

c. Nothing contained in this subparagraph shall be construed to prohibit or limit a court from imposing any other suspension pending prosecution required or permitted by law.

d. Notwithstanding any contrary provision of this chapter, if any suspension occurring under this subparagraph has been in effect for a period of thirty days, the holder may be issued a conditional license, in accordance with section eleven hundred ninety-six of this article, provided the holder of such license is otherwise eligible to receive such conditional license. A conditional license issued pursuant to this subparagraph shall not be valid for the operation of a commercial motor vehicle. The commissioner shall prescribe by regulation the procedures for the issuance of such conditional license.

e. If the court finds that the suspension imposed pursuant to this subparagraph will result in extreme hardship, the court must issue such suspension, but may grant a hardship privilege, which shall be issued on a form prescribed by the commissioner. For the purposes of this clause, "extreme hardship" shall mean the inability to obtain alternative means of travel to or from the licensee's employment, or to or from necessary medical treatment for the licensee or a member of the licensee's household, or if the licensee is a matriculating student enrolled in an accredited school, college or university travel to or from such licensee's school, college or university if such travel is necessary for the completion of the educational degree or certificate. The burden of proving extreme hardship shall be on the licensee who may present material and relevant evidence. A finding of extreme hardship may not be based solely upon the testimony of the licensee. In no event shall arraignment be adjourned or otherwise delayed more than three business days solely for the purpose of allowing the licensee to present evidence of extreme hardship. The court shall set forth upon the record, or otherwise set forth in writing, the factual basis for such finding. The hardship privilege shall permit the operation of a vehicle only for travel to or from the licensee's employment, or to or from necessary medical treatment for the licensee or a member of the licensee's household, or if the licensee is a matriculating student enrolled in an accredited school, college or university travel to or from such licensee's school, college or university if such travel is necessary for the completion of the educational degree or certificate. A hardship privilege shall not be valid for the operation of a commercial motor vehicle.

(f) Notice of charges to parent or guardian. Notwithstanding the provisions of subdivision two of section eighteen hundred seven of this chapter, upon the first scheduled appearance of any person under eighteen years of age who resides within the household of his or her parent or guardian upon a charge of a violation of subdivision one, two and/or three of section eleven hundred ninety-two of this article, the local criminal court before which such first appearance is scheduled shall forthwith transmit written notice of such appearance or failure to make such appearance to the parent or guardian of such minor person; provided, however, that if an arraignment and conviction of such person follows such appearance upon the same day, or in case such person waives arraignment and enters a plea of guilty to the offense as charged in accordance with the provisions of section eighteen hundred five of this chapter, transmittal of notice of his or her conviction as provided in section five hundred fourteen of this chapter shall be sufficient and the notice required by this paragraph need not be given; provided further that the failure of a local criminal court to transmit the notice required by this paragraph shall in no manner affect the validity of a conviction subsequently obtained.

§1194.　Arrest and testing.

1. Arrest and field testing. (a) Arrest. Notwithstanding the provisions of section 140.10 of the criminal procedure law, a police officer may, without a warrant, arrest a person, in case of a violation of subdivision one of section eleven hundred ninety-two of this article, if such violation is coupled with an accident or collision in which such person is involved, which in fact has been committed, though not in the police officer's presence, when the officer has reasonable cause to believe that the violation was committed by such person.

(b) Field testing. Every person operating a motor vehicle which has been involved in an accident or which is operated in violation of any of the provisions of this chapter shall, at the request of a police officer, submit to a breath test to be administered by the police officer. If such test indicates that such operator has consumed alcohol, the police officer may request such operator to submit to a chemical test in the manner set forth in subdivision two of this section.

2. Chemical tests. (a) When authorized. Any person who operates a motor vehicle in this state shall be deemed to have given consent to a chemical test of one or more of the following: breath, blood, urine, or saliva, for the purpose of determining the alcoholic and/or drug content of the blood provided that such test is administered by or at the direction of a police officer with respect to a chemical test of breath, urine or saliva or, with respect to a chemical test of blood, at the direction of a police officer:

(1) having reasonable grounds to believe such person to have been operating in violation of any subdivision of section eleven hundred ninety-two of this article and within two hours after such person has been placed under arrest for any such violation; or having reasonable grounds to believe such person to have been operating in violation of section eleven hundred ninety-two-a of this article and within two hours after the stop of such person for any such violation,

(2) within two hours after a breath test, as provided in paragraph (b) of subdivision one of this section, indicates that alcohol has been consumed by such person and in accordance with the rules and regulations established by the police force of which the officer is a member;

(3) for the purposes of this paragraph, "reasonable grounds" to believe that a person has been operating a motor vehicle after having consumed alcohol in violation of section eleven hundred ninety-two-a of this article shall be determined by viewing the totality of circumstances surrounding the incident which, when taken together, indicate that the operator was driving in violation of such subdivision. Such circumstances may include any visible or behavioral indication of alcohol consumption by the operator, the existence of an open container containing or having contained an alcoholic beverage in or around the vehicle driven by the operator, or any other evidence surrounding the circumstances of the incident which indicates that the operator has been operating a motor vehicle after having consumed alcohol at the time of the incident; or

(4) notwithstanding any other provision of law to the contrary, no person under the age of twenty-one shall be arrested for an alleged violation of section eleven hundred ninety-two-a of this article. However, a person under the age of twenty-one for whom a chemical test is authorized pursuant to this paragraph may be temporarily detained by the police solely for the purpose of requesting or administering such chemical test whenever arrest without a warrant for a petty offense would be authorized in accordance with the provisions of section 140.10 of the criminal procedure law or paragraph (a) of subdivision one of this section.

(b) Report of refusal. (1) If: (A) such person having been placed under arrest; or (B) after a breath test indicates the presence of alcohol in the person's system; or (C) with regard to a person under the age of twenty-one, there are reasonable grounds to believe that such person has been operating a motor vehicle after having consumed alcohol in violation of section eleven hundred ninety-two-a of this article; and having thereafter been requested to submit to such chemical test and having been informed that the person's license or permit to drive and any non-resident operating privilege shall be immediately suspended and subsequently revoked, or, for operators under the age of twenty-one for whom there are reasonable grounds to believe that such operator has been operating a motor vehicle after having consumed alcohol in violation of section eleven hundred ninety-two-a of this article, shall be revoked for refusal to submit to such chemical test or any portion thereof, whether or not the person is found guilty of the charge for which such person is arrested or detained, refuses to submit to such chemical test or any portion thereof, unless a court order has been granted pursuant to subdivision three of this section, the test shall not be given and a written report of such refusal shall be immediately made by the police officer before whom such refusal was made. Such report may be verified by having the report sworn to, or by affixing to such report a form notice that false statements made therein are punishable as a class A misdemeanor pursuant to section 210.45 of the penal law and such form notice together with the subscription of the deponent shall constitute a verification of the report.

(2) The report of the police officer shall set forth reasonable grounds to believe such arrested person or such detained person under the age of

twenty-one had been driving in violation of any subdivision of section eleven hundred ninety-two or eleven hundred ninety-two-a of this article, that said person had refused to submit to such chemical test, and that no chemical test was administered pursuant to the requirements of subdivision three of this section. The report shall be presented to the court upon arraignment of an arrested person, provided, however, in the case of a person under the age of twenty-one, for whom a test was authorized pursuant to the provisions of subparagraph two or three of paragraph (a) of this subdivision, and who has not been placed under arrest for a violation of any of the provisions of section eleven hundred ninety-two of this article, such report shall be forwarded to the commissioner within forty-eight hours in a manner to be prescribed by the commissioner, and all subsequent proceedings with regard to refusal to submit to such chemical test by such person shall be as set forth in subdivision three of section eleven hundred ninety-four-a of this article.

(3) For persons placed under arrest for a violation of any subdivision of section eleven hundred ninety-two of this article, the license or permit to drive and any non-resident operating privilege shall, upon the basis of such written report, be temporarily suspended by the court without notice pending the determination of a hearing as provided in paragraph (c) of this subdivision. Copies of such report must be transmitted by the court to the commissioner and such transmittal may not be waived even with the consent of all the parties. Such report shall be forwarded to the commissioner within forty-eight hours of such arraignment.

(4) The court or the police officer, in the case of a person under the age of twenty-one alleged to be driving after having consumed alcohol, shall provide such person with a scheduled hearing date, a waiver form, and such other information as may be required by the commissioner. If a hearing, as provided for in paragraph (c) of this subdivision, or subdivision three of section eleven hundred ninety-four-a of this article, is waived by such person, the commissioner shall immediately revoke the license, permit, or non-resident operating privilege, as of the date of receipt of such waiver in accordance with the provisions of paragraph (d) of this subdivision.

(c) Hearings. Any person whose license or permit to drive or any non-resident driving privilege has been suspended pursuant to paragraph (b) of this subdivision is entitled to a hearing in accordance with a hearing schedule to be promulgated by the commissioner. If the department fails to provide for such hearing fifteen days after the date of the arraignment of the arrested person, the license, permit to drive or non-resident operating privilege of such person shall be reinstated pending a hearing pursuant to this section. The hearing shall be limited to the following issues:

(1) did the police officer have reasonable grounds to believe that such person had been driving in violation of any subdivision of section eleven hundred ninety-two of this article;

(2) did the police officer make a lawful arrest of such person;

(3) was such person given sufficient warning, in clear or unequivocal language, prior to such refusal that such refusal to submit to such chemical test

or any portion thereof, would result in the immediate suspension and subsequent revocation of such person's license or operating privilege whether or not such person is found guilty of the charge for which the arrest was made; and

(4) did such person refuse to submit to such chemical test or any portion thereof. If, after such hearing, the hearing officer, acting on behalf of the commissioner, finds on any one of said issues in the negative, the hearing officer shall immediately terminate any suspension arising from such refusal. If, after such hearing, the hearing officer, acting on behalf of the commissioner finds all of the issues in the affirmative, such officer shall immediately revoke the license or permit to drive or any non-resident operating privilege in accordance with the provisions of paragraph (d) of this subdivision. A person who has had a license or permit to drive or non-resident operating privilege suspended or revoked pursuant to this subdivision may appeal the findings of the hearing officer in accordance with the provisions of article three-A of this chapter. Any person may waive the right to a hearing under this section. Failure by such person to appear for the scheduled hearing shall constitute a waiver of such hearing, provided, however, that such person may petition the commissioner for a new hearing which shall be held as soon as practicable.

(d) Sanctions. (1) Revocations. a. Any license which has been revoked pursuant to paragraph (c) of this subdivision shall not be restored for at least one year after such revocation, nor thereafter, except in the discretion of the commissioner. However, no such license shall be restored for at least eighteen months after such revocation, nor thereafter except in the discretion of the commissioner, in any case where the person has had a prior revocation resulting from refusal to submit to a chemical test, or has been convicted of or found to be in violation of any subdivision of section eleven hundred ninety-two or section eleven hundred ninety-two-a of this article not arising out of the same incident, within the five years immediately preceding the date of such revocation; provided, however, a prior finding that a person under the age of twenty-one has refused to submit to a chemical test pursuant to subdivision three of section eleven hundred ninety-four-a of this article shall have the same effect as a prior finding of a refusal pursuant to this subdivision solely for the purpose of determining the length of any license suspension or revocation required to be imposed under any provision of this article, provided that the subsequent offense or refusal is committed or occurred prior to the expiration of the retention period for such prior refusal as set forth in paragraph (k) of subdivision one of section two hundred one of this chapter.

b. Any license which has been revoked pursuant to paragraph (c) of this subdivision or pursuant to subdivision three of section eleven hundred ninety-four-a of this article, where the holder was under the age of twenty-one years at the time of such refusal, shall not be restored for at least one year, nor thereafter, except in the discretion of the commissioner. Where such person under the age of twenty-one years has a prior finding, conviction or youthful offender adjudication resulting from a violation of section eleven hundred ninety-two or section eleven hundred ninety-two-a of this article, not arising from the same incident, such license shall not be restored for at least one year or until such person reaches the age of twenty-one years, whichever is the greater period of time, nor thereafter, except in the discretion of the commissioner.

c. Any commercial driver's license which has been revoked pursuant to paragraph (c) of this subdivision based upon a finding of refusal to submit to a chemical test, where such finding occurs within or outside of this state, shall not be restored for at least eighteen months after such revocation, nor thereafter, except in the discretion of the commissioner, but shall not be restored for at least three years after such revocation, nor thereafter, except in the discretion of the commissioner, if the holder of such license was operating a commercial motor vehicle transporting hazardous materials at the time of such refusal. However, such person shall be permanently disqualified from operating a commercial motor vehicle in any case where the holder has a prior finding of refusal to submit to a chemical test pursuant to this section or has a prior conviction of any of the following offenses: any violation of section eleven hundred ninety-two of this article; any violation of subdivision one or two of section six hundred of this chapter; or has a prior conviction of any felony involving the use of a motor vehicle pursuant to paragraph (a) of subdivision one of section five hundred ten-a of this chapter. Provided that the commissioner may waive such permanent revocation after a period of ten years has expired from such revocation provided:

(i) that during such ten year period such person has not been found to have refused a chemical test pursuant to this section and has not been convicted of any one of the following offenses: any violation of section eleven hundred ninety-two of this article; refusal to submit to a chemical test pursuant to this section; any violation of subdivision one or two of section six hundred of this chapter; or has a prior conviction of any felony involving the use of a motor vehicle pursuant to paragraph (a) of subdivision one of section five hundred ten-a of this chapter;

(ii) that such person provides acceptable documentation to the commissioner that such person is not in need of alcohol or drug treatment or has satisfactorily completed a prescribed course of such treatment; and

(iii) after such documentation is accepted, that such person is granted a certificate of relief from disabilities as provided for in section seven hundred one of the correction law by the court in which such person was last penalized.

d. Upon a third finding of refusal and/or conviction of any of the offenses which require a permanent commercial driver's license revocation, such permanent revocation may not be waived by the commissioner under any circumstances.

(2) Civil penalties. Except as otherwise provided, any person whose license, permit to drive, or any non-resident operating privilege is revoked pursuant to the provisions of this section shall also be liable for a civil penalty in the amount of five hundred dollars except that if such revocation is a second or subsequent revocation pursuant to this section issued within a five year period, or such person has been convicted of a violation of any subdivision of section eleven hundred ninety-two of this article within the past five years not arising out of the same incident, the civil penalty shall be in the amount of

seven hundred fifty dollars. Any person whose license is revoked pursuant to the provisions of this section based upon a finding of refusal to submit to a chemical test while operating a commercial motor vehicle shall also be liable for a civil penalty of five hundred fifty dollars except that if such person has previously been found to have refused a chemical test pursuant to this section while operating a commercial motor vehicle or has a prior conviction of any of the following offenses while operating a commercial motor vehicle: any violation of section eleven hundred ninety-two of this article; any violation of subdivision two of section six hundred of this chapter; or has a prior conviction of any felony involving the use of a commercial motor vehicle pursuant to paragraph (a) of subdivision one of section five hundred ten-a of this chapter, then the civil penalty shall be seven hundred fifty dollars. No new driver's license or permit shall be issued, or non-resident operating privilege restored to such person unless such penalty has been paid. All penalties collected by the department pursuant to the provisions of this section shall be the property of the state and shall be paid into the general fund of the state treasury.

(3) Effect of rehabilitation program. No period of revocation arising out of this section may be set aside by the commissioner for the reason that such person was a participant in the alcohol and drug rehabilitation program set forth in section eleven hundred ninety-six of this article.

(e) Regulations. The commissioner shall promulgate such rules and regulations as may be necessary to effectuate the provisions of subdivisions one and two of this section.

(f) Evidence. Evidence of a refusal to submit to such chemical test or any portion thereof shall be admissible in any trial, proceeding or hearing based upon a violation of the provisions of section eleven hundred ninety-two of this article but only upon a showing that the person was given sufficient warning, in clear and unequivocal language, of the effect of such refusal and that the person persisted in the refusal.

(g) Results. Upon the request of the person who was tested, the results of such test shall be made available to such person.

3. Compulsory chemical tests. (a) Court ordered chemical tests. Notwithstanding the provisions of subdivision two of this section, no person who operates a motor vehicle in this state may refuse to submit to a chemical test of one or more of the following: breath, blood, urine or saliva, for the purpose of determining the alcoholic and/or drug content of the blood when a court order for such chemical test has been issued in accordance with the provisions of this subdivision.

(b) When authorized. Upon refusal by any person to submit to a chemical test or any portion thereof as described above, the test shall not be given unless a police officer or a district attorney, as defined in subdivision thirty-two of section 1.20 of the criminal procedure law, requests and obtains a court order to compel a person to submit to a chemical test to determine the alcoholic or drug content of the person's blood upon a finding of reasonable cause to believe that:

(1) such person was the operator of a motor vehicle and in the course of such operation a person other than the operator was killed or suffered serious physical injury as defined in section 10.00 of the penal law; and

(2) a. either such person operated the vehicle in violation of any subdivision of section eleven hundred ninety-two of this article, or b. a breath test administered by a police officer in accordance with paragraph (b) of subdivision one of this section indicates that alcohol has been consumed by such person; and

(3) such person has been placed under lawful arrest; and

(4) such person has refused to submit to a chemical test or any portion thereof, requested in accordance with the provisions of paragraph (a) of subdivision two of this section or is unable to give consent to such a test.

(c) Reasonable cause; definition. For the purpose of this subdivision "reasonable cause" shall be determined by viewing the totality of circumstances surrounding the incident which, when taken together, indicate that the operator was driving in violation of section eleven hundred ninety-two of this article. Such circumstances may include, but are not limited to: evidence that the operator was operating a motor vehicle in violation of any provision of this article or any other moving violation at the time of the incident; any visible indication of alcohol or drug consumption or impairment by the operator; the existence of an open container containing an alcoholic beverage in or around the vehicle driven by the operator; any other evidence surrounding the circumstances of the incident which indicates that the operator has been operating a motor vehicle while impaired by the consumption of alcohol or drugs or intoxicated at the time of the incident.

(d) Court order; procedure. (1) An application for a court order to compel submission to a chemical test or any portion thereof, may be made to any supreme court justice, county court judge or district court judge in the judicial district in which the incident occurred, or if the incident occurred in the city of New York before any supreme court justice or judge of the criminal court of the city of New York. Such application may be communicated by telephone, radio or other means of electronic communication, or in person.

(2) The applicant must provide identification by name and title and must state the purpose of the communication. Upon being advised that an application for a court order to compel submission to a chemical test is being made, the court shall place under oath the applicant and any other person providing information in support of the application as provided in subparagraph three of this paragraph. After being sworn the applicant must state that the person from whom the chemical test was requested was the operator of a motor vehicle and in the course of such operation a person, other than the operator, has been killed or seriously injured and, based upon the totality of circumstances, there is reasonable cause to believe that such person was operating a motor vehicle in violation of any subdivision of section eleven hundred ninety-two of this article and, after being placed under lawful arrest such person refused to submit to a chemical test or any portion thereof, in accordance with the provisions of this section or is unable to give consent to

such a test or any portion thereof. The applicant must make specific allegations of fact to support such statement. Any other person properly identified, may present sworn allegations of fact in support of the applicant's statement.

(3) Upon being advised that an oral application for a court order to compel a person to submit to a chemical test is being made, a judge or justice shall place under oath the applicant and any other person providing information in support of the application. Such oath or oaths and all of the remaining communication must be recorded, either by means of a voice recording device or verbatim stenographic or verbatim longhand notes. If a voice recording device is used or a stenographic record made, the judge must have the record transcribed, certify to the accuracy of the transcription and file the original record and transcription with the court within seventy-two hours of the issuance of the court order. If the longhand notes are taken, the judge shall subscribe a copy and file it with the court within twenty-four hours of the issuance of the order.

(4) If the court is satisfied that the requirements for the issuance of a court order pursuant to the provisions of paragraph (b) of this subdivision have been met, it may grant the application and issue an order requiring the accused to submit to a chemical test to determine the alcoholic and/or drug content of his blood and ordering the withdrawal of a blood sample in accordance with the provisions of paragraph (a) of subdivision four of this section. When a judge or justice determines to issue an order to compel submission to a chemical test based on an oral application, the applicant therefor shall prepare the order in accordance with the instructions of the judge or justice. In all cases the order shall include the name of the issuing judge or justice, the name of the applicant, and the date and time it was issued. It must be signed by the judge or justice if issued in person, or by the applicant if issued orally.

(5) Any false statement by an applicant or any other person in support of an application for a court order shall subject such person to the offenses for perjury set forth in article two hundred ten of the penal law.

(6) The chief administrator of the courts shall establish a schedule to provide that a sufficient number of judges or justices will be available in each judicial district to hear oral applications for court orders as permitted by this section.

(e) Administration of compulsory chemical test. An order issued pursuant to the provisions of this subdivision shall require that a chemical test to determine the alcoholic and/or drug content of the operator's blood must be administered. The provisions of paragraphs (a), (b) and (c) of subdivision four of this section shall be applicable to any chemical test administered pursuant to this section.

4. Testing procedures. (a) Persons authorized to withdraw blood; immunity; testimony. (1) At the request of a police officer, the following persons may withdraw blood for the purpose of determining the alcoholic or drug content therein: (i) a physician, a registered professional nurse, a registered physician assistant, a certified nurse practitioner, or an advanced emergency medical technician as certified by the department of health; or (ii) under the supervision and at the direction of a physician, registered physician

assistant or certified nurse practitioner acting within his or her lawful scope of practice, or upon the express consent of the person eighteen years of age or older from whom such blood is to be withdrawn: a clinical laboratory technician or clinical laboratory technologist licensed pursuant to article one hundred sixty-five of the education law; a phlebotomist; or a medical laboratory technician or medical technologist employed by a clinical laboratory approved under title five of article five of the public health law. This limitation shall not apply to the taking of a urine, saliva or breath specimen.

(2) No person entitled to withdraw blood pursuant to subparagraph one of this paragraph or hospital employing such person, and no other employer of such person shall be sued or held liable for any act done or omitted in the course of withdrawing blood at the request of a police officer pursuant to this section.

(3) Any person who may have a cause of action arising from the withdrawal of blood as aforesaid, for which no personal liability exists under subparagraph two of this paragraph, may maintain such action against the state if any person entitled to withdraw blood pursuant to paragraph (a) hereof acted at the request of a police officer employed by the state, or against the appropriate political subdivision of the state if such person acted at the request of a police officer employed by a political subdivision of the state. No action shall be maintained pursuant to this subparagraph unless notice of claim is duly filed or served in compliance with law.

(4) Notwithstanding the foregoing provisions of this paragraph an action may be maintained by the state or a political subdivision thereof against a person entitled to withdraw blood pursuant to subparagraph one of this paragraph or hospital employing such person for whose act or omission the state or the political subdivision has been held liable under this paragraph to recover damages, not exceeding the amount awarded to the claimant, that may have been sustained by the state or the political subdivision by reason of gross negligence or bad faith on the part of such person.

(5) The testimony of any person other than a physician, entitled to withdraw blood pursuant to subparagraph one of this paragraph, in respect to any such withdrawal of blood made by such person may be received in evidence with the same weight, force and effect as if such withdrawal of blood were made by a physician.

(6) The provisions of subparagraphs two, three and four of this paragraph shall also apply with regard to any person employed by a hospital as security personnel for any act done or omitted in the course of withdrawing blood at the request of a police officer pursuant to a court order in accordance with subdivision three of this section.

(b) Right to additional test. The person tested shall be permitted to choose a physician to administer a chemical test in addition to the one administered at the direction of the police officer.

(c) Rules and regulations. The department of health shall issue and file rules and regulations approving satisfactory techniques or methods of conducting chemical analyses of a person's blood, urine, breath or saliva and to ascertain the qualifications and competence of individuals to conduct and supervise chemical analyses of a person's blood, urine, breath or saliva. If the analyses were made by an individual possessing a permit issued by the department of health, this shall be presumptive evidence that the examination was properly given. The provisions of this paragraph do not prohibit the introduction as evidence of an analysis made by an individual other than a person possessing a permit issued by the department of health.

§1194-a.   Driving after having consumed alcohol; under twenty-one; procedure.

1. Chemical test report and hearing. (a) Whenever a chemical test of the breath, blood, urine or saliva of an operator who is under the age of twenty-one indicates that such person has operated a motor vehicle in violation of section eleven hundred ninety-two-a of this article, and such person is not charged with violating any subdivision of section eleven hundred ninety-two arising out of the same incident, the police officer who administered the test shall forward a report of the results of such test to the department within twenty-four hours of the time when such results are available in a manner prescribed by the commissioner, and the operator shall be given a hearing notice as provided in subdivision one-a of this section, to appear before a hearing officer in the county where the chemical test was administered, or in an adjoining county under such circumstances as prescribed by the commissioner, on a date to be established in accordance with a schedule promulgated by the commissioner. Such hearing shall occur within thirty days of, but not less than forty-eight hours from, the date that the chemical test was administered, provided, however, where the commissioner determines, based upon the availability of hearing officers and the anticipated volume of hearings at a particular location, that the scheduling of such hearing within thirty days would impair the timely scheduling or conducting of other hearings pursuant to this chapter, such hearing shall be scheduled at the next hearing date for such particular location. When providing the operator with such hearing notice, the police officer shall also give to the operator, and shall, prior to the commencement of the hearing, provide to the department, copies of the following reports, documents and materials: any written report or document, or portion thereof, concerning a physical examination, a scientific test or experiment, including the most recent record of inspection, or calibration or repair of machines or instruments utilized to perform such scientific tests or experiments and the certification certificate, if any, held by the operator of the machine or instrument, which tests or examinations were made by or at the request or direction of a public servant engaged in law enforcement activity. The report of the police officer shall be verified by having the report sworn to, or by affixing to such report a form notice that false statements made therein are punishable as a class A misdemeanor pursuant to section 210.45 of the penal law and such form notice together with the subscription of the deponent shall constitute verification of the report.

(b) Every person under the age of twenty-one who is alleged to have operated a motor vehicle after having consumed alcohol as set forth in section eleven hundred ninety-two-a of this article, and who is not charged with violating any subdivision of section eleven hundred ninety-two of this article arising out of the same incident, is entitled to a hearing before a hearing officer in accordance with the provisions of this section. Unless otherwise provided by law, the license or permit to drive or any non-resident operating privilege of such person shall not be suspended or revoked prior to the scheduled date for such hearing.

(i) The hearing shall be limited to the following issues: (1) did such person operate the motor vehicle; (2) was a valid request to submit to a chemical test made by the police officer in accordance with the provisions of section eleven hundred ninety-four of this article; (3) was such person less than twenty-one years of age at the time of operation of the motor vehicle; (4) was the chemical test properly administered in accordance with the provisions of section eleven hundred ninety-four of this article; (5) did the test find that such person had driven after having consumed alcohol as defined in section eleven hundred ninety-two-a of this article; and (6) did the police officer make a lawful stop of such person. The burden of proof shall be on the police officer to prove each of these issues by clear and convincing evidence.

(ii) Every person who is entitled to a hearing pursuant to this subdivision has the right to be present at the hearing; the right to be represented by attorney, or in the hearing officer's discretion, by any other person the operator chooses; the right to receive and review discovery materials as provided in this subdivision; the right not to testify; the right to present evidence and witnesses in his own behalf, the right to cross examine adverse witnesses, and the right to appeal from an adverse determination in accordance with article three-A of this chapter. Any person representing the operator must conform to the standards of conduct required of attorneys appearing before state courts, and failure to conform to these standards will be grounds for declining to permit his continued appearance in the hearing.

(iii) Hearings conducted pursuant to this subdivision shall be in accordance with this subdivision and with the provisions applicable to the adjudication of traffic infractions pursuant to the following provisions of part 124 of title fifteen of the codes, rules and regulations of the state of New York: paragraph (b) of section 124.1 regarding the opening statement; paragraph (b) of section 124.2 regarding the right to representation and to remain silent and paragraphs (a) through (e) of section 124.4 regarding the conduct of the hearing, procedure and recusal; provided, however, that nothing contained in this subparagraph shall be deemed to preclude a hearing officer from changing the order of a hearing conducted pursuant to this subdivision as justice may require and for good cause shown.

(iv) The rules governing receipt of evidence in a court of law shall not apply in a hearing conducted pursuant to this subdivision except as follows:

(1) on the merits of the charge, and whether or not a party objects, the hearing officer shall exclude from consideration the following: a privileged

communication; evidence which, for constitutional reasons, would not be admissible in a court of law; evidence of prior misconduct, incompetency or illness, except where such evidence would be admissible in a court of law; evidence which is irrelevant or immaterial;

(2) no negative inference shall be drawn from the operator's exercising the right not to testify.

(v) If, after such hearing, the hearing officer, acting on behalf of the commissioner, finds all of the issues set forth in this subdivision in the affirmative, the hearing officer shall suspend or revoke the license or permit to drive or non-resident operating privilege of such person in accordance with the time periods set forth in subdivision two of section eleven hundred ninety-three of this article. If, after such hearing, the hearing officer, acting on behalf of the commissioner, finds any of said issues in the negative, the hearing officer must find that the operator did not drive after having consumed alcohol.

(vi) A person who has had a license or permit to drive or non-resident operating privilege suspended or revoked pursuant to the provisions of this section may appeal the finding of the hearing officer in accordance with the provisions of article three-A of this chapter.

(c) Unless an adjournment of the hearing date has been granted, upon the operator's failure to appear for a scheduled hearing, the commissioner shall suspend the license or permit to drive or non-resident operating privilege until the operator petitions the commissioner and a rescheduled hearing is conducted, provided, however, the commissioner shall restore such person's license or permit to drive or non-resident operating privilege if such rescheduled hearing is adjourned at the request of a person other than the operator. Requests for adjournments shall be made and determined in accordance with regulations promulgated by the commissioner. If such a request by the operator for an adjournment is granted, the commissioner shall notify the operator of the rescheduled hearing, which shall be scheduled for the next hearing date. If a second or subsequent request by the operator for an adjournment is granted, the operator's license or permit to drive or non-resident operating privilege may be suspended pending the hearing at the time such adjournment is granted; provided, however, that the records of the department or the evidence already admitted furnishes reasonable grounds to believe such suspension is necessary to prevent continuing violations or a substantial traffic safety hazard; and provided further, that such hearing shall be scheduled for the next hearing date. If a police officer does not appear for a hearing, the hearing officer shall have the authority to dismiss the charge. Any person may waive the right to a hearing under this subdivision, in a form and manner prescribed by the commissioner, and may enter an admission of guilt, in person or by mail, to the charge of operating a motor vehicle in violation of section eleven hundred ninety-two-a of this article. Such admission of guilt shall have the same force and effect as a finding of guilt entered following a hearing conducted pursuant to this subdivision.

1-a. Hearing notice. The hearing notice issued to an operator pursuant to subdivision one of this section shall be in a form as prescribed by the commissioner. In addition to containing information concerning the time, date and location of the hearing, and such other information as the commissioner deems appropriate, such hearing notice shall also contain the following information: the date, time and place of the offense charged; the procedures for requesting an adjournment of a scheduled hearing as provided in this section, the operator's right to a hearing conducted pursuant to this section and the right to waive such hearing and plead guilty, either in person or by mail, to the offense charged.

2. Civil penalty. Unless otherwise provided, any person whose license, permit to drive, or any non-resident operating privilege is suspended or revoked pursuant to the provisions of this section shall also be liable for a civil penalty in the amount of one hundred twenty-five dollars, which shall be distributed in accordance with the provisions of subdivision nine of section eighteen hundred three of this chapter.

3. Refusal report and hearing. (a) Any person under the age of twenty-one who is suspected of operating a motor vehicle after having consumed alcohol in violation of section eleven hundred ninety-two-a of this chapter, and who is not charged with violating any subdivision of section eleven hundred ninety-two of this article arising out of the same incident, and who has been requested to submit to a chemical test pursuant to paragraph (a) of subdivision two of section eleven hundred ninety-four of this article and after having been informed that his license or permit to drive and any non-resident operating privilege shall be revoked for refusal to submit to such chemical test or any portion thereof, whether or not there is a finding of driving after having consumed alcohol, and such person refuses to submit to such chemical test or any portion thereof, shall be entitled to a hearing in accordance with a schedule promulgated by the commissioner, and such hearing shall occur within thirty days of, but not less than forty-eight hours from, the date of such refusal, provided, however, where the commissioner determines, based upon the availability of hearing officers and the anticipated volume of hearings at a particular location, that the scheduling of such hearing within thirty days would impair the timely scheduling or conducting of other hearings pursuant to this chapter, such hearing shall be scheduled at the next hearing date for such particular location.

(b) Unless an adjournment of the hearing date has been granted, upon the operator's failure to appear for a scheduled hearing, the commissioner shall suspend the license or permit to drive or non-resident operating privilege until the operator petitions the commissioner and a rescheduled hearing is conducted, provided, however, the commissioner shall restore such person's license or permit to drive or non-resident operating privilege if such rescheduled hearing is adjourned at the request of a person other than the operator. Requests for adjournments shall be made and determined in accordance with regulations promulgated by the commissioner. If such a request by the operator for an adjournment is granted, the commissioner shall notify the operator of the rescheduled hearing, which shall be scheduled for the next hearing date. If a second or subsequent request by the operator for an adjournment is granted, the operator's license or permit to drive or non-resident operating privilege may be suspended pending the hearing at the time such adjournment is granted; provided, however, that the records of the department or the evidence already admitted furnishes reasonable grounds to believe such suspension is necessary to prevent continuing violations or a substantial traffic safety hazard; and provided further, that such hearing shall be scheduled for the next hearing date. If a police officer does not appear for a hearing, the hearing officer shall have the authority to dismiss the charge. Any person may waive the right to a hearing under this subdivision.

(c) The hearing on the refusal to submit to a chemical test pursuant to this subdivision shall be limited to the following issues: (1) was a valid request to submit to a chemical test made by the police officer in accordance with the provisions of section eleven hundred ninety-four of this article; (2) was such person given sufficient warning, in clear or unequivocal language, prior to such refusal that such refusal to submit to such chemical test or any portion thereof, would result in the revocation of such person's license or permit to drive or nonresident operating privilege, whether or not such person is found to have operated a motor vehicle after having consumed alcohol; (3) did such person refuse to submit to such chemical test or any portion thereof; (4) did such person operate the motor vehicle; (5) was such person less than twenty-one years of age at the time of operation of the motor vehicle; (6) did the police officer make a lawful stop of such person. If, after such hearing, the hearing officer, acting on behalf of the commissioner, finds on any one said issue in the negative, the hearing officer shall not revoke the operator's license or permit to drive or non-resident operating privilege and shall immediately terminate any outstanding suspension of the operator's license, permit to drive or non-resident operating privilege arising from such refusal. If, after such hearing, the hearing officer, acting on behalf of the commissioner, finds all of the issues in the affirmative, such hearing officer shall immediately revoke the license or permit to drive or any non-resident operating privilege in accordance with the provisions of paragraph (d) of subdivision two of section eleven hundred ninety-four of this article. A person who has had a license or permit to drive or non-resident operating privilege suspended or revoked pursuant to the provisions of this section may appeal the findings of the hearing officer in accordance with the provisions of article three-A of this chapter.

§1195. Chemical test evidence.

1. Admissibility. Upon the trial of any action or proceeding arising out of actions alleged to have been committed by any person arrested for a violation of any subdivision of section eleven hundred ninety-two of this article, the court shall admit evidence of the amount of alcohol or drugs in the defendant's blood as shown by a test administered pursuant to the provisions of section eleven hundred ninety-four of this article.

2. Probative value. The following effect shall be given to evidence of blood-alcohol content, as determined by such tests, of a person arrested for violation of section eleven hundred ninety-two of this article:

(a) Evidence that there was .05 of one per centum or less by weight of alcohol in such person's blood shall be prima facie evidence that the ability of such person to operate a motor vehicle was not impaired by the consumption of alcohol, and that such person was not in an intoxicated condition;

(b) Evidence that there was more than .05 of one per centum but less than .07 of one per centum by weight of alcohol in such person's blood shall be prima facie evidence that such person was not in an intoxicated condition, but such evidence shall be relevant evidence, but shall not be given prima facie effect, in determining whether the ability of such person to operate a motor vehicle was impaired by the consumption of alcohol; and

(c) Evidence that there was .07 of one per centum or more but less than .08 of one per centum by weight of alcohol in such person's blood shall be prima facie evidence that such person was not in an intoxicated condition, but such evidence shall be given prima facie effect in determining whether the ability of such person to operate a motor vehicle was impaired by the consumption of alcohol.

3. Suppression. A defendant who has been compelled to submit to a chemical test pursuant to the provisions of subdivision three of section eleven hundred ninety-four of this article may move for the suppression of such evidence in accordance with article seven hundred ten of the criminal procedure law on the grounds that the order was obtained and the test administered in violation of the provisions of such subdivision or any other applicable law.

§1196. Alcohol and drug rehabilitation program.

1. Program establishment. There is hereby established an alcohol and drug rehabilitation program within the department of motor vehicles. The commissioner shall establish, by regulation, the instructional and rehabilitative aspects of the program. Such program shall consist of at least fifteen hours and include, but need not be limited to, classroom instruction in areas deemed suitable by the commissioner. No person shall be required to attend or participate in such program or any aspect thereof for a period exceeding eight months except upon the recommendation of the department of mental hygiene or appropriate health officials administering the program on behalf of a municipality.

2. Curriculum. The form, content and method of presentation of the various aspects of such program shall be established by the commissioner. In the development of the form, curriculum and content of such program, the commissioner may consult with the commissioner of mental health, the director of the division of alcoholism and alcohol abuse, the director of the division of substance abuse services and any other state department or agency and request and receive assistance from them. The commissioner is also authorized to develop more than one curriculum and course content for such program in order to meet the varying rehabilitative needs of the participants.

3. Where available. A course in such program shall be available in at least every county in the state, except where the commissioner determines that there is not a sufficient number of alcohol or drug-related traffic offenses in a county

to mandate the establishment of said course, and that provisions be made for the residents of said county to attend a course in another county where a course exists.

4. Eligibility. Participation in the program shall be limited to those persons convicted of alcohol or drug-related traffic offenses or persons who have been adjudicated youthful offenders for alcohol or drug-related traffic offenses, or persons found to have been operating a motor vehicle after having consumed alcohol in violation of section eleven hundred ninety-two-a of this article, who choose to participate and who satisfy the criteria and meet the requirements for participation as established by this section and the regulations promulgated thereunder; provided, however, in the exercise of discretion, the judge imposing sentence may prohibit the defendant from enrolling in such program. The commissioner or deputy may exercise discretion, to reject any person from participation referred to such program and nothing herein contained shall be construed as creating a right to be included in any course or program established under this section. In addition, no person shall be permitted to take part in such program if, during the five years immediately preceding commission of an alcohol or drug-related traffic offense or a finding of a violation of section eleven hundred ninety-two-a of this article, such person has participated in a program established pursuant to this article or been convicted of a violation of any subdivision of section eleven hundred ninety-two of this article other than a violation committed prior to November first, nineteen hundred eighty-eight, for which such person did not participate in such program. In the exercise of discretion, the commissioner or a deputy shall have the right to expel any participant from the program who fails to satisfy the requirements for participation in such program or who fails to satisfactorily participate in or attend any aspect of such program. Notwithstanding any contrary provisions of this chapter, satisfactory participation in and completion of a course in such program shall result in the termination of any sentence of imprisonment that may have been imposed by reason of a conviction therefor; provided, however, that nothing contained in this section shall delay the commencement of such sentence.

5. Effect of completion. Except as provided in subparagraph nine of paragraph (b) of subdivision two of section eleven hundred ninety-three or in subparagraph three of paragraph (d) of subdivision two of section eleven hundred ninety-four of this article, upon successful completion of a course in such program as certified by its administrator, a participant may apply to the commissioner on a form provided for that purpose, for the termination of the suspension or revocation order issued as a result of the participant's conviction which caused the participation in such course. In the exercise of discretion, upon receipt of such application, and upon payment of any civil penalties for which the applicant may be liable, the commissioner is authorized to terminate such order or orders and return the participant's license or reinstate the privilege of operating a motor vehicle in this state. However, the commissioner shall not issue any new license nor restore any license where said issuance of restoral is prohibited by subdivision two of section eleven hundred ninety-three

of this article. 6. Fees. The commissioner shall establish a schedule of fees to be paid by or on behalf of each participant in the program, and may, from time to time, modify same. Such fees shall defray the ongoing expenses of the program. Provided, however, that pursuant to an agreement with the department a municipality, department thereof, or other agency may conduct a course in such program with all or part of the expense of such course and program being borne by such municipality, department or agency. In no event shall such fee be refundable, either for reasons of the participant's withdrawal or expulsion from such program or otherwise.

7. Conditional license. (a) Notwithstanding any inconsistent provision of this chapter, participants in the program, except those penalized under paragraph (d) of subdivision one of section eleven hundred ninety-three of this article for any violation of subdivision two, three, or four of section eleven hundred ninety-two of this article, may, in the commissioner's discretion, be issued a conditional driver's license, or if the holder of a license issued by another jurisdiction valid for operation in this state, a conditional privilege of operating a motor vehicle in this state. Such a conditional license or privilege shall be valid only for use, by the holder thereof, (1) enroute to and from the holder's place of employment, (2) if the holder's employment requires the operation of a motor vehicle then during the hours thereof, (3) enroute to and from a class or an activity which is an authorized part of the alcohol and drug rehabilitation program and at which his attendance is required, (4) enroute to and from a class or course at an accredited school, college or university or at a state approved institution of vocational or technical training, (5) to or from court ordered probation activities, (6) to and from a motor vehicle office for the transaction of business relating to such license or program, (7) for a three hour consecutive daytime period, chosen by the administrators of the program, on a day during which the participant is not engaged in usual employment or vocation, (8) enroute to and from a medical examination or treatment as part of a necessary medical treatment for such participant or member of the participant's household, as evidenced by a written statement to that effect from a licensed medical practitioner, and (9) enroute to and from a place, including a school, at which a child or children of the holder are cared for on a regular basis and which is necessary for the holder to maintain such holder's employment or enrollment at an accredited school, college or university or at a state approved institution of vocational or technical training. Such license or privilege shall remain in effect during the term of the suspension or revocation of the participant's license or privilege unless earlier revoked by the commissioner.

(b) The conditional license or privilege described in paragraph (a) of this subdivision shall be in a form prescribed by the commissioner, and shall have indicated thereon the conditions imposed by such paragraph.

(c) Upon receipt of a conditional license issued pursuant to this section, any order issued by a judge, justice or magistrate pursuant to paragraph (c) of subdivision two of section eleven hundred ninety-three of this article shall be surrendered to the department.

(d) The commissioner shall require applicants for a conditional license to pay a fee of seventy-five dollars for processing costs. Such fees assessed under this subdivision shall be paid to the commissioner for deposit to the general fund and shall be in addition to any fees established by the commissioner pursuant to subdivision six of this section to defray the costs of the alcohol and drug rehabilitation program.

(e) The conditional license or privileges described in this subdivision may be revoked by the commissioner, for sufficient cause including, but not limited to, failure to register in the program, failure to attend or satisfactorily participate in the sessions, conviction of any traffic infraction other than one involving parking, stopping or standing or conviction of any alcohol or drug-related traffic offense, misdemeanor or felony. In addition, the commissioner shall have the right, after a hearing, to revoke the conditional license or privilege upon receiving notification or evidence that the offender is not attempting in good faith to accept rehabilitation. In the event of such revocation, the fee described in subdivision six of this section shall not be refunded.

(f) It shall be a traffic infraction for the holder of a conditional license or privilege to operate a motor vehicle upon a public highway for any use other than those authorized pursuant to paragraph (a) of this subdivision. When a person is convicted of this offense, the sentence of the court must be a fine of not less than two hundred dollars nor more than five hundred dollars or a term of imprisonment of not more than fifteen days or both such fine and imprisonment. Additionally, the conditional license or privileges described in this subdivision shall be revoked by the commissioner upon receiving notification from the court that the holder thereof has been convicted of this offense.

(g) Notwithstanding anything to the contrary contained in a certificate of relief from disabilities issued pursuant to article twenty-three of the correction law, any conditional license or privilege issued to a person convicted of a violation of any subdivision of section eleven hundred ninety-two of this article shall not be valid for the operation of any commercial motor vehicle. In addition, no such conditional license or privilege shall be valid for the operation of a taxicab as defined in this chapter.

(h) Notwithstanding any inconsistent provision of this chapter, the conditional license described in this subdivision may, pursuant to regulations established by the commissioner, be issued to a person whose license has been suspended pending prosecution pursuant to subparagraph seven of paragraph (e) of subdivision two of section eleven hundred ninety-three of this article.

§1197. Special traffic options program for driving while intoxicated.

"The program", as used in this section, shall mean the special traffic options program for driving while intoxicated, a program established pursuant to this section, and approved by the commissioner of motor vehicles.

1. Program establishment. (a) Where a county establishes a special traffic options program for driving while intoxicated, pursuant to this section, it shall

receive fines and forfeitures collected by any court, judge, magistrate or other officer within that county, including, where appropriate, a hearing officer acting on behalf of the commissioner,: (1) imposed for violations of subparagraphs (ii) and (iii) of paragraph (a) of subdivision two or subparagraph (i) of paragraph (a) of subdivision three of section five hundred eleven of this chapter; (2) imposed in accordance with the provisions of section eleven hundred ninety-three and civil penalties imposed pursuant to subdivision two of section eleven hundred ninety-four-a of this article, including, where appropriate, a hearing officer acting on behalf of the commissioner, from violations of sections eleven hundred ninety-two, eleven hundred ninety-two-a and findings made under section eleven hundred ninety-four-a of this article; and (3) imposed upon a conviction for: aggravated vehicular assault, pursuant to section 120.04-a of the penal law; vehicular assault in the first degree, pursuant to section 120.04 of the penal law; vehicular assault in the second degree, pursuant to section 120.03 of the penal law; aggravated vehicular homicide, pursuant to section 125.14 of the penal law; vehicular manslaughter in the first degree, pursuant to section 125.13 of the penal law; and vehicular manslaughter in the second degree, pursuant to section 125.12 of the penal law, as provided in section eighteen hundred three of this chapter. Upon receipt of these moneys, the county shall deposit them in a separate account entitled "special traffic options program for driving while intoxicated" and they shall be under the exclusive care, custody and control of the chief fiscal officer of each county participating in the program.

(b) Expenditures from such account shall only be made pursuant to the approval of a county program by the commissioner of motor vehicles. The chief fiscal officer of each participating county shall, on a quarterly basis, forward to the commissioner a written certificate of moneys expended from such account.

2. Program organization. (a) Where a program is established by a county, it shall be organized by a coordinator for the special traffic options program for driving while intoxicated, who shall be designated by the chief executive officer of the county, if there be one, otherwise the chairman of the governing board of the county, or in the city of New York, a person designated by the mayor thereof. Where a coordinator is designated, the coordinator shall receive such salary and expenses as the board of legislators or other governing body of such county may fix and properly account for such expenses and shall serve at the pleasure of such appointing body or officer.

(b) In counties having a county traffic safety board, the chief executive officer, if there be one, otherwise the chairman of the governing board of the county or the mayor of the city of New York, may designate the chairman of the board or a member thereof as coordinator of the program.

3. Purposes. (a) The program shall provide a plan for coordination of county, town, city and village efforts to reduce alcohol-related traffic injuries and fatalities.

(b) The program shall, where approved by the county board or other governing body, provide funding for such activities as the board or other body may approve, for the above-described purposes.

4. Duties of the coordinator; reports. (a) It shall be the duty of the coordinator to:

(1) Render annually or at the request of the county legislature or other governing body of the county, a verified account of all moneys received and expended by the coordinator or under the coordinator's direction and an account of other pertinent matters.

(2) Submit annually or upon request of the chief fiscal officer of each county participating in the program, in such manner as may be required by law, an estimate of the funds required to carry out the purposes of this section.

(3) Make an annual report to the commissioner, which shall be due on or before the first day of April of each year following the implementation of said program, and shall include the following:

a. the progress, problems and other matters related to the administration of said program; and

b. an assessment of the effectiveness of the program within the geographic area of the county participating therein and any and all recommendations for expanding and improving said program.

(b) Any annual report shall also contain the following, in a form prescribed by the commissioner:

(1) Number of arrests for violations of section eleven hundred ninety-two of this article and subdivision two of section five hundred eleven of this chapter;

(2) Number and description of dispositions resulting therefrom;

(3) Number of suspensions issued in the county for alleged refusals to submit to chemical tests;

(4) Total fine moneys returned to the participating county in connection with the program;

(5) Contemplated programs;

(6) Distribution of moneys in connection with program administration;

(7) Any other information required by the commissioner.

5. Functions of the coordinator. In addition to the duties of the coordinator as provided in subdivision four of this section, the coordinator shall perform the following functions:

(a) Formulate a special traffic options program for driving while intoxicated and coordinate efforts of interested parties and agencies engaged in alcohol traffic safety, law enforcement, adjudication, rehabilitation and preventive education.

(b) Receive proposals from county, town, city or village agencies or non-governmental groups for activities related to alcohol traffic safety and to submit them to the county board of legislators or other such governing body, together with a recommendation for funding of the activity if deemed appropriate.

(c) Cooperate with and assist local officials within the county in the formulation and execution of alcohol traffic safety programs including enforcement, adjudication, rehabilitation and education.

(d) Study alcohol traffic safety problems with the county and recommend to the appropriate legislative bodies, departments or commissions, such changes in rules, orders, regulations and existing law as the coordinator may deem advisable.

(e) Promote alcohol and drug-related traffic safety education for drivers.

(f) Obtain and assemble data on alcohol-related accident arrests, convictions and accidents and to analyze, study, and consolidate such data for educational, research and informational purposes.

6. County purpose and charge. The provisions of this section and expenditures made hereunder shall be deemed a county purpose and charge.

7. Program approval. The program, including a proposed operational budget, shall be submitted by each county coordinator to the commissioner for approval. The commissioner shall consider the following before approving said program:

(a) The interrelationship of such program with existing drunk driving related programs in areas including, but not limited to, law enforcement, prosecution, adjudication and education.

(b) Avoidance of duplication of existing programs funded or operated by either the state or any municipality including, but not limited to, the alcohol and drug rehabilitation program, established under section eleven hundred ninety-six of this article.

(c) All other factors which the commissioner shall deem necessary.

8. Duties of the commissioner. (a) The commissioner shall compile the reports submitted by the county coordinators and shall issue a comprehensive report on such programs to the governor and to the legislature.

(b) The commissioner shall monitor all programs to ensure satisfactory implementation in conjunction with the established program application goals.

9. Program cessation. When a participating county wishes to cease its program, the coordinator shall notify the commissioner in writing of the date of termination and all money remaining in the fund established by that county pursuant to subdivision one of this section on such date shall be transferred to the general fund of the state treasury. All fines and forfeitures collected pursuant to the provisions of this section on and after the termination date shall be disposed of in accordance with subdivision one of section eighteen hundred three of this chapter.

10. Program audit. The comptroller is authorized to conduct audits of any program established pursuant to this section for the purposes of determining compliance with the provisions of this section and with generally accepted accounting principles.

*§1198. Installation and operation of ignition interlock devices.

1. Applicability. The provisions of this section shall apply throughout the state to each person required or otherwise ordered by a court as a condition of

probation or conditional discharge to install and operate an ignition interlock device in any vehicle which he or she owns or operates.

2. Requirements. (a) In addition to any other penalties prescribed by law, the court shall require that any person who has been convicted of a violation of subdivision two, two-a or three of section eleven hundred ninety-two of this article, or any crime defined by this chapter or the penal law of which an alcohol-related violation of any provision of section eleven hundred ninety-two of this article is an essential element, to install and maintain, as a condition of probation or conditional discharge, a functioning ignition interlock device in accordance with the provisions of this section and, as applicable, in accordance with the provisions of subdivisions one and one-a of section eleven hundred ninety-three of this article; provided, however, the court may not authorize the operation of a motor vehicle by any person whose license or privilege to operate a motor vehicle has been revoked except as provided herein. For any such individual subject to a sentence of probation, installation and maintenance of such ignition interlock device shall be a condition of probation.

(b) Nothing contained in this section shall prohibit a court, upon application by a probation department, from modifying the conditions of probation of any person convicted of any violation set forth in paragraph (a) of this subdivision prior to the effective date of this section, to require the installation and maintenance of a functioning ignition interlock device, and such person shall thereafter be subject to the provisions of this section.

(c) Nothing contained in this section shall authorize a court to sentence any person to a period of probation or conditional discharge for the purpose of subjecting such person to the provisions of this section, unless such person would have otherwise been so eligible for a sentence of probation or conditional discharge.

3. Conditions. (a) Notwithstanding any other provision of law, the commissioner may grant a post-revocation conditional license, as set forth in paragraph (b) of this subdivision, to a person who has been convicted of a violation of subdivision two, two-a or three of section eleven hundred ninety-two of this article and who has been sentenced to a period of probation or conditional discharge, provided the person has satisfied the minimum period of license revocation established by law and the commissioner has been notified that such person may operate only a motor vehicle equipped with a functioning ignition interlock device. No such request shall be made nor shall such a license be granted, however, if such person has been found by a court to have committed a violation of section five hundred eleven of this chapter during the license revocation period or deemed by a court to have violated any condition of probation or conditional discharge set forth by the court relating to the operation of a motor vehicle or the consumption of alcohol. In exercising discretion relating to the issuance of a post-revocation conditional license pursuant to this subdivision, the commissioner shall not deny such issuance based solely upon the number of convictions for violations of any subdivision of section eleven hundred ninety-two of this article committed by such person within the ten years prior to application for such license. Upon the termination

of the period of probation or conditional discharge set by the court, the person may apply to the commissioner for restoration of a license or privilege to operate a motor vehicle in accordance with this chapter.

(b) Notwithstanding any inconsistent provision of this chapter, a post-revocation conditional license granted pursuant to paragraph (a) of this subdivision shall be valid only for use by the holder thereof, (1) enroute to and from the holder's place of employment, (2) if the holder's employment requires the operation of a motor vehicle then during the hours thereof, (3) enroute to and from a class or course at an accredited school, college or university or at a state approved institution of vocational or technical training, (4) to and from court ordered probation activities, (5) to and from a motor vehicle office for the transaction of business relating to such license, (6) for a three hour consecutive daytime period, chosen by the department, on a day during which the participant is not engaged in usual employment or vocation, (7) enroute to and from a medical examination or treatment as part of a necessary medical treatment for such participant or member of the participant's household, as evidenced by a written statement to that effect from a licensed medical practitioner, (8) enroute to and from a class or an activity which is an authorized part of the alcohol and drug rehabilitation program and at which participant's attendance is required, and (9) enroute to and from a place, including a school, at which a child or children of the participant are cared for on a regular basis and which is necessary for the participant to maintain such participant's employment or enrollment at an accredited school, college or university or at a state approved institution of vocational or technical training.

(c) The post-revocation conditional license described in this subdivision may be revoked by the commissioner for sufficient cause including but not limited to, failure to comply with the terms of the condition of probation or conditional discharge set forth by the court, conviction of any traffic offense other than one involving parking, stopping or standing or conviction of any alcohol or drug related offense, misdemeanor or felony or failure to install or maintain a court ordered ignition interlock device.

(d) Nothing contained herein shall prohibit the court from requiring, as a condition of probation or conditional discharge, the installation of a functioning ignition interlock device in any vehicle owned or operated by a person sentenced for a violation of subdivision two, two-a, or three of section eleven hundred ninety-two of this chapter, or any crime defined by this chapter or the penal law of which an alcohol-related violation of any provision of section eleven hundred ninety-two of this chapter is an essential element, if the court in its discretion, determines that such a condition is necessary to ensure the public safety. Imposition of an ignition interlock condition shall in no way limit the effect of any period of license suspension or revocation set forth by the commissioner or the court.

(e) Nothing contained herein shall prevent the court from applying any other conditions of probation or conditional discharge allowed by law, including treatment for alcohol or drug abuse, restitution and community service.

(f) The commissioner shall note on the operator's record of any person restricted pursuant to this section that, in addition to any other restrictions, conditions or limitations, such person may operate only a motor vehicle equipped with an ignition interlock device.

4. Proof of compliance and recording of condition. (a) Following imposition by the court of the use of an ignition interlock device as a condition of probation or conditional discharge it shall require the person to provide proof of compliance with this section to the court and the probation department or other monitor where such person is under probation or conditional discharge supervision. If the person fails to provide for such proof of installation, absent a finding by the court of good cause for that failure which is entered in the record, the court may revoke, modify, or terminate the person's sentence of probation or conditional discharge as provided under law. Good cause may include a finding that the person is not the owner of a motor vehicle if such person asserts under oath that such person is not the owner of any motor vehicle and that he or she will not operate any motor vehicle during the period of interlock restriction except as may be otherwise authorized pursuant to law. "Owner" shall have the same meaning as provided in section one hundred twenty-eight of this chapter.

(b) When a court imposes the condition specified in subdivision one of this section, the court shall notify the commissioner in such manner as the commissioner may prescribe, and the commissioner shall note such condition on the operating record of the person subject to such conditions.

5. Cost, installation and maintenance. (a) The cost of installing and maintaining the ignition interlock device shall be borne by the person subject to such condition unless the court determines such person is financially unable to afford such cost whereupon such cost may be imposed pursuant to a payment plan or waived. In the event of such waiver, the cost of the device shall be borne in accordance with regulations issued under paragraph (g) of subdivision one of section eleven hundred ninety-three of this article or pursuant to such other agreement as may be entered into for provision of the device. Such cost shall be considered a fine for the purposes of subdivision five of section 420.10 of the criminal procedure law. Such cost shall not replace, but shall instead be in addition to, any fines, surcharges, or other costs imposed pursuant to this chapter or other applicable laws.

(b) The installation and service provider of the device shall be responsible for the installation, calibration and maintenance of such device.

6. Certification. (a) The commissioner of the department of health shall approve ignition interlock devices for installation pursuant to subdivision one of this section and shall publish a list of approved devices.

(b) After consultation with manufacturers of ignition interlock devices and the national highway traffic safety administration, the commissioner of the department of health, in consultation with the commissioner and the director of the division of probation and correctional alternatives, shall promulgate regulations regarding standards for, and use of, ignition interlock devices. Such standards shall include provisions for setting a minimum and maximum calibration range and shall include, but not be limited to, requirements that the devices:

(1) have features that make circumventing difficult and that do not interfere with the normal or safe operation of the vehicle;

(2) work accurately and reliably in an unsupervised environment;

(3) resist tampering and give evidence if tampering is attempted;

(4) minimize inconvenience to a sober user;

(5) require a proper, deep, lung breath sample or other accurate measure of blood alcohol content equivalence;

(6) operate reliably over the range of automobile environments;

(7) correlate well with permissible levels of alcohol consumption as may be established by the sentencing court or by any provision of law; and

(8) are manufactured by a party covered by product liability insurance.

(c) The commissioner of the department of health may, in his discretion, adopt in whole or relevant part, the guidelines, rules, regulations, studies, or independent laboratory tests performed on and relied upon for the certification or approval of ignition interlock devices by other states, their agencies or commissions.

7. Use of other vehicles. (a) Any requirement of this article or the penal law that a person operate a vehicle only if it is equipped with an ignition interlock device shall apply to every motor vehicle operated by that person including, but not limited to, vehicles that are leased, rented or loaned.

(b) No person shall knowingly rent, lease, or lend a motor vehicle to a person known to have had his or her driving privilege restricted to vehicles equipped with an ignition interlock device unless the vehicle is so equipped. Any person whose driving privilege is so restricted shall notify any other person who rents, leases, or loans a motor vehicle to him or her of such driving restriction.

(c) A violation of paragraph (a) or (b) of this subdivision shall be a misdemeanor.

8. Employer vehicle. Notwithstanding the provisions of subdivision one and paragraph (d) of subdivision nine of this section, if a person is required to operate a motor vehicle owned by said person's employer in the course and scope of his or her employment, the person may operate that vehicle without installation of an approved ignition interlock device only in the course and scope of such employment and only if the employer has been notified that the person's driving privilege has been restricted under the provisions of this article or the penal law and the person whose privilege has been so restricted has provided the court and probation department with written documentation indicating the employer has knowledge of the restriction imposed and has granted permission for the person to operate the employer's vehicle without the device only for business purposes. The person shall notify the court and the probation department of his or her intention to so operate the employer's vehicle. A motor vehicle owned by a business entity which business entity is all or partly owned or controlled by a person otherwise subject to the provisions of this article or the penal law is not a motor vehicle owned by the

employer for purposes of the exemption provided in this subdivision. The provisions of this subdivision shall apply only to the operation of such vehicle in the scope of such employment.

9. Circumvention of interlock device. (a) No person whose driving privilege is restricted pursuant to this article or the penal law shall request, solicit or allow any other person to blow into an ignition interlock device, or to start a motor vehicle equipped with the device, for the purpose of providing the person so restricted with an operable motor vehicle.

(b) No person shall blow into an ignition interlock device or start a motor vehicle equipped with the device for the purpose of providing an operable motor vehicle to a person whose driving privilege is so restricted.

(c) No person shall tamper with or circumvent an otherwise operable ignition interlock device.

(d) No person subject to a court ordered ignition interlock device shall operate a motor vehicle without such device.

(e) In addition to any other provisions of law, any person convicted of a violation of paragraph (a), (b), (c), or (d) of this subdivision shall be guilty of a Class A misdemeanor.

10. Warning label. The department of health shall design a warning label which the manufacturer shall affix to each ignition interlock device upon installation in the state. The label shall contain a warning that any person tampering, circumventing, or otherwise misusing the device is guilty of a misdemeanor and may be subject to civil liability.　　　　　*(Repealed Eff.9/1/23,Ch.55,L.2021)*

§1198-a.　Special procedures and disposition involving alcohol and substance abuse assessment and treatment.

1. Definitions. For purposes of this section, the following terms shall have the following meanings:

(a) "Alcohol and substance abuse professional" shall mean persons credentialed by the office of alcoholism and substance abuse services to provide alcohol and substance abuse services pursuant to the mental hygiene law and persons licensed by the state education department in an appropriate health field, including licensed clinical social worker, licensed master social worker, licensed mental health counselor, nurse practitioner, physician, physician's assistant, psychiatrist, psychologist, and registered nurse.

(b) "Licensed agency" shall mean an agency licensed by the office of alcoholism and substance abuse services to provide alcohol and substance abuse services pursuant to the mental hygiene law.

2. Procedure. (a) Mandatory screening; when authorized. Upon the arraignment of, or at the discretion of the court, prior to the sentencing of any person who (i) at arraignment is charged with or prior to sentencing convicted of a first violation of operating a motor vehicle in violation of subdivision one, two or three or paragraph (b) of subdivision 2-a of section eleven hundred ninety-two of this article while such person has less than .15 of one per centum by weight of alcohol in the person's blood as shown by chemical analysis of such person's blood, breath, urine or saliva made pursuant to the provisions of

section eleven hundred ninety-four of this article, or in violation of subdivision four of such section eleven hundred ninety-two, or (ii) has refused to submit to a chemical test pursuant to section eleven hundred ninety-four of this article, the court shall order such person to submit to screening for alcohol or substance abuse and dependency using a standardized written screening instrument developed by the office of alcoholism and substance abuse services, to be administered by an alcohol or substance abuse professional.

(b) Mandatory assessment; when authorized. The court shall order a defendant to undergo a formal alcohol or substance abuse and dependency assessment by an alcohol or substance abuse professional or a licensed agency:

(i) when the screening required by paragraph (a) of this subdivision indicates that a defendant is abusing or dependent upon alcohol or drugs;

(ii) following the arraignment of any person charged with or, at the discretion of the court, prior to the sentencing of any person convicted of a violation of subdivision one, two, three, four or four-a of section eleven hundred ninety-two of this article after having been convicted of a violation of any subdivision of section eleven hundred ninety-two of this article or of vehicular assault in the second or first degree, as defined, respectively, in sections 120.03 and 120.04 of the penal law of aggravated vehicular assault, as defined in section 120.04-a of the penal law or of vehicular manslaughter in the second or first degree, as defined, respectively, in sections 125.12 and 125.13 of the penal law or of aggravated vehicular homicide, as defined in section 125.14 of such law within the preceding five years or after having been convicted of a violation of any subdivision of such section or of vehicular assault in the second or first degree, as defined, respectively, in sections 120.03 and 120.04 of the penal law or of aggravated vehicular assault, as defined in section 120.04-a of the penal law or of vehicular manslaughter in the second or first degree, as defined, respectively, in sections 125.12 and 125.13 of the penal law or of aggravated vehicular homicide, as defined in section 125.14 of such law, two or more times within the preceding ten years; or

(iii) following the arraignment of any person charged with or, at the discretion of the court, prior to the sentencing of any person convicted of operating a motor vehicle in violation of subdivision two or three or paragraph (b) of subdivision two-a of section eleven hundred ninety-two of this article while such person has .15 of one per centum or more by weight of alcohol in the person's blood as shown by a chemical analysis of such person's blood, breath, urine or saliva made pursuant to the provisions of section eleven hundred ninety-four of this article or in violation of paragraph (a) of subdivision two-a of section eleven hundred ninety-two of this article.

(c) Mandatory assessment; procedure. The assessment ordered by a court pursuant to this section shall be performed by an alcohol or substance abuse professional or a licensed agency which shall forward the results, in writing, to the court and to the defendant or his or her counsel within thirty days of the date of such order.

3. Authorized disposition. When a sentence of probation or a conditional discharge is imposed upon a person who has been required to undergo an

alcohol or substance abuse and dependency assessment pursuant to subdivision two of this section and where such assessment indicates that such person is in need of treatment for alcohol or substance abuse or dependency, the court shall require, as a condition of such sentence, that such person participate in and successfully complete such treatment. Such treatment shall be provided by an alcohol or substance abuse professional or a licensed agency.

4. Any case wherein a court has accepted a plea pursuant to the provisions of subparagraph (ii) of paragraph (a) of subdivision ten of section eleven hundred ninety-two of this article and such plea includes as a condition thereof that the defendant attend and complete the alcohol and drug rehabilitation program established pursuant to section eleven hundred ninety-six of this article, including any assessment and treatment required thereby, shall be deemed to be in compliance with the provisions of this section.

5. The chief administrator of the office of court administration shall make available to all courts in this state with jurisdiction in criminal cases a list of alcohol and substance abuse professionals and licensed agencies as provided by the office of alcoholism and substance abuse services pursuant to subdivision (g) of section 19.07 of the mental hygiene law.

6. Confidentiality of records. (a) The records and content of all screenings, assessments and treatment conducted pursuant to this section, including the identity, diagnosis and prognosis of each individual who is the subject of such records, and including any statements or admissions of such individual made during the course of such screenings, assessments and treatment, shall be confidential, shall not be disclosed except as authorized by this subdivision, and shall not be entered or received as evidence at any civil, criminal or administrative trial, hearing or proceeding. No person, other than a defendant to whom such records are disclosed, may redisclose such records.

(b) Consistent with Section 290 dd-2 of Title 42 of the United States Code, as such law may, from time to time, be amended, such records and content may only be disclosed as follows:

(i) to a court for the sole purpose of requiring a defendant charged with or convicted of a violation of subdivision one, two, two-a, three, four or four-a of section eleven hundred ninety-two of this article to undergo alcohol or substance abuse or dependency assessment or treatment;

(ii) to the defendant or his or her authorized representative; and

(iii) to medical personnel to the extent necessary to meet a bona fide medical emergency.

7. Effect of completion of treatment. Except as provided in subparagraph nine of paragraph (b) of subdivision two of section eleven hundred ninety-three or in subparagraph three of paragraph (d) of subdivision two of section eleven hundred ninety-four of this article, upon successful completion of treatment ordered pursuant to this section as certified by the alcohol or substance abuse professional or licensed agency which provided such treatment, the defendant may apply to the commissioner on a form provided for that purpose, for the termination of the suspension or revocation order issued as a result of the defendant's conviction. In the exercise of discretion, upon receipt of such

application, and upon payment of any civil penalties for which the defendant may be liable, the commissioner is authorized to terminate such order or orders and return the defendant's license or reinstate the privilege of operating a motor vehicle in this state. However, the commissioner shall not issue any new license nor restore any license where said issuance or restoration is prohibited by subdivision two of section eleven hundred ninety-three of this article.

§1199. Driver responsibility assessment.

1. In addition to any fines, fees, penalties and surcharges authorized by law, any person convicted of a violation of any subdivision of section eleven hundred ninety-two of this article, or any person found to have refused a chemical test in accordance with section eleven hundred ninety-four of this article not arising out of the same incident as a conviction for a violation of any of the provisions of section eleven hundred ninety-two of this article, shall become liable to the department for payment of a driver responsibility assessment as provided in this section.

2. The amount of the driver responsibility assessment under this section shall be two hundred fifty dollars per year for a three-year period.

3. Upon receipt of evidence that a person is liable for the driver responsibility assessment required by this section, the commissioner shall notify such person by first class mail to the address of such person on file with the department or at the current address provided by the United States postal service of the amount of such assessment, the time and manner of making required payments, and that failure to make payment shall result in the suspension of his or her driver's license or privilege of obtaining a driver's license.

4. If a person shall fail to pay any driver responsibility assessment as provided in this section, the commissioner shall suspend such person's driver's license or privilege of obtaining a license. Such suspension shall remain in effect until any and all outstanding driver responsibility assessments have been paid in full.

5. The provisions of this section shall also be applicable to any person convicted of any violation of section forty-nine-a of the navigation law, any person convicted of a violation of section 25.24 of the parks, recreation and historic preservation law, or any person found to have refused a chemical test in accordance with the applicable provisions of either the navigation law or the parks, recreation and historic preservation law not arising out of the same incident as such conviction.

ARTICLE 33
MISCELLANEOUS RULES

Section

1212.   Reckless driving.

§1212.   Reckless driving.

Reckless driving shall mean driving or using any motor vehicle, motorcycle or any other vehicle propelled by any power other than muscular power or any appliance or accessory thereof in a manner which unreasonably interferes with the free and proper use of the public highway, or unreasonably endangers users of the public highway. Reckless driving is prohibited. Every person violating this provision shall be guilty of a misdemeanor.

Accident
   defined 94
Accidents
   leaving scene w/o reporting 137
   police authorities and coroners to report 141
   police to indicate serious physical injury and death 142
Addict
   defined 62
Administer
   defined 62
Agent
   defined 62
Aggravated failure to answer appearance tickets 136
Aggravated unlicensed operation of a motor vehicle 125
Alcohol and substance abuse
   special procedures involving 213
Animal-drawn vehicles 145
Arrest and testing 188
Article 137; Pharmacy 38
   adulterating, misbranding and substituting 42
   misdemeanors 38
   records of shipment 42
   seizure 40
   special provisions 40
Article 19; lic. of drivers 91
Article 19-A; bus drivers 92
   compliance required 95
   conviction from violation 94
   drugs, controlled substance and intoxicating liquor 97
   ill or fatigued operator 97
Article 22; Accidents and Accident Reports 137
Article 23; Obedience to and Effect of Traffic Laws 143
Article 30; speed restrictions 146
   basic rule and maximum limits 146
   maximum speed limits 149
Article 31; Alcohol and Drug-related Offenses 165
Article 33; Miscellaneous Rules 217
Article 33; Controlled Substances 61
Article 6-C; Sex offender reg 1
Authorized internet entity
   defined 4
Blind external proficiency testing
   defined 47
Board
   defined 4
Board of examiners of sex offenders 19
Bus
   defined 93
   operation; not licensed 94
Chemical test evidence 201

Commercial driver's license
    suspension & revocation of 116
Commercial driver's licenses; downgrade 122
Commission
    defined 48
Commission on forensic science 48
    confidentiality... 57
    powers and duties 49
    State DNA identification index 54
Commissioner
    defined 62
Controlled substance
    defined 62, 94
    exemptions 66
    manufacture or distribution 89
    prohibited acts 65
    schedules of 67
    schedules of; exceptions 81
Correction Law 1
Credit card
    defined 59, 60
Debit card
    defined 59
Deliver
    defined 62
Department
    defined 62
Department of motor vehicles
    duties of 97
Designated offender
    defined 47
Dispense
    defined 62
Distribute
    defined 62
Distributor
    defined 62
Diversion
    defined 62
Division
    defined 3
Division; duties of 5
DNA
    defined 47
DNA record
    defined 48
DNA subcommittee
    defined 48
DNA testing methodology
    defined 47

Driver or bus driver
  defined 93
Driver responsibility assessment 216
Driver's licenses; suspension & revocation of 124
Driving after having consumed alcohol
  traffic options program 205
  under 21; procedure 197
Drug
  defined 62, 94
Drugs, controlled substance and intoxicating liquor 97
Education Law 37
  Article 137; Pharmacy 38
  Subarticle 4; Unauthorized Acts 37
Emergency vehicles
  authorized 144
Executive Law 47
  Article 49-B; DNA ID Index 47
Facilitating aggravated unlicensed operation of a motor vehicle 128
Failure of operator to comply w/certain max speed limits 151
Failure of operator to comply; certain max speed limits 158
Federal agency
  defined 62
Federal controlled substances act
  defined 63
Federal registration number
  defined 63
Forensic laboratory
  defined 47
General Business Law 59
  Art. 29-A; credit/debit cards 59
Good behavior allowances 31
Habitual user
  defined 63
Holder
  defined 59
Hospital
  defined 3
Ignition interlock devices
  installation and operation of 208
Ill or fatigued operator 97
Improper use
  defined 59
Indeterminate and determinate sentences
  good behavior allowances 31
Institution of higher education
  defined 4
Institutional dispenser
  defined 63
Internet access provider
  defined 4

Internet identifiers
    defined 5
Intoxicating liquor
    defined 93
Issuer
    defined 59
Law enforcement agency having jurisdiction
    defined 3
Learner's permits; suspension & revocation of 124
Lender
    defined 59
License
    defined 63
Local correctional facility
    defined 4
Manufacture
    defined 63
Manufacture or distribution of controlled substances 89
Maximum speed limits 149
Maximum speed limits, posted; failure of operator to comply 151
Mental abnormality
    defined 4
Merit time allowance 32
Minimum speed regulations 165
Motor carrier
    defined 93
Motor vehicle; operating
    under influence 165
    under influence; under 21 170
MV department; duties of 97
Narcotic drug
    defined 63
New York State Controlled Substances Act 61
Nonresident student
    defined 4
Nonresident worker
    defined 4
Opiate
    defined 63
Opioid overdose prevention 83
Opium poppy
    defined 64
Owner
    defined 131
Person
    defined 59, 64
Pharmacist
    defined 64
Pharmacy
    defined 64

Pharmacy; Article 137 38
Poppy straw
    defined 64
Posted maximum speed limits 158
Practitioner
    defined 64
Predatory
    defined 4
Predicate sex offender
    defined 4
Prescribe
    defined 64
Prescription
    defined 64
Prescription pain medication 86
Probation
    defined 4
Public Health Law 61
    Article 33; Controlled Substances 61
Reckless driving 217
Registration and verification
    duration of 16
Registration and verification requirements 16
Rehabilitation program
    alcohol and drug 202
Secured credit card
    defined 59
Security interest
    defined 132
Seizure and forfeiture of vehicles
    unlicensed operation of 131
Seizure and redemption of unlawfully operated vehicles 129
Sell
    defined 64
Seller
    defined 59
Sex offender
    board of examiners 19
    defined 1
    determination; judicial 23
    discharge of, from facility 12
    duration of registration and verification 16
    duties of the court 9
    duty of register 13
    internet posting 29
    official; immunity from liability 30
    penalty; failure to register 30
    petition for relief or modification 25
    prior convictions 15
    registration and verification requirements 16

relocation; notification 8
retail sales of frozen desserts 31
Sex Offender Registration Act 1
    definitions 1
Sex offense
    defined 1
Sexual predator
    defined 3
Sexually violent offender
    defined 4
Sexually violent offense
    defined 2
Shock incarceration program
    defined 36
Special telephone number 27
State DNA identification index
    defined 47
Termination of the criminal proceeding
    defined 132
U.S. Department of Transp
    exempt carriers 99
Ultimate user
    defined 64
Unauthorized practice 37
Unauthorized use
    defined 59
Unauthorized use of a professional title 37
Vehicle & Traffic Law 91
    Article 19; drivers; licensing 91
    Article 19-A; bus drivers 92
    Article 20; Suspension and Revocation 100
    Article 22; accident reports 137
    Article 23; Obedience to and Effect of Traffic Laws 143
    Article 30; speed restrictions 146
    Article 31; Alcohol and Drug-related Offenses 165
    Article 33; Miscellaneous Rules 217
    suspension, revocation and reissuance of licenses and registrati 100
    violations 91
Violations 91

Notes

Notes

NYS PENAL LAW
OFFENSES AND
CLASSIFICATIONS

NYS
FELONY
SENTENCING
GUIDELINES
and Post Indictment Plea Limitations

Revised and Maintained by
John M. Castellano

Originally written by Bonnie Cohen-Gallet, Esq.

Part IV

Looseleaf
Law Publications, Inc.
43-08 162nd Street
Flushing, NY 11358
www.LooseleafLaw.com   800-647-5547

Current through
Chapter 834
of the
2021 Legislative Session

NEW YORK STATE PENAL LAW
OFFENSES AND CLASSIFICATIONS
Current Through Chapter 834 of the
2021 Legislative Session

Offense	Section(s)
CLASS A-I FELONIES	
Aggravated Enterprise Corruption	460.22
Aggravated Murder	125.26
Arson – 1st Degree	150.20
Attempted Aggravated Murder	110.05(1)/125.26(1)
Attempted Criminal Possession of a Chemical or Biological Weapon – 1st Degree	110.05(1)/490.45
Attempted Criminal Possession of a Controlled Substance – 1st Degree	110.05(1)/220.21
Attempted Criminal Sale of a Controlled Substance – 1st Degree	110.05(1)/220.43
Attempted Criminal Use of a Chemical or Biological Weapon – 1st Degree	110.05(1)/490.55
Attempted Murder – 1st Degree	110.05(1)/125.27
Conspiracy – 1st Degree	105.17
Criminal Possession of a Chemical or Biological Weapon – 1st Degree	490.45
Criminal Possession of a Controlled Substance – 1st Degree	220.21
Criminal Sale of a Controlled Substance – 1st Degree	220.43
Criminal Use of a Chemical or Biological Weapon – 1st Degree	490.55
Domestic Act of Terrorism Motivated by Hate – 1st Degree	490.28
Domestic Act of Terrorism Motivated by Hate – 2nd Degree	490.27
Kidnapping – 1st Degree	135.25
Murder – 1st Degree	125.27
Murder – 2nd Degree	125.25
Operating as a Major Trafficker	220.77
Terrorism - **VFO** (if underlying offense Class B felony)	490.25

CLASS A-II FELONIES	
Attempt to Commit a Class A-II Felony	110.05(2)
Criminal Possession of a Controlled Substance – 2nd Degree	220.18
Criminal Sale of a Controlled Substance – 2nd Degree	220.41
Criminal Use of a Chemical or Biological Weapon – 2nd Degree	490.50
Predatory Sexual Assault	130.95
Predatory Sexual Assault Against a Child	130.96

Offense	Section(s)

CLASS B FELONIES

Aggravated Assault Upon a Police or Peace Officer **(VFO)** 120.11

Aggravated Manslaughter – 1st Degree **(VFO)** 125.22

Aggravated Patronizing a Minor for Prostitution – 1st Degree .. 230.13

Aggravated Sexual Abuse – 1st Degree **(VFO)** 130.70

Aggravated Vehicular Homicide 125.14

Arson – 2nd Degree **(VFO)** 150.15

Assault – 1st Degree **(VFO)** 120.10

Attempt to Commit a Class A-I Felony other than the A-I felonies of Murder – 1st Degree, Aggravated Murder as defined in 125.26(1), Criminal Possession of a Controlled Substance – 1st Degree, Criminal Sale of a Controlled Substance – 1st Degree, Criminal Possession of a Chemical or Biological Weapon – 1st Degree, or Criminal use of a Chemical or Biological Weapon – 1st Degree **(VFO if Att/Murder 2nd Degree, Att/Kidnapping 1st Degree or Att/Arson 1st)** . 110.05(3)

Bribe Receiving – 1st Degree 200.12

Bribery – 1st Degree 200.04

Burglary – 1st Degree **(VFO)** 140.30

Compelling Prostitution 230.33

Conspiracy – 2nd Degree 105.15

Corrupting the Government – 1st Degree 496.05

Course of Sexual Conduct Against a Child – 1st Degree **(VFO)** . 130.75

Criminal Facilitation – 1st Degree 115.08

Criminal Mischief – 1st Degree 145.12

Criminal Possession of a Chemical or Biological Weapon - 2nd Degree **(VFO)** 490.40

Criminal Possession of a Controlled Substance – 3rd Degree ... 220.16

Criminal Possession of a Weapon – 1st Degree **(VFO)** 265.04

Criminal Possession of Stolen Property – 1st Degree 165.54

Criminal Sale of a Controlled Substance – 3rd Degree 220.39

Criminal Sale of a Controlled Substance in or near School Grounds 220.44

Criminal Sale of a Controlled Substance to a Child 220.48

Criminal Sale of a Firearm – 1st Degree **(VFO)** 265.13

Criminal Sexual Act – 1st Degree **(VFO)** 130.50

Criminal Use of a Chemical Weapon or Biological Weapon – 3rd Degree **(VFO)** 490.47

Criminal Use of a Firearm – 1st Degree **(VFO)** 265.09

Enterprise Corruption 460.20

2

Offense	Section(s)
Facilitating a Sexual Performance by a Child with a Controlled Substance or Alcohol	263.30
Gang Assault – 1st Degree **(VFO)**	120.07
Grand Larceny – 1st Degree	155.42
Hate Crime (underlying offense C Felony)	485.05
Health Care Fraud – 1st Degree	177.25
Hindering Prosecution of Terrorism – 1st Degree **(VFO)**	490.35
Incest – 1st Degree **(VFO)**	255.27
Insurance Fraud – 1st Degree	176.30
Intimidating a Victim or Witness – 1st Degree **(VFO)**	215.17
Kidnapping – 2nd Degree **(VFO)**	135.20
Life Settlement Fraud - 1st Degree	176.65
Manslaughter – 1st Degree **(VFO)**	125.20
Money Laundering – 1st Degree	470.20
Money Laundering in Support of Terrorism – 1st Degree	470.24
Obstruction of Governmental Duties by Means of a Bomb, Destructive Device, Explosive or Hazardous Substance	195.17
Promoting Prostitution – 1st Degree	230.32
Rape – 1st Degree **(VFO)**	130.35
Residential Mortgage Fraud – 1st Degree	187.25
Robbery – 1st Degree **(VFO)**	160.15
Sex Trafficking **(VFO if 230.34(5) subdivisions (a) or (b))**	230.34
Sex Trafficking of a Child **(VFO)**	230.34-a
Tampering With a Witness – 1st Degree	215.13
Terrorism - **VFO** (if underlying offense Class C felony)	490.25
Unlawful Manufacture of Methamphetamine – 1st Degree	220.75
Welfare Fraud – 1st Degree	158.25

CLASS C FELONIES

Offense	Section(s)
Aggravated Criminal Possession of a Weapon **(VFO)**	265.19
Aggravated Criminal Sale of Cannabis	222.65
Aggravated Criminally Negligent Homicide **(VFO)**	125.11
Aggravated Grand Larceny of an Automated Teller Machine	155.43
Aggravated Interference with Health Care Services – 1st Degree	240.73
Aggravated Labor Trafficking	135.37
Aggravated Manslaughter – 2nd Degree **(VFO)**	125.21
Aggravated Sexual Abuse – 2nd Degree **(VFO)**	130.67
Aggravated Strangulation	123.13-a
Aggravated Vehicular Assault	120.04-a
Arson – 3rd Degree	150.10

PENAL LAW OFFENSES AND CLASSIFICATIONS

Offense	Section(s)
Assault on a Judge	120.09
Assault on a Peace Officer, Police Officer, Fireman or Emergency Medical Services Professional **(VFO)**	120.08
Attempt to Commit a Class B Felony **(VFO if the underlying crime is a Class B VFO)**	110.05(4)
Attempt to Commit Sex Trafficking of a Child **(VFO)**	230.34-a
Bribe Receiving – 2nd Degree	200.11
Bribery – 2nd Degree	200.03
Burglary – 2nd Degree **(VFO)**	140.25
Computer Tampering – 1st Degree	156.27
Corrupting the Government – 2nd Degree	496.04
Criminal Diversion of Prescription Medications and Prescriptions – 1st Degree	178.25
Criminal Facilitation – 2nd Degree	115.05
Criminal Possession of a Chemical or Biological Weapon – 3rd Degree **(VFO)**	490.37
Criminal Possession of a Controlled Substance – 4th Degree	220.09
Criminal Possession of a Forged Instrument – 1st Degree	170.30
Criminal Possession of a Weapon – 2nd Degree **(VFO)**	265.03
Criminal Possession of Public Benefit Cards – 1st Degree	158.50
Criminal Possession of Stolen Property – 2nd Degree	165.52
Criminal Sale of a Controlled Substance – 4th Degree	220.34
Criminal Sale of a Firearm – 2nd Degree **(VFO)**	265.12
Criminal Sale of a Firearm to a Minor	265.16
Criminal Sale of a Firearm with the Aid of a Minor **(VFO)**	265.14
Criminal Sale of a Prescription for a Controlled Substance	220.65
Criminal Solicitation – 1st Degree	100.13
Criminal Use of a Firearm – 2nd Degree **(VFO)**	265.08
Criminal Usury – 1st Degree	190.42
Forgery – 1st Degree	170.15
Gang Assault – 2nd Degree **(VFO)**	120.06
Grand Larceny – 2nd Degree	155.40
Hate Crime (underlying offense D Felony)	485.05
Health Care Fraud – 2nd Degree	177.20
Hindering Prosecution of Terrorism – 2nd Degree **(VFO)**	490.30
Insurance Fraud – 2nd Degree	176.25
Life Settlement Fraud - 2nd Degree	176.60
Luring a Child *(if the underlying crime is a class A Felony)*	120.70(2)
Manslaughter – 2nd Degree	125.15
Money Laundering – 2nd Degree	470.15
Money Laundering in Support of Terrorism – 2nd Degree	470.23

Offense	Section(s)
Promoting Prostitution – 2nd Degree	230.30
Receiving Reward for Official Misconduct – 1st Degree	200.27
Residential Mortgage Fraud – 2nd Degree	187.20
Rewarding Official Misconduct – 1st Degree	200.22
Robbery – 2nd Degree	160.10
Soliciting or Providing Support for Act of Terrorism – 1st Degree **(VFO)**	490.15
Strangulation 1st Degree **(VFO)**	121.13
Terrorism - **VFO** (*if underlying offense class D felony*)	490.25
Trademark Counterfeiting – 1st Degree	165.73
Unlawful Manufacture of Methamphetamine – 2nd Degree	220.74
Use of a Child in a Sexual Performance	263.05
Vehicular Manslaughter – 1st Degree	125.13
Welfare Fraud – 2nd Degree	158.20

CLASS D FELONIES

Offense	Section(s)
Aggravated Cemetery Desecration – 1st Degree	145.27
Aggravated Criminal Contempt	215.52
Aggravated Identity Theft	190.80-a
Aggravated Insurance Fraud – 4th Degree	176.35
Aggravated Life Settlement Fraud	176.70
Aggravated Patronizing a Minor for Prostitution – 2nd Degree	230.12
Aggravated Sexual Abuse – 3rd Degree **(VFO)**	130.66
Aggravated Unpermitted Use of Indoor Pyrotechnics – 1st Degree **(VFO)**	405.18
Assault – 2nd Degree **(VFO)**	120.05
Attempt to Commit a Class C Felony **(VFO if the underlying felony is a Class C VFO)**	110.05(5)
Auto Stripping – 1st Degree	165.11
Bail Jumping – 1st Degree	215.57
Bribe Giving for Public Office	200.45
Bribe Receiving – 3rd Degree	200.10
Bribe Receiving by a Juror	215.20
Bribe Receiving by a Labor Official	180.25
Bribe Receiving by a Witness	215.05
Bribe Receiving for Public Office	200.50
Bribery – 3rd Degree	200.00
Bribing a Juror	215.19
Bribing a Labor Official	180.15
Bribing a Witness	215.00
Burglary – 3rd Degree	140.20

Offense	Section(s)
Coercion – 1st Degree	135.65
Computer Tampering – 2nd Degree	156.26
Conspiracy – 3rd Degree	105.13
Corrupting the Government – 3rd Degree	496.03
Course of Sexual Conduct Against a Child – 2nd Degree **(VFO)**	130.80
Criminal Diversion of Prescription Medications and Prescriptions – 2nd Degree	178.20
Criminal Manufacture, Sale, or Transport of an Undetectable Firearm, Rifle or Shotgun	265.50
Criminal Mischief – 2nd Degree	145.10
Criminal Possession of a Controlled Substance – 5th Degree	220.06
Criminal Possession of a Forged Instrument – 2nd Degree	170.25
Criminal Possession of a Weapon – 3rd Degree **(VFO if subdivisions (5), (6), (7), (8), (9) or (10))**	265.02
Criminal Possession of Cannabis – 1st Degree	222.40
Criminal Possession of Forgery Devices	170.40
Criminal Possession of Public Benefit Cards – 2nd Degree	158.45
Criminal Possession of Stolen Property – 3rd Degree	165.50
Criminal Purchase or Disposal of a Weapon	265.17
Criminal Sale of a Controlled Substance – 5th Degree	220.31
Criminal Sale of a Firearm – 3rd Degree **(VFO)**	265.11
Criminal Sale of a Ghost Gun – 1st Degree	265.61
Criminal Sale of an Unfinished Frame or Receiver – 1st Degree	265.64
Criminal Sale of Cannabis – 1st Degree	222.60
Criminal Sexual Act – 2nd Degree **(VFO)**	130.45
Criminal Solicitation – 2nd Degree	100.10
Criminal Tampering – 1st Degree	145.20
Criminal Trespass – 1st Degree	140.17
Criminally Using Drug Paraphernalia – 1st Degree	220.55
Disseminating Indecent Material to Minors – 1st Degree	235.22
Endangering the Welfare of a Vulnerable Elderly Person, or an Incompetent or Physically Disabled Person – 1st Degree	260.34
Escape – 1st Degree	205.15
Facilitating a Sex Offense with a Controlled Substance **(VFO)**	130.90
Falsely Reporting an Incident – 1st Degree **(VFO)**	240.60
Forgery – 2nd Degree	170.10
Fraudulent Making of an Electronic Access Device – 2nd Degree	170.75
Grand Larceny – 3rd Degree	155.35
Hate Crime (underlying offense E Felony)	485.05
Health Care Fraud – 3rd Degree	177.15
Hindering Prosecution – 1st Degree	205.65

Offense	Section(s)
Identity Theft – 1st Degree	190.80
Impairing the Integrity of a Government Licensing Examination	200.55
Impairing the Integrity of a Pari-Mutuel Betting System – 1st Degree	180.53
Incest – 2nd Degree	255.26
Insurance Fraud – 3rd Degree	176.20
Intimidating a Victim or Witness – 2nd Degree **(VFO)**	215.16
Labor Trafficking	135.35

(VFO if subdivisions (a) or (b) of 135.35(3))

Offense	Section(s)
Life Settlement Fraud - 3rd Degree	176.55
Luring a Child *(if the underlying crime is a class B felony)*	120.70(2)
Making Terroristic Threat **(VFO)**	490.20
Manufacture, Transport, Disposition and Defacement of Weapons and Dangerous Instruments and Appliances *(depending upon the weapon or instrument)*	265.10(1)(2)(3)(4 *with priors*)&(6)
Menacing a police officer or peace officer **(VFO)**	120.18
Money Laundering – 3rd Degree	470.10
Money Laundering in Support of Terrorism – 3rd Degree	470.22
Obscenity – 1st Degree	235.07
Obstructing Governmental Administration by Means of a Self-Defense Spray Device	195.08
Patronizing a Person for Prostitution – 1st Degree	230.06
Perjury – 1st Degree	210.15
Placing a False Bomb or Hazardous Substance – 1st Degree **(VFO)**	240.62
Placing a False Bomb or Hazardous Substance in Sports Stadium or Arena, Mass Transportation Facility or Enclosed Shopping Mall **(VFO)**	240.63
Possession of Unlawful Gaming Property – 1st Degree	225.80
Prohibited Use of Weapons *(see section for D felony description)*	265.35(2)
Promoting a Sexual Performance by a Child	263.15
Promoting an Obscene Sexual Performance by a Child	263.10
Promoting Prison Contraband – 1st Degree	205.25
Promoting Prostitution – 3rd Degree	230.25
Rape – 2nd Degree **(VFO)**	130.30
Reckless Assault of a Child **(VFO)**	120.02
Reckless Endangerment – 1st Degree	120.25
Residential Mortgage Fraud – 3rd Degree	187.15
Robbery – 3rd Degree	160.05
Sexual Abuse – 1st Degree **(VFO)**	130.65

Offense	Section(s)
Soliciting or Providing Support for an Act of Terrorism – 2nd Degree **(VFO)**	490.10

Offense	Section(s)
Soliciting or Providing Support for an Act of Terrorism – 2nd Degree (VFO)	490.10
Sports Bribing	180.40
Staging a Motor Vehicle Accident – 1st Degree	176.80
Stalking – 1st Degree (VFO)	120.60
Strangulation – 2nd Degree (VFO)	121.12
Tampering with a Witness – 2nd Degree	215.12
Tampering with Public Records – 1st Degree	175.25
Terrorism - VFO (if underlying offense Class E felony)	490.25
Unauthorized Use of a Vehicle – 1st Degree	165.08
Unlawful Fleeing a Police Officer in a Motor Vehicle – 1st Degree	270.35
Unlawful Manufacture of Methamphetamine – 3rd Degree	220.73
Unlawful Possession of Personal Identification Information – 1st Degree	190.83
Unlawful Surveillance – 1st Degree	250.50
Vehicular Assault – 1st Degree	120.04
Vehicular Manslaughter – 2nd Degree	125.12
Welfare Fraud – 3rd Degree	158.15

CLASS E FELONIES

Offense	Section(s)
Abandonment of a Child	260.00
Absconding from a Community Treatment Facility	205.19
Absconding from Temporary Release – 1st Degree	205.17
Advertisement or Sale of Unauthorized Recordings – 1st Degree	275.30
Aggravated Assault upon a Person less than 11 yrs old	120.12
Aggravated Cemetery Desecration – 2nd Degree	145.26
Aggravated Family Offense	240.75
Aggravated Harassment – 1st Degree	240.31
Aggravated Harassment of an Employee by an Inmate	240.32
Aggravated Interference with Health Care Services – 2nd Degree	240.72
Aggravated Patronizing a Minor for Prostitution – 3rd Degree	230.11
Aggravated Sexual Abuse – 4th Degree (VFO)	130.65-a
Aggravated Unpermitted Use of Indoor Pyrotechnics – 2nd Degree	405.16
Arson – 4th Degree	150.05
Attempt to Commit Criminal Possession of a Weapon **(VFO if subds. (5), (6), (7), (8), (9) or (10) as a lesser included offense as defined in CPL 220.20)**	110.05(6)/265.02
Attempt to Commit a Class D Felony	110.05(6)
Auto Stripping – 2nd Degree	165.10
Bail Jumping – 2nd Degree	215.56
Bigamy	255.15

Offense	Section(s)
Cemetery Desecration – 1st Degree	145.23
Coercion – 2nd Degree	135.61
Commercial Bribe Receiving – 1st Degree	180.08
Commercial Bribing – 1st Degree	180.03
Computer Tampering – 3rd Degree	156.25
Computer Trespass	156.10
Concealment of a Human Corpse	195.02
Conspiracy – 4th Degree	105.10
Corrupt Use of Position or Authority	200.56
Corrupting the Government – 4th Degree	496.02
Criminal Anarchy	240.15
Criminal Contempt – 1st Degree	215.51
Criminal Diversion of Medical Marihuana – 1st Degree	179.10
Criminal Diversion of Prescription Medications and Prescriptions – 3rd Degree	178.15
Criminal Facilitation – 3rd Degree	115.01
Criminal Impersonation – 1st Degree	190.26
Criminal Injection of a Narcotic Drug	220.46
Criminal Interference with Health Care Services or Religious Worship – 1st Degree	240.71
Criminal Mischief – 3rd Degree	145.05
Criminal Nuisance – 1st Degree	240.46
Criminal Possession of a Firearm	265.01-b
Criminal Possession of an Undetectable Firearm	265.55
Criminal Possession of a Weapon on School Grounds	265.01-a
Criminal Possession of Cannabis – 2nd Degree	222.35
Criminal Possession of Computer Related Material	156.35
Criminal Possession of Methamphetamine Manufacturing Material in the First Degree	220.71
Criminal Possession of Precursors of Controlled Substances	220.60
Criminal Possession of Precursors of Methamphetamine	220.72
Criminal Possession of Public Benefit Cards – 3rd Degree	158.40
Criminal Possession of Stolen Property – 4th Degree	165.45
Criminal Sale of a Ghost Gun – 2nd Degree	265.60
Criminal Sale of an Unfinished Frame or Receiver – 2nd Degre	265.63
Criminal Sale of Cannabis – 2nd Degree	222.55
Criminal Sexual Act – 3rd Degree	130.40
Criminal Solicitation – 3rd Degree	100.08
Criminal Use of a Public Benefit Card – 1st Degree	158.35
Criminal Use of an Access Device – 1st Degree	190.76
Criminal Usury – 2nd Degree	190.40

Offense	Section(s)
Criminally Negligent Homicide	125.10
Custodial Interference – 1st Degree	135.50
Defrauding the Government	195.20
Directing a Laser at an Aircraft – 1st Degree	240.77
Disseminating Indecent Material to Minors – 2nd Degree	235.21
Dissemination of an Unlawful Surveillance Image – 1st Degree	250.60
Eavesdropping	250.05
Endangering the Welfare of an Incompetent or Physically Disabled Person – 1st Degree	260.25
Endangering the Welfare of a Vulnerable Elderly Person, or an Incompetent or Physically Disabled Person – 2nd Degree	260.32
Escape – 2nd Degree	205.10
Failure to Disclose Origin of Recording – 1st Degree	275.40
Falsely Reporting an Incident – 2nd Degree **(VFO)**	240.55
Falsifying Business Records – 1st Degree	175.10
Female Genital Mutilation	130.85
Forgery of Vehicle Identification Number	170.65
Gaming Fraud – 1st Degree	225.60
Grand Larceny – 4th Degree	155.30
Harassment of Rent Regulated Tenant in the First Degree	241.05
Harming a Service Animal – 1st Degree	242.15
Hate Crime (underlying offense misdemeanor)	485.05
Health Care Fraud – 4th Degree	177.10
Hindering Prosecution – 2nd Degree	205.60
Identity Theft – 2nd Degree	190.79
Illegal Possession of a Vehicle Identification Number	170.70
Immigrant Assistance Services Fraud – 1st Degree	190.89
Impairing the Integrity of a Pari-Mutuel Betting System – 2nd Degree	180.52
Incest – 3rd Degree	255.25
Insurance Fraud – 4th Degree	176.15
Intimidating a Victim or Witness – 3rd Degree	215.15
Issuing a False Certificate	175.40
Killing a Police Work Dog or Police Work Horse	195.06-a
Life Settlement Fraud - 4th Degree	176.50
Luring a Child *(unless underlying crime is a class A or B felony)*	120.70(1)
Making an Apparently Sworn False Statement – 1st Degree	210.40
Manufacture of Unauthorized Recordings – 1st Degree	275.10
Manufacture or Sale of an Unauthorized Recording of a Performance – 1st Degree	275.20
Menacing – 1st Degree	120.13

PENAL LAW OFFENSES AND CLASSIFICATIONS

Offense	Section(s)
Money Laundering – 4th Degree	470.05
Money Laundering in Support of Terrorism – 4th Degree	470.21
Non-Support of a Child – 1st Degree	260.06
Obscenity – 2nd Degree	235.06
Obstructing Governmental Administration – 1st Degree	195.07
Offering a False Instrument for Filing – 1st Degree	175.35
Operating an Unlawful Electronic Sweepstakes	156.40
Patronizing a Person for Prostitution – 2nd Degree	230.05
Patronizing a Person for Prostitution in a School Zone	230.08
Perjury – 2nd Degree	210.10
Persistent Sexual Abuse **(VFO)**	130.53
Placing a False Bomb or Hazardous Substance – 2nd Degree **(VFO)**	240.61
Possessing a Sexual Performance by a Child	263.16
Possessing an Obscene Sexual Performance by a Child	263.11
Possession of Gambling Records – 1st Degree	225.20
Possession of Unlawful Gaming Property – 2nd Degree	225.75
Prohibited Use of Weapons *(see section for E felony description)*	265.35(2)
Promoting a Suicide Attempt	120.30
Promoting Gambling – 1st Degree	225.10
Promoting Prostitution in a School Zone	230.19
Rape – 3rd Degree	130.25
Receiving Reward for Official Misconduct – 2nd Degree	200.25
Reckless Assault of a Child by a Child Day Care Provider	120.01
Rent Gouging – 1st degree	180.57
Residential Mortgage Fraud – 4th Degree	187.10
Rewarding Official Misconduct – 2nd Degree	200.20
Riot – 1st Degree	240.06
Scheme to Defraud – 1st Degree	190.65
Sports Bribe Receiving	180.45
Staging a Motor Vehicle Accident – 2nd Degree	176.75
Stalking – 2nd Degree	120.55
Substitution of Children	135.55
Tampering with a Consumer Product – 1st Degree	145.45
Tampering with a Sports Contest – 1st Degree	180.51
Tampering with a Witness – 3rd Degree	215.11
Tampering with Physical Evidence	215.40
Theft of Services *(certain circumstances, see last para.165.15)*	165.15
Trademark Counterfeiting – 2nd Degree	165.72
Unauthorized Use of a Vehicle – 2nd Degree	165.06

PENAL LAW OFFENSES AND CLASSIFICATIONS

Offense	Section(s)
Unlawful Disposal of Methamphetamine Laboratory Material	220.76
Unlawful Duplication of Computer Related Material – 1st Degree	156.30
Unlawful Fleeing a Police Officer in a Motor Vehicle – 2nd Degree	270.30
Unlawful Grand Jury Disclosure	215.70
Unlawful Imprisonment – 1st Degree	135.10
Unlawful Operation of a Recording Device in a Motion Picture or Live Theater – 1st Degree	275.34
Unlawful Possession of a Skimmer Device – 1st Degree	190.86
Unlawful Possession of Personal Identification Information – 2nd Degree	190.82
Unlawful Surveillance – 2nd Degree	250.45
Unlawful Use of Secret Scientific Material	165.07
Unlawful Wearing of a Body Vest	270.20
Unlawfully Concealing a Will	190.30
Unlawfully Dealing With Fireworks	270.00 (2)(b)(iii)
Unlawfully Using Slugs – 1st Degree	170.60
Unpermitted Use of Indoor Pyrotechnics – 1st Degree	405.14
Use of a Child to Commit a Controlled Substance Offense	220.28
Use of Unlawful Gaming Property	225.85
Vehicular Assault – 2nd Degree	120.03
Welfare Fraud – 4th Degree	158.10

CLASS A MISDEMEANORS

Offense	Section(s)
Absconding from a Furlough Program	205.18
Absconding from Temporary Release – 2nd Degree	205.16
Advertisement or Sale of Unauthorized Recordings – 2nd Degree	275.25
Aggravated Harassment – 2nd Degree	240.30
Arson – 5th Degree	150.01
Assault – 3rd Degree	120.00
Attempt to Commit a Class E Felony	110.05(7)
Auto Stripping – 3rd Degree	165.09
Bail Jumping – 3rd Degree	215.55
Burn Injury and Wounds to be Reported	265.26
Cemetery Desecration – 2nd Degree	145.22
Certain Wounds to be Reported	265.25
Coercion – 3rd Degree	135.60
Commercial Bribe Receiving – 2nd Degree	180.05
Commercial Bribing – 2nd Degree	180.00
Compounding a Crime	215.45
Computer Tampering – 4th Degree	156.20
Conspiracy – 5th Degree	105.05

PENAL LAW OFFENSES AND CLASSIFICATIONS

Offense	Section(s)
Criminal Contempt – 2nd Degree	215.50
Criminal Contempt of a Temporary State Commission	215.65
Criminal Contempt of State Commission on Judicial Conduct	215.66
Criminal Contempt of the Legislature	215.60
Criminal Diversion of Prescription Medications and Prescriptions – 4th Degree	178.10
Criminal Facilitation – 4th Degree	115.00
Criminal Impersonation – 2nd Degree	190.25
Criminal Interference with Health Care Services or Religious Worship – 2nd Degree	240.70
Criminal Mischief – 4th Degree	145.00
Criminal Obstruction of Breathing or Blood Circulation	121.11
Criminal Possession of a Controlled Substance – 7th Degree	220.03
Criminal Possession of a Forged Instrument – 3rd Degree	170.20
Criminal Possession of a Rapid Fire Modification Device	265.01-c
Criminal Possession of a Taximeter Accelerating Device	145.70
Criminal Possession of a Weapon – 4th Degree	265.01
Criminal Possession of Cannabis – 3rd Degree	222.30
Criminal Possession of Methamphetamine Manufacturing Material in the Second Degree	220.70
Criminal Possession of Stolen Property – 5th Degree	165.40
Criminal Retention of Medical Marihuana	179.15
Criminal Sale of a Police Uniform	190.27
Criminal Sale of Cannabis – 3rd Degree	222.50
Criminal Simulation	170.45
Criminal Solicitation – 4th Degree	100.05
Criminal Tampering – 2nd Degree	145.15
Criminal Trespass – 2nd Degree	140.15
Criminal Use of a Public Benefit Card – 2nd Degree	158.30
Criminal Use of an Access Device – 2nd Degree	190.75
Criminally Using Drug Paraphernalia – 2nd Degree	220.50
Custodial Interference – 2nd Degree	135.45
Directing a Laser at an Aircraft – 2nd Degree	240.76
Disruption or Disturbance of Religious Service, Funeral, Burial or Memorial Service	240.21
Disseminating of a False Registered Sex Offender Notice	240.48
Dissemination of an Unlawful Surveillance Image – 2nd Degree	250.55
Divulging an Eavesdropping Warrant	250.20
Endangering the Welfare of a Child	260.10
Endangering the Welfare of an Incompetent or Physically Disabled Person – 2nd Degree	260.24

Offense	Section(s)
Escape – 3rd Degree	205.05
Facilitating Female Genital Mutilation	260.22
Failure to Disclose Origin of Recording – 2nd Degree	275.35
False Advertising	190.20
Falsely Reporting an Incident – 3rd Degree	240.50
Falsifying Business Records – 2nd Degree	175.05
Forcible Touching	130.52
Forgery – 3rd Degree	170.05
Fraud and Deceit Relating to Controlled Substances	178.26
Fraud in Insolvency	185.00(2)
Fraud Involving a Security Interest	185.05
Fraudulent Accosting	165.30
Fraudulent Disposition of Mortgaged Property	185.10
Fraudulent Disposition of Property Subject to a Conditional Sale Contract	185.15
Fraudulently Obtaining a Signature	165.20
Gaming Fraud – 2nd Degree	225.55
Giving Unlawful Gratuities	200.30
Harassment of a Rent Regulated Tenant – 2nd Degree	241.02
Harming a Service Animal – 2nd Degree	242.10
Harming an Animal Trained to Aid a Person with a Disability – 1st Degree	195.12
Hazing – 1st Degree	120.16
Health Care Fraud – 5th Degree	177.05
Hindering Prosecution – 3rd Degree	205.55
Identity Theft – 3rd Degree	190.78
Immigrant Assistance Services Fraud – 2nd Degree	190.87
Inciting to Riot	240.08
Insurance Fraud – 5th Degree	176.10
Issuing a False Financial Statement	175.45
Jostling	165.25
Killing or Injuring a Police Animal	195.06
Licenses to Carry, Possess, Repair and Dispose of Firearms	400.00
Life Settlement Fraud - 5th Degree	176.45
Making a False Statement of Credit Terms	190.55
Making a Punishable False Written Statement	210.45
Making an Apparently Sworn False Statement – 2nd Degree	210.35
Making Graffiti	145.60
Manipulation of Gaming Outcomes at an Authorized Gaming Establishment (if not previously convicted of the same crime)	225.90
Manufacture of Unauthorized Recordings – 2nd Degree	275.05

PENAL LAW OFFENSES AND CLASSIFICATIONS

Offense	Section(s)
Manufacture or Sale of an Unauthorized Recording of a Performance – 2nd Degree	275.15
Manufacture, Transport, Disposition and Defacement of Weapons and Dangerous Instruments and Appliances (*depending upon the weapon or instrument*)	265.10(1), (2), (4 if no priors), (5), (7)
Menacing – 2nd Degree	120.14
Misapplication of Property	165.00
Misconduct by a Juror – 1st Degree	215.30
Misrepresentation by Child Day Care Provider	260.31
Non-Support of a Child – 2nd Degree	260.05
Obscenity – 3rd Degree	235.05
Obstructing Emergency Medical Services	195.16
Obstructing Firefighting Operations	195.15
Obstructing Governmental Administration – 2nd Degree	195.05
Offering a False Instrument for Filing – 2nd Degree	175.30
Official Misconduct	195.00
Patronizing a Person for Prostitution – 3rd Degree	230.04
Perjury – 3rd Degree	210.05
Petit Larceny	155.25
Possession of a Gambling Device	225.30
Possession of Burglar's Tools	140.35
Possession of Eavesdropping Devices	250.10
Possession of Gambling Records – 2nd Degree	225.15
Possession of Unlawful Gaming Property – 3rd Degree	225.70
Possession of Usurious Loan Records	190.45
Prohibited Use of Weapons	265.35(1) & (3)
Promoting Gambling – 2nd Degree	225.05
Promoting Prison Contraband – 2nd Degree	205.20
Promoting Prostitution – 4th Degree	230.20
Prostitution in a School Zone	230.03
Providing a Juror with a Gratuity	215.22
Public Display of Offensive Sexual Material	245.11
Public Lewdness – 1st Degree	245.03
Receiving Unlawful Gratuities	200.35
Reckless Endangerment – 2nd Degree	120.20
Rent Gouging – 2nd Degree	180.56
Residential Mortgage Fraud – 5th Degree	187.05
Resisting Arrest	205.30
Riot – 2nd Degree	240.05
Safe Storage of Rifle, Shotguns, and Firearms (Violation of)	265.45
Scheme to Defraud – 2nd Degree	190.60

15

Offense	Section(s)
Scheme to Defraud the State by Unlawfully Selling Prescriptions	190.70
Sexual Abuse – 2nd Degree	130.60
Sexual Misconduct	130.20
Stalking – 3rd Degree	120.50
Tampering with a Consumer Product – 2nd Degree	145.40
Tampering with a Juror – 1st Degree	215.25
Tampering with a Sports Contest – 2nd Degree	180.50
Tampering with a Witness – 4th Degree	215.10
Tampering with Public Records – 2nd Degree	175.20
Theft of Services	165.15
Trademark Counterfeiting – 3rd Degree	165.71
Unauthorized Radio Transmission	190.72
Unauthorized Use of a Computer	156.05
Unauthorized Use of a Vehicle – 3rd Degree	165.05
Unlawful Dissemination of an Intimate Image	245.15
Unlawful Disposition of Assets Subject to Forfeiture	215.80
Unlawful Fleeing a Police Officer in a Motor Vehicle – 3rd Degree	270.25
Unlawful Imprisonment – 2nd Degree	135.05
Unlawful Manufacture, Sale, Distribution, Marking, Altering or Modification of Equipment and Devices Associated with Gaming (if not previously convicted of the same crime)	225.95
Unlawful Operation of a Recording Device in a Motion Picture or Live Theater – 2nd Degree	275.33
Unlawful Possession of a Large Capacity Ammunition Feeding Device	265.36
Unlawful Possession of a Skimmer Device – 2nd Degree	190.85
Unlawful Possession of Personal Identification Information – 3rd Degree	190.81
Unlawful Use of Credit Card, Debit Card or Public Benefit Card	165.17
Unlawfully Dealing with a Child – 1st Degree	260.20
Unlawfully Dealing With Fireworks and Dangerous Fireworks	270.00(2)(a)(ii) & (2)(b)(ii)
Unlawfully Issuing a Dissolution Decree	255.05
Unlawfully Procuring a Marriage License	255.10
Unlawfully Solemnizing a Marriage	255.00
Unpermitted Use of Indoor Pyrotechnics – 2nd Degree	405.12
Use of Counterfeit, Unapproved or Unlawful Wagering Instruments	225.65
Welfare Fraud – 5th Degree	158.05

Offense	Section(s)

CLASS B MISDEMEANORS

Adultery	255.17
Attempt to Commit a Misdemeanor	110.05(8)
Conspiracy – 6th Degree	105.00
Creating a Hazard	270.10
Criminal Diversion of Medical Marihuana – 2nd Degree	179.11
Criminal Nuisance – 2nd Degree	240.45
Criminal Possession of an Anti-Security Item	170.47
Criminal Tampering – 3rd Degree	145.14
Criminal Trespass – 3rd Degree	140.10
Employer Unlawfully Penalizing Witness	215.14
Failing to Report Criminal Communications	250.35(2)
Failure to Report Wiretapping	250.15
False Personation	190.23
Fortune Telling	165.35
Harassment – 1st Degree	240.25
Harming an Animal Trained to Aid a Person with a Disability – 2nd Degree	195.11
Interference, Harassment or Intimidation of a Service Animal	242.05
Issuing a Bad Check	190.05
Loitering – 1st Degree	240.36
Loitering for the Purpose of Engaging in a Prostitution Offense 240.37(2)- *(with specified prior convictions)*	
Menacing – 3rd Degree	120.15
Misconduct by Corporate Official	190.35
Permitting Prostitution	230.40
Possession of Graffiti Instruments	145.65
Prostitution	230.00
Public Lewdness	245.00
Reckless Endangerment of Property	145.25
Refusing to Aid a Peace or Police Officer	195.10
Rent Gouging – 3rd degree	180.55
Sexual Abuse – 3rd Degree	130.55
Stalking – 4th Degree	120.45
Tampering with Juror – 2nd Degree	215.23
Tampering with Private Communications	250.25
Unauthorized Sale of Certain Transportation Services	165.16
Unlawful Assembly	240.10
Unlawful Collection Practices	190.50
Unlawful Disclosure of an Indictment	215.75
Unlawful Duplication of Computer Related Material – 2nd Degree	156.29
Unlawful Possession of Certain Ammunition Feeding Devices	265.37
Unlawful Possession of Radio Devices	140.40

Offense	Section(s)
Unlawfully Dealing With a Child – 2nd Degree	260.21
Unlawfully Dealing With Fireworks and Dangerous Fireworks and Selling Ammunition	270.00(2)(a)(i) & (5)
Unlawfully Installing a Gas Meter	270.40
Unlawfully Obtaining Communications Information	250.30
Unlawfully Possessing or Selling Noxious Material	270.05(2)
Unlawfully Refusing to Yield a Party Line	270.15(2)
Unlawfully Using Slugs – 2nd Degree	170.55

VIOLATIONS

Appearance in Public Under the Influence of Narcotics or a Drug Other Than Alcohol	240.40
Criminal Solicitation – 5th Degree	100.00
Disorderly Conduct	240.20
Exposure of a Person	245.01
Failing to Respond to an Appearance Ticket	215.58
Harassment – 2nd Degree	240.26
Hazing – 2nd Degree	120.17
Littering on Railroad Tracks and Rights-of-Way	145.50
Loitering	240.35
Loitering for the Purpose of Engaging in a Prostitution Offense	240.37(2)- *(if no specified prior convictions)*
Misconduct by a Juror – 2nd Degree	215.28
Offensive Exhibition	245.05
Promoting the Exposure of a Person	245.02
Report of Theft or Loss of a Firearm, Rifle or Shotgun.	400.10
Theft of Services *(certain circumstances, see last par.165.15)*	165.15
Trespass	140.05
Unlawful Operation of a Recording Device in a Motion Picture or Live Theater – 3rd Degree	275.32
Unlawful Possession of a Weapon Upon School Grounds	265.06
Unlawful Possession of Cannabis	222.25
Unlawful Prevention of Public Access to Records	240.65
Unlawful Sale of Cannabis	222.45
Unlawfully Dealing With Fireworks and Dangerous Fireworks	270.00(2)(b)(i)
Unlawfully Posting Advertisements	145.30

JUVENILE DELINQUENCY

Unlawful Possession of Weapons by Persons Under Sixteen	265.05

NYS FELONY SENTENCING GUIDELINES
Current Through Final Chapter 834
of the 2021 Legislative Session
John M. Castellano & Bonnie Cohen-Gallet, Esq.

TABLE OF CONTENTS

INTRODUCTION 20
  Sentencing Highlights 2020/2021 20
  Sentencing Highlights 2019/2020 20
  Sentencing Highlights 2018/2019 22
  Sentencing Highlights 2017/2018 23
  Prior Legislative Highlights 23
DEFINITIONS 26
CLASS A FELONY – NON-DRUG OFFENSE 29
CLASS B FELONY – NON-DRUG OFFENSE 30
CLASS C FELONY – NON-DRUG OFFENSE 32
CLASS D FELONY – NON-DRUG OFFENSE 33
CLASS E FELONY 36
JUVENILE, ADOLESCENT, AND YOUTHFUL OFFENDERS 38
SENTENCES FOR FELONY SEX OFFENSES PL §70.80 41
SECOND CHILD SEXUAL ASSAULT
  FELONY OFFENDER §70.07 43
OPTIONS AND PROGRAM ELIGIBILITY FOR FELONY DRUG
  OFFENSES 44
  Judicial Diversion 44
  Determinate Sentences 44
  Definite Sentence of Imprisonment 45
  Alternative Sentence 45
  Conditional Sealing 45
  Re-Sentencing 45
CLASS A FELONY – DRUG OFFENSE PL § 60.04 46
CLASS B FELONY – DRUG OFFENSE 47
CLASS C FELONY – DRUG OFFENSE 48
CLASS D FELONY – DRUG OFFENSE 49
CLASS E FELONY – DRUG OFFENSE 50
POST INDICTMENT PLEA LIMITS 51
ADDITIONAL PENALTIES 52
  Financial Penalties 52
  Orders of Protection 52
  Probation and Conditional Discharge 53
FOOTNOTES 54

INTRODUCTION

During the past 25 years, the New York State Felony sentencing structure has grown in complexity. With this booklet, members of the bench and bar will find most of the answers they need. Despite all the numbers, terms, and definitions, the basics have not changed and are easy to learn. With a few exceptions, the maximum term of incarceration for felonies, in ascending order (from E to A) is 4, 7, 15, 25, Life. Take a moment to commit the phrase to memory and then, to ascertain the full sentencing parameters in any given situation, it is my sincere hope that this booklet will provide you with the answers you seek.

Sentencing Highlights 2021/2022

The year 2021 saw many highly significant legislative developments regarding both the sentencing options for particular crimes and the administration of parole and post-release supervision. Perhaps the most dramatic changes in criminal law have to do with the "legalization" of marijuana in New York. *See* L. 2021, ch. 92 (eff. Mar. 31, 2021). Former Article 221 was repealed and replaced with Article 222, under which possession of less than three ounces of marijuana (now denominated "cannabis") is not an offense at all. Possession of up to one pound of cannabis is a violation and not a crime, and as much as five pounds of cannabis can be stored in the home. While there are still restrictions on the possession and sale of cannabis by and to minors, the statutory scheme dramatically reduces the penalties for cannabis-related offenses, including felony possession and sale. And, significantly, the new legislation allows for those convicted under old Article 221, including those convicted of felonies, to apply to lower their sentences in accordance with the new sentencing structure. *See* CPL § 440.46-a.

The Legislature also dramatically circumscribed post-release supervision and parole in its last legislative session. As of March 1, 2022, anyone placed on post-release supervision or on a specified period of parole will earn 30 days of credit for every 30 days in which they are not charged with a violation. *See* L. 2021, ch. 427. Thus, for example, a five-year period of post-release supervision imposed along with a determinate sentence for a violent felony offense could be as short as two and one-half years. These new calculations do not apply to sentences including lifetime parole, such as a sentence of 25 years to life, but they do apply retroactively to afford other individuals on post-release supervision or parole up to two years of credit for "earned time" before the statute takes effect. The Legislature has also established a category of "technical" parole violations (ones that do not constitute new crimes) that will rarely result in reincarceration. Even after several such violations are sustained, the maximum period of re-incarceration is 30 days. Notably, defendants are entitled to a prompt bail hearing in court on any violation, and the standards of proof for establishing a violation have been heightened at the preliminary hearing and final disposition stages.

Other significant changes include a provision allowing those denied youthful offender status to reapply for that designation five years after the offense, if they have no additional convictions. *See* L.2021, ch. 552 (eff. Nov. 2, 2021). And eligibility for judicial diversion was expanded to include additional types of offenses, including cannabis offenses, certain conspiracy offenses, auto stripping, and identity theft. Sentencing courts should also be aware that the Legislature has now required certain notifications at the time of sentence, including notice that a felon's voting rights will be restored when released to parole, *see* L. 2021, ch. 103 (notification requirements effective Sept. 2, 2021), and notice that a defendant sentenced to probation or conditional discharge cannot suffer a violation for curfew violations when at or traveling to and from bona fide employment, *see* L. 2021, ch. 487 (eff. Oct. 22, 2021). Finally, the Legislature scheduled a change, effective at the end of 2022, raising the minimum age of juvenile delinquency from seven to twelve years old, except in the case of certain homicide offenses. L. 2021, ch. 810 (eff. Dec. 29, 2022).

Sentencing Highlights 2020/2021

While few legislative changes were made to sentencing statutes in 2020, the pandemic resulted in several changes in normal sentencing procedures. By Executive Order 202.48, the Governor suspended Criminal Procedure Law provisions that would otherwise prohibit electronic appearances at sentences. As a result, remote sentencings even in felony cases have become quite common, if not the norm, during the pandemic. These changes will likely last well into 2021, and perhaps remain available even beyond. Any statutory or constitutional concerns about in-person appearances at sentencings will likely be obviated where defendant expressly waives his appearance as in *People v. Rossborough*, 27 N.Y.3d 485 (2016).

The Court of Appeals issued some significant rulings during the year as well. In *People ex rel. Johnson v. Superintendent*, 36 N.Y.3d 187 (2020), the Court made clear that defendants convicted of certain offenses may be held beyond the time they would otherwise be released to parole or post-release supervision if they cannot find housing compliant with the Sex Assault Reform Act's requirement that they live more than 1000 feet from school grounds. This applies largely to those who have been convicted of sex or kidnaping offenses against child victims or who have been convicted of such offenses against adults and have been designated Level Three sex offenders under SORA. *See People v. ex rel. Negron v. Superintendent*, 36 N.Y.3d 32 (2020). The Court of Appeals also rejected efforts of defendants to overturn predicate felony convictions as being "illegally lenient" to prevent those convictions from being used as predicate felony offenses in later proceedings. *People v. Francis*, 34 N.Y.3d 464 (2020).

Sentencing Highlights 2019/2020

The most important changes in the felony sentencing scheme in 2019 are the significantly reduced sentences for defendants who have committed crimes in response to domestic violence. While some limited reduced sentences were previously available, amendments to section 60.12 of the Penal Law have dramatically expanded the availability and extent of these reductions. The new law now affords reduced sentences to both second felony offenders as well as first felony offenders, although, as before, certain offenses are excluded, like first-degree murder, aggravated murder, and sex offenses. Also, the reduced sentences are not available for second violent felony offenders or persistent felony offenders. But for the remainder, sentences available after a hearing to determine eligibility include probation for both first B, C, D, and E felonies and second C, D, and E felonies. Prison sentences are limited under the statute, even for a first B felony, to no more than five years. Similarly, reduced sentences are provided for A felonies, including most second-degree murder charges, drug felonies, and violent and ordinary second felony offenders. The new sentencing law is also retroactive, as domestic violence victims convicted prior to the effective date of the new provisions who are serving incarceratory sentences of eight or more years may move to be resentenced under new section 440.47.

In addition, the Legislature has now made those convicted of certain forms of second-degree burglary and second-degree robbery eligible for shock incarceration programs. L. 2019, ch. 55, § 2 (eff. May 12, 2019). The burglary of a dwelling and a robbery in which the defendant is aided by another are now included in section 865 of the Correction Law as eligible for the shortened sentences available upon successful completion of shock-incarceration programs, despite the fact that convictions for other violent felony offenses render inmates ineligible for these programs.

Also, the Court of Appeals held in *People v. Thomas*, 33 N.Y.3d 1, 121 N.E.3d 270, 97 N.Y.S.3d 642 (2019), that the date of the original sentence, rather than any re-sentence, controls for the purpose of determining the date of prior convictions under the second and persistent felony offender statutes. While some courts had previously held that a full re-sentence on a prior conviction changed the date of the prior conviction, which might invalidate a determination that the defendant was a second or persistent felony offender, the Court of Appeals made clear that the date of the original sentence is the relevant date for all second and persistent felony offender issues, unless, of course, the prior conviction itself was overturned.

Other significant sentencing changes pertain to misdemeanors, but are worth noting here. These include the reduction of all definite sentences of one year to 364 days under Part OO of Chapter 55 of the Laws of 2019 (eff. April 12, 2019). The change, designed to avoid provisions of federal law that attach significant immigration consequences to one-year sentences for certain misdemeanors, applies to all one-year sentences on misdemeanors whenever imposed. Also, the Legislature decriminalized up to two ounces of marijuana, subjecting offenders only to penalties for a violation rather than a crime for these amounts. *See* Ch. 131, L. 2019 (eff. Aug. 28, 2019).

Sentencing Highlights 2018/2019

The 2018 legislative session resulted in few changes to the sentencing structure of the state. Perhaps the most notable of those that were enacted involves a collateral consequence to conviction for domestic violence misdemeanors requiring offenders to surrender their firearms, including any rifles and shotguns, upon conviction. While the surrender of many firearms was previously required after felony convictions and certain other "serious offenses," Chapter 60 of the Laws of 2018 (eff. 6/11/18) extends these provisions to a number of misdemeanors commonly committed against family members or members of the same household, regardless of whether a weapon was used as part of the offense. These misdemeanors, now included within the definition of "serious offenses" in section 265.00 of the Penal Law, encompass many offenses commonly charged in domestic violence cases, such as third-degree assault, menacing, unlawful imprisonment in the second degree, harassment in the first degree, aggravated harassment in the second degree, and criminal trespass, or an attempt to commit any of these offenses. The section also extends the surrender provision to include "long guns," such as rifles and shotguns. The defendant is entitled, under C.P.L. § 370.15, to notice that the victim is alleged to be a member of the same household and a hearing to determine the issue.

As its first enactment in 2019, the Legislature passed the Reproductive Health Act, which, among other things, eliminated all liability for the crimes of abortion and self-abortion in all degrees. See L. 2019, ch. 1. The Act substantially revised Article 125 of the Penal Law, removing any mention of abortion, repealing five sections of that article in their entirety, and repealing portions of four others. These sections had criminalized abortions unless done by a licenced physician prior to 24 weeks into the pregnancy, and classified these crimes along with homicides.

While the Legislature was relatively inactive on sentencing issues, two Court of Appeals decisions resolved significant sentencing questions this year. In *People v. Hakes*, 32 N.Y.3d 624 (2018) the Court made clear that a court imposing a condition of probation, including wearing an alcohol monitoring bracelet, may require a defendant to pay for the costs associated with that condition. But, the Court of Appeals warned, courts cannot impose a condition of probation that incurs costs that a particular defendant cannot feasibly meet. Moreover, if a defendant becomes unable to pay after initially accepting the condition, the court must hold a hearing and, if the defendant demonstrates an inability to pay, the court must attempt to fashion a reasonable alternative to incarceration. If the court finds, however, that the defendant willfully refused to pay, it may revoke the defendant's probation and impose a term of incarceration. In *Matter of Teri W.*, 31 N.Y.3d 124 (2018), the Court clarified that a Youthful Offender who has committed a felony sexual assault may be sentenced to a term of ten years' probation, rather than the five years required for an undesignated E felony.

Prior Legislative Highlights

In 2007, the Legislature enacted section 70.80 of the Penal Law, which, in major part, provides for increased determinate sentences for sex offenders. The Legislature also created a new category of "sexually motivated felonies," which converts many ordinary felonies into sex crimes when they are committed for the purpose, in whole or substantial part, of the defendant's sexual gratification. These new sex crimes are subject to the added penalties under section 70.80(4) of the Penal Law. Sexual offenders who prey on children under the age of 15 are, however, sentenced as Second Child Sexual Assault Felony Offenders under section 70.07. The Legislature also provided a mechanism for the civil commitment of certain sex offenders upon the expiration of their sentences.

In 2013, the Legislature, in response to the recent massacre at a Newton, Connecticut, elementary school, enacted the crime of Aggravated Possession of a Weapon, a C violent felony with a mandatory minimum of five years' imprisonment, and Criminal Possession of a Weapon on School Grounds. The aggravated possession crime raised the minimums for weapon possession during the commission of violent felony offense and drug felonies.

In 2014, the Legislature gave judges increased flexibility over most probationary sentences, allowing courts to impose less than the five-year periods previously required for felonies and three-year periods required for misdemeanors. The Legislature provided for some exceptions, such as sexual assaults and higher level drug felonies.

Additionally, in 2014, the Legislature passed the Public Trust Act, creating the crimes of Public Corruption, which raised the punishment for stealing public funds or defrauding the government to one class higher than those applicable to ordinary thefts and fraudulent schemes. The Act also increased the fines on individuals and corporations to three times the amount of financial gain from the crime.

The Death Penalty

The statutory trial procedures established to determine whether the death penalty, life without parole or an indeterminate sentence shall be imposed were ruled unconstitutional by the Court of Appeals (*People v. LaValle*, 3 N.Y.3d 88; 817 N.E.2d 341; 783 N.Y.S.2d 485). No new statutory scheme has been enacted. As a result, the death penalty cannot be imposed in New York State.

Second Child Sexual Assault Felony Offender

In 2000 the legislature enacted the Sexual Assault Reform Act (SARA) effective for crimes committed on or after February 1, 2001, which mandates greatly enhanced penalties for a new category of predicate felony offenders, namely the Second Child Sexual Assault Felony Offender (PL § 70.07). Similar to the procedure for predicate felony offenders, if the defendant has a prior sexual felony conviction against a child under the age of 15, a longer period of incarceration is mandated. A ten year period of probation is also provided for many sexual offenders who will be prohibited from entering schools without prior approval. The chart on page 43 delineates the sentencing parameters for predicate sex offenders who commit these crimes against children.

DEFINITIONS

ARMED FELONY OFFENSES (AFOs) - CPL § 1.20(41) - Any Violent Felony Offense that includes as an element either (a) possession, being armed with or causing serious physical injury by means of a deadly weapon, if the weapon is a loaded weapon from which a shot, readily capable of producing death or other serious physical injury may be discharged; or (b) display of what appears to be a pistol, revolver, rifle, shotgun, machine gun or other firearm.

DEFINITE SENTENCE - A sentence for a specific number of days (or months) up to a maximum of 364 days.

DETERMINATE SENTENCE - A sentence in excess of one year for a set number of years or half years, such as a sentence of 5 years. A determinate sentence must be accompanied by a period of post-release supervision, similar to parole. The permissible range depends on the offense and the offender's history, and is imposed as a definite period, in whole or half years.

DRUG TRAFFICKING FELONY - A specified felony consisting mostly of offense involving the sale of controlled substances that, if committed with a weapon, gives rise to a mandatory minimum of five years imprisonment. *See* Penal Law § 10.00(21). Defendant must be convicted of Aggravated Possession of a Weapon under P.L. § 265.19. Similar enhanced mandatory minimum exists for Criminal Possession of a Weapon (CPW) 3, subdivision 10, possessing an unloaded firearm during the commission of a violent felony offense.

"FOR HIRE" VEHICLE OFFENSE - If the victim was operating a "for hire" vehicle and the defendant commits a crime set forth in PL § 60.07(2), the minimum of an indeterminate sentence may be 3 to 5 years more than otherwise authorized. If a determinate sentence is imposed, the term may be 3 to 5 years more than otherwise authorized (PL § 60.07). A court may decline to impose the higher sentence upon making specific findings. *See* PL § 60.07(1).

HATE CRIME - PL § 485.05 - If convicted of a hate crime and the offense is either a misdemeanor or a class C, D or E felony, the crime shall be deemed to be one category higher. If the conviction is for a class B or A-1 felony, a longer sentence must be imposed. Hate crime prevention counseling may also be required.

INDETERMINATE SENTENCES - A sentence that has both a minimum term that generally must be served before the inmate can be released on parole and maximum term that could be served (without regard to time off for good behavior), such as 3-9 years or 4-8 years.

PAROLE AND POST-RELEASE SUPERVISION – Parole and post-release supervision are two forms of community supervision attached to felony incarceratory sentences. Post-release supervision is a definite period imposed along with determinate sentences, and parole, attached to indeterminate sentences, encompasses the period of time between the defendant's release and the maximum of the indeterminate sentence. Under the Less is More Act, L. 2021, ch. 427 (eff. Mar. 1, 2022), these sentences may be shortened to as little as one-half of the imposed or expected period. For every 30 days that the defendant does not violate his or her period of post-release supervision or parole, the period is shortened by 30 days, except for lifetime parole.

SECOND CHILD SEXUAL ASSAULT FELONY OFFENDER - PL § 70.07 - A defendant who is convicted for a felony sexual assault against a child under PL Article 130, who, within the previous 15 years (minus any periods of incarceration), has a prior felony conviction which is also for a sexual assault against a child. See the chart on page 43 for sentencing parameters.

SEXUAL ASSAULT - PL § 65.00 (3) (To determine the period of probation under PL § 65.00) - Any offense contained in PL Articles 130 and 263 and PL § 255.25, PL § 255.26, PL § 255.27, or an attempt to commit any of the foregoing crimes.

SEXUALLY MOTIVATED FELONY - A person commits a sexually motivated felony when he or she commits a specified offense, including most assault, burglary, robbery, arson, and kidnapping offenses, for the purpose, in whole or substantial part, of his or her own direct sexual gratification. Such offenses are sentenced as sex crimes pursuant to P.L. § 70.80(4).

VIOLENT FELONY OFFENSES (VFOs) - *See* PL § 70.02

CLASS A FELONY – NON-DRUG OFFENSE

Felony	Life Without Parole	Indeterminate Sentence
Murder 1 PL 125.27	Life without Parole -or-	Min: 20 - life Max: 25 - life[1]
A-I Murder in the course of a sex crime with a victim less than 14 years of age	Life without Parole PL 70.00 (3)(a)(i)	NOT ALLOWED
A-I Terrorism with a class A-I specified offense, Possession of a Chemical or Biological Weapon 1 (PL 490.45 or 490.55) or Domestic Act of Terrorism Motivated by Hate 1st Degree (PL 490.28)	Life without Parole[2]	NOT ALLOWED
A-I Aggravated Murder PL 125.26, subd. 1 and *Murder 2°* PL 125.25 (5) only *A-I Aggravated Murder* PL 125.26, subd. 2	Life without Parole PL 70.00 (5)	PL 125.25(5) and 125.26, subd. 1: NOT ALLOWED PL 125.26, subd. 2: Min. 15 to life / Max 25 to life (PL 60.06)
Attempted Murder - only if the conviction is for attempt to commit PL 125.27 (1)(a)(i), (ii) or (iii) or attempted PL 125.26	NOT ALLOWED	Min: 20 to life / Max: 40 to life PL 70.00 (3)(a)(i)
All other **A-I Felonies and all Persistent non-violent felons**	NOT ALLOWED	Min: 15 to life / Max: 25 to life [3] Hate Crimes: Min: 20 to life[4] / Max: 25 to life
A-II Felonies only PL 130.95 & 130.96	NOT ALLOWED	Min: 10 to life / Max: 25 to life *PL 70.00 (3)(a)(ii)*
A-II Felonies except PL 130.95 & 130.96	NOT ALLOWED	Min: 3 to life / Max: 8 ⅓ to life
A-II Felonies Predicate Felons except PL 130.95 & 130.96	NOT ALLOWED	Min: 6 to life / Max: 12½ to life[5]
A-II Felonies Predicate Felons only PL 130.95 & 130.96	NOT ALLOWED	Min: 10 to life / Max: 25 to life PL 70.06(4)
A-II Felonies Persistent Violent Felons only PL 130.95 & 130.96	NOT ALLOWED	25 to life (*see* PL 70.08 (1) & (3) (a))

If the victim was operating a 'for hire' vehicle and the defendant commits specified crimes, the minimum of the indeterminate sentence, or the determinate term, may be 3 to 5 years more than otherwise authorized. PL § 60.07

CLASS B FELONY – NON-DRUG OFFENSE

Felony and Sentencing Status	Indeterminate Sentences	Determinate Term *Whole or half years only*	Straight Probation	"Split" Sentence, Definite Sentence *(Up to 1 Year)*, Conditional Discharge or Intermittent
B Felony Non-Predicate Non-VFO	Min: 1-3 Max: 8⅓-25 [6] except Hate Crimes minimum is 2-6 yrs.	NO	NO	NO
B VFO [7] Non-predicate	*Crime before 10/1/95* Min: 2-6 Max: 8⅓-25[8] if AFO [9] *On or after 10/1/95* Min: 3-6 Max: 12½-25[10]	*Crime on or after 9/1/98 (Determinate not mandatory for certain domestic abuse situations).* [11] Min. Term: 5 yrs. Max Term: 25 yrs.[12] Whole or ½ yrs. only[13] plus from 2½ - 5 yrs. post-release supervision[14] **Criminal Use/Firearm 1°** add a 5 year consecutive sentence. [15] **Hate Crime** Min. Term: 8 years. **Aggravated Manslaughter 1°** and **Aggravated Assault on an Officer** Min Term: 10 years Max Term: 30 years	NO	NO
B Predicate Felon Current conviction is not a VFO	Min: 4½-9 Hate Crime Min. 5-10 Max: 12½-25[16]	NO	NO	NO

If the victim was operating a **"for hire"** vehicle and the defendant commits specified crimes, the minimum of the indeterminate sentence, or the determinate term, may be 3 to 5 years more than otherwise authorized, PL § 60.07.

CLASS B FELONY – NON-DRUG OFFENSE

Felony and Sentencing Status	Indeterminate Sentences	Determinate Term *Whole or half years only*	Straight Probation	"Split" Sentence, Definite Sentence *(Up to 1 Year)*, Conditional Discharge or Intermittent
B Predicate First conviction is not a VFO Current is a VFO	*Crime before 10/1/95:* Min: 4½-9 Max: 12½-25[17]	*Crime on or after 10/1/95* Min Term: 8 yrs. Hate Crime Min Term: 10 yrs. Max Term: 25 yrs.[18] If *on or after 9/1/98*, add 5 yrs. post-release supervision[14]	NO	NO
B Predicate Both convictions VFOs	*Crime before 10/1/95:* Min: 6-12 Max: 12½ to 25[19]	*Crime on or after 10/1/95* Min Term: 10 yrs. Hate Crime Min Term: 12 yrs. Max Term: 25 yrs. Whole or ½ yrs. only.[20] *If on or after 9/1/98* add 5 yrs. post-release supervision.[14]	NO	NO
B Persistent VFO *Mandatory*	*Crime before 10/1/95:* Min: 10-life Max: 25-life[21] *On or after 10/1/95:* Min: 20-life Max: 25-life[22]	NO	NO	NO
B Non-Violent Persistent	*Discretionary*: See sentencing range for all other A-1 felonies above PL §70.10(2)			

CLASS C FELONY – NON-DRUG OFFENSE

Felony and Sentencing Status	Indeterminate Sentences	Determinate Term *Whole or half years only*	Straight Probation	"Split" Sentence, Definite Sentence *(Up to 1 Year)*, Conditional Discharge or Intermittent
C Felony Non-Predicate Non-VFO	If imposed, Min: 1-3 / Max: 5-15;[23], [24] Certain non-VFO, felonies PL 60.05(4)[25] carry a mandatory indeterminate sentence	NO	YES 3,4 or 5 yrs. -except PL 60.05(4) class C *Enumerated* felonies ---------------- Sexual Assault: 10 years probation PL 65.00(3)a(iii)	No intermittent, split or Definite allowed. All *"Enumerated"* Felonies must get an indeterminate sentence. For other non-VFOs, a CD is permitted.
C VFO[26] Non-Predicate Effective 11/1/06 this includes PL 265.03(3) *which was formerly* a class D felony	*Crime before 10/1/95* Min: 1½-4½ Max: 5-15[27] *On or after 10/1/95 but before 9/1/98* Min: 2¼-4½ Max: 7½-15[28]	*Crime on or after 9/1/98 (Determinate not mandatory for domestic abuse situations)*[11] Min: 3½ yrs. Max: 15 yrs.[29] Whole or half yrs. only.[13] **Aggravated Manslaughter 2°** and **Att. Agg. Assault on an Officer** Min:7 yrs. Max: 20 yrs. -------------------- **Agg. Crim. Neg. Homicide** Min: 3½ yrs. Max: 20 yrs. -------------------- **Agg. CPW** Mandatory Min. 5 yrs. *Eff.3/16/13* -------------------- Add from 2½ - 5 yrs. post-release supervision.[14]	NO	NO
C Predicate Current conviction not a VFO	Min: 3-6; Max: 7½-15[30]	NO	NO	NO

If the victim was operating a **"for hire"** vehicle and the defendant commits specified crimes, the minimum of the indeterminate sentence, or the determinate term, may be 3 to 5 years more than otherwise authorized, PL § 60.07.

Felony and Sentencing Status	Indeterminate Sentences	Determinate Term *Whole or half years only*	Straight Probation	"Split" Sentence, Definite Sentence *(Up to 1 Year)*, Conditional Discharge or Intermittent
C Predicate Prior conviction not a VFO Current crime is a VFO	*Crime before 10/1/95* Min: 3-6 Max: 7½-15[31]	*Crime on or after 10/1/95* Min Term: 5 yrs. Max Term: 15 yrs.[32] *If on or after 9/1/98*, add 5 yrs. post-release supervision.[14]	NO	NO
C Predicate Both convictions VFOs	*Crime before 10/1/95* Min: 4-8 Max: 7½-15[33]	*Crime on or after 10/1/95* Min Term: 7 yrs. Max Term: 15 yrs. Whole or half yrs. only.[34] *If on or after 9/1/98*, add 5 yrs. post-release supervision.[14]	NO	NO
C Persistent VFO *Mandatory*	*Crime before 10/1/95* Min: 8-life Max: 25-life[35] *On or after 10/1/95* Min: 16-life Max: 25-life[36]		NO	NO	NO
C Non-VFO Persistent	*Discretionary:* See all other A-1 felonies above, PL §70.10(2).			

CLASS D FELONY – NON-DRUG OFFENSE

Felony and Sentencing Status	Indeterminate Sentences	Determinate Term *Whole or half years only*	Straight Probation	"Split" or Definite Sentence *(Up to 1 Year)*, Conditional Discharge or Intermittent
D Felony Non-Predicate Non-VFO	Min: 1-3 Max: 2⅓-7[37, 38]	NO	YES 3, 4, or 5 yrs. except Att/Promoting Prostitution 2[39] ------------------ Sexual Assault = 10 yrs.	YES, however, no Conditional Discharge is permitted for Att/Promoting Prostitution 2[*][40]
D VFO[41] Non-Predicate (except Handgun VFOs)	*Crime before 10/1/95* Min: 1-3 Max: 2⅓-7 [42] *On or after 10/1/95* Min: 1½-3 Max: 3½-7[43]	*Crime on or after 9/1/98 (Determinate not mandatory for certain domestic abuse situations)*[11] Min: 2 yrs. Max: 7 yrs.[44] Add from 1½ - 3 yrs. post-release supervision.[14] **Menacing an Officer** Min: 2 yrs. Max: 8 yrs. **CPW 3, subdivision 10** Mand. Min. 3½ yrs. *Eff.3/16/13*	YES except Att/Assault 1 *(before 11/96)* and Assault 2[45] ------------------ Sexual Assault = 10 yrs. (PL 65.00(3) (a)(iii)	YES, except no Conditional Discharge Assault 2.[46] If originally an AFO, see footnote 45
D VFO HANDGUNS: Non-Predicate: PL § 265.02 (4)*,(5),(6),(7) and (8) *Repealed 11/1/06	*Crime before 10/1/95* Min: 1-3; Max: 2⅓-7 *On or after 10/1/95* Min: 1½-3 Max: 3½-7[47]	*Crime on or after 9/1/98 (Determinate not mandatory for certain domestic abuse situations).*[11] Min: 2 yrs. Max: 7 yrs.[48] Add from 1½ - 3 yrs. post-release supervision.[14]	YES[49] for PL § 265.02(6) all others if special circumstances exist, see footnote 49	YES for PL § 265.02(6) For all other D Handgun VFOs, less than one year only if special circumstances exist, see footnote 49

---

[*]Probation or conditional discharge with Ignition Interlock Device required for at least 6 months for D felony DWI.

PL §60.21, VTL §1192(1)(b)(ii). DWI split sentences not subject to cap on incarceration contained in PL § 60.01(2)(d). *See* L.2009, ch. 496, §15 for effective date.

CLASS D FELONY – NON-DRUG OFFENSE

Felony and Sentencing Status	Indeterminate Sentences	Determinate Term *Whole or half years only*	Straight Probation	"Split" or Definite Sentence *(Up to 1 Year)*, Conditional Discharge or Intermittent
D Predicate Felon Current conviction is not a VFO	Min: 2-4 Max: 3½ -7[50] or Parole Supervision*[51]	NO	NO	NO
D Predicate Prior conviction not a VFO Current crime is a VFO	*Crime before 10/1/95* Min: 2-4 Max: 3½-7.[52]	*Crime or after 10/1/95* Min Term: 3 yrs. Max: 7 yrs.[53] *If on or after 9/1/98*, add 5 yrs. post-release supervision.[14]	NO	NO
D Predicate Both convictions VFOs	*Crime before 10/1/95* Min: 2½-5 Max: 3½-7[54]	*Crime on or after 10/1/95* Min: 5 yrs. Max: 7 yrs. Whole or half yrs. only.[55] *If on or after 9/1/98*, add 5 yrs. post-release supervision.[14]	NO	NO
D Persistent Violent *Mandatory*	*Crime before 10/1/95* Min: 6-life Max: 25-life[56] *On or after 10/1/95* Min: 12-life Max: 25-life[57]	NO	NO	NO
D Non-VFO Persistent	*Discretionary*: See all other A-1 Felonies, PL §70.10(2)			

If the victim was operating a **"for hire"** vehicle and the defendant commits specified crimes, the minimum of the indeterminate sentence, or the determinate term, may be 3 to 5 years more than otherwise authorized, PL § 60.07.

35

CLASS E FELONY

Felony and Sentencing Status	Indeterminate Sentences	Determinate Term *Whole or half years only*	Straight Probation	"Split" Sentence, Definite Sentence *(Up to 1 Year)*, Conditional Discharge or Intermittent
E Non-Predicate Non-VFO[58] AND ALL YO SENTENCES[59]	Min: 1-3 / Max: 1⅓-4 [60, 61]	NO	YES - 3, 4, or 5 yrs. ------------------ Sexual Assault = 10 yrs.	YES*
***E VFOs*[57]**	*Crime before 10/1/95* Min: 1-3, / Max: 1⅓-4[62] *On or after 10/1/95* Min: 1½-3 Max: 2-4 [63]	*Effective 9/1/98 (Mandatory except for certain domestic abuse situations)[11]* Min: 1½ yrs. Max: 4 yrs.[64] Add from 1½ - 3 yrs. post-release supervision.[14]	YES[65] 3, 4, or 5 yrs. Except PL §265.02(6)	YES Except PL §265.02(6) However, if the sentence is less than 1 year, see footnote 65.
E Predicate Current conviction is not a VFO	Min: 1½-3 / Max: 2-4[66] *or* Parole Supervision*[67] but the max for Aggravated Harassment by an Inmate is 2½-5.[68]	NO	NO	NO
E Predicate Prior conviction not a VFO Current crime is a VFO	*Crime before 10/1/95* Min: 1½-3 Max: 2-4 [69]	*Crime on or after 10/1/95* Min: 2 yrs. Max: 4 yrs.[70] *If on or after 9/1/98*, add 5 yrs. post-release supervision.[14]	NO	NO

*Probation or conditional discharge with Ignition Interlock Device required for at least 6 months for E felony DWI.

PL §60.21, VTL §1192(1)(b)(ii). DWI split sentences not subject to cap on incarceration contained in PL § 60.01 (2)(d). *See* L.2009, ch. 496, §15 for effective date.

CLASS E FELONY

Felony and Sentencing Status	Indeterminate Sentences	Determinate Term *Whole or half years only*	Straight Probation	"Split" Sentence, Definite Sentence *(Up to 1 Year)*, Conditional Discharge or Intermittent
E Predicate *Both convictions VFOs*	*Crime before 10/1/95* The only possible sentence is 2-4 yrs.[71]	*Crime on or after 10/1/95* Min Term: 3 yrs. Max Term: 4 yrs. Whole or half yrs. only.[72] *If on or after 9/1/98*, add 5yrs. post-release supervision.[14]	NO	NO
E Persistent VFO *Mandatory*	Min sentence: 3 to life Max sentence: 4 to life.[73]	NO	NO	NO
E non-VFO Persistent	*Discretionary*: See all other A-1 felonies, PL §70.10(2).			
JO: YO is not available for class A felony convictions. If defendant does not get Y.O. only indeterminate sentences are allowed, PL §70.05.	The felonies for which 13,14 and 15 year olds can be prosecuted and sentenced in Supreme Court are in PL §10.00(18) and PL §30.00(2). *Murder 2* °: If the defendant is 13 years old, the minimum sentence is 5-life and the max is 9-life. If the defendant is 14 or 15, the minimum sentence is 7½-life and the maximum sentence is 15-life. *Arson 1 & Kidnap 1:* Minimum portion of the indeterminate sentence must be set between 4 and 6 years. The maximum portion of the sentence must be set between 12 and 15 years. If Y.O. is not granted for B and C felonies the sentencing range is: *B Felonies:* The minimum sentence is 1-3 years, the maximum sentence is 3⅓-10 years. *Hate Crimes:* Minimum 1⅓-4 years. *C Felonies:* The minimum sentence is 1-3 years, the maximum sentence is 2⅓-7 years.[74] *D Felonies:* The minimum sentence is 1-3 years; the maximum sentence is 1½ - 4 years.			

If the victim was operating a **"for hire"** vehicle and the defendant commits specified crimes, the minimum of the indeterminate sentence, or the determinate term, may be 3 to 5 years more than otherwise authorized, PL § 60.07.

JUVENILE, ADOLESCENT, AND YOUTHFUL OFFENDERS

	Juvenile Offender (JO)	Adolescent Offender (AO)	Youthful Offender (YO)
Defined	13, 14, 15 year-olds who have committed designated offenses, including: 1. If committed at 13, Murder 2 (intentional and depraved), Sexually Motivated Felony 2. If committed at 14 or 15, above plus Felony Murder, Man 1, Kidnapping 1, Rape 1, Arson 1, Assault 1, Robbery 1 & 2, Burglary 1 & 2, and others CPL § 1.20(42)	16 and 17 year-olds charged with a felony Effective after Oct. 1, 2018 if defendant is 16 at time of commission of crime, or Oct. 1, 2019 if defendant is 17 at time of commission CPL § 1.20(44)	16, 17, or 18 year-olds, or child charged in Superior Court as a JO Not eligible under CPL § 720.10 if: - convicted of AI or AII felony - convicted of armed felony, first-degree rape or criminal sexual act, - previously convicted of a felony - previously adjudicated a YO (except, under CPL §§ 170.80, 720.25, if defendant is 16 or 17 and currently convicted of prostitution or loitering for prostitution, defendant is still eligible for YO and no such offense may be used to prevent subsequent YO).
Treatment in Superior Court	As of Oct. 1, 2018, exclusive jurisdiction is in Youth Part of Superior Court, BUT case may, or in some circumstances must, be removed to Family Court: 1. After preliminary hearing: Court must remove if no reasonable cause to believe defendant committed crimes for which a person under 16 is criminally responsible but defendant qualifies as juvenile delinquent under FCA. CPL § 722.20(3)(b).	Exclusive jurisdiction in Youth Part of Superior Court, BUT may, or in some circumstances must, be removed to FC: 1. After preliminary hearing: court must remove if no reasonable cause to believe defendant committed felony. CPL § 722.21(3)(b).	Jurisdiction in any part of Superior Court Sentencing court must consider YO on the record for eligible youths, even if the plea bargain specifies no YO. *People v. Pacherille*, 25 N.Y.3d 1021 (2015). YO finding substituted for conviction of eligible youth upon finding that "the interest of justice would be served by relieving the eligible youth from the onus of a criminal record and by not imposing an indeterminate term of imprisonment of more than four years." CPL § 720.20.

JUVENILE, ADOLESCENT, AND YOUTHFUL OFFENDERS

	Juvenile Offender (JO)	Adolescent Offender (AO)	Youthful Offender (YO)
Treatment in Superior Court (Cont'd.)	2. At DA's request (CPL § 722.20[4]), court remove: if in interests of justice (*see* criteria in CPL § 722.22[2]), BUT if charged with Murder 2, forcible Rape 1, CSA 1, or AFO, court must find mitigating circumstances of crime, defendant's participation was minor, or there are deficiencies in proof; 3. Upon defendant's motion (CPL §§ 722.20[5], 722.22[1]), court may remove if in interests of justice, after considering specified criteria under CPL § 722.22(2).	2. At DA's request or with DA's consent: **Less Serious Felonies** (non-drug A felony, VFO, JO designated offense) court must order removal, CPL § 722.21(4). **More Serious Felonies** (including VFO, non-drug felonies) must remove if in the interests of justice, except that for Murder 2, Rape 1, CSA 1 or AFO court must find mitigating circumstances of crime, defendant's participation was minor, or there are deficiencies in proof. CPL § 722.21(5). 3. By court, following arraignment: **Less Serious Felonies** (excluding non-drug A felonies, VFOs, JO designated offenses, and VTL offenses) court must order removal to Family Court, unless prosecutor moves to prevent within 30 days and shows exceptional circumstances. CPL § 722.23(1). **More Serious Felonies** (including VFO, non-drug A felonies): proceeds as for less serious felonies BUT tried as adult if prosecution establishes that: 1. Defendant caused significant physical injury; 2. Displayed a firearm, shotgun, rifle, or other	

JUVENILE, ADOLESCENT, AND YOUTHFUL OFFENDERS

	Juvenile Offender (JO)	Adolescent Offender (AO)	Youthful Offender (YO)
Treatment in Superior Court (Cont'd.)		deadly weapon in furtherance of offense; 3. Unlawfully engaged in sexual intercourse, oral sexual conduct, anal sexual conduct or sexual contact as defined in PL § 130.00. CPL § 722.23(2).	
Available Sentences in Superior Court	P.L. § 70.05 Must be indeterminate sentence but may include restitution BUT may be eligible for YO treatment	Same sentences as available for adults for same crime, PL § 60.10-a, but may be eligible for YO treatment. BUT Life imprisonment without parole not mandatory for 17 or younger even where mandatory for adult. PL § 70.00(5) (Eff. Oct. 1, 2018)	Conviction replaced with Y.O. adjudication, which is not a crime. Defendant can receive sentence available for E felony (up to 1 1/3 to 4 year indeterminate sentence) or probation up to 5 years or ten years for a felony sexual assault but not conditional or unconditional discharge for drug felony . PL § 60.02

SENTENCES FOR FELONY SEX OFFENSES PL §70.80 *
Effective for Crimes after April 13, 2007

Felony and Sentencing Status	Determinate Term *Whole or half years only* PL § 70.80(4)	Post-release Supervision PL §70.45 2-a	Probation PL §70.80(4)a	"Split" or Definite Sentence *1 year or less* PL §70.80(4)(b)
A-I - if the crime is deemed to be a "sexually motivated felony" pre-existing statutory framework still applicable **Persistent felons** pre-existing statutory framework still applicable				
A-II *predatory sexual assault and predatory sexual assault against a child (PL 130.95 & 130.96)*	*INDETERMINATE SENTENCE* Min: 10 to life Max: 25 to life	not applicable	NO	NO
B *Non-Predicate non-VFOs & VFOs*	Min: 5 yrs. Max: 25 yrs.	Min: 5 yrs. Max: 20 yrs.	NO	NO
B *Predicate Felons - prior conviction is not a VFO*	Min: 8 yrs. Max: 25 yrs.	Min: 10 yrs. Max: 25 yrs.	NO	NO
B *Predicate Felons - prior conviction is a VFO*	Min: 9 yrs. Max: 25 yrs.	Min: 10 yrs. Max: 25 yrs.	NO	NO
C *Non-Predicate non-VFOs & VFOs*	Min: 3 ½ yrs. Max: 15 yrs.	Min: 5 yrs. Max: 15 yrs.	NO	NO
C *Predicate Felons - prior conviction is not a VFO*	Min: 5 yrs. Max: 15 yrs.	Min: 7 yrs. Max: 20 yrs.	NO	NO
C *Predicate Felons - prior conviction is a VFO*	Min: 6 yrs. Max: 15 yrs.	Min: 7 yrs. Max: 20 yrs.	NO	NO

* *Second Child Sexual Assault Felony Offense must be sentenced in accordance with PL §70.07 (see page 43).*

Felony and Sentencing Status	Determinate Term *Whole or half years only* PL § 70.80(4)	Post-release Supervision PL §70.45 2-a	Probation PL §70.80(4)a	"Split" or Definite Sentence *1 year or less* PL §70.80(4)(b)
D *Non-Predicate non-VFOs & VFOs*	Min: 2 yrs. Max: 7 yrs.	Min: 3 yrs. Max: 10 yrs.	YES	YES
D *Predicate Felons - prior conviction is not a VFO*	Min: 3 yrs. Max: 7 yrs.	Min: 5 yrs. Max: 15 yrs.	NO	NO
D *Predicate Felons - prior conviction is a VFO*	Min: 4 yrs. Max: 7 yrs.	Min: 5 yrs. Max: 15 yrs.	NO	NO
E *Non-Predicate non-VFOs & VFOs*	Min: 1½ yrs. Max: 4 yrs.	Min: 3 yrs. Max: 10 yrs.	YES	YES
E *Predicate Felons - prior conviction is not a VFO*	Min: 2 yrs. Max: 4 yrs.	Min: 5 yrs. Max: 15 yrs.	NO	NO
E *Predicate Felons - prior conviction is a VFO*	Min: 2 ½ yrs. Max: 4 yrs.	Min: 5 yrs. Max: 15 yrs.	NO	NO

SECOND CHILD SEXUAL ASSAULT
FELONY OFFENDER §70.07

Effective 2/01/01, applies to a defendant who is convicted of a felony sexual assault against a child less than 15 years old under PL Article 130 and within the previous 15 years (minus any periods of incarceration), has a prior felony conviction which is also for a sexual assault against a child. All sentences must include a term of post-release supervision between 10 and 20 years.

CURRENT CONVICTION	PRIOR QUALIFYING FELONY CONVICTION	
A-II or B felony Sexual Assault against a Child	*A-II, B or C felony Sexual Assault against a Child* Min: 15 - life Max: 25 - life	*D or E felony* Min: 12 years Determinate Term Max: 30 years Determinate Term
C felony Sexual Assault against a Child	*A-II, B or C felony Sexual Assault against a Child* Min: 12 years Determinate Max: 30 years Determinate or, if the court deems warranted Min: 15 - life Max: 25 - life	*D or E felony* Min: 10 years Determinate Term Max: 25 years Determinate Term
D felony Sexual Assault against a Child	Any prior qualifying felony sexual assault conviction Minimum: 5 years Determinate Term Maximum: 15 years Determinate Term	
E felony Sexual Assault against a Child	Any prior qualifying felony sexual assault conviction Minimum: 4 years Determinate Term Maximum: 12 years Determinate Term	

Effective November 1, 2003, if the defendant was less that 18 years old when he committed the prior felony sexual assault against a child, the court *may* treat the defendant as a predicate violent felony offender and may impose a determinate sentence, (PL § 70.07(5)).

CURRENT CONVICTION	POSSIBLE DETERMINATE SENTENCE
Class B felony	Min: 10 years Determinate Term Max: 25 years Determinate Term
Class C felony	Min: 7 years Determinate Term Max: 15 years Determinate Term
Class D felony	Min: 5 years Determinate Term Max: 7 years Determinate Term
Class E felony	Min: 3 years Determinate Term Max: 4 years Determinate Term.

OPTIONS AND PROGRAM ELIGIBILITY
FOR FELONY DRUG OFFENSES

Judicial Diversion – Under Article 216 of the Criminal Procedure Law, courts may direct that a defendant who pleads guilty to a controlled substance or cannabis offense, or certain other offenses specified in CPL §410.91, enter an alcohol or drug treatment program prior to sentence. As of October 7, 2021, diversion may also be obtained for certain conspiracy, auto-stripping, and identity theft offenses. A guilty plea is not required if the prosecution consents or the court finds special circumstances, such as when a defendant would suffer severe collateral consequences from non-participation in the program. Upon successful completion of the program, the court may direct that the defendant serve a period of interim probation or allow the defendant to withdraw any guilty plea and dismiss the indictment. Judicial diversion is available for first and multiple felony offenders convicted of class B or lesser drug offenses. Defendants who have previously been convicted of a Violent Felony Offense, an A felony, second-degree manslaughter, sex offenses, or a limited number of other offenses specified in Correction Law § 803(d)(ii) are not eligible, unless the prosecutor consents or the prior offense is more than 10 years old, excluding periods during which the defendant was incarcerated.

Determinate Sentences – Determinate sentences are available but not mandatory for most drug offenses, including cannabis-related offenses (see accompanying chart). Defendants serving determinate sentences may be eligible for the following programs, substantially altering the nature and term of their sentences.

Shock Incarceration – Under PL § 60.04(7), a court may order the Department of Corrections to enroll a defendant convicted of a controlled substance or marijuana offense in a SHOCK incarceration program – a six-month program of rehabilitation therapy and treatment as defined in Correction Law § 865. Defendants must not have previously been convicted of a VFO, be within 3 years of parole or conditional release, and be under 50 years old. Defendants are not eligible if, along with a qualifying offense, they are currently serving a sentence for certain crimes listed in section 865, including any A-I felony offense, any homicide, a violent felony offense, or a sex crime defined in Article 130. Otherwise, defendants are eligible as indicated in the accompanying chart. Defendants who successfully complete the program are immediately eligible for conditional release.

CASAT – Comprehensive Alcohol and Substance Abuse Treatment – Under PL § 60.04(6), courts may direct the Department of Corrections to enroll a defendant convicted of a drug offense in an alcohol or substance abuse program at a correctional annex designated for this purpose. All defendants convicted of controlled substance offenses are eligible for this program, but a B felony defendant convicted as a multiple felony drug offender must first serve nine months of his sentence.

Parole Supervision – A sentence of imprisonment for a drug offense, as for a number of other offenses specified in CPL §410.91, may be executed as a sentence of parole supervision. This allows a defendant to be placed in the Willard Drug Treatment Campus for 90 days and then released on parole. The option is available, as indicated on the accompanying chart, for most second felony drug offenders and B felony first offenders who have not previously been convicted of a VFO, an A felony, a non-drug class B felony, and who are not subject to an undischarged term of imprisonment.

Definite Sentence of Imprisonment – For certain offenses indicated on the accompanying chart, a court may impose a definite prison term of one year or less. The court must be of the opinion that a determinate sentence of imprisonment in a state facility would be unduly harsh, giving due regard to the circumstances of the crime and the nature and character of the defendant.

Alternative Sentence – In limited circumstances, indicated on the accompanying chart, courts may sentence a felony drug defendant to an "alternative sentence," defined as any other sentence permitted under Penal Law § 60.01. Under this provision, a court may, for example, impose solely a fine or a conditional discharge.

Conditional Sealing – Defendants convicted of drug felonies or certain other crimes listed in CPL § 410.91 may be entitled to a conditional sealing of their convictions after they have completed their sentences. The defendant must have participated in, and fulfilled the conditions of, judicial diversion or a similar treatment program. These defendants may also obtain sealing of up to three misdemeanor drug or marijuana convictions. Those previously convicted of marijuana offenses under the now-repealed Article 221 of the Penal Law may be entitled to have their prior offenses sealed, if the prior offense would not have been a crime under new Article 222, dealing with cannabis offenses. *See* P.L. § 440.46-a.

Re-Sentencing – Under CPL § 440.46, B felony offenders convicted prior to January 13, 2005, may apply for re-sentencing under the current determinate sentencing scheme. Defendants are not eligible if they are serving a sentence on, or have previously convicted of, an exclusion offense, such as a VFO, a non-drug A-I felony, second-degree manslaughter, vehicular manslaughter, or a sex-related offense, prior to the offense on which re-sentencing was sought and the applicable offense occurred within ten years prior to the re-sentencing application. *People v. Golo*, 28 N.Y. 3d 358 (2015). Upon repealing former Article 221 dealing with marihuana offenses and enacting Article 222 of the Penal Law, the Legislature provided a mechanism for re-sentencing those previously convicted under the old law. If the offense would not have been a crime under the new law or would have been subject to a lesser penalty, a defendant can move under CPL § 440.46-a to expunge the conviction or lower the sentence, as appropriate.

Felony and Sentencing Status	Incarceration *Determinate in half or whole years or indeterminate as indicated*	Post-Release Supervision	Probation	Definite Sentence *1 year or less*	Alternate Sentence *Any sentence authorized under PL §60.01*
A-I *with no prior felony convictions*	Determinate: Min: 8 yrs. Max: 20 yrs. *CASAT permitted*	5 years	NO	NO	NO
A-I *with prior felonies but no VFOs*	Determinate Min: 12 yrs. Max: 24 yrs. *CASAT permitted*	5 years	NO	NO	NO
A-I *with prior VFO convictions*	Determinate Min: 15 yrs. Max: 30 yrs. *CASAT permitted*	5 years	NO	NO	NO
A-I *PL §220.77 Major Trafficker*	Indeterminate Min: 15 to life / Max: 25 to life If sentence unduly harsh, then: Determinate Min: 8 yrs. Max: 20 yrs. *CASAT permitted*	*If determinate is imposed* 5 years	NO	NO	NO
A-II *with no prior felony convictions*	Min: 3 yrs. Max: 10 yrs. *CASAT permitted*	5 years	Lifetime *if defendant cooperates & DA consents*	NO	NO
A-II *with prior felonies but no VFOs*	Min: 6 yrs. Max: 14 yrs. *CASAT permitted*	5 years	Lifetime *if defendant cooperates & DA consents*	NO	NO
A-II *with prior VFO convictions*	Min: 8 yrs. Max: 17 yrs. *CASAT permitted*	5 years	NO	NO	NO

Felony and Sentencing Status	Determinate Term *Whole or half years only*	Post-Release Super-vision	Probation	Definite Sentence *1 year or less*	Alternate Sentence *Any sentence authorized under PL §60.01*
B *with no prior felony convictions*	Min: 1 yr. Max: 9 yrs. *Permitted: Parole Supervision (where no prior A or non-drug B) or SHOCK* or CASAT*	1 to 2 years	3, 4, or 5 years	YES	NO
PL §220.48 *or §220.44(2) with no prior felony convictions*	Min: 2 yrs. Max: 9 yrs. *Parole Supervision (where no prior A or non-drug B) except 220.48 or SHOCK* or CASAT*		25 years *if defendant cooperates and DA consents*	YES *except section 220.48*	
B *with prior felonies but no VFOs*	Min: 2 yrs. Max: 12 yrs. *SHOCK* or CASAT permitted*	1½ to 3 years	Lifetime *if defendant cooperates and DA consents*	NO	NO
B *with prior VFO convictions*	Min: 6 yrs. Max: 15 yrs. *with CASAT*	1½ to 3 years	NO	NO	NO

*Must be within 3 years of parole or conditional release and under 50 years old; no prior VFO; excludes certain crimes listed in Correction Law §865(1).

47

CLASS C FELONY – DRUG OFFENSE PL § 60.04

Felony and Sentencing Status	Determinate Term *Whole or half years only*	Post-Release Super-vision	Probation	Definite Sentence *1 year or less*	Alternate Sentence *Any sentence authorized under PL §60.01*
C *with no prior felony convictions*	Min: 1 yr. Max: 5½ yrs. *SHOCK* or CASAT permitted*	1 to 2 years	3, 4, or 5 years	YES	YES
C *with prior felonies but no VFOs*	Min: 1½ yrs. Max: 8 yrs. *Parole Super-vision (where no prior A or non-drug B) or SHOCK* or CASAT permitted*	1½ to 3 years	3, 4, or 5 years	YES	NO
C *with prior VFO convictions*	Min: 3½ yrs. Max: 9 yrs. *CASAT permitted*	1½ to 3 years	NO	NO	NO

*Must be within 3 years of parole or conditional release and under 50 years old; no prior VFO; excludes certain crimes listed in Correction Law §865(1).

CLASS D FELONY – DRUG OFFENSE PL § 60.04

Felony and Sentencing Status	Determinate Term *Whole or half years only*	Post-Release Supervision	Probation	Definite Sentence *1 year or less*	Alternate Sentence *Any sentence authorized under PL §60.01*
D *with no prior felony convictions*	Min: 1 yr. Max: 2½ yrs. *SHOCK** *or CASAT* *permitted*	1 year	3, 4. or 5 years	YES	YES
D *with prior felonies but no VFOs*	Min: 1½ yrs. Max: 4 yrs. *Parole Supervision (where no prior A or non-drug B) or SHOCK** *or CASAT permitted*	1 to 2 years	3, 4, or 5 years	YES	NO
D *with prior VFO convictions*	Min: 2½ yrs. Max: 4½ yrs. *CASAT permitted*	1 to 2 years	NO	NO	NO

*Must be within 3 years of parole or conditional release and under 50 years old; no prior VFO; excludes certain crimes listed in Correction Law §865(1).

CLASS E FELONY – DRUG OFFENSE PL § 60.04

Felony and Sentencing Status	Determinate Term *Whole or half years only*	Post-Release Super-vision	Probation	Definite Sentence *1 year or less*	Alternate Sentence *Any sentence authorized under PL §60.01*
E *with no prior felony convictions*	Min: 1 yr. Max: 1½ yrs. *SHOCK* or CASAT permitted*	1 year	3, 4 or 5 years	YES	YES
E *with prior felonies but no VFOs*	Min: 1½ yrs. Max: 2 yrs. *Parole Super-vision (where no prior A or non-drug B) or SHOCK* or CASAT permitted*	1 to 2 years	3, 4 or 5 years	YES	NO
E *with prior VFO convictions*	Min: 2 yrs. Max: 2½ yrs. *CASAT permitted*	1 to 2 years	NO	NO	NO

*Must be within 3 years of parole or conditional release and under 50 years old; no prior VFO; excludes certain crimes listed in Correction Law §865(1).

FELONY	PLEA LIMITATIONS - See CPL §§220.10, 220.30
Murder 1	C VFO
All other A-1 Felonies	Article 220-With YO: B; Article 220-Without YO: A-II or class B felony -Eff. 1/13/05. Non-drug: C VFO
A-II Felonies	Article 220: B Felony
B Felony	If the top count is a B AFO, the minimum plea must be to a class C VFO. If the top count is a B VFO, the minimum plea must be to a class D VFO. Article 220 cases, the minimum plea is to a D Felony. All other B Felonies, the minimum plea is to an E Felony.
C Felony	C AFO or VFO The minimum plea must be to a D VFO. *All other C Felonies* no downward limit except predicate felons who must plead guilty to at least an E Felony.
D Felony	All Predicate Felons must plead guilty to a Felony. Otherwise no downward limitations except as noted for PL § 265 offenses. *If the top count is § 265.02(4):* If defendant has an A misdemeanor conviction within the prior 5 years, defendant must plead guilty to a D or E VFO. If defendant does not have an A misdemeanor conviction within the previous 5 years, defendant can plead to an E VFO or PL § 265.01(1). *If the top count is § 265.02(5) or § 265.12* the defendant must plead to either a class D or class E VFO, see CPL § 220.10(5)d(iv).
E non-VFO offenses	All Predicate Felons must plead guilty to a Felony. Aggravated Harassment by an Inmate requires a minimum plea to a class E Felony. Otherwise, there are no plea limits.
E VFOs	All predicate felons and all persons charged with PL 240.32 must plead guilty to an E felony. Otherwise, there are no plea restrictions.

ADDITIONAL PENALTIES

Financial Penalties

A Fine can be imposed in addition to any other sentence imposed. (PL Article 80). For *A-I Drug Offenses*, the maximum fine is $100,000.00. For *A-II Drug Offenses*, the maximum fine is $50,000.00. For *B Felony Article 220 cases*, the maximum fine is $30,000.00. In *C Felony Article 220 and 221 cases*, a maximum fine of $15,000.00 can be imposed. Other than Article 220 and Article 221 offenses, the maximum fine for all felonies is $5,000 or double defendant's gain from the commission of the offense, whichever is greater. For corporations, the maximum fine for all felonies is $10,000.00 (PL §80.10). See PL §460.30 for enterprise corruption forfeitures. In prosecutions for money laundering, the fine can be up to twice the amount of the monetary instruments that were the proceeds of the criminal activity.

Reparations and restitution can also be ordered, in addition to any other sentence imposed (PL §60.27 and PL §65.10) and can include a surcharge to cover the cost of collecting the payments. At the time of sentencing of an individual convicted of Identity Theft and its related provisions, the District Attorney shall advise the Court of the extent of economic loss and the court may, *in addition to any other sentence imposed*, mandate that the defendant make restitution.

If the conviction is for Larceny and the property stolen was timber, the court may mandate that the defendant pay treble the stumpage value (PL § 60.27 (12)).

Effective July 1, 2008, the mandatory surcharge for all felonies is $300.00 and the Crime Victim Assistance fee is $25.00. The court may order restitution and the mandatory surcharge and CVA if the defendant has not yet made restitution (*People v. Quinones*, 95 NY2d 349). The CVA fee may be waived for eligible youths (CPL § 420.30(3)).

Two additional fees must be collected in sex offense cases, a sex offender registration fee and a DNA databank fee shall be paid by the defendant (PL § 60.35(1)), but the CVA fee may be waived for eligible youths (CPL § 420.35(2)). Effective 11/1/06 the supplemental sex offender registration fee was raised to $1,000.00.

Neither the sex offender registration fee, the DNA databank fee or the supplemental sex offender victim fee shall be imposed if the conviction is substituted with a youthful offender finding (PL §60.02(3) and PL §60.35(10)).

Orders of Protection

An Order of Protection can be imposed in addition to any other sentence. An Order of Protection issued in conjunction with a felony conviction may generally be imposed for a period of 8 years from the date of the conviction or eight years from the date of the expiration of the maximum term of the sentence. In 2015, the Legislature extended the permissible duration applicable to certain sex offenses to be commensurate with the extended probation available on those sentences. *See* C.P.L. §§530.12, 530.13. As to determinate sentences, the expiration date may be calculated using the aggregate sentence of incarceration and subsequent supervision, without the need to account for any jail time credit a defendant may subsequently receive. *See* N.Y. Session Laws ch. 240 (eff. 10/22/15).

Probation and Conditional Discharge

The conditions of probation and of conditional discharge shall be such as the court, in its discretion, deems reasonably necessary to insure that the defendant will lead a law-abiding life or to assist him to do so. In recent years, the legislature has added specific conditions that can be imposed. In 2008, the legislature set forth a series of conditions, relating to prohibited use of the internet, that must be imposed on sex offenders who receive a sentence of probation. (PL §65.10 (4-a)). Ordinarily, a defendant must stay within the jurisdiction of the court, and even when granted permission to move or travel elsewhere, must sign a waiver of extradition.

1.PL §70.00(3)(a)(i), see *People v. LaValle*, 3 NY3d 88 (2004).

2.PL §60.06 *Eff. 7/23/04.*

3.PL §70.00(2)(a) and (3)(a)(i).

4.PL §485.10 (4).

5.PL § 70.06(3)(a) and (4)(a).

6.PL §70.00(2)(b)and(3)(b). Except for PL §220.44(2), the minimum must be at least 1 year but can be less than 1/3 the maximum.

7.See PL §70.02(1)(a) for all current class B Violent Felony Offenses (VFOs).

8.PL §70.02(3)(a)and(4) before 10/1/95.

9.See CPL §1.20(41) for the definition of an AFO. The minimum must be at least 1/3, but can be up to half the maximum, PL § 70.02(4), before 10/1/95.

10.The minimum must be half the maximum, PL §70.02(3)and(4) eff. 10/1/95.

11.PL §60.12(1) eff. 9/1/98.

12.PL §70.02(3)(a) eff. 9/1/98.

13.PL §70.02(2)(a) eff. 9/1/98.

14.PL §70.45(2)

15.Effective 1996, a 5 year consecutive sentence must be imposed unless "unduly harsh," PL § 265.09(2).

16.PL §70.06(3)(b)and(4)(b).

17.PL §70.06(3)(b)and(4)(b).

18.PL §70.06(6)(a) eff. 10/1/95.

19.PL §70.04(3)(a)and(4) before 10/1/95.

20.PL §70.04(2)and(3)(a) eff. 10/1/95.

21.PL §70.08(2)and(3) before 10/1/95.

22.PL §70.08(2)and(3) eff. 10/1/95.

23.PL §70.00(2)and(3). The minimum shall not be less than 1 year nor more than 1/3 the maximum, PL §70.00(3)b.

24.Except a defendant convicted of Grand Larceny in the Second Degree, a Class C felony, may be sentenced the same as a Class B felon, if the offense is prosecuted as a public corruption crime. PL § 496.07.

25.See PL §60.05(4) for a list of all class C enumerated felonies. First time felony offenders convicted of any class C 'enumerated' felony must receive an indeterminate sentence.

26.See PL §70.02(1)(b) for all current C VFOs.

27.PL §70.02(3)(b)and(4) before 10/1/95.

28.PL §70.02(4) eff. 10/1/95. The minimum must be half the maximum.

29.PL §70.02(3)(b) eff. 9/1/98.

30.PL §70.06(3)(c) and (4)(b).

31.PL §70.06(3)(c) and (4)(b).

32.PL §70.06(6)(b) eff. 10/1/95.

33.PL §70.04(3)(b) and (4) before 10/1/95.

34.PL §70.04(2)and(3)(b) eff. 10/1/95.

35.PL §70.08(2) and (3)(b) before 10/1/95.

36.PL §70.08(2) and (3)(b) eff. 10/1/95.

37.PL §70.00(2)(d)and(3)(b). The minimum must be at least 1 year, but can be less than 1/3 of the maximum, PL § 70.00(3)(b).

38.Except a defendant convicted of Grand Larceny in the Third Degree, a Class D felony, may be sentenced the same as a Class C felon, if the offense is prosecuted as a public corruption crime. PL § 496.07.

39.PL §60.05(5).

40.PL §60.05(5), 70.00(4) and 60.01(2)(d).

41.See PL §70.02(1)(c) for all current D VFOs.

42.PL §70.00(2)(d) and (3)(b).

43.PL §70.02(4) eff. 10/1/95. The minimum must be half the maximum.

44.PL §70.02(3)(c) eff. 9/1/98.

45.PL §60.05(5). If the indictment charged an AFO, only an indeterminate sentence is allowed unless the Court finds mitigating circumstances, defendant's participation was minor or there are deficiencies in the proof, see PL §70.02(4).

46.PL §60.05(5), 70.00(4) and 60.01(2)(d).

47.PL §70.02(4) eff. 10/1/95.

48.PL §70.02(3)(c) eff. 9/1/98.

49. For violations of PL § 265.02 (4), (5), (7) and (8), *but not PL § 265.02(6).* If defendant is not a predicate and does not have any A misdemeanor convictions within the past five years, defendant can receive less than one year if one year in jail would be unduly harsh, PL § 70.02(2)(c)(I). If defendant is not a predicate, but does have an A misdemeanor conviction within the past five years the Court must find either mitigating circumstances, defendant's participation was minor or deficiencies in the People's proof, PL §70.02(2)(c) and PL § 70.02(4)(b) and (c).

50. PL §70.06(3)(d) and (4)(b).

51. PL §70.06(7) and CPL §410.91

52. PL §70.06(3)(d) and (4)(b).

53. PL §70.06(6)(c) eff. 10/1/95.

54. PL §70.04(3)(c) and (4) before 10/1/95.

55. PL §70.04(2) and (3)(c) eff. 10/1/95.

56. PL §70.08(2) and (3)(c) before 10/1/95.

57. PL §70.08(2) and (3)(c) eff. 10/1/95.

58. See PL §70.02(1)(d) for class E VFOs. PLEASE NOTE: The class E felonies of 110/265.02(4), (5), (6), (7) and (8) are only VFOs if pled as a "lesser included" on an indictment that charged a greater offense PL § 70.02(1)(d).

59. PL §60.02 and CPL Article 720.

60. PL §70.00(2)(e) and (3). The minimum must be at least 1 year, but can be less than 1/3 of the maximum, PL §70.00(3)(b).

61. Except a defendant convicted of Grand Larceny in the Fourth Degree or Scheme to Defraud in the First Degree, Class E felonies, may be sentenced as a Class D felon, if the offense is prosecuted as a public corruption crime. PL § 496.07

62. PL §70.00(2)(e) and (3)(b). The minimum must be at least 1 year nor more than 1/3 of the maximum.

63. PL §70.02(4) eff. 10/1/95.

64. PL § 70.02(3)(d) eff. 9/1/98.

65. If the defendant does not have any A misdemeanor convictions within the past 5 years and the Court finds one year in jail would be unduly harsh, PL §70.02(2)(c)(I). If defendant does have an A misdemeanor conviction within the past five years the Court must find either mitigating circumstances, defendant's participation was minor or deficiencies in the People's proof. PL §70.02(4)(b)and(c).

56

66.PL §70.06(3)(e) and (4)(b).

67.PL §70.06(7) and CPL §410.91.

68.PL §70.06 (3)(e).

69.PL §70.06(3)(e) and (4)(b).

70.PL §70.06(6)(d) eff. 10/1/95.

71.PL §70.04(3)(d) and (4).

72.PL §70.04(2)and(3)(d) eff. 10/1/95.

73.PL §70.08(2). The statute is silent regarding the minimum but *People v. Tolbert,* 93 N.Y.2d 86 (1999) created a four year minimum.

74.PL §70.05